South Africa Handbook

Lizzie Williams & Francisca Kellett

❝❞
Everything in Africa bites,
but the safari bug is worst of all.

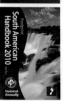

Footprint story

It was 1921

Ireland had just been partitioned, the British miners were striking for more pay and the federation of British industry had an idea. Exports were booming in South America – how about a handbook for businessmen trading in that far away continent? The Anglo-South American Handbook was born that year, written by W Koebel, the most prolific writer on Latin America of his day.

1924

Two editions later the book was 'privatized' and in 1924, in the hands of Royal Mail, the steamship company for South America, it became The South American Handbook, subtitled 'South America in a nutshell'. This annual publication became the 'bible' for generations of travellers to South America and remains so to this day. In the early days travel was by sea and the Handbook gave all the details needed for the long voyage from Europe. What to wear for dinner; how to arrange a cricket match with the Cable & Wireless staff on the Cape Verde Islands and a full account of the journey from Liverpool up the Amazon to Manaus: 5898 miles without changing cabin!

1939

As the continent opened up, The South American Handbook reported the new Pan Am flying boat services, and the fortnightly airship service from Rio to Europe on the Graf Zeppelin. For reasons still unclear but with extraordinary determination, the annual editions continued through the Second World War.

1970s

Many more people discovered South America and the backpacking trail started to develop. All the while the Handbook was gathering fans, including literary vagabonds such as Paul Theroux and Graham Greene (who once sent some updates addressed to "The publishers of the best travel guide in the world, Bath, England").

1990s

During the 1990s the company set about developing a new travel guide series using this legendary title as the flagship. By 1997 there were over a dozen guides in the series and the Footprint imprint was launched.

2000s

The series grew quickly and there were soon Footprint travel guides covering more than 150 countries. In 2004, Footprint launched its first thematic guide: *Surfing Europe*, packed with colour photographs, maps and charts. This was followed by further thematic guides such as *Diving the World*, *Snowboarding the World*, *Body and Soul escapes*, *Travel with Kids* and *European City Breaks*.

2009

Today we continue the traditions of the last 87 years that has served legions of travellers so well. We believe that these help to make Footprint guides different. Our policy is to use authors who are genuine experts who write for independent travellers; people possessing a spirit of adventure, looking to get off the beaten track.

Title page: Game driving in Kruger National Park.
Above: Table Mountain, Cape Town.

South Africa is celebrated, first and foremost, for its incredible natural beauty. It has some of the most varied and extreme environments in the world, from the tropical beaches of KwaZulu Natal to the sweeping emptiness of the Kalahari Desert. Yet it is the people, a fascinating mix of cultures, religions and ethnicities, who are the beating pulse of South Africa, and who give meaning to its nickname, 'Rainbow Nation'. Many visitors come here to see the Big Five – the collective term for the big-bucks players of wildlife spotting: elephant, black rhino, buffalo, leopard and lion. While the choice of excellent game reserves virtually guarantees sightings, the country's vibrant cities are an equally compelling reason to visit. There's the fast-paced sophistication of Johannesburg and Tshwane (Pretoria), the steamy humidity and spicy Indian influence of Durban, or the spectacular setting and quirky beach-side hedonism of Cape Town.

916.804
Flegg
2009

Contents

LIMPOPO
MPUMALANGA
GAUTENG
○ JOHANNESBURG
SWAZILAND
NORTH WEST PROVINCE
FREE STATE
KWAZULU NATAL
LESOTHO
NORTHERN CAPE
EASTERN CAPE
WESTERN CAPE
CAPE TOWN ○
GARDEN ROUTE

• 5

Planning your trip

AGE FOTOSTOCK/SUPERSTOCK

A meerkat family sunbathing
at a burrow in the Kgalagadi
Transfrontier Park.

Where to go

South Africa has more to offer than you could ever hope to manage in one trip. There's an expansive choice of worthwhile destinations around the country and it's a very easy place to get around. The magnificent natural beauty – South Africa's main attraction – is represented in the multitude of game reserves and national parks, which are home to a whole host of wildlife. South Africa's vibrant cities – another major draw – are characterized by the cosmopolitan populations you'd expect from the Rainbow Nation. Here there are numerous exciting urban attractions as well as the best eating

The best way of getting around is to hire a car. This allows the freedom to explore more remote areas and also provides independent access to national parks.

and shopping opportunities on the African continent.

South Africa's history is compelling too, from the early hunter-gatherers to the arrival of the Europeans, the Boer War and the more recent breakdown of Apartheid, reflected in the cave paintings, colonial architecture, lively townships, moving battlefields and contemporary museums.

Being outdoors is also very much a way of life here and you can try hiking and surfing, or opt for one of the booming adrenalin sports such as bungee jumping or whitewater rafting. In short, the choice of destinations, activities and itineraries is virtually inexhaustible, so careful planning is needed to make best use of your time.

South Africa's facilities, food and accommodation tend to be of a very high standard, and there's a wide range of travel options available. Independent travel is one of the most popular ways of seeing the country and South Africa's road and transport network is one of the best on

Opposite page: One of Cape Peninsula's glorious beaches.
Above: Costumed rickshaw pullers, Durban.

the continent. Modern highways, good train and bus networks, and comprehensive internal flights link all the main urban centres. The best way of getting around is to hire a car. This allows the freedom to explore more remote areas and also provides independent access to national parks. There are also ever-expanding choices of organized tours, which take in the national parks and historic sites, focus on sports such as scuba-diving, or are tailored to specific interests such as history or flora and fauna.

The absolute minimum time to spend in South Africa is around two weeks. Rather than cram in too much, try to arrange a visit to a specific region so you can fully appreciate what there is on offer; you can always return to another part of the country at some time in the future.

As arrival in the country will probably be either via Johannesburg, Cape Town or Durban, it's best to stick to the areas accessible from these cities if you are

on a shorter holiday; there are plenty of worthwhile attractions within striking distance of Jozi, the Mother City or Durbs as these three are affectionately known.

If you have more time, venture further afield into the other provinces too, or even other countries. South Africa completely surrounds the mountain kingdom of Lesotho and most of Swaziland and these two countries, along with Namibia and Botswana, allow cars hired in South Africa to cross their borders. Another alternative would be to go on a longer organized tour which might take in several southern African countries. In short, an international flight to South Africa opens up all sorts of opportunities to visit the tip of the African continent.

None of the suggested sample itineraries overleaf are set in stone and the options are far from exhaustible; rather, they are regional suggestions for travellers wishing to explore a certain area of South Africa, or for returning visitors to travel somewhere new.

Itineraries

Two weeks

Cape Town and Western Cape

Spend a minimum of four to six days in Cape Town exploring the sights and enjoying the fine shops and restaurants. The city is home to historic buildings, museums, beautiful beaches, the botanical gardens of Kirstenbosch and the famous Constantia wine estates. Climbing to the top of Table Mountain or riding in the cable car should definitely be on the agenda, while organized and thought-provoking tours to Robben Island and the townships on the Cape Flats will offer a glimpse of South Africa's fragile past. Day trips are available to the Cape of Good Hope and Cape Point via the spectacular Cape Peninsula, the beautiful wine estates around Stellenbosch and, in flower season, to the West Coast to see the spring blooms. From Cape Town spend a week or more following the coast along the Garden Route, stopping off along the way at pretty towns such as Hermanus on the Whale Coast, Knysna or Plettenberg Bay, and at the beautiful Tsitsikamma National Park. Return to Cape Town via the tranquil back country roads surrounded by vineyards through the Western Cape interior, known locally as Route 62. Alternatively, if you have a few more days, at the end of the Garden Route in the Eastern Cape Province is the quirky surfing town of Jeffrey's Bay and the excellent Addo Elephant National Park and its neighbouring private game reserves. Again, you can drive back, but there is also the option of flying back to Cape Town from Nelson Mandela Bay (Port Elizabeth).

KwaZulu Natal

Another two-week itinerary could start with a day or two in Durban where you can stroll along the beachfront and perhaps take an afternoon excursion to the Valley of 1000 Hills,

or go shopping at the massive Gateway Mall before heading north up the tropical coast road to Zululand. At least two days is needed to explore Hluhluwe-Imfolozi Game Reserve, which is home to one of the world's largest rhino populations and has been instrumental in saving this creature from extinction. The lakes and wetlands at iSimangaliso Wetland

Small fishing boats in Hermanus harbour.

Park warrant a day or two, especially the gorgeous beach at Cape Vidal, and divers should head for the coral reefs at Sodwana Bay. Turning inland, go via the mountain reserve of Ithala for one night and then on to Dundee, which is a suitable base for exploring the numerous battlefield sites relating to the Anglo-Boer and Anglo-Zulu wars. Allow a full day to do a guided tour of Isandlwana and Rorke's Drift; longer for the other sites. Then head across the Natal Midlands to the magnificent mountain chain which forms a natural border with Lesotho – the uKhahlamba-Drakensberg National Park. There are plenty of mountain resorts and country hotels to choose from and at least three or four days should be spent here to enjoy the scenery.

Northern provinces

The north is for travellers who want to see more unusual and isolated destinations, but be prepared to spend long stretches behind the wheel. Starting in Johannesburg head north to Sun City, the hedonistic casino and leisure resort next to the Pilanesberg National Park in the North West Province. To appreciate all there is on offer here stay at least two days. Then move on to one of the north's best-kept secrets, the Madikwe Game Reserve, where a number of excellent lodges offer game-watching activities. Moving on east, a long drive brings you to Kimberley in the Northern Cape where you can visit the newly vamped Kimberley Mine Museum and Big Hole to learn all about the diamond wealth that modern South Africa is founded on. Drive further north and spend three or four days in the Kgalagadi Transfrontier Park, a stunning Kalahari wilderness with a unique ecosystem, or the Ai-Ais/Richtersveld Transfrontier Park where the Gariep (Orange) River winds its way towards the ocean between soaring granite cliffs. From the extreme north it's a two-day drive south to Cape Town, though there are a number of distractions along the way such as the Namakwa flowers in season, the Cederberg Wilderness Area and the West Coast. Alternatively, head north to explore southern Namibia and the Fish River Canyon.

Gauteng, Mpumalanga and Swaziland

Another two-week option can start with three or four days in Johannesburg or Tshwane (Pretoria) to take informative township and city tours and visit the historic buildings and museums, such as Pretoria's Voortrekker Monument or Johannesburg's excellent Apartheid Museum and Gold Reef City. Johannesburg in particular is also known for its chic shopping malls and craft markets, varied restaurant districts and happening nightlife, and it regularly hosts major sporting events. From Gauteng head east into Mpumalanga to visit the Kruger National Park, South Africa's premier wildlife destination, which warrants at least four or five days. The area around Kruger is commonly known as the Panorama region because of its stunning mountain scenery.

Game drives in Kruger can be combined with a visit to the Blyde River Canyon, one of the deepest canyons in the world, and the pretty mountain towns of Graskop and Sabie, as well as the historic gold-mining towns of Pilgrim's Rest and Barberton. From here you could head south into Swaziland for a couple of days' relaxation at the Mlilwane Wildlife Sanctuary or one of the lesser-known nature reserves and try some cycling, horse riding or hiking through the tranquil bush.

Three weeks

Free State and Lesotho
In addition to one of the above itineraries, visitors with another week to spare can head south from Johannesburg to the Eastern Highlands and spend a night in the scenic Golden Gate Highlands National Park in Free State. From here you can cross any of the borders into Lesotho and spend two or three days in a resort such as Malealea or Semonkong, hiking or pony trekking in the cool mountain kingdom. This is sufficient time to get a taste of Lesotho, but spend a few more days to see Lesotho's greatest attraction, which are the highlands. Until recently fairly inaccessible, new tarred roads have opened up three spectacular routes: the mountain road from Maseru to Thaba-Tseka; the new tarred road from Hlotse to Katse Dam; and the 'Roof of Africa' road between Butha-Buthe and Mokhotlong. All these roads are in good enough condition during the drier months to attempt in a normal saloon car. If you have a 4WD, the last two routes can be linked in a full circle by the road between Mokhotlong and Thaba-Tseka. There's another stunning drive in the far south of the country between Moyeni (Quthing) and Qacha's Nek and, except for a short section around Sekake, it is accessible by normal car. The options from Lesotho depend on where you are and what border to cross, but both Johannesburg and Durban can be reached in a (long) day.

South Africa highlights & itineraries

See colour maps in centre of book

Two weeks

Cape Town & Western Cape

KwaZulu Natal

Northern provinces

Gauteng, Mpumalanga & Swaziland

One-week extension

Free State & Lesotho

BOTSWANA

Kgalagadi
Transfrontier
Park

NAMIBIA

Kalahari

Green Kalahari

Upington

Ai-Ais/
Richtersveld
Transfrontier
National
Conservation
Park

Diamantveld

Springbok

NORTHERN CAPE

Namaqua

Atlantic Ocean

Great Karoo

Garden Route
Gorgeous beaches, pretty
forests, scenic lagoons
and a number of
attractive seaside towns,
page 305.

Winelands
World-class wines,
rolling vineyards, stark
mountains and historical
Cape Dutch estates,
page 155.

WESTERN CAPE

Tsitsikamma
National
Park

Cape Town   Stellenbosch   Heidelberg   Knysna

Cape Town
Climb Table Mountain,
soak up the culture, shop
up a storm, or lounge on
the pristine beaches,
page 78.

Hermanus

Plettenberg
Bay

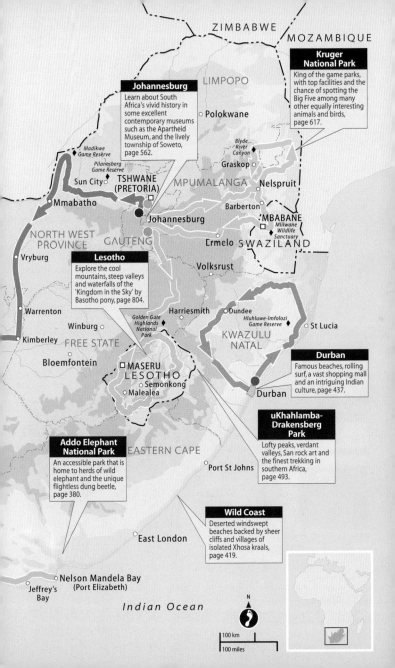

ZIMBABWE

MOZAMBIQUE

Kruger National Park
King of the game parks, with top facilities and the chance of spotting the Big Five among many other equally interesting animals and birds, page 617.

LIMPOPO

● Polokwane

Blyde River Canyon ◆

Johannesburg
Learn about South Africa's vivid history in some excellent contemporary museums such as the Apartheid Museum, and the lively township of Soweto, page 562.

Madikwe Game Reserve ◆

Pilanesberg Game Reserve ◆

Graskop ●

MPUMALANGA

Sun City ●

TSHWANE (PRETORIA) □

Nelspruit ●

Mmabatho ●

Barberton ●

MBABANE □

Mlilwane Wildlife Sanctuary ◆

Johannesburg ●

NORTH WEST PROVINCE

GAUTENG

Ermelo ○

SWAZILAND

Vryburg ○

Lesotho
Explore the cool mountains, steep valleys and waterfalls of the 'Kingdom in the Sky' by Basotho pony, page 804.

Volksrust ●

Harriesmith ●

Dundee ○

Warrenton ○

Hluhluwe-Imfolozi Game Reserve ◆

St Lucia ○

Winburg ○

Golden Gate Highlands National Park ◆

KWAZULU NATAL

Kimberley ○

FREE STATE

Bloemfontein ●

□ MASERU
LESOTHO

Durban
Famous beaches, rolling surf, a vast shopping mall and an intriguing Indian culture, page 437.

Semonkong ○

Malealea ○

Durban ■

uKhahlamba-Drakensberg Park
Lofty peaks, verdant valleys, San rock art and the finest trekking in southern Africa, page 493.

Addo Elephant National Park
An accessible park that is home to herds of wild elephant and the unique flightless dung beetle, page 380.

EASTERN CAPE

Port St Johns ●

Wild Coast
Deserted windswept beaches backed by sheer cliffs and villages of isolated Xhosa kraals, page 419.

East London ○

Nelson Mandela Bay ● (Port Elizabeth)

Jeffrey's Bay ○

Indian Ocean

N

100 km
100 miles

Game reserves

Kruger

Kruger Park is the king of South African game parks and one of the best game-viewing areas in all of Africa. The figures speak for themselves: 507 bird species, 114 reptile, 49 fish, 34 amphibian, 147 mammal and over 23,000 plant species have been recorded here. The region itself is enormous, extending from the Crocodile River in the south to the Limpopo River in the north, from the wooded foothills of the eastern escarpment to the humid plains of the Lowveld. It certainly fulfils most visitors' fantasies of seeing magnificent herds of game roaming across acacia-studded stretches of savannah, and of course it is home to the Big Five.

Pilanesberg

This, the fourth largest national park in South Africa, has imported animals from all over southern Africa: elephant and buffalo from Addo Elephant National Park, black and white rhino from the Natal Parks Board, eland from Namibia, Burchell's zebra and waterbuck from the Transvaal and red hartebeest from the Northern Cape and Namibia. It is also the natural habitat for a number of rare species, including brown hyena, Cape hunting dog and sable antelope. You now have a good chance of seeing all the large animals including rhino, elephant, lion, cheetah, buffalo and even leopard.

Madikwe

Covering over 60,000 ha, this reserve has the second largest elephant population in South Africa. In the 1990s more than 10,000 animals were successfully released into the reserve. Animals now present include elephant, zebra, lion, buffalo, white rhino, spotted hyena, wild dog, steenbok, duiker, kudu, leopard and cheetah. Visitors are able to view these animals during game drives or on morning walks with a guide and experienced tracker. The introduction of community projects is allowing local communities to benefit from, and contribute to, the ecological management of Madikwe.

DAVID PETA/SHUTTERSTOCK

A bull elephant sharing a road with cars in Kruger National Park.

Above left: A male lion with a magnificent mane in Addo Elephant National Park.
Above right: Oryx standing among spring flowers in the Kgalagadi Transfrontier Park.

Addo

With the reintroduction of lion in 2003, it is now possible to see the Big Seven – elephant, rhino, lion, buffalo, leopard, whale and great white shark – in a malaria-free environment. The expansion of the park is one of the most exciting and ambitious conservation projects ever undertaken, and Addo, now home to the densest population of elephant on earth, has become a highlight of the Eastern Cape.

Hluhluwe-Imfolozi

This is one of the best reserves in KwaZulu Natal for seeing wildlife, and one of the finest in the world for seeing rhino. The varied landscapes of Hluhluwe-Imfolozi provide a wide range of habitats which support large numbers of big game. The Big Five are present and there are important populations of three rarely seen animals: the white rhino, the black rhino and the nyala. Despite the thriving hippo populations in nearby St Lucia, there are fewer than 20 hippo in this park because the rivers flow too fast. Over 300 species of bird, including the rare bateleur eagle, have been recorded in Hluhluwe-Imfolozi; bird lists are available from camp offices.

Kgalagadi Transfrontier

Although probably one of the least-visited national parks in the country, the Kgalagadi Transfrontier Park has some of the finest game viewing in Africa. It is remote and relatively undeveloped, with uncomfortably high summer temperatures, but few visitors begrudge the hot dusty roads once they've glimpsed their first lion. The park is famous for its predators, particularly the dark-maned Kalahari lion which can sometimes be spotted lazing in the shade of trees found along the river beds. Other predators to look out for include cheetah, wild dog, spotted hyena, bat-eared fox, black-backed jackal and the honey badger. Leopard are, as always, elusive but are seen relatively regularly in the park. You should also see giraffe, red hartebeest, Burchell's zebra and huge herds of wildebeest and springbok. The birdlife, too, is impressive. Over 200 species have been recorded in the park. The best viewing months are between February and May, especially if the rains have been good.

Spas and retreats

Bushman's Kloof

Set in a remote World Heritage Site renowned for its ancient rock art, and with stunning views across the Cederberg Mountains and rugged plains of the Great Karoo, Bushman's Kloof provides real luxury in the wilderness. For a pampering fix, there's a spa offering facials and Moya therapies which use aromatic, therapeutic and native South African essences to heal, nourish and soothe. Reflexology, aromatherapy, Swedish and deep-tissue massages are also available. There are plenty of hiking routes and the chance to swim in natural rock pools or three pools at the lodge, one of which is heated. Mountain biking, rock climbing and canoeing are also available, or take a game drive to spot antelope, zebra and wildebeest, before watching the sun set from a nearby hilltop with a glass of wine.

Mount Grace

A favourite venue for stressed-out Gautengers set in lovely manicured grounds in the Magaliesburg Mountains, Mount Grace is a fine country house with luxury cottages spread up the hillside with their own plunge pools. The elegant thatched spa is surrounded by tumbling waterfalls and a hydrotherapy garden completely enclosed by trees. Here warm water flows through various features including a reflexology stream where you can walk over small smooth pebbles and pick them up with your feet, a large stone jacuzzi and an enormous indoor flotation pool painted in deep blue, with dim lights, underwater whale sounds and stars on the ceiling.

Lanzerac Manor

This 300-year-old traditional Cape Dutch wine estate 4 km outside Stellenbosch is an excellent luxury hotel offering gourmet food and wine and 'spafaris'. These involve numerous treatments, time in the indoor pool and hydrotherapy area, wine tasting, a walk or golf cart ride around the estate, ending with a massage and picnic under the arms of a huge willow tree. The spa has saunas, steam rooms and wet rooms, it overlooks the vineyards, there's a gazebo

BUSHMANS KLOOF HOMESTEAD

Opposite page: Bushman's Kloof is one of the best places to see San art in South Africa.
Above: The flotation pool at Mount Grace – open to non-residents – has underwater whale sounds.
Right: The 18th-century Lanzerac estate offers spa treatments, wine tastings and cellar tours.

for outdoor treatments and a deck area on the roof for relaxing in the sunshine.

Coach House

This fine country hotel near Tzaneen in Limpopo Province is set in the picturesque Magoebaskloof Mountains and is an ideal stopover to or from Kruger. Here the Agatha Spa is centered around the Sensorium, an open-plan area incorporating a gym, heated hydro-jet pool, saunas, steam rooms and restaurant. This entire space is glass-fronted and has excellent views of the surrounding mountains and valleys. The comprehensive spa menu includes an unusual nougat body wrap and the hotel has a special kitchen dedicated to making nougat, which it sells locally.

Ulusaba

Richard Branson's super luxurious Ulusaba Private Game Reserve lies in the heart of exclusive Sabi Sands in Mpumalanga on the edge of Kruger and features stunning hilltop thatched suites with their own plunge pools. Pampering is in the temptingly named Aroma Boma, where you can try rejuvenating facials including one for the dominant male called the Lion Tamer, which also involves a close shave. After a game drive massages can be taken in the privacy of your own spacious wooden deck with magnificent views over the 13,500 ha of unspoilt game-rich bush.

Etali Safari Lodge

In the North West Province's Madikwe Game Reserve, this luxury and intimate game lodge has suites under thatch with contemporary African furnishings, crisp white linen on the vast beds and double baths. The partially open-air spa with soothing splashes of green and beaded ethnic decor has a gym, steam-room, pool and reflexology walk; treatments include salt rubs and body wraps – the mud one is charmingly named Warthog Hour – and there's a full range of facials, manicures and pedicures.

Wineries

Constantia Uitsig Wine Estate

Constantia Uitsig winery, hotel and restaurants are situated only 20 minutes from Cape Town's city centre, but they could be in another world. In the shadow of the Table Mountain the estate offers an exhilarating eating experience for travelling gourmets. Sixteen garden rooms have glorious views of the Constantia Valley, while a short walk through the gardens leads to the Wine Shop, where the estate's range of fine wines can be sampled.

The luxuries of this hotel, its surroundings, wines, gorgeous spa, top restaurants – Constantia Uitsig, La Colombe (voted Restaurant of the Year in *Eat Out* magazine, and one of the top 50 in the world by the San Pellegrino World's 50 Best Restaurants Awards 2009), and the less formal River Café – make this the perfect destination for visitors with adventurous tastes.

Groot Constantia

The oldest working winery in the Cape was established in 1685 but, until recently, it was worth visiting for everything except its wine. The landmark building was undeniably interesting but the state-owned winery was underperforming woefully. A shift in philosophy and the arrival of a new winemaker have brought huge changes, so that, today, the Gouverneur's Reserve Cabernet Sauvignon is one of the best, most subtle reds in the Cape. The Manor House contains a museum and the Cloete Cellar provides an idea of what winemaking was like here over two centuries ago. There are two restaurants: Simons and the more interesting Jonkershuis, which offers good Cape Malay cooking and estate wines.

Steenberg Vineyards

The history of Steenberg stretches back to the 1600s, when the original name of this area was Swaaneweide, meaning 'the feeding place of swans'. Today, spur-winged geese are found here. In the mid-1800s the estate was sold to the Louw family, who owned it until 1990, when it was purchased by Johannesburg Consolidated Investments, which re-developed

Above: Steenberg Vineyards in the Constantia Valley.
Opposite page left: Al fresco dining at Constantia Uitsig with views across vineyards to Table Mountain.
Opposite page right: A garden guest room at Constantia Uitsig.

it into the impressive vineyard that it is today. There are around 70 ha under vine; 60% is white – mostly Sauvignon Blanc, followed by Chardonnay, Sémillon and Muscat de Frontignan – and the rest is red: a mix of Cabernet Sauvignon, Merlot, Cabernet Franc, Pinot Noir, Shiraz and some Nebbiolo. There's a luxury hotel and spa, Catharina's gourmet restaurant and an 18-hole golf course.

Boschendal

Boschendal estate has been producing wine for 300 years and is today one of the most popular estates in the region, not least for its excellent food and pleasant wine-tasting area underneath a giant oak. The restored H-shaped manor house is one of the finest in South Africa, and is open as a museum to the public. Interestingly, a third of the estate is now owned by a black empowerment consortium. Most of the wine produced on the estate is white; their sparkling wines are highly regarded.

Saxenburg Wine Farm

The Bührer family of Switzerland took over Saxenburg in 1989 and dedicated their time to reviving the family tradition of the estate's historic past, ensuring its growth and development in future years. They also fulfilled their wish to have a sister vineyard in France, acquiring Château Capion, near Montpellier, in 1996. Saxenburg is situated on the hills above Kuils River, between the Atlantic and Indian oceans, where the vineyards enjoy ideal conditions. There are around 90 ha of vines, growing predominantly Shiraz, Cabernet Sauvignon, Sauvignon Blanc, Merlot and Pinotage. The Guinea Fowl Restaurant specializes in fresh seafood, game and a variety of exclusive guinea fowl dishes. The wines are all Saxenburg, with plenty of older vintages . There is a vine-covered terrace giving a Mediterranean feel and wonderful views of the sunset over Table Mountain.

Spier Wine Centre

Located in a beautifully restored 17th-century barn on the main estate, the Spier Wine Centre stocks more than 200 wines. It is a haven for any wine-lover, with rare vintages, collectors' labels, and the estate's own range of wines, including their award-winning Cabernet Sauvignon and Merlot. There is also a range of wine accessories available, a delivery service, and the knowledgeable staff are always keen to help. Tastings are run every day, with the emphasis on communicating the best way to truly appreciate wine. It features Moyo, an outstanding African-themed restaurant, a deli where you can buy picnics to enjoy on the estate, a luxury hotel and family activities, including a cheetah centre.

When to go

South Africa has a moderate climate and long sunny days for most of the year. You will only come across truly tropical conditions in the northeast corner of KwaZulu Natal around Kosi Bay and the border with Mozambique. During summer it rarely gets hotter than 30°C, though Gauteng and KwaZulu Natal get very humid, and parts of the Northern Cape experience temperatures in the region of 45°C – too hot for most people. The coast around Cape Town and the Garden Route is at its best during the spring and summer months, though the best time for whale watching is in winter. During July and August, in the middle of winter, it can get cold at night in Cape Town and the interior mountains in the Drakensberg and Eastern Cape, with frosts and snowfalls. But winter is the best time to visit the northern desert areas around Upington and the Kalahari. Most of the rain falls in the summer months and, when it does rain, there are often very heavy storms. If driving in these conditions, slow down and pull over. Also be on the lookout for flash floods, especially if you're camping.

The best time of year for game viewing is during the winter months, when vegetation cover is at a minimum and a lack of water forces animals to congregate around rivers and waterholes. Winter is also the best time for hiking, avoiding the high temperatures and frequent thunderstorms of the summer months. Despite being cooler, July and August are a popular time for visitors as they coincide with the European school holidays. December and January are by far the busiest months for South African tourism. Be sure to book your car hire and accommodation well in advance during these periods. One major disadvantage of visiting during the summer is that much of the accommodation is fully booked months in advance, and the coastal towns become horribly overcrowded.

For further advice on when to go to South Africa, visit www.weathersa.co.za.

Best of the festivals

If there's one festival you have to attend, it's the National Arts Festival in Grahamstown, South Africa's oldest, biggest and best-known arts festival. It's a 10-day event which takes place in June, with hundreds of performances of theatre, music, song, dance and film. For further information, see Festivals and events, page 53.

South Africa

Activity	J	F	M	A	M	J	J	A	S	O	N	D
See the blanket of spring blooms up the West Coast								★	★	★		
Watch whales from a cliff top in Hermanus							★	★	★	★	★	
Enjoy clear sunny skies in Lesotho		★	★	★				★	★	★		
Dive in the Indian Ocean with ragged-tooth sharks					★	★	★	★	★	★	★	
Relax on glorious beaches on the KwaZulu Natal coast	★	★	★	★						★	★	★
Experience the different seasons in Kruger	★	★	★	★	★	★	★	★	★	★	★	★
Party in sunny Cape Town over the New Year	★											★

Rainfall and climate charts

Cape Town

Month	Average temperature in °C max-min	Average rainfall in mm
Jan	26 - 16	15
Feb	26 - 16	08
Mar	25 - 14	18
Apr	22 - 12	48
May	19 - 09	79
Jun	18 - 08	84
Jul	17 - 07	89
Aug	18 - 08	66
Sep	18 - 09	43
Oct	21 - 11	31
Nov	23 - 13	18
Dec	24 - 14	10

Nelson Mandela Bay

Month	Average temperature in °C max-min	Average rainfall in mm
Jan	26 - 16	31
Feb	26 - 17	33
Mar	24 - 16	48
Apr	23 - 13	46
May	22 - 10	61
Jun	20 - 07	46
Jul	19 - 07	48
Aug	20 - 08	51
Sep	20 - 10	58
Oct	21 - 12	56
Nov	22 - 14	56
Dec	24 - 15	43

Durban

Month	Average temperature in °C max-min	Average rainfall in mm
Jan	27 - 21	109
Feb	27 - 21	122
Mar	27 - 20	130
Apr	26 - 18	76
May	24 - 14	51
Jun	23 - 12	33
Jul	22 - 11	28
Aug	22 - 13	38
Sep	23 - 15	71
Oct	24 - 17	109
Nov	25 - 18	122
Dec	26 - 19	119

Johannesburg

Month	Average temperature in °C max-min	Average rainfall in mm
Jan	26 - 14	114
Feb	25 - 14	109
Mar	24 - 13	89
Apr	22 - 10	38
May	19 - 06	25
Jun	17 - 04	08
Jul	17 - 04	08
Aug	20 - 06	08
Sep	23 - 09	23
Oct	25 - 12	56
Nov	25 - 13	107
Dec	26 - 14	125

Graskop

Month	Average temperature in °C max-min	Average rainfall in mm
Jan	24 - 13	650
Feb	26 - 13	550
Mar	25 - 12	425
Apr	24 - 11	150
May	21 - 06	75
Jun	20 - 05	25
Jul	20 - 04	00
Aug	23 - 06	50
Sep	24 - 08	50
Oct	25 - 10	75
Nov	25 - 11	125
Dec	26 - 10	455

Polokwane

Month	Average temperature in °C max-min	Average rainfall in mm
Jan	28 - 17	74
Feb	28 - 17	55
Mar	27 - 16	42
Apr	25 - 13	17
May	23 - 08	07
Jun	22 - 05	03
Jul	20 - 04	01
Aug	23 - 07	02
Sep	26 - 10	03
Oct	26 - 14	28
Nov	27 - 15	68
Dec	28 - 17	61

Mafiekeng

Month	Average temperature in °C max-min	Average rainfall in mm
Jan	35 - 13	90
Feb	33 - 11	80
Mar	32 - 09	83
Apr	30 - 04	30
May	27 - 11	25
Jun	24 - 10	20
Jul	24 - 09	15
Aug	27 - 11	20
Sep	32 - 02	25
Oct	34 - 07	50
Nov	34 - 08	75
Dec	35 - 10	90

Bloemfontein

Month	Average temperature in °C max-min	Average rainfall in mm
Jan	30 - 16	91
Feb	28 - 15	79
Mar	26 - 13	76
Apr	23 - 08	56
May	19 - 04	25
Jun	17 - 01	08
Jul	16 - 01	10
Aug	19 - 03	20
Sep	23 - 06	20
Oct	26 - 10	51
Nov	27 - 12	66
Dec	29 - 14	61

Springbok

Month	Average temperature in °C max-min	Average rainfall in mm
Jan	42 - 09	00
Feb	42 - 10	00
Mar	39 - 07	01
Apr	38 - 05	03
May	32 - 04	05
Jun	30 - 02	20
Jul	29 - 01	18
Aug	34 - 02	19
Sep	36 - 02	04
Oct	38 - 05	02
Nov	38 - 07	01
Dec	40 - 08	00

Sport and activities

Birdwatching

ⓘ **Southern African Birding**, www.sabird ing.co.za, is a good source of information. Birdwatching tours are offered by **Bird-Watch Cape**, T021-762 5059, www.bird watch.co.za, and **Safariwise**, T023-342 7534, www.birdwatching.co.za.

With over 700 species of bird recorded in South Africa, birdwatching has become a popular pastime that is easily combined with game viewing. The country's incredibly diverse ecosystems, ranging from fynbos and semi-desert to rainforest, support a fascinating variety of birds, including rare species that are endemic to South Africa.

Bungee jumping

ⓘ **Face Adrenalin**, T042-281 1255, www.faceadrenalin.com, operates the Bloukrans Bridge jump.

The most popular location in the country is at the Bloukrans River Bridge between Plettenberg Bay and Tsitsikamma National Park. This claims to be the highest jump in the world, with a drop of 216 m, and they also offer a cable slide across the gorge.

Diving

ⓘ For more information about dive sites and diving holidays visit **www.dive-southafrica.co.za**. Other operators are listed in the relevant places throughout the book.

The convergence of two major ocean environments provides the South African coast with a particularly rich and diverse marine flora and fauna. The Agulhas current continually sweeps warm water down from the subtropical Indian Ocean and meets the cold nutrient-rich waters of the Atlantic. This

A rare golden weaver in Addo Elephant National Park.

mixing of water temperatures has created a marvellous selection of marine ecosystems, ranging from the tropical coral reefs of KwaZulu Natal to the temperate kelp forests around Cape Point. The best time of year to dive the east and southern coast is during the South African winter from April to October when the prevailing wind is from the west. Visibility is generally better and the waters are calmer. Summertime, October to March, is when you can brave the icy waters of the Atlantic for some incredible wreck and kelp dives – visibility often exceeds 20 m. If you want to get away from the crowds, avoid South African holidays whenever possible. Dive schools are listed in the relevant chapters. In KwaZulu Natal Sodwana Bay, just south of the Mozambique border, is very popular with South African divers due to its warm, clear waters, tropical reefs and rare but magical whale sharks. There are common sightings of turtles, reef sharks and stingrays, along with a huge variety of hard and soft corals and colourful reef fish. Aliwal Shoal, 5 km offshore, south of Umkomaas, is famous for its ragged-tooth shark season, while Protea Banks, 8 km off Shelly Beach, is for experienced divers only and is known for its hammerheads. In the Eastern Cape, despite

A diver and dive boat over the reefs in Sodwana Bay.

low visibility, the sites around Port Elizabeth are magnificent and boast coral colours more vivid than tropical waters. It is not unusual to see huge pods of dolphins, African penguins and southern right whales in the bay. Along the Garden Route the Underwater Trail at Storms River Mouth camp, Tsitsikamma National Park, is reasonably protected and there are a number of wreck and lagoon dives around Knysna. The area is notorious for great white sharks and dive briefings include rules for reducing the risk of inviting their attention. Plettenberg Bay is popular for its soft coral reefs and sheltered location. Home to dolphins and seals, the bay also acts as a nursery to the endangered southern right whales, which come to calve in winter and spring (July-December). From Cape Town, kelp diving is very popular: the sealife is prolific and the sighting of playful and inquisitive seals and shy sharks (dogfish) common. If the Cape waters are too cold, you can dive in the tanks of the aquarium at the V&A Waterfront. The tank is surprisingly large, with inquisitive ragged-tooth sharks, stingrays, turtles and large predator fish.

Diving with sharks

Dyer Island is located 10 km off Gansbaai on Walker Bay. Populated by seals, penguins, large gamefish and birds, the area is a natural hunting ground for the protected great white sharks. Shark cage diving raises many questions about teaching sharks to associate humans with food but, for many, cage diving is a chance to witness this magnificent animal in its natural habitat safely. For non-divers there is the opportunity to snorkel at the top of the cage.

Hiking

ⓘ Details of the trails are listed in the relevant chapters.

South Africa has an enormous number of well-developed hiking trails, many passing through spectacular areas of natural beauty. These range from pleasant afternoon strolls through nature reserves to challenging hikes in wilderness areas. Hiking in South Africa does involve some forward planning and permits, but the rewards and the choice of

Hiking in the bush

As experienced walkers will know, good preparation is the key to a successful and enjoyable hike. It is also important to remember that, however short or easy a walk may appear to be, walking in the bush is not like going for a stroll in the park – a few basic steps should be followed. Below is a short checklist of equipment and guidelines for hiking in the bush:

Day hikes Good walking boots or shoes; sunhat; minimum of 2 litres of water per person; first-aid kit; penknife; trail snacks (peanuts, biltong, dried fruit); binoculars, camera and bird-book/gamebook; toilet paper; matches to burn paper.

Additional overnight gear Sleeping bag; fleece or equivalent top (even in summer); torch; lightweight camping stove (it is not always permitted to collect firewood); matches/lighter/firelighters; dehydrated food (pasta, instant soups, etc).

▸▸ Don't leave litter or throw away cigarette butts.
▸▸ Leave everything as you find it; don't pick plants or remove fossils or rocks.
▸▸ Stick to marked trails especially in the bush – it's easy to lose your way.
▸▸ Camp away from waterholes so as not to frighten game away.
▸▸ Never feed the animals.
▸▸ Remember, in the southern hemisphere the sun goes via the north not the south.

trails are well worth the effort. Hiking opportunities begin in Cape Town on Table Mountain and the coastal trails around Cape Point, with a number of longer trails along the Garden Route. Inland, the Cederberg is an excellent and isolated hiking area, but the most popular and best-known region is the uKhahlamba-Drakensberg National Park, bordering Lesotho. This is a national park nearly 300 km long where a network of trails (some climbing to over 3000 m) offers hikers a vast mountain region with possibilities comparable to regions of the Himalayas.

Horse riding

① For information on specialist horse safari operators, contact the **African Horse Safari Association (AHSA)**, www.africanhorse.com.

Horse riding is a popular activity amongst farming communities and in mountainous areas. A good place to try it is the Drakensberg, where hotels can organize anything from a short morning trot to a six-day mountain safari. Longer treks are very popular in Lesotho, where ponies are the main form of transport in rural areas.

Western-style riding in the Maluti Mountains is organized by Bokpoort Farm outside Clarens in the Free State. On the Garden Route you can ride in the ancient forests close to Knysna and on the beaches in the Western Cape.

Kloofing

① **Abseil Africa**, www.abseilafrica.co.za, among other operators.

Kloofing, or canyoning, involves hiking, boulder-hopping and swimming along mountain rivers. One of the most popular kloofing trips is to the Kamikaze Kanyon in the mountains above Gordon's Bay just outside Cape Town.

Mountain biking

① **Mountain Bike South Africa**, www.mtbsa.co.za, has information on trails and events. Cape Town is also well equipped for mountain bikers; contact **Downhill Adventures**, T021-4220388, www.downhilladventures.com, who offer a number of day trips and rent out bikes.

Going on safari

No visit to South Africa is complete without at least one visit to a major game reserve. The game reserves here are not as crowded as the East African game parks and offer visitors the chance of seeing splendid African landscapes and wildlife including the Big Five: elephant, buffalo, rhinoceros, lion and leopard. The optimum times to go viewing are early in the morning and late in the afternoon.

The best season is during the winter months, from July to September, when dry weather forces animals to congregate around waterholes, and vegetation is lower and less dense, making it easier to spot wildlife. Summer weather, from November to January when rainfall is at its highest, also has its advantages as animals will be in good condition after feeding on the new shoots, and there are chances of seeing breeding displays and young animals. The landscape is green and lush, although the thick vegetation and the wide availability of water means that wildlife is far more widespread and difficult to spot.

South Africa's wildlife parks are well organized with good facilities for game viewing, including well-surfaced roads and hides overlooking waterholes. There are numerous safari companies operating out of Johannesburg, Durban and Cape Town, which can arrange accommodation and game-viewing trips as part of a tour. The cost varies, with everything from bargain backpacker tours to expensive luxury safaris. Organized tours can often provide more game-viewing opportunities – quite simply because a group means more pairs of eyes on the lookout. Experienced guides will also be adept at spotting well-camouflaged animals. For malaria-free safaris, stick to the game reserves of Madikwe, Pilanesberg and the Eastern Cape; for nature on a grander scale head to Kruger – but take precautions against malaria.

A male warthog in the bush

Organizations

▶▶ Most of the national parks and game reserves are under the jurisdiction of **South African National Parks** (SAN Parks), T012-428 9111, www.sanparks.org; **Cape Nature Conservation**, T021-426 0723, www.capenature.org.za; **KZN Wildlife**, T033-845 1000, www.kznwild life.com; and **Swaziland Big Game Parks**, T052-83944/3, www.biggameparks.org.
▶▶ If you are travelling independently and planning to visit a number of parks that come under the jurisdiction of SANParks, KZN Wildlife, Cape Nature, or Big Game Parks in Swaziland, then it might be well worth investing in a **Wild Card**. You pay a set fee – currently R940 per individual, R1640 per couple and R2210 for a family of four – and the card lasts for a year and covers all entry fees into the parks and reserves. This can represent great savings, especially if you are spending a considerable amount of time in the parks, but study your itinerary carefully and compare the costs before you buy. For more information, visit www.wildcard africa.co.za.

Paraglider launching from the ridge over the town of Hermanus.

Many nature reserves and wilderness areas have increased their accessibility for mountain bikes, with some excellent routes suitable for all levels of fitness. Some of the best organized regions include De Hoop Nature Reserve in the Overberg, the Tulbagh Valley, Kamiesberg in Namaqualand, Goegap Nature Reserve outside Springbok, and the mountains around Citrusdal.

Paragliding

ⓘ For a full list of clubs offering courses and tandem glides, visit www.paraglide-south-africa.com.

South Africa has several world-renowned paragliding locations; leaping from Lions Head in Cape Town or floating above the Kalahari are two of the most popular options. Cape Town aside, most of the action is around Kuruman in the Northern Cape and Barberton in Mpumalanga. Climatic conditions in South Africa are ideal – good thermal activity allows gliders to climb between 6 and 8 m a second and the cloud base is usually at 5000 m. The best season is between November and February.

Surfing

ⓘ For more information visit www.wavescape.co.za, which has everything you need to know about surfing in South Africa including SMS numbers to get the low-down on local wave action. Spike, who runs the website, is also the author of the book *Where to Surf in South Africa*.

South Africa has quickly established itself as a major surfing hotspot and has some of the best waves in the world. There are, however, two drawbacks to surfing in South Africa. Firstly, the water is cold, especially around the Cape, and full-length wetsuits are generally essential. Second, there is a small risk of shark attack – but remember that attacks on surfers are very rare. Wherever you surf, be sure to listen to local advice, vital not just for safety but also for learning about the best surf spots.

Jeffrey's Bay on the south coast of the Eastern Cape is undoubtedly South Africa's surfing hotspot, known for its consistently good surf and host to the annual Billabong surf championships in July. This is also a good place to learn to surf, with a number of courses available and areas of reliable, small breaks perfect for beginners. The whole southern coast is in fact dotted with good breaks, particularly around Port Elizabeth and East London. Cape Town, too, has an ever-expanding surf scene with some excellent, reliable breaks on the Atlantic and False Bay beaches. Surfing in the Indian Ocean at Durban and the KwaZulu Natal beaches is far warmer than the cool oceans of the Cape, though it's only permitted at designated areas due to the unpredictable currents. The Golden Mile on Durban's beachfront has good surf, well protected by lifeguards and the presence of shark nets. Floodlit night surfing, sometimes arranged in Durban, is equally entertaining for spectators. Many backpacker hostels along the coast offer board rental, escorted surfaris and surfing lessons, and there are dedicated surf schools in Jeffrey's Bay, Durban and Cape Town.

Whale watching

ⓘ www.whaleroute.com has information about whale migration routes and explanations of breaching, blowing, lobtailing and spy hopping. Contact the **Greater Hermanus Tourism Bureau**, T021-3122629, www.hermanus.co.za, for more details.

Whale Coast, along Walker Bay near Cape Town, trumpets itself as the world's best land-based whale-watching spot and with good reason. Between July and November southern right and humpback whales congregate in impressive numbers in the bay to calve. Whales can also be seen in the sheltered bays from Elands Bay on the west coast all the way

round to Mossel Bay and even Tsitsikamma on the south coast. Boat-based whale watching is also popular from points along the KwaZulu Natal coast, especially June-October, when southern right, mink and humpback whales travel from Mozambique to their breeding grounds at the Cape.

Whitewater rafting

ⓘ Details of the operators are listed in the relevant chapters.

There are several excellent rapids in South Africa: the Ash River in Free State; the Gariep (Orange) River by the Augrabies Falls or near Kimberley in the Northern Cape; the Great Usutu River in Swaziland; and the Sabie, Olifants and Blyde rivers in Mpumalanga.

Wine tasting

ⓘ For details of all the routes, visit www.wine.co.za. Also check out Footprint's *Wine Travel Guide to the World*.

The Winelands, near Cape Town, is South Africa's oldest and most beautiful wine-producing area and the most popular tourist destination in the province after Cape Town itself. There are several wine routes criss-crossing the valleys, visiting hundreds of wine estates, which open their doors for tastings, cellar tours and sales. Wine is increasingly grown up the West Coast and there are now established wine routes in this region too.

SENA AKSOY/SHUTTERSTOCK

SEAN NEL/SHUTTERSTOCK

Above left: Vineyard in the Cape Winelands. **Above right**: Surfer at the icy-cold hollow barrel break at Llandudno Beach.

2010 FIFA World Cup™

Back in 2004, when FIFA president Joseph Blatter opened the envelope in Zurich and announced that South Africa had won the bid to host the 2010 FIFA World Cup™, his words were barely audible above the roaring crowd, and a collective cheer rose above South Africa. Sitting next to Blatter, Nelson Mandela couldn't hold back the tears as he raised the 2010 FIFA World Cup™ Official Trophy and said "I feel like a young man of 15". Since then South Africa has been in the throes of organizing the biggest sporting event on earth and the host cities are finalizing their preparations for the tournament, which will take place from 11 June to 11 July 2010. This will be the 19th FIFA World Cup™ and the first to be played on African soil. The final 32 teams will play 64 matches at 10 stadiums in nine host cities. South Africa's team Bafana Bafana ('the boys') automatically qualify, and Africa will have six teams competing in total.

Johannesburg Soccer City has been upgraded to a capacity of 94,700. It is the tournament's principal stadium and will host the opening ceremony, five first-round matches, one second-round match, a quarter-final, the final and the closing ceremony. Ellis Park Stadium has been upgraded to a capacity of 61,000 and will host five first-round matches, a second-round match and a quarter-final.

Durban Moses Mabidha Stadium has been built on the site of the demolished Kings Park Soccer Stadium and has a capacity of 70,000. It will host five first-round matches, one second-round match and one of the semi-finals.

Cape Town Green Point Stadium has been built on the demolished old one, and has a capacity of 68,000. It will host five first-round matches, one second-round match, a quarter-final and the other semi-final.

Tshwane (Pretoria) Loftus Versfeld Stadium has been upgraded to a capacity of 50,000, and will host five first-round matches and one second-round match.

Nelson Mandela Bay (Port Elizabeth) Nelson Mandela Bay Stadium is newly built with a capacity of 48,000, and will

JACO WOLMARANS/ALAMY

Above: Young goal keeper in action near Cape Town's Green Point Stadium when it was under construction. **Opposite page:** 2010 FIFA World Cup™ Official Mascot.

© 2007 FIFA TM

Zakumi

The official mascot for the 2010 FIFA World Cup South Africa™ is Zakumi, a leopard with green hair. His name derives from combining ZA, the international abbreviation for South Africa, and 'kumi', a word that means '10' in several African languages. The story goes that he was born on Youth Day (which commemorates the 1977 Soweto Uprising) in 1994, the same year as the birth of South Africa's democracy, and represents those in South Africa born in a free and democratic society. He will turn 16 on 16 June, which is also South Africa's second first-round match in the tournament. He wears a gold and green football strip, the same colours as not only Bafana Bafana's, but South Africa's Springbok rugby team and Protea cricket team. Zakumi's priority is to turn the 2010 FIFA World Cup South Africa™ into one unforgettable party and show the thousands of international guests the warmth and spirit of the African continent.

host five first-round matches, a second-round match and a quarter-final.

Bloemfontein Free State Stadium has been upgraded to a capacity of 48,000, and will host five first-round and one second-round match.

Polokwane Peter Mokaba Stadium has been built on the site of the demolished old one and now has a capacity of 45,000. It will host four first-round matches.

Nelspruit Mbombela Stadium is newly built and has a capacity of 46,000 and will host four first-round matches.

Rustenburg Royal Bafokeng Stadium has been upgraded to a capacity of 42,000 and will host five first-round and one second-round match.

For more information, visit the websites www.fifa.com or www.sa2010.gov.za.

How big is your footprint?

Sustainable or ecotourism has been described as "ethical, considerate or informed tourism where visitors can enjoy the natural, historical and social heritage of an area without causing adverse environmental, socio-economic or cultural impacts that compromise the long-term ability of that area and its people to provide a recreational resource for future generations and an income for themselves". South Africa is a beautiful, wild country but also a living, working landscape and a fragile, vulnerable place. By observing certain guidelines outlined in the box, opposite, and behaving responsibly you can help to minimize your impact and protect the natural and cultural heritage of this wonderful country.

Environmental legislation plays its part in protecting tourist destinations. CITES (Convention on International Trade in Endangered Species of Wild Fauna and Flora) aims to control the trade in live specimens of endangered plants and animals and also "recognizable parts or derivatives" of protected species. International trade in elephant ivory, sea turtle products and the skins of wild cats is illegal. Restrictions have also been imposed on trade in reptile skins, coral and certain plants and wild birds. If you feel the need to purchase souvenirs derived from wildlife, it would be prudent to check whether they are protected. Importation of CITES-protected species can lead to heavy fines, confiscation of goods and even imprisonment.

Go green: six ways to skip the flights

▸▸ Take a ferry from southern Spain to Morocco (www.trasmediterranea.es) and drive yourself to South Africa.
▸▸ Board a freight ship from the UK to Cape Town (www.strandtravel.co.uk).
▸▸ Sail in style on Cunard from Southampton to Cape Town (www.cunard.co.uk).
▸▸ Avoid internal flights and drive yourself around South Africa.
▸▸ Hop on and off the Bas Bus (www.bazbus.com) from Cape Town to Durban and on to Tshwane (Pretoria).
▸▸ Sit back and relax on the Shosholoza Meyl train linking the major South African cities (www.spoornet.co.za).
For more ideas, see www.seat61.com.

W.WONK/SHUTTERSTOCK

Above: Traditional homesteads in rural South Africa. **Opposite page:** Safari-goers watching a solitary cheetah.

Travelling light

▸ Keep on the well-marked roads and track; off-road driving is harmful because smoke, oil and destruction of the grass layer cause soil erosion.

▸ Do not drive through closed roads or park areas. It is mandatory to enter and exit the parks through the authorized gates.

▸ For your own safety, stay in your vehicle at all times. Your vehicle serves as a blind or hide since animals will not usually identify it with humans. In all the parks that are visited by car, it is forbidden to leave the vehicle except in designated places, such as picnic sites or walking trails.

▸ Stick to the parks' opening hours; it is usually forbidden to drive from dusk to dawn unless you are granted a special authorization. At night you are requested to stay at your lodge or campsite.

▸ Never harass the animals. Make as little noise as possible; do not flash lights or make sudden movements to scare them away; never try and attract the animals' attention by calling out or whistling. Never chase the animals and always give way to them; they always have right of way.

▸ Do not feed the animals; the food you provide might make them ill. Once animals such as elephants learn that food is available from humans they can become aggressive and dangerous when looking for more and will eventually have to be shot. If camping at night in the parks, ensure that the animals cannot gain access to any food you are carrying.

▸ Do not drop any litter, used matches and cigarette butts; this not only increases fire risk in the dry season, but also some animals will eat whatever they find.

▸ Do not disturb other visitors: they have the same right as you to enjoy nature. If you discover a stopped vehicle and want to check what they are looking at, never hinder their sight or stop within their photographic field. If there is no room for another car, wait patiently for your turn; the others will eventually leave and the animals will still be there. If there is a group of vehicles, drivers should take it in turns to occupy the prime viewing spot. Always turn the engine off when you are watching game at close range.

▸ Do not drive too fast; the speed limit is usually 40 kph. Speeding damages road surfaces, makes more noise and increases the risk of running over animals.

▸ Wild animals are dangerous; despite their beauty their reactions are unpredictable. Don't expose yourself to unnecessary risks; excessive confidence can lead to serious accidents.

South Africa on page and screen

Books to read

Probably the best-known South African novelist is John Coetzee, whose books include *Dusklands, In the Heart of the Country, Waiting for the Barbarians, Life & Times of Michael K* (winner of the 1983 Booker Prize), *Age of Iron, Foe* and *The Master of Petersburg*. He won the Booker Prize again in 1999 for his novel, *Disgrace*, and was awarded the Nobel Prize for Literature in 2003, only the fourth African author to do so and the second South African after Nadine Gordimer. His style is stark and intellectual, but surprisingly accessible. He is one of the most brilliant commentators on the effects of Apartheid.

Another award-winning South African novelist is Nadine Gordimer whose books include *A Guest of Honour, The Conservationist* (winner of the 1974 Booker Prize), *Burger's Daughter, July's People, A Sport of Nature, My Son's Story, None to Accompany Me* and *Get a Life*. Her beautifully written work tends to concentrate on the way wider political/social events impact on individual lives and she won the 1991 Noble Prize for Literature. *Playing the Enemy; Nelson Mandela and the Game that made a Nation* by John Carlin is about when South Africa won the 2005 Rugby World Cup. When Nelson Mandela embraced captain Francois Pienaar wearing a Springbok green and gold jersey, it was a moment that melted the hearts of all South Africans. It's currently being made into a film directed by Clint Eastwood, starring Matt Damon as Pienaar and Morgan Freeman as Mandela. For more books, see page 896.

Films to watch

Given its turbulent history, there have been a number of films made about South Africa. The epic *Zulu* (1964), starring Stanley Baker and a young Michael Caine was about the battle of Rorke's Drift, while *Zulu Dawn* (1979), with Peter O'Toole and Burt Lancaster, depicts the battle of Isandlwana. Movies covering the Apartheid regime include *Cry Freedom* (1987), the true story of black activist Stephen Biko (Denzel Washington), who mysteriously died in police custody and whose story was taken up by white journalist Donald Woods (Kevin Klein). *Mandela & DeKlerk* (1997) covers the negotiations between the two men who broke down Apartheid and stars Sidney Poitier and Michael Caine, while *Goodbye Bafana* (2007) follows the relationship of imprisoned Mandela (Dennis Haysbert) and his Afrikaner warder (Joseph Fiennes). *Stander* (2004) is the remarkable true story of Andre Stander (Thomas Jane), a 1970s South African police captain who robbed banks during his lunch hour then returned to the scene of the crime to lead the investigation. Home-grown South African film and Best Foreign Language Film in the 2005 Academy Awards, *Tsotsi* (2005) was filmed entirely in Tsotsi-taal, a township gangster rap, and is a powerful story of life for a troubled gang member in a Soweto slum.

Contents

Footprint features

Essentials

Getting there

Air

The three main international airports in **South Africa** are OR Tambo International Airport in Johannesburg, and Cape Town and Durban International Airports. OR Tambo (renamed from Johannesburg International Airport in 2006 after the late anti-Apartheid activist Oliver Tambo) is the regional hub with numerous daily flights to Europe, North America, Asia and Australia. Although most flights arrive in to Johannesburg, a fair number of carriers fly directly to Cape Town. There is a huge choice of routes and flights, but for the best fares you need to book three or four months in advance, especially over Christmas.

If you are flying through Johannesburg be sure to allow at least a couple of days to explore the attractions of Johannesburg or Tshwane (Pretoria) at the beginning or end of your trip.

South African Airways (SAA), operates the route between Moshoeshoe I International Airport in **Lesotho** and Johannesburg's OR Tambo International Airport, and there are daily flights. **South African Airways** (SAA), in conjunction with **SA Airlink** operates the route between Matsapha International Airport in **Swaziland** and Johannesburg's OR Tambo International Airport, again there are daily flights.

From Europe

British Airways, **Virgin** and **South African Airways** are the main operators with daily flights between London Gatwick or Heathrow and Johannesburg or Cape Town. Flying time is 10½ hours to Johannesburg and 11 hours to Cape Town. During peak season, a direct return flight can cost as much as US$1800 but in low season this can drop to below US$1000. Deals can be found if you book well in advance. Other European carriers include **Air France**, **Air Portugal**, **Alitalia**, **Austrian Airlines**, **Iberia**, **KLM**, **Lufthansa**, and **Swiss International** (LX). Indirect flights from other airlines can also be good value: **Kenya Airways** flies between London and Johannesburg, via Nairobi; **Air Namibia** flies between Frankfurt and London to Johannesburg and Cape Town via Windhoek; and **Emirates** flies daily to Johannesburg via Dubai from just about anywhere else in the world.

Jet lag is not an issue if flying from Europe to South Africa as there is only a minimal time difference.

From North America

Delta Airlines has code share agreement with **South African Airways**, who run daily direct flights from Atlanta to Johannesburg with connections to Cape Town. Flight time is around 17 hours. **American Airlines** has an agreement with **British Airways**, with flights to Johannesburg and Cape Town via London Heathrow.

From Australia, New Zealand and Asia

Qantas code shares with **South African Airways**, and between them they run a direct daily flight to and from Perth and Johannesburg, flying time 10 hours, with connections from across Australia. Flights run approximately four times per week and on some the same flight continues on from Perth to Sydney. **Air Mauritius** flies between Perth and Johannesburg once a week with a touchdown on Mauritius. **Singapore Airlines** offers regular flights between Sydney and Johannesburg via Singapore, and has a code sharing agreement with **Air New Zealand** (which means that flights from Wellington to Johannesburg have

Packing for South Africa

A good rule of thumb is to take half the clothes you think you'll need and double the money. Laundry services are cheap and reliable in South Africa, you shouldn't need to bring too many clothes. A backpack or travelpack (a hybrid backpack/suitcase), rather than a rigid suitcase, covers most eventualities and survives the rigours of a variety of modes of travel well. A lock for your luggage is strongly advised – there are cases of pilfering by airport baggage handlers the world over. Light cotton clothing is best, with a fleece or woollen jumper for evenings. Hikers will need comfortable walking boots that have been worn in. Those going on camping safaris will need a sleeping bag, towel and torch. During the day you will need a hat, sunglasses and high factor sun cream. Everything you could need on holiday is available to buy in South Africa. Before you leave home, send yourself an email to a web-based account with details of your passport, driver's licence, traveller's cheques, credit cards and travel insurance numbers. Be sure that someone at home also has access to this information.

two stops). **Malaysia Airlines** has regular flights from Perth, Melbourne, Sydney and Darwin in Australia and Auckland in New Zealand to Kuala Lumpur, connecting with a flight to Johannesburg three times a week, which continues on to Cape Town and then Buenos Aires (Argentina). **Cathay Pacific** flies to Johannesburg from Hong Kong once a week.

From Africa and the Middle East

Johannesburg and, in some instances, Cape Town are served by a number of regional airlines that link all the major cities of Africa. These include **Air Botswana**, **Air Madagascar**, **Air Mauritius**, **Air Malawi**, **Air Namibia**, **Air Seychelles**, **Air Zimbabwe**, **Egypt Air**, **Ethiopian Airlines**, **Ghana Airways**, **Kenya Airways**, **Kulula.com** and **South African Airways** and its subsidiaries **SA Express** and **SA Airlink**. **Emirates** connects Johannesburg with the Middle East.

Airport information

South Africa's international airports are modern and efficient, with food courts, shops, banks and ATMs, post offices, car and mobile phone rental desks, and shuttle services into the respective cities. Although there are some direct flights to Cape Town, the majority of international flights arrive in Johannesburg, and then connect on to Durban, Cape Town and the other cities. Johannesburg International Airport has undergone a major upgrade in the last few years and now has a brand new departures terminal in-between the international and domestic arrivals terminals. Regardless of your eventual destination, immigration is done at Johannesburg, which usually means you have to pick up your luggage from the international arrivals terminal and check in again at domestic departures. Remember to put locks on your bags – there have been many incidents of things going missing from luggage en route through Johannesburg airport. For information on airport facilities T011-921 6262 and for flight arrivals T086-727 7888 or www.acsa.co.za.

Lesotho's **Moshoeshoe I International Airport** is 21 km south of Maseru along the Main South Road. **Matsapha International Airport** is 8 km from Manzini in Swaziland's Ezulwini Valley. ▸▸ *For further details, see Ins and outs, pages 78, 437, 560 and 789, and Transport, pages 131, 455, 587 and 792.*

Border crossings

There are good road connections between South Africa and Namibia, Botswana, Mozambique, Lesotho, Swaziland and Zimbabwe. In total, South Africa shares 55 border crossings with neighbouring countries. They are generally open daily 0600-1800, though quieter borders will have shorter hours, while the principal border crossings on the main highways are open 24 hours.

South Africa–Botswana
Pioneer Gate and **Ramatlabana** are the main crossings and are in striking distance of Botswana's capital, Gaborone, which lies not far over the border. For those coming from the Cape and the interior of South Africa the border at Ramatlabana (6000-2000), 26 km north of Mafikeng on the R503, is the most logical (see page 699), while from Gauteng, Pioneer Gate (24 hour) is on the N4, 56 km northwest of Zeerust. **Makgobistad** (24 hour), 70 km west of Mafikeng, and **Tlokweng Gate** (6000-2200), next to Madikwe Game Reserve and 101 km north of Zeerust on the R49, are alternative border posts. Crossings are usually swift and efficient.

South Africa–Lesotho
Caledonspoort (T058-223 8400, South Africa, daily 0600-2200), see page 798, is the logical border post for visitors arriving in their own transport from Gauteng or northern KwaZulu Natal. **Ficksburg/Maputsoe Bridge** (T051-933 2760, South Africa, 24 hours daily), see page 729, is one of the busiest crossings. **Maseru Bridge** (T051-924 4300, South Africa, 24 hours daily), page 788, is usually less crowded and is used by visitors arriving from Bloemfontein. **Van Rooyen's** (T051-583 1525, South Africa, daily 0600-2200), page 810, is between Mafeteng and the small Free State town of Wepener. **Makhaleng Bridge** (T051-673 1484, South Africa, daily 0800-1600), page 815, is close to Mohales Hoek and on the South African road to Zastron. **Tele Bridge** (T051-633 1099, South Africa, daily 0600-2200), page 815, the southernmost border, is close to the town of Moyeni (Quthing).

There are five road crossings from the eastern mountains of Lesotho into the uKhahlamba-Drakensberg Park. **Monontsa Pass** (T058-713 1600, South Africa, daily 0800-1600) is a little-used crossing between the Lesotho settlement of Libono and the South African village of Phuthaditjaba near to the Golden Gate National Park (see page 731) in the Free State. This is the most northerly border crossing and can only be accessed by 4WD. **Sani Pass** (T033-702 1169, South Africa, daily 0800-1600), page 800, is a well-known scenic crossing, with poor roads only passable by 4WDs, though presently this road on the South African side is being tarred (should be completed by end of 2010). **Qacha's Nek** (T039-2564391, daily 0600-2200), page 811, is now tarred and is accessible by a normal car, and traffic here is increasing. Two border crossings into the Drakensberg are totally unmanned on the Lesotho side and you can only walk or ride a horse across them: **Ongeluksnek** (T039-256 7001, South Africa, daily 0800-1600) and **Nkonkoana–Bushman's Nek** (T033-701 1212, South Africa, daily 0800-1600), page 812. If you enter Lesotho at either of these, you are required to present yourself at the nearest immigration office in Qachas Nek or Quthing to complete formalities.

South Africa–Mozambique
The journey between South Africa and Maputo has improved considerably since the completion of a toll road between Nelspruit and Maputo via the border at **Lebombo–Ressano Garcia** at Komatipoort, page 608. There's a smaller crossing at **Ponta do Ouro**, in Maputaland, page 549, which, while being accessible by road in a normal car on the South African side, requires a 4WD in Mozambique. Visas for Mozambique are available at the border for US$25, which can also be paid in rand.

South Africa–Namibia
The main crossing point is **Vioolsdrift** (24 hours), page 778, 714 km north of Cape Town along the N7. Less frequently used borders are at **Nakop–Ariamsvlei** west of Upington, page 759, and **Rietfontein** and **Mata Mata**, page 764.

South Africa–Swaziland
The principal entry points from South Africa are **Ngwenya–Oshoek** (daily 0700-2200), page 838, is the busiest and most convenient for Gauteng; **Mahamba** (daily 0700-2200), page 834, east of Piet Retief in Mpumalanga; and **Lavumisa–Golela** (daily 0700-2200), page 834, the most convenient for Durban. Minor entry points tend to have shorter opening hours, such as **Bulembu/Josefsdal** (daily 0800-1600), see page 839.

South Africa–Zimbabwe
The only border crossing is at **Beitbridge** (24 hours), page 674, a notoriously slow crossing during peak periods, with long queues and thorough searches.

Swaziland–Mozambique
The **Lomahasha–Namaacha** border (0700-2000) is 98 km northeast of Manzini on the road that goes through Hlane Royal National Park and is the only crossing between Swaziland and Mozambique. Visas for Mozambique can be obtained at the border. Maputo is 75 km away on a newly tarred road. See page 835.

Airlines

From the UK and Europe
Air Namibia, T0870-774 0965 (UK), www.airnamibia.com.na.
British Airways, T0870-850 9850 (UK), www.britishairways.com.
Emirates, T0870-243 2222 (UK), www.emirates.com.
Kenya Airways, T01784-888233 (UK), www.kenya-airways.com.
KLM, T0204-747747 (Netherlands), www.klm.com.
Lufthansa, T01805-838426 (Germany), www.lufthansa.com.
South African Airways, T0870-747 1111 (South Africa), www.flysaa.com.
Virgin, T0870-574 7747 (UK), www.virgin-atlantic.com.

From North America
Delta, T1800-221 1212 (USA), www.delta.com.
United Airlines, T1800-538 2929 (USA), www.united.com.

From Australia, New Zealand and Asia
Cathay Pacific, T0852-2747 1888 (Hong Kong), www.cathaypacific.com.
Qantas, T131313 (from anywhere in Australia), www.qantas.com.au.
Singapore Airlines, T065-6223 8888 (Singapore), www.singaporeair.com.

Air Malaysia, T0603-7843 3000 (Malaysia), www.malaysia-airlines.com.
Air Mauritius, T+230-207 7070 (Mauritius), www.airmauritius.com.
Air New Zealand, T0800-737000 (New Zealand), www.airnewzealand.com.

In North America
Air Brokers International, T1800-883 3273, www.airbrokers.com.
Airtech, T1212-219 7000, www.airtech.com.
STA Travel, T1800-781 4040, www.statravel.com.
Travel CUTS, T1866-246 9762 (Canada), www.travelcuts.com.

Discount flight agents

In the UK and Ireland
Flightbookers, T0871-223 5000, www.ebookers.com.
Flight Centre, T0870-499 9931, www.flightcentre.co.uk.
STA Travel, T0871-230 0040, www.statravel.co.uk.
Trailfinders, T0845-058 5858, www.trailfinders.com.
Travelbag, T0800-804 8911, www.travelbag.co.uk.

In Australia and New Zealand
Flight Centre, T133-133 (Australia), www.flightcentre.com.au.
Skylinks, T02-9223 4277, www.skylink.com.au.
STA Travel, T134-782, www.statravel.com.au (Australia), T0800-474400, www.statravel.com.nz (New Zealand).
Travel.com.au, T1300-130482, www.travel.com.au.

Rail

There are trains between Johannesburg and Komatipoort, from where buses on the Mozambique side of the border operate services to and from Maputo. The journey to the border is 12½ hours and is overnight in both directions. This is very slow compared to the direct bus journey between the two cities, which takes less than eight hours. Accommodation is in two or four-sleeper compartments and there's a restaurant car franchised to a fast-food chain. Although there is a railway, trains no longer run between Zimbabwe and South Africa. Passenger trains are run by **Shosholoza Meyl**, T0860-00888 (in South Africa), T011-774 4555 (from overseas), www.shosholozameyl.co.za, which is part of South Africa's national railway company Spoornet.

Namibia's railway company, **Transnamib Starline Passenger Services**, T+264 (0)61-298 2175, www.transnamib.com.na, runs a service between Upington in South Africa and Windhoek twice a week. However, as Namibia's trains are primarily used for freight, it is slow going with a lot of stops. Despite this the passenger compartments are comfortable with airline-like seats, videos are shown and there are vending machines for drinks and snacks.

Road

South Africa

Bus The three main coach companies cover routes across South Africa's borders and some services go as far as Malawi. All bus tickets can be booked online at www.computicket.com. **Translux**, T0861-589282 (in South Africa), T011-774 3333 (from overseas), www.translux.co.za, runs services from Johannesburg and Tshwane (Pretoria) to Blantyre, Bulawayo, Harare, Lusaka, and Maputo. **Intercape**, T0861-287287 (in South Africa), T012-380 4400

(from overseas), www.intercape.co.za, runs coaches from Johannesburg/Tshwane (Pretoria) to Gaborone, Windhoek and Maputo, and from Cape Town to Livingstone in Zambia (via Namibia). **Greyhound**, T083-915 9000 (in South Africa), T011-276 8550 (from overseas), www. greyhound.co.za, runs coaches from Tshwane (Pretoria) to Maputo, Harare and Bulawayo.

Car If crossing any international borders in a private car, you must have a registration document, insurance and a driving licence printed in English with a photograph. With the exception of Zimbabwe, you should be able to take a hire car into all the bordering countries, though check with the rental company first. You will need a letter of permission to take a car across a border if it is not registered in your name, and a ZA sticker (available from any AA shop). Botswana, Namibia, Lesotho, Swaziland, Mozambique and South Africa are all part of SADC's (Southern Africa Development Community) joint customs agreement, so if you are in your own car travelling on a carnet, you only have to produce this when crossing your first or last border to the SADC countries. ▸▸ *For border crossings, see box, page 36.*

Lesotho and Swaziland
Lesotho The most common way of entering and leaving Lesotho is by road. There is a R5 entry and departure tax on all vehicles. For driving licence and insurance requirements and for driving across international borders, see above.

Swaziland There are 12 border posts in total, 11 with South Africa and one with Mozambique. Visas for Mozambique are now issued at the border. The border posts are open every day of the year, including public holidays, and immigration and customs formalities take about 30 minutes. There is an E50 road tax on all vehicles entering Swaziland and cars hired in South Africa are usually permitted into Swaziland. ▸▸ *For further details, see Transport, page 829.*

Getting around

South Africa has an efficient transport network linking its towns and cities. The road systems and flight networks are the best in Africa, making travelling the considerable distances a straightforward experience. Affordable domestic flights link the cities, a sophisticated army of private coaches criss-crosses the country, and the train system, although painfully slow, offers another way of getting from A to B. City transport, however, is a problem. South Africa's cities universally lack safe and reliable urban public transport, often making private transport the only option. Though this is improving in line with requirements for the 2010 FIFA World Cup™, and new transport systems will be up and running in time for the tournament. Presently, Integrated Bus Systems are being laid out along some main roads in Johannesburg and Cape Town. The system will work in a similar way to a light railway or tram and will have stations. The buses will run on dedicated lanes that can also be used by cyclists. The new vehicles will be similar to the 'bendy buses' in London in the UK.

Air

South Africa
There is a far-reaching and efficient domestic service and regular daily flights connect Johannesburg with other major towns, all of which can be reached within a couple of

hours' flying time. On popular routes where there is some competition, such as Durban–Johannesburg or Johannesburg–Cape Town, a single ticket is usually only a little more expensive than a bus ticket.

Airlines

By booking early online, good deals can be found with all the airlines. You can either book directly, or through Computicket (www.computicket.com) which represents all the domestic airlines.

1Time, T0861-345345 (in South Africa), T011-928 8000 (from overseas), www.1time.aero, is another budget carrier that flies between Johannesburg, Cape Town, Durban, George, Port Elizabeth and East London. They have rather stylish planes with spacious leather seats, bought from a bankrupt airline. They now have a weekly flight between Johannesburg and Zanzibar.

British Airways Comair, T011-441 8600, www.britishairways.com, has daily flights between Johannesburg and Cape Town, Durban and Port Elizabeth, as well as flights between Johannesburg and Mauritius, Windhoek, Livingstone, Victoria Falls and Harare.

Kulula.com, T0861-585852 (in South Africa), T011-921 0111 (from overseas), www.kulula.

com, also owned by British Airways, is a hugely successful no-frills airline and fun to travel with (when you get off the plane the crew in their jeans and T-shirts tell you not to forget to take your husband and children with you). Daily services between Cape Town, Durban, Johannesburg, Port Elizabeth and George. Also now flies to Mauritius, Windhoek and Harare on a code-share agreement with BA.

Mango, T0861-162646 (in South Africa), T011-359 1222 (from overseas), ww5.flymango.com, is the newest of the no-frills operators with daily flights between Johannesburg, Cape Town, Durban and Bloemfontein.

South African Airways (SAA), central reservations T0861-359722 (in South Africa), T011-978 5313 (from overseas), www.flysaa.com, cover most of the country as well as other southern African cities in conjunction with both **SA Airlink**, www.flyairlink.com, and **SA Express**, www.saexpress.co.za.

Rail

All the major cities are linked by rail and while this is a comfortable and relaxing way to travel, it is very slow. The trains are run by **Shosholoza Meyl**, part of the national network **Spoornet**, T0860-008888 (in South Africa), T011-7744555 (from overseas), www.shosholozameyl.co.za. Timetables and fares can be found on the website. Shosholoza means 'to push forward' or 'to strive' and is the name of a popular traditional African song favoured particularly by hard-working men whose job it was to lay railway lines. All the trains travel overnight, the Cape Town–Durban service over two nights, so they arrive at some stations en route at inconvenient times. There are sleeping carriages, with coupés that sleep four or six people, with a wash basin, fold-away table and bunk beds. The 'sitter' carriages are not recommended for long journeys as there is only open coach seating. Always book well in advance for sleeping compartments, especially during local holidays. Refreshments are available from trolleys or dining cars, but these have been franchised to burger-type chains, so don't expect brilliant food. Note that all trains have a problem with security: if you leave your compartment, make sure a train official locks it after you. Accompanied children under four travel free; children between seven and 12 years travel for half price.

Routes include: **Johannesburg–East London** (Sunday to Tuesday, Thursday and Friday in both directions, 19 hours); **Johannesburg–Musina** (Sunday to Friday in both directions,

14 hours); **Johannesburg–Komatipoort** (Sunday to Friday in both directions, 13 hours); **Johannesburg–Bloemfontein** (Wednesday, Friday and Saturday in both directions, 12 hours); **Johannesburg–Durban** (Sunday, Monday and Wednesday to Friday in both directions, eight hours); **Durban–Cape Town** (Wednesday), **Cape Town–Durban** (Monday, 38 hours), **Tshwane (Pretoria)–Cape Town** (daily in both directions, 29 hours); **Johannesburg–Port Elizabeth** (Sunday, Monday and Wednesday to Friday in both directions, 18 hours).

    Spoornet also operate a more upmarket service, the **Premier Classe**, T0860-008888 (in South Africa), T011-774 5247 (from overseas), www.premierclasse.co.za, between Johannesburg and Cape Town (25 hours), Johannesburg and Durban (14 hours), both twice a week, and Cape Town and Port Elizabeth (25½ hours). The carriages are a lot nicer than the regular train, with proper food in a sit-down dining car, and extras in the coupés like toiletries and dressing gowns. Fares include all meals.

    There are a number of short excursions on restored vintage steam trains through amazing scenery. These are described in the relevant chapters.

Luxury trains

If the journey is more important than the destination, then experience a trip on an old-fashioned luxury train, which operate much like five-star hotels on wheels. The **Blue Train**, T021-334 8459, www.bluetrain.co.za, is considered to be southern Africa's premier luxury train with 18 carriages that can accommodate 84 passengers. The wood-panelled coaches feature luxury coupés with en suite bathrooms, elegant lounge cars and fine dining in the restaurant car. It runs scheduled services between Tshwane (Pretoria) and Cape Town, one day and one night with a stop at Kimberley to visit the Kimberley Mine Museum and Big Hole (see page 745), and occasional trips to Durban and Pilanesberg Game Reserve. A similar luxury train experience is the **Pride of Africa**, operated by Rovos Rail, T012-315 8242, www.rovos.co.za, which also runs between Tshwane (Pretoria) and Cape Town with occasional trips to Victoria Falls. Check out the websites for routes and prices.

Metro commuter trains and high-speed rail links

Many of the larger cities such as Tshwane (Pretoria), Johannesburg and Cape Town have a network of metro commuter services linking the suburbs to the business districts. These should generally be avoided as there have been many cases of robbery. Avoid the metro around Johannesburg and Tshwane (Pretoria) at all costs. Some tourists use the Cape Town metro, www.metrorail.co.za, on selected routes; namely from the city to Simon's Town on the Cape Peninsula, and experience no problems. If you do use it, stick to first class, travel only during rush hour (0600-0800, 1600-1800) and avoid it at weekends.

    The **Gautrain** – a high-speed rail link between Johannesburg, Tshwane (Pretoria) and OR Tambo International Airport – is currently being built in Gauteng. It is due to be completed by the 2010 FIFA World Cup™. See page 563 or visit www.gautrain.com for details of its progress.

Road

South Africa

Intercity coaches **Greyhound**, T083-915 9000 (in South Africa), T011-276 8550 (from overseas), www.greyhound.co.za; **Intercape**, T0861-287287 (in South Africa), T012-380 4400 (from overseas), www.intercape.co.za; and **Translux**, T0861-589282 (in South Africa), T011-774 3333 (from overseas), www.translux.co.za, are the three major long-distance bus companies that run between towns and popular destinations, with a large number of buses on each route. All have online booking and seats can be reserved several months in advance. You can also book through Computicket, www.computicket.com, online or at any of their kiosks in the shopping malls or any branch of Checkers supermarket. The coaches are air-conditioned and have a toilet; some sell refreshments and show videos. They will stop at least every three to four hours to change drivers and give the passengers a chance to stretch their legs. For long journeys the prices are reasonable (though always compare fares with the no-frills airlines), but short routes are expensive for budget travellers. However, they are an efficient and a safe way of travelling and, on night routes, bear in mind that you will be saving the cost of a hotel room. Note that the long distance buses take 10 hours to do the same route as opposed to around 24 hours on the train.

Baz Bus The Baz Bus, T021-439 2323, www.bazbus.com, is a hop-on, hop-off bus that offers a convenient and sociable alternative to the main bus services. It is specifically designed for backpackers visiting South Africa and remains one of the most popular ways of seeing the country on a budget. One of the best aspects of the service is that the bus collects and drops off passengers at their chosen backpacker hostel. There are a few exceptions such as Hermanus, Coffee Bay and Sani Pass, where the bus will drop you off at the closest point on the main road, and the hostels will then meet you for an extra charge, though you must arrange this in advance. The Baz Bus route is Cape Town–Durban along the coast, and Durban–Tshwane (Pretoria) on two routes via either Swaziland or the Drakensberg. Visit the website for the full timetable.

Tickets are priced per segment, for example from Cape Town to Durban. You are allowed to hop off and on the bus as many times as you like in the given segment, but must not backtrack. This is where the savings are made, since other commercial buses, such as Translux and Greyhound, charge high prices for short journeys. However, note that for long distances without stops, the mainline buses are better value. YHA and ISIC card holders are entitled to a 5% discount on Baz Bus tickets.

The Baz Bus drivers are a great source of information, both about the places of interest along the route and what to expect at each hostel. The buses are fairly cramped Mercedes vehicles, although a trailer at the back has space for rucksacks, surf boards and other luggage.

Car hire Hiring a car for part, or all, of your journey is undoubtedly the best way to see the country. The roads are generally in good condition and, away from the major urban centres, there is little traffic. South Africans are, however, notoriously bad drivers – speeding and drink-driving are common. Do not drive at night for safety reasons. The advantage of hiring a car is that you get to explore more isolated areas, as well as seeing the national parks and nature reserves at a more leisurely pace without being tied to a tour. For budget travellers, hiring a car is ideal for carrying camping equipment and costs come down considerably if you share with three or four people. Petrol, not a major expense, is available 24 hours a day along the national highways. Driving is on the left side of the road and speed limits range from 60 kph in built-up areas to 120 kph on the main highways. The police are cracking down on drink-driving and while many locals still disregard the laws, speed traps with on-the-spot fines are employed. Also remember that if you are caught by a speed camera, the fine will go to the hire car company who have every right to deduct the amount from your credit card, even if it is some time after you have left South Africa.

It is worth asking at hostels or hotels for recommended local car hire companies, and be sure to shop around. Car hire companies have a range of vehicles, from basic hatchbacks and saloon cars, to camper vans and fully equipped 4WD vehicles. In general there are two types of deal on offer: a short weekend package including free mileage; or longer-term deals for a week or more. In the first case you can get very good rates for a Group A car, although you might want a larger vehicle for long journeys – bear in mind that during a two- to three-week holiday you're likely to clock up over 3000 km. The extra engine power and space of a Group B car will make for more comfortable and safe driving. In summer, air conditioning is also well worth the extra but make sure it works before you sign.

Tourist offices usually recommend large international organizations such as Avis or Budget, but there are a number of reliable local companies, usually with a good fleet of cars and follow-up service. Backpacker hostels are often a useful source of information and can offer competitive rates.

If you are intending to visit more remote areas, such as Maputaland, the Kalahari and the Richtersveld, consider hiring a 4WD vehicle. There are specialist companies in Cape Town and Johannesburg that hire out fully equipped safari Land Rovers or pickups with all necessary camping equipment. Fully equipped camper vans or motorhomes represent excellent value for a group or a family as money is saved on accommodation, and if self-catering, food too.

For emergency breakdown and traffic update information contact the **Automobile Association of South Africa**, T083-84322, www.aa.co.za.

Make sure you have the correct documents from the rental company if you wish to take the car into one of the neighbouring countries. See Getting there by road, page 38.

Car hire companies

All of the large firms now have toll free phone numbers which can be dialled from anywhere within South Africa, and most of them have kiosks at the airports. Be sure to book in advance through the websites for the high season. See also the Transport sections under individual towns. Some of the larger companies partner with the airlines, so it's also possible to book a car online with your flight.

Aroundabout Cars, T021-422 4022, www.aroundaboutcars.com, is a good national agent for local car hire and they know where to find the best deal. They also have their own fleets in Cape Town and Namibia and can now organize 4WDs with camping equipment, and allow vehicles over the borders.

Avis, T0861-113748 (in South Africa), T011-923 3660 (from overseas), www.avis.co.za.
Budget, T0861-016622 (in South Africa), T011-398 0123 (from overseas), www.budget.co.za.
Britz Africa, T011-396 1445, www.britz.co.za. Contact for camper vans and motorhomes for travel in and beyond South Africa. Good all-inclusive deals.
Europcar, T0801-131000 (in South Africa), T011-574 1000 (from overseas), www.europcar.co.za.
Hertz, T0861-600136 (in South Africa), T021-935 4800 (from overseas), www.hertz.co.za.
Leisuremobiles, T011-475 2902, www.africanleisure.co.za. Camper vans and fully equipped safari 4WDs.

Buying your own car If you want to stay in the country for a while, or plan a grand tour of southern Africa, buying your own car may be a sensible option. Johannesburg, Cape Town or Durban are the best places to buy or sell. Check the local press for private sales, or visit a second-hand car dealership. Be sure to discuss the possibility of selling back to you dealer.

For car insurance contact **Outsurance**, T0860-006000 (in South Africa), T012-673 3000, who can organize insurance instantly if you have a credit or debit card. Alternatively consider buying a car on a buy-back scheme. There are companies that will sell you a car with a buy-back guarantee once you have finished with it. Work out the costs, though, and compare them to long-term car hire. Sometimes the price difference is minimal and with the buy-back scheme you don't get the back up of a car hire company in the case of an emergency. The following websites are useful: www.drivesouthafrica.co.za, www.drive southernafrica.com, www.resqrentacar.co.za.

Hitchhiking Hitchhiking is not common in South Africa and is not recommended as it can be very dangerous. Women should never hitch, under any circumstances, even in a group. If you have to hitch, say if your vehicle has broken down, be very wary of who you are accepting a lift from; a car with a family or couple in may be fine, but avoid getting into a vehicle with a group of men. In rural areas, especially in Lesotho, you may be expected to pay if a lorry or a pickup gives you a lift.

Minibus taxis The majority of South Africa's population travel by minibus taxis and, in many areas, including inner cities, they are the only way of getting around. However, the accident rate of such vehicles is notoriously high, with speeding, overcrowding and lack of maintenance being the main causes. There is also the problem of possible robbery, especially at the taxi ranks, so many visitors and locals remain wary of using them.

Nevertheless, minibus taxis remain the cheapest and most extensive form of transport in the country. Many routes have experienced little or no crime, but you should exercise extreme caution and always ask people in the know before using them. In central Cape Town minibus taxis provide an efficient (and relatively safe) means of transport into the city centre from places such as Observatory, Camps Bay, Sea Point, Rondebosch and Claremont.

Taxis Except in the major cities there are few taxi ranks in South African towns so it's generally a better idea to order a taxi in advance. Any hotel, hostel or restaurant will make a booking for you. Taxis are metered and charge around R9.50 per kilometre. Larger groups should request a Toyota Venture if available as these carry nine people. They can also accommodate wheelchairs. Travelling by taxi, especially at night, is one of the safest ways to cross city centres when visiting a restaurant or nightclub; don't walk just to save a few cents.

Lesotho

Many of Lesotho's main roads have been upgraded to tarmac in recent years (a direct result of the Lesotho Highlands Water Project) making getting around much easier than it used to be when roads were little more than rough gravel tracks. The main route running north-south along the lowland strip is tarred and in good repair. Other tarred routes include the road from Maseru to Roma, Maseru to Mohale Dam, Leribe/Hlotso to Katse dam, and Butha-Buthe to Mokhotlong. The quality of gravel roads varies considerably: the 'mountain road' to Thaba Tseke and the road to Semonkong are both in good condition while the routes from Thaba Tseke to Mokhotlong or Qacha's Nek are very poor in parts and get very slippery in the wet.

Petrol is readily available in the lowland centres but if you are travelling into the mountains make sure you have plenty of fuel before you leave. Distances between filling stations are long and supplies are not always reliable. You will definitely need to put anti-freeze in your car radiator in the colder months as it can freeze overnight.

Car If driving yourself through Lesotho, take local advice regarding the time a journey may take, and the possible need for 4WD and chains. The tourist office in Maseru can assist with this and can give detailed instructions of the exact route to be taken. Remember that while there have been major improvements to Lesotho's roads in recent years, all road conditions deteriorate rapidly after heavy rains, they get icy in the cooler months, and some may be blocked by snow in the winter. It is worth considering carefully what time of the year to go if you are driving. It's recommended that you carry two spare wheels and a couple of spare inner tubes if possible, though many of the villages offer cheap tyre-mending services.

Road safety in Lesotho usually leaves a lot to be desired, as the death of the King in an accident in 1996 on the Main South Road indicates. Taxi drivers are often in direct competition for passengers so rush to get to stops ahead of other drivers – which often means they take huge risks. Be especially careful when driving behind taxis as they often brake sharply to pick up passengers. Drink-driving is also a problem, especially at weekends, bank holidays and at the end of the month when people have just been paid. It is probably best to avoid driving at these times. Wear your seat belt at all times, and always be wary of pedestrians, cyclists and livestock at the sides of the road.

Hitchhiking As taxis are cheap and frequent and most drivers will charge the same fare as a taxi anyway, hitchhiking in the lowlands is not usually worth the trouble. In more remote areas more or less every passing vehicle acts as a de facto taxi service – somewhat blurring the distinction between hitching and taking a taxi. There are certain routes, however, where hitchhiking is the only alternative to walking, for example over Sani Pass into KwaZulu Natal or from Qacha's Nek into the Eastern Cape. If you are hitchhiking in the mountains make sure you have a jacket or blanket (or both) to hand – most lifts will be on the back of a pickup or a truck and it can get very cold, especially on winter evenings. Although it's usually safe to hitchhike in Lesotho, remember to avoid hitchhiking alone.

Taxis and buses The lowland towns and villages are linked together by a regular and cheap (if hair-raising) taxi service. These consist of minibuses with about 16 seats or sometimes, in remote districts, of converted 4WDs. There is no set timetable for taxis; they simply set off when they are full. It is important to remember, however, that taxis stop running very early in the evening and it is more or less impossible to get one after sunset. There is also very little space for baggage. The first passengers to arrive get the most comfortable seats next to the driver, though the downside is that you'll have a full view of Lesotho driving habits. Unlike most of South Africa, people talk to each other in taxis.

Larger buses cover the longer routes, especially over the gravel mountain roads. To most towns there is at least one bus a day to and from Maseru or another larger lowland centre. They usually leave between 0600 and 1000 depending on the distance but timetables vary with the number of passengers.

Other transport Horses and ponies are the main form of transport other than foot for most Basotho in the mountains. You can hire ponies from a number of centres.

Swaziland

The easiest way of getting around is by car and, in such a little country, everything of interest is within a couple of hours' drive. Petrol stations are frequent and are open 0700-1800. Roads are well signposted and tarred, though beware of drink-driving in the evenings and at weekends (the laws are far less stringent here than in South Africa).

Note the law requires that all vehicles move to the side of the road and stop when approached by an official (usually royal) motorcade led by police escorts. Also beware of livestock on the road in the rural areas. The **Baz Bus** offers an efficient and frequent service through Swaziland. Regular minibus taxis ply the road through the Ezulwini Valley between Mbabane and Manzini.

Maps

The best map and travel guide store in the UK is **Stanfords** ① *12-14 Longacre, Covent Garden, London WC2E 9LP, T020-7836 1321, www.stanfords.co.uk,* with branches in Manchester and Bristol. Within South Africa, the **Shell Road Atlas to Southern Africa**, available at all Shell service stations, is comprehensive and includes maps of major tourist areas, marking sights and some accommodation facilities, and detailed city maps. The **Automobile Association of South Africa**, www.aa.co.za, has shops in all major cities selling national, regional and touring maps. The **Map Studio**, www.mapstudio.co.za, produces a wide range of maps covering much of Africa. South African bookshops such as **Exclusive Books** and **CNA** carry a full range of maps.

Sleeping

South Africa offers a wide variety of accommodation from top-of-the-range five-star hotels, game lodges and tented camps that charge US$300-1000 or more per couple per day, to mid-range safari lodges and hotels with self-contained air-conditioned double rooms for US$150-300, to guesthouse or B&Bs that charge US$75-150 and dormitory beds or camping for under US$15 a day. Generally, accommodation booked through agents in Europe will be more expensive than if you contact the hotel directly by email or book online. Make sure you keep a copy of all correspondence and reconfirm your bookings once you arrive in the country. Comprehensive accommodation information can be found on the regional tourism websites listed in each area. All accommodation in South Africa is graded a star value by the **Tourism Grading Council of South Africa** and the website has comprehensive lists in all categories; www.tourismgrading.co.za. In the main cities, hotels often remain a practical option, although note that Cape Town and Johannesburg suffer from a shortage of hotel beds, and you should always book well in advance.

Hotels Every small town has at least one hotel of two- or three-star standard but, where tourists are not expected, the service can be poor and dismissive. These hotels tend to be aimed at business travellers and may be characterless buildings with restaurants serving bland food. However, there are lots of alternatives and there are some delightful family-run and country hotels, and in the cities boutique hotels with stylish interiors and, for those who enjoy the anonymity of a large hotel, chains such as **Holiday Inn** and **Protea**.

Guesthouses Guesthouses can offer some of the most characterful accommodation in South Africa, with interesting places springing up in both cities and small towns. Standards obviously vary enormously; much of what you'll get has to do with the character of the owners and the location of the homes. Some are simple practical overnight rooms, while at the more luxurious end, rooms may be in historic homes filled with antiques, and offering impeccable service. Breakfast is almost always included and, in some, evening meals

Sleeping price codes

Hotels and guesthouses

L	over R2550	C	R641-850
AL	R1871-2550	D	R301-640
A	R1271-1870	E	R131-300
B	R851-1270	F	under R130

Prices refer to the cost of a double room, not including service charge or meals unless otherwise stated. See page 65 for exchange rates.

Private game reserves

L4	over R7650	L2	R3831-4680
L3	R4681-7650	L1	R2550-3830

Prices are based on two people sharing accommodation and are inclusive of all meals and game drives.

can be prepared if you phone ahead. For further information contact the **Guest House Association of Southern Africa**, T021-762 0880, www.ghasa.co.za, or the **Portfolio Collection**, T021-689 4020, www.portfoliocollection.com.

Bed and breakfast B&B accommodation is hugely popular in South Africa; even the smallest town will usually have one private home that rents out rooms, and B&Bs in townships are catching on fast. Local tourist offices are the best source of information for finding B&Bs. Assuming you get on with your hosts, they can offer a valuable insight into local life. In rural areas, farmhouse B&Bs are often in beautiful settings where guests will have access to a garden and swimming pool as well as to hikes and horse riding. Increasingly, some establishments are providing TVs, air-conditioning or fans, and have separate entrances for those who want more privacy away from the owners. The breakfasts are almost always good and in large enough quantities to fill you up for the day. Full English breakfasts are usually served but it is increasingly common to have a choice of continental breakfast or even a traditional South African breakfast of boerewors, mince on toast and mealie porridge.

Backpacker hostels Apart from camping, backpacker hostels are the cheapest form of accommodation, and a bed in a dormitory will cost as little as R90 a night. Some also have budget double rooms with or without bathrooms, while others have space to pitch a tent in the garden.

While hostel standards can obviously vary, stiff competition means that most hostels are clean and have good facilities. You can usually expect a self-catering kitchen, hot showers, a TV/DVD room and internet access. Many hostels also have bars and offer meals or nightly braais, plus a garden and a swimming pool. Most hostels are a good source of travel information and many act as booking agents for bus companies, budget safari tours and car hire. On the whole, hostels are very safe and security is not a problem. Your fellow travellers remain the greatest threat, especially in dormitories in the busy city hostels. The **Baz Bus** (see page 42) caters for backpackers and links most hostels along the coast between Cape Town and Durban, and Durban and Johannesburg via either the

Drakensberg or Swaziland. For information, visit **Backpacking South Africa**, www.btsa.co.za, or **Coast to Coast**, www.coastingafrica.com, which publishes a free annual backpackers' accommodation guide and is available in all the hostels.

Camping and caravan parks Camping is the cheapest and most flexible way of seeing South Africa. Every town has a municipal campsite, many of which also have simple self-catering chalets. These vary in quality and facilities, from basic rondavels with bunks, to chalets with a couple of bedrooms and fully equipped kitchens. They can be excellent value and are often the only budget accommodation available in a town.

As camping is very popular with South Africans, sites tend to have very good facilities, although they may be fully booked months in advance, especially during the school holidays in the most popular game reserves and national parks. Even the most basic site will have a clean washblock with hot water, plus electric points and lighting. All sites have braai facilities, with charcoal, wood and firelighters available in campsite shops. Some sites also have kitchen blocks. At the most popular tourist spots, campsites are more like holiday resorts with shops, swimming pools and a restaurant – these can get very busy and are best avoided in peak season.

Camping equipment is widely available in South Africa and usually at lower prices than in the UK. If your time is limited, you should bring your own tent and sleeping bag, but if you're not on a tight schedule you may want to shop around once you've arrived. Lightweight tents, sleeping bags, ground mats, gas lights, stoves and cooking equipment can be bought at good prices in all the major cities and some car hire companies rent out equipment.

Self-catering apartments Self-catering apartments (and in some cases cottages) are particularly popular with South African holidaymakers and there is an enormous choice, especially along the coast. Prices vary with the seasons: Christmas is the most expensive time of year, but off season many resorts are virtually empty and discounts can be negotiated. If you are travelling in a group, a flat could cost as little as US$20 per person per day and these are ideal for families on a budget.

National park accommodation While the larger rest camps in Kruger have supermarkets, launderettes, post offices and banks, most camps are rather more basic. All have at least a small shop selling maps, basic food provisions and firewood. Most accommodation is self-catering, but larger camps may have restaurants. Petrol is often available at larger camps and road conditions between them are usually good. Reception is usually located within the shop or office, where you can arrange guided walks and game drives. Both are highly recommended for learning about and spotting wildlife. Some parks also offer night drives where visitors have the chance of seeing unusual nocturnal animals. National parks across the country are under the jurisdiction of **South African National Parks (SANParks)**, central reservations T012-428 9111, www.sanparks.org, which also has drop-in offices in Tshwane (Pretoria), T012-428 9111, two offices in Cape Town, at the Clock Tower Centre and the V&A Waterfront, T021-405 4500, or at the Cape Town tourist office on the corner of Burg and Castle streets T021-487 6800, and at the Tourist Junction in Durban, T031-304 4934. In the Western Cape, the game reserves are managed by **Cape Nature Conservation**, T021-659 3500, www.capenature.org.za, and in KwaZulu Natal, **KZN Wildlife**, T033-845 1000, www.kznwildlife.com.

The central reservations offices are a good source of advice and can help plan your trip in advance. In peak season, it's wise to book a month or two before you arrive.

Lighthousing

A relatively new initiative by South Africa's National Ports Authority is the SA Lighthouse Tourism. Due to modern technology and automation, only 15 of the 45 lighthouses along South Africa's 3700-km coastline are still manned. The authority has opened up many of the remaining 30 lighthouses as self-catering accommodation in what was once the light keepers' quarters. These lighthouses are found at Cape Columbine on the West Coast in the Saldanha Bay area, Danger Point near Gansbaai on the Atlantic side of Cape Agulhas, Cape St Blaize at Mossel Bay, Great Fish Point in Port Alfred and North Sand Bluff in Port Edward, both on the KwaZulu Natal coast.

Contact the central reservation office, T021-449 2400, or visit the National Ports Authority website, www.transnetnationalportsauthority.net.

All bookings can be made over the telephone, by email or through the websites. Most international credit cards are accepted. If you are already staying in a park, the reception can make advance bookings for other parks.

Luxury game lodges The most famous luxury game lodges are on private game farms adjoining Kruger National Park, although there are others around the country. Their attraction is the chance to combine exclusive game viewing in prime wilderness areas, with top-class accommodation, fine dining, vintage wines and a spectacular natural setting.

The cost of staying in a luxury game lodge varies from US$250 to over US$1000 per person per night. This includes all meals, drinks and game-viewing trips. In order to get the most from the experience, guests tend to stay for at least two nights. The lodges are often isolated and not easily accessible by road so many reserves have their own airstrips where light aircraft can land. Charter flights save time and avoid long dusty journeys, and can be booked through the game lodge or from Johannesburg, Durban or Cape Town.

» For details of the luxury reserves around Kruger National Park, see pages 639-640.

Lesotho

Hotels There is no star-grading in Lesotho and don't expect the high standards of accommodation found in South Africa. Most main centres have one or two formal and rather soulless hotels. These often look dilapidated from the outside but are often kept reasonably clean inside. They rarely have more than a handful of guests, so you are usually able to benefit from close attention from hotel staff. Nearly all of them have restaurants and they are often the only choice for eating, but don't expect anything other than plates of basic chicken and rice or stew and pap. As these hotels are often the centre of the town's nightlife for local professionals, it is usually best to ask for a room away from the bar area, especially at weekends. Cheaper accommodation can be found in various farming training centres, missions, or education centres. In these you'll usually get a dorm bed, a (not always hot) shower, and perhaps a simple meal. Most are very basic but nonetheless friendly and very cheap. Lesotho has a number of well-run lodges in the mountains and foothills that provide excellent value accommodation, namely the **Trading Post**, **Semonkong Lodge**, **New Oxbow Lodge** and the **Malealea Lodge**. These are a much better alternative to the bland town hotels and it is in these resorts that you are going to get the most out of a visit to Lesotho as they also organize hiking and pony trekking.

Maseru has two international standard hotels (both part of the **Sun International** chain). Neither are outstanding, but they are comfortable with a range of facilities, though expensive. There are few budget travellers' hostels in Maseru and those that are available are not very nice. For the budget traveller it is a good idea to arrive in Maseru early in the morning, spend the day in the city before heading out to cheaper accommodation in the outlying districts, some of which is only 20-30 km away. This avoids having to pay the high prices for the city hotels. Remember that most accommodation outside Maseru only accepts cash for payment.

Camping Away from the main towns, camping is very easy if you are completely self-sufficient, but remember it can get cold, even during summer nights. You should always get permission to set up camp from the chief of the nearest village.

In the densely populated lowlands it is more difficult to find a suitable camping site and you also run the risk of losing your belongings to the crowds of children who inevitably gather. Ask around at the churches and missions for permission to camp in their grounds or at the local police station.

Eating and drinking

South Africa

Food

South African food tends to be fairly regional, although a ubiquitous love of meat unites the country. In and around Cape Town visitors will find many restaurants offering Cape Malay cuisine, a blend of sweet and spicy curries and meat dishes cooked with dried fruit. Seafood along the coast is excellent and usually very good value. KwaZulu Natal is famous for its Indian curries, especially the delicious bunny chow, served in a hollowed-out loaf of bread. Portuguese influences, thanks to neighbouring Mozambique, are strong – spicy peri-peri chicken or Mozambiquan prawns are widespread. Meat, however, is universal and South Africa offers plenty of opportunities to try an assortment of game, from popular ostrich or springbok to more acquired tastes such as crocodile or warthog. Two local meat products which travellers invariably come across are biltong and boerewors. Biltong is heavily salted and spiced sun-dried meat, usually made from beef but sometimes made from game such as ostrich, kudu or impala. Boerewors is a strongly seasoned beef sausage usually grilled on a braai. The staple diet for much of the black South African population is a stiff maize porridge known as pap, served with a stew. Pap tends to be rather bland, although the accompanying stews are often quite tasty.

Supermarkets usually have a similar selection of groceries to that found in Europe. South Africa is a great source of fresh fruit, and during the summer months you should be able to get a good range of exotic fruits from the better supermarkets (Woolworth's is always a good bet). Local produce such as apples in Ceres or pineapples along the Wild Coast will always be excellent. Meat is generally significantly cheaper than in Europe, and as most fruit and vegetables are grown in South Africa, their price changes depending on season. An avocado for example, (grown all over South Africa), can be as low as US$0.50 in season, and US$2 out of season when they are imported from Israel.

Eating price codes

🍴🍴🍴 over R260   🍴🍴 R130-260   🍴 under R130

Prices refer to the cost of a two-course meal for one person including one soft drink, beer or glass of wine and tax.

Drink

South Africa is a major player in the international market and produces a wide range of excellent wines. The Winelands in the Western Cape have the best-known labels (see pages 155-186) but there are a number of other wine regions dotted around the country. South Africa also produces a range of good beer. Major names include Black Label, Castle and Amstel. Windhoek, from Namibia, is also widely available and more popular than some of the South African beers. Home-brewed beer, made from sorghum or maize, is widely drunk by the African population. It has a thick head, is very potent and not very palatable to the uninitiated. Bitter is harder to come by, although a good local variety is brewed at Mitchell's Brewery in Knysna and Cape Town and can be found at outlets along the Garden Route.

No liquor may be sold on Sundays (and public holidays) except in licensed bars and restaurants. The standard shop selling alcohol is known as a bottle store, usually open Monday-Friday 0800-1800, Saturday 0830-1400 (some may stay open until 1600). Supermarkets do not sell beer or spirits, stop selling wine at 2000, and don't sell alcohol on Sundays. Note that despite drink-driving being a very serious offence, it remains a problem, especially in rural areas.

Soft drinks Tap water in South African towns is chemically treated and safe to drink. Bottled mineral water and a good range of fruit juices are available at most outlets including petrol stations – the Ceres and Liquifruit brands are the best. Another popular drink is Rooibos tea, literally red bush tea. This is a caffeine-free tea with a smoky flavour, usually served with sugar or honey. The main area producing Rooibos is around Clanwilliam by the Cederberg in the Western Cape.

Eating out

Restaurants and cafés vary widely in quality and service, depending largely on where you are. Small-town hotels tend to serve bland meals focusing on standard meat-and-two-veg dishes, while town restaurants are often part of a chain. The main cities, however, have an excellent variety of restaurants and South Africa is fast gaining a reputation as a culinary hotspot. Cape Town in particular has experienced a boom in top-class restaurants, from traditional Cape Malay cooking to cordon bleu seafood, all at incredibly good prices. Johannesburg and Tshwane (Pretoria) also have a wide selection of smart restaurants in the more affluent suburbs. Some of the best restaurants in the country are found in the Winelands around the Western Cape, many of which are part of historic wine estates. Franschhoek has a particularly good reputation, with a number of excellent French restaurants, while the Garden Route offers fresh, good-value seafood. Because of the Indian influence in KwaZulu Natal, the best curries are found in Durban and the authenticity of the dishes is better than you would expect in Europe. Meat is almost always of a high standard wherever you are, and a number of restaurants offer a variety of game such as springbok, ostrich and kudu.

Vegetarians, however, will find their choice rather limited. South Africa is a meat-loving country and menus rarely include anything but the most basic dishes for vegetarians. Away from the major cities, you'll have to make do with salads, pasta and chips. Cape Town, Tshwane (Pretoria) and Johannesburg have a better range for vegetarians, with some trendy meat-free restaurants appearing on the scene in recent years. Self-catering is often a better option.

Eating out continues to be very good value, despite the strengthening rand. Outside the cities and major tourist centres, people eat early and many kitchens will close around 2100, except at the weekend. Private restaurants are often closed on Sunday evenings, when hotel dining rooms or fast-food outlets may well be the only choices for eating out. A great starting point for choosing a restaurant is buying the latest edition of *Eat Out*, which features South Africa's best choice of restaurants and is available at CNA and Exclusive Books. Alternatively, www.dining-out.co.za provides hundreds of reviews and contact details for restaurants throughout the country.

Braais

One of the first local terms you are likely to learn will be braai, which quite simply means barbecue. The braai is incredibly popular, part of the South African way of life, and every campsite, back garden and picnic spot has a braai pit. Given the excellent range of meat available, learning how to cook good food on a braai is an art that needs to be mastered quickly, especially if you are self-catering, and is part of the fun of eating in South Africa. Once you have established a core of heat using firelighters and wood or charcoal (charcoal is more eco-friendly and less smoky but wood makes for a wonderful fire), wrap up potatoes, sweet potatoes, squash, butternut, etc, in heavy-duty foil and cook them in the coals for an hour or so. Set beside a good piece of meat, with a sauce and a cold beer, and you will be living the South African dream. To check whether your braai is the right heat to cook on, hold your hand over the braai grill and count to 10. If you have to pull your hand back before 10 it's too hot, any later than 10 then it's too cold.

Lesotho

Food

Every village will have a small shop selling basic tinned and dried foods. The larger villages have small supermarkets, though more luxury items and fresh food like cheese or vegetables and fruit (other than those grown locally) can only be found in supermarkets in major towns, or should be purchased in South Africa prior to coming to Lesotho. Maize is the staple food of most Basotho. It is usually made into a stiff porridge, pap, and eaten with stew twice or even three times a day. It is fairly tasteless but if properly cooked and accompanied by a flavoursome stew it is enjoyable and very filling.

In the mountain areas where wheat is grown, bread forms an important part of the staple diet. The bread is baked in huge saucepans greased with mutton fat over fires – delicious.

In most towns, a profusion of street vendors can be found selling a wide variety of goods from home-made fried cakes called *makoenya* to pap and barbecued meat. Outside Maseru most restaurants serve boring but filling meals. Vegetarians will have a very limited choice. After experiencing excellent high levels of service in restaurants in South Africa, you may find the pace somewhat slower in Lesotho. Rather than complaining, try to enjoy the laid-back atmosphere.

Drink

All the major South African beers are available throughout the country and there is also a decent commercial local variety, Maluti Beer. Maize beer is brewed by many women as an additional source of income: a white flag (usually made from a faded maize bag) is hung outside the house when this beer is for sale. The beer has a thick, almost porridge-like head and is usually not enjoyed by visitors, though it is well worth the experience. South African wine can be purchased in Maseru and some of the larger towns but is not widely drunk by Basotho. Whisky is popular and sold at many bars.

Swaziland

Food

Basic staples include pap and stew; roasted cobs of maize are popular roadside snacks. Restaurants in Swaziland serve much the same food as those in South Africa given that all ingredients are imported from there. Like KwaZulu Natal it has the added advantage of being close to Mozambique's coastline; fresh seafood arrives daily and Mozambique's peri-peri (spicy) style of cooking is popular. There are few independent restaurants; most of the hotels feature restaurants and the best choice is along the Ezulwini Valley.

Drink

There's a full range of South African wines, beers and soft drinks. Ceremonial beer made from sorghum is reserved for special occasions and Swazi festivals. Another home-brewed concoction is marula, an intoxicating drink made from the fruit of the marula tree. Although it was banned in Swaziland in 2002 (it was thought to be responsible for a high number or road deaths caused by drunken drivers), it is still drunk surreptitiously.

Festivals and events

South African school holidays are mid-December to mid-January; mid-April to early May; early August to early September. During these times prices of accommodation are often higher and most of the popular destinations become fully booked. The government lists the exact dates for the school calendar on their website; www.info.gov.za.

Festival calendar

2 Jan Karnaval. Begins in the Bo-Kaap district and ends up near the Green Point Stadium, it includes a procession of competing minstrel bands, complete with painted faces, straw boaters and bright satin suits.

Feb FNB Dance Umbrella, Johannesburg, www.at.artslink.co.za. A festival of contemporary choreography and dance from community-based dance troupes to international companies.

Feb Prickly Pear Festival, Uitenhage, Eastern Cape, www.nmbt.co.za. A day of traditional food such as ginger beer, pancakes, *potjiekos*, home-made jam, a spit braai and fish braai, bunny chow and home-made puddings.

Mar Cape Town Carnival, Cape Town, www.capetowncarnival.com. New to the mother city, this annual event will be first held on the 3rd weekend of Mar in 2010. Copying the model of the Rio Carnival, it will include a 1-km procession of floats, dancers and musicians and there will numerous balls, beach and street parties over the weekend.

Mar Lambert's Bay Kreeffees, Lambert's Bay, West Coast, http://kreeffees.com. Crayfish festival and rock concerts by some of South

Africa's Afrikaans musicians. Bungee jumping, aerial displays, a half-marathon, beer tents.

Mar Splashy Fen, Underberg, KwaZulu Natal, www.splashyfen.co.za. A musical gathering on a farm close to Underberg. This is a mix of popular sounds and jazz bands from all walks of life, akin to the summer festivals held in Europe, with camping and fringe activities.

Apr Cape Town Jazz Festival, Cape Town, www.capetownjazzfest.com. 2-day festival featuring some 40 international and African acts performing on 5 stages at the Cape Town International Convention Centre to an audience of 15,000. The night before, a free concert is held in Greenmarket Sq.

Apr Morija Arts and Cultural Festival, Lesotho, www.morijafest.com (see page 809).

Apr Pink Loerie Mardi Gras, Knysna, www.pinkloerie.com. A gay festival with parade and 4 days of non-stop entertainment for anyone who enjoys a party.

Apr Prince Albert Olive, Food and Wine Festival, Prince Albert, Western Cape, www.patourism.co.za. 2-day festival with an art exhibition, beer tents, live music, wine and olive tastings, a cycle race, an olive pip-spitting competition and live entertainment.

Apr Sasol Scifest, Grahamstown, Eastern Cape, www.scifest.org.za. The 7-day festival features 600 events: game drives, laser shows, robotics competitions, science olympics and a film festival. Attendance now exceeds 40,000 visitors a year, most of which are school children.

Jun-Jul National Arts Festival, Grahamstown, Eastern Cape, www.nafest.co.za. South Africa's oldest, biggest and best-known arts festival. A 10-day event with hundreds of performances of theatre, music, song, dance and film. If there's one South African festival you have to attend, this is it.

Jul Knysna Oyster Festival, Knysna, Western Cape, www.oysterfestival.co.za. Oyster braais, oyster tasting, oyster-eating competitions and other molluscular activities; there's live entertainment and lots of sporting events – cycling, running, canoeing, downhill racing and sailing.

Aug Joy of Jazz, Johannesburg, www.joyofjazz.co.za. Jo'burg's biggest annual jazz festival with over 200 local and international performers at different venues across the city, particularly in Newtown.

Aug Oppikoppi Bushveld Festival, Northam, North West, www.oppikoppi.co.za. Popular rock festival that has helped establish many South African musicians' careers. This is real bushveld: hot, dry and covered in red dust and thorn trees. Expect to shower a lot when you get home. (Oppikoppi also hosts an Easter Festival in Mar/Apr.)

Sep Arts Alive, Johannesburg, www.artsalive.co.za. 4-day festival with over 600 performers in dance, visual art, poetry and music at venues in the Jo'burg inner city area; the main concert is held at the Johannesburg Stadium.

Sep Hermanus Whale Festival, Hermanus, Western Cape, www.whalefestival.co.za. An entertainment-packed festival, with the best land-based whale watching in the world.

Sep Macufe, Bloemfontein, Free State, www.macufe.co.za. 10-day African cultural festival, featuring jazz, gospel, kwaito, hip-hop, R&B, rock and classical music, as well as dance, drama, musical theatre, poetry, fine art and traditional arts and crafts.

Nov Woodstock, Harrismith, Free State, www.woodstock.co.za. 4-day youth-oriented music and lifestyle festival, with bands and a market of crafters and alternative lifestyle products.

Dec Spier Summer Festival, Stellenbosch, www.spier.co.za. At the amphitheatre on the Spier Estate, 4 months of music, opera, dance, stand-up comedy and theatre from Dec to Mar.

Public holidays

South Africa

When a public holiday falls on a Sun, the following Mon becomes a holiday. Most businesses will close but shopping malls and large supermarkets in city centres remain open and public holidays are some of their busiest days – especially if a holiday weekend coincides with month-end pay day.

1 Jan New Year's Day
21 Mar Human Rights' Day
Mar/Apr Good Friday; Family Day
(Mon following Easter Sun)
27 Apr Freedom Day
1 May Workers' Day
16 Jun Youth Day
9 Aug National Women's Day
24 Sep Heritage Day
16 Dec Day of Reconciliation
25 Dec Christmas Day
26 Dec Day of Goodwill

Lesotho
1 Jan New Year's Day
11 Mar Moshoeshoe's Day
4 Apr Heroes' Day
Mar/Apr Good Friday; Easter Monday
1 May Workers' Day
17 May Ascension Day
25 May Heroes' Day
17 Jul King's Birthday
4 Oct National Independence Day
25 Dec Christmas Day
26 Dec Boxing Day

Swaziland
1 Jan New Year's Day
Mar/Apr Good Friday; Easter Monday
25 Apr National Flag Day
1 May Workers' Day
22 Jul Public Holiday
2-3 Sep Umhlanga Dance
6 Sep Independence Day
25 Dec Christmas Day
Dec/Jan Incwala Day

Essentials A-Z

Accident and emergency

South Africa Police, T10111; **Medical**, T10177; **Fire**, T10111. All emergencies from a cell phone, T112.
Lesotho Police, T123/124; **Ambulance**, T121.
Swaziland Police, T999.

Children

Inform the airline in advance that you are travelling with a baby or toddler and check out the facilities when booking as these vary with each aircraft. Also useful is www.babygoes2.com.

South Africa is a popular family holiday destination; in Dec and Jan accommodation in the parks and along the coast is packed with South African families during the school holidays. In the main towns with supermarkets, you will find plentiful supplies of all you need to feed and look after your little ones. Hygiene throughout the country is of a good standard; stomach upsets are rare and the tap water everywhere is safe to drink. Be sure to protect your children from the sun's intense rays, and be aware of the potential dangers of wild animals, snakes and insects in the bush. Most of the accommodation options welcome families; many have either specific family rooms or adjoining rooms suitable for families, and there are plenty of family chalets or bungalows, especially in the parks. Children get significant discounts on accommodation and entry fees. South Africa has a great appeal for children: animals and safaris are very exciting for them (and their parents), especially when they catch their first glimpse of an elephant or lion. However, small children may get bored driving around a hot game reserve or national park all day if there is no animal activity. If you travel in a group, think about the long hours inside the vehicle sharing the small space with other people. Noisy and bickering children can annoy your travel mates and scare the animals away. Many travel agencies organize family safaris that are especially designed for couples travelling with children, and there is also the option of self-drive, which is ideal for families.

Customs and duty free

The official customs allowance for visitors over 18 years includes 200 cigarettes, 50 cigars, 250 g of tobacco, 2 litres of wine, 1 litre of spirits, 50 ml of perfume and 250 ml of eau de toilette. Tourists can reclaim the 14% VAT on purchases bought in South Africa whose total value exceeds R250. You can do this when departing, at the VAT reclaim desks at airports in Johannesburg and Cape Town or border posts. Refunds are given by cheque in South African rand, which can be paid into home bank accounts (or at the airports cashed for rand at the bureaux de changes). Goods need to be shown to the refund officer as proof of purchase with VAT receipts, so be sure to ask for these when you buy something, and at the airport this needs to be done before you check in your luggage. The procedure is simple enough at the airports but allow plenty of time, especially if your flight is at night. At the border crossings such as Beitbridge (Zimbabwe) or Ramotswa (Botswana) the procedure is painstakingly slow, as there are few customs officials to check goods against receipts. Expect lengthy queues. Refunds only apply to items taken out of the country and not on services rendered, such as accommodation or goods consumed or used within the country. For example, if you are buying clothes, keep the shop tags on them to prove that you haven't worn them in South Africa and you'll get the tax back. To save time at the airport or border, you can also go to one of the pre-processing offices, at the Clock Tower at Cape Town Waterfront and at Sandton City shopping mall in Johannesburg. At these offices you will be required to submit the receipts to be checked off against goods you will be exporting from South Africa, as well as presenting your passport and air ticket. They will stamp your receipts for verification but cannot give out refunds. This still has to be done at the airport or border on departure. For more information visit www.taxrefunds.co.za.

Disabled travellers

South Africa
Facilities for disabled travellers are generally of a high standard in South Africa and the 3 main airports in Johannesburg, Cape Town and Durban are fully wheelchair accessible and can provide wheelchairs for less mobile travellers. Smaller domestic airports may not be as reliable. Many of the more modern hotels have specially adapted rooms and it is worth asking about these even in smaller or more remote places when enquiring about accommodation. Facilities vary from hotel to hotel and some are more accessible than others. At the best you can expect wider doors, larger bathrooms, lowered light switches and mirrors, and roll-in showers with flip-down seats and grab rails. Modern shopping malls, and many restaurants, museums and other attractions are accommodating, but as with hotels, it's always a good idea to check in advance. Safaris should not pose too much of a problem either, given that most of the time is spent in the vehicle; wheelchair-bound travellers may want to consider a camping or tented camp safari which provides easy access to a tent at ground level. Some tourist attractions have been developed with disabled visitors in mind, such as the Braille Trail at Kirstenbosch Botanical Gardens, or the easily accessible cable car to the top of Table Mountain. Others, such as the new

museum located in the old jail at Johannesburg's Constitutional Hill, are now fully accessible for wheelchairs via ramps and lifts. The fact that South Africa is a very car-friendly country should make getting to the major sights no problem and most places have disabled parking right by the entrance.

Lesotho
Apart from the Sun hotels in Maseru, few hotels have specific facilities for disabled travellers, though it's always worth enquiring if there is a room that can be negotiated by a wheelchair. The nature of the rugged terrain means that travellers with physical impairments cannot take advantage of Lesotho's hiking or pony trekking but driving through the mountains poses no additional problems.

Swaziland
Most larger modern hotels have at least 1 room that is wheelchair accessible and again it's worth phoning ahead to see if smaller places can accommodate your needs.

Useful contacts
Endeavour Safaris, T021-556 6114, www.endeavour-safaris.com. Organizes tours for not only the mobility disabled, but for those with hearing disability, visual impairment, and people on regular kidney dialysis treatment or oxygen. They can also organize equipment hire.
Epic Enabled, T021-782 9575, www.epic-enabled.com. Offers an excellent range of tours for disabled travellers, using fully modified overland trucks, camp assistants and wheelchair-friendly accommodation. Not specifically for the disabled, and caters for accompanying friends and family too.
Flamingo Tours, T021-557 4496, www.flamingotours.co.za. Established Western Cape tour operator specializing in disabled travel; tailor-made tours are led by a registered guide and nurse (if necessary).

Rolling SA, T033-330 4214, www.rollingsa.
co.za. Organizes tours throughout South
Africa specifically for wheelchair users.
Titch Tours, T021-713 0296, www.titch
tours.co.za. Custom-designed itineraries
according to travellers' needs.

Dress

Dress in South Africa tends to be casual
and most people on holiday wear shorts,
sandals and a T-shirt. If you intend to do
any game viewing, clothes in dark green,
muted browns and khaki colours are
best. In general, bars and restaurants
are casual, though some of the more
upmarket establishments have dress
codes where sandals, vest and shorts
are not appreciated.

Drugs

Although marijuana, locally known as
dagga, is grown in rural areas, such as the
Wild Coast and Lesotho, and smoking it is
relatively widespread, it is illegal and strict
penalties apply. Traditionally, poor people
have smoked a lethal cocktail of mandrax
(*buttons*) and *dagga*, which will almost
instantly comatose inexperienced users.
Another highly potent drug, *tik*, or
methamphetamine, which is part of the
amphetamine group of drugs, has also
more recently become a major problem
in urban areas, especially on the Cape
Flats in Cape Town. Hard drugs such as
cocaine and heroin, along with their
associated problems, are also prevalent.
Since independence there has been an
alarming growth in drug-related crime
and inner-city areas of Cape Town,
Johannesburg and, more recently, Durban
have become major transit points for drugs
en route to Europe and America.

Embassies and consulates

South Africa
Australia, Corner Rhodes Pl and State Circle,
Canberra, T02-6272 7300, www.sahc.org.au.
Canada, 15 Sussex Drive, Ottawa, T613-744
0330, www.southafrica-canada.ca.
France, 59 Quai d'Orsay, Paris 75007,
T01-5359 2323, www.afriquesud.net.
Germany, Tiergartenstr 18, 10785 Berlin,
T030-220730, www.suedafrika.org.
Netherlands, 36 Wassenaarseweg 2596
CJ, The Hague, T070-3105920,
www.zuidafrika.nl.
UK, South Africa House, Trafalgar Sq,
London WC2N 5DP, T020-7451 7299,
www.southafricahouse.com.
USA, 3051 Massachusetts Av NW,
Washington, DC 20008, T1202-232 4400,
www.saembassy.org; there are also
consulates in Los Angeles and New York.

Lesotho
South Africa, 391 Anderson St, Menlo Park,
Tshwane (Pretoria) 0001, T012-460 7648.
UK, 7 Chesham Pl, Belgravia, London,
T0207-235 5686.
USA, 2511 Massachussets Av, Washington DC
20008, T0202-797 5533, www.lesothoemb-
usa.gov.ls.

Swaziland
South Africa, 715 Government Av,
Arcadia, Tshwane (Pretoria) 0083, T012-
344 1910, www.swazihighcom.co.za.
UK, 20 Buckingham Gate, London SW1E 6LB,
T020-7630 6611, www.swaziland.org.uk
US, 1712 New Hampshire Av, NW
Washington DC 20009, T202-234 5002,
www.swazilandembassyus.com.

Gay and lesbian travellers

The South African constitution is one of the
most gay-friendly and progressive in the
world and the government legalized same-
sex marriages in Nov 2006 (at the time, the

5th country in the world to do so). Cape Town is the self-proclaimed Pink Capital of Africa and has a flourishing scene, with a yearly **Gay Pride** week, usually held in Feb, www.cape townpride.co.za. Other annual events in Cape Town are the popular gay and lesbian film festival in Aug known as **Out in Africa**, www.oia.co.za; and the annual **Mother City Queer Project**, www.mcqp.co.za, a costume dance event in Dec which is a highlight on the city's social calendar attracting local celebs and TV cameras. Up the coast, the **Pink Loerie Mardi Gras** is held in Knysna in May, www.pinkloerie.com.

The *Pink Map* of the city, available at the tourist offices, lists gay friendly/oriented accommodation, restaurants and nightlife, tour operators, and even health spas and launderettes. Away from Cape Town, Johannesburg and Durban also have burgeoning gay scenes but, outside these cities, South Africa, like **Lesotho** and **Swaziland**, remains deeply conservative. Overtly affectionate behaviour between gay and lesbian couples may elicit a disapproving response – from both black and white communities – particularly in more remote rural parts. It is wise for gay visitors to be discrete. By doing so you should encounter no problems.

Useful contacts
www.exit.co.za Leading gay and lesbian online newspaper.
www.mask.org.za A website dedicated to gay and lesbian affairs throughout Africa.
www.oia.co.za Out in Africa organizes annual gay film festivals in Cape Town and Johannesburg.
www.q.co.za South Africa's main gay and lesbian website with travel and entertain- ment news, chat rooms and a dating service.

Health

See your doctor or travel clinic at least 6 weeks before your departure for general advice on travel risks, malaria and recommended vaccinations. Make sure you have travel insurance, get a dental check (especially if you are going to be away for more than a month), know your own blood group and if you suffer a long-term condition such as diabetes or epilepsy make sure someone knows or that you have a Medic Alert bracelet/necklace with this information on it (www.medicalert.co.uk).

Vaccinations
Confirm your primary courses and boosters are up to date. Courses or boosters usually advised: diphtheria; tetanus; poliomyelitis; hepatitis A. Vaccines sometimes advised: tuberculosis; hepatitis B; rabies; cholera; typhoid. The final decision on all vaccinations, however, should be based on a consultation with your GP or travel clinic. A yellow fever certificate is required if over 1 year old and entering from an infected area. If you don't have one, you'll be required to have one at the airport before being permitted entry.

If you need to have a vaccination or buy malaria prophylactics in South Africa, visit one of the Netcare Travel Clinics in the major cities, www.travelclinic.co.za.

For further information, visit www.fitfortravel.nhs.uk.

A-Z of health risks

Altitude sickness
Acute mountain sickness can strike from about 3000 m upwards and takes a few hours or days to come on and presents with heachache, lassitude, dizziness, loss of appetite, nausea and vomiting. Insomnia is common and often associated with a suffocating feeling when lying down in bed. You may notice that your breathing tends to wax and wane at night and your face is puffy in the mornings – this is all part of the syndrome. If the symptoms are mild, the treatment is rest and painkillers (preferably not aspirin-based) for the headaches. Should the symptoms be severe and

prolonged it is best to descend to a lower altitude immediately and reascend, if necessary, slowly and in stages. The symptoms disappear quickly – even after a few hundred metres of descent. The best way of preventing acute mountain sickness is a relatively slow ascent. When trekking to high altitude, some time spent walking at medium altitude, getting fit and acclimatizing is beneficial.

Bites and stings

This is a very rare event indeed for travellers, but if you are unlucky (or careless) enough to be bitten by a venomous snake, spider, scorpion or sea creature, try to identify the culprit, without putting yourself in further danger. Snake bites in particular are very frightening, but in fact rarely poisonous – even venomous snakes bite without injecting venom. Victims should be taken to a hospital or a doctor without delay. Reassure and comfort the victim frequently, immobilize the limb with a bandage or a splint and get the patient to lie still. Do not slash the bite area and try to suck out the poison. This does more harm than good. You should apply a tourniquet in these circumstances, but only if you know how to. Do not attempt this if you are not experienced.

Certain tropical fish inject venom into bathers' feet when trodden on, which can be exceptionally painful. Wear plastic shoes if such creatures are reported. The pain can be relieved by immersing the foot in hot water (as hot as you can bear) for as long as the pain persists.

Cholera

There have been occasional outbreaks of cholera in the northeast of the country, the most recent being in early 2009, which was possibly linked to the far more serious endemic in neighbouring Zimbabwe. The main symptoms of cholera are profuse watery diarrhoea and vomiting, which in severe places may lead to dehydration and death. However, most travellers are at extremely low risk of infection and the disease rarely shows symptoms in healthy well-nourished people. The new cholera vaccine, Dukoral, is only recommended for certain high-risk individuals such as health professionals or volunteers.

Dengue fever

This viral disease is spread by mosquitoes that tend to bite during the day. The symptoms are fever and often intense joint pains, also some people develop a rash. Symptoms last about a week but it can take a few weeks to recover fully. Dengue can be difficult to distinguish from malaria as both diseases tend to occur in the same countries. There are no effective vaccines or antiviral drugs though, fortunately, travellers rarely develop the more severe forms of the disease (these can prove fatal). Rest, plenty of fluids and paracetamol (not aspirin) is the recommended treatment.

Diarrhoea and intestinal upset

Diarrhoea can refer either to loose stools or an increased frequency of bowel movement, both of which can be a nuisance. Symptoms should be relatively short-lived but if they persist beyond 2 weeks specialist medical attention should be sought. Also seek medical help if there is blood in the stools and/or fever. Adults can use an antidiarrhoeal medication such as loperamide to control the symptoms but only for up to 24 hrs. In addition keep well hydrated by drinking plenty of fluids and eat bland foods. Oral rehydration sachets taken after each loose stool are a useful way to keep well hydrated. These should always be used when treating children and the elderly.

Bacterial traveller's diarrhoea is the most common form. Ciproxin (Ciprofloxacin) is a useful antibiotic and can be obtained by private prescription in the UK. You need to take one 500 mg tablet when the diarrhoea starts. If there are no signs of improvement after 24 hrs the diarrhoea is likely to be viral and not bacterial. If it is due to other organisms such as those causing giardia or amoebic dysentery, different antibiotics will be required.

The standard advice to prevent problems is to be careful with water and ice for drinking. If you have any doubts then boil the water or filter and treat it. Food can also transmit disease. Be wary of salads (what were they washed in, who handled them), re-heated foods or food that has been left out in the sun having been cooked earlier in the day. There is a simple adage that says wash it, peel it, boil it or forget it. Also be wary of unpasteurized dairy products as these can transmit a range of diseases. On the positive side, very few people experience stomach problems in South Africa and standards of hygiene are very high, although less so in the rural areas and Lesotho.

Hepatitis

Hepatitis means inflammation of the liver. Viral causes of the disease can be acquired anywhere in the world. The most obvious symptom is a yellowing of your skin or the whites of your eyes. However, prior to this all that you may notice is itching and tiredness. Pre-travel hepatitis A vaccine is the best bet. Hepatitis B (for which there is a vaccine) is spread through blood and unprotected sexual intercourse, both of which can be avoided.

HIV/AIDS

Southern Africa has the highest rates of HIV and AIDS in the world; Swaziland is currently 1st, Lesotho 3rd and South African 5th. Efforts to stem the rate of infection have had limited success, as many of the factors that need addressing such as social change, poverty and gender inequalities are long-term processes. Visitors should be aware of the dangers of infection from unprotected sex and always use a condom. Do not inject non-prescribed drugs or share needles; avoid having a tattoo or piercing, electrolysis or acupuncture unless you're sure the equipment is sterile. If you have to have medical treatment, ensure any equipment

used is taken from a sealed pack or is freshly sterilized. It may even be worth taking your own sterlized needles as part of a first-aid kit. If you have to have a blood transfusion, ask for screened blood.

Malaria

In **South Africa**, there is a seasonal (Oct-May) risk of malaria in the east of the country, particularly in Ndumu and Tembe game reserves. **Swaziland** has malaria risk in all lowland areas. For a map of malaria regions in South Africa, visit www.malaria.org.za. **Lesotho**'s high altitude makes it a healthier place than many African countries; malaria is non-existent and other tropical diseases are rare.

Malaria can cause death within 24 hrs and can start as something just resembling an attack of flu. You may feel tired, lethargic, headachy, feverish; or more seriously, develop fits, followed by coma and then death. Have a low index of suspicion because it is very easy to write off vague symptoms, which may actually be malaria. If you have a temperature, visit a doctor as soon as you can and ask for a malaria test. On your return home, if you suffer any of these symptoms, have a test as soon as possible. Even if a previous test proved negative, this could save your life.

Treatment is with drugs and may be oral or into a vein depending on the seriousness of the infection. Remember ABCD: **Awareness** (of whether the disease is present in the area you are travelling in), **Bite avoidance, Chemo-prohylaxis, Diagnosis**.

To prevent mosquito bites wear clothes that cover arms and legs, use effective insect repellents in areas with known risks of insect-spread disease and use a mosquito net treated with an insecticide. Repellents containing 30-50% DEET (Di-ethyltoluamide) are recommended when visiting malaria endemic areas; lemon eucalyptus (Mosiguard) is a reasonable alternative. The key advice is to take the correct anti-malarials and finish the recommended course. If you are popular target for insect bites or develop lumps quite soon after being bitten use antihistamine tablets and apply a cream such as hydrocortisone. Remember that it is risky to buy medicine, and in particular anti-malarials, in some developing countries. These may be sub-standard or part of a trade in counterfeit drugs.

Rabies
Rabies is endemic throughout certain parts of the world so be aware of the dangers of the bite from any animal. Rabies vaccination before travel can be considered but if bitten always seek urgent medical attention – whether or not you have been previously vaccinated – after first cleaning the wound and treating with an iodine-base disinfectant or alcohol.

Sun
Take good heed of advice regarding protecting yourself against the sun. Overexposure can lead to sunburn and, in the longer term, skin cancer and premature skin aging. The best advice is simply to avoid exposure to the sun by covering up, wearing a hat and staying out of the sun if possible, particularly between late morning and early afternoon. Apply a high-factor sunscreen (greater than SPF15) and also make sure it screens against UVB. Be aware of sunburn at high altitudes too; it might feel cool, but the sun can be strong in the rarefied air of the mountains.

A further danger in tropical climates is heat exhaustion, or more seriously heat stroke. This can be avoided by good hydration, which means drinking water past the point of simply quenching thirst. Also when first exposed to tropical heat take time to acclimatize by avoiding strenuous activity in the middle of the day. If you cannot avoid heavy exercise it is also a good idea to increase salt intake.

Tuberculosis
Tuberculosis is most commonly transmitted via droplet infection. Ensure that you have been immunized, especially those mixing closely with the local population and those at occupational risk, eg health care workers. Check with your doctor or nurse.

Underwater health
If you plan to dive make sure that you are fit do so. The **British Sub-Aqua Club (BSAC)**, T01513-506200, www.bsac.com, can put you in touch with doctors who will carry out medical examinations. Check that any dive company you use is reputable and has appropriate certification from BSAC, **Professional Association of Diving Instructors (PADI)**, www.padi.com, or the **National Association of Underwater Instructors (NAUI)**, www.nauisa.org.

Other diseases
There are a range of other insect-borne diseases that are quite rare in travellers, but worth finding out about if going to particular destinations. Examples are sleeping sickness, river blindness and leishmaniasis. Fresh water can also be a source of diseases such as bilharzia and leptospirosis and it is worth investigating if these are a danger before bathing in lakes and streams.

Further information

Websites
British Travel Health Association (UK), www.btha.org. This is the official website of an organization of travel health professionals.
Fit for Travel (UK), www.fitfortravel.nhs.uk. This site provides a quick A-Z of vaccine and travel health advice requirements for each country.
Foreign and Commonwealth Office (FCO) (UK), www.fco.gov.uk. This is a key travel advice site, with useful information on the country, people and climate, and lists of the UK embassies/consulates. The site also promotes the concept of 'Know Before

You Go' and encourages travel insurance and appropriate travel health advice.

Medical Advisory Service for Travellers Abroad (MASTA) (UK), www.masta.org. Provides a quick A-Z of vaccine and travel health advice requirements for each country.

Medic Alert (UK), www.medicalert.co.uk. This is the website of the foundation that produces bracelets and necklaces for those with existing medical problems.

Travel Screening Services (UK), www.travelscreening.co.uk. A private clinic dedicated to integrated travel health that gives vaccine and travel health advice.

World Health Organization, www.who.int.

Books

Lankester T, *Travellers' Good Health Guide*, 2e, 978-0859699914, Sheldon Press, 2006.

Insurance

Before departure, it is vital to take out full travel insurance. There is a wide variety of policies to choose from, so shop around. At the very least, the policy should cover personal effects and medical expenses, including repatriation to your own country in the event of a medical emergency. Make sure that it also covers all activities that you might do while away, trekking or skydiving for example. There is no substitute for suitable precautions against petty crime, but if you do have something stolen whilst in South Africa, report the incident to the nearest police station and ensure you get a police report and case number. You will need these to make any claim from your insurance company.

Internet

There are plenty of internet cafés in all major urban centres. Many hotels, guesthouses or backpacker hostels offer internet access as a service. Wireless internet (Wi-Fi) is available at some hotels, as well as the 3 major airports and at many coffee shops in the cities. Costs are little more than US$1 per hr. In **Lesotho** internet facilities are generally only available in Maseru. In **Swaziland** Wi-Fi is available at the airport and the large hotels, and there are business centres and internet cafés in the shopping malls in Mbabane and Manzini.

Language

South Africa

There are 11 official languages in South Africa: English, isiZulu, isiXhosa, Afrikaans, Venda (Tishivenda), siSwati, North Sotho (Sesotho sa Leboa), South Sotho (Sesotho), Setswana, isiNdebele and Tsonga. Afrikaans is spoken by 60% of white South Africans and the majority of the Cape coloured population. In addition to this, there are 6 Asian languages spoken, mostly in KwaZulu Natal. English is widely spoken and understood and is the language used in education and business, but it is always a good idea to learn at least a couple of basic phrases in the predominant language of the area that you're travelling in – a simple 'hello' in isiXhosa (Molo) or 'thank you' in Afrikaans (dankie) can go a long way. *Lekker* is an Afrikaans word for 'very good' or 'things are going well'.

Lesotho

Lesotho has 2 official languages, Sesotho, which is spoken everywhere, and English. Both are taught in schools from the 5th year of primary education so while English is spoken in Maseru and the bigger towns; in remote areas there will usually be somebody, often a school child, who speaks some English. See also Glossary, page 900.

Swaziland

The 2 main languages are siSwati, which is similar to the Zulu language, and English. English is the language used in education and business while parliament works with both languages. English is widely spoken and understood in urban areas; in the more isolated rural areas siSwati is prevalent. Knowing and using a couple of Siswati greetings is considered polite. *Sawubona* means 'hello' and is also the name of South African Airways inflight magazine. See also Glossary, page 900.

Media

Magazines

There are a number of publications that travellers will find useful in South Africa. The annual *Eat Out* lists the best restaurants in the country, although it tends to concentrate on the more upmarket eateries. *Time Out Cape Town* is a useful annual magazine with good nightlife and culture listings. Similar content can be found in the monthly *Cape Etc*, which also has interesting articles on shopping, day trips and eating out. The monthly *Getaway* is aimed at outdoorsy South Africans, but has excellent travel features and ideas, as well as reviews of accommodation alternatives and activities throughout southern Africa. *Africa Geographical* is a glossy monthly with high-quality photographs, which publishes regular articles on southern Africa's parks, reserves and wildlife. Its sister magazine, *Africa, Birds & Birding*, also monthly, is a must for anyone with an interest in bird-watching in South Africa. For inspiration before you leave home, pick up a copy of *Travel Africa*, www.travelafricamag.com.

Newspapers

The *Sunday Times* and *Sunday Independent* are weekly English-language papers with national coverage, although several editions are produced for different areas. The excellent weekly *Mail & Guardian* (with close links to the British *Guardian*) provides the most objective reporting on South African issues and has in-depth coverage of international news. Daily English-language newspapers include: *The Star* and *The Citizen* (Johannesburg); *The Daily News* and *The Natal Mercury* (Durban); *The Argus* and *The Cape Times* (Cape Town). The *Sowetan* provides a less white-oriented view of South African news and has the best coverage of international soccer. There are also a number of newspapers published in Afrikaans, isiZulu and isiXhosa.

Radio

Radio is available even in the most remote corners of the country. The **South African Broadcast Corporation** (SABC) has numerous national stations catering for the 11 official languages. The corporation has an agreement with the BBC, which means that listeners can hear BBC news and programmes at certain times of day. 5FM is the SABC national pop music station, while Metro FM offers R'n'B, hip-hop and Kwaito. There is also an abundance of local commercial and community radio stations, such as Good Hope FM in Cape Town, Jacaranda FM in Tshwane (Pretoria) or Highveld FM in Johannesburg.

In Lesotho, the BBC World Service has a relay station near Maseru, and there are 6 local radio stations, 3 of which broadcast primarily in English. South African radio can also be picked up. Swaziland has 3 radio stations (one of them a Christian broadcaster) but again most people tune in to South African stations.

Television

The **SABC** – the state broadcaster – has significantly restructured its service in the last decade to accommodate all 11 official languages. The majority of programmes are in English, followed by Afrikaans, isiZulu and isiXhosa. There are 4 free channels – SABC 1, 2 and 3, and E TV. The latter is the most popular and tends to have better news and entertainment programmes, although SABC 3 is pretty similar and both import shows from the US. The paying channel, M-Net offers a range of sport, sitcoms and movies, and most hotels also have satellite

TV, known as DSTV, with sports, movie and news channels.

Lesotho TV has news and current affairs programmes that are broadcast (in English and Sesotho) every evening at 1730-1900. At other times South African TV channels are shown and DSTV is available at the larger hotels. Swaziland has 2 TV stations, Swazi TV and Channel Swazi, both covering local news and events, but hotels subscribe to South African DSTV.

Money

→ *US$1 = R7.5; £1 = R13; €1 = R11 (Jul 2009).*

Currency
South Africa
The South African currency is the **rand** (R) which is divided into 100 *cents* (c). Notes are in 200, 100, 50, 20 and 10 R, and coins are in 5, 2, 1 R and 50, 20, 10 and 5 c. You can carry your funds in traveller's cheques (TCs), credit cards, rands, US dollars, euros or pounds sterling.

There is no restriction on the amount of rand cash brought into the country and any surplus on departure can be changed at banks and bureaux de changes at the airport. If you plan on visiting neighbouring countries, note that most of their currencies can only be purchased within South Africa and not before you leave home. However, rand can easily be exchanged in all South Africa's neighbouring countries and in some cases, such as Lesotho, Swaziland, Namibia and Mozambique, is used interchangeably alongside the local currency. Since the collapse of the Zimbabwean dollar in 2009, rand can now be used in Zimbabwe.

Lesotho
The standard unit of currency is the *maloti*, divided into 100 *lisente*. It is exactly equivalent to the rand, and the 2 are inter-changeable, so you can pay in either currency. Bring sufficient rand with you from South Africa, as this will considerably reduce

money-changing hassles. While the rand is interchangeable with the maloti in Lesotho this is not the case in South Africa. If you are due to leave Lesotho in a few days, try to get change in rand and when you change money ask for the cash in rand.

Swaziland
The standard unit of currency is the **lilangeni** (plural emalangeni, E) and is equivalent to the South African rand. TCs can be changed in Mbabane but the process is slow. You are better off bringing in cash in the form of South African rand. Both the rand and the emalangeni are accepted currencies everywhere in Swaziland but again emalangeni is not a convertible currency so make sure you change any back into rand before leaving the country.

Changing money
South Africa
All the main high street banks offer foreign exchange services. You can also change money at branches of **Master Currency**, www.mastercurrency.co.za, which has branches at the airports and large shopping malls in Johannesburg, Durban and Cape Town. **American Express Foreign Exchange Service**, www.americanexpress.co.za, has offices in the larger cities and offers a poste restante service to card holders. Larger hotels offer exchange facilities, but these often charge exorbitant fees.

Lesotho
There are 3 main banks in Lesotho: the **First National Bank**, **Nedbank** and **Standard Bank**. All change money, although it usually involves filling out paperwork and long queues (especially on Fri). There are now several ATM machines in Maseru, which offer a hassle-free way of getting hold of local currency. Outside Maseru, most banks do not have a separate foreign-exchange counter.

Swaziland
There are 4 main banks in Lesotho: the **First National Bank**, **Nedbank**, **SwaziBank** and

Standard Bank. It is not worth changing your rand into emalangeni for just a short visit, but you can change money at the banks in Mbabane and Manzini have foreign exchange facilities and ATMs.

Credit and debit cards
Lost or stolen cards: **American Express**, T0800-990123; **Diners Club**, T0800-112017; **MasterCard**, T0800-990418; **Visa**, T0800-990475.

South Africa
You can get all the way around South Africa with a credit or debit card. Not only do they offer a convenient method of covering major expenses but they offer some of the most competitive exchange rates when withdrawing cash from ATMs. They are particularly useful when hiring a car – indeed, many companies will only hire a car to foreign visitors if they have a credit card. The chip and pin system is beginning to feature for holders of foreign cards. Note that credit cards are not accepted as payment for petrol, which can only be purchased with cash or local debit cards. ATMs are everywhere; Plus, Cirrus Visa, Mastercard, American Express and Diners' Club are all accepted. The amount you can withdraw varies between systems and cards, but you should be able to take out at least R1000 a day. Note that theft during or immediately after a withdrawal can be a problem, so never accept a stranger's help at an ATM, be aware of your surroundings and avoid using street-side ATMs. Instead, go into a bank or shopping mall, where guards are often on duty.

Lesotho
Credit cards are accepted at the large international Sun hotels and can be used at ATM machines in Maseru and at the few banks in the regional towns. Some of the main branches of the banks in Maseru can advance local currency off a credit card, but this is a lengthy process.

Swaziland
Major credit cards such as **Visa**, **MasterCard** and **American Express** are accepted in hotels, large town chainstores, some restaurants, and the national parks and game reserves for accommodation, though you are advised to use cash for smaller items and services. ATMs are available in Mbabane and Manzini; credit cards can be used to withdraw cash, either through the machine or from a teller.

Useful websites
www.americaexpress.com
www.mastercard.com
www.visa.com
For up-to-the-minute exchange rates, visit www.xe.com

Traveller's cheques
The major advantage of TCs is that if they are lost or stolen there is a relatively efficient system for replacement. Make sure you keep a full record of the cheques' numbers and value and always keep the receipts separate from the cheques. The drawback is that replacement cheques can usually only be collected from banks in major cities. Another disadvantage is the time it takes to cash them and the commission charged, which ranges from 0.2% to 2%. The most widely accepted are American Express, Thomas Cook and Visa.

Cost of travelling
South Africa is fairly good value for money for tourists spending US dollars, pounds sterling or euro. If you are travelling independently and propose to hire a car, you will need to budget R250-400 per day, depending on the season, type of vehicle and equipment included. If this is shared among a group of 4 it's the most affordable way to get around. The cost of fuel is about half of what Europeans are used to, but distances travelled can be considerable so longer holidays will run up a hefty fuel bill.

Accommodation will represent your other principal daily expense. In first-rate luxury lodges, tented camps or guest farms expect to pay in excess of R1000-2000 per night for a double, rising to R6000-7000 per person per night in the most exclusive establishments. For this you will get impeccable service, cuisine and decor in fantastic locations. If staying in simple B&Bs and hotels, budget R350-1000 per couple per night. By camping or staying in backpacker dorms, you can bring this down to R100-150 on average per person per night. See also Sleeping, page 47.

Food and drink is still good value in southern Africa and a 2-course evening meal with wine in a reasonable restaurant will cost under R300 for 2 people, and you can be pretty assured of good food and large portions. For the budget traveller there are plenty of fast-food outlets, and almost every supermarket has a superb deli counter serving hot and cold meals. Costs can be brought down by self-catering. Food in supermarkets is considerably cheaper than, say, in Europe, especially meat and fresh fruit and vegetables, and a bottle of wine and beer are an affordable R30 and R10 respectively. See also Eating, page 51.

Opening hours

South Africa
Banks Mon-Fri 0900-1530, Sat 0830/0900-1030/1100. **Businesses** Mon-Fri 0830-1700, Sat 0830-1400. **Post offices** Mon-Fri 0830-1600, Sat 0800-1200, minor branches have slightly shorter hours. **Shops and supermarkets** Mon-Fri 0800-1800, Sat 0800-1300, Sun 0900-1300. Larger branches of the supermarkets stay open until late in the evening. Large shopping malls in the cities may stay open until 2100.

Lesotho
Banks Mon-Fri 0900-1530, Sat 0830/0900-1030/1100. **Businesses** Mon-Fri 0830-1700, Sat 0830-1400. **Government offices** Mon-Fri 0830-1300, 1400-1630. **Post offices** Mon-Fri 0830-1600, Sat 0800-1200.

Shops Mon-Fri 0800-1800, Sat 0800-1300, Sun 0900-1300.

Swaziland
Banks Mon, Tue, Thu and Fri 0830-1530, Wed 0830-1300, Sat 0830-1130. **Post offices** Mon-Fri 0800-1600, Sat 0800-1100. **Shops** Mon-Fri 0830-1700, Sat 0830-1300. Some larger supermarkets are open on Sun mornings.

Post

South Africa
Both domestic and international mail is generally reliable. If you are sending home souvenirs, surface mail to Europe is the cheapest method but will take at least 6 weeks. Letters to Europe and the US should take no more than a few days, although over the busy Christmas season can take longer. There is a 'speed service', but this costs significantly more. Parcels have been known to disappear en route, so it's probably best to use registered mail for more valuable items so that you can track their progress. Courier services are useful for sending valuable items. Contact DHL, T0860-345000 (in South Africa) or T011-921 3666 (from overseas), for the nearest branch, or visit www.dhl.co.za.

You can send faxes from post offices and there are a number of private companies such as **Postnet**, www.postnet.co.za, usually found in the shopping malls that offer fax, mail and business services.

Lesotho
The main post office is on central Kingsway in Maseru, where you will spend a very long time in a queue to purchase a stamp. The international postal service is fairly quick and reliable.

Swaziland
Mbabane's main post office is on Warmer St, to the east of the Swazi Plaza and there are

small post offices in the regional towns. The postal service is reliable.

Safety

South Africa has had more than its fair share of well-publicized crime problems. In the 1980s and 1990s Johannesburg was frequently dubbed the most dangerous city in the world, although crime rates are declining there today. Despite the statistics, much of the serious, violent crime is gang-based and occurs in areas that tourists are unlikely to visit, such as Mitchells Plain in Cape Town's townships, or the inner-city ghettos such as Hillbrow in Johannesburg or Point Road in Durban. Dangers facing tourists are on the whole limited to traditional mugging or, on occasion, carjacking. Guns are widely available and you should be aware that your assailant may well be armed and any form of resistance could be fatal.

Nevertheless, visitors need not worry about their safety outside the inner cities any more than they would in any foreign country. The most simple points to remember are to avoid altogether what are considered to be dangerous areas, not to walk about any urban centres at night and to avoid driving after dark. If you are going to be travelling alone in a car, it's a good idea to bring (or hire) a mobile phone; useful in any case if you break down. For specific advice for women travellers, see page 73.

Drink-driving is a big problem in South Africa, and although it is illegal, the laws are routinely ignored by locals. Be especially wary on the roads at Christmas when the number of road deaths soar dramatically. Reputedly there are more deaths caused by road accidents in Dec in South Africa, than there are in a whole year in Australia.

Bear in mind that safety is not just a matter of avoiding crime. South Africa has a severe HIV epidemic and travellers should always take precautions, see page 61.

Problem areas

City centres Horror stories abound among travellers passing through Johannesburg. The city centre, Hillbrow, and Yoeville have the worst reputation and the crime rate remains high. There are few facilities or accommodation options in these areas, so it is feasible to avoid them altogether and visit the sights only on an organized tour. Travellers arriving at the Park City Transit Centre in Johannesburg should not walk into town. Instead, take a taxi directly to your hotel. The crime rate in Johannesburg's suburbs, where most of the hotels, hostels, nightlife and shops are located, has improved greatly in recent years, due mainly to an increase in security measures, and you should experience few problems in these areas.

Apart from Johannesburg, city centres are generally safe during daylight hours, although listen to advice from locals about which areas to avoid. Closed-circuit cameras (CCTV) and private security guards have made Cape Town and Durban city centres as safe as European cities, but the likelihood of being mugged increases sharply after dark. The safest way to travel around cities at night is to take a taxi directly to and from your destination.

Townships While by no means out of bounds to tourists, it would not be wise to wander into a township by yourself. On the other hand, if you know a local or have friends living and working in South Africa who know their way around, a trip to a township market or nightclub can be an interesting and rewarding experience. Alternatively, go on a township tour which will undoubtedly give you a different picture of the way a very large number of urban South Africans live.

Carjacking This remains a problem in South Africa, although the number of incidents is constantly declining thanks to collaboration with neighbouring countries to crack down on stolen cars crossing borders.

The favoured location for this crime is at red traffic lights on a junction. It is a good idea to travel with the windows closed and the doors locked. When faced with a suspicious situation at a junction, it is general practice to jump the lights and get away as fast as possible. Incidents can also happen on quiet rural roads, so be vigilant at all times. Again, it is important to remember that carjackers are almost always armed and will use their weapons when faced with resistance. Note that the insurance on hire cars in South Africa is correspondingly high.

Student travellers

Anyone in full-time education is entitled to an **International Student Identity Card (ISIC)**. These are issued by student travel offices and travel agencies across the world and offer special rates on all forms of transport (including the **Baz Bus**) and other concessions and services. Visit www.isic.org for up-to-date information on cards and local contact details. **Youth Hostel Association (YHA)** cards also attract discounts at some of the backpacker hostels, for information visit www.hihostels.com.

Telephone

South Africa → *Country code: +27; international direct dialling code 00; directory enquires T1023; international operator T0009; international enquires T1025.*
You must dial the full 3-digit regional code for every number in South Africa, even when you are calling from within that region.

The telephone service is very efficient. Card and coin phones are widespread and work well – even in remote national parks there are usually card phones from which one can dial direct to anywhere in the world. Note that hotels usually double the rates and even a short international call can become very expensive.

Blue call boxes are coin-operated telephones but these are becoming rare as green card phones take over. Phone cards are sold for R10, R20, R50 and R100. They are available in larger supermarkets, newsagents, some chemists and Telkom vending machines. A R50 card is sufficient to make an international call to Europe for a few mins.

Lesotho → *Country code: +266.*
The local telephone system is reasonable in the lowlands but there is poor coverage in the mountain areas. There are no area codes. International calls are very expensive and only possible from the larger centres. Note that some accommodation options in Lesotho have reservation telephone numbers in South Africa; if you are calling these in Lesotho, you must dial the country's access code (00) followed by the code for South Africa (27).

Swaziland → *Country code: +268.*
When making a call within the country there are no area codes. When calling from South Africa, dial the international access code 00, followed by Swaziland's country code (+268), then the telephone number. Direct dialling for international calls is possible from coin and card phones in the urban and tourist areas. All the luxury hotels have an efficient telephone system but they charge very high rates for international calls.

Mobile phones
South Africa
South Africa uses the GSM system for mobile phones and overseas visitors should be able to use their mobiles on roaming. Alternatively, you can buy a local SIM card and start-up pack from any of the phone shops in the super-markets and at the 3 international airports, which also offer phone and SIM hire. For anyone travelling alone by car, especially women, it is essential to hire 1 for emergencies.

Lesotho

Reception is improving steadily even in the most remote places. This is largely due to the fact that a number of mobile phone towers have been put in place in outlying areas during the Lesotho Highlands Water Project.

Swaziland

If your mobile phone has international roaming it will work throughout Swaziland, otherwise local SIM and top-up cards are available for the only cell phone provider, Swazi MTN.

Time

South Africa, Lesotho and Swaziland have only 1 time zone: GMT +2 hrs (+1 during UK Summer Time Mar-Oct), 8 hrs ahead of USA Eastern Standard Time, 1 hr ahead of Europe; 8 hrs behind Australian Eastern Standard Time. There is no daylight saving.

Tipping

Waiters, hotel porters, stewards, chambermaids and tour guides should be tipped 10-15%, according to the service. When leaving tips make sure it goes to the intended person. It is common practice to tip petrol pump attendants, depending on their service – up to R5 for a fill up, oil and water check and comprehensive windscreen clean. It is also customary to tip car guards R2-5 if parking on the street. These are usually identified by a work vest or badge. On safari you are expected to tip guides. If in any doubt, ask the company that you booked with for advice on how much to tip.

Tour operators

UK and Ireland

Abercrombie & Kent, T0845-070 0600, www.abercrombiekent.co.uk.
Acacia Adventure Holidays, T020-7706 4700, www.acacia-africa.com.
Africa Explorer, T020-8987 8742, www.africa-explorer.co.uk.
Africa Travel Centre, 3rd floor, New Premier House, 150 Southampton Row, London WC1B 5AL, T0845-450 1520, www.africatravel.co.uk.
Africa Travel Resource, T01306-880770, www.africatravelresource.com.
Amazing Voyages Ltd, 52 Brook St, London W1K 5DS, T020-7268 2053, www.amazing voyages.co.uk. Luxury travel specialists.
Cedarberg African Travel, T020-8898 8510, www.cedarberg-travel.com.
Expert Africa, T020-8232 9777, www.expertafrica.com.
Explore, T0870-333 4001, www.explore.co.uk.
Global Village, T0844-844 2541, www.globalvillage-travel.com.

Odyssey World, T0845-370 7733,
www.odyssey-world.co.uk.
Rainbow Tours, T020-7226 1004,
www.rainbowtours.co.uk.
Somak, T020-8423 3000, www.somak.co.uk.
South African Affair, T020-7381 5222,
www.southafricanaffair.com.
Steppes Africa, T01285-880980,
www.steppestravel.co.uk.
Tim Best Travel, T020-7591 0300,
www.timbesttravel.com.
Wildlife Worldwide, T0845-130 6982,
www.wildlifeworldwide.com.

Rest of Europe

**Iwanowski's Individuelles Reisen
GmbH**, T+49 (0)21-332 6030, www.afrika.de.
Jambo Tours, T+49 (0)29-357 9191,
www.jambotours.de.

North America

Adventure Center, T1800-228 8747,
www.adventure-center.com.
Africa Adventure Company, T1800-882 9453,
T1954-491 8877, www.africa-adventure.com.
Bushtracks, T1707-433 0258,
www.bushtracks.com.
Maupintour, T1800-255 4266,
www.maupintour.com.

Australia and New Zealand

African Wildlife Safaris, T+61-(0)3-9249
3777, www.africanwildlifesafaris.com.au.
Africa Exclusive, T+61-(0)7-5474 8160,
www.africaexclusive.com.
Classic Safari Company, T+61-(0)2-9327
0666, www.classicsafaricompany.com.au.
Intrepid, T61-(0)3-9473 2626,
www.intrepidtravel.com.
Peregrine Adventure, T+61-(0)3-9662
2700, www.peregrine.net.au.

Tourist information

South Africa

South African Tourism (SATOUR) has a very
useful website with information on special
interest travel, maps, latest travel news,
airlines, accommodation and national parks.
The website is published in 15 languages and
each version provides specific information
for people coming from each individual
country, T011-895 3000, www.southafrica.net.
SATOUR also has offices around the world
(see below), which are useful for pre-travel
information. Regional (see below) and local
tourist boards are some of the best sources
of information once in the country; even
the smallest town will have a publicity
bureau with details of local sights and
accommodation. Local tourist offices
are listed under individual towns.

Tourist offices overseas

Australia Level 1, 117 York St, Sydney, NSW
2000, T02-9261 5000, bangu@southafrica.net.
France 61 Rue La Boetie, 75008 Paris,
T01-4561 0197, info.fr@southafrica.net.
Germany Friedensstr. 6-10, Frankfurt 60311,
T069-280950, info.de@southafrica.net.
Italy Via Mascheroni 19, 5th floor,
20145 Milano, T02-4391 1765,
info.it@southafrica.net.
Netherlands Jozef Isralskade 48 A,
1027 SB Amsterdam, T020-471 3181,
info.nl@southafrica.net.
UK 6 Alt Grove, London SW19 4DZ,
T020-8971 9350, info.uk@southafrica.net.
USA 500 5th Av, 20th floor, Suite 2040,
New York NY 10110, T1212-730 2929,
newyork@southafrica.net.

Regional tourist boards

**Cape Town and Western Cape
Tourism**, www.tourismcapetown.co.za.
Eastern Cape Tourism,
www.ectourism.co.za.
Free State Tourism,
www.freestatetourism.org.
Gauteng Tourism Authority,
www.visitgauteng.net.
Limpopo Province Tourism Board,
www.limpopotourism.org.za.
Mpumalanga Tourism Authority,
www.mpumalanga.com.

Northern Cape Tourism Authority, www.northerncape.org.za.
North West Province, www.tourismnorthwest.co.za.
Tourism KwaZulu Natal, www.zulu.org.za.

Websites

There are thousands of websites about travel in South Africa in a number of languages, and these days even the tiniest *dorps* (villages) have their own website. These are listed in the relevant chapters.

www.africaguide.com Everything you need to know about African travel, also sells holidays and reviews guidebooks.

www.exploresouthafrica.net General overview of the main tourist attractions.

www.fco.gov.uk UK Foreign Office, for the official advice on latest political situations.

www.gardenroute.org Wide-reaching website covering one of the most popular regions in South Africa.

www.go2africa.com Accommodation and holiday booking service, with useful practical information and links to overland companies.

www.southafrica.co.za General information and travel advice.

www.overlandafrica.com A variety of overland tours offered throughout Africa.

www.sanparks.org Full details of all the national parks, including online booking.

Lesotho

Tourist Information Centre, Basotho Shield building opposite the Basotho Hat building on Kingsway in Maseru, T2231 2427, Mon-Fri 0800-1700, Sat 0800-1300, is extremely helpful and stocks a range of brochures and maps.

If you are crossing into the country through Maseru Bridge be sure to drop in at the **Maloti Tourist Office** in Ladybrand, which also covers Lesotho in its jurisdiction (see page 729).

Useful websites

www.ltdc.org.ls Lesotho Tourism Development Corporation website has basic information for tourists.

www.lhwp.org.ls Information about the Lesotho Highlands Water Project; also has information about the new national parks.

Swaziland

Tourist information office, Swazi Plaza, Mbabane, T404 2531, www.welcometo swaziland.com, Mon-Fri 0800-1700, Sat 0830-1230.

There's a second tourist information office at the **Ngwenya border**, T442 4206, daily 0800-1700. Although this office isn't always manned, there are useful leaflets to pick up. You can also pick up leaflets at the **Mantenga Craft Centre**.

Visas and immigration

South Africa

Most nationalities including EU nationals and citizens from the USA, Canada, Australia and New Zealand don't need visas to enter South Africa. On arrival, visitors from these countries are granted temporary **visitors' permits**, lasting up to 90 days. You must have a valid return ticket or voucher for onward travel and at least one completely empty page in your passport to get a permit; without these you maybe denied entry.

It is possible to apply for an extension to the permit at one of the offices of the **Department of Home Affairs**, Cape Town T021-462 4970; Durban T031-308 7930; Johannesburg T011-836 3228; Tshwane (Pretoria) T012-314 8109; Nelson Mandela Bay (Port Elizabeth) T041-487 1026; www.home-affairs.gov.za. This can take up to 10 days and costs R425. You will need to produce documentation to show when you are leaving the country, such as a flight ticket or tour confirmation voucher, as well as proof of funds such as a credit card or TCs. Citizens of countries other than those listed above should consult the South African embassy or consulate in their country for information on visa requirements, or visit www.home-affairs.gov.za/visa_countries.asp.

Note that going to Lesotho or Swaziland and returning to South Africa is not a valid way to extend your holiday visa or permit. On re-entering South Africa, immigration officials will scan your original South African entry stamp for its date of departure. If this date has passed while you are in Lesotho or Swaziland, South African immigration will extend your visa for 2-4 weeks, during which time you are expected either to leave the country or to extend your visa. See www.home-affairs.gov.za, to find out the nearest office.

Lesotho

Most nationalities, including EU nationals and citizens from the USA, Canada, Australia, New Zealand and South Africa don't need visas to enter Lesotho, and will be given a 1 month permit with their entry stamp (although it is possible to ask for longer if you have proof of funds). Citizens of countries other than those listed above should consult the Lesotho embassy or consulate in their country for information on visa requirements. You must have at least 2 blank pages in your passport to enter.

Visitors who need a visa can wait until they are in South Africa and then contact the **Lesotho High Commission**, 391 Anderson St, corner of Thomas Edison St, Menlo Park, Tshwane (Pretoria) 0001, T012-460 7648, visa office Mon-Fri 0900-1630. In a few cases you can contact the Lesotho Overseas High Commission in your own country. When applying for a visa you must fill in an application form and provide a passport photo; processing takes 24 hrs. A single entry, valid for 1 month, costs R500. Alternatively the immigration regulations allow the border officials to let you enter Lesotho, and give you 72 hrs to present yourself to the immigration office in Maseru to get a visa. **Lesotho Immigration Department**, Transport Building, Assissi Rd, Maseru, T2232 3771. This is also where you can extend your permit but it's also worth asking at the larger border posts if they will extend it for you.

Swaziland

Most nationalities, including EU nationals and citizens from the USA, Canada, Australia, New Zealand and South Africa don't need visas to enter Swaziland, and 30-day permits can be obtained on arrival at any of the borders. They can also be extended at any of the borders.

Voltage

South Africa

Voltage 220/230 volts AC at 50 Hz, except for Tshwane (Pretoria), where it is 250 volts AC. Most plugs and appliances are 3-point round-pin (one 10 mm and two 8 mm prongs). Hotels usually have 2-pin sockets for razors.

Lesotho

Voltage 220/230 volts AC at 50 Hz.

Swaziland

Voltage 220-240v.

Weights and measures

The metric system is used in South Africa, Lesotho and Swaziland.

Women travellers

Although South Africa has an unusually high incidence of rape, tourists are, as a rule, not targeted and South Africa is a relatively safe country for women to travel in. However, the usual rules of not travelling alone after dark, never hitchhiking and avoiding quiet areas always apply. While women are not usually confronted with prejudice when checking into hotels or trying to be served, it is worth remembering that there is a strong macho element in most South African communities. Women may experience some unwanted attention from men, but nothing that can't be dealt with assertively. It is often a good idea to cover up in more conservative or rural areas – avoiding tight, revealing tops and short skirts should help.

Working in South Africa

There are no opportunities for travellers to obtain casual paid employment in South Africa, Lesotho and Swaziland and it is illegal for a foreigner to work without an official work permit. Most foreign workers in the country are employed through embassies, development or volunteer agencies or through foreign companies. For the most part these people will have been recruited in their countries of origin. A number of NGOs and voluntary organizations can arrange placements for volunteers, usually for periods ranging from 6 months to 2 years, visit www.volunteerafrica.org.

Contents

Footprint features

Cape Town & the Winelands

At a glance

◉ **Getting around** Buses, taxis, car hire or day tours recommended for the Cape Peninsula and Winelands.

◉ **Time required** Minimum 3 days for central Cape Town, 1 day for Cape Peninsula, 1-2 days for the Winelands.

☀ **Weather** Chilly in Jul and Aug. Best in Nov and Feb.

✖ **When not to go** Avoid the Christmas South African school holidays.

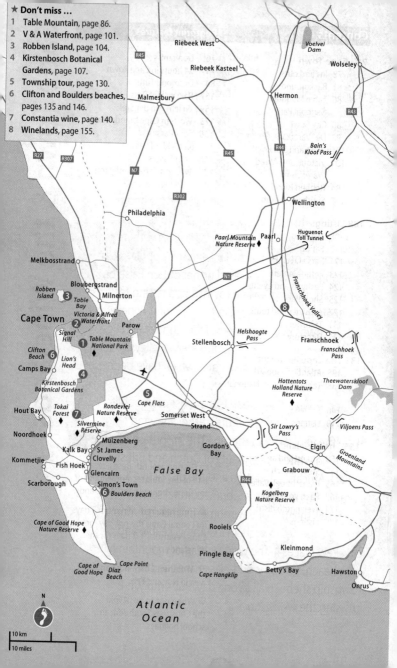

Voelvei
Dam

Riebeek West

Wolseley

Riebeek Kasteel

R45

Hermon

Malmesbury

R43

Bain's
Kloof Pass

R44

R45

Wellington

N7

R302

Philadelphia

Huguenot
Toll Tunnel

Paarl Mountain
Nature Reserve   Paarl

R27   R307

Melkbosstrand

N1

Franschhoek Valley

Bloubergstrand

Robben
Island   3   Table
              Bay

Milnerton

Table Bay

Helshoogte
Pass

Franschhoek

Victoria & Alfred
Waterfront

Cape Town   2

Parow

Stellenbosch

Franschhoek
Pass

Signal
Hill   1   Table Mountain
              National Park

Clifton
Beach   6   Lion's
              Head

Hottentots
Holland Nature
Reserve

Theewaterskloof
Dam

Camps Bay

4

Kirstenbosch
Botanical Gardens

Cape Flats

5

Hout Bay   Tokai   7
            Forest

Rondevlei
Nature Reserve

Somerset West

Sir Lowry's
Pass

Viljoens Pass

Noordhoek   Silvermine
             Reserve

Strand

Gordon's
Bay

Elgin

Groenland
Mountains

Kalk Bay

Muizenberg

Kommetjie   Fish Hoek   St James
                          Clovelly

False Bay

Grabouw

R44

Scarborough   Glencairn

Simon's Town

6   Boulders Beach

Kogelberg
Nature Reserve

Cape of Good Hope
Nature Reserve

Rooiels

Kleinmond

Pringle Bay

Hawston

Cape of
Good Hope   Cape Point
             Diaz
             Beach

Cape Hangklip

Betty's Bay

Onrus

N

Atlantic
Ocean

10 km
10 miles

South Africa's 'Mother City', dominated by Table Mountain and surrounded by the wild Atlantic, has unquestionably one of the most beautiful city backdrops in the world. Despite being a considerable urban hub, its surroundings are surprisingly untamed, characterized by a mountainous spine stretching between two seaboards and edged by rugged coast and dramatic beaches.

Central Cape Town with its grandiose colonial buildings and beautiful public gardens crammed up against modern skyscrapers lies in the steep-sided bowl created by Table Mountain. Atmospheric Victorian suburbs stretch around the lower slopes, while the Atlantic Seaboard with its promenade and dense crop of holiday flats and the popular V&A Waterfront development hug the coast. Further out on False Bay are the Cape Flats, their sprawling townships a lasting testimony of the Apartheid era. Beyond, in the beautiful Winelands region, the old towns of Stellenbosch, Franschhoek and Paarl nestle in a range of low mountains and scenic valleys covered by the vineyards of historic wine estates which have been cultivating grapes for some 300 years.

Cape Town's population is the most cosmopolitan in the country, with a mix of cultures, ethnicities and religions that drive the very pulse of the city. The mishmash of people, including white descendants of Dutch and British settlers, a black African population and the distinctive 'Cape Coloured' community, results in a vibrant cultural scene.

It is this mixture of environments and communities that makes Cape Town such an instantly likeable and captivating city. Few places in the world can offer mountain hiking, lazing on a beach, tasting world-class wines and drinking beer in a township shebeen all in one day. Put simply, it is a city worth crossing the world for.

Cape Town

To get the best idea of Cape Town's layout, head to the top of Table Mountain. From its summit, the city stretches below in a horseshoe formed by the mountains: Table Mountain is in the centre, with Devil's Peak to the east and Lion's Head and Signal Hill to the west. Straight ahead lies the City Bowl, the central business district backed by leafy suburbs. This is also the site of Cape Town's historical heart and where all the major museums, historical buildings and sights are. Further down is the Victoria & Alfred Waterfront, a slick development of shopping malls and restaurants. Following the coast around to the west, you come to the modern residential districts of Green Point and Sea Point which is now dominated by the enormous Green Point stadium currently being built for the 2010 FIFA World Cup™. In the opposite direction the southern suburbs stretch west and south, dipping from the mountain's slopes, and here, under a blanket of trees, are Cape Town's largest mansions as well as beautiful Kirstenbosch Botanical Gardens. ➤➤ For listings, see pages 108-134.

Ins and outs ➤➤ Colour map 8, B1.

Getting there

Cape Town International Airport ① airport enquiries, T021-9371200, flight information T0867-277888, www.acsa.co.za, is 22 km east of the city centre, or, out of rush hour a 20-minute drive. Shuttle services run from kiosks in the international arrivals hall. Alternatively you can pre-book one through your hotel, guesthouse or backpacker hostel; directly through **Magic Bus** ① T021-505 6300, www.magicbus.co.za, that drops off at hotels and guesthouses; or the **Backpacker Bus** ① T021-4397600, www.backpackerbus. co.za, that takes you to the backpacker hostel. This costs from R150 per person. Taxis running between the airport and town centre should have a special airport licence and they must use their meter by law; expect to pay around R250 to the city centre. Public transport from the airport is presently being put in place as part of the Integrated Rapid Transport (IRT) plan and will be operational by 2010 (see page 80). At the airport, there are presently two terminal buildings; for domestic and international arrivals and departures, but by the end of 2009, these will be linked by the new Terminal 2010, which will provide a centralized check-in for both domestic and international flights, as well as a new retail mall. Within international arrivals, **Cape Town Tourism** ① daily 0700-1700, can arrange accommodation and has a number of maps and leaflets to give out. The **Master Currency** exchange counter remains open for international arrivals and

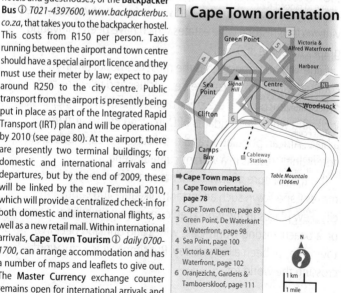

1 Cape Town orientation

➡ **Cape Town maps**

1 km
1 mile

24 hours in Cape Town

Start the day with an early-morning jog or stroll along the wide promenade that runs the length of **Mouille Point** and **Sea Point**. Take in some fresh ocean air and admire the huge ships in **Table Bay** waiting to get into Cape Town's harbour. Look out for the mammoth construction site of the new **Green Point Stadium** that dominates Cape Town's skyline and is being built for the 2010 FIFA World Cup South Africa™ that has been awarded to South Africa (see pages 28-29). Then take in the views of Table Mountain while enjoying a full English or healthy breakfast in the sunshine at any of the **V&A Waterfront**'s many al fresco restaurants.

After breakfast, browse the upmarket boutiques and curio shops in the **Victoria Wharf shopping mall**, and look for seals splashing around in the harbour. Alternatively, spend an hour or so in the **Two Oceans Aquarium**, where the highlight is the giant predators' tank that is home to ragged-tooth sharks and huge eagle rays. At the **Nelson Mandela Gateway** board the **Robben Island ferry** for the 3½-hour informative excursion to the famous island prison, 12 km offshore in **Table Bay**. Once there, the tour includes a bus ride around the island with great views back on to Table Mountain, a guided tour of the ex-maximum security complex and a peek into Nelson Mandela's former cell.

Back at the V&A Waterfront jump on the **Sightseeing Cape Town** hop-on, hop-off, bright red, open-topped double-decker bus for a ride through the city bowl to the **Table Mountain Lower Cableway Station**. The bus stops at the excellent **District Six Museum**, dedicated telling the story of the forced removals in Cape Town during Apartheid, and the imposing **Castle of Good Hope**, the oldest colonial building in South Africa, among many other of the city centre's museums and attractions. Ride the rotating cable car to the top of **Table Mountain** for the dizzying views of the **City Bowl**, Camps Bay and **Robben Island**, and grab a snack or toast your ascent with a glass of champagne at the highest restaurant in Cape Town, 1073 m above the city. If you're feeling fit, set off early and walk up; this takes about three hours. Back at the **Lower Cableway Station** jump on the bus and continue the drive over **Kloof Nek** and down into the fashionable suburb of **Camps Bay** on the Atlantic Seaboard. Here you can join the beautiful people at any one of the bars along **Victoria Road** for a cocktail and admire the swathe of perfect white-sand beach and pounding waves.

In the evening dine at one of the city's popular African restaurants: **Mama Africa**, **Marco's African Place** or the **Africa Cafe**, which all serve up authentic and tasty dishes such as grilled game meat and Cape Malay curries. Alternatively, opt for freshly caught Cape seafood and build your own platter at the **Cape Town Fish Market**, **The Codfather** or **Baia**, and be sure to accompany your meal with a good bottle of South African wine from Cape Town's Winelands. Those that want to see some local theatre or comedy should check out what's on at **Artscape**, the **Baxter Theatre** or the **Theatre on the Bay**. Nightcaps can be enjoyed in any of the late bars in Green Point or Camps Bay and late night revellers should head for the lively clubs at the top end of Long Street or the more sophisticated **Hemisphere** on the 31st floor of the ABSA building in the city centre or **Rhodes House** in Gardens. Late-night nibbles can be found at **Mr Pickwicks** on Long Street or the **Obz Cafe** in Observatory, which are both open until 0200-0300.

there are ATMs. You can hire mobile phones at **Vodacom's Rentaphone desk** ① *T021-934 4951, www.vodacom.co.za*, at domestic departures, or from **MTN's Cell Place** ① *T021-934 3261, www.mtnsp.co.za*, outlet at international departures. Both are open 0600-2300. Look out for joint deals between car hire companies and mobile phone companies.

The main **railway station** is in the centre of town and is also the terminus for the longcoach companies, Greyhound, Intercape and Translux. The complex is presently being redeveloped in line with the 2010 FIFA World Cup South Africa™ requirements. ➤➤ *For further details, see Transport, page 131.*

Getting around

Most of Cape Town's oldest buildings, museums, galleries and the commercial centre are concentrated in a relatively small area and best explored on foot. However, to explore more of the city, and to visit Table Mountain, the suburbs or the beaches, it's a good idea to rent a car. Otherwise, taxis are affordable, particularly if you use **Rikki**'s shared taxis (see page 133).

Alternatively, **Sightseeing Cape Town** ① *T021-5116000, www.citysightseeing.co.za, daily from 0830*, is a red, double-decker, open-top, hop-on hop-off bus that follows a 2¼-hour route around the city. There are two routes; the Red Route has 13 stops and a bus comes by every 20 minutes, while the Blue Route has 13 stops and buses come by every 50 minutes. Audio-commentary is available in eight languages and there's a special kids channel. The main ticket kiosk is outside the Two Oceans Aquarium at the V&A Waterfront, however you can buy tickets online and join anywhere on the routes. It's ideal if you don't want to drive, and stops include the Lower Cableway Station, Camps Bay, Kirstenbosch, all the city centre museums, and as far south as Hout Bay on the peninsula. A one-day ticket costs R120, children R60, and a two-day ticket is R200/R120. The buses are wheelchair friendly.

Public transport is in the way of Golden Arrow buses, which depart from the bus station in the city centre next to the Grand Parade and follow all the major routes where bus stops are clearly denoted, and minibus taxis which also ply the main roads and can be flagged down on the side of the street (see page 133). The latter are not particularly recommended to visitors, as there is the danger of petty crime on the crowded vehicles, but nevertheless they are cheap. However public road transport in Cape Town is about to go through a transformation as the city's **Integrated Rapid Transport (IRT)** plan develops. The first phase will be operational by 2010 when one route will link the airport with the city centre and a second route will link the West Coast through the city to Hout Bay. Further phases will continue after 2010. Transport will be in large buses, which will have their own exclusive dedicated traffic lanes with stations on the main roads, and will therefore operate in a similar way to trams or light railways. The vehicles and stations will be equipped for wheelchairs and prams, and will have CCTV and security guards.

Tourist information → *Phone code: 021. Postal code: 8000.*

Cape Town Tourism ① *The Pinnacle, corner of Burg and Castle streets, T021-487 6800, www.tourismcapetown.co.za, Mon-Fri 0800-1900, Sat 0830-1400, Sun 0900-1300, closes 1 hr earlier in winter (Apr-Sep)*, the official city tourist office, can help with bookings and tours throughout the Western Cape. It is an excellent source of information and a good first stop in the city. In addition to providing practical information about Cape Town, it can help with accommodation bookings and has plenty of information on nightlife and events. It is also home to **Western Cape Tourism** (same contact details) and there is a

South Africa National Parks (SANParks) desk ⓘ www.sanparks.org, where you can make reservations for the parks. There's also a café, gift shop and internet access. There are 18 other branches/desks throughout the Cape, the most useful of which is at the **Victoria & Alfred Waterfront** ⓘ T021-4054500, daily 0900-2100.

If you are planning a trip to Namibia, it is well worth picking up maps and brochures at the **Namibian Tourist Office** ⓘ underneath Cape Town Tourism, in the Pinnacle, T021-422 3298, www.namibiatourism.com.na, Mon-Fri 0800-1700. There's also a Namibia Wildlife Resorts desk where you can pre-book accommodation in Namibia's national parks (see Footprint Namibia).

Background

First people
The first evidence of human inhabitants in the Cape has been dated back to nearly 30,000 years ago. Rock art found in the area was created by nomadic San people (also known as Bushmen), a hunter-gatherer group which roamed across much of southern Africa. Some San groups survive today, mostly in Namibia and Botswana, despite continuing persecution. The original San were replaced about two thousand years ago by Khoi groups, a semi-nomadic people who settled in the Cape with herds of sheep and cattle.

First landing
António de Saldanha, a Portuguese admiral who lost his way going east, landed in Table Bay in 1503. They called the bay Aguada da Saldanha (it was renamed Table Bay in 1601 by **Joris van Spilbergen**). Saldanha and a party of the crew went ashore in search of drinking water. They followed a stream to the base of Table Mountain and then proceeded to climb to the top. From here Saldanha was able to get a clear view of the surrounding coastline and the confusion caused by the peninsula. On their return they found the crew unsuccessfully trying to barter with local indigenous Khoi for livestock. The trade quickly developed into a row which ended in bloodshed. There was another battle between the Portuguese and the Khoi in March 1510. On this occasion the Khoi had struck back after children and cattle were stolen by the sailors. Seventy-five Portuguese were killed, including **Dom Francisco de Almeida**, who had just finished five years as the first Portuguese Viceroy to India. Few Portuguese ships landed in Table Bay after this.

The Dutch and the VOC
By the end of the 16th century British and Dutch mariners had caught up with the Portuguese and they quickly came to appreciate the importance of the Cape as a base for restocking ships with drinking water and fresh supplies as they made their long journeys to the East. Indeed, seafarers found that they were able to exchange scraps of metal for provisions to supply a whole fleet.

The first moves to settle in the Cape were made by the Dutch, and on 6 April 1652 **Jan Van Riebeeck** landed in Table Bay. His ships carried wood for building and some small cannons, the first building to be erected being a small fort at the mouth of the Fresh River. The site of the original fort is where Grand Parade in the centre of Cape Town is today. Van Riebeeck was in charge of the supply station that belonged to the Dutch East India Company (Vereenigde Oost-Indische Compagnie or VOC). After the fort was built, gardens for fruit and vegetables were laid out and pastures for cattle acquired. As the settlement slowly grew, the Khoi people were driven back into the interior. Surprisingly, the early settlers were forbidden from enslaving the Khoi; instead, slaves were imported by the VOC from Indonesia and West Africa. Although many died, these slaves were the origin of the Cape Malay community.

In 1662 Jan van Riebeeck was transferred to India. Because of rivalries in Europe, the VOC was worried about enemy ships visiting the Cape, so work started on a new stone fort in 1666. Over the next 13 years several governors came and went. During this time the French and British went to war with Holland, but the British and the Dutch East India companies joined in a treaty of friendship in March 1674, and then in July of the same year a ship arrived with the news that the British and Dutch had made peace. In October 1679 one of the most energetic governors arrived in the Cape, **Simon van der Stel**. For the next 20 years van der Stel devoted his energies to creating a new Holland in southern Africa. During his period as Governor, van der Stel paid particular attention to the growth and development of Cape Town and the surrounding farmlands. The company garden was replanted, nursery plots were created and new experimental plants were collected from around the world. North of the gardens he built a large hospital and a lodge to house VOC slaves. New streets were laid out which were straight and wide with plenty of shade. New buildings in the town were covered in white limewash, producing a smart and prosperous appearance. In 1685, in appreciation for his work, he was granted an estate by the VOC, which he named **Constantia**. During his life he used the estate as an experimental agricultural farm and to grow oak trees which were then planted throughout the Cape.

One of his more significant contributions was the founding of the settlement at Stellenbosch. He directed the design and construction of many of the town's public buildings, and then introduced a number of the crops to be grown on the new farms. For many years he experimented with vines in an effort to produce wines as good as those in Europe. He was particularly pleased when in 1688 French Protestant Huguenot refugees arrived in the Cape. He saw to it that they were all settled on excellent farmlands in what became to be known as **Franschhoek** (French glen), the upper valley of the Berg River. In 1693 he had the foresight to appoint the town's first engineer to tackle problems of a clean water supply, and the removal of rubbish. Van der Stel died in June 1712 at Constantia.

Under the British

The next period of Cape Town's history was closely related to events in Europe, particularly the French Revolution. The ideas put forward by the Revolution of Liberty, Fraternity and Equality were not welcome in colonies such as the Cape. The Dutch East India Company was seen to be a corrupt organization and a supporter of the aristocracy. When the French invaded Holland, the British decided to seize the Cape to stop it from falling into French hands. After the Battle of Muizenberg in 1795, Britain took over the Cape from the representatives of the Dutch East India Company, which was bankrupt. In the Treaty of Amiens (1803) the Cape was restored to the Batavian Republic of the Netherlands. In 1806 the British took control again at the resumption of the Anglo-French wars.

When the British took over power it was inevitable that they inherited many of the problems associated with the colony. The principal issue was how to manage European settlement. The Dutch East India Company had only encouraged settlement as a cheap and efficient means of supplying their base in Cape Town. Thereafter they were only interested in controlling the Indian Ocean and supplying ships. By the time the British arrived, the Dutch settler farmers (the Boer) had become so successful that they were producing a surplus. The only problem was high production costs due to a shortage of labour. To alleviate the situation, a policy of importing slaves was implemented. This in turn led to decreased work opportunities for the settler families. Gradually the mood changed and the Boer looked to the interior for land and work. They were not impressed by the British administration and in 1836 the Great Trek was under way.

The growth of the city and the port

Industrialization in Europe brought great change, especially when the first steamship, the *Enterprise*, arrived in Table Bay in October 1825. After considerable delay and continual loss of life and cargoes, work began on two basins and breakwater piers. The first truckload of construction rocks was tipped by Prince Alfred, the 16-year-old son of Queen Victoria, on 17 September 1860. The Alfred Basin was completed in 1870 and a dry dock was added in 1881.

No sooner had the first basin been completed than diamonds and gold were discovered in South Africa. Over the next 40 years Cape Town and the docks were to change beyond recognition. In 1900 work began on a new breakwater which would protect an area of 27 km. After five years' work the **Victoria Basin** was opened. This new basin was able to shelter the new generation of ships using Table Bay but was unable to cope with the increase in numbers during the **Anglo-Boer War**. A third basin was created to the east of Victoria Basin in 1932 and for a while this seemed to have solved the problem, but fate was against Cape Town. In January 1936 the largest ship to visit South Africa docked with ease at B berth in the new basin. The boat, which was being used to help promote tourism in South Africa, was filled with wealthy and famous visitors. The morning on which she was due to sail, a strong southeasterly wind blew up and pressed the liner so firmly against the quay that she couldn't sail. In one morning all of the new basin's weaknesses had been exposed.

The next phase of growth was an ambitious one, and it was only completed in 1945. The project involved the dredging of Table Bay and the reclaiming of land. The spoil from the dredging provided 140 sq km of landfill, known as Foreshore. This new land extends from the present-day railway station to **Duncan Dock**. As you walk or drive around Cape Town today, remember that just over 50 years ago the sea came up to the main railway station. ⏩ *For the best record of the vibrant community that once thrived here, visit the excellent District Six Museum, see page 93.*

Impact of the Apartheid years

The descendants of the large and diverse slave population have given Cape Town a particularly cosmopolitan atmosphere. Unfortunately, Apartheid urban planning meant that many of the more vibrant areas of the city in the earlier part of this century were destroyed. The most notorious case is that of District Six, a racially mixed, low income housing area on the edge of the City Bowl. The Apartheid government could not tolerate such an area, especially so close to the centre of the city, and the residents, most of whom were classified as 'Coloured', were moved out to the soulless townships of the Cape Flats, such as Mitchell's Plain. The area was bulldozed but few new developments have taken place on the site: this accounts for the large areas of open ground in the area between the City Bowl and the suburb of Woodstock. Happily, the government recently handed over the first pocket of re-developed land to a small group of ex-residents of District Six and their descendants. What the area will become remains to be seen – the issue remains controversial as many ex-residents feel the open, barren land should remain as a poignant testimony to the forced removals.

Other reminders of the cosmopolitan history of Cape Town can be experienced in the area to the west of Buitengracht Street. This district, known as **Bo-Kaap**, is still home to a small Islamic (Cape Malay) community that somehow managed to survive the onslaught

Desmond Tutu

Like Nelson Mandela, Desmond Tutu is accepted as an influential and respected figure far beyond the borders of South Africa. His powerful oration and his simple but brave defiance of the Apartheid state has impressed the world. Tutu first caught the international headlines as an outspoken secretary general of the South African Council of Churches in the late 1970s, especially with his call for the international community to stop buying South African goods. But it was the award of the Nobel Peace Prize in 1984 that really established him as an international figure.

Desmond Tutu was born on 7 October 1931 in Klerksdrop and was educated in local mission schools and the Johannesburg Bantu High School in the Western Native township. After obtaining a BA and teaching diploma he taught at a high school in Krugersdorp before going to St Peter's Theological College to train as an Anglican priest. After being ordained he moved to London with his wife and young family, living in Golders Green, while he studied for both a BA and an MA in Theology. In 1966 he returned to South Africa.

After a spell teaching in the Eastern Cape, Tutu became a lecturer at the National University of Lesotho. He was in England again for three years in the early 1970s, before taking an appointment as the Anglican Dean of Johannesburg, but then quickly moved back to Lesotho to become Bishop. In 1978 he moved to Johannesburg once again, now as the secretary general of the South African Council of Churches. It was at about this time that the press began to take notice of Tutu's forceful anti-Apartheid statements.

In response to Tutu's comments about Apartheid the South African government took away his passport to prevent him speaking at international conferences, though he was occasionally allowed temporary travel documents and was able to address some important meetings and hold discussions with other religious leaders. Tutu made it clear that he believed that economic sanctions on South Africa were essential to make the Apartheid state introduce reforms at a faster pace. These comments obviously annoyed the South African government and Tutu was regarded as a dangerous opponent. The government was, however, always wary of treating him as cruelly as they treated many of their other opponents, as they knew that any mistreatment would lead to an enormous international outcry. This was especially so

of Apartheid urban planning. The coloured population of Cape Town has historically outweighed both the white and African populations, hence the widespread use of Afrikaans in the city. This balance was maintained by Apartheid policies that prevented Africans from migrating into the Western Cape from the Eastern Cape and elsewhere. This policy was not, however, able to withstand the pressure of the poor rural Africans' desire to find opportunities in the urban economy. Over the past couple of decades there has been an enormous growth in the African population of Cape Town. Many of these new migrants have been forced to settle in squatter areas, such as the notorious Crossroads Camp next to the N2 highway. During the Apartheid era these squatter camps were frequently bulldozed and the residents evicted but as soon as they were cleared they sprang up again. Crossroads was a hotbed of resistance to the Apartheid state and much of the Cape Flats area existed in a state of near civil war throughout much of the 1980s.

after 1984, when he was awarded the Nobel Peace Prize.

In February 1985 Tutu was made Bishop of Johannesburg and finally, in April 1986, he was elected Anglican Archbishop of Cape Town. His election was not popular with many white rank and file members of the Anglican Church who believed his calls for economic sanctions were harming their economic interests. The Anglican Church's white congregation have tended to come from the English-speaking sections of the community who regard themselves as more liberal than the Afrikaners. They did not want to be seen to oppose Tutu on grounds of race. Furthermore, it would have appeared unchristian to complain too vocally about how their privileged pockets had been affected by his stance on sanctions. Opposition was, therefore, most commonly expressed through the criticism that he was mixing religion with politics. This claim was not easy to sustain, however, as Tutu always brought a strictly moral and Christian approach to all his 'political' interventions. He often headed protest marches dressed in his Archbishop's robes, though this did not stop him being arrested on a couple of occasions and even tear-gassed.

Since the end of Apartheid in South Africa Tutu has continued to play a prominent, though not quite as central, public role. During 1996 he chaired the hearings of the Truth and Reconciliation Committee and argued forcibly that the policy of granting amnesty to all who admitted their crimes was an important step in healing the nation's scars. His continued espousal of a Christian philosophy of forgiveness has at times angered some of the families of the victims of Apartheid, who emphasize instead the need for justice, but few could deny the sincerity of Tutu's belief in what was undisputedly a healing process.

In recent years, Tutu has used his voice in international conflict resolution such as those in Zimbabwe, the Gaza Strip and Kenya. In 2007, Nelson Mandela, Graça Machel and Desmond Tutu convened a group of world leaders to contribute their wisdom, independent leadership and integrity to tackle some of the world's toughest problems. This new group is known as The Elders, and Tutu is presently chairman. Nelson Mandela once said of him, "sometimes strident, often tender, never afraid and seldom without humour, Desmond Tutu's voice will always be the voice of the voiceless".

Today, Cape Town remains the most cosmopolitan city in South Africa. The official colour barriers have long since disappeared and residential boundaries are shifting. The economic balance, too, is beginning to change: a black middle class has emerged in recent years, and the coloured middle class is strengthening.

Like the other host cities, since it was announced that South Africa is to host the 2010 FIFA World Cup™, development across Cape Town has gone into overdrive. The unmissable Green Point Stadium now dominates the skyline and the surrounding development of the Green Point commons is well under way, which includes new roads, sports fields, an 18-hole golf course (to replace the one the stadium has been built on) and infrastructure associated with the stadium. Elsewhere in the city, the airport is being extended, the railway station is being refurbished, and the N1 and N2 highways are being widened and improved with additional access roads and lanes being added for the IRT.

Table Mountain National Park

ⓘ *www.sanparks.org. The most popular ascent of the mountain directly above the City Bowl is described below; other parts of the park are covered later in the chapter.*

Cape Town is defined, first and foremost, by Table Mountain. Rising a sheer 1073 m from the coastal plain, it dominates almost every view of the city, its sharp slopes and level top making it one of the world's best-known city backdrops. For centuries, it was the first sight of Cape Town afforded to seafarers, its looming presence visible for hundreds of kilometres. Certainly, its size continues to astonish visitors today, but it is the mountain's wilderness, bang in the middle of a bustling conurbation, that makes the biggest impression. Table Mountain sustains over 1400 species of flora, as well as baboons, dassies (large rodents) and countless birds. The Table Mountain National Park encompasses the entire peninsula stretching from here to Cape Point. Between September and March you have the additional pleasure of seeing the mountain covered in wild flowers. The most common vegetation is fynbos, of which there is an extraordinary variety, but you'll also see proteas plus the rare silver tree, *Leucadendron argenteum*.

Aerial Cableway

ⓘ *Tafelberg Rd, information line T021-424 8181, www.tablemountain.net; the first car up is at 0830, the last car down varies from 1800 to 2200 depending on the time of year, both the information line and the website has up-to-the-minute details of times and, given Cape Town's unpredictable weather, will tell you if the cableway is open or not (always check before going up to the Lower Cableway Station). Return ticket for adults R145, children 4-18 R76, family ticket, 2 adults and 2 children R370; one-way ticket for adults R74, children under 18 R38. Under 4's go free. Also check the website for special offers; 2 for the price of 1 on summer evenings to watch the sunset for example. Quite uniquely, the cableway is free to South African citizens on their birthdays. Note, you cannot pre-book tickets because of the weather factor and the cableway can close immediately without notice. In the summer season, Dec-Jan, this can mean queues. The cableway is closed for annual maintenance for 2 weeks end Jul/beginning Aug (check the website for exact dates). There are a number of options of getting to the lower cableway station; you can drive and parking is along Tafelberg Rd on either side of the station, go by taxi and once you come back down there is a taxi rank at the station, by Rikki taxi, by the Cape Town City Sightseeing bus, or by regular Golden Arrow bus from the city centre to Camps Bay and get off at Kloof Nek, from where it is a 1.5 km walk up Tafelberg Road to the station.*

The dizzying trip to the top in the Aerial Cableway is one of Cape Town's highlights. The first cableway was built in 1929, and since then has had three upgrades, the latest being in 1997. It's estimated to have carried up some 18 million people to date. There are two cars, each carrying up to 65 passengers, and as you ride up the floor rotates, allowing a full 360° view. Journey time is just under five minutes. In the base of each car is a water tank that can carry up to 4000 litres of fresh water to the top. There is the Table Mountain Café at the top station, which also has a deli for takeaway sandwiches, cheese and sushi platters and other light meals. To conserve water, they've recently introduced compostable plates and containers. An extensive network of paths has been laid out from the top station, allowing walks of various lengths, leading to different lookout points with stunning views of the City Bowl, Cape Flats, Robben Island and back along the peninsula. There are also free guided walks daily at 1000 and 1200.

Hiking → *Mountain Rescue: T10177.*

The entire area is a nature reserve, and the mountain is protected as a national monument. There are numerous paths climbing to the top. The most popular route starts 1.5 km beyond the Lower Cableway Station and follows a course up Platteklip Gorge; there's another path from Kirstenbosch Botanical Gardens. Both take about two to three hours to the top, although they are both fairly tough and should not be taken lightly. Given Table Mountain's size and location, conditions can change alarmingly quickly. The weather may seem clear and calm when you set out, but fog (the famous 'Table Cloth' which flows from the top) and rain can descend without warning. Numerous people have been caught out and the mountain has claimed its fair share of lives. There have also been recent muggings in Platteklip Gorge, though authorities are presently doing their best to address the problem.

Before venturing out, make sure you have suitable clothing, food and water. Take warm clothes, a windbreaker, a waterproof jacket, a hat, sunscreen, sunglasses, plenty of water (2 litres per person) and energy foods. Never climb alone and inform someone of which route you're taking and what time you should be back. Also be aware that if the weather is too unfavourable for the cableway to be open, don't rely on it being open to take you back down, so allow enough daylight hours to make the descent on foot. A detailed map is essential – these can be purchased at the tourist office. For those wanting to spend more time on the mountain, an 100 km overnight trail – the **Hoerikwagga Trail** (meaning 'sea mountain' in Khoi) – was introduced in 2005. The name means 'mountains in the sea' in an indigenous language. The six-day trek involves sleeping in tented camps and renovated forester houses dotted along the top of the mountain, and food and overnight gear is carried by porters. It starts in central Cape Town and ascends Platteklip Gorge and then follows the spine of the peninsula down to Cape Point. For full details, contact the tourist office or SANParks (see Tourist information, page 80). If you're interested in learning about the mountain's flora and fauna, take a guide or a tour (see Activities and tours, page 127).

Signal Hill

Signal Hill's summit offers spectacular views of the city, the Twelve Apostles (the mountainous spine stretching south from Table Mountain) and the ocean. It is possible to drive to the 350-m summit, which means that it can get pretty busy with tour groups around sunset. Nevertheless, watching the sun dip into the Atlantic from this viewpoint with a cold sundowner in hand is a highlight of a visit to Cape Town. Avoid being there after dark, as there have been reports of muggings, although the presence of security officers has now reduced this considerably. From the town centre, follow signs for the Lower Cableway station and take a right at Kloof Nek opposite the turning for the cableway station. On the lower slopes above Bo-Kaap is the Noon Gun which is fired electronically at noon every day, except Sunday. There is also a *karamat* (Islamic tomb) on the hill.

Lion's Head

Halfway along the road up Signal Hill you pass Lion's Head, a popular hiking spot. The climb to the peak is fairly easy going, and takes about two hours, and the 360° views from the top are incredible. There are two routes to the top: the easier of the two winds around the mountain; the quicker one involves climbing up a couple of drops with the aid of chains. Both are signposted. Hiking to Lion's Head is especially popular at full moon, when Capetonians watch the sunset from the peak and then descend by the light of the moon. Take plenty of water and a torch, and always climb in a group.

From the Lower Cableway Station, you look out over the central residential suburbs of Tamboerskloof (Drummers' Ravine), Gardens, Oranjezicht (Orange View) and Vredehoek (Peaceful Corner), and beyond here lie the high-rise blocks of the business district. Together these form the City Bowl, a term inspired by the surrounding mountains. Closest to the mountain is **Oranjezicht**, a quiet district with a good selection of guesthouses and B&B accommodation. Up until 1900 the area was a farm of the same name. On the boundary with Gardens is the **De Waal Park** and **Molteno Reservoir**. Originally built as a main storage facility for the city in 1881, the reservoir now provides a peaceful wooded spot from where you can enjoy a view of the city. Close by, on the corner of Prince Street and Sir George Grey Street, is an **old iron pump**. Such pumps were once dotted about the city for people to draw water for domestic use.

There is nothing peaceful about **Vredehoek** today, as the De Waal Drive (M3) brings rush hour traffic into the top end of town from the southern suburbs and beyond. Most of the area has been given over to ugly high-rise apartments, though the residents benefit from some excellent views. This was the area in which many Jewish immigrants from Eastern Europe settled, and have to a large part remained.

Gardens is a lively neighbourhood with a choice of quality restaurants and comfortable guesthouses. Cape Town's best-known hotel, the **Mount Nelson**, is situated here in its own landscaped gardens. The grand gateway to the hotel was built in 1924 to welcome the Prince of Wales. From here the land slopes gently towards the Waterfront, with the commercial heart of the city laid out in between. This was the area where the Dutch East India Company first created fruit and vegetable gardens to supply the ships' crews who suffered greatly from scurvy. Across Orange Street from the entrance to the Mount Nelson Hotel is the top end of **Government Avenue**, a delightful pedestrian route past Company Gardens and many of the city's main museums. Originally sheltered by lemon trees, it is now lined with oaks and myrtle hedges, and is one of Cape Town's most popular walks. It was declared a national monument in 1937.

South Africa Museum and Planetarium

ⓘ *25 Queen Victoria St, at the top end of Company's Garden, T021-4813800, www.iziko. org.za. Daily 1000-1700, R15, children under 16 free, free on public holidays. There's a shop and café in the museum.*

This, the city's most established museum, specializes in natural history, ethnography and archaeology, and is a good place to take children. There are extensive displays of the flora and fauna of southern Africa, including the popular Whale Well and interactive Shark World area, but the highlight is the 'IQe – the Power of Rock Art' exhibition. The displays of ancient San rock art have been in the museum for almost 100 years but, following a process of consultation and dialogue with Khoi-San communities, they have been re-interpreted in a far more sensitive and illuminating manner. The exhibits focus on the significance and symbolism of San rock art, with some fascinating examples including the beautifully preserved Linton panel, which depicts the trance experiences of shamans. Other themes explored include rainmaking and the significance of animal imagery; the eland, for example, appears more often than any other animal in San rock art, and it holds a central role in all major rituals, from teenage initiation to marriage and rainmaking. The whole exhibition, although short, is beautifully arranged and accompanied by the sound of San singing, a disjointed and haunting sound.

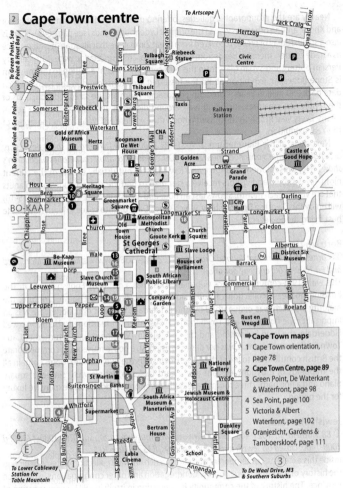

2 Cape Town centre

To Artscape

Jack Craig

Hertzog

Hertzog

Oswald Pirow

To Green Point, Sea Point & Hout Bay

To 2

Long

Heerengracht

Tulbagh Square

Riebeeck Statue

Civic Centre

Hans Strijdom

Chiappini

Bree

Prestwich

SAA

Thibault Square

Somerset

Buitengracht

Riebeeck

Lower Burg

CNA

Taxis

Railway Station

Waterkant

Gold of Africa Museum

Hertz

Koopmans-De Wet House

Burg

St George's Mall

Adderley St

Golden Acre

Strand

Castle

Castle of Good Hope

Castle St

Grand Parade

To Green Point & Sea Point

Strand

Hout

Heritage Square

Darling

Berg

Shortmarket St

Greenmarket Square

Longmarket St

Plein

City Hall

Longmarket St

BO-KAAP

Rose

Church

Bree

Metropolitan Methodist Church

Old Town House

Groote Kerk

Church Square

Corporation

Parade

Caledon

Wale

St Georges Cathedral

Albertus

Bo-Kaap Museum

Slave Lodge

District Six Museum

Dorp

Slave Church Museum

South African Public Library

Houses of Parliament

Barrack

Leeuwen

Commercial

Roeland

Upper Pepper

Pepper

Loop

Company's Garden

St Johns

Hope

Bloem

Keerom

Buitengracht

New Church

Bulten

Queen Victoria St

Parliament

Rust en Vreugd

Orphan

St Martin

Baths

National Gallery

Vrede

Paddock

Buitensingel

Lion

Bryant

Jordaan

Whitford

South Africa Supermarket

South Africa Museum & Planetarium

Jewish Museum & Holocaust Centre

Government Av

Dunkley Square

Carlsbrook

Bertram House

Rheede

Orange

Kloof St

Faure

Park

Labia Cinema

Hatfield

School

Annandale

To Lower Cableway Station for Table Mountain

Up Buitengracht

New Church

To De Waal Drive, M3 & Southern Suburbs

➡ Cape Town maps

1 Cape Town orientation, page 78
2 Cape Town Centre, page 89
3 Green Point, De Waterkant & Waterfront, page 98
4 Sea Point, page 100
5 Victoria & Albert Waterfront, page 102
6 Oranjezicht, Gardens & Tamboerskloof, page 111

200 metres

200 yards

Sleeping
Backpack 1 E1
Cape Diamond 18 C2
Cape Heritage 8 B1
Cape Town Hollow 3 D2
Cat & Moose
Backpackers 5 D2
Daddy Long Legs 16 C1
Grand Daddy 12 B1
Inn Long Street 14 D1
Long St Backpackers 11 D2
Park Inn 10 B2
Protea Hotel Fire & Ice 4 E1
Tudor 17 C2
Urban Chic 19 D1
Westin Grand Cape Town
Arabella Quays 2 A1

Eating
Africa Café 1 C1
Biesmiellah 9 C1
Caveau 10 C1
Five Flies 3 C2
Mama Africa 5 D1
Marco's African Place 6 B1
Mr Pickwicks 7 D1
Rcaffé 13 C1
Royale 12 D2
Savoy Cabbage 2 B1
Simply Asia 10 C1

Sundance 10 C1

Bars & clubs
Chrome 14 D1
Hemisphere 16 B2
Jo'burg 17 D1
Marvel 18 D1
Vertigo 15 C1
Zula 19 D1

Nearby are the ethnographic galleries, offering interesting displays on the San, Khoi and Xhosa, among others, as well as the original Lydenburg Heads (see page 649). There is also a small display of pieces recovered from Great Zimbabwe that illustrate its importance as a trade centre – there are beads from Cambay, India, Chinese Celadon ware, 13th-century Persian pottery and Syrian glass from the 14th century. A recent addition to the museum is Stone Bones, an exhibition about the fossilized skeletons found in the Karoo, which date back 250 million years – predating dinosaurs. There are life-sized reproductions of the reptile-like creatures, including walk-around dioramas and examples of the actual fossils. Every year in spring the museum hosts the excellent BBC Wildlife Photographer of the Year exhibition.

Next door, at the **Planetarium** ⓘ *T021-481 3900, www.iziko.org.za, show times vary depending on what's on; check the website, R20, children R6, adult chaperones at children's shows R10,* presentations change every few months, but usually a view of the current night sky is shown and visitors receive a star map to find the constellations and planets that are visible each month. Shows last an hour and are fascinating. Children (aged 5-10) will enjoy the Davy the Dragon show, which sends Davy off into space to learn how to the best flying dragon ever.

Bertram House
ⓘ *Corner of Government Av and Orange St, T021-424 9381, www.iziko.org.za, Mon, Wed and Fri 1000-1700, entry by donation.*
This early 19th-century red-brick Georgian House has a distinctly English feel to it. The building houses a collection of porcelain, jewellery, silver and English furniture, the majority of which was bequeathed by Ann Lidderdale. Winifred Ann Lidderdale was an important civic figure in Cape Town in the 1950s. After her marriage to Henry Maxwell Lidderdale, she lived in England and the USA, but in 1951 the couple returned to Cape Town for their retirement. It was her desire to establish a house museum to commemorate the British contribution to life at the Cape. Downstairs the two drawing rooms contain all the trappings of a bygone elegant age – card tables, a Hepplewhite settee, a square piano and a fine harp. Three rooms have wallpaper from London, a very expensive luxury for the period.

Jewish Museum
ⓘ *88 Hatfield St, T021-465 1546, www.sajewishmuseum.co.za, Sun-Thu 1000-1700, Fri 1000-1400, closed on Jewish and public holidays, R35, children R15.*
Inside this excellent, contemporary museum is a rich and rare collection of items depicting the history of the Cape Town Hebrew Congregation and other congregations in the Cape Province. The history of the community is interesting in itself: in 1841 a congregation of 17 men assembled for the first time in Cape Town to celebrate Yom Kippur. At the meeting they set about the task of raising funds to build a synagogue, and in 1862 the foundation stone was laid for the first synagogue in southern Africa. The following year the building was completed and furnished – quite a feat for such a small community at the time. On display upstairs are bronze Sabbath oil lamps, *Chanukkah* lamps, *Bessamin* spice containers, *Torah* scrolls, *Kiddush* cups and candlesticks. There is a beautiful stained-glass window depicting the Ten Commandments in Hebrew. From here a glass corridor leads you to a newer section of the museum that is devoted to the history of Jewish immigration to the Cape, mainly from Lithuania. A lot of thought has been put into the displays, which include photographs, immigration certificates, videos and a full

reconstruction of a Lithuanian *shtetl*, or village. There are special displays outlining the stories of famous Jewish South Africans, including Helen Suzman and Isie Maisels. The museum complex also houses a library, café and bookshop.

Holocaust Centre
ⓘ *88 Hatfield St, T021-462 5553, www.ctholocaust.co.za, Sun-Thu 1000-1700, Fri 1000-1300, entry by donation.*

An intelligent and shocking examination of the Holocaust can be found next door at this modern museum. Exhibits follow a historical route, starting with a look at anti-Semitism in Europe in previous centuries, and then leading to the rise of Nazism in Germany, the creation of ghettos, death camps and the Final Solution, and liberation at the end of the war. Video footage, photography, examples of Nazi propaganda and personal accounts of the Holocaust produce a vividly haunting and shocking display. The exhibits cleverly acknowledge South Africa's recent emergence from Apartheid and draw parallels between both injustices, as well as looking at the link between South Africa's Greyshirts (who were later assimilated into the National Party) and the Nazis. The local context is highlighted further at the end of the exhibition, with video accounts of Jews who survived the Holocaust and moved to Cape Town.

National Gallery
ⓘ *Government Av, T021-467 4660, www.iziko.org.za, Tue-Sun 1000-1700, R15, children (under 16), free.*

The National Gallery is one of the city's finest museums, housing a permanent collection but also hosting some excellent temporary exhibitions that include the best of the country's contemporary art. The original collection was bequeathed to the nation in 1871 by Thomas Butterworth Bailey, and features a collection of 18th- and 19th-century British sporting scenes, portraits and Dutch paintings. Far more interesting are the changing exhibitions of contemporary South African art and photography. Check the website to see what's on. There's a good souvenir shop on site.

Rust en Vreugd
ⓘ *78 Buitenkant St, T021-464 3280, Tue-Thu 1000-1700, entry by donation. Note this is temporarily closed until late-2009 while they install access for wheelchairs.*

A few hundred metres east of the National Gallery, hidden behind a high whitewashed wall, is this 18th-century mansion. It was declared a historical monument in 1940, and was subsequently restored to its original finery. Today it houses six galleries displaying a collection of watercolours, engravings and lithographs depicting the history of the Cape. Of particular note are Schouten's watercolour of Van Riebeeck's earth fort (1658), watercolours by Thomas Baines (a British artist who travelled extensively in South Africa and Australia) of climbing Table Mountain, lithographs by Angas of Khoi and Zulus, and a collection of cartoons by Cruikshank depicting the first British settlers arriving in the Cape. These are all part of the William Fehr Collection. Commercial exhibitions are held in the galleries upstairs.

Company's Garden
ⓘ *Daily 0700-1900, closes 1800 Jun-Aug.*

Running alongside Government Avenue are the peaceful Company Gardens, situated on the site of Jan van Riebeeck's original vegetable garden, which was created in 1652 to grow produce for settlers and ships bound for the East. It is now a small botanical garden, with lawns, a variety of labelled trees, ponds filled with Japanese koi and a small aviary. It's a popular spot with office workers at lunchtime. The grey squirrels living amongst the oak trees were introduced by Cecil Rhodes from America. There are also a couple of statues here: opposite the South African Public Library at the lower end of the garden, is the oldest statue in Cape Town, that of Sir George Grey, governor of the Cape from 1854 to 1862. Close by is a statue of Cecil Rhodes, pointing northwards in a rather unfortunate flat-handed gesture, with an inscription reading, "Your hinterland is there", a reminder of his ambition to paint the map pink from the Cape to Cairo. There is a café in the garden, serving drinks and snacks beneath the trees.

South African Public Library

ⓘ *5 Queen Victoria St, behind St George's Cathedral, T021-424 6320, www.nlsa.ac.za, Mon, Tue, Thu, Fri 0900-1700, Wed 1000-1700.*

Adjoining the gardens is the South African Public Library, which opened in 1818. It is the country's oldest national reference library and was one of the first free libraries in the world. Today it houses an important collection of books covering South Africa's history. The building also has a bookshop and an internet café.

Houses of Parliament

ⓘ *Entry via Parliament St gate, T021-403 2266, www.parliament.gov.za, public gallery tickets available during parliamentary sessions Jan-Jun, overseas visitors must present their passports, phone ahead for tours of the chambers and Constitutional Assembly.*

On the other side of the avenue are the Houses of Parliament. The building was completed in 1885, and when the Union was formed in 1910 it became the seat for the national parliament. In front of the building is a marble statue of Queen Victoria, erected by public subscription in honour of her Golden Jubilee. It was unveiled in 1890.

St George's Cathedral

ⓘ *5 Wale St, T021-424 7360, www.stgeorgescathedral.com. Mon-Fri 0800-1600 and during services in the evenings and at weekends.*

The last building on Government Avenue and on the corner of Wale Street is St George's Cathedral, best known for being Archbishop Desmond Tutu's territory from 1986 until 1996 (see box, page 84). It is from here that he led over 30,000 people to City Hall to mark the end of Apartheid, and where he coined the now universal phrase 'Rainbow Nation'. The building was designed by Sir Herbert Baker in the early 20th century. Inside, some of the early memorial tablets have been preserved, while over the top of the stairs leading to the crypt is a memorial to Lady D'Urban, wife of Sir Benjamin D'Urban, the Governor of the Cape from 1834 to 1838. Under the archway between the choir and St John's Chapel is a bronze recumbent statue of Archbishop West Jones, the second Archbishop of Cape Town (1874-1908). The Great North window is a fine piece of stained glass depicting the pioneers of the Anglican church. There is a small café, **The Crypt**, open during the day for light snacks and breakfasts. The Cathedral's choir is superb and they regularly perform at evensong and at organ recitals. Check the website for the music programme.

Slave Lodge

ⓘ *T021-460 8242, www.iziko.org.za. Mon-Sat 1000-1700, R15, children under 16 free.*

On the corner of Adderley and Wale streets is Slave Lodge, the second oldest building in Cape Town. The building has had a varied history, but its most significant role was as a slave lodge for the VOC (see page 81) – between 1679 and 1811 the building housed up to 1000 slaves. Local indigenous groups were protected by the VOC from being enslaved; most slaves were consequently imported from Madagascar, India and Indonesia, creating the most culturally varied slave society in the world. Conditions at the lodge were appalling and up to 20% of the slaves died every year.

It has now been developed into a museum chartering the history of the building and slavery in South Africa. At the entrance to the exhibition is a slick cinema room, with two flat-screen TVs showing a 15-minute film on the history of slavery in the Cape, highlighting the rules under which slaves lived, the conditions in which they were imported and sold, and the fundamental role slavery played in the success of Cape Town. Beyond here, the museum has a series of displays, including a model of a slave ship and images and sounds of what life was like in the lodge. The top floor houses a muddle of British and VOC weapons, household goods, furniture and money, as well as relics from Japan and ancient Rome, Greece and Egypt.

Groote Kerk
ⓘ T021-422 0569, www.grootekerk.org.za. Daily 1000-1900, free guided tours available.
Nearby is one of Cape Town's older corners, **Church Square**, site of the Groote Kerk. Up until 1834 the square was used as a venue for the auctioning of slaves from the Slave Lodge, which faced onto the square. All transactions took place under a tree – a concrete plaque marks the old tree's position.

The Groote Kerk was the first church of the Dutch Reformed faith to be built in South Africa (building started in 1678 and it was consecrated in 1704). The present church, built between 1836 and 1841, is a somewhat dull, grey building designed and constructed by Hermann Schutte after a fire had destroyed most of the original. Many of the old gravestones were built into the base of the church walls, the most elaborate of which is the tombstone of Baron van Rheede van Oudtshoorn. Inside, more early tombstones and family vaults are set into the floor, while on the walls are the coats of arms of early Cape families. Note the locked pews, which were rented out to wealthy families in the 19th century. Two of the Cape's early governors are buried here – Simon van der Stel (1679-1699) and Ryk Tulbagh (1751-1771).

District Six Museum
ⓘ 25A Buitenkant St, T021-466 7200, www.districtsix.co.za. Mon 0900-1500, Tue-Sat 0900-1600, entry by donation. There is a small café and a bookshop in the museum.
This small museum, housed in the Methodist Church, is one of Cape Town's most powerful exhibitions and gives a fascinating glimpse of the inanity of Apartheid. District Six was once the vibrant, cosmopolitan heart of Cape Town, a largely coloured inner city suburb renowned for its jazz scene. In February 1966, P W Botha, then Minister of Community Development, formally proclaimed District Six a 'white' group area. Over the next 15 years, an estimated 60,000 people were given notice to leave their homes and were moved to the new townships on the Cape Flats. The area was razed, and to this day remains largely undeveloped. Over the years there has been much talk about relocating some of those who were originally displaced to new housing in the area, but as yet there has been no progress.

The museum contains a lively collection of photographs, articles and personal accounts depicting life before and after the removals. There are usually a couple of musicians at the back, tinkering away at their guitars and tin pipes and adding immeasurably to the atmosphere of the place. Highlights include a large map covering most of the ground floor on which ex-residents have been encouraged to mark their homes and local sights. The **Namecloth** is particularly poignant: a 1.5-m-wide length of cloth has been provided for ex-residents to write down their comments, part of which hangs by the entrance. It has grown to over 1 km, and features some moving thoughts. A display in the back room looks at the forced removals from the Kirstenbosch area.

City Hall and Grand Parade

From Adderley Street, a short walk down Darling Street will take you to the City Hall and the Grand Parade. The latter is the largest open space in Cape Town and was originally used for garrison parades before the castle was completed. In 1994, after his release from prison, Nelson Mandela made his first speech from City Hall to over 100,000 people. Today the oak-lined parade is used as a car park and twice a week it is taken over by a colourful market (see page 126). It is presently being re-landscaped in preparation for the 2010 FIFA World Cup™ when it will serve as the city's principle fan-park. The neoclassical City Hall, built to celebrate Queen Victoria's golden jubilee, overlooks the parade. Its clock tower is a half-size replica of Big Ben in London. In 1979 the municipal government moved to a new Civic Centre on the Foreshore, a dominant tower block which straddles Hertzog Boulevard. The hall is now headquarters of the Cape Town Symphony Orchestra and houses the **City Library**.

Castle of Good Hope

① *Buitenkant St, entry from the Grand Parade side, T021-464 1260, www.castleofgoodhope. co.za, www.iziko.org.za. Daily 0930-1600, R20, children (5-16) R10, ½ price on Sun. Free guided tours Mon-Sat 1100, 1200 and 1400. Expect to have any bags checked since the castle is still used as the regional offices for the National Defence Force.*

Beyond the Grand Parade, on Darling Street, is the main entrance of South Africa's oldest colonial building, the Castle of Good Hope. Work was started in 1666 by Commander Zacharias Wagenaer and completed in 1679. Its original purpose was for the Dutch East India Company to defend the Cape from rival European powers, and today it is an imposing sight, albeit a rather gloomy one. Under the British, the castle served as government headquarters and since 1917 it has been the headquarters of the South African Defence Force, Western Cape.

Today the castle is home to three museums. The **William Fehr Collection** is one of South Africa's finest displays of furnishings reflecting the social and political history of the Cape. There are landscapes by John Thomas Baines and William Huggins, 17th-century Japanese porcelain and 18th-century Indonesian furniture. Upstairs is an absurdly huge dining table which seats 104, in a room still used for state dinners.

To the left of the William Fehr Collection is the **Secunde's House**. The Secunde was second in charge of the settlement at the Cape, responsible for administrative duties for the Dutch East India Company. None of the three rooms contain original furniture from the castle, but they do recreate the conditions under which an official for the Dutch East India Company would have lived in the 17th, 18th and early 19th centuries. The third museum is the **Military Museum**, a rather indifferent collection depicting the conflicts of early settlers. More absorbing are the regimental displays of uniforms and medals.

The free guided tours are informative and fun, although a little short. Tour highlights include the torture chambers, cells, views from the battlements and Dolphin Court, where Lady Anne Barnard was supposedly seen bathing in the nude by the sentries. While waiting for a tour you can enjoy coffee and cakes at a small café, or explore van der Stel's restored wine cellars, where you can taste and buy wines. There is full ceremonial changing of the guard at noon, which coincides with the firing of the Noon Gun from Signal Hill.

Adderley Street and Heerengracht

Adderley Street is one of the city's busiest shopping areas, and is sadly marred by a number of 1960s and 1970s eyesores, but it does still boast some impressive bank buildings. On the corner of Darling Street is the **Standard Bank Building** (1880), a grand structure built shortly after the diamond wealth from Kimberley began to reach Cape Town. Diagonally across is the equally impressive **Barclays Bank Building** (1933), a fine Ceres sandstone building which was the last major work by Sir Herbert Baker in South Africa. At the corner of Adderley Street and Strand Street stands a modern shopping mall complex, the **Golden Acre**. On the lower level of the complex the remains of an aqueduct and a reservoir dating from 1663 can be viewed. The line of black floor tiles close to the escalator which links the centre with the railway station mark the position of the original shoreline before any reclamation work began in Table Bay. Continuing down towards the docks, Adderley Street passes Cape Town Railway Station. At the junction with Hans Strijdom Street is a large roundabout with a central fountain and a bronze statue of **Jan van Riebeeck**, given to the city by Cecil Rhodes in 1899. At the bottom end of Adderley Street on the foreshore are statues of Bartholomew Dias and Maria van Riebeeck, donated respectively by the Portuguese and Dutch Governments in 1952 for Cape Town's tercentenary celebrations.

In front of the Medical Centre on Heerengracht is the **Scott Memorial**. What is on show is in fact a bronze replica; the original, a stone argosy, was smashed by vandals. Its location has barely changed, but when it was unveiled in 1916 it was on the approach to a pier at the foot of Adderley Street, a further indication of how much additional land has been reclaimed from Table Bay over the years. The palm trees once graced a marine promenade in this area. Up until the 1850s there was a canal running the full length of Heerengracht and Adderley streets. This was covered over as the city prospered and traffic congestion became a problem.

Greenmarket Square

A couple of blocks south of the junction of Strand Street and St George's Mall is Greenmarket Square, the old heart of Cape Town and the second oldest square in the city. It has long been a meeting place, and during the 19th century it became a vegetable market. In 1834 it took on the significant role of being the site where the declaration of the freeing of all slaves was made. Today it remains a popular meeting place, with a busy daily market selling African crafts, jewellery and clothes.

Most of the buildings around the square reflect the city's history. Dominating one side is a **Park Inn** hotel, housed in what was once the headquarters of Shell Oil – note the shell motifs on its exterior. Diagonally opposite is the **Old Town House** (1751) ① *T021-481 3933, www.iziko.org.za, Mon-Fri 1000-1700, Sat 1000-1600, entry by donation*, originally built to house the town guard. It became the first town hall in 1840 when Cape Town became a municipality. Much of the exterior remains unchanged, and with its decorative plaster mouldings and fine curved fanlights, it is one of the best preserved Cape baroque exteriors in the city. The first electric light in Cape Town was switched on in the Old House on 13 April 1895. Today the white double-storeyed building houses the Michaelis Collection of Flemish and Dutch paintings, as well as the **Courtyard Café** which serves snacks. At the entrance to the house is a circle set into the floor which marks the spot from which all distances to and from Cape Town are measured. Next to the **Tudor Hotel** is the second oldest building on the square – the **Metropolitan Methodist Church** (1876). This, the only high Victorian church in Cape Town, has a tall spire decorated with an unusual series of miniature grotesques. The church was designed by Charles Freeman and is regarded as one of the finest in the country.

If you walk out of the square past the Methodist church to Church Street, you'll come to the area between Burg and Long streets, which is the venue for a daily (except Sunday) **antiques market**.

Koopmans-De Wet House

ⓘ *Strand St, T021-481 3935, www.iziko.org.za, Tue-Thu 1000-1700, R10, under 16s free.*
Just off St George's Mall, a pedestrianized road lined with shops and cafés, is the delightfully peaceful Koopmans-De Wet House. The house is named in memory of Marie Koopmans-De Wet, a prominent figure in cultured Cape Society who lived here between 1834 and 1906. The inside has been restored to reflect the period of her grandparents who lived here in the late 18th century. All of the pieces are numbered and a small catalogue gives a brief description. Though not too cluttered, there is a fascinating collection of furnishings which gives the house a special tranquil feel. Look out for the early map of the Cape coastline at the head of the stairs, dating from 1730 – Saldanha Bay and Cape Agulhas are clearly visible. At the back of the house is a shaded courtyard and the original stables with the slave quarters above.

Gold of Africa Museum

ⓘ *96 Strand St, T021-405 1540, www.goldofafrica.com, Mon-Sat 0930-1700, R25, children R15.*
A few blocks west of Koopmans-De Wit House is the **Lutheran Church**, and next door is the **Martin Melck House**, now home to the Gold of Africa Museum. Originally the house served as a clandestine Lutheran church, as in the 18th century the Dutch authorities refused to tolerate any churches other than those belonging to the Dutch Reformed Church. The present museum houses a slick display of the history of gold mining, outlining the first mining by Egyptians in 2400 BC and the subsequent development of trade networks across Africa. There are comprehensive displays of 19th- and 20th-century gold artworks from Mali, Ghana and Senegal, including jewellery, masks, hair ornaments and statuettes. It's a reasonable collection, but you need a real interest in precious metals to stay for long. Downstairs there's a shop and workshop where you can watch goldsmiths at work. In the courtyard is the **Gold Restaurant** ⓘ *T021-421 4653, www.goldrestaurant.co.za, daily 1000-2300*, and if you are visiting for dinner, evening guided tours are available of the museum for R40 per person which includes a glass of wine sprinkled with gold leaf. This is a nice option and the restaurant serves good traditional South African cuisine and drummers entertain.

Long Street

One of the trendiest stretches in Cape Town, Long Street gets particularly lively at night. Lined with street cafés, fashionable shops, bars, clubs and backpacker hostels, it has a distinctly youthful feel about it, although a clutch of new boutique hotels, posh apartment complexes and upmarket restaurants are injecting the area with a new sophisticated edge. Long Street is also home to some fine old city buildings. One of Cape Town's late Victorian gems is at No 117, now an antiques shop. On the outside is an unusual cylindrical turret with curved windows; inside is a fine cast-iron spiral staircase leading to a balustraded gallery.

The **Slave Church Museum** ① *No 40, T021-423 6755, Mon-Fri 0900-1600, free*, is the oldest mission church in South Africa, built between 1802 and 1804 as the mother church for missionary work carried out in rural areas. Fortunately the building was saved from demolition in 1977 and restored to its present fine form. Though utilized by directors and members of the South African Missionary Society, it was more commonly used for religious and literacy instruction of slaves in Cape Town; by 1960 most of its congregation had been moved to the Cape Flats. Inside are displays of missionary work throughout the Cape, and behind the pulpit are displays showing early cash accounts and receipts for transactions such as the transfer of slaves.

Heritage Square

A few blocks north of Long Street is this renovated block of 17th- and 18th-century townhouses, which include one of the city's oldest blacksmiths, but is better known for its excellent restaurants and the **Cape Heritage Hotel** (see Sleeping, page 109). In the centre is a cobbled courtyard holding the Cape's oldest living grape vine, which was planted in 1781.

Bo-Kaap and the Bo-Kaap Museum

About 600 m west along Wale Street is Bo-Kaap, Cape Town's historical Islamic quarter and one of the city's most interesting residential areas. The area was developed in the 1760s and today feels a world away from the nearby CBD. Here the streets are cobbled and tightly woven across the slopes of Signal Hill, and the closely packed houses are painted in bright hues of lime, pink and blue. The name means 'upper Cape' and it developed as a working class district for freed slaves, who were mostly imported by the Dutch from Malaysia, Indonesia and other parts of Asia. Today's Cape Malay community in Bo-Kaap are the descendents of these. It was this community who also introduced Islam to South Africa and the Owal Mosque on Dorp Street, built in 1794, is the oldest mosque in the country and there are nine other mosques in the district. The air here rings with muezzin calls before the five daily prayers. Opposite the museum on Wale Street, **Atlas Trading** is a shop worth stopping by to see the shelves stacked with relishes and pickles and at the back the wooden boxes of spices used in Cape Malay cooking. You can do a great half day tour of Bo-Kaap with **Andulela Experience** (see page 130), which includes a walkabout, a visit to the museum and a cookery class and lunch in a local family's home. To the west, Bo-Kaap blends into the trendy new gay area of De Waterkant.

The **Bo-Kaap Museum** ① *71 Wale St, T021-481 3939, www.iziko.org.za, Mon-Sat 1000-1700, R10, under 16s free*, housed in an attractive 18th-century house, is dedicated to the Cape's Malay community and contains the furnishings of a wealthy 19th-century Muslim family. There are antique furnishings and Islamic heirlooms such as an old Koran and *tasbeh* beads set in front of the mihrab alcove, while the back room has displays dedicated to the input that slaves had in the economy and development of Cape Town. The photos are the most interesting articles, giving a fascinating glimpse of life in the Bo-Kaap in the early 20th century. At the back is a community centre, with temporary photographic exhibitions. The house itself is one of the oldest buildings in Cape Town surviving in its original form. It was built by Jan de Waal for artisans in 1763 and it was here that Abu Bakr Effendi started the first Arabic school and wrote important articles on Islamic law. He originally came to Cape Town as a guest of the British government to try and settle religious differences amongst the Cape Muslims.

De Waterkant, Green Point and Sea Point ⊜❷❶ ▸▸ *pp108-134.*

These suburbs are the closest seaside residential areas to the city, and are undergoing rapid transformation. De Waterkant – until fairly recently a run-down area of flaking bungalows – is now Cape Town's most fashionable district, with beautifully restored Victorian homes painted in bright hues crammed into a tight cobbled grid of streets, climbing up towards Signal Hill. This is the city's main gay area, with excellent nightlife and a wide choice of super-trendy restaurants, bars and boutiques. Most of these are in the Cape Quarter, a shopping/dining complex with a charming outside piazza with a central water feature and trees with twinkly lights. This is currently being extended to cover a large block from Waterkant Street to Somerset Road, and the Victorian façades on Somerset Road are being incorporated into the complex. About 500 m beyond, along Somerset Road, is the start of Green Point, where there was a large roundabout with a turning northeast to the V&A Waterfront. This has temporarily been taken out as the road development around the new Green Point Stadium is being built, which includes a new

③ Green Point, De Waterkant & Waterfront

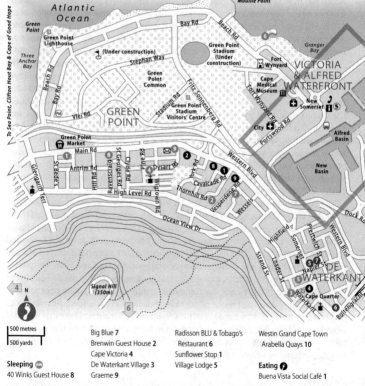

road being ploughed through from the stadium to the V&A Waterfront. It is expected that parts of Somerset Road and Waterkant Street will be developed as a 'Golden Mile' from Cape Town Railway Station, which will be the city centre terminus for the new Integrated Rapid Transport (IRT), see page 80. Work on this will continue until 2010. At the time of writing the unmissable new Green Point Stadium for the 2010 FIFA Football World Cup™ was 80% complete and should be finished by the time you read this. Presently the area is teaming with the Team Green Point construction workers in their distinctive red and yellow uniforms decorated with football emblems. As a spin off to being close to the stadium, there's presently a massive wave of development along Somerset/Main Road which runs from the centre of Green Point the length of Sea Point, and the buildings are developing into a series of high-rise apartment blocks and shopping and restaurant malls. Green Point Common to the left of the stadium is presently a pile of rubble and is being developed into sports fields and a new 18-hole golf course.

The **Green Point Stadium Visitor's Centre** ① *T021-430 0410, www.greenpoint stadiumvc.co.za, tours Mon-Fri 1000 and 1400, Sat 1000 and 1200, R40, children R20,* is housed in a still-standing section of the old Green Point Stadium, which was all but knocked down. It is clearly signposted from Main Road. The new state-of-the-art Green Point Stadium will be 52 m high and will accommodate 68,000 spectators, have an underground car park for 1200 cars and be surrounded by 60 ha of parkland. The 60-minute tours include a display on the history of football in South Africa; information about the building of the stadium; an entertaining theatre performance about the history of Green Point; a virtual tour of the stadium on film, which is just as interesting for architects and engineers as it is for football fans; and a visit to a viewing deck overlooking the construction site. Since this facility opened in 2007, it's had over 25,000 visitors, including many school children, so hopefully they'll keep it going in some form or other when the stadium is completed. There was some controversy about the location of the new stadium – it's on South Africa's oldest golf course and not directly on the site of the old stadium – but it was built here because every television shot of it will have Table Mountain as a backdrop. There couldn't be better publicity for Cape Town.

Running parallel to Main Road is Beach Road which winds its way from the V&A Waterfront and around Mouille Point, where there is another smart row of apartment

➡Cape Town maps
1 Cape Town orientation, page 78
2 Cape Town Centre, page 89
3 Green Point, De Waterkant & Waterfront, page 98
4 Sea Point, page 100
5 Victoria & Albert Waterfront, page 102
6 Oranjezicht, Gardens & Tamboerskloof, page 111

Giovanni's Deliworld 2
Mano's 9
Miss K Food Cafe 8
Nose 4
Tank 4

Bars & clubs 🍸
Bronx Action 5
Fireman's Arms 6
Loft Lounge 7

blocks and the red and white candy-striped **Green Point Lighthouse**. This is the oldest working lighthouse on the South African coast, built by Herman Schutte (a German builder) in 1824, which was electrified in 1929. From Green Point, both Main Road and Beach Road then continue on their parallel journey through Sea Point and merge on their way to Clifton. There's a pleasant promenade the length of Beach Road, which is intercepted by short stretches of beach and has an adjoining strip of park where there are

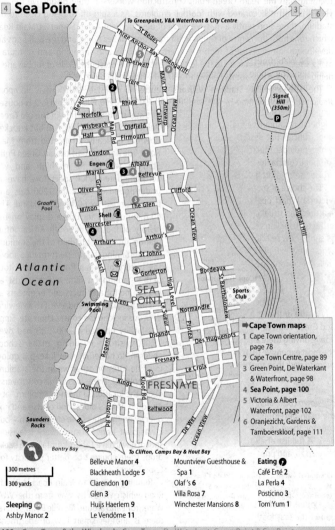

Sleeping 🛏
Ashby Manor **2**
Bellevue Manor **4**
Blackheath Lodge **5**
Clarendon **10**
Glen **3**
Huijs Haerlem **9**
Le Vendôme **11**
Mountview Guesthouse & Spa **1**
Olaf's **6**
Villa Rosa **7**
Winchester Mansions **8**

Eating 🍴
Café Erté **2**
La Perla **4**
Posticino **3**
Tom Yum **1**

a few attractions for children such as a mini-train, mini-golf and playgrounds. Primarily it's a place where local people jog, rollerblade or walk their dogs and there are good views of Table Bay and some surf spots below the promenade wall. The beach is unsafe for swimming, although there are a couple of rock pools, including Graaf's Pool (men only) and Milton's Pool. The centre of Sea Point on Main Road has a bit of a scruffy reputation, but the numerous new developments are giving it a facelift and bringing in a number of upmarket shops and restaurants. There's a good open-air swimming pool on the beachfront in Sea Point (see page 129).

Victoria and Alfred Waterfront ⬤🅿🛈 ▶ pp108-134.

The V&A Waterfront, Cape Town's original Victorian harbour, is the city's most popular attraction. The whole area was completely restored in the early 1990s, and today it is a lively district packed with restaurants, bars and shops. Original buildings stand shoulder to shoulder with mock-Victorian shopping malls, museums and cinemas, all crowding along a waterside walkway with Table Mountain towering beyond. Prices are a little higher in restaurants and bars here and many have argued that the area is over-sanitized and artificial. But despite being geared towards tourists it remains a working harbour, which provides much of the area's real charm. To explore the harbour and beyond, there are boat companies along Quay 5 in front of Victoria Wharf offering all manner of boat cruises, from short half hour harbour tours to two hour sails to Camps Bay by schooner.

The choice of shops, restaurants and entertainment is unrivalled. When the main mall **Victoria Wharf** opened, it was similar to any other South African shopping mall and featured the usual chain stores. Over the years and with growing popularity – today it attracts 10 million visitors a year – the quality of shops has shifted upmarket. The majority of shops now sell clothes, souvenirs, jewellery and specialist items. In November 2007, a whole new extension of Victoria Wharf was opened, with 70 more shops and a fashion gallery featuring the likes of Gucci, Jimmy Choo and Burberry.

Ins and outs

Getting there To get here there is a bus that runs from outside the railway station in the city centre or there's a Golden Arrow bus service that runs along Beach Road in Sea Point and Green Point to the V&A. **City Sightseeing** has its ticket office outside the aquarium. If you're driving there are several multi-storey car parks. The one underneath Victoria Wharf is the most expensive (R10 per hour) – put it this way, if you went to see a movie, it would cost more to park than the price of a movie ticket. The other car parks are half the price.

Tourist information There is a **tourist information office** ⓘ *T021-405 4500, www.tourism capetown.co.za, daily 0900-2100*, in the Clock Tower Centre across the swing bridge from the main development. They stock a good selection of maps and guides for the whole country; there are also desks for car hire and safari companies, and a **SANParks** booking desk. A full list of all the shops, amenities and attractions can be found at www.water front.co.za, and printed guides can be picked up throughout the V&A.

Background

The V&A Waterfront derives its name from the two harbour basins around which it is developed. Construction began in 1860, when Prince Alfred, Queen Victoria's second son, tipped the first load of stone to start the building of the breakwater for Cape Town's harbour. Alfred Basin could not handle the increased shipping volumes and subsequently a larger basin, the Victoria Basin, was built. A number of original buildings remain around the basins and are an interesting diversion from the razzmatazz of the shops and restaurants.

5 Victoria & Alfred Waterfront

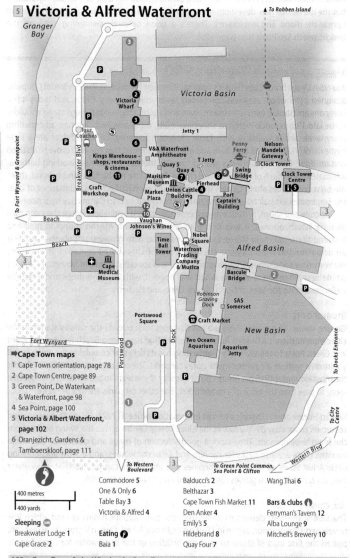

➡ **Cape Town maps**
1 Cape Town orientation, page 78
2 Cape Town Centre, page 89
3 Green Point, De Waterkant & Waterfront, page 98
4 Sea Point, page 100
5 **Victoria & Albert Waterfront, page 102**
6 Oranjezicht, Gardens & Tamboerskloof, page 111

400 metres
400 yards

Sleeping 🛏
Breakwater Lodge 1
Cape Grace 2

Commodore 5
One & Only 6
Table Bay 3
Victoria & Alfred 4

Eating 🍴
Baia 1

Balducci's 2
Belthazar 3
Cape Town Fish Market 11
Den Anker 4
Emily's 5
Hildebrand 8
Quay Four 7

Wang Thai 6

Bars & clubs 🍸
Ferryman's Tavern 12
Alba Lounge 9
Mitchell's Brewery 10

Clock Tower

At the narrow entrance to the Alfred Basin, on the Berties Landing side, is the original Clock Tower, built in 1882 to house the port captain's office. This is in the form of a red octagonal Gothic-style tower and stands just in front of the **Clock Tower Centre**, a modern mall with a collection of shops, offices and restaurants. The Clock Tower Centre houses the Nelson Mandela Gateway to Robben Island, from where you catch the main ferry to the island. This side of the Waterfront is connected the bulk of the area by a swing bridge, which swings open every 10 minutes to allow boats to pass underneath.

Union Castle Building

Walking across the swing bridge (look out for the Cape fur seals on a landing to your right as you cross), you come to the stocky square building known as **Union Castle Building** (1919), designed by the firm of architects owned by Sir Herbert Baker. The Union Steamship Company and the Castle Line both ran monthly mail ships between Britain and South Africa in the late 19th century. In 1900 they amalgamated and from then on mail was delivered every week. The last Union Castle ship to sail to England with the mail was the *Windsor Castle* in 1977. This is now home to the **Maritime Museum** ① *T021-405 2880, www.iziko .org.za, daily 1000-1700, entry by donation*, a collection of model ships and objects associated with the era of mail ships. It also holds an archive of over 19,000 photographs of ships that visited Cape Town from the 1920s to the 1960s. Nearby is the museum ship, the *SAS Somerset*, a boom defence vessel that is permanently moored for public viewing.

Opposite the Union Castle Building is the **Victoria and Alfred Hotel**. Now a luxury four-star hotel and shopping mall, the building was originally a coal store before being converted into Union Castle's warehouse and customs baggage store. It used to have a third floor but this was destroyed in a fire in 1939. This was the first hotel to be opened at the Waterfront and it is an important part of the success of the whole venture.

To the south of the hotel is **Nobel Square** ① *www.nobelsquare.com*, which was opened on 16 December 2006, the Day of Reconciliation, and pays tribute to four of South Africa's Nobel Peace Prize laureates – the late Nkosi Albert Luthuli (1961), Archbishop Desmond Tutu (1984) and FW de Klerk and Nelson Mandela who jointly won it in 1993. Slightly larger than life-size statues of the four formidable men stand next to each other with a backdrop of Table Mountain and, in front of the sculpture, the Laureates' preferred quotations engraved in their chosen language. In the middle of the square, the Peace and Democracy sculpture – a narrative work of a jumble of people and faces on top of each other – represents the contribution made by women and children to the attainment of peace in South Africa.

Time Ball Tower

Heading west, on the other side of Dock Road above the car park, is the 1894 Time Ball Tower; its purpose was to act as an accurate reference for ships' navigators who set their clocks as the ball on the roof fell. Correct time was vital for navigators to be able to determine precise longitude. Beside the tower is a 110-year-old dragon tree, *Dracaeno draco*, from the Canary Islands, and next to the tree is the original **harbour master's residence** (1860).

Two Oceans Aquarium

① *Entrance is on Dock Rd, by the Waterfront Craft Market, T021-418 3823, www.aquarium. Co.za. Daily 0930-1800, R85, children (4-13) R40, (14-17) R65, under 4s free.*

Focusing on the unique Cape marine environment created by the merging of the Atlantic and Indian Ocean, this aquarium is the top attraction on the Waterfront. The display begins with a walk through the Indian Ocean, where you'll follow a route past tanks filled with a multitude of colourful fish, turtles, seahorses and octopuses. Highlights include giant spider crabs and phosphorescent jellyfish floating in a mesmerizing circular current. Then you walk past touch pools, where children can pick up spiky starfish and slimy sea slugs. Free puppet shows and face painting keep children busy at the **Alpha Activity Centre** in the basement. The main wall here looks out into the water of the actual harbour, and you can watch Cape fur seals dart and dive before the glass. The seals are fed at 1100 and 1400. Upstairs is a vast tank holding the Kelp Forest, an extraordinary tangle of giant kelp that sways drunkenly in the artificial tides. The highlight is the Predators exhibit, a circular tank complete with glass tunnel, holding ragged-tooth sharks, eagle rays, turtles and some impressively large hunting fish. There are daily feeds at 1500 and, with an Open Water diving certificate, you can arrange to dive with the sharks. The aquarium also has a new conservation programme, where it tags and releases ragged tooth sharks back into the sea, providing valuable data on their movements.

Cape Medical Museum
ⓘ *T021-418 5663, Tue-Fri 0900-1600, entry by donation.*
Close by the Waterfront, at the City Hospital Complex on Portswood Road, the medical achievements of South Africa's doctors are celebrated in this interesting display, a must for any medical students doing their elective in Cape Town. There are turn-of-the-20th-century reconstructions of a consulting room and dispensary, dentist's room, operating theatre and hospital ward plus a collection of medical instruments.

Robben Island

Tours to the island are run by the **Robben Island Museum** ⓘ *T021-413 4220, www.robben-island.org.za.* The Nelson Mandela Gateway at the Clock Tower Centre is the embarkation and disembarkation point for tours. The Gateway also houses a shop, the ticket office and a small museum with photographic and interactive displays on Apartheid and the rise of African nationalism, open 0730-2100. An air-conditioned catamaran completes the half-hour journey to the island. Tickets cost R180, children under 18 R90. Tours begin with a 45-minute drive around the key sites, including Sobukwe's house, the lime quarry where Mandela was forced to work, the leper cemetery and the houses of former warders. Tours around the prison are conducted by ex-political prisoners, who paint a vivid picture of prison life here. Departures are daily at 0900, 1100, 1300 and 1500, and the whole excursion lasts 3½ hours. You must remain with your guide throughout the tour. Be sure to book a day ahead (or several days in peak season) as tickets sell out quickly, and always phone ahead to see if the ferry is running in bad weather. Do not drink any tap water on the island.

Lying 12 km off Green Point's shores, Robben Island is best known as the notorious prison that held many of the ANC's most prominent members, including Nelson Mandela and Walter Sisulu. It was originally named by the Dutch, after the term for seals, 'rob' – actually a misnomer as none are found here. The island's history of occupation started in 1806, when John Murray was granted permission by the British to conduct whaling from the island. During this period the authorities started to use the island as a dumping ground for common convicts; these were brought back to the mainland in 1843, and their accommodation was deemed suitable only for lepers and the mentally ill. These were in turn moved to the mainland between 1913 and 1931, and the island entered a new era as a military base during the Second World War. In 1960 the military passed control of the island over to the Department of Prisons, and it remained a prison until 1996. On 1 December 1999 the island was declared a World Heritage Site by UNESCO.

Robben Island's effectiveness as a prison did not rest simply with the fact that escape was virtually impossible. The authorities anticipated that the idea of 'out of sight, out of mind' would be particularly applicable here, and to a certain extent they were correct. Certainly, its isolation did much to break the spirit of political prisoners, not least Robert Sobukwe's. Sobukwe, the leader of the Pan African Congress, was kept in solitary confinement for nine years. Other political prisoners were spared that at least, although in 1971 they were separated from common law prisoners, as they were deemed a 'bad' influence. Conditions were harsh, with forced hard labour and routine beatings. Much of the daily running of the maximum security prison was designed to reinforce racial divisions: all the wardens, and none of the prisoners, were white; black prisoners, unlike those deemed coloured, had to wear short trousers and were given smaller food rations. Contact with the outside world was virtually non-existent – visitors had to apply for permission six months in advance and were allowed to stay for just half an hour. Newspapers were banned and letters were limited to one every six months.

Yet despite these measures, the B-Section, which housed Mandela and other major political prisoners, became the international focus of the fight against Apartheid. The last political prisoners left the island in 1991.

) *As a prison, the area was strictly protected allowing the fish and bird populations to flourish. There are over 100 species of bird on the island, and it is an important breeding site for African penguins.*

Southern suburbs ●❷👣 ›› pp108-134.

Primarily encompassing the more affluent residential areas of Cape Town, the suburbs, stretching southeast from the centre, are an interesting diversion to the usual tourist spots. Although a car is the best way to visit them, it's possible to reach all by train – the metro service between the city centre and Simon's Town runs through the suburbs, but safety can be an issue; avoid the trains when it's not busy. ›› *For further details, see Transport, page 131.*

Woodstock and Observatory

The first suburb, **Woodstock**, is a mixed commercial and residential area, historically a working-class coloured district. Today it is somewhat run down and depressing, although the back streets are an attractive mesh of Victorian bungalows, some of which have been taken over by fashionable bars and restaurants. **Observatory** is an appealing area of tightly packed houses, narrow streets and student hangouts. Being close to the university, there is a good range of trendy bars, cafés and restaurants catering for a mixed scene of students, bohemian types and backpackers. The observatory after which the suburb is named is where Station Road intersects Liesbeeck Parkway. The first Astronomer Royal to work at the Royal Observatory was also a clergyman, the Reverand Fearon Fellowes. Aside from making astronomical observations the observatory was responsible for accurate standard time in South Africa. It has also been an important meteorological centre and has a seismograph which records earthquakes around the world. Observatory is also where you'll find the **Groot Schuur Hospital** on Main Road, the site of the world's first heart transplant performed by Professor Christiaan Barnard. A small **museum** ⓘ *T021-404 5232, Mon-Fri 0900-1400, R5,* in the hospital commemorates the transplant with a restored theatre built to look as it did when the transplant took place in 1967.

Mowbray, Rosebank and Rondebosch

The next suburbs of Mowbray, Rosebank and Rondebosch lie just below the **University of Cape Town**. Again, they are popular with students and have a good selection of restaurants and shops. **Mowbray** was originally known as Driekoppen, or three heads, after the murder by three slaves of a European foreman and his wife in 1724. On their capture they were beheaded and their heads impaled on stakes at the farm entrance to act as a deterrent. **Rondebosch**, conversely, has for some time been associated with education. Aside from the university, several important schools were founded in the district. The area was also important from a practical point of view: in 1656 Van Riebeeck realized that Company's Garden was exposed to a damaging southeast wind. His first choice of a more sheltered spot was Rondebosch. This proved a success and a grain storage barn was built. Early accounts describe the area as wild country, with the farmers frequently losing livestock to hyenas, lions and leopards – an image that is hard to imagine as you sit in the evening rush hour on Rhodes Drive. Also in Rondebosch is **Groot Schuur**, the Prime Minister's official residence; **Westbrooke**, home of the State President; and the original residence of the Cape Governor over 200 years ago, **Rustenburg**.

Irma Stern Museum

ⓘ *Cecil Rd, Rosebank, T021-685 5686, www.irmastern.co.za, Tue-Sat 1000-1700, R10, children R5.*

A lesser-known but fascinating attraction in the area is this museum. Irma Stern was one of South Africa's pioneering artists and her lovely house displays a mixture of her own works, a collection of artefacts from across Africa and some fine pieces of antique furniture from overseas, including 17th-century Spanish chairs, 19th-century German oak furniture and Swiss *mardi gras* masks. Her portraits are particularly poignant and those of her close friends are superb, while her religious art is rather more disturbing. Stern's studio, complete with paint brushes and palettes, has been left as it was when she died. The most important African items were collected in the Congo and Zanzibar. Of particular note is the Buli Stool, one of only 20 known carvings by a master carver from southeast Zaire. The kitchen houses a collection of Chinese ceramics including two fine Ming celadon dishes.

Rhodes Memorial

ⓘ *T021-689 9151, www.rhodesmemorial.co.za, Nov-Apr 0700-1900, May-Oct 0800-1800.*

The best-known attraction in the area is the Rhodes Memorial, off Rhodes Drive, by the Rondesbosch turning. The imposing granite memorial to Cecil John Rhodes (Cape Prime Minister from 1890 to 1896) was designed by Francis Masey and Sir Herbert Baker. Four bronze lions flank a wide flight of steps which lead up to a Greek Temple. The temple houses an immense bronze head of Rhodes, wrought by JM Swan. Above the head are the words "slave to the spirit and life work of Cecil John Rhodes who loved and served South Africa". At the base of the steps is an immense bronze mounted figure of *Physical Energy* given to South Africa by GF Watts, a well-regarded sculptor of the time; the original stands in Hyde Park, London. Other than the memorial, the great attraction here is the magnificent view of the Cape Flats and the southern suburbs. Behind the memorial are a number of popular trails leading up the slopes of Devil's Peak. Also tucked away here is an excellent little tea house set in a garden of blue hydrangeas that serves breakfasts, light meals and excellent cheesecake and cream teas.

South of Rondesbosch

By this point the southern suburbs have reached right around Devil's Peak and the shadowy mountains now dominating the views represent an unfamiliar view of Table Mountain. The suburb of **Newlands** backs right up to the slopes of the mountain and is probably best known for being the home to Western Province Rugby Union and the beautiful Newlands cricket Test Ground. The first recorded cricket match in Africa took place between officers in the British army in Cape Town in 1808, and the Newlands cricket oval opened in 1888. In 2003 it hosted the Cricket World Cup opening match. The first official rugby match at Newlands was played in 1890 and the stadium was a venue for 1995 World Cup matches. There are several good hotels and guesthouses in the area. On Boundary Road in Newlands is the **Rugby Museum** ① *T021-659 6700, Mon-Fri 0830-1700, free,* housed in the Sports Medical Research Institute Building. The somewhat chaotic collection commemorates the history of the sport in the country and is also home to the Currie Cup, the premier domestic competition trophy.

Also on Boundary Road, **Josephine Mill** ① *T021-686 4939, www.josephinemill.co.za, Mon-Fri 1000-1600, Sat 1000-1400, R10, milling demonstrations Mon-Fri 1100 and 1500, R20,* the only surviving watermill in Cape Town, has been restored as a working flour mill; note the massive iron waterwheel. The building is in the style of a Cornish red-brick mill, built by a Swede, Jacob Letterstedt in 1840, and named in honour of his Crown Princess, Josephine. The mill is tucked away near the rugby stadium and has a shop selling organic stone-milled flour and bread and a peaceful tea garden and deli.

Claremont offers little of interest. On the main road is the upmarket **Cavendish Square Complex**, another shopping mall. There are two good cinema complexes here – the Ster-Kinekor Commercial, on the second floor, shows big releases, while the Ster-Kinekor Nouveau specializes in alternative and foreign-language films.

Nearby are **Ardene Gardens** ① *0800-1630,* a Victorian park first planted in 1845 by Ralph Arderne, who was so charmed by the Cape while en route for Australia that he decided to settle here instead. He succeeded in creating a garden that would represent the flora of the world. When his son died the estate was split up but fortunately in 1927 the Cape Town Municipality bought 4.5 ha of the garden. Today the arboretum is probably the best collection of trees in South Africa. An obelisk marks the site from which the famous astronomer, Sir John Herschel, carried out his research from 1834 to 1838.

A little further along the main road takes you to **Wynberg**. Apart from a few curio shops, the main attraction is the well-preserved 19th-century homes known as **Little Chelsea**. South of Wynberg the countryside opens up. To the west lie the fertile and prosperous valleys of Constantia and Tokai; due south the road quickly brings False Bay (page 140) and the coastal resort of Muizenberg into view. To the east lie the exposed high-density suburbs on the Cape Flats – Crossroads, Guguletu, Khayelitsha, Langa and Mitchells Plain.

Kirstenbosch Botanical Gardens

① *T021-799 8783, www.sanbi.org, Sep-Mar 0800-1900, Apr-Aug 0800-1800, R32, children (6-17) R10. By far the easiest way of getting here is by hire car. Otherwise there are trains to the nearest station at Mowbray, 10 mins from the city centre. From here there is an erratic bus service or a very long walk. Alternatively, take a Rikki taxi – they will pick up and drop off at any time other than rush hour. Most of the organized city tours also include the gardens on their itinerary and the City Sightseeing buses stop here.*

Kirstenbosch, 5 km south of Rondesbosch is South Africa's oldest, largest and most exquisite botanical garden. The gardens stretch up the eastern slopes of Table Mountain, merging seamlessly with the fynbos of the steep slopes above. Cecil Rhodes bought Kirstenbosch farm in 1895 and promptly presented the site to the people of South Africa with the intention that it become a botanical garden. It was not until 1913 that it was proclaimed a National Botanical Garden – the Anglo-Boer War had caused the delay. The first director of the gardens was Professor Harold Pearson, who died just three years after the garden's creation. A granite Celtic Cross marks his grave in the Cycad garden. There is a fitting epitaph: "If ye seek his monument, look around you." The real development was under Professor RH Compton, who cared for the gardens for 34 years. The herbarium, named after him, houses over 250,000 specimens, including many rare plants.

A great deal of time and effort has been put into making the gardens accessible to the general public, ensuring they provide pleasure for both serious botanists and families enjoying a day out on the slopes of Table Mountain. In the **Fragrance Garden** herbs and flowers are set out so as to make appreciating their scents effortless. On a warm day, when the volatile oils are released by the plants, there are some rather overpowering aromas. The plaques are also in Braille. The **Dell** follows a beautifully shaded path snaking beneath ferns and along a stream. Indigenous South African herbs can be inspected in the **Medicinal Plants Garden**, each one identified and used by the Khoi and San peoples in the treatment of a variety of ailments. The plants' uses are identified on plaques, and it seems that most ailments are covered – kidney trouble, rheumatics, coughs, cancer, piles and bronchitis. For a sense of the past, it is worth visiting what is known as **Van Riebeeck's Hedge**. Back in 1660 a hedge of wild almond trees (*Brabejum stellatifolium*) was planted by Van Riebeeck as part of a physical boundary to try and prevent cattle rustling. Segments still remain today within the garden. The **Skeleton Path** can be followed all the way to the summit of Table Mountain. It starts off as a stepped path, but becomes fairly steep near the top. It involves a climb up a rocky waterfall; take special care in the wet season.

Perhaps the most enjoyable way of experiencing the gardens is at one of the Sunday sunset concerts held throughout summer (see Music, page 124). Also available for a small fee are eco-adventure tours, and tours by motorized golf cart. Just beyond the entrance is a shop and café on the courtyard terrace. The shop has the usual collection of curios, along with a good choice of books on South Africa and a selection of indigenous plants. The café serves overpriced sandwiches and cakes; better value and with far nicer views is the **Silver Tree and Fynbos Deli** inside the gardens, which serves good meals (until 2200). And, for a reasonable price, you can have a ready-made picnic with wine and join the Capetonians on the lush lawns.

◉ Cape Town listings

Hotel and guesthouse prices

L over R2550 **AL** R1871-2550 **A** R1271-1870
B R851-1270 **C** R641-850 **D** R301-640
E R131-300 **F** under R130

Restaurant prices

♔♔♔ over R260   ♔♔ R131-260   ♔ under R130
See pages 46-53 for further information.

⌷ Sleeping

Cape Town has an excellent selection of accommodation from large flashy 5-star

hotels to good value small guesthouses and backpackers hostels. During peak periods, be sure to call in advance to check availability, and book well ahead for Christmas and the New Year when Cape Town is especially popular with domestic tourists.

Several agencies specialize in **medium- and long-term holiday lets** of private homes, self-catering flats or home swaps. These are good value for families or groups. Try www.capehomes.co.za, or www.capeletting.com. **International Home Exchange**, www.home linksouthafrica.com, is affiliated to HomeLink International in the UK and has a home swap directory in over 50 countries.

City Bowl p88, maps p89 and p111

AL Cape Heritage Hotel, 90 Bree St, Heritage Sq, T021-424 4646, www.cape heritage.co.za. Charming hotel set in a rambling renovated town house dating from the late 17th century. 15 huge rooms, each individually styled, with muted coloured walls (avocado, rust-red, eggshell blue), some with 4-poster beds. All have large windows and sound-proofing to protect from busy Bree St, plus newly renovated bathrooms, minibar, a/c, M-Net TV. Breakfast served under a historical vine in the courtyard, or in the airy black-and-white breakfast room. Good location close to Long St. Friendly management. Recommended.

AL Cape Town Hollow, 88 Queen Victoria St, T021-423 1260, www.capetownhollow.co.za. Pleasant newish hotel overlooking Company's Garden with 56 rooms with fairly bland but comfortable furnishings, spotless bathrooms, fantastic views of the mountain from front-facing rooms. Small, sunny pool deck on 1st floor, some gym equipment, conference centre and spa. Smart Italian restaurant on the ground floor with adjoining bar.

AL Urban Chic, corner of Long and Pepper streets, T021-426 6119, www.urbanchic.co.za. Italian-owned hotel in a trendy corner block with 20 rooms spread over several floors (prices rise the higher you go, as the views of the mountain improve). Beautiful, airy decor, with pale colours, modern art on the walls, large stone-clad bathrooms, some with sliding partition walls to the bedroom. Stylish bar attached, and on the 1st floor is the **Gallery Café** with a large fusion menu, for-sale art on the walls and understated, spacious seating, including in a covered balcony over Long St.

AL Westin Grand Cape Town Arabella Quays, Convention Sq, Lower Long St,

T021-412 9999, www.starwoodhotels.com. A fairly new addition to the city, this huge grey-glass structure overlooks the convention centre and has 483 rooms, in modern and minimalist style, with huge beds, floor-to-ceiling windows, stone bathrooms, satellite TV and internet. Facilities include popular rooftop spa, gym and pool, 5 restaurants and bars, and service is impressively swift and efficient. Rates start from R1885 per night.

A Grand Daddy, 38 Long St, T021-424 7247, www.daddylonglegs.co.za. Long St's newest and most eccentric boutique hotel, with 45 double rooms. Like its sister hotel, **Daddy Long Legs** (below), it is decorated throughout by local artists and the design element is simply stunning. Talk of the town are the 7 vintage Airstream trailers on the roof that are again wonderfully individually theme decorated. They are a rather unique way to sleep in Cape Town. The **Daddy Cool** bar is a sexy and stylish cocktail bar and the **Showroom Cafe** offers good food with an organic and low calorie slant. Highly recommended.

A Park Inn, 10 Greenmarket Sq, T021-423 2050, www.parkinn-capetown.com. City centre hotel set in the historical Shell building right on bustling Greenmarket Sq. 166 rooms with pleasant neutral decor and functional, attractive bathrooms (shower only). Small pool deck with sauna and gym with view of Table Mountain. Good steak restaurant – **The Famous Butcher's Grill** – on the ground floor with tables overlooking the market, plus pleasant, if dark, cigar bar. Excellent service, good central location and secure parking. A practical and comfortable choice.

B Cape Diamond, corner of Longmarket and Parliament streets, T021-461 2519, www.cape diamondhotel.co.za. In a great location just round the corner from Government Av and a short walk from Long St. 60 double rooms and 3 self-catering apartments, with contemporary decor, understated colours and the occasional splash of bright. Rooftop jacuzzi, bar, **Patat** restaurant specializing in Cape cuisine. Owner-run, good value.

B Protea Hotel Fire and Ice, corner of New Church and Victoria streets, T021-488 2555, www.proteahotels.co.za. Fashionable place with spacious modern lobby with trendy cocktail bar, swinging chairs, restaurant specializing in gourmet burgers and a cheeky smoking room where seats are fashioned as coffins. Rooms are small but neat with all mod cons. The unique pool here has one wall that forms part of the restaurant. Room prices work in the same way as budget airlines – price goes up as availability goes down.

C Daddy Long Legs, 134 Long St, T021-422 3074, www.daddylonglegs.co.za. South Africa's first art hotel with 13 rooms spread across a town house, offering funky, artistic rooms – each is individually themed and designed, with walls covered in art works. Rooms are small, but the stylish, original decor makes up for it. Breakfast is offered in the café downstairs. Good value and refreshingly different. Also offers self-catering apartments on Long St, with exposed brick walls and polished wood floors.

C Tudor Hotel, Greenmarket Sq, T021-424 1335, www.tudorhotel.co.za. This historic building, right on bustling Greenmarket Sq, has 26 rooms, choice of doubles and family rooms, with TV, some a/c, modern with contemporary decor, trendy bathrooms with shower. Breakfast served in stylish downstairs café, off-street parking R60 per day. Great location, friendly staff.

D-F Cat & Moose Backpackers, 305 Long St, T021-423 7638, www.catandmoose.co.za. A little tatty but cheap and a bright set-up, and central location in an atmospheric old town house. Dorms and doubles, those at front can be noisy, some have balconies overlooking Long St, lovely courtyard with sun deck and braai, good bar, small travel centre, TV/DVD lounge, breakfast available, laundry room.

D-F Inn Long Street, 230 Long St, T021-424 1660, www.innlongstreet.co.za. Run by young, friendly South Africans, this hostel has a great location on Long St, with a wide wrap-around balcony overlooking the goings on. 3 dorms with 6 beds, and 7 private rooms

(sleeping 2-4), all with polished wooden floors, simple decor. Pleasant, airy TV lounge and bar. Self-catering kitchen and laundry room. Some rooms have views of Table Mountain. One of the friendliest on Long St.

E-F Long St Backpackers, 209 Long St, T021-423 0615, www.longstreetbackpackers. co.za. Sociable, vaguely pretentious hostel spread around leafy courtyard, 80 beds in small dorms and doubles which feel cramped, fully equipped kitchen, TV/video lounge, pool room, internet access, travel centre, free pickup. Great mosaics in some of the bathrooms. Good security with 24-hr police camera opposite. Lively atmosphere, occasional parties organized and weekly communal braais; can be noisy.

Oranjezicht, Gardens and Tamboerskloof

L Alta Bay, 12 Invermark Cres, Higgovale, T021-487 8800, www.altabay.com. Quiet, secluded choice in fashionable Higgovale, nestled on leafy slopes just below Table Mountain. Beautifully designed rooms use a pale palette, beige and cream fabrics, and warm wood furniture. Each room has its own private terrace, flat-screen TV and large stone bathroom. Plunge pool with peaceful sun deck, huge healthy buffet breakfast served in airy room or overlooking pool. Free bar and high-ceilinged lounge area. Recommended.

L Kensington Place, 38 Kensington Gardens, Higgovale, T021-424 4744, www.kensington place.co.za. Cape Town's original boutique hotel in a quiet, leafy area. Small and well-run with excellent and friendly service. 8 beautiful and good-sized rooms, each individually styled with Afro-chic furnishings, big bath-rooms, lots of light from the large windows, great views over the city, bar, small pool and tropical gardens, breakfast served on a leafy veranda, excellent restaurant.

L Mount Nelson, 76 Orange St, Gardens, T021-483 1737, www.mountnelsonhotel. co.za. Cape Town's famous colonial hotel with 131 luxurious rooms and 31 'Oasis' gards. Emphasis is on traditional decor – lots of floral fabrics, antique-style furniture, heavy curtains, but all in bright, airy colours. Set in beautiful landscaped parkland with heated swimming pool, tennis courts, squash court and beauty centre. Rates vary widely from R400-11,000 depending on room and season. Celebrated

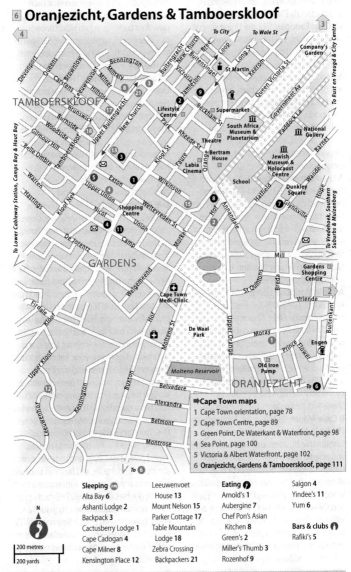

➡Cape Town maps
1 Cape Town orientation, page 78
2 Cape Town Centre, page 89
3 Green Point, De Waterkant & Waterfront, page 98
4 Sea Point, page 100
5 Victoria & Albert Waterfront, page 102
6 Oranjezicht, Gardens & Tamboerskloof, page 111

Sleeping 🛏		Eating 🍴	
Alta Bay **6**	Leeuwenvoet House **13**	Arnold's **1**	Saigon **4**
Ashanti Lodge **2**	Mount Nelson **15**	Aubergine **7**	Yindee's **11**
Backpack **3**	Parker Cottage **17**	Chef Pon's Asian	Yum **6**
Cactusberry Lodge **1**	Table Mountain	Kitchen **8**	
Cape Cadogan **4**	Lodge **18**	Green's **2**	**Bars & clubs** 🍸
Cape Milner **8**	Zebra Crossing	Miller's Thumb **3**	Rafiki's **5**
Kensington Place **12**	Backpackers **21**	Rozenhof **9**	

Cape Colony Restaurant serves Cape specialities and contemporary fare to live jazz. The Oasis Restaurant (worth visiting for the daily cream teas on the veranda) and the trendy Planet Champagne Bar.

AL Cape Cadogan, 5 Upper Union St, Tamboerskloof, T021-480 8080, www.cape cadogan.com. Ultra-elegant 2-storey mansion with 12 rooms, spacious with grass mat flooring, private terraces, subtle lighting and decor, large 4-poster beds, interesting touches like driftwood chandeliers, fabulous bathrooms, some with enormous stone walk-in showers for 2. Shady courtyard with small pool, all-white dining room with pleasant breezes. Also has 4 self-catering mews houses.

A Leeuwenvoet House, 93 New Church St, Tamboerskloof, T021-424 1133, www.lee uwenvoet.co.za. Pronounced Loo-en-Foot, this historical guesthouse has 12 double rooms, all with traditional, attractive decor, a/c, TV and telephone. Excellent breakfasts, swimming pool, off-street secure parking, close to shops and restaurants but retains a peaceful atmosphere.

A Table Mountain Lodge, 10a Tamboers-kloof Rd, T021-4230042, www.table mountainlodge.co.za. Characterful house with 7 beautifully decorated rooms, stripped wooden floors, white linen, large spotless bathrooms, breezy and very comfortable, small garden with even smaller pool, breakfast room, tiny bar called Jock's Trap, owned by the very friendly and welcoming Diana and Janne Dagh. Recommended.

B Cape Milner, 2a Milner Rd, Tamboerskloof, T021-426 1101, www.capemilner.com. Fashionable business-oriented hotel, popular with media types, with 57 rooms spread through a modern building on a busy road, all have neutral pale grey decor and slick dark wood furniture, plus tiled bathrooms (bath and shower), and M-Net TV. Lovely pool area, with sun deck, small infinity pool and bar, popular local meeting place, and decent restaurant serving good Capetonian cuisine. Laid-back, media-savvy choice.

B Parker Cottage, 3 Carstens St, Tamboers-kloof, T021-424 6445, www.parkercottage. co.za. Award-winning B&B, stylish and atmospheric set in a restored Victorian bungalow, 8 bedrooms, bathrooms with claw-foot baths, polished wood floors, lots of antiques, flamboyant colours with a Victorian touch, good breakfasts, friendly service, gay-friendly. Recommended.

C Cactusberry Lodge, 30 Breda St, Oranjezicht, T021-461 9787, www.cactus berrylodge.com. Friendly guesthouse in a converted Victorian cottage with Oregon pine floors and high ceilings, with 6 bright and airy rooms, 2 with kitchenettes, modern decor of bright white linen and muted colours, small splash pool in the courtyard, off street parking, honesty bar, Dutch spoken.

D-E Ashanti Lodge, 11 Hof St, Gardens, T021-423 8721, www.ashanti.co.za. One of Cape Town's best-known and most popular hostels, not least for its party atmosphere. Medium-sized dorms and small doubles in huge old house with polished wooden floors, high ceilings, large windows and communal balconies. Some rooms surround a courtyard and small pool and there are a couple of spaces for camping. Lively bar serving good snacks, with pool table and M-Net TV, plus good booking centre, internet access and DVD room. Not to everyone's liking as it is firmly on the busy overland truck route and can be very noisy, but perfect if you're looking for people to travel or party with. Also has a guesthouse (D) nearby with smart en suite double rooms and spotless kitchen.

D-E The Backpack, 74 New Church St, T021-423 4530, www.backpackers.co.za. Cape Town's first hostel and today one of the most comfortable and best run in town. Set across several houses with spotless dorms, doubles and singles. Polished wood floors, upmarket decor, tiled courtyard and linked gardens with pool, lovely bar with TV, meals and snacks served throughout the day, one of the best backpacker travel centres around. Recommended.

D-E Zebra Crossing Backpackers, 82 New Church St, T021-422 1265, www.zebra-crossing.co.za. Quiet, friendly backpacker hostel straddling 2 Victorian bungalows, spotless dorms plus small double rooms, good views of Table Mountain, internet access and travel centre, shady courtyard café and bar serving great breakfasts, snacks and meals, helpful.

De Waterkant and Green Point
p98, map p98

L-AL Radisson BLU, Beach Rd, Granger Bay, T021-441 3000, www.radissonblu.com/hotel-capetown. Quality large hotel in an unbeatable location right on the ocean's edge and a short walk from the V&A Waterfront. All 177 rooms are spacious with sunny decor and crisp white linen and have all mod cons including Wi-Fi. **Tobago's** restaurant and bar is very popular for sundowners and outside tables are set around the stunning infinity pool and there's a state-of-the-art spa and fitness centre.

L-C De Waterkant Village, 1 Loader St, De Waterkant, T021-430 4444, www.villageandlife.com. Village and Life own over 50 historical Bo-Kaap style houses and apartments in the trendy Waterkant area, each stylishly and individually decorated in either cutting-edge modern decor or traditionally with antiques, sleeping 1-6, many have delightful roof terraces. They also have **Waterkant House**, a guesthouse with 9 chic rooms with all mod cons, a splash pool, beautiful lounge and terrace. Their other main property is **The Charles**, www.thecharles.co.za, a gay-friendly guesthouse with 9 lovely bright rooms, some with Victorian bath, and good views from the spacious wooden decks. Also has a fantastic range of properties across Cape Town in stylish and historical buildings. Recommended.

A The Village Lodge, 49 Napier St, De Waterkant, T021-421 1106, www.thevillagelodge.com. Relative newcomer to the area, offering 15 double rooms spread across 2 converted houses. Decor is trendy greys and white, with shimmery black stone

bathrooms (shower only), some with a/c, all M-Net TV, but they feel a little cramped. Attractive restaurant, **Soho**, attached, serving Thai food in slick black surrounds. Also has a choice of cottages and apartments in the area. Good location, but overpriced.

B 40 Winks Guest House, 2 Ravenscraig Rd, Green Point, T021-434 7936, www.40winks guesthouse.co.za. Comfortable set-up in a brightly painted family house set on a quiet street above Green Point. 7 rooms plus 1 self-catering cottage next door sleeping 4-6, garden with pool, pleasant dining room where cooked breakfasts are served, off-street parking, friendly management.

B Brenwin Guest House, 1 Thornhill Rd, Green Point, T021-434 0220, www.brenwin.co.za. Guesthouse with 13 large, well-appointed rooms with en suite bathrooms, wooden floors, simple, airy decor, shady patio overlooking tidy tropical garden with swimming pool, within easy walking distance of the Waterfront. Also rents out 3 self-catering apartments each sleeping 4.

B Cape Victoria, 13 Torbay Rd, Green Point, T021-439 7721, www.capevictoria.co.za. A mix of exclusive hotel service and the privacy of a guesthouse. 10 tastefully furnished rooms with antiques and African touches, bathrooms, TV, minibar and views of the sea or Table Mountain, swimming pool, booking essential. Run by the affable Lilly. Rates drop in low season.

C Hotel Graeme, 107 Main Rd, Green Point, T021-434 9282, www.hotelgraeme.co.za. Smart hotel set on the busy Main Rd, a few mins' walk to the Waterfront and directly opposite the stadium. 31 double rooms and 5 self-catering suites sleeping 2-6, all with TV, phone, DVD, small pool deck at back, gym, secure off-street parking, laundry, internet access, business centre. Breakfast served in a glazed courtyard; also has a bar/café and an ice cream shop facing onto the street.

D-F Big Blue, 7 Vesperdene Rd, Green Point, T021-439 0807, www.bigbluebackpackers.hostel.com. Spotless and airy backpacker hostel set in a gorgeous mansion dating from 1885. Offers 86 beds in spacious dorms with bunks, single and double rooms (or shared bathrooms), all with polished yellow-wood floors, high ceilings, ceiling fans, yellow and orange walls and framed pictures. The doubles have great extras such as complimentary toiletries, and some have coffee-making facilities and free chocolates. Pleasant breakfast room, bar with outdoor section leading onto small pool, internet café, travel centre, TV room, spotless kitchen.

D-F Sunflower Stop, 179 Main Rd, Green Point, T021-4346535, www.sunflower stop.co.za. Dorms with a bit more room than most, smallish doubles, clean place with a huge kitchen. Pleasant garden with swimming pool, bar, satellite TV, tours and travel advice. Good location close to restaurants and bars.

Sea Point p98, map p100

This area has a holiday resort feel but has far less character than other areas in town. It does have an excellent range of accommodation, though, and there is some good nightlife towards Green Point.

L Le Vendôme, 20 London Rd, T021-430 1200, www.le-vendome.co.za. Large, well-designed luxury hotel with a French theme and traditional and very comfortable rooms and suites with a/c, TV and internet facilities. Attractive courtyard with pool, 1 restaurant overlooks the pool and serves snacks and lunch, the other is for fine dining. Secure parking.

AL Winchester Mansions, 221 Beach Rd, T021-434 2351, www.winchester.co.za. A well-run family hotel with 76 rooms with TV, bathroom with separate shower, some with views of the Atlantic. Pleasant pool deck and Ginkgo Spa. All rooms overlook a large courtyard where meals are served beneath the palms. Also has **Harvey's** restaurant, offering fusion cuisine and jazz brunches on Sun.

A The Clarendon, 67 Kloof Rd, T021-439 3224, www.clarendon.co.za. Luxurious Italian-style guesthouse with 10 spacious rooms spread across main house and gards, plus extra house further up the street. Rooms are large and grandly furnished with posh bathrooms, some with great views of Lion's Head. Attractive garden with large pool shaded by banana trees, breakfast served on terrace, beautiful lounge, off-street parking. Also has a similar upmarket guesthouse in Bantry Bay at 158 Kloof St.

A The Glen, 3 The Glen, T021-439 0086, www.glenhotel.co.za. Gay boutique hotel in an Italian-style villa with views of Signal Hill. Classy decor and super-trendy stone bathrooms some of which have double showers. Tropical garden with palm trees and pool, Moroccan-themed steam room with splash pool. Secure parking. Special rates out of season.

A Huijs Haerlem, 25 Main Drive, T021-434 6434, www.huijshaerlem.co.za. 2 beautifully converted neighbouring houses with 4 rooms in each, connected by well-tended gardens. All rooms are and extremely comfortable, with solid antique furniture, brass beds (some 4-poster), big bathrooms, fabulous sea views. Solar-heated saltwater swimming pool. Both houses have breakfast rooms and lounge. Rates go up considerably in summer.

A-B Blackheath Lodge, 6 Blackheath Rd, T021-439 2541, www.blackheathlodge.co.za. 7 smart, large doubles in a Victorian mansion with TV, internet and minibar, attractive decor with muted colours, off-street parking, palm-fringed patio, good-sized swimming pool, no children. Good for couples.

B Olaf's, 24 Wisbeach Rd, T021-439 8943, www.olafs.co.za. Relaxed guesthouse with 8 individually decorated rooms with shower, telephone, a/c, Wi-Fi and DSTV, mix of antiques and animal prints, breezy communal areas, breakfast served on sunny patio, small pool. Well run and friendly. German spoken.

D Ashby Manor, 242 High Level Rd, T021-434 1879, www.ashbyaccommodation.co.za. 10 simple self-catering apartments in a medium-sized rambling Victorian house.

Secure and clean rooms with kitchen facilities, some with shared bathrooms and balconies, large communal lounge and dining area, limited off-road parking, 5-min walk from Sea Point's Main Rd.

C Bellevue Manor, 5 Bellevue Rd, T021-434 0375, www.bellevuemanor.co.za. Beautiful Victorian town house that is a National Monument with doubles and self-catering rooms on a quiet side street. Wrought-iron balconies and fine palm trees. All rooms have homely decor, bathrooms, TV and laundry.

C Mountview Guesthouse and Spa, 208 High Level Rd, T021-434 3335, www.mountviewspa.co.za. Friendly and intimate set-up with just 6 rooms and generous health breakfasts, the garden has a pool, jacuzzi and good mountain views, and decor features stylish African touches. Facilities include a sauna and massages can be arranged.

C Villa Rosa, 277 High Level Rd, T021-434 2768, www.villa-rosa.com. Rose-coloured Victorian villa with 8 bright and comfortable rooms, traditional, appealing furnishings, original fireplaces, new stone-tiled bathrooms, all rooms with TV, some with fridges, 1 family room and 1 'flatlet'. Brilliant breakfasts served with home-made breads and jams. Off-street parking, pleasant veranda with sea views. Friendly, welcoming and relaxed place to stay. Recommended.

V&A Waterfront *p101, map p102*

Generally hotels at the V&A Waterfront are aimed at the high-spending foreign visitor, and all are expensive. For cheaper accommodation within walking distance of the Waterfront, although not at night, consider Green Point, above.

L Cape Grace, West Quay Rd, driving access is from the Clock Tower side of the Waterfront, T021-410 7100, www.capegrace.com. This has become one of the most luxurious hotels in Cape Town. Large development, just a short walk from the main waterfront shops and restaurants, with 122 spacious, comfortable rooms with all the mod cons,

traditional and plush decor, balconies have views of the waterfront or the mountain. Service and food is excellent, 2 bars and the celebrated **one.waterfront Restaurant**. Attractive swimming pool and deck with bar opens out from the restaurant and there's a lovely rooftop spa. Room rates from R5750.

L The Commodore, Portswood Rd, T021-415 1000, www.legacyhotels.co.za. 236 elegantly furnished rooms and suites designed for comfort, quality and luxury. Rooms have recently been refurbished and offer a/c, DSTV and all mod cons. Facilities include a swimming pool, gym and steam room. The **Clipper Restaurant** offers superb breakfasts and à la carte dining in a tranquil setting.

L One&Only, Dock Rd, T021-431 5215, www.oneandonlyresorts.com. This 131-room super luxury hotel is Sol Kerzner's (of Sun City fame) new offering and Africa's first 6-star hotel and as you can imagine it is stunning. All spacious rooms have balconies or terraces overlooking Table Mountain or the ocean, 2 islands in the marina have a clutch of villas – if you are in this league you can park your yacht outside – plus a vast heated swimming pool (the largest in Cape Town) and a tranquil spa. The giant lobby has a cocktail bar, which is also used for high tea, a branch of famed Japanese restaurant **Nobu**, and Gordon Ramsey's gourmet **Maze** restaurant, which has a wall of 5000 bottles of wine. Other top-class facilities include the **Neo** boutique, where labels like Stella McCartney and Matthew Williamson are available in South Africa for the first time. Refreshingly, despite the fact that it's expensive (rooms start from R6800) and Mariah Carey, Sharon Stone, Robert de Niro and Matt Damon were at the opening party, it's not like the other One&Only resorts which are private enclaves for the rich and famous on beaches or islands. In Cape Town, facilities are open to all.

L The Table Bay, Quay 6, Waterfront, T021-780 7878, www.suninternational.co.za. Enormous luxury offering from the Sun International Group, 329 top-notch rooms. What they lack in character they make up for in facilities and comfort. Large pool and sun deck, health club and spa, bar and good restaurant. Expensive by Cape Town standards, efficient service but feels ostentatious (note the sculpture by the main entrance commemorating the stays of celebrities and politicians). **AL Victoria & Alfred**, Pierhead, Waterfront, T021-419 6677, www.vahotel.co.za. Stylishly converted warehouse with 96 rooms, spacious with cool and comfortable furnishings, king-size beds, a/c, TV with DVD player, minibar, dramatic mountain views, large marble and stone bathrooms with separate WC, some rooms have jacuzzis on the balconies. Excellent restaurant serving seafood and steaks, fashionable, airy bar attached. Friendly and efficient service. Recommended. **C Breakwater Lodge**, Portswood Rd, Waterfront, T021-406 1911, www.protea hotels.com, www.breakwaterlodge.co.za. This hotel, managed by the **Protea** group, fills what was once the notorious Breakwater Prison (1859) and is today aimed at the tour group market. The 268 rooms are fairly small but comfortable, with functional decor. Cheaper rooms share a shower and toilet with the neighbouring room. 2 restaurants, bar, conference centre. Overpriced for what you get but cheapest option in the Waterfront. Breakfast is extra for US$13.

Southern suburbs p105

These suburbs extend east of the city, along the Eastern Blvd and around Devil's Peak towards Constantia, in the following order: Woodstock, Observatory, Mowbray, Rosebank, Rondebosch, Newlands, Claremont, Kenilworth and Wynberg. All suburbs are a short drive or train journey from the city centre. Each district has its own character and plenty of shops and restaurants close by.

Woodstock and Observatory p105
D Koornhoop Manor House, 24 London Rd, Observatory, T021-448 0595, www.geocities. com/koornhoop. Converted Victorian home in a large, peaceful garden, with 8 rooms,

all with TV, floral and homely decor, lounge and breakfast room, off-street parking. Also has 2 huge and extremely good-value self-catering apartments with 3 bedrooms, open-plan kitchens, TV lounges, private entrance and access to garden. Run by friendly English couple Vic and Trish. **D-E The Green Elephant**, 57 Milton Rd, Observatory, T021-448 6359, www.hostels. co.za. A full-on backpacker joint set in an old Observatory mansion, plenty going on in the area away from the city centre, dorms plus 3 double rooms, some en suite, with rustic 4-poster beds in a separate house, also a long-stay house, garden with pool and jacuzzi, small bar, pool table, TV room, laundry facilities.

South of Rondesbosch p107
L Andros, corner Phyllis and Newlands roads, Upper Claremont, T021-797 9777, www.andros.co.za. Grand old Cape Dutch house built in 1908 by Herbert Baker set in neat parkland, elegant and homely ambience. 8 well-appointed rooms with TV, bathrooms, under-floor heating, white and cream decor, smart breakfast room, terrace and swimming pool set in gardens, gym, sauna and beauty treatments on offer. Picnic hampers and meals arranged on request. Swiss-owned, several languages spoken. **AL The Vineyard Hotel & Spa**, Colinton Rd, off Protea Rd, Newlands, T021-657 4500, www.vineyard.co.za. 175 a/c rooms with Wi-Fi set around an 18th-century house; the decor is a mix of Cape Dutch with yellow-wood furniture and modern. The oldest part was originally built as a country house for Lady Anne Barnard in 1799. There are indoor and outdoor heated pools, 2 restaurants, 2 cafés, spa and gym. A new wing of rooms is presently under construction. **B Harfield Guest Villa**, 26 1st Av, Claremont, T021-683 7376, www.harfield.co.za. Award-winning, elegant B&B with 8 individually designed rooms. All are spacious, with TV, minibar and views of Table Mountain. Lounge/bar, sun deck and swimming pool,

bicycle hire, secure off-street parking. Relaxing ambience during the winter months when log fires keep guests warm. Recommended.

❶ Eating

Capetonians like to eat out, a fact which is reflected in its multitude of restaurants – and the extent to which they get packed out. Booking ahead is often a good idea.

City Bowl *p88, maps p89 and p111*

₩₩₩ The Africa Café, Heritage Sq, 108 Short-market St, T021-422 0221, www.africacafe. co.za. Mon-Sat 1830-2300. African-themed restaurant geared at tour groups, offering an excellent introduction to the continent's cuisines. The menu is a set 'feast' and includes 13 dishes from around Africa, such as Egyptian-smoked fish, Kenyan patties, Cape Malay mango chicken curry and springbok stew. The price includes as many dishes you like, as well as coffee and dessert. Excellent service, but it's pricey and very touristy.

₩₩₩ Five Flies, 14 Keerom St, T021-424 4442, www.fiveflies.co.za. Mon-Fri 1200-1500, daily 1900-2300. A long-standing local favourite in a historic setting. Lovely string of dining rooms, excellent 2-4 course menu of traditional food with a modern slant. The preferred haunt of lawyers and judges but also attracting well-heeled media types.

₩₩₩ Savoy Cabbage, Heritage Sq, 101 Hout St, T021-4242626, www.savoycabbage.co.za. Mon-Fri 1200-1430, Mon-Sat 1900-2230. Widely regarded as one of the best restaurants in Cape Town, serving beautifully prepared contemporary South African cuisine. The menu changes daily, and includes dishes such as gemsbok carpaccio, free-range duck breast and a gorgeous soft-centred chocolate pudding. Good wine list too, especially on reds. Bookings essential.

₩₩₩ Caveau, Heritage Sq, 92 Bree St, T021-422 1367, www.caveau.co.za. Mon-Sat 0800-late. Laid-back, stylish deli and restaurant with stone-clad walls, comfy banquettes and

tables overlooking Bree St. Menu changes daily, but includes tapas, excellent cheese and meat platters, salads and adventurous mains, and on Tue evening is a sushi and wine pairing event.

₩₩ Mama Africa, 178 Long St, T021-424 8634, www.mamaafricarest.net. Mon-Sat 1900-late. Popular restaurant and bar serving 'traditional' African dishes often with great live music. Looking a little faded around the edges, but remains popular with tourists, tasty food if overpriced and notoriously slow service. Centrepiece is a bright green carved Mamba-shaped bar. Somewhat tacky but a fun place nevertheless.

₩₩ Marco's African Place, 15 Rose St, T021-423 5412, www.marcosafricanplace.co.za. Tue-Sat 1200-late, Sun 1500-late. Good-value 'African' menu covering everything from slow-roasted Karoo lamb to samp and beans, plus popular Pan-African platter with assortment of grilled game. Huge place with a friendly atmosphere, tasty starters but main courses can be disappointing. Live music in the evening when a cover charge is added to the bill.

₩ Biesmiellah, 2 Upper Wale St, T021-423 0850, www.biesmiellah.co.za. Mon-Sat 1200-1500, 1800-2200. One of the better-known and well-established Malay restaurants, serving a delicious selection of Cape Malay dishes. This is the place to come for sweet lamb and chicken curries and sticky malva pudding. There's also a kiosk for takeaways. A treat for any fan of spicy food. No alcohol.

₩ Mr Pickwicks, 158 Long St, T021-423 3710. Mon-Sat 0830-late. Trendy spot, a favourite with pierced and tattooed Long St locals, serving the best milkshakes in town. Excellent baguettes, toasties, quiche of the day, healthy salads, large pasta portions. Pumps out loud funk and dance tunes, licensed, gets very busy with an after-work crowd, open late. Also sells tickets to Cape Town's major club nights and gigs.

₩ Rcaffé, 138 Long St, T021-424 1124. Mon-Fri 0630-1700, Sat 0830-1630. Airy, high-ceilinged café serving great Italian coffees and a delicious range of cakes and pastries baked on the premises – the double-chocolate muffins are to die for. Also serves light lunches, such as butternut quiche and feta salads. Friendly service. Wi-Fi hotspot.

♥ **Royale**, 273 Long St, T021-422 4536. Open 1200-late. Ultra-trendy eatery specializing in gourmet burgers – try the 'Miss Piggy' with bacon and guacamole, served with sweet potato fries. Attractive decor with booths and tables spilling onto the pavement. Friendly service, popular place, expect to queue (no bookings). The **Royale Kitchen**, upstairs, has the same menu and does take bookings.

♥ **Simply Asia**, Heritage Sq, 94 Shortmarket St, T021-426 4347, www.simplyasia.co.za. Daily 1200-2200. Outlet of a popular noodle chain, with a long list of freshly prepared stir-fries, Thai curries, noodles and sweet and spicy soups. Tables spill outside in summer, overlooking Shortmarket St. Other branches are in the shopping malls.

♥ **Sundance**, Heritage Sq, 59 Buitengracht St, T021-424 1461. Bare brick walls, an airy mezzanine and brisk service make this a popular choice for stylish Capetonians after a quick caffeine fix. Great choice of coffees, and excellent sandwiches on a variety of interesting breads. Wi-Fi hotspot.

Oranjezicht, Gardens and Tamboerskloof

♥♥♥ **Aubergine**, 39 Barnet St, Gardens, T021-465 4909, www.aubergine.co.za. Tue-Fri 1200-1400, Mon-Sat 1900-2230. Sophisticated and award-winning menu, modern slant on classical European dishes such as foie gras and quail, excellent wine list. One of the best in town. Stylish shaded courtyard, lounge/bar, good service.

♥♥♥ **Cape Colony**, Mount Nelson Hotel, 76 Orange St, T021-483 1000, www.mount nelson.co.za. Open 1830-2300. One of Cape Town's finest restaurants in the impressive setting of the Mount Nelson. Dishes are a mix of traditional British (think sensible roasts) and Cape classics, such as Bo-Kaap chicken and prawn curry, plus lots of game. Impeccable service, live jazz most evenings. The hotel also serves fabulous cream teas in the lounge and on the terrace every afternoon for R150 (under 12s, R75) from 1430-1730. This is a fabulous experience and bookings are essential.

♥♥♥ **Miller's Thumb**, 10b Kloof Nek Rd, T021-424 3838. Tue-Fri 1230-1430, Mon-Sat 1830-2230. Beloved by locals, bookings essential, this place serves delicious and good value seafood, plus steaks and some veggie choices, lots of spices and a Creole or Mozambique twist on some dishes. A friendly laid-back place but not as good value as it used to be.

♥♥♥ **Rozenhof**, 18 Kloof St, T021-424 1968. Mon-Fri 1230-1700, Mon-Sat 1900-2200. Smart restaurant set in an attractive 18th-century town house, decorated with local artwork and chandeliers, with cool wooden floors. Look out for seasonal dishes such as asparagus and springbok and they are well known for their roast duck, good choice for vegetarians.

♥♥♥ **Saigon**, corner of Camp and Kloof streets, T021-424 7670. Sun-Fri 1200-1430, daily 1800-2230. Superb Vietnamese cuisine, very popular place set on a corner overlooking busy Kloof St, brilliant crystal spring rolls, barbecued duck and caramelized pork with black pepper. Good choice for vegetarians. Book ahead. Recommended.

♥♥♥ **Yindee's**, 22 Camp St, Tamboerskloof, T021-422 1012. Mon-Fri 1230-1430, Mon-Sat 1830-2300. An excellent Thai restaurant serving authentic spicy curries, stir-fries, soups and unusual deep-fried coconut ice cream for dessert. Served in a sprawling Victorian house with traditional low tables. Service can be very slow, but the place is always popular, so book ahead.

♥♥-♥ **Chef Pon's Asian Kitchen**, 12 Mill St, Gardens, T021-465 5846, www.chefpons asiankitchen.co.za. There's a long menu of favourite dishes from across Asia, and everything arrives freshly cooked and sizzling hot but it's the Thai food that wins hands down. Decor is simple and dark, but cosy on a winter's night, and lingering after your meal is discouraged if they need the table (which they frequently do).

Arnold's, 60 Kloof St, Gardens, T021-424 4344, www.arnolds.co.za. Open 0745-2300. Popular good-value breakfast and lunch spot on busy Kloof St, good salads, pasta and more substantial meals like ostrich steak. Fast, friendly service. Happy hour 1630-1830. May have to queue for a table for breakfasts at weekends.

Green's, 9 Park Rd, Gardens, T021-422 4415. Mon 0800-1700, Tue-Sat 0800-2300. Pleasant café and bar in a Victorian house with sunny tables on the patio, breakfasts and light meals during the day and a more sophisticated menu in the evening. Try the freshly baked scones and cakes, crunchy salads or quiche of the day.

Yum, 2 Deer Park Drive, Vredehoek, T021-461 7607, www.yumrestaurantct.co.za. Sat-Sun 0930-2200, Mon-Fri 1800-220. Stylish deli and restaurant serving excellent sandwiches, salads and original pasta dishes, such as roast lamb tortellini or goat's cheese and roasted pepper lasagne. Good service, relaxed young crowd, delicious pickles and chutneys on sale. Arrive early if you want to try their legendary weekend brunches. Recommended.

Cafés Vida e Caffe, 34 Kloof St, Gardens, T021-426 0627, www.vidacaffe.co.za. The original of what has become the city's most successful coffee chain. Retains its quirky atmosphere, serving excellent coffees and a choice of muffins and melting hot paninis. The minimalist red and white interior is packed throughout the day.

De Waterkant and Green Point
p98, map p98

Tank, Cape Quarter, Waterkant St, T021-419 0007, www.the-tank.co.za. 1100-late. Airy, super-fashionable seafood restaurant serving the best rated sushi in the city with attractive tables spilling out onto the piazza. Inside, tables are dotted around 2 rooms, with a huge central aquarium. Good menu, daily specials, slightly pretentious clientele.

Buena Vista Social Café, 81 Main Rd, T021-433 0611, www.buenavista.co.za. Open 1200-0200. Cuban-themed bar and restaurant in a great location with balconies overlooking Main Rd. Fashionable crowd tuck into a mix of Cuban and Tex-Mex-style dishes washed down with mojitos. DJ for Latin music at weekends and salsa dancing on Sun nights.

Mano's, 39 Main Rd, Green Point, T021-434 1090. Mon-Sat 1200-2200. The affable Mano oversees this small Mediterranean restaurant with simple decor and outside terrace tables and a short but pleasing menu. The steak and pommes frites and lamb cutlets are always popular and there's a good choice of cocktails and wine.

The Nose, Cape Quarter, Waterkant St, T021-425 2200, www.thenose.co.za. Mon-Sat 0900-late. Wine bar with tables leading onto the Waterkant piazza, serving a wide range of wines accompanied by excellent seafood (the mussels in white wine and cream are especially good), steaks and burgers. Cosy interior, dishes can be ordered in large or small portions.

Giovanni's Deliworld, 103 Main Rd, Green Point, T021-434 6593. Open 0730-0900. Cape Town's best and busiest deli, this is a favourite with regulars who come to chat at the coffee bar and buy the imported cheese, cold meats and olives, fresh bread and pastries and hard to come buy groceries from Italy and the UK. The delicious ready meals can be eaten here or taken away.

Miss K Food Cafe, 65 Main Rd, Green Point, T021-439 9559, www.missk.co.za. Tue-Sun 0730-1700. A fashionable hangout for breakfast is this all-white café and on a Sun morning expect to queue. Later in the day light meals include buffet salads, home-made pies and decadent creamy cakes and tarts. Not licensed but you can BYO.

Sea Point *p98, map p100*

La Perla, corner Church and Beach roads, T021-434 9538, www.laperla.co.za. Opened in 1969, but recently completely refurbished, this is a long-term Sea Point favourite, with an extensive Italian menu with over 200 dishes specializing in seafood. Excellent anitpasto, plenty of vegetarian options, and wonderful desserts.

Tom Yum, 72 Regent Rd, T021-434 8139. Open1200-1430, 1800-2230. Simple, popular Thai restaurant serving delicious noodle and rice dishes including great seafood and ostrich stir-fries, very spicy, great tom yum soup and crispy duck with pancakes.

Posticino, 323 Main Rd, T021-439 4014, www.posticino.co.za. Popular with local residents and always has a buzzy atmosphere, this good value Italian is well known for its thin-based pizzas and you can make up your own pasta sauce. Sit on the terrace in summer and bag a table next to the fire in winter.

Cafés Café Erté, 265 Main Rd, Sea Point, T021-434 6624, www.cafeerte.com. Open 1000-0400. Tiny but trendy café/bar playing loud trance and techno, serves a vegetarian only menu of salads, sandwiches and snacks, plus cocktails and shooters, and has several internet terminals.

V&A Waterfront *p101, map p102*
With over 70 restaurants and cafés, the Waterfront is one of the most popular districts in Cape Town for eating out and gets very busy. There is a wide range of places to eat but prices are steeper than elsewhere.

Baia, top floor, Victoria Wharf, T021-421 0935. Open 1200-1500, 1900-2300. Fine seafood restaurant spread over 4 terraces with moody, stylish decor and lighting. Very smart (and expensive) venue, delicious seafood dishes following a Mozambique theme – try the spicy beer-baked prawns. Very stylish with views of Table Mountain, slightly erratic service. Book ahead.

Belthazar, Victoria Wharf, T021-421 3753, www.belthazar.co.za. Open 1200-2300. Top-of-the-range steakhouse with tables overlooking the harbour. Excellent Karan dry- and wet-cured steaks, plus range of seafood and with a staggering 600 South African wines to choose from, including 100 wines by the glass – this claims to be the world's largest wine bar.

Cape Town Fish Market, ground floor, Victoria Wharf, T021-413 5977, www.ctfm.co.za. Open 1100-2300. Fish restaurant, but the reason to come here is the revolving sushi bar, serving excellent sushi and sashimi. Dishes are limited but very fresh and good value.

Den Anker, Pierhead, T021-419 0249, www.denanker.co.za. Daily 0900-2300. Popular Belgian restaurant and bar with a continental feel, high ceiling flying the various duchy flags, airy bar, views across Alfred Basin of Table Mountain, civilized atmosphere. Good menu serving French and Belgian dishes, lots of seafood and an impressive selection of imported bottle beers.

Emily's, Clock Tower Centre, T021-421 1133. Mon-Sat 1200-2200. Very smart restaurant attached to a catering school serving excellent French-style cuisine, superb wine list, has won several awards, great views from balcony overlooking the Waterfront, polite service, slightly fussy but popular.

Balducci's, Victoria Wharf, T021-421 6002, www.balduccis.co.za. 0900-2230. Popular, elegant Italian restaurant with seats over-looking the harbour. Good choice of pasta dishes and mains ranging from ostrich steak and luxury lamb burgers, to confit de canard and blackened kingklip.

Hildebrand, Pierhead, T021-425 3385, www.hildebrand.co.za. Open 1100-2300. Well-established Italian seafood place right on the harbour's edge, superb handmade pasta and good antipasto platters, plus traditional Italian deserts. Good reputation, but touristy given the location.

Quay Four, Quay 4, T021-419 2008, www.quay4.co.za. Open 1800-2230. Popular bistro above the more relaxed pub downstairs (open all day and evening). Great views over the Waterfront, seafood is the focus but also has grills and vegetarian options. Cheaper food downstairs on the deck, calamari and fish and chips served in giant frying pans and beer on tap.

¶ Wang Thai, Victoria Wharf, T021-421 8702, www.wangthai.co.za. Open 1130-2300. Great Thai restaurant serving mouth-watering stir-fries, well known for its spicy curries with coconut milk and lemon grass. Decor is all things Buddha inspired. Reservations advised.

Cafés
Mugg & Bean, Victoria Wharf, T021-419 6451. Open 0830-2330, also branches in Cavendish Sq, Claremont. Café serving mouth-watering muffins, cakes and sandwiches and good bottomless coffee. Service can be slow.

Southern suburbs p105

Woodstock and Observatory p105
¶ Don Pedro's, 113 Roodebloem Rd, Woodstock, T021-447 4493. Informal, bustling restaurant serving huge portions of South African food, pasta and pizza at cheap prices. Very popular, focal point of the community, great mixed crowd, book ahead.
¶ Pancho's, Lower Main Rd, Observatory, T021-447 4854. Open 1200-late. Mexican dishes in a lively atmosphere, all the usual tacos and fajitas, good home-made nachos, big portions, nothing fancy but a fun place. Tasty cocktails – try the strawberry margarita.

Cafés
Obz Café, 115 Lower Main Rd, Observatory, T021-448 5555, www.obzcafe.co.za. Open 0700-2400. Popular student haunt open all day for light meals, coffee or cocktails, great salads and sandwiches, also main meals in the evenings and occasional live music.

South of Rondesbosch p107
¶¶¶ Myoga, Vineyard Hotel, Colinton Rd, Newlands, T021-657 4545, www.vineyard. co.za. Mon-Sat 1130-1500, 1830-2230. A very smart award-winning hotel restaurant with a great global fusion menu run by acclaimed chef Mike Bassett. Lunch is buffet style with a weigh-by-plate charging system and dinner is à la carte. Booking always advised.

¶¶¶ Barristers Grill, corner of Kildare and Main streets, Newlands, T021-671 7907, www.barristers.co.za. Mon-Sat 0930-2300, Sun 1730-2300. A popular steakhouse that has expanded into a bistro/café during the day with plenty of alfresco tables. Great steaks and ribs, plus veggie choices. Still retains the mock-Tudor timber decor of the steakhouse.

⚙ Bars and clubs

City Bowl *p88, maps p89 and p111*
The *Cape Times* and *Argus* newspapers have good listings sections, as does *Cape etc* magazine, out twice a month. Nightlife around Long St is generally fairly grungy and studenty and exercise caution on the streets after dark. The best source of advice in Long St is **Mr Pickwicks** café (see page 117) as the waiting staff are in the know about clubbing and you can pick up fliers. The more sophisticated bars and clubs are in Green Point, the V&A Waterfront and Camps Bay.
Chrome, Pepper St, between Long and Loop streets, T021-422 3368, www.chromect.com. Wed-Sun, doors open 2200. One of Cape Town's newest clubs, aimed firmly at the serious dance crowd, mostly hip hop and R&B, large dance floor, sophisticated lighting and sound system, VIP lounges with smoother music, over 25s.
Hemisphere, ABSA Centre, 2 Riebeek St, T021-422 3368, www.hemisphere.org.za. Thu and Sat doors open at 2200, Fri 1630 (for sundowners). Super-sophisticated night spot in an incredible location on the 31st floor of the ABSA Centre with great night time city views. Very attractive oval bar, glassed VIP section, plush furnishings and frequented by models and local celebs. Need to dress up and no under 25s.
Jo'burg, 218 Long St, T021-422 0142, www.joburgbar.com. 0900-0330-late. Trendy bar with industrial decor serving pints and cocktails to a mixed crowd, gay-friendly, relaxed during the week but gets very busy

at weekends when live bands play in the early evening followed by DJs who spin funky house and drum 'n' bass. Recommended.

Mama Africa, 178 Long St, T021-424 8634, www.mamaafricarest.net. Mon-Sat 1900-late. Great live music played by the large green mamba snake bar every night, usually marimba, but more popular with tourists than locals.

Marvel, 236 Long St. Another fashionable watering hole, less busy than Jo'Burg, with vinyl booths, a dimly lit bar and chilled out tunes. The pace picks up in the evenings, when überkool kids arrive to hang out on the pavement outside.

Vertigo, 96 Long St, T072-323 7621. Wed-Sat 2200-late. Spacious club with red walls, bar and sofas, hip hop, house and R&B, casual dress, also offers salsa classes on Tue from 1930.

Zula, 196 Long St, T021-424 2242, www.zula bar.co.za. Tue-Sat 1200-late. Fashionable bar and cocktail lounge with several small rooms, big sofas, hip-hop on most nights, great balcony overlooking Long St, and occasional live music.

Oranjezicht, Gardens and Tamboerskloof

Mercury Live & Lounge, 43 de Villiers St, T021-465 2106, www.mercuryl.co.za. Wed, Fri, Sat 2100-late. Live music venue and club nights, rock and hip hop acts play regularly, also holds weekly hip-hop parties and 'nostalgia' alternative rock nights. Cape Town's leading live music venue, lively, young crowd.

Rafiki's, 13 Kloof Nek Rd, T021-426 4731, www.rafakis.co.za. 1200-0200. Popular bar overlooking Kloof Nek with a huge wrap-around balcony perfect for a sundowner. Relaxed atmosphere, friendly crowd, DJs and occasional live music in the evenings, simple food like pizzas and burgers.

Rhodes House, 60 Queen Victoria St, Gardens, T021-424 8844, www.rhodes house.com. Fri-Sat 2100-late. Rated as one of the best nightclubs in the city. Swanky lounge with dancefloor and alfresco courtyard, super-trendy decor, good music, fantastic but pricey cocktails.

Green Point *p98, map p98*
The area around De Waterkant and Green Point is the focus of Cape Town's gay and lesbian scene, with a number of trendy bars and clubs with mixed crowds.

Bronx Action Bar, 35 Somerset Rd, corner Napier St, T021-419 9216, www.bronx.co.za. 2000-late. Cape Town's best known and most popular gay bar and club, gets packed out at weekends, mostly men but women welcome, live DJs spin out thumping techno every night.

Buena Vista Social Café, Main Rd, T021-433 0611, www.buenavista.co.za. Mon-Fri 1200-0200, Sat and Sun 1700-0200. Cuban-themed bar and restaurant catering to a well-heeled crowd. Latin music, live bands at weekend, tasteful decor and a relaxed atmosphere, nice balcony overlooking Main Rd, great spot for sophisticated cocktails on a hot evening.

Café Manhattan, 74 Upper Waterkant St, T021-421 6666, www.manhattan.co.za. 1000-late. Cape Town's most established gay venue in a bright red building with a wrap-around balcony and long bar, popular with regulars, good varied food, especially the burgers, perfect venue to start an evening out in Green Point.

Fireman's Arms, 25 Mechau St, T021-419 0207, www.firemansarms.co.za. Mon-Sat 1200-2300. Historic pub set in what was Cape Town's first fire station built in 1864, still complete with fire pole and fireman's hats. Best known as a place to watch sports and its get packed out on rugby match days. Good homely menu of pub grub like liver and onions or bangers and mash.

Loft Lounge, 24 Napier St, De Waterkant, T021-425 2647, www.loftlounge.co.za. Wed-Sun 1900-late. Stylish and sophisticated gay bar in a new building designed to look like an old converted warehouse to keep with the architecture of the area with large windows and views of Table Mountain. Plush couches and chaise longs, art from local artists on the walls, balcony, lounge music and DJs later in the night.

Tobago's, Radisson SAS Hotel, Beach Rd, T021-441 3000, www.radissonsas.com. Super-stylish hotel bar set around an infinity pool, with great ocean views, a long list of cocktails and giant wicker chairs with cushions. A perfect spot for sundowners and attracts a mixed crowd of tourists and after work drinkers.

V&A Waterfront *p101, map p102*
Alba Lounge, Pier Head, T021-425 3385, www.albalounge.co.za. 1700-late. Sophisticated cocktail lounge above the Hildebrand restaurant with a quiet ambience, comfortable couches and good harbour views. Food includes hot canapés or larger Italian meals, and the chocolate martini is to die for.
Ferryman's Tavern, East Pier Rd, T021-419 7748, www.ferrymans.co.za. 1100-2300. A popular haunt with restaurant upstairs, huge outside seating area, TV continually showing sports action, a lively mixed crowd.
Mitchell's Brewery, East Pier Rd, T021-419 5074. Open 1100-2300. Next door to **Ferryman's** this is an English-style wood panelled pub and it brews its own beer including bitter and stout, which are not common in South Africa. The cloudy Forester's lager is also good. Upstairs sports are shown on TV and there's simple pub fare on offer.
Quay Four, see Eating, page 120. Open 1100-2400. Large shady deck overlooking the water, popular with well-heeled locals and tourists, good value meals and great draught beer, and there's often live music in the evening.

Southern suburbs *p105*
Observatory is the city's alternative nightlife centre and the place to head for laid-back bars and clubs with a bohemian feel, while Rondebosch and Claremont have plenty of sports bars popular with sporty types.

Woodstock and Observatory *p105*
A Touch of Madness, Pepper Tree Sq, Nuttal Rd, Observatory, T021-448 2266, www.cafeatom.co.za. 1500-late. Flamboyant bar with series of rooms decked out with tongue-in-cheek opulence, eccentric regulars, great atmosphere, good light meals, live Irish music on Thu nights.
Café Ganesh, 46 Trill Rd, Observatory, T021-448 3435, www.cafeganesh.co.za. Mon-Sat 1800-late. Lively little café and bar serving hearty Cape dishes and plenty of vegetarian options and ice-cold beers in a leafy courtyard leading to a characterful interior. Very friendly, great place to meet local people.

South of Rondesbosch *p107*
Forester's Arms, Newlands Av, T021-689 5949. 1100-late. Old fashioned English-style pub, popular with weird mix of suited types on their way home from work and studenty sports jocks. A fun-loving, boozy scene with a leafy beer garden and fire inside in winter.
Oblivion, corner 3rd Av and Chichester Rd, Harfied Village, between Claremont and Kenilworth, T021-671 8522, www.oblivion.co.za. Daily 1130-0200. No under 23s. Laid-back wine bar and restaurant, which turns into a raucous dance venue later on. Good selection of snack platters, nachos and pizzas and an impressive wine list.
Tiger Tiger, The Atrium, Main Rd, Claremont, T021-683 2220, www.tigertiger.co.za. Tue, Thu-Sat doors open at 2030. Age restriction changes depending on the night – check the website. This is the Southern Suburbs most commercial and modern nightclub with several bars, plenty of seating areas, a large sunken dance floor and mainstream pop music. Attracts the odd local rugby or cricket star and Prince Harry used to woo Chelsy here.

🎭 Entertainment

Cinema
The 2 major cinema groups are **Nu Metro**, www.numetro.co.za, and **Ster-Kinekor**, www.sterkinekor.co.za. New films are released on Fri. Evening shows are very popular, booking advised especially at week-ends (you can do this through the websites).

Daily newspapers and the bi-monthly *Cape etc* have full listings. There are multi-screen cinemas at Century City, the V&A Waterfront and Cavendish Sq. The latter 2 also have a separate **Cinema Nouveau**, which screens international and art-house films (information and bookings also at Ster-Kinekor). For film festivals, see below.

Labia on Orange, 68 Orange St, Gardens, and **Labia on Kloof**, Lifestyle Centre, Kloof St, T021-4245927, www.labia.co.za. Perhaps Cape Town's most enjoyable cinema, showing independent international films in a historic building that used to be a ballroom, with a café serving good pre-movie snacks. **Labia on Kloof** is the mainstream version, with 2 screens showing Hollywood releases. Both are licensed, so you can take your glass of wine into the movie.

Music
See also Bars and clubs, page 121, for live music venues.
Green Dolphin, V&A Waterfront, T021-421 7471. Open 1200-1500, 1800-2400. Restaurant and jazz venue featuring top local jazz groups that play in the evening while you eat, when bookings are advised. There's a varied international menu with lighter meals at lunchtime.
Kirstenbosch Summer Concerts, www.sanbi.org, Nov-Mar every Sun at 1700. Idyllic setting, picnics on the lawns, concerts varying from folk and jazz to classical and opera, plus Carols by Candlelight at Christmas. Recommended.
V&A Waterfront Amphitheatre. Outdoor venue on the Waterfront with daily concerts and live performances, mainly jazz.

Theatre
All tickets can be purchased from **Computicket**, T021-340 8000, www.computicket.com. There are kiosks at the V&A Waterfront and Cavendish Sq and the other larger malls, as well as in Checkers supermarkets.
Artscape, DF Malan St, Foreshore, T021-410 9800, www.artscape.co.za. Major complex offering opera, ballet, theatre and music.

Baxter, Main Rd, Rondebosch, T021-685 7880, www.baxter.co.za. Long-established involvement in black theatre, good reputation for supporting community theatre, international productions and musicals.
Theatre on the Bay, Link St, Camp's Bay, T021-4833301, www.theatreonthebay.co.za. Slightly alternative shows, licensed so you can take your drinks in, interesting mix of plays, comedy and musicals. The restaurant here is good and there's the option of a pre-show dinner and then dessert in the interval.

⊛ Festivals and events

Celebrations are a serious business in Cape Town, and during the summer months you'll be hard pressed to find a free weekend. Street carnivals and festivals compete with cultural and sporting events, although publicity is often limited. See *The Cape Times* or www.tourismcapetown.co.za, for listings.
2 Jan Karnaval. Begins in the Bo-Kaap district and ends up near the Green Point Stadium, this includes a procession of competing minstrel bands, complete with painted faces, straw boaters and bright satin suits.
Jan J&B Metropolitan Handicap, last Sat in Jan, www.jbmet.co.za. South Africa's major horse racing meet at Kenilworth Race Course, where everyone is expected to dress up. The 2009 theme was glitz and glam.
Feb/Mar Cape Town Pride, www.capetown pride.co.za. The biggest gay event in town, floats and a parade around Green Point culminating in a street party in De Waterkant.
Mar Cape Town Carnival, www.capetown carnival.com. New to the mother city, this annual event will be first held on the 3rd weekend of Mar in 2010. Copying the model of the Rio Carnival, it will include a 1 km procession of floats, dancers and musicians and there will be numerous balls, beach and street parties over the weekend.
Mar Cape Town Festival, www.capetown festival.co.za. Week-long arts and cultural festival at the end of Mar, various venues.

Mar Cape Town International Jazz Festival, International Convention Centre, www.capetownjazzfest.com. 5 stages with a huge array of local and international jazz artists, last weekend in Mar.

Mar Cape Argus Pick 'n' Pay Cycle Tour, www.cycletour.co.za. World's largest timed cycling event taking an impressive 109-km route around Table Mountain and along the shores of the peninsula. It's open to international cyclists and attracts some 40,000 participants each year.

Mar Two Oceans Marathon, www.two oceansmarathon.org.za. 56-km race with over 9000 competitors, last weekend in Mar.

Apr Start of Rugby season, at Newlands, www.wprugby.com.

Jul Encounters Documentary Film Festival, www.encounters.co.za. Films screened at Nu Metro at the V&A Waterfront.

Aug Cape Times Wine Festival, V&A Waterfront, www.waterfront.co.za. You can taste 300 wines from 85 estates, and there's a cheese hall, last weekend in Aug.

Sep Out in Africa Festival, www.oia.co.za. Annual gay and lesbian film festival, with screenings at Nu Metro on the V&A Waterfront.

Sep Hermanus Whale Festival, www.whale festival.co.za. Marks beginning of calving season of southern right whales, excellent viewing, last week in Sep, an easy day trip from Cape Town.

Oct Cape Town Comedy Festival, Baxter Theatre, www.comedyfestival.co.za. A week-long festival with local and international talent.

Nov Cape Times/Discovery Health Big Walk, www.bigwalk.co.za. World's largest timed walk started in 1903 attracting 25,000 on walks from 5-80 km.

Dec Obz Festival, Observatory, www.obz festival.com. Huge street party with stalls, live music and all-nights parties.

Dec Kirstenbosch Summer Concerts, www.sanbi.org. Every Sun until Mar. Picnics on the lawns, concerts varying from folk and jazz to classical and opera.

O Shopping

Arts, crafts and curios

African Image, 52 Burg St, T021-423 8385, www.african-image.co.za. Excellent alternative to the tired souvenir shops, this gallery sells contemporary African art, such as bags made from traditional weavings, beautiful baskets, old township signs, photography, plus quirky souvenirs like coke-bottle-top bags and chickens made from colourful plastic bags. Also has an outlet in Victoria Wharf, V&A Waterfront.

Greenmarket Square Market. Lively market selling crafts, textiles and clothes from across the continent. Be prepared to take part in some cheerful haggling.

Monkeybiz, Rose St, Bo-Kaap, T021-426 0636, www.monkeybiz.co.za. Something of a local sensation, **Monekybiz** creates employment for women (many of them HIV positive) in the townships of Mandela Park and Khayelitsha. The women create beautiful and quirky one-off bead works, including figures, animals and accessories.

Out of This World, V&A Waterfront, T021-419 3246. One of many African arts and crafts shops at the Waterfront, better value and a more tasteful selection than many.

The Pan African Market, Long St, T021-426 4478, www.panafrican.co.za. 2-storey centre set in a converted Victorian house, selling crafts from across the continent, good local crafts made from recycled material, beadwork, ceramics. Café specializing in African food, plus a book shop and holistic healing area.

Red Shed Craft Workshop, part of Victoria Wharf shopping centre. Handful of local craftsmen, goods are of suspect taste, kitsch embroidery and satin cushions.

Streetwires, 77 Shortmarket St, T021-426 2475, www.streetwires.co.za. Building housing a wire sculpture cooperative, useful place to browse these interesting South African craft works without feeling under pressure from the usual street vendors.

Books and maps

Clarke's Bookshop, 211 Long St, T021-423 5739, www.clarkesbooks.co.za. A mass of antiquarian, 2nd-hand and new books in a muddled old shop, a must for any book lover.

CNA (Central News Agencies). A city-wide chain of shops carrying a reasonable stock of guide books, glossy coffee-table publications, some colourful maps, foreign newspapers and magazines.

Exclusive Books. A more upmarket chain with branches at Victoria Wharf at the V&A Waterfront and Cavendish Sq Mall. Good for travel and coffee-table books.

The Map Studio, www.mapstudio.co.za. Tourist maps of towns and regions as well as official survey maps. For sale in **Exclusive Books**.

Select Books, 232 Long St, T021-424 6955, www.selectbooks.co.za. Something of a local institution, with a pleasantly ordered interior and vast range of books on southern Africa including great contemporary choices.

Wordsworth Books, Gardens Centre, T021-461 8464, and at Victoria Wharf at the V&A Waterfront, T021-425 6880. Knowledgeable staff assist in this comprehensive bookstore. They branch in the V&A Waterfront has a section dedicated to guide books, maps and books about South Africa.

Clothes

Long St and Kloof St in the City Bowl have become the powerhouse of Cape Town's fashion scene, and have a good choice of kooky boutiques selling one-offs and locally designed clothes and accessories. For better-known clothes chains and upmarket boutiques, head to the shopping malls. Particularly popular with the young and well-heeled are the shops in Victoria Wharf, at the Waterfront, T021-408 7600, www.water front.co.za, and Cavendish Sq, in Claremont, T021-657 5620, www.cavendish.co.za. Prices here are only marginally cheaper than in Europe.

Markets

Church St Antiques Market, on Church St, between Long and Burg streets, Mon-Sat 0900-1400. Offbeat antiques, nautical equipment, crockery and jewellery.

Grand Parade Market. Mon-Sat 0800-1400. General market at the large parade ground in front of the old City Hall, selling clothes, fabrics and flowers.

Greenmarket Square. Mon-Sat 0900-1600. A lively arts and crafts market on a picturesque cobbled square, goods from across Africa, formerly a fruit and vegetable market, flanked by several terrace cafés.

Green Point Market, beside Green Point Stadium (although presently at a temporary spot on Green Point Common). Sun 0800-1700. Good mixture of curios, one lane of food stalls, plenty of buskers.

Music

The African Music Store, 134 Long St, T021-426 0857, www.africanmusicstore.co.za. Stocks an excellent choice of albums by major southern African artists as well as compilations and reggae. The staff are incredibly helpful and are happy to let you listen to any number of CDs before purchasing.

Mabu Vinyl, 2 Rheede St, Gardens, T021-423 7635, www.mabuvinyl.co.za. A relative Aladdin's Cave of vinyl LPs and 12"s, cassettes, turntables, comics and new CDs of independent South African artists and can ship around the world.

Musica, www.musica.co.za. The biggest music shop chain, selling all the latest CDs, videos and DVDs. It can be found in every shopping centre and along high streets. It has a massive branch at the V&A Waterfront just south of Nobel Sq in its own building, which is particularly strong on African music.

Supermarkets

Each of the suburbs has its own shopping complex with a branch of one of the major supermarket chains – **Checkers, OK Bazaar, Pick 'n' Pay, Shoprite** and **Spar**. For high-quality groceries head to **Woolworths** which is much the same as Marks & Spencer in Britain, with equivalent prices.

▲▲ Activities and tours

With its equitable climate and outdoor lifestyle, Cape Town's adventure sports scene has boomed in recent years. Most backpacker hostels promote a huge choice of activities, particularly the more action-packed ones such as kloofing, abseiling or paragliding.

Abseiling
Abseil Africa, T021-4244760, www.abseil africa.co.za. Operates one of the world's highest and longest commercial abseils – 112 m down Table Mountain – R495 excluding cable car fee. Also runs day trips to other abseil points around the Cape and kloofing trips.

Cricket
In the southern suburb of Newlands is the famous **Sahara Park Cape Town Test Match Ground**, 161 Camp Ground Rd, for fixtures contact, T021-657 2003, www.cricket.co.za, tickets Computicket, T011-340 8000, www.computicket.com. Despite considerable redevelopment, a few of the famous old oak trees remain and it is still possible to watch a game from a grassy bank with Table Mountain as a backdrop. Some of the public seats are very exposed – wear a hat and have plenty of sun cream to hand. Since the demolition of the old Green Point Stadium, it's also become the venue for rock concerts.

Fishing
The most common catches are mako shark, long-fin tuna and yellowtail, but there are strict rules governing all types of fishing. The simplest way of dealing with permits and regulations is through a charter company. **Hooked on Africa**, T021-790 5332, www.hookedonafrica.co.za. Deep-sea tuna trips, in-shore light tackle and fly fishing and crayfish charters. Leaves from Hout Bay. 4 boats to choose from, all gear supplied. **Nauticat Charters**, T021-790 7278, www.nauticatcharters.co.za. Game fishing and boat charters, also operates from Hout Bay.

Golf
For further details contact the **Western Province Golf Union**, T021-712 6910, www.wpgu.co.za. Expect to pay green fees of around R3-350 for 18 holes. The following golf clubs are open to overseas visitors:
Milnerton Golf Club, Bridge Rd, Milnerton, T021-552 3108, www.milnertongolf.co.za. 6011 m, par 72. This is a true links course in the shadow of Table Mountain, watch your par when the wind blows. A popular course set between the Atlantic Ocean and a river.
Mowbray Golf Club, Ratenberg Rd, Mowbray, T021-685 3018, www.mowbray golfclub.co.za. One of the oldest clubs, hosts national championships, a par-74 course with plenty of trees, bunkers and water holes.
Rondebosch Golf Club, Klipfontein, Rondebosch, T021-689 4177, www.ronde bosch-golf-club.co.za. A tidy course with the Black River flowing through it.
Royal Cape Golf Club, 174 Ottery Rd, Wynberg, T021-761 6551, www.royalcape golf.co.za. Length: 6174 m, par 74. An old course that has been the venue for major professional tournaments.
Simon's Town Country Club, T021-786 1233, www.simonstowngolf.co.za. A 9-hole, 18-tee, links course on the seafront, just by the turning for Boulders Beach. This is a narrow course and is a real test for anyone not used to playing in very windy conditions.

Hiking
Downhill Adventures, T021-422 0388, www.downhilladventures.com. Guided half-day hikes on Table Mountain for R450.

Horse riding
The 8-km beach at Noordhoek is popular. **Imhoff Equestrian Centre**, Imhoff Farm, Kommetjie, T082-774 1191, www.horse riding.co.za. 2-hr beach rides at Noordhoek, no children under 12.
Sleepy Hollow Horse Riding, T021-789 2341, www.sleepyhollowhorseriding.co.za. Noordhoek beach rides, no children under 14, have horses suitable for novice riders.

Kiteboarding

The Cape's strong winds have made it a very popular site for kiteboarding. The best spot is Dolphin Beach at Table View, north of the city centre where winds are strong and waves perfect for jumping.

Cabrinha, T021-556 7910, www.cabrinha. co.za. Rents out equipment to experienced kiteboarders and offers 2-hr lessons at Table View for R495. Affiliated to the International Kiteboarding Organization (IKO).

Downhill Adventures, T021-422 0388, www.downhilladventures.com. Beginners tuition from R650 per 2-hr lesson and recommends 3 sessions before going alone.

Kloofing

Kloofing (canyoning) involves hiking, boulder-hopping and swimming along mountain rivers. It is very popular on and around Table Mountain; many of the tour operators listed on page 129 organize daily excursions.

Mountain biking

Downhill Adventures, T021-422 0388, www.downhilladventures.com. Organizes a range of mountain-biking excursions, including the popular Table Mountain double descent (90% downhill), rides around Cape Point and the Winelands Meander. Also offers bike and helmet rentals for R140 per day.

Homeland, 305 Long St, T021-426 0294, www.homeland.co.za. Mountain-bike rentals cost R140 for 24 hrs; cheaper rates the longer you hire. Also rents out surf boards, paddle skis, wet suits and camping equipment.

Paragliding

Paragliding from Lion's Head is very popular, with gliders landing by the sea between Clifton and Camps Bay. For tandem paragliding sessions contact **Para-Pax**, T082-881 4724 (mob), www.parapax.com. Flights cost R950 and include drinks and refreshments. Pick-up/drop-off from hotels is R100 extra and for R150 you get photos and video.

Rugby

International games are played at the **Western Province Rugby Football Union** ground, Boundary Rd, Newlands, T021-659 4600, www.wprugby.co.za. Tickets for major games can be bought through **Computicket**, T011-340 8000, www.computicket.com.

Sailing

Regattas are regularly held in Table Bay. **Royal Cape Yacht Club**, Small Craft Harbour, Duncan Rd, T021-421 1354, www.rcyc.co.za. The club is for members only, but accommodates visitors if they are a member of an affiliated international club. They will also let you in to look at the notice board, which advertises placements for crew members.

Table Bay is not a bad place to learn to sail and **Yachtmaster**, T021-788 1009, www.yachtmaster.co.za, offers a number of courses. For charters and day-trips, see Boat tours, page 130.

Sandboarding

Try the latest addition to board sports on sand dunes. It is not a very fast sport and can be frustrating if you're used to snow, but it can be a fun day out.
Downhill Adventures, T021-422 0388, www.downhilladventures.com. Day trips to dunes about 1 hr from Cape Town.

Scuba-diving

The Cape waters are cold but are often very clear and good for wreck and kelp diving. The best season for diving is during the winter months when the weather ensures the sea is flat as the prevailing winds blow offshore. Water temperatures are between 12°C-18°C; visibility is usually between 5-10 m. When the winds change direction in the summer months visibility can be reduced to almost zero. There are a number of interesting wreck dives along the coast and most sites can be reached direct from the shore. A number of dive companies also specialize in great white shark cage dives.

Dive Action, 22 Carlisle St, Paarden Island, T021-511 0800, www.scubadivecape town.co.za. Full dive shop and training centre offering a range of wreck, shore and coral dives around the Cape.

Great White Ecoventures, T021-530 0470, www.white-shark-diving.com. Runs cage diving trips to see great white sharks in Gansbaai, a 2-hr drive away. Non-divers can snorkel at the top of the cage. Costs R1500 inclusive of transfers from Cape Town.

Scuba Shack, 289 Long St, T021-424 2233, www.scuba-shack.co.za; also in Kommetjie on the peninsula, T021-785 6742. Well-run local scuba-diving school. Full range of PADI-instruction and equipment hire, as well as organized tours to the best dive sites and great white shark cage dives. Also arranges snorkelling with the seals trips for non-divers.

Table Bay Diving, Quay 5, V&A Waterfront, T021-419 8822, www.tablebaydiving.com. Dive charters and full range of PADI courses, and sells scuba and snorkelling gear.

Skydiving
Skydive Cape Town, T082-800 6290 (mob), www.skydivecapetown.za.net. Offers tandem jumps on the West Coast for R1450; extra R570 for video and photos. Also runs and static-line courses.

Surfing
Surfing is a serious business in Cape Town, and there are excellent breaks catering for learners right through to experienced surf rats. Some of the best breaks are on **Long Beach, Kommetjie, Noordhoek, Llandudno, Kalk Bay, Muizenberg** and **Bloubergstrand**. Daily surf report: T082-234 6370.

Downhill Adventures, T021-422 0388, www.downhilladventures.com. Organizes day and multi-day courses from R655 per day as well as 'Secret Surf Spots' tours.

Homeland, 305 Long St, T021-426 0294, www.homeland.co.za. Rents out surf boards and wet suits (essential) to experienced surfers.

Swimming
The beaches on the Atlantic seaboard are almost always too cold to swim in – even during the hottest months, the water temperatures rarely creep above 16°C. Camps Bay has a tidal pool and shady, grassy areas, see page 136. Noordhoek is too rough for swimming, but is a great place for kite-flying or a horse ride, see page 137. False Bay is always a good 5°C warmer, and the main swimming spot is Seaforth Beach, see page 145. You can't swim at Boulders Beach but it is one of the most attractive beaches on the False Bay seaboard and is the best place for spotting African penguins, see page 146. Fish Hoek has a pleasant beach with small waves and a playground, see page 145. Additionally, a number of beaches have artificial rock pools, which although rather murky can be perfect for paddling children.

Sea Point Swimming Pool, Beach Rd, Sea Point, T021-434 3341. Daily Oct-Apr 0700-1900, May-Sep 0830-1700, R10, children R6. Some (probably Cape Town people), regard this as being the most stunning location for a public swimming pool in the world. Indeed, it is a sparkling bright blue outdoor Olympic-sized pool built right on the rocks next to the ocean with superb mountain and sea views. It has 2 splash pools for kids and a springboard diving pool.

Tour operators
For information about a city tour in an open-top bus with **Sightseeing Cape Town**, visit www.citysightseeing.co.za, or see Getting around, page 80. There are a diverse range of day tours in and around Cape Town available through the operators below. Expect to pay in the region of R350 for a ½-day tour and R600 for a full day. The 3 most popular are tours of the Cape Peninsula, the Winelands and the townships. Peninsula tours generally go down the west side to Hout Bay and offer an optional boat trip to see the seals on Duiker Island, then go over Chapman's Peak Drive (if its open) and into the Table Mountain National Park to Cape Point. They return to

the city on the eastern side with a stop to see the penguins at Boulders Beach. Winelands tours take in about half a dozen vineyards in the Stellenbosch and Paarl regions. Township tours usually begin at the District Six Museum and continue to Langa and Khayelitsha, and companies work with the communities they visit, putting back some of the proceeds. If you want to combine a ½-day township tour with the excursion to Robben Island, all operators will drop off at the ferry. For a full list of tour operators, visit www.tourismcapetown.co.za.

Day tours

Andulela Experience, T021-790 2590, www.andulela.com. Very different township tours that focus on music and poetry, jazz and soccer and a day trip in Bo-Kaap that includes a walking tour, Cape Malay cookery lessons and meals.

Cape Capers, T021-448 3117, www.tour capers.co.za. Range of trips, including ½-day tours looking at Cape Town's slave history, District Six and Bo-Kaap tours and the Cape Care Route that goes to social and environmental projects on the Cape Flats. Recommended.

Cape Rainbow Tours, T021-551 5465, www.caperainbow.com. Tours in many European languages to the townships, Winelands, Peninsula and, in season, to the West Coast to see the flowers and Hermanus for whales.

Day Trippers, T021-511 4766, www.day trippers.co.za. Peninsula tours which include 1 or 2 hrs of cycling at Cape Point, Winelands, township, Table Mountain hike and the Whale Coast. Good value and fun, popular with backpackers.

Downhill Adventures, T021-422 0388, www.downhilladventures.com. Rents out bikes and organizes adventure tours on Table Mountain, Cape Point, along the coast and in the Winelands.

Endeavour Safaris, T021-556 6114, www.endeavour-safaris.com. All Cape Town day trips for the frail and physically challenged, with specially adapted vehicles and trained

guides, for peninsular, Robben Island and District Six, Table Mountain and Kirstenbosch, and Winelands tours. They can also arrange tours for the deaf, blind and people needing oxygen or regular kidney dialysis.

Footsteps to Freedom, T083-452 1112, www.footstepstofreedom.co.za. Mon-Sat 1030-1330, R120, R60 children (under 12). Starting at the tourist office this is a historical walking tour of central Cape Town which goes to the Castle, District Six Museum and Company's Garden and can be combined with a township minibus tour later in the afternoon. English and German spoken. Recommended to get the most out of the city centre's attractions.

Friends of Dorothy, T021-465 1871, www.friendsofdorothytours.co.za. Gay-friendly tours, including a Four Passes tour, Peninsula, Winelands and whale-watching trips. Gay drivers and guides, max 6.

Homeland, T021-426 0294, www.home land.co.za. Cape Point Classic tour, which includes biking, a braai lunch and transport in an open-sided overland truck for R350 per person and it runs on Mon, Wed, Fri and Sun.

Hylton Ross, T021-511 1784, www.hylton ross.com. Full range of day tours, Cape Point with optional boat ride to see the seals from Hout Bay, winelands, township, and longer trips to the Garden Route.

Boat tours

See also page 104 for Robben Island Tours and page 148 for boats trips from the Peninsula. There are more than 20 boats of varying types and sizes operating from Quay 5, the Pierhead or the Clock Tower at the V&A Waterfront (a couple are listed below). Just take a stroll around and the touts at the various kiosks will tell you what's on offer and when the next departure is. Alternatively, visit www.water front.co.za and go to the 'play' section where it lists all the options. Departures are throughout the day and in some cases early evening and you can choose from a sail on a schooner to Camps Bay, a quick ferry trip across one of the docks, a guided tour of the working harbour, a sunset cruise with champagne, or a fast inflatable jet boat ride.

Drumbeat Charters, T021-791 4441, www.drumbeatcharters.co.za. Daily boat trips from Hout Bay Harbour to see the seals on Duiker Island, R50, children R25. Boats leave at 0830, 0915, 1000 and 1045 and the round trip takes about 30 mins.

Nauticat, T021-790 7278, www.nauticat charters.co.za. Daily cruises from Hout Bay to see the seals at Duiker Island in a glass-bottomed boat.

Spirit of Just Nuisance, Simonstown T082-257 7760 (mob), www.boatcompany.co.za. Short tours around the harbour area, which include a special visit to the naval dockyard. Also organizes longer trips to Seal Island and Cape Point, and can be chartered for private cruises. Departs regularly from the main pier.

Tigger Too, Quay 5, V&A Waterfront, T021-790 5256, www.tiggertoo.co.za. Upmarket outfit with daily departures from the Waterfront, sunset cruises and day trips, booking advised during peak periods.

Waterfront Boat Company, Quay 5, V&A Waterfront, T021-418 5806, www.waterfront boats.co.za. 6 boats to choose from including a large catamaran and stylish schooner called the Spirit of Victoria, and a range of boat tours including around (not to) Robben Island, whale watching, sunset and dinner cruises. Prices from R200 for 1½-hr sunset cruise, jet boat from R350, 1-hr.

Helicopter flights

Cape Town looks quite incredible from the air and a helicopter flight is a great way to get a grip of the geography of Table Mountain. The company offices are at Quay 5 at the V&A Waterfront from where passengers are ferried to the helipad beyond the Table Bay Hotel. The standard 15-min flight along the coast as far as Camps Bay and then back through Kloof Nek to see the top of Table Mountain and the City Bowl start from R500 pp. Longer 20-, 30- and 60-min flights take in other parts of the peninsula.

The Hopper, Quay 5, V&A Waterfront, T021-419 8951, www.thehopper.co.za. Standard 3-seated choppers suitable for anyone from children to grandmothers.

The Huey Helicopter Co, Quay 5, V&A Waterfront, T021-419 4839, www.thehuey helicopterco.com. Flights in an ex-US Army Huey that served during the Vietnam War – as the sides are open this is more of an adrenalin activity.

Whale watching

The whale-watching season is Jul-Nov. Rules surrounding trips to the see the whales are very stringent, and only 1 boat a year is given a permit to run whale-watching cruises. This is presently held by the **Simon's Town Boat Company**, Simon's Town jetty, T083-257 7760, www.boatcompany.co.za. Trips go out daily at 0900, 1200 and 1430 in season, R650, children (under 12), R400, booking essential. Weather permitting, they also offer fast speed boat rides to Cape Point for R350, children (under 12) R200, and the round 2½-hr trip includes a stop on the seaward side of Boulders Beach (see page 146) to watch the penguins in the water.

Windsurfing

Langebaan has the best reputation for surfable winds on the Cape; the southeasterly roars between Sep and Apr. In Mar there is a **Boardsailing Marathon** in False Bay, while Big Bay at Blouberg is a good spot for wave-jumping. Daily windsurf report: T082-234 6324 (mob). For more information visit www.capetownwindsurf.com.

Milnerton Aquatic Club, T021-557 7090, www.windsurfingcapetown.com. Offers equipment and tuition and a 2-day beginner's course costs R500.

⊖ Transport

Air

See also Ins and outs, page 78, for details of getting to/from the airport. Departure tax is included in the ticket price.

South African Airways (SAA) and its subsidiaries have numerous flights every day to every city in South Africa. **British Airways/Comair** has several flights/day to **Johannesburg**. Kulula flies to **Port Elizabeth**, **Durban** and **Johannesburg**. Mango has daily flights to **Bloemfontein**, **Johannesburg** and **Durban**. 1Time has flights to **East London**, **Johannesburg**, **Port Elizabeth** and **Durban**.

Airline offices
All air tickets can be booked online at www.computicket.com. 1Time, www.1time. aero. SA Airlink, www.flyairlink.com. British Airways Comair, www.britishairways.com. Kulula, www.kulula.com. Mango, ww5.fly mango.com. SA Express, www.saexpress. co.za. South African Airways (SAA), central reservations T0861-359722 (in South Africa), T011-978 5313 (from overseas), www.flysaa.com.

Bus
Intercape, Greyhound and Translux all depart from/arrive at Adderley St, next to Cape Town railway station. Booking offices are also here. Buses head north up the N7 to **Upington** and **Windhoek** in Namibia, east along the N2 to **Knysna**, **Port Elizabeth** and **Durban**, and northeast up the N1 to **Bloemfontein**, **Kimberley**, **Johannesburg** and **Tshwane** (**Pretoria**). Full timetables can be found on the websites and tickets can be booked online at www.computicket.com.

Budget buses
The **Baz Bus** has a daily service from Cape Town to **Port Elizabeth**. The service continues from Port Elizabeth to **Durban**, the following day, for where there are 2 routes to **Johannesburg** and **Tshwane** (**Pretoria**). See page 42 for details.

Bus companies
Baz Bus, www.bazbus.com. Greyhound, www.greyhound.co.za. Intercape, www.inter cape.co.za. Translux, www.translux.co.za.

Car hire
Cape Town and the surrounding Winelands are best explored in a hired car. The cheapest local car hire companies change frequently – it's a good idea to check at hotels and backpacker hostels to see which ones they recommend. See page 42 for further advice on car hire and driving.
Around About Cars, T021-422 4022, www.aroundaboutcars.com.
Atlantic Car Hire, T021-934 4600, www.atlanticcarhire.co.za.
Avis, T0861-021 111 (in South Africa, T011-923 3660 (from overseas), www.avis.co.za.
Budget, T0861-016622 (in South Africa) T011-398 0123 (from overseas), www.budget.co.za.
Britz Africa, T021-982 5107, www.britz.co.za. Contact for camper vans and motorhomes for travel in and beyond South Africa. Good all-inclusive deals.
Camper King, T021-558 2203, www.camper king.co.za. Campers and motor homes.
Cape Car Hire, T021-383 0445, www.cape carhire.co.za.
Europcar, T0861-131000 (in South Africa), T011-574 1000 (from overseas), www.europcar.co.za.
Hertz, T0861-600136 (in South Africa), T021-935 4800, www.hertz.co.za.

Metro
The suburban train service, **Metrorail**, T0800-656463, www.capemetrorail.co.za, serves the suburbs. Services run as far as Simon's Town, but also go out as far as Strand. These trains are fine to use in rush hour (0700-0800 and 1600-1800), but are best avoided at quieter times due to safety issues and avoid the routes to the east, which pass through the Cape Flats.

Motorbike hire
There are a number of places to hire bikes around the city and they are a great way to get around in summer but remember you'll need a licence. **Cape Town Scooter**, T082-450 9722, www.capetownscooter.co.za,

rents out scooters and delivers to your hotel, and **La Dolce Vita Biking**, T083-528 0897, www.la-dolce-vita.co.za, rents out scooters from their shop at 13 Kloof Nek Rd, Gardens. **Cape Sidecar Adventures**, 2 Glengariff Rd, Sea Point, T021-434 9855, www.sidecars. co.za, rents out vintage ex-Chinese Red Army motorbikes with sidecars, and **Harley Davidson Cape Town**, 9 Somerset Rd, Green Point, T021-446 2999, www.harley-davidson-capetown.com, rents out Harleys and provides route maps for day tours.

Taxi

There are several ranks dotted around town – the most useful ones are outside the train station at Adderley St, in Greenmarket Sq, and on Long St. If you are outside the city centre, you will have to call one in advance or ask your hotel or restaurant to call one for you. **Rikki Taxis**, T0861-745547, www.rikkis.co.za. Can be seen buzzing around all over Cape Town. The small, shared people-carriers have now been replaced by a fleet of London black cabs. They are a cheaper alternative to regular taxis for getting around the city. You need to call one, but they pick up several people along the route, which brings down costs. They operate 24 hrs, and costs vary from R20-35 depending on the distance. They only operate in the City Bowl and Atlantic Seaboard as far as Camps Bay, but a few people can charter one to get to somewhere like Kirstenbosch, for example. There is also another fleet of Rikki's that operates in the Hout Bay area, T021-786 2136, Mon-Thu 0630-0200 and Fri-Sun 24 hrs, daily 0700-1700. Back in the city, there are now more than 20 **Rikki phones** at some backpacker hostels, supermarkets and petrol stations, from where you can phone a **Rikki** for free. If you see 1 in the street, you can flag it down.

Minibus taxis

These serve all areas of the city on fixed routes, and leave from the minibus terminal accessed from the top floor of the railway station on Adderley St. They can also be flagged down from the street. Minibuses to the Atlantic Seaboard usually leave from the corner of Strand and Plein St. Most trips cost around R5. Minibuses stop running at 1900. These are generally safe to use, although you'd be advised to do your best not to look like a tourist and leave all valuables at home. Avoid taking them on the highways, too, as they have high accident rates.

Train

Cape Town has 1 main railway station in the centre of town. Long-distance and suburban services leave from here. Leaflets with train times and fare structure are available in the concourse. The rail network is run by **Spoornet**, www.spoornet.co.za. For more details of train travel, including luxury services between Cape Town and Tshwane (Pretoria), see page 40.

● Directory

Banks

Only change money in hotels as a last resort: their exchange rates are unbelievably poor. There are plenty of 24-hr ATMs throughout the city, and most banks cash TCs. All the main branches are open Mon-Fri 0830-1530 and Sat 0800-1100.

The 2 main bureaux de change are: **American Express**, T021-4218920, lower level, Victoria Wharf V&A Waterfront, open Mon-Sat 0900-2100, who will receive and hold mail for card holders. There are also several branches of **Master Currency** at the V&A Waterfront which stay open until 2100.

Embassies and consulates

Foreign representatives have their embassies in Tshwane (Pretoria), but some have consulates in Cape Town, although most cannot deal with passport-related issues and you will have to go through Tshwane (Pretoria). **Australia**, Standard Bank Centre, Hertzog Blvd, T021-4211440. **France**, 78 Queen Victoria St, Gardens, T021-423 1575, www.consulfrance-lecap.org.

Germany, Triangle House, 22 Riebeek St, T021-405 3000, www.kapstadt.diplo.de. **Mozambique,** 45 Castle St, T021-426 2944, visas issued within 24 hrs. **Netherlands,** 100 Strand St, T021-421 5660, www.dutch consulate.co.za. **UK,** Southern Life Centre, 8 Riebeeck St, T021-405 2400. **USA,** 2 Reddam Av, Westlake, T021-702 7300, www.south africa.usembassy.gov.

Emergencies
Fire, 107; **Medical,** 10177; **Police,** 10111; **Sea rescue:** T021-4344011. **All emergencies from a cell phone,** T112.

Internet
Access is available at hotels and backpacker hostels, **Postnet** branches (see Telephone, below) or at the dozens of internet cafés around the city (including one at the main tourist office). There are also internet cafés in all the shopping malls and Wi-Fi at many of the chain coffee shops and at the airport.

Medical services
Hospitals facilities are available at **City Park,** Longmarket St, T021-480 6111, 24 hrs; and **Cape Town Medi-Clinic,** 21 Hof St, Gardens, T021-464 5500, www.capetownmc.co.za. **Netcare Travel Clinic,** 11th floor, Picbel Parkade, Strand St, T021-419 3172, www.travelclinic.co.za.

Newspapers
Cape Town has an English morning paper, the *Cape Times,* and an evening paper, the *Argus.* Both are good sources of what's going on in the city, with daily listings and entertainment sections. There is also a daily paper in Afrikaans, *Die Burger.*

Post office
Post offices are found in the principal shopping malls and are generally open Mon-Fri 0800-

1630, Sat 0800-1200. A branch locater can be found on www.sapo.co.za.

Radio
Radio KFM: 94.5 FM, contemporary music, mix of old classics and new hits. **Radio Good Hope FM:** 94-97 FM, teenage pop music, current hits. **Cape Talk:** 567 MW, news and talk station with plenty of phone-in debates.

Telephone
Postnet is a useful chain found throughout the city, usually in shopping malls. The main branch is in the Union Castle Building, 6 Hout St, T021-426 0839, www.postnet.co.za, open Mon-Fri 0830-1700, Sat 0830-1300. Services include sending parcels, internet access, fax sending and receiving, phonecards, passport photos and couriering. Again a store locater can be found on the website.

Tickets
Computicket: T011-340 8000, www.compu ticket.com, for nationwide bus tickets, theatre, concerts and sport events. Book online or kiosks are in the shopping malls or branches of Checkers supermarkets and the one at Victoria Wharf at the V&A Waterfront is open daily 0900-2100.

Weather
Weather reports: T082-233 9900, www.weathersa.co.za.

Wildlife and conservation
Cape Nature Conservation, T021-659 3500, www.capenature.co.za. **South African National Parks (SANParks),** www.sanparks.org. Has desks at the main tourist office and at the office in the Clock Tower Centre at the V&A Waterfront.

The Cape Peninsula

The most popular day trip from central Cape Town is a leisurely loop around the Cape Peninsula. The stunning coast road winds its way through the city's swanky suburbs on the Atlantic Seaboard on the western side, down to Cape Point and the Cape of Good Hope at the southern tip of the peninsula, and then up again through the quaint fishing settlements on the False Bay coast on the eastern side. This can be done under your own steam and a day's hire car is an ideal way to explore at your own pace; alternatively, all the tour operators offer the excursion – some take mountain bikes too, for a spot of cycling in the Table Mountain National Park. As well as fine ocean and mountain views, there are a number of attractions to stop for including the boat trip from Hout Bay to see the seals on Duiker Island, the spectacularly scenic Chapman's Peak Drive, climbing to the lighthouse at Cape Point, and the penguins at Boulders Beach. There are also ample places to stop for lunch, be it simple fish and chips or a gourmet meal, and there are many tourist shops, art galleries and roadside stalls to grab your attention along the way. ▶▶ *For listings, see pages 148-154. See also Activities and tours, page 127, and Transport, page 131.*

Atlantic Seaboard ⊜🕭🏠 ▶▶ *pp148-154. Colour map 8, B1.*

The Atlantic Seaboard refers to Cape Town's wealthy suburbs on the west side of the peninsula. Exclusive Clifton, Camps Bay and Llandudno have some of Cape Town's most sought after properties and whitewashed modern mansions and luxury apartments with their brilliantly blue swimming pools climb up the hillsides, while the pristine beaches are popular with the beautiful people. Further south the road winds its way above the rocky shoreline and below the magnificent Twelve Apostles, the spine of mountains from the back of Table Mountain, before dropping into Hout Bay and the back end of the Constantia Valley, before continuing south towards Cape Point.

Ins and out

The tour operators take the Atlantic Seaboard route on Cape Peninsula day tours, but a car is a logical option if you want to stop. Some minibus taxis from central Cape Town go beyond Green Point and Sea Point as far as the police station on the main seaside strip of Camps Bay. Golden Arrow buses also ply this route and some (roughly one an hour) continue on to Hout Bay. The Sightseeing Cape Town bus (see page 80) goes as far as Hout Bay on its Blue Route.

Clifton Beach

Cape Town's best-known beaches stretch along Clifton, and are renowned as the play-ground of the young and wealthy – this is the place to see and be seen. Other than being hotpots of high society, Clifton's four sheltered beaches are stunning, perfect arches of powder-soft white sand sloping gently into turquoise water. The beaches, reached be a series of winding footpaths, are divided by rocky outcrops and are unimaginatively named First, Second, Third and Fourth. Each has a distinct character – if you're bronzed and beautiful, head to First beach. More demure visitors may feel more comfortable on Fourth, which is popular with families and has been an award-winning Blue Flag beach for many years now. The sunbathing and swimming are good on all the beaches and life guards are on duty, but note that the water is very cold – usually around 12°C. Most of the relatively small-scale, high-luxury development has been behind the beaches (some impressive houses can be glimpsed from the winding steps leading down). Be warned that there is limited parking in high season, so get here early.

Camps Bay

Following the coast south, you soon skirt around a hill and come out over Camps Bay, a long arch of sand backed by the Twelve Apostles. This is one of the most beautiful (and most photographed) beaches in the world and it also has Blue Flag status, but the calm cobalt water belies its chilliness. The sand is also less sheltered than at Clifton, and sunbathing here on a windy day can be painful. But there are other distractions; the beachfront is lined with excellent seafood restaurants, and a sundowner followed by a superb meal is quite the perfect ending to a day in Cape Town.

The drive between Camps Bay and Hout Bay runs along the slopes of the Twelve Apostles and is beautiful. Apart from the turning to Llandudno, there is no easy access to the coast until you reach Hout Bay. **Llandudno** itself is a small, exclusive settlement with only one road in and out and no shops, and a fine beach and excellent surf but again parking can be difficult on a sunny day.

Hout Bay

Hout Bay, a historical fishing harbour with an attractive beach, attracts swarms of South African families during peak season. Most come for the seafood restaurants and boat trips, but the best reason for heading here is for spectacular Chapman's Peak Drive (see below), which begins just outside town. As the sun sets in the summer months every pullover along the road is filled with spectators, drink in hand.

Hout Bay itself is fairly attractive, with a busy fishing harbour at the western end of the bay; at the other end is a collection of shops and popular restaurants. By the

Cape Peninsula

harbour is a commercial complex known as **Mariners Wharf**, a popular attraction, although looking a little wind-worn these days. It is based upon Fisherman's Wharf in San Francisco, with a whole string of fish 'n' chips restaurants, souvenir shops, boats for hire and a fish market known as **Snoekies Fresh Fish Market**, close to the harbour gates. Even if you're not intending to buy anything it is worth a quick look to see the huge variety of fish that are caught off this coast. Boats run from here to see the seals on **Duiker Island** (see Boat tours, page 130).

Back in the town, next to the **tourist office** ① *T021-791 8380, www.tourismcapetown. co.za, Mon-Fri 0830-1730, Sat-Sun 0900-1300*, is the **Hout Bay Museum** ① *4 Andrews Rd, T021-790 3474, Tue-Sat 1000-1230, 1400-1630, R5*, with displays on the history of the area, aimed at visiting school groups. More popular with families is **The World of Birds** ① *Valley Rd, T021-790 2730, www.worldofbirds.org.za, daily 0900-1700, R59, children R37*, with over 400 species of birds housed in impressive walk-through aviaries. There's also the **Monkey Jungle**, populated with squirrel monkeys.

Chapman's Peak Drive

It is worth hiring a car for a day just to drive along Chapman's Peak Drive, a breathtaking 9-km route with 114 curves, carved into the cliffs 600 m above the sea. The route was re-opened a couple of years ago, following extensive repairs and the rigging of giant nets to catch falling rocks. It's now a toll road, costing R24 per car. Although the road up to the toll gates is fairly busy with groups pulled over in view points, the Drive itself is remarkably quiet, allowing outstanding and uninhibited views of the craggy coastline and thrashing ocean. The best time to drive along here is close to sunset in the summer, but the views of the crescent of white sand at Hout Bay on one side, and the vast stretch of Noordhoek on the other, are recommended at any time. The Drive sometimes closes in bad weather, and at the time of writing was closed temporarily for engineering work, check its status at www.chapmanspeakdrive.co.za.

Noordhoek

The greatest attraction here is the 8-km-long deserted beach, backed by a couple of tidal lagoons which offer excellent birdwatching. There's very little to the village itself, but the **Noordhoek Farm Village** on Beach Road is a pleasant spot for a coffee or light lunch, with two family restaurants and a couple of shops selling antiques, crafts and organic produce. The beach also offers the Cape's finest setting for horse riding along the shore (see Activities, page 127).

Kommetjie → *Colour map 8, B1.*

Driving along the Atlantic side of the peninsula, you could miss Kommetjie altogether. The name means 'little basin', a reference to the natural inlet in the rocks which has been developed into a tidal pool. The settlement is small with a pub, restaurant, caravan park and little else. It is, however, a major surfing spot and Long Beach to the north is always busy with surfers, even in winter. There is also an interesting walk along Long Beach to the wreck of the *Kakapo*, offering a rare opportunity to examine a wreck at close quarters without having to don full scuba equipment. The *Kakapo* is a steamship which was beached here in May 1900 on her maiden voyage when the captain apparently mistook Chapman's Peak for Cape Point during a storm. The boiler and shell are still intact about 100 m above the high tide mark.

Scarborough

Scarborough consists of a scattering of weekend and holiday homes on the hillside overlooking the Atlantic. The beach is broad and long but swimming is not a good idea as the water is cold and there are strong currents. Just outside Scarborough, close to the entrance to the Table Mountain National Park, is the **Cape Point Ostrich Farm** ① *T021-780 9294, www.capepointostrichfarm.com, daily 0930-1730, R30, children R10*, which is worth visiting for its in-depth tours, describing the lifecycle of the ostrich; during breeding season you can watch eggs hatching. There's a pleasant tea garden on site.

Table Mountain National Park ➤ ⊖ ➤ *pp148-154. Colour map 8, B1.*

① *T021-701 8692, www.sanparks.org, www.capepoint.co.za, Oct-Mar 0600-1800, Apr-Sep 0700-1700, R70, children R20.*

Formerly the Cape of Good Hope Nature Reserve, this is now part of Table Mountain National Park, and was established to protect the unique flora and fauna of this stretch of coast. In 1928 the area came under threat from developers who were looking to build seaside resorts. Those in favour of a reserve persuaded local families to sell their land, and in 1939 the reserve came into existence. Some game animals were introduced and the land has since been left to its own devices. Today, it is a dramatically wild area of towering cliffs, stupendous ocean views, some excellent hiking and, to top it all off, beautiful, deserted beaches.

Ins and outs

Getting there Given its location at the southern tip of the peninsula, you can approach the reserve from two directions: along the False Bay shoreline via Muizenberg and Simon's Town; or by the quieter M65 via Kommetjie and Scarborough. It is about 70 km from Cape Town centre to the reserve gates. There is no public transport to the reserve.

Getting around We strongly recommend you come with your own transport to see the reserve; alternatively, there are several companies that organize good day trips from the city. A **funicular railway** ① *0800-1700, R40 return, R30 single, R15/12 children (under 16)*, takes visitors up from the main car park to the original lighthouse where there are a series of paved footpaths and viewpoints. The walk is about half a kilometre and is fairly steep and takes about 20 minutes, depending on how fit you are. Next to the car park is the **Two Oceans Restaurant** ① *T021-780 9200, www.two-oceans.co.za, 0900-1700*, specializing in seafood but also serving steak, chicken dishes and salads. Between December and March it is advisable to book a table. There is also a takeaway cafeteria which sells hamburgers, sandwiches, cold drinks, tea and coffee, as well as an information centre, curio shop, toilets and telephones (card and coins).

Around the reserve

The Cape of Good Hope is an integral part of the Cape Floristic Kingdom, the smallest but richest of the world's six floral kingdoms. A frequently quoted statistic is that within the 7750 ha of the reserve there are as many different plant species as there are in the whole of the British Isles. In addition to all this there are several different species of antelope: eland, bontebok, springbok, cape grysbok, red hartebeest and grey rhebok, as well as the elusive cape mountain zebra, snakes, tortoises and pesky baboons.

Although the strong winds and the low-lying vegetation are not ideal for birds, over 250 species have been recorded here, of which about 100 are known to breed within the reserve. There are plenty of vantage points where you can watch open sea birds such as Cape gannet, shy albatross, sooty shearwater, white-chinned petrel, Sabine's gull and Cory's shearwater. In the Strandveld vegetation along the coast you can expect to see many fruit-eating birds such as the southern boubou, Cape robin and bully canary. Around Sirkels Vlei you will find freshwater birds. Finally there are few rarities: the white-rumped sandpiper from South America, macaroni penguins from Antarctica, and the purple gallinule from the US have all been spotted. The **Vlei Museum** issues a checklist of 100 birds. Alongside each name is a code telling you the typical habitat and the bird's resident status.

Cape Point

Cape Point Lighthouse is nothing special in itself, but the climb is well worth it for spectacular views of the peninsula. On a clear day the ocean views stretching all around are incredible – as is the wind, so be sure to hold on to hats and sunglasses. You can take the funicular to the top, but the 20-minute walk allows better views of the coast. There are plenty of viewpoints, linked by a jumble of footpaths.

The first lighthouse came into service in May 1860, but it quickly became apparent that the most prominent point on a clear day was far from ideal in poor weather. It was quite often shrouded in cloud while at sea level all was clear. In 1872 the Lighthouse Commission decided on a lower site, but it was only after the Portuguese ship, the *Lusitania*, struck Bellows Rock in April 1911, that work started on a new lighthouse. This was built just 87 m above sea level, close to Diaz Rock and remains the Cape's most important lighthouse today. The current beam can be seen up to 63 km out to sea, and 18 km out there is a red lamp that warns ships that they are in the danger zone.

From the top point of the railway there are still approximately 120 steps to the old lighthouse where you get some of the finest views. If you are reasonably fit and have a good head for heights, there is a spectacular walk to the modern lighthouse at Diaz Point. From the renovated old lighthouse you can see the path running along the left side of the narrow cliff that makes up the point. The round trip takes about 30 minutes, but do not attempt it if it is windy – the winds around the Cape can reach up to 55 knots.

As you look down from the lighthouse at Cape Point it is easy to see how ships could suffer on a dark night in a storm, especially before the lighthouse was built. There are 23 wrecks in the waters around the Cape, but only five can be seen when walking in the reserve: *Thomas T Tucker* (1942); *Nolloth* (1964); *Phyllisia* (1968); *Shir Yib* (1970), at Diaz Beach and the *Tania* (1972), the most recent wreck which can be seen at Buffel's Bay. The first wreck was the *Flying Dutchman* in 1680, which has since become famous as a ghost ship. The most famous sighting was by midshipman King George V in 1881.

Diaz Beach

Apart from visiting Cape Point and the Cape of Good Hope there are a few minor attractions dotted about the reserve as well as three excellent walks, probably the best way of appreciating the splendour of the coastline. You can drive down to the Cape of Good Hope and then walk to beautiful **Diaz Beach** via Maclear's Peak, a very steep walk in parts. You can also approach Diaz Beach via a 253-step staircase. **Diaz Cross**, further inland, is a memorial to the explorer Bartholomew Diaz. Note how it is painted black on one side so that sailors can see it against the horizon.

Hiking around the Cape of Good Hope

Hiking is encouraged within the reserve. There are several marked paths and maps are available from the information centre. One of the most spectacular routes is along the coast from Rooikrans towards Buffels Bay. Look out for the wreck of *Tania* (1972). On the west side close to Olifants Bay there are a couple of walks; one to the inland lake, Sirkels Vlei, the other along the coast where you can see the wrecks of the *Thomas Tucker* (1942) and *Nolloth* (1964). You can light a braai at one of the designated areas at Buffels Bay and Bordjiesrif, but again watch the baboons.

False Bay ⊜⦿ ⇥ pp148-154. Colour map 8, B1.

On the eastern side of the peninsula lies False Bay, a popular stretch of coast thanks to the warmer waters – temperatures can be as much as 8°C higher. The area is also more sheltered and better developed for tourism, although some of the landscape seems almost dull after the Atlantic seaboard. Nevertheless, the area has some excellent beaches and gets busy with domestic tourists in summer. In spring, False Bay is the favoured haunt of calving whales, offering excellent opportunities to see southern right, humpback and Bryde whales. There are also some interesting fishing villages. False Bay is also known for its population of white sharks. A shark watch service operates from Muizenberg, signalling alerts when sharks come in proximity of bathers and surfers.

Ins and outs

False Bay is easily accessed from the city centre by the M3, which runs around the mountain and along the coast. There are also two routes across the mountainous spine linking the roads that hug the coast around the peninsula: you can cross from Noordhoek to Fish Hoek via the M65 and Sun Valley or, further south, take the Red Hill road from Scarborough to Simon's Town. Each route is convenient if your time is short, but the most scenic route is to follow the M65 along the coast from the Atlantic seaboard to False Bay. It is impossible to get lost as there is only one road along the shoreline.

Alternatively, the **metro** ① *for up-to-date times, T0800-656463, www.capemetrorail. co.za*, continues through the southern suburbs to Simon's Town – the stretch following False Bay is spectacular. Trains go as far as Simon's Town and leave every 30 minutes, with the last trains leaving Simon's Town at around 2000. There have been some reports of crime on the trains, so it's best to avoid them at quieter times and in the evening.

Constantia

South of Kirstenbosch Botanical Gardens and the city's southern suburbs, lies the verdant area of Constantia and its winelands. This historical district was the first site of wine-making in South Africa and today it is an attractive introduction to the country's wines, as well as offering some fine examples of Cape Dutch architecture. There are five estates here, of which Groot Constantia (see below) is the best known and definitely worth a visit. **Buitenverwachting** ① *T021-794 5190, www.buitenverwachting.co.za*, is a working estate with an excellent restaurant (see page 152) that also offers picnic baskets during the summer (November-April) from 1200-1600. **Klein Constantia** ① *T021-794 5188, www.klein constantia.com*, is a beautiful hilly estate with a great tasting centre, and is famed for its dessert wine, Vin de Constance, allegedly Napoleon's favourite wine. **Constantia Uitsig** ① *T021-794 1810, www.constantia-uitsig.com*, has excellent wines, luxury accommodation and two restaurants (see page 149). **Steenberg** ① *T021-713 2222, www.steenberghotel.com*, also offers superb wines as well as having luxurious lodgings, a good restaurant and a golf course (see page 149).

Groot Constantia
ⓘ T021-794 5128, www.grootconstantia.co.za. Mon-Fri 0900-1800, Sat-Sun 1000-1800, free entrance to the main estate and orientation centre, museum R10, R2 children (under 16). 2 restaurants: Jonkershuis has traditional Cape food; Simon's serves burgers, salads and sea-food. Wine tastings at the sales centre, R25 for 5 wines; cheese platters available. Cellar tours every hour on the hour.

This old wine estate has some of the finest Cape Dutch architecture in South Africa, and with its rolling, vineyard setting and wine-tasting centre is a delightful place to spend an hour or two – although it does get swamped with tour buses in high season.

The main Manor House was originally home to Cape Governor Simon van der Stel between 1699 and 1712. He named the estate after Constantia, the daughter of the company official who had granted the land to him. Before his death, van der Stel planted most of the vines, but it was not until 1778 that the estate became famous for its wines. During this period the estate was unable to meet the demand from Europe, especially France. The house is now a museum full of period furniture and a booklet is available giving a brief description of the objects on show. The magnificent wine cellar behind the main house was designed by the renowned French architect, Louis Thibault, and today has displays on brandy and wine making. There are two impressive giant oak vats each with a capacity of over 4000 litres. The **Orientation Centre** near the car park has some interesting storyboards on the history of the estate.

Tokai Forest
ⓘ Take the M3 out of town towards the southern suburbs. Just before Muizenberg, turn right into Tokai St and follow the signs for Tokai Manor House, T021-712 7471. Open daily during daylight hours, R5.

Tokai was set up as a forest nursery in 1883 to start a programme of reforestation. Due to this, large parts of the Constantiaberg Mountains are covered in pine trees and as they are non-indigenous there is some debate on whether they should remain. Today, the forest is part of Table Mountain National Park. The arboretum contains 40 tree species – there are two walking trails, and horse riding and mountain biking are possible in the low-lying section (permits from the main gate).

Rondevlei Nature Reserve
ⓘ From Cape Town take the M5, Prince George Drive, turn left into Victoria Rd in Grassy Park, and then right into Fisherman's Walk, 17 km from the town centre, 6 km from Muizenberg, T021-706 2404, www.rondevlei.co.za. Open 0730-1700, on summer weekends 0730-1900, R5, children R2 (under 13).

This 220-ha reserve was originally established to protect the birdlife and the coastal fynbos vegetation. Today it is an important environmental education centre for local schools and, despite being surrounded by suburban sprawl, it is one of the best bird-watching spots around Cape Town. Only the northern shore of the lake is open to the public. A path follows the vlei's edge, along which there are two lookout towers equipped with telescopes. There are several hides along the water's edge, and cuts within the reeds allow views across the water. The best time to visit the reserve is from January to March when many European migrants can be seen. Over 230 bird species have been recorded; on a good day visitors should be able to see more than 65 species including white pelican, greater flamingo, African spoonbill and Caspian tern. There are a few small, shy mammals in the reserve, plus a small population of hippos. Inside the reserve is a small **aquarium** showing the freshwater fish that inhabit the area and a snake and amphibian house.

Muizenberg

Travelling out from the city centre on the M3, Muizenberg is the first settlement you reach on False Bay and as such has long been a popular local bathing spot. The Battle of Muizenberg was a small but significant military affair that began in June 1795 and ended three months later with the (first) British occupation of the Cape. Cecil Rhodes bought a holiday cottage here in 1899 and many other wealthy people followed, building some fine Victorian and Edwardian cottages along the back streets and attracting the likes of Agatha Christie and Rudyard Kipling to its shores. Although the resort had decayed significantly over the last decade, various recent regeneration projects have meant that the area is starting to look like its old cheerful self again. The beach certainly remains beautiful: a vast stretch of powdery white sand sloping gently to the water. It is safe for swimming as there is no backwash, and it is very popular with surfers who head out to the bigger breakers. At low tide you can walk into the shallow sea for more than 300 m without having to swim.

The walk along Main Street towards St James is known locally as the **Historic Mile** and will take you past a number of interesting old buildings. Some of these are national monuments, but most are closed to the public. The first of note is the **Station building**, a fine example of art-deco architecture built in 1912. Further along on the right is **Het Post Huijs (The Post House)** ① *186 Main Rd, T021-788 7972, Mon-Fri 0800-1530, Sat 0900-1300, Sun 1400-1700, entry by donation*, thought to be the oldest building in False Bay, dating back to 1742 and built by the Dutch East India Company as a toll-house to levy taxes on farmers passing by to sell their produce to ships moored in Simon's Bay. One of the early post holders was Sergeant Muys, from whom Muizenberg is thought to have got its name. The building itself is a picturesquely squat stone house, with thick whitewashed walls and a thatched roof. Inside are exhibits on the history of Muizenburg, with photos of the resort in its heyday and displays on the Battle of Muizenburg of 1795. There are original English canonballs which the cheery curator will happily let you lift.

Rhodes Cottage ① *246 Main St, T021-788 9140, daily 1000-1600, entry by donation*, is surprisingly small and austere for someone as wealthy as Cecil Rhodes. It has been restored and now contains many of his personal items, including his diamond-weighing scale and the chest in which he carried his personal belongings, and there are displays on his life and achievements. It's a pleasant place to wander around, with a lovely garden around the side. This is where he died on 26 March 1902, and his body was transported by train with great ceremony to the Matobo Hills outside Bulawayo in Zimbabwe, where he was buried in a giant rock outcrop. The volunteers that keep the place open make charismatic and enthusiastic guides.

Graceland, further along Main Road, is one of the largest and most impressive mansions along the coast. It was the home of John Garlick, a well-known merchant at the turn of the 20th century. The house has a Spanish feel to it, with arched balconies and glazed clay roof tiles. Unfortunately the house is not open to the public. Just before you reach St James you pass another grand house, with palm trees in the garden, known as

Stonehenge. Built in the style of an Italian villa this house once belonged to HP Rudd of De Beers Consolidated Mines.

St James

Just beyond Muizenberg lies the more upmarket resort of St James, an appealing village with characteristic brightly coloured bathing huts lining the tidal pool. The village is named after a Roman Catholic church which was built here in 1854 to save Catholics having to travel as far as Simon's Town to attend services – interestingly, some of the early settlers were Catholic Filipino fishermen. There is a small sheltered beach and reasonable surf off **Danger Beach** and the tidal pool is a safe place for a swim.

St James is also a suitable starting point for a hike in the excellent Silvermine section of the Table Mountain National Park. A path starts on Boyes Drive and climbs up through the Spes Bona Forest to Tartarus Cave. The views alone are worth the hike (see page 144 for further details of hiking in the reserve).

Kalk Bay

Kalk Bay is one of the most attractive settlements on False Bay, with a bustling fishing harbour and a bohemian vibe. The town is named after the lime kilns that produced kalk from shells in the 17th century. An important local product, the lime created the white-walled appearance of many houses in the Cape, especially amongst the Bo-Kaap community. Kalk is derived from the Dutch for lime. Until the arrival of the railway in 1883, the local fishermen hunted whales, seals and small fish. Today it remains a fishing harbour, worked mainly by a coloured community which somehow escaped the Group Areas Act under Apartheid. It is one of the few remaining coloured settlements on the peninsula.

Main Road is an appealing spot, lined with bric-a-brac and antiques shops and a handful of arty cafés. The beach is sandy and safe for swimming, with a couple of tidal pools for children to explore. Between June and July the harbour is busy with the snoek season, one of the most plentiful local fish harvests. Look out for returning deep-sea fishing boats around the middle of the day, as there's a daily impromptu quayside auction. You can buy a variety of fresh fish at the counters and for an extra small fee get them to gut them for you too. Another attraction is **Seal Island**, an important breeding ground for birds and seals, the latter attracting hungry great white sharks. Cruises run from Simon's Town (see page 145). In the harbour itself you can also see seals, who cheekily hop up to try and get to the fish at the counters. Also at the harbour, **Kalky's** (see Eating, page 153), is in a colourful wooden shed and serves up great fish and chips.

You should look out for the **Holy Trinity Church** on Main Road. It has a thatched roof, but its appeal is its windows, considered to be some of the finest in the Cape. On Quarterdeck Road is a tiny mosque built in the 1800s. If you fancy browsing for local art and antiques, take your pick from Main Road, where a dozen shops vie for custom – **Kalk Bay Gallery**, **Cape to Cairo** and **Railway House** have the most intriguing offerings. On the other side of the road is the entrance to Kalk Bay's most popular attraction, the **Brass Bell**, a simple seafood restaurant and pub wedged between the railway tracks and the water (see Eating, page 152).

High up behind the town is **Boyes Drive**, a scenic route connecting the bay with Muizenburg. It's a spectacular route offering sweeping views of False Bay and the Atlantic, and takes just 10 minutes to complete – look out for the signs from Main Road as you head out of Kalk Bay towards Simon's Town.

Clovelly

Continuing along the main road, the next settlement you reach is Clovelly, tucked between the waters of False Bay and the mountains of the Silvermine reserve. Along the main street are several shops and places to have a snack. Anyone visiting from the West Country in Britain will be interested to know that this community is named after the village in Devon. Golf enthusiasts should head a little way inland for the **Clovelly Country Club** ① www.clovelly.co.za.

Silvermine

This is a popular local reserve, now part of the Table Mountain National Park, but not often visited by overseas visitors. Table Mountain and Cape Point tend to dominate the open-air attractions, and rightly so, but this reserve is well worth a visit if you enjoy hiking, plus there are great views across False Bay and the Atlantic Ocean.

Like much of the Cape, the reserve encompasses one of the oldest floral kingdoms in the world. Over 900 rare and endangered species have been recorded in the mountains, including many types of proteas, ericas and reeds. In addition to the plants there are a couple of patches of indigenous forest in the Spes Bona and Echo valleys. Ornithologists should look out for black eagles, ground woodpeckers, orange-breasted sunbirds and rock kestrels. If you're extremely lucky, you may also come across small shy mammals such as lynx, porcupine and various species of mongoose.

Ins and outs The reserve is split into two sections by the Ou Kaapseweg Road as it crosses the Kalk Bay Mountains – the eastern sector and western sector. There is no public transport along this road. By car you can approach either from the Cape Town side or from Noordhoek and Fish Hoek. Driving out from Cape Town, follow the M3 from Newlands to its very end and then take a right. After 2 km turn left into Ou Kaapseweg Road, M64. Note that this road is windy and has one of Cape Town's highest accident rates, so take care when driving.

A variety of footpaths from Muizenberg, St James, Kalk Bay and Chapman's Peak Drive lead into the reserve and make a pleasant day trip from Cape Town. Access into the reserve is allowed between sunrise and sunset. Toilet facilities are found at Silvermine Reservoir, Hennies Pool, Bokkop Peak, and at the car park near Maiden Peak in the eastern sector of the reserve. Braais are only permitted within the Hennies Pool, Silvermine Reservoir and Bokkop picnic areas.

Around the reserve A tarred road leads from the western sector gates to the Silvermine Reservoir built in 1898 to supply Kalk Bay and Muizenberg with water until 1912. There is a shady picnic site under some pine trees close to the dam. One of the more popular walks from here is to **Noordhoek Peak** (754 m), a circuit of about 7 km from the dam. The path is marked by stone cairns. At the summit there are spectacular views of the Sentinel and Hout Bay. Another interesting walk is from the car park to **Elephant's Eye Cave** covered with ferns and hanging plants. En route you pass the **Prinz Kasteel waterfall**. Allow about three hours for the round trip. The cave can also be reached from Tokai Manor through the Tokai Forest.

The eastern sector of the reserve has plenty of sandstone caves to explore, while the views from the peaks here are across False Bay. One of the popular trails is to **Steenberg Peak** (537 m) via the Wolfkop picnic site. If you have made your way to the top without a car, try an interesting walk which drops down to Muizenberg or St James via the **Spes Bona Valley**. Be careful if exploring any of the caves as there are dangerous deep drops.

Fish Hoek

Fish Hoek is one of the most conservative settlements on the coast, not least because the sale of alcohol is prohibited here. It does, however, have a fine beach – perhaps the best for swimming after Muizenberg – which stretches right across the Fish Hoek valley. Swimming is safe at the southern end of the bay, but avoid the northern end where a small river enters the sea, as there is the danger of quicksand. From mid-August to October, there is a good chance of catching a glimpse of whales from here. The valley which stretches behind the town joins with Noordhoek beach on the Atlantic coast. In recent geological times this was flooded and all the lands towards Cape Point were in fact an island.

Glencairn

It is easy to drive through this coastal resort without realizing you've actually been here, although it does have one of the best mid-range hotels in False Bay (see Sleeping, page 150). There is a small beach by the railway station but it is exposed to the southeast winds. Be wary of the cross currents close to the inlet where a small river enters the sea. At low tide you can occasionally see the remains of a steamship, the *Clan Stuart*. She was blown aground on 20 November 1914 while the crew drank in the local hotel.

Simon's Town

This is the most popular town on False Bay, with a pleasant atmosphere and numerous Victorian buildings lining Main Street. If you want a break from Cape Town, this makes for a good alternative base from which to explore the southern peninsula. It's also a good place to spot whales in False Bay and notice the statue of a real-size southern right whale on the quayside of the waterfront. For information, contact the **tourist office** ① *111 St George's St, T021-786 8440, www.simonstown.com, Mon-Fri 0900-1700, Sat-Sun 0900-1300.*

The town is fairly quiet for most of the year but becomes very busy with families during the summer school holidays. Whenever you visit, take some time to wander up the hill away from the main road – the quiet, bougainvillea-bedecked houses and cobbled streets with their sea views are a lovely retreat from the bustling beaches. The main swimming spot is **Seaforth Beach**, not far from Boulders. To get there, turn off St George's Street into Seaforth Road after passing the navy block to the left. The beach is the second on the right, on Kleintuin Road. A little further towards Cape Point are two other popular bathing beaches, **Windmill** and **Fisherman's**. Seaforth Beach has changing and toilet facilities, snack bars, restaurants and a clean stretch of shady lawn bordering the beach with some picnic spots and bench seats. The swimming is safe, there is no surf due to offshore rocks which protect the beach. For children there is a water slide and a wooden raft in the water. Look out for some giant pots, a legacy from whaling days, when they were used for melting whale blubber.

Simon's Town is named after Simon van der Stel, who decided that an alternative bay was needed for securing ships in the winter months as Table Bay suffered from the prevailing northwesterly. However, because of the difficult overland access, the bay was little used in the early years. It was not until 1743 that the Dutch East India Company finally built a wooden pier and some barracks here. In 1768 the town transferred into British hands, and following the end of the Napoleonic Wars in Europe, the British decided to turn Simon's Town into a naval base. It remained as such until 1957 and is now a base for the South African Navy.

Just before you hit the town centre, the **Simon's Town Museum** ① *Old Residency, Court Rd, T021-786 3046, Mon-Fri 0900-1600, Sat 1000-1300, Sun 1100-1500, entry by donation,* guided walks along the 'Historical Mile' on request, has displays related to the town's history as a naval base for the British and South African navies. Several displays are dedicated to Just Nuisance, a great dane who became something of a local hero in the 1930s. He was officially registered as personnel aboard *HMS Afriander* and is the only dog in history to have been given a full military burial on his death. His favourite spot was to lie on the deck on the brow at the top of the gangplank. No one could easily get past him and he was loathe to move, hence the name. His image has become Simon's Town's unofficial mascot, and there's a bronze statue of him on Jubilee Square. Also of interest is the **Peoples of Simon's Town Exhibit**, a collection referring to the forcible removal of coloured families from the area in the 1960s and 1970s, photographs, family trees and household goods. The building itself was built in 1777 as the winter residence of the Governor of the Cape.

Nearby, the **South Africa Naval Museum** ① *Court Rd, T021-787 4686, daily 1000-1600, entry by donation*, includes a collection of model ships, gunnery displays, information on mine-sweeping, a modern submarine control room plus relics from the Martello Tower.

In the centre of town, the **Quayside Centre** is a smart development on Wharf Street, next to Jubilee Square in the centre of town, which has greatly enhanced the seafront. Above the shops and restaurants is a comfortable new hotel, the **Quayside Lodge**. Cruises in the harbour can be booked here.

Just round the corner from Jubilee Square, and worth a quick peek, is the **Warrior Toy Museum** ① *St George's St, T021-786 1395, daily 1000-1600, entry by donation*, a tiny museum with an impressive collection of model cars, trains, dolls and toy soldiers. This is a great little place and definitely worth a stop – nostalgic for adults and fun for kids. New and old model cars are also for sale.

The nearby **Heritage Museum** ① *Amlay House, King George's Way, T021-786 2302, Tue-Fri 1100-1600, Sat 1100-1300, entry by donation*, faithfully charts the history of the Muslim community in Simon's Town. The town was designated a 'white' area during the Group Area Act and over 7000 people classified as coloured were relocated. The Amlay family were the last to be forcibly removed from Simon's Town in 1975 and were the first to return in 1995 – today the Muslim community has all but disappeared here, although there is still an attractive working mosque up behind Main Road. The exhibition consists mainly of pictures and artefacts dating back to the turn of the 20th century. There is a traditional bridal chamber, with wedding clothes and a display in the Hadj room.

Mineral World ① *Dido Valley Rd, T021-786 2020, www.scratchpatch.co.za, Mon-Fri 0830-1645, Sat and Sun 0900-1730*, is an important gemstone factory where you can watch the different stages of polishing and buy the finished product. There is also the 'Scratch Patch', a large landscaped yard covered with a deep layer of polished stones, and an old mine shaft to explore.

Boulders Beach

About 2 km south of Simon's Town is a lovely series of little sandy coves surrounded by huge boulders (hence the name).

The attraction here is the colony of African penguins that live and nest between the boulders. **Boulders Visitors Centre** ① *T021-786 2329, www.sanparks.org, R30, children R10, Apr-Sep 0800-1700, Oct-Mar 0700-1900*, has been created to protect the little creatures, and their numbers have flourished. One of the highlights of a visit to Cape Town is watching them happily go about their business of swimming, waddling and braying (their characteristic braying was the reason they were, until recently, known as Jackass penguins). This is one of two colonies on mainland Africa, the other being in Betty's Bay (see

Glencairn, Simon's Town & Boulders Beach

page 244). The best time to see large numbers of penguins is just before sunset, when they return from a day's feeding at sea, but you're guaranteed to see them at any time of day. While visitors used to be able to walk on the beach it is now a protected area (as part of Table Mountain National Park) and from the visitor's centre a (wheelchair accessible) boardwalk leads you down to viewpoints over the beach. Look out for the little concrete half moon huts that have been recently installed for the penguins to nest in and look up from the beach where you're likely to see a single penguin contemplating life from the top of a boulder. Every visitor gets a leaflet telling the story of the colony – it started from just two breeding pairs in 1985 and now numbers some 3000 penguins – and the shop sells all things 'penguiney'. If you want swim, go to the adjoining Seaforth Beach, which is a lovely sandy cove with a picnic lawn and you may bump into a stray penguin in the water.

Miller's Point

This is the last easy access to the sea on this side of the peninsula. Beyond **Partridge Point** the main road cuts into the hillside, and access to the beach is via steep footpaths. Miller's Point has two sandy coves and a tidal pool. There is a large caravan site here plus a picnic area and a good restaurant, the **Black Marlin** (see Eating, page 153), which is a popular lunch stop for coach tours of the Cape Peninsula. The beach itself is mainly used for speedboat launches; there are a few scuba-dive sites off shore and the Cape Boat and Ski-Boat Club is located here. The road then climbs above the sea before rounding the mountains by **Smitswinkel Bay**. On a clear day you can look back to a perfect view of the cliffs plunging into the sea. A short distance from the shore is the Table Mountain National Park entrance to Cape Point and the Cape of Good Hope entrance.

Beyond Miller's Point be on the lookout for baboons. They are not shy and will approach cars. Wind windows up and remember they can be vicious.

A number of **boat trips** to the Cape of Good Hope originate from Simon's Town harbour. Taking a trip from here allows views of the spectacular coastline and its hinterland from a different angle. In addition to straightforward sightseeing tours, there are several options for viewing bird life, seals and whales during the right season. ⟩⟩ *For Boat tours, see page 130.*

◉ The Cape Peninsula listings

For Sleeping and Eating price codes and other relevant information, see pages 46-53.

● Sleeping

Camps Bay *p136*
L The Bay, Victoria Rd, T021-438 4444, www.thebay.co.za. Set just across the road from the beach, with 78 modern de luxe a/c rooms all with views across the bay, pleasant contemporary feel, large pool with deck, wellness spa that also offers cosmetic procedures and beach-facing restaurant with a good reputation. Excellent service, a well-known place for the rich and famous.
A Bay Atlantic, 3 Berkley Rd, T021-438 4341, www.thebayatlantic.com. Family-run guesthouse with some of the best views in Cape Town. 6 individually decorated rooms, TV, light and airy with terracotta tiles and white linen, some with private balcony. Quiet garden with good-sized pool, breakfast served on balcony overlooking the bay, relaxed atmosphere. Run by welcoming Smith family.
B Whale Cottage Guesthouse, 57 Camps Bay Drive, T021-438 3840, www.whalecottage.com. Small tasteful place with marine decor, 11 sunny en suite double rooms, breakfast deck overlooking the beach, good views of the Twelve Apostles, satellite TV and internet access, 5 mins' walk to the restaurants and beach. Also has properties in Hermanus, Franschhoek and Plettenberg Bay.

Hout Bay *p136*
A-B Chapmans Peak Hotel, Chapmans Peak Drive, T021-790 1036, www.chapmanspeakhotel.co.za. This traditional hotel has

10 double rooms in the original historical building and 21 stylish more expensive rooms in a new block, with simple, contemporary decor, large windows, some with sea views. Good restaurant which is well known for its excellent calamari and popular bar with seating on veranda, great location just across from the beach and at the start of Chapman's Peak Drive.
B Froggs Leap, 15 Baviaans Close, T021-790 2590, www.froggsleap.co.za. Converted 'plantation' house with stunning veranda overlooking the bay, 3 double rooms with bathroom, TV, minibars and airy decor with a seaside feel, wicker furniture, and a large collection of ornamental frogs on display. Good breakfasts served on veranda.
C Sorgh Vliet Lodge, 3060 Valley Rd, T021-790 2767, www.sorghvlietlodge.com. 2 self-catering cottages and 2 B&B cottages set in peaceful gardens with mountain views. Bright and comfortable with wooden floors, cane furniture, open-plan kitchens, access to gardens, patio and pool, small terraces at back. Breakfast on request. Wheelchair and child friendly and can provide cots.

Noordhoek *p137*
A Monkey Valley, Mountain Rd, T021-789 1391, www.monkeyvalleyresort.com. Resort with self-catering thatched log cottages set in woodland overlooking Noordhoek Beach. Each sleeps 4-8, with 2 or 3 bedrooms, kitchen, lounge and bathroom, log fires, plus secluded veranda with superb views. There's also a good restaurant.
B De Noordhoek, at the Noordhoek Farm Village, at the junction of Chapman's

Peak Drive and Village Lane, T021-789 2760, www.denoordhoek.co.za. Newly built but in traditional Cape Dutch style architecture, this has 21 sleekly modern a/c rooms with satellite TV and internet, a comfortable lounge with bar and fireplace. Restaurants are in the farm village. Strong on environmental policies – water is heated by solar energy, everything is recycled, the gardens have been designed in a water-wise way and staff all live within a 10-km radius.

C-D Goose Green Lodge, Briony Close, T021-789 2933, www.goosegreen.co.za. B&B accommodation in main house, also has 5 self-catering cottages in converted family homes dotted around pretty gardens, sleeping up to 8, very comfortably furnished, close to Chapman's Peak and the beach.

Kommetjie p137

L The Long Beach Villa, 1 Kirsten Av, T021-799 6561, www.thelongbeach.com. 6 modern luxury suites with views over Long Beach, spacious airy decor in pale blues and pinks, internet access, a/c and DSTV, lunch and dinner on request, stunning swimming pool right on the sand dunes, bar, rates include all drinks.

D-F Imhoff Caravan Park, Wireless Rd, T021-783 1634, www.imhoff.co.za. Large site with 100 camping and caravanning sites, all grass, electric points, well lit, 2 brick self-catering chalets sleeping up to 6, laundry, games room, TV lounge, 500 m from beach, aimed at families.

Constantia p140

The original Cape Dutch homestead and vineyard that gave the area its name is today surrounded by one of Cape Town's most exclusive suburbs, dotted with luxury hotels.

L The Cellars-Hohenort Hotel, 93 Brommersulei Rd, T021-794 2137, www.cellars-hohenort.com. Part of the **Relais & Chateaux** group. One of the most luxurious hotels in Cape Town, set in 2 converted manor houses on a wine estate, with 13 spacious suites and 33 individually decorated double rooms, plus

the Madiba Presidential Suite, a 2-storey house with private pool, and the Dove Cote suite overlooking the golf green. 2 excellent restaurants (see Eating, page 152). 2 swimming pools, tennis court, golf course, set in 3.5 ha of mature gardens which overlook False Bay, impeccable service.

L Constantia Uitsig, Spaanschemat, River Rd, T021-794 6500, www.constantia-uitsig.com. On the well-known wine estate, with 16 luxurious and spacious cottages set in neat gardens with views across vineyards to the mountain. Plush furnishings, private verandas, activities include horse riding and vineyard walks and there's a stunning spa, and 2 excellent restaurants of which **La Colombe** (see Eating, page 152) is considered one of the best in South Africa.

L Steenberg Country Hotel, Tokai Rd, T021-713 2222, www.steenberghotel.com. Luxurious country hotel with 30 elegant, traditional rooms furnished with beautiful antiques, in converted farm buildings overlooking manicured gardens and working vineyards. Swimming pool, gym, spa and steam room, horse riding and 18-hole golf course. The award-winning **Catharina Restaurant** (see Eating, page 152) has an excellent reputation. Relaxed and friendly atmosphere.

A Alphen Hotel, Alphen Drive, T021-794 5011, www.alphen.co.za. 21 spacious rooms on an elegant 18th-century Cape Dutch estate. Suites and rooms are decorated with fine antiques and have polished floors and log fires. Lunches in the pub or in the gardens during the summer, popular restaurant in the manor house, swimming pool.

Muizenburg p142

D Sonstraal Guest House, 4 Axminster Rd, T021-788 1611, www.sonstraalguesthouse.com. Pleasant, old-fashioned guesthouse a short walk from the beach and seafront, with 7 rooms in the main house, 5 of which are en suite, plus self-catering cottages sleeping 4-6 and studios sleeping 2. Simple decor, sunny breakfast room, plant-filled courtyard, pool.

Kalk Bay *p143*

C The Inn at Castle Hill, 37 Gatesville Rd, T021-788 2554, www.castlehill.co.za. Elegant restored Edwardian house with wrought-iron balconies and veranda offering fine sea views. 6 comfortable rooms with white linen and fresh flowers, guest lounge and breakfast room, veranda is the most pleasant part of the house and perfect for whale watching during the season. Secure parking, well run.

Fish Hoek *p145*

C Sunny Cove Manor, 72 Simon's Town Rd, T021-782 2274, www.sunnycovemanor.com. Friendly, well-run family B&B in a solid old manor house overlooking False Bay, with 4 rooms, some have wide ocean views, breakfast room and lounge. Recommended for families.

C Tudor House by the Sea, 43 Simon's Town Rd, T021-7826238, www.tudorhouse.co.za. 5 slightly old-fashioned but comfortable self-catering apartments with 1-3 bedrooms, friendly and very reasonably priced, sea views, secure parking, secluded gardens, ideal for a longer break for those wishing to explore the area. Very popular in season, advance reservations necessary.

Glencairn *p145, map p147*

C Southern Right, 12-14 Glen Rd, T021-782 0314, www.southernright.info. Delightful hotel in turn-of-the-20th-century building set a short walk from the sea. 8 double and twin rooms with high ceilings, dark polished wood floors, subtle decor, some with 4-poster beds and baths only, others with shower and bath. Stylish bar and restaurant serving pub meals, seafood and grills and 3 boules pistes in front of the hotel with regular matches on Fri and Sun afternoons (guests can join in). Fashionable place but family friendly. Recommended.

Simon's Town *p145, map p*

AL British Hotel Apartments, 90 St George St, T021-786 2214, www.britishhotelapartments.co.za. Despite the unpromising name, this is one of the best places to stay in False Bay. Converted characterful Victorian hotel with 4 elegant self-catering apartments. Each apartment is enormous, stretching over 2 open-plan floors, with 3 bedrooms, all with delightful Victorian bathrooms. Polished wood floors throughout, attractive mix of maritime antiques, art deco and stylish modern furnishings, open-plan kitchen and lounge, separate TV room, great views of the bay from magnificent balconies, breakfasts available on request. Highly recommended.

B Quayside Hotel, Jubilee Centre, St George's St, on the seafront, T021-786 3838, www.relaishotels.com/quayside. A smart, modern development in a great central location overlooking the harbour, with 26 spacious double rooms, comfortable marine blue and white decor, bright and sunny with good views. Book well in advance during local holidays. Within walking distance of several restaurants.

C Lord Nelson Inn, 58 St George's St, T021-786 1386, www.lordnelson.co.za. Old fashioned traditional hotel with faded charm and comfortable individually decorated rooms with TV, some with private patios or balconies with harbour views. The homely dark wood English-style pub serves the likes of cottage pie, bangers and mash and ploughman's platter, and has a pool table.

C-D Roman Rock, 21 Dorries Drive, past Simon's Town on way to Cape Point, T021-786 3431, www.simonstown-accommodation.com. Comfortable and modern self-catering apartments sleeping 2-6, in a secluded setting overlooking the beach and sea, cool tiled interiors, large balconies, braai facilities, 3 mins' walk to beach, parking.

D Rocklands, 25 Rocklands Rd, Murdoch Valley South, T021-786 3158, www.rocklandsbnb.com. Cool and comfortable B&B, airy tiled rooms with TV and balconies overlooking the sea, simple furnishings, sunny breakfast room, short walk to the beach. Also offer self-catering apartments and holiday homes.

D-F Simon's Town Backpackers, 66 St George's St, T021-786 1964, www.cape pax.co.za. 38-bed backpacker joint spread across cramped dorms and fairly pleasant doubles, brightly painted walls and bush-camp-style furniture, small kitchen, honesty bar, braai on balcony overlooking the main street and harbour, bikes for hire and can organize sea kayaking.

Boulders Beach p146, map p147
A Boulders Beach Lodge, 4 Boulders Pl, T021-786 1758, www.bouldersbeachlodge.com. One of the most relaxing places you could stay in the area. This friendly, well-run beachside guesthouse is a firm favourite, with 9 double rooms and 2 family rooms with bathrooms, most arranged around a paved yard without sea view, good-sized beds and baths, simple, refreshing design. At night you're likely to see penguins exploring the grounds after everyone has gone home. Good restaurant and souvenir shop. Recommended.

⊖ Eating

Clifton p135
¶¶¶ **Salt**, 34 Victoria Rd, Bantry Bay, T021-439 7258, www.saltrestaurant.co.za. Open 1200-1500, 1830-2200. Sophisticated formal restaurant with contemporary decor and magnificent ocean views from the floor to ceiling windows, especially at sunset. The menu changes regularly but expect the likes of slow-roasted pork, braised duck leg or rib eye steak. Free valet parking.

Camps Bay p136
¶¶¶ **Blues**, Victoria Rd, T021-438 2040, www.blues.co.za. 1200-late. Popular and well-known restaurant and lounge/bar with superb views and Californian-style seafood menu served to a beautiful crowd, but you pay for the restaurant's reputation. The newly revamped interiors are luxurious and the long cocktail menu features the signature Blues Bellini.

¶¶¶ **The Codfather**, corner of Geneva Drive and The Drive, T021-438 0782. Open 1200-2300. One of the best seafood restaurants in Cape Town, stylish laid-back place offering a range of superbly fresh seafood. No menu – the waiter takes you to a counter and you pick and choose whatever you like the look of. Also has an excellent sushi bar. Highly recommended.

¶¶ **Ocean Blue**, Victoria Rd, T021-438 9838. Open 1000-late. Friendly seafood restaurant on Camps Bay trendy strip overlooking the beach. Good fresh seafood, especially daily specials, superb grilled prawns and butterfish kebabs. Less pretentious than many of the restaurants in the area. Recommended.

¶¶ **Tuscany Beach**, 41 Victoria Rd, T021-438 1213, www.tuscanybeachrestaurant.com. 0700-2300. Italian seafood place overlooking the beach, open all day from breakfast. Delicious seafood specials – don't miss the kingklip espetadas or the paella. Also serves wood-fired pizzas, salads, burgers and steaks. Trendy place, gets very busy for sundowners.

Hout Bay p136
¶¶ **Chapman's Restaurant**, Chapman's Peak Hotel, T021-790 1036. Open 1100-2200. A lively restaurant and bar with wood panelled interior, serving good seafood dishes in frying pans, also grills and pub fare. The outside terrace gets packed in summer. Be sure to book ahead.

¶¶ **Dunes**, Hout Bay Beach, T021-790 1876. Open 0900-late. Sprawling restaurant over-looking the dunes behind the beach, very popular with families, large menu, quick service but the food can disappoint – stick to the tasty fish and chips. Book ahead at weekends or you'll be stuck in the hot court-yard instead of the breezy balcony tables.

¶ **Fish on the Rocks**, Harbour Rd (beyond Snoekies Market), T021-790 1153. Open 1000-1900. Simple and delicious fresh fish and chips, deep-fried calamari and prawns, overlooking harbour. No frills, and getting popular with big tour groups.

Constantia *p140*

Buitenverwachting, Klein Constantia Rd, T021-794 5190, www.buitenverwachting.co.za. Mon-Sat 1200-1500, 1830-2200. Fine dining with a cosmopolitan menu of flawless Italian, French and South African dishes from an award-winning chef. Good service, upmarket, prices reflect the quality of the food.

Catharina's, Steenberg Country Hotel, Spaanschemat River Rd, T021-713 2222. Open 0700-2130. The principal restaurant in a 5-star hotel (see Sleeping, page 149). Breakfast is served in the conservatory, lunch and dinner under the oaks or at indoor tables set next to a roaring fire. Elegant hotel restaurant serving excellent South African fare such as West Coast mussels, Knynsa oysters and springbok loin on polenta. Fine wine list. One of the finest restaurants in the area.

The Greenhouse, The Cellars-Hohenort Hotel, see Sleeping, page 149. Open 0730-2200. One of 2 highly rated restaurants at this 5-star hotel, set in a pretty conservatory with white wicker furniture. The Michelin-trained chef produces top-quality fare – mostly modern South African, so expect fresh fish and game, and divine desserts. Excellent wine list to match.

La Colombe, Constantia Uitsig, see Sleeping, page 149. Mon-Sat 1230-1430, 1930-2130. This is a foodie shrine and was 2009 winner in *Eat Out* magazine as South Africa's best restaurant. Excellent French menu with strong Provençal flavours and some Asian influences, and you can expect the likes of rabbit, duck, fish and game dishes, with emphasis on rich sauces, jus and foams. The fine food is paired with wine on the 7-course tasting menus. In fine weather you can sit outside overlooking the gardens and a pool. Highly recommended. Also here is the **Constantia Uitsig Restaurant** and the **River Café**.

Silver Tree, Kirstenbosch Botanical Gardens, T021-762 9585, www.kirstenboschrestaurant.com. 0830-2200. Lovely terrace with views of the gardens and mountain looming behind. Decent Cape menu, including a great sweet and spicy bobotie, butternut ravioli, ostrich burgers, plus breakfasts, sandwiches and salads and there's a carvery on Sun. Also offers a picnic hamper service. There's access at night from the car park after the gardens have closed.

Muizenburg *p142*

Gaylords, 65 Main Rd, T021-788 5470. Wed-Sun 1200-1430, Wed-Mon 1830-2200. Unpretentious, bustling Indian restaurant set in a Victorian cottage with tacky decor. Good value, highly rated north and south Indians curries. Recommended for vegetarian dishes.

Balmoral On Beach, Beach Rd, T021-788 6441. Wed-Mon 0900-1700. Despite the grand name, this is little more than a stylish café serving healthy breakfasts and surfer-friendly fry-ups as well as light lunches such as butternut risotto cakes.

Empire Café, 11 York Rd, T021-788 1250. Tue-Sat 0700-2100, Sun and Mon 0700-1600. Eatery serving eclectic breakfasts and lunchtime fare, including interesting salads and omelettes (try the famous bacon, banana and honey) and some seafood specials. Popular with local surfers and trendy day-trippers.

Kalk Bay *p143*

Cape to Cuba, Main Rd, T021-788 1566. Open 1100-2300. Atmospheric Cuban restaurant and cocktail bar serving good-value seafood with Caribbean flavours. Great setting on water's edge with tables overlooking the harbour, funky decor, Cuban music, good cocktails and cigars for sale. Bar open till 0200.

Brass Bell, by the railway station, T021-788 5455. Mon-Fri 1100-2300. A well-known and very popular pub and restaurant in a great location. Simple set-up serving pub meals and good pizzas and fish and chips. Downstairs gets packed with a young crowd, very busy around sunset, great for a cool beer outside close to the waves. More expensive restaurant upstairs serves fresh fish and steak.

Kalky's, Kalk Bay Harbour, T021-788 1726. Open 1000-2000. Simple seafood and chips at plastic tables, very popular and freshly cooked, counter service and then listen for your number to be called out. You'll rub shoulders with Kalk Bay's characterful fishermen here.

Olympia Café & Deli, 134 Main Rd, T021-788 6396. 0700-2100. Another Kalk Bay institution, this laid-back café serves some of the freshest bread on the peninsula, plus light lunches, fabulous cakes and fresh daily specials. Great atmosphere and good value, but expect to chalk your name on the blackboard and queue for a table at weekends.

Sirocco, 82 Main Rd, T021-788 1881. Stylish restaurant set right on the main road, with blue and white tables on a shady terrace with lots of plants and an area to relax on cushions. Seafood, steaks, good spot for coffee and all-day breakfasts, try the salmon omelette.

The Timeless Way, 106 Main Rd, T021-788 5619. Open 1200-2200. An excellent, old-fashioned restaurant with polished wooden floors serving Cape cuisine, steaks and seafood. The bobotie is good, as is the pasta, gourmet burgers and Sun roast lunch.

Simon's Town *p145, map p147*

Black Marlin, Miller's Point, 2 km from Simon's Town, T021-786 1621, www.black marlin.co.za. 1200-1600, 1800-2100. Set in an old whaling station, this place is well known for its excellent seafood and is a good lunch stop on the way to or from Cape Point. Fabulous sea views and wide range of fresh seafood – try the delicious crayfish and oysters or the signature king-klip skewers, Great wine list. Recommended, but it can get busy with tour buses in summer and reservations are essential.

Bon Appetit, 90 St George's St, T021-786 2412. Tue-Sat 1200-1400, 1830-2200. One of the finest restaurants on the peninsula specializing in top-notch French cuisine – the chef is Michelin-trained. Excellent set menus and imaginative main meals

such as ravioli of rabbit plus French staples like confit de canard. Popular and quite small. Book ahead.

Bertha's, Jubilee Sq, Wharf Rd, T021-786 2138. Open 0700-2130. 0700-2200, sushi only served at lunch and dinner. A seafood grill in a prime location overlooking the yacht harbour. During the day the outside terrace is a good place to enjoy good fresh seafood and watch the goings on in the harbour. Inside is a dining area perfect for large family meals. Great selection of fresh seafood dishes, good value.

Quarterdeck, Jubilee Sq, T021-786 3825. Open sat-Thu 0800-1900, Fri 0800-2300. Simple café with great views over the harbour, serving sandwiches, burgers and interesting salads like avocado with smoked chicken and biltong. Also has a Cape Malay buffet on Fri evenings.

Salty Sea Dog, next to Quayside Centre, T021-786 1918. Mon-Sat 1000-2100, Sun 1000-1630. Cheap and cheerful place serving fresh fish and chips with seats overlooking the harbour. Good value, friendly and swift service. Popular with groups.

The Two and Sixpence, 88 St George's St, next to the **British Hotel**, T021-786 5735. Open 1000-2400. Local British-style pub serving standard bar food such as burgers, bangers and mash, ploughman's, plus Yorkshire pudding specials, Sun roasts and curry nights. Also has pool tables and occasional live music.

Boulders Beach *p146, map p147*

Boulders Beach Restaurant, Boulders Beach Lodge, T021-786 1758, www.boulders beachlodge.com. 0800-1115, 1200-1500, 1800-2130. Homely place with wooden floors and fireplace and broad outside deck, serving good English breakfasts, cocktails (including Pickled Penguins), delicious seafood platters and daily specials like lamb rump is soy sauce or prawn ravioli, plus salads for a light meal. Dishes are beautifully presented.

♪ Bars and clubs

Clifton p135

La Med, Glen Country Club, Victoria Rd, T021-438 5600, www.lamed.co.za. 1100-late. Something of a Cape Town institution, hugely popular meeting place for locals, busy bar overlooking the sea, good pub food, great for a sundowner when you'll be hard pressed to find a seat, turns into a raucous club later on. Also a venue for watching rugby matches on giant TVs and is well known for its New Year's Eve party.

Camps Bay p136

Baraza, Victoria Rd, T021-438 1758, www.baraza.co.za. 1200-late-0200, closes some days out of season. Stylish bar with ocean and sunset views, popular for sundowners, glamorous decor in muted earthy colours with African touches, long list of cocktails and imported bottled beers and you can order food from **Blues** (see Eating, page 151) next door.

Café Caprice, Victoria Rd, T021-438 8315. Open 0900-late. Popular café and bar with outdoor seats, great fresh fruit cocktails. Gets packed and very noisy around sunset, loud house music played until late by a DJ every night in season and at the weekends in winter.

Dizzy Jazz Café, 41 The Drive, T021-438 2686. Open 1130-late. Busy bar and music venue, popular at the weekend, mostly jazz but has everything from funk to rock, comfortable couches, low tables, food includes sushi and pizza.

Sandbar, 31 Victoria Rd, T021-438 8336, www.sandbar.co.za. 0930-late. Popular for sundowners at one of the shady tables looking onto the beach. Small place so get here early if you want to secure a table, menu includes wraps, sandwiches and nachos.

▲ Activities and tours

For information on Activities and tours, see Cape Town, page 127.

⊖ Transport

Table Mountain National Park p138
Car

From the entrance to the reserve take a left and follow the M65 along the edge of the reserve. After 8 km the road divides; the right turn winds over the Swartkopberge to **Long Beach** and **Simon's Town**. Known as Red Hill (M66), this is a quicker route back to **Cape Town** if your time is short. There are 2 picnic spots with braai facilities along here. The road to the left leads down to **Scarborough**, and then along the coast to **Kommetjie**, 18 km from the reserve gates. There is a craft centre just after the junction, on the right.

The Winelands

The Winelands is South Africa's oldest and most beautiful wine-producing area, a fertile series of valleys quite unlike the rest of the Western Cape. It is the Cape's biggest attraction after Cape Town, and its appeal is simple: it offers the chance to sample several hundred different wines in a historical and wonderfully scenic setting.

This was the first region after Cape Town to be settled, and the towns of Stellenbosch, Paarl and Franschhoek are some of the oldest in South Africa. Today, their streets are lined with beautiful Cape Dutch and Georgian houses, although the real architectural gems are the manor houses on the wine estates. While the wine industry flourished during the 18th and 19th centuries, the farmers built grand homesteads with cool wine cellars next to their vines. Most of these have been lovingly restored and today can be visited as part of a Winelands tour – many have even been converted into gourmet restaurants or luxury hotels. ▶▶ *For listings, see pages 175-186.*

Ins and outs

Getting there The N2 highway goes past Cape Town International airport, 22 km east of the city, and then continues along the northern fringes of the Cape Flats, home to the sprawling townships of Mitchells Plain, Nyanga and Khayelitsha. Beyond these the R310 left turning is the quickest route to Stellenbosch, the heart of the Winelands, 16 km from the N2. The N2 continues east splitting the towns of Strand and Somerset West before climbing over the Hottentots Holland Mountains into the Overberg via Sir Lowry's Pass (see page 166). The R44 is an alternative route from Strand to Stellenbosch. Paarl and Wellington are best accessed by the N1 from Cape Town, and Franschhoek by either route. The wine estates in the region are far too numerous to list in full, but on an organized tour (see page 185) or a self-drive trip, there is ample opportunity to visit several estates in one day.

Tourist information Tourist offices in Cape Town (see page 80) can provide brochures and maps; also visit www.tourismcapewinelands.co.za. For a list of tour operators offering day tours to the Winelands from Cape Town, see page 129. Wine estates charge a small tasting fee of about R5-20, which often includes a free wine glass.

Background

The Cape's wine industry was started in earnest by Simon van der Stel in 1679. Previously, vines had been grown by Van Riebeeck in Constantia, Company's Garden and in the area known today as Wynberg. The first wine was produced in 1652, and there was soon a great demand from the crews of ships when they arrived in Table Bay as red wine was drunk to fight off scurvy and it kept better than water. As the early settlers moved inland and farms were opened up in the sheltered valleys, more vines were planted. Every farmer had a few plants growing alongside the homestead, and by chance the soils and climate proved to be ideal. Van der Stel produced the first quality wines on Constantia estate, with the help of Hendrik Cloete. These were mostly sweet wines made from a blend of white and red Muscadel grapes, known locally as *Hanepoot* grapes. The industry received a boost in 1806 when the English, at war with France, started to import South African wines. However, under Apartheid, sanctions hindered exports and the Kooperatieve Wijnbouwers Vereniging (KWV) controlled prices and production quotas. Since the lifting of sanctions, the KWV has lost much of its power, allowing the industry to experiment and expand. Today, South Africa has 120,000 ha of vineyards and produces some 800 million litres of wine each year.

Today, all major wine grape varieties are grown in South Africa, plus the fruity red Pinotage, a variety produced in Stellenbosch in 1925 by crossing Pinot Noir and Cinsault. Wine is now produced as far north as the Orange River Valley in the Northern Cape.

1 Winelands

➡ **Winelands maps**
1 Winelands, page 156
2 Franschhoek Valley, page 167
3 Paarl Winelands, page 172
4 Wellington district, page 174

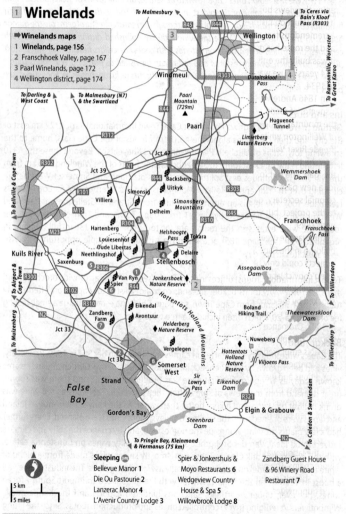

Sleeping
Bellevue Manor **1**
Die Ou Pastourie **2**
Lanzerac Manor **4**
L'Avenir Country Lodge **3**

Spier & Jonkershuis &
Moyo Restaurants **6**
Wedgeview Country
House & Spa **5**
Willowbrook Lodge **8**

Zandberg Guest House
& 96 Winery Road
Restaurant **7**

Bain's Kloof Pass

No matter which direction you take when leaving the Cape by road you will at some stage have to cross the mountains via a spectacular pass. Bain's Kloof is regarded as one of the greatest passes; as you drive through, enjoy the views but also take note of its construction history. The pass was a tremendous feat of engineering and the route has not changed since it was built; the only change made in 154 years of use was to tar the road in 1934.

In 1846 Andrew Geddes Bain, the inspector of roads, noticed a gap in the mountain range in the direction of Wellington while working in the Breede River Valley. A few months later, he traversed the mountains via the 'gap' and put forward a proposal for a new pass. John Montagu, the colonial secretary, gave his full backing to the project, but work did not start until 1849.

This was the greatest period of road building in the Cape, but these ambitious projects could only be afforded by using convict labour. On his arrival in the Cape, John Montagu had been shocked by the conditions on Robben Island, where convicts were incarcerated. In 1847, Ordinance 7 was promulgated, for the "discipline and safe custody of convicts employed on public roads". This was Montagu's plan to reform prison conditions and ways of punishment. The first pass to be constructed under the new system was Mitchell's Pass in 1846. From then until 1888 all the major roads and passes were built using the convict system. It was considered a great success, but the labour was hard and the prisoners wore chains. The only tools available were picks, shovels, sledgehammers, rock drills and gunpowder.

Before work could start at Bain's Kloof, neat stone barracks were built to house over 200 convicts. Conditions were better than in prison and local farmers were contracted to supply fresh straw for palliasses on a weekly basis. The total cost of Bain's Kloof Pass was £50,000; the convicts were paid 60 pence per month, but the cost of their daily rations, seven pence, was deducted from this; Bains was paid an annual salary of £300; the head warders and chaplains were paid £100 per annum, while the ordinary warders received £12 per annum plus rations. The cost of gunpowder used was £1223 – over 10 km of rock had to be blasted out.

The pass took 1608 days to complete, a considerable achievement considering the terrain and the tools available. Most of the labour was unskilled (at the outset) and yet retaining walls, culverts, aqueducts and drains were built – all using drystone masonry techniques. What's more, all these features are still in place and in use today. The pass was opened by Petrus Borchardus Borcherds, chairman of the Central Roads Board, Cape Town, on 14 September 1853, amidst great celebrations. The new route between Cape Town and Worcester was 57 km shorter and it saved two days' travel.

In total, Andrew Geddes Bain built eight passes in South Africa during the first half of the 1800s. His son Thomas Charles John Bain built another 24 major mountain roads and passes in the Cape during the second half of the 1800s. These include Prince Alfred's Pass from Knysna to Uniondale (1865), Seven Passes road from George to Knysna (1882) and Swartberg Pass from Oudtshoorn to Prince Albert (1888).

Strand and around ●❷❸ ►► pp175-186. Colour map 8, B1.

Although principally an industrial area, Strand is a popular seaside resort and commuter town with an excellent 5-km white-sand beach. It mainly caters for domestic tourists and, despite its proximity to Cape Town, the Winelands and the Whale Coast, it holds little appeal. Further inland, **Somerset West** is a prosperous town and again a major commuter centre. It has a beautiful location on the slopes of the Helderberg Mountains, with unimpeded views of False Bay and, occasionally, Cape Point.

Vergelegen Estate

① *T021-847 1334, www.vergelegen.co.za. Daily 0930-1600, R10, children (under 16) R5, wine tasting R30. From Somerset West take the R44, turn right at the traffic lights and after 1 km turn left into Lourensford Rd; the estate is 4 km on the right. There is a shop, displays on the history of the estate, a smart wine-tasting room and 2 restaurants: Lady Phillips Restaurant is à la carte, teas and coffees are served 1000-1145 and 1430-1600, lunch 1200-1430, booking essential for lunch T021-847 1346; the Rose Terrace is an open-air light lunch spot, Nov-Apr 1000-1600. There is also a picnic hamper service.*

This is one of the Cape's finest estates and the highlight is a visit to the magnificent manor house filled with beautiful period furniture and historical paintings, similar to the collection at Groot Constantia. At the front of the house are five **Chinese camphor trees** that were planted by Willem van der Stel between 1700 and 1706. They are the oldest living documented trees in South Africa and are now a national monument. Behind the house is a walled octagonal garden – many of the plants were planted here by Lady Phillips (wife of Sir Lionel Phillips, owner for 25 years from 1917), who wished to recreate a typical English garden, complete with herbaceous border. Look out for the collection of roses next to the main house. The surrounding parkland, much of it similar to an English country estate, is also open for exploration.

Stellenbosch ●❷❸❹❺❻⊙▲❼❽ ►► pp175-186. Colour map 8, B1.

Stellenbosch, the centre of the Winelands, is the oldest and most attractive town in the region, with a large university giving it a liveliness which is lacking in other nearby towns. The centre has a pleasing mix of architectural styles: Cape Dutch, Georgian, Regency and Victorian houses line broad streets, dappled with shade from centuries-old oak trees, and furrowed with water ditches which still carry water to the gardens. It's a fairly large place but, with its handful of good museums and fun nightlife, is a perfect base for visiting the wine estates.

Ins and outs

The town is served by the suburban Metro railway from Cape Town, But for safety reasons, this is best avoided. Hiring a car is the best way of getting here as you then have the freedom to explore the surrounding wine estates. The trip from Cape Town takes about an hour, either along the N1 or the N2. Stellenbosch itself is perfect for exploring on foot as many of the interesting sights are concentrated in a small area along Church, Dorp and Drostdy streets. **Stellenbosch Tourist Office** ① *36 Market St, T021-883 3584, www.stellenboschtourism.co.za, Mon-Fri 0800-1800, Sat 0900-1700, Sun 1000-1600 (in Jun and Aug the office opens 1 hr later and closes 1 hr earlier)*, is a professional and helpful office, which provides maps and can help with accommodation bookings, tour information and

Willem van der Stel

Two of the farms on the banks of the Lourens River, Parelvallei and Vergelegen, belonged to two sons of Simon van der Stel, Governor of the Cape. When the governor retired, he went to live on his estate of Constantia. The directors of the Dutch East India Company honoured his works in the Cape by appointing his son, Willem Adriaan, as his successor to the governorship. This proved to be a disaster since Willem principally devoted his energies to building up his estate, Vergelegen. Over the next six years he acquired most of the land in the valley and used the Cape's resources to improve the estate. He was not unskilled at farming and, before he was found out, Vergelegen was regarded as one of the most gracious and successful country estates in the Cape.

However, in 1707 the Dutch East India Company was made aware of the corrupt nature of Willem's dealings and he was recalled to the Netherlands. Vergelegen was confiscated, divided into four farms and sold. Since Simon van der Stel died at Constantia on 24 June 1712 there have been no Van der Stels in the Cape.

wine routes. **Stellenbosch On Foot** ① *T021-887 9150, or book at the tourist office, R80 per person (minimum 3 people)*, offers 90-minute guided walks that leave from the tourist office every day at 1100 and 1500.

Background

In November 1679 Simon van der Stel left Cape Town with a party of soldiers in order to explore the hinterland. There was already a great need for additional land to be brought under cultivation to supply both Cape Town and passing ships calling for fresh supplies. On the first night the group camped beside a stream they named the Kuilsrivier. The stream turned out to be a tributary of a much larger river, the Eersterivier. As they followed the Eersterivier towards the mountains they found themselves in a fertile alluvial valley. There was no sign of human habitation, the waters were cool and clean and everything seemed to grow in abundance – exactly the type of land Van der Stel had been sent to discover. Several days after entering the valley the group camped under a large tree on an island formed by two branches of the Eersterivier. The camp was named Van der Stel se Bosch (Van der Stel's Wood).

Six months later, in May 1680, eight families from Cape Town moved into the area, tempted by the offer of as much free land as they could cultivate, and by the summer of 1681 Stellenbosch was a thriving agricultural community. This became the first European settlement in the interior of southern Africa. By the end of 1683 more than 30 families had settled in the valley, a school had been built and a *landdrost* (magistrate) had been appointed. Throughout his life, Simon van der Stel maintained a close interest in the development of the town. One of his greatest legacies was to order the planting of oak trees along the sides of every street. Canals were also built to bring water to the town gardens. Today, a number of the original oaks are still standing and some have been proclaimed national monuments.

It is difficult to picture it today, but at the end of the 17th century this new settlement was a frontier town. For the next 100 years the magistracy had dealings with the explorers, hunters, adventurers and nomadic peoples who lived beyond the Cape, and the authority extended over 250,000 sq km. In the meantime, the town prospered as an agricultural centre and also emerged as a place of learning. In 1859 the Dutch Reformed Church started a Seminary which in 1866 became the Stellenbosch Gymnasium, renamed Victoria College in 1887. After the creation of the Union of South Africa in 1910, there was pressure on the new government to establish a single national university. By this stage Victoria College had emerged as a respected Afrikaner school, and Stellenbosch itself was regarded as an important centre of Afrikaner culture. In 1915 a local farmer, Johannes Marais died and left £100,000 towards higher education in Stellenbosch. This bequest finally persuaded the government to yield to public pressure and in April 1918 the Victoria College became the University of Stellenbosch.

Sights

Stellenbosch offers two approaches to sightseeing: walking around the town centre viewing public buildings, oak-lined streets and stately homes; or going on a wine tour,

Stellenbosch

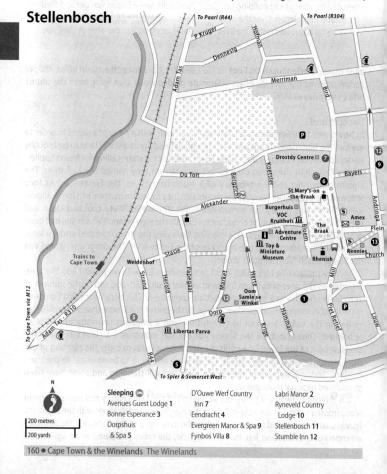

Sleeping
Avenues Guest Lodge **1**
Bonne Esperance **3**
Dorpshuis
& Spa **5**

D'Ouwe Werf Country
Inn **7**
Eendracht **4**
Evergreen Manor & Spa **9**
Fynbos Villa **8**

Labri Manor **2**
Ryneveld Country
Lodge **10**
Stellenbosch **11**
Stumble Inn **12**

visiting any number of the roughly 130 wineries and private cellars. Spend a couple of days in Stellenbosch and you'll get to do both. No other town in South Africa has such an impressive concentration of early Cape architecture. However, like Swellendam (see page 269), many of the earliest buildings were lost to fires in the 18th and 19th centuries; what you see today is a collection of perfectly restored buildings. Following each fire, the destroyed buildings were recreated with the help of photographs, original plans and sketches, although the technology and materials of the day were used. This is perhaps why they appear to have survived in such good condition. This restoration process is not unusual: the town of Tulbagh in the Breede River Valley was completely destroyed by an earthquake in 1969, but today it has the look and feel of an unspoilt quaint Victorian village.

Dorp Street, which runs east-west in the southern part of town, has all the classic features – an avenue of oak trees, running water in open furrows and carefully restored white-walled buildings. A walk from the **Libertas Parva** building to the Theological

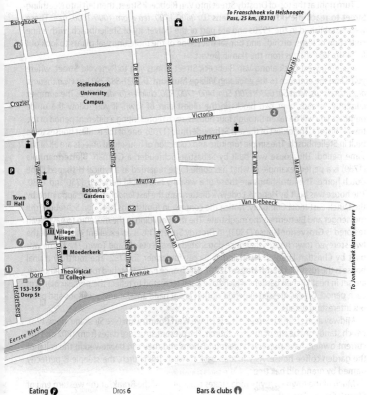

College takes you through the oldest parts of town and past some of the best-preserved old buildings. Libertas Parva is a beautifully restored classic H-shaped manor house built in 1783. Today it serves as an **art gallery** ⓘ *Mon-Fri 0900-1245, 1400-1700, Sat 1000-1300, 1400-1700*, with pictures of Cape Town. The cellar behind the house has a small wine and cork museum. Continue east along Dorp Street, where you'll pass the famous **Oom Samie se Winkel** (No 82), a Victorian-style general store that is still functioning as a shop today. Of particular note are the town houses just past the junction with Helderberg Street. **Hauptfleisch House** (No 153), **Bakker House** (No 155), **Loubser House** (No 157), and **Saxenhof** (No 159), are regarded as the best-preserved street façades in old Stellenbosch.

Branching off from Dorp Street is Drostdy Street, dominated by a building with a tall tower. Also in this street is the town church, the **Moederkerk**; its current steeple church was designed by Carl Otto Hagen and built in 1862. Inside, it is worth admiring the pulpit and the unusually thick stained-glass windows.

Turn right at the top of Drostdy Street into Van Riebeeck Street, then left into Neethling Street to reach the **Botanical Gardens** ⓘ *0800-1700, tea room 1000-1700, free*. These were established in the 1920s and are part of the University of Stellenbosch, with a fine collection of ferns, orchids and bonsai trees. One of the more unusual plants to look out for is the *Welwitschis* from the Namib Desert.

Heading west back along Van Riebeeck Street brings you to Ryneveld Street, where you'll find the entrance to the engaging **Village Museum** ⓘ *T021-887 2902, www.museums.org.za/stellmus, Mon-Sat 0930-1700, Sun 1400-1700, R20, children (under 14) R5*. The complex currently spreads over two blocks in the oldest part of town. If you follow the guide numbers you will be taken through four houses, each representing a different period of the town's history. The oldest of these is **Schreuderhuis** (1709), one of the earliest houses to be built in Stellenbosch. The simple furniture and collection of household objects are all of the same period. The house was built by Sebastian Schreuder, a German. **Blettermanhuis** (1789) is a perfect example of what has come to be regarded as a typical H-shaped Cape Dutch home. The furnishings are those of a wealthy household between 1750 and 1780. The house was built by Hendrik Lodewyk Bletterman, the last *landdrost* to be appointed by the Dutch East India Company. Notice the contrast in furnishings between Schreuder the messenger and Bletterman the magistrate. The third building in the museum to have been restored is **Grosvenor House** (1803), in Drostdy Street. This is an excellent example of the two-storeyed town houses that once dominated the streets of Cape Town. The home was built by Christian Ludolph Neethling, a successful farmer, in 1782. The fourth and final house is the fussy **OM Bergh House** (1870), which once had a thatched roof. All four houses are set in neat kitchen gardens which have been recreated to reflect the popular plants of each period. Guides dressed in period clothes are at hand answer any questions and point out interesting details.

Midway along Church Street is the **D'Ouwe Werf Country Inn** (see Sleeping, page 176), which stands on the site of the first church. The present structure dates from 1802 and the current owners have preserved the foundations and they can be viewed in the cellar of the garden coffee house. As you look back towards the church, the steeple is perfectly framed by grand old oak trees.

Much of the town's activity today takes place around the **Braak**, at the western end of Church Street. This is the original village green, and one-time military parade ground. On the western edge by Market Street is the **VOC Kruithuis** ⓘ *T021-887 2902, Sep-May, Mon-Fri 0930-1300, R2*, or Powder House, built in 1777 as a weapons store. Today it is a military museum. A short distance north, on the corner of Alexander Street, is the **Burgerhuis**

ⓘ *T021-887 0339, www.museums.org.za/burgerhuisstel, Mon-Fri 0800-1630, Sat 1000-1300, 1400-1600, free*, a classic H-shaped Cape Dutch homestead built by Antonie Fick in 1797, that is now decorated to represent the house of a well-to-do Stellenboscher in the Victorian era.

Two churches overlook the Braak, **Rhenish Church**, built in 1832 as a training school for coloured people and slaves, which has a very fine pulpit, and **St Mary's-on-the-Braak**, an Anglican church completed in 1852. A little to the west, on Market Street just behind the tourist office, is the **Toy and Miniature Museum** ⓘ *T021-887 2948, Mon-Sat 0930-1700, Sun 1400-1700, R5, children (under 14) R1*, a small but fairly diverting collection of antique toys including a working model of the Blue Train, and a set of rooms devoted to miniatures. Most interesting are the tiny replicas of furniture, clothes and household items for dolls' houses that you can buy in the shop.

Stellenbosch wine route
ⓘ *Maps and brochures on the wine route can be picked up at the tourist offices in Stellenbosch and Cape Town or visit www.wineroute.co.za. Remember the drink-drive laws in South Africa: when wine tasting, you may be offered up to 15 different wines to sample at each estate, so make sure one of you stays sober.*

This was the first wine route to open in South Africa, in April 1971. It was the idea of three local farmers: Neil Joubert, Frans Malan and Spatz Sperling. It has been hugely successful, attracting tens of thousands of visitors every year, and today the membership comprises around 130 private cellars. It's possible to taste and buy wines at all of them, and the cellars can arrange for wine to be delivered internationally. Many of the estates have excellent restaurants as well as providing very popular picnic lunches – at weekends it is advisable to book in advance.

Delaire ⓘ *T021-885 1756, www.delairewinery.co.za, sales and tastings: Mon-Fri 0900-1700, Sat 1000-1700, Sun 1000-1600.* This small estate has some of the best views in the valley, and has produced some very high-standard wines. Their flagship Merlot is very popular, while the Chardonnay remains a favourite export label. The **Green Door** restaurant serves lunch Tuesday to Sunday; picnic hampers are available. On a clear day visitors are rewarded with views of the Simonsberg Mountains.

Delheim ⓘ *T021-888 4600, www.delheim.com, sales and tastings: Mon-Fri 0900-1700, Sat 0900-1600, Sun 1030-1600 (Oct-Apr only), cellar tours: Mon-Fri 1030 and 1430, Sat 1030, restaurant: Mon-Sat 0930-16300, Sun (Oct-Apr only) 0930-1630.* This is one of the more commercially oriented estates and may seem a little too impersonal. However, the restaurant has a beautiful setting with views towards Cape Town and Table Mountain, and serves breakfasts, lunches and teas. Tastings are conducted in a cool downstairs cellar.

Eikendal ⓘ *T021-855 1422, www.eikendal.com, sales and tastings: Oct-Apr, Mon-Sat 0900-1630, Sun 1000-1600, May-Sep, 1000-1600; cellar tours: Oct-Apr, Mon-Fri, 1000 and 1430, May-Sep, on request.* The microclimate on the western slopes of the mountain is ideal for viticulture, and there is a wide selection of both whites and reds. Lunch is served in the wine-tasting room or the gardens; Swiss owned so expect unusual European dishes on the menu.

Hartenberg ⓘ *T021-865 2541, www.hartenbergestate.com, sales and tastings: Mon-Fri 0900-1715, Sat 0900-1500, lunches: 1200-1400.* This privately owned old estate, founded in 1692, is off the Bottelary Road, 10 km north of Stellenbosch. During the summer, lunches are served in the shade and peace of the gardens; come winter the tasting room doubles up as a restaurant with warming log fires. A number of red and white wines are produced, but their reds seem the most successful – past award winners include their 2003 Shiraz and Pinotage.

Neethlingshof ① T021-883 8988, www.neethlingshof.co.za, sales and tastings: Mon-Fri 0900-1700, Sat-Sun 1000-1600, cellar and vineyard tours: by appointment, meals are served in 2 restaurants, Lord Neethling and Palm Terrace, 0900-2100. With its fine restaurants, Cape Dutch buildings and grand pine avenue (which now features on the labels of the estate wines), this estate is a very pleasant one to visit. The first vines were planted here in 1692 by a German, Barend Lubbe, and the manor house was built in 1814 in traditional Cape Dutch H-style. Today this has been converted into the **Lord Neethling** restaurant renowned for its venison and veal. Neethlingshof has won a clutch of awards – the Lord Neethling Pinotage is a consistent trophy winner.

Saxenburg ① T021-903 6113, www.saxenburg.co.za, sales and tastings: Mon-Fri 0900-1700, Sat 1000-1700, Sun 1000-1600 (Sep-May only). The Guinea Fowl restaurant is open Wed-Mon for lunch and Wed-Sat for dinner. Saxenberg has a long history, starting in 1693 when Simon van der Stel granted land to a freeburgher, Jochem Sax. Sax planted the first vines and built the manor house in 1701, and the estate has been producing ever since. It produces a small number of cases each year; its Private Collection of red wines is very good. The restaurant attracts most of the visitors.

Spier ① Welcome Centre, T021-809 1100, www.spier.co.za, sales and tastings: daily 1000-1630. Meals are available throughout the day and evening at 4 on-site restaurants (book several days ahead); picnics and a deli are also available. Accommodation is in The Village at Spier (see Sleeping, page 177). This is the Winelands' most commercial wine estate, offering a vast array of activities and wine tastings – of both Spier's own wines and those of other Stellenbosch estates. Spier wines are well regarded, and their Private Collection Chenin Blanc and Chardonnay are especially good and frequently win awards. As well as wine tasting, there is a cheetah outreach programme (although the creatures seem rather lacklustre) and a birds of prey area, plus horse riding, fishing, an 18-hole golf course and the Camelot spa. There are four superb restaurants on site including a riverside pub, the outdoor 'African' **Moyo** BBQ, and the **Jonkershuis**, which has superb (if expensive) Cape Malay buffets. These are hugely popular with tourists and are listed separately under Eating. An annual music and arts festival is held at the open-air amphitheatre during the summer months.

Simonsig ① T021-888 4900, www.simonsig.co.za, sales and tastings: Mon-Fri 0830-1700, Sat 0830-1600, cellar tours: Mon-Fri 1000 and 1500, Sat 1000. This large estate has been in the Malan family for 10 generations, and in recent years has produced some exceptionally fine wines. There is an attractive outdoor tasting area with beautiful views out over the mountains. One wine worth looking out for is the Kaapse Vonkel, a sparkling white considered the best of its kind in South Africa. Their Chardonnay is consistently very good and not badly priced too.

Villiera ① T021-865 2002/3, www.villiera.co.za, sales and tastings: Mon-Fri 0830-1700, Sat 0830-1500. Villiera is highly regarded and produces some of the best wines in the Cape. There are plenty of classic wines to choose from, including their Merlot and Sauvignon Blanc. They don'tconduct cellar tours, but allow self-guided tours.

Franschhoek Valley ◎❷◐▲ »» pp175-186. Colour map 8, B2.

Franschhoek

This is the most pleasant of the Wineland's villages, with a compact centre of Victorian whitewashed houses backed by rolling vineyards and the soaring slopes of the Franschhoek Mountains. It does, however, have an artificial feel to it as most of the attractions here have been created to serve the tourist industry. The outlying wine estates all have their individual appeal, but the village itself is made up of restaurants and touristy craft shops. Nevertheless, Franschhoek is famed for its cuisine and dubs itself the 'gastronomical capital of the Western Cape', so a visit here should guarantee an excellent meal accompanied by a fine glass of wine.

Ins and outs Franschhoek is 71 km from Cape Town (via the N1), 26 km from Paarl and 31 km from Stellenbosch. There is no regular public transport so you will need a car. Most of the tour operators offering Winelands tours don't usually include Franschhoek. The **tourist office** ① *70 Huguenot Rd, T021-876 3603, www.franschhoek.org.za, Mon-Fri 0900-1800, Sat 1000-1700, Sun 1000-1600*, has helpful staff with a good knowledge of accommodation and restaurants. The office also has the Franschhoek wine route desk (see page 167) and a wine and cheese tasting area, and there's a plant nursery at the back.

Background Although the first Huguenots arrived at the Cape in 1688, the village of Franschhoek only took shape in 1837 after the church and the manse had been built. The first immigrants settled on farms granted to them by Simon van der Stel along the Drakenstein Valley at Oliphantshoek in 1694. Franschhoek is built on parts of **La Motte** and **Cabrière** farms. The village became the focal point of the valley but the oldest and most interesting buildings are to be found on the original Huguenot farms and estates.

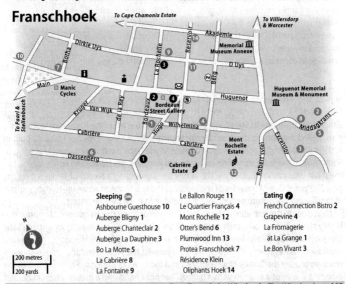

Franschhoek

Sleeping ⏍		Eating ❼
Ashbourne Guesthouse 10	Le Ballon Rouge 11	French Connection Bistro 2
Auberge Bligny 1	Le Quartier Français 4	Grapevine 4
Auberge Chanteclair 2	Mont Rochelle 12	La Fromagerie
Auberge La Dauphine 3	Otter's Bend 6	at La Grange 1
Bo La Motte 5	Plumwood Inn 13	Le Bon Vivant 3
La Cabrière 8	Protea Franschhoek 7	
La Fontaine 9	Résidence Klein	
	Oliphants Hoek 14	

Four Passes

One of the popular recommended day drives from Cape Town is known as the Four Passes route. This takes you through the heart of the Winelands, and, as the name suggests, over four mountain passes. It is a wonderful day out from Cape Town, especially if combined with fine wine and gourmet food in Franschhoek. The first stop on the drive is Stellenbosch. From here you take the R310 towards Franschhoek. Driving up out of Stellenbosch you cross the first pass – **Helshoogte Pass**. After 17 km you reach a T-junction with the R45: a left turn would take you to Paarl, 12 km, but the route continues to the right. This is a pleasant drive up into the Franschhoek Valley. The road follows a railway line and part of the Berg River. After passing through Franschhoek, take a left in front of the Huguenot Monument and climb out of the valley via the **Franschhoek Pass**. This pass was built along the tracks formed by migrating herds of game centuries earlier, and was originally known as the Olifantspad (elephant's path). One of the more surprising aspects of this drive is the change in vegetation once you cross the lip of the pass, 520 m above the level of Franschhoek. As the road winds down towards Theewaterskloof Dam, you pass through a dry valley full of scrub vegetation and fynbos – gone are the fertile fruit farms and vineyards.

Take a right across the dam on the R321 towards Grabouw and Elgin. An alternative but much longer route back to Cape Town is to take a left here, onto the R43. This is the road to Worcester, 50 km, the principal town in the Breede River Valley (see page 216). From Worcester follow the N1 back to Cape Town.

The Four Passes Route continues across the Theewaterskloof Dam and then climbs **Viljoens Pass**, the third of four. To the right lies the Hottentots Holland Nature Reserve, a popular hiking region. The country around here is an important apple-growing region. At the N2 highway turn right and follow the road back into Cape Town. The fourth and most spectacular pass is **Sir Lowry's Pass**, which crosses the Hottentots Holland Mountains. From the viewpoint at the top you will be rewarded with a fine view of the Cape Flats with the brooding Cape Peninsula behind.

Sights The **Huguenot Memorial Museum** ⓘ *T021-876 2532, www.museum.co.za, Mon-Sat 0900-1700, Sun 1400-1700, R10, children (under 16) R5*, is housed in two buildings either side of Lambrecht Street. The main building, to the left of the Huguenot Monument, is modelled on a house designed by the French architect, Louis Michel Thibault, built in 1791 at Kloof Street, Cape Town. The displays inside trace the history of the Huguenots in South Africa. There are some fine collections of furniture, silverware and family bibles, but the most interesting displays are the family trees providing a record of families over the past 250 years. One of the roles of the museum today is to maintain an up-to-date register of families, so that future generations will be able to trace their ancestors.

Next door to the museum is the rather stark and unattractive **Huguenot Monument**, a highly symbolic memorial built to mark 250 years since the first Huguenots settled in the Cape. It is set in a peaceful rose garden with the rugged Franschhoek Mountains providing a contrasting background. The three arches represent the Trinity, and the golden sun and cross on top are the Sun of Righteousness and the Cross of Christian Faith. In front of the arches, a statue of a woman with a bible in her right hand and a broken chain in her left symbolizes freedom from religious oppression. If you look closely at the globe you can see objects carved into the southern tip of Africa: a bible, harp, spinning wheel, sheaf of corn and a vine. These represent different aspects of the Huguenots' life, respectively their faith, their art and culture, their industry and their agriculture. The final piece of the memorial, the curved colonnade, represents tranquillity and spiritual peace after the problems they had faced in France.

Franschhoek wine route

All the vineyards lie along the Franschhoek Valley, making it one of the most compact wine routes in the region. What makes this such a rewarding route is that many estates have opened their own excellent restaurants and several also offer luxury accommodation. There are now 43 wine estates on the route, with more being added every year. All the valley's wine can be tasted at the **Vignerons de Franschhoek** ① *at the tourist office, 70 Huguenot St, T021-876 2086, www.franschhoek.org.za/drink.co.za, Mon-Fri 0930-1700, Sat 1000-1600, Sun 1100-1500*, on the right just before you enter the village when approaching from Stellenbosch. Maps and information on all the estates are available here.

Allée Bleue ① *T021-874 1021, www.alleebleue.com, sales and tastings: daily 0900-1700.* This estate is a good place to drop in for some quick wine tasting if you haven't the time to

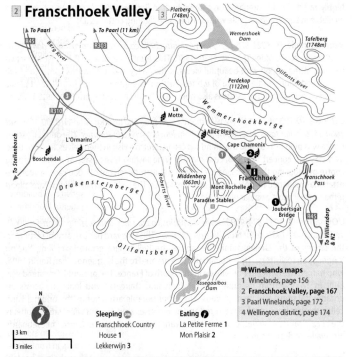

2 Franschhoek Valley

To Paarl
R45
Berg River
To Paarl (11 km)
R303
Platberg (748m)
Wemershoek Dam
Tafelberg (1748m)
Olifants River
R310
La Motte
Perdekop (1122m)
Wemmershoekberge
L'Ormarins
Allée Bleue
Cape Chamonix
To Stellenbosch
Boschendal
Drakensteinberge
Roberts River
Middenberg (663m)
Franschhoek
Franschhoek Pass
Mont Rochelle
Paradise Stables
Joubertsgat Bridge
R45
To Villiersdorp & N2
Olifantsberg
Assegaaibos Dam

N
3 km
3 miles

Sleeping 🛏
Franschhoek Country House 1
Lekkerwijn 3

Eating 🍴
La Petite Ferme 1
Mon Plaisir 2

➡ **Winelands maps**
1 Winelands, page 156
2 **Franschhoek Valley, page 167**
3 Paarl Winelands, page 172
4 Wellington district, page 174

see a whole vineyard. There is a small, fashionable restaurant and deli set just off the R45 towards Franschhoek at the entrance, serving light meals 0830-1730. Tastings include four wines accompanied by four cheeses to offset the flavours.

Boschendal ① *T021-870 4272, www.boschendal.com, sales and tastings: daily 0830-1830, vineyard tours: 1030 and 1130, by appointment. The restaurant serves an excellent buffet lunch; between Nov-Apr Le Pique Nique offers picnic hampers in the gardens. Le Café is open daily for snacks and afternoon teas.* Boschendal estate has been producing wine for 300 years and is today one of the most popular estates in the region, not least for its excellent food and pleasant wine-tasting area underneath a giant oak. The estate started life as two farms in 1687, and was bought in 1715 by Abraham de Villiers. The restored H-shaped manor house (1812) is one of the finest in South Africa, and is open as a museum to the public. Interestingly, a third of the estate is now owned by a black empowerment consortium. Most of the wine produced on the estate is white; their sparkling wines are highly regarded.

Cape Chamonix ① *T021-876 2494, www.chamonix.co.za, sales and tastings: daily 0930-1630, cellar tours: by appointment.* This is one of the largest farms in the valley, with an underground cellar providing pleasantly cool tours at the height of summer. Wine tastings are held in the Blacksmith's Cottage; you can also try their fruit schnapps or the Chamonix mineral water. The **Mon Plaisir** restaurant (see Eating, page 182) is family friendly and highly rated. Food is prepared on a stove built in Paris in 1908. Accommodation is also available in seven comfortable whitewashed self-catering cottages (**D**).

Mont Rochelle ① *T021-876 2770, www.montrochelle.co.za, sales and tastings: daily 0930-1800, cellar tours: Mon-Fri 1100, 1230, 1500.* This estate has one of the most attractive settings in the region with beautiful views of the valley and it produces some good full bodied red wines and a couple of whites. Tastings are informal and friendly and picnic baskets are available. The estate is also home to a hotel and restaurant (see page 177).

La Motte ① *T021-876 3119, www.la-motte.co.za, sales and tastings: Mon-Fri 0900-1630, Sat 1000-1500, cellar tours: by appointment, light lunches served in summer.* The original manor house was built in 1752 and the grand old cellars, worth a visit in themselves, are now used as a classical concert venue once a month. Wine tasting takes place in a smart tasting centre overlooking the cellars. As a relatively small producer, only 15,000 cases a year, the estate has managed to create some excellent wines. The La Motte Millennium Claret blend remains their most popular wine.

L'Ormarins ① *T021-874 9000, www.lormarins.co.za, sales and tastings: Mon-Fri 0900-1630, Sat 1000-1430, cellar tours: by appointment.* This vineyard has a beautiful setting on the slopes of the Drakensteinberge, above the Bellingham estate (excellent, but no longer open to visitors). The original land was granted to the Huguenot, Jean Roi, in 1694, who named the farm after his village in the South of France. The present homestead was built in 1811 – from its grand marble halls and staircases you look out across an ornamental pond and neat gardens. The other notable attraction is the original wine cellar; this has been carefully restored and now houses a set of giant wine vats. On offer is the classic range of wines, plus the Italian varietal range, Terra del Capo. Cheeseboards are available during summer.

Paarl

While Paarl is home to two of South Africa's better-known wine estates, KWV and Nederburg (see page 172), the town itself is not as interesting as Stellenbosch or as fashionable as Franschhoek. All of the attractions and restaurants are strung out along Main Street at the base of Paarl Mountain. When the first European arrival, Abraham Gabbema, saw this mountain in October 1657 it had just rained; the granite domes sparkled in the sunlight and he named the mountains *paarl* (pearl) and *diamandt* (diamond). The first settlers arrived in 'Paarlvallei' in 1687 and, shortly afterwards, the French Huguenots settled on four farms, **Laborie**, **Goede Hoop**, **La Concorde** and **Picardie**. The town grew in a random fashion along an important wagon route to Cape Town. Several old buildings survive, but they are spread out rather than concentrated in a few blocks as in Stellenbosch. There is a helpful **tourist office** ⓘ *216 Main St, T021-877 0860, www.paarlonline.com, Mon-Fri 0800-1700, Sat 0900-1400, Sun 1000-1400.*

Sights The 1-km walk along Main Street will take you past some of the finest architecture in Paarl. Here you'll find one of the oldest buildings, the **Paarl Museum** ⓘ *303 Main St, T021-876 2651, www.museums.org.za/paarlmuseum, Mon-Fri 0900-1700, Sat 0900-1300, R5.* This 18th-century U-shaped Cape Dutch former parsonage houses a reasonably diverting collection of Cape Dutch furniture and kitchen copperware plus some more delicate silver. There is also a small section outlining Paarl during Apartheid, although the fact that Nelson Mandela spent his final years in prison near Paarl is barely mentioned. Only a few hundred metres away, in Gideon Malherbe House, the **Afrikaans Language Museum** ⓘ *Pastorie St, T021-872 3441, www.taalmuseum.co.za, Mon-Fri 0900-1600, Sat 0900-1300, R12, children (under 16) R5*, gives a detailed chronicle of the development of the Afrikaans language and the people involved. The house itself was built in 1860 by a wealthy wine farmer of the same name and the downstairs rooms have been decorated with period furniture donated by his descendents. Between the two museums is **Zeederberg Square**, a 19th-century square with a fine mix of restored buildings and lively restaurants. Further south on Main Street is the **Strooidakkerk**, a thatched church consecrated in 1805 and still in use.

On the east bank of the Berg River is a 31-ha **arboretum** ⓘ *open during daylight hours.* From the tourist office, go down Market Street and cross the river; the arboretum is on the right. It was created in 1957 to mark the tercentenary of the discovery of the Berg River Valley. To help establish the parkland the town treasurer asked other municipalities in South Africa to contribute trees and shrubs from their region. The response was excellent and when the arboretum was inaugurated there were trees from 61 different regions. Today there are over 700 different species and around 4000 trees.

☾ *Nelson Mandela spent his final years in prison near Paarl. His first steps of freedom were from Victor Verster Prison, 9 km south of town on the road to Franschhoek.*

Paarl Mountain Nature Reserve

ⓘ *Jan Philips Mountain Drive, T021-872 3658. Daily 0700-1900 in summer, 0700-1800 in winter. There is a small entrance fee to the reserve but only at weekends, and you do not need to obtain further permits for hiking. The tourist office should be able to give you a clear colour map which has details of access roads and footpaths. There are several car parks with toilets and braai spots. If you wish to fish in one of the dams you need to go to the municipality for a permit.*

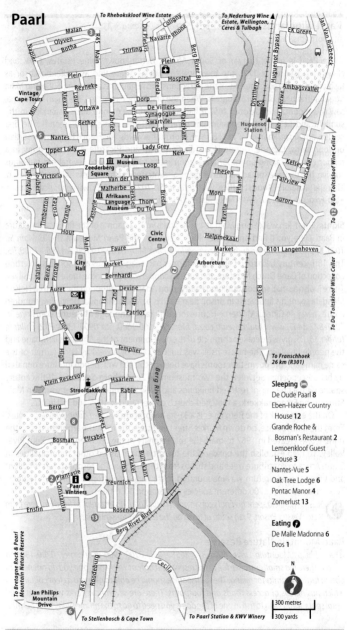

Paarl

To Rhebokskloof Wine Estate

To Nederburg Wine Estate, Wellington, Ceres & Tulbagh

EK Green

Jan Van Riebeeck

Malan
Olyven
Botha
Napier
Main
R45
Stirling
Du Plessis
Navarre
Rhone
Coligny
Plein
Hospital
Berg River Blvd
Ambagsvallei
Van der Merwe
Huguenot Bypass

Vintage Cape Tours

Plein
Reyneke
Alexander
Louie
Ottawa
Bethel
Mill
Dorp
Vester
Fabriek
De Villiers Synagogue
Swartvlei
Castle
Waterkant
Distillery
Huguenot Station

Nantes
Upper Lady
Zeederberg Square
Paarl Museum
Loop
Van der Lingen
Lady Grey
New
Breda
Thesen
Kelsey
Fairview
Muscadel
Kloof
Victoria
Myburgh
Queen
Durr
Protea
Orania
Timberon
Hour
Malherbe Afrikaans Language Museum
Dexter
Thom
Du Toit
Breda
Moni
Elland
Aurora
Textile
Pastorie
Main

To & Du Toitskloof Wine Cellar

Civic Centre
Faure
Helpmekaar
Market
Arboretum
R101 Langenhoven
R303

To Du Toitskloof Wine Cellar

City Hall
Market
Bernhardi
Faldie
Berea
Protea
Auret
Devine
1st
2nd
3rd
4th
Zion
Pontac
Patriot
High
Rose
Templier

To Franschhoek 26 km (R301)

Klein Reservoir
Strooidakkerk
Haarlem
Rabie
Berg
Elisabet
Eeufees
Brug
Bosman
Skakel
Elba
Bulkkant
Berg River

Plantasie
Paarl Vintners
Constantia
Treurnich
Rosendal
Enslin
Roodeburg
R45
Berg River Blvd
Cecilia

To Bretagne Rock & Paarl Mountain Nature Reserve

Jan Philips Mountain Drive

To Stellenbosch & Cape Town

To Paarl Station & KWV Winery

Sleeping
De Oude Paarl **8**
Eben-Haëzer Country House **12**
Grande Roche & Bosman's Restaurant **2**
Lemoenkloof Guest House **3**
Nantes-Vue **5**
Oak Tree Lodge **6**
Pontac Manor **4**
Zomerlust **13**

Eating
De Malle Madonna **6**
Dros **1**

N

300 metres
300 yards

Paarl runs along the eastern base of Paarl Mountain, a giant granite massif, which in 1970 was declared the Paarl Mountain Nature Reserve. Within the 1900-ha reserve is a network of footpaths, a circular drive and a couple of dams. The vegetation differs from the surrounding countryside because of the bedrock – the granite mass is not as susceptible to veld fires and many of the fynbos species grow exceptionally tall.

The domed summit is easy to climb, and near the top is an old cannon dating from the early days of the Cape Colony. On the summit are three giant granite rocks. The highest point is 729 m and there is a chain to help you up the last steep incline. Nearby is **Gordon's Rock**, named after Colonel Robert Jacob Gordon who commanded the British troops at the Cape from 1780 to 1795. This rock is dangerous and should only be tackled by experienced climbers. The third rock is known as **Paarl Rock**. Just below the summit a mountain stream flows through the **Meulwater Wild Flower Reserve**. This garden was created in 1931, and contains specimens of the majority of flowers found around Paarl Mountain including 15 species of proteas.

Set high on the slopes of Paarl Mountain amongst granite boulders and indigenous trees stands the controversial **Afrikaanse Taalmonument** ① *daily 0800-1700*, three concrete columns linked by a low curved wall. This is the Afrikaans Language Monument, inaugurated in October 1975 and designed by Jan van Wijk. Built to celebrate 100 years of Afrikaans being declared as a different language from Dutch, it is thought to be on the only monument in the world dedicated to a language. Each column represents different influences in the language. The phrase 'Dit is ons erns', roughly meaning 'this is our earnestness' is inscribed on the pathway leading up to the monument. The **coffee shop** ① *Mon 0830-1700, Tue-Sun 0830-2200*, has excellent views across the Berg River Valley.

The best views of the surrounding countryside are from Bretagne Rock; on a clear day you can see False Bay, Table Mountain and all the vineyards.

Those with little children in tow may wish to visit **Butterfly World** ① *Klapmuts, T021-875 5628, www.butterflyworld.co.za, daily 0900-1700, R35, children (3-16) R20, family of 4 ticket R90*, the largest such park in South Africa, with butterflies flying freely in colourful landscaped gardens. They are at their most active on sunny days. There are also spiders, scorpions and meerkats to see and you can buy packets of seeds for children to feed the goats, ducks and chickens in the garden. There is a craft shop and the **Jungle Leaf Café** on site.

Paarl wine route
① *The wine route information office can be found at Paarl Vintners at 86 Main Rd, T021-863 4886, www.winecountry.co.za.*

The route was set up in 1984 by local producers to help promote their wines and attract tourists into the area. The programme has been a great success and some of the estates have opened their own restaurants. All of the estates have tastings and wine sales on a daily basis. Today there are 35 members, but only the largest estates conduct regular cellar tours. Below is a short selection.

Boland ① *T021-862 6190, www.bolandwines.co.za, sales and tastings: Mon-Fri 0800-1700, Sat 0900-1400, cellar tours: by appointment.* The estate has an excellent wine cellar, and offers one of the most interesting cellar tours. Their Shiraz and Merlot won many gold medals in 2008.

Fairview ① *T021-863 2450, www.fairview.co.za, wine and cheese sales and tastings: Mon-Fri 0830-1700, Sat 0830-1600, Sun 0930-1600.* This popular estate has a rather unusual attraction in the form of a goat tower, a spiral structure which is home to two pairs of goats. In addition to a variety of good wines (look out for the popular Goats do Roam and Bored Doe blends – a humorous dig at French wines) visitors can taste delicious goat cheeses, which are now produced from a herd of 600 goats and sold in South African supermarkets. Their Camembert has won awards as the best in the world at the World Cheese Awards held in London. A new addition is the Goatshed restaurant.

The Laborie ① *T021-807 3390, www.labo rie.co.za, sales and tastings: daily 0900-1700, Sun 1100-1500 Apr-Sep, cellar tours: by appointment.* Part of KWV (see below), this is a beautifully restored original Cape Dutch homestead – in many ways the archetypal wine estate, and developed with tourism firmly in mind. It's an attractive spot, with a tasting area overlooking rolling lawns and vineyards, and a highly rated restaurant.

KWV ① *T021-807 3007, www.kwvwineempor ium.co.za, sales and tastings: Mon-Sat 0900-1600, Sun 1100-1600, cellar tours: Mon-Sat 1000, 1015 (in German), 1030, 1415.* A short distance from the Laborie estate is the famous **KWV Cellar Complex** which contains the five largest vats in the world. Th#e **Ko-operative Wijnbouwers Vereniging van Zuid-Afrika** (Cooperative Wine Growers' Association) was established in Paarl in 1918 and is responsible for exporting many of South Africa's best-known wines. They are also well known for their brandy and tastings are served with Belgium chocolates.

Nederburg ① *T021-862 3104, www.neder burg.co.za, sales and tastings: Mon-Fri 0830-1700, Sat 1000-1600, Sun 1100-1600; cellar tours are available in English, German and French but must be booked in advance; picnic lunches are available (vegetarian and children's menu available) or enjoy a 2-hr 3-course lunch where the food is matched to a selection of 6 wines.* This is one of the largest and best-known estates in South Africa. Their annual production is in excess of 650,000 cases. As such a large concern they are involved in much of the research in South Africa to improve the quality of the grape and vine. Every April the annual Nederburg Auction attracts buyers from all over the world and is considered one of the top five wine auctions in the world. The homestead was built in 1800, but throughout the 19th century the wines were not considered to be

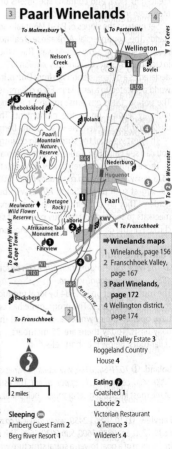

Paarl Winelands

➡ Winelands maps
1 Winelands, page 156
2 Franschhoek Valley, page 167
3 Paarl Winelands, page 172
4 Wellington district, page 174

Palmiet Valley Estate 3
Roggeland Country House 4

Eating 🍴
Goatshed 1
Laborie 2
Victorian Restaurant & Terrace 3
Wilderer's 4

Sleeping 🛏
Amberg Guest Farm 2
Berg River Resort 1

Western Cape brandy route

South Africans consume over 45 million litres of brandy each year. There are a dozen or so cellars on the Western Cape brandy route around Stellenbosch, Wellington and Worcester. For more information visit www.sabrandy.co.za.

Avontuur Estate, R44, 3 km from Somerset West, T021-855 3450, www.avontuurestate.com, Mon-Fri 0830-1700, Sat-Sun 0900-1600. Produces a five-year-old copper-distilled brandy and a 10-year-old limited edition made from Chenin Blanc grapes.

Backsberg, R44 towards Paarl, T021-875 5141, www.backsberg.co.za, Mon-Fri 0800-1700, Sat 0930-1400, Sun 1030-1630. A well-known wine estate producing brandies in a state-of-the-art still imported from the Cognac region of France.

Louiesenhof, R304, 4 km outside Stellenbosch towards the N1, T021-865 2630, www.louiesenhof.co.za, Mon-Fri 0900-1700, Sat-Sun 1000-1700. Produces anything special.

alambic-distilled 16-year-old blend brandies made using an antique distilling kettle that was built in Stuttgart in 1930.

Tokara, at the top of the Helshoogte Pass (R310), 5 km from Stellenbosch, T021-808 5900, www.tokara.co.za, Mon-Fri 0900-1700, Sat-Sun 1000-1500. A wine estate that produces a five-year-old brandy matured in French oak vats.

Uitkyk, R44 towards Paarl from Stellenbosch, T021-8844 416, Mon-Fri 0900-1700, Sat-Sun 1000-1600. Produces one of South Africa's finest 10-year-old estate brandies in a lovely setting on the slopes of the Simonsberg Mountain.

Van Ryn Brandy Cellar, Vlottenburg, 8 km from Stellenbosch, T021-881 3875, www.vanryn.co.za, tours Mon-Fri 1000, 1130 and 1500, Sat 1000, 1130. This is the oldest working cellar in the Cape, where you can view the distillation process and the workshop where the coopers make the maturation barrels from French oak.

anything special. This all changed in 1937 when Johann George Graue bought the estate. Riesling and Cabernet Sauvignon vines were planted, and the cellars completely modernized. Today their wines win countless annual awards. To get there from the centre of Paarl, cross the Berg River and take the R303 towards Wellington as you leave town, the estate is signposted to the right.

Nelson's Creek ① T021-869 8453, www.nelsonscreek.co.za, sales and tastings: Mon-Fri 0800-1800, Sat 0900-1400, restaurant is open during the summer months, picnic baskets also available for lunches on the estate. This is a very pleasant estate to spend the afternoon exploring. Its most recent owner, Alan Nelson, has been successfully producing wines since 1987. In 1996, he donated part of his estate to his farm labourers who now produce wines under the 'New Beginnings' label. A farmers' market is held here on the first Saturday morning of the month.

Rhebokskloof ① T021-869 8386, www.rhebokskloof.co.za, sales and tastings: daily 0900-1700, the Victorian Restaurant serves breakfast, lunches and teas and dinner Fri-Sun. This old estate is now a thoroughly modern outfit, informal tastings are accompanied by cheese and biscuits, or pre-booked formal guided tastings by a variety of snacks to bring out the flavours of the wines and a cellar tour. The terrace café is popular with tour groups and on Sundays they offer a family buffet lunch with children's entertainment.

Wellington

Wellington, like the other Winelands towns, is surrounded by beautiful countryside and has a number of fine historic buildings, with the added bonus of far fewer tourists thronging the streets. Nevertheless, there is little in the town to keep visitors for long – there are a few wine estates in the surrounding area, but the town is best known for its dried fruit. (The other important fruit centres, Ceres and Tulbagh, are on the eastern side of the Limietberg. They can be visited via the magnificent Bain's Kloof Pass, see page 157). To the north, the countryside opens up into the rolling Swartland, an important wheat region. A short drive to the south reveals steep hills where all the farmland is given over to vines. The staff at **Wellington Tourism Bureau** ① *104 Main St, housed in the Old Market Building next to the Dutch Reformed Church, T021-873 4604, www.wellington.co.za, Mon-Fri 0800-1700, Sat 0900-1400, Sun 1000-1300*, are helpful and well organized and there is a good selection of local wines on sale.

The Murray Jubilee Hall and Samuel House were once an institute for training Dutch Reformed Church missionaries; they are now part of **Huguenot College**. The shady **Victoria Park** in Church Street is notable for its roses. Look out for the archway which was built to commemorate the coronation of King Edward VII in 1902. The fountain in **Joubert Square** was unveiled in 1939 as a memorial to the Huguenot settlers in the valley. The **Wellington Museum** ① *Church St, T021-873 4710, Mon-Fri 0900-1700, Oct-Feb, Sun 0900-1300, R5, children (under 16) free*, has a small collection on the history of the town and the Huguenot farms in the district. The archives of the Huguenot Seminary are kept here. Oddly, there are a few ancient Egyptian relics on display.

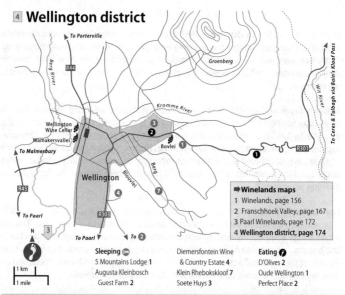

4 Wellington district

To Porterville

Berg River

R44

Groenberg

Kromme River

Wit River

To Ceres & Tulbagh via Bain's Kloof Pass

Wellington Wine Cellar

Wamakersvallei

To Malmesbury

Bovlei

R301

Blouvlei

Berg

R45

Wellington

To Paarl

R303

To Paarl

To

N

1 km
1 mile

➡ Winelands maps
1 Winelands, page 156
2 Franschhoek Valley, page 167
3 Paarl Winelands, page 172
4 **Wellington district, page 174**

Sleeping ●
5 Mountains Lodge **1**
Augusta Kleinbosch
Guest Farm **2**

Diemersfontein Wine
& Country Estate **4**
Klein Rhebokskloof **7**
Soete Huys **3**

Eating ●
D'Olives **2**
Oude Wellington **1**
Perfect Place **2**

Wellington wine route

This is one of the smallest routes in the area, with only 26 members. Much of the farmland in the district is devoted to the production of wheat, and grapes used for dried fruit. The following is a selection of winemakers who open their doors to the public.

Bovlei ① *T021-873 1567, www.bovlei.co.za, sales and tasting: Mon-Fri 0800-1700, Sat 0830-1230, out of town on the R301 towards Bain's Kloof Pass.* Established in 1907 and with a completely modernized cellar, Bovlei produces mainly white wines, although the Shiraz won a gold award in 2008.

Wamakersvallei ① *T021-873 1582, www.wamakersvallei.co.za, sales and tasting: Mon-Fri 0800-1700, Sat 0830-1230, north of town on the R44.* This is one of the largest wine producers on the Wellington route. It has won several awards in recent years, for its Cabernet Sauvignon and Pinotage varieties amongst others.

Wellington ① *T021-873 1163, www.wellingtoncellar.co.za, sales and tasting: Mon-Fri 0800-1300, 1400-1700, cellar tours by appointment, close to the railway station.* This is another award-winning cellar; Chenin Blanc is their most important white cultivar, and the Pinotage is the most popular red. It's worth a visit to see some of the most advanced wine-making technology in the region.

◉ The Winelands listings

For Sleeping and Eating price codes and other relevant information, see pages 46-53.

◉ Sleeping

Strand and around *p158, map p156*
A Willowbrook Lodge, Morgenster Av, Somerset West, T021-851 3759, www.willowbrook.co.za. Homely country lodge set in a beautiful garden, 12 large, well-appointed rooms with a/c, TV, private patio, good restaurant offering gourmet food, beautician, swimming pool, pleasant setting on outskirts of Somerset West.
A Zandberg Guest House, 96 Winery Rd, just out of Somerset West towards Stellenbosch, T021-842 2945, www.zandberg.co.za. Guest-house on a working wine estate, with 11 luxury cottages set in immaculate gardens, some have fireplaces, all have private terraces and contemporary decor. Swimming pool, braai, fine restaurant, beauty treatments. Rates drop considerably in winter. Recommended.
B Die Ou Pastorie, 41 Lourens St, Somerset West, T021-850 1660, www.die-ou-pastorie.

com. Restored parsonage originally built in 1819. 16 luxurious rooms with comfortable, traditional furnishings, TV, some rooms in separate complex, mature Victorian gardens, swimming pool. Attached restaurant is popular and has won national awards for its food and wine list (see Eating, page 181).

Stellenbosch *p158, map p160*
The Winelands has a fine selection of accommodation, much of it in historic buildings furnished with antiques, but room rates are very high. However Stellenbosch has an excellent backpacker hostel, which enables budget travellers to explore this region on an overnight stay.

In town
A Dorpshuis & Spa, 22 Dorp St, T021-883 9881, www.proteahotels.com. A very smart Victorian townhouse with 27 a/c rooms, some of which are suites, all have TV, marble-clad bathrooms, heavy fabrics and dark furniture, private patios, antiques, large breakfasts with plenty of choice, neat

gardens, swimming pool. The spa is also open to day visitors.

A D'Ouwe Werf Country Inn, 30 Church St, T021-887 4608, www.ouwewerf.com. Converted Georgian house with 31 a/c rooms, all individually decorated with antique furnishings and polished floors. Off-street parking, good-sized pool, beauty salon and vine-shaded terrace where breakfast and lunch are served. **Café Cuba** has an excellent reputation (see Eating, page 183). Recommended as a treat.

A Eendracht, 161 Dorp St, T021-883 8843, www.eendracht-hotel.com. Housed in a reconstruction of what was one of Stelllen-bosch's oldest houses, this boutique hotel has 12 rooms with modern understated decor and luxuries like silk-filled duvets, a/c, DSTV, wireless internet, pool, bar, lounge. The small restaurant serves traditional South African dishes such as water-blommetjiebredie.

A Evergreen Manor & Spa, 29 van Riebeeck St, T021-886 6343, www.evergreenmanor. co.za. Stylishly converted corner house with 5 attractive a/c double rooms in the main building, and 4 in garden units, individually decorated, some with 4-poster beds, big sofas, antiques, free-standing baths, TV, lovely sunny courtyard. Close to botanical gardens and town centre. The spa offers a full range of treatments. Welcoming place to stay. Recommended.

B Fynbos Villa, 14 Neethling St, T021-883 8670, www.fynbosguesthouse.co.za. Converted family home with garden extension, with 14 a/c rooms, all with TV, en suite bathroom and kettle. 1 self-catering cottage sleeping up to 4. Large courtyard, pool, private parking, friendly, homely feel, though rather fussy decor in velvets and florals. Short walk to town centre. German spoken.

B Labri Manor, 71 Victoria St, T021-886 5652, www.labrimanor.co.za. 10 luxury rooms with beautiful decor, polished wooden floors, huge 4-poster beds, subtle yellow walls and dark wood antiques. Spacious Victorian-style bathrooms, TV lounge, spa room, cobbled courtyard, dinner and picnic baskets on request, extras include fresh flowers and a glass of port, a fine Victorian house. Recommended.

B Ryneveld Country Lodge, 67 Ryneveld St, T021-887 4469, www.ryneveldlodge.co.za. B&B in a smart Victorian house with 15 a/c rooms with TV and minibar, (some in more expensive cottages with additional kitchenettes suitable for families). Beautiful house full of antiques with breakfast room, shady terrace, small pool, secure parking.

B Stellenbosch Hotel, 162 Dorp St, T021-887 3644, www.stellenbosch.co.za/hotel. Central hotel with 27 a/c rooms and 2 apartments in a national monument building. Each room has TV, minibar and pleasant bathroom, although the decor could do with an update. Friendly bar popular with locals, bright dining room with tables on terrace overlooking the street, serving game and seafood (see Eating, page 181).

C Avenues Guest Lodge, 32 The Avenue, T021-887 1843, www.theavenues.co.za. 8 rooms, some non-smoking, wooden floors and bright, simple furnishings. The garden-facing room (No 5) is the nicest, with original fittings in the bathroom. TV lounge, small pool, secluded gardens (can be noisy from traffic), huge breakfasts served.

C Bonne Esperance, 17 Van Riebeeck St, T021-887 0225, www.bonneesperance.com. Appealingly rambling Victorian townhouse with wrap-around veranda, opposite the botanical gardens. 15 comfortable rooms with high ceilings and an English feel to the decor, DSTV, Wi-Fi, sunny and spacious breakfast room, lovely garden with plunge pool.

D-F Stumble Inn, 12 Market St, T021-887 4049, www.stumbleinnstellenbosch. hostel.com. Popular hostel in 2 separate Victorian bungalows. Spacious double rooms, cramped dorms and camping. Original house has attractive garden, bar, TV room, kitchen, hammocks, shady cushion banks; other house has small pool, kitchen. Very relaxed and friendly place. Excellent value **Easy Rider Wine Tours** (see page 185), bicycles to hire, remains by far the best budget option in town.

Out of town

L Lanzerac Manor, 2 km from town centre towards Jonkershoek Reserve, Jonkershoek Rd, T021-887 1132, www.lanzerac.co.za. Very expensive but fittingly luxurious hotel set around an 18th-century Cape Dutch manor house on a wine estate, tastings and cellar tours on offer. 48 suites, some around a patio and swimming pool, spacious and plush with all mod cons. 2 restaurants: the formal **Governor's Hall**, which is rather fussy with slow service; and the relaxed and more enjoyable **Lanzerac Terrace** for al fresco dining during summer. New addition is an extensive wellbeing centre and beauty spa with a separate pool overlooking the vines.

AL The Spier Hotel, Spier Wine Estate on the R44, T021-809 1100, www.spier.co.za. Probably the Winelands' most commercial wine estate, but a thoroughly enjoyable place to stay. Accommodation is in condo-style buildings set around courtyards with private pools for each section. The 155 rooms are enormous and very comfortable, with neutral, stylish decor, trendy polished concrete floors, huge beds, lots of windows, TV, minibar, beautiful bathrooms stocked with aroma-therapy products. 4 restaurants on site. See page 164 for details of the wines and all the activities on offer. Recommended if you only have a day in the Winelands and check the website for package specials.

AL Wedgeview Country House & Spa, The Bonniemile, 5 km south of town, T021-881 3525, www.wedgeview.co.za. Attractive thatched farmhouse with 11 garden thatched luxury suites and 1 family cottage with Wi-Fi and DSTV, main house has snooker room, bar, drawing room, breakfast room, all set in 1.5 ha of attractive gardens surrounded by vineyards, 2 swimming pools, jacuzzi and wellness and beauty spa. Light lunches and snacks available but dinner on request.

A L'Avenir Country Lodge, 5 km north of Stellenbosch off the R44 towards the N1 and Paarl, T021-889 5001, www.lavenir.co.za. A peaceful setting on a smart wine farm with 9 luxury bedrooms with contemporary

African decor, flat screen TVs, a/c, Wi-Fi, honeymoon suite has private heated splash pool. Price includes breakfast and wine tasting, meals arranged on request. Substantial discounts are available off season. Well-run, peaceful and elegant place to experience the Winelands. Recommended.

B Bellevue Manor, 5 km south of Stellenbosch on the R44, T021-880 1086, www.bellevuestellenbosch.co.za. Purpose-built a/c cottages in Cape Dutch style with thatched roofs, pleasant country-style furnishings, TV, fireplace, bathroom, honesty bar fridge, private terrace, good-sized pool with braai area, close to 2 golf courses. Rates drop in winter. Debi, the onsite therapist offers de-stress treatments such as reiki and reflexology.

Franschhoek *p165, map p165*

L Le Quartier Français, 16 Huguenot Rd (accessed from Wilhelmina St), T021-876 2151, www.lequartier.co.za. An elegant country house with 17 enormous en suite rooms all with fireplaces, beautiful bathrooms, plush furnishings and views over the gardens. Small central swimming pool and peaceful, shady courtyard. The attached restaurant (see Eating, page 182) is rated as one of the best in South Africa. A superb hotel with impeccable service, child-friendly. Recommended.

L Mont Rochelle, Dassenberg Rd, T021-876 2770, www.montrochelle.co.za. 24 luxury suites and rooms set in the main manor house or in garden units, elegantly decorated with enormous bathrooms, superb award-winning restaurant (see Eating, page 182) cigar bar, swimming pool, gym and sauna, attentive service, good mountain views and pleasant rolling gardens. Rates vary considerably depending on room and season.

AL La Cabrière, Middagkrans Rd, T021-876 4780, www.lacabriere.co.za. Small luxurious and stylish guesthouse set just outside town in formal lavender and herb gardens. 6 a/c rooms with Provençal decor, limed-wood furniture, grass matting floors and large stone en suite bathrooms, some rooms have fireplaces and views of vineyards and mountains, swimming pool. Within walking distance of restaurants.

A Ashbourne Guesthouse, 47 Huguenot Rd, T021-876 2146, www.ashbourne.co.za. Beautifully restored Victorian town house with sunny wooden deck around a swimming pool, 6 spacious double rooms with tiled floors, neutral decor, DSTV and a/c. Set on main road just a brief walk from the shops and restaurants. No children under 16.

A Auberge Chanteclair, 500 m behind the Huguenot Monument on Middagkrans Rd, T021-876 3685, www.chanteclair.co.za. 6 beautiful, spacious rooms with and old-fashioned decor and DSTV, in a Victorian farmhouse. Comfortable lounge, swimming pool, secluded gardens set among 30 ha of orchards and vineyards. Birdwatcher's should head for the farm's lake. A superior B&B with attentive service to match. Recommended.

A La Fontaine, 21 Dirkie Uys St, T021-876 2112, www.lafontainefranschhoek.co.za. One of the finest guesthouses in Franschhoek, with 12 rooms set in a Victorian house near the village centre, elegant decor with antiques and fine wooden floors, some rooms set in garden around pool with tasteful ethnic decor. Friendly, efficient and a beautiful place to stay. Highly recommended.

A Plumwood Inn, 11 Cabrière St, T021-876 3883, www.plumwoodinn.com. 7 individually styled rooms, each with private entrance, DSTV, Wi-Fi, country-style furniture and brightly painted walls, breakfast served in the well-kept garden by a small swimming pool, dinner available on Tue and Thu.

A-B Auberge Bligny, 28 Van Wijk St, T021-876 3767, www.bligny.co.za. A beautifully restored house dating from 1861, with 9 double rooms, including a special honey-moon suite which opens onto a shaded veranda, and 1 wheelchair-friendly room. TV, lounge with a small library and open fire in winter, neat gardens, swimming pool, friendly management, German spoken.

B Auberge La Dauphine, at La Dauphine Wine Estate off Excelsior Rd, T021-876 2606, www.ladauphine.co.za. One of the most peaceful locations in the valley, with 6 luxury a/c rooms each with a spacious lounge and patio in a carefully restored and converted wine store, surrounded by beautiful gardens and vineyards. There is a large swimming pool, guided tours of the farm available, plus mountain bike trails and horse riding in the nearby mountains.

B Protea Hotel Franschhoek, 34 Huguenot Rd, T021-876 3012, www.proteahotels.co.za. 8 spacious and good-value self-catering apartments set on the main road, each sleeping 2-3. A quality offering from the Protea Hotel group and in an excellent location right in the village centre, though there are more atmospheric places to stay. The 30 spacious rooms are individually decorated, have Wi-Fi, DSTV and a/c, and are arranged in a double storey block around the swimming pool, and there's a decent restaurant and bar.

B-C Bo La Motte, Middagkrans Rd, T021-876 3067, www.bolamotte.co.za. A good and affordable family option with 4 fully equipped self catering cottages sleeping 2-4 with fireplaces, braais, TV, DVD, shared pool, great views of the mountains. English-run. Peaceful spot on a working wine farm just outside the village. Fly-fishing available on the farm's dams. Can also provide baby-sitters if parents want to eat out.

B-C Le Ballon Rouge, 7 Reservoir St, T021-876 2651, www.ballon-rouge.co.za. 8 double rooms set in a converted Victorian bungalow with wrap-around shady veranda offering private entrances to the rooms, which are small but nicely and individually decorated, swimming pool, no children under 12. The large loft room is the best and has a Victorian bath.

B-C Résidence Klein Oliphants Hoek, 14 Akademie St, T021-876 2566, www.klein oliphantshoek.com. A very fine guesthouse close to the centre of Franschhoek which was built originally as a missionary hall in 1888, with 6 comfortable and old-fashioned a/c double rooms with TV (M-Net), some have their own plunge pools. The vast, high-ceilinged lounge, once the original meeting hall, is filled with antiques, big sofas and has a fireplace. Good-sized pool, small restaurant and cigar bar. Recommended.

C-E Otter's Bend, Dassenberg Rd, T021-876 3200, www.ottersbendlodge.co.za. Budget accommodation in 5 small en suite log cabins, 1 flat sleeping 4 or camping on the lawns in a lovely wooded spot around a swimming pool. Communal fully equipped kitchen with fireplace and braai and a unique table fashioned out of a giant wine barrel. Breakfast extra.

Out of town

AL Franschhoek Country House, a few kilometres to the west of town on the Paarl road, T021-876 3386, www.fch.co.za. Very elegant boutique hotel with 14 rooms and 12 suites, some with fireplace, underfloor heating, private verandas, the new suites are 100 sq m and very luxurious, French-style furniture, dramatic drapes and candelabra, 2 swimming pools, spa treatment room, lovely fountains in the grounds, excellent restaurant.

C Lekkerwijn, 10 mins' drive from the centre of Franschhoek, heading towards Paarl, just before the junction with the R310 to Stellenbosch, T021-874 1122, www.lekkerwijn.com. A fine B&B in an old Cape Dutch homestead close to Boschendal wine estate, in fine park-like gardens with peacocks and guinea fowl. 3 double rooms and 1 single, plus a cottage suitable for a family of 4. The bedroom wing was designed by Herbert Baker and is arranged around a private pillared courtyard, tastefully furnished lounge and swimming pool.

Paarl Winelands *p169, maps p170 and p172*
L Grande Roche, Plantasie St, T021-863 5100, www.granderoche.co.za. An 18th-century manor which has established itself as one of the top hotels in South Africa. The 34 luxury a/c suites, non-smoking rooms, are set in a collection of restored farm buildings that stand in peaceful gardens, surrounded by vineyards, 2 floodlit tennis courts, 2 swimming

pools, gym. **Bosman's** restaurant is regarded as one of the best in the country (see Eating, page 183). Will collect from Cape Town airport.

A Pontac Manor Hotel, 16 Zion St, T021-872 0445, www.pontac.com. Elegant fully restored Victorian manor house with manicured gardens full of oak trees that are home to an army of squirrels. 22 spacious individually decorated rooms (one is wheelchair accessible), TV and a/c, a mix of African and antique decor, the 5 rooms in the pool annexe also have microwave and fridge and there's a 5-bed cottage with kitchenette. Smart bar, lounges with fat armchairs and very good restaurant (see Eating, page 183).

B De Oude Paarl, 132 Main St, T021-872 1002, www.deoudepaarl.com. Swanky hotel in a set of national monument buildings dating back to 1700 on the main road, with 26 a/c individually designed rooms, with a nod at 'boutique' hotel style, a swimming pool, 2 excellent restaurants (see Eating, page 183), and friendly, efficient service.

B Lemoenkloof Guest House, 396a Main St, T021-872 3782, www.lemoenkloof.co.za. Luxurious converted country house on northern edge of town, with 20 a/c rooms and a family unit grouped in several buildings set around gardens and palm-shaded pool. Each room has TV, minibar, floral fabrics, fresh flowers in vases, black-and-white tiled bathrooms, separate entrance. Large breakfasts, evening meals on request for big groups, friendly owners. Recommended.

C Eben-Haëzer Country House, Sonstraal Rd, T021-862 7420, www.eben-haezer.co.za. Original Cape Dutch homestead, 7 large and very comfortable double rooms, individually decorated with antiques and with Victorian-style bathrooms, 1 self-catering cottage, swimming pool, breakfast served under oak trees in the tea garden or in the 18th-century dining room, beautiful whitewashed chapel for weddings. Friendly management, also offers fishing in the dam.

C Nantes-Vue, 56 Mill St, T021-872 7311, www.nantes-paarl.co.za. Elegant B&B set in a Victorian house in the centre of town, with 5 double rooms and 1-bedroom cottage in garden, all with high ceilings and TV, understated decor, iron bedheads, enormous showers and free-standing baths. Breakfast room has country farm feel to it and there's a splash pool. Good value. Recommended.

C Oak Tree Lodge, 32 Main St, T021-863 2631, www.oaktreelodge.co.za. 18 modern rooms with TV, set in a large family home, underfloor heating, children well catered for, rather twee decorations, sunny breakfast room, garden, large pool, secure parking, central location.

C Zomerlust, 193 Main St, T021-872 2117, www.zomerlust.co.za. 14 rooms in a restored historic country house in the centre of town. All rooms are en suite, with TV, fireplace and decked out in antiques. Some rooms are in converted stables. Courtyard, terrace, swimming pool, library and cellar pub. Check for winter discounts. Recommended.

Out of town

L-AL Palmiet Valley Estate, 1 km north of junction 62 on the N1, T021-862 7741, www.palmiet.co.za. A restored 1642 historic Cape Dutch homestead located on a wine estate to the east of the town centre, surrounded by vines and giant oak trees, with 10 spacious doubles and 1 honeymoon suite with TV, CD player, each decorated with antiques, private balconies or terraces, neat garden, swimming pool, very good food served in the dining room or terrace. Popular wedding venue.

AL Roggeland Country House, Roggeland Rd, Dal Josafat, 7km northeast of Paarl, follow the signs off the R303, T021-868 2501, www.roggeland.co.za. A fine Cape Dutch farmhouse (declared a national monument) with 10 spacious luxury rooms, large en suite bathrooms, Cape-style furnishings, mature gardens, swimming pool. Highlight of a stay here is the excellent cuisine: lodging prices include 4-course dinner, bed and breakfast.

C Amberg Guest Farm, Klein Drakenstein, T021-862 0982, www.amberg.co.za. Good budget option on farm, spectacular setting.

5 self-catering cottages sleeping 2-6 with a/c and TV, gardens, pool, braai facilities, friendly Swiss owners (German and French spoken).

D-E Berg River Resort, 5 km out of town towards Franschhoek (R45), south side of the N1, T021-863 1650, www.bergriver resort.co.za. Self-catering chalets of varying comfort sleeping 2-6, caravan and camping space available (first-come, first-served basis), hot water, electric points, swimming pool, mini-golf, kiosk for snacks and drinks, nice spot next to the river and ideal for families.

Wellington district *p174, map p174*

A 5 Mountains Lodge, east of town on the R301 towards Bain's Kloof, T021-864 3409, www.exclusiveescapes.com/5mountains. Mix of luxurious garden cottages and suites in original homestead, stylish bedrooms with 4-poster beds, private deck with beautiful views, breakfast served by the pool or in an attractive dining room, meals on request. Very friendly, family-run, excellent choice for a relaxing night. Recommended.

B Augusta Kleinbosch Guest Farm, south of the town off the R303 (close to Paarl), T021-868 2481, www.kleinbosch.de. German-run guesthouse in a fine Cape Dutch home-stead and converted Afrikaans school set among orchards on a working wine and guava farm. 9 spacious and elegant rooms, with mini-fridges, CD players, 4-poster beds, some with TV. An à la carte restaurant, swimming pool, walks around the vine-yards possible.

B Diemersfontein Wine and Country Estate, Van Riebeck Drive, off the R303, T021-864 5050, www.diemersfontein.co.za. A classic luxury country house set in beautifully tended gardens on a wine estate, with 17 rooms, either in the main house or in garden annexe, traditional, plush furnishings, elegant teak-panelled lounge, grand veranda, swimming pool, very good restaurant, beauty spa and horse riding. Wine tasting daily 1000-1700.

C Klein Rhebokskloof, 4 km out of town, off Berg St, T021-873 4115, www.wine-estate-hildenbrand.co.za. Old country guesthouse

set on an olive and wine farm, with 4 double rooms, simple and comfortable with TV, ceiling fans, private terrace, plus 2 self-catering apartments, shared lounge, swimming pool with sun deck and beautiful garden, children will enjoy the farm animals.
D Soete Huys, 1 Stadsig, T021-864 3442, www.soetehuys.com. Beautiful converted family house, 4 en suite double rooms, and 2 4-bed family units, pleasant furnishings with wrought-iron beds, terracotta-tiled floors, good breakfasts served, garden and pool, quiet location on the outskirts of town.

❶ Eating

Strand and around *p158, map p156*
🍴 **96 Winery Road**, Zandberg Wine Estate, 96 Winery Rd, just out of Somerset West on the Stellenbosch road, T021-842 2020, www.zandberg.co.za, www.96winery road.co.za. 1200-1500, 1900-late, Sun closed in the evening. An excellent award-winning restaurant in an informal farmhouse setting. Very good grills, and some fish such as Norwegian salmon, and specials like guinea fowl or duck and cherry pie. Also has luxury overnight cottages on the estate (see Sleeping, page 175). Recommended.
🍴 **Die Ou Pastorie**, 41 Lourens St, Somerset West, T021-852 2120, www.dieoupastorie. com. Tue-Sat 1200-1400, Mon-Sat 1900-2130. French restaurant set in a luxury lodge in a gracious Victorian parsonage. Changing menu of traditional French cuisine, also has good vegetarian options and makes good use of game. Silver service, award-winning wine list. Booking advised.

Stellenbosch *p158, map p160*
As well as the restaurants in town, most of the wine estates on the Stellenbosch wine route also have restaurants that are especially nice for lazy lunches in a picturesque setting. Recommended for the overseas visitor are the restaurants at **Spier Estate**, which are a very special dining experience. You may

even want to consider making a reservation before your arrival in South Africa.
🍴 **Jan Cats**, 162 Dorp St, T021-887 3644. Open 0700-2200. Part of the **Stellenbosch Hotel** and well known for its game dishes. Just about everything from the African bush is served up, from crocodile kebabs to kudu steaks. Also has specials like ostrich cottage pie or warthog ribs, plus some seafood including excellent fresh crayfish. Cheaper pub lunches available.
🍴 **Jonkershuis**, **Spier Estate**, on the R44, T021-809 1159. Open 1230-1530, 1830-2230. Atmospheric Cape Malay restaurant set in restored farmhouse decorated with fine antiques, outside tables in the shade of oak trees, spicy bredies, curries, seafood, home-made breads and soups, baked puddings and biscuits, huge variety of food buffet style – a good opportunity to try all of South Africa's unique recipes. Recommended but book well in advance.
🍴 **Moyo**, **Spier Estate**, on the R44, T021-809 1133, www.moyo.co.za. 1200-1600, 1800-2300. Consistently fully booked so make a reservation at least a week ahead. Superb restaurant in a beautiful location and a highlight of a trip to South Africa. Arranged in Bedouin tents with outside tables in delightful tree houses or wrought-iron gazebos lit by candles. The vast buffet has just about everything imaginable from hot mussels to fine cheese and pan-African food. As well as wine and food, each table is entertained by women who decorate your face with traditional Xhosa white paint, Zimbabwean musicians, jazz bands and township opera singers. Allow extra time to browse in the superb souvenir shop. Touristy yes, but the atmosphere is unbeatable. A magical experience and highly recommended. Other branches in Johannesburg and Durban.
🍴 **Volkskombuis**, Aan de Wagen Rd, T021-887 2121, www.volkskombuis.co.za. 1200-1430, 1830-2130, closed Sun during winter. High standards of food and service, with a focus on traditional Cape cooking. Try the home-made oxtail or springbok pies.

Housed in a characterful building – a restored Herbert Baker Cape Dutch homestead, with views across the Eerste River. A sensibly priced treat.

Brazen Head, 62 Andringa St, T021-882 9672. Open 1100-late. Friendly, informal Irish-themed pub and restaurant with beer garden, Guinness and Kilkenny on tap, Irish whiskies, long varied menu including a 1-kg steak, seafood platter and traditional Irish stew, children's menu and a roast at Sun lunch.

The Coachman, Ryneveld St next to the Village Museum, T021-883 2230. Open 1200-2400. Cobbled courtyard with a beer garden feel, serving light meals and Cape specialities such as bobotie, springbok stew and lamb chops. Convenient location but can get very busy with tour groups.

Dros, corner of Bird and Alexander streets, T021-886 4856, www.dros.co.za. 0800-2200. A large bar-cum-restaurant with outdoor seating in a lively square. Popular chain serving standard pub fare such as burgers, steaks, ribs, pizza. Good value, but portions are on the small side.

Fishmonger, corner of Plein and Ryneveld streets, T021-887 7835, www.fishmonger. co.za. 1200-2200. Portuguese-style seafood restaurant serving a great choice of fresh Cape seafood – kingklip, calamari, tiger prawns, oysters and the like – including taster platters for those who can't decide. Also has a sushi chef, and a choice of vegetarian dishes. Good service, booking essential. Recommended.

Wijnhuis, Andringa St, T021-887 5844, www.wijnhuis.co.za. 0800-late. Bustling wine bar and wine shop, pretty outside eating in a courtyard, menu offers of steak, some seafood, and venison, delicately presented, and over 20 wines available by the glass.

Blue Orange, 77-79 Dorp St, T021-887 2052. Mon-Sat 0700-1800, Sun 0830-1700. Delicious range of breakfasts, good-value snacks and sandwiches plus light lunches such as quiche and pasta. Interesting mix of students, well-coiffed locals and back-packers. Also has an attached deli selling local produce such as jams, bread, fruit and veg.

Café Nouveau, corner of Plein and Ryneveld streets, T021-887 5627. Open 0700-1700. Lovely old-fashioned café with gilt mirrors and tightly packed tables serving sandwiches, light meals, coffee and cakes throughout the day.

Franschhoek p165, map p165

Franschhoek is dubbed 'gourmet capital of South Africa', and for good reason. There are some superb restaurants here. Booking ahead, especially at the weekends, is advised.

Mon Plaisir, 1 Uitkyk St, T021-876 2393, www.montplaisir.co.za. Tue-Sat 1200-1430, 1900-2100. Highly rated upmarket country-style restaurant set on a wine estate (see page 168) with great views and a warming fire inside in winter. Ideal for a long lazy lunch with a fine selection of South African and French dishes, so expect the likes of frogs legs, foie gras and snails, and it's well known for its whole roasted duck with potatoes to share.

Ici at Le Quartier Français, 16 Huguenot Rd, T021-876 2151, www.lequartier.co.za. 0730-1030, 1200-1530, 1800-late. Rated as one of the best restaurants in the Western Cape with a chef trained in New York. French and South African dishes, best known for their lamb burgers and slow-roasted pork with sage mash, plus seared tuna and salmon. Nice decor with bright orange walls, expensive but a place for a treat.

La Petite Ferme, on Franschhoek Pass Rd, T021-876 3016, www.lapetiteferme.co.za. Daily for lunch 1200-1600. Spectacular views over the Franschhoek Valley from this smart 'boutique' winery. The restaurant is well known for its wholesome country fare as well as delicate fusion dishes like gourmet pork and fig burgers with beetroot chutney, or hearty braised rabbit with parsnips. Good desserts and wine list, too.

Mange Tout, Dassenberg Rd, T021-876 2770, www.montrochelle.co.za. 1200-1500, 1900-2130. Small, formal restaurant based at the ultra-smart **Mont Rochelle Hotel** and wine estate. Perfect setting overlooking the vineyards, excellent gourmet menu with separate vegetarian section, light lunches are proving popular, also arranges picnics and offers 5-course dinners, long wine list. A pianist plays a white baby grand piano.

¶¶¶ Monneaux, Franschhoek Country House, Main Rd, T021-876 3386, www.fch.co.za. 0800-1000, 1200-1430, 1900-2100. Highly rated restaurant serving contemporary fusion cuisine, more up-to-date than many restaurants in Franschhoek, attractive outdoor terrace and cosy dining room. Lots of game and fish with strong spicing; to whet your appetite consider confit of guinea fowl and beef in vanilla bean béarnaise or smoked duck breast with watermelon and feta salad. Good local wine list.

¶¶¶-¶¶ Le Bon Vivant, 22 Dirkie Uys St, T021-876 2717, www.lebonvivant.co.za. Thu-Tue 1200-1500, 1830-2100. Small garden restaurant with tables set in dappled shade, serving delicious light lunches (don't miss the local smoked trout sandwich) and a 5-course dinner which is paired with wine and has had excellent reports. Recommended.

¶¶ The French Connection Bistro, 48 Huguenot Rd, T021-8764056, www.french connection.co.za. 1200-1530, 1830-2145. French bistro serving refreshingly unfussy food such as steamed mussels, steak-frites or Toulouse sausages and mash. Good food at sensible prices and generous portions. Pleasant bustling atmosphere and you can watch the chef at work in the kitchen behind glass.

¶¶ The Grapevine, Huguenot Rd, T021-876 2520. Open 0800-2100, closed Sun evening. Family restaurant serving big breakfasts, light lunches (try the tasty butternut soup) and steaks and pizzas in the evening. Also some good Cape Malay dishes like the ever-popular bobotie, and warming hot chocolate with a shot of brandy in it.

¶¶ La Fromagerie at La Grange, 13 Daniel Hugo St, T021-876 3420, www.lagrange.co.za. Daily for lunch 1200-1600. Excellent deli specializing in cheese with 40 varieties for sale, set up in a 200-year-old barn, salads and quiches, soups and all things cheesy such as soufflé and pasta, recommended is the Camembert with caramelized pears.

Paarl Winelands *p169, maps p170 and p172*
¶¶¶ Bosman's, Grande Roche Hotel, Plantasie St, T021-863 2727, www.granderoche.co.za. Aug-May 0700-1030, 1200-1400, 1900-2100. Award-winning international cuisine of the highest standard in a grand vineyard-fringed setting. Popular 3-course set lunch, but the real treat is the celebrated 5-course 'Flavours of the Cape' menu (R620), offering superbly created examples of Cape cuisine. Good choice of vegetarian dishes, award-winning wine list. Regarded as one of the finest restaurants in South Africa and it is Africa's only Relais Gourmands (Relais & Chateax) establishment.

¶¶¶ Laborie, Taillefer St, T021-807 3095, www.laborierestaurant.co.za. Daily 1000-1700, Wed-Sun 1830-2200. Closed in Jul. Gourmet restaurant on wine estate with pleasant seating under giant oak trees. Delicious Cape and Mediterranean dishes, lots of contemporary choices such as lamb cutlets with wasabi mash, as well as Cape specialities like bobotie and some vegetarian options. Smart but relaxed atmosphere, good service. Recommended.

¶¶¶ Pontac, Pontac Manor Hotel, 16 Zion St, T021-872 0445, www.pontac.com. 1200-1400, 1900-2200. Informal and friendly restaurant in a cosy setting in a 17th-century manor house, serving traditional and beautifully presented dishes (lots of game), weekly specials and imaginative vegetarian options, everything on the menu is available in full or half portions. Good service.

¶¶ Café Cuba, De Oude Paarl Hotel, see Sleeping, page 179. Mon-Sat, 1200-2300. Fashionable, moodily lit restaurant, light lunches served in the courtyard, or informal suppers indoors in the Cuban decorated interior. The menu offers small tapas-sized dishes, which are ideal to share of chicken or beef skewers, chorizo sausage, prawns and calamari. Short but good wine list. The hotel also has the **Butcher's Steakhouse (¶¶)**, for all things meaty and a good line of desserts.

¶¶ Dros, Main Rd, T021-863 0350. Open 0900-late. Outlet of pub-style chain serving steaks, ribs and pasta dishes in a cellar atmosphere. Also has a good choice of beers at the bar.

♦♦ **Victorian Restaurant and Terrace**, Rhebokskloof Estate, T021-869 8606, www.rhebokskloof.co.za. Daily 0800-1700, also open for dinner Sep-May, Thu-Mon. Wonderful views from the terrace over farmland and giant oaks, where light lunches are served. The club sandwiches and salads are good, as is the Sun starter buffet. Old-fashioned interior is the setting for a heavier international evening menu.

♦♦ **Wilderer's**, Wilderer's distillery, 3 km outside Paarl on R45, T021-863 3555, www.wilderer.co.za. Tue-Sun 1100-1700. Relaxed lunchtime French restaurant in a schnapps distillery, speciality is *lammkuchen*, a type of pizza from Strasbourg. Finish off with a shot of their pear or fynbos schnapps. Live jazz on the 1st Sun of the month.

♦♦-♦ **The Goatshed**, Fairview, T021-863 3609, www.fairview.co.za. 0900-1700. A fairly new offering at this popular wine and cheese farm, which can sometimes be overrun with tour groups but don't let that put you off as the food is excellent and there's a pretty terrace. Cheese platters with freshly baked bread are the highlight, but the mains of duck, lamb, veal and trout will appeal to the hungrier. Naturally the baked cheesecake is superb.

♦ **De Malle Madonna**, 127 Main Rd, T021-863 3925. Tue-Sun 0830-1730. Cool and kooky café serving creamy quiches, huge sandwiches, burgers and wraps, plus towering cakes and muffins in the afternoon. Refreshingly modern.

Wellington district *p174, map p174*
♦♦ **Oude Wellington**, R303, Bain's Kloof Pass, 5 km south of town, T021-873 1008, www.kapwein.com. 1200-late. Lovely spot in an old whitewashed farmstead with 2 fireplaces, outside seating in the grounds with dogs, peacocks and ostriches roaming around, good country-style cooking, home-made bread, pasta and ice cream, also a wine estate.

♦ **D'Olives Restaurant and Tea Garden**, 41 Church St, T021-864 3762. Mon-Sat 0800-2200, Sun 0900-1500. Pleasant restaurant with cool terracotta-tiled floor and wrought-iron furniture, short but good menu of salads, pasta, grills and fish, best known for their waffles and pancakes.

♦ **Perfect Place**, 66 Church St, T021-873 6620. Mon-Fri 0800-1700, Sat 0800-1500. Charming old-world coffee shop in a Victorian house with corrugated-tin roof and decorated with lace, sweet and savoury stuffed pancakes, try the pear, nuts and caramel one, also serves wine and sells antiques.

● Bars and clubs

Stellenbosch *p158, map p160*
Bohemia Pub, corner of Andringa and Victoria streets, T021-882 8375, www.bohemia.co.za. 1000-late. One of the main student haunts with an eccentric brightly coloured interior and attractive wrap-around veranda. This popular bar gets very busy with a young clientele who come for the cold beers, relaxed atmosphere and occasional live music.

Dros, see Eating, page 182. Open 0800-2400. The restaurant turns into a noisy bar later at night. Tables spill out onto the square and get crowded with backpackers and students.

Fandango, Shop 11, Drostdy Centre, T021-887 7506, www.fandango.co.za. 0900-0100. Café and bar offering internet access with tables outside on the square, popular for after-work cocktails, occasional live music. Also rents out bicycles.

● Entertainment

Stellenbosch *p158, map p160*
Theatre
Dorp Street Theatre, T021-886 6107, www.dorpstraat.co.za. Local productions, plays in Afrikaans, and jazz on Sun.
Endler Hall, at the university, T021-808 2340, www.sun.ac.za/music. Classical music concerts and university productions.

Oude Libertas Amphitheatre, on a wine estate just west of the centre off the R306, T021-808 7473, www.oudelibertas.co.za. Outdoor events from Nov-Mar, and there's a farmers market here every Sat morning.
Spier Amphitheatre, T021-809 1100, www.spier.co.za. Open-air summer concerts, jazz events, plays and comedy on the wine estate. The amphitheatre here is a great venue.

⊛ Festivals and events

Stellenbosch *p158, map p160*
Aug The Stellenbosch Wine Festival, www.wineroute.co.za, in the first week of Aug. An annual event to promote local award-winning wines along with traditional rural cuisine, music and arts.

O Shopping

Stellenbosch *p158, map p160*
Oom Samie se Winkel (Uncle Sammy's Shop), 84 Dorp St, T021-887 0797, Mon-Fri 0830-1730, Sat-Sun 0900-1700. Has been trading since 1791. The first owner, Pieter Gerhard Wium, traded in meat, but the shop became famous between 1904 and 1944 when the store was owned and run by Samuel Johannes Volsteedt. He stocked virtually everything you could need, and was known throughout the town. Today the shop still sells a wide range of goods and it has retained its pre-war character with items hanging from all corners, and old cabinets full of bits and pieces. It has all the makings of a tourist trap, but unlike many others it is genuine.

Franschhoek *p165, map p165*
Bordeaux Street Gallery, Huguenot Rd, T021-876 2165, bordeauxgallery@saol.com. Series of rooms on 2 storeys selling local arts and crafts, including antique furniture, Massai jewellery, woven baskets, fabrics and batiks.

▲ Activities and tours

Stellenbosch *p158, map p160*
Bicycle hire
Adventure Centre, 36 Market St, next to the tourist office, T021-882 8112, www.adventure shop.co.za. R30 per hr or R120 per day and they'll drop off bikes at hotels or you can arrange to pick them up at the office.
Fandango, see Bars and clubs, page 184. This bar also rents out bicycles.
Stumble Inn, 12 Mark St, T021-887 4049, www.stumbleinnstellenbosch.hostel.com. Good advice and bike hire.

Horse riding
Spier Horse Trails, Spier wine estate on the R130, T021-881 3683. Expect to pay R160 per hr. The horses are well trained and can take complete novices. Pony rides for children and carriage rides for non-riders are also on offer.

Wine tours
As well as those listed below, many Cape Town tour operators organize day trips to the Winelands, see page 129.
Easy Rider Wine Tours, T021-886 4651, www.stumbleinnstellenbosch.hostel.com. Hugely popular day-long wine tour organized by **Stumble Inn** (see Sleeping, page 175). Good-value tours take in 5 estates, with several tastings in each, and include lunch in a farm restaurant and cheese tasting. Remember they are aimed at backpackers so things can get a little messy towards the end of the day.
Vine Hopper, T021-882 8112, www.vine hopper.co.za, or book through the Adventure Centre (above). A useful hop-on, hop-off bus that tours between some estates and the tourist office in town, costing R160 per person. There are 2 routes – 1 to the north and 1 to the south – of town and 6 estates on each are visited.

Franschhoek *p165, map p165*
Bicycle hire
Manic Cycles, La Gare Centre, Huguenot St, T021-876 4956, www.maniccycles.co.za.

A range of bikes for hire for self tours of the village and wine farms including mountain bikes, hybrids, a tandem, children's bikes and bikes with baby seats.

Horse riding
Paradise Stables, outside the village on the Robertsvlei Rd, T021-876 2160, www.paradise stables.co.za. Guided trails through the vineyards with stops at 2 estates for wine tasting for R450 (including tastings) or hourly rides for R150. Beginners welcome, children over 12.

Tour operators
Winelands Experience, T021-876 4042, www.winelands-experience.com. Daily scheduled food and wine tours.

Paarl Winelands *p169, map p170*
Bicycle hire
Bike Point, T021-863 3901, www.bike point.org. Organizes fun rides in the region, as well as renting out bikes and providing route maps.

Tour operators
Vintage Cape Tours, T082-656 3994, www.vintagecape.co.za. Specialist wine tours, historical walking tours and hiking. More suited to the older client.

⊖ Transport

Strand and around *p158*
Somerset West is 50 km from central Cape Town and 31 km from Cape Town International Airport along the N2. The only public transport at the moment is the Metrorail, though this is not advised for visitors as it runs through the townships on this route and petty theft is a problem. The Integrated Rapid Transport (IRT) will run as far as the airport from Cape Town and may well be extended to Strand and Somerset West in the future.

Stellenbosch *p158, map p160*
Taxi Let's Go Taxis, T021-852 5835.

Paarl Winelands *p169, maps p170 and p172*
Taxi Paarl Radio Taxis, T021-872 5671.

Train The **Cape Town–Johannesburg** service stops in Paarl on Sun, Mon, Wed, Fri. Departs Paarl 1125 for **Cape Town** (75 mins), and departs Cape Town at 1230. See www. spoornet.co.za for timetables. Huguenot station is across the river from Lady Grey St.

Wellington district *p174, map p174*
Car 72 km to **Cape Town**, 131 km to **Saldanha**, 49 km to **Stellenbosch**. To return to **Cape Town** take the R44 around Paarl Mountain, and turn right after 20 km onto the N1. The R45 to Malmesbury continues west towards Saldanha Bay and the Atlantic. Alternatively, travel north on the R44 to Porterville and join with the N7 before it starts to climb Grey's Pass. From the top of the pass you descend into the Olifants River Valley.

Train The service between **Cape Town** and **Johannesburg** stops in Wellington on Sun, Mon, Wed and Fri. Departs Wellington 1110 for **Cape Town** (90 mins), departs Cape Town 1230. See www.spoornet.co.za for timetables.

❶ Directory

Stellenbosch *p158, map p160*
Banks The main South African banks are here, all with ATMs. The following **Bureaux de Change** are open Mon-Fri 0830-1700, Sat 0900-1200: **Rennies Foreign Exchange** (local representatives of Thomas Cook), Mill St, T021-8865259; **American Express**, 4 Plein St, T021-8870818. **Internet** Fandango, Shop 11, Drostdy Centre, T021-887 7506, www.fand ango.co.za, 0900-0100, café and bar offering internet access; you can also check your email at the **tourist office** on Market St and at hotels. **Medical services** 24-hr private Medi-Clinic, corner Saffraan and Rokewood avenues, T021-883 8571, www.stellenboschmc.co.za. **Post office** Main post office, Plein St.

Contents

Western Cape

At a glance

🚌 **Getting around** Buses on major routes, car hire.

🕐 **Time required** At least 1 week for major sites.

☼ **Weather** Chilly in Jul and Aug. Best in Nov and Feb.

✕ **When not to go** The Karoo gets very cold in winter, Jun-Aug.

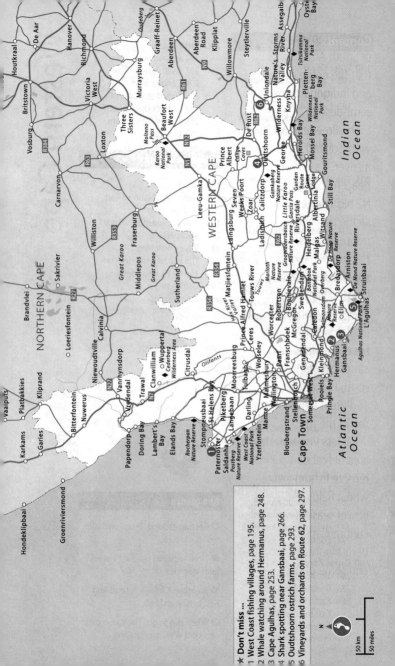

★ Don't miss ...

1 West Coast fishing villages, page 195.
2 Whale watching around Hermanus, page 248.
3 Cape Agulhas, page 253.
4 Shark spotting near Gansbaai, page 266.
5 Oudtshoorn ostrich farms, page 293.
6 Vineyards and orchards on Route 62, page 297.

50 km
50 miles

N

The Western Cape is arguably the most beautiful and varied of South Africa's nine provinces. It has just about everything that the entire country can offer, from endless beaches and indigenous forests to historic wine estates and scorched semi-desert.

The Breede River Valley is best known for its farming, with isolated settlements tucked away along the banks of its river. It's dotted with vineyards and fruit orchards and the peaceful country roads make a pleasant alternative to the N2 highway en route to the famed Garden Route. Further east lie the parched plains of the Karoo, their shimmering horizons peppered with craggy mountains and lonely farmsteads. Hemmed in by impressive mountain ranges crossed by spectacular mountain passes, the Little Karoo offers hiking, the popular Cango Caves and, of course, ostriches, who peer over every fence around Oudtshoorn. The southern coast begins with Walker Bay, which claims to have the best land-based whale watching in the world; in season, sightings are almost guaranteed from the clifftops in Hermanus. Further south the waters around Gansbaai are home to seals, penguins and great white sharks, while the lighthouse at Cape Agulhas marks the most southerly point of Africa.

Far less visited is the west coast, north of Cape Town: a wild area of fynbos-covered sand dunes, sun-bleached beaches and remote fishing villages. Inland, the undulating landscape of wheat fields and low grassy hills are tinged with colour during flower season, while the higher mountains attract snow (and curious Capetonians) during winter. Further north the Cederberg Mountains are a rugged range with ancient San rock art and some of the best hiking in the country.

West Coast

The West Coast is vastly different from the more-visited Garden Route – a wild, bleak stretch lashed by the icy Atlantic and backed by rolling dunes covered in coastal fynbos; it's far removed from the lush green landscape full of rivers and waterfalls found in the south. It has now become a standard fixture for tourists, who are attracted by both the sun-bleached coast and the spectacular flowers that blanket the area in spring. The cold Benguella of the Atlantic also brings with it some of the most nutrient-rich waters found on the planet. This fertile sea supports an enormous wealth of marine life; the fishing is superb and the coast is famous for its excellent seafood. Inland lies a fertile farming region, the Swartland, known for its grain and wine. Further north, the N7 highway passes along the magnificent Cederberg, a wilderness area with some of the best hiking in South Africa. ▶▶ *For listings, see pages 198-203.*

Ins and outs

Getting there Driving out of Cape Town, follow the N1 through Durbanville and the northern suburbs for the West Coast. If time is not an issue, turn off the N1 at the Maitland junction, signposted Milnerton M5, and follow the signs for the R27. This is the old coast road which runs all the way north to Velddrif, north of the West Coast National Park. If you are pressed for time, take a left at Acacia Park and follow signs for the N7. This is the main highway from Cape Town to Namibia, which runs up the west coast through the Northern Cape Province.

Tourist information For information on the West Coast, visit www.capewestcoast.org.

Best time to visit While the sea may be too cold for swimming, the region's climate is very favourable. As you travel north from Cape Town the summer temperatures are higher, and the rainfall is less. The air is dry and, even in winter, providing the winds aren't blowing, it can be very warm. Most of the rain falls between June and September. Whales start arriving along the West Coast around May and the mating pairs and family pods remain until December.

Cape Town to Vanrhynsdorp via the coast ●🕐 ▶▶ *pp198-203.*

Darling → *Colour map 8, A1.*

Less than an hour's drive north of Cape town, the first settlement of note is Darling, a small, thriving town, named after a Lieutenant Governor of the Cape, Sir Charles Henry Darling. It's the sort of town where it's not unusual to see a gaggle of geese waddling down the streets. Reflecting the prosperity of the surrounding area, it is in typical **Swartland** country, surrounded by vast expanses of wheat fields and lush irrigated pastures for dairy herds. Few visitors will spend much time here, except during the spring months of August and September, when the wild flowers on the veld are blooming – a **Wild Flower Show** has been held here during the third weekend of September since 1917. The most common flowers found in the area include daisies, nemesias, vygies and lilies. There are four vineyards in the Darling region which are all open for tastings and sales. The **tourist information office** ① *in the museum on Pastorie St, T022-492 3361, www.darlingtourism.co.za, www.tourismdarling.co.za, Mon-Fri 0900-1300, 1400-1600, Sat-Sun 1000-1300, 1400-1600,* is a good source of local information especially when the wild flowers are in bloom. The **museum** has a typical small-town collection devoted to depicting the region's history. The slightly unusual display traces the history of the butter industry in Darling. Staff at the museum will direct you to local farms which are open for viewing wild flowers during spring.

More recently, Darling has become well known as the home of Evita Bezuidenhout, a sort of Afrikaans Dame Edna created by comedian Pieter Dirk-Uys. Evita is something of a South African gay institution, and hosts lively cabaret shows at her **Evita se Perron** café-theatre in the tiny old railway station (see Eating, page 201). This is also worth visiting during the day as it's home to a number of good craft shops and stalls and the decor in and out of the railway station is quite eclectic.

At Kraalbosdam farm, 6 km to the north, stands the **Hildebrand Memorial**. This commemorates the southernmost confrontation of the Anglo-Boer War (1899-1902). There is a memorial and the gravestone of Hildebrand, a Boer Commando who was killed here. The local farm, Oudepost, is famous for its orchid nursery, the largest in South Africa. These amazing blooms are available locally, but the majority are for the export market.

Yzerfontein → *Colour map 8, A1.*
Driving north from Cape Town (85 km) on the R27, Yzerfontein is the first settlement of any size along the West Coast, still with distant views of Table Mountain in clear weather. It is named after a local spring rising from an ironstone formation. The village sits on the edge of an exposed rocky headland which in turn forms a sheltered bay. The harbour has a slipway suitable for the launching of small fishing boats, popular for the abundant shoaling snoek found off the coast. At times it may be possible to see whales sheltering in the bay, although there are better spots along this coast for whale watching. To the south of the village is an excellent sandy beach which is safe for swimming, although the water is always cold. A further attraction is the strong swell in the bay which makes it great for surfing. For information, contact the Yzerfontein **Tourism Bureau** ⓘ *46 Main Rd, T022-451 2366, www.tourismyzerfontein.co.za, Mon-Fri 0830-1230, weekends in season 1000-1400.* Many of the local holiday homes stand empty and the town can be very quiet out of season. Most of the local amenities are concentrated around the petrol station.

Dassen Island
Dassen Island, is 9 km to the southwest, and is the largest along the west coast, and is the peak of an underwater mountain. When Jan van Riebeeck first visited here in 1654, the island was home to hundreds of seals. These have long since been hunted out, but there remain large cormorant and African penguin breeding populations. A caretaker lives on the island's lighthouse but it is not open to the public.

Langebaan ⬤🄟🄞🄐🄒 ›› *pp198-203. Colour map 6, B1.*

A little more than an hour by road from Cape Town (125 km), this is a very popular family resort which has been all but spoilt by heavy development. Situated on the sheltered waters of the beautiful **Langebaan Lagoon**, it is an ideal centre for watersports – sailing conditions are reputedly the best along the Western Cape coastline. The beach is also good and sheltered so it's not too cold for swimming. The **Langebaan Tourism Association** ⓘ *corner of Breë and Oostewal streets, T022-772 1515, www.langebaaninfo.com, Mon-Fri 0900-1700, Sat 0900-1300,* is in the municipality.

Today it is impossible to picture the town's origins as a small fishing village in the 1880s. The hillside is a mosaic of new houses and vacant plots waiting for the next

West Coast National Park birdwatching

The main attraction in the park is the varied and impressive birdlife, and there are a number of hides allowing good viewing. Almost 250 species of bird have been recorded: flamingos from the Etosha Pan in Namibia; an estimated 50% of the world's population of swift terns during season; 25% of the world's Cape gannets, and a sizeable population of rare African black oystercatchers. Other rare species to look out for are the black harrier, great-crested grebe and the silver gull. Each year over 65,000 waders visit the lagoon – many of these birds started life in the Siberian marshlands. The greatest influx occurs between September and April. It takes the birds about six weeks to complete the 15,000-km journey from Siberia to Langebaan. It is vital that the habitat of the lagoon is protected; otherwise it is uncertain where these birds could or would migrate to.

building to obstruct the view of an earlier speculator. The town is dominated by the hideous-looking **Club Mykonos** timeshare complex and hotel, a collection of elaborate pastel-coloured town houses built to look like so-called Greek tavernas where holiday-makers from Cape Town spend their allotted two weeks of time share, parking their ski boats in the little harbour, and gambling in the on-site 24-hour casino. In October the annual **Langebaan Mussel Festival** includes good food, wine tasting and arts and crafts stalls.

The first Europeans to visit the region were French whale and seal hunters in the 17th century who stored their booty – whale oil and seal skins – on an island in the lagoon known as Isle la Biche. This was renamed by the first Dutch settlers as **Schaapen Island**. It was not until 1870 that a village began to take shape. Prior to this, Langebaan was put on the map by Lord Charles Somerset, Governor of the Cape in the 1820s, who built a hunting lodge on a private farm overlooking the lagoon. The growth of the village was slow due to a shortage of fresh water, a problem which was only solved after the Second World War when a pipeline was built to bring water from the Berg River to the northeast.

The lagoon is an important feature of the region. The northern part, opening onto the Atlantic Ocean, is known as **Saldanha Bay** and is the deepest and safest natural harbour in South Africa. Not surprisingly, it has been fully utilized by the South African navy. More recently, mining interests have built a large iron-ore wharf and steel mill on the bay, a real eyesore which is visible from all angles. In contrast, the southern shores and waters are part of the fascinating **West Coast National Park** (see below) – a rather precarious situation, as heavy ore carriers and naval boats frequenting the lagoon threaten the fragile marine environment.

West Coast National Park ⬤🏍 ➤➤ pp198-203. Colour map 8, A1.

ⓘ *Jun-Sep 0700-1830, Oct-Apr 0600-2000. R72, children (under 16) R36 in flower season (Aug-Sep); R40, children R36 (under 16) during other months.*

Although it may not seem very remarkable at first sight, this park remains unmatched in South Africa. Covering 30,000 ha, it was established in 1985 to protect the rich marine life in the lagoon and the rare coastal wetlands. It extends from just north of Yzerfontein to Saldanha Bay, and includes the Postberg Nature Reserve, Langebaan Lagoon and the islands – Malgas, Jutten, Marcus and Schaapen. The diversity of species here is impressive, but the main attraction is the excellent variety of birdlife.

Ins and outs

Getting there You can enter the park from two directions: from the south (look out for the signs along the R27); or by driving south out of Langebaan town. If you don't mind paying the small entrance fee, it is a pleasant alternative to drive through the park when travelling between Langebaan and Cape Town. All the roads are surfaced.

Tourist information **SANParks** ① *T022-772 2144, www.sanparks.org.* The main **information centre** ① *just before the entrance to the park (follow the signs from Langebaan centre),* has maps and information on the area. Within the park, a beautiful farmstead dating from 1744 has been fully restored and turned into an **environmental centre and restaurant** ① *T022-772 2134, www.geelbek.co.za, daily 0900-1700,* which today is a popular wedding venue. This is

Saldanha Bay & West Coast National Park

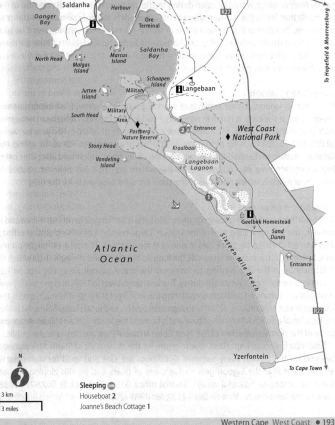

To Paternoster, Stompneusbaai & St Helena Bay

To Velddrift & Lamberts Bay

Danger Bay

Saldanha

Harbour

Ore Terminal

North Head

Marcus Island

Malgas Island

Saldanha Bay

Jutten Island

Schaapen Island

Langebaan

Military

South Head

Military Area

Postberg Nature Reserve

Entrance

West Coast National Park

Stony Head

Kraalbaai

Vondeling Island

Langebaan Lagoon

Atlantic Ocean

Geelbek Homestead

Sand Dunes

Sixteen Mile Beach

Entrance

Yzerfontein

To Cape Town

To Hopefield & Moorreesburg

R45

R27

R27

N

3 km

3 miles

Sleeping
Houseboat **2**
Joanne's Beach Cottage **1**

found at the southern end of the lagoon and is known as the **Geelbek Homestead**. Most visitors, including tour groups, stop here and the food on offer is traditionally South African cuisine – babotie, snoek salad, ostrich burgers, Cape Malay curries – and some of the recipes are 300 years old There are some interesting displays on the different ecosystems found in the park and a good curio shop. Several walks start from here, leading to simple hides in amongst the reed beds and the mud flats.

Postberg Nature Reserve

Apart from the prolific birdlife in the park the other major attraction is its wild flowers which bloom after the first spring rains. Because of the variety of soil types, you can see many different flowers within a small area. The most colourful spreads are frequently found in Postberg Nature Reserve. Since 1987, this private nature reserve has been administered by the national park, while the actual lands remain the property of farmers. Three farms make up the reserve: Nieuwland, Kreeftebaai and Oude Post. Between 1838 and 1966 the land was used as winter grazing for cattle. In 1969 it was declared a private nature reserve which would be open during the flower season. It is found at the tip of the peninsula that forms the western shore of the lagoon. It is still only open from August to September, but during the spring it is one of the best places to see wild flowers. The land has also been stocked with eland, zebra, hartebeest, kudu and wildebeest. There are three picnic sites with toilets. Allow sufficient time to exit the park at the end of the day as it is a long drive all the way round the lagoon.

Langebaan Lagoon

The beautiful lagoon, a wide expanse of sparkling turquoise water, is an important and integral part of the park. It is rich in nutrients – twice a day the tides replenish the lagoon with cold plankton-rich water – and home to thousands of birds. Every year between 50,000 and 70,000 birds fly more than 15,000 km from northern Russia to spend the summer feeding on Langebaan lagoon. Looking down from a high vantage point helps you appreciate how exceptionally clear the waters are. This has been attributed to colonies of mussels which filter the microscopic particles brought in by the tide.

Saldanha → *Colour map 6, B1.*

At the northern end of Langebaan Lagoon, Saldanha is the largest town in the area and is certainly the less appealing part of the lagoon. Large numbers of fishing vessels offload their harvests here to be processed in one of three factories. The greatest blight on the area, however, is the massive steel mill, the long iron ore jetty and the bulk ships which sit complacently in the bay waiting to transport the ore. Aquaculture in the lagoon has grown into a very important local industry. The first harvest was in 1984, and the quality was exceptional – surprising perhaps, considering the vicinity of the jetty. The main crop is the Mediterranean blue mussel, along with Japanese oysters and local clams. Saldanha is also the location of a South African naval base and is home to the South African Military Academy. Some of the northern reaches of the West Coast National Park are closed to the public.

Saldanha is also an important tourist centre for the thousands of South Africans who descend on the lagoon every summer. Conditions are safe and ideal for watersports, which means that the lagoon gets its fair share of boats and jet skis zipping up and down the otherwise peaceful waters. **Tourist office** ⓘ *Van Riebeeck St, T022-714 2088, www.saldanhabay.co.za, Mon-Fri 0830-1630, Sat 0900-1200.*

Sishen–Saldanha railway

Anyone driving north from Saldanha Bay is likely to follow a route close to the Sishen–Saldanha railway. This was purpose-built between 1973 and 1976 to transport high-grade iron ore from the Northern Cape to a new deep-water harbour in Saldanha Bay. The line is 861 km long and only has three bends. It has earned a place in the Guinness Book of Records. In 1989 a world record was set when the longest and heaviest train covered the route. It was 7.3 km long, had 660 loaded trucks weighing 71,210 metric tonnes and was pulled by 16 locomotives. You can see segments of a train in the marshalling yards just outside the harbour. When there is a waiting train the road to Langebaan is diverted.

Coastal fishing villages ⊜❶ ➻ pp198-203. Colour map 6, B1.

Running in a clockwise direction to the north of Vredenburg are the small fishing communities of Paternoster, Stompneusbaai, St Helena Bay, Laaiplek and Dwarskersbos. None of these have much to keep visitors in the area for long, but offer a view of quiet coastal life. Given that it is and easy drive from Cape Town, in recent years, especially Paternoster, they've grown considerably with holiday homes built by wealthy Capetonians.

Paternoster

Paternoster was once a typical fishing village 15 km northwest of Vredenburg. It's very pretty with whitewashed homes with bright red and blue roofs and a wide expanse of sandy beach with rows of photogenic brightly coloured fishing boats. Today the village has mushroomed with holiday homes that stretch along the beach, but thanks to strict development regulations, the style of the architecture is all the same so it retains its character. It's quiet here out of season, but on summer weekends gets very busy and is a popular spot for lunch and a stroll on the beach for people from Cape Town. At the waterfront is a fairly new development where you can buy fresh fish and seafood or traditional fish and chips. The fishing community is supported by a thriving Cape lobster export business. The name means 'Our Father' in Afrikaans and it is believed that this stretch of coast was the first place in Africa that the Lord's Prayer was uttered by Vasco de Gama and his sailors. **Tourist office** ① *at the entrance to the village on the right hand side before the 4-way stop, T022-752 2323, www.paternoster.info, Mon-Fri 0830-1630, Sat (and Sun in season) 0900-1200*. They can help find self-catering accommodation in the village.

At the south end of Paternoster Bay is a working lighthouse built in 1936 marking the treacherous **Cape Columbine**, which has wrecked many ships. *Columbine* was in fact a barque wrecked in 1829. It's 80 m tall and its beam is visible for about 50 km. You can visit the **lighthouse** ① *T022-752 2705, May-Sep Mon-Fri, Oct-Apr daily 1000-1500, R14, children (under 12) R7*, and now you can also sleep in it (see box, page 49). The lands around here make up the **Columbine Nature Reserve** ① *T022-752 2718, 0700-1900, minimal entrance charge*. This area of protected coastline has a rich mix of wild flowers in the spring, also Karoo succulents and nesting seabirds, and there is a simple beach camp here (see Sleeping, page 200).

Stompneusbaai

Meaning Blunt Nose Bay, Stompneusbaai is a similar coastal village. The presence of a fish-processing factory detracts somewhat from the attractive local fishermen's cottages, but it is an important source of income for the village. This is also the area where Vasco da Gama landed in 1497 after three months at sea, the first voyage he had made this far south. The modern monument commemorating this is hardly worthy of his feat.

St Helena Bay

A surfaced road links Stompneusbaai with St Helena Bay, an important centre of South Africa's commercial fishing industry, especially for lobster. Remember it is illegal to buy lobster directly from the fishermen. The bay was named by Vasco da Gama who anchored here with four vessels on 7 November 1497, St Helena Day. A granite monument commemorating this event stands on the shore near Sandy Point.

Rocherpan Nature Reserve → *Colour map 6, A1.*

① *Sep-Apr daily 0700-1800, May-Aug daily 0800-1700, T022-952 1727, www.capenature. org.za. There are no staff at the small interpretive centre next to the gate, but visitors should sign in and drop their fee (R25, children 3-13 R12) into the honesty box. You can also pick up an excellent bird checklist with map from here. The reserve office is another 100 m into the reserve. There are 2 sturdy bird hides beside the freshwater lake. Behind the car park a footpath leads across the dunes to the desolate beach.*

This important and rarely visited bird sanctuary is 12 km beyond Dwarskersbos. More often than not, you'll have it to yourself with an endless beach and only the sound of thousands of feeding birds. The 914-ha reserve was established in 1967 around a seasonal *vlei*. In 1988 the boundaries were extended to include all the area up to the shore of the Atlantic Ocean. When fully flooded the *vlei*, fed by the Papkuils River, is nearly 3 km long, although it is unable to drain into the sea because of the sand dunes. The reserve maybe closed to the public when this happens. This mix of protected habitats provides excellent breeding and feeding conditions for over 180 bird species. Nearly 70 varieties of waterbirds have been recorded, including some endangered species. If you are lucky you might spot the African black oystercatcher, one of the rarest endemic breeding coastal birds in South Africa. During its breeding season (November to March), listen out for its high-pitched call, designed to startle intruders. It usually feeds at low tide, looking for mussels and limpets. White pelicans, Cape shovellers and flamingos are often seen here. There is also the chance of spotting a few of the resident small mammals such as steenbok, duiker, water mongoose and the shy African wild cat.

Elands Bay → *Colour map 6, A1.*

There are three very good reasons for visiting this small and isolated coastal community, which makes it all the more surprising to find that tourism has barely made its mark. First, it is a good location for whale watching – this is about the furthest north that southern right and humpback whales can be seen from the shore. Second, it is well known for its good surfing conditions. Finally, it lies at the mouth of **Verlorenvlei**, a stream with marshlands that support a large, varied aquatic bird population. Over 240 species have been recorded in the area. There's an interesting walk out to Baboon Point with good views of the bay. Ask for directions to the cave which has some San paintings. All activities are concentrated around an open square by the **Eland's Bay Hotel**, which also acts as the local **tourist information office**. There is a post office, bottle shop, supermarket and a cheap café.

Nearby, on the way to Lambert's Bay, is **Wadrif Salt Pan**. After rains there are a couple of shallow ponds here, providing an excellent chance of seeing flamingos. Take a left by the railway bridge and follow the line to Lambert's Bay. Wadrif Salt Pan is by the railway line.

Lambert's Bay ⊜🕏🛦🕒 ➤➤ pp198-203. Colour map 6, A1.

Once a small fishing village, Lambert's Bay is now a popular holiday town and gets very busy in summer. Between July and November you have a good chance of seeing the southern right whale migrating north. The excellent **Muisbosskerm** restaurant (see page 203) played an important role in drawing visitors to the region, but the bay has appeared on maps for many years – it was the last point at which Bartholomew Diaz went ashore before sailing around the Cape in 1487. The village is named after the British admiral, Sir Robert Lambert, who produced detailed charts of this coastline between 1826 and 1840. In 1918 Axel Lindstrom established the **Lambert's Bay Canning Co** and the future of the fishing community was assured. **Lambert's Bay Tourism Bureau** ⓘ *Main St, T027-432 1000, www.lambertsbay.co.za, Mon-Fri 0900-1300, 1400-1700, Sat 0900-1230 (open Sun during the flower season).*

The town itself is modern and rather unattractive, although it has one absorbing, if pungent, attraction – **Bird Island**. No longer an island, this 3-ha rock outcrop is now joined to the land by a concrete jetty. It is an important breeding ground for Cape gannets and, to a lesser extent, cormorants, and it attracts Cape fur seals. Although the birds make for interesting viewing, their cantankerous screeching and overpowering smell leaves a rather longer-lasting impression. Quite unexpectedly during the 2005 gannet breeding period, seals began to attack gannets on the island (although not unheard of, it's very unusual for seals to attack birds on dry land). Cape Nature estimated that they found over 2000 gannet carcasses and the gannets all but abandoned the island, their nests and eggs. In an attempt to entice them back, the Lamberts Bay Bird Island Action Committee commissioned 50 plaster of paris decoys from local artist Gerrit Burger – these are sort of half-moon-shaped protective shelters under which the birds can build their nests. Within an hour of placing the decoys the gannets started coming back. From the end of the jetty there are good views of the fishing fleet and more sea birds. Note that around high tide, breakers crash across the jetty as you walk out to the island. Wear shoes with grip, as the surface is very slippery and uneven. The **Bird Island Interpretation Centre** ⓘ *T022-931 2900, daily 0800-1700*, has exhibits on the birds and a feature on the history of collecting guano, traditionally used as fertilizer, plus a mini aquarium, and a rather sad-looking penguin pool. There's also a hide to watch the gannets from a little further inland.

Lambert's Bay to Vredendal

Doring Bay is a small fishing village based around a crayfish factory. The rocky coastline and deep coastal waters make this an ideal spot for crayfish to live in. Diamond boats can sometimes be seen around the jetty. There is a good restaurant here, **The Cabin**, on the seafront which is worth a visit (see Eating, page 203). Note that the only petrol station here is closed on Sunday.

About 8 km further on is the northernmost village on the coast, **Strandfontein**. This is a delightful settlement built on the slopes of a small basin. The coastline is quite rocky and mountainous along here with a clean white-sand beach with excellent surfing conditions. Although usually quiet, the village is very popular during the school holidays when there are full-time lifeguards present on the beach. There are strong cross currents so only swim in front of the town where there is a tidal pool for children. The earliest residents got their drinking water from a spring on the beach, and Strandfontein means beach fountain.

Papendorp, close to the estuary of the Olifants River, is more of a cluster of fishermen's cottages than a village. There is a small island in the middle of the river mouth, and at low tide there are thousands of waterbirds on the mud flats. As an important wetland reserve, it is being considered as a future world RAMSAR site. From this point the road turns inland towards Lutzville (20 km from Strandfontein), a small farming village, and on to Vredendal.

Vredendal → *Colour map 6, A1.*

Despite the fact that it is some distance west of the main N7, Vredendal is the main commercial centre in the northwestern Cape. It is a modern town which owes its existence entirely to the Olifants River irrigation scheme. The first settlers came to the region as early as 1732 when the Dutch East India Company granted a farm to Pieter van Zyl, but it was only when the Bulshoek Dam was built that new farmers were attracted to the area. In 1925 a bridge was built across the Olifants River and the town grew rapidly into its present form. The region is also home to several quarries which extract dolomite and limestone. For tourist information contact the **Vredendal Information Office** ① *11 Church St, T027-201 3330, www.tourismvredendal.co.za, Mon-Fri 0800-1300, 1400-1700, Sat 0830-1300.*

◉ West Coast listings

For Sleeping and Eating price codes and other relevant information, see pages 46-53.

◉ Sleeping

Darling *p190*

C Darling Lodge, 22 Pastorie St, T022-492 3062, www.darlinglodge.co.za. A comfortable, restored 19th-century town house. Stream running through the garden and 6 double rooms, 3 in the house with Victorian bathrooms, and 3 pool deck rooms, a shared lounge with TV and fridge, swimming pool, generous breakfasts.

C Trinity Guest Lodge, 19 Long St, T022-492 3430, www.trinitylodge.co.za. Beautifully converted family home, with 4 stylish, understated bedrooms, each with their own entrance, goose-down duvets and hand-embroidered linen, old-fashioned Victorian bathrooms, lovely bright restaurant also open to non-guests, swimming pool, friendly owners Shaun and Debbie.

Yzerfontein *p191*

A Villa Pescatori, 316-Mile Beach, T022-451 2782, www.villapescatori.co.za. Perched right above the beach with gorgeous views, this upmarket guesthouse set in a Tuscan-style villa has 4 immaculately decorated rooms with DSTV and fridge. Generous breakfasts and a lovely pool with sun loungers overlooking the ocean.

C-D Kaijaiki Guest House and Restaurant, 36 Park Rd, T022-451 2858, www.kaijaiki.co.za. Comfortable, homely guesthouse with 1 self-catering room sleeping 4, 1 family room and 2 doubles, each has own fireplace and separate entrance, decorated with old photos and antiques, good restaurant attached serving West Coast traditional food. German, Dutch and French spoken. Recommended.

D Caravan Park, Park St, T022-451 2211. Good facilities, next to the dunes on the main beach with sweeping ocean views, bungalows and caravans for hire, and sheltered campsites behind hedges and the dunes.

Langebaan *p191*

There are plenty of options, given the town's popularity on the domestic holiday front, but many of these choices are for a minimum period of a week and are closed in the winter. Nevertheless, visitors have considerable bargaining power in the winter months. As with all South African coastal resorts advance booking is necessary during the school holidays, especially Dec and Jan.

A-B The Farmhouse, 5 Egret St, T022-772 2062, www.thefarmhouselangebaan.co.za. A smart and cosy converted Cape Dutch farmhouse, with 18 rooms, some with fireplace, TV, good restaurant with pine furnishings and a crackling fire open to non-guests, provides picnic baskets, swimming pool, a lovely bright white spa, library, no young children, overlooks Langebaan Lagoon. Recommended.

B Langebaan Beach House, 44 Beach Rd (entrance from Jacoba St), T022-772 2625, www.langebaanbeachhouse.com. Small guesthouse in idyllic setting right on beach overlooking the lagoon, with 4 tastefully furnished rooms, understated with terracotta-tiled floors, white linen, TV, private lounge or veranda overlooking beach, cooked breakfasts served on terrace, neat gardens and pool, no children under 12. Recommended.

C-D Falcon's Rest, 21a Zeeland St, T022-772 1112, www.falconsrest.co.za. Large converted family home with 12 double rooms with TV, several lounges, panoramic views from the garden, large pool, sun deck, attentive service but 1.5 km from the beach.

C-D Oliphantskop Farm Inn, opposite turning for **Club Mykonos**, T022-772 2326, www.oliphantskop.co.za. Set in converted farm buildings, 17 en suite rooms plus some self-contained chalets, sleeping 2-6, set around a lovely swimming pool designed to look like a rock pool. In the low season backpackers are put in main rooms for budget rates, making it extraordinarily good value. Stables on the farm specialize in horse trails. Candlelit restaurant set in long barn with log fires, choice of good-value seafood and steaks, beer garden.

West Coast National Park *p192, map p193*

SANParks run a couple of options within the park's boundaries. Reservations through SANParks Tshwane (Pretoria) office, T012-428 9111, www.sanparks.org. Bookings can also be made in person at the offices in Cape Town and Durban (see page 48). Cancellations or reservations under 72 hrs in advance contact the park directly, T022-772 2144.

B Houseboat, permanently moored in the lagoon. Can accommodate 4 adults and 2 small children, with gas-operated kitchen, shower, flush toilet, braai and parking. There's also a larger houseboat that sleeps 22 but this is more suited to corporate groups than holidaymakers. These have their own website, www.houseboating.co.za.

B Joanne's Beach Cottage, Churchaven, within walking distance of the lagoon. 8-bed fully equipped self-catering cottage, no electricity but solar lighting and gas appliances. Linen, towels and all cooking equipment provided, you just need to bring food and firewood.

Saldanha *p194, map p193*

B Blue Bay Lodge and Resort, Gracillaria Crescent, T022-714 1177, www.blouwater baai.com. 20 1- to 3-bed fully equipped, self-catering cottages with TV, simple furnishings but big views from the large windows, patio and lawn in front leading to the beach, 16 more luxurious rooms in the whitewashed hotel, swimming pool, tennis, windsurfing, full range of beauty treatments on offer, restaurant and bar overlooking Saldanha Lagoon. Check there's not a large conference on.

C Protea Hotel Saldanha Bay, 51 Main Rd, T022-714 1264, www.proteahotels.co.za. Standard chain hotel in centre of town, 58 rooms, some non-smoking, satellite TV, restaurant, swimming pool, secure parking. One of the less characterful Proteas but recently refurbished to high standards, reasonable value and offers weekend specials.

E-F Saldanha Holiday Resort, Camp St, T022-714 2247. Large, grassy camping and caravan site close to the beach, plus 48 simple self-catering chalets sleeping 4-6 people in bunk beds, with bathroom and kitchen with hotplate, microwave, fridge, kettle and basic utensils. Very busy at Christmas with families.

Paternoster *p195*
There are a number of holiday cottages in the village, contact **Stay in Paternoster**, T022-752 2048, www.stayinpaternoster.co.za.
C Paternoster Hotel, St Augustine St, T022-752 2703, www.paternosterhotel.co.za. 10 spacious rooms, with 1 double and 1 single bed, DSTV, 4 have balconies with sea view, great pub with crackling fire, restaurant open to all serving good range of seafood including crayfish. Also lets out self-catering cottages in the village, which are good for families.
E Beach Camp, Cape Columbine Nature Reserve, T082-926 2267, www.beach camp.co.za. A-frame huts and tents with beds, you'll need to bring your own sleeping bag. Lovely setting in the nature reserve, hot communal showers, self-catering facilities, bar and *lapa* area, also serves seafood dinners and can arrange sea kayaking and boat trips. A bit like a backpackers on the beach and an excellent budget option.

St Helena Bay *p196*
B Oystercatcher Lodge, 1st Av, T022-742 1202, www.oystercatcherlodge.co.za. An upmarket B&B, all the rooms have panoramic views of the bay, with stylish all-white decor, underfloor heating for chilly winter nights, terrace and swimming pool with sun loungers, bar, comfortable lounge with fireplace and DSTV, a good base for exploring the region, no small children. They also operate 5 self-catering apartments within walking distance of the lodge.
E-F Laingville Caravan Park, Strand St, T022-736 1684. Standard holiday park with 7 very basic and bare self-catering chalets (no bedding) and caravan and camping sites and ablution block. Quiet until the school holidays, when it gets far too crowded.

Elands Bay *p196*
D-F Eland's Bay Hotel, Beachfront, T022-972 1640, www.elandsbayhotel.co.za.

Comfortable rooms with sea views, large and airy seafood restaurant, TV lounge, braai facilities, the principal building in the village, cheap backpacker beds are in an annexe with shared bathrooms and there's campsite with newly built ablution block.
E-F Eland's Bay Caravan Park, right on beachfront in the village centre, T022-972 1736. Small municipal site, windy but low thick hedges provide some shelter, it's an ideal spot for surfers and a short walk from the **Eland's Bay Hotel**.

Lambert's Bay *p197*
C Lambert's Bay Hotel, Voortrekker St, T027-432 1126, www.lambertsbayhotel.co.za. Standard 3-star hotel with 47 large rooms, the ones at the front have a mixed view of the scenic harbour and ugly fish-processing factory – do NOT open your windows when the factory is working. Popular **Waves** restaurant specializes in fresh, quality seafood, lively bar, within walking distance of shops plus Bird Island, ask about whale-watching boat trips.

Camping
E-F Lambert's Bay Caravan and Camping Park, T027-432 2238. Overlooks the main beach, a bit exposed, very busy in peak season, communal laundry and kitchen facilities, a kid's playground and kiosk.

Lambert's Bay to Vredendal *p197*
C Die Anker, Doring Bay, T027-215 1016, www.doringbaai.com. Main local hotel, mix of accommodation including B&B rooms in the main house, self-catering units and some camping space, all with sea views and within walking distance of the beach. Fully licensed restaurant serves a good selection of seafood and meat dishes.
C-E Strandfontein Resort, Kreef Rd, Strand-fontein, T027-215 1169. A well-equipped park which is a bit hectic when all 150 stands are occupied during the holidays. At quieter times, this is a relaxing spot to have a break. It is situated next to the beach, with 4- and 6-bed self-catering chalets, power points,

tidal swimming pool, café open all year plus a small kiosk (open in peak season).

Vredendal *p198*

C Tharrakamma Guesthouse, 18 Tuin St, T027-213 5709, www.tharrakamma.co.za. 5 double rooms, 2 family self-catering chalets, a/c, TV, non-smoking available, lovely wooden African furniture, beautiful house with wide verandas, pretty garden full of palms, meals on request, award-winning guesthouse. Recommended.

D Vredendal Hotel, 11 Voortrekker St, T027-213 1064, www.vredendalhotel.co.za. Main hotel in town, old-fashioned 2-storey brick building with 51 a/c rooms with TV, **Saddles Steak Ranch** restaurant, bar with pool table, swimming pool.

⦿ Eating

There are several very popular open-air restaurants along the West Coast specializing in seafood. These are weather dependent so always phone ahead on the day and most require pre-booking. Also be aware that some do not have credit card facilities; check first.

Darling *p190*

♥ Evita se Perron, in the old railway station, T022-492 2831, www.evita.co.za. Open for breakfast and lunch, Tue-Sun 1000-1600 and dinner when performances are on – check out the website. A range of entertainments set in the old railway building, including a restaurant, coffee shop and famous cabaret shows performed by Evita Bezuidenhout (see page 191). Good range of South African dishes such as bobotie and bredies and excellent entertainment, although it's often South African politically biased, which may not appeal to the overseas visitor.
♥ Trinity, **Trinity Guest Lodge** (see Sleeping, page 198). Dinner by arrangement only. A Victorian building with outside tables next to the pool, home-cooked food using produce from their own garden, variable and innovative

menu depending on what's in season. Debbie the chef is well known for her pear and chocolate tart. Occasional wine-tasting evenings.
♥ Marmalade Cat, 19 Main Rd, 022-492 2515. Open 0800-1630. A small decor shop with a café serving simple country fare such as chicken pie, savoury tarts, salads and apple pie. It's also open on Fri nights when it serves pizza and salads.

Yzerfontein *p191*

♥♥♥ Die Strandkombuis, 16-Mile Beach, T082-575 9683, www.strandkombuis.co.za. Sep-May open for lunch daily 1300-1500, and dinner by arrangement only, also weather dependent so phone first. Open-air seafood braai, one of many beach seafood set-ups popular on the west coast. Start with seafood soup, and move on to smoked snoek, mussels and crayfish all cooked over hot coals. If it's chilly you can hire heaters. Bookings essential.
♥♥ Beaches, corner of Beach Rd and Ninth St, T022-451 2200. Lunch Tue-Sun 1200-1530. À la carte restaurant on the beach specializing in seafood, also serves steaks and some vegetarian dishes, both the seafood curry and seafood *potjie* are worth a try, also has 'lite bites' and pizzas in the bar, all with ocean views.

Langebaan *p191*

♥♥♥ Boesmanland Plaaskombuis, on the beach at Club Mykonos, T022-772 1564, www.boesmanlandfarmkitchen.com. 1200-1400, 1900-2100. Another open-air buffet restaurant on the beach, although this is covered, tables strewn out on the sand lit by paraffin lamps in the evening. As well as crayfish, prawns, snoek and mussels, there's farm-style roast lamb and chicken, and South African desserts like melktart and koeksisters. Bookings are essential.
♥♥♥ Die Strandloper, follow signs for **Club Mykonos**, on the beach, T022-772 2490, www.strandloper.com. Daily in season, lunch 1200, dinner 1800, out of season Sat-Sun, again weather dependent, phone first. Casual, romantic surroundings with wooden tables under sunshades, cooking is done

in a central fire pit, excellent seafood buffet, award-winning, light guitar music, bar or BYO. Mussels are served for starters, then the empty mussel shells are used as cutlery for the 10 courses of fish served in the West Coast tradition with home-made bread and apricot jam. The final course is half a crayfish. Cost is R175 per head and children (under 12) are charged by height. Charming, one of the best eating experiences in South Africa. Highly recommended. Bookings essential.

The Farmhouse, in the guesthouse (see Sleeping, page 199), 5 Egret St, T022-772 2062. Open 0700-2300. Good lamb steaks, fresh seafood, quality food, vegetarian menu, Sun roasts, views across the bay from an 1860s farmstead, crackling fires in winter. The pub has a cheaper menu of sandwiches, fish and chips and lasagne.

Pearly's, 46 Beach Rd, T022-772 2095, www.pearlys.co.za. 0930-late. Right next to the beach with an outside deck, this offers fresh seafood and excellent thin based pizzas, as well as breakfasts and light meals. Very popular, be prepared to wait during busy periods since all the dishes are fresh. Relaxing views across the lagoon. Recommended.

Spinnakers, Langebaan Waterfront Centre, Breë St, T022-772 1278. Open 0830-2300. Excellent views of the lagoon from the terrace and a homely interior, this is open daily from breakfast when you can choose a full fry-up or South African favourite mince on toast, and a long menu of light meals, sandwiches, burgers, grills, pizzas and seafood including creamy West Coast mussels.

Lagoon Fisheries, Breë St. Fast-food joint dishing out tasty fish and chips.

Saldanha p194, map p193

Blue Bay Cafe, see Sleeping, page 199. Open 0700-2200. Stylish dining room serving up some surprising dishes for such a remote location, Moroccan lamb with chorizo sausage, truffles, and duck, very popular with people from Cape Town, booking essential.

Mussel Cracker, 51 Main Rd, T022-714 1264. Open 0630-1030, 1230-1430, 1900-2200.

Part of **Protea Hotel**, smart seafood restaurant with views across bay, good fresh fish, crayfish and mussels, also steak combos such as rump with calamari. Good seafood buffet on Sat night and a carvery on Sun lunchtime.

Slipway, Main Harbour, T022-714 4235, www.slipway.co.za. 0900-late. Seafood, vegetarian and pasta dishes, steak and seafood combos are recommended, as are the unusual mussels in coconut cream, all overlooking the yachts at the jetty, and they can arrange sails around the harbour before or after your meal on their own yacht.

Paternoster p195

The Noisy Oyster, 62 St Augustine Rd, T022-752 2196. Wed-Sun 1200-1500, Wed-Sat 1800-2100. A fantastic location on the beach with a wooden deck and arty clutter on the walls, serving West Coast fare such as oysters, spicy calamari and freshly caught linefish as well as gourmet burgers and specials like crispy duck or ostrich steaks. Bookings are essential on summer weekends as its popular for lunch with visitors from Cape Town. Consistently packed so service can be a little slow.

Lambert's Bay p197

Bosduifklip, 4 km out of town towards Clanwilliam, T027-432 2735, www.bosduifklip.co.za. Opening times depend on weather and number of customers; call in advance to check. Set outside amongst some rock formations on Albina farm. Another popular open-air restaurant serving buffet meals in West Coast style, bar or bring your own drink, booking essential at weekends and holidays. Enjoy a tasty selection of seafood dishes including mussels, crayfish, smoked snoek and pickled fish, and farm cuisine such as lamb on the spit and venison stew, which go well with the home-made breads and butter.

Isabella's, next to the entrance to Bird Island, T027-432 2235. Open 0900-2100. An excellent seafood restaurant serving quality shellfish – you can select your own crayfish from the tank. Has an extensive range of grilled or battered fish, plus calamari and mussels and a good selection of wines. Decor consists of plastic tables among fishing nets in a light easy-going atmosphere.

††† **Muisbosskerm**, 5 km towards Elands Bay, T027-432 1017, www.muisbosskerm.co.za. Summer lunch 1230, dinner 1830; winter lunch 1200, dinner 1800. This was the first of the open-air, no-frills seafood braai-style restaurants on the West Coast and has been operational for 23 years. For a fixed price of R175 you have a wide choice of seafood dishes cooked over a braai, baked and.smoked, eat as much as you like, meals last about 3 hrs, bring your own drink, small corkage fee, book even out of season. During peak periods there can be more than 150 people eating here – it can become a bit of a scrum around the braais.

Lambert's Bay to Vredendal *p197*

††† **The Cabin**, on the edge of Doring Bay village, T027-215 1016, www.doringbaai.com. Open 1200-1500, 1800-2100. Run by a family team, the outside tables are on a wrecked boat hull; inside you can sip sherry by a roaring fire in a decor of fishing nets and life belts. Well known for its fish soup and calamari and, for meat eaters, the spare ribs are good. There's a separate pub with pool table, dart board, TV.

O Shopping

Langebaan *p191*

Freeport is a large shopping and accommodation development with a supermarket, bakery, bottle store and café. All other shops and restaurants are in Breë St, close to the town hall. Here you will find a bookshop, launderette, **Standard Bank** and curio shops.

▲ Activities and tours

Langebaan *p191*

Boat trips and fishing

Bugaloo Adventures, Club Mykonos jetty, T022-772 0277, www.bugalooadventures. co.za. Power boat rides around the islands in

the lagoon from R350 pp plus guided jet-ski rides from R600.

Langebaan Fishing Adventures, Club Mykonos jetty, T083-266 0231, www.fishing trips.co.za. Game fishing is very popular along this stretch of coast, as is collecting crayfish. Fishing permits are issued by the post office. This operator can organize fishing in the lagoon by ski-boat from R650 per person, including bait and tackle, as well as sight-seeing boat cruises to see the seals on Dassen Island (see page 191).

Golf

Langebaan Country Estate, 1 Oostewal Rd, 2 km before town, T022-772 2112, www.lan gebaanestate.co.za. A fairly new 18-hole golf course and time share resort on the edge of the lagoon. Accepts visitors, green fees R300.

Watersports

Cape Sports, on the beach on the northern reaches of town, T022-772 1114, www.cape sport.co.za. Organizes windsurfing, kitesurfing and watersports with full instruction per hr or per day. Also rents out surfboards.

Lambert's Bay *p197*

Tour operators

Lambert's Bay Boat Charters, office at the harbour, T082-922 4334, www.sadolphins. co.za. A strongly recommended boat trip to see dolphins, seals, whales (and sharks if you're lucky), and excellent for birdwatchers, expect to pay in the region of R350 per person.

● Directory

Langebaan *p191*

Emergencies Police, T022-772 2111; Sea rescue, T082-990 5966. **Medical services** West Coast Private Hospital, T022-719 1030.

Lambert's Bay *p197*

Emergencies Police, T027-432 1122. **Banks** Standard Bank in Church St is the best place to change money, with an ATM.

The N7 to the Northern Cape

If your time is short or you want to get to the Northern Cape, the quickest way out of Cape Town is to take the N7 highway. The first part of the route passes through rolling wheat country known as the Swartland, or 'Black Country', named after the dark hue of the rhinoceros bush, which once covered the area. Most of the towns in the region are small, prosperous farming communities, with little in terms of sights, despite their long history. The principal centres of the wheat industry are Malmesbury and Moorreesburg. Around this region and clearly signposted, are the vineyards that are part of the Swartland wine route (www.swartlandwineroute.co.za). Further north the eastern boundary of the Olifants River valley is made up of the spectacular Cederberg Mountains, a striking wilderness area offering some of the best hiking in South Africa. Both Citrusdal and Clanwilliam are a two- to three-hour drive from Cape Town and make good bases for exploring the area, their irrigated valleys providing a powerful contrast to the seemingly barren Cederberg. ▸▸ *For listings, see pages 211-214.*

Malmesbury → *Colour map 8, A1.*

About 50 km north of Cape Town the N7 passes Malmesbury, the centre of the surrounding wheat industry and the principal settlement in the Swartland. The sleepy town lies in a shallow valley close to the Diep River. For information visit **Malmesbury Tourism Bureau** ⓘ *1 Church St, T022-487 2989, www.tourismswartland.co.za. Mon-Fri 0900-1600.*

The town was given its current name in 1829 when the British Governor, Sir Lowry Cole, visited and renamed it in honour of his father-in-law, the Earl of Malmesbury. Today the skyline is dominated by the unsightly grain silos and huge flour mills. **Swartland Cellars**, 4 km outside town, produces a full-bodied red wine and the famous Hanepoot, with its strong honey flavour, is popular as a dessert wine. The winery has won a number of awards, despite the fact that experts claim local climatic conditions are far from ideal. One of the grandest buildings in town is the **Dutch Reformed Church** on Church Street, opposite the city hall. Although the original building was completed in 1751, the present form dates from around 1899 when the church was enlarged by building the existing transepts. The magnificent heavy church bell isn't rung for fear of the vibrations damaging the structure – instead, a recording is played at services.

Moorreesburg → *Colour map 8, A1.*

Further north on the main N7, 102 km north of Cape Town, is this important farming and railway centre in the heart of the Swartland. Like Malmesbury, the surrounding area is devoted to wheat fields and sheep farming. Close to the railway are enormous grain silos and flour mills – wheat has been grown in the area since 1752. The settlement was founded in 1879 as a church centre, on a farm called **Hooikraal**. The town was named after the Reverend HA Moorrees. For information contact the **tourist office** ⓘ *Municipality building, corner of Plein and Retief streets, T022-433 1072, www.tourismmoorreesburg.co.za. Mon-Fri 0900-1600.*

Wheat Industry Museum ⓘ *Main Rd, T022-433 1093, Mon-Thu 0800-1700, Fri 0800-1600, small entrance fee.* Located in an old Dutch Reformed Mission Church, this proudly proclaims that it is one of only three in the world and has a fairly diverting collection that traces the history of the crop. Some of the early harvesting and threshing machines are well worth a look; they are reminiscent of kit models, which in many ways is what they are, having been shipped out from England in pieces.

Piketberg → Colour map 6, B2.

After 31 km the N7 passes the turning for Velddrif and the small town of Piketberg. The Piketberg hills rise as a large massif to the east as the road heads across the plains to the Olifants River Mountains. Before the road starts to climb, you pass the turning on the right for Porterville. This is the R44 and takes you back towards Paarl and Cape Town. Piketberg is another typical agricultural town, with a few old buildings and churches in the centre surrounded by modern suburbs, which in turn give way to rolling wheat fields. Look out for an old cannon in the grounds of the high school. There was once a series of cannons along the mountain slopes all the way to Cape Town, which were fired to let farmers know when a new ship was arriving in Table Bay to take on board fresh supplies. The cannon was also used to warn of the approach of Khoi-San people. The name of the town dates back to 1792 when a lookout post was set up on Honigberg Farm to protect the local farmers from looting by the Khoi-San. The actual word is derived from the French word *picquet*, referring to a small group of soldiers on the lookout. For information, contact the local **tourist office** ⓘ *Kerk St, T022-913 2063, www.piketberg.com, Mon-Fri 0830-1630.*

Like most of the small towns in the region, the dominant building is the **Dutch Reformed Church**, built 1880-1882. It is a striking building, neo-Gothic in style with plenty of turrets and plastered panels. There is an obelisk in its grounds commemorating the 1838 Great Trek. In 1938 the building was declared a national monument.

Piketberg Museum ⓘ *10 Kerk St, Mon-Fri 0900-1300, free,* is a small museum housing antiquities donated by the community, and an exhibition about the Anglo Boer War in Piketberg history.

Olifants River Valley ◉◉ ⏵ pp211-214.

As you drop down from the Piekenierskloof Pass, the scenery changes significantly with the arrival of the Olifants River. Although not one of South Africa's largest rivers, it is of vital importance to the region, irrigating over 12,000 ha of farmland. This is most immediately obvious in the brilliant green citrus farms interspersed with vineyards. Marking the east of the valley are the stark and magnificent Cederberg Mountains.

Citrusdal → Colour map 6, A2.

As the name implies, this modern rural town is the centre of the local citrus industry, nestling in a valley filled with citrus farms. During spring, the air is heavy with the scent of orange blossom and from May hundreds of thousands of oranges are packed up and exported. Even more striking is the town's setting at the southern edge of the Cederberg Mountains. Along with Clanwilliam, Citrusdal makes an ideal base for exploring the wilderness of the mountains, though there are no roads from Citrusdal into the Cederberg; from here you will have to continue along the N7 to the turning to Algeria. The **tourist office** ⓘ *39 Voortrekker St, T022-921 3210, www.citrusdal.info, Mon-Fri 0900-1630,* is housed in a recently built example of a typical Sandveld dwelling.

Clanwilliam, lying at the northern edges of the Cederberg, is a peaceful agricultural centre and one of the oldest towns in South Africa. During the spring, the profusion of wild flowers that blanket the area attract a large number of visitors, many of whom travel up from Cape Town (240 km). Just off the N7, Clanwilliam is a good base for exploring the Cederberg, and more peaceful and picturesque than Citrusdal. **Clanwilliam Tourism Bureau** ① *Main Rd, just to the left of the Old Jail, T027-482 2024, www.clanwilliam.info, Mon-Fri 0830-1700, Sat 0830-1230 (longer hrs during flower season)*, a very helpful, friendly office, is worth a visit, although for more detailed advice on hiking in the area, you'll have to go to the office in Algeria in the Cederberg Wilderness Area (see page 212).

Background

The entire area of the Cederberg was populated by nomadic San people for over 20,000 years, and a profusion of rock art bears testament to their presence and displacement from the area. The land was first settled by white farmers in 1726; Jan Dissels started one of the first farms here, building a homestead close to the wagon track route from Table Bay. At the time, this spot was referred to as *Aan de Renoster Hoek*, literally, 'By the Rhinoceros Corner'. Similar names in the region refer to *olifants* and *seekoei*, elephant and hippopotamus, providing further evidence of the wildlife that once roamed the area.

In 1808 a garrison was constructed to try to deal with the problem of cattle rustling by Khoi people. The hot and arid farming conditions further dissuaded families from settling here, and the first British settlers were in fact brought here by the British government to create a human buffer in a grand scheme to stabilize the border from further tribal incursions. Only six families remained and, when the village was renamed in 1814, there were only 16 families living in the area. The new name was given by Sir John Cradock, the Governor of the Cape, in honour of his father-in-law, the Earl of Clanwilliam. Despite being a strong Afrikaner region, the name has stuck.

Sights

The majority of South Africans come to Clanwilliam to make use of the sporting facilities on and around the beautifully situated **Clanwilliam Dam**, though there are a couple of sights worth seeing in town. **Old Jail** ① *Mon-Fri 0800-1230, during flower season (Aug-Sep) daily 0800-1700, R5.* This stocky white fort-like building overlooking the main street was built in 1808. The first part of the museum is devoted to the works of Clanwilliam's two famous residents: Dr P le Fras Nortier, who worked on citrus and the rooibos bush; and Louis Leipoldt, a well-known nature poet. There are also some displays on the rooibos (red bush) and cedar industries. At the back of the museum is an incredible giant threshing machine which was shipped out to South Africa in parts from Ipswich, England.

The rooibus tea industry originally flourished during the Second World War when teas from the Far East were difficult to obtain in Europe. After the war the market collapsed, but in recent times it has grown in popularity since it is caffeine-free and low in tannin. Today it is the biggest industry in the area and the tea is a refreshing, if acquired, taste. For a cup of tea and a video show contact the **Rooibos Tea Factory** ① *on the road to the right of the Old Jail, T027-482 2155.* Further along the same road is the **Clanwilliam Dam Resort**, part of which is the **Ramskop Nature Reserve** ① *mid-Jul to Oct,* worth visiting in season to view its magnificent wild flowers in bloom, of which there are over 400 species. There are well-laid-out paths through the reserve to the dam wall with good views of the mountains.

The Cederberg is famous for its rugged scenery, stunning rock formations and ancient rock art, all of which make it fantastic walking country. There are over 250 km of paths in the mountains, passing streams and waterfalls and bizarre mountain flora. The highest peaks are Snow Peak (2028 m) and Table Peak (1969 m), while the most notable sandstone features include the **Wolfberg Arch**, the **Maltese Cross**, the **Wolfberg Cracks**, **Lot's Wife**, the **Town Hall** and the **Valley of the Red Gods**.

Ins and outs

Getting there and around   All of the roads into the Cederberg Mountains are gravel, with steep and twisting sections, although some of the steeper parts have been covered with tarmac. The principal administrative centre for the wilderness is Algeria. Approaching from Citrusdal, the quickest route to Algeria is north along the N7; after 27 km take a right, signposted Kriedouwkrans and Algeria. You will cross the Olifants River via a low-level bridge and then descend into Algeria via Nieuwoudt Pass. The bridge crossing is sometimes flooded during winter. Contact the Algeria office to enquire about road conditions before setting off.

Best time to visit   Climate is an important factor to bear in mind when planning a hike. During the summer months daytime temperatures are high, most streams and pools are dry, and you will need to carry plenty of water. Conversely, in the winter there can be heavy snowfalls, so you must carry the appropriate equipment. The best months for hiking are March to April and September to December. January and February are very hot and few people walk during these months; between June and August you can expect to encounter snow on the high ground.

Tourist information   The **Cape Nature Conservation office** ⓘ *T027-482 2403, www.cape nature.co.za, R35, children (2-13) R22 per day, R60 children (2-13) R30 per overnight in the wilderness area*, in Algeria, is the best source of information, and issues hiking permits and maps. The region is divided into three areas and 50 people are allowed in each area per day, but you shouldn't have to book permits in advance, even in peak season.

Hiking

As an officially declared wilderness, you are allowed to walk and camp anywhere in the mountains. There are, however, important rules to observe. No fires are allowed, so gas or paraffin stoves must be carried on overnight hikes. All waste material must be taken away – if you come across other people's rubbish, don't ignore it but carry it with you. Finally, while you are allowed to swim in the streams and pools, **do not wash with any form of soap** in the waters. The idea behind a wilderness is that the entire watershed is left to its own devices with minimal interference from man. There are few areas, even in South Africa, where you can wander so freely, so enjoy it and respect the rules. While there are recognized trails, these are not always easy to follow. Anyone planning a hike of more than one day should buy the excellent Cederberg map available at the Cape Nature Conservation office, and always carry a compass.

Warning   There are 16 species of snake found in the mountains. Hikers may encounter a snake sunning itself on a path and although they are not aggressive it's best to wear strong

Cederberg Wilderness Area

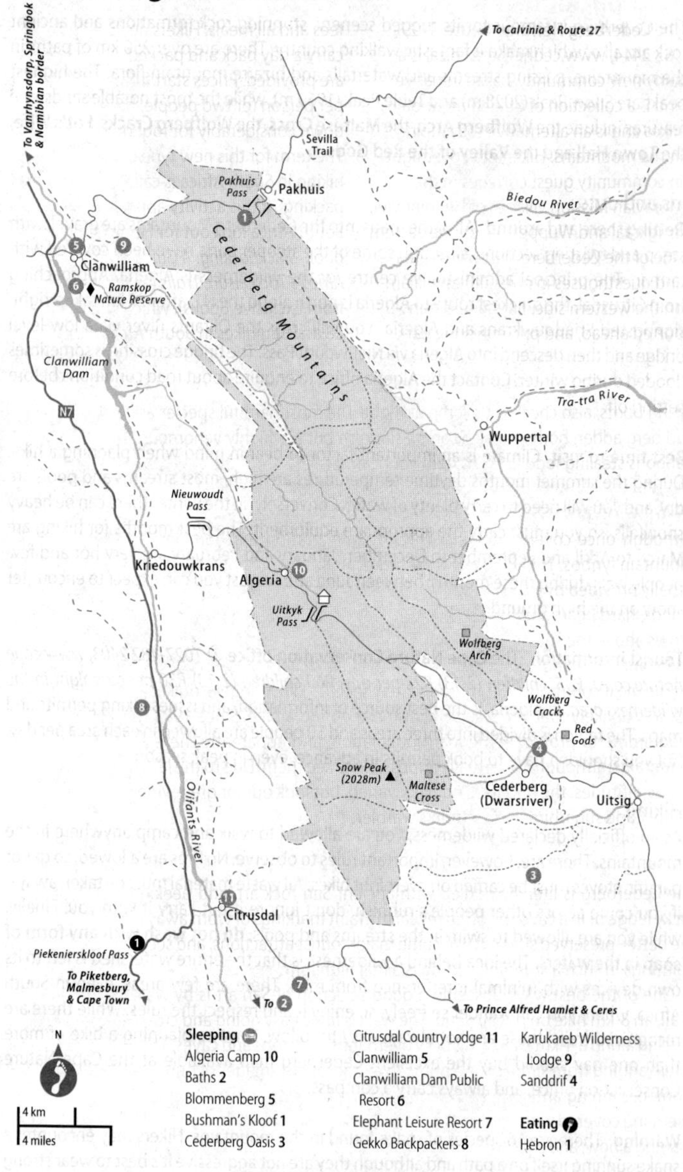

Slackpacking

The **Cederberg Heritage Route**, T027-482 2444, www.cedheroute.co.za, is a fairly new community-based initiative and is a collection of guided multi-day hikes and is an alternative to camping in the mountains. Hikers stay overnight in community guest cottages in the Moravian Mission villages of Heuningvlei, Brugkraal and Wupperthal on the eastern side of the Cederberg Wilderness area and guesthouses in or near Clanwilliam on the western side. Luggage is transported ahead, and prices include park fees and all meals. Hikers need only to carry a day pack and packed lunches are provided. Prices start from R3000 per person for two people, but come down considerably for four or six people. The term for this new type of assisted hiking in South Africa is called 'slackpacking'. If this activity appeals, once in South Africa look out for Fiona McIntosh's book, *Slackpacking: A Guide to South Africa's Top Leisure Trails* (available from Exclusive Books), which details 28 assisted hikes in South Africa.

hiking boots; also check your camp at night. The most harmful species are the puff adder and berg adder, both of which can be sluggish but are highly venomous. Beware, too, of baboons stealing food at night from your camp.

Vegetation and wildlife

Although once covered in cedar trees, the vegetation that remains is predominantly mountain fynbos. There are few trees found along the major hikes – shade and shelter is usually provided by rock overhangs. In the wetter gullies and valleys you will find yellowwoods, hard pears and the Cape beech. The rare endemic snow protea, *Protea cryophila*, grows above the snowline. It is only found in a few locations but these are kept a secret. There are some photos of the flowers in the Clanwilliam museum.

The most common antelope found here include klipspringers, duiker and grey rhebok, but it is unlikely that you'll see any of these during a hike. Since 1988 there has been a programme to protect the leopard population, and apparently there are plenty in the mountains, although it is virtually impossible to see them. Due to the lack of vegetation at higher altitudes, the birdlife is not very varied, but look out for grey-wing francolin, Cape siskin, Cape sugarbird and Victorin's warbler.

Rock art

The Cederberg is literally riddled with ancient San rock art, and peeking underneath a rocky ledge or in a cave will often reveal the faint markings of worn away images. Some of the better-preserved sites have become major tourist attractions, and seeing these ancient paintings in such a stunning setting is a real highlight.

One of the best ways of seeing a good selection of San art is by walking the **Sevilla Trail**, an 8-km hike on private land. The walk is fairly easy going and crosses a rocky plain, passing along a 4-km stretch of rocky overhangs, outcrops and caves. There are 10 sites in total, ranging from simple hand prints to extraordinary images of hunters, processions of women, running antelope and elephants. The highlight of the hike is Site Five, a rocky overhang covered with images in various stages of erosion, with a beautifully clear hunter carrying a bow, and a painting of a zebra foal, perfectly embodying its first uncertain steps.

Even those with just a passing interest in San art will find this walk thoroughly absorbing. The stunning rock formations, silent bush and shimmering mountains add to the atmosphere. The trail begins at **Traveller's Rest Farm** ① *34 km from Clanwilliam on Wuppertal Rd, over the Pakhuis Pass, T027-482 1824, www.travellersrest.co.za.* Permits are issued at the farm and there are also 12 self-catering cottages. If your interest in rock art isn't satiated and you've got plenty of cash, spend a day or two at **Bushman's Kloof** (see Sleeping, page 213).

North of Cederberg ⊖● » *pp211-214.*

Calvinia → *Colour map 6, A2.*

Although Calvinia is actually in the Northern Cape, it is relatively far from most sights in the north, and therefore usually visited as part of the Western Cape. It is a typical hot, sleepy Karoo town that most people just pass through, perhaps stopping for petrol and a cool drink. It has a beautiful setting though, at the foot of the Hantams Mountains. It's also an important sheep-farming centre, though, given the vast size of the farms, chances are you won't see any sheep. It also has clear star-filled skies at night 80% of the time, and attracts many South African astronomers.

The **tourist office** ① *T027-341 1043*, is in the **Calvinia Museum** ① *44 Church St, T027-341 8500, Mon-Fri 0800-1300, 1400-1700, Sat 0800-1200, small entry fee.* The mildly interesting museum is located in an art deco synagogue built in the 1920s, and relates to the early history of the region, made up of photographs and farming implements and stuffed sheep. In the garden is a horsemill, which are still in use on farms in the depths of the Karoo.

Calvinia's best known quirky attraction is the giant red post office box that stands in the main street. It's 6.2 m high and is actually a painted disused water tank. If you post a letter in it, it will get a special flower frank, but to do this you somehow have to reach the slot at the top.

Vanrhynsdorp → *Colour map 6, A1.*

This town is known as the gateway to arid Namakwa region (see the Northern Cape chapter). North from here the countryside seems a thousand miles from the fertile Cape. The town is named after Petrus Benjamin van Rhyn, the first representative for Namaqualand to sit in the old Cape Legislative Council. Although the region was first visited by Pieter Crythoff in 1662 it was only settled in the 1740s. The town itself first took shape in 1887 with the building of a church. The **tourist office** ① *Van Riebeeck St, T027-219 1552, www.tourismvanrhynsdorp.co.za, Mon-Fri 0800-1700, sometimes Sat in flower season,* is near the old jail.

The green-fingered may want to visit the **Kokerboom Succulent Nursery** ① *74 Voortrekker St, T027-219 1062, Mon-Fri 0800-1700, small entrance charge,* on the outskirts of town. Gardeners come here from afar, and it's worth a visit if you're here out of the flower season. It claims to be the largest such nursery for the distinct kokerboom (aloe) trees in South Africa. **Latsky Radio Museum** ① *close to the post office at 4 Church St, T027-209 1032, Mon-Sat 0900-1200, 1400-1700,* is a private collection of over 200 domestic radios covering the period 1915-1965.

For Sleeping and Eating price codes and other relevant information, see pages 46-53.

⊜ **Sleeping**

Malmesbury *p204*

C Orchard Country House, Long St, T022-487 2377, www.orchardhouse.co.za. A neat guesthouse with 7 rooms in a Herbert Baker designed house built in 1936. Some rooms have Victorian claw-foot baths and 4-poster beds, and facilities include a cigar lounge and bar with full-size snooker table, pool, and restaurant that serves breakfasts, lunches and afternoon teas to passing trade and dinner on request for guests.

D Bergzicht, 43 Bergzicht St, T022-482 4274, www.bergzichtlodgings.co.za. Comfortable B&B with 4 double rooms and 4 garden self-catering units sleeping 2-4, next to the swimming pool, pretty courtyard with a fountain, full English breakfasts.

Piketberg *p205*

B-C Dunn's Castle, T022-913 2470, www.dunnscastle.co.za. Dunn's Castle was built in the 1890s for George Dunn and was designed by Sir Herbert Baker. It has 5 pretty double rooms in the castle with Victorian finishes, country decor, fireplaces and freestanding bathtubs, plus 20 self-catering cottages in the grounds, swimming pool, restaurant and bar.

Citrusdal *p205*

Plenty of farms in the region provide accommodation, convenient for hiking. Full lists are available from the tourist office.

C Elephant Leisure Resort, 7 km from Citrusdal in the shadow of the Cederberg Mountains, T021-921 2884, www.elephant leisure.co.za. 10 well-equipped cottages on a private nature reserve with views of

the valley and nearby dam. Each cottage sleeps 2-4, with a/c, TV, fridge, cooking facilities (including microwave), fireplace, braai area and veranda. Rather unusually each has a 4-seater jacuzzi and there's a swimming pool.

C The Baths, 18 km to the south of Citrusdal, the well signposted turning is between the N7 and the town, T022-921 8026, www.the baths.co.za. A popular and long-established site at a natural hot-water spring surrounded by citrus groves, the first resort was opened here in 1739 and the main Victorian stone buildings survive. 16 well-equipped chalets, 18 flats and 15 camping pitches, all self-catering. Depending on the unit, bedding is included in some or you can rent it, but you'll need to bring towels, shop on site but buy fresh groceries in Citrusdal, restaurant and bar, hot and cold swimming pools, tennis courts, mountain biking, hiking trails, individual spa baths/jacuzzis, all set in a tract of indigenous woodland. A lovely peaceful spot, no TVs or mobile phone coverage. Recommended.

D Citrusdal Country Lodge, 67 Voortrekker St, T022-921 2221, www.cedarberglodge. co.za. This is a family-run town hotel with 26 a/c rooms, TV with M-Net, swimming pool, full-size billiard table, gardens and gym. **Tangelo's** restaurant has a good reputation, mix of usual steaks with country cooking, pub with big-screen TV showing sports.

E-F Gekko Backpackers, 20 km north of Citrusdal on the N7, turning to left is signposted, T022-921 3721, www.gekko.co.za. Excellent backpacker lodge on a citrus farm. Double rooms, dorms, camping. If you don't have a sleeping bag, bedding can be hired. Brightly painted bathrooms, large kitchen, bar, meals on request, table-tennis room, small lounge, hammocks strung underneath trees for relaxing on the lawns. Access to swimming holes in river and added bonus of San rock art on the farm. Popular with overlanders, so can be lively, but usually very peaceful. Will pick up from the Intercape bus in Citrusdal by prior arrangement. Highly recommended.

Clanwilliam p206

B Karukareb Wilderness Lodge, 1 km from Clanwilliam towards Calvinia, turn right at the Boskloof turn off, the lodge is 13 km, T027-482 1675, www.karukareb.co.za. 5 colonial-style rooms or 5 luxury permanent safari tents with claw foot baths, very stylish with a/c, wooden floors, lovely restaurant and bar in a thatched *lapa*, swimming pool, lots of activities from hiking trails to horse riding. Rates include breakfast, dinner and mountain bikes. An excellent base to explore the Cederberg, but no young children permitted.

C Blommenberg, 1 Graafwater Rd, T027-482 1851, www.blommenberg.co.za. Comfortable set of 12 units, 4 of which are self-catering, M-Net TV, a/c, minibar, breakfasts served in a dining room full of antiques, lovely gardens, braai areas, pool, hard to miss on the right-hand side just before town.

C Clanwilliam Hotel, Main St, T027-482 1101, www.clanwilliamhotel.co.za. Friendly, homely and recently refurbished 3-star town hotel, large comfortable rooms, en suite, a/c, TV, good restaurant and tea room, swimming pool, sauna, good value and excellent service. Across the road from **Reinhold's Restaurant**.

D-F Clanwilliam Dam Public Resort, 1 km out of town beside the dam, T027-482 8000. Huge resort with 180 grassy caravan and tent stands on tiers up the hillside, modern but plain self-catering chalets, plenty of trees offering shade, electric and gas points, gets very busy and noisy in season when you should watch security. Out of season you should be able to turn up on the day and find space. No restaurant, bar or shop.

Cederberg Wilderness Area p207, map p208

Outside Citrusdal and Clanwilliam are a host of private farms. The list includes those closest to the mountains. If you are self-catering, stock up in advance. Basic groceries can be bought at a shop just before Algeria.

C Sanddrif, 25 km south of Algeria, T027-482 2825, www.cederbergwine.com. 15 chalets, a choice of standard self-catering chalets, luxury chalets or a grassy and shady campsite (**F**), bring bedding and towels. The standard chalets have no shade but views of the mountains, and all are close to the river. 20 mins' walk downstream is Maalgat, an 8-m-deep pool popular with divers. There are power points at the campsite, and campers can use the deep freeze in the office at Dwarsriver. The farm sells fresh milk, butter and their own wine. The advantage of staying here is that you can easily visit the Maltese Cross, Wolfberg Cracks and the Wolfberg Arch on a day's walk from the camp without having to drive anywhere, and hiking permits are available from the office. Recommended.

C-E Algeria Camp, run by **Cape Nature Conservation**, reservations through their Cape Town office, T021-659 3500, www.capenature.co.za. Take the N7 27 km north of Citrusdal, turn right on Algeria Rd; it is 18 km to the camp on a dirt road. The camp is in a beautiful setting on the edge of a pine forest by a mountain stream and swimming hole. It is exceptionally clean, well run and very popular; book in advance especially for school holidays. Self-catering stone cottages sleep 4-8, all fully equipped, plus 48 shady camping spots, some with electric points. At the foot of Uitkyk Pass, 5 km to the south of Algeria, are 4 more **cottages**, sleeping 4-6. These are very basic, with solar electricity, although there is a gas-run fridge and stove, and hot water. Bbedding is provided but you'll need to bring towels and extra candles with you. The helpful information office and camp reception is open 0730-1600; you must arrive before 1600 to collect keys for accommodation. It also issues hiking permits and maps for some of the longer trails in the Cederberg Mountains starting from the camp. There is a card and coin phone next to reception and firewood is available. Guests can swim in the nearby river. Note that accommodation is more expensive at the weekend and on public holidays.

D-F Cederberg Oasis, 30 km south of Algeria and 67 km from the turn-off for Algeria on the N7, T027-482 2819, www.cederbergoasis. co.za. A well-placed backpacker hostel for many of the major hikes, and is part of the Cederberg conservancy. Good-value cottages, some with dorms, self-catering, camping, restaurant, bar, swimming pool and internet access. Maps and information available. A good friendly family-run set-up.

Private lodges and camps

L2 Bushman's Kloof, Wupperthal Rd over the Pakhuis Pass, central reservations, T021-685 2598 (Cape Town), www.bushmans kloof.co.za. This private reserve claims to have the 'world's largest open-air rock art gallery', and it certainly is one of the best places to see San art in South Africa with over 130 sites, dating back as far as 10,000 years. Animals present include Cape mountain zebra, klip-springer, baboon and smaller mammels. Accommodation is in luxurious cottages and in the main building. All rooms are a/c, with 4-poster beds, tasteful decor, log fires and wooden decks overlooking a lake. There are 4 swimming pools, sauna, beauty spa, excellent restaurant with outdoor terrace, gift shop, library, billiard room and wine cellar. An overnight itinerary begins with check-in at 1400, followed by afternoon tea, an evening game drive and dinner; the next morning is an excursion to the rock art followed by lunch and check out at 1200. Prices include all meals, game drives and tours but starting from R5200 per night for 2 people the experience does not come cheap; ask about specials Apr-Jun. Air and road transfers can be arranged from Cape Town.

Calvinia *p210*

B-C Hantem House, 44 Hoop St, T027-341 1606, www.calvinia.co.za. Several converted Victorian houses in the village, with luxury rooms, wooden floors, antique furniture, cosy traditional kitchens, full of old-world charm and no TVs, the only modern amenities are the electric blankets on the beds. Overall very smart and of a high standard. Light meals can be arranged in the house kitchens or eat at the main restaurant at **Hantem House** (¥¥), which is a restored 19th-century homestead and the oldest surviving building in the village, and the best place to try traditional Karoo cuisine, plus excellent breakfasts. Recommended.

D Hantam Hotel, Kerk St, T027-341 1512, www.hantamhotel.co.za. A large solid building with great shady verandas, 17 rooms with a/c and TV, **Busibee** restaurant serving predominantly steaks and a bar popular with local farmers. The principal town hotel but with far less character than the Victorian houses above.

Vanrhynsdorp *p210*

D Namaqualand Country Lodge, Voortrekker St, T027-219 1633, www.namaqua lodge.co.za. Some old rooms plus new rooms in block at back, comfortable TV lounge and open central courtyard decorated with wood carvings, used by tour groups. Steakhouse-style restaurant, small bar, swimming pool. The smart external appearance is let down by ordinary faded rooms.

D Van Rhyn Guest House, Van Riebeeck St, T027-219 1429, www.vanrhyngh.co.za. 11 comfortable en suite rooms, non-smoking, in a pleasant old Victorian 1-storey house built in 1916 in gardens full of trees. Pool, TV room, fully licensed and offers wine from the Olifants River region, dinner on request. Doubles up not only as an art gallery but as the local hairdressers.

🍴 Eating

Malmesbury *p204*
🍴🍴 **Die Herehuis**, 1 Loedolf St, T022-487 1771.
Open 0730-1400, 1800-2100, closed Sun
evening. Enormous choice on the à la carte
menu, 4-course set menu at Sun lunchtime
includes a local roast with fresh vegetables.
Friendly service, garden setting, oil lamps
and roaring fires in winter. Recommended.

Citrusdal *p205*
🍴🍴 **Hebron**, on Piekenierskloof Pass, before
you descend into the Citrusdal Valley, T022-
921 2595. Open 0730-1600. Lovely terrace
setting and good gourmet breakfasts and
lunches for this remote location. Freshly
ground coffee, home-made bread and rolls,
fresh vegetables, chickpea stew or beef
with couscous, and lots of sticky puddings.
You can also pick home-made jams and
marmalade at the farm stall.
🍴🍴 **Patrick's**, 77 Voortrekker St, T022-921 3062.
This used to be a pub and restaurant with
an Irish theme and some of the best food
in town. At the time of writing it was closed
for a complete refurbishment but may
have reopened by the time you read this.

Clanwilliam *p206*
🍴🍴 **Reinhold's**, opposite Clanwilliam Hotel,
T027-482 1101, Tue-Sat 1900-2100. Smart
à la carte, dinner only, small bar and cosy
atmosphere, good range of steaks, fish
and pasta, the best option in the area.
🍴 **Nancy's Tearoom**, 33 Main St, T027-482
1101. Mon-Fri 0830-1630, Sat 0830-1430.
Classy tea room set in beautiful gardens
with blue and gold decor, serving good
sandwiches and cakes and specials for
lunch like babotie, quiches and burgers.
🍴 **Olifantshuis Pizzeria**, Main St, T027-982
2301. Mon-Sat 1700-late, daily in flower
season. Popular and informal pub serving
steaks, grills, salads and good pizzas with
garden tables and friendly atmosphere.

🏔 Activities and tours

Clanwilliam *p206*
Tour operators
Blue Yonder, T083-232 4306, www.blue
yonder.co.za. Adventure trips using 4WD
and 'Xumbugs', small 4WD go-carts, into
the Cederberg mountains.
Cederberg Travel, T027-482 2444,
www.cedarberg-travel.com. A broad-
based Southern and East African travel
agent but can organize 4- to 5-day tours
from Cape Town to the Cederberg.

🚍 Transport

The N7 to the Northern Cape *p204*
Bus
Intercape, www.intercape.co.za. There is a
daily service in both directions between
Cape Town and **Namibia** along the length
of the N7. However, only passengers starting
their journey in one country and finishing it
in another are permitted to use this service.
   There is another service between **Cape
Town** and **Upington**, the bus turns off the
N7 at **Vanrhynsdorp** and on to **Calvinia**.
The bus stops in **Malmesbury** outside
Malmesbury Motors; **Moorreesburg** outside
Swartland Motors; **Citrusdal** outside Sonop
Motors; **Clanwilliam** outside Cedar Inn;
Vanrhynsdorp outside Turck's Garage at
the junction with the N7. The Namibia
service runs along the N7 during the day
but the Upington service arrives and
departs in the middle of the night.

🗂 Directory

Calvinia *p210*
Banks ABSA, 25 Hoop St; Standard,
21 Hoop St.

Breede River Valley

Only 310 km long, the Breede River (also known as the Breë, meaning 'broad') is one of the most important rivers in the Cape, and its valley is a beautiful boundary zone. Fed by streams from the mountains, the river is a major source of water for a large number of orchards and vineyards. Leaving the mountains behind at Ceres, the river passes through the Bontebok National Park and then flows across an undulating coastal terrace, meandering through the wheat fields of the Overberg before entering the Indian Ocean at St Sebastian Bay.

Worcester is the principal town of the region. Along the broad valley are important farming centres such as Ceres, Prince Alfred Hamlet, Ashton and Bonnievale and the picturesque villages of Tulbagh, McGregor and Montagu. These old settlements are surrounded by vineyards and fruit farms that undergo beautiful colour changes through the seasons. Behind the farms are mountains rising to 2000 m with challenging hiking trails and hidden valleys, their peaks capped with snow in the winter. The valley acts very much as the dividing line between two contrasting regions of South Africa. To the southwest are the verdant Winelands and populous Cape Town, both very fertile and prosperous districts. To the northeast is the start of the Karoo, a vast expanse of semi-desert, dotted with the odd sheep farm or isolated Victorian town.
▶▶ *For listings, see pages 233-242.*

Ins and outs

Since the opening of the Huguenot Toll Tunnel in 1988 it has been possible to drive to Worcester from Cape Town in less than an hour. Worcester lies just to the south of the N1, and is the largest town in the Breede Valley. From here you can continue your journey in three different directions. Firstly, the main N1 highway continues for another 1300 km to Johannesburg. Locals regard this road as dull and something to be got over with as quickly as possible. The road passes through the southern margin of the Great Karoo, known as the Koup. While most people only pause here to refuel or stay overnight, this is a wonderful region to explore with a couple of beautiful Victorian towns as well as the superb Karoo National Park outside Beaufort West.

Heading north from Worcester along the R43, you quickly reach the N7 highway. The N7 is the main road between Cape Town and Namibia, running up the West Coast. This route will take you to the upper reaches of the Breede River Valley and the agricultural centres of Tulbagh and Ceres.

The final direction you could take when leaving Worcester is to follow the R60 along the Breede River Valley as far as Swellendam in the Overberg and then head east along the N2 highway to the Garden Route and Port Elizabeth.

The 3.9-km-long Huguenot Toll Tunnel reduces the journey through the mountains by 11 km. As you emerge on the Cape Town side, the road is perched high on a viaduct with superb views of Paarl Mountain, its hillsides covered with ordered vineyards – a sharp contrast to the countryside at the other end of the tunnel. Much of this region is part of the successful Route 62 tourism initiative which provides an alternative route to the N2 between Cape Town and the Garden Route, along the back roads through fruit farming and vineyard country; tourist information and maps can be found at the very detailed www.route62.co.za.

This medium-sized farming centre is the capital of the Breede River Valley, a prosperous town with many interesting historic buildings and a fine collection of museums. The excellent Karoo Desert National Botanical Garden is well worth visiting, particularly during the flowering months of August to October, and there's a wine route to explore.

Ins and outs

Tourist information **Worcester Wine and Tourism** ⓘ *25 Baring St, T023-348 2795, www.worcestertourism.com, Mon-Fri 0800-1700, Sat 0830-1230*, provides a walking-tour booklet that can also be downloaded from the website.

Background

The first Europeans to settle in the region were farmers, and when it became necessary to build a settlement, their land had to be acquired. The streets were laid out and the first plots were sold in 1820; the new settlement was named after the Marquess of Worcester, the eldest brother of the Governor of the Cape, Lord Charles Somerset. One of the first buildings to emerge was the local *drostdy* (magistracy), which was one of the finest Cape buildings in South Africa. Today it is part of the Drostdy Technical High School. The wealth in the region is almost entirely derived from agriculture, a fact that is easy to appreciate while travelling past the numerous vineyards and orchards of the valley. Many of the neat farms visible from the roadside depend upon irrigated waters. The highly fertile neighbouring Hex River Valley is in effect the last of the productive Cape farmlands. In contrast, driving east from the valley one quickly comes to the dry and arid Karoo.

Sights

If time permits, a short walk around the centre is very pleasant. The main sights are central and close together, and the grid street pattern makes it easy to find your way about. There are some fine Victorian town buildings, although the main road is made up of mostly modern shops and fast-food outlets. Many of the old buildings are along **Church Street**, most of which were built between 1840 and 1855. Also in Church Street is the **Congregational Church**, housing some fine original examples of wooden church furnishings and standing in a well-kept garden. The **Dutch Reformed Church** dates from 1832, a Gothic-style building which dominates the town skyline. Its spire has an interesting history: the original was considered to be too squat and was replaced by a cheap tin version in 1899. The current spire was built in 1927 after the tin one had twice been blown down by the summer gales from the southeast.

Next to Church Square is a **Garden of Remembrance** which contains some monuments commemorating local residents. It was designed by one of the town's more famous citizens, the artist Hugo Naudé. Each Saturday morning a **Flea Market** is held on Church Square.

Worcester is well known throughout South Africa as being the home of two important institutes for the disabled set up by the Dutch Reformed Church. In 1881 an **Institute for the Blind** ⓘ *www.blind-institute.org.za*, was opened, and a few years later an **Institute for the Deaf** ⓘ *http://deafnet.co.za*, was founded in De la Bat Street. Each institute has opened a shop in the town centre selling crafts made by members (see Shopping, page 241). The institutes are also open to visitors who wish to learn more about the pioneering work undertaken with blind and deaf people. Unlike most South African towns, the pedestrian crossings in Worcester emit sounds for the blind.

On the corner of Baring and Church streets is **Beck House** ① *T023-342 0936, Mon-Fri 0830-1630, small entrance fee*, built in 1841 in typical Cape Dutch style. It has an interesting display depicting the town life of an important Worcester citizen, Cornelius Beck. There are some excellent examples of late 19th-century furnishings – the quality of the yellow-wood and stinkwood furniture is regarded as some of the best in South Africa. Look out for the bath house, the delightful herb garden and the Cape cart in the old coach house. It is also home to a small coffee and gift shop.

The interesting **Hugo Naudé & Jean Welz Gallery** ① *115 Russell St, T023-342 5802, Mon-Fri 0830-1630, Sat 0900-1200*, is home to a mixed collection of works by prominent South African artists. The first collection is of sculptures by Bill Davis, displayed in the garden. Inside are paintings by Jean Welz, Paul de Toit and Hugo Naudé. Hugo Naudé was a pioneer painter who also designed this large two-storey building and had it built as his home in 1904. He lived and worked here until his death in 1941.

There are 18 cooperative wine cellars, three wine estates, and several brandy distilleries in the Worcester region. **KWV Brandy Cellar** ① *Church St, T023-342 0255, www.kwv.co.za, Mon-Fri 1000-1500 for tastings, guided tours of the distillery in English Mon-Fri at 1000 and 1400, tours in other languages organized on request*, is the largest in the world under a single roof. There are 120 copper pot stills producing 10- and 20-year-old brandies.

🌙 Look out for the Braille labels on some of the local wine – these are the only Braille wine labels in the world.

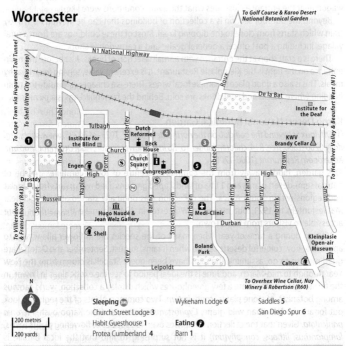

Worcester

To Golf Course & Karoo Desert National Botanical Garden

N1 National Highway

To Cape Town via Huguenot Toll Tunnel
To Shell Ultra City (Bus stop)
To Villiersdorp & Franschhoek (R43)
To Hex River Valley & Beaufort West (N1)
To Overhex Wine Cellar, Nuy Winery & Robertson (R60)

Rabie · Tulbagh · Adderley · Dutch Reformed ④ · Roux · De la Bat · Institute for the Deaf · Institute for the Blind · Church · Beck House · KWV Brandy Cellar · Brown · Engen · Church Square · ③ · Riebeeck · High · Congregational · ⑤ · High · Drostdy · Napier · ⑥ · Baring · Stockenstroom · Fairbain · Metring · Sutherland · Murray · Combrink · Smith · Somerset · Russell · Hugo Naudé & Jean Welz Gallery · Medi-Clinic · Durban · Shell · Grey · Boland Park · Kleinplasie Open-air Museum · Leipoldt · Caltex

N · 200 metres · 200 yards

Sleeping 🛏
Church Street Lodge 3
Habit Guesthouse 1
Protea Cumberland 4
Wykeham Lodge 6
Saddles 5
San Diego Spur 6

Eating 🍴
Barn 1

Kleinplasie Open-air Museum

ⓘ *Robertson Rd, T023-342 2226, www.kleinplasie.co.za, Mon-Sat 0900-1630, R12, children (under 16) R5.*

Kleinplasie is an open-air museum depicting the lifestyle of the early pioneer farmers. The collection is a series of old farm buildings, many with traditional skills on show such as tobacco rolling. There is also an indoor collection of smaller tools and implements as well as a tea room. In addition, Kleinplasie is the home of **Worcester Winelands** ⓘ *T023-342 8710, www.worcesterwineroute.co.za,* which is very helpful in giving information on the surrounding winelands, as well as offering tastings and sales of local wines. Allow at least two hours to look around all the exhibits. The first part of the display comprises 26 buildings which have been furnished or equipped in the styles of the period 1690-1900. Only the tobacco shed is an original structure, dating from 1900; all the other buildings are reconstructions, but good ones. Several rural skills are demonstrated using traditional methods and tools. You can watch an ironmonger at work, or view the grinding of flour and baking of bread, plus cheese- and candle-making. Walking around the buildings gives one the feel of being on an old working farm: there are horses, cattle, pigs and geese in pens, not to mention all the farmyard smells and sounds. The second part of the collection is indoors and equally interesting. Most of the displays are of old farm implements and home industry pieces. All are clearly displayed and well labelled. A couple of items worth a closer look include the early example of a fruit grader, and a mean-looking self raker from the 1860s which was used in the wheat industry. The painted Voortrekker wagon near the entrance illustrates what the living conditions were like.

Beyond the outdoor section is a collection of buildings that can be viewed from a toy train which starts from close to the dipping kraal. Most of these buildings are from a rural village, including a post office, a general dealer and a cartwright's shop.

There is a craft shop at the entrance with a small selection of books. Just before the main entrance on the right is the **Kleinplasie Restaurant**. It is excellent value, serving fresh healthy meals. This is also a good place to sample local wines. There is a cheaper café inside the main building where snacks and cool drinks are sold. Behind the farm buildings is a picnic site.

Karoo Desert National Botanical Garden

ⓘ *Off Roux St beyond the golf club on the north side of the N1, T023-347 0785, www.sanbi.org, daily 0700-1800, free, R14, children (under 16) R6 in the flower season, Aug-Oct. Plant shop and Kokerboom Restaurant (1000-1700).*

This garden, hidden away from the commercial centre of town, combines 144 ha of natural semi-desert plants and 11 ha of landscaped gardens filled with plants from similar arid regions within South Africa. The collection was originally started at Whitehill near Matjiesfontein in 1921, but moved to Worcester in 1946 to make the gardens more accessible to visitors from Cape Town.

Visiting during a time of year when many of the species are in flower allows you to appreciate how colourful deserts can be when it rains. August, September and October are good months to go, assuming the rains have been good. Stapelias bloom from the New Year through to mid-March, and June is the ideal period to see the exotic aloes in flower. In the formal gardens there are a few greenhouses which display a collection, world-famous among botanists, of stone plants, *conophytum*. Two common plants of the region to look out for are the Namibian wild grape, *Cyphostemma juttae*, and the Karoo bush, *Pteronia paniculata*. Given that the collection comprises over 400 species of flowering plants (*aloes, lampranthus, lithops, conophytum*) it is not surprising to find that the local birdlife is exceptionally rich. Over 70 species have been recorded in the gardens. There are also several short trails, including an excellent 1-km-long **Braille Trail**, and much of the gardens are wheelchair accessible. Children will especially enjoy the porkwood plant maze.

Worcester wine route

There are 21 estates listed as part of the Worcester wine route. All are fairly local, and some of them offer tastings, tours and sales to visitors. Unlike many of the more visited wineries around Stellenbosch, most of the cellars here were founded in the 1940s – the farm buildings therefore lack much of the history and beauty found elsewhere. Furthermore, the countryside is not as dramatic as that around Paarl, and none of the cellars yet offers the excellent meals available on the Franschhoek Valley estates. That's not to say that the route is not worth visiting – one major advantage it has is that it is far less commercial than the Winelands and, by comparison, relatively tourist-free.

Listed below are some of the more interesting cellars. The **Worcester Winelands office** in the Kleinplasie Open-air Museum (see page opposite) is a good starting point. They can provide you with additional information on other members of the wine route and also offer tastings and sales of the area's best wines.

Botha Cellar ① *T023-355 1740, www.bothakelder.co.za, sales and tastings: Mon-Fri 0800-1700, Sat 1000-1300, cellar tours: by prior arrangement, 20 km along the R43 towards Ceres.* This is a pleasant cooperative with a neat tasting centre beside a colourful rose garden. The cellar is known for its Chardonnay, Hanepoort Jerepiko and port. Several varieties are on sale including some dessert wines and very good grape juice.

Worcester wine route

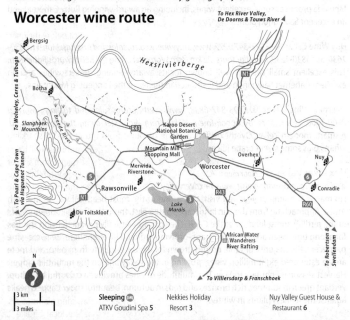

Bergsig Estate ① T023-355 1603, www.bergsig.co.za, sales and tastings: Mon-Fri 0800-1700, Sat 0900-1700, cellar tours: by prior arrangement, 40 km along the R43 towards Ceres. This is the oldest estate in the region and Bergsig has belonged to the Lategan family for six generations – the first vine was planted in 1843. It is a friendly estate with some good off-dry and semi-sweet whites. The **Bistro** (see Eating, page 239) offers breakfast, tea and cake and light lunches.

Conradie Private Cellar ① T023-342 7025, www.conradie-vineyards.co.za, sales and tastings: Mon-Sat 0900-1700, Sun 1000-1400, cellar tours: by appointment, 19 km from Worcester along the R60 towards Robertson. This is a young cellar but well known for its reds including Cabernet Sauvignon, Shiraz, and Merlot and an affordable range of whites. You can eat at the restaurant and enjoy their wine in the **Nuy Valley Guest House** (see Sleeping, page 233) across the road.

Du Toitskloof Winery ① 20 km from Worcester along the N1 towards Cape Town, T023-349 1601, www.dutoitskloof.com, sales and tastings: Mon-Fri 0900-1700, Sat 0900-1230, cellar tours: by prior arrangement. Some of the best award-winning local wines are produced here, on one of the most progressive estates in the country. It has a mixture of red wines, semi-sweet whites, dessert wines and grape juices.

Merwida Riverstone Vineyards ① T023-349 1144, www.merwida.com, sales and tastings: Mon-Fri 0800-1230, 1330-1700, Sat 0900-1300, cellar tours: by appointment, 10 km from Worcester off the road to Rawsonville. Despite being a small and relatively young cellar, Merwida produces some excellent wines, including an award-winning Ruby Cabernet and an excellent Sauvignon Blanc.

Nuy Wine Cellar ① T023-347 0272, www.nuywinery.co.za, sales and tastings: Mon-Fri 0830-1630, Sat 0830-1230, no cellar tours, 22 km from Worcester along the R60 towards Robertson. This excellent small cellar is well known for its award-winning dessert wines and an excellent Cabernet Sauvignon and is situated in the lee of the Langeberg Mountains.

Overhex Wine Cellar ① T023-347 6838, www.overhex.com, sales and tastings: Mon-Fri 0800-1700, cellar tours: by appointment, 6 km from Worcester along the Robertson Rd. A smart, modern cellar, Overhex offers a range of wines from muscadets to sparkling whites plus some sweet grape juices.

Hex River Valley → Colour map 8, A2.
① For more information visit www.hexrivervalley.co.za.
No matter the time of year you visit, this is one of the most beautiful valleys in South Africa. Approaching from the arid landscapes of the east, this is the first glimpse one gets of the fertility and splendour of the Cape. The soils are naturally productive and this has for a long time been an important grape-growing region. Although there are some wine producers, the majority of table grapes grown for export originate from here, and there are an estimated eight million vines growing in the valley and on the mountain slopes. Harvest season is February to May. This multitude of vines provides a colourful backdrop: verdant green in summer, rich bronzes and reds in autumn, beautiful snow-capped peaks against the leafless plants in winter.

De Doorns → *Colour map 8, A2.*

Heading towards the interior, 32 km along the N1 from Worcester, is this small settlement lying in the centre of a major grape-producing region. The name meaning 'the thorns' in Afrikaans refers to the local Acacia thorn bush. Information is available from the **tourist office** ① *Voortrekker St, T023-356 2041, www.tourismdedoorns.co.za, Mon-Fri 0800-1700, Sat 0800-1200.*

De Doorns Wine Cellar ① *T023-356 2100, www.dedoornscellar.co.za, Mon-Fri 0800-1230, 1330-1700, Sat 0800-1200, next to the N1*, is a large co-op in an old Cape Dutch building. In addition to producing a popular Hanepoort Jerepigo, there are refreshing red or white grape juices for sale, plus sherries and an alcohol-free sparkling wine. This is also a good stop for tourist information as there are many brochures on display. Nearby are a couple of farm stalls selling a good range of fresh local produce including table grapes in season. From De Doorns the N1 continues northeast through the Hex River Pass to Touws River and the Aquila Private Game Reserve (see page 281).

North from Worcester ⬤🍴🏵️▲ ▸▸ *pp233-242.*

The R43 follows the Breede River Valley to Wolseley and the major fruit-producing regions. Most of the farms can be visited on a day visit from Worcester, but there is a greater variety of choice in places to stay on the farms around Tulbagh and Ceres. The road follows the Breede River flows as it flows through the vineyards towards its source.

Wolseley → *Colour map 8, A2.*

This small town is in a unique position on the watershed of two rivers, one flowing into the Atlantic Ocean, the other into the Indian Ocean. Given the beauty of the surrounding countryside and the variety of tourist sights in Tulbagh and Worcester, there is no reason to spend much time here aside from a lunchtime meal. The few interesting old buildings that had survived through time were destroyed in the same earthquake that caused much of the damage in Tulbagh in 1969.

Tulbagh → *Colour map 8, A2.*

Tucked away in the Tulbagh Valley, surrounded by the Winterhoekberg, Witsenberg and Saronsberg Mountains, is this small village with a beautifully preserved centre of traditional Cape buildings. Along with Swellendam in the Overberg, it rates as one of the best examples of a rural Victorian settlement in South Africa. Like Swellendam, however, the state of the buildings is somewhat artificial because much of the settlement was destroyed by a sudden earthquake on 29 September 1969. This was a significant local tragedy: nine people died and considerable damage was done to property. However, the earthquake gave rise to the largest restoration project in South Africa's history. Many of the old buildings had been in a bad state of repair and some were practically derelict, but the village underwent massive restoration and became the fine settlement you see today.

The original name of the valley was Land van Waveren, an outpost of the Dutch East India Company dating from 1699. In the early days of Dutch rule the western hinterland, stretching as far north as present-day Piketberg and Porterville, was known as Waveren. The first settlers arrived in the valley on 31 July 1700 but it was another 40 years before permanent structures appeared and a village took shape. As with many settlements in the Cape, Tulbagh is named after a former Governor of the Cape, Ryk Tulbagh (1751-1771).

Today Tulbagh is a prosperous and peaceful settlement, isolated from Cape Town by several intervening mountain ranges. North of the town, the upper valley of the Little Berg River is a centre for some small wine estates and fruit farms. Sheep and wheat farming are also important to the local economy.

The **tourist office** ① *4 Church St, T023-230 1348, www.tulbaghtourism.org.za, Mon-Fri 0900-1700, Sat 1000-1600, Sun 1100-1600*, is enthusiastic and friendly, with some interesting and useful leaflets covering the area. There is an attached restaurant and coffee shop with outdoor seating overlooking beautiful Church Street. The office is in one of the houses which is part of the museum; tickets for all the museum buildings are sold here.

Tulbagh Valley

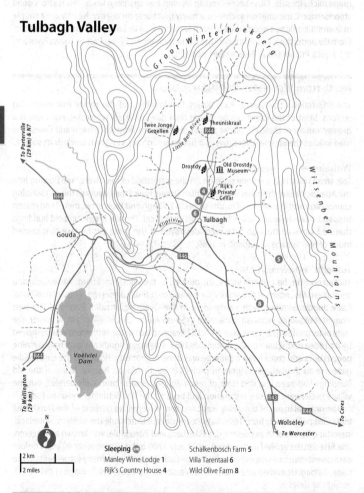

Sleeping 🛏
Manley Wine Lodge 1
Rijk's Country House 4

Schalkenbosch Farm 5
Villa Tarentaal 6
Wild Olive Farm 8

Sights in the town The main attraction is the delightful tree-lined **Church Street**; 32 of its original buildings were restored after the earthquake, and the whole street feels like a living museum. The majority of the buildings are in private ownership, but three are part of the town museum (see below) and a couple have been converted into B&Bs. The old slave lodge is now the **Paddagang** ('frog passage') **Restaurant** (see Eating, page 239), overlooking lush lawns. In complete contrast, the main commercial centre, Van der Stel Street, is a straight line of dull modern buildings saved by a colourful municipal garden.

If your time is short, the one place to visit in Tulbagh is the **Oude Kerk Volksmuseum** ① *2 Church St, T023-230 1041, Mon-Fri 0900-1700, Sat 0900-1600, Sun 1100-1600, R10, children R2*, which has one of the most interesting collections of Victorian furniture and objects in the Cape. The high ceiling and good light of the church makes it an ideal display case and it's a popular venue for weddings. There is also interesting information about the 1969 earthquake.

Sights outside the town The **Old Drostdy Museum** ① *T023-230 0203, Mon-Fri 1000-1700, Sat 1000-1400, R7, children R2, wine tasting R8*, is built on one of the early settler farms, Rietvlei, 4 km out of town. Designed by Louis Thibault, it has been restored and now houses a fine collection of sherry vats in the cellars, plus a museum devoted to antique furniture upstairs. Nearby is the **Drostdy Wine Cellar** ① *www.drostdywines.co.za*, where local wines and sherries are made (see below). The Old Drostdy building appears on their wine labels. For a small extra fee, their fortified wines can be tasted in the atmospheric, candle-lit cellars.

Wine route
This area is in fact better known for its fruit production – Ceres, the centre of the fruit industry, is only 35 km away. For more information about the vineyards in this region visit www.tulbaghwineroute.com. **Rijk's Private Cellar** ① *Sales and tastings: Mon-Fri 1000-1600, Sat 1000-1400, cellar tours: by appointment*. This is a young farm and vines were only planted in 1997, but it now produces an acclaimed variety of reds, and is the location of the excellent and luxurious **Rijk's Country House** (see Sleeping, page 234). North of Tulbagh is **Theuniskraal Estate** ① *T023-230 0688, www.theuniskraal.co.za, sales and tastings: Mon-Fri 1000-1200, 1300-1600, Sat 0900-1300, tours by appointment only*, which has been in the hands of the Jordaan family since 1927. Their white wines have won several awards. Their Riesling, with John Platter's seal of approval, is highly acclaimed. **Twee Jonge Gezellen** ① *T023-230 0680, www.houseofkrone.co.za, sales and tastings: Mon-Fri 0900-1600, Sat 1000-1400, cellar tours: Mon-Fri 1100 and 1500, Sat 1100*, has the only underground Méthode Cap Classique (South Africa's version of champagne) cellar in South Africa and there's a restaurant open during peak season. To get there take a left turn at the north end of Church Street. The tourist office can provide all the details of other estates in the valley.

Ceres → *Colour map 8, A2.*
Anyone travelling for some time in South Africa will undoubtedly try one of two brands of fruit juice – Liquifruit or Ceres, both of which are packed in Ceres. This is the most important fruit-growing centre in the country, and all types of soft fruits are grown and processed in the valley. Surrounded by the harsh and rugged Skurweberg Mountains, this attractive farming centre was founded in 1854 and aptly named after the Roman goddess of agriculture. During the winter months there can be heavy snowfalls in the mountains, enough at times for some limited winter sports. Snow is such a novelty in South Africa

that when there is snow on the ground, curious Capetonians visit here in droves: cars line the country roads and the local farmers' fields are trampled by thousands of people. When the snows melt, the Dwars, Koekedouw and Titus rivers become the perfect environment for trout fishing. For information visit **Ceres Tourism** ⓘ *Owen St, T023-316 1287, www.ceres.org.za, Mon-Fri 0830-1600*, in the town library.

One of the town's first magistrates, JA Munnik, was responsible for planting numerous trees around the town to provide shade. Fortunately, this tradition has been maintained and, as a result, there are plenty of mature trees lining the roads and the banks of the Dwars River, which flows through the town centre and the gardens of the **Belmont Hotel**.

Togryers' Museum (Transport Riders' Museum) ⓘ *8 Oranje St, T023-312 2045, Mon-Fri 0900-1300, 1400-1700, R7*, houses a fine collection of horse-drawn vehicles. All types of wagons and carriages are on show, celebrating the town's past importance as a centre for making these vehicles. Before the railways arrived, the fruit produced here had to be transported to the Cape in such wagons. Some excellent photographs capture the spirit of the time.

The following fruit packhouses and factories allow visitors to look around on tours – a sort of 'fruit route', if you like. It is surprisingly interesting to see how life starts for a peach or a potato that is going to end up on a local or even international supermarket shelf. Note that most of the factories insist on visitors wearing closed shoes and long trousers for hygiene purposes. **Ceres Fruit Growers** (CFG) is worth visiting to see its vast cold-storage facilities. This is one of the larger cooperatives specializing in deciduous fruits. **Ceres Fruit Juices** (CFJ) is home to the award-winning juices found on supermarket shelves around South Africa. **Ceres Potatoes** is a similar operation but with a crop of onions and potatoes. Tours run twice a day Monday to Friday at 1000 and 1400 depending on demand but they must be booked in advance through **Ceres Tourism** (see above); two-hour tours cost R60 per person. During the fruit season, December to March, they can also organize tours to working fruit farms or drying yards in the Ceres region.

Prince Alfred Hamlet → *Colour map 8, A2.*

This small village is the second most important farming centre in the Warm Bokkeveld Valley. It was named after the second son of Queen Victoria, who was the first member of the British royal family to visit South Africa. In 1865 he went on a hunting expedition in this region. North from here the road skirts along the western fringes of the arid Karoo for over 100 km, without passing through any settlements of note. The farmlands in this area are very productive, so much so that a rail link was specially built from Ceres to transport fruits and vegetables. Apples, peaches, plums, nectarines and pears are grown in the valley, and the short drive north from Ceres (R303) is particularly enjoyable during the spring when the orchards are in full blossom. Popular activities include fruit tours and trout fishing. Continuing north towards the Cederberg Mountains and Citrusdal, the road leaves the valley through **Gydo Pass**, R303. This is yet another pass built by Andrew Bain, this time while he was also working on the more important Michell's Pass. It was completed in 1848, and remained as a gravel road until the 1950s. The settlement is also the junction to the **Swartberg Pass** or R328 to 'The Hell', Oudtshoorn and the Cango Caves (see page 294). This is a good place to stop for a cool drink before climbing the scenic mountain pass. For local tourist information you're best off contacting the Ceres office, as Prince Alfred falls under their control.

Kagga Kamma Private Game Reserve

① *Off the R303 north of Prince Alfred Hamlet, T021-872 4343, www.kaggakamma.co.za.*

Kagga Kamma Private Game Reserve is 90 minutes' drive from Ceres, on the fringe of the Cederberg Mountains. It is a nature reserve devoted to the history of the San people who lived here, the remarkable rocky landscape dotted with their ancient rock art. The reserve did have a resident San village within its boundaries, but the villagers have moved back to their ancestral lands in the Kalahari. They drop in periodically to sell traditional wares. The area is one of outstanding natural beauty and the best way of exploring it is on foot. Resident anthropologists accompany visitors to rock art sites to explain their meaning, and are also very knowledgeable about the traditions, lifestyle and beliefs of the San.

It is possible to go on game drives and quad-bike safaris in the reserve, which has a good variety of antelope including eland, gemsbok, bontebok, springbok and kudu. There are also lynx, caracal and leopard, but these are very elusive. If you're in a hurry and

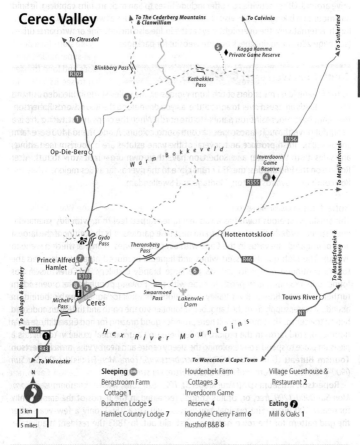

Ceres Valley

To Citrusdal
To The Cederberg Mountains & Clanwilliam
To Calvinia
To Sutherland

R303
Blinkberg Pass
Kagga Kamma Private Game Reserve 5
Katbakkies Pass

3
Op-Die-Berg
Warm Bokkeveld
R356
Inverdoorn Game Reserve 4
R355
To Matjiesfontein

Gydo Pass
Theronsberg Pass
Hottentotskloof
To Matjiesfontein & Johannesburg

Prince Alfred Hamlet 7
R303
8 i 2
Swaarmoed Pass
Lakenvlei Dam
R46
6
Touws River
N1
To Worcester & Cape Town

Michell's Pass
Ceres
To Tulbagh & Wolseley

R46
1
R43
To Worcester
Hex River Mountains

N
5 km
5 miles

Sleeping	Houdenbek Farm	Village Guesthouse &
Bergstroom Farm Cottage 1	Cottages 3	Restaurant 2
Bushmen Lodge 5	Inverdoorn Game Reserve 4	**Eating**
Hamlet Country Lodge 7	Klondyke Cherry Farm 6	Mill & Oaks 1
	Rusthof B&B 8	

have money to burn, you can fly the 260 km from Cape Town in just 40 minutes. Access to the reserve is by overnight stay at the lodge (see Sleeping, page 235), or day trips can be arranged for R995 per person (September-April) or R795 per person (May-August), including a rock art tour, lunch and a quad-bike safari. Visit the website for package deals.

Inverdoorn Game Reserve
ⓘ T021-434 4639, www.inverdoorn.com.
Inverdoorn Game Reserve is 55 km from Ceres. Follow the R46 for Touws River and the N1. Take the R355 turning for Calvinia and almost immediately after join the R356 for Sutherland. The entrance is on the left. This is a private 3500-ha game reserve specializing in 4WD game safaris to view its range of wildlife, which includes rhino, buffalo, giraffe, zebra, wildebeest, eland, kudu and impala. A pair of lions and seven cheetahs were introduced a few years ago. The area is a typical Karoo landscape and quite beautiful to drive around. Other activities on offer include hikes to San rock art, birdwatching, fishing and mountain biking. The day visit starts at 1000 and includes a two-three hour safari and lunch. Alternatively, the overnight stays at the lodge also include one or two game drives (see page 236), or again, check out the website for packages.

South from Worcester ⬤�🚹🏃🔺⬤🅒 ➤➤ pp233-242.

As the Breede River meanders south from Worcester, the valley starts to broaden out and the level lands are given over to agriculture. As you drive along the R60 towards Robertson, the Langeberg mountains run parallel to the north. When the crops are maturing this is a beautiful drive through landscapes of contrasting colours. Along the roadside are farm shops selling fresh produce and several of the wine estates are open for wine tastings and sales. Both Worcester and Robertson have their own organized wine routes. After Robertson the R60 divides; the R317 runs close to the river as far as Bonnievale, while the R60 continues towards Ashton, Montagu and Swellendam.

Robertson → Colour map 8, B2.
This small, prosperous town has a vaguely time-warped feel to it, with tidy jacaranda-lined streets, orderly church squares and neat rose gardens. It is the centre of the largest area of irrigated vineyards in the Cape with over 20 wineries, many of which have won awards. The high-quality dessert wines and liqueurs produced here have ensured the town's continued prosperity, as has the large brandy distillery. The town itself was founded in 1852 as a new parish to cope with the growing population of Swellendam further down the Breede River Valley. Conditions are ideal for agriculture as there is an abundant water supply from the Langeberg Mountains to the north and the Riviersonderend hills to the south. The lime-rich soil here provides good grazing for horses and there are a number of stud farms in the region. While there isn't a great deal to see in town, it is a pleasant place to spend a day exploring the sleepy centre and nearby vineyards. **Robertson Tourism Bureau** ⓘ T023-626 4437, www.robertsonr62.com, Mon-Fri 0900-1700, Sat-Sun 0900-1400, is on the corner of Reitz and Voortrekker streets.

Robertson Museum ⓘ 50 Paul Kruger St, T023-626 3681, www.robertsonmuseum.org, Mon-Sat 0900-1200, free, or 'Druids Lodge', remained in the hands of the same family for nearly 100 years. The original house was built circa 1860, only a few years after the grid pattern for the town had been first laid out. In 1883 the resident magistrate,

Mr WHD English, bought the house and it remained the property of the family until 1976, when the last living member, Miss Violet English, died. The municipality bought the house and set up a museum. Most of the collection is devoted to the lives of William Henry Dutton English and his offspring, as well as the history of Robertson and the area. Of particular note is a beautiful collection of lace. Here you can pick up a useful guide for a historical walk around the village that takes in the villas built during the ostrich feather boom.

Klipdrift Brandy is as iconic to South Africa as biltong is and few South African's have not heard of or use regularly the expression 'klippies and coke'. It was first distilled by Kosie Marius on his farm in 1938 and the distillery in Robertson opened in the 1940s. **Robertson Klipdrift Distillery** ① *4 Voortrekker Rd, T023-626 3027, www.kilpdrift.co.za, Mon-Fri 0800-1700, Sat 0900-1600*, has an interesting visitors centre which displays the history of the popular tipple and you can go on tours of the distillery and see the giant copper vats and of course taste brandy. The good **Brandewyntuin** restaurant (see Eating, page 240) serves breakfast and lunch.

Robertson Valley wine route
① *T023-626 3167, www.robertsonwinevalley.co.za.*
The Robertson Valley is home to 10% of South Africa's vineyards, and produces excellent Chardonnays and several good Muscadets. Ask about the **Food and Wine Festival** held every October; it's an excellent chance to sample the region's varied fresh produce.

This wine route follows the Breede River Valley and embraces the districts of Robertson, McGregor, Bonnievale and Ashton. In total there are 48 cooperatives and estates open to the public. The greatest concentration is found along the R317 as it follows the Breede River between Robertson and Bonnievale.

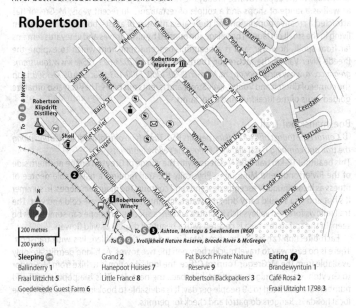

Robertson

Sleeping 🛏
Ballinderry 1
Fraai Uitzicht 5
Goedereede Guest Farm 6

Grand 2
Hanepoot Huisies 7
Little France 8

Pat Busch Private Nature
Reserve 9
Robertson Backpackers 3

Eating 🍴
Brandewyntuin 1
Café Rosa 2
Fraai Uitzight 1798 3

One of the most welcoming estates along the wine route is **Van Loveren** ① *T023-615 1505, www.vanloveren.co.za, Mon-Fri 0830-1700, Sat 0930-1300*. Try their Blanc de Noir wines. Tastings are conducted in a restored rondavel set in the middle of a colourful garden. Guests are allowed to taste the full range and someone is always close at hand to assist with any queries.

The **Bon Courage Estate** ① *9 km from Robertson along the R317, T023-626 4178, www.boncourage.co.za, Mon-Fri 0800-1700, Sat 0900-1500*, is best known for their award-winning Chardonnays and wine tasting is in an old Cape Dutch whitewashed building or on the lawns. **Café Maude** is open for lunch. **Robertson** ① *T023-626 3059, www.robertson winery.co.za, Mon-Fri 0800-1700, Sat-Sun 0900-1500*, is the oldest winery in the area. The shop and processing plant are located on Voortrekker Road. During the harvest time you can see tractor loads of grapes being delivered to the town.

McGregor → *Colour map 8, B2.*

This picturesque village lies off the beaten track in the lee of the Riviersonderend Mountains. The village is made up of a collection of perfectly preserved, whitewashed thatched cottages which radiate out from a **Dutch Reformed Church** which is in turn surrounded by a neat, colourful garden. Originally, McGregor was known as Lady Grey, after the wife of Sir George Grey, a former governor of the Cape Colony. In 1903 it was renamed, as there was another town in the province with the same name. The new name came from the Reverend Andrew McGregor, a Scottish minister who had worked in the district during the formative years of the village. Dr Mary Cooke, a local historian, described McGregor as "easily the best-preserved and most complete example of mid-19th-century townscape in the Cape Province". Today the village has a good choice of accommodation, as well as a range of shops and a couple of restaurants. In recent years, McGregor has attracted a creative population and there are a number of artists, potters and craftsmen living in the small cottages. The village surrounded by olive groves and vineyards remains far from spoilt, however, and is a beautiful, peaceful spot from which to explore the Breede River Valley. The **McGregor Tourism Bureau** ① *T023-625 1954, www.tourismmc gregor.co.za, www.mcgregor.org.za, Mon-Fri 0900-1300, 1400-1630, Sat-Sun 0900-1300*, is on the corner of Church and Voortrekker Street and it rents out bikes. They can also organize guided tours of the local fruit and dairy farms.

Boesmanskloof Trail

① *Contact the tourist office for hiking permits R50. There is no official accommodation along the trail and camping is not allowed. Follow the yellow footprints.*

This beautiful 16-km trail links McGregor with the village of **Greyton** on the northern side of the Riviersonderend Mountains. Physically the trail requires a reasonable degree of fitness as it continuously ascends, descends and contours the mountain slopes. In summer it's hot and you should carry drinking water. In winter, conditions are cold and wet. The trail follows forested valleys rich in protea and erica species. Antelope can sometimes be seen. In the spring this area is covered with a beautiful display of wild flowers.

Each direction can easily be completed in a day – the problem lies with transport. There is no easy way to travel quickly between the two towns. As hiking permits are only available from the **McGregor Tourism Office**, the logical option is to hike from McGregor to Greyton, stay overnight, and then hike back the next day. This is a popular trail and numbers are restricted to 50 people per day. It is advisable to book in advance during the local holidays. Rangers do patrol and check for permits.

Vrolijkheid Nature Reserve

① *Enquiries T021-659 3500, www.capenature.co.za, R25, children (2-13) R12.*

Vrolijkheid Nature Reserve lies 15 km south of Robertson on the McGregor road. The landscape is rugged and strikingly scenic, with sandstone and underlying shale formations. Small mammals such as klipspringer, grysbok and springbok are fairly common, and if you are very lucky you may see a caracal, a type of wildcat. The terrain lends itself to raptors and there are often buzzards or goshawks circling the arid landscape during the summer months. Despite the fact that the reserve lies in an area a good distance to the west of the Karoo, many of the plants and trees are identical to those growing there. Grasses are scarce on the rocky lands, but there are plenty of succulents, and during September the land is covered with a colourful blanket of wild flowers, assuming the spring rains have been good enough.

Two hiking trails have been clearly marked out, known as the **Heron Trail** and the **Rooikat Trail**. The Heron Trail is a simple 3-km walk to a couple of dams where there are some bird hides. Waterbirds can always be seen on the lakes. A rare attraction for enthusiastic herpetologists is the Robertson dwarf chameleon. The office at the gate has species lists and can help you with suggestions of what to look out for, and where. The Rooikat Trail is a much more strenuous 19 km and requires you to carry at least 2 litres of water per person (none is available en route). The terrain is rocky in parts and proper hiking boots should be worn. This is a circular walk through the Elandsberg Mountains, taking in a few peaks of over 500 m with views of the Langeberg and Riviersonderend Mountains. Allow at least eight hours. From November to March temperatures are high and precautions should be taken against sunstroke. Wear a hat and drink plenty of fluids before and during the walk. A pamphlet available at the gate contains a good scale map with contours shown, which will help you plan your day. There is also an 8-km circular mountain-bike route in the reserve.

Bonnievale → *Colour map 8, B2.*

This small town is known for its wines and cheese, and is the site of the main Parmalat dairy factory, a brand that becomes very familiar to visitors in South Africa. The settlement was founded by one of the first farmers to appreciate fully the agricultural potential of the area, Christopher Rigg, who arrived in the valley and immediately set about building an ingenious system of canals to irrigate it. Most of the land is devoted to grape and wine production today, but you will also find several fruit orchards, including peaches, navel oranges, clementines and apricots. The **Bonnievale Tourism Office** ① *Main St, T023-616 3563, www.bonnievale.co.za, Mon-Fri 0800-1700*, is a well-organized and helpful office covering the whole Breede River region.

In the town itself the only real tourist attraction is the **Myrtle Rigg Memorial Church**, which is kept locked but keys can be obtained from the tourist office during working hours. This church has a rather sad story behind it. Two of the Rigg's children died when they were still very young, and their third child, Myrtle, died at the age of seven, in 1911. Before her untimely death, Myrtle asked that her parents build a small church to remember her by. This little Gothic-style building was constructed using the finest materials from around the world, including roof tiles from Italy and a fine carved door from Zanzibar. It was consecrated in 1921, but fell quickly into disrepair after the Riggs' deaths. Fortunately, the municipality saw fit to restore it in 1977. The **Parmalat cheese factory**, which produces 40 tonnes of Gouda and Cheddar each day, is another legacy of Mr Rigg and today many Parmalat dairy products are found on South African supermarket shelves. The shop sells cheese, butter, milk, yoghurt and cottage cheese.

Bonnievale wine cellars

The following is a small selection of wine estates close to Bonnievale, open for tastings and purchases. They are all members of the Robertson Valley wine route (see page 227 for further details).

De Wetshof① *T023-615 1853, www.dewetshof.co.za, Mon-Fri 0830-1630, Sat 0930-1300, cellar tours by prior arrangement*, a well-known export label, is a short drive from the town on the far side of the Breede River. This was the first registered wine estate in the region and is known for its excellent white wines, especially its award-winning Chardonnay. **Langverwacht**① *T023-616 2815, Mon-Fri 0800-1230, 1330-1700*, has good Riesling and Colombard. **Viljoensdrift**① *T023-615 1901, www.viljoensdrift.co.za, Mon-Fri 0830-1700, river cruise R35, children (3-16) R15*, is a relatively new member of the wine route which resumed producing wine after a 30-year gap. In addition to wine tastings you can enjoy a one-hour cruise on a raft on the river that departs at 1200 and make up a picnic from items on their deli menu to take with you. **Weltevrede Estate**① *T023-616 2141, www.weltevrede. com, Mon-Fri 0830-1700, Sat 0900-1530*, has a restaurant and self-catering cottages (see Sleeping, page 237, and Eating, page 240) and has a good range of whites and Rieslings.

Ashton and around → *Colour map 8, B2.*

The small settlement of Ashton is rather an odd place, dominated as it is by two major canning factories. Pass through here on a weekday, and it seems that the entire population of the town is dressed in either green or blue uniforms, depending upon which factory they work in. There is little of interest in town, although there are a couple of wine cooperatives. The **Tourism Bureau**① *Main Rd, T023-614 2471, www.montagu-ashton.info, Mon-Sat 0900-1700, Sun 0930-1230*, is next door to a finely preserved steam locomotive built in 1919, and used on the Worcester–Mossel Bay line until 1983.

A large proportion of local wine production is handled by the **Ashton Wine Cooperative Wine Cellar**① *T023-615 1135, sales and tastings: Mon-Fri 0800-1230, 1330-1700, Sat 0900-1300, guided tours by prior arrangement*, who are also well known for their excellent grape juice. If you are keen on your wines, the pleasant **Zandvliet Estate**① *T023-615 1146, www.zandvliet.co.za, Mon-Fri 0900-1700, Sat 0930-1300*, on the banks of Cogmans River, is well worth a visit. Although the cellar's first wine, a Shiraz, was initially produced as recently as 1975 it has won many prizes and is highly regarded in wine-producing circles. The estate has invested heavily in the latest techniques to help grow and produce quality wines. The estate house is a fine example of a traditional thatched Cape Dutch homestead.

If you have taken the main road, the R60, between Robertson and Ashton you will pass **Sheilam Cactus Farm/Nursery**① *T023-626 4133, www.sheilamnursery.com, Mon-Sat 0900-1700, R10, children (under 16) free*, or 'Little Mexico', as it is now known, where you can admire some of the 3000 cactus plants and succulents. It rates itself as the biggest cactus nursery in the southern hemisphere. Plants and seeds can be bought here and sent home.

Montagu and around → *Colour map 8, B2.*

Although Montagu is very much a Karoo town, it is usually visited by people exploring the Breede River Valley. It is 245 km from Oudtshoorn, the administrative centre for the Little Karoo, and only 15 minutes' drive from Ashton and the Breede River. It is a delightful place in a stunning setting, its long streets lined with oak trees and whitewashed Cape Dutch houses, sitting humbly beneath jagged mountain peaks. Founded in 1851, the settlement was named after John Montagu who, as the colonial secretary from 1843 to 1853, had been responsible for the first major road-building programme in the Cape. The greatly improved road network enabled previously remote settlements such as Montagu to thrive and grow. From its early days the region was recognized as ideal for fruit and wine production. The valley was fertile and the climate ideal for vines. In 1940 the Langeberg Co-op was formed, which proved to be the necessary boost for the local economy. Within 10 years, local production of apples and pears had doubled, while over a period of 16 years the wine produced increased by fivefold.

More recently, in November 2008 Montague and to some extent Ashton, Barrydale and Robertson, witnessed severe flooding. Bridges were washed away, which for a while left the village stranded, and there was extensive damage at the Avalon Springs Resort. Nevertheless, today bridges providing access to the town have been repaired and the resort reopened in early 2009.

The exceptionally helpful and enthusiastic **Montagu Tourism Bureau** ⓘ *24 Bath St, T023-614 2471, www.montagu-ashton.info, www.tourismmontagu.co.za, Mon-Fri 0830-1730, Sat-Sun 0900-1700*, has several useful leaflets including one about the historic homes in the area. The **Montagu Market** ⓘ *Bath St, opposite the tourist office, Sat 0980-1300*, is good for crafts, food and collectables.

Joubert House ⓘ *25 Long St, T023-614 1774, museum: Mon-Fri 0900-1300, 1400-1630, Sat-Sun 1030-1230, R5*, the oldest building in the town, is now part of the museum (housed further along Long Street). The house has a collection of late 19th-century furnishings and ornaments and part of the garden has been turned into an indigenous medicinal plant collection.

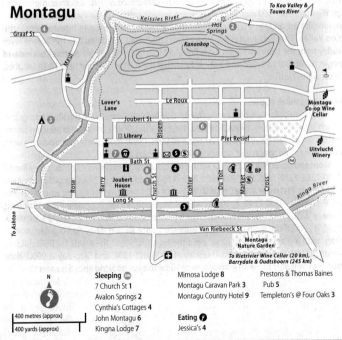

Montagu

Sleeping ◉
7 Church St **1**
Avalon Springs **2**
Cynthia's Cottages **4**
John Montagu **6**
Kingna Lodge **7**

Mimosa Lodge **8**
Montagu Caravan Park **3**
Montagu Country Hotel **9**

Eating ◉
Jessica's **4**

Prestons & Thomas Baines
Pub **5**
Templeton's @ Four Oaks **3**

Long Street, a popular attraction, has 14 national monuments along its length. With so many well-preserved buildings, it is easy to get a vivid impression of how the settlement would have looked in its early days and the tourist office sells a booklet about the houses.

The **Montagu Nature Garden** ① *Van Riebeeck St, T023-614 2590, daily, small entrance fee, teas served on Tue and the first Sat of the month, May-Nov, the best time to visit is spring (Aug-Oct)*, on the south side of the Kinga River off Van Riebeeck Street, has the largest collection of mesembryanthemums in the country.

Just 3 km from the town centre are the hot mineral springs at the **Avalon Springs Resort** ① *T023-614 1150, R25, R18 child, see Sleeping, page 238, for resort details*, which have been used for over 200 years for their healing powers. There are two indoor pools and five outdoor pools, all at different temperatures. At the weekends and holidays it gets very busy so try to go early in the morning or in the evening when it's cooler. The waters are radioactive and have a steady temperature of 48°C. In 1980 Montagu suffered a tragic setback when continued heavy rains in the Langeberg resulted in a flash flood down the Keisie River. It was a local catastrophe and 13 people were killed. The hotel was filled with several metres of sand and debris and the hot springs were covered with mud, but the town itself was barely touched. Again in 2008, the resort was damaged by flooding, though this time the town did not fare as well and some houses, trees and vehicles were washed away but thankfully there were no human victims.

Tractor rides ① *Protea Farm, from Montagu, take the R318 towards Matroosberg, after 30 km the road descends the Burger Pass into the Koo Valley, book at the tourist office T023-614 2471, or through the website, www.proteafarm.co.za, R70, R35 child, trips usually go Wed and Sat 1000 and 1400 if there are enough takers*, to the top of the Langeberg mountains are on offer from Neil Burger, a local farmer; the trip leaves from his farm in the **Koo Valley**. There are impressive views across the Karoo and down into the Breede River Valley from the summit. For an extra R80 (R50 for children) you get an excellent meal of *potjie*, home-baked bread and a drink. Note that the tractor does not operate in October. Wear warm clothes.

Montagu wine route

The Montagu cellars are best known for producing white wines with the Muscadel grape, which tend to be fairly sweet, fortified dessert wines. There are several wineries in the district which can be visited for tastings and sales. Cellar tours are by appointment only. For further information visit www.kleinkaroowines.co.za.

Montagu Co-op Wine Cellar ① *T023-614 1125, www.montaguwines.co.za, sales: Mon-Fri 0800-1230, 1330-1700, Sat 0900-1200*, is next to the golf course, heading out of town via Bath Street. **Rietrivier Wine Cellar** ① *T023-614 1705, www.rietrivier.co.za, sales: Mon-Thu 0800-1700, Fri 0800-1500*, is 20 km east of Montagu on the Barrydale road. **Uitvlucht Winery** ① *T023-6141340, www.uitvlucht-wines.co.za, sales: Mon-Fri 0800-1730, Sat 0830-1330*, is just off the main road not far from the police station. They also organize tractor rides, with a glass of wine in hand, from the tourist office to the estate for R65, children (under 16) R40 on Tuesday and Thursday at 0900 and 1500, and Saturday at 0900. Note that they will only run with a minimum of 10 people, so booking ahead is advised.

● Breede River Valley listings

For Sleeping and Eating price codes and other relevant information, see pages 46-53.

● Sleeping
Some of the rates are per cottage – if there are 4 or more of you staying, they're good value. Many of the ones located on remote farms don't take credit cards so check first.

Worcester and around *p216,*
maps p217 and p219
There are few hotels in the town itself; most of the private accommodation is on farms in the surrounding valleys. These are all very pleasant and in most cases good value.

In town
B Protea Hotel Cumberland, 2 Stockenstroom St, T023-347 2641, www.protea hotels.com, www.cumberland.co.za. 55 comfortable a/c rooms, breakfast extra, smart à la carte **Gallery** restaurant, plus a daytime coffee shop and poolside cocktail bar, immaculate swimming pool, health complex including a gym, sauna, spa bath, squash courts and a tennis court. Check for special offers.
C-D Church Street Lodge, 36 Church St, T023-342 5194, www.churchst.co.za. A modern guesthouse with 21 rooms, with extras such as coffee facilities, fridge and satellite TV, comfortable lounge areas with fat leather sofas, swimming pool set in peaceful grounds with fountains.
D Habit Guesthouse, 6 Porter St, T021-342 3538, www.thehabit.co.za. Quaint historic home built in 1837 with wrap-around veranda, polished wooden floors and lovely established gardens with swimming pool, 8 rooms and 2 3-bed self-catering garden cottages, guest lounge with honesty bar. It used to be home to Catholic nuns; hence the name.
D Wykeham Lodge, 168 Church St, T023-347 3467, www.theguesthouse.ch. A pleasant B&B set in a lovely thatched 1835 homestead at the quieter end of Church St on the edge

of town overlooking open parkland. 7 double rooms with TV, private balconies, secure off-street parking, small bistro restaurant for guests, pretty gardens.

Out of town
B-D ATKV Goudini Spa, 22 km from the town centre just off the N1 at Rawsonville, T023-344 3013, www.goudinispa.co.za. A dated but popular family resort and warm mineral water spa. It has 154 fully equipped self-catering rondavels and duplex flats with 2-8 beds, 53 camping and caravan pitches (**E**), plus excellent facilities, outdoor pools, tennis courts, mini-golf and jacuzzis, in beautiful setting in the lee of Slanghoek Mountains, surrounded by vineyards. Rates are higher at the weekends.
C Nekkies Holiday Resort, 4.5 km from Worcester on Lake Marais, T023-343 2909, nekkies@breedevallei.gov.za. 14 self-catering log chalets built on stilts overlooking the lake, with 2 bedrooms and 2 bathrooms, fully equipped kitchen, balcony and fireplace, good for families. You can also camp (**F**) here on grassy sites and there are good ablution facilities and braai pits.
D-E Nuy Valley Guest House, 19 km from town off the R60 towards Robertson, T023-342 1258, www.nuyvallei.co.za. A large, well-kept guesthouse in an 1871 Cape Dutch building close to the river on a wine estate in the countryside, 27 en suite rooms, à la carte restaurant, self-catering kitchen, swimming pool, neat gardens with rose trees and ornamental ponds. A walk will take you to a refreshing waterfall. Call ahead to check if a wedding or conference is on. The wine cellar, nearby, has been converted into cheaper rooms for backpackers with shared bathrooms. Outstanding value, recommended.

Hex River Valley *p220*
Given the excellent choice of places to stay in the valley, De Doorns is usually only visited when driving through.

D Arbeid Adelt Guest House, Voortrekker Rd, T023-356 2204, www.arbeidadelt.co.za. Late 18th-century Victorian house on a grape farm where you can pick your own grapes and visit the packing shed during harvest time, with 5 double rooms, 1 self-catering cottage sleeping 6, 3 caravan/camping pitches, B&B, dinner on request, tea garden with lawns and ornamental fountain, pretty veranda to take in the mountain views.

D De Vlei Country Inn, 5 km out of town on Voortrekker Rd, T023-356 3281, devlei countryinn@telkomsa.net. A well-restored Cape Dutch coach house, peaceful location, 5 well-appointed double chalets with under-floor heating in pretty gardens surrounded by vines, good restaurant and bar in an old barn, dinner on request French spoken.

Wolseley p221

C White Bridge Farm, 9 km from Wolseley towards Ceres, take the R46 and turn right on to the R43, T023-231 0705, www.white bridge.co.za. Farm accommodation in 1 B&B double room or 3 attractive self-catering cabins sleeping 4-6 built from natural materials such as stone, reeds and bamboo, swim in the pool or in the river among orchards of citrus fruits, pearsand plums.

Tulbagh p221, map p222
In town

B-E Tulbagh Country Manor, 24 Church St, T023-230 1171, www.tulbaghguesthouse. co.za. Delightful renovated 1809 Cape Dutch house, complete with thatched roof, pool and neat flower garden, with 4 attractive, comfortable en suite rooms with polished wood floors and antique furnishings. Huge breakfasts are served up in an appealing dining room. Also acts as an art gallery. There are 5 self-catering rooms in neighbouring houses and on the 1st floor of Tulbagh's old bank, backpacker accommodation in bright sunny en suite doubles or dorms with shared bathroom, communal kitchen and lounge with DSTV and board games, and light breakfasts. Perfect for a night in a historic

Tulbagh home for most budgets. Recommended.

C De Oude Herberg, 6 Church St, T023-230 0260, www.deoudeherberg.co.za. 4 en suite rooms with French windows onto the pretty veranda in a national monument Cape Dutch building, TV, ideal for walking to main town attractions, **Pielows** restaurant (closed Mon), sheltered sunny courtyard, swimming pool, laundry service, can arrange sundowner trips to the mountains.

Out of town

AL Rijk's Country House, follow Van der Stel St north of town for 2 km, T023-230 1006, www.africanpridehotels.com, www.rijks.co.za. Luxury development that was extended and reopened in 2008 on a wine estate on the outskirts of town, with 15 suites in a stunning, thatched Cape-style buildings, overlooking vineyards and a dam. Swimming pool, excellent restaurant, bar, extensive gardens full of roses, wine tasting and cellar tours. Recommended.

A-B Manley Wine Lodge, 2 km from Tulbagh, T023-230 0582, www.manleywine lodge.co.za. 13 en suite double rooms in Cape Dutch style cottages plus 2 luxury suites with spa baths and DVD and CD players, B&B, swimming pool surrounded by lawns and gardens full of rose bushes, wine-tasting and cellar tours, and walks around the farm. There's also a chapel for weddings.

C Villa Tarentaal, Van der Stel St, 1 km north of town, T023-230 0868, www.villatarentaal. com. 2 attractive self-contained 2-bedroom a/c cottages set on farm, with open-plan kitchen, lounge, fireplace, DSTV, veranda and beautiful mountain views, braai area, rates include breakfast which is served in your cottage. Professional beautician Christine offers aromatherapy massages, reflexology and facial treatments.

C-D Wild Olive Farm, 7 km south of Tulbagh turn-off on the R46, T023-230 1160, www.wildolivefarm.com. 6 self-contained cottages, each with a different configuration, ranging from a basic room with hot plate to

2-bedroom cottage with kitchen, lounge, TV and fireplace. Also 10 caravan sites and 15 camping pitches with shared ablution block and use of gas braais and a fridge/freezer. The whole set-up is on a working farm with lovely mountain views.

D Schalkenbosch Farm, on the Wolseley road, 800 km from Tulbagh turn left at the sign and follow the road 6.5 km through the farm, T023-230 0654, www.schalkenbosch. co.za. Historic manor house (1792) on a wine farm, declared a national monument, in the lee of the Witsenberg Mountains with 3 pretty fully equipped self-catering cottages with fireplaces, DSTV and braais and, views across Tulbagh Valley. No young children.

Ceres *p223, map p225*
There is a surprisingly small choice of accommodation or restaurants in the town, and the main town hotel closed and was recently demolished, but there are several excellent places in the nearby countryside.

In town
D Village Guesthouse and Restaurant, 64 Vos St, T023-316 2035, www.ceres.org.za/VillageGuest. Comfortable guesthouse with 12 spacious individually decorated rooms with TV, a/c and private entrances set around a courtyard, swimming pool, bar and simple meals in the restaurant, including some traditional South African dishes.

D-F Rusthof B&B, 71 Lyelle St, T023-312 3622, www.rusthofbb.co.za. Neat set-up with 3 B&B rooms with pastel coloured furnishings and bright white linen, and a 2-bed apartment with kitchenette in the loft with a separate entrance. Pretty gardens and a wide peaceful veranda.

Out of town
B-D Houdenbek Farm Cottages, 55 km from Ceres, follow the R303 towards Citrusdal up the Gydo Pass, turn right in the village of Op-Die-Berg (the road is surfaced as far as Sand River, but the last few kilometres are gravel), T023-317 0749, www.houdenbek.co.za. 2 fully

equipped self-catering cottages each sleeping 4, and 1 fully equipped house sleeping 11, rates average R180 per person per night, B&B and evening meals available on weekdays, and breakfast baskets available at the weekend. A beautiful and remote spot on the Môrester Estate, a working fruit and vegetable farm. Worth spending a few days here walking in the mountains. Trout fishing and canoeing.

B-E Bergstroom Farm Cottage, 67 km from Ceres, off the Citrusdal Rd (R303), T023-317 0628, www.ceres.org.za/Bergstroom. 2 pleasant self-catering cottages in the mountains of the Koue Bokkeveld sleeping 6 and 8, with kitchen, lounge, large fireplace, rates are R150 per person per night. Good base for hiking trails, and there's a lovely waterfall with natural rock pools for swimming on the farm. Popular in winter with South Africans for the novelty of seeing snow.

C-D Klondyke Cherry Farm, T023-312 1521, www.cherryfarm.co.za. 3 homely self-catering cottages sleeping 2, 4 and 8 on farm with superb views of the mountains, rates are higher at the weekend, camping also possible under pine trees with ablution block. Ideal for keen walkers, bass fishing in the farm dams, cherry picking mid-Nov to early Jan. Again be prepared for snow in winter.

Prince Alfred Hamlet *p224*
There is only 1 hotel here, but there are several farms in the region that offer accommodation. See above for details.

D Hamlet Country Lodge, Voortrekker St, T023-313 3070, hamletlodge@telkomsa.net. Typical old town hotel, 6 spacious old-fashioned rooms, some with a/c or fans and coffee-making machines, bar and **Taylor's Grill** restaurant, permits and gate keys issued from the hotel to those wishing to go trout fishing on Lakenvlei Dam.

Kagga Kamma Private Game Reserve *p225*
L-AL Bushmen Lodge, T021-872 4343 (Cape Town), www.kaggakamma.co.za. 18 chalets built into caves in the rock, or free-standing

and a new outdoor bedroom set in the rocks where you can sleep in good weather. Voted one of the world's best honeymoon lodges, with stunning views, a pool, spa, open-air boma restaurant and bar, rates include all meals, game drives, a visit to the rock art and sundowners at a 500-m-deep canyon. Rates drop significantly in low season; May-Aug.

Inverdoorn Game Reserve *p226*
A Luxury chalets, T023-316 1264, www.inverdoorn.com. 7 a/c chalets with fireplace, and 2 100-year-old farmhouses with 2 bedrooms for families, all sumptuously decorated. Excellent restaurant on site serving French cuisine, several lounges, pool and deck, library, mini-gym, curio shop, all rates include meals and game drives, and there is a landing strip and helipad for those who want to arrive in style. 50% discounts for children under 11.

Robertson *p226, map p227*
In town
C Ballinderry, 8 Le Roux St, T023-626 5365, www.ballinderryguesthouse.com. Smart villa with 6 spacious a/c rooms with stylish modern decor, fireplaces and wooden floors, champagne breakfast, 3-course dinners, pool, internet and bar. Run by a friendly Belgium couple.
D The Grand, 68 Barry St, T023-626 3272, www.grandhotel.co.za. Reasonable Victorian old-style town hotel on a corner of leafy White St, with 10 double rooms with en suite bathrooms and TV, and 4 cheaper but simpler rooms in an adjoining building, a good restaurant, bar with an L-shaped pool table, swimming pool, helpful staff.
E-F Robertson Backpackers, 4 Dordrecht St, T023-626 1280, www.robertsonbackpackers. co.za. Located in an old 1880s Victorian house, with pretty garden full of chill-out hammocks to enjoy the mountain views, dorms and doubles with huge duvets or camping on the lawn. 3 meals a day or self-catering in the kitchen, can organize local activities including wine tours and boat trips on the Breede River.

Out of town
B Fraai Uitzicht, 13 km from Robertson on the Ashton road, T023-626 6156, www.fraai uitzicht.com. Restored farm cottages on a wine estate, luxurious decor but rooms on the small side, with embroidered linen and nice works of art, beautiful spot surrounded by orchards and vines, excellent award-winning restaurant (see Eating, page 240) that occasionally hosts live music. Several languages spoken.
C-D Pat Busch Private Nature Reserve, 15 km from Robertson, off the R60 heading towards Ashton, T023-626 2033, www.pat busch.co.za. Self-catering accommodation in 3 cottages, Peach, Fig and Oak, plus 2 simple farm houses located in the foot-hills of the Langeberg Mountains. There is a 40-km network of circular walks which follow the kloofs between the hills. The vegetation consists of a mix of proteas and ericas, with lilies and ferns along the streams. This is an excellent spot for birdwatching and a few small antelope have been introduced. A peaceful place to really get away from it all.
D Goedereede Guest Farm, T023-626 4173, www.goedereede.co.za. Converted farm buildings just out of town on a fruit farm through which the Breede River flows, 4 self-catering cottages with 2, 4, or 6 beds and TV overlooking a picturesque dam, good farm breakfasts and dinners on request. Activities include hiking, fishing, canoeing on the river (free for overnight guests) and there's a swimming pool.
D Hanepoot Huisies, 9 km from Robertson off the Worcester road, T023-626 4139, www.hanepoothuisies.co.za. 9 restored old farm cottages set on a 190-ha farm, hidden away among vines and fruit trees, nicely decorated and well priced with a/c, electric blankets and tea and coffee stations. Plenty of activities can be organized including boat trips and fishing and there's a pool and braai facilities. The farm has a number of resident owls. Breakfast and supper extra and on request. Recommended.

D Little France, 5 km from Robertson on the Worcester Rd, T023-626 4142, www.little france.co.za. Attractive modern building with stylish furnishings, with 6 tasteful and comfortable rooms with polished wooden floors, brass beds with bright white linen. Dining room, lounge, large pool and deck, good breakfasts served by pool or log fire in dining room, dinner on request. Recommended.

McGregor *p228*

C Green Gables Country Inn, Voortrekker Rd, T023-625 1626, http://greengables countryinn.co.za. A delightful old town house that was once a trading store, with 8 en suite double rooms in the garden with separate entrances, B&B. Also has a splash pool, small lounge decorated with silverware and chandeliers and good restaurant (see Eating, page 240). Also rents out a charming thatched self-catering cottage in the village. Recommended.

C Old Mill Lodge, Mill St, T023-625 1841, www.oldmilllodge.co.za. This beautifully restored 1860s lodge is at the far end of the village among vineyards and fruit orchards. Accommodation is in 4 cottages, each with 2 bedrooms and en suite bathrooms. The central building has a comfortable lounge with an open fireplace, much needed during the winter, and a bar and dining room looking out over the vineyard. There's a swimming pool tucked away and beauty treatments are also on offer. The restaurant, which is open to non-guests, is excellent value and the evening meals take on a French twist. There's an old watermill in the grounds. Recommended.

C Whipstock Guest Farm, 8 km from the village on the far side from the Robertson Rd, T023-625 1733, www.whipstock.za.net. Choice of 6 converted farm cottages, each with a different style and sleeping 2-6. **Rietvlei Cottage**, which sleeps 6, is the oldest building. There is no electricity, but oil lamps and candles help create a peaceful atmosphere in the evenings. Hot water for

the bathroom comes from a gas geyser. Excellent wholesome and generous farm breakfasts and dinners are included in the rate and lunch packs are available for hikers – don't miss the home-made bread. An excellent place to bring children as this is a working farm with plenty to see and do each day like collecting eggs or milking cows.

D McGregor Country House, Voortrekker St, T023-625 1656, mcgcountry@telkomsa.net. 3 double rooms and 1 family room with small kitchenette, shared TV lounge, swimming pool, decorated in a Georgian theme, good value. Located in the same building as the local pub, **The Overdraught**.

Bonnievale *p229*

There are several places within the town centre, although staying on one of the many farms along the banks of the Breede River is more enjoyable. On most farms the river flows through the land, and there are often boats available for hire to explore this beautiful stretch as it winds its way through vineyards, orchards and stud farms.

B Merwenstein Guest Farm, 6 km from town centre off the Swellendam Rd, T028-616 2806, www.merwenstein.co.za. An old fruit and vegetable farm with the Breede River running through, with 3 double rooms with en suite bathrooms, rates include breakfast, dinner and tour of the farm, hearty home-made meals or take the whole house as a self-catering option, swimming pool, birdwatching trips on the river. German spoken. Recommended.

C Weltevrede Wine Estate, T023-626 2141, www.weltevrede.com. A beautiful and peaceful location on the wine estate 5 km to the east of the town; follow signs to Robertson. 2 self-catering cottages between the vines, fully equipped, sleep 2-4, swimming pool, rose gardens, small art gallery selling work by local artists, estate restaurant open for lunch Tue-Sat, farm produce available to buy, excellent value.

C-D Toy Cottages, 6 km from town centre off R60, T023-616 2735, www.toycottages.

com. 3 a/c self-catering cottages with modern interiors, each sleeps up to 6 people so price depends on size of group, DSTV, swimming pool, fishing, canoe hire, set among vineyards right on the banks of the Breede River. A tranquil spot.

D Bonnies B&B, Van Zyl St, T023-616 2251, www.bonniesb-b.co.za. 5 rooms with en suite bathrooms and rather flowery decor, DSTV, separate entrances leading into the garden with swimming pool. Evening meals available on request, healthy breakfasts served with freshly baked bread. Bicycles for hire, braai facilities. Good value. German-speaking hosts.

Montagu and around *p230, map p231*
Ask at the tourist office for details of budget accommodation suitable for hikers on surrounding farms.

A Kingna Lodge, 11 Bath St, T023-614 1066, www.kingnalodge.co.za. 6 rooms in an atmospheric 1898 Victorian house, some with private patio, TV, non-smoking lounge with collection of art and books, generous breakfast is served in an elegant black and gold dining room, swimming pool and jacuzzi in private gardens. Ex presidents Mandela and de Klerk both once stayed here. Recommended.

B Mimosa Lodge, Church St, T023-614 2351, www.mimosa.co.za. Excellent hotel owned by a Swiss-German chef with 11 rooms (those upstairs have balconies), 11 garden suites, 3 guest lounges, library, very stylish decor with original 1920s art deco items, neat gardens, restaurant, bar, heated swimming pool. The restaurant menu reflects the wide variety of locally grown fresh produce. Recommended.

B Montagu Country Hotel, 27 Bath St, T023-614 3125, www.montagucountryhotel.co.za. A well-established central hotel in a 1920s art deco building, with 33 large rooms with a/c, TV, a smart dining room with open log fires during the winter, swimming pool, heated mineral pool, beauty treatments, secure parking. Rents out a number of chauffeur driven cars for wine tours, including a classic Cadillac and Mercedes convertible. Recommended.

A-B Avalon Springs, 3 km from town centre, Uitvlucht St, T023-614 1150, www.avalonsprings.co.za. A well-developed resort that was renovated after devastating floods in 2008 centred on the hot springs with a range of self-catering apartments and chalets and hotel rooms, conference facilities and a health spa, 2 restaurants, 3 bars, shops, several hot and cold swimming pools, 60-m water slide, jacuzzis and spa baths, gym and sauna, tennis courts. Comfortable and in a peaceful spot, but inconvenient for those wishing to explore the town. Check their website for out-of-season special rates.

B 7 Church St, T023-614 1186, www.7churchstreet.co.za. Beautiful views from this stylish, friendly guesthouse, set in a restored Victorian home, with 1 large family room with a mezzanine floor under vaulted thatch, 2 other rooms and 2 garden suites, with TV and extras such as embroidered linen and fresh flowers, large lounge, good English breakfast, rose and herb garden, off-road parking, swimming pool. Recommended.

C Cynthia's Cottages, 3 Krom St, T023-614 2760, www.cynthias-cottages.co.za. Delightful restored self-catering country cottages with thatched roofs, and the brass beds add to the homely atmosphere. Suitable for 2-6 people, each with own garden and braai, some have fireplaces and outdoor spa pool.

D The John Montagu, 30 Joubert St, T023-614 1331, www.johnmontagu.co.za. 5 tastefully decorated rooms with antique furnishings, small pool and bar in the gardens at the back, sunny breakfast room, off-street parking. The perfect place to relax after exploring the area. Recommended.

D-F Montagu Caravan Park, west end of Bath St, across the Keissies River, T023-614 3034, www.montagucaravanpark.co.za. Well laid out with camping and caravan sites, budget 4-bed self-catering en suite log cabins, swimming pool, TV room, boating and fishing on the dam. Short walk into the town centre.

🍴 Eating

Worcester and around p216, maps p217 and p219

Surprisingly for a town with a reasonable population, Worcester has few restaurants, apart from the usual takeaways and family steakhouses: both **Saddles** (₸), T023-342 7779, and the **San Diego Spur** (₸), are on High St.

₸₸ **The Barn**, 170 Church St, T023-342 8136. Sun and Mon 0900-1700, Tue-Fri 0900-late, Sat 0900-1400, 1830-late. There is an interesting collection of hand-blown glass objects here, with demonstrations by the master glass-blower, David Reede. The shop and restaurant are situated in a renovated wine cellar, unusual and delicious menu, such as mushroom filo parcels or butternut risotto, and lots of dishes using fresh herbs. A lighter and cheaper menu during the day and wine and olive tastings are offered.

Wolseley p221

₸₸ **Mill & Oaks**, 7 km from Tulbagh, take the R46 and turn right onto the R43, T023-231 0860, www.millandoaks.co.za. Tue-Sat 0900-2130, closed Sun evening. Serves some beautifully presented food at lunch and dinner on a patio with mountain views, try the oven-roasted duck or mushroom risotto followed by the crème brûlée for dessert, and there are breakfasts and snacks and pizzas throughout the day. You can swim in the pool and there is a jungle gym for kids. Also has 3 a/c B&B rooms (**D**).

₸ **Bergsig Bistro**, on the Bergsig Estate (see page 220) 40 km along the R43 towards Ceres, T023-355 1603, www.bergsig.co.za. Mon-Fri 0800-1700, Sat 0900-1700. There are expansive views over the vineyards from this top floor bistro, which is open for breakfasts, tea and cake and lunches, which change seasonally but often feature traditional South African baboties or bredies, and hearty fare in winter like oxtail or lamb shanks.

Tulbagh p221, map p222

₸₸₸ **Rijk's Country House**, follow Van der Stel St north of town for 2 km, T023-230 1006. Open 0730-2230. Very smart country hotel set on wine estate, with excellent restaurant and wine cellar. The usual steaks, salads and pasta and more unusual offerings such as pork fillet with blue cheese and cider sauce and crêpes suzettes for dessert. Delicious food in a stylish environment and in summer you can sit on the vine covered terrace. Recommended.

₸₸ **Paddagang**, 23 Church St, T082-324 4463. Open Sun-Thu 0900-1700, Fri-Sat 0900-2200. Set in well-kept tranquil gardens with tables under vines this is very popular and serves a selection of Tulbagh wines. Good for late breakfasts, quality fresh Cape cuisine like babotie and waterblommetjiebredie, plus a full range of steaks, pastas and salads, try the malva pudding with apricot jam and custard for dessert. Recommended.

₸₸ **Pielows**, De Oude Herberg, see Sleeping page 234, T023-230 0432. Tue-Sat 1800-2200, closed May-Sep. Set in a historic home with tables outside under an oak tree, the short but imaginative menu offers the likes of roasted pork belly glazed in honey with caramelized apples, or chicken tandoori with fennel mayonnaise, and some sticky puddings for dessert. The Pielows are attentive hosts and were part of a 2005 TV documentary about relocating their restaurant business from Ireland to South Africa.

₸₸ **Readers**, 12 Church St, T023-230 0087. Wed-Sun 1230-1500, 1900-2130. Quality home cooking in a pleasant old dining room in the oldest house in Tulbagh (1754), decorated with colourful exhibits from the local art school. Varied and interesting menu with tempting specials on the blackboard, and in summer there is a rather unusual range of home-made ice cream with sweet and also savoury flavours – cumin, sesame or garlic.

₸ **The Things I Love**, 61 Van der Stel St, T023-230 1742, www.thingsilove.co.za. 0800-1700, stays open later on Fri-Sat in season. A deli, restaurant and wine boutique, with a sunny terrace, there's plenty of choice of local produce, handmade chocolates and home-baked bread, pastries and pies. Meals include lasagne, moussaka, chicken pies and healthy salads, finished off with traditional desserts like apple crumble.

Robertson *p226, map p227*

The town lacks a good choice of restaurants – only a handful are worth trying:

¶¶¶ Fraai Uitzicht 1798, 13 km from Robertson on the Ashton road, T023-626 6156, www.fraaiuitzicht.com. Wed-Sun 1200-1500, 1800-2030, closed mid-Jun to end of Aug. Award-winning restaurant set on the historic wine estate in beautiful herb, bamboo and rose gardens. Very good food, choose the 7-course set menu with accompanying wines, or individual dishes such as springbok medallions with rosemary and orange marmalade or rabbit in white wine sauce and desserts made from Belgian chocolate, good service.

¶¶¶ Brandewyntuin, Robertson Klipdrift Distillery, see page 227. Mon-Fri 0800-1700, Sat 0900-1600. Breakfasts and light meals at lunchtime and famous for their Klipdrift burger with potato wedges. During summer you can sit outside in the neat gardens and in winter a blazing log fire greatly adds to the atmosphere. Also offers brandy tasting.

¶ Café Rosa, Robertson Nursery, 9 Voortrekker Rd, T023-626 5403. Mon-Sat 0800-1730. Nice setting among the plants in the nursery, serving tea, coffee, wine, breakfasts, light lunches and home-made cakes, friendly service.

¶ The Grand Hotel, 68 Barry St, T023-626 3272. Very faded and old fashioned decor, but exceptionally good country food, popular carvery on Sun when all the townsfolk seem to eat out after church, good-value set-menu lunches, there's a pub next door.

McGregor *p228*

The popularity of the village as a day-trip destination is reflected in the choice of a few good places to grab a meal or have

afternoon teas in. Most overnight guests will take their evening meal at their guesthouse or self-cater.

¶¶¶ Green Gables, at Green Gables Country Inn, Voortrekker St, T023-625 1626, http://greengablescountryinn.co.za. 0900-late. Popular family-run local restaurant serving light lunches and teas, and good country fare such as roast dinners or steak and kidney pie in the evenings. Eat in the cosy pub or on the candle-lit garden terrace. Recommended.

¶ Tebaldi's, corner of Bree and Voortrekker streets, T023-625 1115. Tue-Sun 0900-1630. Espresso, ciabatta, bruschetta, pasta, all things Italian, in a lovely garden setting with a duck pond and you can take away items from the deli. Thu is pizza night and at the weekend the menu is extended with dishes like beef goulash or coq au vin.

Bonnievale *p229*

¶¶¶ Under the Vines, at the Weltevrede Wine Estate on the R317, T023-626 2141, www.weltevrede.com. Tue-Sat 0100-1530. Pleasant country setting, wine available, daily blackboard specials, game pies, thick soups, salads and good cheese platters served with fresh farm bread. In summer sit outside under trailing vines and in winter inside next to the roaring fire.

Montagu and around *p230, map p231*

Montagu has a surprisingly large number of good restaurants, with a fine variation of cuisines – not just the usual steaks and pizzas.

¶¶¶ Templeton's @ Four Oaks, 46 Long St, T023-614 2778. Mon-Sat 1230-1430, 0700-2200, open Sun lunch in season. Good local cuisine and Mediterranean deli items in the historic setting of an 1855 farmhouse, slow-cooked oxtail, lamb curry and good home-made burgers, lovely garden and tables in a courtyard under 100-year-old pear trees, cosy bar serving bubbly and oysters, chef used to work at the **Mount Nelson Hotel** in Cape Town. It's possible to stay as there are 4 rooms next door (**D**).

♚♚-♚♚ **Jessica's**, 47 Bath St, T023-614 1805, www.jessicasrestaurant.co.za. 1830-2200, closed on Tue in low season. A slightly off-beat place with bright pink walls and decorated with loads of pictures and ceramic statues of dogs. A good opportunity to sample the best of South African ingredients washed down with good local wines. Known for their rich creamy sauces, try springbok in mushroom sauce, and finish with fruit and white chocolate sauce. Recommended.

♚ **Prestons & Thomas Baines Pub**, 17 Bath St, T023-614 3013. Open 1030-1430, 1730-late. Popular à la carte menu, tasteful decor with a small outside courtyard, friendly hosts. Try the Prestons platter or the Karoo lamb, all served with excellent salads. The pub, which has a cosy wood bar and tables and outside terrace for warm days, stays open after the kitchen closes at 2145. Recommended.

♚ **Wild Apricot**, Montagu Country Hotel, 27 Bath St, T023-614 3125, www.montagu countryhotel.co.za, 0730-2200. Excellent Sun lunch of roast meat and veg, traditional South African bobotie, cheeses and desserts. À la carte menu of local dishes such as tomato bredie and Karoo lamb chops, all set in the bright pink art deco hotel.

🎵 Bars and clubs

McGregor p228
Overdraught Pub, Voortrekker St, T023-625 1656. A tiny, old-fashioned bar with an English pub feel that can only accommodate about a dozen people. Serves a selection of draught beers including Guinness and Caffery's imported from Ireland and a number of British bitters.

⊛ Festivals and events

Tulbagh p221, map p222
Jun Christmas in Winter. Held along Church St, which is festooned with Christmas decorations and has craft and food stalls. Christmas dinners are served in restaurants.

Sep The local **Agricultural Show**, held on the banks of the Kliprivier. This is the oldest show of its kind in South Africa.

○ Shopping

Worcester and around p216, maps p217 and p219
Curios
Blind Shop, 126 Church St. Furniture, woodwork and woven products made by the visually impaired and sold from this outlet. Visits to the workshop are possible.
Deaf Shop, De la Bat St. Handicrafts such as ceramics, cane work and art curios – some excellent pieces at very reasonable prices. Again it is possible to visit the workshop.

Shopping malls
Mountain Mill Shopping Mall, on the N1 at the turn-off to town. Mon-Sat 0900-1800, Sun 1000-1600. The largest mall in the region and a good place to stock up if self-catering in cottages along the Breede River, with 117 shops, including chain stores and supermarkets, and a NuMetro cinema.

⛰ Activities and tours

Worcester and around p216, map p217
Canoeing
African Water Wanderers, T021-976 3924, www.africanwaterwanderers.co.za. River rafting trips on the Breede River (Oct-Mar) from R395 per person, the launching site is on the R43 about 14 km south of Worcester.

Golf
Worcester Golf Club, 3 km north of town across the N1, T023-342 7482, www.worcester golfclub.co.za. The club was founded in 1895. The present 18-hole course designed by the Gary Player Group is over 10 years old and has some large greens of tournament standard. The mountains are a perfect backdrop. The wmodern club-house has a good restaurant.

Prince Alfred's Hamlet *p224*
Horse riding
Hamlet Equestrian Centre, T083-287
7751, www.ceres.org.za/hamlethorseriding.
Offers ½-hr (R70) and hr (R100) rides through
farmland and fruit orchards. No experience
needed and children welcome. Book ahead.

Robertson *p226, map p227*
Sky diving
Skydive @ Robertson, T021-462 5666,
www.skydive.co.za. Offers tandem jumps
from 10,000 ft with a 35-second freefall
for R1400, from Robertson Airfield.
Viljoensdrift, wine estate 12 km from
Robertson on the Bonnievale road on the
banks of the Breede River, T023-615 1901,
www.viljoensdrift.co.za. Relaxed cruises on
their river boat, R35, children (3-16) R15.
You can pick up a picnic basket and a
bottle of wine from their shop.

Bonnievale *p229*
Boat trips
The *Breede River Goose*, a 2-storey pontoon
with a tender boat for fishing, runs daily
trips on the river with additional braais;
book in advance, T023-616 2175.

◎ Transport

Worcester and around *p216, maps p217
and p219*
Worcester is 112 km from **Cape Town**,
60 km from **Ceres**, 50 km from **Paarl**,
and 117 km from **Swellendam**.

Bus
All services arrive/depart from the Breede
Valley Shell Ultra City on the N1 and the
railway station. Each of the major long-
distance luxury bus services stop here as they
head inland from the Cape to **Bloemfontein**
(11 hrs), **Johannesburg** and **Tshwane**
(**Pretoria**) (16 hrs), but they do not offer good
value for the 2-hr journey to **Cape Town**.

Bus companies All bus tickets can be
booked online at www.computicket.com.
Greyhound; www.greyhound.co.za;
Intercape, www.intercape.co.za; and
Translux, www.translux.co.za. For details,
see Getting around, page 41.

Train
The station is off Tulbagh St to the north of
the centre. The service between **Cape Town**
and **Johannesburg** stops in Worcester on
Sun, Mon, Wed and Fri. Departs Worcester
0940 for **Cape Town** (2½ hrs), and departs
Cape Town at 1230. Central reservations,
Shosholoza Meyl, T0860-00888 (in South
Africa), T011-774 4555 (from overseas),
www.shosholozameyl.co.za, timetables
and fares are published on the website.

Robertson *p226, map p227*
48 km to **Worcester**, 67 km to **Swellendam**.

Bus
Robertson has surprisingly poor transport
connections and at the time of writing
was only accessible by Translux bus. **Cape
Town** (2½ hrs): daily, via **Worcester**
(45 mins). **Port Elizabeth** (9 hrs) daily
via **Swellendam** and the **Garden Route**.
Bus companies Translux, T0861-589
282, www.translux.co.za. Bus tickets are
booked at www.computicket.com.

◎ Directory

Worcester *p216, maps p217 and p219*
Medical services Medi-Clinic, Russell St,
T023-348 1500, www.worcestermc.co.za.

Montagu and around *p230, map p231*
Banks ABSA, Bath St; Standard, Market St,
both have ATMs. **Medical services**
Hospital, Hospital St, T023-614 1133.

Overberg and the Whale Coast

The evocatively named Whale Coast lives up to its title from July to November, when large numbers of whales seek out the sheltered bays along the coast for breeding. Whales can be seen close to the shore from False Bay all the way east to Mossel Bay, but by far the best place for whale spotting is Hermanus as the whales favour the sheltered Walker Bay, and daily sightings are guaranteed in August and September. Elsewhere along the coast there are opportunities to see the fearsome great white shark. There are seaside towns with miles of sandy beaches and rock pools, plus the southernmost point in South Africa, Cape Agulhas.

More than 120 ships have been wrecked along this coast (the first recorded wreck dates from 1673); there are hazardous reefs, headlands and rocks all the way to Cape Infanta and the Breede River estuary. A museum in Bredasdorp traces the misfortunes of the wrecked ships. In addition to whale watching, this coast offers some of the best fishing in South Africa and an opportunity to dive historic shipwrecks. ▶▶ For listings, see pages 257-266.

Gordon's Bay to Hermanus ⊜❻ ▶▶ pp257-266.

The most beautiful and exhilarating stretch of the coast is between Gordon's Bay and Hermanus, where the mountains plunge into the ocean forming a coastline of steep cliffs, sandy coves, dangerous headlands and natural harbours. This is an area of much beauty and also botanical significance and in 1998 it was the first UNESCO-declared Biosphere Reserve in southern Africa and is now known as the Kogelberg Nature Reserve. It's known for its fynbos and over 1700 species of plant has been recorded here. This route is often compared to the spectacular Chapman's Peak Drive on the Cape Peninsula, and rightly so.

Gordon's Bay, Rooiels and Pringle Bay → Colour map 8, B1.

Set in the lee of the Hottentots Holland Mountains at the eastern end of False Bay, away from the more glamorous beaches of Cape Town, is the popular family seaside resort of Gordon's Bay. There are two sandy beaches, **Bikini** (which has been awarded Blue Flag status) and **Main**, both of which are safe for swimmers. The rocky shoreline, a short walk from the seafront, is popular for fishing. The most likely catch includes mackerel, steenbras and kabeljou. The beach road is lined with a number of seafood restaurants and this is a popular lunch spot at the weekends for people from Cape Town.

Following the R44 south, the first small coastal resort after Gordon's Bay is **Rooiels** (19 km), a cluster of holiday homes at the mouth of a small river. The beach has a strong backwash, so be wary if children are swimming. There's a large troop of chacma baboons in this region that move between Rooiels and Betty's Bay and they can sometimes be seen on the beach. Continuing towards Hermanus, the road leaves its precipitous course and climbs the hills inland. After 5 km turn right to **Pringle Bay**, which is dominated by a large rock outcrop known as the Hangklip, 454 m. This is the rock you see when standing by the lighthouse at Cape Point looking across False Bay. Hangklip was formerly known as 'Cabo Falso' ('false cape'), because of its resemblance to Cape Point. It prompted sailors from the east to turn north earlier than they should have done into what is now known as False Bay. The gravel loop road around **Cape Hangklip** is a scenic distraction; another track leads to Hangklip. The road rejoins the R44 just before Silver Sands.

Betty's Bay → *Colour map 8, C1.*

This small holiday village, midway between Strand and Hermanus, is known for its penguin colony and botanical garden. The community was named after Betty Youlden, the daughter of a local businessman who had plans to develop the Cape Hangklip area in the 1930s. Fortunately little came of the idea and today the village remains an untidy collection of holiday homes in a beautiful location. At Stoney Point there is a **reserve** ① *0900-1700, R5,* to protect a small breeding colony of African jackass penguins, one of the few places where you are guaranteed to see these birds breeding on the mainland. A boardwalk has been constructed to allow visitors good views of the penguins without disturbing them. Also here are the remains of a whaling station plus the hulk of a whaler, the *Balena*. Behind the village are the well-known **Harold Porter Botanic Gardens**, worth a visit if time permits. Along the main beach is another area of protected land, the **HF Verwoerd Coastal Reserve**. There is safe swimming close to the kelp beds, and the dunes above Silver Sands are a popular spot for sandboarding. For sandboarding operators, see Cape Town chapter, page 128.

☾ *African jackass penguins mate for life and return to the same nest each year to breed.*

Harold Porter Botanic Gardens
① *T028-272 9311, www.sanbi.org. Mon-Fri 0800-1630, Sat-Sun 0800-1700, R15, children (5-16) R5, the garden is signposted from the main road, just outside Betty's Bay. There is the*

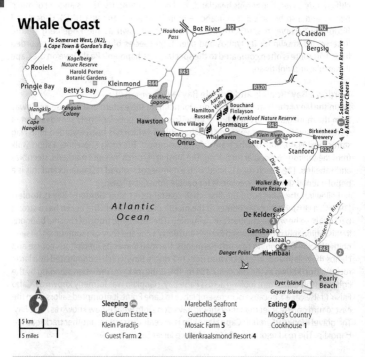

Whale Coast

To Somerset West, (N2),
▲ Cape Town & Gordon's Bay

Houhoek Pass
Bot River N2
Caledon N2
Bergsig

Kogelberg Nature Reserve
Harold Porter Botanic Gardens
Rooiels
Pringle Bay
Betty's Bay
Kleinmond R44
R43

Hangklip
Penguin Colony
Cape Hangklip

Bot River Lagoon
Hemel-en-Aarde Valley
Hamilton Russell
Bouchard Finlayson ①
Wine Village
Hermanus
Hawston
Vermont
Onrus
Whalehaven
R320
Fernkloof Nature Reserve
R43
Klein River Lagoon
Gate ⑤

Salmonsdam Nature Reserve
To Salmonsdam Nature Reserve & Klein River Cheese

Birkenhead Brewery
Stanford R326

Die Pi't

Atlantic Ocean

Walker Bay Nature Reserve ♦

De Kelders
Gate

Gansbaai
Franskraal ④
Danger Point
Kleinbaai

Paardenberg River
R43 ②

Dyer Island
Geyser Island
Pearly Beach

N
5 km
5 miles

Sleeping 🛏
Blue Gum Estate **1**
Klein Paradijs
Guest Farm **2**

Marebella Seafront
Guesthouse **3**
Mosaic Farm **5**
Uilenkraalsmond Resort **4**

Eating 🍴
Mogg's Country
Cookhouse **1**

pleasant Sugarbird Tearoom and a gift shop by the entrance gate, 0900-1630. To the left of
the entrance is a picnic site and toilets. Guided tours should be arranged in advance.

This garden, lying between mountains and coast, was originally acquired in 1938 by Harold Porter, a keen conservationist. In his will he bequeathed the grounds to the nation. There are 10 ha of cultivated fynbos garden and a further 191 ha of natural fynbos which has been allowed to flourish undisturbed. [Fynbos is the term given to a type of vegetation that is dominated by shrubs and comprises species unique to South Africa's southwestern and southern Cape.] The reserve incorporates the whole catchment area of the Dawidskraal River. The garden has many fynbos species, including proteas, ericas, legumes, buchus and brunias. Another draw is the chance of seeing red disa flowering in its natural habitat – this usually occurs from late December to late January. More than 88 species of bird have been identified; of special interest are the orange-breasted sunbird and the rare protea canary, which is only seen in fynbos environments. The best time to visit is from September to November, although it can still be cool and windy at this time.

There are three longer paths which lead from the formal grounds into the surrounding mountains. Disa Kloof has a small dam and a waterfall; Leopard's Kloof takes you several kilometres into the Kogelberg; and a contour path starts by the Harold Porter memorial stone, from which there are excellent views of the ocean and the gardens. Fire prevention is an important issue, especially from January to March when the terrain is dry and the wind prevails from the southeast. Fynbos contains resin and oils which are highly flammable.

Kleinmond, Vermont and Onrus → *Colour map 8, B1/C2.*

Kleinmond is a popular summer resort in Sandown Bay that has been frequented by the wheat farmers of the interior since 1861 and is today a sizeable resort. Exercise caution when swimming at Kleinmond as the sandy beach is steep; children should be watched at all times. The name Kleinmond refers to the 'small mouth' of the Bot River lagoon. The settlement is overlooked by the magnificent Kogelberg Mountains which in the spring are full of flowering proteas. Information is available from the helpful **Hangklip-Kleinmond Bureau** ① *signposted, 14 Harbour Rd, just off the R44, T028-271 5657, www.eco scape.org.za, Mon-Fri 0830-1700, Sat 0900-1400, Sun 1000-1400.* The Harbour Road area has an intriguing collection of shops. To the east of the town is the Bot River Lagoon, a popular sailing and canoeing area. Where the Bot River meets the sea is a large marsh which is home to thousands of waterfowl. This is a birdwatchers' paradise, especially at low tide. The more common species are spoonbills, herons, pelicans, gulls, terns, kingfishers and geese and a pair of fish eagles breed at the lagoon. There is also a small herd of wild horses that roam the marshlands; after several attempts to cull them in the 1950s, they are now protected.

After Kleinmond the R44 joins the R43, which then continues along the coast to the next sizeable settlements of **Vermont** and **Onrus**, these days more or less suburbs of Hermanus, before arriving in Hermanus proper. Vermont, named after the American state, was founded by CJ Krige who became the first speaker of the South African parliament. The beach here is sheltered by high dunes and is safe for children. Onrus, meaning 'restless', lying on the east bank of the mouth of the Onrus River, was named by the first European settlers because of the perpetual noise made by the waves along the rocky coastline. The Onrus River forms a small lagoon with a short sandy beach which is also safe for children to swim from. The beach is popular with surfers too.

Hermanus has grown from a rustic fishing village to a much-visited tourist resort famed for its superb whale watching. It is the self-proclaimed world's best land-based whale-watching site, and indeed Walker Bay is host to impressive numbers during the calving season (July to November). However, don't expect any private viewings – Hermanus is very popular and has a steady flow of binocular-clutching visitors. While this means it can get very busy, there is also a good range of accommodation and restaurants, making it a great base for exploring the quieter reaches of the Overberg and, while you may find it far too crowded at Christmas, at other times it reverts to its small-town calm. Alternatively, being only a few hours from Cape Town, Hermanus is an easy day trip from the city.

Ins and outs

Hermanus is 120 km from Cape Town (via N2). Despite being a popular destination, none of the three major coach companies runs a service via Hermanus. One of the easiest ways to visit, if you don't have a car, is to travel on the **Baz Bus** from Cape Town to Bot Rivier on the N2, which is 23 km from Hermanus. From here you can arrange to be collected by your hosts for a small fee, but this must be arranged in advance. **Splash Shuttle and Tours** ① T028-316 4004, splash@hermanus.co.za, can arrange a car shuttle service to and from Cape Town.

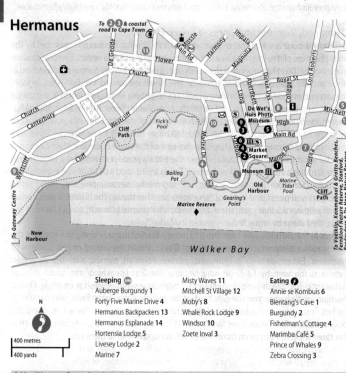

Hermanus

Sleeping 🛏️
Auberge Burgundy 1
Forty Five Marine Drive 4
Hermanus Backpackers 13
Hermanus Esplanade 14
Hortensia Lodge 5
Livesey Lodge 2
Marine 7

Misty Waves 11
Mitchell St Village 12
Moby's 8
Whale Rock Lodge 9
Windsor 10
Zoete Inval 3

Eating 🍴
Annie se Kombuis 6
Bientang's Cave 1
Burgundy 2
Fisherman's Cottage 4
Marimba Café 5
Prince of Whales 9
Zebra Crossing 3

The **Greater Hermanus Tourism Bureau** ① *Old Station Building, Mitchell St, T028-312 2629, www.hermanus.co.za, Mon-Fri 0800-1800, Sat 0900-1700, Sun 0900-1500 (shorter hours in winter)*, is extremely helpful and has lots of information on the surrounding area, plus an accommodation booking service.

Background
The town is named after Hermanus Pieters, an old soldier who set up camp in the bay while looking for better pastures for his animals during the hot summer months. The presence of a freshwater spring persuaded him to spend the summer here. Soon other farmers arrived with their families from the interior. Almost by accident it became a holiday destination – the herds required little attention, so the men turned their attention to fishing while the women and children enjoyed themselves on the sandy beaches. When the farmers returned inland to the winter pastures, it was the fishermen who remained and settled here.

In the 1920s the town gained a reputation as an excellent location for convalescing, and even doctors from Harley Street in London were recommending the 'champagne air' of Hermanus. As it became popular with the gentry, so suitably smart hotels were built to accommodate them. After the Second World War the construction of a new harbour stimulated the expansion of the fishing industry and there are now three canning factories in Walker Bay.

Sights
The **Old Harbour** is a national monument and a focal point for tourist activities. A ramp leads down the cliff to the attractive old jetty and a group of restored fishermen's cottages, including the **Old Harbour Museum** ① *T028-312 1475, www.old-harbour-museum.co.za, Mon-Sat 0900-1300, 1400-1700, small entry fee*. The displays are based on the local fishing industry and include models of fish, a whale skeleton, some shark jaws, fish tanks and early fishing equipment. One of the most interesting features is the recordings of calls between whales. There are also telescopes to watch the whales further out. An information plaque helps identify what you see. Outside the museum on the harbour ramp is a collection of small restored fishing boats, the earliest dating from 1855. Also on show are the drying racks for small fish and cement tables which were once used for gutting fish.

The **De Wet's Huis Photo Museum** ① *Market Sq, T028-313 0418, Mon-Fri 0900-1300, 1400-1700, Sat 0800-1300, 1400-1600, small entry fee*, houses an interesting collection of photography depicting the historical development of Hermanus. The building is interesting in itself as it was a Sunday school next to the Dutch Reformed Church, and it was carefully dismantled stone by stone and re-erected in Market Square.

Outside the old harbour is a memorial to those who died in the First World War. Set in the stonework is a barometer and the words "to help to protect the lives of present and future fishermen". Either side of the beehive-shaped monument are two ship's cannons. The new harbour, to the west of the old harbour in Westcliff, is still a busy fishing port. It's a great idea to head down to the dockside to buy fresh crayfish, mussels or linefish from the fish shop. The staff will be happy to advise you on how best to cook your selection.

Walks around Hermanus
The excellent **Cliff Path** starts at the new harbour in Westcliff in the west and follows the shore all the way round Walker Bay to the mouth of the Klein River in the east, a distance of just over 10 km. Between cliffs the path goes through stands of milkwood trees and

Whale watching

The WWF acknowledges Hermanus as one of the 12 best places in the world to view whales. It is the ideal destination if you wish to see whales from land without bobbing around in a boat. The town promotes itself as the 'heart of the Whale Coast', and during the season most visitors should not be disappointed. The town's advantage is that whales can come very close to the shore. The combination of low cliffs and deep water at the base of the cliffs means that you are able to look down from above into clear water and see the outlines of whales from as close as 10 m.

To add to the excitement there is a whale crier who between 1000 and 1600 during September and October strolls around the town centre blowing a kelp horn to announce the arrival of each whale in Walker Bay. The whale crier is easily identified: he wears a giant Bavarian-style hat and carries a sandwich board which records the daily sightings of whales from different vantage points around Walker Bay. You can phone him directly on his cell phone, T079-301 4665 to ask if there are whales in the bay.

The first southern right whales start to appear in Walker Bay from June onwards. By the end of December most have returned to the southern oceans. The whales migrate north to escape heavy winter storms in the oceans around Antarctica. In August and September most of the calves are born in the calm sheltered bays, where the cows then stay with their young for a further two months. They can travel up to 2000 km to and from Antarctica on this continuous annual cycle. Out of an estimated world population of only 7000 southern right whales, up to 80 have been recorded mating and calving in Walker Bay. The best months are September and October when daily sightings are almost guaranteed. You would be unlucky not to see some sign of whale action during this period, though of course they are just as likely to be in the middle of the bay as up close to one of the vantage points along the cliff path.

The southern right whale is distinguished from other whales by its V-shaped 'blow', produced by a pair of blowholes, and callosities which appear randomly on and around the oval head. The callosities are growths of tough skin in patterns which help to identify individuals. Southern right whales are basically black with occasional streaks of grey or white on the back. Their flippers are short, broad and almost square. They are thought to live for up to 100 years, and a fully grown adult can weigh as much as 80 metric tonnes.

They are so-named because they were regarded as the 'right' whale to catch. The carcass yielded large quantities of oil and baleen, and the task of collecting the booty was made all the more easy by the fact that the whale floated in the water when killed. The northern right whale is virtually extinct, and the southern right has shown only a slight increase in numbers since international legislation was introduced to protect the species. The South African coastline is the most likely place in the world to see them in coastal waters.

takes you around the sandy beaches. The most popular viewpoints are Dreunkrans, Fick's Pool, Gearing's Point, the Old Harbour, Die Gang, Siever's Punt, Kwaaiwater and Platbank. On an ideal day allow at least a morning for the walk. Bench seats are provided at the prime viewpoints, which make them good spots for a picnic.

Beaches

There are some good beaches a short distance in either direction from the town centre. The best beaches to the west are found at Onrus and Vermont (see page 245). Heading east towards Stanford and Gansbaai, there are long, open beaches or secluded coves with patches of sand and rock pools. **Grotto Beach** is the largest, best developed and most popular for swimming and is one of South Africa's 20 Blue Flag beaches. The fine white sands stretch beyond the Klein River Lagoon, and there are changing facilities, a restaurant and a beach shop. Slightly closer to the town centre is **Voëlklip Beach**, a little run down, but with well-kept lawns behind the sand. Conditions are good for swimming and surfing. The most popular spot for surfers is **Kammabaai** next door to Voëlklip beach. There are braai facilities under the shade of some milkwood trees, an ideal setting for beach parties.

Fernkloof Nature Reserve

ⓘ *T028-313 8100, www.fernkloof.com, 24 hrs, free. The visitors' centre, 500 m from the entrance, has a display of the most common plants you are likely to see when walking in the reserve. All the hiking trails start from here.*

Set in the hills behind Hermanus, the reserve has a 60-km network of trails through an area rich in protea and coastal fynbos. Access is from the east end of Hermanus – just before the Main Road crosses Mossel River, turn up Fir Street. The reserve gates are just beyond the botanical society buildings. The diversity of plants in the reserve is due to the long period it has been under protection, plus its range of elevation from 60 to 850 m. With such a diverse plant population, there is also a wide range of bird and animal species including mongoose, dassie and baboon. Higher up in the mountains, look out for breeding black eagles. Small patches of indigenous forest remain in some of the moist ravines.

Hermanus wine route

Hidden away in the **Hemel-en-Aarde Valley** behind Hermanus are a few vineyards producing some surprisingly good wines, mostly Burgundy varieties based around Pinot Noir and Chardonnay grapes. Rarely crowded, three vineyards are open to the public and have tastings in their cellars. **Hamilton Russell Vineyards** ⓘ *T028-312 3595, www. hamiltonrussellvineyards.com, tastings: Mon-Fri, 0900-1700, Sat-Sun 0900-1300*, is the oldest and one of the more picturesque estates and dubs itself both the most southerly wine estate in Africa and the closest to the sea. The cellar and tasting room are set beside a small trout lake. Follow the R43 out of Hermanus towards Cape Town, after 2 km take a right turn marked Caledon, R320; there is a signpost and right turn 5 km along this gravel road.

　　Whalehaven Wines ⓘ *T028-316 1633, www.bottegafamilywine.co.za, tastings: Mon-Fri 0930-1700, Sat-Sun 1030-1430*, is one of the newest vineyards in the valley, so all their wines are quite young – the Pinot Noir is their flagship wine. The cellars and production rooms are open to visitors. Take the R320 turning for Caledon, as above. The winery is almost immediately on the right after turning off the R43.

　　Bouchard Finlayson Wines ⓘ *T028-312 3515, www.bouchardfinlayson.co.za, tastings: Mon-Fri 0900-1700, Sat 1930-1230*, on the Caledon road 1 km beyond the Hamilton Russell Vineyard, has won several awards.

Stanford, the next town along the R43 17 km east of Hermanus, is a peaceful Victorian village set inland from the Atlantic, which has become a popular centre for artists and craftsmen. It is an attractive spot, with some well-restored Victorian thatched cottages and a beautiful setting on the Klein River. This is also the nearest village to the small **Salmonsdam Nature Reserve**. The **Stanford Tourism Bureau** ① *17 Queen Victoria St, T028-341 0340, www.stanfordinfo.co.za, Mon-Fri 0900-1300, 1400-1600*, is next to the library. Information can also be found at www.stanfordvillage.co.za.

Sights

Some of the more notable buildings include **Bachelor's Hope** ① *19 Morton St*, which was built in 1902. In the 1930s it was dubbed Bachelor's Hope because it was home to the village's lady teachers and many a local bachelor found his wife there. The **Anglican Church** on the corner of Longmarket and Morton streets dates from 1872. The **Dutch Reformed Church** on the corner of Queen Victoria and Church streets was built in 1926 but was replaced in the 1960s by the present hall. However, the original church tower, clock and organ remain and have recently been restored. **Market Square**, between Shortmarket and Longmarket streets, is one of the few remaining market squares left undeveloped in South Africa.

Birkenhead Brewery ① *just out of the village off the R326 towards Caledon, T028-341 0183, www.birkenhead.co.za, tours at 1100 and 1500, R20*, is the most popular sight in the area. Six beers are brewed and sold, of which the tastiest is Birkenhead Premium Lager, a slow-brewed beer using rich malted two-rowed barley and aromatic Hallertau and Saaz hop cones. Many of the ingredients are grown on the site and you can take a tour of the hop garden before going inside the modern buildings. Wine is also on sale and can be tasted. The restaurant and pub on the site is open for lunch daily but closes Monday and Tuesday out of season.

Klein River Cheese ① *from the R43, take the left turn onto the R326 opposite the turning to Stanford and follow the signposts, T028-341 0693, http://kleinrivercheese.co.za, Mon-Fri 0900-1700, Sat 0900-1300, picnics can be bought mid-Sep to mid-May, 1100-1500*, is another popular place to stop. The factory specializes in making Gruyère and other cheeses using Jersey and Friesland milk. Visitors can watch cheese being made, taste the produce in the shop, or enjoy a delicious picnic lunch on the banks of the Klein River. Baskets are filled with home-made breads, crackers, pâtés, pickles, cold meats, salads and a selection of cheese. Good for kids too as special picnic baskets are available, there's a playground, and they can visit the farm animals. Also rents out a 3-bed cottage on the farm (**C-D**).

Walker Bay Nature Reserve

① *T028-314 0062, www.capenature.co.za. 0700-1900, R25, children (2-13) R12.*

Driving out of Hermanus to the east you pass through the suburb known as **Voëlklip**. If you are planning to visit the Walker Bay Nature Reserve you must collect your entry permit from the **office** ① *corner of 7th St and 17th Av, Voëlklip, Mon-Fri 0800-1600*. The reserve stretches from the Klein River estuary to De Kelders just before Gansbaai and covers about 1000 ha with a coastline of 17 km. It features a long beach, known as **Die Plaat**, with white sands and rocky limestone outcrops to the east. Vegetation is coastal fynbos and along the Klein River Lagoon are tracts of milkwood trees. Most of the mammals in the reserve are shy, but the tracks of Cape clawless otter, bushbuck, duiker, grysbok and steenbok are occasionally seen. Offshore, whales can be spotted in season and the reserve is home to numerous species of seabirds, including the striking African black oystercatcher. Visitors can explore the coast on hikes though swimming is not recommended as the sea can be rough. There is no overnight accommodation in the reserve. There are two entrances, one to the west of Stanford on a back road, and one further south off the R43 just north of De Kelders.

Salmonsdam Nature Reserve

① T028-341 0018, www.capenature.co.za. 0700-1800, R25, children (2-13) R12. There are 3 basic cabins and a campsite (see Sleeping, page 259). The reserve is 33 km from Hermanus and 16 km from Stanford. It can easily be visited as a day trip from either of these towns. On reaching Stanford, turn right on to the R326. A few kilometres up this road turn right onto a gravel road. The reserve is clearly signposted.

This small reserve was established in 1962 and was named after Captain Robert Salmon of the ill-fated HMS Birkenhead, which sank at Danger Point in 1852 with a loss of 454 lives. It covers 834 ha of the mountains which form part of the catchment area for the Paardenberg River. The main attraction here is the opportunity to view how the Overberg region would have appeared before much of it was cleared by farmers. As you either drive or walk up to the main viewpoint, **Ravenshill**, you pass by several deep, lush valleys which retain a number of indigenous trees. An added attraction is several waterfalls, best viewed after the rains. There are three distinct vegetation zones to look out for, each of which hosts different bird species. The high areas are covered with mountain fynbos – disas, waboom and ground proteas. Around the campsite and in the low-lying, flooded vleis are reeds, water heath and fountain bush. Between the high and low areas, stands of lush indigenous forest fill the kloofs formed by streams running off the mountains. These forested areas are the most rewarding parts to walk in (there are three easy short trails of 2, 3 and 4 km, which start behind the camping area. Look out for small antelope such as steenbok, grey duiker, grey rhebuck, klipspringer and bontebok.

Gansbaai and around ◉❼🅰️🄿 ⤞ pp257-266. Colour map 8, C2.

The R43 reaches Gansbaai 22 km south of Stanford. The history of this popular fishing centre dates back over a century to when a local youth from Hermanus decided to make his home here. The story goes that in 1881 Johannes Cornelis Wessels walked across the sand dunes between Stanford and Gansgat. He found the fishing to be very good and the natural cove provided a safe and sheltered landing spot for the small fishing vessels in use at the time.

The bay was named by fishermen who used it for protection against large storms. The original name gansgat ('goose hole') refers to the colony of Egyptian geese, which used to nest in the reeds that surrounded a natural spring in the bay. These days the village is a prosperous fishing harbour with a modern deep-water wharf and several fish-canning factories. It has, however, managed to retain the character of a small community and busy fishing harbour, albeit with strong ties to the tourist industry. A number of Capetonians have second houses along this coast.

Ask at **Gansbaai Tourism Bureau** ① Gateway Centre, Kapokblom St, T028-384 1439, www.gansbaaiinfo.com, for details of the best operators for shark diving. The office also produces some good maps of the coastline showing the area's walking routes. Further information on this region can be found at www.danger-point-peninsula.co.za.

Sights

Like Hermanus at the other end of Walker Bay, there are some excellent vantage points for whale watching. The southern right whales come close inshore to the sheltered deep waters to calve between June and November each year. A couple of kilometres up the coast at **De Kelders** are tall cliffs which are perfect whale-watching vantage points and quickly give way to a large white-sand beach.

Offshore, **Dyer Island** is named after Samson Dyer, a black American who lived on the island collecting guano around 1806. The Portuguese first named it Isla de Fera ('Island of Wild Animals') and the name is still applicable. Today the island is an important breeding spot for African penguins and many other sea birds. On nearby **Geyser Island** there is a breeding Cape Fur seal population thought to number 50,000. Both are protected by Cape Nature and you are not allowed on to the islands, but they can be visited on boat tours (see Activities and tours, page 266) The area between the two islands is known as Shark Alley, as great white sharks are attracted to the breeding seals. For details of great white shark cage diving see page 266.

South from Gansbaai

From Gansbaai the R43 continues southeast along the coast, passing through the small resorts of Kleinbaai, Franskraal, Pearly Beach and on to Die Dam at Sandbaai. Few visitors venture this far into the Overberg, although it is the area's relative isolation that is much of its appeal. **Franskraal**, 4 km from Gansbaai, has a long sand-beach crossing the outlet of the Uilkraals River Estuary, a known birding hotspot. To the southwest, a gravel road connects Kleinbaai along the rugged coast with many rock pools to the **lighthouse** at **Danger Point**. The lighthouse is 18 m tall and on weekdays from 1000 to 1500, the lighthouse keeper will give you a **tour** ① *R14, children (under 12) R7*. There's also a self-catering cottage here that sleeps four (**C**). For more details about accommodation in lighthouses see box, page 49. In May 1852 the *HMS Birkenhead* sank here with a loss of 445 lives, though every woman and child on the ship escaped unharmed in the lifeboats and this is where the phrase 'women and children first' was thought to be originated. It took the sinking of a further 20 ships before a lighthouse came into operation in 1895. Further on along the R43, **Pearly Beach** starts with some rocky outcrops and then opens up to a large expanse of smooth sand and is ideal to enjoy long and lonely beach-walks. From Sandbaai, the road turns inland and cuts across wild countryside that remains virtually untouched. During the spring the fields are full of wild flowers, and throughout the year the area is rich in varieties of fynbos. Follow signs for Wolvengat, formerly known as Viljoenshof, and continue on to Elim.

Elim → *Colour map 8, C2.*

Founded by German missionaries in 1824, this is one of the best-known Moravian mission stations in South Africa. The settlement is named after the spot where, in Exodus 15:27, the Israelites rested after crossing the Red Sea. To live here you must be a member of the local Moravian church and your livelihood must come from the earth. A new industry has emerged in recent years, based upon two long-lasting species of wild flower – helipterum and helichrysum – which are now successful export crops. Once dried, they are very popular for wreaths in Germany, keeping the historical connections alive today.

The whole village has been declared a national monument, so it is not surprising that there are a variety of quaint old buildings still standing and in use. One attraction is a restored **watermill** dating from 1833. It has a huge Burmese-teak wheel, which replaced the original stone wheels. The mill was reopened in 1990 to produce wholewheat flour. The **Old Mill Tea Room** serves delicious Elim biscuits and other items made from the mill's flour. Two other old buildings worth looking out for are the **parsonage** and the original **mission church**, which has a thatched roof and a clock. The church has a clock that dates back 235 years and still keeps good time. It was acquired for Elim in 1914 but has been working since 1764 when it was built in Germany for a church in Herrenhut.

Bredasdorp and around ⊖❼ ⇥ pp257-266. Colour map 8, C2.

This is South Africa's first *dorp*, founded in 1837 by Michiel van Breda, an important local figure. From his farm, Zoetendalsvlei, he played an active role in the development of the Merino sheep industry throughout South Africa and was the first mayor of Cape Town in 1840. Sheep farming, as well as wheat, remains the mainstay of the local economy.

Sights
Despite its age, there is little to keep you in town for long. Worth a peek is the **Shipwreck Museum** ⓘ *6 Independent St, T028-424 1240, Mon-Fri 0900-1645, Sat-Sun 1100-1545, small entry fee*, which houses a collection of odd bits and pieces salvaged from along the coast, 24 km away. The whole display is greatly enhanced by the sound effects. In the Shipwreck Hall you hear the distinct shrieks of seagulls and the thunderous sound of waves on a stormy night. Four wrecks are featured: the *Queen of the Thames*, *HMS Birkenhead*, the *Oriental Pioneer* and HMS *Arniston*. In the coach house are some old horse-drawn carts and a fire engine.

South from Bredasdorp
Driving south on the R319 for a further 36 km takes you to **Cape Agulhas**. Before reaching the coast, the road runs close to some large *vleis* (marshes): Karsrivier and Soetendals. These are important breeding grounds for aquatic birds, and there is a good chance of seeing flamingos. At the coast the road passes through **Struisbaai** before ending at the Agulhas National Park. A second road going south from Bredasdorp, the R316, ends at Arniston.

Malgas
This small settlement on the banks of the Breede River was a vital point in the transport route in the mid-19th century of the famous Overberg tycoon, Joseph Barry. Until the roads east from Cape Town were improved and the many mountain passes negotiated, the majority of goods were brought into the Overberg region through Malgas. The Barry family had a 158-ton vessel, *Kadie*, especially built to transfer goods from Cape Town to Port Beaufort. From here the cargo was transferred to river boats and taken upstream as far as Malgas, before the final stage of transportation was completed by ox wagon. Today the settlement is famous for having the last manually operated pontoon in South Africa. Cars are carried across the river during daylight hours.

Struisbaai and L'Agulhas
Strisbaai is an attractive fishing village surrounding by a sprawling a collection of holiday and retirement homes homes, safe swimming in the bay and a 14-km white-sand beach.

L'Agulhas just to the south and at the end of the road is a rather wind-blown settlement of a few houses and shops. The principal attraction in this region is nearby **Cape Agulhas**. This is the southernmost point in Africa, but it is rather disappointing and lacks the grandeur one might hope for. Aside from the lighthouse, the surroundings are rather dull and the beach is very rocky, although it's excellent for fishing. This is where the warm waters of the Indian Ocean meet the cooler waters of the Atlantic Ocean, although most visitors seem to think they meet at Cape Point. However, it doesn't happen in a straight line and the warm waters of the Indian Ocean do reach as far west as False Bay. At the end of the 15th century the early Portuguese seafarers christened this tip Cabo das Agulhas, which means 'Cape of Needles' and refers to the needle of the compass which at this point shows no real deviation between true north and magnetic north.

Cape Agulhas Lighthouse ① *1 km east of the tip of Africa, T028-435 6078, 0900-1700, R14, children (3-13) R7*, was built in 1848 and was modelled on the Egyptian pharaohs' light in Alexandria. It now houses a pleasant tea room, decorated with antiques and museum pieces, which serves breakfast and light lunches. If you climb up the 70-odd stairs there are good views over the unforgiving ocean that has claimed many ships and lives.

 ❍ *The official position of the southernmost tip of Africa is 34°49'58" south and 20°00'12" east and is found approximately 1 km west of the Cape Agulhas Lighthouse. The location is marked by a simple cairn.*

Agulhas National Park

① *For information contact T028-435 6222, www.sanparks.org, free entry.*
The park encompasses a large area of coastland centred around Cape Agulhas, and it was created to help protect the rugged coastline and the immediate hinterland, known as the Agulhas Plain, which forms the southernmost area of Africa. The Agulhas Plain is home to almost 2000 species of indigenous plants, of which 100 are endemic to the area. A large part of the area is taken up by a variety of wetlands which attract more than 21,000 migrant and resident birds annually. The park also protects a couple of islands found just offshore which are home to seals and seabirds, as well as the whales which frequent this part of the coastline in spring and early summer. Finally, the area is important in archaeological terms, and several ancient habitation sites have already been discovered. At present, there are limited tourist facilities in the park (a couple of toilets and little else), but for a while now SANParks has been considering building a 60-bed accommodation facility. The quickest route from Cape Town (230 km) is to take the N2 highway as far as Caledon and then turn onto the R406 for Bredasdorp. From Bredasdorp follow the signs for either Struisbaai or L'Agulhas. At present these are the two closest settlements to the park with accommodation facilities.

Arniston

This tranquil fishing village, which is sometimes still known to locals by its Afrikaans name, *Waenhuiskrans* (wagon house cliff), is made up of a jumble of whitewashed, thatched cottages. Some of these are the homes of poor fishermen who put their brightly painted boats (chukkies) to sea early each morning, while others have been renovated into smart holiday homes. The appeal of the place is its beaches – the water is noticeably warm and turquoise here on the Indian Ocean side, and is backed by bone-white dunes making the effect all the more startling. Just to the west of the village is **Waenhuiskrans Cave**, a huge cavern overlooking the sea, which can be explored at low tide. The cavern goes back into the cliffs and is named after the ox wagons which it once held.

The town's other name is derived from the wreck of the *Arniston* (1815), which lies about 1 km from the slipway. Items salvaged from the wreck are on display in the **Bredasdorp Shipwreck Museum** (see page 253). The wreck can be dived, but there is a heavy swell. There is a monument to the deceased near the beach; only six of the 378 passengers survived. There are two beaches, **Slipway** in front of the **Arniston Hotel**, and **Bikini Beach**. The waters are warm and bright blue, with some good snorkelling. At low tide a couple of rock pools are exposed on Bikini Beach and are fun for children to explore. A few shops in the village stock the basics for self-catering. You can only reach here in your own vehicle; there is no public transport.

De Mond Nature Reserve

① *26 km south of Bredasdorp, T028-424 2170, www.capenature.co.za. 0700-1800, office hours 0700-1600, R25, children (2-13) R12. Vehicles are not allowed in the reserve and there is a car park next to the office by the main gate from where the Sterna Trail begins, and a 3-bedroom cottage to rent (see Sleeping, page 261). The best time to visit is Oct-Mar.*

This pleasant small reserve is centred around the mouth of the Heuningnes River. Two former farms were designated as a nature reserve in 1986. About 10 km of the shoreline is also protected, although most of the land remains inaccessible to the public. A 7-km hike known as the **Sterna Trail** starts from the office and in the most part follows the beach. This is an easy path that winds through a range of different coastal habitats, including dune forest, stabilized dunes, riverine vegetation and some salt marshes.

De Hoop Nature Reserve ●❷ ▸▸ *pp257-266. Colour map 8, C3.*

① *T028-542 1253, www.capenature.co.za. 0700-1800, Fri 0700-1900, office hours 0800-1700, R25, children (2-13) R12. Accommodation in the reserve has recently been privatized (see Sleeping, page 261).*

This is an important coastal reserve which extends 5 km out to sea, protecting the shoreline and marine life. It is divided into two sectors. The **western region** is for hiking, game viewing and birdwatching while the **eastern section** is for mountain biking. The region enjoys a Mediterranean climate with mild winters and warm summers. August is the wettest month, with some morning fogs. The sea has strong currents and can be dangerous for swimming. Consult the reserve office for advice on safe spots to swim.

The reserve covers an exceptionally varied and rich environment – seven different ecosystems are found within the 34,000-ha reserve. De Hoop is a large freshwater *vlei* surrounded by marshlands which stretch for 15 km. The coastline is a mix of sandy beaches, rocky headlands and cliffs with wave-cut platforms. Further inland are giant sand dunes, some as high as 90 m, and behind these are limestone hills and the Potberg Mountains. The higher ground is clearly divided by kloofs covered with indigenous vegetation. It has been estimated that over 1500 plant species grow here, of which 34 are endemic to the reserve, including rare lowland fynbos species. Details of the rarer plants are displayed at the environmental education centres and the reserve offices at De Hoop and Potberg.

Ins and outs

Getting there Coming from Bredasdorp, follow the R319 towards Swellendam. After 8 km is a signposted right turn onto a gravel road. After 40 km you reach **Ouplaas** – take a right for the western section or continue straight on for another 10 km for the entrance to the eastern section. The office and car park are at Potberg. Approaching from the N2, the quickest route is to take the Witsand (see also page 273) turning 12 km east of Swellendam. After 23 km turn right for Malgas and then follow the signs. The last 50 km or so on both of these routes is on gravel roads.

Reserve information There are information displays at De Hoop and Potberg offices introducing the visitor to the environment and the diversity of species to be found in the reserve. The closest shops and petrol are in Ouplaas, 15 km from the De Hoop office. There are two drives in the reserve, one 11 km circular drive and a 15 km drive to the coast. Visitors are permitted to leave their cars anywhere on the side of the roads and go for a walk.

Wildlife

With such a variety of terrain in a relatively small area, the region supports a diverse range of wildlife. Over 250 species of bird have been recorded here, while elusive leopard, bontebok and Cape mountain zebra roam around, along with the more common eland, grey rhebok, baboon and klipspringer. The last known breeding colony of the Cape vulture in the southwestern Cape is close to Potberg, and you may glimpse them circling high in the skies. The **Windhoek Cave** is home to a large colony of bats which have attracted their fair share of research interest. Other rare species that you might see include black oystercatchers, which forage amongst the dunes. Finally, there is a chance of seeing southern right whales, which calve in the shallow waters and can be seen between July and December (see page 248). Although the whales found here are often in larger concentrations than elsewhere, they are difficult to see as they remain beyond the breakers.

Hiking The reserve is traversed by a number of self-guided hiking trails, and they have been designed for all levels of fitness and with different interests in mind. There are four one-day walks close to the camps and car parks and the **Vlei Trail** follows the banks of the De Hoop Vlei where you'll find masses of waterbirds. A new 55 km five-day **Whale Trail** follows the coast and well-equipped overnight huts are found at suitable intervals. This trail needs to be pre-booked through Cape Nature and is limited to groups of six or 12. The cost of R1250 per person includes a shuttle service back to your car at the beginning at Potberg, and for an additional fee you can organize for your gear to be portaged to the next overnight stop.

Mountain biking Cyclists are permitted to use any of the management roads in the western sector of the reserve. There is also the **De Hoop Mountain Bike Trail** laid out in the eastern sector (bookings essential). A hut at **Cupidoskraal** is used as an overnight base for cyclists on the trail. The trail varies in difficulty and cyclists will need to allow two to three days to complete it. Numbers are limited to 12 cyclists per day. The hut provides comfortable overnight accommodation for 12 people, with storage space for bicycles, gas, fireplace, but no bedding. The only drinking water available is by the overnight hut, so make sure you carry enough for each day. Beware of dehydration and cramp when cycling in the heat. Always carry a rudimentary first-aid kit; you will quickly appreciate how isolated you are in the reserve.

For Sleeping and Eating price codes and other relevant information, see pages 46-53.

⊜ Sleeping

Gordon's Bay *p243*

B Berg en Zee, 131 Beach Rd, T021-856 3095, www.bergenzee.co.za. Stylish, intimate guesthouse in a whitewashed house with wooden floors, 6 rooms and 1 honeymoon suite with white furnishings and bedding. Terrace, splash pool, bar, within walking distance of restaurants, beauty treatments on offer, and the host, a registered guide, offers local day tours.

B Celtic Manor, 22 Suikerbossie Drive, T021-856 1907, www.celticmanor.co.za. High up on the hill above Gordon's Bay with sweeping views of False Bay, this boutique guesthouse has 6 rooms and 1 self-catering apartment sleeping 4, arranged around the hillside. Guests share dinner around a large dining table, there is a comfortable lounge and bar, swimming pool and separate spa with 2 therapists.

Pringle Bay *p243*

A Moonstruck on Pringle Bay, 264 Hangklip Rd, T028-273 8162, www.moonstruck.co.za. Intimate guesthouse with large windows overlooking the ocean and mountains, 4 spacious rooms, stylish decor, balconies and fireplaces, pool with wooden deck, 100 m from the beach reached by a private path through the fynbos.

Betty's Bay *p244*

D Buçaco Sud, Clarence Drive, T028-272 9750, www.bucacosud.co.za. Spanish-style villa with 6 tastefully decorated rooms, terracotta tiles, fireplaces in public areas, all rooms have either mountain or coastal views, breakfast served in attractive courtyard with pool, no children under 10.

D Waterlilly Lodge, on the R44, Porter and Angler Drive, T028-272 9378, www.waterlilly lodge.co.za. 6 stylish rooms with bright white bedding, some with wooden floors, pretty garden and patio with sea and mountain views, attentive host who's an ex-South African Airways steward, good wholesome breakfasts.

Onrus *p245*

C On the Vermont Guest House, 21 Tiptol Cres, T028-316 2873, www.hermanus-onrus-accommodation.co.za. Smart modern lodge in a Tuscan-style villa with 4 comfortable rooms, 1 completely wheelchair accessible with lift and roll in shower, balconies, DSTV, swimming pool and patio.

D Flick's Places, 8 Beach Rd, T028-316 2998, www.flicksplace.co.za. Friendly B&B, owned by a well-known local caterer, 200 m from the beach, with comfortable double rooms, with private entrances and satellite TV, excellent breakfasts. Also organizes holiday house rentals in the area.

Hermanus and around *p246, map p246*

There are hundreds of accommodation options in Hermanus and we only have room to list a few examples. For a full listing visit www.hermanus.co.za or visit the tourist office on arrival. Be sure to book well ahead during whale season and school holidays.

L The Marine, Marine Drive, T028-313 1000, www.marine-hermanus.co.za. Part of the Relais & Chateaux group, a historic hotel and one of the finest in the country. 42 luxurious rooms, some with stunning ocean views, all with exceptionally fine furnishings – silk curtains, plush carpets, pale suede armchairs and marble bathrooms. A/c, satellite TV, fresh flowers, 4-poster beds, some have his 'n' hers bathrooms. Rates drop significantly in winter. Also has a spa, heated swimming pool, shop, internet and 2 restaurants; the seafood restaurant has won many awards (see Eating, page 262). Impeccable service. Highly recommended for a treat.

B Auberge Burgundy, 16 Harbour Rd, T028-313 1201, www.auberge.co.za. Provençal-style villa in the heart of Hermanus. 17 rooms, a mix of luxury doubles and suites, the penthouse can sleep 6, all set around a sumptuous inner courtyard with a swimming pool, private terraces or balconies, some with fine views across Walker Bay. Also owns the **Burgundy** restaurant, opposite (see Eating, page 262).

B Misty Waves, 21 Marine Drive, T028-313 8460, www.hermanusmistybeach.co.za. Luxury hotel in a spacious modern building on 2 levels with ample decks and roof terraces, suites have ocean views, spa baths, swimming pool, restaurant, while the annex next door offers elegant B&B accommodation with 4-poster beds and chandeliers in smart white blocks, in rooms that have all the mod cons.

B Mitchell St Village, 56-60 Mitchell St, T028-312 4560, www.56.co.za. 11 rooms, all very differently designed (the owner is an interior decorator), some have private court- yards or balconies and fireplaces, 2 swimming pools, attractive lounge and breakfast rooms. Crayfish dinners can be arranged in season.

B Whale Rock Lodge, 26 Springfield Rd, T028-313 0014, www.whalerock.co.za. Well-appointed B&B with 11 double rooms, en suite, TV, set in a thatched building decorated with antiques and oil paintings, close to the new harbour and a short walk from the cliff path. Garden with pool, lounge, no children under 6.

B Windsor Hotel, 49 Marine Drive, T028-312 3727, www.windsor-hotel.com. Large and popular, this is Hermanus's oldest hotel built in 1896, set on cliffs overlooking the ocean, with 60 en suite rooms with TV. Pay considerably more for the ones with sea views. Excellent views across Walker Bay from the glazed lounge, though a slightly plain restaurant. Frequently used by tour groups.

C Forty Five Marine Drive, and **Hermanus Esplanade**, 45 and 63 Marine Drive, T028-312 3610, www.45marinehermanus.com. Jointly managed self-catering accommodation in large white blocks in a commanding position

above the rocks and waves, 2- to 3-bedroom fully equipped apartments with kitchen and lounge, underfloor heating, TV, lock-up garages, not very stylish but modern and functional with great views and good value for families.

C Hortensia Lodge, 66 Mitchell St, T028- 312 4358, www.hortensialodge.co.za. Small comfortable guesthouse set in neat gardens with swimming pool, 5 rooms, en suite with TV and views of the garden, simple decor. German, French and Hungarian spoken, no children under 14.

C Livesey Lodge, 13 Main Rd, T028-313 0026, www.liveseylodge.co.za. Friendly guesthouse with 6 double rooms set around garden with good-sized pool. Spacious and bright, all have separate entrances, individual decor, TV, mini-fridge, huge beds, nice touches like books in all the rooms. Off-street parking. Location a little outside town is a drawback, but otherwise it's a good value and well-run place.

D-F Moby's, 9 Mitchell St, T028-313 2361, www.mobys.co.za. Backpacker joint offering a good range of rooms: doubles, dorms sleeping 6-8, family rooms, all are en suite. Pub with DSTV, large garden with pool, daily braais, internet access, TV lounge, fully equipped kitchen. Friendly and laid-back place, and organizes cheap shark dives, wine tasting, sandboarding and the usual excursions. Will meet the Baz Bus at **Bot River Hotel** for a small fee.

D-F Zoete Inval, 23 Main Rd, T028-312 1242, www.zoeteinval.co.za. Excellent budget choice with 7 double B&B rooms, and another double, 1 family room, and 2 dorms in a converted loft, which has self-catering facilities. Pleasant TV lounge, laundry, sunny deck with jacuzzi, internet access, secure parking. Will meet the Baz Bus at **Bot River Hotel** for a small fee. Friendly and good value.

E-F Hermanus Backpackers, 26 Flower St, T028-312 4293, www.hermanusback packers.co.za. Well positioned behind Main Rd, dorms, doubles/twins with or without bathrooms, vibey atmosphere, bar with pool table, TV lounge with DVD library, nightly braai, pickup from Baz Bus for a small fee, will book all activities and give out maps of the area.

Stanford and around *p250*
AL Mosaic Farm, 11 km west of Stanford on the edge of the Klein River Lagoon, T028-313 2814, www.mosaicfarm.net. Luxury accommodation in 5 stone and thatch chalets with stunning views of the mountains and lagoon, large bathtubs, outdoor showers, wooden decks, swimming pool. Rates are all-inclusive of breakfast and dinner and activities such as sundowner drives and kayaking, lunch and quad-biking extra. There are also 2 self-catering cottages or eat at the restaurant for extra.
A Blue Gum Estate, 7 km from Stanford on the R326, T028-341 0116, www.bluegum. co.za. Country-style lodge set on a working farm which the Klein River runs through, with rooms in the manor house or garden suites with colonial decor, wooden floors, DSTV, 4-poster beds and private verandas. The restaurant offers gourmet cuisine and generous buffet and hot breakfasts. Lots of walks around the farm, plus croquet on the lawns and a pool.
C-D Springfontein, T028-341 0651, www.springfontein.co.za. A collection of comfortable self-catering cottages, sleeping 2-6, some of them thatched, on a working farm 4 km from Stanford. Excellent value for families, with pool, gardens, beautiful setting surrounded by farmland and a small vineyard.
D Stanford Hotel, Queen Victoria St, T028-341 0900, www.stanfordvillage.co.za. Attractive historic inn set in the heart of Stanford. Recently renovated, with 6 rooms of varying sizes, all en suite with wooden floors, wicker furniture, brass beds, simple and comfortable. Popular pub attached serving evening meals Wed and Thu and weekend braais. Good value. Recommended.

Salmonsdam Nature Reserve *p251*
E Salmonsdam Cabins, reservations T021-659 3500, www.capenature.co.za. 3 basic overnight cabins, 1 sleeps 6 with 3 rooms, living area, kitchen and bathroom, the other 2 sleep 2 in bunk beds, shared ablution block, suitable for hikers, no electricity but gas fridge, stove, cooking and eating utensils, visitors need to bring bedding and food. There are also 10 camping sites and a small cement swimming pool.

Gansbaai and around *p251*
B Marebella Seafront Guesthouse, De Kelders, T028-384 2665, www.marebella.co.za, 3 km along Walker Bay towards Hermanus from Gansbaai. Smart and comfortable B&B with 3 en suite rooms, shared lounge with satellite TV, breakfast and dinner served on large deck overlooking the sea, private garden leads down to the water. Stunning location perched high up on the cliff, the perfect location for whale watching in the bay Jun-Nov.
C The Great White House, 5 Geelbek St, T028-384 3273, www.white-house.co.za. Popular thatched house with 3 'fishermen's cottages' with fireplaces, wooden floors, en suite, pleasant African-themed decor, range of activities including whale watching and shark diving arranged, restaurant popular with the shark dive companies where they do their briefings, good location close to the harbour.

South from Gansbaai *p252*
A Klein Paradijs Guest Farm, off the R43, 21 km southeast of Gansbaai at Pearly Beach, T028-381 9760, www.kleinparadijs.co.za. A pleasant farm just inland from the beautiful white-sand beach, with 5 individually decorated rooms, newly refurbished, with thatched ceilings, elegant table d'hôte dining room, superb food from a Swiss-trained chef and unique pool with a grassy island in the middle of it. Also has 5 much cheaper self-catering cottages dotted about the farm (**D**) and guests can still eat in the restaurant. Recommended.

D-F Uilenkraalsmond Resort, 5 km
along the coast from Gansbaai at Franskraal,
T028-388 0200, www.uilenkraalsmond
resort.co.za. A vast modern resort and
caravan park with 40 self-catering family
chalets, wash blocks, grassy, limited shade,
sea breeze can be a problem at times.
Plenty of facilities for children, supertube,
trampoline, crazy golf, swimming in the
lagoon, and access to a beautiful stretch of
sandy beach. Very busy during local school
holidays, but for the rest of the year it is quiet.

Bredasdorp and around *p253*
C Firlane Guesthouse, 5 Fir Lane, T028-425
1192, www.afriscape.co.za/firlane. Historic
1926 mansion with gleaming wooden floors
and high ceilings with scrolled cornices,
3 double rooms, individually decorated,
spacious and luxurious bathrooms, 1 has
a Victorian claw foot bath, breakfast served
in a smart dining room or in the garden,
or if you want, in bed.

Struisbaai *p253*
D Harbour Lights, 5 Kusweg, T028-435 6053,
www.capeagulhas.co.za. Smart bright-yellow
B&B within walking distance of the harbour.
5 comfortable rooms with fans, TV, fridge
and electric blankets, bar, evening meals
available, no children under 12.
D-F Cape Agulhas Backpackers, corner
of Main and Duiker streets, Struisbaai,
T082-372 3354, www.capeagulhas
backpackers.com. Double and quads
with or without bathrooms and dorms
in a brightly decorated house with lots
of warm colours, or camping in the
spacious garden. Bedding and towels
included, kitchen for self-catering or all
meals are available, internet, bar with pool
table, pool and can organize local activities.
D-F Struisbaai Caravan Park, Main Rd,
T028-435 6538. Camping and 16 self-catering
chalets, good shade, laundry, shop and café
within walking distance, overlooks the sea,
short walk to lighthouse. All ablution
facilities have been modernized.

L'Agulhas *p253*
A Agulhas Country Lodge, Main Rd, T028-
435 7650, www.agulhascountrylodge.com.
An unusual building made of limestone set
amongst the rocks with broad ocean views,
8 rooms with balconies and complimentary
sherry, some with jacuzzis, restaurant, bar
with nautical and aviation theme, cigar bar.
Rates drop in winter months.
B Villa@Cape Agulhas, 17 Golf St, T028-
435 6917, www.villacapeagulhas.co.za. Very
stylish upmarket B&B with views of the lighthouse, the walls in the communal areas are
painted bright orange, pink and lime green, funky
furniture, fireplaces, rooms have TV, sea views
and fridge. Jacuzzi, no smoking or credit cards.

Arniston *p254*
A Arniston Spa Hotel, Beach Rd, T028-445
9000, www.arnistonhotel.com. An elegant
seaside hotel, 40 rooms, thoughtfully
decorated, small bathrooms, TV, sea-facing
rooms have private balconies but are more
expensive than the pool/courtyard-facing
ones, restful reception rooms with fireplaces.
Good restaurant, bar built around a fish tank,
swimming pool, sheltered garden. The newest
addition is the spa, which has a long menu of
treatments and spa packages are on offer.
C Arniston Lodge, 23 Main Rd, T028-445
9175, www.arnistonlodge.co.za. Appealing
thatched cottage which blends in well with
the traditional fishermen's cottages. 4 double
en suite rooms, characterful upstairs rooms
have thatched ceiling and views across the
beach, sheltered swimming pool, lounge with
log fireplace, evening meals can be arranged,
a welcome peaceful retreat, German spoken.
D Arniston Seaside Cottages, Huxham St,
T028-445 9772, www.arniston-online.co.za.
Compact development set among the dunes
with 20 whitewashed thatched self-catering
cottages, with log fireplaces, reed ceilings,
pine furnishings, most with sea views from
private balcony, cottages are serviced every
day, all facilities close by, buy fresh fish from
the boats as they land. Recommended
and good value.

De Mond Nature Reserve *p255*
D De Mond Cottage, T021-659 3500 (Cape Town), www.capenature.co.za. The cottage is located near the entrance to the reserve among milkwood trees and coastal fynbos and has ocean views. Self-catering with 3 bedrooms, 2 single beds in each, electricity, hot water, shower, braai, stove, fridge, toaster and kettle, bring food and bedding.

De Hoop Nature Reserve *p255*
A variety of accommodation is within the reserve; check out the website for all the options. In 2008 **De Hoop Collection**, T0861-334667, www.dehoopcollection.co.za, took over management and have upgraded and refurbished all the accommodation.
AL Koppie Alleen, whitewashed thatched farmhouse situated right by the beach with wonderful ocean views. This is relatively luxurious self-catering and sleeps 8 people (minimum 6 at R750 per person) in 4 rooms with 4-poster beds, 2 bathrooms with guest toiletries, gas stove, fridge and geysers but no electricity, lighting is by paraffin lamps and candles, fully equipped kitchen, comfortable lounge with fireplace. Nice decor throughout, and outside, sun loungers and umbrellas.
   Opstal This area on the western edge of the reserve right on the edge of the vlei, has the most accommodation (**A-E**). There are dozens of self-catering chalets, rondavels and houses to choose from. All have recently been given a complete overhaul and are now very nicely decorated, are fully equipped and have extras like toiletries in the bathroom. Expect to pay in the region of R450-750 per person per night. The campsite here has basic facilities, with views over the vlei and set under milkwood trees. A communal kitchen and electric points may be operational by the time you read this. Firewood is available from the office. The **Vlei Trail** starts in the camp and 2 paths follow a route around the freshwater lake. Facilities near the reserve's office shared by all guests in the area include a swimming pool, tennis court and boules pitch.

🍴 Eating

Gordon's Bay *p243*
🍴 **Bertie's Moorings**, Harbour Island, T021-856 3343, www.berties.co.za. 1000-2400. Lively pub serving light meals and good seafood on the waterfront. Also a venue for stand-up comedy and live bands at the weekends. The furniture and the bar were handcrafted from wine barrels by owner Bertie Reed.
🍴 **Harbour Lights**, Gordon's Bay Harbour, T021-856 1830. Tue-Sun 1200-1500, 1800-2200. Excellent seafood and good views of the yacht basin at night. Popular place, especially with families in the holidays, serving daily specials, linefish and seafood platters, plus a good wine list and a collection of rare whiskies.
🍴 **Miguel's Al Fourno Pizzeria**, 33 Beach Rd, T021-856 4021. Open 1000-2200. Pleasant spot with outside wooden deck with umbrellas, overlooking the beach, fairly comprehensive Italian menu of standard pastas and pizzas, but slow service. Next door in the blue building is **Trawlers** for takeaway seafood.

Pringle Bay *p243*
🍴 **Hook, Line & Sinker**, 382 Crescent Rd, T028-273 8688, www.hooklineandsinker.co.za. Lunch 1200, dinner 1900. Lunch is beer-battered hake and chips wrapped in newspaper, while dinner and Sun lunch is an ever-changing chalkboard menu cooked by owner and chef Stephan in the open-plan kitchen. Most nights it's seafood, but on Wed and Sun nights he also cooks steak, and there's a single dessert of crème brûlée, which is finished off by blow torch at your table. This only seats 26 people so reservations are essential.
🍴 **Miems**, Hangklip Rd, T028-273 8764. Wed-Sun 1130-1500, Tue-Sat 1800-2100. Cosy village pub serving good-value seafood and pub grub, hearty portions, a good place to hole up on a cold day.

Kleinmond *p245*

Europa, 1 Harbour Rd, T028-271 5107. Open 0800-2200. Large seafront restaurant and coffee shop, good views from the deck, light meals like open sandwiches and freshly baked cakes, plus seafood, spare ribs and steaks, long wine and spirit menu.

Potters Garden, 14 Harbour Rd, T028-271 5505. Open 0800-1700. Look out for the giant blue teapot in front. Light meals, coffees and snacks, big breakfast served all day, Sun lunch popular with the locals.

Onrus *p245*

Milkwood, Atlantic Drive, Onrus, T028-316 1516. Open 0900-2230. Standard breakfast and lunch menu, tea cakes in the afternoon followed by more upmarket dinners, good seafood including fresh grilled calamari and linefish plus venison and steaks, excellent views of the beach.

What the Dickens, Onrus Trading Post, Main St, Onrus, T028-316 3946. Open 1000-late. Well-known and good-value pub lunches with a full menu in the evenings.

Hermanus and around *p246, map p246*

The tourist trade in Hermanus supports an enormous number of restaurants and cafés, far too many to list. It's just a case of wandering around town until you find something that takes your fancy, though it's advisable to book ahead in season.

The Burgundy, Market Sq, Marine Drive, T028-312 2800, www.burgundy restaurant.co.za. 0830-1700, 1900-2200. Restored rural cottage set back from the old harbour. One of the top restaurants in town but relaxed, with tables spilling onto a shady terrace outside. Excellent seafood including superb grilled crayfish and good poultry too like chicken stuffed with dates or duck with orange sauce. Recommended.

Seafood at the Marine, Marine Drive, T028-313 1000, www.marine-hermanus.co.za. 1200-1400, 1900-2100. This superb award-winning establishment serves the freshest seafood in stylish surrounds. The menu is refreshingly unfussy, and includes a crayfish platter, seafood bunny chow, 'Rich man's' fish and chips and gorgeous prawn and leek ravioli with lobster bisque. The wine list is excellent and the service friendly and fast. Highly recommended.

Annie se Kombuis, Warrington Arcade, 8 Harbour Rd, T028-313 1350. Tue-Sun 1000-late. Unusual menu of South African dishes such as waterblommetjies, babotie, oxtail, chicken pie, ostrich, venison and seafood, served up in a homely atmosphere with farm-style furnishings.

Bientang's Cave, T028-312 3454, www.bientangscave.com. Access is via steps from the car park on Marine Drive, between the village square and **Marine Hotel** – look out for the Bientang Seaworld sign. Open 1130-1600, 1900-2130, out of season only open Fri-Sat for dinner. The name doesn't lie, it's an actual cave with an extended deck overlooking the waves. Superb spot for whale watching during season. Excellent seafood buffets and famous bouillabaisse soup, simple wood benches and long tables, very popular, book ahead.

Fisherman's Cottage, Old Harbour, T028-312 3642. Open 1100-1500, 1800-2200. Tiny place set in an old thatched cottage serving excellent seafood, simple dishes such as seafood *potjie*, half and full portions available, charming setting. Choose a veranda table in good weather. Known as the smallest pub in town. No credit cards.

Marimba Café, Royal Arcade, off Main Rd, T028-312 2148. Open 1100-late, closed Sun out of season. Fun 'African' restaurant with dishes from across the continent, including good seafood gumbo, Moroccan lamb shanks and Cape Malay curries. Also has daily specials and occasional live music.

Mogg's Country Cookhouse, Hemel-en-Aarde Valley, 11 km from Hermanus centre, take R43 out of town for Cape Town, after 2 km turn onto the R320 for Caledon, T028-312 4321, www.moggscookhouse.com. Wed-Fri and Sun 1230-1400, Sat 1930-2100.

Farm restaurant in an old farm labourer's cottage with a seasonal menu. From the bread to the ice cream, every dish is home-made and freshly prepared and served in a lovely rustic setting. Likely dishes include lamb shank, seafood risotto or ostrich fillet. Great spot for lunch if you're visiting the vineyards and take your own wine as they don't charge corkage. Recommended.

Prince of Whales, Astoria Village, T028-313 0725. Mon-Fri 0815-1700, Sat 0815-1330. Excellent breakfasts, filled pancakes, sandwiches, cakes and fresh croissants.

Zebra Crossing, corner of Long St and Main Rd, T028-312 3906. Mon-Sat 0900-0200, Sun 1000-0200. Lively pub with zebra-print theme, serving breakfasts, burgers, steaks, salads and ploughman's lunches. Turns into a popular drinking haunt later at night.

Stanford and around *p250*

Blue Gum Estate, see Sleeping, page 259. Open 1900-2200. Smart restaurant set on a luxurious country estate, stylish dining room and beautiful terrace, delicious local cuisine that is delicately and lovingly presented, and good wine list.

Hennie's Pub & Grill, 20 Queen Victoria St, T028-341 0701. Mon-Sun 1100-1400, 1700-late. Informal and friendly pub with signed rugby star photos on the wall, with a simple country menu, big on steaks and the T-bones are enormous and do try their delectable onion rings.

Mariana's Home Deli and Bistro, 12 Du Toit St, T028-341 0272. Thu-Sun 0900-1600. Deli stocked with local products, cheeses, stuffed olives and chutneys. Also serves bistro-style meals on the vine-shaded terrace. The mussels are particularly good. Much of the produce is grown in the back garden.

Gansbaai and around *p251*

The Great White House, see Sleeping, page 259. Open 0730-1600. Daytime restaurant serving filling breakfasts, light lunches and snacks. The pan-fried calamari is very good. At Sun lunch the menu expands to include steaks. This is where cage shark divers warm up in front of the fireplace after their excursion.

Bredasdorp and around *p253*

Blue Parrot, Dirkie Uys St, T028-425 1023. Mon-Sat 1130-late. Popular family restaurant, cosy candlelit tables in a Victorian house, reliable food with standard steaks, pasta and salads, and local wine list.

Julian's, 22 All Saints St, T028-425 1201. Mon-Sat 0900-late. Unusual purple and orange building next door to a ceramics factory that is worth a browse, the crockery is used and sold in the restaurant. Grills and seafood, sandwiches, pancakes and burgers, plenty of choice for vegetarians, and more ambitious specials like duck or pork dishes. Best known for their baked chocolate cheesecake.

Struisbaai and L'Agulhas *p253*

Agulhas Country Lodge, Main Rd, T028-435 7650, www.agulhascountrylodge.com. 0800-2200. Elegant restaurant set in a guest-house which serves excellent fresh seafood – crayfish and Cape Malay prawn curry are specialities, and also well known for its local lamb. Finish off a meal with nightcap in the cigar lounge.

Arniston *p254*

Arniston Spa Hotel, Beach Rd, T028-445 9000, www.arnistonhotel.com. 0700-1000, 1230-1500, 1800-2200. Great ocean views from the large airy dining room and broad outside terrace, and has a long menu of seafood, grills and vegetarian options. Try the oven-baked linefish with horseradish or springbok medallions with mango relish. Cheaper light meals are available all day at the bar.

De Hoop Nature Reserve *p255*

In Opstal, **The Fig Tree Restaurant** and a deli serve 3 meals a day as well as snacks and teas and coffees and there is also the option of getting ready meals delivered to your accommodation or ordering picnic baskets.

❂ Festivals and events

Hermanus and around *p246, map p246*
Aug Hermanus Food and Wine Festival,
www.hermanuswineandfood.co.za. Wine
tasting from over 70 vineyards, plus cheese,
olives and sushi in the gourmet food tent,
and a coffee and brandy tasting lounge.
Sep Hermanus Whale Festival, T028-313
0928, www.whalefestival.co.za. Primarily
an arts festival which attracts theatre and
singing acts along with children's events
and a craft market, and also the best time
of the year to spot whales in Walker Bay.

◎ Shopping

Hermanus and around *p246, map p246*
As befits a popular tourist town there are
plenty of curio shops and speciality boutiques.
Market Sq has a small, daily craft, curio and
clothes market. A popular shopping mall is
the **Village Square**. To the west of the town
centre is the larger **Gateway Centre**. This has
all the high street shops as well as restaurants
and amusements for children.

Wine
Wine Village, at the entrance to the Hemel-
en-Aarde Valley, corner of the R43 and the
R320 on the way into town, T028-316 3988,
www.wine-village.co.za. Mon-Fri 0900-1800,
Sat 0900-1700, Sun 1000-1500. Advertises
itself as the biggest wine shop in South Africa
and sells wine from over 600 estates. Can also
organize international shipping.

▲ Activities and tours

Hermanus and around *p246, map p246*
Diving
In addition to coral reef and kelp forest dives,
there are 3 stimulating wreck dives between
here and Arniston. In Walker Bay, the most
rewarding dives close to the shore are at
Tamatiebank, which has been recommended

for snorkelling, and The Haksteen, a pinnacle
with steep drop-offs, 26 m. A short boat trip
from the new harbour is Whale Rock, or Table
Top. Conditions are quite calm, maximum
depth is 40 m. Expect to see seafans and corals.
From the high-tide mark to 500 m out to sea is
a marine reserve. No marine animals may be
collected or disturbed. **Warning** You are not
allowed to dive when whales are in the bay. If
you come within 300 m of a whale, either in a
boat or the water, there are heavy fines and
visitors will be deported. Enjoy them from
the cliff vantage points instead. For shark
cage diving see under Gansbaai, page 266.
Scuba Africa, New Harbour, T028-316 2362,
www.scubaafrica.com. Equipment hire, dive
courses (NAUI) and daily organized dives.

Fishing
For many local visitors the principal reason
for coming to Hermanus is the excellent sea
fishing. There are strict regulations concerning
what you can catch, the bait you use and the
actual season. Permits are available from any
post office for R50. Most of the coastline in
front of the town centre is a marine reserve
so, although angling is allowed, nothing else
may be removed from the sea in this area.
Chartered fishing trips start from the new
harbour; check with the tourist office for
which charters are operating. Rock angling
is popular with local fishermen; steenbras,
cob, red roman, silver fish, red stumpnose
and John Brown are often caught. Deep-
sea angling is more popular with foreign
tourists, who hope to catch tuna, the local
snoek and Cape salmon. Crayfish and
perlemoen are a big draw for divers, but
are subject to stringent regulations due
to a problem with poaching.

Golf
Hermanus Golf Club, Main Rd, T028-312
1954, www.hermanusgolfclub.com. This
is a beautiful par-73 course in the lee of the
mountains with heather-lined fairways,
some holes have sea views, visitors welcome.

The crucial whale lexicon

Blowing This is the sight we are all familiar with, the spout of water vapour accompanied by an echoing sound as air is expelled from the whale's lungs through the blowhole. Seasoned whale watchers will be able to identify the species from the shape of the spout. The vapour is created by condensation when the warm breath comes in contact with the cooler outside air.

Breaching Probably the most spectacular sight, this is when whales lift their entire body out of the water in an effortless arc, creating a huge splash as they fall back into the sea. Not an isolated event, a whale will often leap several times so keep your binoculars trained. The experts have yet to agree on why the whale does this, and the whales aren't giving much away.

Grunting Just a loud grunting sound which carries a long way over water, a moving noise when heard on a calm moonlit night. No translations available.

Lobtailing The action of the whale slapping the surface with its tail producing a loud clap. This can be seen repeatedly over a long period. Interpreted as some form of warning or social communication.

Sailing The whale lifts its tail clear of the water for long periods. There are several theories about this action: to use the wind to 'sail' through the water (dubious), to feed on the sea-floor, or as a means of temperature control. Diehard watchers reckon the whales are just showing off.

Spyhopping When the whale lifts its head and part of its body above the water vertically. This gives the whale a 360° view of the sea.

Hiking

There is a 10-km cliff path marked around Walker Bay that starts in the New Harbour and ends at Grotto Beach, with plenty of benches at potential whale-viewing spots. There are also well-maintained trails in Fernkloof Nature Reserve.

Swimming

On a calm summer day Walker Bay looks cool and inviting from the cliff paths, but it has its dangers. There are strong undercurrents, so look out for warnings and advice, especially at spring tides. During the holidays all the popular swimming beaches have lifeguards on duty. Don't swim alone in isolated coves. There are several tidal pools which offer safe bathing for children and a fun place to snorkel for the first time. Below the Marine Hotel is the **Marine Tidal Pool** (*Bietang se Baaigat*), which always has plenty of sealife and fish. Along Westcliff Rd is a smaller pool known as **Fick's Pool**. This is a sheltered spot and has the bonus of a sandy bottom. There

are toilets and changing rooms close by. Out of town there is a tidal pool at the Onrus River campsite which is open to day visitors.

Tour operators

Hermanus Whale Cruises, office in the New Harbour, T028-313 2722, www.hermanus-whale-cruises.co.za. Daily 2-hr whale-watching cruises in season, with 5 departures throughout the day, R550, children (under 12) R200, including snacks and soft drinks. As a permit holder, they are allowed to get the boat within 50 m of the whales.

Southern Right Charters, office in the New Harbour, T082-353 0550, www.southern rightcharters.co.za. Again boat-based 2 hr whale watching in season with a hydrophone on board allowing you to listen to the whales too and also permitted to get within 50 m of the whales.

Walker Bay Adventures, just out of town towards Gansbaai at Prawn Flats, T028-314 0925, www.walkerbayadventures. co.za. Daily cruises on the lagoon, weather permitting, for larger groups and canoe and sea-kayaking trips.

Stanford and around *p250*
Boat cruises up the Klein River are a great way of enjoying the birdlife on the banks – there are around 130 species.
Klein River Cruises, T082-781 1704 (mob), www.stanfordvillage.co.za.

Gansbaai and around *p251*
Cage diving
One of the most popular activities here is cage diving to see great white sharks. Several companies offer trips to view the sharks, and people with a diving certificate can see them from an underwater cage. Non-divers can still do it, but they first have to spend a day doing a course. The boats used are motorized catamarans and trips last 3-7 hrs. Alternatively you can go on a long shark-diving day trip from Cape Town. This has become one of South Africa's booming tourist industries and viewing a great white at such close quarters is certainly an amazing experience. However, conservationists argue that these trips can be harmful to the sharks as they interfere with their natural eating patterns and can encourage them to equate humans with food (contrary to popular belief, we do not feature on their standard menu). If you are considering viewing the sharks off Dyer Island, check with the tourist offices in Cape Town or locally to find out which is currently the best company running trips, and try to choose one which is taking part in conservation and research into the species. Expect to pay in the region of R1100 plus extra for transfers to and from Cape Town.
Shark Diving Unlimited, Gansbaai, T028-384 2787, www.sharkdivingunlimited.com.

Shark Lady, Kleinbaai, T028-312 3287, www.sharklady.co.za.
White Shark Adventures, 13 Main Rd, Gansbaai, T028-384 1380, www.white sharkadventures.com.
White Shark Diving Co, Kleinbaai, T021-461 1583 (Cape Town), www.sharkcage diving.co.za.

Tour operators
Dyer Island Cruises, T028-384 0406, www.dyer-island-cruises.co.za. Boat trips to Dyer Island to see penguins and seals. All cruises depart from Kleinbaai harbour near Gansbaai and, during the season, whales and sharks may be spotted too, R500, R300 children (5-12) R300, under 5's free, more expensive in whale season.

⊖ Transport

Hermanus and around *p246, map p246*
Hermanus is 120 km from Cape Town (via N2). None of the 3 major coach companies runs a service via Hermanus. For transport options to and from Hermanus, see Ins and outs, page 246.

❶ Directory

Hermanus and around *p246, map p246*
Banks ABSA, 67 Main Rd; Standard Bank, 99 Main Rd, there are also ATMs in all the shopping centres and arcades. **Internet** Great White Internet Shop, 2 Harbour Rd, T028-313 0215. **Medical services** Hermanus Medi-Clinic, Hospital St, T028-313 0168, www.hermanusmc.co.za.

Overberg interior

While most South Africans can tell you where the Overberg is, they might have difficulty defining its limits. It is a vague term which generally refers to the area to the east of the Hottentots Holland Mountains extending as far as Mossel Bay. To the north are the Langeberg Mountains and to the south the ocean.

Having climbed the spectacular Sir Lowry's Pass from Somerset West, the N2 highway cuts east across the interior of the Overberg towards Mossel Bay and George. The landscape is immediately very different on this side of the mountains – the road passes through forested hills before opening onto the endless dry, orange plains of the Overberg. To the north lie the Langeberg Mountains, their smooth foothills and sharp peaks providing a serene backdrop to the route. Most of the towns en route are quiet farming centres, and were some of the first areas settled by white farmers as they ventured east of Cape Town in search of new farmlands.

Most visitors choose to stick to the main road, and it is easy to pass quickly through the region without taking much in. If you are keen to get to the Garden Route, George can be reached in three hours, but there are several sights worth lingering over on the way. One centre that deserves a stopover is Swellendam, the third-oldest town in the Cape. Nearby are a couple of nature reserves, and the town has some well-preserved examples of early Cape architecture. ➤➤ *For listings, see pages 274-279.*

East to Caledon on the N2 ⊖⊘ ➤➤ *pp274-279.*

Ten kilometres from Sir Lowry's Pass is a turning signposted Villiersdorp, R321. This takes you back into the heart of the Winelands, or north to the Breede River Valley. A short loop takes you to the undistinguished twin towns of **Grabouw** and **Elgin**. Regional information is available from **Elgin Valley and Grabouw Tourism** ⓘ *T021-848 9838, www.tourism elginvalley.co.za, Mon-Sat 0900-1700, Sat 0900-1400,* at the Peregrine Farm Stall on the N2. (Grabouw is the centre of South Africa's apple industry and is where the popular fizzy drink Appletizer is made.) Continuing east, the N2 crosses the Houhoek Pass where there is a famous watering hole, the **Houw Hoek Inn**, always worth a stop (see Sleeping, page 274). At Bot River is the turning for Hermanus. It is a further 23 km on the N2 to the regional capital of the Overberg, Caledon.

Hottentots Holland Nature Reserve → *Colour map 8, B1.*
ⓘ *The entrance to the reserve is at Nuweberg, high in Viljoen's Pass between Grabouw and Villiersdorp. To get there turn left at Elgin, on to the R321. After about 10 km, at the bottom of Viljoens Pass past Nuweberg Dam, turn left to the Nuweberg Forest Station and reserve office. Reserve information: T028-841 4826, www.capenature.co.za, R25, children (2-13) R12. There is an information centre in the car park. Note that at the time of writing there was no access to the reserve after it suffered extensive fire damage in 2009, when many of the overnight hiking huts were destroyed. The fire lasted for 2 weeks and destroyed many thousands of hectares of vegetation. Check with Cape Nature about the status of the reserve.*

The Hottentots Holland Mountains are the southern end of a continuous mountainous chain which extends inland as far as Ceres and beyond, effectively cutting the Cape off from the rest of South Africa, and overlooking False Bay. The 42,000-ha reserve stretches from Elgin in the south to beyond Villiersdorp in the north, and from the Stellenbosch Mountains in the west, eastwards to the Groenland Mountains. It's an important conservation area for mountain fynbos: over 1300 species have been recorded here, including some rare and endemic plants. There are also small populations of rhebuck, klipspringer, duiker and grysbok.

Being so close to Cape Town makes this an important and popular hiking region. Various restrictions are in force to help protect the flora and fauna as well as the physical landscape. The main trail in the reserve is the **Boland Hiking Trail**. The full circuit is 50 km and takes three days to cover. The shorter hikes are known as the **Nuweberg Circuit** and the **Riviersonderend Canyon**. Due to flooding, all hiking trails are closed from July to the end of August. There are also two mountain bike trails; the 6 km **Hottentants Holland Trail** is fairly easy and family orientated, while the 22 km **Groenlandberg Trail** is a little more challenging.

🌓 *In the early days of settlement, people would refer to the area beyond the Hottentots Holland as 'over the berg'. It was not until the construction of Sir Lowry's Pass that the region began to be cultivated.*

Caledon and around 🏨🚗❄️🍴 ›› *pp274-279. Colour map 8, B2.*

The regional capital of the Overberg, 120 km from Cape Town, lies just off the N2 at the foot of the Swartberg Mountains. It is a typical rural town – small and quiet, with a couple of sights, but only really worth an hour or two; it's best to press on to Swellendam for an overnight stay. The town is famous for its six naturally occurring hot springs, which produce over 800,000 litres per day. The water has a high ferrous carbonate content. Not surprisingly the first European settler, Ferdinandus Appel, sought to develop the springs. He was granted an 18-ha freehold, on the condition that he built baths and accommodation. Word of the water's healing powers spread quickly and distinguished guests from the Dutch East India Company frequented the springs. At the turn of the 20 th century the Caledon Mineral Baths and Sanatorium was built to cash in fully on their popularity. For 40 years they continued to be an attraction until a fire destroyed the complex in 1946. It was only in 1990 that a new hotel, **The Caledon** (see Sleeping, page 275), was built. Day visitors can use the spa's facilities, which include a waterfall and a series of pools. The pool at the top is the hottest, with water temperatures averaging 40°C. There are additional saunas, gym, cold pool and steam room, and treatments such as massages and facials are available.

Today the prosperity of the town and the region is based on agriculture. Caledon was the centre of a major development in wool production with a new breed of sheep, the merino. For information, visit **Cape Overberg Tourism Association** ① *22 Plein St, T028-214 1466, www.tourismcapeoverberg.co.za, Mon-Fri 0830-1600, Sat 0830-1230.*

The **Caledon House Museum** ① *11 Constitution St, T028-212 1511, Mon-Fri 0800-1700, small entrance fee*, is based in a Victorian house that was originally the Freemasons' Lodge. It has displays on local history, domestic items and crafts. There is a working kitchen where bread is baked every few days. For a small fee the curator will show you around and make the items on display a bit more interesting. The museum shop in Donkin Square is full of local farm produce and curios. **Mill Street** has a collection of historic buildings which have been declared national monuments. The Holy Trinity Church on Prince Alfred Drive is a small, neat church dating from 1855. Outings to local wetlands and the nearby nature reserves can be arranged for bird enthusiasts; contact the tourist office for details. Look out for the endangered blue crane which is found in the area on open farmland. Due to their vulnerable status, an Overberg Crane Group was created in 1991 by Cape Nature Conservation to devise a protection programme. (75% of South Africa's blue cranes, the national bird, are found in the Overberg.)

Caledon Nature Reserve

This small reserve, 214 ha, is just on the edge of town. Since 1892 the annual wild flower show has been held in the grounds, usually in September. Part of the reserve was turned into the **Victoria Wild Flower Garden** ① *0700-1700*, by Cecil Young and CW Meiring in 1927, local enthusiasts who had the foresight to protect the amazingly rich local flora. Of the 630 known species of *erica* in the world, over 200 grow in the Caledon district. This may not be everyone's cup of tea (56 ha of the reserve were converted into formal gardens with ponds, shaded paths and picnic spots) but for the botanist it is a fascinating attraction. Within the reserve there is a 10-km walk, the **Meiring Trail**, a good chance to appreciate the many species of fynbos and birds of the area. There is no shelter and hikers must bring all their drinking water. Allow up to five hours for the full circuit. A leaflet from the tourist office has a simple map of the hiking trail.

Greyton → *Colour map 8, B2.*

Just a short drive north of the main N2 highway, the quiet village of Greyton is a popular place to retire and attracts many artists. The mixture of restored old buildings and streets, lined with oaks, have helped create a low-key and peaceful atmosphere. When the first streets were laid out in 1854, the settlement was named after Sir George Grey, who had served two periods as governor of the Cape Colony. To the north lie the **Riviersonderend Mountains**, which in winter often have snow on their peaks – Kanonberg (1466 m) is the tallest peak overlooking the village. The **Greyton Nature Reserve** is at the edge of town on the southern slopes of the Sonderend Mountains. The best time to visit is from September to November. There is a short 20-minute walk to the **Noupoort Gorge**, which can be followed close to the Kanonberg summit. There are a number of streams running off the hills through forested valleys, with the occasional waterfall which can be reached by paths. Greyton is at the end of the well-known **Boesmankloof Hiking Trail**. This 16-km trail links Greyton with the village of **McGregor** on the northern side of the Riviersonderend Mountains (see page 228 for further details). For tourist information, contact **Greyton Tourism** ① *29 Main St, T028-254 9564, www.greyton.net, Tue-Fri 1000-1630, Sat 1000-1600.*

Swellendam and around ⊖𝟶🅰⊖❶ ›› *pp274-279. Colour map 8, B3.*

Founded in 1745, Swellendam is the third oldest European town in South Africa, and it is also one of its most picturesque. The main centre bears witness to its age with an avenue of mature oak trees and whitewashed Cape Dutch homesteads. Unfortunately, before the town fully appreciated their inherent charm and tourist potential, many of the trees and older buildings were knocked down in 1974 to widen the main street. Nevertheless, the town is very pretty and has an appealing, quiet atmosphere, which, combined with the rural setting and beautiful views, makes it a very pleasant spot to spend a day or two. Swellendam also acts as an important base for exploring the region, with the Breede River Valley, the Little Karoo and the coast all within easy reach, and it is roughly halfway between Cape Town and the Garden Route.

Tourist information is available at **Swellendam Tourism** ① *Oefeningshuis, Voortrek St, T028-514 2770, www.swellendamtourism.co.za, Mon-Fri 0900-1300, 1400-1700, Sat 0900-1200.* This office produces a leaflet called *Swellendam Treasures*, which outlines the interesting Cape Dutch buildings still standing today.

Background

Swellendam started as a trading outpost for the Dutch East India Company. The new settlement was named after Governor Hendrik Swellengrebel and his wife, Ten Damme. Once established, all sorts of characters passed through looking for their fortunes or more land. One of the most successful was Joseph Barry who, in the 1800s, had a virtual monopoly on all trade between Cape Town and the new settlements in the Overberg and Little Karoo.

In 1795 a particularly strange event took place. Just at the point when British soldiers were bringing an end to Dutch rule in the Cape, the burghers of Swellendam declared themselves to be an independent republic, in a reaction to the mal-administration and corruption of the Dutch East India Company. Hermanus Steyn was president from 17 June to 4 November 1795 but, once the British had set up a new regime in Cape Town, the republic was quietly forgotten about. During the 19th century the town prospered and grew as the agricultural sector gradually expanded. This came to an abrupt halt in May 1865, when a fire that started in a baker's destroyed 40 of the town's finest old buildings. Even greater harm was caused by a prolonged drought and when, in 1866, the influential Barry Empire was declared bankrupt the whole region's fortunes declined. Today the town is a prosperous community, and many of the old buildings are still standing, or have been restored.

Sights

Of all the old Cape buildings in town the **Drostdy Museum** ① *18 Swellengrebel St, T028-514 1138, www.drostdymuseum.com, Mon-Fri 0900-1645, Sat-Sun 1000-1545, R15, children (under 16) R2, which covers entrance to a number of buildings*, is the most impressive and is often described as one of the country's great architectural treasures. The main building dates from 1747, built as the official residence and seat for the local magistrate or *landdrost*. Originally built in the shape of a T, the addition of two wings changed the form to an H. Inside, some of the floors have been preserved; what was the lounge has a lime-sand floor, while the kitchen floor is made from cow dung, which helps keep the room cool. The museum concentrates on local history, with a well-preserved collection of 18th- and 19th-century furniture. Within the grounds is a restored Victorian cottage, **Mayville**, which has an antique rose garden plus the original gazebo and is today home to a coffee shop.

Close by is an open-air display, on the Crafts Green, of many of the early farm tools, charcoal burners, wagons and a horse-driven mill complete with threshing floor. Opposite the museum is the **Old Gaol building** ① *T028-514 3847*, which housed both prisoners and local government officials, including the jailer who was also the postmaster. In the middle of all the cells was one without windows, known as the 'black hole'. Today, this is a local arts and crafts centre, with a good café (see Eating, page 278).

Not far from the town centre are more restored buildings from the town's early days. The **Oefeningshuis** (1838) first served as a place for the religious instruction of freed slaves; it now houses the tourist office. Note the painted plaster clock face, which reads 1215, set above a working clock. This was designed for illiterate churchgoers – if the painted face was the same as the clock's, it was time for service. Worth a look is the fine, domineering **Dutch Reformed Church**. This large whitewashed building has a tall central clock tower and a mix of architectural styles. Just next to the church, on **Church Square**, are some fine examples of early two-storey town houses built by wealthy farmers who used to visit the town for holy communion. The square had to be large enough to hold their ox wagons. Another grand town house is the **Auld House** dating from 1802 which for many years was the family home for the Overberg trader, Joseph Barry. Inside is some furniture, originally fitted on a steamer which used to sail between Cape Town and Port Beaufort. Also worth a visit is the small **Church of St Luke** built in 1865. Finally, look out for the shop **Buirski & Co**, built in 1880. It has one of the finest examples of Victorian wrought-iron balconies and fittings in the town.

Swellendam is an ideal base for exploring this part of the Overberg. Close by is the small Bontebok National Park, and the larger Marloth Nature Reserve. They have only simple accommodation and both can easily be visited on a day trip.

Bontebok National Park → *Colour map 8, B3.*
Although this is one of South Africa's 21 national parks, it has less of interest than other parks. Nevertheless, it is a good place to spot several species of antelope, and has a pleasant riverside setting. Most of the park is accessible by car, and there are two 2-km self-guided nature trails which you can walk at any time without a permit or booking. Guided walks are organized when there is sufficient demand. Swimming and fishing are both possible in the Breede River, but only within the confines of the campsite. An angling licence must be shown.

Ins and outs The park is 238 km from Cape Town and 6 km from Swellendam. The turning off the N2 is clearly signposted, on the George side of Swellendam. There is a 5-km gravel road from the highway to the entrance. Information is available at the **SANParks office** ① *T028-514 2735, www.sanparks.org, Oct-Apr 0700-1900, May-Sep 0700-1800, R40, children (under 16) 20.* There is a new restcamp here, named Lang Elsie's Kraal after a female chief who lived here with her clan in the 18th century.

Background At the beginning of the 20th century the bontebok was the rarest species of antelope in Africa. It had been hunted and driven off its natural habitat by the settler farmers in the Overberg. Fortunately, something even scarcer came to their rescue – a group of local conservation-minded farmers, who recognized the need to set up a protected area to save the remaining animals. In 1931 the first reserve was established, but it was not until the herd was moved to a more suitable environment beside the Breede River in 1960 that the numbers started to recover significantly. This has proved to be a success but, although no longer endangered, there are still not many places where the bontebok can be seen in the wild. Today, other antelope indigenous to the Overberg have been introduced to the reserve including red hartebeest, steenbok and duiker plus the rare Cape mountain zebra.

Marloth Nature Reserve → *Colour map 8, B3.*
This mountain reserve encompasses a number of the peaks and forested valleys of the Langeberg Mountains. Looking at the peaks from the centre of Swellendam, locals claim to be able to tell the time between 0700 and 1300 by the shadows cast by seven of the **Clock Peaks**. There is a variety of hiking trails, including a rewarding six-day route. Small stands of indigenous forest have been preserved. These are very important when you consider that the mountains were once forested all the way along this coast from Cape Town to Port Elizabeth and beyond. Today, only a few small pockets of forest remain. Some of the more common indigenous trees which can be seen in the reserve include yellowwood, red alder, hard pear, spoon wood, Cape beech and cherrywood. The wildlife is confined to mountain species – look out for klipspringer standing on rock outcrops, and if you're lucky you may glimpse bushbuck in the cooler, darker patches of forest. The colourful Cape sugarbird is a common sight on flowering aloes and ericas.

Ins and outs

Follow the signs to the forest station, 3 km to the north of Swellendam. The ideal time to visit is in the spring (September and October) when the flowers are at their best. The wettest months are March and Octofber. Permits for the six-day walk or climbing the peaks are issued from the **park office** ① *T028-514 1410, www.capenature.co.za, Mon-Fri 0800-1600, R25, children (2-13) R12.* For more information on accommodation options within the reserve, see Sleeping, page 276.

Hiking The **Swellendam Trail** is the principal hiking trail in and around Marloth Reserve. The complete circular route is 74 km long and hikers are advised to allow six days for the full circuit. This was the first trail designed in the Cape to return hikers to their starting point without having to backtrack. Hiking conditions require a medium level of fitness, as there are strenuous segments when the trail goes around several peaks. Each day's walking passes through montane forest as well as open fynbos terrain. Be wary of the sun and carry plenty of water. The six overnight huts are fitted out with bunks, toilets and drinking water. Hikers must bring their own food, gas stoves, cooking and eating utensils, and bedding. Do not walk in heavy rain or misty conditions.

Shorter day walks are possible in the vicinity of the entrance gate by the forest station. Six trails have been defined, ranging from an easy stroll to the picnic site in a sheltered valley known as the **Hermitage**, to an all-day trail taking in two of the peaks closest to Swellendam. The most difficult day walk climbs from the car park to the **Tienuurkop peak** (1195 m), along a ridge to **Twaalfuurkop** (1428 m), and then zigzags back down to the entrance. The walk is 9 km and takes at least eight hours. The other day walks are on the lower slopes and can be completed in less than three hours. Day walks do not require permits or pre-booking.

Heidelberg to Albertinia ●● » pp274-279. Colour map 7, B1.

Continuing east from Swellendam along the N2 highway, the road passes several small agricultural towns which have little of interest to detain tourists. One of these settlements is **Heidelberg**, which is dominated by its Dutch Reformed church on the banks of the Duivenhoks River. The first settlers arrived in the valley in 1725, and in 1855 it was named Heidelberg after the city in Germany. To the north in the Langeberg Mountains is the Grootvadersbosch Nature Reserve (see below). The Anglican church, St Barnabas, has some wood sculptures of note and particularly fine rose windows. **Tourist information** ① *25 Van Riebeeck St, T028-722 2700, www.heidelberginfo.co.za, Mon-Fri 0900-1600, Sat 0900-1200.*

Grootvadersbosch Nature Reserve → Colour map 8, B3.

① *All advance details and reservations are made through the manager, T028-659 3500, www.capenature.co.za, permits for hiking and mountain biking (R35) are available on arrival, but note that the trails have a limit of 12 people so it is a good idea to pre-book.*

This 250 ha of preserved forest is the finest remaining cover of indigenous forest in the southwestern Cape. There is an excellent hiking trail (see below) and paths which provide easy access to the forest. The early settlers in the Overberg managed to satisfy the huge demand for hardwoods at the turn of the 20th century throughout South Africa, but in doing so almost totally destroyed the unique forests in the Cape. Grootvadersbosch was established to preserve the area and restore it to its former beauty. Between 1896 and 1913 alien trees such as ash, bluegum, Californian redwood, Australian blackwood and camphor were planted on the slopes which had been cleared of indigenous forest. Efforts are now being made to reclaim these areas. The wilderness areas remain untouched and this is reflected in the richness of wildlife and birdlife one encounters while walking here. There is a good chance of seeing the shy bushbuck in the forest.

Ins and outs The reserve is 22 km northwest of Heidelberg on the R322 towards Tradouw Pass. Coming from Swellendam, take the R324 turning for Suurbraak then keep heading in the direction of Heidelberg – the left turning for the reserve is 27 km further on. There is a simple campsite by the entrance gates with 10 camping pitches and two cottages, communal ablution block and thatched braai area with fridge. Look out for a bird hide 500 m into the reserve. The nearest comfortable accommodation is in Swellendam, 40 km away.

Hiking The **Bushbuck Trail** is a series of paths allowing you to choose a route between 2 km and 10 km without having to backtrack too often. The paths weave between the moist and dry forest of the slopes of the Langeberg Mountains. The best periods for walking are May to July and December to January.

Witsand → *Colour map 8, B3.*
Just outside Swellendam is the R324 turning to Witsand, which can also be reached from Heidelberg on the R322, and from De Hoop Nature Reserve via the pont at Malgas (see page 253) a quiet, picturesque seaside town at the mouth of the Breede River. The area is best known for its land-based whale watching and its excellent fishing, but there is little other reason to come here. The town is small and peaceful, and as such attracts mainly older couples wanting to escape the bustle of larger resorts. From June to November southern right whales come to the bay to calve and rear their young and the town is frequently dubbed the 'whale nursery' by the regional tourist boards. In 2005 a count by helicopter recorded 94 whales including 43 calves in the bay on one day during the season. In town, one building of note is the wool store built for the Barry family business. The neighbouring settlement of **Port Beaufort** was built by Joseph Barry, a businessman from Swellendam who, for a period, dominated all forms of trade in the Overberg (see page 270). Large boats from Cape Town unloaded their cargo here, which was then transferred to river boats and taken upstream as far as Malgas. The Barry family built a church in the village in 1859, which is now a national monument. For tourist information contact the **Witsand Tourism Bureau** ⓘ *T028-537 1010, www.witsandtourism.co.za, on the main street, Mon-Fri 0830-1600, Sat 0900-1200.*

Riversdale → *Colour map 8, B3.*
Back on the N2, Riversdale is a small farming centre based around wheat, wool and potatoes. There is little in town for visitors other than fuel and food, although there is the small **Julius Gordon Africana Museum** ⓘ *Long St, Mon-Fri 0800-1300*, which outlines the lives of several local characters and is home to some paintings by Thomas Baines and Peter Wenning. Around the town are no fewer than 15 stone churches, the oldest being the St Matthew's Anglican Church, built in 1856. The district is well known for the growing of Agathosma shrubs which emit a very strong aroma. For anyone with an interest in wild flowers the **Van Riebeeck Garden** has a superb collection of aloes and vygies. The best time to visit is in May and June when the flowers are in full bloom. The road to Ladismith in the north crosses the spectacular Garcia Pass before entering the Little Karoo. The **tourist office** ⓘ *T028-713 1996, www.riversdaler.co.za, Mon-Fri 0830-1730, Sat 0900-1200*, is on the N2 as you drive through.

Still Bay → *Colour map 8, B3.*

This small fishing village 26 km from the N2 is in a beautiful spot straddling both sides of the Goukou River. On the west bank is a fishing harbour, while the east bank holds a cluster of holiday cottages and shops. The beach is sandy and safe for swimmers. Surfers speak of good waves here, while the river is ideal for small pleasure boats. The bridge joining the two settlements was opened in 1955, replacing a pontoon that had been in use since 1930. Like many South African seaside towns, Still Bay remains eerily quiet for much of the year, but during the school summer holidays the place comes alive with families. Next to the **tourist office** ① *on the east bank, T028-754 2602, www.stilbaai tourism.com*, there's a fountain where eels are fed Monday to Saturday at 1100.

Albertinia → *Colour map 7, B1.*

Being only a few hours from Cape Town and tantalizingly close to the Garden Route, few people stop here. The predominant business is still wheat and sheep farming, although the local economy was able to diversify following the discovery in the 1920s of large ochre deposits. Another unusual product collected around Albertinia is the juice from aloe plants, *Aloe ferox*, which is an important ingredient in medicine and cosmetics. You can visit the **Alcare Aloe Factory** ① *T028-735 1454, www.alcare.co.za, 0900-1700*, just outside town. They conduct free daily tours and sell a variety of aloe skincare products and there's a coffee shop.

   Garden Route Game Lodge ① *7 km east of Albertinia off the N2, T028-735 1200, www.grgamelodge.co.za, day visitors 0730-1630, 2 hr game drives 1100 and 1400, R350*, is a private game lodge that has been stocked with a number of species of large game including giraffe, white rhino, lion, elephant, kudu, zebra, wildebeest and buffalo. It's a popular overnight stay from Cape Town and one of the nearest places to the city for wildlife viewing. Transfers from Cape Town can be arranged. There is luxurious accommodation at the lodge but day visitors are also welcome for game drives, which must be pre-booked, and lunch in the à la carte restaurant. As well as game drives, tours of the reptile centre are on offer where the resident herpetologist (reptile man) will share his knowledge of snakes, crocodiles and other cold-blooded creatures. You can also visit the cheetah-breeding centre and there are a variety of programmes for children, including bush survival skills, children's game drives and guided bush and insect walks. ➧ *See Sleeping, page 277.*

◉ Overberg interior listings

For Sleeping and Eating price codes and other relevant information, see pages 46-53.

● Sleeping

East to Caledon on the N2 *p267*
A Villa Exner, 11 Essenhout Av, Grabouw, T021-859 3596, www.villaexner.com. Country retreat with 4 suites in the main whitewashed manor house and 2 garden units, elegantly furnished with art and designer pieces, flat screen TVs, wireless internet, 2 lounges with fireplaces, library and dining rooms, swimming pool in rolling lawns, close to the Hottentots Holland Nature Reserve. No children under 14.
B Houw Hoek Inn, off N2 12 km past Grabouw, T021-284 9646, www.houwhoe kinn.co.za. The oldest licensed hotel in South Africa, with 50 a/c rooms in an elegant country hotel, the oldest section dates from 1779, the upstairs was built in 1860, while there's a newer block of modern rooms. All the rooms have en suite bathrooms, the dining room is in a converted farm building, and is very popular at weekends

when dinner dances are held on Sat night and there's a traditional roast Sun lunch. The gardens are dominated by large old oak and blue gum trees. Swimming pool.

B Wildekrans Country House, **Houw Hoek Farm**, turn left at Houw Hoek Inn sign, follow road round to left, the farm is on your right, T021-284 9827, www.wildekrans.co.za. 6 B&B rooms, or self-catering cottages with TV and log fires, dinner on request, swimming pool, wild farm gardens with lots of rose bushes, national monument, quiet setting on a working farm.

Hottentots Holland Nature Reserve *p267*

At the time of writing there was no accommodation in the reserve as some hiking huts were destroyed by fire in 2009. Check with Cape Nature (www.capenature.co.za).

Caledon and around *p268*

B The Caledon Hotel, Spa & Casino, 1 Nerina Av, T028-214 5100, www.cnty.com/casinos/caledon, 1 km out of town just off the N2. Unattractive modern complex based at the historic springs, with a flashy casino, 95 a/c rooms and 3 restaurants, including an Italian one. There is a pub with log fires, extensive gardens, a number of hot and cold pools, a beauty clinic, mountain bikes for hire, full-size snooker tables, 18-hole putting golf and the excellent Victorian hot-spring baths enclosed by a pavilion. Most people come here for the brash casino.

Greyton *p269*

B The Post House, 42 Main Rd, T028-254 9995, www.theposthouse.co.za. A high-quality country guesthouse, 13 rooms with a Beatrix Potter theme, the honeymoon suite is called Two Bad Mice. Each room has an open fire and a private veranda. The oldest parts of the building, which was once a post office, date back to 1860. Good food and service in the restaurant and pub, picnic baskets, colourful gardens, swimming pool, quiet setting, easy access to the village. Recommended.

C Greyton Lodge, 52 Main St, T028-254 9876, www.greytonlodge.com. 15 rooms, some with 4-poster beds, in a renovated 1882 trading store that has also served as a police station, excellent restaurant open to non-guests from 0800-late, swimming pool, gardens, comfortable country lodge feel, a neat whitewashed building with a corrugated-iron roof and small veranda.

Swellendam and around *p269*

A De Kloof, 8 Weltevreden St, T028-514 1303, www.dekloof.co.za. Elegant and luxurious thatched Cape Dutch homestead (1801) set in a neat garden, 6 double rooms with en suite bathroom, contemporary African and Asian decor, TV lounge, library and cigar bar, gym with mountain views, garden, swimming pool, champagne breakfasts included in the rate, evening meals available, very friendly. Recommended.

A-B Klippe Rivier Country House, from the N2 take the R60, left at crossroads, 2 km, T028-514 3341, www.klipperivier.com. 6 double rooms in and around a restored Cape Dutch homestead (1820), declared a national monument. Large rooms with brass beds, wooden floors, some with cosy fireplaces and under thatch, superb restaurant (see Eating, page 278), swimming pool, a peaceful and superior location, look out for owls in the oak trees, family owned and managed, no children under 8. Recommended.

B Adin & Sharon's Hideaway, 10 Hermanus Steyn St, T028-514 3316, www.adinbb.co.za. Award-winning B&B in the centre of town, with 5 spacious, comfortable en suite rooms with a/c, in a Victorian cottage, overlooking a neat, shady garden with 600 rose bushes and an indoor heated pool. Excellent breakfasts, very friendly hosts. Recommended.

B Old Mill Guest House & Restaurant, 241 and 243 Voortrek St, T028-514 2790, www.oldmill.co.za. En suite rooms in a beautiful listed building set in a spacious garden with a stream flowing through, superb meals served in the restaurant, which is well known for its Belgian pancakes and waffles. Slightly overpriced, but still recommended.

C Coachman Guesthouse, 14 Drostdy St, T028-514 2294, www.coachman.co.za. Lovely whitewashed converted historic homestead with 3 double rooms with separate entrances, plus 2 thatched garden cottages with log fires. TV lounge, laundry, evening meals available, swimming pool.

C Moolmanshof, 217 Voortrek St, T028-514 3953, www.annascollection.com. A homestead built in 1798 and full of character with 3 en suite rooms, furnished with antiques, plus 3 self-catering units in the converted barn, guest lounge with TV, swimming pool, mature gardens, extra beds available for children, farm breakfasts. Recommended.

C Swellengrebel, 91 Voortrek St, T028-514 1144, www.swellengrebelhotel.co.za. Large, bland and modern hotel set on the main road, with 48 rooms, some with mountain views, restaurant with good food, swimming pool, pool room, jacuzzi, sauna and gym, noisy public bar. Comfortable, but seems a shame to stay somewhere so characterless compared to most of the B&Bs in town. Ask about weekend discounts.

D-F Swellendam Caravan Park, Glen Barry Rd, T028-514 2705. Caravan park with 20 fully equipped thatched chalets, 4 beds, bring your own linen, 100 well-grassed and shady tent and caravan stands. A beautiful and peaceful setting with good mountain views within walking distance of town centre, popular during school holidays.

E-F Swellendam Backpackers, 5 Lichtenstein St, T028-514 2648, www.swellendamback packers.co.za. An excellent hostel with a small dorm in the main house, plus individual Wendy houses and safari tents (no electricity but paraffin lamps) in secluded corners around the garden, lots of camping space, internet, well-organized kitchen, home-cooked breakfasts and dinners. Can arrange local tours, hiking in the mountains and visits to the nearby Bontebok National Park. The Baz Bus calls here twice a day.

Bontebok National Park *p271*
C Lang Elsie's Kraal Rest Camp reservations through **SANParks** Tshwane (Pretoria) office, T012-428 9111, www.san parks.org. Bookings can also be made in person at the offices in Cape Town and Durban (see page 48). For cancellations and bookings under 72 hrs, for campsite reservations, and for general enquiries, phone the camp reception direct, T028-5142735. In a pleasant location next to the Breede River, there are 10 new fully equipped self-catering chalets sleeping 4, 2 of which are totally disabled accessible with ramps, hand rails and specially adapted bathrooms, and there are good views of the Langeberg Mountains from the outside terraces. The shop at the park entrance sells some groceries and beer but stock up on fresh food in Swellendam.

Camping
There are a number of shady camping and caravan sites along the river, some with electric points, and a new ablution block.

Marloth Nature Reserve *p271*
For reservations, T021-659 3500, www.capenature.co.za.

Cottages
There are 2 basic self-catering cottages (**C**), 1 sleeping 8, the other 5, good value for families or groups, fully equipped kitchens with microwave, stove, fridge and all utensils, bedding and towels provided, comfortable option especially for the night before tackling the Swellendam Hiking Trail.

Hiking huts
6 basic hiking huts (**E**) are available, equipped with bunks, bush toilets and drinking water, which can accommodate 22 hikers. If you stay in these huts bring all your provisions, they only provide a roof and a mattress. Firewood is only provided at 2 of the huts, Koloniesbos and Wolfkloof, but you are not permitted to light fires elsewhere in the reserve. Bring a gas stove for cooking.

Grootvadersbosch Nature Reserve p272

D Scolopia, reservations through Cape Nature Conservation T021-659 3500, www.capenature.co.za. 500 m from the entrance gate, the name of this wooden cottage is a type of pear tree, sleeps 6, living room with fireplace, fully equipped kitchen with microwave, and outside braai.

Camping

10 sites, ablution block (cold/warm water), and a thatched lapa for cooking, which also has a fridge. You'll need to bring firewood.

Witsand p273

A Breede River Lodge, T028-537 1631, www.breederiverlodge.co.za. Comfortable en suite lodges and hotel cabins overlooking the river, well furnished, some with dining area and kitchenette, great views, bar, restaurant serves fresh seafood (see Eating, page 278). Boats and fishing tackle for hire for trips up the river.

C Big Cob Chalets, 104 Main Rd, T028-537 1942, bigcob@telkomsa.net. Neat gardens around 4 self-catering chalets with 3 rooms, each room has twin beds, fully equipped, thatched roof, braai area, secure parking.

Riversdale p273

D Sleeping Beauty, 3 Long St, T028-713 1651, www.sleepingbeautyguesthouse.com. A Victorian guesthouse built as a parsonage in 1880 with 6 double rooms, home-made breads for breakfast, lush gardens and double-storey veranda.

Still Bay p274

D Papillon, corner of Perlemoen and Seebreis St, T082-774 8381, www.papillonstilbaai.co.za. Beachfront cottage sleeping 6 and a separate flat that sleeps 2, both with fully equipped kitchens, bright and airy decor, gardens rolling down to beach, views of the bay, braai area, TV and video, internet, wheelchair friendly.

Albertina p274

L Garden Route Game Lodge, 7 km east of Albertinia off the N2, transfers from Cape Town can be arranged, T028-735 1200, www.grgamelodge.co.za. Accommodation in main lodge or in secluded thatched chalets, decorated with an African theme, superb restaurant serving local dishes, comfortable bar, swimming pool, rates include game drives and meals, special activities for children, horse riding and quad-biking also on offer.

D Albertinia Country Hotel, Main St, T028-735 1030, www.albertiniahotel.co.za. Comfortable town hotel with friendly service, 16 small but neat rooms with TV, good traditional restaurant, pub that sometimes hosts parties at the weekend, the very affordable rates are for B&B. If you are not staying the pub lunches are recommended on your way through.

🍴 Eating

East to Caledon on the N2 p267

Several local farms have small stalls selling a variety of fresh juices and other fruit products.
🍴 **Houw Hoek Farm Stall**, by the Houw Hoek Inn, see Sleeping, page 274, T021-284 9015, www.houwhoekfarmstall.co.za. 0800-1800. A full-blown shop and café serving light lunches, coffee and picnic hampers, and it's open on Fri nights for dinner. They also have 3 dams on the farm stocked with trout, and rent out fishing tackle for fly-fishing. Look out for fresh trout on the menu.

Caledon and around p268

🍴🍴 **Dassiesfontein**, on the N2 between Caledon and Bot River, T028-214 1475, www.dassies.co.za. 0830-1730. Country restaurant and farm stall selling home-made bread (they grind their own flour), cheese and biltong, tables in the cottage decorated with antiques, local dishes such as bobotie and bredie, good chicken and game pies, buffet lunch on Sun. For breakfast try the fried slice of bread with apricot jam. Recommended.

Greyton p269

Abbey Rose, 19 Main Rd, T028-254 9470. Mon-Fri 0800-1700, Tue, Fri-Sat also stays open later for dinner. Housed in an old trading store with a lovely garden out back with its own miniature replica English-style abbey, which is used for weddings, the day-time menu includes light lunches or afternoon teas, don't miss the freshly baked scones, and more sophisticated country cooking in the evening like lamb shank or oxtail.

Swellendam and around p269

Most local restaurants are closed Sun evening; be prepared to eat by 2100.

Klippe Rivier Country House, see Sleeping, page 275, T028-514 3341. Open for breakfast and dinner, booking essential. Popular restaurant, delicious Cape haute cuisine using fresh ingredients like home-grown asparagus and mushrooms picked from the estate, served in a classic Cape Dutch manor with manicured gardens, good wine list. Recommended.

The Connection, 132 Voortrek St, T028-514 1988. Open 1200-2100, closed Wed and Sun afternoon. Pleasant restaurant serving light lunches, and meatier dinners such as venison, hearty soups, some Italian dishes, outdoor tables on terrace.

Herberg Roosjie van de Kaap, 5 Drostdy St, T028-514 3001, www.roosjevandekaap. com. Tue-Sun, breakfast 0800-1000, dinner 1900-2130. Local word has this down as the best place to eat in town. Booking essential for dinner. Cosy atmosphere in a candlelit room with thick walls and a low roof. Superb gourmet pizzas plus hearty South African fare, good steaks and seafood, fine wines. Recommended.

Koornlands, 5 Voortrek St, T028-514 3567, www.koornlandsrestaurant.co.za. Jul-Apr Mon-Sat 1900-2200. A historic Cape Dutch cottage serving local food such as crocodile steaks, ostrich fillets, loin of kudu, guinea fowl and freshwater trout, washed down with local wines. Desserts include a delicious Cape brandy tart. Recommended.

Mattsen's, 25 Swellengrebel St, T028-514 2715. Open 1100-2200. Busy restaurant serving excellent, good-value steaks, plus pizzas and traditional South African dishes, popular with tour groups, open the latest of all Swellen-dam's restaurants, attractive outside wooden deck under oak trees. Recommended.

Old Mill Restaurant and Tea Garden, 241 Voortrek St, T028-514 2790, www.old mill.co.za, see Sleeping. Open 0700-2100. Good afternoon teas, syrupy waffles and cinnamon pancakes, outside tables in pretty gardens with chickens pecking around, romantic candlelit tables inside for dinner, South African dishes such as Karoo lamb or local curries.

Coffee Shop at the Old Gaol, Drostdy Museum, T028-514 3847, www.oldgaol restaurant.co.za. Daytime licensed café serving breakfasts, light meals, hot soup in winter, coffee and cakes, home-made lemonade, and local specialities such as melktert.

La Belle Alliance, Swellengrebel St, T028-514 2252. Open 0800-1700. Good place for a lazy lunch in a lovely setting under the trees by the stream. Popular giant breakfasts, good sandwiches, fully licensed.

Witsand p273

Breede River Lodge, see Sleeping, page 277. Open 0730-2200. Hotel dining room with good views over the Breede River estuary under a timbered roof, roaring fire in winter, broad menu specializing in seafood. The lodge's **Coffee Shack** serves light meals and coffee and cake.

⊛ Festivals and events

Caledon and around p268

Mar Beer and Bread Festival. A sort of harvest festival, rather unusual. Held in a large marquee near the Wild Flower Garden. Live music is laid on in the evenings, and plenty of local farm produce is available.
Sep Wild Flower Festival. To coincide with the annual bloom of wild flowers. An excellent

opportunity to see the plants which make up the Cape fynbos, including protea, erica, gladioli and iridaceae. The principal display hall is in Hope St, a short walk from the town museum, and tractor rides are on offer to see flowers on local farms.

▲ Activities and tours

Swellendam and around p269
Golf
9-hole 72-par course, Andrew Whyte St, in the lee of the Langeberg Mountains, T028-514 1026, www.swellendamgolfcourse.co.za.

Tour operators
Breede River Dream Cruises, T028-542 1049, www.rivercruises.co.za. A range of houseboats with onboard sleeping, aimed at fishermen, can negotiate 50 km of the river.
Felix Unite River Adventures, T021-670 1300 (Cape Town office), www.felixunite.co.za. Professional outfit that runs trips from Cape Town to the Breede River, with overnight stays in bush camps, restored Voortrekker ox wagons, or A-frame houses.
Umkulu, T021-853 7952 (Cape Town), www.umkulu.co.za. Another operator that will take you to the Breede River from Cape Town for a day's float, some wine tasting, and an overnight at a local lodge.

⊖ Transport

Caledon and around p268
Bus
Greyhound, Intercape and Translux serve Caledon and **Swellendam**. Buses stop at the Caledon Hotel and Spa and the Swellengrebel Hotel in Swellendam

and run daily to **Cape Town** (2 hrs); and **Durban** (24 hrs) via **Port Elizabeth** (9 hrs).

Bus companies All bus tickets can be booked online at www.computicket.com. Greyhound, www.greyhound.co.za. Intercape, www.intercape.co.za; and Translux, www.translux.co.za. For details, see Getting around, page 41.

Car
Continuing east from Caledon, the N2 passes through rolling wheat fields towards **Mossel Bay**. From Caledon you can also deviate inland to the villages of **Genadendal** and **McGregor**; the R406 makes a convenient loop. Alternatively, take the R316 south towards **Bredasdorp** into the heart of Overberg country. The R319 rejoins the N2 just before **Swellendam**.

Swellendam and around p269
240 km to **Cape Town**, 225 km to **George**, 560 km to **Port Elizabeth**, 270 km to **Knysna**.

Bus
The Baz Bus stops daily in Swellendam and can take you as far as **Port Elizabeth** in a day. From **Cape Town** it arrives about 1200 allowing plenty of time to see the sights in the afternoon. From **Port Elizabeth** it arrives around 1800.

Bus companies Baz Bus, T021-439 2323, www.bazbus.com.

❻ Directory

Swellendam and around p269
Banks ABSA, 14 Voortrek St; Standard Bank, 32a Voortrek St. **Medical services** Hospital, Drostdy St, T028-514 1140.

Great Karoo

→ www.centralkaroo.co.za.

From Cape Town the N1 heads northeast through the Great Karoo, a vast, ancient plateau that covers nearly a third of the total area of the country. It is a beautiful and extraordinary region, as much for its history as for its remarkable emptiness. Today, the landscape is a parched expanse of baked red earth inhabited by tough merino sheep and their even tougher owners. Endless plains stretch between stark mountain ranges, with little but the characteristic steel windmills peppering the horizons. Hundreds of millions of years ago, however, this was an enormous swamp inhabited by dinosaurs, making it a key palaeontological site. More recently, the region has played a significant historical role, as the Voortrekkers penetrated the interior with their ox wagons, evidence of which can be seen in a handful of perfectly preserved Victorian settlements. The name Karoo comes from karusa, a Khoi word meaning dry, barren, thirstland.
▶▶ *For listings, see pages 287-289.*

The Koup ● ▶▶ pp287-289.

The 'Koup' refers to the southern districts of the Great Karoo, traversed by the N1 highway between Cape Town and Johannesburg. Travelling east from the **Hex River Valley**, the countryside quickly becomes arid and seemingly barren, with vast stretches of uninhabited semi-desert stretching to all horizons. Despite the area's arid appearance there is a surprisingly abundant supply of underground water, brought to the surface by the windmills which dot the plains. The most common vegetation is the Karoo bush, which forms the staple diet of the merino sheep bred here. Most of the farms are used for sheep, although more and more are being converted into game farms for game viewing and hunting. The sheer scale of the area is remarkable – the average farm size is over 20,000 ha, which makes popping round to the neighbours an arduous task. The isolated Karoo towns have a great sense of history, with many preserved 19th-century buildings, as well as a delightfully slow pace of life. Although rather off the beaten track, visitors often end up spending the night in one of these towns while en route to Cape Town or Johannesburg. None of them warrant a special visit, but have an hour or two's worth of distractions if you want to take a break from driving. Note that if you arrive in South Africa in either Johannesburg or Cape Town and tour the country, the likely route back to your starting point (to meet return or onward flights) will be along the N1. If you don't want to fly, you can negotiate this route by returning a hire car or travelling by mainline bus.

Climate

The dry summer months are oppressively hot. During and after the rains, however, the countryside takes on an entirely different appearance. The first rains arrive in the winter months, although centres such as Graaff-Reinet and Colesberg receive their rains in late summer. If you plan to hike in the region remember that summer daytime temperatures frequently exceed 40°C, while in the winter the nights get very cold and snow can fall on the mountain peaks.

Touws River → Colour map 8, A2.

As the railways moved further inland from Cape Town, this became an important depot for locomotives, bringing about the growth of the town in the 1870s. However, since electrification its importance as a railway centre has all but vanished. The area has become a graveyard for old **steam engines** – an impressive if somewhat eerie open-air museum. In its early days the station was known as Montagu Road; its present name was adopted in 1883. In addition to the steam engines, look out for a pair of concrete pillars behind the town hotel, the Loganda. They were used to mount astronomical instruments to view the transit of **Venus**. On 6 December 1882 a British astronomer took readings to help calculate the distance between the sun and earth.

Aquila Private Game Reserve
ⓘ *Off the R46 south of Touws River, T021-431 8400 (Cape Town), www.aquilasafari.com.*
In the last few years this private game reserve has had a rather staggering R25 million spent on it, mostly through the relocation of large animals. It's also the closest game reserve to Cape Town (less than two hours' drive) with lion, giraffe, elephant and rhino. It is set among 4500 ha of mountains, rivers, valleys and kloofs which make up the southern Karoo highlands and is now home to a wide range of species, many of which were relocated from other parts of the country. As well as the above, there are buffalo, black and blue wildebeest, zebra, a variety of antelope, bat-eared fox, mountain leopard, crocodile, ostrich, black-backed jackal and hippo. It has the largest breeding herd of white rhino in the Cape and, in February 2005, the first white rhino was born at the reserve, thought to be the first rhino born in the Cape for over 200 years. Aquila also has a huge natural wetland, which is home to 172 species of bird including several breeding pairs of the rare and endangered black eagle. There is luxury accommodation on the reserve (see Sleeping, page 287) but you can also visit for the morning, which begins with breakfast, then a three-hour game drive, followed by a buffet lunch, for around R1800 per person, R1100 if you're in your own car. Other options are horseback or quad-bike safaris, or combine these with the standard game drive for a full day of activities.

Before the arrival of Aquila, the unemployment rate in Touws River was 97%. Today the reserve is the single biggest employer in the region and provides for around 180 families. It also sponsors the local cricket team, school teachers and helped establish Touws River's supermarket and coordinates regular fundraising activities in Cape Town to provide blankets, clothes and basic necessities for the people of Touws River.

Matjiesfontein → *Colour map 8, A3.*
In 1975 the entire village of Matjiesfontein was declared a national monument – small surprise considering the excellent state of repair of its Victorian houses. There is little to the town itself, other than a couple of dusty streets lined with perfectly preserved period houses, the highlight of which is the famous **Lord Milner Hotel**, resplendent with turrets and adorned balconies. The history of the settlement is a reflection of the life of a young Scot, Jimmy Logan, an official on the Cape Government Railways in the 1890s. He originally came here hoping that the dry air would cure a chest complaint. He found the climate so beneficial that he decided to settle permanently. As an ex-railwayman he quickly saw the opportunity to supply water to steam trains from his farm. While the engines took on water, he served the passengers cool drinks and meals as back then the trains had no dining cars. Today, the luxurious **Blue Train** still stops here for lunch. So successful was his business that he built the fashionable **Lord Milner Hotel**, attracting rich and influential guests who suffered from lung complaints. These included Cecil Rhodes and the Sultan of Zanzibar. During the Anglo-Boer War the town became a military headquarters and a marshalling ground for troops. Logan financed a regiment and served in the war – the

The N1 to Johannesburg

The N1 covers the distance between Cape Town and Johannesburg via Bloemfontein in just over 1400 km, the majority of which runs through the Great Karoo. With a couple of drivers the journey can be made in one very long day but you need to leave early to arrive in either Cape Town or Johannesburg before dark. Most people, however, break their journey in one of the regional towns in either the Free State or Western Cape, which have no shortage of accommodation for motorists on this route. Recommended overnight stays are Beaufort West (roughly a third of the way from Cape Town), Colesberg (approximately halfway), or Kimberley and Bloemfontein (almost two-thirds of the distance from the Cape to Gauteng). The road is long and straight, and much of the Karoo scenery is featureless – be wary of getting tired behind the wheel and take frequent breaks. The towns have large petrol stations with toilets, shops and a restaurant such as Wimpy, but remember there are some big distances between the centres so fill up with fuel when you can. The road is heavily used by trucks and mainline buses and at times can be very busy – over the few days at the beginning of the Christmas holidays some 500 cars an hour leave Jo'burg with Gauteng families bound for the Cape. Finally, if you are driving through the 'boring' Karoo – pull over to the side of the road, switch off the engine of your car and take a moment before the next truck comes rumbling by. The space and silence is deafening.

hotel's turrets were used as lookout posts. Jimmy Logan lived here until his death in July 1920. Another famous resident was the writer and feminist Olive Schreiner, whose first novel *The Story of an African Farm* was set in the Karoo. She lived in a Matjiesfontein cottage from where she corresponded with friends including George Bernard Shaw and William Gladstone.

Today the town is a popular stopover for travellers between the Cape and Johannesburg. There is a small town museum, the **Marie Rawdon Museum**, in the old jail under the railway station, and a newer shed displaying some vintage cars, train carriages and a penny farthing bicycle just to the east of the hotel. The **cemetery**, 11 km to the west, has some interesting monuments and tombstones dating from the 1900s. Visit the hotel for **tourist information** ⓘ *T023-561 3011, www.matjiesfontein.com*, which also provides access to the above sights.

Laingsburg → *Colour map 6, B3.*

Laingsburg, another small town on the N1, started life as a staging post for coaches on a farm belonging to Stephanus Greeff. When the railway arrived, plans for a town were drawn up and in 1879 it was named Laingsburg after the John Laing, a Cape government official. Sadly, little of the original centre remains after a huge flood in 1981 washed away most of the town, though the magistrate's court and the old post office survived. The library contains a collection of photographs taken after the flood. The town hosts an 80-km ultra-marathon through the Karoo in September. For information visit the **Municipality offices** ⓘ *Van Riebeeck St, T023-551 1019, www.centralkaroo.co.za/laings burgdistrict.htm, Mon-Fri 0900-1600.*

N1 northeast

After crossing the Dwyka River, you reach the small settlement of **Prince Albert Road**. Turning south on the R328 takes you to Prince Albert (45 km), over the **Swartberg Pass**, and to the secluded **Gamkaskloof Valley**, known as 'The Hell' (see page 296). The next settlement of note along the N1 is **Leeu-Gamka**. The name means 'lion', a sad reminder that the last Cape Lion was shot here in 1857, rendering the species extinct.

Beaufort West ●❶❷❸ » pp287-289. Colour map 7, A2.

This is the largest and oldest of the Central Karoo towns, but despite its history it is an unattractive place. Most of its energies seem devoted to servicing those travelling from Johannesburg to Cape Town – the N1 passes right through town, lined with petrol stations and fast-food joints. It is known as the 'oasis' town, hard to believe when you see hot, dusty streets but, thanks to the presence of the Nuweveld Mountains to the north, its 150 mm annual rainfall is far higher than other towns in the Karoo. Beaufort West was named after the fifth Duke of Beaufort, father of the Cape governor, Lord Charles Somerset. It was established in 1818 to try and control gun smuggling and general lawlessness in the region. In 1837 it became South Africa's first municipality. Before the railway reached the town in 1880, all of the locally produced merino wool had to be transported to the coast by wagon across the Swartberg Mountains. The earliest route was via Meiringspoort Pass (see page 299), one of several magnificent passes which link the Great Karoo with the Little Karoo.

The country around Beaufort West is home to the largest variety of succulents in the world. In the town itself, there are more different species than in all of Great Britain. Pear trees – some of the which date back to the 1830s – provide welcome shade as you walk along the pavements. The **Beaufort West Tourism Bureau** ① *57 Donkin St, T023-415 1488, www.beaufortwestsa.co.za, Mon-Fri 0900-1700, Sat 0900-1200,* is an efficient, well-run office and they have prepared some useful material on the region and its major sights.

Sights

The tourist office provides a *Stroll Through Our Town* leaflet that takes about an hour and covers the main sights. The old Town Hall (1867) on Donkin Street houses the **Beaufort West Museum** ① *T023-415 2308, Mon-Fri 0830-1245, 1345-1645, Sat 0900-1200, R5.* This has a couple of above-average collections relating to two of the town's most famous past residents – Dr Christiaan Barnard and Dr Eric Louw. Dr Louw was the MP for Beaufort West for many years and rose through the government's ranks to become South Africa's Foreign Minister between 1957 and 1963. The late Dr Barnard is known throughout the world for his pioneering work with heart transplants. He performed the world's first at Groot Schuur Hospital in Cape Town in 1967. The displays include awards and trophies given to each, along with some of their personal effects. There is also a replica of Dr Barnard's heart transplant theatre. Next door is the **Dutch Reformed Mission Church** and the **parsonage** in which Dr Barnard spent his childhood. After his death in 2001, his ashes were scattered in the garden. In the next street are some fine examples of Karoo Victorian single-storey houses. These are all private homes; similar buildings can be seen in Matjiesfontein and other Karoo towns. In the **cemetery** is the grave of Stefanus Marais, a member of a group of Voortrekkers from Beaufort West who fought in the 1838 Battle of Blood River in Natal, as well as the graves of several British soldiers killed during the Anglo-Boer War.

Karoo National Park ● ↦ pp287-289. Colour map 7, A2.

Only 5 km from Beaufort West, this national park was created to conserve a representative area of the unique Karoo environment. There are two other conservation areas in the Karoo, each preserving a slightly different ecosystem: the Camdeboo National Park near Graaff-Reinet, and the Karoo Mountain Zebra Park at Cradock. Despite limited human presence the environment of the Great Karoo has undergone radical change during the past 150 years and the protected areas are now recognized as important conservation centres as well as popular tourist destinations. Springbok are present in large numbers – a reminder of the once-massive herds that could stretch for several kilometres, which used to cross the Karoo on annual migrations.

Ins and outs

Getting there The main entrance is signposted off the N1 highway 5 km southwest of Beaufort West. The entrance gate is beside the highway and the road takes visitors straight to the park office and accommodation facilities. The gates are open 0500-2200; it is 7 km from the main entrance to the reception office, T023-415 2828, which is open 0730-1900. The daily conservation fee per person, which also covers the vehicle, is R88, children R44. Next to the office is the **Rest Camp** (see Sleeping page 288), which has a **restaurant** ① *0700-1000, 1800-2100*, open for breakfast and dinner, and a **shop** ① *0730-2000*, selling frozen meat, firewood and booze. The office has trail and park maps, as well as pamphlets detailing the main attractions within the park, and every evening except Sunday there is a slideshow. There is a bird hide near the dam close to the camp.

Climate The Karoo is semi-desert, which means extremes – very hot days in summer (average for January is 32°C) with temperatures often reaching over 35°C, and warm days in winter but very cold nights (from June to August frost is common, and snow falls on the mountain peaks). March and April are regarded as the wet months, although the rainfall only averages 250 mm annually.

Background

The 70,000-ha national park was proclaimed in September 1979 after a lengthy and concerted effort by local residents to conserve the Karoo environment before farming practices totally destroyed it. The success of the campaign was primarily due to the efforts of a local farmer, William Quinton. The municipality donated over 7000 ha, and funds raised by the Nature Foundation were used to purchase two farms, Stolshoek and Puttersvlei. The success of the park is attributed to the efforts of the first warden, Bruce Bryden and his wife Helena. Between 1977 and 1980 they saw to the removal of all the old farm fences and ripped out as much alien vegetation as possible. This was not without opposition; local farmers feared the reserve would become a protected breeding ground for predators which would then prey upon their sheep. The numbers of caracal and jackal have increased, but so too have the smaller mammals they traditionally prey on, so they now have less need to hunt the farmers' sheep. The park has modern chalets and camp-sites in a scenically situated camp.

The current boundaries of the park encompass an area of Karoo plains, which merge into mountain slopes and a high plateau. The **Nuweveld Mountains** in the north of the park are nearly 2000 m high. The vegetation in the low-lying areas is a mixture of grasses and shrubs such as honey-thorn and the common acacia karroo. On the steep slopes a sourgrass known as renosterbos (*Elytropappus rhinocerotis*) and harpuis flourish. The flora can be studied along the specially laid out Bossie Trail (see below). Note the difference in vegetation cover between areas within the park and the neighbouring farms. The overgrazed farms have little grass cover and small, unpalatable shrubs.

Wildlife

There is a surprisingly diverse range of game and smaller wildlife in the park. Records list 174 species of birdlife, 38 species of reptile, 37 types of gecko and lizard, and five different species of tortoise (this is the largest number in a conservation area in the world). In another effort to help restore the area to its previous state, antelope such as eland, black wildebeest, gemsbok, Cape mountain zebra, springbok and red hartebeest have been moved into the park. The reserve is also home to two endangered species: the **black rhino** and the **riverine rabbit**. While the statistics are impressive, actually spotting most of these animals requires a degree of patience, effort and, of course, luck. Look out for the tent tortoise; it is well camouflaged and looks like an inverted egg box.

Hiking in the park

There are three short day walks known as the **Fossil Trail**, 400 m, the **Pointer's Hiking Trail**, 10 km, and the **Bossie Trail**, 800 m. Each of these explores a different aspect of the park. The most interesting is the the Fossil Trail along which you can see fossils in situ. It has been adapted for the blind as well as people in wheelchairs: Braille boards tell the 250-million-year tale of the region. The trails all start from near the environmental educational centre where further information about the park is on display.

Driving in the park

Visitors in 4WDs are allowed on certain short tracks in the park. The park also has its own vehicle for hire, and day trips with a nature guide and lunch included can be organized. Other trips on offer include night drives and overnight tours. The trails are rough, slippery and steep in parts and previous experience with a 4WD is essential. There are a few rough roads open for game viewing, but given the mountainous conditions you cannot go too far. Walking remains the best way to enjoy the park.

East to Colesberg 🚌 ➤➤ *pp287-289. Colour map 7, A2/3.*

This tiny settlement of **Three Sisters** is 78 km north of Beaufort West and there's nothing here except an Ultra City for petrol and refreshments. It is however the junction of the N1 and N12. The N1 continues to Johannesburg via Bloemfontein whilst the N12 goes to Johannesburg via Kimberley. The N1 is shorter as far as mileage is concerned. If you want to break the journey by exploring one of these two cities, it is at Three Sisters that you will have to choose which road to follow.

If you decide to continue on the N1 via Bloemfontein, then **Hanover** is the midway point between Cape Town and Johannesburg, and there is a sign marking its geographical importance. Once you have reached here during a long day on the road, remember it is another 700 km in either direction.

Colesberg ⬤⬤ ⟫ pp287-289. Colour map 4, B2.

Colesberg actually lies in the Northern Cape but for ease of reference it is included here. The town is situated at the base of a distinctive landmark, **Cole's Kop** (1700 m), visible from 40 km away. This rounded rock outcrop was a very important landmark for early settlers, who moved inland across a largely featureless region. In those days it was called Toringberg – Towering Mountain – although some insist it meant Magic Mountain. The town was then named after Sir Lowry Cole, Cape Governor in 1830.

The town is an important junction between the N9, which heads south towards Port Elizabeth and George, and the N1, which cuts right through the centre of town. Many of the town's oldest buildings are found along here, and turning off the N1 takes you to further clusters of Victorian houses tucked between a couple of picturesque hills. In its early days, this was a classic frontier town with illicit trade in a wide range of commodities, especially gunpowder and liquor. During the Anglo-Boer War it was close to the front and several battles were fought in the vicinity. The surrounding hills are named after the British regiments who held them: Suffolk, New Zealand, Worcester and Gibraltar. The town itself was captured by the Boers and for four months was part of the Free State territory.

Today Colesberg is the centre of two very successful businesses: horse breeding and sheep farming. Many champion racehorses have been bred around the town, due mainly to the soil type which yields high-quality grasses and other fodder. The legendary golfer Gary Player owns a nearby stud farm. The majority of visitors are just passing through along the N1 – the town springs to life in the early evening as people arrive, there is a burst of action as bills are settled and fuel tanks filled in the morning, and then Colesberg reverts to a peaceful farming town for the rest of the day. The **tourist office** ① *T051-753 0678, www.colesberginfo.co.za, Mon-Fri 0900-1500*, is on Murray Street.

Sights

There are a few historic buildings mainly along **Bell Street**. The flat-roofed cottages which line the street were built between 1860 and 1870, and have today been attractively restored. There is also an old flour mill which was operated by horses and was the country's last working horse mill until it was turned into a pub a few years ago. The street is named after Charles Bell, a surveyor who is known in philatelic circles for designing a rare Cape Triangular stamp issued in September 1853. There are four churches around town. The most interesting is the **Church of the Province** (1848), designed by the wife of the first Bishop of Cape Town, Lady Grey. She had intended it to be a cathedral, but only the chancel was built. The **Dutch Reformed Church** (1866) is a characteristically grand, whitewashed building.

The **Colesberg Kemper Museum** on Bank Square is a short walk from the Central Hotel, and contains an interesting photo collection, objects relating to the Anglo-Boer War and a 19th-century toy collection. It is a fine, solid two-storey structure built in 1862 to house the Colesberg District Bank, later absorbed by the Standard Bank. Look out for the pane of glass in the museum on which the letters 'DP' have been scratched. In 1866 John O'Reilly, a diamond trader and transport rider from the Northern Cape diamond fields, brought a stone to the Colesberg magistrate, Lorenzo Boyes, who told O'Reilly that the scratching seemed to confirm that the stone was indeed a diamond. This was the first recognized stone to be found in South Africa. The diamond was 21.25 carats, and was bought for £500 by the Cape's governor, Sir Philip Wodehouse.

From Colesburg, the N1 enters the Free State and heads north to Bloemfontein.

Great Karoo listings

For Sleeping and Eating price codes and other relevant information, see pages 46-53.

Sleeping

Aquila Private Game Reserve *p281*
L3 Aquila Game Lodge, off the R46 west of Touws River, T021-405 4513 (Cape Town), www.aquilasafari.com. Tastefully decorated luxury cottages with stone baths, outdoor showers, ceiling fans, fireplaces, and minibars. Family units are available. Raw materials such as rock, river pebbles, natural wood, reeds and thatch have been used wherever possible to maintain a natural look. There is the **Cigar Bar** and **Boma Restaurant**, and horseback safaris or traditional game drives are included in the price, check the website for details of packages. The rates are in the **L1** category if you have your own transport, so it's worth considering hiring a car and the driving out here through the Hex River Valley (see page 280) is attractive.
D Loganda, T023-385 1130, www.loganda lodge.com. The main town hotel, in a 1960s dreary-looking block. 15 fairly comfortable rooms, some with a/c. Restaurant, beer garden, cosy pub with DSTV and swimming pool.

Matjiesfontein *p281*
B Lord Milner, T023-561 3011, www.matjies fontein.com. The original old Victorian town hotel is very much part of the town's history. The 53 large rooms are filled with antiques, as is the lounge and entertainingly old-fashioned dining room, which serves good-value meals. There are some family rooms and 4 self-catering cottages in the garden. Don't miss the wonderfully atmospheric old bar. The Union Jack is still raised daily from one of the hotel's turrets. Recommended.

Beaufort West *p283*
During peak seasons all the best-value lodges and hotels are fully booked months in advance by families from Gauteng, especially at the beginning and end of the long Christmas holidays. For the rest of the year trade is much quieter, although there is a continual flow of people driving between the Cape and Gauteng. Room rates increase during school holidays.
B Beaufort Manor, 13 Bird St, T023-415 2175, www.beaufortmanor.co.za. 16 modern and attractive rooms with private entrances opening onto a courtyard where there is a swimming pool, 5 open-plan self-catering cottages with a/c sleeping up to 4 which are good value for a family, located next to a pond with ducks and swans, very good restaurant and bar, 3-course Karoo dinners, famous for their lamb.
B Lemoenfontein Game Lodge, 2 km north of Beaufort West and 4.5 km off the N1 on the De Jager's Pass road, T023-4152 847, www.lemoenfontein.co.za. A luxury lodge with 13 en suite rooms with modern decor, swimming pool, country cooking in the dining room on a wooden deck, game drives and hiking on the farm where giraffe and zebra are present as well as a number of antelope.
C-D Matoppo Inn, corner of Meintjies and Bird streets, T023-415 1055, www.matoppo inn.co.za. Set in a quiet residential street, this was originally the 1834 *drostdy* (magistrate's house), now converted into a luxury guest-house with high ceilings, beautiful yellow-wood floors, comfortable rooms furnished with antiques, traditional Karoo candlelit dinners, neat garden with swimming pool. Cecil Rhodes stayed here on the way to what was then Rhodesia. Excellent value, recommended.
C-E Wagon Wheel Country Lodge, 500 m north of town centre on the N1, T023-414 2145, www.wagonwheel.co.za. Friendly country motel with simple rooms to suit most groups and some camping pitches with a kitchen block, TV, bar, cheap restaurant with filling meals, swimming pool, disabled facilities, laundry service. Booking essential

Western Cape Great Karoo Listings ● **287**

as it's a popular and good-value stopover for motorists on the N1.

D Karoo Gateway Guesthouse, based in Beaufort West's old airport terminal building, 12 km north on the N1, T023-414 3444, www.karoogateway.co.za. 6 pleasantly decorated en suite rooms, and 2 family self-catering unit, with a/c and tea and coffee stations. TV lounge with free internet access, restaurant serving wholesome breakfasts and dinners (must be pre booked), and rather uniquely enjoy sundowners in the control tower with great views over the Karoo. The airport is still operational for private planes.

D Young's Budget Accommodation, 56 Donkin St, T023-414 3878, www.wagon wheel.co.za/youngs. 36 en suite budget rooms sleeping up to 5 people decorated in country style, with TV, coffee-making facilities, fans and heaters, 24-hr security and reception, safe parking, big swimming pool, braai facilities and excellent **Mac Young's Restaurant**, see Eating page 289. Recommended.

Karoo National Park *p284*

B-E Rest Camp, reservations through **SAN-Parks** Tshwane (Pretoria) office, T012-428 9111, www.sanparks.org. Bookings can also be made in person at the offices in Cape Town and Durban (see page 48). For cancellations and bookings under 72 hrs, for campsite reservations, and for general enquiries, call camp reception direct, T023-415 2828. The camp is at the entrance gate to the park, there is a shop selling basic groceries, an à la carte restaurant, laundry and a bright-blue swimming pool. The accommodation here is superb, even by **SANParks** standards.

36 spacious self-catering thatched cottages (**C**) in Cape Dutch style, grouped around the swimming pool, sleeping 2-6 people, kitchen, lounge with highly unusual furnishings for parks accommodation – ornate clocks on the wall, Persian rugs, bellows and coal scuttles by the fireplace. 2 cottages are wheelchair-friendly and one is also kitted out for visually impaired visitors. Breakfast is included in the rates.

Camping
24 grassy caravan and camping sites, good clean ablution blocks, kitchen unit, power points, maximum of 6 per site.

East to Colesberg *p285*

D Hanover Lodge, corner of Queen and Mark streets, Hanover, T053-643 0019, www.hanover. co.za. Excellent family-run hotel and guest- house, good-sized rooms, some in garden rondavels, extras like hot water bottles in winter, secure parking, DSTV in pub and guest lounge, restaurant serves good bar meals even for late arrivals. Discounts available out of season.

Colesberg *p286*

D Colesberg Lodge, 32 Church St, T051-753 0734, www.colesberglodge.co.za. A large, old, blue town hotel with 52 double or family rooms with a/c or fan, rather faded and old-fashioned but adequate, restaurant serving standard but filling meat and veggie dishes, swimming pool.

D The Lighthouse, 40 Church St, T051-753 0043, www.karoolighthouse.co.za. Popular good-value guesthouse with 11 comfortable en suite rooms, furnished with antique farm furniture, well managed, good reports, booking essential, swap driving tales in the communal lounge, breakfast (extra) is served on the patio or in bed.

D Van Zylsvlei, Philippolis road 6 km north of town, T051-753 0589, www.vanzyls vlei.co.za. Roadside motel with 19 rooms in rondavels, hearty farm breakfasts and dinner on request. Swimming pool and bar, 6 stands for caravans or tents (**F**), grassy and shady, electric points, shops at nearby petrol station.

❶ Eating

Town hotels have restaurants and welcome non-residents for evening meals. Most of the guesthouses offer dinner given sufficient notice.

Beaufort West p283

King Pie, Wimpy and **KFC** are along the main street

†† **Mac Young's**, 156 Donkin St, T023-414 4068. Open 0630-1000, 1700-2130. Bustling restaurant decorated in tartan, including the carpet, serving steaks from a charcoal grill, plus pizza, pasta and seafood. One of their more unusual dishes is haggis, the last dish you'd expect to find in the middle of the Karoo.
†† **Wagon Wheel Country Lodge**, see Sleeping, page 287. Open 0700-2200. Light lunches, bar snacks and quality à la carte evening meals, huge menu, big portions and great value. The bar has a fireplace and TV, good place to wind down after a day's driving.

⊙ Transport

Beaufort West p283
Bus
None of the towns along the N1 make interesting destinations in their own right, so if you travelling between **Cape Town** and **Johannesburg** by bus, it's better to do the 19-hr overnight journey in 1 hit. **Greyhound, Intercape** and **Translux** all stop at Beaufort West (and the other Karoo towns along the N1) on the Cape Town–Johannesburg route, though they often arrive and depart at awkward times during the night. The towns are surprisingly quiet from as early as 2100, it is unlikely anyone will be around to help if you haven't reserved a seat. Buses stop at the Engen Garage. **Cape Town** (6 hrs) daily via **Worcester** (4 hrs). **Johannesburg** and

Tshwane (Pretoria) (12 hrs) daily via **Bloemfontein** (6 hrs) or via **Kimberley** (6 hrs).

Bus companies All bus tickets can be booked online at www.computicket.com. **Greyhound**, www.greyhound.co.za; **Intercape**, www.intercape.co.za; and **Translux**, www.translux.co.za. For more information, see Getting around, page 41.

Train
Central reservations, **Shosholoza Meyl**, T0860-00888 (in South Africa), T011-774 4555 (from overseas), www.shosholoza meyl.co.za, timetables and fares are published on the website. Daily to **Cape Town** (9 hrs), Tue to **Durban** (27 hrs) via **Bloemfontein** and **Harrismith**. Daily to **Tshwane (Pretoria)** (17 hrs) via **Kimberley** (7½ hrs). Trains stop here for almost 30 mins.

Colesberg p286
It's 778 km to **Cape Town**, 226 km to **Bloemfontein**, 625 km to **Johannesburg**.

Bus
Again many services depart at awkward times in the middle of the night. Buses arrive in Colesburg 4 hrs after leaving Beaufort West and stop at the Shell Ultra City for 20 mins.

Train
See above for contact details. There is a daily service between **Johannesburg** and **Port Elizabeth**. Change at Bloemfontein for other services to **Durban, Kimberley** and **Cape Town. Johannesburg** (10 hrs) via **Bloemfontein** (6 hrs) and **Port Elizabeth** (7 hrs).

Little Karoo

Unlike the Great Karoo to the north, the Little Karoo is not a flat, dry and empty landscape; instead, it is made up of a series of parallel fertile valleys, enclosed by the Swartberg Mountains to the north and the Langeberg and Outeniqua Mountains to the south. It is an especially rewarding region to explore and much of it is hardly visited by tourists. The Cango Caves are a big attraction, as are the ostrich farms, which are often visited as a detour off the Garden Route, but further afield lies spectacular and peaceful countryside, dotted with a multitude of small, historic villages. Here are some of the most dramatic kloofs and passes in South Africa (there are 14 in all) with excellent hiking and the springtime allure of bright patches of flowers.

The majority of the passes, constructed in the late 19th century, were surveyed and built by Thomas Bain, a truly remarkable engineer. Perhaps the greatest testament to his work is that almost every pass he constructed is still in use today along almost identical lines. Like the Breede River Valley (see page 215) this region is also mostly part of the Route 62 tourist initiative; www.route62.co.za. ⟩⟩ For listings, see pages 299-304.

Ins and outs

Climate
The climate of the Little Karoo is markedly different from that of the coastal Garden Route, and yet it is no more than 30 km further inland. The principal reason for this is the mountains which act as a barrier to the weather moving inland. In the summer it is hot and dry and daytime temperatures of 40°C are not uncommon. During the winter you can expect to see snow on top of the Swartberg Mountains. Average annual rainfall is about 300 mm; water has to be carefully managed and farmers need to irrigate crops.

Vegetation and wildlife
There are several nature reserves managed by Cape Nature Conservation in the region, including Anysberg, Towerkop, and Swartberg. For the botanist, it is one of the best environments in the world for succulents. There are many fascinating small plants which have adapted to the scorching hot sunshine, erratic limited rainfall and rocky shallow soils. Aloes, lilies, geraniums and fynbos vegetation dot the landscape. A rare red variety of protea (*Aristata protea*) grows only in the Seweweekspoort Valley. The guided tours in Gamkaberg Nature Reserve are some of the most informative outings, and will leave you with a greater appreciation of the unique nature of the Karoo landscape.

Around Oudtshoorn, you'll see ostrich peering at you over fences everywhere you turn. When explorers from the Cape first came to the valley, they found it to be teeming with buffalo, elephant, rhino, lion, hippo, kudu and the now-extinct quagga. Today only a few leopard remain in the remote hills; the more common antelope can be found in the reserves. The **Gamkaberg Nature Reserve** is home to the rare Cape mountain zebra, as well as antelope such as steenbok and klipspringer. Antelope can also be seen in the **Swartberg Nature Reserve**.

By far the largest settlement in the Little Karoo, this is a pleasant administrative centre which still retains much of the calm of its early days. It is a major tourist centre thanks to the nearby Cango Caves and the countless ostrich farms surrounding the town. Oudtshoorn itself is appealing, with broad streets, smart sandstone Victorian houses, many of which are now B&Bs, and a good choice of restaurants.

Oudtshoorn Tourist Bureau ⓘ *Baron van Rheede St, T044-279 2532, www.oudtshoorn. com, Mon-Fri 0800-1800, Sat 0830-1300*, has a well-informed, enthusiastic and helpful team and is worth a visit for details on accommodation and the less well-known sights of the Karoo.

Background
In 1838 a small church was inaugurated on the Hartebeestrivier Farm to serve the farmers who had settled along the banks of the Olifants and Grobbelaars rivers. Nine years later

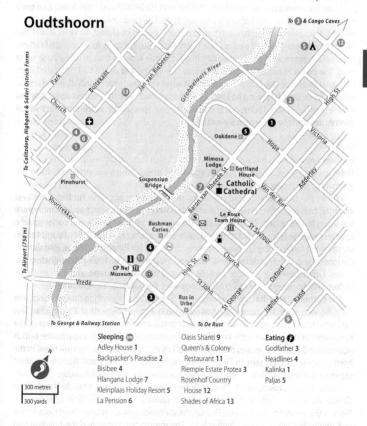

Oudtshoorn

To ③ & Cango Caves

Sleeping ⊜
Adley House 1
Backpacker's Paradise 2
Bisibee 4
Hlangana Lodge 7
Kleinplaas Holiday Resort 5
La Pension 6

Oasis Shanti 9
Queen's & Colony
Restaurant 11
Riempie Estate Protea 3
Rosenhof Country
House 12
Shades of Africa 13

Eating ❼
Godfather 3
Headlines 4
Kalinka 1
Paljas 5

the village of Oudtshoorn was founded when land was subdivided and sold by the surveyor J Ford. The town was named after Baron Van Rheede van Oudtshoorn, who died on his way to the Cape to take up the post of governor in 1773. In 1858 the first group of British immigrants settled in the village.

When visiting during the dry season it is easy to see how for many years the supply of water to the new settlement restricted its growth. A severe drought in 1865 persuaded many established farmers to move on and most made the long trek to the Transvaal. In its early days, water was brought to the town in barrels and then sold to households at sixpence a bucket. But the local farmers learnt to cope with this handicap and many of South Africa's early irrigation experts came from the region. When you cross the Grobbelaars River in the centre of town during the dry season, all the bridges and culverts seem redundant but they provide ample evidence of how much water can pass through when it rains. If you have time, walk across the Victorian **Suspension Bridge** where Church Street crosses the river; this is now a protected national monument.

It was the advent of two ostrich-feather booms (1865-1870 and 1900-1914) that truly established the town, and led to the erection of the fine sandstone buildings and 'ostrich palaces' that now line Oudtshoorn's streets. For a period of almost 40 years it was the most important settlement east of Cape Town. At the peak of its fortunes, ostrich feathers were selling for more than their weight in gold – little wonder that so many birds were bred. The boom attracted a large Jewish community, most of which had emigrated from Lithuania to escape the Tsarist pogroms. But when the good years finished, few chose to remain. While ostrich farming no longer brings in as much wealth, it remains an important business in the Karoo. Today, it is the production of specialized agricultural seed which contributes most to the region's wealth.

Sights

The two major reasons for coming here are the ostrich farms and the superb Cango Caves. There are also several nature reserves and scenic drives, which are introductions to the diversity of the landscape.

Within the town limits there is little to see aside from appreciating the sandstone Victorian buildings. There are several **ostrich palaces** in town, which unfortunately are not open to the public. They are still worth a look from the outside since their ornate exteriors were very much part of their design. Most examples are in the old part of town on the west bank of the Grobbelaars River. Look out for **Pinehurst**, on St John Street, designed by a Dutch architect, and **Gottland House**, built in 1903 with an octagonal tower. Other buildings of note include **Mimosa Lodge**, **Oakdene** and **Rus in Urbe**. Unfortunately, many fine Victorian buildings were demolished in the 1950s.

The **Catholic Cathedral**, on Baron von Rheede Street, is a fascinating modern cruciform building with splendid stained-glass windows and a chapel beneath the main altar. The cathedral houses two notable works of art: the first is a painting given by Princess Eugenie in memory of her brother – the last of the Bonapartes, who died fighting with the British against the Boers. The second is a replica of a Polish icon incorporating childhood items from refugee children sent to Oudtshoorn during the Second World War; the children returned bearing the gift to celebrate the 50th anniversary of their evacuation.

In the centre of town, next to the old Queen's Hotel on Baron van Rheede Street, is the **CP Nel Museum** ① *T044-272 7306, www.cpnelmuseum.co.za, Mon-Fri 0800-1700, Sat-Sun 0900-1700, small entrance fee.* This fine sandstone building with its prominent clock tower was originally built as a boys' high school. The masons who designed the building had

Ostrich trivia

→ The ostrich (*Struthio camelus*) has been around since the Pliocene period, and has changed little in the intervening eight million years.

→ A giant ostrich-feather fan was discovered in Tutankhamen's tomb.

→ The Oudtshoorn area has 97% of the world's ostrich population.

→ The shell of an ostrich egg can withstand the weight of a human adult.

→ Incubation, 42 days, is carried out by both birds; the male sits at night, the female during the day.

→ Each egg can weigh more than 1 kg, they make good omelettes, and can feed 20 people in one go.

→ It takes two years for the chick to mature.

→ The best-quality feathers are produced by birds aged between three and 12 years.

→ Plucking occurs every nine months: about 1 kg of feathers is removed.

→ Over 80% of the feathers are exported.

→ Their skin makes excellent handbags and wallets.

→ The meat once used only for biltong is now popular in Europe and America because it is almost fat free.

→ The male bird has a vicious kick and a sharp toenail – beware!

been brought to Oudtshoorn by the 'feather barons' to build their grand mansions. The displays include a reconstructed trading store, synagogue and chemist, plus an interesting section on the history of the ostrich boom and the characters involved. The rest of the collection of historic objects was bequeathed to the town by CP Nel, a local businessman. A short walk away is **Le Roux Town House**, at 146 High Street, which is part of the CP Nel Museum. This classic town house was built in 1908 and provides a real feel for how the wealthy lived in the fine ostrich palaces of Oudtshoorn. The interior and furnishings are in art nouveau style and the furniture was shipped from Europe between 1900 and 1920. During the summer, teas are served in the garden. **Arbeidsgenot**, Jan van Riebeeck Road, is the former home of Senator Cornelius Langenhoven, a leading figure in the history of the Afrikaans language who wrote the old national anthem of South Africa.

Around Oudtshoorn

Visiting an ostrich farm in the area can be great fun, although the appeal of riding ostriches, feeding ostriches, buying ostrich eggs and leather, or eating ostrich-egg omelette can fade quickly. To keep visitors for longer, some farms have introduced different species. Visiting the farms or the Cango Caves without your own transport can be surprisingly tricky. There are no tour companies that organize daily trips, although it is possible to find a guide through the tourist office. Otherwise, you might want to hire a car for the day.

Cango Ostrich Farm ① *T044-272 4623, www.cangoostrich.co.za, daily 0800-1700, R56, children R27, tours every 20 mins, duration 45 mins*, in the Shoemanshoek Valley 14 km from Oudtshoorn, is particularly convenient as it is on the way to and from the Cango Caves. The farm attractions are also within walking distance of each other. You can interact directly with the birds, sit on or ride them, buy local curios and sample Karoo wines and cheeses.

Wilgewandel Holiday Farm ① *T044-272 0878, www.wilgewandel.co.za, daily 0800-1500, camel rides R25, children (3-13) R15*, is also in the Shoemanshoek Valley, 2 km before the Cango Caves. It offers you the chance to ride a camel around the farm – a pleasant change from all those ostriches. There are also lots of attractions for children such as farmyard animals, a pet area, trampolines, bumper boats, donkey cart rides, and a restaurant serving anything from tea and scones to crocodile and ostrich steaks.

Highgate Ostrich Farm ① *T044-272 7115, www.highgate.co.za, daily 0800-1700, R40, children R26, tours every 15 mins, duration 1½ hrs,* is 10 km from Oudtshoorn off the R328 towards Mossel Bay. This very popular show farm, named after the London suburb of Highgate, has been owned by the Hooper family since the 1850s. It has won prizes in the last few years for its high standards, and is very well run and better organized than other farms. You will learn everything there is to know about the bird, and can then try your hand at riding (or even racing) them. Snacks and drinks are served on the porch of the homestead. As well as English, guides speak German and Dutch.

Safari Ostrich Farm ① *T044-272 7311, www.safariostrich.co.za, daily 0730-1700, adults R46, children R24, tours depart every 30 mins, duration 1 hr,* 6 km from Oudtshoorn on the Mossel Bay road, has the usual array of ostrich rides, educational exhibits and curio shops. There is also a smart homestead known as Welgeluk. The house was built in 1910, and is a perfectly preserved example of an ostrich palace. There are roof tiles from Belgium, teak from Burma and expanses of marble floors, proof of the wealth and influence the short-lived boom brought to Oudtshoorn families. Unfortunately, the house is closed to visitors; the closest you can get is the main gate.

Cango Wildlife Ranch ① *T044-272 5593, www.cango.co.za, daily 0800-1700, R95, children (4-15) R60, tours every 40 mins, duration 1 hr,* is 3 km from Oudtshoorn along the R328 towards Cango Caves and is a popular stop for tour groups. There are mixed opinions on this place since it is, in effect, a zoo which stocks animals including white lions, leopards, cheetahs and, oddly, jaguars, pumas and two rare white Bengal tigers that produced three cubs in 2003. There is even an albino python. However, the ranch is a leading player in conservation and breeding, particularly with cheetah and wild dog, and the enclosures are very spacious. After walking safely above the animals, you have the choice of paying a little more to pet a cheetah, or you can visit the restaurant. A new attraction here is the **Valley of the Ancients**, a well-forested string of lakes and enclosures connected by boardwalks that are home a number of unusual animals. The pools are home to Nile crocodiles, pygmy hippos, monitor lizards and otters, while birds include flamingos and marabou storks. You can watch the crocodiles being fed by hand and this is probably the only place in the world that offers cage diving with crocodiles (R240; children must be over 12).

Following the R328 north, the road passes several ostrich farms and then follows the Grobbelaars River Valley towards the Cango Caves (see below). The little village of **Schoemanshoek**, 15 km from Oudtshoorn, is in a lush valley with small farms and homesteads and has some good places to stay.

Cango Caves ➤ *Colour map 7, B2.*

Tucked away in the foothills of the Swartberg Mountains 28 km from Oudtshoorn, the Cango Caves are a magnificent network of calcite caves, recognized as among the world's finest dripstone caverns. In 1938 they were made a national monument. Despite being seriously hyped and very touristy, they are well worth a visit. Allow a morning for a round trip if based locally; if you have a car it is possible to visit them and Oudtshoorn on a day trip from towns along the Garden Route such as Mossel Bay, George and Wilderness.

Ins and outs

The caves are 28 km north of Oudtshoorn along the R328, clearly signposted from the centre of town. The road goes straight to the caves; you have to turn left for the Swartberg Pass and Prince Albert. A range of facilities has been developed in the middle of this sparsely inhabited wilderness. There is a restaurant, a crèche, several curio shops and a small money exchange. The caves are usually around 20°C, so a T-shirt and shorts will be fine. Wear shoes with reasonable grip, as after rain the floors can become a little slippery. It is a criminal offence to touch or take anything from inside the caves. Please adhere to these rules and be careful not to touch the rock formations – the acidity of the human sweat that is left from by wandering hands has already caused considerable damage. Eating, drinking and smoking are also forbidden inside. The caves are open daily 0900-1700; you can only enter on a tour (see Oudtshoorn Activities and tours, page 304) – these run until 1600. During the holidays it gets very crowded and nearly 200,000 people pass through the caves each year. Each tour has a maximum number of people, so you may have to wait an hour or more. It's a good idea to get here early in the morning to avoid queues.

Cave tours

ⓘ *T044-272 7410, www.cangocaves.co.za. There are 2 tour options: the standard tour starting every hour on the hour from 0900, with the last tour at 1600, 1 hr, R55, R30 children, and the adventure tour starting at half past every hour 0930-1530, 1½ hrs, R70, children R45.*

The only access to the caves is on a guided tour: the short tour takes in two chambers and provides a brief insight into the cave complex; the most popular tour takes in six caves, while the adventure tour follows narrow corridors and involves some crawling. During the tours, each section is lit up and the guide points out interesting formations and their given names. Although one small chamber is still lit in gaudy colours, the rest are illuminated with white light to best show off the formations. These are turned off behind you as you progress further into the system as research has shown that continued exposure to light causes damage to the caves.

The caverns are not just a beautiful series of bizarre formations, but represent over a million years of slow chemical processes. The Cango cave system is known as a phreatic system, the term given to caves which have been chemically eroded by underground water. Once the caves had been exposed to air, the first deposits started to form – these now make up the incredible stalagmites, stalactites and flowstones visitors can see. The timescale of some of the formations is mind-boggling; many of the pillars took hundreds of thousands of years to form, while the oldest flowstone is over a million years old.

The standard one-hour tour is a good introduction to the caves and allows you to see the most impressive formations. It is, however, aimed at tour groups, so visitors with a special interest may find it rather simplistic. The adventure tour lasts for 1½ hours, is over 1 km long and there are over 400 stairs. This can be disturbing for some people, since it involves crawling along narrow tunnels, and at the very end climbing up the Devil's Chimney, a narrow vertical shaft. It leads up for 3.5 m and is only 45 cm wide in parts – definitely not for broad people. If at any stage you feel you can't go on, inform the guide who will arrange for you to be led out. Although strenuous, this tour allows you to see the most of the caves, and gives a real feeling of exploration.

Just before the Cango Caves is the turning for the Swartberg Pass and Prince Albert that travels through the Swartberg Nature Reserve. The reserve encompasses 1,291,000 ha of mostly state-owned land and includes the area around Swartberg Pass and the Gamkaskloof Valley (see below). The main attractions here are the mountain fynbos and a varied birdlife. Animals likely to be spotted include kudu, baboon, klipspringer and dassie. Leopard and caracal also occur in the region but are rarely seen. The mountains behind the Cango Caves are 2000-3000 m high and have a maze of trails snaking through them. The longest trail, the **Swartberg Hiking Trail**, is 60 km long and takes five days and is fairly strenuous. There are three overnight huts at Ou Tol, Bothashoek and Gouekrans, with bunks and cold showers but no fires are permitted so hikers need to bring their own gas stoves. The trail may be closed in winter because of snowfall. Permits and maps are issued by **Cape Nature** ① *T021-659 3500, www.capenature.co.za*. Water has to be carried between huts during the day.

Swartberg Pass → *Colour map 7, B1.*
One of the most spectacular passes in South Africa, the Swartberg Pass is a national monument in recognition of the engineering genius of Thomas Bain (see pages 157 and 290). Following severe floods in 1875 which closed Meiringspoort and Seven Weeks Poort and washed away parts of the road, farmers in the region petitioned the government in Cape Town to build a reliable road across the Swartberg. After the first contractor went bankrupt Bain finished the job. It was built between 1881 and 1888 using convict labourers. The route is 24 km long; the top of the pass is 1585 m and the summit is often closed in winter due to snow. The road today follows much the same route and care must be taken. It is very steep, climbing 1000 m within 12 km, and there are very sharp, blind hairpins. As you descend towards Prince Albert there are plenty of shaded picnic sites to pause at and enjoy the views.

Gamkaskloof Valley: 'The Hell'
① *3 km past the summit of Swartberg Pass, coming from Oudtshoorn, is a gravel road to the left signposted 'The Hell' in the Gamkaskloof Valley. The Otto du Plessis road is suitable for a saloon car but be sure to take care driving here. The road is narrow and steep in parts and there are many blind bends. In all, it is 58 km to the start of the valley; allow at least 1½ hrs each way. Note that there are no shops or fuel, but some of the original cottages in the valley have been restored as accommodation by Cape Nature, see Sleeping, page 301.*
Gamkaskloof Valley is 16 km long with two seasonal rivers criss-crossing the road. This is one of the more unusual places to visit in South Africa. It is an isolated valley, which is hidden away in the mountains, and whose residents have managed to avoid the change going on all around them. For more than 50 years these European immigrants were the forgotten people. They paid no taxes, had no schoolteachers and made their own clothes. It was only in 1963, 126 years after the first Europeans built their homes here, that a road was built connecting the valley to the outside world. Prior to this all provisions had been brought in by pack donkeys from Prince Albert.

It was during the Great Trek that farmers searching for a place free of the influence and interference of British officials decided to settle in the kloof. Amongst the last people to leave the valley were their descendants. The last farmer, Piet Swanepoel, left the valley in 1991. An account written in 1955 in Karoo, by L G Green, relates an accurate image of conditions in the valley: "Calitzdorp is the nearest village, but 'The Hell' can be reached in comfort only by helicopter. It has no road, nothing but a track for pack-donkeys. As there are only about 20 families living in the kloof, the road-makers have by-passed this solitude. You must leave your car at Matjiesvlei farm and struggle along the Gamka River banks on foot for two or three hours, sometimes knee-deep in water, to meet white people who have never seen the outside world."

Prince Albert → Colour map 7, B1.

This old village lies on the edge of the Swartberg Mountains and only 2 km from the start of the scenic Swartberg Pass. Canals from these hills bring water to the gardens, helping to give an oasis feel to the settlement. There is an old watermill on the edge of town. A few minutes walking about the village quickly gives one an impression of life at the turn of the 20th century during the hot summers of the Karoo. Fortunately, many of the homes from this period have survived in a good state of repair. Reflecting the richness of the landscape is the **Frans Pienaar** collection of fossils, one of the largest in the world, housed in the local **museum** ① *T023-541 1172, Mon-Fri 0900-1230, 1400-1700, Sat 0900-1200, Sun 0900-1030, R10, children R2.* There is also an excellent display of Victorian items, including a fully made-up bedroom of furniture, and information about the building of the Swartberg Pass. Tourist information for the area can be found next door to the **Frans Pienaar Museum** ① *Church St, T023-541 1366, www.patourism.co.za*, and there is also a super-market, some general shops and a couple of restaurants. On Saturday mornings there is an excellent market next to the museum selling home-made cheese, pickles, olives, dried fruit, bread and cakes. The town holds the annual **Olive Food and Wine Festival** on the last weekend of April with a street market, music, a half marathon, cycle races, a strongman competition and an olive spitting contest.

West of Oudtshoorn ●● ▸▸ pp299-304.

The main road through the Little Karoo to the west of Oudtshoorn is the R62, a beautiful stretch, now marketed as **Route 62**. After 52 km you reach Calitzdorp, a small farming centre. Take the old road which follows the Olifants River to visit the **Gamkaberg Nature Reserve** and **Calitzdorp Spa**. North from Calitzdorp is a gravel road to Groenfontein along the Nels River Valley. This route is narrow and full of tight bends, and should not be travelled after heavy rains in an ordinary vehicle. Eventually it joins up with the R328, Oudtshoorn– Prince Albert road. A loop back to Oudtshoorn via the Cango Caves is a possible circuit. Continuing west from Calitzdorp, the R62 crosses the Dwyka River. After 24 km is a turning north to Seven Weeks Poort. Soon after this you pass the mission stations of Amalienstein and Zoar. It is another 21 km to Ladismith. The area around Ladismith is good for hiking.

Calitzdorp → Colour map 7, B1.

Until the branch line from Oudtshoorn arrived in 1924, this settlement remained a small service stop for farmers. The village is now a successful agricultural centre and an important area for port production in South Africa. It is possible to visit a couple of port farms, and a port festival is held every May. At harvest time, fresh fruits are sold along the wide roads of the village. The village is also known for the warm healing waters at **Calitzdorp Spa**, 22 km towards Oudtshoorn on the old cement road (see above). When the first farms were established in the area, the surrounding plains were full of game. Sadly today only the early farm names survive as a reminder. The helpful **tourist office** ① *Voortrekker St, T044-213 3775, www.calitzdorp.co.za, Mon-Fri 0900-1700, Oct-Apr also open Sat-Sun 1000-1500*, has some good leaflets on the area as well as information about the wineries.

Anysberg Nature Reserve

This is one of the newer reserves in the region, reflecting the need to protect the Karoo. Created in 1988, the area covers 34,000 ha and has a rich and varied fauna and flora along with some well-preserved Khoisan paintings in the Anysberg hills. The further you explore into the wilderness, the more likely you are to see elusive wildlife such as scrub hare, black-backed jackal and the caracal. There are some spectacular gorges which are home for birds such as the black eagle and the pale chanting goshawk. During dry periods the dams provide a focal point for animals and birds. Walking is allowed but no trails have been marked out.

Ins and outs The reserve is on the northern fringe of the Little Karoo. There are two possible routes to the campsite and offices. From the north, travelling along the N1 highway between Touws River and Beaufort West, take the turning at Laingsburg. For the first 25 km the road is surfaced. Take a right turning onto a good dirt road (signposted Ladismith). After another 25 km another right turning takes you into the hills towards the nature reserve. The camp is 23 km from here. From Calitzdorp it is about 120 km to the reserve via the small settlement of Ladismith on the R323 dirt road. This is a beautiful drive as the road climbs up into the Swartberg Mountains over the Seven Weeks Poort and Garcia passes. In wet weather the gravel roads on the approach to the reserve are only suitable to 4WDs; check their status with Cape Nature before driving there.

Barrydale → Colour map 8, B3.

This is the centre of a small farming community set in a fertile valley between the Little Karoo and the Breede River Valley. It's a quiet rural town where the odd cow or sheep can occasionally be seen munching on someone's garden lawn. The surrounding farmland is a colourful mix of vineyards and wild flowers, and in the spring the hillsides are covered with mesembryanthemums. The area also produces peaches, apricots, apples and brandy. The local wine cooperative has been a great success and any meal eaten in the locality should be accompanied by their Chardonnay. For tastings visit the **Barrydale Wine Cellar** ① *on the R62 towards Montagu, T028-572 1012, www.barrydalewines.co.za, Mon-Fri 0800-1700, Sat 0900-1500*. For information contact the **Barrydale Information Office** ① *1 Van Riebeeck St, T028-572 1572, www.barrydale.co.za, Mon-Fri 0800-1600, Sat 0800-1200*.

Tradouw Pass

Running parallel to the Langeberg Mountains, the R62, or Route 62, continues west along the course of the Kingna River to Montagu, 66 km. To the south, the R324 passes over the spectacular Tradouw Pass through the Langeberg Mountains to join the N2 11 km west of Swellendam. When opened in 1873, the pass provided an important trade link for the farmers of the Little Karoo with Port Beaufort at the mouth of the Breede River. As with many civil engineering projects of the time, convict labour was used to build the road, under the direction of road engineer Thomas Bain (Bain built 13 road passes in the southern Cape in the 1800s). Halfway up the remains of the prisoners' camp can still be seen.

East of Oudtshoorn ●● ▸▸ pp299-304.

De Rust → Colour map 7, B2.

This well-preserved village 35 km from Oudtshoorn along the N12 has a number of classic Karoo homes. Surprisingly it is world renowned for its rare pelargoniums from which geraniums were first grown. If you have time, the wine farm and farm stall **Domein**

Anysberg Horse Trail

This is a gentle two-day circular horse trail through the Anysberg Nature Reserve, suitable for inexperienced riders. At first glance the horses appear to be feral as they spend their days grazing on the mountainside, but a whistle from a staff member will soon have them reporting to the tack room for duty. This is a unique experience. The trail goes through traditional Karoo countryside with the ever-present backdrop of the looming mountains. In the relative silence of clipping hooves, you are likely to get close to mammals and the big raptors that inhabit the reserve. At the overnight spot, where water is available and meals are cooked over an open fire, you sleep on a mattress under the stars in a makeshift camp next to your mount. Cooking equipment, mattresses and firewood are included in the price but you bring your own food. Everyone is responsible for their own horse, including cleaning and feeding it. Riders are restricted to a body weight of 95 kg and 5 kg of luggage. The ride is limited to six riders and costs R680 per person. Reservations through T021-659 3500, www.capenature.co.za.

Doornkraal ⓘ *T044-251 6715, Mon-Fri 0900-1700, Sat 0800-1300*, has tastings and sales, and along with Barrydale Wine Cellar and a handful of other farms in the region, is part of the **Klein Karoo Wine Route** ⓘ *www.kleinkaroowines.co.za*. Information is available from the **tourist office** ⓘ *2 Schoeman St, T044-241 2109, www.derust.org.za, Mon-Fri 0900-1600, Sat 0900-1200*, which is also a curio shop and internet café.

Continuing along the N12, the road through the **Meiringspoort Pass** in the Swartberg Mountains is worth the petrol; so too is the 60-m **Meiringspoort waterfall**. This can be reached via a short path from the car park. The road through the mountains was built by AG de Smidt, the son-in-law of the famous road builder Thomas Bain. It was opened in 1857, but because it more or less followed the course of the River Groot, it suffered considerable damage during the rains and by 1885 had been completely washed away. Funds collected at the toll gate were never sufficient to pay for repairs. The tar road still survives today along the base of the gorge, and crosses the river 30 times. The 17-km drive is one to be savoured as the vast sandstone cliffs loom above you. After the pass, the road splits; the N12 continues to Beaufort West approximately 120 km away, and the R407 eventually ends up at **Prince Albert**, 90 km away. You can then return to Oudtshoorn (72 km) via the scenic Swartberg Pass along the R328.

⚜ Little Karoo listings

For Sleeping and Eating price codes and other relevant information, see pages 46-53.

🛏 Sleeping

Oudtshoorn *p291, map p291*
For a town slightly off the main tourist trail, Oudtshoorn has a good and varied choice of accommodation. However, if you plan to stay at a guesthouse or B&B, book in advance.

AL Rosenhof Country House, 264 Baron van Rheede St, T044-272 2232, www.rosenhof.co.za. 12 a/c rooms with DSTV, swimming pool, beautiful rose garden, beauty spa, gym, jacuzzi, sauna, and there's fine food in the restaurant. Great thought and care has gone into choosing the furnishings of this restored Victorian house, and the fabrics and the ornaments create a comfortable homely atmosphere. For total privacy the 2 executive suites are 100 m from the main house and have their own pools. Recommended.

A-B Adley House, 209 Jan van Riebeeck Rd, T044-272 4533, www.adleyhouse.co.za. A comfortable B&B in a fully restored 1905 house built during the ostrich boom, set in large grounds a short distance from the town centre. 14 rooms, all with, M-Net TV, minibar, heaters in winter, home-made bread at breakfast and excellent 3-course evening meals available, 2 swimming pools. Recommended.

B Hlangana Lodge, 51 North St, T044-272 2299, www.hlangana.co.za. An excellent lodge with 19 rooms in a pretty, low building surrounded by palm-filled gardens, a/c, TV, safe, minibar, saltwater pool, free car wash, attentive and friendly hosts. The expansive breakfast buffets (including ostrich sausage) will keep you going all day. Recommended.

B Riempie Estate Protea, Baron van Rheede St, 3 km from town centre, T044-272 6161, www.riempieestate.co.za, www.protea hotels.co.za. Mix of thatched rondavels and double chalets surrounded by farmland, 40 rooms in total, with a/c and tea and coffee stations, 1 with roll-in shower for wheelchair users. The restaurant offers tasty country cuisine, the thatched bar has a cosy fireplace, and the swimming pool is in mature shady gardens.

B Queen's Hotel, 5 Baron van Rheede St (next to **CP Nel Museum**), T044-272 2101, www.queenshotel.co.za. Historic hotel set in tidy gardens in the centre of town, with 40 a/c stylish and comfortable rooms with antique furniture. Good restaurant on 1st floor with balcony, which serves a buffet lunch on Sun and some interesting South African dishes, swimming pool, tennis courts, curio shop, laundry service and secure parking. A comfortable and friendly hotel which is owned and run by the Barrow family. Good value with discounts during quiet periods. Recommended.

B Shades of Africa, 238 Jan van Riebeeck Rd, T044-272 6430, www.shades.co.za. A new building which has been decorated with some fine examples of African art and

textiles, with 4 very stylish double rooms by the swimming pool set in indigenous gardens, a/c, TV, wireless internet, country or vegetarian breakfasts, use of the kitchen, bar, no children under 12.

C La Pension, 169 Church St, T044-279 2445, www.lapension.co.za. Well-furnished guest-house set in a lovely large garden with shady fruit trees, with 4 B&B rooms in the Cape Dutch-style house built in 1914, plus 1 family self-catering unit, and one 2-bed self-catering garden cottage, TV, sauna, swimming pool.

C-D Bisibee, 171 Church St, T044-272 4784, www.bisibee.co.za. Large colonial home with 5 rooms, and another 6 units in the garden full of mature trees, swimming pool, braai, Wi-Fi, very friendly hosts, breakfast and evening meals extra and must be pre-booked.

D Kleinplaas Holiday Resort, 171 Baron van Rheede St, T044-272 5811, www.kleinplaas. co.za. 56 simple brick-built fully equipped self-catering chalets sleeping 2-6 people, each with M-Net TV, own braai and carport, plus caravan and camping pitches with plenty of shade and electric points. Swimming pool, shop, laundry, and break-fast room for full buffet breakfasts (extra) if you don't want to prepare your own.

D-E Backpacker's Paradise, 148 Baron van Rheede St, T044-272 3436, www.back packersparadise.hostel.com. Spotless lodge set over 4 houses, with a mix of dorms and en suite doubles, camping, volleyball court, well-stocked kitchen, pub with pool table, nightly ostrich braais, splash pool, internet, within walking distance of shops, free town pickup, and a daily pickup from the Baz Bus in George. Plenty of activities can be organized from here including bike hire. Recommended.

E-F Oasis Shanti, 3 Church St, T044-279 1163, www.oasisshanti.com. Clean and quiet hostel with a good range of rooms, including singles, doubles, triples and uncrowded dorms (bedding provided but not towels) as well as some space for camping. Swimming pool with braai area, ostrich-egg breakfasts, nightly ostrich braais and also vegetarian meals, TV lounge, kitchen, internet, good travel advice especially about hiking in the region.

Around Oudtshoorn p293
A Altes Landhaus, 13 km north of Oudtshoorn towards the Cango Caves, T044-272 6112, www.alteslandhaus.co.za. Award-winning guesthouse in a Cape Dutch homestead, 10 en suite double rooms, some with a/c and TV. Each room is decorated with antiques and has its own special character, evening meals with fine wines available on request, salt pool in garden with pool bar, German spoken. Recommended.

B De Opstal, 12 km north of Oudtshoorn off the road to Cango Caves, T044-279 2954, www.deopstal.co.za. A working ostrich farm that offers tours. 20 rooms, some of which are converted farm buildings and stables circa 1830 with plenty of character, some have a/c and/or fireplaces, swimming pool with sun loungers, restaurant and bar. Check first there's not a wedding on.

C Oue Werf, 13 km north of Oudtshoorn, T044-272 8712, www.ouewerf.co.za. Old 1857 farmhouse with 8 comfortable en suite rooms with private entrance, TV, a/c, swimming pool, boating on farm dam, 4-course evening meals on request; an ideal base from which to explore the area.

D Cango Mountain Resort, 7 km before Cango Caves is a turning off the R328, the resort is 3 km down the road (the road follows the Oude Murasie Valley and can be followed all the way to De Rust, see page 298), T044-272 4506, www.cangomountainresort.co.za. A large resort with 21 fully equipped self-catering 4-6 bed chalets with TV, 70 caravan and 40 camping sites, electric points, shop and 3 swimming pools, one of which is suitable for children. A peaceful spot next to the Koos Raubenheimer Dam, where there are some pleasant braai spots among the oak trees.

Swartberg Nature Reserve p296
Efforts have been made by **Cape Nature Conservation** to restore some of the houses scattered throughout the Gamkaskloof Valley, also known as 'The Hell'. Reservations, T021-659 3500, www.capenature.co.za.

Self-catering cottages
These cottages (**D**) sleeping 4-8 are very good value for families or groups. For a detailed description of each cottage, and a little bit of history about the individual former residents, check out www.cape nature.co.za. Each has solar lighting, gas stoves and fridges but no electricity. Bedding and cooking and eating equipment are provided but you need to bring food and towels. Rates are higher at the weekends.

Camping
There are 10 camping sites with a braai and cold showers, tents only, caravans cannot access here. You can swim in the Gamka River. All-round recommended for a rustic and remote few days.

Prince Albert p297
Although there is little choice, this is an ideal base for the many hiking trails in the area.
B-C Saxe-Coburg Lodge, 60 Church St, T023-541 1267, www.saxecoburg.co.za. A well-preserved Victorian house with 4 a/c rooms and 5 cottages in the garden, honeymoon room has spa bath and swimming pool. The pub lounge is a relaxing place to end the day by the fire. Richard and Regina can offer advice on hiking. French and German spoken.

C Dennehof, 5 mins from the village on the R328, T023-541 1227, www.dennehof.co.za. Large garden with views of the Swartberg, swimming in the summer months in a country dam. The main house, a well-preserved Cape Dutch farmhouse, the oldest in the village, has 3 en suite rooms, there's 2 garden cottages and the farm's wagon shed has been converted into the honeymoon suite, evening meals on request. The friendly and helpful hosts, who are also tour guides, can arrange tours to 'The Hell'. Recommended.

C Swartberg Hotel, 77 Church St, T023-541 1332, www.swartberg.co.za. 13 rooms plus 5 garden rondavels, delightful restored Victorian home, over 150 years old, with antiques, restaurant, South African dishes a speciality, bar with roaring fire in the winter, swimming pool. Recommended.

Calitzdorp p297
C Port Wine Guest House, 7 Queen St, T044-213 3131, www.portwine.net. A smart guesthouse in a historic Cape thatched building from the 1830s surrounded by vines. 8 en suite double rooms with a complimentary decanter of port, 4-poster beds and open fires, 1 room accessible for wheelchairs, swimming pool, evening meals available on request taken under the vines. The owners can tell you all you need to know about the region. If you have the time, try to arrange a visit to their ostrich farm. Recommended.
D Welgevonden Guest House, St Helena Rd, T044-213 3642, www.welgevondenguest house.co.za. A peaceful country guesthouse. 4 rooms with chintzy furnishings and en suite bathrooms, communal lounge and kitchenette. Lush gardens, swimming pool, part of a Chardonnay farm, enjoy the comfort of a family home, evening meals by arrangement.

Anysberg Nature Reserve p298
D Anysberg Cottages, reservations through Cape Nature Conservation T021-659 3500, www.capenature.co.za. 5 restored labourer's cottages with no electricity, light is from candles and lamps, gas fridge, basic kitchen, braai, and communal ablution block, bedding is provided but bring towels and food. This is where the Anysberg horse trails start (see box, page 299).

Camping
A grassy area under the shade of eucalyptus trees near the office has 2 caravan/camping sites with ablution block.

Barrydale p298
B Rietfontein Guest Farm, off the R62 between Barrydale and Ladismith, 12 km from the main road, T028-551 2128, www.rietfontein.co.za. Lovely rural retreat set in the foothills of the Touwsberg Mountains on a working apricot, port wine, almond and olive farm, 5 self-catering cottages sleeping 5-6, well furnished and equipped, just bring food and drink, the swimming pool pump is powered by solar energy.
D Dandelion Guest House, 12 Van Riebeeck St, T028-572 1539, jberry@mweb.co.za. Delightful Cape Dutch-style thatched cottage with outside wooden stairs to rooms in the roof, 2 comfortable but tiny en suite rooms with lots of character, 1 garden rondavel, swimming pool, B&B, evening meals on request.

De Rust p298
B De Gat, 7 km from De Rust on the R341, T044-241 2406, www.diegat.co.za. B&B with 5 en suite rooms in garden units separate from the main house, which is a lovely farm homestead dating back to around 1800 and a national monument. It's also possible to sleep overnight in the ox wagon. Traditional Karoo dinners on request. There's a swimming pool and Anton can take guests out on the farm by landrover for a bush braai.
B Housemartin Guest Lodge, 6 Kerk St, T044-241 2214, www.housemartin.co.za. 12 smart modern B&B rooms in the garden of a 110-year old Victorian house, with under-floor heating, private verandas, complimentary port and home-made biscuits, pool and the very good **Plough** restaurant (see Eating page 303). The owners are avid birdwatchers and will advise on what species can be seen in the region.
D Olivier's Rust, 9 Schoeman St, T044-241 2258, www.derust.org.za. 8 self-catering, fully equipped modern brick chalets sleeping 2-4, garden, pool, braai area, attached **Herrie's** coffee shop where you can get a light meal until 2100 and home-made bread.

🍴 Eating

Oudtshoorn *p291, map p291*
Most of the hotels have their own bar and restaurant, which tend to stay open a little later than the restaurants in town.
🍴🍴 Colony, **Queen's Hotel**, 5 Baron van Rheede St, T044-279 2414, www.queens hotel.co.za. Open 1800-2300. Excellent restaurant set in this historic hotel. Menu has a very wide range of local dishes, such as Karoo lamb, springbok steak and ostrich. Balcony overlooking the main street, good atmosphere and service, crisp white linen and bar with fireplace. Recommended.
🍴 The Godfather, 61 Voortrekker Rd, T044-272 5404. Mon-Sat 1800-2300. Good game menu with springbok steaks and ostrich, plus pizza and good Italian fare, tasty meals but a little more expensive than elsewhere. The bar here is also a good place for a nightcap.
🍴 Headlines, Baron van Rheede St, T044-272 3434. Mon-Sat 0830-1500, 1745-2300, Sun 1100-1500. Coffee shop and restaurant decorated in an odd mixture of sports and railway memorabilia specializing in ostrich dishes of all kinds from ostrich-egg omelettes to ostrich-liver pâté. The Bushmen kebab is a favourite, with ostrich, venison, crocodile, pork/beef fillet and chicken all on one skewer.
🍴 Kalinka, 93 Baron van Rheede St, T044-279 2596. Open 1800-late. A fine menu served in a cosy converted sandstone town house with a clutch of small dining rooms. Variety of ostrich dishes including good steaks, plus dishes with an unusual twist like caviar pancakes or mussels in coconut broth.
🍴 Paljas, 109 Baron van Rheede St, T044-272 0982. Open 1700-2300. Pan-African cuisine, a good selection of Cape Malay curries, Karoo roasts, West Coast seafood, and a few unusual Zulu and Xhosa dishes, extensive wine list, a good place to try a 3-course meal with a lot of different flavours. Interesting African-style decor and a sting quartet plays in the background. Recommended.

Calitzdorp *p297*
🍴 Rose of the Karoo, 21 Voortrekker Rd, T044-213 3133, www.roseofthekaroo.co.za. Mon-Sat 0700-2200. A group of buildings surrounding a vine-covered courtyard with a cosy restaurant with fireplace open all day until 2200 for freshly home-cooked food and famous for their chicken pie and rosemary lamb. Pick up home-made preserves and dried fruit in the delicatessen, and there's a curio shop, and 2 overnight family en suite rooms sleeping 4 (**D**) with fridge and kettle.

Barrydale *p298*
🍴 Jam Tarts, on the R62 as it goes through town, T028-572 1173. Open 0830-1630. Attached to an eccentric gift shop and fashioned from a former petrol station, **Jam Tarts** sells home-made jams and deli products including chilli jam and olive bread. The varied day time menu includes Spanish omelettes, Moroccan dishes, organic salads, and good thin-based pizzas.

De Rust *p298*
🍴 The Plough, **Housemartin Guest Lodge**, see Sleeping, page 302. Tue-Sat 0800-1100, 1200-1500, 1800-2100, Sun 0800-1100, 1200-1500. A good spot for Karoo lamb and traditional dishes, fresh salads and vegetables, old-fashioned sticky desserts and excellent farm-style breakfasts from a full English to a bowl of highland oats with brown sugar, fresh cream and a tot of whiskey! It's run by Christina Martin who has a cooking school so cooking and service is provided by her students.

🛍 Shopping

Oudtshoorn *p291, map p291*
Baron van Rheede St is lined with curio shops selling every ostrich by-product imaginable, from expensive leather purses to feather dusters and tacky enamelled eggs. One such emporium is **Bushmen's Curios**, 76 Baron van Rheede St, T044-272 4497, www.bushmancurios.co.za.

▲ Activities and tours

Oudtshoorn *p291, map p291*
Backpacker's Paradise, 148 Baron van
Rheede St, T044-272 3436, www.backpackers
paradise.hostel.com. Plenty of activities can
be organized from this backpacker hostel.
Mountain biking to the Swartberg Pass
leaves daily at 0830: you are driven to
the top and enjoy the long ride downhill.
On the way back to Oudtshoorn, you
can stop at the Cango Caves and all the
other attractions along the R328. They
can also organize overnight trips to the
'The Hell', wine tastings and cave trips.
TBI Adventures, 56 St Saviour St, T082-
926 9389, www.tbiadventures.co.za. Local
company that can arrange a number of
activities in the Swartberg region, including
quad-biking and mountain biking through
the Swartberg Pass, abseiling, hiking
and kloofing.

⊖ Transport

Oudtshoorn *p291, map p291*
It's 172 km to **Beaufort West**, 510 km
to **Cape Town**, 60 km to **George**, 245 km
to **Montagu**, 93 km to **Mossel Bay**.

Bus
Translux buses depart Queen's Riverside Mall.
Daily to **Knysna** (2 hrs), **Johannesburg** and
Tshwane (Pretoria) (14 hrs) via **Kimberley**
(7 hrs) or via **Bloemfontein** (5 hrs). Intercape
run a daily service to **Johannesburg** and
Pretoria (14 hrs) via **Kimberley** (7 hrs) or via
Bloemfontein (5 hrs).

Bus companies All bus tickets can be
booked online at www.computicket.com.
Greyhound, www.greyhound.co.za;
Intercape, www.intercape.co.za; and
Translux, www.translux.co.za. For more
information, see Getting around, page 41.

⊙ Directory

Oudtshoorn *p291, map p291*
Banks Branches of the major banks
are along High St or Baron van Rheede St.
Medical services Private hospital,
Medi-Clinic, 185 Church St, T044-272
0111, www.kleinkaroomc.co.za.

Contents

Footprint features

Garden Route

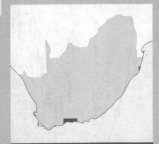

At a glance

⊜ **Getting around** Buses and Baz Bus on major routes, car hire, tours start and finish in Cape Town.

⊚ **Time required** 3-5 days.

☼ **Weather** Chilly Jul and Aug, reasonably pleasant rest of the year.

⊗ **When not to go** Christmas and Easter South African school holidays.

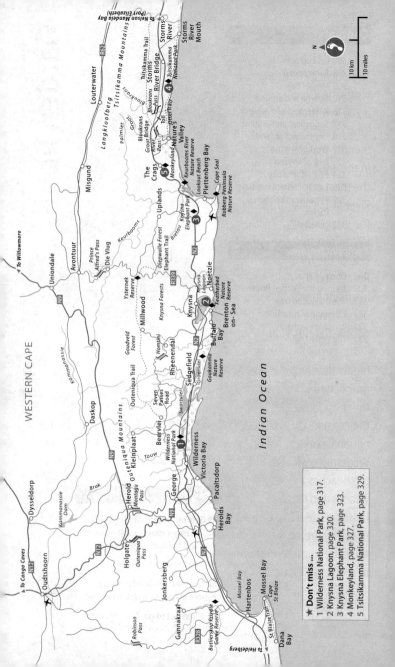

WESTERN CAPE

To Willowmore
To Cango Caves

To Nelson Mandela Bay (Port Elizabeth)

To Heidelberg

Indian Ocean

N

10 km
10 miles

★ Don't miss ...
1 Wilderness National Park, page 317.
2 Knysna Lagoon, page 320.
3 Knysna Elephant Park, page 323.
4 Monkeyland, page 327.
5 Tsitsikamma National Park, page 329.

Dysseldorp
Oudtshoorn
Kammanassie Dam
Daskop
Kommanassie
Uniondale
Avontuur
Louterwater
Misgund
Langkloofberg
Tsitsikamma Mountains

Mossel Bay
Cape St Blaize
Hartenbos
Dana Bay
Mossel Bay
Gannakraal
Robinson Pass
Botlierskop Private Game Reserve
Jonkersberg
Holgate
Outeniqua Pass
Herolds Bay
Pacaltsdorp
George
Montagu Pass
Herold
Kleinplaat
Bedrvlei
Outeniqua Mountains
Seven Passes Road
Outeniqua Trail
Swartvlei
Touw
Victoria Bay
Wilderness
Wilderness National Park
Rheenendal
Horipi
Goudveld Forest
Millwood
Knysna Forests
Ysternek Reserve
Prince Alfred's Pass
Die Vlug
Keurbooms
Sedgefield
Groenvlei
Goukamma Nature Reserve
Buffalo Bay
Brenton-on-Sea
Knysna Lagoon
Knysna
Featherbed Nature Reserve
Noetzie
R339
Diepwalle Forest
Elephant Trail
Bitou
Kranshoek
Elephant Park
Uplands
The Crags
Monkeyland
Nature's Valley
Keurbooms River Nature Reserve
Lookout Beach
Plettenberg Bay
Robberg Peninsula Nature Reserve
Cape Seal
Great River
Groot River Pass
Bloukrans Pass
Bloukrans River Bridge
Toll
Tsitsikamma Trail
Storms River Bridge
Tsitsikamma National Park
Storms River
Storms River Mouth

R62
N9
N12
N2
R328

The Garden Route is probably South Africa's most celebrated area, a stretch of coast heralded as one of the country's highlights. The publicity it receives has made it hugely popular and few visitors to Cape Town miss it. The area is undeniably beautiful: a 200-km stretch of rugged coast backed by mountains, with long stretches of sand, nature reserves, leafy forests and tourist-friendly seaside towns. Officially the route runs from Heidelberg in the west to the Tsitsikamma National Park in the east, though the most popular stretch is the coast from Mossel Bay to Storms River in Tsitsikamma National Park. The region is separated from the interior by the Tsitsikamma and Outeniqua mountain ranges. In contrast to the dry and treeless area of the Karoo on the interior side of the mountains, rain falls all year round on the Garden Route, and the ocean-facing mountain slopes are covered with luxuriant forests. It is this dramatic change in landscape, which occurs over a distance of no more than 20 km, that prompted people to refer to the area as the Garden Route.

The larger towns, such as Plettenberg Bay and Knysna, are highly developed tourist resorts, while other areas offer untouched wilderness and wonderful hikes, including one of the most famous in the country, the Otter Trail. This runs along the coast in Tsitsikamma National Park, one of the most popular national parks in South Africa. There is a second national park, Wilderness, which is also very popular. If hiking isn't your scene, the beaches are stunning, offering a mix of peaceful seaside villages and livelier surfer spots, and there are various attractions hugging the N2 to distract the motorist. Finally, the Garden Route is coming into its own as an adventure destination and there are numerous activities on offer from bungee jumping to mountain biking.

Ins and outs

Getting there

The most direct route from Cape Town to the Garden Route is along the N2, and it's an easy 365-km drive and you may break your journey in the attractive town of Swellendam for at least lunch. Alternatively, there is the option of travelling from Cape Town away from the N2 via either the Whale Route or Breede River Valley/Route 62 if you have the extra time. See the Western Cape chapter for details.

Getting around

To get the most out of the Garden Route you really need a car, and whilst it's quite easy to drive the full length of the Garden Route in a day, most visitors either choose a base for exploring the area, or spend a day or two in several places of interest along the way. Many of the attractions are in between the major resorts so it's good to have the flexibility to stop when you want. ▶ *For touring the Garden Route on public transport, see box, page 309, and Transport, page 349.*

Best time to visit

The area's popularity means that good-value accommodation is difficult to find, and gets booked up months in advance, especially during peak season. It is advisable to avoid the area during the two weeks over Christmas and the New Year, and at Easter. For the rest of the school holidays most of the self-catering accommodation will still be fully booked, but bed and breakfasts or hostels should have a free room – call in advance to be sure. For more information about the Garden Route visit www.gardenroute.co.za or www.garden route.org.za. ▶ *For listings, see pages 332-352.*

Background

Travelling along the coast, the vegetation is lush and green compared to the interior, but this hides the fact that the majority of the Knysna and Tsitsikamma forest was completely destroyed by the early settlers. What remains today is only a small fraction of the indigenous forest, and this is threatened by the encroachment of alien species. The recent history of the region is closely linked with the search for timber for the growing population in the Cape. It only took a few years for the small patches of forest in Hout Bay, Rondebosch, Newlands and Kirstenbosch to be depleted, and the first white colonists to reach Mossel Bay in 1711 came looking for wood. During the 1850s the forests around the Humansdorp area were exploited, but it was not until a road was cut through to the Keurbooms River in 1867 that the Tsitsikamma forest came under threat.

In 1880, Comte De Vasselot de Regne, a French forestry scientist of international repute, introduced the idea of preserving the indigenous forest. However, it wasn't until 1938, when all remaining woodcutters were pensioned off, that over-exploitation ceased to be a problem. The first exotic species were planted in 1891; red gum and cluster pine were planted near Bloukrans to replace sections of the forest damaged by the great fire. The supply of timber for the industry is now based entirely upon fast-growing exotic species such as slash pine, monterey pine, karri gum and Australian blackwood. However, these species are having a negative effect on indigenous species – their fast water absorption has starved other trees, in effect suffocating indigenous species. Some areas have started to remove the exotic aliens in order to control the problem. Today only

Touring the Garden Route

If you don't want to self drive, there are a number of other options for exploring the Garden Route. **Baz Bus**, T021-439 2323, www.bazbus.com, offers a very adequate service and drops and picks up at Garden Route hostels every day. Mainline buses operate a daily service, but most departures and arrivals are in the middle of the night and it's not as economical as the Baz Bus.

For those on a budget and short of time, the **Bok Bus**, T082-320 1979, www.bokbus.com, is a comprehensive award-winning five-day tour of all the major attractions along the Garden Route starting and finishing in Cape Town. The tour visits most of the

adventure activities (optional extras) and accommodation is in hostels or you can upgrade to guesthouses. Prices start at R4450 and include breakfasts, most dinners and entrance fees. There are numerous other coach and minibus operators running short tours from Cape Town along the Garden Route that appeal to a wide range of age groups and offer a variety of accommodation alternatives. These include: **African Eagle**, T021-464 4266, www.daytours.co.za; **Cape Rainbow**, T021-551 5465, www.caperainbow.com; **Eco-Tours**, T021-788 5741, www.ecotours sa.co.za; and **Springbok Atlas**, T021-460 4700, www.springbokatlas.co.za.

65,000 ha of the original forest remain along the Garden Route, most of which is in Tsitsikamma National Park and around Knysna.

Mossel Bay ⊙⊙⊘⊙▲⊙⊙ ▸ pp332-352. Colour map 7, B2.

Built along a rocky peninsula which provides sheltered swimming and mooring in the bay, Mossel Bay is one of the larger and less appealing seaside towns along the Garden Route. During the school holidays the town is packed – it receives one million domestic visitors in December alone – but for the rest of the year it is just another dull coastal town. A fact often overlooked in promotional literature is that since the discovery of offshore oil deposits, Mossel Bay is also the home of the ugly Mossgas natural gas refinery and a multitude of oil storage tanks. The town has a number of Portuguese flags and names dotted around, thanks to the first European to anchor in the bay – Bartolomeu Dias, who landed in February 1488. His efforts to communicate with local herdsmen were met with stone throwing, but Vasco da Gama, who moored in the bay in 1497, had more luck; he managed to establish trading relations with them. The bay's safe anchorage and freshwater spring ensured that it became a regular stopping-off point for other seafarers. The town was named by a Dutch trader, Cornelis de Houtman, who in 1595 found a pile of mussel shells in a cave below the present lighthouse.

Ins and outs

Getting there All mainline buses stop at the Shell Truck Stop at Voorbaai, on the N2 7 km from Mossel Bay. The **Baz Bus** is the only service that goes right into town.

Tourist information **Mossel Bay Tourism Bureau** ① *corner of Church and Market streets, T044-691 1067, www.visitmosselbay.co.za, Mon-Fri 0800-1800, Sat-Sun 0900-1700,* provides information and acts as a central reservations office for accommodation. Cage diving to see great white sharks is possible in Mossel Bay; see page 347.

Sights

Many of the local attractions relate to the sea and reflect the bay's importance to early Portuguese navigators and Dutch explorers. All the museums are on one site known as the **Bartolomeu Dias Museum Complex** ① *T044-691 1067, www.diasmuseum.co.za, Mon-Fri 0900-1645, Sat-Sun 0900-1545, R25, children (under 12) R8.* Here you'll find the Culture Museum, the Shell Museum, an Aquarium, the Maritime Museum, some Malay graves, and the original freshwater spring that attracted the early sailors and which still flows into a small dam. There's also a tea shop on site in a restored 1830s cottage. The displays in the Maritime Museum are arranged around a full-size replica of Bartolomeu Dias's caravel. Also here is a tree with a fascinating past, the **Post Office Tree**, a giant milkwood situated close to the freshwater spring. History relates that in 1500 a letter was left under the tree by a ship's captain. A year later it was retrieved by the commander of the Third East India Fleet en route to India. Messages were also left carved in rocks and left in old boots tied to the branches. The tree has been declared a national monument and it is still possible to send a postcard home from here – all mail dispatched from the Post Office Tree is franked with a special commemorative stamp and makes a great souvenir. The Outeniqua Choo-Tjoe steam train now stops at the station (see page 314).

In the middle of the bay is **Seal Island** which can be visited by cruises departing from the harbour. The island is inhabited by colonies of African penguins and Cape fur seals (the best month to see seal pups is November). It's also possible to see great white sharks

Mossel Bay

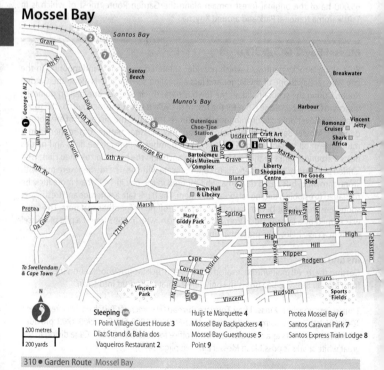

Sleeping
1 Point Village Guest House **3**
Diaz Strand & Bahia dos
 Vaqueiros Restaurant **2**
Huijs te Marquette **4**
Mossel Bay Backpackers **4**
Mossel Bay Guesthouse **5**
Point **9**
Protea Mossel Bay **6**
Santos Caravan Park **7**
Santos Express Train Lodge **8**

and small hammerhead sharks which prey upon the seals. Between September and November the warm waters of the bay are often visited by southern right, humpback and brydes whales while calving. Another vantage point for viewing whales and dolphins is **The Point** at the end of Marsh Street. Close by is the 20-m high **St Blaize Lighthouse** ① *Mon-Fri 1000-1500, R14, children (under 12) R7, for details on sleeping in the lighthouse see box, page 49*, built in 1864, one of only two remaining continuously manned lighthouses in South Africa.

St Blaize Trail

The St Blaize Trail is a perfect introduction to the stunning coastline that you are likely to encounter along the Garden Route. This is a 13.5-km walk along the cliffs and rocky coast west from Mossel Bay. The official trail starts from Bats Cave, just below the lighthouse; the path is marked by the white image of a bird in flight. As you walk further from the town the scenery becomes more and more spectacular. You can leave the coast at Pinnacle Point, and follow a path inland to Essenhout Street. This cuts about 5 km off the walk. The path ends by a group of houses in Dana Bay. From here you will have to organize your own transport back into town, so it helps to have a mobile phone to call a taxi from Mossel Bay. A helpful map is available from the tourism office. You are rightly warned to be careful in places during strong winds, as there are some precipitous and unprotected drops from the cliff tops. Some years ago Khoi-San articles dating back 80,000 years were discovered in **Cape St Blaize Cave**, also known as Bats Cave, which are now in the museum. You can visit the cave, where this a boardwalk, some reproduction Khoi-San huts, and restaurant with open deck.

Botlierskop Private Game Reserve

① *T044-696 6055, www.botlierskop.co.za. To get there turn off the N2 on to the R401 to the northeast of Mossel Bay, the Klein Brakrivier turn-off, and follow signs for 25 km.*
This private reserve is situated on a 2400-ha game farm, which is home to 24 different species of animals and a wide variety of birds. A former farm, Botlierskop was bought in 1996, and the new owners saw the opportunity to reintroduce wildlife in this area. After four years of recovering from domestic farming, it was opened in 2000. The land has been restocked and wildlife includes the rare black impala, rhino, elephant, lion, buffalo, giraffe, mountain zebra and eland. Activities include game drives, nature walks, picnics and helicopter flips (rides). The most exciting activity is elephant riding and expect to pay in the region of R550, no children under six. The two elephants are orphans who survived a

Mossel Bay

Huckle
Daley
Bland
Lower Cross
Marsh
Upper Cross
Montagu
Khoof
Beach
Mui
Lazaretto Cemetery
Lazaretto
Point
St Blaize Lighthouse
Bats Cave
Cape St Blaize
The Point

Indian Ocean

Eating ⑦
Café Gannet **4**
Jazzbury's **5**
Kingfisher & Delfino's **6**

Pavilion **7**
Stonehill **1**

culling program in the Zambezi Valley in Zimbabwe. There is luxurious accommodation available (see Sleeping, page 333) or you can visit for the day, though booking is essential. Check out the website for prices and programmes.

George and around 🔊🏨🍴⛰🏖 ▸▸ pp332-352. Colour map 7, B2.

Often referred to as the gateway to, or the capital of, the Garden Route, George owes its status to the fact that it has an airport. It is also an important junction between the N2 coastal highway and the N9 passing through the Outeniqua Pass into the Karoo. It lies in the shadow of the Outeniqua Mountains, but unlike the majority of towns along the Garden Route, it is not by the sea. The town itself is a mostly modern grid of streets interspersed with some attractive old buildings and churches. While it is pleasant enough, it has little appeal compared to other towns along the coast; the main reason overseas visitors come here is to play golf. George has several outstanding golf courses and received worldwide attention in November 2003 when it hosted the President's Cup Golf Tournament. More recently it hosted the inaugural Women's World Cup of Golf.

Ins and outs

Getting there **George Airport** is 10 km from the town centre, T044-876 9310, www.acsa. co.za. It was fully upgraded in 2007 and now features banks, ATMs and restaurants. The main car rental companies have desks in the terminal building.

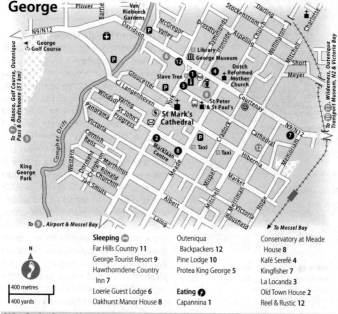

George

Sleeping 🛌
Far Hills Country 11
George Tourist Resort 9
Hawthorndene Country
Inn 7
Loerie Guest Lodge 6
Oakhurst Manor House 8
Outeniqua
Backpackers 12
Pine Lodge 10
Protea King George 5

Eating 🍴
Capannina 1

Conservatory at Meade
House 8
Kafé Serefé 4
Kingfisher 7
La Locanda 3
Old Town House 2
Reel & Rustic 12

The milkwood tree

Four white milkwood (*Sideroxylon inerme*) trees in South Africa have been proclaimed as national monuments. All milkwoods are protected to such an extent that a permit is required before an individual can even prune a tree on his or her land. Their name is derived from the milky latex found in the fruit and the bark. The flowers have a very distinctive smell which attracts insects, which in turn attract birds. The trees also bear fruit which, when ripe, turns a purple colour and is eaten by birds and baboons. These beautiful shade trees are found all along the Pacific coast in many shapes and sizes. In the harshest of conditions they may only grow into a shrub-like bush; the largest tree is on

a farm near Bredasdorp: it has a spread of 20 m, a trunk girth of over 3 m, and is thought to be over 1000 years old. The most famous specimen is the Post Office Tree in Mossel Bay which must be at least 500 years old. Milkwoods were one of the species that early settlers singled out for commercial use: their wood is hard and durable and was used for building boats, bridges and homes. These days the threat to their survival comes from alien vegetation in the forests. During a bush fire, alien plants burn fiercely and any milkwoods close by may die as a result of the intensity of the heat. Thick alien growth also prevents the germination of milkwood seeds and the growth of the saplings.

Tourist information There's a very helpful **Tourism Bureau** ⓘ *124 York St, T044-801 9295, www.tourismgeorge.co.za, Mon-Fri 0800-1700, Sat 0900-1300*, with a wide range of information on the Garden Route. But, like many offices along the Garden Route, they only promote accommodation which pays a fee to the office.

Background

The first settlement appeared here in 1778 as a forestry post to process wood from the surrounding forests. In 1811 it was formally declared a town, and named after King George III. It was at this time that its wide tree-lined streets – Courtenay, York and Meade – were laid out. For the next 80 years the town remained the centre for a voracious timber industry. Much of the indigenous forest was destroyed supplying wood for wagons, railway sleepers and mine props. Some of the trees, which are endemic to South Africa, came to be known as **stinkwoods** because of their odour when freshly cut. Few remain today, although they are slow growing back.

Sights

Within the town itself there are only a few sights of interest. On the corner of Cathedral and York streets, **St Mark's Cathedral**, consecrated in 1850, has an unusually large number of stained-glass windows for its size; many were designed by overseas artists of limited fame. In 1911 a bible and royal prayer book were given to the church by King George V. The interior of the **Dutch Reformed Mother Church** at the north end of Meade Street reflects the town's early history as a centre for the timber industry. The pulpit is carved out of stinkwood and took over a year to create. The ceiling was built from yellowwood, and six yellowwood trunks were used as pillars. The mountains create an impressive backdrop to the church when viewed from the corner of Courtenay and Meade streets.

Outeniqua Choo-Tjoe

Until 2006, the most enjoyable way to travel between George and Knysna was on the Outeniqua Choo-Tjoe, a historic steam train. This picturesque branch line was opened in 1928 and the 67-km journey gave passengers an extraordinary view of some spectacular coastal scenery and forests, passing through Wilderness National Park and along the Goukamma Valley. The journey ended by crossing Knysna Lagoon via a long bridge. Unfortunately, landslides caused by bad weather in August 2006, damaged the line beyond repair and it is now closed.

However, it still runs on an alternative line between George and the Dias Museum Complex in Mossel Bay and now follows a scenic route traversing the farmlands outside George with the Outeniqua Mountain in the background, before descending to the Indian Ocean. It runs every day except Sunday from 1 April and 30 September, and on Friday only between 1 May and 31 August. The train departs from the Railway Museum in George at 1000, gets to Mossel Bay at 1200, leaves again at 1415 and arrives back in George at 1615; return R140, children (3-12) R70, children under 3 free; one-way R110, children (3-12) R60, children under 3 free. Reservations and information, George Railway Museum, T044-801 8288.

In front of the tourist office, housed in the King Edward VII library, is an ancient oak tree known as the **Slave Tree**. It is one of the original trees planted by Adrianus van Kervel in the early 1800s and has been declared a national monument. The tree acquired its name because of the chain embedded in the trunk with a lock attached to it. The story of the chain can be traced back to when a public tennis court was in use next to the library (now the information office), and the court roller was secured to the tree to prevent playful children from rolling it down the street. Housed in the old Drostdy, the **George Museum** ① *Courtenay St, T044-702 3523, Mon-Fri 0900-1630, Sat 0900-1230, small entry fee, coffee shop*, has displays on the timber industry as well as musical instruments and a collection of old printing presses. In the Sayer's Wing is an exhibition devoted to former President PW Botha, who was a member of parliament for George for 38 years. The **Outeniqua Transport Museum** ① *2 Mission Rd, just off Knysna Rd, T044-801 8288, Mon-Sat 0800-1700, R20, children (3-12) R10*, has an interesting display outlining the history of steam train travel including 13 steam locomotives, a 1947 Royal Mail coach, and a room dedicated to model railways, as well as a collection of vintage cars and flight memorabilia. It is adjacent to the new platform from which the **Outeniqua steam train** departs (see box, above).

Victoria Bay → *Colour map 7, B2.*

If you are based in George and wish to spend a quiet day by the sea, this small resort is only 9 km or 15 minutes' drive away. Victoria Bay, 2 km off the N2, is an excellent place to surf during the winter. It has a narrow cove with a broad sandy beach, a grassy sunbathing area, and a safe tidal pool for children. There's only one row of houses with some of the best-positioned guesthouses in the region.

Little Karoo and Montagu Pass

The N2 continues from George to Wilderness, but if you have been travelling along the coast from Cape Town, a short diversion into the Little Karoo is well worth the effort. Starting in George, the most direct route is the N9 via the **Outeniqua Pass**. Having reached the summit (799 m) it quickly becomes apparent why the narrow coastal belt is referred to as the Garden Route. The dry, undulating terrain is in stark contrast to the lush coastal region, no more than 15 km away. From the top of the pass it is 35 km to **Oudtshoorn**, the capital of the Little Karoo, known for its ostrich farms and the **Cango Caves** (see page 294).

Returning from Oudtshoorn, an alternative and scenic route through the mountains is via **Montagu Pass**, the fourth pass over the Outeniqua range. It was opened in 1847 and took over four years to complete. Travelling on the N12 from Oudtshoorn, look out for a left turn just before the road starts to climb up to Outeniqua Pass. This is the N9 and will be signposted to Uniondale and Willowmore. After several kilometres, look out for a right turn for Herold and Montagu Pass. Before the road starts to climb it goes through a fertile valley full of hops and fruit trees. The area is ideal for hop growing since it is sheltered from strong winds and rarely has hail. Harvest time is during February and March. This road is gravel so take care after rain. For much of the route there is a low stone wall along the side of the road, and several stretches are single track. Fortunately, very little local traffic uses this road. Near the summit the road passes under a narrow bridge – the railway line linking George with Oudtshoorn – an amazing engineering feat when you look out across the valley below. Halfway along the road are the ruins of a blacksmith's shop and, before the road links up with the N12 back into George, you'll see the old toll house.

Seven Passes Road

One of the most enjoyable drives in the region, the Seven Passes Road (or the Old Passes Road), is the name given to the original route between George and Knysna. It starts 3 km out of George, just before Pine Lodge. The route was surveyed and built by Thomas Bain in 1867 and, like so many of his engineering projects, is still in use today. Much of the road follows the foothills of the Outeniqua Mountains. When it was built the engineers had to cut their way through dense forest and negotiate the fast-flowing rivers coming out of the mountains. The seven passes which give the road its name are: the Swart River, Kaaimans, Touw River, Hoogekraal, Karatara, Homtini and Phantom. At each pass the road winds down the gorges to a narrow bridge at the bottom. The stone bridges over the Silver and Kaaimans rivers have been declared national monuments.

After crossing the Swart River, which flows out of the Garden Route dam, the road rises through the forest onto a plateau. Some 5 km from the turning is the entrance to **Saasveld**, a college of forestry founded in 1905. The descent to the Kaaimans River was a major obstacle for Bain in 1867. Loaded wagons slid on their brake shoes to the bottom before being hauled up by 32 oxen on the other side, the ground so soft that the wheels had gouged out 3-m-deep channels. Shortly after the road crosses the Silver River, there is a junction with White Road for **Wilderness**. After crossing the fourth river, Touw, the road reaches turnings to Woodville, Bergplaas and Kleinplaat forest stations. Just before Woodville there is a turning north leading to a giant yellowwood tree which is thought to be more than 800 years old. It is 31 m high and has a girth of 9 m. A picnic site and a short trail into the forest have been laid out close by. At Bergplaas there is a right turning which leads down to the lakes, **Langvlei** and **Rondevlei**, before joining the N2 outside Sedgefield.

The next two passes are the **Hoogekraal** and **Karatara**. The village of Karatara was established in 1941 as a centre for woodcutters who could no longer practice their skills as attitudes towards the forests and trees changed. The **Homtini Pass** is a beautiful wooded valley which ends by the turning for the village of Rheenendal. After another kilometre there is a left turning signposted for Millwood, Goldfields and Bibby's Hoek. The rest of this route into Knysna is described in the West of Knysna section (see page 321).

This appealing little town is an ideal base for exploring the Garden Route and has a superb swathe of sandy beach. Check locally for demarcated areas for swimming and surfing. Children should be supervised in the sea as there are strong rip currents. One of the safest spots for swimming is in the Touw River mouth. Except for the few hectic weeks at Christmas and New Year, Wilderness is generally very relaxed and has an excellent range of accommodation. The advantage of staying here is that you are also within a day's drive of all the interesting sights of the Little Karoo. The highlight, however, is Wilderness National Park, a quiet, well-managed park, with three levels of self-catering accommodation and a campsite.

The town itself doesn't have much of a centre, but stretches instead up the lush foothills of the Outeniqua Mountains and along leafy streets by the lake and river. The supermarket, restaurants, post office and tourist office are by the petrol station, where the N2 crosses the Serpentine channel.

Ins and outs

Wilderness Tourism Bureau ① *Leila's Lane, turn left by the post office, T044-877 0045, www.tourismwilderness.co.za, Mon-Fri 0800-1700, Sat 0900-1300,* is a very helpful office, especially when it comes to finding good-value accommodation during the peak season.

Background

The first European to settle in the district was a farmer, Van der Bergh, who built himself a simple farmhouse in the 1850s. It was in 1877 that the name was first used, when a young man from Cape Town, George Bennet, was granted the hand of his sweetheart only on condition that he took her to live in the wilderness. He purchased some land where the present-day **Wilderness Hotel** stands and promptly named it 'wilderness' (of dense bush and forest) to appease his new father-in-law. At this time the only road access was from the Seven Passes Road between George and Knysna. Bennet cut a track from this road to his new farmhouse. In 1905 Montagu White bought the homestead from Bennet and converted it into a boarding house. It wasn't a great success: the area was undoubtedly

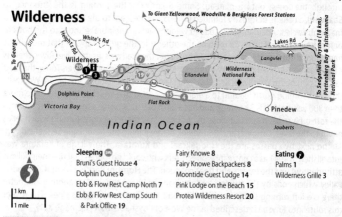

Sleeping 🏨		
Bruni's Guest House 4	Fairy Knowe 8	Eating 🍴
Dolphin Dunes 6	Fairy Knowe Backpackers 8	Palms 1
Ebb & Flow Rest Camp North 7	Moontide Guest Lodge 14	Wilderness Grille 3
Ebb & Flow Rest Camp South	Pink Lodge on the Beach 15	
& Park Office 19	Protea Wilderness Resort 20	

beautiful, but the swimming was dangerous and access was still a problem. When the property changed hands in 1921 the farmhouse/boarding house underwent further alterations and the Wilderness Hotel came into being. In 1907 the railway line from Mossel Bay reached George and six years later, Oudtshoorn. It wasn't until 1928 that the link between George and Knysna was completed. By 1928 a second hotel, now known as the **Fairy Knowe Hotel**, had been built by the river. In 1985 the original Wilderness Hotel was destroyed in a fire – the new building is the smart four-star hotel of the same name.

Wilderness National Park → *Colour map 7, B2.*
ⓘ *The camp reception, T044-877 1197, www.sanparks.org, 0700-2000, has a map of the camp and useful information on the surrounding countryside. The daily conservation fee is R72, children R36. The nearest supermarkets and restaurants are in Wilderness.*

Since the accommodation is provided by SANParks it is excellent value, especially for four or more people, and this is one of the most relaxing places to stay along the Garden Route. The main attraction is the water and the birdlife in the reed beds but there are some excellent hikes and a beautiful sandy beach. Each of the accommodation units has a folder with maps and details of all the possible hikes and routes in the park.

Four kilometres east of Wilderness, off the N2, a gravel road drops down the edge of the hill to the main camp next to a river. The park covers 2612 ha and incorporates five rivers and four lakes as well as a 28-km stretch of the coastline. The series of freshwater lakes is situated between the Outeniqua foothills and sand dunes which back onto a beautiful, long sandy beach. As this is such a stunning and unique ecosystem, the land around the national park is also protected by SANParks – this area is referred to as the National Lake Area. The four lakes are known as Island, Langvlei, Rondevlei and Swartvlei. There are bird hides on Langvlei and Rondevlei.

There are two ways in which to enjoy the beauty of the surroundings, on foot or in a canoe. You can cover more ground by walking, but canoeing is ideal for seeing birds. There are five trails in the park. The **Pied Kingfisher Trail**, a 10-km circular route, can be completed in four hours. It follows the river in one direction and the beach on your return. The other walks are also forest walks, except for the 3-km **Dune Molerat Trail** which takes you through dune fynbos where you may see proteas in flower in season.

The main camp has canoes and pedalos for hire – these should be arranged through **Eden Adventures** (see page 347). One of the more interesting short routes is to continue up the Touw River past the Ebb and Flow Camps. This quickly becomes a narrow stream and you have to leave your canoe. A path continues along the bank of the stream through some beautiful riverine forest. Eden Adventures also have mountain bikes, some with child seats, to rent out for use on the trails in the park.

Sedgefield and around ●●● ▸▸ *pp332-352. Colour map 7, B2.*

Unless you turn off the N2, all that can be seen of Sedgefield is a collection of curio shops, supermarkets and snack bars. Between the main road and the beach is the **Swartvlei Lagoon**, South Africa's largest natural inland saltwater lake, most of which lies on the inland side of the N2. The lake is a popular spot for watersports and birdwatching, although the two pastimes don't always go well together. Around Sedgefield's lakes and forests look out for the secretive starred robin, the blue mantle flycatcher, the difficult-to-see Victorian warbler and the rare African finfoot.

The village itself is of little interest, but the country around the lakes is spectacular and very peaceful. On the Knysna side of Sedgefield is another lake, **Groenvlei**, a freshwater lake lying within the Goukamma Nature Reserve. **Sedgefield Tourism Bureau** ⓘ *30 Main Rd, T044-343 2010, www.tourismsedgefield.co.za, Mon-Fri 0800-1700, Sat 0830-1100*, has good information on accommodation.

Goukamma Nature Reserve

ⓘ *T044-802 5310, www.capenature.org.za. Gates open 0800-1800, entry for day visitors R25, children (2-13) R12.*

The reserve was established to protect 2230 ha of the hinterland between Sedgefield and Buffalo Bay. This includes Groenvlei or Lake Pleasant, a large freshwater lake, and a 13-km sandy beach with some magnificent sand dunes covered in fynbos and patches of forest containing milkwood trees. The **Goukamma River** estuary in the eastern part of the reserve has been cut off from the sea by the large sand dunes. The lake is now fed by natural drainage and springs, and is surrounded by reed beds which are excellent for bird-watching; more than 75 species have been identified. To get there, look out for the turning for the Lake Pleasant Hotel, just east of Sedgefield. Beyond the hotel the road divides; take the left turning by the dunes to the bushcamp and the Groenvlei office. A 4-km hiking trail starts close by which runs along the lake shore. If you are feeling energetic, there is a 14-km trail starting from the same point, which takes you across the reserve to the Goukamma River in the eastern sector, although this leaves you with the problem of return transportation. On any of the walks in the reserve, always carry plenty of drinking water and keep an eye out for snakes, especially among the sand dunes. The second point of access is much closer to Knysna. Look out for the Buffalo Bay signpost where the N2 crosses the Goukamma River, and the railway crosses the N2. There is Cape Nature accommodation in both the western and eastern ends of the reserve (see Sleeping, page 336).

Knysna and around 🚌🏧🚲🅿️🏕️📶 ➤ *pp332-352. Colour map 7, B2.*

Knysna (the 'K' is silent) is the self-proclaimed heart of the Garden Route. It is no longer the sleepy lagoon-side village it once was – far from it – but is nevertheless a pleasant spot to spend a day or two. The town itself is fully geared up for tourists, which means a lot of choice in accommodation and restaurants, as well as overcrowding and high prices. It remains quite an arty place, though, and many of the craftspeople who have gravitated to the region display their products in craft shops and galleries. Nevertheless, development is booming, with a slick waterfront complex, complete with souvenir shops and fast-food outlets, setting the pace. If you're trying to choose between Knysna and Plettenberg Bay as a base, Knysna offers more amenities and activities, while Plett is far more relaxed and has the better beach. Both get very busy during high season.

Ins and outs

Getting there and around Knysna can easily be accessed by road as it lies on the N2 between Cape Town (500 km) and Port Elizabeth (260 km). **Baz Bus** has a daily service between Cape Town and Port Elizabeth, from where it continues to Durban five times a week. Mainline buses stop at Knysna daily on the route between Cape Town and Durban. **Translux** has a service between Knysna and Johannesburg and Tshwane (Pretoria) via Bloemfontein. The centre of town is compact and it is easy to find your way about, although you'll need transport to see the sights. ➤ *For further details see Transport, page 351.*

Tourist information **Knysna Tourism** ⓘ *40 Main St, T044-382 5510, www.tourism knysna.co.za, Mon-Fri 0800-1700, Sat 0830-1300, hours extended in high season*, can make reservations for accommodation, tours and public transport. It's a helpful and professional office, well clued-up on the region. For more information on Knysna, visit www.knysna.org.

Background

The Hottentots named a local river in the area by a word that sounded like Knysna to the early Europeans, and it's generally believed to mean a place of wood or leaves. In 1804 George Rex, a timber merchant, purchased the farm Melkhoutkraal, effectively taking owner-ship of all the land surrounding the lagoon. It was rumoured he was the first and illegitimate son of England's King George III. By 1817 the Knysna Lagoon was being used by ships to bring in supplies, and later to take away timber. The vast, indigenous forests just outside Knysna became an invaluable source of timber for buildings, ships and wagons. In 1870, Arnt Leonard Thesen and his family moved from Norway to Knysna and set up the first trading store and counting house, and by 1881 the settlements of Melville and Newhaven united to form the new town of Knysna. The timber industry continued well into the 20th century

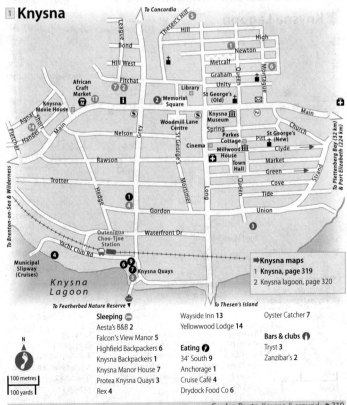

1 Knysna

Knysna maps
1 Knysna, page 319
2 Knysna lagoon, page 320

Sleeping 🛏
Aesta's B&B **2**
Falcon's View Manor **5**
Highfield Backpackers **6**
Knysna Backpackers **1**
Knysna Manor House **7**
Protea Knysna Quays **3**
Rex **4**
Wayside Inn **13**
Yellowwood Lodge **14**

Eating 🍴
34' South **9**
Anchorage **1**
Cruise Café **4**
Drydock Food Co **6**
Oyster Catcher **7**

Bars & clubs 🍸
Tryst **3**
Zanzibar's **2**

and unfortunately wiped out much of the natural forest on the coast, so whilst there are still tracts of Knysna forest, the region undoubtedly looks very different to from 150 years ago.

Sights

Although there are a couple of sights and museums in the town, Knysna's highlights are its natural attractions. The main feature of the town is the **lagoon**, around which much of Knysna life revolves. **The Heads**, the rocky promontories that lead from the lagoon to the open sea, are quite stunning. The **Knysna National Lakes**, over 15,000 ha of protected area, are also wonderful to explore, comprising islands, seashore and beach. This fragile ecosystem is bound to suffer from the ever-expanding tourist industry; of particular concern is the rich variety of aquatic life in the lagoon. This has not been helped by the construction of large retirement residential suburbs, such as Belvidere Estate, Thesen Island and Leisure Island – the latter two should never have been built upon. One of the striking features of Knysna is the location of the sprawling township, which is at the top of the hills above the town. From a boat trip on the lagoon you can look back at the town; all the sleek modern and luxurious development in the foreground and, quite by contrast, the tight cluster of shacks at the very top of the hill.

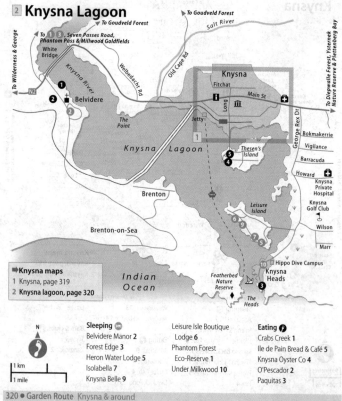

2 Knysna Lagoon

Knysna maps
1 Knysna, page 319
2 Knysna lagoon, page 320

Sleeping
Belvidere Manor 2
Forest Edge 3
Heron Water Lodge 5
Isolabella 7
Knysna Belle 9

Leisure Isle Boutique
Lodge 6
Phantom Forest
Eco-Reserve 1
Under Milkwood 10

Eating
Crabs Creek 1
Ile de Pain Bread & Café 5
Knysna Oyster Co 4
O'Pescador 2
Paquitas 3

South African Wildlife

Introduction

A large proportion of people who visit South Africa do so to see its spectacular wildlife. This colour section is a quick photographic guide to some of the more fascinating mammals you may encounter. We give you pictures and information about habitat, habits and characteristic appearance to help you when you are on safari. It is by no means a comprehensive survey and some of the animals listed may not be found throughout the whole country. For further information about South Africa's mammals, birds, reptiles and other wildlife, see the Land and environment section of the Background chapter, page 887.

The Big Nine

It is fortunate that many of the large and spectacular animals of Africa are also, on the whole, fairly common. They are often known as the 'Big Five'. This term was originally coined by hunters who wanted to take home trophies of their safari. Thus it was, that, in hunting parlance, the Big Five were elephant, black rhino, buffalo, lion and leopard. Nowadays the hippopotamus is usually considered one of the Big Five for those who shoot with their cameras, whereas the buffalo is far less of a 'trophy'. Equally photogenic and worthy of being included are the zebra, giraffe and cheetah. But whether they are the Big Five or the Big Nine, these are the animals that most people come to Africa to see and, with the possible exception of the leopard and the black rhino, you have an excellent chance of seeing them all.

■ **Hippopotamus** *Hippopotamus amphibius*. Prefers shallow water, grazes on land over a wide area at night, so can be found quite a distance from water, and has a strong sense of territory, which it protects aggressively. Lives in large family groups known as 'schools'.

■ **Black rhinoceros** *Diceros bicornis*. Long, hooked upper lip distinguishes it from white rhino rather than colour. Prefers dry bush and thorn scrub habitat and in the past was found in mountain uplands. Males usually solitary. Females seen in small groups with their calves (very rarely more than four), sometimes with two generations. Mother always walks in front of offspring, unlike the white rhino, where the mother walks behind, guiding calf with her horn. Their distribution has been massively reduced by poaching and work continues to save both the black and the white rhino from extinction. You might be lucky and see the black rhino in Kruger, Shamwari and Pilanesberg national parks and private reserves like Mala Mala and Londolozi.

■ **White rhinoceros** *Diceros simus*. Square muzzle and bulkier than the black rhino, they are grazers rather than browsers, hence the different lip. Found in open grassland, they are more sociable and can be seen in groups of five or more. More common in southern Africa due to a successful breeding program in Hluhluwe/Umfolozi National Park.

Opposite page:
Leopard with a kill.
Above left: Black rhinoceros.
Above right: White rhinoceros.
Right: Hippopotamus.

■ **Common/Masai giraffe** *Giraffa camelopardis*. Yellowish-buff with patchwork of brownish marks and jagged edges, usually two different horns, sometimes three. Found throughout Africa in several differing subspecies.

■ **Reticulated giraffe** *Giraffa reticulata*. Reddish-brown coat and a network of distinct, pale, narrow lines. The patches tend to be much larger than those found in East Africa and have well-defined outlines, although giraffes found in the desert margins of Namibia are very pale in colour and less tall – probably due to a poor diet lacking in minerals.

■ **Common/Burchell's zebra** *Equus burchelli*. Generally has broad stripes (some with lighter shadow stripes next to the dark ones) which cross the top of the hind leg in unbroken lines. The true species is probably extinct but there are many varying subspecies found in different locations across Africa, including Chapman's (east across southern Africa to Kruger National Park).

■ **Leopard** *Panthera pardus*. Found in varied habitats ranging from forest to open savannah. They are generally nocturnal, hunting at night or before the sun comes up to avoid the heat. You may see them resting during the day in the lower branches of trees.

■ **Cheetah** *Acinonyx jubatus*. Often seen in family groups walking across plains or resting in the shade. The black 'tear' mark is usually obvious through binoculars. Can reach speeds of 90 kph over short distances. Found in open, semi-arid savannah, never in forested country. Endangered in some parts of Africat. More commonly seen than the leopard, they are not as widespread as the lion (*Panthera leo*).

Opposite page left:
Common giraffe.
Opposite page right:
Reticulated giraffe.
Top left: Burchell's zebra.
Top right: Grevy's zebra.
Above: Cheetah.
Right: Leopard.

■ **Lion** *Panthera leo* (see page i). The largest (adult males can weigh up to 450 pounds) of the big cats in Africa and also the most common, lions are found on open savannah all over the continent. They are often not at all disturbed by the presence of humans and so it is possible to get quite close to them. They are sociable animals living in prides or permanent family groups of up to around 30 animals and are the only felid to do so. The females do most of the hunting (usually ungulates like zebra and antelopes).

■ **Buffalo** *Syncerus caffer*. Considered by hunters to be the most dangerous of the big game and the most difficult to track and, therefore, the biggest trophy. Generally found on open plains but also at home in dense forest, they are fairly common in most African national parks but, like the elephant, they need a large area to roam in, so they are not usually found in the smaller parks.

■ **Elephant** *Loxodonta africana*. Commonly seen, even on short safaris, elephants have suffered from the activities of war and from ivory poachers. However overall numbers have recovered to around 18,000 leading to problems of over population. As a result culling programmes are being vi considered by the South Africa government.

Larger antelopes

■ **Gemsbok** *Oryx gazella*, 122 cm. Unmistakable, with black line down spine and black stripe between coloured body and white underparts. Horns (both sexes) straight, long and look v-shaped (seen face-on). Only found in arid, semi-desert country. ■ **Nyala** *Tragelaphus angasi*, 110 cm. Slender frame, shaggy, dark brown coat with mauve tinge (males). Horns (male only) single open curve. The female is a different chestnut colour. They like dense bush and are usually found close to water. Gather in herds of up to 30 but smaller groups more likely. Found in Kruger National Park. ■ **Common waterbuck** *Kobus ellipsiprymnus* and **Defassa waterbuck** *Kobus defassa*, 122-137 cm. Very similar with shaggy coats and white marking on buttocks. On the common variety, this is a clear half ring on rump and around tails; on Defassa, the ring is a filled-in solid white area. Both species occur in small herds in grassy areas, often near water.

Top: Gemsbok. **Bottom left:** Nyala. **Bottom right:** Common waterbuck.

■ **Sable antelope** *Hippotragus niger*, 140-145 cm and **Roan antelope** *Hippotragus equinus*, 127-137 cm. Both are similar in shape, with ringed horns curving backwards (both sexes), longer in the sable. Female sables are reddish brown and can be mistaken for the roan. Males are very dark with a white underbelly. The roan has distinct tufts of hair at the tips of its long ears. Sable prefers wooded areas and the roan is generally only seen near water. Both species live in herds.

■ **Greater kudu** *Tragelaphus strepsiceros*, 140-153 cm. Colour varies from greyish to fawn with several vertical white stripes down the sides of the body. Horns long and spreading, with two or three twists (male only). Distinctive thick fringe of hair running from the chin down the neck. Found in fairly thick bush, sometimes in quite dry areas. Usually live in family groups of up to six, but occasionally larger herds of up to about 30.

■ **Topi** *Damaliscus korrigum*, 122-127 cm. Very rich dark rufous, with dark patches on the tops of the legs and more ordinary looking, lyre-shaped horns.

Top: Greater kudu. **Middle:** Sable antelope. **Bottom:** Topi.

Hartebeest In the hartebeest the horns arise from a bony protuberance on the top of the head and curve outwards and backwards. There are three sub-species: **Coke's hartebeest** *Alcephalus buselaphus*, 122 cm, is a drab pale brown with a paler rump; **Lichtenstein's hartebeest** *Alcephalus lichtensteinii*, 127-132 cm, is also fawn in colour, with a rufous wash over the back and dark marks on the front of the legs and often a dark patch near shoulder; and the **red hartebeest** *Alcephalus caama*.

Brindled or **blue wildebeest** or **gnu** *Connochaetes taurinus*, 132 cm. Found only in southern Africa and is often seen grazing with zebra.

Eland *Taurotragus oryx*, 175-183 cm. The largest of the antelope, it has a noticeable dewlap and shortish spiral horns (both sexes). Greyish to fawn, sometimes with rufous tinge and narrow white stripes down side of body. Occurs in groups of up to 30 in grassy habitats.

Top: Blue wildebeest. **Middle:** Red hartebeest.
Bottom: Eland.

Smaller antelope

■ **Bushbuck** *Tragelaphus scriptus*, 76-92 cm. Shaggy coat with white spots and stripes on the side and back and two white, crescent-shaped marks on front of neck. Short horns (male only) slightly spiral. High rump gives characteristic crouch. White underside of tail noticeable when running. Occurs in thick bush, near water. Either seen in pairs or singly.

■ **Klipspringer** *Oreotragus oreotragus*, 56 cm. Brownish-yellow with grey speckles and white chin and underparts with a short tail. Has distinctive, blunt hoof tips and short horns (male only). Likes dry, stony hills and mountains.

■ **Bohor reedbuck** *Redunca redunca*, 71-76 cm. Horns (males only) sharply hooked forwards at the tip, distinguishing them from the oribi (see page xiii). It is reddish fawn with white underparts and has a short bushy tail. They usually live in pairs or otherwise in small family groups. Often seen with Oribi, in bushed grassland and always near water.

■ **Steenbok** *Raphicerus campestris*, 58 cm. An even, rufous brown colour with clean white underside and white ring around eye. Small dark patch at the tip of the nose and long broad ears. The horns (male only) are slightly longer than the ears: they are sharp, have a smooth surface and curve slightly forward. Generally seen alone, prefers open plains, often found in arid regions. Usually runs off very quickly on being spotted.

■ **Springbuck** *Antidorcas marsupialis* or **springbok**, 76-84 cm. The upper part of the body is fawn, and this is separated from the white underparts by a dark brown lateral stripe. It is distinguished by a dark stripe which runs between the base of the horns and the mouth, passing through the eye. This is the only type of gazelle found south of the Zambezi River. You no longer see the giant herds the animal was famous for, but you will see them along the roadside as you drive between Cape Town and Bloemfontein. They get their name from their habit of leaping stiff-legged and high into the air.

■ **Common (Grimm's) duiker** *Sylvicapra grimmia*, 58 cm (see page xii). Grey-fawn colour with darker rump and pale colour on the underside. Its dark muzzle and prominent ears are divided by straight, upright, narrow pointed horns. This particular species is the only duiker found in open grasslands. Usually the duiker is associated with a forested environment. It's difficult to see because it is shy and will quickly disappear into the bush.

■ **Oribi** *Ourebia ourebi*, 61 cm (see page xiii). Slender and delicate looking with a longish neck and a sandy to brownish-fawn coat. It has oval-shaped ears and short, straight horns with a few rings at their base (male only). Like the reedbuck it has a patch of bare skin just below each ear. They live in small groups or as a pair and are never far from water.

■ **Suni** *Nesotragus moschatus*, 37 cm (see page xiii). Dark chestnut to grey-fawn in colour with slight speckles along the back, its head and neck are slightly paler and the throat is white. It has a distinct bushy tail with a white tip. Its longish horns (male only) are thick, ribbed and slope backwards. This, one of the smallest antelope, lives alone and prefers dense bush cover and reed beds.

■ **Impala** *Aepyceros melampus*, 92-107 cm. One of the largest of the smaller antelope, the impala is a bright rufous colour on its back and has a white abdomen, a white 'eyebrow' and chin and white hair inside its ears. From behind, the white rump with black stripes on each side is characteristic and makes it easy to identify. It has long lyre-shaped horns (male only). Above the heels of the hind legs is a tuft of thick black bristles (unique to impala) which are easy to see when the animal runs. There's also a black mark on the side of abdomen, just in front of the back leg. Found in herds of 15 to 20, it likes open grassland or sometimes the cover of partially wooded areas and is usually close to water.

Above: Bohor reedbuck

Top: Klipspringer. **Bottom:** Steenbok

xii **Top:** Springbuck. **Bottom:** Common (Grimm's) duiker

Top left: Oribi. **Top right:** Suni. **Bottom:** Impala

Other mammals

There are many other fascinating mammals worth keeping an eye out for. This is a selection of some of the more interesting or particularly common ones.

■ **African wild dog** or **hunting dog** *Lycacon pictus*. Easy to identify since they have all the features of a large mongrel dog: a large head and slender body. Their coat is a mixed pattern of dark shapes and white and yellow patches and no two dogs are quite alike. They are very rarely seen and are seriously threatened with extinction (there may be as few as 6000 left). Found on the open plains around dead animals, they are not in fact scavengers but effective pack hunters.

■ **Brown hyena** *Hyaena brunnea*. High shoulders and low back give the hyena its characteristic appearance. The spotted variety, larger and brownish with dark spots, has a large head and rounded ears. The brown hyena, slightly smaller, has pointed ears and a shaggy coat, and is more noctural. Although sometimes shy animals, they have been know to wander around campsites stealing food from humans.

Top: African wild dog. **Middle:** Brown hyena. **Bottom:** Chacma baboon.

■ **Warthog** *Phacochoerus aethiopicus*.
The warthog is almost hairless and grey with a very large head, tusks and wart-like growths on its face. It frequently occurs in family parties and when startled will run away at speed with its tail held straight up in the air. They are often seen near water caking themselves in thick mud which helps to keep them both cool and free of ticks and flies.

■ **Chacma baboon** *Papio ursinus*.
An adult male baboon is slender and weighs about 40 kg. Their general colour is a brownish grey, with lighter undersides. Usually seen in trees, but rocks can also provide sufficient protection, they occur in large family troops and have a reputation for being aggressive where they have become used to the presence of humans.

■ **Rock hyrax** *procavia capensis*. The nocturnal rock hyrax lives in colonies amongst boulders and on rocky hillsides, protecting themselves from predators like eagle, caracal and leopard by darting into the rock crevices.

■ **Caracal** *felis caracal*. Also known as the African lynx, it is twice the weight of a domestic cat, with reddish sandy colour fur and paler underparts. Distinctive black stripe from eye to nose and tufts on ears. Generally nocturnal and with similar habits to the leopard. They are not commonly seen, but are found in hilly country.

Top: Warthog. **Middle:** Rock hyrax.
Bottom: Caracal.

The **Knysna Museum** ① *Queen St, T044-302 6320, Mon-Fri 0930-1630, Sat 0930-1230, free but donations accepted*, is housed in the Old Gaol – the first public building erected by the colonial government in the 1870s. Most of the collection focuses on fishing methods used along the coast, with a variety of nets and tackle on display. Unless you are a devoted angler this is not going to take up too much of your time. The highlight is in fact a fish, or to be more precise, a coelacanth. This is a prehistoric fish that was believed to be extinct, but a live specimen was famously caught by a fisherman in 1938. There is also an art gallery, tearoom and gift shop.

Millwood House ① *Mon-Fri 0930-1630, Sat 0930-1230*, is a single-storey wooden building similar to those that once made up the gold-mining community of Millwood (see page 322). The house was originally built in sections and re-erected here. It is now a national monument and houses the local history museum, including a display depicting the goldrush days. Next door is **Parkes Cottage**, a similar wooden house, which was moved three times before arriving at its present site. Originally erected in Millwood village, it was moved into Knysna when the gold ran out. In 1905 it was moved to Rawson Street, and then finally in 1992 it was moved to its present site.

There are two **St George's Churches** in Knysna, the old and the new. Both ran into financial difficulties during construction. To complete the old church the Bishop of the Cape Colony, Robert Gray, persuaded six local businessmen to come up with the necessary £150. The church was consecrated in October 1855. The interior has a timbered ceiling and a fine yellowwood floor. In the 1920s it was decided that a second church needed to be built to accommodate the local congregation. It was 11 years between the foundation stone being laid and the church being consecrated by Bishop Gwyer of George in April 1937. Construction had been delayed due to lack of funds. The community was very proud of the fact that all the materials used in the construction were local – the stone for the walls was quarried from the other side of the lagoon in the Brenton hills. Most of the interior fittings are made from stinkwood, and commemorate local worthies.

Featherbed Nature Reserve ① *T044-382 1693, www.knysnafeatherbed.com, daily 1000, 1115, 1230, R375, children R180 (including lunch), 1430, R260, children R100 (without lunch)*. This is a private nature reserve in the unspoilt western side of the **Knysna Heads**, which can only be reached by the **Featherbed Co** ferry which runs from the John Benn Jetty, at the Knysna Quays. The reserve is home to South Africa's largest breeding herd of blue duiker (*Cephalophus monticola*), an endangered species. Also of interest is a cave once inhabited by the Khoi, which has been declared a national heritage site. This four-hour excursion includes return ferry trip, 4WD vehicle ride up the western promontory of the Knysna Heads and an optional 2 km guided nature walk through the forest, onto the cliffs, into the caves and along the spectacular coastline. It ends with a buffet lunch under some Milkwood trees before returning to Knysna. This is an excellent family excursion. The Featherbed Co also offers 1½-hour cruises around the lagoon on a paddle cruiser at 1230 for R150, children R65 or at 1815, which includes a three-course buffet dinner, R350, children R180. In addition, they run the **Cruise Café** at the boat departure point at the Knysna Quays (see Eating, page 344).

West of Knysna ● ▶▶ *pp332-352*.

Belvidere, Brenton and Brenton-on-Sea
These villages, 12-14 km from town on the western shores of the lagoon, are in many ways really smart suburbs of Knysna. Brenton has the great attraction of having the nearest sandy beach (Brenton-on-Sea), making it very popular during the school holidays.

Invisible elephants

No guide to Knysna would be complete without a mention of the Knysna elephants. They have come to represent the last stand of wildlife against man in the region. The elephants live deep in the forest and few people have ever seen them. Little is known about their numbers or their characteristics. They belong to the same species as the savanna elephant but as a result of living in the forest their lifestyle and habits have changed, and they are thought to now resemble the forest elephant found in the equatorial jungle of Central Africa.

In 1876, several hundred elephants were recorded in the region, but under heavy pressure of ivory hunters they were reduced to 20 to 30 individuals by 1908. In 1970 the Knysna elephant population was estimated at 11, and by 1994, only one Knysna elephant was known to survive, an elderly female. In the same year, three young elephants from the Kruger National Park were introduced

into the range of the elderly female in an effort to increase numbers. Unfortunately, one of them died of stress-related complications soon after release. The remaining two elephants joined up with the elderly female for only short periods before choosing to spend 80% of their time in mountainous fynbos habitat beyond the Knysna forest. In 1999 they were then recaptured and relocated to the Shamwari Private Game Reserve in the Eastern Cape. Then, after a study in 2007, conservation geneticists from the US University of Missouri-Columbia announced that there could be several elephants in Knysna Forest. By extracting DNA samples from dung, they established that there were five individual females and at least one bull, and possibly a calf was born recently. They also established that these were not related to the reintroduced Kruger elephants. Happy hiking – you may just see more than the Knysna lourie.

There is a fine hotel and a limited selection of seaside cottages. Belvidere is primarily a leafy residential suburb along the banks of the river where it enters the lagoon. A large proportion of the village is made up of the relatively new Belvidere Estate, a prestigious development on 67 ha, made up of large houses and gardens.

The small village church, **Belvidere Church**, is a popular attraction in the area and is a miniature replica of a Norman church. It was built in 1855 from local stone and timber, with picturesque stained-glass windows and stinkwood fittings. The rose window on the west side was installed in 1955. Further along the road is the seaside resort of Brenton-on-Sea.

Knysna Forest and Millwood Goldfields

On the southern slopes of the Outeniqua Mountains, behind Knysna, are the remnants of the grand forests that first attracted white settlers to the region. No longer a single expanse, the patches go under a variety of names which can be confusing: Diepwalle Forest, Ysternek Reserve, Goudveld Forest, and Millwood Creek (and Jubilee Creek) Nature Reserve. As a whole, these state forests are often referred to as the **Knysna Indigenous Forests**. The indigenous forests are noteworthy for the variety of birdlife and their magnificent trees. Species of special interest include the yellowwood, assegai, stinkwood, red alder, white alder and the Cape chestnut. A variety of short walks has been laid out in the forests. In some areas horse riding and mountain biking is allowed. The tourist office produces a good trail map.

About 25 km from Knysna, in the **Goudveld Forest**, are the remains of an old mining town, **Millwood** ① *sunrise-sunset*. This was the site of a minor goldrush in the 1880s, just before the gold was discovered at Pilgrim's Rest and Johannesburg. The first gold was discovered here in 1876 when a local farmer picked up a nugget in the Karatara River. This triggered the usual manic influx, and by 1887 Millwood had a court building, three banks, 32 stores, six hotels and three newspapers. By 1900 most people had left as the reefs became too difficult to mine. Today only one building survives, along with some mining machinery which has remained untouched for over 60 years. To reach the mine, take the Phantom Pass road out of Knysna, just before the village of Rheenendal take a right turn, signposted for Millwood, Goldfields and Bibby's Hoek.

Further up the slope is the shaft and a short Co-Co Pan rail track. In addition to the mine buildings, there are a few picnic spots and short paths leading into the forest; you only have to walk a few metres before being completely enveloped by trees.

East of Knysna ◉ ⏵ *pp332-352*.

Diepwalle Forest and Elephant Trail

① *Before setting out you must sign in at the forest station where maps are on offer. There is no charge but the hike is only open 0600-1800.*

Starting from the Diepwalle forest station is the 20-km Elephant Walk, an easy-going, level hike that gives a clear insight into the forest environment. The trail is marked by elephant silhouettes and takes around seven hours to complete. The hike is made up of three loops, but it is possible to shorten the walk by completing only one or two loops. The three paths are simply known as Routes I, II and III, and are 9-, 8- and 6-km long, respectively. Apart from the (very slim) possibility of spying the rare Knysna elephant (see box, page 322), of which there are three on record at present, the main attractions are the giant forest trees, particularly the Outeniqua yellowwood. There are eight such trees along the full trail – the largest, at 46 m, is known as the **King Edward VII Tree**, and stands just off the R339 by the Diepwalle picnic spot at the end of Route I and the start of Route II. The end of the **Outeniqua Trail** meets with Route III.

To get there from Knysna, follow the N2 towards Plettenburg Bay. After 7 km turn onto the R339 and the Diepwalle forest station is about 16 km on a gravel road. The R339 passes through the middle of the forest en route to Uniondale via the Prince Alfred's Pass.

Noetzie and Brackenhill Falls

Noetzie is a small village on the coast with an outlandish collection of holiday homes built to look like castles from medieval Europe, complete with towers and battlements. On the curiosity scale they rate quite high, but unfortunately you can only see them from the outside, as they are all private homes. A further 5 km beyond the Noetzie turning is another turning to the right; a gravel road passes through a eucalyptus and pine plantation to a picnic spot which overlooks the Brackenhill Falls. This is where the Noetzie River plunges into a narrow gorge with flourishing plants growing in the spray on the steep sides.

Knysna Elephant Park

① *T044-532 7732, www.knysnaelephantpark.co.za. Daily, tours every 30 mins, 0830-1630, R160, children (3-12) R83, bookings not required; elephant riding 0930, 1030, 1500, 1600, R682, children (6-12) R330, children under 6 not permitted, booking essential.*

On the N2, 20 km from Knysna and 10 km before Plettenburg Bay, this small park is a refuge for orphaned elephants. Visitors are taken on tours around the forest area and are allowed to touch and play with the little elephants. Although the animals are 'free range' they are very used to human contact, making it a wonderful experience for children. Longer walks with the elephants can also be arranged and the newest option here is elephant riding, which is a two-hour excursion through the bush ending with refreshments. Sleeping with the elephants is also on offer, and six rooms have been built above the elephants' boma where they sleep at night (see Sleeping, page 338). This is also the only realistic chance you'll have of seeing elephants in the area – the fabled indigenous ones are far too elusive.

Plettenberg Bay ☺❶❷❸▲❹❺ ⇒ pp332-352. Colour map 7, B2.

Plettenberg Bay, or 'Plett', as it is commonly known, is one of the most appealing resorts on the Garden Route. Although it is modern and has little of historical interest, the compact centre is attractive and the main beach beautiful. Plett has now become fashionable and, during the Christmas season, the town is transformed. Wealthy families descend from Johannesburg and the pace can get quite frenetic – expect busy beaches and long queues for restaurant tables. For the rest of the year the pace is calmer and the resort becomes just another sleepy seaside town. There are three beaches that are good for swimming, but the coastline is spoilt by a multi-storey hotel built without much thought on a sandbar between two of the three beaches.

Ins and outs

Getting there For short trips to other towns along the Garden Route the **Baz Bus** represents the best value and most convenient schedule and has a daily service in either direction between Cape Town and Port Elizabeth. Mainline buses stop at the Shell Ultra City out of town on the N2. ⇒ For further details, see Transport, page 351.

Best time to visit Avoid Plett on the last week of November and the first week of December. This is the end of Matric (final school exams) in South Africa, when thousands of young people descend on the resort to celebrate – known locally as 'The Plett Student Rage'.

Tourist information **Plettenburg Bay Tourism** ① Melville's Corner shopping centre, Main St, T044-533 4065, www.plettenbergbay.co.za, Mon-Fri 0900-1700, Sat 0900-1300, slightly longer hours during the peak summer season, is a helpful office with quite a detailed website.

Background

In 1630 a Portuguese vessel, the **San Gonzalez**, was wrecked in the bay. This was 20 years before Jan van Riebeeck's arrival at the Cape. The survivors stayed here for eight months, during which time they built two smaller boats out of the wreckage, and one of the boats managed to sail up the coast to Mozambique. The survivors were eventually returned home to Lisbon, but they left behind a sandstone plaque on which they had inscribed the name *Baia Formosa*. Today a replica can be seen in Plett in the same place that the first was left by the sailors. (The original is now on show in the South African Museum in Cape Town.) The Portuguese had a number of names for the bay, but none stuck for very long. Later the Dutch also gave the bay several different names, such as Content Bay and Pisang River Bay; it was only in 1778 when Governor Joachim van Plettenberg opened a timber post on the shores of the bay, and named it after himself, that a name stuck.

Plettenberg Bay

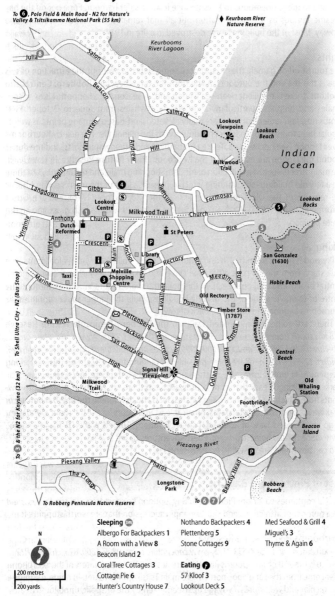

To **6**, Polo Field & Main Road - N2 for Nature's
Valley & Tsitsikamma National Park (55 km)

♦ Keurboom River
Nature Reserve

Keurbooms
River Lagoon

Indian
Ocean

Lookout
Viewpoint

Lookout
Beach

Milkwood
Trail

Lookout
Centre

Milkwood Trail

Anthony
Dutch
Reformed

Church

St Peters

Lookout
Rocks

5

San Gonzalez
(1630)

Hobie Beach

Library

Taxi

Melville
Shopping
Centre

Old Rectory

Timber Store
(1787)

Central
Beach

Sea Witch

Signal Hill
Viewpoint

Milkwood
Trail

Old Whaling
Station

Footbridge

Beacon
Island

Piesangs River

Piesang Valley

Pharos

The Prongs

Longstone
Park

To **6 7**

Robberg
Beach

To Robberg Peninsula Nature Reserve

To Shell Ultra City - N2 (Bus Stop)

To **3** & the N2 for Knysna (32 km)

N

200 metres
200 yards

Sleeping
Albergo For Backpackers **1**
A Room with a View **8**
Beacon Island **2**
Coral Tree Cottages **3**
Cottage Pie **6**
Hunter's Country House **7**

Nothando Backpackers **4**
Plettenberg **5**
Stone Cottages **9**

Eating
57 Kloof **3**
Lookout Deck **5**

Med Seafood & Grill **4**
Miguel's **3**
Thyme & Again **6**

Plettenberg remained an important timber port until the early 1800s when the Dutch decided to move operations to Knysna since it was a safer harbour. For a period the bay became famous as a whaling station but all that remains is a blubber cauldron and slipway. Most of the buildings were destroyed in a fire in 1914.

Sights

The tourist office gamely tries to promote some sights to visit but the attraction of this area is the sea and the outdoors. Aside from the three beaches, **Robberg**, **Central** and **Lookout**, there is excellent deep-sea fishing and, in season, good opportunities to spot whales and dolphins, particularly southern right whales from June to October. Plett climbs up a fairly steep hill; there are many elevated land-based vantage points as well as regular boat tours offering closer encounters with the marine life. The nearby **Keurbooms River lagoon** (see below) is a safe area for bathing and other watersports, and the dunes around the lagoon are now part of the **Keurboom River Nature Reserve**. In town itself, the main streets are just a collection of modern shopping malls and restaurants, but there are a few old buildings still standing which represent a little of the town's earlier history: the remains of the Old Timber Store (1787), the Old Rectory (1776), and the Dutch Reformed Church (1834). Also look out for the polo field with its lush grass and stylish white pavilion.

Hiking

Milkwood is a 3- or 5-km trail in and around the town. Follow the yellow footprints. The walk starts from the car park off Marine Drive and takes you via Piesangs River lagoon, Central beach, and Lookout beach. At this point the shorter route turns back through the centre of town via some of the historic buildings, while the longer route continues via Keurbooms Lagoon and round the back of town.

There are some recommended walks in the **Robberg Peninsula Nature Reserve** ① *8 km south from Plett on the old airport road, T044-533 2125, www.capenature.org.za, Feb-Nov 0700-1700, Dec and Jan 0700-2000, permits are available at the entrance gate, R25, children (2-13) R12*. There are three possibilities ranging from 2-9 km on this loop along the peninsula which forms the western boundary of Plettenberg Bay. Follow the 'seal' markers. Walking is easy thanks to boardwalks, and there are plenty of prominent viewpoints from which it is possible to see whales, seals and dolphins in the bay, but beware of freak waves along the coastal paths. Allow at least four hours for the full route. If you want to go on a guided walk of Robberg, contact **Robberg Guided Walks** ① *T044-533 2632, www.robbergwalks.homestead.com*. **Eden Adventures** based in Wilderness (see page 347) also can arrange 45-m abseiling in the reserve.

East of Plettenberg Bay ◉▲▲ ›› pp332-352.

The N2 continues east from Plettenberg Bay, but don't expect to travel too fast as there are a number of attractions and sights in rapid succession that are worth stopping for.

Keurbooms River Nature Reserve

① *7 km east of Plett, T044-533 2125, www.capenature.co.za. 0800-1800, R25, children R12.*
First up is the 750 ha Keurbooms River Nature Reserve. The headwaters of the Keurbooms River come from the Langkloof, north of the main Tsitsikamma mountain range. Its gorge is spectacular and well worth a voyage upstream to enjoy the unspoilt, unpolluted beauty.

A variety of habitats are conserved, including the relatively unspoilt riverine gorge, patches of Knysna forest along the flood banks and in protected kloofs, coastal fynbos, and dune fields. The reserve is named after the Western Keurboom (*Virgilia oroboides*) or choice tree, which grows in the coastal forest edges. The environment attracts a number of birds, and look out for the Knysna lourie, malachite and giant kingfisher, Narina Trogan fish eagle, white-breasted cormorant and various sunbirds. Taking a sailing trip upstream on the **Keurbooms River Ferry** (see Activities and tours, page 349, for further details) is a great way to spend a few hours. You are ferried 5 km along the river through a spectacular gorge overhung by indigenous trees and other flora. At the furthest point from the jetty there is an optional 30-minute walk, with a professional guide, through the forest. This is the ultimate eco-experience and a relaxing way to be introduced to the plants, sights and sounds of the forest. Make sure you are wearing sturdy footwear if you intend to join the walk.

The Keurbooms River is also a safe designated area for canoeing and waterskiing and it is possible to hire canoes from the **Cape Nature office** ⓘ *on the east side of the Keurbooms River Bridge on the N2, T044-533 2125, a double canoe costs R90 per day, if you just want to picnic next to the Keurbooms River it's R5 per person.*

Monkeyland and Birds of Eden
ⓘ *T044-534 8906, www.monkeyland.co.za, www.birdsofeden.co.za. Daily 0830-1700, a guided tour for each attraction costs R125, children (3-12) R62.50; a combo ticket for both is R200, children R100. To get here, turn off at the signpost on the N2 at the Forest Hall turning, Monkeyland and Birds of Eden are a further 2 km down the road.*

At the settlement known as The Crags 16 km east of Plettenburg Bay (just after the BP filling station) is the well-signposted turning to Monkeyland. As the name suggests, this is a primate reserve with lemurs, apes and monkeys from several continents where the attractions are free to move about in the living indigenous forest. Most are rescued pets. Visitors are advised to join a guided walk which takes in various waterholes in the forest. Guides have a keen eye for spotting animals. One of the highlights here is the Indiana Jones-style rope bridge that spans 118 m across a canyon, offering glimpses of species that spend their entire lives in the upper reaches of the forest. The primates themselves also use this bridge (supposedly the longest of its kind in the southern hemisphere). If you don't wish to join a tour, the day centre has a good viewpoint and the restaurant serves a tasty lunch. Great for kids. **Birds of Eden** is a 2.3-ha mesh dome spanning more of the same forest with 1.2 km of walkways, 900 m of which is elevated, that go past waterfalls and dams. Along the same principle as Monkeyland, previously caged birds have been released into a natural environment and visitors, who are permitted to wander around without a guide, can get a bird's eye view of macaws, cockatoos, parrots and louries.

If you are in a hurry, stay on the N2 – this is a good stretch of road, although there is a toll of around R10. The more spectacular route is via the village of Nature's Valley along the old R102, a beautifully forested road that branches off the N2 just after The Crags. Look out for ververt monkeys in the trees.

Nature's Valley → *Colour map 7, B3.*
This small village has one of the most beautiful settings along the Garden Route. Since the N2 toll road was opened in 1984, most traffic bypasses this sleepy community. The village is surrounded on three sides by the western section of the **Tsitsikamma National Park** (see page 329). The approach by road is particularly spectacular. The R102, dropping 223 m to sea level via the narrow Kalanderkloof Gorge, twists and turns through lush green coastal

forest. At the bottom is a lagoon formed by the sand dunes blocking the estuary of the **Groot River**. A right turn leads into the village, made up of a collection of holiday cottages and one shop that is an all-in-one restaurant, bar and **tourist information bureau** ① *T044-270 7077, www.natures-valley.com*. Note that there are no banks in Nature's Valley. There are several braai spots on the sandy beach, but be warned that swimming in the sea is not safe. Canoes, rowing boats and yachts can all be used on the Groot River and lagoon, but powerboats are prohibited.

Groot River and Bloukrans Passes

As the road starts to climb out of the Groot Valley it passes the **Nature's Valley Rest Camp** on the right. This is the only camp at the western end of the Tsitsikamma National Park (see page 341 for booking details). Many visitors will find themselves here because it is one end of two of the Garden Route's most spectacular hiking trails, the **Tsitsikamma Trail** and the **Otter Trail**. From the top of the Groot River Pass the road continues for 6 km before crossing a second river valley, the Bloukrans Pass. Here it descends 183 m into the narrow gorge before crossing the river and climbing up again. The R102 rejoins the N2 highway 10 km further on and crosses the **Bloukrans River Bridge**. Just after the bridge is a turning to the left that leads to a viewpoint at the top of the Bloukrans Gorge. The bridge is apparently the highest in Africa, and the drop into the gorge is quite spectacular. But the main reason for stopping is the **Bloukrans Bungee Jump** ① *T042-281 1458, www.face adrenalin.com, daily from 0900-1700, booking not essential but recommended, bungee jump R620 which includes the bridge walk*. At 216 m it is the highest commercial bungee in the world. The first rebound is longer than the previous holder of the record, the 111-m bungee jump at Victoria Falls. It's a hugely exhilarating experience and the free fall once you've leapt from the bridge lasts seven seconds, travelling over 170 kph before you reach the maximum length of the bungee cord. The new event at Bloukrans is the **Flying Fox** ① *R170*, a 200-m cable slide from a platform on land to the centre of the bridge arch. If you cannot muster the courage to do either of these, you can go on a guided bridge walk for R90. This involves walking out to the bungee platform along the caged walkway underneath the bridge, where a guide tells you how the bridge was built and a little bit about the surrounding area. This is not for anyone who suffers from vertigo, but if you want to support a mate who's doing a jump, it's a great way to feel some of the fear they are experiencing when standing on the lip of the bungee platform. Also at the top of the gorge is the **Tsitsikamma Forest Village**, a fairly new sustainable initiative to help local people make and sell curios to the many passing tourists. Shops are in a collection of attractive reed Khosian huts, and you can buy items such as candles or home-made paper.

Storms River Bridge → *Colour map 7, B3.*

Storms River Bridge is a further 5 km along the N2 from Bloukrans. There is a viewing platform to look down into the river gorge. Next to the bridge is the **Petro-Total Village**, a popular stopover with petrol pumps, curio shops, a restaurant, small museum and the **Tsitsikamma Information office** ① *T042-280 3561, www.tsitsikamma.info, daily 0830-1630*. It is worth stopping here briefly to pick up some local tourist leaflets, especially if you have plans to hike in the region. It is a helpful office and can provide information and local bookings for a whole variety of adventure activities. This is also an official stop for the mainline buses that travel along the Garden Route. Note that Storms River Village is a further 8 km along the N2, not to be confused with Storms River Mouth which is in the Tsitsikamma National Park.

Tsitsikamma National Park ⊜▲ᛏ *pp332-352. Colour map 7, B3.*

This is one of the most popular national parks in the country, second only to Kruger. It consists of a beautiful 80-km stretch of lush coastal forest and is known for its excellent birdlife. Not only is the forest protected, but the park boundaries reach out to sea for 5.5 km in the eastern sector. No boats are allowed in this area, nor is spearfishing permitted and no shells (even dead ones) may be removed or disturbed.

Ins and outs

Getting there There are two access points into the park depending on which rest camp you are staying in, although day visitors generally enter through the Storms River Mouth entrance, where there are better facilities for those on day trips. The turn-off for **Storms River Rest Camp** is on a straight stretch of the N2, about 4 km after the Storms River Bridge, easy to miss if driving fast. A surfaced road leads down to the reception centre on the coast. The last part of this drive is a beautiful, steep descent through lush rainforest, a marked contrast to the coniferous plantations along the N2 toll road. If you are travelling along the R102, the turning is just beyond the sawmill at Boskor. If you are approaching from the Port Elizabeth side, the turning is 4 km after the small village of Storms River.

The **Nature's Valley Rest Camp** is 40 km west of Storms River Mouth and can only be reached from the R102; when approaching from Knysna take the Nature's Valley turning at Kurland (R102). If you miss this turning you cannot turn off the N2 toll road until it meets with the other end of the R102, at which point you are only 8 km from the turning for Storms River camp. When approaching from Port Elizabeth look out for signs for Nature's Valley, R102. Nature's Valley Rest Camp is clearly signposted 3 km outside the village of the same name.

Best time to visit The best time to visit is between November and February. Bear in mind that, although this is midsummer, you can expect rain at any time. Annual rainfall is in excess of 1200 mm; June and July are the driest months, while May and October are the wettest.

Park information Gates open 0700-1900, office hours 0730-1800, T042-281 1607. The daily conservation fee including vehicles is R88, children R44. At the Storms River Rest Camp a shop is open daily 0800-1800, it stocks gift items as well as groceries, wine and beer. There's **Tiger's Eye Restaurant** ① *0730-1000, 1200-1500, 1800-1930*, where you need to make reservations for evening meals by 1700, and other facilities include a swimming pool, card telephone and occasional film shows on the park ecology.

Background

The park stretches 80 km along the coast between Nature's Valley and Oubosstrand. For most of its length it is no more than 500 m wide on the landward side. At the western end, where the Otter Trail reaches the Groot River estuary, the park boundary extends 3 km inland. It was established on 4 December 1964 in response to an appeal for the creation of more marine parks and reserves, made during the First World Conference on National Parks in Seattle in 1962. The main administrative office is at Storms River Rest Camp, which is almost the midpoint of the park. The park is the location for the famous 42-km **Otter Hiking Trail** (see box, page 331), which follows the coastline between Storms River Rest Camp and Nature's Valley Rest Camp. The trail can be hiked in either direction.

Vegetation and wildlife

A cross-section of the coastlands would reveal the Tsitsikamma Mountains (900-1600 m), whose slopes level off into a coastal plain or plateau at about 230 m, and then the forested cliffs which plunge 230 m into the ocean. The slope is only precipitous in a few places; elsewhere along the coast it is still very steep, but there is enough soil to support the rainforest which the park was in part created to protect. The rainforest is the last remnant of a forest which was once found right along this coast between the ocean and the mountains. The canopy ranges between 18 m and 30 m and is closed, which makes the paths nice and shady. The most common species of trees are milkwood, real yellowwood, stinkwood, Cape blackwood, forest elder, white pear and candlewood, plus the famous Outeniqua yellowwood, a forest giant. All are magnificent trees which combine with climbers such as wild grape, red saffron and milky rope to create an outstandingly beautiful forest.

In the forest itself 35 different bird species have been recorded, while in the park as a whole over 220 species have been identified. The most colourful bird in the forest is the Knysna lourie (*Tauraco corythaix*). Its call is a korr korr korr, and in flight it has a flash of deep red in its wings, with a green body and distinctive crest. In the vicinity of the Storms River campsite and the Groot River estuary you will see an entirely different selection of birds: over 40 species of seabird have been recorded here. The most satisfying sighting is the rare African black oystercatcher, with its black plumage and red eyes, beak and legs.

With such steep slopes and dense forest you will only come across a few small mammals. The species that do occur include caracal, bushbuck, blue duiker, grysbok, bushpig and the Cape clawless otter. The blue duiker is the smallest antelope in South Africa – the adult male stands less than 30 cm high and weighs about 4 kg, although the female is slightly bigger. They live in forest and thick bush along the coast, feeding on forest fruits and flowers that are dropped from the canopy by feeding monkeys, or birds such as the Knysna lourie or rameron pigeons. Each animal lives alone in a territory of about 6 ha in extent. The most likely time to see them is at dawn or dusk in an open clearing – ask the park rangers about recent sightings. The Cape clawless otter is also very rare and considered an endangered species. It feeds on fish and sea crabs, emerging from its den in the early evening. You will be very lucky to catch a glimpse of either of these mammals.

Hiking in the park

Nature's Valley Rest Camp Across the Groot River from the camp are six trails in the Grootkloof Forest. There are a number of large trees here and the birdlife is excellent, although there's the usual problem of catching sight of them in the first place. The best spots are in clearings and along streams. Note that there are a large number of streams in the forest which can be difficult to cross after heavy rains. South of the camp the river estuary broadens into a lagoon which is a popular spot for watersports. Fortunately no powerboats are allowed on the water, and exploring the limits by canoe is great fun.

Storms River Camp There are four different trails in the vicinity of the camp. The most popular, and strongly recommended, is a 1-km walk along a raised boardwalk from the restaurant block to the mouth of the Storms River. The last part of the walk involves a steep descent – there is a solid handrail, but the wooden steps can be slippery after rains, as can other parts of the walk. At the bottom is the suspension bridge which appears in many pictures promoting the Garden Route. The views from this point are excellent, especially at midday when there is a clear view of the narrow river gorge extending back inland. The path continues on the other side of the bridge, and from here you can climb the hill for

The Otter Trail

This is one of South Africa's best hiking trails, managed by South African National Parks (SANParks), and it was also the first of its kind to be laid out. The 42.5-km trail is unidirectional; it runs between Storms River Mouth restcamp in the Tsitsikamma National Park and the village of Nature's Valley at the western end of the national park. It takes five days and four nights to complete, and closely follows the coast – care should be taken near the cliffs. None of the sectors are that long, but it is still fairly strenuous in parts since you have to cross 11 rivers and there are steep ascents and descents at each river crossing. Apart from the natural beauty and the birdlife, the trail passes some fine waterfalls and Strandloper caves. Look out for the fine large old hardwood trees which have escaped the dreaded axe.

This is a very popular hike and booking opens 13 months in advance, though it's always worth asking about cancellations. Permits are available from SANParks, Tshwane (Pretoria), T012-426 5111, www.sanparks.org. Bookings can also be made in person at the offices in Cape Town (see page 48) and Durban. The offices also provide excellent maps which are packed full of background information and advice to help make your experience an enjoyable one. The route is marked with painted otter footprints.

Distances: **Day 1** = 4.8 km (± 2 hours); **Day 2** = 7.9 km (± 4 hours); **Day 3** = 7.7 km (± 4 hours); **Day 4** = 13.8 km (± 6 hours); **Day 5** = 6.8 km (± 3 hours).

Total distance = 42.5 km. Only 12 people can start the trail each day; groups should consist of a minimum of four. It costs R595 per person, which includes four nights in the hiking huts as well as the permit.

The four overnight camps are Ngubu, Scott, Oakhurst and André. At each site there are two log huts, each sleeping six people in bunk beds; mattresses and firewood are provided. Each hut has a braai place with a sturdy steel grill but hikers need to provide their own pots for cooking. There are numerous streams and springs throughout the length of the Otter Trail that are suitable for drinking. However, it may be wise to use purification tablets especially if you are not used to this water and where streams/rivers pass through communities such as the Coldstream/Witels River (3.6 km mark of Day 4) and the Lottering River (7.5 km mark of Day 4). There are rainwater tanks at each overnight hut that may also be used. The Bloukrans River crossing presents the most problems. Check tide tables; you will at least have to wade, or even swim across. Waterproofing for your rucksack is vital. If you are unable to cross the river, you can take the escape route, which branches to the right of the trail, where it climbs steeply to the top of the plateau and leads to the N2. Take time to enjoy the trail, relish the scenery and the solitude, respect the environment and leave with positive and happy memories.

superb views; there are over 300 steps and the path is narrow and steep. Look out for identification labels on the trees as the path winds through the forest. This is a great opportunity to see the trees which a century ago were in great demand for household furniture and building projects – much of the reason for the extensive deforestation in the area. Allow at least an hour for the walk to the bridge and back.

The other trails close to the camp are the **Lourie Trail**, 1 km through the forested slopes behind the camp; the **Blue Duiker Trail**, 3.7 km further into the forest; and the **Waterfall**

Trail, a 3-km walk along the first part of the Otter Trail (see page 331); hikers without a permit have to turn back at the waterfall.

The latest addition to the park is the **Dolphin Trail** ① *information and reservations T042-280 3588, www.dolphintrail.co.za*, a three-day guided trail to the east of Storms River Rest Camp and in the opposite direction to the Otter Trail. This is a far more upmarket hike – luggage is transported from one night stop to the next, accommodation is in luxurious lodges, all meals are included (pre-packed picnics for lunch), and the hike is professionally guided. This trail is also much more expensive, at R4200 per person for three days.

Behind the restaurant is the rather unusual **Underwater Trail**, which can be completed with scuba equipment or a mask and snorkel. You can see a good cross-section of the marine life found along the south coast, but conditions are not ideal, so few people complete the trail. If you do want to give it a go, the best time of year is in the summer, although conditions are rough for most of the year and visibility is rarely more than 10 m. The water is fairly cold, so be sure to wear a wetsuit.

Storms River Village → *Colour map 7, B3.*

Storms River Village lies 8 km east of the Storms River Bridge, 4 km from the entrance to Tsitsikamma National Park, and 1 km south of the N2. Administratively, this is the first settlement in the Eastern Cape Province, but it is also regarded as the first and last town along the Garden Route, hence its inclusion here. This small village of around 40 houses has several accommodation options catering for visitors to the park, and hikers wishing to head for the inland mountains. It's also a stop-off for the **Baz Bus** and the starting point for many of the adventure activities in the region. The small supermarket and liquor store are useful for those self-catering at Tsitsikamma. Note that the village is nowhere near the sea.

◉ Garden Route listings

For Sleeping and Eating price codes and other relevant information, see pages 46-53.

◎ Sleeping

Mossel Bay *p309, map p310*
During busy periods, contact the **Mossel Bay Tourism Bureau**, T044-691 2202, to confirm overnight accommodation. It acts as a central reservations office for registered members. In Dec it's essential to pre-book.
A Diaz Strand, Santos Beach, T044-692 8400, www.diazbeach.co.za. Luxury hotel in a commanding position on Santos Beach overlooking the waves, 86 spacious rooms in a modern block, all with balconies and ocean views. Facilities include outdoor rim-flow pool, indoor heated Olympic-sized pool and wellness centre, a water theme park with tubes and a lazy river, live entertainment and the highly regarded **Bahia Dos Vaqueiros** restaurant (see Eating, page 342).

B Huijs te Marquette, 1 Marsh St, T/F044-691 3182, www.marquette.co.za. A comfortable house which has been very thoughtfully decorated with 12 rooms, relaxed atmosphere, small snug bar and lounge with fireplace, evening meals on request, swimming pool, secure parking, wheelchair friendly. Recommended.
B The Point, Point Rd, T044-691 3512, www.pointhotel.co.za. Large, ugly construction but in an unbeatable location, right on the rocks below the lighthouse. All 52 rooms have satellite TV, internet, sea views and private balconies. **The Lighthouse** restaurant and bar caters for most. The rock pool just outside is good for swimming.
B Protea Hotel Mossel Bay, corner of Church and Market St, T044-691 3738, www.oldpost tree.co.za, www.proteahotels.com. This is part of the museum complex and was formerly known as the **Old Post Office Tree Manor**.

Comfortable hotel rooms and self-catering suites in a smart manor house which is the 3rd-oldest building in Mossel Bay. Outdoor dining area with views across bay, swimming pool, popular and always recommended by visitors, check for seasonal discounts.

C Mossel Bay Guesthouse, 61 Bruns Rd, T044-691 2000, www.mosselbaygh.co.za. Friendly guesthouse with 4 double rooms, sea views and M-Net TV. Heated pool and wooden deck with ocean views where breakfast is served in summer, and small pub. The house is tucked back from the town centre up the hill.

D 1 Point Village Guest House, Bland St East, T044-690 7792, www.pointguest house.co.za. Good location near the Point, this neat guesthouse has 6 rooms, some with sea views, individually decorated in fresh colours. Heated swimming pool in courtyard, braai area and generous break-fasts, also rents out modern self-catering holiday cottages nearby sleeping 4-8, which are good value for families and groups.

D-F Mossel Bay Backpackers, 1 Marsh St, T044-691 3182, www.gardenroute adventures.com. Part of Huijs te Marquette, dorms and double rooms, TV room, break-fasts and dinners available, self-catering kitchen, pool, convenient location 300 m from the beach and close to some bars, travel centre can organize activities, popular.

D-F Santos Caravan Park, on the George road 2 km from town centre, T044-691 2915. Large well-grassed park with 54 camping and caravan sites, limited shade, some self-catering chalets, not the place to stay when full, but fine at the quiet time of year, on the beach.

E Santos Express Train Lodge, Santos Beach T044-691 1995, www.santosexpress.co.za. Converted train carriages set 30 m from the sea, with tiny cabins sleeping 4, shared hot showers, sun deck and an onboard pub and restaurant serving seafood, lamb on the spit and braais. Baz Bus stop.

Botlierskop Private Game Reserve *p311*
Private lodges and camps
L3 Botlierskop Private Game Reserve, T044-696 6055, www.botlierskop.co.za. 19 luxury tented suites on wooden platforms, good views over river and mountains, some have private jetties for fishing, decorated in a colonial theme with 4-poster beds swathed in mosquito nets. Rates include game drives, walks and all meals. An all-round safari experience close to the Garden Route.

George and around *p312, map p312*
L Fancourt Hotel and Country Club, 6 km from George airport, T044-804 0010, www. fancourt.com. This is an exclusive upmarket resort and thanks to the President's Cup being hosted here in Nov 2003, it is one of the world's leading golf destinations. Set on more than 500 ha of land, Fancourt encompasses 4 outstanding 18-hole golf courses, 2 of which were designed by Gary Player. There are 150 rooms in the 19th-century manor house or garden suites and studios overlooking the golf courses. Health spa, gym, tennis courts, 2 outdoor pools, 1 indoor heated pool, 6 superb restaurants. Golf open to members and guests only. Special packages are sometimes published on the website. Golfer Ernie Els sponsors a golf academy here for talented young South Africans who could not under normal circumstances afford to participate in the sport. Room rates drop significantly in low season (1 Apr-31 Aug).

A-B Far Hills Country Hotel, off the N2 towards Wilderness, T044-889 0000, www.far hillscountryhotel.co.za. A large comfortable country hotel in the lee of the Outeniqua Mountains, with 51 tastefully decorated rooms with fireplace and balcony, some with superb views across the forest, but a bit cramped, 2 restaurants and – rather surprisingly – a sushi bar, open terrace, lounge, bar and swimming pool. Very attentive service for such a big hotel.

B Oakhurst Manor House, corner of Meade and Cathedral streets, T044-874 7130, www.oakhursthotel.co.za. Luxury town inn in the design of a classic Cape Dutch house with thatched roof, 25 smart, individually decorated rooms, large restaurant, lounge, ladies' bar and swimming pool. Professionally run but aimed at the business traveller.

B Protea Hotel King George, King George Drive, T044-874 7659, www.proteahotels.com. Smart Victorian hotel situated close to the 11th fairway of the George Golf Course, 60 comfortable rooms, good restaurant, pub, 2 swimming pools, the usual quality of service expected in a Protea.

B-C George Tourist Resort, York St, T044-874 5205, www.george-tourist-resort.co.za. Huge complex with self-catering chalets sleeping up to 8, smaller rondavels and shady camping and caravan sites with power and water, indoor pool and outdoor heated pool, gym, sauna, tennis courts, crazy golf, shop, laundry, room for 300 caravans. Double the price during peak season.

D Hawthorndene Country Inn, Langenhoven Rd, T044-874 4160, www.hawthorndene.co.za. Family-run, good value country inn with 26 neat rooms, pool, good restaurant and bar with log walls and crackling fire, big TV screen and live music at the weekends.

D Loerie Guest Lodge, 91 Davidson Rd, T044-874 4740, www.loerielodge.co.za. Modern buildings with 22 large and comfortable en suite rooms, a neat garden with a swimming pool and sun deck, pub on the 1st floor with a deck for good views of the mountains. Alright for an overnight stop, but predominantly a conference venue. Also rents out a 5-bedroom house nearby.

D Pine Lodge, Knysna Rd, close to Pick 'n' Pay, T044-871 1974, www.pinelodgegeorge.co.za. Large resort close to Victoria Bay, suitable for families, with 46 self-catering chalets with 1-3 bedrooms, M-Net TV, Wi-Fi, telephone and braai area. Restaurant, the **Courtyard Grill**, bar, tennis courts and swimming pool. There are a few budget rooms without kitchens.

D-F Outeniqua Backpackers, 115 Merriman St, T082-216 7720, www.outeniqua-backpackers.com. Newish hostel with 20 dorm beds and a couple of doubles, bright and airy, some with mountain views, braai area, breakfasts, DSTV and internet. Only backpacker option in town. Baz Bus stop and free pick-ups from George Airport. You can hire bikes and they'll drop you off at the top of Montagu Pass for the ride back down.

Victoria Bay *p314*
B Lands End, The Point, T044-889 0123, www.vicbay.com. 2 double en suite rooms with TV, 3 self-contained apartments with sun deck, self-catering or breakfasts served on an open veranda only 6 m from the ocean, beautiful location, fishing and surf equipment hired out, golf at Fancourt can be arranged. Laundry, wine cellar, glass of sherry on arrival.
B The Waves, 6 Beach Rd, T044-889 0166, http://thewavesvictoriabay.co.za. A superior B&B right on the beach, 3 double rooms with en suite bathroom, balconies and sea views, 1906 historic building, friendly, low-key place, a more pleasant location than the centre of George, 2 separate family cottages available (B&B or self-catering). Recommended.
D Sea Breeze, 300-m walk to the beach, T044-889 0098, www.seabreezecabanas.co.za. 36 units, modern development of self-catering flats and chalets with M-Net TV, bedding supplied but you have to bring your own towels and dishcloths. The beach has a safe tidal pool, good for families.

Wilderness and around *p316, map p316*
A Dolphin Dunes, Buxton Close, approaching from George, turn right off the N2, 2.5 km after the Caltex petrol station T044-877 0204, www.dolphindunes.co.za. A fine upmarket purpose-built guesthouse with 8 tasteful, double rooms, some with wheelchair access, fridge, TV, telephone, splash pool, private access to the beach on a boardwalk. Also rents out a fully equipped modern holiday villa sleeping 8-10.
A-B Moontide Guest Lodge, Southside Rd, T044-877 0361, www.moontide.co.za. 7 en suite thatched cottages, one of them a honeymoon suite, set under milkwood

trees in a beautiful garden overlooking the lagoon. Each cottage has been tastefully decorated with kilims and fine furniture. Easy access to the hiking trails in the national park, a short walk from the beach and a good spot for birdwatchers. A well-appointed and well-run guesthouse. Recommended.

B The Pink Lodge on the Beach, 45 die Duin, T044-877 0263, www.pinklodge.co.za. B&B or self-catering in a great position right on the beach, 7 spacious, a/c, en suite rooms, 1 with self-catering facilities, all facing the ocean, spot whales or dolphins from your bed, rolling lawns, a very relaxing spot. Shame about the hideous bright pink colour.

B Protea Wilderness Resort, George Rd (N2), T044-877 1110, www.proteahotels.com. Smartest hotel in the area, with 155 stylish rooms with TV and a/c, restaurant, beauty spa, 2 swimming pools, bowling green, giant chess board in the grounds, great views all-round. If you are not staying here, pop in for the very good-value Sun lunch (1230-1500), when you can also try Knysna oysters.

C Fairy Knowe, Dumbleton Rd, T044-877 1100, www.fairyknowe.co.za. 42 rooms, some thatched rondavels, peaceful forested location on Touw River, close to Wilderness National Park, birdwatchers will enjoy regular visits by the Knysna lourie and there are a couple of resident Cape spotted eagle owls, restaurant, bar, canoes, pedalos and tennis.

D Bruni's Guest House, 937 8th Av, Wilderness East, T044-877 0551, www.brunis.co.za. 4 en suite double rooms in a thatched house perched on the dunes with sweeping views of the ocean from the glassed-in breakfast room. German spoken, no children under 12.

D-F Fairy Knowe Backpackers, Dumbleton Rd, just off Waterside Rd, T044-877 1285, www.wildernessbackpackers.com. A great set-up in 2 farmhouses surrounded by gardens and milkwood trees, clean attractive rooms, dorms and doubles, camping space in the garden, bar, great breakfasts, nightly camp fires and braais. Also has a travel desk. A very relaxing place to rest up for a few days. Baz Bus stops here. Recommended.

Wilderness National Park *p317, map p316*

Accommodation is laid out in 2 camps divided by the railway and the Serpentine River channel: **Ebb & Flow Rest Camp, North** and **Ebb & Flow Rest Camp, South**. All the park's accommodation must be vacated by 0900. Arriving visitors can have access from 1200. Reservations through SANParks Tshwane (Pretoria) office, T012-428 9111, www.sanparks.org. Bookings can also be made in person at the offices in Cape Town and Durban (see page 48). For reservations under 72 hrs or cancellations contact the park reception directly, T044-877 1197.

Ebb and Flow Rest Camp, South

This Rest Camps is on the Touw River close to Wilderness village, and has 34 units in total, including cottages (**C**) with 2 bedrooms and sofa bed, bathroom, partially equipped kitchen, lounge, modern bungalows with no appeal when you compare them with the log cabins; self-catering log cabins (**C**) on stilts, all with views across the river and the reed beds, 2 bedrooms, bathroom, kitchen, comfortable lounge area and a veranda, lots of character, good value for 4 people especially with a seasonal discount; and forest cabins (**D**) sleeping 2 or 4, fairly basic but with bathroom and partially equipped kitchen, communal kitchen also available.

Camping There is an excellent campsite in thick grass with patches of good shade on the banks of the river. Beautiful setting and good facilities, 59 caravan and camping sites, full of character as long as it is not too busy.

Ebb & Flow Rest Camp, North

A short walk from the office, this is a smaller camp beside the Touw River where it emerges from the hills. A beautiful and peaceful spot but its geography means that cold air collects in the narrow valley and the sun only reaches the camp for a few hours.

There are 12 huts (**D**), 1-room rondavels with 2 single beds, 2-plate electric stove, fridge, cooking equipment, plus a shower, for 2 people, or a cheaper option with communal ablutions.

Camping On the banks of the Touw River there are 45 caravan and camping sites. Plenty of grass and shade, wash block, no communal kitchen but braais, some sites with electric points.

Sedgefield and around *p317*
As with all villages along this stretch of coast, prices are considerably higher at Christmas and rooms need to be booked well in advance. There is a choice of overnight stops and holiday cottages in the village and around the lakes.

A Lake Pleasant, east of Sedgefield on the edge of Groenvlei, T044-349 2400, www.lake pleasanthotel.com. This comfortable 5-star hotel has had a major overhaul and now belongs to the South African Mantis chain of luxury hotels. Set right on the lake, with 36 rooms, opening onto gardens, all with lake views. Smart lounge furnished with antiques, library, cigar bar, restaurant with a menu to match the setting – great lunch stop if you're passing through. Swimming pool, tennis court, gym, health spa. Perfect for birdwatchers with some hides by the lake, rowing boats for hire. Recommended.

D Lake Pleasant Chalets & Lodges, on the lakeshore, follow the Buffalo Bay signs from the N2, T044-343 1985, www.lake-pleasant. co.za. Well-maintained, fully-equipped self-catering timber chalets sleeping 6, with TV, braais and plenty of shade from milkwood trees, plus smaller brick cottages sleeping 4. Peaceful location overlooking the lake, swimming pool, pub/restaurant, kiddies playground and you can hire mountain bikes, canoes and basic fishing tackle and can buy bait.

D Sedgefield Arms, Pelican Lane, off the N2 in the village centre, T044-343 1417, www.sedgefieldarms.co.za. A comfortable mix of self-catering cottages suitable for 2-6 people with patio and braai, or B&B.

Attached restaurant and lively English theme pub, good spot for lunch on the lawn, bar with big sports screen, swimming pool, all set in leafy gardens, good value and fun atmosphere. Rates drop significantly out of season.

Goukamma Nature Reserve *p318*
For reservations, T021-659 3500, www.cape nature.org.za.

D Groenvlei & Muvubu Bushcamps, on the western side of the reserve, hidden away in the milkwood forest. 2 thatched family houses sleeping 8-9, with living area and kitchen linked by boardwalks, furnishings made from wood or reeds. Both a short walk to the lake where you can swim and watch the sun set. Bedding is supplied but bring your own food and towels. A beautiful setting with particular attention paid to the environment. Recommended and good value for 4 or more.

D Musselcracker House, 300 m from the river and 4 km from the sea in the eastern side of the reserve. 3 rooms sleeping 7 people, 2 bathrooms, fully equipped kitchen and braai area. Bedding is supplied but bring your own food, firewood and towels.

E Rondavels, 300 m from the river and 4 km from the sea in the eastern side of the reserve. Also here are 3 cheaper thatched rondavels sleeping 2-5, each with its own braai area but with shared kitchenette and bathroom. Again, bedding is supplied but bring your own food, firewood and towels.

Knysna and around *p318, maps p319 and p320*
It is difficult to find accommodation during the Christmas and New Year period unless you book 6 months in advance. As one of the most popular holiday centres along the Garden Route, there is plenty of choice of accommodation, both in type and location, but it's generally more expensive than in other towns along the Garden Route. The list below is far from comprehensive. Remember you'll be paying a premium to stay over school holiday periods. The centre of Knysna

is on the northern margin of the lagoon. To the east of town, George Rex Dr leads to Leisure Island and the Knysna Heads. Along and off this road are a number of guesthouses and B&Bs. For something different, and especially recommended for families, **self-catering houseboats (A)** are available for hire on the Knysna Lagoon. All eating and sleeping equipment is included, and you can hire fishing tackle, and you do not need to have any nautical experience. They are very easy to operate and allow you to explore the lagoon at leisure. Contact **Lightleys Holiday Houseboats**, T044-386 0007, www.houseboats.co.za.

AL Falcon's View Manor, 2 Thesen Hill, T044-382 6767, www.falconsview.com. You can book online through the African Pride hotel group; www.africanpridehotels.com. Small upmarket hotel in a classic Victorian house. 9 spacious double rooms (non-smoking) with DSTV, tastefully decorated and furnished to an exceptional level of comfort. There's a relaxing veranda overlooking the lagoon, swimming pool, neat gardens and intimate bar. Recommended.

A Leisure Isle Boutique Lodge, 87 Bayswater Drive, Leisure Isle, T044-384 0462, www.leisu reislelodge.co.za. Award-winning guesthouse with 11 spacious rooms, comfortable lounge and bar, heated swimming pool, views across bay, gardens stretch to waterfront, no children under 12, superb food in the elegant restaurant, spa for massages and treatments a short drive from Knysna Heads.

A Rex Hotel, 8 Grey St, T044-302 5900, www.rexhotel.co.za. Super stylish in an architectural gem of a modern building, with 30 spacious luxury rooms, in muted browns and creams, with kitchenettes, a/c, DSTV, DVD players, Wi-Fi and balconies. The **Dish Restaurant** is well regarded for its gourmet food, the bar is popular with Knysna's elite.

A Under Milkwood, at the end of George Rex Drive, T044-384 0745, www.milkwood. co.za. 16 self-catering log chalets at Knysna Heads set in a grove of milkwood trees, can sleep 6, excellent kitchen facilities. Not all have

views of the lagoon. Plenty of light, relaxing sun deck, recommended if you plan to spend a week in the district. Also has comfortable B&B rooms in the main building (**B**). Out of the town, but still close to all the amenities. Dec-Jan rates take a significant hike.

B Isolabella, Cearn Drive, Leisure Isle, T044-384 0049, www.isolabella.co.za. Italian-run villa with wrap-around balconies in a commanding position overlooking the lagoon, with 3 rooms decorated in luxurious cream carpets and fresh flowers. Breakfast served on the balcony or in your private lounge.

B Knysna Belle, 75 Bayswater Drive, Leisure Isle, T044-384 0511, www.knysnabelle.co.za. 7 very stylish individually decorated rooms, 1 with a Victorian bath tub, very good breakfasts, swimming pool, lovely balconies to relax and enjoy the views of the lagoon, mountain bikes and a rowing boat available to rent out, no children under 6.

B Knysna Manor House, 19 Fitchat St, T044-382 5440, www.knysnamanor.co.za. A peaceful Victorian stone house with good views of the lagoon, a short walk from town centre. 13 rooms with TV, decor is a bit frilly.

B Protea Hotel Knysna Quays, Knysna Quays, T044-382 5005, www.proteahotels. com. Usual large state-of-the-art hotel, with 123 comfortable a/c rooms, restaurant, cocktail bar, lounge, attractive swimming pool and Wi-Fi. Great location next to the Waterfront and within walking distance of restaurants.

B Yellowwood Lodge, 18 Handel St, T044-382 5906, www.yellowwoodlodge.co.za. Lovely guesthouse in one of Knysna's older houses with 10 thoughtfully decorated rooms. Ask for an upstairs room – they have relaxing balconies with views of the lagoon and Heads. Delicious buffet breakfasts, immaculate garden, swimming pool, strictly non-smoking household, no children under 10. Loses some of its appeal when full, look out for the flagpole.

C Wayside Inn, 48 Main St, T044-382 6011, www.waysideinn.co.za. Smart set-up in the centre of town with a Victorian theme.

15 luxury rooms with iron beds and sisal carpets, fans, fine African art on show, private balconies, wicker furniture, TV, superior picnic hampers can be made to order. Several readers have commented on the lack of a lounge area and breakfast is served in the rooms or on the patio, weather permitting. Friendly staff.

D Aesta's B&B, 21 Fitchat St, T044-382 4849, www.aestas.co.za. Nice views from several spacious and attractive rooms, swimming pool, walking distance from the tourist office and shops and restaurants on the main road, well-run medium-sized B&B, children under 6 sharing with parents free.

D Heron Water Lodge, 33 Cearn Drive, Leisure Isle, T044-384 0624, www.garden route.co.za/knysna/heron. A friendly and comfortable B&B just 20 m from the lagoon with 4 plain but spacious en suite double rooms, 2 overlook the lagoon in a separate wing. Sun deck, bar, pool, generous filling breakfasts, mountain bikes available to rent.

E-F Highfield Backpackers, 2 Graham St, T044-382 6266, www.highfieldsbackpackers. co.za. Quiet backpacker hostel set in 2 town houses, dorms and doubles, shared bathrooms, bar with pool table, kitchen, courtyard with pool, travel centre. A bit of a rabbit warren but the new owners have done much to spruce up the place. Baz Bus stop.

E-F Knysna Backpackers, 42 Queen St, T044-382 2554, www.knysnabackpackers. co.za. Large dorms, clean bathrooms, TV room, well-stocked kitchen, travel centre, set in a large rambling Victorian mansion in established gardens, which are good for camping, and views across the lagoon from the wide veranda. Baz Bus stop.

Belvidere *p321*

A Belvidere Manor, 169 Duthie Drive, Belvidere, T044-387 1055, www.belvidere.co.za. 34 smart cottages arranged around a pool in shady gardens, sleeping 2-4 people. Private verandas with views across the lagoon, kitchens, DSTV and DVD players. Some have a study; all are individually

furnished and have log fires. The manor house, from 1834, houses the reception and the elegant dining room. **The Bell** pub is housed in an old farm cottage and the highlight here is seeing the wine cellar underneath the glass floor. Friendly and attentive staff.

Knysna Forest *p322, map p320*

L Phantom Forest Eco-Reserve, T044-386 0046, www.phantomforest.com. Signposted from the Phantom Pass road. This lodge offers ultra-stylish accommodation in a superb collection of 14 luxurious and eco-friendly 'tree suites' set in the forest high above the lagoon. Each has a private terrace and luxurious bathroom – the showers are open to the forest. Individual houses are connected by walkways to the excellent restaurant, bar, lookout points, gorgeous beauty spa with Moroccan decor, and stunning pool on the edge of a wooden deck. Attentive, helpful staff, the perfect place to experience the forest. Highly recommended.

D Forest Edge, just past the Rheenendal Post Office, turn right at the Bibby's Hoek sign. At the entrance to the state forest, turn left for 1.5 km, the lodge is the last property on this road, T082-456 1338, www.forestedge.co.za. 3 holiday cottages with delightful names – Field Mouse, Froggy Pond and Fire Fly, self-contained and fully equipped, sleeping 4-5 people, overlooking a picturesque dam. Linen and towels are provided and there is a fireplace, telephone, braai facilities and outdoor hot shower. Mountain bikes available for hire, you can walk straight into the forest from here.

Knysna Elephant Park *p323*

B Elephant Lodge, T044-532 7732, www.knysnaelephantpark.co.za. 5 newly refurbished twin rooms and 1 large family flat sleeping 6 over the boma where the elephants sleep, so you can fall asleep to their nightly sounds (and smells!), and see them when they are out and about. Modern and comfortable with DSTV and a spacious lounge with large picture windows.

Plettenberg Bay *p324, map p325*
During Christmas it is difficult to find a bed unless you have booked well in advance. Along with Knysna, there is an unbelievable transformation here during the midsummer holiday rush. For the rest of the year, hotels and B&Bs cry out for guests. In an effort to attract visitors during the winter months, discounts are offered so it's worth checking these out when choosing somewhere to stay.
L Hunter's Country House, 10 km towards Knysna, T044-532 7818, www.hunterhotels. com. 21 luxury individually decorated thatched suites with fireplace, antique furnishings and private patio, 2 swimming pools, conservatory, antique shop, forest chapel for weddings, childcare service. One of South Africa's top country hotels and part of the Relais & Chateaux group, which has won awards for food and service, a special place to treat yourself to. Recommended.
L The Plettenberg, 40 Church St, Lookout Rocks, T044-533 2030, www.plettenberg.com. 40 a/c rooms, lounge and dining rooms furnished with antiques, superb food and wine, swimming pool, beauty spa, smartest in area, another Relais & Chateaux property, everything you would expect in a small, exclusive top-class, 5-star hotel, but very expensive. Request a room with ocean views, some of them look over the car park. Rates double in high season.
A Beacon Island, Beacon Island Cres, T044-533 1120, www.southernsun.com. Multi-storey building dominating the bay, right on the water between 2 beaches, 200 rooms, 4 excellent restaurants, swimming pool, tennis, also a timeshare resort. A superb location but an eyesore on Plett's sweeping beach.
B Cottage Pie, 16 Tarbet Ness Av, T044-533 0369, www.cottagepie.co.za. Homely but upmarket guesthouse offering 8 well-appointed rooms, very comfortable and cosy with TV and minibar. Pool, bougainvillea-bedecked terrace. Slightly out of town, but

only 100 m to Robberg Beach. Pricey in the height of season when rates double.
B Stone Cottages, corner of Harker and Odland streets, T044-533 1331, www.stone cottage.co.za. Beautifully restored 19th-century cottage, tastefully decorated rooms with high ceilings and gleaming wooden floors, antiques and old photographs, fully equipped for self-catering, sleeps 5 in 3 bedrooms, panoramic views of the ocean, deck with jacuzzi over-looking the main beach. Close by are 3 smaller modern, cheaper self-catering cottages for 2, with TV and DVD in the lounge, decor in the same theme as the older cottage. A good option for families or friends travelling together, and price per person is reasonable.
C A Room with a View, 5 Julia Av, T044-533 1836, www.roomwithaview.co.za. Near the beach with, as the name suggests, good views, an unusual building arranged in blocks up the hill with 3 en suite rooms and 1 suite with extra kitchen, with TV, fridge, heater and fan, special touches like fruit bowls and glasses of sherry, lovely garden terraces where you can take breakfast.
C-D Coral Tree Cottages, off the N2 11 km from Plett towards Knysna, T044-532 7822, www.coraltreecottages.co.za. Good self-catering option if you have a car, 6 spacious and nicely furnished thatched cottages with 1 or 2 bedrooms, satellite TV, fully equipped kitchen, patio and braai area, set in lovely green woodlands full of flowers, breakfast on request. They also can arrange quad-bike safaris and there's a small water park with lazy river and slide. An excellent base for families for a few days as Knysna is only 25 km away.
D-F Albergo For Backpackers, 8 Church St, T044-533 4434, www.albergo.co.za. Centrally located hostel with sea views. Dorms, double rooms and camping area, garden with hammocks and bonfires, 2 kitchens, travel centre, TV room, bar and pool table, surf-boards for hire. Baz Bus stop.
D-F Nothando Backpackers, 5 Wilder St, T044-533 0220, www.nothando.co.za. Camping, dorms, double rooms, B&B, in a central location, cheap and friendly, with

extras like hairdryers in the bathrooms, plus offering plenty of activities with discounts. Beds have duvets, some rooms are en suite, small kitchen, large TV lounge, kitchen, bar with braai and pool table. Baz Bus stop.

East of Plettenberg Bay p326
L Hog Hollow Country Lodge, 18 km east of Plettenberg Bay at the Crags off the N2 main road, T044-534 8879, www.hog-hollow.com. Closed Jun. One of the finest lodges along the Garden Route set in a private nature reserve, with 15 suites, all with ceiling fans, minibar decorated with locally made wall hangings and woodcarvings, each with its own wooden deck with hammock overlooking the Matjies River gorge and Tsitsikamma Mountains. There is a spacious lounge with open fireplace for log fires in the winter months. Good evening meals are served around a communal table in a relaxed manner. Swimming pool with stunning views, library/lounge in the main house. Special touches include a glass of milk and gingerbread man for children at bedtime. The lodge also organizes 3-hr boat trips around the bay to view whales and dolphins, and there are a number of walking trails through the forest surrounding the lodge which are very popular with birdwatchers. Recommended.
B Protea Hotel Keurbooms River, on Keurbooms River 8.5 km east from Plett, T044-535 9300, www.proteahotels.com. Modern and functional but very comfortable hotel set in indigenous gardens, 61 rooms with TV and kettles, some with kitchenettes and adjoining rooms can make up 2 or 3 bedroom flats, swimming pool, bar and restaurant with wooden deck with outstanding river views.
C Forever Resorts Plettenberg, 6 km east of Plett on the Keurbooms River, T044-535 9309, www.foreversa.co.za. 30 neat timber or brick self-catering chalets nestled along the riverbank, plus 112 camping and caravan spots (**F**) with excellent facilities, swimming pool, canoes and pedalos for hire, tennis and volleyball courts, good all-round family

option but gets horribly busy during school holidays when rates are considerably higher.

Nature's Valley p327
Surprisingly Nature's Valley has hardly any accommodation, though there is always the option of the Nature's Valley Rest Camp in the Tsitsikamma National Park, which is accessed from the village (page 341).
A Tranquility Lodge, 130 St Michaels Av, next to the Nature's Valley shop and pub, T044-531 6663, www.tranquilitylodge.co.za. Lovely reed-and-timber lodge in pretty gardens, with 7 rooms, 4 of which is a honeymoon suite with spa bath, double shower and fireplace, very nicely decorated throughout with lots of lounging areas. The owner is also a chef and meals can be taken together with other guests in the dining room, or alone on the wooden deck. There's a swimming pool, outside hot pool, each room gets its own double kayak to explore the lagoon, a complimentary bridge walk at the nearby Bloukrans Bridge is included in the price, and finally it's registered with BirdLife as a birder-friendly establishment. No children under 16. Recommended.
D Hiker's Haven, 411 St Patrick's St, T044-531 6805, www.hikershaven.co.za. A large stone guesthouse with thatched roof, 7 comfortable individually decorated rooms, 5 en suite and 3 share a bathroom, TV lounge, kitchenette, pool table, beach and lagoon a 200-m walk away. Operates a shuttle service to take hikers back to their cars at the opposite ends of the Tsitsikamma and Otter trails and provides hearty breakfasts for hikers starting these trails from Nature's Valley.

Groot River and Bloukrans Passes p328
The Baz Bus stops at the site below, though a car is a necessity as there are no amenities in the vicinity and only a coffee shop on site. Despite being comfortable inside the chalets and backpacker lodge, this is a bleak spot in winter. There is also a caravan park with electricity points and shared ablutions.

D Tsitsikamma Forest Village, off the N2 next to the Bloukrans bungee jump, T042-281 1450, www.tsitsikamma.org.za. 16 self-catering log chalets, some on stilts with kitchen, braai area, lounge and veranda, suitable for families.

E-F Bloukrans Backpackers Lodge, see above. A good range of accommodation, including 2 dorms sleeping 8, and some double rooms, modern and comfortable communal kitchen and lounge area with DSTV and a pool table.

Tsitsikamma National Park *p329*

This is a very popular national park, particularly with South Africans, so during the school holidays it is almost impossible to find accommodation here. Reservations must be made up to 12 months in advance. Fortunately there is plenty of accommodation along the Garden Route. If you're staying in Knysna, for example, it is a 1-hr drive to the park. There are also several private lodges close to the main entrance (see below).

All the park's accommodation must be vacated by 0900. Arriving visitors have access from 1200. There are 2 rest camps in the park: **Storms River Mouth**, the main camp with a full range of facilities; **Nature's Valley**, a very basic camp close to the settlement of the same name. Reservations, through the **SANParks** office in Tshwane (Pretoria), T012-428 9111, www.sanparks.org. Bookings can also be made in person at the offices in Cape Town and Durban (see page 48). For cancellations and reservations under 72 hrs contact Storms River Mouth camp directly, T042-281 1607. Credit card bookings are accepted over the phone. Seasonal discounts apply to all accommodation in May-Aug.

Storms River Mouth

On a narrow strip of land between ocean and forested hills, this is one of the most beautiful settings of all the national parks.

There are log cabins (**B-C**), with 2 bedrooms sleeping a maximum of 6 people, fully equipped kitchen with fridge and stove,

bedding provided, bathroom, lounge area; Oceanettes (**C**) with 2 bedrooms, fully equipped kitchen, bathroom, lounge, a little less smart and comfortable, but ideal when you are likely to spend most of the day outdoors; very basic but self-contained Forest Cabins (**C-D**) sleeping 2, with bathroom and kitchen facilities, generally, these can only be booked on a nightly basis as they are used for accommodation on the Dolphin Trail (see page 332) but enquire with SANParks when booking; and very basic Forest Huts (**D**) sleeping 2, with shared ablution block.

Camping Terraced lawns in a beautiful location right on the shoreline, but exposed when the wind blows. There are a few shady trees, and it is a real thrill to peer out of your tent at dawn and watch the waves crashing on the rocks right in front of you. There are twice as many places for caravans as for tents, braai sites but no electric points, laundry and central wash blocks.

Nature's Valley Rest Camp

This camping and caravan site is 40 km west of Storms River Mouth. The site is set in an indigenous forest on the banks of the Groot River, and in recent years has been upgraded. On top of the accommodation rates, there is a daily conservation fee of R88, children R44 to enter this section of the park. Accommodation is in Forest huts (**D**), which are very basic with 2 beds and electricity, or in campsites (**E**). Both of these share the wash block, hot water, laundry, no electricity, no shop or restaurant, all supplies can be bought in Nature's Valley village, 3 km away.

Storms River Village *p332*

A-B Tsitsikamma Lodge, 2 km east of village along the N2, T042-280 3802, www.tsitsikamma.com. Luxurious selection of 32 timber log cabins, including several honeymoon suites, each with spa bath (perfect after a long hike), fridges and braais, set in forested grounds and colourful gardens. Restaurant serving buffet lunches, swimming

pool. The whole complex is of a high standard and well run, the ideal base from which to start the Otter Trail as the management will transport you to the start and collect you at the end after 4-5 days for a small fee, a very useful service. Special offers in low season.
B The Armagh, 24 Fynbos Av, T042-281 1512, www.thearmagh.com. Comfortable guest-house with 6 double rooms including a free-standing cottage, all with en suite facilities and private patios, guest lounge, craft shop, spa treatment room and pool. Views and walks from the lodge are good and the garden is full of birds. Attached **Rafters** restaurant has a good local reputation with tasty buffets.
D-F Tube 'n Axe, corner of Darnell and Saffron streets, T042-281 1757, www.tube naxe.co.za. 4-bed dorms, doubles and some pre-erected tents on wooden platforms, set in a forested garden with plenty of room for camping and overland vehicles. The rustic bar has a pool table and braai pit. Breakfast and dinner available or self-catering kitchen. Shuttles to the Bloukrans Bridge Bungee, they rent out quad bikes and mountain bikes, and operate the popular **Blackwater Tubing** (see page 349) in the Tsitsikamma National Park. The **Stormsriver Adventures** office is a stone's throw away so there's plenty to keep the adventurer occupied for a couple of days. Baz Bus stop, picks up from mainline buses at the Petro-Total Village at Storms River Bridge.

● Eating

Mossel Bay p309, map p310
¶¶¶ **Admirals**, in the **Garden Route Casino** at Pinnacle Point south of Mossel Bay off the N2, T044-693 3910, www.admirals.co.za Open 1200-1500, 1800-2300. Great-value buffet in the main casino restaurant, over 120 dishes, plus Mongolian stir-fry bar where you make up your own plate of food before the chef cooks it in front of you, plenty of seafood and roasts, cold meat and cheese platters, and desserts including home-made ice cream. Recommended for the very hungry.

¶¶¶ **Bahia Dos Vaqueiros**, Diaz Strand, see Sleeping, page 332. Open 0700-1030, 1900-2200. Dominated by a giant frieze on the ceiling of the Portuguese landing on the coast and sweeping ocean views, an upmarket spot with cigar bar, walk-in wine cellar and attentive service. Interesting combinations of taste such as pork medallions with red cabbage and blue cheese or quail with apricots.
¶¶¶ **Stonehill**, Little Brak River, 6 km east of Mossel Bay off the N2 on the R107, T044-696 6501, www.stonehill.co.za. Mon-Sat 1800-2300, Sun 1130-1500. Set in a 1920s farmhouse with contemporary decor, this upmarket country French restaurant makes for a romantic night out. The chef uses organic herbs and vegetables grown on the farm, and free range meat. There's a pricey but excellent seafood platter for 2 or try the likes of beef fillet with foie gras, lobster thermidor, fish fillets in saffron butter, and finish off with a traditional crème brûlée.
¶¶ **Café Gannet**, Bartholomeu Dias Museum Complex, Market St, T044-691 1885, www.cafegannet.co.za. 0700-2300. A well-established seafood restaurant, popular all year round since the tour buses stop here, seafood grills and pizza from a wood oven, enjoyable bay views from a shady outdoor terrace, mixed reports on quality of the food but efficient and prompt service.
¶¶ **Jazzbury's**, 11 Marsh St, T044-691 1923. Open 1800-2300. Popular restaurant serving good-value traditional meals such as *potjes* and bredies, ostrich steaks, seafood and a delectable dessert trolley. Eat at tables on the patio or inside the cosy bar. Decor is striking, orange and deep purple. Recommended.
¶¶ **Kingfisher**, The Point, T044-690 6390, www.thekingfisher.co.za. 1030-2300. Modern development overlooking the beach, seafood platters and combos, good grilled fish served with rice and chips, some meat dishes, indifferent service. **Delfino's**, T044-690 5247, is an attached pizza and pasta restaurant that also does sandwiches during the day.

Pavilion, Santos Beach, T044-690 4567. Open 1000-2300. The ideal spot for lunch, just stroll up straight from the beach onto the old wooden veranda and enjoy a steak, burger, pizza or light lunch while watching the boats in the bay. Bustling atmosphere.

George and around *p312, map p312*
As well as the town restaurants, **Fancourt Hotel and Country Club** has several superb top-range restaurants open to non-guests.
Reel and Rustic, corner of York and Courtenay streets, T044-884 0707. Open 1230-1430, 1830-late, closed Sat lunch. Popular seafood restaurant with smart decor of velvet drapes and candelabras in a historical building serving good fresh Cajun and Creole dishes and unusual stuffed fish dishes and decadent desserts. Limited menu for vegetarians. Award-winning wine list.
Capannina, 122 York St near the tourist office, T044-874 5313. Mon-Fri 1100-1400, 1800-2200, Sat-Sun 1800-2200. Popular and homely Italian with local art on the walls and outside tables. Long menu of pizza, pasta, grills and fish and daily specials such as veal masala or marinated tuna. Good vegetarian choice.
The Conservatory at Meade House, 91 Meade St, T044-874 1938. Mon-Fri 0800-1600, Sat 0830-1500, Wed-Sat 1830-2200, Sun 1200-1500. Quality restaurant set in one of the oldest homes in George, dine in the conservatory or in the pretty gardens, very extensive à la carte from cakes and muffins to full meals of steak and grilled fish. Open for breakfast, lunch, afternoon teas, and dinner on some nights, also has a well-stocked shop of gifts and books.
Kafé Serefé, 60 Courtenay St, near the museum, T044-8742046. Mon-Fri 0930-1630, Mon-Sat 1900-late. Elegant interiors with Persian rugs and Arabic lamps, this Turkish restaurant serves a range of mezzes, some melt-in-the mouth kebabs and aged steaks, and for breakfast, bacon and egg shwarmas or Turkish breakfasts of cold meat, boiled egg, cucumber and tzatziki. Diners are entertained by a belly dancer on Wed and Sat nights.

Kingfisher, 1 Courtenay St, T044-873 3127, www.thekingfisher.co.za. 1200-2230. Fresh seafood dishes, renowned for prawns and fish and chips, some meat dishes including good ostrich, also has a fine selection of pasta and pizzas and a sushi bar. Good range of wine and whiskies.
La Locanda, 124 York St, T044-874 7803, www.lalocanda.co.za. Mon-Fri 1100-2200, Sat 1700-2200. Home-style Italian cooking from genuine Italian chefs who make their own pasta and cure their own cold meats, and there's a long menu of over 60 dishes, plus weekly specials using well-researched recipes from Italy. Homely interior and pleasant courtyard tables outside, South African and Italian wine.
Old Town House, corner of Market and York streets, T044-874 3663. Mon-Fri 1200-1500, 1800-late, Sat dinner only. Housed in one of George's oldest buildings dating to 1848, local specialities include lamb shank and venison pie, plus steak, seafood and grills. Home-made desserts, good-value wine list.

Wilderness and around *p316, map p316*
Wilderness does not have a large choice of restaurants but most of the accommodation offers meals. The majority of domestic visitors will self-cater.
The Palms, corner of George and Owen Grant roads, Central location off the N2, T044-877 1420, www.palms-wilderness.com. Open daily for set 4-course dinners from 1900, reservations essential, tables in the thatched restaurant or under umbrellas, wine is matched to the food. The menu changes daily but there is a choice from 2 starters and 2 mains which are finished off by the likes of petit fours and cheese. Aimed at people who want a change from self-catering accommodation in Wilderness.
Wilderness Grille, George Rd, T044-877 0808. Open 0800-2200. Seafood, steaks and pizza, good breakfasts, light meals like stuffed bagels, outdoor leafy terrace, pop in throughout the day and you'll get something substantial to eat, though service is somewhat slow.

Knysna and around p318, maps p319 and p320

Knysna is well known for its seafood, especially its excellent oysters which are cultivated in the lagoon. During the peak season, it is not uncommon to wait an hour or more before getting a table – be sure to book ahead at the better-known restaurants.

O'Pescador, Brenton Rd, Belvidere, T044-386 0036. Mon-Sat 1830-late. Long-established and popular Portuguese restaurant, traditional cosy decor, Mozambique prawns or try the spicy fish dishes, peri peri chicken or grilled sardines. Portuguese wines. Booking advised in season. Recommended.

Cruise Café, 400 m west of the Knysna Quays, T044-382 1693. Mon-Sat 0800-2200, Sun 0800-1700. Great views of fishing boats on the lagoon, best known for seafood, plus good breakfasts and simple lunches like ploughman's platters and fish and chips; more sophisticated and pricier menu in the evening like prawn and crab risotto or roast duck, long wine and cocktail list.

34' South, Knysna Quays, T044-382 7268, www.34-south.com. 0830-2330. Snacks and meals daily in a deli-style seafood restaurant, try the sushi, seafood platter or paella, make up a meal from the packed fridges or buy takeaway items, including cook books, wine and home-made goodies, laid-back sunny deck overlooking the quays. Recommended.

Anchorage, 11 Grey St, T044-3822230. 1830-late, from 1200 in season. Seafood platters, prawns, oysters and steaks all washed down with excellent draught Mitchell's beer and a good choice for vegetarians too, some outside tables on the patio.

Crabs Creek, 8 km from Knysna, 200 m off the N2 on the Belvidere road, T044-386 0011. Open 1100-late. A mock-Tudor building beside Knysna River, secluded country pub with pleasant outdoor terrace overlooking the river, sensible prices, good selection of wines and several beers on tap, standard pub grub, mostly seafood. Sat afternoon is popular for watching sport on the giant TV screens and there's live music in the evening.

Drydock Food Co, Knysna Quays, at the Waterfront, T044-382 7310, www.drydock. co.za. 1130-2200. Modern restaurant with good views from the 2nd floor, mostly seafood but steaks and vegetarian options too. Oysters, fish with pickles, slightly different twists on standard dishes, try west coast mussels with white wine or the kingklip espetada.

Knysna Oyster Co, Thesen's Island, T044-382 6942, www.knysnaoysters.co.za. 1000-1900. This restaurant is right next to the oyster farm that has been in operation since 1949; you need to drive across the causeway to get there from town. Once on the island, take a left just after the Boatshed retail complex. The seafood restaurant is perhaps the best place to try a dozen of Knysna's famous raw or cooked oysters washed down with a glass of champagne. It's one of Kynsna's must-dos but unfortunately the service can be poor. Despite this, it's recommended.

Oyster Catcher, Knysna Quays, T044-382 9995. Open 1000-2130. Another place to try oysters, at working quays with a backdrop of busy boats coming and going. If oysters aren't your thing, try the tapas or nachos. Good cocktails and vegetarian choices.

Paquitas, George Rex Drive, Knysna Heads, T044-384 0408. Open 1200-2200. Relaxed family restaurant and vibey pub, burgers, pizza, pasta, seafood and steaks, but the main reason for coming here is for the stunning views of the Knysna Heads and the long beach where kids can play.

Ile de Pain Bread & Café, The Boatshed, Thesen's Island, T044-302 5707, Tue-Sat 0800-1500, Sun 0900-1330. Superb bakery and coffee shop emitting lovely warm smells of freshly baked goodies, such as croissants and pastries. The bakers live upstairs and start baking at 0200. Good coffee, fresh fruit salad, cheeses and olives, good spot for a light brunch or lunch.

Plettenberg Bay p324, map p325

All the hotels have their own restaurants and bars, and you can pre-order meals at the backpacker hostels.

¶¶¶ **Hunter's Country House**, see Sleeping, page 339. Open 0730-1030, 1230-1430, 1900-2100. Excellent gourmet food served in a rambling thatched house, 3 dining rooms with silverware and china on the tables, pricey but worth it, recommended for special occasions, booking essential. Tea on the veranda is quite special. The **Summer House** restaurant in the garden serves simpler meals like tapas, salads and gourmet burgers.

¶¶ **57 Kloof**, Melville Shopping Centre, corner of Main St and Marine Drive, T044-533 5626. Open 0830-late. Modern decor and floor-to-ceiling windows highlighting great views, good range of meat and fish dishes, some with an Asian slant, large fresh salads, unusual breakfasts such as eggs hollandaise, and excellent vegetarian menu.

¶¶ **The Lookout Deck**, perched on the rocks above Lookout Beach, T044-533 1379, www.lookout.co.za. 0900-2300. Popular family seafood restaurant, perfect location, excellent seafood, soups, salads and steak, also has a busy bar, lively, bustling atmosphere. From the terrace you can watch surfers share a wave with a dolphin. Recommended.

¶¶ **The Med Seafood and Grill**, Village Sq, T044-533 3102, www.med-seafoodbistro. co.za. Mon-Fri 1230-1500, Mon-Sat 1800-late, open 7 days in high season. Established 20-year-old European-style bistro with alfresco dining on the leafy patio. À la carte seafood, good light lunches, huge seafood platters, excellent duck with orange sauce and slow-cooked lamb shanks, plus the odd vegetarian dish. Nice ambience.

¶¶-¶ **Miguel's**, Melville Shopping Centre, corner of Main St and Marine Drive, T044-533 5056, www.miguels.co.za. 0900-late. Excellent breakfasts, sandwiches and salads, good coffee, more sophisticated meals for dinner like seafood and grills, and a sushi chef works over lunch and dinner, shady seating on outdoor terrace overlooking bustle of Marine Drive.

¶ **Thyme and Again**, N2 opposite the Keurboom River turning, T044-535 9432. Open 0800-1600. Great farm stall with tables on a vine-covered stoep, serving breakfasts and light meals like inventive wraps and salads, plus teas and cakes and there's a delicious selection of still warm breads, pies and pastries from the bakery. You can buy a bottle of wine from the shop, or try the home-made ginger beer. Stock up on fresh food items here if self-catering.

❶ Bars and clubs

Knysna and around *p318, maps p319 and p320*

Tryst, in the industrial area, Lower Queen St, T044-382 0590, www.tryst.co.za. Wed-Sat 2100-late. Dance club, with local and visiting DJs, cocktail bar, pool tables, big screen TVs to watch sport, moody blue and pink lighting and comfortable leather sofas.

Zanzibar's, Main Rd, T044-382 0386. Terraces overlooking Main Rd, dance floor and pool tables. Tue-Sat 1900-0200 in season, tribal decor, occasional DJs and live music, upstairs quieter cocktail lounge.

❻ Entertainment

Knysna and around *p318, maps p319 and p320*
Cinema
Knysna Movie House, Pledge Sq, 50 Main St, T044-382 7813, www.knysnamoviehouse. co.za. Restored art deco independent movie house with daily shows of new releases.

❑ Shopping

Mossel Bay *p309, map p310*
Arts and crafts
Craft Art Workshop, Market St, next to the tourist office. Mon-Fri 0900-1700, Sat 0900-1500. Sells African curios from all over the continent and you can watch artists at work.

The Goods Shed Indoor Fleamarket, 68 Bland St, T044-691 2104, Mon-Fri 0900-

1700, Sat 0900-1500, also Sun in high season 1000-1600. Sells a variety of items including clothes, jewellery, arts and crafts, home-made food and hand-crafted furniture in interesting historical railway goods shed built in 1902.

Shopping malls
The **Liberty Shopping Centre** on Bland St contains most of the shops you'll need, including chemists, bookshops, a wine store and a **Pick 'n' Pay** supermarket.

George and around p312, map p312
Arts and crafts
Strydom Gallery, Marklaan Centre, 79 Market St, T044-874 4027, www.artaffair. co.za. Mon-Sat 0900-1700. An art shop with interesting exhibits as well as pieces for sale from a cross section of South African artists and sculptors, organizes delivery worldwide.

Shopping malls
Garden Route Mall,out of town on the junction with the N2, www.gardenroute mall.co.za. A 125-store mall with all the usual South African chain stores, restaurants, multi-screen Ster-Kinekor cinema and exhibition space.
Marklaan, between Market and Meade streets. Mall in converted store rooms arranged around 2 open squares. There is a coffee shop plus a couple of curio shops. A **farmers' market** is held in the square Fri 0700-1000.
St George's Mall, at the southern end of York St. New slick mall with clothes and food shops, Ster-Kinekor cinema and restaurants.

Sedgefield and around p317
Arts and crafts
Scarab Art and Craft Village, on the N2 next to the Engin petrol station, T044-343 2455. Well worth a stop for the interesting craft shops and stalls including one that demonstrates making handmade paper, the **Num Num Café** and a nursery.

Knysna and around p318, maps p319 and p320
Keeping in tune with Knysna's reputation as a cultural arts and crafts centre are a number of galleries and craft shops. Check at the tourist office for special exhibitions. There is a good **African craft market** on the side of the road as you enter Knysna on the N2 from George, with an extensive range of carvings, baskets, drums and curios. There is also a cluster of expensive curio shops and a daily fleamarket at the **Knysna Quays**.
Birds of Africa, 12 Waenhout St, T044-382 5660 www.birdsofafrica.co.za. Unusual carved wooden birds.
Bitou Craft, Woodmill Lane Centre, Main St, T044-382 3251. Local arts and crafts. There's another branch at Knysna Quays.
Metamorphosis, 12 Main Rd, T044-382 5889. Interesting selection of items made from recycled cans and other materials, mostly by artists from Knysna's townships.
Model Shipyard, Knysna Quays, T044-691 1531. Hand-crafted model ships and maritime antiques. There's another branch at the Waterfront in Cape Town.

Shopping malls
Woodmill Lane Centre, corner Main and Long streets, www.woodmillane.co.za. Mon-Fri 0900-1800, Sat 0830-1300. An open-air shopping centre built around a restored Victorian timber mill built in 1919. 75 shops, fountains and trees in the squares, and regular performing artists and buskers. There are several boutiques and arts and crafts shops and a branch of **Pick 'n' Pay** supermarket.

Plettenberg Bay p324, map p325
There is a wide range of souvenir shops reflecting the town's popularity with domestic visitors. The only products which could be regarded as a speciality of the area are those made from wood and paintings.
Lookout Art Gallery, Lookout Centre, Main St, T044-533 2210, www.lookout-art-gallery. co.za. Antiques and artwork from local artists and ships overseas.

Old Nick's, N2 3 km outside Plettenberg Bay going east, T044-533 1395, www.oldnick village.co.za. 1000-1700. Group of galleries, craft workshops and studios, with a weaving museum, shops and a restaurant. Look out for the ceramics and Zimbabwean sculpture at the **Porcupine**.

▲ Activities and tours

Mossel Bay p309, map p310
Diving
The best time for diving is between Dec and the end of Apr. During this period the sea is at its calmest and conditions in the bay are clear and safe. Close to Santos Beach are 4 recognized dive sites but none could be considered spectacular. All can be reached from the shore. For experienced divers, the **Windvogel Reef**, 800 m off Cape St Blaize, is highly recommended. The reef is fully exposed to the ocean and should therefore only be dived when the sea is calm. There are drop-offs and a few caves. Soft corals and colourful sponges are plentiful. Maximum depth is 27 m. **Electro Dive**, T044-6981976, www.electro dive.co.za. Equipment hire and boat charters, also offer PADI courses.

Shark cage diving
Shark Africa, Mossel Bay Harbour, T044-6913796, www.sharkafrica.co.za. Offers cage diving and snorkelling in pursuit of a great white shark on a 15-m catamaran aptly named *Shark Warrior*. The trip costs R1200 and is 4-5 hrs long and includes lunch and drinks.

Tour operators
Romonza, T044-6903101, www.mosselbay. co.za/romonza. Runs daily pleasure cruises from Vincent Quay in the harbour off Bland St. Look out for the blue tent. The most popular outings are to Seal Island (see page 310), a boat carrying up to 50 people leaves on the hour 1000-1600, advanced booking is advised. The sunset cruise (Nov-Apr) lasts 2 hrs and there's a cash bar. **Romonza** also offers the

only licensed boat-based whale watching in Mossel Bay (Jun-Oct).

George and around p312, map p312
Golf
Fancourt Hotel and Country Club, T044-804 0030, www.fancourt.com. 4 gold courses including the par 71, 5935-m, championship links course designed by Gary Player, open to members and hotel guests only. The President's Cup tournament was played here in 2003.
George Golf Club, Langenhoven St, T044-873 6116, www.georgegolfclub.co.za. Par 72, 18 holes, 5852-m course surrounded by trees. Visitors welcome.

Hiking
There are over 20 recognized hiking trails around George and Wilderness, many on private farmland. Check out www.tourism george.co.za for contact details.

Tour operators
Outeniqua Adventure Tours, T044-871 1470, www.outeniquatours.co.za. Minibus tours to sights along the Garden Route or Klein Karoo, can also organize cycling tours.
South Cape Travel, 111 York St, T044-874 6930, www.southcapetravel.co.za. Very helpful local travel agent. Book flights, bus seats, local tours.

Wilderness National Park p317, map p316
Paragliding
Windmaster Paragliding, T072-1526093, www.paraglidingsa.com. There are many thermic sites around Sedgefield and Wilderness, which are perfect for paragliding. Best conditions are Oct-Jun, though training conditions are best Jan-Apr. This company offers introductory courses, tandem flights and the full pilot's course that takes 2 weeks. They can arrange accommodation.

Tour operators
Eden Adventures, T044-877 0179, www. eden.co.za. A good-value adventure tour

operator that organizes daily trips to the national park. Offer kayaking, kloofing, mountain biking, abseiling, rock climbing and walking tours. The guides are very knowledgeable about the environment and are happy to answer endless questions. They now offer abseiling in Plettenberg Bay's Robberg Nature Reserve. Recommended.

Knysna and around p318, maps p319 and p320

Diving

Hippo Dive Campus, George Rex Drive, T044-384 0831, www.hippodivecampus.co.za. PADI courses from their dive centre at Knysna Heads, equipment rental, daily trips to reefs and to the *Paquita* wreck in the lagoon.

Golf

Knysna Golf Club, George Rex Drive, T044-384 1150, www.knysnagolfclub.com. 18-hole, par 73 course. Visitors welcome, booking advised.

Tour operators

Knysna Forest Tours, T044-382 6130, www.knysnaforesttours.co.za. ½- and full-day guided hikes and mountain bike trails, or overnight trails along the coast or in Knysna Forest and local nature reserves, plus canoeing on the Goukamma River.
Mountain Biking Africa, T044-382 0260, www.mountainbikingafrica.co.za. Guided mountain-bike trails around the forests in the area, easy rides, lots of downhills, bikes and refreshments included.
Springtide Charters, Knysna Quays, South Jetty, T082-470 6022 (mob), www.spring tide.co.za. 3-hr sunset cruises on a 50-ft sailing boat including a stop for a swim. Departs Dec-Jan 1700, Feb-Apr and Oct-Nov 1600, May-Sep 1500, R5600 including sushi and seafood snacks and champagne. Maximum of 12 people per trip. Can also arrange 4-hr lunch excursions for R700 and the boat is available for charter overnight for honeymooners to stay in the lovely master cabin and you can get married on the yacht.

Plettenberg Bay p324, map p325

Diving and snorkelling

Conditions are best for diving during the winter months of Sep and Oct. The average water temperature is 16-18°C with visibility 5-10 m. There are not many tropical fish but due to an abundance of planktonic matter there is a colourful reef life. One of the more exciting dive sites is **Groot Bank**, about 12 km northeast of Hobie Beach. The reef is 35 m offshore and is best reached by boat. The maximum depth is 25 m and there is a whole variety of rock formations to explore, including tunnels and caves. There is a good chance of seeing parrotfish, ragged-tooth sharks and steenbras. At the southern end of Plettenberg Bay is the wreck of the *MFV Athina*, a Greek trawler sunk in 1967. It should only be dived in the calmest of conditions. For those who enjoy snorkelling, there is a popular spot in front of the Beacon Isle Hotel known as **Deep Blinders**; behind the reef is a sandy area where you might see stingrays.
Pro-Dive, T044-533 1158, www.prodive. co.za, in the **Beacon Island Hotel**. Runs daily dives and rents equipment.

Fishing

There are several good rock-angling sites along the coast – Beacon Island, Robberg Beach, Lookout Rocks and Nature's Valley. Elf, galjoen and steenbras are the most frequent catch. Deep-sea fishing is also possible.
Coastal Fishing Charters, T072-330 7296, www.coastalfishingcharters.co.za. Rock and surf angling from R750 per day, or boat fishing from R900, includes tackle and bait; contact John Adelaine.

Golf

Goose Valley Golf Estate, T044-533 5082, www.goosevalley.net. A challenging 72 par, 6000-m, 18-hole golf course on the banks of Keurbooms Lagoon designed by Gary Player with good ocean views.

Plettenberg Bay Country Club, T044-533 2132, www.plettgolf.co.za. Lush 18-hole course in the middle of a private nature reserve, Piesang Valley. Tennis and bowls also available. The Knysna loerie and woodpeckers are often seen on the course. Priority bookings for members Dec-Jan, visitors welcome the rest of the year.

Horse riding
Equitrailing, Wittedrift Rd, T044-533 0599, www.pletthorsetrails.co.za. Lessons as well as trails through the forest from 1 hr to overnight. Note horse riding is not permitted on the beaches around Plett.

Whale and dolphin watching
Several companies organize whale-watching trips in season (Jun-Nov), about 2 hrs and R650, children (under 12) R350. Both the companies below are permitted to get within 50 m of the whales. Out of season there are cheaper (R400, children (under 12) R200) trips to see seals, dolphins and marine birds.
Ocean Blue Adventures, T044-533 5083, www.oceanadventures.co.za. Can also organize sea-kayaking.
Ocean Safaris, T044-533 4963, www.oceansafaris.co.za.

East of Plettenberg Bay *p326*
Boat Trip
Keurbooms River Ferries, T044-532 7876, www.ferry.co.za. Daily summer trips, 1100, 1400 and 1700, boat trip plus walk and swim lasts for 2½ hrs, adults R120, children (3-12) R50, breakfast, lunch or picnic baskets can be organized in advance and there's a cash bar. The ferry departs from the jetty on the east side of the Keurbooms River Bridge on the N2, each ferry can carry up to 30 people, they are shaded and have a toilet on board, highly recommended for nature lovers. The company also rents out self-drive motor boats for R95 per hour, which carry 4 and you get a lesson on how to use them.

Bungee jumping
Bloukrans Bungee Jump, see page 328 for details.

Storms River Village *p332*
Tour operators
Black Water Tubing, Tube 'n Axe Backpackers, see Sleeping, page 342. R495. This starts with a briefing at Tube 'n Axe, before a short a drive through the Tsitsikamma forest, then a steep descent by rope ladder to the Storms River canyon followed by a float on a giant inner tube to the suspension bridge within the Tsitsikamma National Park. The 'black water' refers to a stretch of river where you float under 2 overhangs of rock so close together, it's like floating through a cave.
Tsitikamma Canopy Tour, T042-281 1836, www.tsitsikammacanopytour.co.za. A fantastic way to see the forest from a new angle, which involves climbing up into the trees and gliding between 10 different platforms on a steel rope, the longest of which is 80 m, giving extraordinary views from high above the ground. Excellent for birdwatching, and the Knysna loerie may be spotted. Suitable for all ages from 7 years old. Departure times are every 45 mins Sep-May 0700-1600, Jun-Aug 0800-1530, the excursion lasts around 3 hrs, costs R395 and includes light refreshments. For the less active, 4WD tours of the forest are available.

⊖ Transport

Mossel Bay *p309, map p310*
It's 394 km to **Cape Town**, 55 km to **George**, 116 km to **Knysna**, 80 km to **Oudtshoorn**, 206 km to **Tsitsikamma**, 375 km to **Port Elizabeth**. The N2 bypasses Mossel Bay, almost halfway between Cape Town and Port Elizabeth.

Bus
Greyhound, **Intercape**, and **Translux** all stop here daily on the Cape Town–Durban route.

Cape Town (6 hrs), Durban (19 hrs) via Port Elizabeth and East London (13 hrs).

Intercape and Translux, also have a daily service between Mossel Bay and Johannesburg and Tshwane (Pretoria) (16 hrs).

Towards Cape Town the Baz Bus arrives in Mossel Bay 1500-1600, towards Port Elizabeth, 1330-1430.

Bus companies All bus tickets can be booked online at www.computicket.com. Greyhound, www.greyhound.co.za; Intercape, www.intercape.co.za; and Translux, www.translux.co.za. For more information, see Getting around, page 41.

George and around *p312, map p312*

It's 420 km to **Cape Town**, 320 km to **Port Elizabeth**, 61 km to **Knysna**, 55 km to **Mossel Bay**, 93 km to **Plettenberg Bay**, 151 km to **Tsitsikamma**, 60 km to **Oudtshoorn**.

Air

George Airport is 10 km from the town centre, T044-8769310, www.acsa.co.za. You'll need to pre-arrange a shuttle with your hotel or take a taxi, **Eden Taxis**, T044-587 8490. The main car rental companies have desks in the terminal building (see below).

SAA have daily flights between George and **Cape Town** (1 hr), **Durban** (2½ hrs), and **Johannesburg** (1 hr 45 mins).**Kulula** and **1Time** have daily flights between George and **Johannesburg** (1 hr 45 mins).

Airline offices All air tickets can be booked online at www.computicket.com. **1Time**, www.1time.aero. **Kulula**, www.kulula.com. **South African Airways (SAA)**, ww2.fly saa.com. For further details, see Essentials, page 40.

Bus

All buses stop in St Mark's Square. **Greyhound**, **Intercape** and **Translux** run daily to **Cape Town** (6 hrs) and **Durban** (18 hrs) via **Knysna** (1 hr), **East London** (9 hrs) and **Port Elizabeth** (4 hrs).

Translux and **Intercape** also have a daily service between George and **Johannesburg**

(14 hrs) and **Tshwane (Pretoria)** (16 hrs) via **Bloemfontein** (9 hrs).

Baz Bus runs daily in both directions between **Cape Town** and**Port Elizabeth**. Drops off at Outeniqua Backpackers. Towards Cape Town it arrives around 1500-1600, and towards Port Elizabeth 1430-1530.

Bus companies All bus tickets can be booked online at www.computicket.com. Greyhound, www.greyhound.co.za; Intercape, www.intercape.co.za; and Translux, www.translux.co.za. For more information, see Getting around, page 41.

Car hire

The car hire companies all have desks at the airport. **Avis**, T044-876 9314, www.avis.co.za; Budget, T044-8769204, www.budget.co.za; Hertz, T044-801 4700, www.hertz.co.za; Tempest, T044-8769250.

Taxi

George Taxis, T044-870 8146.

Train

The railway station is in the town centre at the east end of Market St. The **Outeniqua Choo-Tjoe** runs between George and **Mossel Bay**, T044-8018288 (see page 314 for details).

Wilderness and around *p316, map p316*

Bus

Translux, **Greyhound** and **Intercape** all stop at Wilderness, 20 mins before or after **George**. The daily **Baz Bus**, T021-439 2323, www.baz bus.com, collects and drops off at Fairy Knowe Backpackers. From **Port Elizabeth** it arrives 1345-1415 and from **Cape Town** 1500-1600.

Sedgefield and around *p317*

Bus

Greyhound, **Intercape** and **Translux** services stop at the Shell garage, 15 mins to **Knysna**. See Knysna transport, below, for timetable and contact details. The **Baz Bus**, T021-439 2332, www.bazbus.com, will stop in Sedgefield if requested in advance. See Knysna transport for details.

Knysna and around p318, maps p319 and p320

It's 932 km to **Bloemfontein**, 500 km to **Cape Town**, 61 km to **George**, 1350 km to **Johannesburg**, 100 km to **Mossel Bay**, 120 km to **Outdshoorn**, 32 km to **Plettenberg Bay**, 244 km to **Port Elizabeth**, 90 km to **Tsitsikamma National Park**.

Bus

All buses stop outside the railway station near the Knysna Quays. **Greyhound**, **Intercape** and **Translux** run daily to **Cape Town** (8 hrs), **Port Elizabeth** (3½ hrs), and **Durban** (18 hrs). Intercape and Translux also have a daily service between Knysna and **Tshwane** (**Pretoria**) and **Johannesburg** (14 hrs), via **Bloemfontein** (11 hrs).

Baz Bus runs a daily service in either direction between **Cape Town** and **Port Elizabeth**. Heading towards Cape Town expect to be picked up around 1230-1330, towards Port Elizabeth 1630-1730. Drops and picks up at all the hostels.

Bus companies All bus tickets can be booked online at www.computicket.com. Greyhound, www.greyhound.co.za; Intercape, www.intercape.co.za; and Translux, www.translux.co.za. For more information, see Getting around, page 41.

Taxis

Crown Cabs, T044-3821890.

Train

The **Outeniqua Choo-Tjoe** steam train between Knysna and **George** (2½ hrs) is no longer running due to landslides destroying part of the line in 2006 (see page 314). In the event it starts up again, the station is on Remembrance Av close to the lagoon.

Plettenberg Bay p324, map p325

It's 525 km to **Cape Town**, 93 km to **George**, 32 km to **Knysna**, 171 km to **Mossel Bay**, 236 km to **Port Elizabeth**, 55 km to **Tsitsikamma National Park**.

Bus

Mainline buses depart from the Shell Ultra City on the N2 out of town. Arrange a taxi with your hotel, but remember that some buses pass through in the early hours.

Greyhound, **Intercape** and **Translux** all stop here daily on the Cape Town–Durban route. **Cape Town** (8½ hrs) daily, **Durban** (17½ hrs) daily via **Port Elizabeth** (3½ hrs).

Intercape has a service between Plettenberg Bay and **Tshwane** (**Pretoria**) and **Johannesburg** (14 hrs) daily via **Oudtshoorn** (2 hrs), and **Bloemfontein** (11 hrs).

Baz Bus has a service towards Cape Town, expect to be picked up 1200-1300, and to Port Elizabeth, 1730-1800.

Bus companies All bus tickets can be booked online at www.computicket.com. Greyhound, www.greyhound.co.za; Intercape, www.intercape.co.za; and Translux, www.translux.co.za. For more information, see Getting around, page 41.

❶ Directory

Mossel Bay p309, map p310
Emergencies Sea Rescue T082-990 5954 (mob). **Medical services** Bayview Private hospital, corner Alhof and Ryk Tulbach streets, T044-6913718, www.bay viewprivatehospital.com.

George and around p312, map p312
Banks All the principal banks, **First National**, **Nedbank**, **Standard** and **ABSA Bank** are in York St and the shopping malls. **Internet** J & D Internet Kafee, corner of Cradock and Courtenay streets, T044-8740 008, internet café with full range of digital services. **Medical services** Medi Clinic, corner Gloucester and York streets, T044-803 2000, www.georgemc.co.za. **Post office** York St.

Knysna and around p318, maps p320 and p319
Banks All banks have branches on Main St and ATMs can be found in the Knysna Quays

and other shopping centres. **Emergencies** Police, T10111, T044-302 6600; Sea rescue, T044-3840211. **Internet** Internet access can be found at a few spots around town including the tourist office, the Knysna Movie House, at the Knysna Quays and at all the backpacker hostels and hotels. **Medical services** Knysna Private Hospital, Hunters Drive, T044-384 1083, casualty department.

Plettenberg Bay *p324, map p325*
Banks First National, 22 Main St; Nedbank, Nedbank Pl, Main Rd; **Standard**, 17 Main St. **Internet** There is an Internet Café, just next to the Melville Shopping Centre, on Main Rd. **Post office** Plettenberg St, by police station.

Contents

Footprint features

At a glance

⊖ **Getting around** Buses and
Baz Bus on major routes, car hire.

◉ **Time required** Minimum
3-5 days to do the coastal route,
extra time to head inland.

☀ **Weather** Chilly Jul and Aug,
best for beaches Nov-Feb.

✖ **When not to go** Traffic can
be heavy on the N2 over Christmas
when many people return home
from Cape Town.

★ Don't miss ...
1 Surfing at Jeffrey's Bay, pages 374 and 379.
2 Addo Elephant National Park, page 380.
3 Shamwari Game Reserve, page 383.
4 National Festival of Arts in Grahamstown, page 396.
5 Valley of Desolation, page 402.
6 Wild Coast by landrover, bike and canoe, page 419.
7 Nelson Mandela National Museum, page 425.

The Eastern Cape, although far less visited than many parts of South Africa, is a fascinating region of wild, empty beaches, forested mountains and the sun-baked plains of the Karoo. Nelson Mandela Bay (Port Elizabeth), a major industrial centre, has surprisingly good beaches, and acts as a gateway to the Garden Route, the lush coast stretching towards Cape Town, and Tsitsikamma National Park. A short drive from here is Jeffrey's Bay, where the long beach and perfect waves attract surfers from around the world.

To the north is a variety of game reserves and national parks, including the extended Addo Elephant National Park, the third largest game reserve in the country, where lions have been introduced among its famously large herds of elephant. It's now the only place in South Africa where you can see the Big Seven – elephant, lion, rhino, buffalo, leopard, whale and shark. Nearby, a clutch of newly created private game reserves have been restocked with animals not seen in the region for more than 150 years. Further inland lie the mystical landscapes of the Amatola Mountains and the Mountain Zebra National Park, which is a haven for the endangered mountain zebra. In the north is the sharply contrasting Karoo, with its surreal semi-desert conditions and quirky 19th-century towns.

During the Apartheid era the eastern region was referred to as the Transkei, the former homeland for the Xhosa people. These days the area is known as the Wild Coast because of its rugged, virtually deserted coastline. The area is far less developed than much of South Africa's coast, and most of the people live in rural settlements and work on the land. Instead of full-blown resorts, there are small seaside villages backed by protected stretches of verdant coastal forest and windswept dunes.

Getting around

Compared to the other provinces in South Africa, a little planning ahead is needed if you are travelling around the Eastern Cape by public transport. The Eastern Cape is bisected neatly by the N2, which runs closely along the coast on its route from the Western Cape to KwaZulu Natal. At most it is only 100 km from the coastal resorts. Try to avoid driving along the N2 at night as facilities such as service stations are sparse and domestic animals on the road can cause accidents. You will need a car if you want to visit the more remote villages in the Karoo as there is no public transport – the **Owl House Backpackers** in Nieu Bethesda sums it up very eloquently in their advertising material: 'No street lights. No Baz Bus. No crime'. The **Baz Bus** runs along the N2 five days a week between Nelson Mandela Bay (Port Elizabeth) and Durban. It picks up and drops off at the most convenient hostels along this route; for the more out of the way backpacker hostels, you should be able to arrange shuttles from Baz Bus stops but you must book ahead. The mainline buses all stick to the N2. Many hotels also offer shuttle services but again these need to be pre-arranged.

Best time to visit

The coastal area of the Eastern Cape is a further extension of the subtropical Western Cape that rises inland to the plains of the Great Karoo, a mountainous semi-desert. The two experience very different climates. In the northeast, along the Wild Coast, towns like Port St Johns have long, hot summer months and moderate winters, while up towards the Free State, at towns such as Lady Grey and Aliwal North, the rise in altitude causes the lowering of temperatures and conditions here are favoured more by skiers than sunbathers. In general, the weather along the coast is kind to visitors. Nelson Mandela Bay (Port Elizabeth) enjoys a daily average of seven hours of sunshine annually and the region rightly earns its title as the Sunshine Coast. It's only in the Karoo regions that the weather reaches extremes, from the height of the harsh Karoo summer to the icy winters.

Tourist information

There are plenty of sources of tourism information for the Eastern Cape. Search on the internet and you will find a whole bunch of websites, many of which we have listed under the relevant destinations. The official government **Eastern Cape Tourism Board** ① *Tourism Centre, corner of Longfellow and Aquarium roads, Quigney, T043-701 9600, www.ectourism.co.za*, is based in East London, with other branches in Nelson Mandela Bay (Port Elizabeth) and Mthatha. Their website is a good source of information before you leave home.

Nelson Mandela Bay (Port Elizabeth)

→ *Colour map 7, B4. Phone code: 041.*

Nelson Mandela Bay – until recently Port Elizabeth – is a major port and industrial centre, the biggest coastal city between Cape Town and Durban. The centre of town, known as 'Central', is an attractive grid of Victorian houses and green spaces (burnt brown in summer) but the rest of the city – a modern sprawl of shopping malls, office blocks and apartments – is less aesthetically pleasing. The main tourist area is along the long beaches of Algoa Bay, and although the endless soft-sand beaches are enticing, the holiday flats and apartment blocks creeping onto the flat land behind them are less so. Nevertheless, Nelson Mandela Bay is celebrated for its long hours of sunshine and the warm waters of the bay, making it a good place to try some watersports.

The city's other great draw is its proximity to a number of game reserves. The most popular, open for game viewing, are the Addo Elephant National Park and the Shamwari Game Reserve. These offer the opportunity to see the Big Five without having to worry about malaria. Although Shamwari is a private reserve only open to guests at the very smart camps, there are other similar private game reserves nearby that open to the public for day visits as long as you book in advance (see page 371). Combine this with the fact that you can fly back to Cape Town in less than an hour and it becomes obvious why Nelson Mandela Bay is rapidly growing as a popular tourist destination. ►► *For listings, see pages 364-372.*

Ins and outs

Getting there
Port Elizabeth Airport, 4 km from the city centre along Alister Miller Drive, T041-507 7319, www.acsa.co.za, receives several flights daily from major South African cities. The airport has restaurants, ATMs and a tourist information desk in arrivals. Visitors staying at Humewood Beach and Summerstrand can reach the airport without having to negotiate the city centre by way of an elaborate ring road and flyover system. Most major hotels provide a courtesy bus from the airport or alternatively, there are taxis. Several car hire groups also have a desk in the terminal. The mainline **railway station** is on the edge of the town centre on Station Street, by the harbour. Nelson Mandela Bay (Port Elizabeth) is served by **Greyhound**, **Intercape** and **Translux** buses, and it is the overnight spot for the **Baz Bus** on the route between Cape Town and Durban, which calls in at most of the backpacker hostels. ►► *For further details, see Transport, page 371.*

Getting around
Local buses depart from Market Square Bus Station, beneath the Norwich Union Centre Building on Strand Street. The **Algoa Bus Company** ① *T080-142 1444 (toll free)*, operates a regular service between the beachfront, city centre, St George's Park, Rink Street, Greenacres and the Bridge Shopping Complex – Route O.

Best time to visit
Southern right whales visit the bay from June to November, while humpback whales calve and feed their young between May and December.

Tourist information

Nelson Mandela Bay Tourism ⓘ *Donkin Lighthouse Building, Belmont Terr, T041-585 8884, www.nmbt.co.za, Mon-Fri 0800-1630, Sat-Sun 0930-1530 (there's also an office in the Boardwalk, T041-583 2030)*, is a useful office that can book accommodation and advise on nightlife, tours and travel throughout the Eastern Cape. **Eastern Cape Tourist Board** ⓘ *Boardwalk Centre, T041-585 7761, www.ectourism.co.za*, has excellent regional information and their website is very informative. **Eas'capism.com** ⓘ *Boardwalk Centre, beach entrance, T041-507 7912, www.eascapism.co.za, daily 0800-2200*, is a private tourism information service with an **Avis** car hire desk on site. It has a very comprehensive website and can book tours, transfers and accommodation.

Background

In 1497, Vasco da Gama noted the 'Bay' on one of his voyages. It was later named Baia de Lagoa, referring to the lagoon situated at the mouth of the Baakens River. For hundreds of years, however, Nelson Mandela Bay (Port Elizabeth) was referred to on navigational charts only as "a landing place with fresh water". The city was established in 1820 when the first British settlers arrived. The town became a port and a trading centre catering

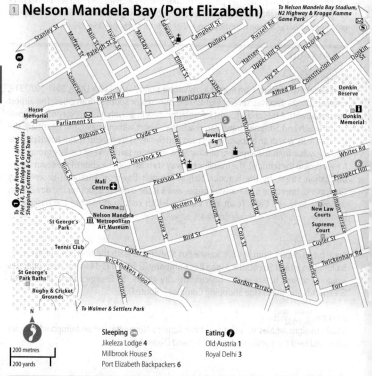

1 Nelson Mandela Bay (Port Elizabeth)

Sleeping
Jikeleza Lodge 4
Millbrook House 5
Port Elizabeth Backpackers 6

Eating
Old Austria 1
Royal Delhi 3

200 metres
200 yards

for the early settlers who were gradually moving inland. During the first half of the 20th century, Port Elizabeth expanded and became an important trading and manufacturing city. The main exports were mineral ores, citrus fruits and wool. Ford General Motors opened its first assembly plants here in the 1920s. Today, with a population of around 1.3 million, it is South Africa's fifth largest city, and one that is currently reinventing itself as 'Nelson Mandela Bay', which is its new formal name. As an industrial city it is understandable that tourists don't want to spend a great deal of time here. However, with the massive growth in tourism along the Garden Route, the city has become a convenient point for visitors to start or finish their journey. The new Nelson Mandela Bay stadium, a venue for 2010 FIFA World Cup™, is around 1 km north of the city centre at North End.

Sights

Central Nelson Mandela Bay

The 5-km **Donkin Heritage Trail** has been created to show visitors the most important monuments, buildings, gardens and churches around the city centre. An excellent guidebook, available from the information office, contains 47 places of historical interest. A few of the more interesting buildings are mentioned below – they are not in the order you might

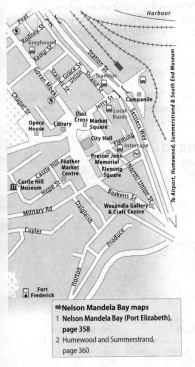

⇒**Nelson Mandela Bay maps**
1 Nelson Mandela Bay (Port Elizabeth), page 358
2 Humewood and Summerstrand, page 360

come across them on the trail. The trail starts in Market Square opposite the City Hall, simply follow the useful signs.

Market Square is probably Port Elizabeth's most attractive corner, with a couple of fine buildings and the beginning of bustling Govan Mbeki Avenue. **City Hall** was built between 1858 and 1862; the clock tower was added in 1883. While part of the hall is still used by the council, it is also now a lecture and concert hall for public performances. Look out for a replica of the Diaz Cross in Market Square. This was donated by the Portuguese Government to commemorate the arrival of Bartholomeu Diaz in Algoa Bay in 1488. The **Main Public Library** ① *T041-585 8133, Mon-Fri 0900-1700*, dominates the northwestern corner of Market Square. This fine early Victorian building, with its terracotta façade shipped out from the UK, dates from 1835 and started life as a courthouse. It was not until 1902 that it was officially opened as the public library. Outside by the road is a fine marble statue of Queen Victoria, erected in 1903. Once inside, visitors have the opportunity to view some beautiful early books.

The **Prester John Memorial** stands in Fleming Square, behind City Hall. It is dedicated to the mythical king-priest and the Portuguese explorers who discovered South Africa. It was unveiled in 1886 and is thought to be the only monument in the world depicting Prester John. The monument is in the form of a large Coptic cross.

The **Campanile** ① *Strand St, Tue-Sun 0900-1230, 1330-1400*, is a 53-m bell-tower close to the docks down by the railway station. It was built to commemorate the landing of the 1820 settlers and was once the highest structure in Port Elizabeth. The views of the city and harbour remain impressive, and if you're fit you can climb up 204 stairs to the observation room at the top. It contains the largest carillon of bells in the country as well as a chiming clock, and the tower is a useful reference point on the coast. Note this is in a rough area and it's advised to visit in a group.

South of City Hall is the **Wezandla Gallery and Craft Centre** ① *27 Baakens St, T041-585 1185, www.wezandla.com, Mon-Fri 0900-1700, Sat 0900-1300*, hard to miss with its brightly painted exterior. This is an interesting collection of African art: wire and wood sculptures, woven baskets, pottery, crafts and curios. Many of the items are the work of local craftsmen and there are a reputed 25,000 items for sale.

Donkin Reserve is a public park in Central, high up on a hill with views of Govan Mbeki Avenue and the harbour. On the inland side of the park is the fine façade of the **Edward Hotel**; on the other side is a lighthouse and an unusual pyramid. The lighthouse dates from 1861 and is today home to the **Nelson Mandela Bay tourist office**. The rest of the lighthouse building can be opened on request. The odd-looking pyramid is actually a memorial erected by Sir Rufane Donkin in memory of his wife, Elizabeth, after whom the city was named. Local folklore is rather more sinister and suggests that her heart was buried in the pyramid. Rufane Donkin, a British colonialist and former Cape Governor, was sent to administer Port Elizabeth in the late 19th century, but his wife Elizabeth never saw the town.

South of Donkin Reserve, **Castle Hill Museum** ① *7 Castle Hill Rd, T041-582 2515, Mon-Fri 1000-1300, 1400-1600, R9, children (under 12) R5*, is housed in one of the oldest buildings in the city. It was built in 1827 for the Reverend Francis McCleland as the Rectory.

2 Humewood & Summerstrand

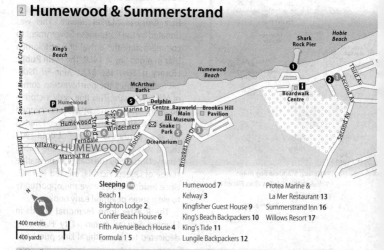

Sleeping	Humewood 7	Protea Marine &
Beach 1	Kelway 3	La Mer Restaurant 13
Brighton Lodge 2	Kingfisher Guest House 9	Summerstrand Inn 16
Conifer Beach House 6	King's Beach Backpackers 10	Willows Resort 17
Fifth Avenue Beach House 4	King's Tide 11	
Formula 1 5	Lungile Backpackers 12	

The cottage has been restored to look like an early-Victorian home, complete with a slate roof, yellowwood floors and 19th-century furniture and household goods.

Continuing south on Belmont Terrace, is **Fort Frederick** ① *daily, sunrise to sunset, free.* This was the first stone building in the Eastern Cape, completed in 1799. From its high point it overlooks the mouth of the Baakens River. It was built to stop any French troops from landing in the rivermouth but had the effect of helping the rebels at Graaff-Reinet. No shot has ever been fired from, or at, the fort.

Running through the town is the Baakens River Gorge which is surrounded by the well-kept, 54-ha **Settlers Park** – not what you would expect to find in the middle of South Africa's fifth largest city. The valley runs for 7 km and is full of interesting birds, plants and even some small buck. Unfortunately, despite the tranquil setting, there are occasional muggings, so don't come alone. The park has three entrances: How Avenue, just off Park Drive; Chelmsford Avenue, just off Target Kloof; and Third Avenue, Walmer. Look out for the recommended walks by each entrance, such as the 8-km **Guinea Fowl Trail**, which starts in the car park at Third Avenue. **Birdlife Eastern Cape** ① *T041-379 3201*, meet here at 0800 on the first Saturday and third Thursday of each month for birdwatching walks; visitors are welcome.

On the western fringes of the city centre is **Nelson Mandela Metropolitan Art Museum** ① *1 Park Drive, T041-586 1030, www.artmuseum.co.za, Mon and Wed-Fri 0900-1700, Tue, Sat-Sun 1400-1700, 1st Sun of every month 0900-1400, free.* Formerly the King George VI Art Gallery, most of the collection on display is of 19th- and 20th-century British art, but there are also some good monthly contemporary exhibitions, accompanied by films and lectures. Other displays include a collection of oriental miniatures as well as pottery and sculpture.

The **Horse Memorial** standing on the corner of Russell and Cape roads was created after the Boer War. Between 1899 and 1902 thousands of horses died, more often through fatigue and starvation than from being slain in battle. The inscription on the memorial reads: "The greatness of a nation consists not so much in the number of its people or the extent of its territory as in the extent and justice of its compassion." The statue shows a man kneeling in front of a horse with a bucket in his hands making as if to feed or quench the horse's thirst.

Outside Central Nelson Mandela Bay

Most visitors head for Nelson Mandela Bay (Port Elizabeth)'s beaches, which lie to the east of the city centre in the suburbs of **Humewood** and **Summerstrand**, where there are a number of typical seaside attractions and facilities. There are also other beaches and a couple of game reserves within striking distance of the city.

In Humewood, **Bayworld** ① *off Marine Drive, T041-586 0650, www.bayworld.co.za*, comprises the Main Museum, Oceanarium and Snake Park. ① *daily 0900-1630, R45, children (under 12) R20, dolphin and seal shows daily 1100 and 1500, coffee shop*. The Main Museum has exhibits on natural and

→ Nelson Mandela Bay maps
1 Nelson Mandela Bay (Port Elizabeth), page 358
2 Humewood and Summerstrand, page 360

Eating ❼
Dizzy Dolphins Café **1**
Ginger **2**
Island Grill & Bar **3**
Up the Khyber **5**

All other restaurants are in the large entertainment centres, marked on the map cultural history. Look out for the southern right whale skeleton and the fully rigged models of early sailing ships. There is also a collection of objects collected from wrecks in and around Algoa Bay. The rest of the collection focuses on fossils and early man. The **Oceanarium** has over 40 species of fish, as well as a ragged tooth shark tank, rays, turtles and African penguins. The most interesting part of the complex is the dolphin research centre, with seal and dolphin presentations which children will enjoy. The snake park has recently opened after refurbishment and has a number of snakes, tortoises, lizards and baby crocodiles.

Also in Humewood is the **South End Museum** ① *corner of Humewood Rd and Walmer Blvd, T041-582 3325, www.southendmuseum.co.za, Mon-Fri 0900-1600, Sat-Sun 1000-1500, free*. This museum is dedicated to the South End suburb, which was destroyed when the Group Areas Act in 1950 led to the forcible removal of the cosmopolitan population of the area. South End was one of the prime areas of the city because it was close to the centre of town, the beachfront and the harbour. During Apartheid, not only the blacks, Indians and coloureds were forcibly relocated from the city, but the Chinese too.

Midway between Humewood and Summerstrand on Marine Drive, opposite Shark Rock Pier, is the **Boardwalk Casino and Entertainment World**, also known as the **Boardwalk Centre** ① *T031-566 1802* which has added a whole new dimension to leisure in the city. The complex is set around a series of man-made lakes and beautiful gardens lit by some 40,000 lights after dark. There are numerous entertainment venues in the centre, including the Tsitsikamma Conference Centre, the Supersport Arena and the Boardwalk Amphitheatre. The casino offers 700 slot machines and 20 gaming tables, and there's a selection of restaurants (see Eating, page 366), specialist shops and a five-screen cinema.

Townships

The townships around Nelson Mandela Bay (Port Elizabeth) can be visited on a tour (see page 371). The New Brighton township has been in existence since the region was mostly farmland. In 1903, land 8 km north of Port Elizabeth was earmarked for the establishment of a large 'model native settlement'. The outbreak of bubonic plague in 1901 was used as an excuse to gain government assistance for forced removals to this new 'location'. Over time New Brighton became known as the Red Location and takes its name from a series of corrugated-iron barracks, brought down here from a defunct concentration camp at Uitenhage as well as the Imperial Yeomanry Hospital at de Aar. Both had been used in the South African War of 1899-1902. In time, these sheds eventually rusted and turned deep red. After the ANC's armed wing Umkhonto we Sizwe went underground in 1960, Red Location was used for hiding political fugitives. Well-hidden cells were erected between shack floors and the ground where these fugitives could hide from the security police. Today the township is home to the new **Red Location Museum** ① *corner Olof Palme and Singaphi streets, T041-408 8400, www.freewebs.com/redlocationmuseum, Mon-Fri 0900-1600, Sat 0900-1500, R12, children (under 16) R6*. Opened in 2006, the striking, industrial warehouse-styled complex uses space, corrugated iron, wood and steel to echo its shanty town surrounds and has already won three major international architectural awards, including the Royal Institute of British Architects' inaugural Lubetkin Prize for the most outstanding work of architecture outside the UK and Europe. It tells the history of the township and its part in the struggle, and includes a series of 'memory boxes' or galleries of photos and exhibits. There's a shop and café, and outside is a vast space for public events.

Other townships surrounding the city are **Swartkops**, **Kwa-Zakhele** (meaning 'place to build yourself' in Xhosa) and **Motherwell** on the road to Addo, which is reputedly the

Sunshine Coast beaches

A combination of natural conditions and man-made developments means that the Algoa Bay beaches around Nelson Mandela Bay (Port Elizabeth) form one of the most popular stretches of coast in South Africa. The water is clean, warm and calm for most of the year, making it an ideal spot for watersports.

The two main northern beaches are **New Brighton** – good for swimming and fishing, with changing rooms, lifeguards and a promenade – and **Bluewater Bay** – a long stretch of white sand with good swimming, but the lifeguards are only present during summer. To get to there by car, take the N2 towards Grahamstown and follow the signs.

The southern beaches come right up to the city centre. **King's Beach** is the closest, lying between the harbour and Humewood. Being so close to the city it can get very busy, but the swimming is safe, boogie-boarding is allowed and

there are lifeguards and changing facilities. This is probably the best beach for families as there is a go-kart track, mini-golf, children's playground, swimming-pool complex, and plenty of kiosks and snack bars. In contrast, **Humewood** is a quieter beach, which has been awarded the Blue Flag, the swimming is good and there is plenty of shade. The next stretch, **Hobie Beach**, is marked by Shark Rock Pier. In the evenings this is a busy area due to the presence of The Boardwalk, an entertainment centre (see Bars and clubs, page 368). The swimming is safe and throughout the year there are local body surfing, beach volleyball and boardsailing competitions. Next up, **Pollock Beach** is one of the better surfing spots. Beyond the lighthouse at Cape Recife, **Sardinia Bay** is the most beautiful beach near the city and a marine reserve popular for snorkelling and scuba-diving. Dolphins are often seen close to the shore on this stretch of coastline.

largest township in the Eastern Cape, dating back to the 1980s when the city's population swelled with people looking for work.

> In 2006, at the opening of the museum there was a reburial ceremony of anti-Apartheid activists Raymond Mhlaba and Govan Mbeki. They are now laid to rest in the mausoleum within the museum complex.

Game parks

Kragga Kamma Game Park ① *A 15-min drive from Nelson Mandela Bay on the Kragga Kamma road off the N2, T041-379 4195, www.kraggakamma.com, 0800-1700, self-drive R45, children (5-18) R20, under 5s free, guided 2-hr game drives R150 per person,* is a private game reserve is in a lush tract of coastal forest where all the animals roam free. These animals include rhino, buffalo, giraffe, zebra, cheetah and a number of antelope, including the shy nyala. The resident bird of prey is the jackal buzzard and other species include fish eagles, yellow-billed kites and Knysna loeries. You can drive around the small network of gravel roads in your own car or alternatively take a two-hour guided game drive. There's a café, some picnic sites and accommodation in safari tents and log cabins (See Sleeping, page 366).

The **Seaview Game and Lion Park** ① *25 km west of Nelson Mandela Bay, signposted off the N2, the park is 7.5 km towards the sea, T041-378 1702, www.seaviewgamepark.co.za. 0900-1700, lion feeding Sun 1200, R45, children (under 18) R20,* is a wildlife park with around 40 species of animal, including giraffe, zebra, wildebeest, impala, duiker and monkeys. But it is the lions that most people come to see. In total there are 55, all hand reared, including 13 white lion and, for an extra fee, visitors can get close up to a lion cub and possibly cuddle one. Except for the lions, many of the animals arrive at the park as orphans or have been injured and wherever possible are rehabilitated and returned to the wild. There are nature trails and self game drives, a restaurant and curio shop, and a few stands for caravans and tents.

◉ Nelson Mandela Bay (Port Elizabeth) listings

For Sleeping and Eating price codes and other relevant information, see pages 46-53.

● Sleeping

During the last few years Nelson Mandela Bay (Port Elizabeth) has experienced a rapid expansion in tourist accommodation. Much of this has been in the seaside suburbs of Humewood and Summerstrand, and if you're looking for something close to the beach, it's perfect.

Central Nelson Mandela Bay *p359, map p358*

D Millbrook House, 2 Havelok Sq, T041-582 3774, www.millbrookhouse.co.za. A delightful B&B in a leafy square in the centre of town. Victorian house with wrought-iron balconies, peaceful setting, perfect for seeing the sights. Family-run with 4 charming en suite rooms, with ceiling fans, TV with M-Net, clean, bright and airy. Small garden with splash pool, lounge, the owners are very friendly and welcoming. Recommended.

E-F Jikeleza Lodge, 44 Cuyler St, T041-586 3721, www.highwinds.co.za/jikeleza.htm. Double rooms, dorms, 1 family room, kitchen, pleasant backyard, internet access, free pick up from across town, close to shops and some restaurants. Helpful set-up, keen to organize transport and tours, Baz Bus stop.

E-F Port Elizabeth Backpackers, 7 Prospect Hill, T041-586 0697, www.pebackpackers. za.org. Attractive old Victorian building with bright and airy dorms, some doubles, well-equipped kitchen, meals available. Spacious lounge with fireplace, good location, small backyard, good travel centre, Baz Bus stop.

Outside Central Mandela Bay *p361, maps p358 and p360*

Walmer and Mill Park

The leafy suburb of Walmer is on the far side of St George's Park and southwest of the centre and is convenient for the airport, but not for the beach.

L Hacklewood Hill Country House, 152 Prospect Rd, Walmer, T041-581 1300, www.hacklewood.co.za. Luxurious guesthouse in a late-Victorian manor house full of antiques and paintings, with 8 a/c tasteful double rooms, each with massive en suite bathrooms and DSTV. In the beautiful gardens is a swimming pool and tennis court, plus secure covered parking. Elegant dining room where you'll need to brush up on the use of silverware, and some special touches which make this a fine choice: guests, for example, are encouraged to select their wine from the impressive cellar. Advance booking essential during the peak season. No children under 14.

B King George Guesthouse, 2 King George Rd, Mill Park, close to the cricket ground in St George's Park, T041-374 1825, www.king george.co.za. A mock-Tudor upmarket guesthouse built in 1915 with Oregon pine doors and beamed ceilings and stain-glass windows. 8 double rooms with en suite bathroom, minibar and TV. There is a study and a lounge, plus sizeable gardens with a swimming pool. Extra meals available on request.

B Lemon Tree, 14 Mill Park Rd, Mill Park, T041-373 4103, www.lemontreelane.co.za. A little bit off the beaten track but convenient for the shopping centres. Homely award-winning guesthouse with spacious rooms decorated with antiques and opening up on to the gardens. DSTV, wireless internet, minibar, swimming pool, German spoken.

D Oak Tree Cottages, 112 Church Rd, Walmer, T041-581 3611, www.oaktree-accommodation.co.za. A well-run B&B with 5 good-value double rooms set in the garden with private entrances with en suite bathroom, TV, kettle, fridge, and microwave, swimming pool, shady gardens, laundry, secure parking, dinner on request.

Humewood and Summerstrand

A The Beach, Marine Drive, Summerstrand, T041-583 2161, www.pehotels.co.za. Luxurious, low-rise hotel right on the beach. 58 well-appointed rooms, 3 good restaurants, bar with ocean views from the patio, large pool, laundry, secure parking, tidy gardens, good service, just across the road from Shark Rock pier and adjacent to the Boardwalk Centre, a short drive from the centre.

B The Kelway Hotel, Brook's Hill Drive, T041-584 0638, www.thekelway.co.za. An unusual all timber structure with 61 spacious rooms with bright white linen and dark wood stylish furniture. Balconies, some with ocean views. There's a small pool and good restaurant, cosy pub and cigar lounge.

B King's Tide, 16 Tenth Av, Summerstrand, T041-583 6023, www.kingstide.co.za. PE's first luxury boutique hotel, very stylish with 10 beautifully decorated suites, extravagant bathrooms, DSTV, internet access, good gourmet breakfasts, dinner on request, bar, unusual swimming pool with a rocky waterfall feature, comfortable and friendly.

B Protea Hotel Marine, Marine Drive, Summerstrand, T041-583 2101, www.proteahotels.com. Large, unattractive high-rise block just across from the beach, but with 98 a/c rooms with DSTV, comfortable and recently refurbished, some of the 34 rooms in the loft extension have upstairs bedrooms and additional kitchenettes and lounges downstairs, 2 swimming pools, one on the roof with great views of Pollock Beach and Algoa Bay. The **La Mer** restaurant has a good local reputation.

B-C Humewood, 33 Marine Drive, T041-585 8961, www.humewoodhotel.co.za. Attractive old-fashioned seaside building right on King's Beach. 91 plain but adequate rooms, most of which are sea-facing with small private balconies. Restaurant, bar, the morning coffee shop has a pleasant ambience and some seats on a terrace overlooking the street, though lacks a proper garden for children to enjoy.

C Brighton Lodge, 21 Brighton Drive, Summerstrand, T041-583 4576, www.brightonlodge.co.za. A very comfortable guesthouse where each of the 11 bedrooms has been decorated on a different period, all have en suite bathrooms, microwave, fridge, DSTV, wireless internet and a private entrance. Swimming pool, walking distance from the Boardwalk and the beach, and breakfast can be served in bed. Recommended.

C Kingfisher Guest House, 73 Brighton Drive, Summerstrand, T041-5832150, www.kingfisherpe.co.za. Family-run B&B close to the beach, with 8 individually decorated double rooms with en suite bathrooms, private entrance and patio, TV, fridge, microwave and toaster, lounge, disabled facilities, laundry, swimming pool and peaceful garden to relax in.

C Summerstrand Inn, Marine Drive, Summerstrand, T041-583 3131, www.hotsummer.co.za. Large hotel with 235 spacious and recently nicely refurbished rooms, with a/c and TV, views of Humewood Golf Course, leafy gardens offer privacy around the pool area. **Satis** restaurant serves buffet meals; cosy **Boodles** bar; courtesy bus offered.

C-D Fifth Avenue Beach House, 3 5th Av, Summerstrand, T041-583 2441, www.fifthave.co.za. Guests can stay in the main house or in a neat complex with a balcony overlooking 2 palm-fringed swimming pools. 10 double rooms with TV, garden has a tropical feel with several mature palm trees, 200 m from the beach. A friendly and good-value set-up. Recommended.

D Conifer Beach House, 39 Windermere Rd, Humewood, T041-585 5959, www.conifer.co.za. Pretty house and garden with 4 self-catering units with private entrances and patios, wood floors, stylish furniture, TV, gourmet breakfasts available, friendly hosts. German and Dutch spoken.

D Formula 1, Marine Drive, next to Ocean-arium, Spur restaurant and McDonald's, T041-585 6380, www.formule1.co.za. Soulless basic modern accommodation units where the shower and loo are in a sort of cubicle in the corner, but clean and good value in an emergency. 88 basic rooms, same price for 1-3 people, breakfast packs can be bought in the lobby.

D-E Willows Resort, Marine Drive 15 km from the city centre, Schoenmakerskop, T0861-177 177, www.willows.madibabayresorts.co.za. A large, self-contained complex with more than 70 caravan sites, and 70 sea-facing self-catering chalets and rondavels with TV. Café serves snacks on the site during the day, plenty of extras for children: tidal pool, trampolines, mini-golf, children's playground, rock fishing, tractor rides, quad bikes, tennis courts and, in season, a crèche. Very popular in summer.

E-F King's Beach Backpackers, 41 Winder-mere Rd, Humewood, T041-585 8113, kingsb@agnet.co.za. Set 2 blocks back from the beach and close to restaurants, bars and clubs. Comfortable dorms, slightly cramped double rooms set in individual buildings in the garden, and camping space on the lawn. Excellent kitchen facilities, TV and video lounge, internet access, laid-back bar, travel centre, Baz Bus stop.

E-F Lungile Backpackers, 12 La Roche Drive, Humewood, T041-582 2042, www.lungile backpackers.co.za. Lively lodge set in a fine modern house about 10 mins' walk from Humewood Beach and the beachfront night-life. Camping space, dorms in the main house and double rooms in separate wooden cabins at the back, some with TV. Also has a garden with pool, TV and video lounge, bar, pool table, laundry, and a clean kitchen. Free use of surfboards. Great value. Recommended.

Game parks *p363*

D Kragga Kamma Game Park, 15-min drive from PE on the Kragga Kamma road off the

N2, T041-379 4195, www.kraggakamma.com. Self-catering thatched lodges and chalets, with lounge, kitchen and undercover braai area, good for families. Also cheaper pre-erected tents on platforms also with self-catering facilities. All scattered around a pretty forest area where overnight guests are likely to encounter animal activity during the night.

🍴 Eating

There are 2 purpose-built entertainment centres, **Brooke's Hill Pavilion** and **The Boardwalk**, where you will find a wide selection of restaurants and bars under one roof. These are similar to modern shopping malls – there is ample parking and visitors can feel more secure than they would wandering the streets at night.

Central Nelson Mandela Bay *p359, map p358*

¶¶¶ Old Austria, 24 Westbourne Rd, T041-373 0299. Mon-Sat 1200-1500, 1800-2230. Set in a restored Victorian whitewashed rectory, with chandeliers, polished wooden floors and grandfather clocks, the menu features seafood and Austrian fare such as schnitzel and apple strudel. There's also good fish and seafood, including poached sole and grilled prawns.

¶¶¶ Royal Delhi, 10 Burgess St, T041-373 8216. Open 1200-2330, Sat 1600-2330. Very popular local curry house serving a full range of Indian dishes, famous for its messy crab curry and home-made samosas and fish cakes. Non-Indian food eaters, can choose the likes of lamb shanks, steak or fish. Large groups can eat in their own separate dining room.

Outside Central Nelson Mandela Bay *p361, maps p358 and p360*

¶¶¶ Ginger, Marine Drive, Summerstrand, T041-583 2161, www.ginger-restaurant.co.za. New gourmet offering to the city, with chic stylish decor, an outside deck, sleek bar and beautifully presented and imaginative cuisine. A sample menu could be seared scallops with leek and sherry risotto, followed by roast duck with pineapple sauce and crêpes suzettes.

Hacklewood Hill Country House, 152 Prospect Rd, Walmer, T041-581 1300. Open 0700-1000, 1245-1400, 1900-2130. Elegant dining room in a luxury guesthouse, offering candlelit 4- to 5-course dinners (you'll need to know how to use the silverware), with wine suggestions for each course and waiters wearing white gloves. Very romantic and intimate. Recommended as a special treat for couples.

Kyoto, 56 Boardwalk Centre, T041-583 1160. Wed-Sun 1200-1400, 1800-2200, Mon-Tue 1800-2200 only. PE's only upmarket Japanese restaurant, with Japanese-inspired decor. Sit in a tatami – low tables in booths with cushions on the floor – or eat at the sushi bar. Comprehensive menu and excellent service, and as is customary you can watch the chefs at work.

La Mer, Protea Hotel Marine, see Sleeping, page 365. Open 0700-1000, 1800-2100. A quality and smart hotel restaurant with a nautical theme, offering delicious better-than-average buffets for breakfast and dinner, when soups and starters are followed by the likes of roast, beef, venison pie or calamari steak, and finished off with some decadent desserts and port and cheese.

34' South, 29 Boardwalk Centre, T041-583 1085. Open 1000-2130. Fabulous deli and sister branch to the one at the Knysna Waterfront, with all sorts of treats from olives to cookery books. Chrome and glass decor, you can make up meals from the counters or choose a selection of tapas and seafood snacks, tables outside on the wooden deck.

Lai Kung, Boardwalk, Summerstrand, T041-583 1123. Open 1130-2300. Large Chinese restaurant specializing in Cantonese cuisine with a huge range of good-value dishes. Plenty for vegetarians, quick service.

Mauro's, McArthur Baths Centre, Humewood, T041-582 4910. Mon-Fri 1200-1430, Mon-Sat 1800-2230. Fashionable seafood restaurant overlooking the beach, modern airy decor, good grilled fish, calamari, baked crab and giant prawns, also pasta and some meat dishes, lighter lunches served on the spacious deck with outdoor tables and bar, good service.

Piccolo Blackbeards, Brookes Hill Pavilion, corner of Marine Dr and Brookes Hill Drive, Summerstrand, T041-585 5567. Mon-Sat 1800-late. An à la carte seafood restaurant, which has been run by the same family for 3 generations. Great ocean views and impressive fish tank displays, extensive range of seafood, steak, Italian, vegetarian and poultry dishes. Recommended.

The Island Grill & Bar, Cape Recife, Summerstrand, opposite to the entrance of Humewood Golf Club, T041-583 3789. Open 1100-late. Built to resemble a Bali beach shack with reed ceilings and hessian covered walls, this has an informal atmosphere and a broad wooden deck overlooking the sand dunes. The menu has sensibly priced seafood, good value 'baskets' of calamari or chicken and chips and the like, and plenty of cocktails.

Dizzy Dolphins Café, 1 Shark Rock Pier, T041-583 4536. Open 0800-2200. Trendy cocktail bar and restaurant serving good value breakfasts, seafood, steaks and salads. Popular with a young, lively crowd.

Up the Khyber, McArthur Baths complex, King's Beach, T041-582 2200. Mon-Sat 1000-2200. Cheap curries, burgers and steaks in a great setting right above the beach with casual wooden tables on the veranda. Try the rather unusual oxtail curry.

Café Dulce, Boardwalk, Summerstrand, T041-583 1193. Open 0900-2200 Great coffee shop open selling tasty sandwiches, salads, milkshakes, ice creams; gets more alcoholic as the day gets longer.

🖸 Bars and clubs

Nelson Mandela Bay (Port Elizabeth)
p357, map p358 and p360
Nelson Mandela Bay (Port Elizabeth) has a good choice of late-night bars and clubs,

often offering meals in the early evening and live music or DJs later. As in all cities, clubs change regularly – for up-to-date information about which is the happening venue, ask at one of the backpacker hostels or the waiters at Tapas al Sol. Some places have dress codes – this usually means no shorts, vests or sandals.

Most of the nightlife is focused at 2 major entertainment centres, **The Boardwalk**, on Marine Dr by Shark Rock Pier, and **Brookes Hill Pavilion**, on the corner of Beach Rd and Brooke's Hill Dr in Summerstrand. These areas are safe to walk about at night, which is much of their appeal.

Barney's Tavern, The Boardwalk, T041-583 4500. Open 0830-late. Infromal steak restaurant during the day and livens up at night into an atmospheric bar with live music every night as well as on Sat-Sun afternoons on 'The Deck'. Also as popular spot to watch sport on the big screen TVs.

Tapas al Sol, Brookes Hill Pavilion, T041-586 2159, www.tapas.co.za. Mon-Sat 1200-late. As the name suggests, bar and pub serving tapas. Extended happy hour on Thu, spacious balcony, DJs on Fri and Sat, and is the city's top venue for performances by South Africa's most popular rock bands.

⊙ Entertainment

Nelson Mandela Bay (Port Elizabeth)
p357, map p358 and p360
Cinema
All the latest releases from Europe and the US are shown, check the local newspapers for screenings. The main cinemas are: **Cinema Starz**, Boardwalk Complex, T041-583 2000, www.starz.co.za; **Nu-Metro**, Walmer Park Shopping Centre, T041-367 1102, www.nu metro.co.za; and **Ster-Kinekor**, The Bridge at Greenacres, Langenhoven Drive, T041-363 0577, www.sterkinekor.com.

Theatre
There are regular concerts and plays performed by local musical and performance

groups. Check out the press for details or contact the Computicket call centre, T041-586 3177, www.computicket.co.za. The most popular venues in the city are: **The Feather Market Centre**, Baakens St, Central, T041-585 5514; **The Opera House and Barn**, Whites Rd, Central, T041-586 2256; and the **Vodacom Amphitheatre**, at the Boardwalk Centre, Marine Drive, Summerstrand, T041-507 7777.

⊛ Festivals and events

Nelson Mandela Bay (Port Elizabeth)
p357, map pp358 and p360
Feb Shakespearian Festival, a selection of plays are put on at the Mannville Open-Air Theatre in St George's Park. The theatre is named after the late Helen and Bruce Mann, who instituted the festival in 1970. A most enjoyable way to pass a summer's evening.
Feb Prickly Pear Festival, in Uitenhage, 34 km northwest of Nelson Mandela Bay (Port Elizabeth). With over 250 products on sale, crowds of over 25,000 turn up each year to enjoy food such as pancakes, ginger beer, *potjiekos*, jam, spit-braais, fish braais, curry bunnies and home-made pudding.
Mar/Apr Splash Festival, www.splash festival.com. A 4-day beach festival over the Easter weekend, with watersports, surfing competitions, live music and fireworks. Very popular annual event that attracts 200,000 daily. Fundraiser for the Community Chest.
Oct Addo Rose Show, Valentine Hall, Addo, www.addorose.co.za. Aa massive display with over 25,000 blooms on show, including new varieties. An enjoyable day out for anyone keen on gardens.

⊙ Shopping

Nelson Mandela Bay (Port Elizabeth)
p357, map p358 and p360
Flea markets
Art in the Park, St George's Park, located along Park Dr. An open-air exhibition of craft

stalls and local art on 1st Sun of every month.
Humewood Beachfront, between the King's
Beach parking area and McArthur's Baths. Sat
and Sun but everyday over school holidays.

Shopping malls
Like all South African cities, Nelson Mandela
Bay (Port Elizabeth) has its share of modern
shopping malls where not just shops but
banks and post offices are located. Most
well-known chain stores have relocated
from the city centre to these malls. **Greenacres Shopping Centre**, adjacent to The
Bridge at Greenacres (see below), www.
greenacres.co.za, which together result in
a mall 1 km long; **Pier 14 Shopping Centre**,
444 Govan Mbeki Av, North End, a central
location but more downmarket than the
others; and **Walmer Park Shopping Centre**,
Main Rd, Walmer, has aNu-Metro cinema.
The Bridge at Greenacres, Langenhoven
Drive, Greenacres, www.thebridgepe.co.za. A
giant upmarket centre, built over a main road
with great views from its elevated position.
There are 8 cinemas, ATMs, restaurants, coffee
shops and fast-food outlets, plus a smart
fashion mall for those with spare cash.

▲ Activities and tours

Nelson Mandela Bay (Port Elizabeth)
p357, map p358 and p360
Nelson Mandela Bay (Port Elizabeth) has
excellent facilities catering for sports, especially
watersports, golf, tennis, yachting and
athletics. It is also a great city in which to
watch sport and is often dubbed by locals
as 'SPort Elizabeth'.

Boat trips
Algoa Bay is world renowned in sailing circles
and the prestigious yacht club in the city, the
Algoa Bay Yacht Club, www.abyc.org.za, is
based at the harbour. There are 2 prevailing
winds which produce either very rough and
choppy conditions or calm and flat conditions.
Southern right whales mate and calve

between Jul and Oct in the bay, humpback
whales pass by during Jun-Jul, and again in
Nov-Dec, and the sardine-eating Bryde's whale
is present throughout most of the year. Also
be on the lookout for Cape fur seals, penguins,
bottlenose dolphins, gannets and cormorants.
Arctic Storm, at the harbour, T078-510
3443, www.arcticstorm.co.za. Offers breakfast and sunset cruises and can arrange
dinner at the Yacht Club (see above) after
the evening cruise. Can also arrange deep
sea fishing charters.
Raggy Charters, at the harbour, T041-378
2528, www.raggycharters.co.za. Runs marine
life-watching trips into the Algoa Bay and to
islands that form the marine section of the
Addo National Park. Beachfront cruises from
1½-3 hrs, and ½- or full-day fishing trips
using a variety of craft.

Cricket
Nelson Mandela Bay (Port Elizabeth) is
home to the **Eastern Province Cricket
Board**. Matches are played at **St George's
Park Sahara Oval**, also now known as the
'Crusaders Ground', tickets from www.com
puticket.com, information about fixtures,
T041-585 1646, www.epcricket.co.za. The first
Test match played here was between South
Africa and England on 12 Feb 1889, which
was also the first Test match to be played in
Africa. St George's is a pleasant old stadium
with a capacity for 22,000 and an enjoyable
venue to watch cricket. The 2 ends are known
as the Duckpond End and the Park Drive End.
There has been a cricket club here since 1843.
There is some interesting cricket memorabilia
on display in glass cases in the Khaya Majola
Room in the Centenary Pavilion at St George's.

Football & Rugby
The new **Nelson Mandela Bay Stadium** has
been built for the 2010 FIFA World Cup™ and
it occupies a site overlooking the ocean, 1 km
north of the city centre at North End. It seats
48,000 and was the first of the country's new
stadiums to be completed in Jun 2009 and
was host to the British and Irish Lions Tour.

Diving in Nelson Mandela Bay

There are a number of good dive sites around Nelson Mandela Bay (Port Elizabeth) and the best time for diving is during the winter months of May to September when average visibility is 8-15 m. There are a variety of dive sites from colourful reefs and drop-offs to shipwrecks and soft corals. The best diving in the area is around **St Croix Islands**, 20 km from Nelson Mandela Bay (Port Elizabeth) harbour. The average dive is along a slope with a maximum depth of 30 m, where there are a few caves and gullies. The islands and the surrounding waters are protected: fishing and spearfishing are not permitted and it is forbidden to land on the islands. A consequence of this has been a flourishing population of African jackass penguins, gulls, terns and cormorants on land, while the surrounding waters are rich in marine life, providing a plentiful diet for the birds. Other popular local dives are **Thunderbolt Reef, Sardinia Bay, Devil's Reef, Roman Rock** and **Philip's Reef**. There are also some good wreck dives at the **Pati**, on Thunderbolt Reef; the **Inchcape Rock** wreck (this steel hull from 1902 suffers from poor visibility); the **Western Knight** wreck (experienced wreck divers only); and the **Haerlem** wreck (a navy vessel sunk in 1987 to 21 m specifically for divers). The following dive operators can organize daily trips: **Ocean Divers International**, 10 Albert Rd, Walmer, T041-581 5121, www.odipe.co.za. **Pro Dive**, Main Rd, Walmer, opposite the Walmer Park Shopping Mall, T041-581 1144, www.prodive.co.za. Pro Dive can also organize cage diving in the shark tank at the Oceanarium.

In 2006, when Jospeh Blatter, FIFA's boss, visited Nelson Mandela Bay (Port Elizabeth) to inspect progress of the stadium, the Nelson Mandela Metropolitan University awarded him an honorary doctorate. This was in recognition that the chief of South Africa's 2010 Local Organising Committee, Danny Jordaan, comes from Nelson Mandela Bay (Port Elizabeth).

Golf

There are several golf courses in and around the city, but the best bet for visitors are: **Humewood Golf Club**, Marine Drive, Summerstrand, T041-583 2137, www.hume woodgolf.co.za. A challenging links course, rated as 1 of the top 10 courses in the country. 18 holes/72 par with a very elegant clubhouse. **Port Elizabeth Golf Club**, accessed from Westview Drive, Mill Park, T041-374 3140, www.pegolf.co.za. A 100-year-old beautifully maintained 18-hole/par 72 course.

Horse racing

There are 2 major racecourses, **Arlington**, Schoenmakerskop Rd, Walmer, T041-366 1666; and **Fairview**, Draaifontein Rd, Green-bushes, T041-372 1859. Both are managed by Phumelela, www.phumelela.com. There are races every Fri afternoon at both of the 2 courses throughout the year.

Surfing

Good waves on this stretch of coast aren't restricted to Jeffrey's Bay. The Pipe in Algoa Bay is one of the most popular spots, as is Millars Point further to the west. Drawback of the waves closer to town are the crowded beaches and the industrial backdrop.

Swimming

The beaches around Nelson Mandela Bay (Port Elizabeth) are very clean, but the sea temperature rarely gets above 21ºC. Away from the large hotels there are a couple of excellent municipal swimming pools.

McArthur Baths, King's Beach Promenade, T041-586 3412. Sep-Apr daily 0700-1700. Tidal pool, children's waterchute, splash pool, freshwater pool, permanent lifeguard, restaurants and snack bar.

St George's Park Baths, St George's Park, T041-585 7751. Sep-Apr Mon-Fri 0700-2100, Sat 0900-1800, Sun 1030-1800. Olympic-sized pool with diving facilities, children's pool, restaurant and snack bar.

Tour operators

In general, there are 3 types of tours on offer: historical town tours which may involve walking; township tours, which are growing in popularity; and wildlife tours, with visits to one or more of the local game reserves such as Addo Elephant National Park. For a full list of tour operators and to book a tour, contact the tourist office, see page 357.

Calabash Tours, 8 Dollery St, Central, T041-585 6162, www.calabashtours.co.za. Excellent city tours, including visits to various townships, visits to local artists and self-help projects, and evening shebeen tours. Also runs tours to Addo Elephant National Park and visits to the beaches. Minimum 2 people. Good value, highly recommended.

East Cape Tours, T041-581 6260, www.east capetours.com. Day tours around Nelson Mandela Bay, including ½-day township visits and good-value full-day tours of Addo for R600 including lunch and entrance fees.

Highwind Tours, T041-586 3721, www.high winds.co.za. 3-hr city tours for R350, can also guide visitors around the city's Donkin Heritage Trail, plus townships and night-time shebeen visits.

Shield Tours, T082-381 0235, www.shield tours.co.za. Historical city tours and trips to the game parks.

Windsurfing

Experienced windsurfers have the opportunity to go out at Noordhoek, where they are totally exposed to the ocean swell, but it is important to check the tides. There are excellent reef breaks and cross-shore

conditions when the southwest wind blows. Off Hobie Beach the conditions are much calmer, particularly when there is a southwest wind. Be careful at all times to avoid the designated public bathing areas. The Swart-kop River Mouth is a good area for beginners as the conditions are calm. Some of the hotels on the beach front in Summerstrand and Humewood have equipment to rent to guests.

⊖ Transport

Nelson Mandela Bay (Port Elizabeth)
p357, map p358 and p360

It's 72 km to **Addo Elephant National Park**; 643 km to **Bloemfontein**; 763 km to **Cape Town**; 295 km to **East London**; 124 km to **Grahamstown**; 246 km to **Graaff-Reinet**; 79 km to **Jeffrey's Bay**; 1050 km to **Johannesburg**; 150 km to **Port Alfred**; 74 km to **Shamwari Game Reserve**.

Air

Nelson Mandela Bay (Port Elizabeth) airport is 4 km from the city on Alister Miller Drive, T041-507 7319, www.acsa.co.za. There are several daily connections with the other major cities on **South African Airways (SAA)**, **Kulula**, **Comair** and **1Time**.

Airline offices All air tickets can be booked online at www.computicket.com. **1Time**, www.1time.aero. **British Airways Comair**, www.britishairways.com. **Kulula**, www.kulula.com. **South African Airways (SAA)**, www.flysaa.com. or further details, see Essentials, page 40.

Bus

Baz Bus provides the best budget bus travel service along the coast between Cape Town and Durban. Nelson Mandela Bay (Port Elizabeth) is the midway point where the bus stays overnight. In other words, if you start the day in Cape Town and are heading towards Durban, Nelson Mandela Bay (Port Elizabeth) is the furthest you can get in a single day. There is a daily service to and from **Cape Town** and it runs 5 days a week to and from **Durban**. The Baz Bus arrives in Nelson Mandela Bay (Port Elizabeth) from both Cape Town and Durban 2130-2230 and departs 0645-0715.

The 3 mainline bus companies have daily departures linking the other major cities. **Greyhound**, buses depart from the rear car park, 107 Govan Mbeki Av, and in front of Edgars at the Greenacres Shopping Centre. **Intercape** buses depart from the office in the Flemming Building behind the Old Post Office, corner of Flemming and North Union streets. **Translux** buses start their journey by the railway station in the centre of town, then stop at the office, Ernst and Young Building, Ring Rd, Greenacres. If arriving by bus check with your hotel which is the most convenient stop for their location.

Bus companies All bus tickets can be booked online at www.computicket.com. Baz Bus, T021-439 2323, www.bazbus.com; Greyhound, www.greyhound.co.za; Intercape, www.intercape.co.za; and Translux, www.translux.co.za. For more information, see Getting around, page 41.

Car hire

Avis, airport, T041-501 7200, www.avis.co.za; Budget, airport, T041-581 4242, www.budget.co.za; Dollar Thrifty, airport, T041-581 4774, www.thrifty.co.za; Europcar, airport, T041-581 1268, www.europcar.co.za; Tempest/Sixt Car Hire, airport, T041-581 1256, www.tempestcarhire.co.za.

Taxi

Hurters Radio Cabs, T041-585 5500. Local company that rather astonishingly has been operating in Port Elizabeth for 75 years.

Train

The railway station is in the town centre on Station St, just off Strand St which runs parallel to Govan Mbeki Av. Central reservations, **Shosholoza Meyl**, T0860-00888 (in South Africa), T011-774 4555 (from overseas), www.shosholozameyl.co.za, timetables and fares are published on the website. There are services between Port Elizabeth and **Johannesburg** and **Bloemfontein**.

❻ Directory

Nelson Mandela Bay (Port Elizabeth)
p357, map p358 and p360
Banks American Express, Boardwalk Centre, T041-583 2025. **Emergencies** Surf and Sea Rescue, T041-507 3911. **Immigration** corner of Stone and Lavinia streets, T041-487 1026, for visa extensions, Mon-Fri 0800-1500. **Internet** Internet access at all the backpacker lodges and hotels; Boardwalk Internet Café, Boardwalk Centre, T041-583 4725. **Medical services** Netcare Greenacres Hospital, Cape Rd, Greenacres, T041-390 7000, private hospital. St George's Hospital, Park Drive, Central, T041-392 6111.

West of Nelson Mandela Bay

From Nelson Mandela Bay (Port Elizabeth) the N2 heads west for around 190 km to Storms River and the Tsitsikamma National Park at the eastern end of the Garden Route. Although Tsitsikamma is officially in the Eastern Cape and Storms River marks the provincial boundary, we deal with it in the Western Cape chapter along with the rest of the Garden Route. This stretch of road is nowhere near as scenic as the Garden Route itself, though there are a few attractions if you veer off the N2. These include the modern town of Jeffery's Bay, internationally famous for its good surf, a few interesting nature reserves and the tranquil village of St Francis Bay and its neighbour, the upmarket resort of Cape St Francis. ▶▶ *For listings, see pages 376-379.*

Van Stadens Wild Flower Reserve

ⓘ *T041-956 0155, the reserve has a visitor centre, nursery and a picnic site, 0800-1700.*

The N2 from Nelson Mandela Bay (Port Elizabeth) to Humansdorp passes directly through the middle of the wild flower reserve. The turning into the reserve is 35 km from Nelson Mandela Bay (Port Elizabeth). Established to protect and propagate indigenous flora, the area is also worth visiting for its butterflies and birds. The best time to visit is between February and August when many of the plants are in bloom. Plants to look out for include ground orchids and proteas. The southern part of the reserve is an interesting area of forest with ironwood and wild pomegranate trees, as well as a rare tree species, the Cape star-chestnut.

There are two short walks through the different ecosystems of the reserve: the **River Walk**, 4 km, passes the nursery and follows the course of the Van Stadens River; the **Forest Walk**, 6 km, enters an area that has been replanted with proteas. From the highest point of the walk there are views of riverine forest in the valleys and gorge below.

Langkloof

Three mountain ranges lie to the north of the N2 and Jeffrey's Bay: the **Kouga**, the **Baviaanskloof** and the **Grootwinterhoek**, known collectively as the 'Langkloof'. At 270,000 ha, the Langkloof is the third largest wilderness region in South Africa. It became the meeting point of the Khoisan – San hunter-gatherers and Khoi pastoralists. Their rock art in overhangs and caves throughout the area stands testament to their existence.

One of the most fascinating routes to take through the Langkloof is to follow the N2 for 92 km west of Nelson Mandela Bay (Port Elizabeth) to Thornhill, and then the R331 and R332 along the Baviaanskloof River Valley between Patensie and Willowmore. However, it is a narrow, steep, gravel-surfaced, winding road and the distance to Willowmore is approximately 200 km, which can take aobut six to eight hours. A 4WD vehicle is preferable. There are also no shops or fuel in the valley. The road meanders through a landscape dominated by the red sandstone hills on either side. The hills are rich in proteas, ericas, orchids and the 'drie-bessie-bos', an endemic plant which can only be seen in this area. As the road climbs further up the river valley, the scenery becomes more rugged with the mountains rising to over 1600 m. The mountains are a maze of cliffs and ravines inhabited by baboons and tortoises; the trails here pass through thick areas of woodland where you can see the unique Baviaanskloof cedar. From the top of the mountains there are views over the acacia woodland to the fruit farms in the valleys below. Eland and Cape mountain zebra have now been reintroduced, and kudu, bushbuck, klipspringer and baboon are present.

This region offers some of the wildest areas for hiking in the Eastern Cape; hikes here are strenuous and involve some long climbs. Summers here are too hot for long hikes so it makes sense simply to drive through the area. March to November is cooler and more suitable for hiking. For information check out www.baviaans.co.za, www.baviaans.net, www.baviaanskloof.net, or go to the **Tolbos Country Shop and Restaurant** ① *T042-283 0437*, on the R331 in the Gamtoos Valley, roughly 30 km north of the N2.

Jeffrey's Bay ⊜🖉▲⊖ ›› pp376-379. Colour map 7, B4.

Jeffrey's Bay, or 'J-Bay' as it's known locally, is surf central. Home to the 'perfect wave', this is an internationally acclaimed surfing spot and a major playground for self-respecting surf rats. In the evenings, the local bars buzz with talk of supertubes and perfect breaks. Waves can get big, sometimes as high as 3 m giving rides of over three minutes, but J-Bay is surprisingly renowned for its safety. Unsurprisingly, it attracts more than its fair share of long-term resident travellers but, away from the beach, there's little going on in town.

There are numerous surf shops selling a wide range of boards and wetsuits, as well as Billabong and Quiksilver factory outlets, but when surf's up don't be surprised to find many of the local businesses closed.

Ins and outs
Getting there If you don't have a car the **J-Bay Cabs**, T083-611 1003, will bring you here on request from Nelson Mandela Bay (Port Elizabeth). The town is served by the **Baz Bus** (for further details, see Transport, page 379). The nearest drop-off for the mainline buses (**Greyhound** and **Translux**) is in Humansdorp.

Tourist information **Jeffrey's Bay Tourism** ① *Da Gama Rd, Shell Museum complex, T042-293 2923, www.jeffreysbaytourism.org, Mon-Fri 0830-1700, Sat 0900-1200*, are helpful and enthusiastic, but backpacker hostels offer the best practical information about surfing.

Background
The origins of Jeffrey's Bay date to 1894, when a trading post was established here by Joseph Avent Jeffrey, a whaler from the island of St Helena. The trading post received goods by sea and supplied settlers living inland in the Langkloof. Little of the original settlement remains and today Jeffrey's Bay is a sprawl of unattractive bungalows and holiday homes. Out of season in summer,

Sleeping 🛏
African Perfection 5
Beach Cabanas 3
Diaz 15 House on the Beach 1
Dolphin View Guest House 6
Dolphin View Beach House 7
Island Vibe 9
Jeffrey's Bay Backpackers 2
Misty Lodge Backpackers 8
Supertubes 4

Eating 🍴
3 Fat Fish 4
De Viswijf 2
Die Walskipper 6
Kitchen Windows 1
Le Grotto 3
Sunflower Café 5

when most of the coast is at its liveliest, the resort is a quiet and desolate place and there's little of the surfing scene or nightlife you might expect. In winter, however, when the waves are at their best, the town comes back to life. July is also when the **Billabong Pro J-Bay** surf competition (www.billabong pro.com) is held – with prize money amounting to US$250,000 – which draws surfers from across the globe, and the town gets packed out. This is a major surfing event, and you'll get to see some of the best surfers in the world compete.

Sights

The waves here are definitely the main attraction, but as an alternative, the **Shell Museum** ① *T042-293 1945, Mon-Sat 0900-1600, Sun 0900-1300, R5 per person*, makes for an interesting visit. The collection is incredibly large and has many rare examples of Indo-Pacific and southern Cape shells found on nearby beaches. The position of Jeffrey's Bay along the coast happens to coincide with the meeting point of two opposing ocean currents, which explains why so many unusual shells have been found on the local beaches. Some shells have been carried all the way down the western coast of Africa. The collection was put together over a 30-year period and left to the town by Charlotte Kritzinger.

Aston Bay, **Paradise Beach** and the **Kabeljous River Estuary** are only a short drive away and make a pleasant change from the main beach in Jeffrey's Bay.

St Francis Bay and Cape St Francis ⊜❼ ↠ *pp376-379. Colour map 7, B4.*

The adjoining villages of St Francis Bay and Cape St Francis are 20 km from Humansdorp, just off the R330. Less than 40 years ago there was nothing here except fine, white-sand beaches and a mule track which ran from Humansdorp to the lighthouse at Cape St Francis. These days a prosperous collection of whitewashed, thatched holiday homes line the beach just south of the Krom River Mouth, alongside an 18-hole golf course and a shopping centre.

A modern marina development, **The Canals**, is constructed around the largest man-made web of canals in the country. The only privately owned harbour in South Africa, it is full of smart yachts and *chokka* (calamari) fishing boats. A highlight of any visit is eating fresh calamari on the quayside. The nearby dam, the Churchill, supplies Nelson Mandela Bay (Port Elizabeth) with much of its water.

The **Cape St Francis lighthouse**, also known as **Seal Lighthouse** ① *T042-298 0428, 0900-1615, R14, children (under 12) R7*, was built in 1878 and, at a height of 27.75 m, is the tallest stonework tower on the South African coast. You can go on a tour of the lighthouse, where there is also a small coffee shop. Also based at the lighthouse is an **African penguin rehabilitation centre** ① *T042-298 0100, www.penguin-rescue. org.za, donations welcome*, run by **Ajubatus Marine and Wildlife Rescue**, which treats and re-releases sick and injured penguins and cleans up those damaged by oil slicks. They have a small centre with a penguin pool and visitors can look through the large windows. All marine birds are extremely vulnerable to oil pollution, but penguins even more so than flying birds. Once oiled, their insulation becomes severely compromised and they cannot enter the sea to hunt, and as a result slowly starve to death or die of exposure/hypothermia.

The bay, with its 16-km beach, is famous for its waves and attracts surfers from all over the world. In 1963 the surfing movie *Endless Summer* was filmed here, as well as the remake *Endless Summer II* in 1992. For information, contact **St Francis Bay Tourism** ① *corner of Lime Rd South and St Francis Drive, T042-294 0076, www.stfrancistourism.co.za, Mon-Fri 0900-1600, Sat 1000-1400.*

St Francis Bay was named after the patron saint of sailors by the Portuguese explorer Manuel Perestrelo in 1575.

Maitland Nature Reserve

Facing St Francis Bay, the reserve is a small strip of coastal forest near the estuary of the Maitland River. This was the site of a number of lead mines in the 19th century but as these were abandoned so was the whole area, giving the forest a chance to recover. The reserve is now renowned for its birdlife and is an excellent place to see paradise flycatchers and Knysna louries. One of the best months to visit is October, when many of the forest plants are either flowering or in fruit.

The 3-km **Sir Peregrine Maitland Trail** is a leisurely walk through forest along an old wagon trail; the 9-km **De Stades Trail** covers the length and breadth of the reserve, passing through small areas of dune forest and open grassland.

◉ West of Nelson Mandela Bay listings

For Sleeping and Eating price codes and other relevant information, see pages 46-53.

● Sleeping

Jeffrey's Bay *p374, map p374*

As the best-known surfing spot in South Africa, Jeffrey's Bay attracts large numbers of surfers from all over the world. Consequently, there is a good range of budget accom-modation here. Each backpacker place has its own scene and you're bound to come across people who are staying there for the whole season. The tourist office can help with booking a number of holiday flats around the town.

A Diaz 15 House on the Beach, 15 Diaz Rd, T042-293 1779, www.diaz15.co.za. 8 luxury self-catering apartments with 2 or 3 bed-rooms, fully equipped kitchens with microwave, large lounge with open balcony overlooking the beach, 2 bathrooms, TV with M-Net, breakfast included, rim-flow pool, perfect for families looking for a high standard of comfort. Right on the beach, walking distance to the shops and restaurants. Very popular, so you'll need to book several months in advance.

A Supertubes, 10-12 Pepper St, T042-293 2957, www.supertubesguesthouse.co.za. Laid-back B&B set 30 m from the beach and supertubes wave, 14 en suite double rooms

with balcony, or more luxurious suites with extras like a/c and heated towel rail, set across 2 houses, and also rents out 2 nearby self-catering houses sleeping up to 8. Meals are available on request or there's a kitchen and dining area for guests' use, as well as hanging space for wetsuits and boards for surfers.

B African Perfection, 20 Pepper St, T042-293 1401, www.africanperfection.co.z. 8 very spacious individually decorated B&B rooms with lounge areas, picture windows, wooden balconies with views over the Supertubes, minibar, DSTV and surfboard racks. Generous breakfasts and dinner on request. Also rents out a 5-bed self-catering holiday home.

C-D Dolphin View Guest House, Dogwood Circle, Wavecrest, T042-296 0594, www.dolphin-view.com. 4 neat B&B rooms with good ocean views located in the Noorse Kloof Nature Reserve, which is a peaceful area not far from shops and beach, with indoor pool, TV lounge and beautiful gardens which are lit up in the evening. Also has 3 guest rooms 50 m from the beach at the **Dolphin View Beach House**, 13 Akasia St.

D Beach Cabanas, 118 Da Gama Rd, T042-293 2820, www.beachcabanas.co.za. Located 150 m from the beach, small attractive swimming pool surrounded by palms, 16 smart modern flats on 2 storeys with kitchenette, heater, fan, TV, good breakfasts, motel-style parking. One reader reports excellent service and friendly and helpful owners.

D-E Jeffrey's Bay Backpackers, 12 Jeffrey St, T042-293 1379, www.jeffreysbayback packers.co.za. This was the first backpacker place to open in Jeffrey's Bay. It is well run and popular, and is in a good location in the centre of town, close to Main Beach. Small dorms, 5 double rooms, camping in garden, off-street parking, reductions can be negotiated for long stays, well-stocked and clean kitchen, bedding provided, hires out surfboards and bikes. Baz Bus stop and pickups can be arranged from Humansdorp.

D-F Island Vibe, 10 Dageraad St, T042-293 1625, www.islandvibe.co.za. This hostel is in an excellent location at the top end of Jeffrey's Bay, perched high up on the dunes with views across 2 beaches and steps down to the beach. Dorms, doubles and camping, kitchen, bar, café serving set evening meals and good breakfasts. The place has a big surfer scene, so don't expect to get much sleep. Music from the bar pumps out through the night. Very popular and perfect for a couple of day's partying. The new and quieter **Beach House** has en suite doubles and open-plan kitchen and lounge with great sea views. Rents out bikes, canoes, fishing rods and, of course, surfboards. Offers walking tours to the local township and has a good travel centre and internet access. Also the location of **Jeffrey's Bay Surf School** (see Activities and tours, page 379). If you stay here you get 10% off in the Billabong factory shop. Offers a free pickup from buses in Humansdorp and is a Baz Bus stop. All in all, recommended to get a genuine feel of what J-Bay is all about.

D-F Misty Lodge Backpackers, 17 Flame Cres, Wavecrest, T042-293 1878, www.mistylodge.co.za. Variety of accom- modation available: a self-contained thatched cottage which can sleep up to 6, with a fully equipped kitchen and TV; a honeymoon suite with an oval bath and champagne on arrival in your room; 3 double rooms with bathrooms; a dorm; and camping space. Set in a secure walled garden with bar and braai, close to the beach and a shopping centre. The owner offers excellent advice, information and hospitality.

St Francis Bay and Cape St Francis *p375*

While Jeffrey's Bay, appeals to the budget traveller, by contrast St Francis Bay has a few establishments in the luxury bracket.

AL The Beach House, 4 Frank Rd, T042-294 1225, www.stfrancisbay.co.za/thebeach house. Beautiful guesthouse set right on the beach, with 4 luxurious and stylish rooms under thatch, 2 with ocean views, 2 overlooking the pool. DSTV and broad wooden patios, excellent breakfasts, also evening meals by prior arrangement. Attentive, unfussy service. Recommended.

AL The Sands @ St Francis, 8 Frank Rd, T/F042-294 1888, www.thesands.co.za. Smart, comfortable guesthouse just a few mins from the beach, set in an attractive thatched house with 5 en suite a/c rooms. Bathrooms have jacuzzi baths and separate showers, each with its own timber deck overlooking the beach, some with private outside shower and jacuzzi. Swimming pool, sun deck, steam room, beauty therapies on request, breakfast and gourmet dinners served in a very unusual octagonal restaurant with thatched roof and glass walls with a 360° view. Gold clubs and mountain bikes available for guests. Recommended, but pricey.

AL-A Cape St Francis Resort, Da Gama Rd, Cape St Francis, T042-298 0054, www.cape stfrancis.co.za. Upmarket holiday village with a range of accommodation: 3 luxury villas perched on the dunes sleeping up to 12; superior thatched cottages with 3 bedrooms, kitchen and lounge; and en suite apartments with 1 bedroom and kitchen around the swimming pool, **Park Off Pub** and **Joe Fish Restaurant**. The on-site adventure centre can organize a number of activities, from boat rides to deep-sea fishing.

B-C Thatchwood, 63 Lyme Rd, T042-294 0082, www.stfrancisbay-accommodation. co.za. Smart and comfortable thatched guesthouse overlooking the local golf course with private access across the fairways to the beach. 7 double rooms with en suite bathroom and TV, meals served on the lawn or from an open dining room, bar.

C Port View Place, Leighton Hullet Drive, Port St Francis, T042-294 1553, www.port viewplace.co.za. Towards the back of the marina development, small B&B with 6 tastefully, individually decorated en suite rooms, and 4 self-catering family apartments, all with DSTV. Spacious lounge, breakfast on balcony with harbour views, walking distance to restaurants

D St Francis Bay Lodge, 7 Kansies Rd, St Francis Bay, T0846-701131, www.stfrancis baylodge.co.za. Situated behind the Police Station, this lovely B&B is 10 mins' walk from the sea. 4 airy and spacious 2- and 3-bedroom apartments, and 3 B&B rooms. Swimming pool in peaceful gardens, dinners on request, honesty bar with log fire. The couple that run the lodge are very friendly and can organize local activities.

⦿ Eating

Jeffrey's Bay p374, map p374
¶¶ 3 Fat Fish, 27 De Gamma Rd, T042-293 4147. Mon-Sat 1000-late. Contemporary interior with polished wood floors and exposed beams, plus an outside deck. This bistro/bar offers a varied menu using only organic produce and free range chicken and eggs. Gourmet wraps, burgers and pizzas, and some interesting meat and fish dishes like chicken with smoky bacon mash or prawn, artichoke and chorizo sausage pasta.
¶¶ De Viswijf, 55 Diaz Rd, T042-293 3921, www.deviswijf.co.za. 1100-1500, 1700-late, closed Sun evenings. Enclosed deck overlooking the surf and fishing boats, wide selection of seafood and steaks, specials such as *potjies*, and unusual dishes such as curried tripe and occasional game meat. Award-winning wine list.

¶¶ Die Walskipper, Marina Martinique Harbour, out of town towards St Francis Bay, T042-292 0005, www.walskipper.co.za. Tue-Sat 1200-2100, Sun 1200-1500. As befits a popular surfing venue, this open-air restaurant with a corrugated-iron roof and shade cloth attracts a fun crowd on the beach. During the winter months the owners bring coal stoves to the beach. The menu consists of good local dishes with fresh ingredients and home-made breads. Steaming seafood platters with plenty of 'white gold' (calamari) is the go, served up on enamel plates, and drinks are distributed in tin mugs. Recommended.
¶¶ Kitchen Windows, 23 Diaz St, T042-293 4230. Tue-Sun 1130-1400, 1800-late. Informal spot with chunky wooden furnishings and terracotta floors, ocean views from the deck, good seafood including kingklip with oysters and shrimps baked in the pizza oven, steaks and sauces, and pasta. Long menu.
¶¶ Le Grotto, Jeffrey's St, T042-293 2612. Mon-Sat 1100-late, Sun 1100-1600. Popular corner restaurant serving fresh seafood, steaks and burgers, good catch of the day, famous for its 1-kg steaks.
¶ Sunflower Café, 20 Da Gama Rd, T042-293 1682. Open 0800-2300. Café and restaurant serving great range of light meals, including plenty for vegetarians. Delicious milkshakes and home-made cakes, good evening meals such as grilled calamari or pasta. Internet access and local artwork on permanent display. Recommended.

St Francis Bay and Cape St Francis p375
There are several coffee shops and restaurants in the **Village Shopping Centre** on St Francis Dr in the middle of St Francis Bay.
¶¶ Chokka Block, at the harbour, St Francis Bay, T042-294 1615. Open 1200-1500, 1800-2200, closed Sun dinner. Overlooking the port and decorated in a coastal theme with a large collection of shells on display, this restaurant is renowned for its seafood, especially its chokka (calamari), and also has

a good range of meat dishes like steaks and lamb shanks.

♜ Joe Fish, Cape St Francis Resort, see Sleeping, page 377. Open 1130-late. Excellent seafood, especially the calamari steaks, or try the spare ribs, alfresco terrace around the swimming pool or cosy pub with fireplace.

♜ Trattoria San Francesco, Village Centre, St Francis Drive, T042-294 0819. Tue-Sun 1200-1430, 1800-2200. Affordable trattoria-style Italian on the 2nd floor of the shopping centre, good range of pasta and rich sauces, and crisp wood-fired pizzas.

▲▲ Activities and tours

Jeffrey's Bay p374, map p374
Horse riding
Papiesfontein Beach Rides, on the farm of the same name 10 km to the east of Jeffery's Bay off the R102, T082-574 9396, www.horsetrails.co.za. For a small extra fee will pick up from town if you don't have a car. Suitable for novices and instruction is given, 2-hr rides depart daily at 0930 and 1500, R200, booking advised. A 13-km circular trail goes to the Gamtoos River and then leads over the picturesque dunes at the Gamtoos River mouth to the beach. From here, there's 6 km of coastline for galloping or splashing through the waves.

Sandboarding
JayBay Sandboarding, T042-296 2974, or book through the tourist office. There are some big dunes around Jeffrey's Bay – perfect for sandboarding. Trips run daily and include boards and tuition.

Surfing
Jeffrey's Bay Surf School, based at Island Vibe Backpackers, T042-293 1625, www.islandvibe.co.za. Beginner lessons run daily year-round and include wetsuits, beginners' boards and tuition. Advanced lessons use video sessions to see what you did right or wrong. Lessons are R150-250 for 1½ hrs or ask about the 7-day learn to surf packages which include accommodation and meals.

⊖ Transport

Jeffrey's Bay p374, map p374
It's 78 km to **Nelson Mandela Bay (Port Elizabeth)**, 20 km to **Cape St Francis**, 20 km to **Humansdorp** (N2), 206 km to **Knysna**, 1062 km to **Durban**.

Bus
Baz Bus, T021-439 2323, www.bazbus.com. Backpackers' budget service that calls in at hostels to collect/drop off. They should have room to carry your surfing equipment but let them know in advance. Coming from Cape Town, Jeffrey's Bay is the last drop-off, arriving 2030-2100, before the bus crew spend the night in Nelson Mandela Bay (Port Elizabeth). If you want to travel further east than Nelson Mandela Bay (Port Elizabeth), you'll have to leave from there the next morning. Travelling from Jeffrey's Bay to **Cape Town** the Baz Bus picks up 0830-0900 and arrives in Cape Town later that night.

Greyhound and **Translux** pick up and drop off at **Humansdorp**, 20 km from Jeffrey's Bay on the N2 on the service between **Cape Town** and **Durban**. From here, you take a local taxi. J-Bay Cabs, T083-611 1003 operates a shuttle service between Port Elizabeth, Jeffrey's Bay, Humansdorp, St Francis Bay and Cape St Francis. It may be possible to arrange for your accommodation to collect you for a small charge but remember some departure and arrival times are either late at night or in the early hours of the morning.

Nelson Mandela Bay to East London

There are two routes to East London from Nelson Mandela Bay (Port Elizabeth). The quickest is on the N2 via Grahamstown. An alternative route is to take the R72 coastal road, but there are three very compelling reasons for following the N2: to explore the wonderful Addo Elephant National Park; to visit the string of new private game reserves, including the superb Shamwari Game Reserve; and to see the old colonial town of Grahamstown. ▸▸ *For listings, see pages 390-397.*

Addo Elephant National Park ●▲▲ ▸▸ *pp390-397. Colour map 7, B4.*

The original elephant sector of the Addo Elephant National Park, proclaimed in 1931, covered 12,000 ha, when only 11 elephants remained in the area. Since 2000, the park has undergone a process of expansion and new land purchase has been made possible by funds from the government and overseas donors. Today the park covers 292,000 ha and is the third largest conservation area in South Africa. The park now encompasses five neighbouring game reserves and wilderness areas and stretches from the Indian Ocean to the Little Karoo and incorporates five different habitat biospheres.

At the coast is a belt of coastal dunefields and forest. The 200-m Alexandria Dunefield, the largest active dunefields in the world after the Namib Desert, now falls within the park and the 120,000-ha marine reserve adjoining Addo includes many islands that are home to the largest population of African gannets and the second largest population of penguins. With the reintroduction of lion in 2003, it is now possible to see the Big Seven – elephant, rhino, lion, buffalo, leopard, whale and great white shark – in a malaria-free environment. This expansion of the park is one of the most exciting and ambitious conservation projects ever undertaken, and Addo, now home to the densest population of elephant on earth, has become a highlight of the Eastern Cape.

Today this finely tuned ecosystem is sanctuary to a breeding herd of over 450 elephants, 400 Cape buffalo, 48 black rhino, hippo, cheetah, leopard, lion, spotted hyena, a variety of antelope species, as well as the flightless dung beetle – unique to the park and found wherever there's elephant dung. Over 185 species of bird have been recorded here. The relative flatness of the bush and the large number of elephant mean that they are easily seen. To add to this, there are a couple of waterholes which can be accessed by car. Visitors will often see several herds drinking at one time – this can mean watching over 100 elephant – a magnificent experience. Although you'll see them at any time of year, one of the best times to visit is in January and February, when many of the females will have recently calved.

Ins and outs
Getting there Most visitors head for the area where the elephants are found, which is south of the main camp at the main park entrance, 72 km from Nelson Mandela Bay (Port Elizabeth). It can be reached by taking the R335, which is well signposted off the N2 from Nelson Mandela Bay (Port Elizabeth) to Grahamstown. A new access road into the park has been constructed that feeds off the N2 highway near Colchester, and goes through the new Matyholweni Gate and Camp in the new southern block of the park before joining up with the existing network of tourist roads in the park. To get there from Nelson Mandela Bay, take the N2 highway towards Grahamstown, and after 40 km where the road crosses the Sundays River Bridge, turn left at the 'Camp Matyholweni' sign. Follow this

road for about 3 km until you enter Matyholweni Gate at Camp Matyholweni. Follow the southern access road inside the park for 36 km to Addo's main camp. Coming from the Grahamstown direction, either take this new southern route, or from the N2 turn on to the N10 towards Cradock/Cookhouse, 80 km east of Grahamstown. Then, after 22 km, take the R342 to the left when you get to the intersection with Paterson on your right, which leads into the park and continues on to the main camp. Within the park there is a network of good gravel roads if you are in your own car or you can book day and night drives, game walks, and horse rides through reception. Booking ahead is essential. The coastal section and Alexandria Dunefield is south of the N2, and there are access points to the beach off the R72. The northern section is best visited from the **Darlington Lake Lodge**, see page 391.

Best time to visit The weather here is usually warm and dry, and visits to the park are enjoyable all year round.

Park information T042-233 0556, www.sanparks.org, R130, children (under 12) R65, gates open daily 0700-1900; the wildlife viewing area is open 0600-1800 in summer and 0700-1730 in winter, though times vary according to season so check with reception; office 0700-2000. There's a restaurant open 0800-2100, that serves light snacks and meals and a shop open 0800-1900 that sells a selection of groceries, meat, bread and wines. Petrol (no diesel) 0730-1700; laundry, telephone and postal services also available. There is a swimming pool and tennis court at the main camp and a hide at a game-viewing waterhole that is floodlit at night. The park's other hide tends to be busier as it is near the restaurant, but it overlooks a small dam and is good for birdwatching. Note that in the elephant-watching area it is illegal to leave your vehicle anywhere other than at signposted climb-out points.

Alexandria Trail
ⓘ *Permits for the Alexandria Trail are available through SANParks, www.sanparks.org. Alternatively, contact the main reception office at Matyholweni Rest Camp, T042-233 8621. Maximum 12 people; it's a popular trail over weekends. Take precautions against ticks.*

On the coast to the south of Alexandria between the Bushman's River and the Sundays River mouths is the part of the park that is dunes and coastal forest. There are many easy trails passing along the beach and into the forest. The longest hike, for which permits are necessary, is the Alexandria Trail. It is 36 km long and is a marked two-day circular track – be warned that the markers can be blown over in strong wind and get buried in the sand. The trail starts at the Woody Cape offices of the park, near the town of Alexandria. Turn right out of the park entrance towards Paterson. At the Paterson intersection, turn right towards Nelson Mandela Bay (Port Elizabeth). Once you reach the N2, take the R72 to Port Alfred. Just before entering the town of Alexandria, take the gravel road to the right, marked with the park signboard, to the office, T046-653 0601.

There is no large game here but this is the habitat of the hairy-footed gerbil which is endemic to this area. The forests are good for birdwatching and along the coast it is possible to see dolphins and the Damara tern. The first day takes you from the base camp at Langebos through forest down to the coastal dunefield which extends for 120 km up the coast. The hiking can be tough along the windy dunes but worth it for the fine isolated beaches. One night is spent in the hut at Woody Cape. In the morning the trail then heads back across farmland in the Langevlakte Valley and back to Langebos.

Schotia Safaris

ⓘ *To the east of Addo, 55 km from Nelson Mandela Bay (Port Elizabeth), and just north of the junction of the N2 and N10, T042-235 1436, www.schotia.com.*

This is a private game reserve on the edge of Addo with 15 types of antelope, several smaller species such as warthog, monkeys and genets, and lion, hippo, giraffe and rhino. Schotia is also known for its huge open-air dining *lapa* – reputedly the largest in South Africa – built of reed and thatch, which is supported by several large Schotia trees. The lodge here has three double units (see Sleeping, page 391) and if you are staying overnight all game activities are included; day and night game drives into Addo are also available. It is also possible to visit as a day visitor between 1600-2200 and the package includes afternoon and evening game drives and a buffet dinner and drinks for R660. Alternatively,

Addo & around

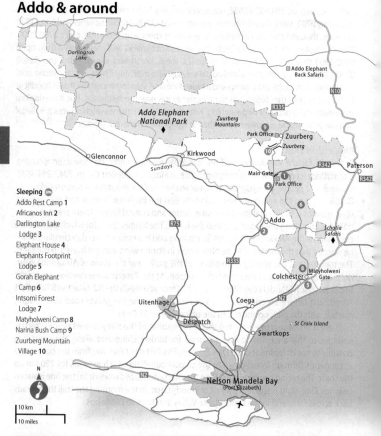

Sleeping 🛏️
Addo Rest Camp **1**
Africanos Inn **2**
Darlington Lake
  Lodge **3**
Elephant House **4**
Elephants Footprint
  Lodge **5**
Gorah Elephant
  Camp **6**
Intsomi Forest
  Lodge **7**
Matyholweni Camp **8**
Narina Bush Camp **9**
Zuurberg Mountain
  Village **10**

you could combine the above day visit with a morning safari to Addo for R1320. Pickups can be arranged from Nelson Mandela Bay (Port Elizabeth) if you don't have a car. Check out the website for options.

Shamwari Game Reserve → Colour map 7, B5.

ⓘ *From Nelson Mandela Bay (Port Elizabeth), follow the N2 towards Grahamstown. After 65 km take a left turn, signposted Shamwari. This gravel road is the R342; after 7 km take a right turn. It is then a further 2 km to the entrance. From Grahamstown, the R342 turning is about 58 km along the N2, T041-407 1000, www.shamwari.com.*

This is a privately owned 20,000-ha reserve which in many aspects resembles the reserves of Mpumalanga along the boundary of Kruger National Park. In 1990 Adrian Gardiner, a successful businessman from Port Elizabeth, bought the property and read up on historical accounts of the Eastern Cape, which described the region as one of the richest wildlife

zones in Africa. Reports dating back to the 18th century indicate a time when vast herds of Cape buffalo and zebra, wildebeest, black rhino, leopard and lion freely roamed the hills and valleys. However, by 1853 early settlers had wiped out most of the game and cleared vast areas of forest for farmland. When Gardiner bought the property all that remained was a dry, eroded dust bowl, but in the last 20 years natural grasses and bush flora have been planted and many species of game reintroduced. Once decimated by overgrazing and drought, the landscape has been transformed into big game country. Today the reserve has been well stocked with game from all over the region including black rhino, elephant, buffalo, leopard, lion and antelope of all sizes. Wild dog, last seen in the area over 200 years ago, have also been reintroduced. Day visitors are not permitted, but there are six superluxurious lodges within the reserve, and overnight packages include all meals and game activities (see Sleeping, page 392).

Amakhala Game Reserve

ⓘ *Off the N2 approximately opposite the turning for Shamwari Game Reserve (see above); the road is well signposted, T046-636 2750, www.amakhala.co.za.*

This is another of the Eastern Cape's successful new game reserves. The 6000-ha reserve was created in 1999 as a joint conservation venture between neighbouring farms and today has six independently owned lodges.

All are owner-managed by the descendants of the original families who arrived here as British settlers from 1820. The lodges offer various styles of accommodation: there are two colonial homesteads, two classic bush lodges, a historic inn and a settler farmhouse (see Sleeping, page 392, for details). The reserve is now another Big Five destination and has been stocked with rhino, elephant, cheetah, lion, buffalo, giraffe, black wildebeest, zebra and over 16 antelope species. Leopard is on the property but is rarely seen. Day and night drives and game walks are arranged from the lodges for overnight guests. There is also the opportunity to go on a cruise or canoe trip on the Bushman's River. Day visitors are welcome and safaris commence around midday with a two-hour game drive followed by a buffet lunch and then an afternoon cruise on the Bushman's River with cheese and wine; and the excursion ends with a short early evening game drive, all for R980 per person. The day visit is not recommended for children under six due to the long programme.

🌙 *Amakhala means aloe in Xhosa, named after the vibrant orange flower that is common in the area.*

Lalibela Game Reserve
ⓘ *22 km from Shamwari and 24 km east of Grahamstown off the N2, T041-581 8170, www.lalibela.co.za.*

This is a another private game reserve covering 7500 ha and spanning four ecosystems that are home to the Big Five as well as cheetah, hyena, hippo, giraffe, zebra, warthog and numerous species of antelope. Wild dog were released here in 2006. Day visitors are not permitted but there are three luxury lodges (see Sleeping, page 393).

Grahamstown ⊙🍴🏠🛏️🏞️⊙🛒 ➤➤ *pp390-397. Colour map 7, B5.*

Grahamstown is first and foremost a student town. At the top end of the high street is one of the country's major centres of learning, **Rhodes University**, which has 70 major buildings on a 195-ha campus with approximately 3200 students and 1800 staff. The presence of the university has a significant impact on this small town and during term time the pubs and bars are packed with students. It is a pleasant enough place to wander around and there are a number of interesting little shops along the high street.

Despite the English feel to the town centre the other side of the valley is dominated by a poor, dusty and badly serviced township where the majority of the African residents live. The proximity of the two sides of town makes the contrast more apparent than in some of the bigger towns and cities, where the townships are some distance from the centre.

Ins and outs
Getting there The town is served by some mainline buses on the route between Nelson Mandela Bay (Port Elizabeth) and Durban. The **Baz Bus** does not stop here, though, as it deviates off the N2 after Nelson Mandela Bay (Port Elizabeth) and goes via Port Alfred on the coast. ➤➤ *For further details, see Transport, page 397.*

Tourist information **Grahamstown Tourism** ⓘ *63 High St, T046-622 3241, www.grahams town.co.za, Mon-Fri 0830-1700, Sat 0900-1300,* is a well-organized centre with accommodation-booking facilities for the entire region. The staff can arrange and book a variety of local tours. There is also a **Translux** desk. A worthwhile local scheme is 'Step-On Guides' under which locally registered guides join you in your own vehicle and show you around the sights.

Background

Grahamstown was established around a fort which had been built here after the Fourth Frontier War. It was founded in 1812 and named after Colonel Graham. Within two years it was a busy border settlement. The 1820 settlers began to arrive after the end of the Fifth Frontier War, during which Grahamstown had been besieged by Xhosa warriors. Despite the continual threat of armed conflict and problems of security, the town had evolved into the second largest settlement in the whole of southern Africa by 1836.

One factor behind the town's rapid growth was that the majority of the 1820 settlers were ill-prepared to be farmers, let alone in an environment of which they had no knowledge. As soon as they realized farming was not going to bring them wealth and security they gave it up and returned to the town to take up the jobs they were trained to do. Grahamstown quickly established a thriving industry based around blacksmiths, carpenters, millers and gunsmiths. Having settled back in the town, the skilled settlers quickly built a series of elegant stone buildings which remain grand specimens of the

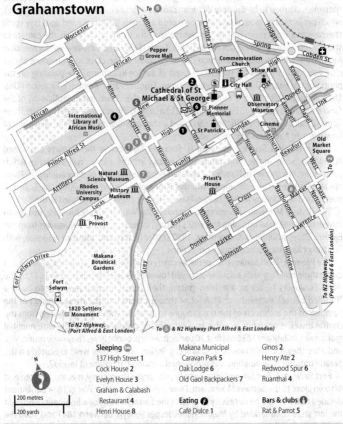

Grahamstown

Sleeping
137 High Street 1
Cock House 2
Evelyn House 3
Graham & Calabash
Restaurant 4
Henri House 8

Makana Municipal
Caravan Park 5
Oak Lodge 6
Old Gaol Backpackers 7

Eating
Café Dulce 1

Ginos 2
Henry Ate 2
Redwood Spur 6
Ruanthai 4

Bars & clubs
Rat & Parrot 5

era's architecture today. Of particular note are the buildings around Church Square, but elsewhere there are churches and fine private homes. The culmination of all this is a smart town centre with a distinctly English atmosphere.

Sights

When you look at a map or walk about the town centre you quickly come across a variety of different museums: the Observatory Museum, Natural Science Museum and the History Museum, along with Fort Selwyn and the Provost. These displays are all part of one museum, the **Albany Museum** ① *T046-622 2312, Tue-Fri 0900-1300, 1400-1700, Sat 1000-1400, Observatory Museum also open Mon, entry to each is about R5-10,* which celebrated its 150-year anniversary in 2005. The collection has grown as the town has developed and presents a fairly complete picture of its history.

The **Observatory Museum** ① *on the right-hand side of Bathurst St, as you look up towards the City Hall,* is a unusual building. It contains a collection of Victorian furniture, household goods and silver, but the highlight is the entertaining camera obscura (a rare specimen, claimed to be the only Victorian camera obscura in the southern hemisphere), which projects an image of Grahamstown onto a screen. Visitors are led up a tiny spiral staircase to a small room on the roof, where an enthusiastic guide pivots the camera to show a 360° view, pointing out major sights. There is also an observatory and a meridian room, from which astronomical time can be calculated. The clock is a miniature of one that was made in 1883 for the Royal Courts of Justice in London. The painting on the pendulum of *Father Time* is by the well-known Frontier Artist, Frederick Timpson I'Ons. The building, which itself is loosely connected with the drawn-out identification of the *Eureka* diamond back in 1869 (see page 743), has a magnificent presence. There are three floors of balconies, each with ornately carved arches and railings, enough to give a hint of how it would have looked in its heyday.

At the **Natural Science Museum** ① *Somerset St,* most of the displays are aimed at children. Some of the more interesting exhibits include a large iron meteorite which came down in a shower in Namibia, a Foucault pendulum and some dinosaur fossils. There are regular temporary exhibitions, and this is one of the main venues for the **Scifest**, a science and technology festival held in March. There is a café in a courtyard at the back.

The **History Museum** ① *Somerset St, opposite the Natural Science Museum,* houses an interesting collection outlining the area's history, including beadwork displays from the Eastern Cape, traditional Xhosa dress, 1820 settler history and some art galleries, with regularly changing contemporary exhibitions.

The **Provost** ① *off Somerset St, at the western end of town in the botanical gardens,* is a quadrangle building with a double-storeyed tower at its apex. It was built in 1837 by the Royal Engineers to act as a military prison; their actual instructions were to build a "fortified barrack establishment". A lot of thought went into the overall design of the complex as the architects of the time sought to come up with a design where, from the central tower, it would be possible to view as many prisoners as possible with minimal manpower. In January 1838 the first 20 convicts were brought here. They were mutineers, and after they had shot one of their officers, Ensign Crowe, they were executed on the parade grounds. The building was proclaimed a national monument in 1937.

Fort Selwyn ① *Fort Selwyn Drive, open by prior appointment only,* is at the western end of town close to the Settlers Monument. During the sixth Frontier War in 1834 parliament decided that it would be necessary to protect the barracks. The Royal Engineers who built the fort were commanded by Major Charles Jasper Selwyn. Between 1841 and 1868 the fort was used as an artillery barracks and a semaphore link – a mast was erected in the northeast corner – but then the army gave up using the building in 1870. During the Anglo-Boer War the fort served in the defence of Grahamstown, but by the 1920s it had once more been left to become run down and overgrown. It was not until the 1970s, when it was proclaimed a national monument, that the building finally got the restoration work it deserved. Although it stands on the property of the Department of Nature and Environmental Conservation, it was given to the Albany Museum to use as exhibition space to further promote the history of Grahamstown.

The **1820 Settlers Monument** is, oddly, a large modern office block with rather a totalitarian feel to it. There are a series of rooms which includes a conference hall, theatre and a restaurant and it's another principal venue for the **Grahamstown Arts Festival**. It overlooks the city and completely dominates its surrounds on Gunfire Hill. It was opened in July 1974, but in 1994 disaster struck and fire gutted the whole complex and it was restored in 1996. The memorial is surrounded by the **Makana Botanical Gardens** ⓘ *daily 0800-1630, free*, which were laid out in 1853 with displays of indigenous plants. The botanical garden has a recreation of a nostalgic old English garden, but more interestingly there is a huge collection of aloes, cycads, proteas and tree ferns. Assuming you're not afraid of ghosts, try to catch a glimpse of Lady Juana Smith, the Spanish wife of Sir Harry Smith who reputedly haunts the gardens.

Part of the university, the **International Library of African Music (ILAM)** ⓘ *Prince Alfred St, T046-603 8557, http://.ilam.ru.ac.za, by appointment only, Mon-Fri 0830-1245, 1400-1700*, is a university research centre for traditional African music, and houses a fascinating collection, with over 200 traditional African instruments from across the continent. To get there, follow signs from the gate opposite Rhodes University Theatre.

The **Cathedral of St Michael and St George** occupies its rightful position in the centre of town on Church Square. The style of this building is early English Gothic, a 13th-century style which the Victorians chose to revive in the late 19th century. Like similar buildings in Europe, the cathedral took generations to complete. Work started in 1824 and the first usable form was opened in 1830 as a single-room church. In 1952 the Lady Chapel was completed and so the cathedral had taken 128 years to build. Look out for the memorial tablets which together provide a vivid history of Grahamstown as the frontier of the empire.

The **Priest's House**, on Beaufort Street, was built as a residence for the bishop and the clergy of the Catholic church. It is one of the finer buildings in Grahamstown and like the Observatory Museum has a connection with the identification of the *Eureka* diamond (see page 743). Because of this connection, the De Beers Group rescued the house in 1981, helped to partially restore the building and then oversaw the establishment of the **National English Literary Museum** ⓘ *T046-622 7042, Mon-Fri 0900-1230, 1430-1630*. These days the research carried out behind the scenes is proving to be an important component in the understanding of the role of English as a national language of South Africa. There is a comprehensive collection of scholarly books, articles and press-clippings as well as a good bookshop. A small display gallery presents temporary exhibitions focusing on a particular writer, literary period or theme. The house is also of interest. The façade is typical of the Cape during the 1800s – flat, with a colonnaded neo-Georgian portico.

The **Shaw Hall** is behind the Observatory Museum, but still in the High Street. It was inaugurated in 1832 as a Methodist Church, with three galleries and room for over 800 members. Once the Commemoration Church had been completed in 1850, the first building was turned over for use as a meeting hall. The Reverend William Shaw was a local missionary worker. The most important role the building played was on 25 April 1864 when the Governor of the Cape Colony, Sir Philip Wodehouse, convened a session of parliament in the hall. This was part of a programme of tacit support for a movement that was trying to break away from the western part of the province and set up an independent government. Although nothing ever came of the idea, it was a clear indication of how serious the government took the threats of secession, since this was the only time that the Cape parliament ever sat outside of Cape Town.

Thomas Baines Nature Reserve

ⓘ *12 km from town off the N2 towards Nelson Mandela Bay (Port Elizabeth), T046-622 7216, www.ecparks.co.za, free.*

The Thomas Baines Nature Reserve offers canoeing, fishing, sailing and windsurfing at Settlers Dam. The reserve is named after the famous 19th-century artist who left a valuable record of the rich diversity of fauna and flora in the region, including the now-extinct quagga. There are 15 km of dirt tracks which pass through fynbos and bushveld inhabited by bontebok, black wildebeest, an impressive herd of 45 buffalo, eland and impala. There's a short 15 km drive around the reserve and picnic sites with braai facilities and toilets are provided at Settlers Dam.

Port Alfred to King William's Town 🌐🖨️🔺🌐🅲 ➤➤ *pp390-397. Colour map 7, B5-B6.*

Port Alfred

Port Alfred can be reached along the R72 coast road from Nelson Mandela Bay (Port Elizabeth) or on the R67 from Grahamstown. It consists almost entirely of holiday homes and bungalows nestling into dunes. It is one of the largest holiday resorts on this stretch of coastline and overlooks large expanses of water in all directions: the Kowie River, the lagoon and the smart Royal Alfred Marina, where many local people keep their powerboats. The town's history is closely linked to the 1820 settlers and there is a small **Methodist Church** 1 km out of town whose cemetery makes for an interesting visit. Many of the names on the gravestones are those of original settlers.

The weather on this coast is mild all year round and Port Alfred has a wide range of facilities to offer tourists. Walks through the dune forests are always pleasant but for the more intrepid, there is a scuba-diving school which organizes trips to nearby reefs, as well as facilities for canoeing and game fishing. The **Fish River Casino** and **St Francis Spa** are both nearby and are popular excursions from town. For information contact **Port Alfred Tourism Information Centre** ⓘ *Causeway St, T046-624 1235, www.portalfred.co.za, Mon-Fri 0800-1630, Sat 0830-1200.* This is a very helpful and brightly painted office which also offers internet access and sells crafts. Port Alfred gets fairly busy at the weekends during term time when students from Grahamstown University come to the coast to play.

The **World's Biggest Pineapple** ⓘ *just outside Bathurst, off the R67, 15 km north of Port Alfred, T046-625 0515, 0900-1630, R10, children (3-16) R5, under 3 free,* is a copy of the giant pineapple on Australia's Sunshine Coast in Queensland but at 16.7 m high it's 70 cm taller than the original. It comes as quite a surprise to discover a giant yellow pineapple, topped with a bright green stalk standing in the middle of a field. Made of fibreglass, on the three floors inside you'll learn everything imaginable about pineapples. On the ground floor is a gift shop selling among other pineapple-related items, home-made jams and chutneys, on the second floor is information about growing, canning and selling pineapples, while on the third floor a continuous DVD explains about the Eastern Cape pineapple industry. If nothing else, it's worth climbing for unbeatable views of the rolling fields and the Indian Ocean.

Huberta the hippo

Huberta the hippo is one of the most famous wild animals in South African history. She was born in the Mhlatuze Lagoon near the modern-day port of Richard's Bay in Zululand, and in 1928 inexplicably decided to head off on an 800-km trek down the coast. This incredible journey took three years and her story was followed by newspapers around the world. She walked through the middle of Durban, looking into shop windows while pedestrians dived for cover, and astounded holidaymakers when she walked on to Durban's beach and swam in the sea. She continued south down what is today the Wild Coast and arrived in Port St Johns in March 1930.

She seemed to like it – she stayed for six months and lived in the river. Despite its name (Mzimvubu, meaning 'home of the hippo') none of her ilk had been seen in the river for years. It was a lively six months for the residents of the town as Huberta wandered through gardens, grazed on lawns, upset a few boats, and things only calmed down after her departure in September. There was national mourning at the end of the year when news flashed around the world that a pair of trigger-happy farmers had shot Huberta in a river in the Eastern Cape. Her remains can be seen at the Amathole Museum in King William's Town. There has never been another hippo in the Mzimvubu River.

Kowie Nature Reserve
ⓘ *About 5 km from Port Alfred on the Bathurst road, T046-624 1235, 0900-1600, hike permits at the gate.*

This reserve lies along the banks of the Kowie River, and it passes through a thickly forested canyon and offers an 8 km walking trail that takes about two hours. Look out for the small mammals found here, such as duiker and bushbuck, vervet monkeys, mountain tortoises, the Cape clawless otter and various other small carnivores: though most are shy and well camouflaged. There are a number of picnic sites, braai facilities and toilets.

King William's Town → *Colour map 7, B6.*
King William's Town, more commonly known simply as King, is 56 km northeast of East London. The London Missionary Society established a mission station here in 1826 and over the years the town has grown into an important commercial centre. The town is best known as the birth and burial place of Apartheid activist Steven Biko who was put under house arrest in the town between 1974 and 1977 before he was arrested at a road block near Grahamstown, outside his restricted area. After his arrest he was taken to Port Elizabeth and intensively interrogated until he died of a brain haemorrhage in police custody on 12 October 1977. The police first claimed he had starved himself to death while on a hunger strike. They later changed their story to say Biko had hit his head against a wall in a scuffle. Finally, 20 years later, the police admitted before the Truth and Reconciliation Commission that they had killed Biko. Diplomats from 13 counties joined mourners at his funeral in King William's Town but not a single South African was made accountable for his death. His grave, with a lovingly tended polished tombstone, lies in the **Steve Biko Remembrance Garden** on the edge of town on the road to Nelson Mandela Bay (Port Elizabeth). To reach the grave, follow Cathcart Street south of King William's Town and turn left down a dirt track that is signposted to the garden. It's a moving place and the grave is much humbler than expected for such an important figure in South African history. The **Amathole**

Museum ① *Alexander St, T043-642 4506, www.museum.za.net, Mon-Fri 0900-1630, Sat 0900-1300, R5, children (under 15) free,* is a good place to get a feel for Xhosa history with displays on how the British crushed the Xhosa during the various frontier wars. There's also some contemporary art, including bus, bikes and cars made from wire, and some dusty old stuffed mammals, including Huberta the hippo (see box, page 389). There's a good selection of local crafts for sale in the museum shop.

◉ Nelson Mandela Bay to East London listings

For Sleeping and Eating price codes and other relevant information, see pages 46-53.

● Sleeping

Addo Elephant National Park *p380*
Some of the accommodation is run by **SAN-Parks**, while others are private concessions within or at the edge of the park.

SANParks accommodation
Reservations through **SANParks**, T012-428 9111, www.sanparks.org, see page 48 for details. Bookings need to be made well in advance, especially during school holidays. For late bookings or cancellations less than 72 hrs, phone Addo reception direct, T042-233 0556.

AL-D Addo Rest Camp, next to the main entrance gate and park reception. There are 61 units in total each fully equipped for self-catering, some have a/c and braai facilities. Some are equipped for wheelchair users. The 2 guest cottages (**AL**), Hapoor and Domkrag, have 6-beds with 2 en suite a/c bedrooms, a fully equipped kitchen and a living room. The bungalows (**B**) are suitable for 4 people and have a bathroom and kitchen. The 2-bed huts (**C**) are simple units with a shower, fridge and toilet, and there is a fully equipped communal kitchen. The five, 2-bed Safari Tents (**D**) have bedding, towels, fan, fridge and braai, use of communal ablutions and kitchen. There is also camping available, a maximum of 6 people can occupy any 1 campsite. The grounds are well grassed and there is plenty of shade. Communal kitchens have hot plates, power points and hot water. Facilities include a swimming pool,

waterhole with hide, restaurant and curio shop which also sells some frozen food. Guided day and night drives and new 2-hr horse-riding trails can be booked at reception.

A Narina Bush Camp, is next to the Witriver in the Zuurberg Mountains approximately 22 km (gravel road, 40 mins' driving) from the main rest camp and park reception. This is a tented camp with 4 tents (2-bed) and must be booked as 1 unit, towels and bedding are provided, open lapa/braai area, kitchen with gas stove, fridge, paraffin lamps, cutlery, crockery and cooking utensils, 1 shower with hot water from a paraffin cylinder geyser, and 1 toilet. Because of no electricity the guests have to arrive at least 2 hrs before sunset but no later than 1800 as they still have to carry their food and clothing to the camp from the car park, crossing a river and walking 400-500 m through the forest. A torch is essential. The camp can also be reached on horseback on Basuto pony/Boer-perd crossbreeds. All the necessary equipment is provided, but it is important to book in advance through reception at the park entrance, T042-233 0556. If you want to go on horseback, departure time is no later than 1100 from the top of the Zuurberg Mountain, approximately 16-km gravel road from the main rest camp (25 mins' driving).

C Matyholweni Camp, in the south of the park, 3 km from the N2 at the Sundays River Mouth, and accessed through Matyholweni Gate, T042-233 8621. Nearest restaurants, shops and fuel are in Colchester. Small camp with 12 brand new SANParks en suite cottages sleeping 2, some have extra sofa bed suitable for children only, open-plan with kitchenette, braai facilities.

E Alexandria Hiking Huts, on the Alexandria Trail, see page 381. There are 2 huts, both sleeping 12 people on bunks and mattresses. Fridge, stove and braai; the hut at base camp has toilets and hot showers; at the overnight hiking hut at Woody Cape you'll be using rainwater to wash.

Private lodges and camps

L4 Gorah Elephant Camp, central reservations T044-5011 111, www.hunterhotels.com. This luxurious camp is a Relais & Chateaux property and has a private concession covering 4500 ha but can also access the rest of the park. Accommodation is in 11 huge, luxurious tents with a colonial theme, complete with 4-poster beds, en suite bathrooms and terraces overlooking the park. Relaxing boma area with rock swimming pool, meals are served in a superbly renovated coach house, overlooking a waterhole frequented by elephant, buffalo and antelope. The price includes all meals, guided game drives and night drives.

L1 Intsomi Forest Lodge, Alexandria Forest at Woody Cape, T046-653 8903, www.intsomi.com. All-inclusive luxury lodge with 8 suites, open walls, African decor, opulent bathrooms, swimming pool, wellness centre, and large deck overlooking a waterhole where antelope and zebra drink. The staff will put on dancing and game drives take in the sweeping views of the Alexandria Dunefield and ocean.

Private accommodation

L1 Elephant House, on the left of the R355, 5 km before Addo's main gate, T042-233 2462, www.elephanthouse.co.za. Exclusive 9-room lodge decorated with the owner's private collection of antiques and Persian rugs. Good food. Qualified guides conduct excellent daily game drives into the park on open Land Cruisers as well as day visits to the various private game reserves in the area. Rates drop significantly in winter.

A Darlington Lake Lodge, next to Darlington Dam in the northern tip of Addo, 180 km north of Nelson Mandela Bay (Port Elizabeth) on the R75 to Graaff Reinet, T/F042-243 3673.

6 double rooms and 7 safari tents with en suite facilities furnished in colonial style, meals are served outdoors in a traditional boma. Wide range of activities on offer around the dam, including walking trail, horse rides, 4WD game-viewing trips, fishing and boat cruises. A tranquil spot to enjoy the little-visited furthest reaches of the new part of the park.

A Zuurberg Mountain Village, 32 km north of the main entrance on the Zuurberg Mountain Pass, access on the R335, T042-233 0583, www.addo.co.za. There are 36 double rooms; 5 are in the original 1850s manor house while the rest are delightful individual spacious lodges under traditional thatch in the Zuurberg Village. Restaurant and pub with magnificent views, swimming pool, tennis, chapel for weddings, game drives. Check out the packages on the website that include dinner and game activities.

B Elephants Footprint Lodge, 1 Riverside Drive, Colchester, 2 km from Matyholweni Gate, T041-468 0499, www.elephantsfootprint.co.za. 12 spacious en suite rooms under thatch, additional outdoor shower, crisp white linen, muted cream and brown decor, large communal lounge with leather furniture, log fire and TV, restaurant swimming pool and wooden deck with sun loungers. Game drives to both the main section of the park and the Alexandria dune-fields.

C Africanos Inn, corner of Main and Zuurberg roads, Addo, 10-min drive from the park gate, T042-233 0605, www.africanos-inn.co.za. An excellent, fairly new spot to stay if you cannot get accommodation in the park. 10 very spacious and modern motel-style rooms, each with lounge area, tea tray and DSTV, the barn is used for weddings and sometimes live music, great restaurant and bar with a long menu, swimming pool. Can organize day and night drives into the park. Recommended.

Schotia Safaris p382

Private lodges and camps

AL Bush Lodges, east of Addo National Park, 55 km from Nelson Mandela Bay

(Port Elizabeth), just north of the junction of the N2 and N10, T042-235 1436, www.schotia.com. 2 double en suite chalets with fireplaces, hidden in the bush that are very private and aimed at honeymooners. A 3rd chalet has 4 beds suitable for families. All meals and game drives included in the price, transfers from Nelson Mandela Bay (Port Elizabeth) can be arranged. No electricity, but lamps will be lit for you in the evening.

Shamwari Game Reserve *p383*
Private lodges and camps
There are 7 luxury camps within the reserve – all are expensive. Each is completely self-contained and independent of the others. Rates are all-inclusive of meals, morning and evening game drives, walking safaris with an armed guard, and visits to the Shamwari/Born Free Conservation Centre. Current rates per person are R3500-R6800 depending on season. Reservations T041-407 1000, www.shamwari.com.

L4 Bayethe Tented Lodge. A tone-walled and thatch-roofed main lodge with viewing deck and dining boma. 9 double, a/c, tented suites, with en suite bathroom, outside shower, private plunge pool and deck.

L4 Bushman's River Lodge, at the centre of the reserve. A small lodge with 4 double rooms, beautifully decorated in an ethnic theme and set in restored settlers' cottages. Plunge pool and a personal ranger service. This is best suited for a group.

L4 Eagles Cragg Lodge, the most central of the 7 camps. This is a restored settler's cottage which has been divided into 9 suites with twin beds and an en suite bathroom, private deck and plunge pool. Lodge facilities include a dining area, library, business centre, lounge, bar and beauty spa.

L4 Lobengula Lodge, at the northern extremity of the reserve. The most luxurious of the 6 complexes, with thatched roof and decorated to the highest standard. 6 rooms, a maximum of 12 guests can stay here. 5 rooms have en suite bathroom and outside shower plus a/c and underfloor heating; the

6th room is the most expensive option in the whole reserve – the Chief Suite. It has a separate lounge with super a/c and fan, plus underfloor heating, private plunge pool and outside shower. The swimming pool has a sunken cocktail bar and there's a small gym, beauty spa and steam bath.

L4 Long Lee Manor, the Edwardian manor house near the main entrance on the western side of the reserve. Largest of the 7 camps, although it never feels crowded. The 18 rooms have underfloor heating, ceiling fans, a/c, TV, telephone. Facilities include 2 swimming pools, a floodlit tennis court, a beauty spa and down by the Bushman's River at a point known as the hippo pool, is a covered *lapa* where guests can watch the animals drink while they enjoy a meal.

L4 Riverdene Lodge. 9 a/c en suite rooms, with separate, elegantly furnished, lounges. Sunroom, a rim flow swimming pool with sun deck and poolside bar. Dining room opens onto a spacious outdoor barbecue area.

L4 Sarili Lodge, in the south of the reserve overlooking the Bushman's River. The latest addition to Shamwari, an architecturally pleasing 2-storey wooden and slate structure with 5 elegant suites. This is probably the best option for children, with child-minders, kid-friendly pool, special menus and activities.

Amakhala Game Reserve *p383*
Private lodges and camps
Game activities such as walks, drives or cruises are included in the rates, which are full board and in most you eat with the host families. All of them have swimming pools. Reservations for all the lodges T046-636 2750, www.amakhala.co.za.

L3 Cararvon Dale. An 1857 farm where guests are accommodated in the historic farmhouse or the elegantly restored Edwardian cottage, rooms with wrought-iron beds, some with fireplaces, private lounges, farm-style meals.

L3 Leeuwenbosch Country Lodge. Built in 1908 and set in its own lovely garden, traditional country house with 4 en suite doubles and 1 suite, cellar pub with full-size antique billiards table.

L3 Reed Valley Inn. 4 en suite rooms in historic buildings that were once the rest stop for the mail wagon in the 19th century. A working farm, farm-style breakfasts and 3-course dinners in the main dining room, no children under 12.

L3 Safari Lodge. Intimate thatched lodge with stylish safari decor, 11 luxurious huts with double baths and outdoor showers, outside terraces with open fire in the evening, rim flow pool.

L3 Shearers Lodge, set in the grounds of Leeuwenbosch. Originally built in 1930 and used for shearing and classing wool, and now beautifully converted into 4 luxury en suite bedrooms, 1 with a private lounge. All the rooms open on to a wide colonial veranda overlooking the gardens and chapel.

L3 Woodbury Lodge. 6 modern stone and thatched cottages designed to blend in with the natural surroundings. Good views from the wooden decks, central dining room and braai area, lounge and bar.

Lalibela Game Reserve *p384*
Private lodges and camps
Rates for all the 3 luxurious lodges in the reserve are all-inclusive of meals, drinks and game drives. Each lodge has a large lounge, viewing deck, pool, and an outdoor dining 'boma' and indoor dining area. There are special arrangements for children who are kept entertained by child-minders whilst parents go on game drives and are offered their own kid's game drives. Reservations T041-581 8170, www.lalibela.co.za.

L3 Lentaba Lodge. 8 thatched chalets with large beds, safari decor and antique African art throughout. Good views from the hilltop location, the outdoor eating boma overlooks a waterhole that has a spotlight at night.

L3 Mark's Camp. Thatched and stone cottages sleeping 20 in 4 doubles, and 3 family units. Private decks overlooking a waterhole, pool, a fire is lit at the outside boma to sit around with drinks after dinner.

L3 Tree Tops. 5 luxury safari tents perched high on thatched platforms at 'tree top' level, joined by raised walkways with fantastic views. Really feels as if you are staying in a treehouse, open-air dining deck overlooking a small waterhole, swimming pool.

Grahamstown *p384, map p385*
Some residents in Grahamstown township offer overnight accommodation in their homes (**D**). Most is in brick houses with a hospitable Xhosa family. The tourist office can arrange this. If you want to attend the **Grahamstown Arts Festival**, accommodation needs to be booked months in advance.

A Evelyn House, 115 High St, T046-622 2366, www.afritemba.com. A very fine guesthouse in a local landmark building dating from the 1800s, with 9 luxury suites, 1 with jacuzzi. A/c, laundry service, DSTV, swimming pool, sauna, gym, secure off-street parking. Well-appointed. Recommended.

B The Cock House, 10 Market St, T046-636 1287, www.cockhouse.co.za. Beautifully restored 1820s national monument with 9 double rooms with en suite bathrooms, 4 self-catering flats, special touches include electric blanket and home-made biscuits. Luxurious guesthouse with a good à la carte restaurant attached, comfortable lounge and library. Peter and Belinda have clearly made a good impression – Nelson Mandela has stayed here 3 times and South African author Andre Brink was a former resident. The 1st-floor veranda is a particularly fine feature. Recommended.

B Graham Hotel, 123 High St, T046-622 2324, www.afritemba.com. Rather unattractive building but in a good location, with 33 en suite, DSTV and lounge. **Calabash** restaurant has a good local reputation, cocktail bar with pool table and darts, laundry service, secure parking, comfortable town hotel within a short walk of the shops and sights.

C 137 High Street, 137 High St, T046-622 3242, www.137highstreet.co.za. Stylish, attractive hotel in a good location close to restaurants and sights. 8 luxurious rooms, en suite bath or shower. Good service, restaurant serves excellent breakfasts and freshly made cakes and scones, as well as more substantial meals for dinner.

D Henri House, 64 Henry St, T046-622 8845, www.henrihouse.co.za. Beautifully restored former rector's house, a fine example of a villa built in the 1850s, with 2 elegant family self-catering flats with DSTV and heaters. The neat gardens with plunge pool complement the house, breakfasts served on a veranda. Good value, recommended.

D Oak Lodge Hotel, 95 Bathurst St, T046-622 9123, www.afritemba.com. Large old building with 20 rooms. Simple pine furniture, DSTV, gardens, swimming pool, braai area, bar, secure parking. Tours arranged. A short walk from the town centre.

D-F Makana Municipal Caravan Park, Grey St, on the outskirts of town on the N2 heading towards Nelson Mandela Bay (Port Elizabeth), T046-603 6072. An easy walk to town, with shady sites for tents or caravans, and family cottages and cabins, a swimming pool, kid's playground. Excellent and fresh facilities as it was completely rebuilt in 2008.

D-F Old Gaol Backpackers, Somerset St, opposite **Albany Museum**, T046-636 1001, www.oldgaol.co.za. An unusual and excellent place to stay. This is the only backpacker place in Grahamstown, and is housed in an old Victorian jail. Double rooms are in individual cells, complete with thick stone walls, domed ceilings and tiny barred windows. The dorms are in the communal cells. There is a lounge with kitchen, TV room, the **Gallows** pub and restaurant, and you can sunbathe in the old exercise yard. The building is listed, so no work can be done on the original structure. While this gives the place a run-down (and rather too authentic) feel with original prisoners' graffiti on the walls, the cells are spotless and the beds comfortable. Highly recommended as an atmospheric and unique backpackers.

Port Alfred *p388*

AL Halyards, Royal Alfred Marina, off Albany Rd, T046-604 3300, www.riverhotels.co.za.

Smartest hotel in Port Alfred, provides luxury accommodation with a nautical theme for the wealthy during peak holiday periods. Out of season, however, rates drop considerably (**B**). 49 spacious a/c rooms with all mod-cons, good views of the marina. restaurant, bar, swimming pool, gym, wooden decks, pleasant grounds. However, poor reports from readers recently.

C Royal St Andrews Lodge, 19 St Andrews Rd, T046-624 1379, www.royalstandrews lodge.co.za. Across the road from the golf course, Tudor mock exterior with 14 bright and modern rooms, doubles and family rooms, and self-catering chalets. Swimming pool with wooden deck, **Thistle** restaurant and **Highlander** pub, good-value small, friendly hotel. Entertained the Prince of Wales in 1925, hence the royal title.

D The Residency, 11 Vroom Rd, T046-624 5382, www.theresidency.co.za. Turn-of-the-20th-century settler's house, with wooden floors and ball and claw baths, 4 en suite rooms furnished with cottage-type items, breakfasts are taken on the wrap-around veranda, German spoken.

D-E Medolino Caravan Park, 23 Stewart Rd, T046-624 1651, www.medolino.co.za. This is a medium-sized park with 48 camping and caravan sites, well grassed and plenty of shade, electric points, electric lights, well-equipped laundry and 2 heated pools. 5 self-catering log cabins sleeping 2-4, disabled access, a short stroll though the dunes to the beach. The dam here is alive with birds and check-lists are available at reception.

D-F Station Backpackers, 1 Pascoe St, T046-624 5869, www.thestation.co.za. A fairly new backpacker place housed in Port Alfred's old station, which is now a national monument. Doubles, dorms, **The Station** restaurant and bar which is very popular locally, internet access, the Baz Bus will drop you here.

King William's Town *p389*

C-D The Lavender House, 57 King's Rd, T046-642 2531, www.thelavenderhouse.co.za. 7 comfortable en suite rooms in a restored historical house, with polished wooden floors and high ceilings, some with Victorian baths and antiques. DSTV, fans and heaters, set in established gardens with swimming pool, excellent meals prepared by Cordon Bleu chef.

D Dreamers Guest House, 29 Gorden St, Hospital Hill, T043-642 3012, www.dreamers guesthouse.com. Neat house on a quiet street in the suburbs, with colourful gardens, 4 en suite rooms and 1 family unit. Lunch and dinner on request, large pool and patio area. The lounge has antiques, wooden floors and an organ dating from 1867.

❼ Eating

Grahamstown *p384, map p385*
Many of the quality restaurants in town are in the main hotels. There are also plenty of cheap cafés and takeaways catering to the large student population, and the town features the usual **Wimpy** and **KFC**.

♉ Calabash, Graham Hotel, see Sleeping page 393. Open 0700-2300. Popular traditional South African restaurant specializing in Xhosa hotpots, various South African dishes and a regular menu of seafood, steaks and venison. Generous breakfasts, daily lunch specials.

♉ Ginos, 8 New St, entrance is from the car park behind on Hill St, T046-622 7208. Mon-Sat 1100-late. 20-year-old family-run restaurant with Tuscan murals on the walls, good selection of pizza and pasta dishes, and some meat dishes and regular specials. Very popular, especially with students.

♉ Henry Ate, 8 New St, T046-622 7208. Mon-Sat 1700-2300. adjoining **Ginos** (see above) and all dishes from there can be ordered here too. Dark wood furniture, central fireplace, medieval theme with a large portrait of Henry VIII, large portions of steaks, burgers, ribs, some vegetarian dishes and a children's 'jester' menu, separate ladies bar.

♉ Norden's, The Cock House, see Sleeping, page 393. Open 1200-1430, 1900-late, closed Mon lunch. Excellent restaurant, part of a smart town guesthouse. Plenty of attention

is given to presentation and quality of the country cuisine. If you don't fancy eating then enjoy a beer in the cosy yellowwood bar with a light snack. One of the most popular spots in town so booking advised.

♉ Redwood Spur, 97 High St, T046-622 2629. Open 1100-2200. Predictable steak, ribs, Tex Mex, chain restaurant, one of the few options open Sun. Good service from clean-cut students working here part time.

♉ Café Dulce, 112 High St. Mon 0800-1700, Tue-Sun 0800-2200. Café and ice cream parlour, excellent sandwiches made to order, ice cream sundaes, milkshakes and salads.

♉ Ruanthai, 7 New St, T046-622 6788. Tue-Fri 1200-1430, Tue-Sat 1800-2300. Popular and good value Thai restaurant with traditional Asian kitschy decor, serving a wide range of authentic noodle dishes, unusually some good salads, and specials like shrimp omelette. No licence so BYO. Also does takeaways.

Port Alfred *p388*
♉ Butlers Riverside Restaurant, 25 Van der Riet St, T046-624 3464. Wed-Mon 1100-late. Restaurant-cum-pub with a lively atmosphere. Pub snack menu served on the open deck overlooking the river, or eat inside in a slightly more formal setting with a more expensive menu. Fresh fish is excellent, menu and blackboard items change with the chef's whims.

♉ Guido's on the Beach, West Beach Drive, T046-624 5264. Open 1100-2200. Serves great pizza and pasta dishes, along with seafood and steaks. There's a children's menu and play area. Busy and boozy bar upstairs with deck over the Kowie River and views across the waves.

♉ The Links, 14 Wesley Hill, T046-624 4533. Mon-Sat 1230-1630, 1730-2130. Central location and good views of the marina from the upstairs bar deck and informal African-inspired decor. The menu is varied and includes predictably good pizzas, grills and seafood, plus specials like lamb shank pie or warthog carpaccio. There's a good choice of vegetarian and gluten-free dishes.

Bars and clubs

Grahamstown *p384, map p385*
Rat & Parrot, 59 New St. Mon-Sat 1100-late.
A popular bar which is big with students on
Wed and Sat nights, gets quite rowdy after
a few rounds of shooters. Wide range of beers
and alcoholic drinks, big-screen TV for major
sports, bar snacks including good *potjies*.

Festivals and events

Grahamstown *p384, map p385*
Check with the local tourist office for the
exact dates and programme details.
Mar Scifest, T046-603 1106, www.scifest.org.
za. Features some 5500 events: lectures, game
drives, laser shows, robotics competitions,
science olympics, interactive exhibitions
and a film festival. Attendance now exceeds
68,000 a year, mostly school children.
Jun-Jul National Festival of Arts, T046-603
1103, www.nafest.co.za. Famous 10-day
festival, one of the top cultural events in the
country. Over 50,000 visitors are attracted
to the town to watch a range of shows, which
include theatre, dance, fine art, films, music,
opera and an increasing variety of traditional
crafts and art, plus a huge range of fringe
shows. There's something for everyone from
techno raves to medieval banquets. The
centre of the festival is the 1820 Settlers
Monument. During this period
accommodation gets booked very quickly, so
make reservations several months ahead, or
phone the tourist office to check if any private
homes are letting out rooms. During the
festival the whole atmosphere of the town
changes, so if you are in the country
at this time it is well worth a visit.

Activities and tours

Addo Elephant National Park *p380*
Addo Elephant Back Safaris, in the north
of the Addo Elephant National Park in the

Zuurberg Mountains, on the Toevlugt Farm.
1.5 km before Addo's main gate, turn left at
the Zuurburg sign, the farm is 34 km from
this turn-off, T042-235 1400, www.addo
elephantbacksafaris.co.za. 3-hr excursion
0800, 1100, and 1530, R875, children (under
12) R440 but must be accompanied by a
parent on top of the elephants. There's the
opportunity to walk with 3 tame elephants
through the bush and forest. The walk is at an
enjoyable pace and not strenuous and allows
visitors to observe the elephants' habits close
up and in their natural surroundings. After
the walk you can ride the elephants to the
waterhole, where you can watch them swim
and it's not unusual for visitors to get sprayed
by water from their trunks. Snacks or lunch
are provided. There's comfortable accommodation in log and canvas-sided cabins,
and accommodation packages (**L2**) which
include the elephant experience as well as a
game drive in Addo, a game walk, all meals
and some drinks, and accompanying the
elephants to their stables at bedtime.

Grahamstown *p384, map p385*
There are several local registered guides who
will take you on historical tours, birdwatching
or game viewing, on foot or in your own
vehicle. Also on offer are ½-day tours to the
large township in Grahamstown which is
known as **Rhini**, or Grahamstown East, and
lies to the east of the town across the river.
Not surprisingly, most local whites will never
have visited this part of their town and will
know very little about it. Tourists, however,
are offered a choice of township tours, with
visits to a 'traditional' Xhosa family for a meal,
as well as visiting craft centres and shebeens.
Contact tourist office for recommendations.
Alan Weyer Tours, T046-622 7896, www.
alanweyerstours.co.za. Acclaimed SATOUR
registered guide who won South Africa's Tour
Guide of the Year in 2005. Anyone with an
interest in the history of the Eastern Cape could
do no better that spend a day listening to his
entertaining tales. ½-day historical tours in and
around Grahamstown start from R895.

Port Alfred *p388*
Diving
Keryn's Dive School, small boat harbour, T082-433 5662, www.kerynsdiveschool.com. Fishing charters and dive courses available, plus daily dives for certified divers. The nearby reef has some fine corals and there are some popular wreck dives, but the water is not warm, nor the visibility that good.

Golf
The Royal Port Alfred Golf Course, T046-624 4796, www.rpagc.co.za. Magnificent view of the sea. This 18-hole, 72 par course was laid out between 1907 and 1915 and was given royal status by King George V. A new clubhouse was built in 2007.

Hiking
Sunshine Coast Hiking, T046-624 5295, www.sunshinecoasthikingtrails.co.za. Offers two, 5-day assisted ('slack-packing') hikes along the coast; the Three Sisters Trail from Port Alfred to Hamburg and the Dias Cross Trail from Port Alfred to Woody Cape in the coastal region of the Addo Elephant National Park. Although roughly 70 km long, both trails are along the beach so they are not challenging, and this is a great way to appreciate the beauty of the coastline. Nights are spent in comfortable lodges and luggage is transported.

Horse riding
The roads that access the most beautiful and remote beaches and river valleys are poor, which means that horses are often the best mode of transport. If you have never ridden before, this is a good place to learn.
Fish River Horse Safaris, 15 mins' drive from Port Alfred on the Fidh River, T082-433 5662, www.fishriverhorsesafaris.co.za. Trails through rolling hills, milkwoods, dunes and along beaches. Experienced guides, can pace to any level including children. Prices from R250 for a 2-hr beach ride.

☎ Transport

Grahamstown *p384, map p385*
Bus
Greyhound and **Translux** coaches depart from outside the Frontier Hotel, Bathurst St. Buses stop in Grahamstown on the **Cape Town–Durban** route.

Bus companies All bus tickets can be booked online at www.computicket.com. The **Baz Bus**, reservations T021-439 2323, www.bazbus.com; **Greyhound**, www.grey hound.co.za; **Translux**, www.translux.co.za. For more information, see Getting around, page 41.

Port Alfred *p388*
Bus
The **Baz Bus** stops at Station Backpackers 5 times a week.

King William's Town *p389*
Bus
Greyhound coaches depart from the Engen One Stop (Wimpy), Cathcart St. **Translux** coaches depart from the BP service station on Alexander Rd. Buses stop in King William's Town on the **Cape Town–Durban** route.

Bus companies All bus tickets can be booked online at www.computicket.com. The **Baz Bus**, reservations T021-439 2323, www.bazbus.com; **Greyhound**, www.grey hound.co.za; **Translux**, www.translux.co.za. For more information, see Getting around, page 41.

☎ Directory

Grahamstown *p384, map p385*
Banks and internet All the major banks have branches in the **Pepper Grove Mall** on African St, where there are also internet cafés.

Port Alfred *p388*
Banks Standard Bank and First National, both in Govan Mbeki Av.

Eastern Cape Karoo

The surreal Karoo landscape, clear air and desert sunsets are evocative of the very heart of South Africa. The archaic scenery, created from sedimentary rock around 250 million years ago, is rich in fossils and San paintings. This is an area of vast open spaces studded with scrub and cacti, craggy mountains looming in the distance. Despite its barren appearance, this is mainly a farming area, known for its sheep, cattle, angora goats and horses. The most beautiful place to experience the Karoo is in the Valley of Desolation next to the historic town of Graaff-Reinet. The fastest route north into the Karoo is via the N2 from Nelson Mandela Bay (Port Elizabeth) past Addo, which connects with the N10 heading to Cradock and Middelburg. The R63 leaves the N10 at Cookhouse and heads west to Somerset East and Graaff-Reinet. For more information on the region visit www.karooheartland.co.za. ➡ *For listings, see pages 402-405.*

North of Nelson Mandela Bay ⊖❷➋▲⊜ ➡ *pp402-405.*

Somerset East → *Colour map 7, A4. Phone code: 042.*

Somerset East, a neat agricultural town typical of the Karoo, is 180 km north of Nelson Mandela Bay (Port Elizabeth). It was founded on a farm that produced horse fodder for the cavalry on the frontline of the many skirmishes going on at the time, and was and named after Lord Charles Somerset, Governor of the Cape in 1815. The town has a few historical buildings and faces the Bosberg Mountains. The **Somerset Museum** ⓘ *Mon-Fri 0800-1700, R5, children (under 16) R2*, recreates the atmosphere and lifestyle of a Victorian parsonage. It is set among beautiful rose gardens and the rose petals are used to make jam, which is on sale in the museum shop. The **Walter Battiss Art Museum** ⓘ *Mon-Fri 1000-1600, free*, is also here and has the world's largest collection of work by this South African artist, who was a friend of Pablo Picasso. For information contact **Blue Crane Tourism** ⓘ *88 Njoli Rd, T042-243 1333, www.somerseteast.co.za, Mon-Fri 0830-1200, 1330-1600.*

Cradock → *Colour map 7, A4. Phone code: 048.*

This small Karoo town is made up of an attractive grid of wide roads lined with Victorian bungalows. It was once a frontier town and has three Victorian churches. The **Dutch Reformed Church** on Stockenstroom Street was opened in 1868 and is based upon London's St Martin in the Fields. Cradock is now better known for its connections with Olive Schreiner who wrote *The Story of an African Farm*. **Olive Schreiner House** ⓘ *9 Cross St, T048-881 5251, Mon-Fri 0800-1245, 1400-1630, R7, children (under 12) R4*, illustrates aspects of her life.

The **Great Fish River Museum** ⓘ *behind the town hall, T048-881 4509, Mon-Fri 0800-1600, Sat 0800-1200, R5, children (under 16) free*, is in a restored parsonage built in 1849, today a national monument. It depicts early pioneer history and on display are old ox wagons and horse carts, including a hearse. **Cradock Spa** ⓘ *4 km from Cradock on the Marlow road, T048-881 2709, 0645-1930, R7*, is a series of indoor and outdoor pools set around natural sulphurous springs. From here, there are two short circular hiking trails. The 10-km **Fish River Trail** follows the river into town, crossing over the bridge and returning on the opposite bank. The **Eerstekrantz Trail**, 4.5 km, is a hike up the mountain opposite the spa resort. Note the silver windmills, a distinguishing feature of the Karoo, on the surrounding farmland.

For information contact **Cradock Tourism** ⓘ *municipality building, J A Calata St, T048-801 5000, www.cradocktourism.co.za, Mon-Fri 0830-1230, 1400-1600.* The office is very helpful and has a good collection of maps and accommodation listings.

Mountain Zebra National Park → *Colour map 7, A4.*

ⓘ *T048-881 2427, www.sanparks.org. Gates open Oct-Apr 0700-1900, May-Sep 0700-1800, R88, children (under 12) R44. The park is 280 km from Nelson Mandela Bay (Port Elizabeth) and 25 km west of Cradock in the foothills of the Bankberg. The reserve is signposted from the Cradock to Middelburg road.*

The plains and mountains of this Karoo landscape support a wide variety of mammals, including black wildebeest, kudu, eland, mountain zebra, red hartebeest, springbok, buffalo, black rhino and caracal. The Rooiplat Plateau is a particularly good area for seeing the zebra. Over 200 species of bird have been recorded here, including many raptors and the endangered blue crane. Less appealingly, this is also the home of the giant earthworm. Buffalo were introduced in 1998 and black rhino in 2001, which put a stop to hiking in the reserve. Game viewing can be done by car during the day on the 37 km of tracks which cross the reserve.

The national park was established in 1937, when the mountain zebra was facing extinction and there were only five left on 65 sq km of land, four of which were male. There are now over 300 of them here, making it the largest herd of mountain zebra in the world. After breeding, many are relocated to other parks in South Africa.

There is a park camp with a fully licensed à la carte restaurant (open 0700-1900), which also serves snacks, and a shop (open 0700-1900), which sells a good range of groceries, wines, curios, books and firewood. The camp also has two swimming pools (one for day visitors), telephones and petrol. If you don't want to drive yourself, guided game drives can be booked at reception. For accommodation details, see Sleeping, page 403.

Nieu Bethesda → *Colour map 7, A3.*

Nieu Bethesda was founded in 1874 on a farm, Uitkyk, by a group of farmers who wanted a church that was closer than the one at Graaff-Reinet, several hours' ride away on horseback. Uitkyk belonged to BJ Pienaar – on his gravestone is engraved *De ouers van de dorp* (the parents of the town). Even today, many people in and around Nieu Bethesda carry the same surname. The first church services were held in a wagon shed, until the Dutch Reformed Church was built in 1905. Even today, this is still lit by gas chandeliers that pre-date the arrival of electricity to the village, and has an imposing white steeple with a clock that chimes accurately on the hour.

This small village has become best known through the work of Helen Martins and her **Owl House** ⓘ *T049-841 1603, www.owlhouse.co.za, 0900-1700, R25 per person*. Helen was a local eccentric who lived a hermit-like existence, devoting her time to her art and the study of Eastern philosophies. She was born in the house in 1898, and when she reached her fifties and when her parents died, she embarked on an extraordinary 25-year transformation of the house. Then in old age with crippling arthritis and poor eyesight – and considering her decoration of her house complete – she took her own life in 1971. Most of the surfaces on the inside of the house are decorated with finely ground glass of many colours, and in the pantry are rows of jars of crushed glass that Helen carefully graded by colour and weight. The light and colour of the glass is highlighted further by the many candles, lamps and strangely shaped mirrors. At the back of the house is an enclosed area known as the Camel Yard, filled with hundreds of sphinxes, camels and other figures made from cement and glass. Her remarkable house and its grounds, along with much of her art is now a museum, which attracts some 13,000 visitors a year.

The village has a collection of other artists' galleries, one shop, four restaurants, and no street lights. If you are self-catering it is better to stock up elsewhere and there is no petrol available here. There are a couple of good accommodation options or, as it is only 50 km from Graaff-Reinet, it can easily be visited in a day though you'll need to have your own transport. There is an **information office** ① *T049-841 1401, www.nieubethesda.co.za.*

Graaff-Reinet 😑🕐🔺😑 ▶▶ *pp402-405. Colour map 7, A3.*

Founded in 1786, Graaff-Reinet, the oldest town of the Eastern Cape, lies between the Sneuberg Mountains and the Sundays River. The town was originally described as "nothing more than a collection of mud huts", but years of prosperity from farming are reflected in the local architecture – over 220 of the town's historical buildings have been declared national monuments. Today it is surprisingly smart, with row upon row of perfectly restored houses, leafy streets and a quiet, bustling atmosphere. Nevertheless, Graaff-Reinet remains a small provincial town in deep Karoo country, so don't expect much in the form of entertainment.

The town was originally established as an administrative centre to control the frontier districts for the government in the Cape. Mauritz Woeke was sent as governor or landrost in 1785. He chose the site of Graaff-Reinet because of its water supplies and fertile soils. The town grew to become an important trading centre on the new frontier and there was a boom in sheep farming during the 1850s, when English settlers first brought merino sheep to the region. The **Graaff-Reinet Publicity Association** can provide **tourist information** ① *7 Church St, T049-892 4248, www.graaffreinet.co.za, Mon-Fri 0800-1700, Sat 0900-1200, Sun 1000-1200.*

Sights
① *All of the town's museums are open Mon-Fri 0900-1300, 1400-1700, Sat-Sun 0900-1200, unless otherwise stated, T049-892 3801. Combination tickets for all of them are purchased at Reinet House, R25, children (under 16) R12. All the sights can easily be explored by foot.*

The earliest surviving historic buildings, mostly square and originally thatched but now roofed with corrugated iron, are on **Cradock Street**. The buildings are typical of Karoo architecture and were designed to be cool during the blistering summer heat. They have thick whitewashed walls and shuttered windows.

A walk down Parsonage Street and Church Street passes many of Graaff-Reinet's most interesting historical buildings. The **Drostdy Hotel** is a fine example of classical Cape architecture designed by Louis Thibault. It was built in 1806 and was the site of the local council for 40 years. In 1855 it was bought by Captain Charles Lennox Stretch and converted into a hotel. The modern Drostdy Hotel was restored in 1977.

Reinet House on Parsonage Street was completed in 1812 and became the parsonage for the Dutch Reformed Church. It was opened to the public as a historic museum in 1956. It is still decorated with original yellowwood and stinkwood furniture and boasts the world's largest vine, planted in 1870. The most recent addition to the complex is a brandy still, built in 1990, now used to demonstrate the distillation of *withond*, a local brand of fire-water from the early settler days.

Opposite is the **Old Residency Museum** ① *Mon-Sat*, which was originally a townhouse built early in the 19th century. It became the magistrate's residence in 1916. Today it houses the Jan Felix Lategan Memorial collection of sporting rifles as well as Middellandse Regiment memorabilia. On the same street, the **John Rupert Little Theatre** was originally the church of the London Missionary Society. It became an art gallery in the 1970s and is now a theatre.

On Church Street, the **Old Library Museum** was built in 1847 and has displays of period costumes and a collection of fossils, and quite by contrast, an exhibition dedicated to the life and work of Robert Sobukwe, founder of the Pan Africanist Congress. The tourist information office is also here. Next door, the **Hester Rupert Art Museum** makes a pleasant change from the nostalgia of other museums. The art gallery has a collection of South African contemporary art.

The **Graaff-Reinet Pharmacy** on Caledon Street is a Victorian chemist's shop which still has many of its original fittings. There are a number of Victorian chemists, which have been converted into tourist attractions in South Africa, but this is considered to be among the finest.

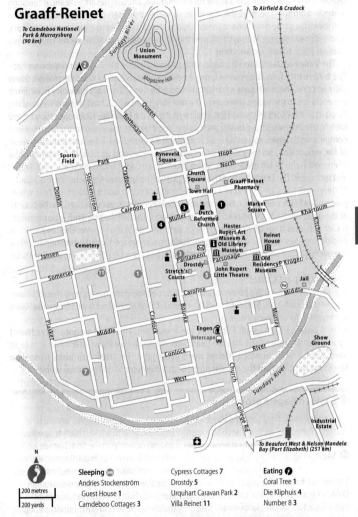

Graaff-Reinet

To Airfield & Cradock

To Camdeboo National Park & Murraysburg (90 km)

Sundays River
Union Monument
Magazine Hill

Queen
Rothman
Park
Stockenstrom
Cradock
Donkin

Sports Field

Ryneveld Square
Hope
North

Church Square
Town Hall
Graaff Reinet Pharmacy

Caledon
Muller
Dutch Reformed Church
Hester Rupert Art Museum & Old Library Museum
Reinet House
Market Square
Khartoum
Kitchner

Cemetery
Jansen
Somerset
Plasket

Parliament
Drostdy
Stretch's Courts
Parsonage
John Rupert Little Theatre
Old Residency Museum
P Kruger
Jail
Middle

Caroline
Bourke
Cradock
Middle
Conlock
West

Engen
Intercape
River
Sundays River
Church
College Rd

Show Ground

Industrial Estate

To Camdeboo National Park & Murraysburg

To Beaufort West & Nelson Mandela Bay (Port Elizabeth) (251 km)

N
200 metres
200 yards

Sleeping
Andries Stockenström Guest House 1
Camdeboo Cottages 3
Cypress Cottages 7
Drostdy 5
Urquhart Caravan Park 2
Villa Reinet 11

Eating
Coral Tree 1
Die Kliphuis 4
Number 8 3

Around Graaff-Reinet

Camdeboo National Park → *Colour map 7, A3.*

ⓘ *Gates open 0600-2000, T049-892 3453, R88, children (under 12) R44. The Driekoppe Trail must be booked in advance through SANParks, T012-428 9111, www.sanparks.org.*

Formerly the Karoo Nature Reserve, the Camdeboo National Park is now administered by SANParks and covers 14,500 ha and virtually surrounds Graaff-Reinet. The landscape is typical of the Karoo, with spectacular rock formations, peculiar desert flora and interesting game and birdlife. There are three main areas within the reserve: the Valley of Desolation to the west; a game drive area to the north; and the eastern hiking area. To reach the park, take the road towards Murraysburg past the 1000-ha dam, which has picnic sites and is a popular place to sail and windsurf.

The **Valley of Desolation** is a national monument within the Camdeboo National Park. The bizarre rock formations were formed millions of years ago by weather erosion. Sheer cliffs and precariously balanced columns of dolerite rise 120 m from the valley floor. From the entrance to the valley, drive up to the first viewpoint which has fabulous views of the Karoo in all directions to the horizon. Looking out over the harsh landscape gives you a good idea of the overwhelming obstacles that the Voortrekkers managed to overcome. If you continue up the road, you come to a car park and a short 1.5-km hike, with stunning views of the mountains and the chance of seeing black eagles and dassies. Back down off the main road, is the 19-km game drive, where you may see Cape buffalo, kudu, mountain zebra and springbok. The **Eerstefontein Day Walks** start at the Spandau Kop Gate. There is a choice of three walks of 4 km, 11 km or 14 km. The walks pass through a wilderness area where you can see black wildebeest, kudu and springbok. Permits are required and can be bought at the gate; the trails are marked by lizard emblems. The **Driekoppe Trail** is an overnight trail that passes through the mountainous eastern area of the reserve. This area is rich in wildlife, and hikers can see klipspringers, kudu, mountain reedbuck and mountain zebra. The overnight hut sleeps eight hikers. The trail must be booked in advance through SANParks.

Kalkkop Impact Crater

ⓘ *Follow the N9 towards Aberdeen for about 30 km; at Aberdeen, turn left onto the R338 until you reach a right-hand turn marked as Aberdeen Rd. From here there is a dirt track that leads to the crater, follow the signs.*

A short distance from Graaff-Reinet are the weathered remains of a giant crater created by a meteorite more than 200,000 years ago. Research has shown the original hole to have been several hundred metres deep. Over time the crater has been filled with limestone deposits, but the circular ridge, with a diameter of 640 m, is still visible.

◉ Eastern Cape Karoo listings

For Sleeping and Eating price codes and other relevant information, see pages 46-53.

◉ Sleeping

Somerset East *p398*

D Glen Avon Farm, 12 km from Somerset East, off the R63 towards Cookhouse, T042-

243 3628, www.glenavonfarm.co.za. Lovely picturesque farm offering hikes to streams and interaction with the farm animals for children. 2 comfortable guest rooms in the main farmhouse and 2 self-catering cottages (3-bed) with yellowwood floors, wrought-iron beds. **Hart Cottage** is a restored 1817 thatched, wattle-and-daub building. Pool,

tennis court, fresh farm produce for breakfast or for sale to self-caterers. Peaceful retreat.

D Somerset Hotel, 83 Nojoli St, T/F042-243 0557, www.somerseteast.co.za/somerset hotel. Simple town hotel built in the 1800s with tin roof, plain but good-value doubles and singles with TV, cheaper rooms without bathrooms, friendly pub where you can meet Karoo farmers, adequate restaurant on site.

Cradock p398

B Die Tuishuise, 36 Market St, T048-881 1322, www.tuishuise.co.za. Characterful guesthouse based in a series of historical buildings on Market St, each restored and decorated to reflect the British and Dutch settlers' lifestyles a century ago. All houses have a fully equipped kitchen and lounge and are ideal for families or 2 couples travelling together. En suite bathrooms and the staff are very friendly and helpful. Delicious, huge breakfasts are served in a Victorian dining room. A good evening meal can be found in the **Victoria Manor Hotel** (see below) at the end of the street. Has won numerous awards, recommended, almost worth a detour alone.

B Victoria Manor Hotel, corner of Market and Voortrekker streets, T048-881 1650, reservations also through www.tuishuise. co.za. Lovely old town inn set in a 3-storey Victorian building built in 1840. Full of character, with old-fashioned furnishings, a very good restaurant serving Karoo dinners, bar, tea room and attached curio shop.

C Heritage House, 45 Bree St, T048-881 3210, www.heritagehousecradock.com. Delightful 170-year-old farmhouse with 7 comfortable en suite rooms in the main house or in garden cottages set on wide lawns. TV, electric blankets and heaters. Good breakfasts, friendly owners, the perfect spot to relax and soak up the Karoo atmosphere.

D Palm House, 26 Market St, T048-881 4229, metcalf@eastcape.net. Victorian bungalow with 3 rooms, en suite, no smoking, old-style furnishings, high ceilings, log fires in winter, lovely old dining room, TV lounge, good breakfasts, very friendly owners.

Mountain Zebra National Park p399

Reservations through **SANParks**, T012-428 9111, www.sanparks.org. See page 48 for details. For late bookings or cancellations within 72 hrs of arrival, phone the reception direct on T048-881 2427.

A Doornhoek Guest House. A restored Victorian farmhouse built in 1836, registered as a national monument. The house sleeps up to 6 people in 2 cast-iron double beds and 2 single beds; all en suite. The house is decorated in Victorian style, with pine floors, stained-glass windows, open fireplaces, fully equipped kitchen. To complete the feeling of isolated luxury, it's set in its own valley.

D Cottages. 19 self-catering cottages, rather more functional. Each has 2 bedrooms, bathroom, living room, partially equipped kitchen.

Camping

20 caravan and camping sites set amongst good shade trees but it can get dusty as lawn-type grass cannot grow in the park. There is a communal wash block and kitchen facilities. A maximum of 6 people are allowed on each site. Some sites have power points.

Nieu Bethesda p399

D House Number One, 1 Cloete St, T049-841 1700. Attractive old-style fully equipped self-catering house. 3 very comfortable spacious rooms sleeping 7 in total, antique furnishings, polished wooden floors, 2 bathrooms, lounge with a full-size snooker table, kitchen, dining room and veranda with braai. At less R200 per person per night, it's good value for a group.

D-F Owl House Backpackers, Martin St, T049-841 1642, www.owlhouse.info. Pleasant budget alternative with creatively decorated dorms and double rooms, cottage, camping, kitchen, bar and home-cooked meals using produce from their garden. The friendly owners can organize tours to the Valley of Desolation and the Mountain Zebra National Park, and for a small fee they will pick up/drop off in Graaff-Reinet. Recommended.

Graaff-Reinet *p400, map p401*
Has a superb collection of guesthouse accommodation in historic buildings.
A Andries Stockenström Guest House, 100 Cradock St, T049-892 4575, www.asg house.co.za. This guesthouse was originally built in 1819 and has been restored and lavishly decorated. 6 en suite, a/c double rooms. Superb dining room (residents only, closed Sun, ♥♥♥) serving imaginative selection of haute cuisine Karoo meals, including kudu, springbok, ostrich and guinea fowl with a French twist. The chef was trained at the **Ritz** in Paris. Swimming pool.
A Drostdy Hotel, 30 Church St, T049-892 2161, www.drostdy.co.za. Beautifully restored building designed by Louis Thibault in 1804. There are 51 rooms, all en suite and with a/c, the rooms at the back of the main house are in an appealing complex of 19th-century cottages known as **Stretch's Courts**, originally the homes of emancipated slaves. Public areas are decorated with antiques and paintings. The **Camdebo** and **Court Room** restaurants have a good reputation (see Eating, below). There's a secluded garden where you can have pre-dinner drinks, a pool and secure off-street parking. Recommended.
B Villa Reinet, 83 Somerset St, T049-892 5525, www.villareinet.co.za. A guesthouse set in an old church hall, with high ceilings and comfy furnishings. There are 2 a/c double rooms with en suite bathroom and large French doors leading onto a garden and splash pool, and 6 a/c garden cottages with hammocks. Breakfast is served in the cosy kitchen or under a pear tree in the garden.
C Camdeboo Cottages, 16 Parliament St, T049-892 3180, www.camdeboocottages. co.za. A group of centrally located national monument 19th-century buildings, which have been converted into 8 self-catering cottages built around a courtyard with a swimming pool and braai. Meals available on request. Hot-water bottles provided in winter, coffee shop on the premises.
C Cypress Cottages, 80 Donkin St, T049-892 3965, www.cypresscottage.co.za. 2 white-

washed Karoo single-storey cottages facing each other across the street, 3 en suite bedrooms in each, communal lounge and dining room full of antiques, large garden, good for families, B&B.
D-E Urquhart Caravan Park, at the edge of town next to the Camdeboo National Park, T049-892 2136. Large park with clean, modern facilities for campers and caravans. There are a 5 chalets next to the Sundays River, some with kitchen, and very simple but excellent value rondavels that share ablutions with campers, though you need to bring your own bedding and towels.

⑦ Eating

Cradock *p398*
Cradock has its fair share of chain restaurants. Alternatively, you can eat in the lovely dining room of the **Victoria Manor Hotel** (see page 403), part of the Die Tuishuise Guesthouse, to sample traditional Karoo cuisine.

Nieu Bethesda *p399*
♥ **Die Waenhuis Pub & Grub**, corner of Hudson and Martin streets, T049-841 1627. Mon-Thu 1100-1430, 1700-late, Fri-Sat 1100-late. Cosy pub with fireplace, stews and pies, traditional desserts like apple crumble, hearty country cooking and big portions, large TV screen for important sports matches.
♥ **The Brewery and Two Goats Deli**, Pienaar St, T049-841 1602. Open 1100-1500. Simple rustic café with wooden benches, known for its home-brewed beer and fresh goat's cheese, excellent ploughman's platters with pickles, cheese and cold meat, in winter there are warming stews and soups, eat in or take away.

Graaff-Reinet *p400, map p401*
One of the best restaurants is at the **Andries Stockenström Guest House** (see Sleeping, above), but you have to stay there to eat.
♥♥♥ **Die Kliphuis**, 46 Bourke St, T049-892 2345, kliphuis@lantic.net. 0730-0930, 1800-2200. One of Graaff-Reinet's most beautiful historic

buildings (1857), serves dinners of Karoo lamb or springbok in a traditionally decorated dining room with a roaring fire. They grow their own vegetables and herbs. There are also 2 rooms here (**B**), with Victorian bathrooms, overlooking a Karoo garden with fruit trees and a pomegranate hedge.

††† **Drostdy Hotel**, see Sleeping, above. This historic hotel has 2 excellent, romantic and elegant restaurants. Beautiful setting with high ceilings, polished wooden floors and candle light. Great nightly buffets with a fine range of local Karoo dishes, the à la carte menu is much more expensive but superb. Need to dress up a bit or there is a light more casual menu in the garden.

††† **Coral Tree**, 3 Church St, T049-892 5947. Mon-Sat, closed for a couple of hours each afternoon. Great location opposite the church, this very popular restaurant serves a good range of typical Karoo dishes – try the Karoo lamb or kudu steaks – and traditional desserts like melktart. Recommended.

††† **Number 8**, 8 Church St, T049-892 4464. Mon-Sat 12-late. Very popular pub and grill house in a Victorian building. Good simple steaks, fish and chips, and more adventurous Mozambique prawns or Portuguese *espetadas*, TV showing sports, special kids' room with toys, busy local watering hole. The owner is an avid collector of memorabilia from the Springboks (rugby) and Proteas (cricket) teams, and there are many signed shirts, balls, etc on display.

▲ Activities and tours

Nieu Bethesda p399
Tour operators
Ganora Excursions, T049-841 1302, www. ganora.co.za. Small operator that specializes in trips to view ancient San rock art, as well as walking trails and fossil walks on their farm 7 km from Nieu Bethesda towards Middleburg. They also rent out a large stone cottage that sleeps 6.

Graaff-Reinet p400, map p401
Tour operators
Karoo Connections, 7 Church St, T049-892 3978, www.karooconnections.co.za. Well-organized local tour operator offering a wide range of trips, including guided historical town walks, township tours, trips to San rock art, and excursions to Camdeboo National Park.

⊖ Transport

Cradock p398
Bus
Intercape, and Translux, stop at Struwig Motors on Main St, and Cradock is on the **Nelson Mandela Bay–Johannesburg** route.
  Bus companies All bus tickets can be booked online at www.computicket.com. Intercape, www.intercape.co.za; Translux, www.translux.co.za. For more information, see Getting around, page 41.

Train
Cradock is on the **Nelson Mandela Bay (Port Elizabeth)–Johannesburg** train route. Central reservations, **Shosholoza Meyl**, T0860-00888 (in South Africa), T011-774 4555 (from overseas), www.shosholoza meyl.co.za, timetables and fares are published on the website.

Graaff-Reinet p400, map p401
It's 251 km to **Nelson Mandela Bay (Port Elizabeth)**, 90 km to **Murraysburg**.

Bus
Intercape and Translux buses stop in Graaf-Reinet daily on the **Cape Town– Queenstown – East London** route. Buses stop at the Engen garage on Church St.
  Bus companies All bus tickets can be booked online at www.computicket.com. Intercape, www.intercape.co.za; Translux, www.translux.co.za. For more information, see Getting around, page 41.

Cape Midlands and East London

From King William's Town the N2 heads back to the coast and East London. To the north of the city is the mountainous region lying between Stutterheim and Fort Beaufort, which is a beautiful area of rolling hills, lush indigenous forests and waterfalls. These are the Amatola Mountains and the region is referred to as the Cape Midlands. Sadly, some areas have now been replaced with pine plantations. Nevertheless, there remains an abundance of unharmed forest, criss-crossed with trails and perfect for hiking. The principal centre of the region is the coastal city of East London. It's predominantly an industrial city, and fairly run-down, though is useful for stocking up on provisions before travelling up the Wild Coast.
▶▶ *For listings, see pages 413-418.*

Ins and outs

Getting there From King William's Town to Queenstown there are two routes. The first follows the R63 west to Fort Beaufort and then heads north along the R67 to Queenstown. The second route heads north via Stutterheim and Cathcart via the N6. The Amatola Mountains can be reached from both sides. Further south the N2 runs through East London on its way to the Wild Coast. East London and Queenstown are connected by bus services running inland along the N6 from East London to Bloemfontein and Johannesburg.
▶▶ *For further details, see Transport, page 417.*

Best time to visit The mountains are at their best in spring or autumn; in winter it can get very cold and it is not unusual to have snow in May. Most of the rain tends to fall during the summer months. On the coast the climate is mild and sunny all year round.

Hogsback ●●●●● ▶▶ *pp413-418. Colour map 7, A5.*

→ *Altitude: 1200 m.*

The quiet village of Hogsback lies in the centre of the Amatola Mountains, surrounded by rolling hills covered in forest reserves. The beautiful surroundings and slow pace of life make it a delightful spot to rest up for a few days and explore the forests. The village itself has no real centre, but is made up of a string of cottages, hotels, tea gardens and craft shops dotted along several kilometres of gravel road. Tucked away down the side lanes are some beautiful gardens, more reminiscent of rural England than inland Africa. Among the early settlers was Thomas Summerton, a market gardener from Oxford, and his attempts to recreate the English countryside can still be seen in apple orchards, avenues lined with hazelnut, berry fruits and the flowering plants that have spread throughout the area. It's one of the few places in South Africa where berries thrive: red, white and black currents, blackberries, raspberries, loganberries, strawberries and English gooseberries. As you can imagine the local people have gone into bottling overdrive and there are some delicious jams for sale in Hogsback's crafts shops. The **Hogsback Spring Festival** is held over two weekends in September when there's a craft market and many residents open their gardens to visitors.

Look out for **Oak Avenue**, an avenue of grand oak trees planted in the 1880s, which are still used for church services at Easter and Christmas when worshippers are seated on logs placed across the road. A new attraction in Hogsback is the labyrinth at **The Edge** (see Sleeping, page 413), which is an 11-circuit labyrinth, similar in design to the labyrinth at Chartres

Cathedral in France. The total distance of the walk to the centre of the maze and out is 1.4 km and the circumference is 91 m. There is a helpful **tourist office** ① *Stormhaven Crafts, Main Rd, T045-962 1050, www.hogsbackinfo.co.za, Mon-Fri 1030-1230, 1500-1700, Sat 1030-1230.*

There are several theories as to how the area got its name. One is that a peak in the Hogsback range resembles the back of a hog when viewed from a particular angle. The other is that the founder was a Captain Hogg who had been based at Fort Mitchell. The Xhosa name for the peaks is *Belekazana* (to carry on the back), as another view from a different angle resembles a woman carrying a child on her back. Three peaks can be seen from the village, **Hog One** (1836 m), **Hog Two** (1824 m) and **Hog Three** (1937 m). The highest peak in the region lies to the north of Hogsback and is known as **Elandsberg** (2019 m).

Local hikes

The spectacular waterfalls are a highlight in the surrounding forests. The most popular falls are known as Madonna and Child, Kettle Spout and the 39 Steps. The **Madonna and Child** falls are a 30-minute walk from a car park on Wolfridge Road, 5 km from the village centre. The easiest falls to visit are the **39 Steps**, which are 10 minutes' walk from the end of Oak Avenue. Look out for a green pig with a red triangle. If you're staying at **Away with the Fairies** (see Sleeping, page 413), there's a good one-hour walk to the **Swallowtail Falls**, where you'll pass an impressive 'big tree' and see plenty of vervet monkeys and birdlife.

A short distance from the centre of the village is the church of **St Patrick on the Hill**. The original chapel dates from 1935, and today's neat thatched building is set in a

Hogsback

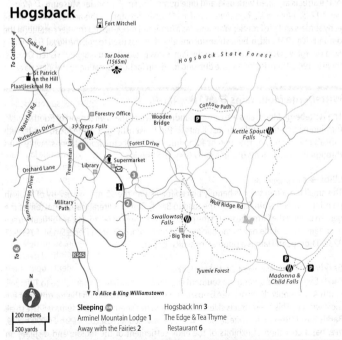

Sleeping
Arminel Mountain Lodge 1
Away with the Fairies 2

Hogsback Inn 3
The Edge & Tea Thyme
Restaurant 6

beautiful garden full of rhododendrons and azaleas. The door is on a latch, so you are welcome to peek inside. Just beyond the church is a track off to the right, Gaika Road, which leads up to the viewpoint **Gaika Kop** (1963 m). The path is not very easy to follow – get a local map from one of the hotels before you set off.

Some of the finest views are from **Tor Doone** (1565 m), weather permitting. The easiest path follows the fire break at the end of Oak Avenue. Look out for markers with a yellow pig and a single green stripe; the contour path is marked with a green pig and yellow dot. Allow a minimum of two hours to get to the top.

Note that if you are here during the winter months the weather gets very cold at night. Even in summer, the nights are cold and a warm clear morning can quickly develop into low cloud and thunderstorms which may take a day or two to clear. If in doubt, check with local people who should be able to interpret the vagaries of the weather.

Queenstown → *Colour map 7, A5.*

Queenstown, the largest town in the Cape Midlands, was named after Queen Victoria. Like many settlements in the area, it only started to thrive once the Frontier Wars had ended. However, the central square in the town was designed with defence in mind. Known today as the Hexagon, the square has six main streets radiating off it like spokes on a wheel. The idea was that defenders would have a clear line of fire to the outskirts of town from the fortified central square. There are several fine buildings in and around the square, including the town hall, court house and public offices and the Anglican church of St Michael. Many of the streets are lined with oaks and blue gums. The small **Frontier Museum** ① *Mon-Fri 0800-1245, 1400-1600, R5, children(under 16) R2,* is devoted to the achievements of the early settlers and the Frontier Wars and has a furnished mock-up of a frontier cottage. In the grounds is a 1921 British-built steam locomotive that was used to pull the Royal Train when King George VI, Queen Elizabeth and the Princesses Elizabeth and Margaret visited Queenstown in 1947. There is also a stone drinking fountain for horses, dating to the Victoria era.

Witteberge Mountains ●▲● ›› *pp413-418.*

The Witteberge Mountains are rather grandly known as the 'Switzerland of South Africa', forming part of the southernmost limits of the Drakensberg. It is the location of South Africa's only ski resort. The road heading into the Witteberge from Queenstown passes through the small towns of Elliot, Lady Grey and Rhodes.

Elliot → *Colour map 7, A6.*

This small mountain town is handily placed for visiting the 32-m-long gallery of Khoisan paintings on **Denorbin Farm**, on the road to Barkly East. It is literally at the bottom of the garden behind the farm house and the paintings are finely detailed, but are difficult to see at certain times of the day as the background rock is dark. Contact Denis Small, T045-931 2232. **Thompson Dam** is a popular local picnic spot.

Barkly East → *Colour map 4, C4. Altitude: 1183 m.*

Barkly East is nestled among the southern Drakensberg foothills. It's very close to Tiffindell, South Africa's only ski resort (see below), and there are snowfalls on the mountains here most winters. This area attracts skiers in the winter and fly fishermen in the summer. The small **Barkly East Museum** ① *White St, T045-971 0724, www.barklyeast.co.za, Mon-Fri 0900-1600, free,* has a collection of exhibits of the early settlement of the region, and displays on the Boer War and some Xhosa beadwork and weapons. The museum also provides tourist information.

Rhodes → *Colour map 4, C5.*

Rhodes is a peaceful little mountain village overlooked by **Ben MacDhui** (3000 m), with a stone school house designed by Herbert Baker, a Victorian hotel, a general store and one pay phone. If you arrive here in winter bring lots of warm clothes – while electricity did arrive a few years ago, there is still no central heating, though hotels will provide electric blankets. The road from Barkly East to Rhodes is gravel, and although usually in good condition, drive with care as there are many hairpin bends. In heavy rains or snow it can become treacherous, so always phone hotels in Rhodes ahead to check on weather and road conditions. For information contact **Rhodes Hotel** (see Sleeping, page 414). Mountain bikers arrive here every October to compete in the 87-km **Rhodes Mountain Challenge**.

Originally known as Rossville, the village was renamed by town leaders after the mining magnet and imperialist, Cecil John Rhodes, in the hope that he would make a substantial contribution to the town's finances. He obliged by donating a wagonload of pine trees that still decorate the streets, and £500 which disappeared at the same time as the town clerk.

Tiffendell

ⓘ *T045-974 9004, www.skisouthafrica.co.za.*

Tiffendell is the only ski resort in South Africa, but the skiing is not up to much compared to other places in the world and the main slope is only 650 m long. Nevertheless it's a reasonable place to learn to ski and fun for children. It is located on the slopes of the highest mountain in the Eastern Cape, the 3001-m Ben Mc Dhui on the border with Lesotho, and is a one-hour drive north from Rhodes on a dirt track. The drive to Tiffendell through some scenic mountain passes is passable by a 2WD (with a powerful engine) in good weather, but only accessible by 4WD in snow. Enquire about the shuttle service, which runs between the **Walkerbouts Inn** (see Sleeping, page 414) and the resort, R250 per person, which operates during the skiing season. You leave your car in a safe, under-cover facility in Rhodes. The resort also has a helicopter, so the other option is to arrange transfers by helicopter from Rhodes (eight minutes) or Barkly East (18 minutes).

At the resort, there is a ski lift, snow-making machines and ski hire. Depending on the snow the resort is usually open from the end of May to the beginning of September and usually sustains a season of about 100 days. The **Snow Festival** takes place at the end of July, when there are skiing and snowboarding races. Accommodation is available at the resort (see Sleeping, page 414), and three- and four-night packages are inclusive of bed, breakfast, ski and snowboard equipment hire and ski pass, as well as emergency medical assistance and resort entertainment. Instruction is also available for beginners.

The resort is popular during the summer for fly fishing, mountain biking, horse riding, grass skiing and hiking, all of which can be arranged at the resort's reception the day before.

Lady Grey → *Colour map 4, B4.*

Lady Grey lies in a forested sandstone valley surrounded by the high peaks of the Witteberge, often covered with snow in winter. The town dam is used for picnics, swimming and trout fishing. Tourist information is available at the **Home Coffee Shop** ⓘ *T051-603 0176, www.ladygreytourism.co.za, Mon-Sat 0900-1530.* The **Karringmelkspruit Vulture Reserve** is 12 km south of Lady Grey on the road to Barkly East. Over 500 Cape vultures breed on the cliffs of this reserve.

Aliwal North → *Colour map 4, B4.*

Aliwal North, on the south bank of the Orange River, was founded by Sir Harry Smith, governor of the Cape, in 1849 and named after his victory over the Sikhs at Aliwal in India. The 'north' bit was added, as at one time Mossel Bay on the coast was to be named Aliwal South. It marks the border between the Eastern Cape and the Free State on the other side of the river. In the south of the town is a **Concentration Camp Memorial** commemorating the 715 Afrikaner people (mostly children) who died in terrible conditions in the camps set up by the British during the Boer War. The town is also known for its hot springs and the rather pungent waters are supposedly therapeutic for rheumatism and arthritis. In the 1960s, they were incorporated into the **Aliwal Spa** ① *T051-633 2951, daily 0800-2200, www.aliwalspa.co.za, R18, children (under 13) R12*, with Olympic-size outdoor pool, curly waterslide, indoor hot pools, saunas and a gym. There's also some basic accommodation and a campsite here (see Sleeping, page 414). **Aliwal North Nature Reserve** adjoins the resort, where a limited number of antelopes can be seen.

◗ *Aliwal North is on the site of what was a strategic ford on the Orange River used by the Voortrekkers on their great trek north from the Cape. This was upgraded with a pontoon in 1872 and, much later, by a bridge.*

East London ●❼❶▲❺❻ ⏪ *pp413-418. Colour map 7, B6.*

East London is South Africa's only river port and a major industrial centre, with an economy based on motor assembly plants, textile and electronics industries. Nevertheless, the city centre has a handful of attractive historical buildings, and there are some good beaches which surprisingly get very busy with domestic tourists over Christmas. Nahoon Beach is best known for its excellent surfing, and the city has attracted a real surfing community in recent years. Despite this, it's not a very attractive place and most travellers only pass through on their way to other coastal resorts or to the Amatola Mountains.

Ins and outs

Getting there **East London Airport** is 11 km west of the city centre off the R347, T043-706 0306, www.acsa.co.za. It's nowhere near as busy as the other regional airports (although it is a busy hub for the exportation of Eastern Cape pineapples). **SAA** connects East London with a number of other cities, and **1Time** flies between East London and Johannesburg and Cape Town. **East London Bus Shuttles** ① *T082-569 3599, www.elbus shuttle.com*, operates an airport shuttle service to the centre of town. **East Coast Shuttle** ① *T043-740 3060*, operates from the airport to the resorts from Gonubie to Kobb Inn on the Wild Coast. The larger car hire companies have desks at the airport. The **train station** ① *T043-700 2129*, is on Station Street. There are bus services to most South African cities with **Greyhound**, **Intercape**, and **Translux**. The **Baz Bus** also stops here. ⏪ *For further details, see Transport page 417.*

Tourist information The main tourist office covers the region from East London to King William's Town and is known as **Buffalo City Tourism** ① *91 Western Av, Vincent, T043-721 1346, www.tourismbuffalocity.co.za, Mon-Fri 0815-1630, Sat 0900-1400, Sun 0900-1300.* The main office of **Eastern Cape Tourism Board** ① *King's Entertainment Centre, Esplanade, T043-701 9600, www.ectourism.co.za, Mon-Fri 0830-1630.*

Background

East London was originally founded as a military camp on the banks of the Buffalo River in 1847 and its strategic position as a port was soon recognized. Sir Harry Smith, the British governor, ambitiously named it London, and its two main thoroughfares are still Fleet Street and Oxford Street. Later it was renamed Port of East London, and then simply as East London – not after London's East End but because the port was on the eastern bank of the river.

Sights

The town centre is a modern, bustling place, though it's fairly run down so exercise caution away from the beach. However, there are several historical monuments: the **Colonial Division Memorial** is in front of the City Hall; the **German Settler Memorial** is on the Esplanade; and there are **War Memorials** on Oxford Street.

East London

To 1, Umtata, Durban, N2 & Beacon Bay

To Ann Bryant Art Gallery, East London Museum, Vincent, Nelson Mandela Bay (Port Elizabeth), N2, Buffalo City Tourism & Airport

Buffalo Park (Cricket)

To 10 10 & Nahoon Beach

Indian Ocean

To West Bank Village

N
200 metres
200 yards

Sleeping 🛏
Blue Lagoon 1
Esplanade 2
Garden Court 3
Kennaway 4
Loerie Hide 10

Niki-Nana Backpackers 7
Premier King David 5
Sugar Shack 9

Eating 🍴
Al Mare 1

Buccaneers 2
Ernst's Chalet Suisse 3
Grazia Fine Food & Wine 4
Le Petit 10
Quarterdeck 8

Coelacanth – back from the dead

The discovery of a living coelacanth off the coast of East London in 1938 provided scientists with a link to pre-historic times. At first it was thought that they shared a common connection with lungfish and land vertebrates; on closer examination it became obvious that the fish had hardly changed since the Devonian period, 350 million years ago. It had been assumed that it had become extinct after some 290 million years. The fact that a living specimen was trawled from the deep destroyed this theory but the fish became known as a living fossil.

Named *Latimeria chalumnae*, this lobe-finned fish grows to about 1.5 m and can weigh 68 kg. It is bright blue and produces large quantities of oil and slime. Its four fins resemble legs and these have some rotating movement which allows them to crawl along the seabed. They have very powerful jaws.

More of these fish have been found near the Comoros Islands, to the north of the Mozambique Channel between Madagascar and mainland Africa. After all the excite-ment, it turned out that the Comores had been eating coelacanth for years. So much for coming back from the dead!

The **Ann Bryant Art Gallery** ⓘ *St Marks Rd off Oxford St, T043-722 4044, www.ann bryant.co.za, Mon-Fri 0900-1700, Sat 0900-1200, free,* is in an interesting Edwardian building dating from 1905. The collection was originally mostly of British artists but now has many fine contemporary South African works. An arts and crafts fair is held here on the first and second Sunday of every month.

The highlights of the **East London Museum** ⓘ *319 Oxford St, T043-743 0686, Mon-Fri 0930-1630, Sat 1000-1300, Sun and public holidays 1000-1500, R10, children (under 16) 3, coffee shop,* include the world's only dodo egg and the coelacanth that was trawled up off the Chalumna River in 1938. The coelacanth, known as the fossil fish, was thought to have been extinct for 80 million years until it was 'rediscovered' earlier this century (see box, above). The museum also has some good displays on Xhosa culture and customs, and a section devoted to Nguni beadwork. In the garden is an impressive collection of cycads.

Also on Oxford Street, the **City Hall** dates from1897, and the design of the clock on **Victoria Tower** was modelled after London's Big Ben. Inside, the marble staircase was constructed from marble directly imported from Carrar in Italy. Outside, is a monument to honour Steven Bantu Biko, which was unveiled by Nelson Mandela on 12 September 1997 to mark the 20th anniversary of his death while in police custody.

Gately House ⓘ *1 Park Gates Rd, T043-722 2141, Mon, Wed-Fri 0930-1630, Sat 1100-1600, R10, children (under 16) R3,* was built in 1876 by John Gately, one of East London's first mayors. The house was donated to the city in 1966 and is now a town house museum decorated with original Victorian furnishings.

Established in 1931, the **East London Aquarium** ⓘ *Esplanade, T043-705 2637, www.el aquarium.co.za, 0900-1700, R20, children (3-18) R13, under 3s free,* is the oldest aquarium in the country with over 400 freshwater and marine species on display. There's a seal show twice daily at 1130 and 1530, and feeding times are half an hour before. There's also a whale deck with a telescope – a blue flag flies when whales are sighted.

The **Lock Street Gaol Shopping Complex** is on Fleet Street. Built in the 1800s, this was South Africa's first women's jail, whose most famous inmates were Winnie Madikizela-Mandela (ex-wife of Nelson Mandela) and Daisy de Melker, who was accused of poisoning two husbands and a son. The original gallows can still be seen. It now houses shops and offices; check out the African curio shops for a good selection of items to take home.

West Bank Village

West Bank Village is the oldest surviving area of East London with some interesting old buildings on Bank Street and near the entrance to the harbour. **Hood Point Lighthouse** ① *T043-700 3056, Mon-Fri 1000-1500, also Sat-Sun Oct-Apr, R14, children (under 12) R7*, was built in 1895 and is a typical Victorian lighthouse with a steel upper gallery and keyhole windows. **Fort Glamorgan** is a vaulted brick building on Bank Street, which now serves as a prison. The fort was built in 1848 during the Seventh Frontier War to defend the supplies that were being sent to the inland garrisons from the Buffalo River Mouth.

⊚ Cape Midlands and East London listings

For Sleeping and Eating price codes and other relevant information, see pages 46-53.

⊖ Sleeping

Hogsback p406, map p407

In addition to the options listed below there are more than 20 different self-catering establishments. If you plan to hike in the region, these may be more convenient than staying in a lodge or hotel where meal times are fixed. Contact the local tourist office for further details. Be sure to book ahead during local school holidays.

B-D The Edge, off Woodside Rd, T045-962 1159, www.theedge-hogsback.co.za. 12 self-catering rondavels and 4 B&B rooms with log fires and feather duvets in a stunning setting perched on a cliff with spectacular views, surrounded by waterfalls and meadows filled with mushrooms and butterflies. If not staying, visit the **Tea Thyme** tea room to enjoy home-made goodies and the mountain views. Recommended.

C Arminel Mountain Lodge, Main Rd, T045-962 1005, www.arminelhogsback.co.za. 31 en suite log cabins, excellent restaurant serving meals based on local fresh produce, room rates include breakfast and evening meals. Extensive gardens with great mountain views, swimming pool, tennis. The management is very friendly and keen to further promote this beautiful area, which few overseas travellers visit. Recommended.

C Hogsback Inn, Main Rd, T045-962 1006, www.hogsbackinn.co.za. Old-fashioned rural retreat with 28 comfortable rooms and 2 self-catering family cabins. There is a good restaurant and a cosy, traditional pub. Swimming pool and tennis court, all set in 7 ha of grounds with the Tyume River flowing through. Log fires greatly add to the ambience. Very friendly and a good place to meet locals.

D-F Away with the Fairies, Ambleside Close, T045-962 1031, www.awaywiththefairies. co.za. A friendly, relaxed and well-run place, with well-kept, brightly painted dorms, en suite double rooms, well-equipped kitchen, clean bathrooms and cosy lounge with fireplace. The rooms are named after characters in *Lord of the Rings*. The surrounding gardens are beautiful and a nesting ground for the Cape parrot – of which there are only 300 left in the world – with plenty of camping space and a gate that leads to forest trails. There's a lively bar, great breakfasts and evening meals, daily guided walks and sundowner trips, regular shuttles to East London and Chintsa most days of the week, which get to East London in time to hook up with buses. Everyone feels very welcome and there's always plenty to do from rock climbing to mountain biking. Recommended.

Queenstown p408

C Heritage Guest House, corner of Frost and Fletcher streets, Top Town, opposite Queens College Boys High School, T045-839

4927. Very smart B&B, with 11 rooms in a Victorian house built in 1890, all en suite with private entrances, TV, heaters and fans, covered patios and braais and well-established gardens. Farmhouse breakfasts are included and dinner on request. Swimming pool, secure parking, braai facilities, ask for Linda or Bridget.

D Hazelmere Country Lodge, off the N6, 57 km towards Aliwal North, 4 km south of Penhoek Pass, T045-966 9622. Comfortable B&B with en suite rooms, in a farmhouse on a sheep farm. Lounge with TV, dinner (but needs to be prearranged), tennis court, swimming pool and croquet lawn.

Witteberge Mountains p408

A Tiffindell Ski Resort, T045-974 9004/5, www.skisouthafrica.co.za. 144 guests are accommodated in centrally heated wooden cabins or lodge rooms, each with balcony and DSTV, within 100 m of the ski slope and the main restaurant and bar. In winter, 3-night skiing packages (minimum stay), including all meals, skiing and equipment start from R4500 per person. However, skiers need to bring their own goggles, and of course plenty of thick socks and warm clothes. Lessons are extra. The pub offers plenty of schnapps and glüwein.

B Rhodes Hotel, corner of Miller and Sauer streets, Rhodes, T045-974 9305, www.rhodes hotel.co.za. Charming old-style hotel restored to resemble the original hotel of more than a century ago. 9 en suite rooms with antiques and electric blankets, rates include breakfast and dinner in the **Partridge Pot** restaurant and pub. Good home cooking, tennis court, local tours, fly-fishing and horse riding.

C Siskin's B&B, 43 Graham St, Barkly East, T045-974 9900. A rambling old home with wood floors, high ceilings, fireplace and TV lounge. Rooms with shared bathroom in the house or 2 en suite rooms in a restored outbuilding. Good food as owner is a cordon bleu chef, rates include dinner. Also offers self-catering accommodation in a nearby farmhouse and cottage.

C Umtali Country Inn, 47 Dan Pienaar Av, Aliwal North, T/F051-633 2400. Smart lodge with 33 newly renovated rooms, a/c, under-floor heating, DSTV, lovely swimming pool and generous meals served in the restaurant with fireplace.

C Walkerbouts Inn, 1 Vorster St, Rhodes, T045-974 9290, www.walkerbouts.co.za. 6 comfortable and spacious en suite rooms with electric blankets, B&B, cosy pub with the only satellite TV in the village, 2 pizza ovens, local beer on tap, and good 3-course dinners. Also rents out self-catering cottages in the village and can organize trout fishing.

D Aliwal Spa, Aliwal North, T051-633 2951, www.aliwalspa.co.za. 10 simple brick self-catering chalets, which have recently been refurbished, with braais. Camping and caravan sites with a newly built ablutions block. Not the most attractive of sites, but useful to use the indoor and outdoor hot and cold pools, which are open 24-hrs for overnight guests. The resort's **Calabash** restaurant serves uninventive but adequate meals.

D Mountain View Country Inn, 36 Botha St, Lady Grey, T051-603 0421, www.ladygrey. co.za. A pleasant rural retreat in a Victorian building with a lovely view over the town towards the mountains. 12 family and double rooms with en suite bathrooms, nicely decorated with antiques. Excellent home-made food, especially the scones and marmalade, and friendly pub where you can meet the locals.

East London p410, map p411

There's not a lot of interesting accommodation and most is in old beachside block hotels. The majority of backpackers staying in East London are here to surf. Others tend to move on to the far nicer Chintsa, 38 km up the coast.
B Blue Lagoon, Blue Bend Pl, Beacon Bay, T043-748 4821, www.chakelahotels.com. 76 en suite rooms in what used be a time-share resort on the Beacon Bay headland overlooking the sea and estuary with stunning views. Some 2-bedroom apartments and 3-bedroom townhouses with kitchenette

and lounge set in large grounds full of palms, 2 restaurants and bars, swimming pool, squash and tennis courts.

B Garden Court, corner of Esplanade and Moore streets, T043-722 7260, www.southern sun.com. This was a **Holiday Inn** which has been rebranded. Modern block set back from the beach, 173 standard a/c rooms, with balcony, some have views of the beach. Restaurant, coffee shop, bar, pool, gym, curio shop, secure parking and it's the seafront.

B Kennaway Hotel, Esplanade, T043-722 5531, www.kennawayhotel.co.za. A large, modern block overlooking Orient Beach, with 96 rooms with a/c and DSTV, non-smoking room available. Restaurants, bar, lounge, a bit impersonal and avoid if there's a conference on but has fine ocean views.

B Premier King David Hotel, 27 Inverleith Terr, T043-722 3174, www.premierhotels. co.za. Comfortable city-centre option aimed at business travellers with 80 rooms, some more luxurious and thus more expensive, DSTV. **Motombo** restaurant serves table d'hôte dishes and a good-value Sun carvery lunch, also **East London** restaurant for coffee and light lunches, 3 bars, secure covered parking.

C Esplanade, 6 Clifford St, Beachfront, T043-722 2518. Offers 74 rooms in a family holiday-style hotel. Dated building, but completely refurbished inside, standard facilities with 2 bars and a dining room but a little dull. In a good location overlooking the beach, with undercover parking.

C Loerie Hide, 2b Sheerness Rd, Bonnie Doon, T043-735 3206, www.loeriehide.co.za. B&B (1 room) in the main house with antique bathroom. 3 thatched cottages for 2 with fridge, TV, and a safari look complete with leopard-skin bedspread, tucked away in a beautiful garden. The grounds border the Nahoon riverine forest. Swimming pool, close to the beaches, a short drive from city centre.

E-F Niki-Nana Backpackers, 4 Hillview Rd, T043-722 8509, www.nikinana.co.za. Friendly set-up with dorms, doubles and camping in the garden. Swimming pool, bar, internet, spacious self-catering kitchen, the whole place is decorated in a zebra theme, including the roof which is painted with unmissable zebra stripes. The Baz Bus stops here.

E-F Sugar Shack, Esplanade Rd, Eastern Beach, T043-722 8240, www.sugarshack.co.za. The best backpackers in East London, in a lively location by the beach. Always popular and has parties most nights. Dorms, doubles, some en suite, well-stocked kitchen, free town pickup, free surf and boogie boards, 20 m away from a whale- and dolphin-watching tower, and offers surfing lessons directly below on the beach. Ideal location with a number of local pubs and clubs within walking distance. Baz Bus stop. Recommended.

🍴 Eating

Hogsback *p406, map p407*
The main hotels include dinner in their room rate, so there is not much of a choice for eating out at night. If staying at a guesthouse, check if evening meals are available, otherwise eat at one of the hotels.

🍴 **Hogsback Inn**, Main Rd, T045-962 1006, www.hogsbackinn.co.za. 1200-1430, 1830-2030. The pub stays open later. Charming country-style restaurant and friendly pub, a good range of meals: steaks, schnitzels and the like, and good salads and vegetable dishes using locally grown produce. Worth coming here for the good value roast lunch on Sun.

🍴 **Tea Thyme**, Edge, see Sleeping, page 413. Open 0800-1700. Informal tea garden with stunning views, serving breakfasts, light lunches, home-made cakes and scones with fresh farm cream, and wholesome dinners on request. On cold days offers hot chocolate and glüwein inside, in front of the fire.

Queenstown *p408*
The usual chain restaurants are in the **Pick 'n' Pay Mall** on Cathcart St, near the tourist office.

East London p410, map p411

East London has a fair smattering of good places to eat and, thanks to the youthful edge the surfers bring to town, many places double up as restaurants during the early evening and then bars, some with live music, as the night wears on. Oddly, East London has 2 Swiss restaurants.

♥♥♥ Ernst's Chalet Suisse, Orient Beach, T043-722 1840. Mon-Fri 1200-1430, 1800-2300, Sat dinner only, Sun lunch only. Probably the best food in town, friendly and efficient service in a 30-year-old East London institution. Local fish and traditional Swiss dishes available, daytime views of the pier and harbour at Orient Beach, romantic night-time dining overlooking a floodlit tropical garden, good-value Sun lunch buffet.

♥♥♥ Le Petit, 54 Beach Rd, Nahoon, T043-735 3685. Mon-Fri 1200-1430, 1800-2230, Sat 1800-2230. A formal Swiss-themed restaurant, with Swiss and French dishes, including aged steaks, frogs' legs and South African dishes using ostrich and crocodile. À la carte or good-value 3-course set menu or cheaper meals in the pub. It's fun watching the chef prepare flambé dishes.

♥♥ Al Mare, at the aquarium complex on the Esplande, T043-722 0287. Mon-Fri 1200-1500, Mon-Sat 1800-late. With modern decor and good ocean views, it offers daily specials chalked-up on blackboards, Mediterranean-influenced dishes, pizza and pasta. For dieters, there are calorie-controlled 'skinny' options, and for non-dieters, rich and sticky desserts.

♥♥ Buccaneers, Eastern Beach, Esplanade, T043-743 5171, www.buccaneers.co.za. 1100-late. Popular pub and grill house serving steaks, seafood and salads. The mood at lunch is more business-orientated but then it gets very lively at night with live music on 2 stages, inside and out, and a thumping bar. Very popular with surfers and backpackers, on the beach close to the **Sugar Shack**.

♥♥ Grazia Fine Food & Wine, Upper Esplan-ade, Beach Front, T043-722 2009, www.grazia finefood.co.za. Tue-Sat 1200-2200. Good location with great views over Orient Beach

and a sunny patio. This offers a well-thought out menu with an Italian bias, good choice of pasta, especially for vegetarians, mains include pork fillet, lamb shank and veal, and save room for the delicious tiramisu.

♥♥ Quarterdeck, Orient Pavilion, Esplanade, T043-743 1840, Mon-Fri 1200-1430, 1800-2300, Sat 1800-2300. A busy seafood dining room and bar with German beer on tap and live music Wed, Fri and Sat. Shares a kitchen with the more upmarket **Ernst's Chalet Suisse**. Great if you're on a tight budget but want to eat well.

○ Shopping

Hogsback p406, map p407

There is a supermarket, a bottle store and a petrol station in the village (but no banks), as well as several craft shops which sell gifts and delicious locally-made jams. When you first arrive you are likely to be greeted by local Xhosas selling their crafts. Look out for the clay animals: kudu, horses and hogs are the most common. These items are not found elsewhere in South Africa.

East London p410, map p411

Vincent Park Centre, Devreux Av, 5 km from the city centre, follow Oxford St and turn right onto Devreux Av just after the museum. This is a modern South African shopping mall where you will find a full complement of shops, plus banks, post office, multi-screen cinema showing the latest blockbuster releases and restaurants. It holds an arts and crafts market every Sun 0900-1300.

▲ Activities and tours

Rhodes p409

Trout fishing is popular in the dams and rivers belonging to the Wild Trout Association, 50 farmers in the region who allow access to their land for fishing. Fly fishing can be arranged through a day-permit system run from **Walkerbouts Inn**, T045-974 9290, www.wildtrout.co.za.

East London *p410, map p411*
Cricket
The East London cricket ground, **Buffalo Park**, is South Africa's newest international venue. It is a short distance from the beach and is the smallest of the current Test Match grounds in the country, with a capacity of 28,000. It's home to local team the Border Bears. Fixture information www.borderbears.co.za, ticket sales Computicket, www.computicket.com.

Surfing
The best-known surf break is Nahoon Reef, with a reputation for having the most consistent break in the country. Easterns, in front of the Sugar Shack backpackers, is the most consistent beach break in the area, with regular tubes. The best surf information is to be found at the Sugar Shack and the other backpacker hostels, most of which will hire out surfboards and offer lessons to beginners.

Tour operators
Imonti Tours, T083-497 8975, www.imonti tours.co.za. Professional operator offering ½-day city and township tours, visits to Xhosa villages, and can also arrange tours to the Nelson Mandela National Museum at Qunu, up the N2 (see page 425).

⊖ Transport

Queenstown *p408*
Bus
Buses depart from Shell Ultra City on Cathcart St. Queenstown is on the **Johannesburg–East London** route.

Bus companies All bus tickets can be booked online at www.computicket.com. For details of bus companies, see Getting around, page 41.

Train
Queenstown is on the **Johannesburg–East London** route, Mon, Tue, Thu, Fri and Sun. Central reservations, **Shosholoza Meyl**, T0860-00888 (in South Africa), T011-774 4555 (from overseas), www.shosholoza meyl.co.za, timetables and fares are published on the website.

Witteberge Mountains *p408*
Bus
Buses depart from Balmoral Hotel, Somerset St in **Aliwal North**. Contact details for **Greyhound**, and **Translux**, same as for Queenstown, above. Aliwal North is on the **Johannesburg–East London** route.

Bus companies All bus tickets can be booked online at www.computicket.com. Greyhound, www.greyhound.co.za; Translux, www.translux.co.za. For more information, see Getting around, page 41.

East London *p410 map p411*
From East London it is 584 km to **Bloemfontein**, 1099 km to **Cape Town**, 674 km to **Durban**, 395 km to **Graaff-Reinet**, 1002 km to **Johannesburg**, 310 km to **Nelson Mandela Bay** (**PE**), 207 km to **Queenstown**, 235 km to **Mthatha**.

Air
1Time flies daily between East London and **Johannesburg** (1 hr 45 mins) and **Cape Town** (1 hr 35 mins). SAA flies daily between East London and **Durban** (1 hr 10 mins), **Johannesburg** (1 hr 45 mins), **Nelson Mandela Bay** (**PE**) (50 mins), and **Cape Town** (1 hr 35 mins).

Airline offices All air tickets can be booked online at www.computicket.com. 1Time, www.1time.aero; SAA, reservations, T011-978 1111, www.flysaa.com. For further details, see Essentials, page 40.

Bus
Baz Bus runs a hop-on, hop-off service for backpackers between **Nelson Mandela Bay** (**PE**) and **Durban**, 5 days a week. The bus

will collect and drop off at any of the local backpacker hostels. From Nelson Mandela Bay (PE) it arrives around 1100-1130 and from Durban around 1800-1830.

All the long-distance buses arrive and depart from both the railway stations and Windmill Park on Moore St. **Greyhound** and **Translux** both have services to **Durban** (9 hrs) daily via **Mthatha**, **Kokstad** and **Port Shepstone**; to **Cape Town** (14 hrs) daily via **Nelson Mandela Bay** (**PE**) and **Knysna**; and to **Johannesburg** and **Tshwane** (**Pretoria**) (14½ hrs) daily via **Bloemfontein** (7 hrs). Intercape has a service to **Cape Town** (14 hrs) via **Nelson Mandela Bay** (**PE**) (4 hrs). There is no direct service to **Johannesburg/Tshwane** (**Pretoria**) but you can change buses in Nelson Mandela Bay (PE).

Bus companies All bus tickets can be booked online at www.computicket.com. The Baz Bus, reservations T021-439 2323, www.bazbus.com; Greyhound, www.greyhound.co.za; Intercape, www.intercape.co.za; Translux, www.translux.co.za. For more information, see Getting around, page 41.

Car hire

Avis, airport T043-736 1344, www.avis.co.za; Budget, airport T043-736 2364, www.budget.co.za; Hertz, airport T043-702 5700, www.hertz.com; Tempest, airport T043-736 1320, www.tempestcarhire.co.za.

Taxi
Border Taxi, T043-722 3946.

Train
The railway station is in the town centre on Station St, which runs parallel to Oxford St. Information T043-700 2719. There are services between East London and **Johannesburg** (20 hrs), via **Queenstown** (4½ hrs) and **Bloemfontein** (13 hrs). Central reservations, Shosholoza Meyl, T0860-00888 (in South Africa), T011-774 4555 (from overseas), www.shosholozameyl.co.za, timetables and fares are published on the website.

🌐 Directory

East London *p410, map p411*
Banks Branches of **Standard Bank**, **First National** and **ABSA** have ATMs and exchange facilities along Oxford St and in the shopping malls. Get cash here, as on the Wild Coast there are no banks in small resort towns and check in advance if your chosen resort accepts credit cards. **Internet** There are a few spots around town or try **Cyber Lounge**, 58 Beach Rd, **Nahoon** or the hotels and backpacker hostels. **Medical services** East London Private Hospital, 32 Albany St, T043-722 3128.

Wild Coast

The coastline region that stretches roughly 280 km from East London to the Umtamvuna Nature Reserve next to Port Edward in KwaZulu Natal was once the former Transkei independent homeland during the Apartheid years. These days it is known as the Wild Coast and is a largely rural area of rolling grasslands wedged between the Great Kei River in the south and the Umtamvuna River in the north. Its inland borders are the Drakensberg and the Stormberg mountains, and dotted between are small villages, brightly painted kraals and endless communal pastureland. It remains a traditional area populated by the Xhosa, who still practise customs such as dowry payments and initiation ceremonies. The Great Kei River was originally the border between South Africa and the Transkei and, as the N2 crosses the Kei River 65 km north of East London, the difference in the standard of living between the two areas is striking. Years of overpopulation and under-investment have taken their toll in the former Transkei. The landscape is deforested and seriously eroded and, away from the N2, and the roads leading to the resorts, the roads are in poor condition compared to the rest of the country. There are few tourist amenities here and you will get a more realistic picture of the poverty that still blights South Africa. Nevertheless it is a beautiful region and the coastline itself is rugged and peaceful, with a number of caves, beaches, cliffs and shipwrecks to explore. ▸▸ *For listings, see pages 427-432.*

Ins and outs

Getting there and around The N2, the Wild Coast's main road, is well surfaced. However, it doesn't run along the coast but rather from East London up to 100 km inland until it meets the coast again at Port Shepstone in KwaZulu Natal, from where it heads north to Durban. The towns along the N2 have thriving economies based around transport. There are abundant petrol stations, basic supermarkets and one or two small hotels, but these are mainly for commercial clientele so there are very few frills. Consequently the towns along the N2 are utilitarian and scruffy and always thronged with traffic. The long-distance buses stick to the N2, and the **Baz Bus** only deviates to Port St Johns. The coast itself is the area's main attraction and there is a fine selection of isolated seaside accommodation between East London and Port St Johns. A number of roads lead from the N2 to the coastal resorts, often by way of ramshackle villages, and although there has been a lot of road resurfacing going on in the Eastern Cape in the last few years, many of these are gravel. If driving, it is always a good idea to check on the latest state of the road, as the region is prone to seasonal flooding. **Note** Before heading for the coast from the N2, remember to stock up on petrol, food, cash and everything you think you will need – the nearest shop or bank could be 100 km away.

Tourist information Arriving at a resort without a reservation is not a good idea as they are often at the end of long and difficult roads. Remember most resorts are fully booked during the holiday season. All towns along the N2 have public telephones, so even with a last-minute decision it is possible to phone ahead and check on the condition of the road. For more information visit www.wildcoast.co.za.

    Wild Coast Holiday Reservations ⓘ *T043-743 6181, www.wildcoastholidays.co.za*, is an excellent central reservations service that can advise on and book accommodation and hiking trails along the coast. This can be very useful when trying to find out about some of the more remote hotels. An excellent way of seeing the most inaccessible areas of the Wild Coast is by doing a tour of the rural regions. ▸▸ *For further details, see Activities and tours, page 432.*

Wild Coast

To Durban

Oribi Gorge
Nature Reserve

Port Shepstone

To Ixopo & Pietermaritzburg

R56

KWAZULU NATAL

Harding

Mtamvuna

Franklin

To Underberg &
Sani Pass
(Lesotho)

Mount
Currie
Nature Reserve

Kokstad

N2

Brooks Nek

Port Edward

R61

Bizana

Magusheni

Amadiba Trails

Mkambati
Nature Reserve

Mt Ayliff

Mzimvubu

Mzimhlava

Flagstaff

Msikaba

Port Grosvenor
Grosvenor
1782

To Qacha's Neck & Lesotho

Mt Frere

R61

Lusikisiki

Embotyi

Tina

Qumbu

Mzimvubu

Port St Johns

Tsolo

Libode

Silaka Nature Reserve

Tsitsa

R396

Mpande

Inxu

Mtata
Dam

Nelson Mandela
National Museum

Mthatha

Coffee Bay

Hole in the Wall

Viedgesville

Santo Alberto
1593

Mqanduli
Qunu

Nelson Mandela
Youth &
Heritage Centre

Ngqungqu

Elliotdale

Coghlan

R61

Alderley

R393

Engcobo

Xuka

Mbashe River Mouth

Mbashe

N2

Dutywa

Frontier III
1939

Willowvale

Qhorha Mouth

Mazeppa Bay

R364

Nxaxo Mouth

Jacaranda
1971

Tsomo

Gcuwa
(Butterworth)

Centane

Qholorha Mouth

R366

Kei Mouth

Cofimvaba

R61

Kei Mouth
Strandloper Trail

Morgan's Bay

To Queenstown &
Bloemfontein (N6)

Komga

R349

Nyara
Forest

Haga-Haga

Mooiplaas

R63

Inkwenkwezi
Game Reserve

Cefane Mouth

To Bisho (R63)

To East London

Chintsa

20 km
20 miles

The coast immediately to the north of East London has been named the 'Romantic Coast' by the local tourist board, and its relative wildness makes the statement ring true. Although the coast is being developed for tourism there are still considerable stretches of the coastline which are protected nature reserves. There are thick dune forests and windswept open beaches stretching to wild waves. The coastal resorts nearest to East London can get crowded during the South African school holidays, but for the rest of the year it is quite surprising how isolated and quiet this coast really is. **Note** Do not drive through the former Transkei (roughly East London to Port Shepstone) after nightfall. Some of the roads are rough and even on the N2 there is the danger of hitting a stray animal.

Ins and outs

Getting around The resorts of Gonubie, Chintsa, Haga-Haga, Morgan's Bay and Kei Mouth are all within an hour's drive of East London. Public transport to these resorts is virtually non-existent, but as the hoteliers on the coast regularly visit East London to collect supplies, you can often get a lift to the coast by telephoning ahead. The **East Coast Shuttle** ① *T043-740 3060*, runs a service from East London to the coastal resorts as far as Kobb Inn but requires a minimum of six passengers.

Gonubie → *Colour map 7, B6.*

This tourist resort overlooks the Qunube (Gonubie) River and the lagoon. It is only 20 km northeast of East London and 8 km off the N2 and has become a popular suburb with commuters. The beach here has large dunes, is safe for swimming in the sea and in the tidal pool, and it's possible to spot dolphins and whales from the 500-m boardwalk overlooking the beach. For information visit www.gonubieinfo.com.

Kwelera Nature Reserve lies 10 km to the north of Gonubie and is an area of sand dunes and dune forest facing the sea. The highest dune here rises just over 250 m above sea level. The forests are inhabited by vervet monkeys, bushbuck and numerous forest birds. There is a small picnic site which is popular with local visitors who come here to fish and surf. This nature reserve is part of the Strandloper Trail, see page 423.

Inkwenkwezi Game Reserve

① *T043-734 3234, www.inkwenkwezi.com. 33 km from East London, take the N2 towards Mthatha and after 25 km out of East London, turn right at the Inkwenkwezi/Chintsa signpost, the reserve is 8 km on the right.*

This private 100-sq-km coastal game reserve has a combination of forest dunes and bushveld, and is home to an impressive range of imported game, including rhino, elephant, lion, wildebeest, giraffe, warthog, Eastern Cape kudu and an abundance of birdlife. The best time of year for spotting birds is from September to November; the wild flowers are best from August to September. Visitors leave their cars at the entrance and are transported around the reserve by 4WD. A range of trips can be organized, including night drives, horse riding, mountain and quad-biking, and walking trails. Day visitors can expect to pay around R600 for a four-hour game drive with lunch, and R700 for a four-hour night drive with dinner. Meals are served in a restaurant with a terrace overlooking the reserve and accommodation is available (see Sleeping, page 427). New to the reserve is the elephant experience when guests get to interact with two tame elephants (one hour costs R125) or ride them (a one-hour ride is R500).

Chintsa → *Colour map 7, B6.*

The combined villages of Chintsa East and Chintsa West nestle on lush hills rolling down to a lagoon and a wide stretch of deserted beach. (It takes about 10 minutes to walk from Chintsa West to Chintsa East along the beach, but nearly 30 minutes to drive between them around the lagoon.) Although popular during the Christmas holidays, the resort is blessedly isolated for the rest of the year and offers relaxing outdoor activities such as canoeing and horse riding, though the main appeal here is lazily exploring the shell-strewn beach, forests and tranquil lagoon. Construction of the large Chintsa River Golfing Estate on the west bank is underway and the project is to include an 18-hole golf course, 650 holiday/time-share homes and a large hotel. Time will tell how it will change the face of this peaceful coastal settlement.

Haga-Haga → *Colour map 7, A6.*

Further along the coast lies this tiny seaside resort, 72 km from East London and 27 km from the N2. The road travels through fields of pineapples. There are two theories on how this resort got its name. One is that it is derived from the sound the waves make as they wash the shoreline. The other is that the village was started in the early 1920s when farmers from the hinterland would bring their livestock here for winter grazing, the smaller animals by ox wagon. To cross the beach they would unspan one team of oxen and hook them onto the other team, hence the word *haka haka* which is isiXhosa for 'hook on'. The rocky coastline, good beaches and lagoon where you can swim, make it ideal for hiking and fishing and, with only one shop and a hotel, this is a peaceful spot to spend a few days and lose track of time.

Morgan's Bay → *Colour map 7, A6.*

This is a perfect resort, 90 km from East London, for a peaceful beach break and a taste of the Wild Coast. The village itself is tiny and somewhat isolated and has little more than a couple of resorts and campsites, the local store, a bottle shop, a couple of curio shops and a petrol pump. The surrounding countryside is a nature reserve and is a great place for hiking along the cliffs or strolling along the miles of white sandy beach where deep currents wash up unusual shells. The bay is regarded as one of the most beautiful in the country. Called Double Mouth, it consists of a lagoon formed by two small rivers backed by a line of sandstone cliffs. The beach with a lighthouse was voted one of the top 10 beach walks of South Africa by the South African outdoor magazine *Getaway*.

Kei Mouth → *Colour map 7, A6.*

This quiet seaside resort has a collection of shops, a petrol station, a couple of resorts and a clutch of holiday homes.

The **Kei River** used to be the border between the two former homelands of Ciskei and Transkei, now all part of the Eastern Cape. The river is navigable upstream for a short distance by boat or canoe, although sandbanks make it difficult at times. A popular river trip is to **Picnic Rock**, about 8 km upstream. The journey passes a private game reserve where it is possible to spot game. The cliffs around **Cob Hole** on the eastern side of the river are quite dramatic and the patches of forest further on are rich in birdlife. There is a spot on the eastern bank of the river with a small creek and a landing stage. The path from here climbs up a riverbed through forest and at the end of the trail is a deep pool with two waterfalls where you can swim – this is Picnic Rock.

Strandloper Trail

The term Strandloper derives from the Dutch *strand*, meaning beach, and *loper*, meaning walker. This is a popular five-day, 55-km hike along the coast from Kei Mouth to Gonubie, over-nighting in huts. It's an ideal walk for anyone looking for a peaceful but energetic few days along the coast and the trail passes through Kwelera Nature Reserve so there is a good chance of seeing some wildlife.

The trail runs in one direction and starts at the manager's station at Cape Morgan at Kei Mouth where you are issued with a permit. The trail is clearly marked with painted yellow footprints and can be walked at any time of year, though the best weather is between February and May, which have warm windless days. Hikers are issued with a tide table to assist in crossing the Quko, Kwenxura, Kwelera and Gonubie rivers.

You need to take strong watertight bags and rope in your pack.

The four huts along the trail; Beacon Valley, Cape Henderson, Pumphouse and Double Mouth, have water and ablution facilities. All have braai places except Cape Henderson, which is in a state forest and no fires are permitted. Take all necessary equipment. The huts are included in the cost of the trail, but there's the option to upgrade and stay in resorts at Morgan's Bay and Haga-Haga, or at the backpacker hostel in Chintsa.

The trail is limited to 12 people and costs R400 per person. It is managed by the **Strandloper Ecotourism Board**, T043-841 1046, www.strandloper trails.org.za, bookings can be made online. There are several other hikes along the Wild Coast, www.wildcoastwalk.co.za for information.

North from Kei Mouth ● ⟫ *pp427-432.*

There are two possible routes leading on from Kei Mouth. The Pont is a **car ferry** ① *0630-1730, R30 per car*, which crosses the Kei River. After crossing on the Pont, the R366 heads uphill for 9 km where it joins the R48/1 at Centane. The road then divides, heading inland to Gcuwa (Butterworth) or seawards to Qholorha Mouth.

Centane

Centane itself is a tiny settlement but it has a huge history. It was the site of the final battle of the Frontier Wars between the Xhosa and the settlers in 1878. The Xhosa warriors had been told by their witch doctor that he had made them impervious to bullets. Therefore they stormed a fort of colonial troops but were mown down by heavy fire. Three hundred warriors died, with a loss of only two of the English forces.

Gcuwa (Butterworth) → *Colour map 7, A6.*

Recently renamed with a Xhosa name, this is the first town that the N2 passes on its way through the old Transkei. It is a hectic and unappealing stretch of supermarkets and discount stores, and has little to keep you there for long. Founded as a Wesleyan mission station in 1827, it is the oldest town in the Transkei, although little of its history is evident today. At the end of the Frontier Wars in 1878, traders began to settle here and the town has grown to become a small industrial centre. Just outside of town, there is one attraction worth stopping for: the **Bawa Falls** on the Qholorha River are spectacular after the rains when the water drops over 100 m. From Gcuwa (Butterworth), the N2 continues north to Mthatha, 135 km.

Qholorha Mouth → *Colour map 7, A6.*

Qholorha Mouth has a private airstrip and is accessible by light aircraft. The alternative is to travel the 16 km from the Pont over the Kei River or come directly from Gcuwa (Butterworth). There are two holiday resorts here on a beautiful stretch of headland overlooking a spacious beach and the Qholorha Lagoon where the Qholorha River widens before spilling into the sea. There is a hike up the **Gxara River Heads**, 4 km inland, to the pool where Nongqawuse, a young Xhosa girl, saw visions and communed with her ancestral spirits. She heard voices telling her that the dead would rise and destroy the European invaders if the Xhosa destroyed all their cattle and crops. This disastrous prophesy lead to the deaths of thousands of people through starvation, and Nongqawuse had to spend the rest of her life in hiding. She is buried on a farm near Alexandria.

Nxaxo Mouth → *Colour map 4, C5.*

The road heading north from Centane goes to the one resort at Nxaxo Mouth, which lies at the confluence of the Nxaxo and Nqusi rivers. The area has a lagoon and is dotted with swamps and islands. The estuary is rich in birdlife and there are hiking trails through a small strip of coastal forest to a colony of crowned cranes. Listen for the distinctive calls of groups of trumpeter hornbills which inhabit the forest.

Mazeppa Bay → *Colour map 4, C5.*

This small holiday resort is named after the *Mazeppa*, a coastal trading ship that ran aground here in 1842 on its way from Port Natal. There is a suspension footbridge to the island from where you can see Clan Lindsay Rocks, the site where the *Clan Lindsay* was wrecked in 1898. **First Beach** is good for swimming, and the waves on this stretch of coast attract local surfers. Just back from the beach are the shell middens left by strandlopers. August is a busy month when many people come here for the shark fishing. The nearby **Manubi Forest** has 7 km of trails passing through patches of yellowwood and sneezewood trees. A 4-km hike north along the coast leads to the grounded wreck of the *Jacaranda*, a 2000-ton Greek ship that ran aground in 1971.

Qhorha Mouth → *Colour map 4, C5.*

The N2 highway continues north from Gcuwa (Butterworth) until it reaches Dutywa. There is a turning at Dutywa to Willowvale, 32 km, from where there is a road which passes the village of Nyokana and leads to Qhorha Mouth, 66 km from Dutywa. This road is tarred as far as Willowvale. Despite what some maps say, there is no road from Mazeppa to Qhorha Mouth. To get between the two, you have to go via the N2. Qhorha Mouth is a small collection of houses, hardly large enough to be called a village, and is known for its kob fishing. The rivermouth here marks the ecological boundary between the sundu palms whose habitat lies to the south of the river and are characteristic to KwaZulu Natal, and the lala palms which only grow to the north. At the mouth of the river is a lagoon and a fine swathe of beach.

Coffee Bay → *Colour map 4, C6.*

There are some very rough tracks further north from Qhorha Mouth to Coffee Bay which are only suitable for a 4WD. Instead you'll need to go back to Dutywa on the N2, and 67 km towards Mthatha, take the right turn on to a tarred road and its 75 kilometres to Coffee Bay. At the mouth of the Nenga River, Coffee Bay is well known for its good surf, making it a major stop on many backpacker routes. Nevertheless, development has been low key and it remains a quiet and laid-back place. The name Coffee Bay comes from the coffee trees which grew here briefly in the 1860s after a ship ran aground with a cargo of coffee beans. The **Hole In The Wall** is a famous natural feature and well worth a visit. An enormous tunnel has been eroded by the sea through a cliff which lies just offshore. The local Xhosa call it *izi Khaleni*, which means 'place of thunder'. At high tide the sound of the waves clapping can be heard throughout the valley. A small holiday resort has sprung up by the beach here.

Mthatha ⊜⊜⊜ ▶▶ pp427-432. Colour map 4, C5.

It is believed that a clan of the Tembu tribe had a custom interring their dead by casting them into the river with the entreaty '*mThate Bawo*' (Take him, Father) and that this was the origin of the name of the river on which Mthatha was founded. Today Mthatha is an impoverished, sprawling, unattractive modern town full of cheap supermarkets and discount liquor stores with a small grid of historical buildings at its core. Founded in 1871, it was the capital of Transkei from 1976 to 1994 and has grown to be a busy administrative centre. The N2 passes through the city centre where some of the oldest buildings are located, including the City Hall built in 1908 and the Bhunga (parliament) Building dating from 1927. The latter is now home to the **Nelson Mandela National Museum**, the town's only sight, but definitely worth a stop for an understanding of how homelands such as the Transkei were created under the Apartheid system, and to learn more about the man.

Sights

The former site of the Transkei parliament, is the **Nelson Mandela National Museum** ⓘ *Bhunga Building, Owen St, T047-532 5110, www.nelsonmandelamuseum.org.za, Mon-Fri 0900-1600, Sat 0900-1230, free.* It was officially opened by the great man himself on 11 February 2000, to coincide with the 10th anniversary of his release from prison. The displays provide a moving insight into Mandela's life and his struggle against Apartheid, focusing on his autobiography, *Long Walk to Freedom*. There are extracts of the book complemented by photography, personal items, letters and video footage, including a short excerpt from a rare interview he gave in 1961 before being imprisoned. Other displays include international awards and honorary degrees that he received, portraits and sculptures of him and diplomatic gifts he received during his term of office. There's even a boxing glove signed by Mohammed Ali and George Foreman (Mandela used to box in his youth).

Other components of the museum are Mandela's primary school and birthplace. The **school** consists of two rondavels and a hut in the tiny rural village of **Qunu**, where Mandela lived as a youth. The graves of his parents and his son and daughter are also here, along with his new house, which can be photographed from the outside but not visited. Today the rondavels form the **Nelson Mandela Youth and Heritage Centre**. Mandela's **birthplace** at the former Transkei village of **Mvezo** is on the other side of the N2. There are remains of the homestead where he was born and some photographs on display, including one of Mandela burning his pass book. The staff at Mthatha are very enthusiastic about the museum and are happy to answer questions. If you don't have your own transport, they will also arrange a tour from Mthatha to Qunu and Mvezo, a short drive south on the N2. A recommended experience.

Port St Johns ⊜⊘ ▶▶ pp427-432. Colour map 4, C6.

This small, peaceful coastal town is 94 km east of Mthatha on a tarred road and lies on the banks of the Mzimvubu River. It has a laid-back atmosphere which may have something to do

isiXhosa

Most of the Eastern Cape is populated by the Xhosa and the predominant language is isiXhosa. In the Wild Coast region, the former Transkei homeland during the Apartheid years, isiXhosa is spoken by approximately 7.9 million people, about 18% of the South African population. Several letters of the language are represented by a click and even the word *isiXhosa* has a click in it. There are three main clicks; the first is the dental click, which is made with the tongue on the back of the teeth, the second is the lateral alveolar click, which is made by the tongue at the sides of the mouth, and the third is the postalveolar click, which is made with the body of the tongue on the roof of the mouth.

The spelling of place names in South Africa, especially in the more remote areas, can sometimes be inconsistent. Place names are derived from so many languages, which then have often become corrupted or Anglicized. It is not unusual to find the same place having slight variations in spelling in different books or maps and on signposts. Also, in the Eastern Cape some places have reverted to their isiXhosa spellings, though this may take a while to reflect on road signs and maps. Cintsa is now spelt Chintsa, Qolora Mouth and Qolora River is now Qholorha, Qora is now Qhorha, and Umtata is now spelt Mthatha. While on the Wild Coast, and especially off the beaten track, you will invariably encounter the Xhosa people. They will be most delighted if you try out a few words of isiXhosa.

English	isiXhosa
Hello	Molo
Good morning	Intsasa emnandi
Good night	Ubusuku obumnandi
How are you?	Unjani?
Good-bye	Sala kakuhle
Please	Enkosi
Thank you	Enkosi kakhulu
Yes	Ewe
No	Hayi

with it being a major cannabis-growing area. Its bohemian feel has attracted many artists and, more recently, backpackers. Consequently, there's a good selection of budget accommodation here, much of which is self-catering. There aren't many restaurants but local produce such as papaya, avocado pears, pecans, macadamia nuts and fresh fish is sold on the beach.

Portuguese ships stopped here to pick up water on their journeys up the coast and the town itself is named after the *São João*, which was wrecked here in 1552. A trading post was built in 1846, and in 1878 the British established a military outpost here and built Fort Harrison. When the Transkei was an independent homeland, much of Port St John's 'green gold' (cannabis) was sent to the gold mines of Johannesburg.

First Beach is at the mouth of the Mzimvubu River but swimming is not advised as there is the threat of sharks which are attracted to the calmer waters of the estuary. **Second Beach** is the most attractive beach: a beautiful stretch of soft sand, backed by smooth, forested hills. It is safe for swimming as it has a very gentle slope, and there are lifeguards present. As a pleasant contrast to most beaches visited by tourists, the majority of sunbathers and swimmers here are black. There are two nature reserves within easy reach of town: Silaka (see below) and **Mount Thesiger**, which has a small herd of wildebeest belonging to an unusual sub-species which has no mane. The warm, sulphurous springs at **Isinuka** are just outside town.

The **tourist office** ① *T047-564 1187, www.portstjohns.org.za, Mon-Fri 0830-1600, Sat 0900-1300*, is on Town Entrance Square, just to the right as you enter the town.

Silaka Nature Reserve → *Colour map 4, C6.*

ⓘ *Open to day visitors 0600-1800. For overnight stays, see Sleeping, page 431.*

This reserve is on a gravel road 6 km south from Port St Johns and lies in a forested valley that stretches from Second Beach to Sugarloaf Rock. Although the reserve is small, the tropical atmosphere of the trails weaving through the tangle of thick forest is unmissable. Blesbuck, blue wildebeest and Burchell's zebra have been reintroduced. There is a beautiful stretch of rugged coastline and just off the beach is Bird Island, a breeding colony for sea birds. Interesting rock pools occur on the shore surrounding the island, which may be reached at low tide. At the estuary opposite Bird Island, an attractive pebble beach is surrounded by driftwood and aloes, which grow almost to the sea.

North to Port Edward and Durban ⊜▲▲ ⇢ *pp427-432.*

Mkambati Nature Reserve → *Colour map 5, C1.*

ⓘ *Sunrise to sunset, for overnight stays see Sleeping, page 431.*

The coastal reserve covers an area of 8000 ha between the Msikaba and Mtentu rivers. The grasslands here are known for their gladioli, ground orchids and watsonias. Large numbers of grazing herbivores such as eland, red hartebeest, blue wildebeest, blesbuck and gemsbok, have been introduced into the reserve, although only the first two species are indigenous to the area. Of the many streams running through the reserve, the Mkambati is perhaps the most beautiful with its crystal-clear pools and series of spectacular waterfalls, the impressive **Horseshoe Falls** drop down several metres into the ocean. The forested ravines along the Msikaba River are lined with thick riverine forest and the unique Pondo coconut or Mkambati palm. This is the only place in the world where it grows. Cape vultures nest on the cliffs above the Msikaba River gorge. Gurney's sugarbird, the greater double collared sunbird, the red-shouldered widow and many other woodland birds can be seen here. Canoe trips, horse riding and hiking are the best way to see this area of forested ravines and coastal grasslands.

The reserve lies on the coast and is accessed off the R61 between Port St Johns and Port Edward. The road from Port St Johns passes through the villages of Lusikisiki, Flagstaff and Holy Cross. There are plans to surface the road to Mkambati, but until that happens it is best to do the journey in a 4WD.

◉ Wild Coast listings

For Sleeping and Eating price codes and other relevant information, see pages 46-53.

⊜ Sleeping

Gonubie *p421*
C-F PSA Holiday Resort, Quenera Rd, T043-732 1022, www.psaresort.co.za. 105 caravan and camping sites set in forested dunes full of birds, a few mins' walk from the beach. Ablution blocks and kitchen units, 5 fully equipped self-catering chalets that offer a bit more than the usual caravan park chalets with cushions, tablecloths and TV.

Overlooking the Quenera rivermouth, pool. To be avoided during school holidays and long weekends but quiet at other times.
D Amanda's B&B, 2 Hart St, T043-740 4691, daphneb@mweb.co.za. 5 luxury sea-facing en suite rooms with floor-to-ceiling windows and spacious balcony or terrace. Bright white decor, fresh flowers, swimming pool, braai, modern set-up overlooking the beach.

Inkwenkwezi Game Reserve *p421*
Private lodges and camps
L1-L2 Inkwenkwezi Tented Camp, T043-734 3234, www.inkwenkwezi.com. Luxury

tents or chalets, some with fireplaces and fridges, bathrooms set in a cave-like environment with showers to look and feel like a waterfall, rates include meals and game drives. The **Emthombeni** restaurant and bar serves Eastern Cape cuisine overlooking the valley.

Chintsa *p422*

B Cintsa Lodge, 684 Fish Eagle Drive, Chintsa East, T043-738 5146, www.cintsalodge.com. Attractive, modern complex with picture windows, smart pool, terraces, balconies with ocean views and private walkway to the beach. 5 bright and spacious doubles in the main house, 2 family chalets in the gardens. DSTV, breakfast included, dinner on request.

D-F Buccaneer's Backpackers, Chintsa East, T043-734 3012, www.cintsa.com. Superb backpacker lodge set in forests overlooking the lagoon and beach. A 2-km dirt track leads to the secluded site, with a choice of dorms, doubles, fully equipped self-catering cottages and camping on platforms beneath trees. There is a lively bar, pool, kitchen, volleyball court, climbing wall, horse riding on the beach, beauty treatments and massages, free canoes and surfboards, excellent home-cooked evening meals and free daily activities. Also home to **African Heartland Journeys**, an ecotourism initiative for exploring the Wild Coast (see Activities and tours, page 432). Very relaxing spot in a beautiful setting and well run. Baz Bus stop. Recommended.

Haga-Haga *p422*

B-C Haga-Haga Hotel and Cabanas, 155 Mariner's Way, T043-841 1670, www.haga hagahotel.co.za. A large family-run complex situated on a rocky headland, with 15 twin or double hotel rooms and 30 self-catering cabanas sleeping 4. Seafood restaurant, bar with pub grub, TV lounge, swimming pool, tennis, fishing, safe tidal pools. Good rates are for full board. A recommended family option.

Morgan's Bay *p422*

B Morgan's Bay Hotel, Beach Rd, T043-841 1062, morgansbay@telkomsa.net. This is a family-run hotel which markets itself as an affordable family resort, great if you are travelling with kids. It was voted one of the top 10 family holidays by the South African outdoor magazine *Getaway*. There are 33 good-value rooms; prices vary with the tourist season but the service maintains its high standard throughout the year and off-season is excellent value. Swimming pool, views across the bay, gardens which extend down to the beach. Inside there is a comfortable lounge, a quiet reading room, a dining room with an extensive breakfast buffet and an à la carte menu in the evenings, both inclusive in the rates. Travellers with children have the option of a separate dining room and child minders. There is also a caravan and camping park with 31 sites.

C-D Mitford Lodge, follow the beach road past the **Morgan's Bay Hotel**, T043-841 1510, www.morgansbay.co.za. Excellent choice of comfortable en suite rooms and self-catering chalets, sleeping 2-6, to suit most budgets. The **Krans Kombuis Bar and Restaurant** offers home-cooked meals, speciality burgers and seafood, pub, outside deck and internet access.

F Yellowwood Forest Campsite, in forest above the village, follow the track next to the river for 1 km, T043-841 1598, www.yellow woodforest.co.za. Lovely forest environment, though a 1 km walk to the beach, with shady grassy sited under enormous trees full of birdlife. Can hire tents and there are a couple of beds in the loft above the curio shop. Rock and thatch ablution blocks, daytime tea garden with pizza oven, if you're not self-catering you can go to the other hotels for dinner. Children's playground and rabbits, ducks and dogs wander around.

Kei Mouth *p422*

There is a large resort here, the former **Kei Bay Hotel**, which is presently being refurbished into a time-share resort, so it remains to be seen if it will offer hotel accommodation.

C Thatches, T043-841 1102, www.thethat ches.co.za. 10 well-equipped self-catering thatched chalets with TV, braai and patio, sleeping 4-6, some with a/c, bring own towels. Communal lapa next to the pool, pleasant gardens dotted with palms, short stroll to the beach.

Qholorha Mouth p424

B Seagulls Beach Hotel, T047-498 0044, www.seagullshotel.co.za. Beachfront hotel with 29 double rooms with en suite bathroom, TV, private patio, some with sea views, and direct access to sandy beach. The rooms are in small, single-storey units dotted around the grounds with swimming pool. The **Anchor Inn** is a bar, restaurant and disco in season. Guests can enjoy canoeing, windsurfing and fishing in the nearby lagoon. Rates are inclusive of breakfast and dinner, or ask about 7-day packages.

B Trennery's, T047-498 0004, www.trennerys.co.za. 45 thatched chalets set in large shady gardens full of mature trees. Seafood restaurant, pool, canoeing, golf, boating, tennis, fishing, bowls, snooker table and a small shop. Excellent value given that breakfast and dinner are included in the rates and there are good-value weekly specials. An all-round holiday resort in one of the finest settings along this stretch of coast. Recommended.

Nxaxo Mouth p424

B Wavecrest, T047-498 0022, www.wavecrest.co.za. An excellent family resort in a beautiful setting on the edge of a lagoon, with 35 thatched bungalows, bar, seafood restaurant, tennis, watersports, deep-sea fishing, spa with steam rooms and jacuzzi, and private airstrip. Off-season full-board packages start from around R520 per person, good value, recommended.

Mazeppa Bay p424

B Mazeppa Bay Hotel, T047-498 0033, www.mazeppabay.co.za. Accommodation is a mix of doubles, family rooms and rondavels, all with sea views and private surrounds. The central building has a restaurant (the **Red Blanket** bar, which serves snacks), a TV lounge,

snooker table and terrace. The whole complex sits on a green ridge covered with tropical vegetation, overlooking a broad sandy beach. Also prides itself on having its own island, accessible by an ancient swing bridge. Anglers have a choice of rock, lagoon or river fishing and tackle can be hired. Again, good value and 3 meals a day are included in the rates.

Qhorha Mouth p424

B Kob Inn, T047-499 0011, www.kobinn.co.za. Isolated, comfortable hotel set on rocks above the sea. Accommodation is in 10 thatched cottages with 1 or 2 bedrooms and en suite bathroom. There is a restaurant specializing in seafood, and a bar. The swimming pool is perched on rocks overlooking the ocean, and the extensive gardens are surrounded by coastal forest. There are a couple of shady beaches nearby, plus the Qhorha River which is ideal for canoeing. Deep-sea fishing trips can be organized from the hotel. Substantial discounts for children under 10.

Coffee Bay p424

All accommodation is well-signposted when you arrive in the village.

B Ocean View Hotel, perched on a headland above the main beach, T047-575 2005, www.oceanview.co.za. Comfortable set-up, 29 double rooms with terraces and sun loungers, 50 m from the beach. Swimming pool, kid's activities, bar, restaurant, rates include breakfast and dinner. Golf and horse riding nearby, deep-sea fishing charters. Trips can be arranged to a traditional Xhosa village.

B-E Hole In The Wall Hotel and Holiday Village, 8 km south of the village, T047-575 0009, www.holeinthewall.co.za. Set by the beach, this large resort has a selection of accommodation to suit all budgets, 26 en suite double rooms in garden thatched rondavels, 28 self-catering white-washed units with 2 bedrooms sleeping up to 8, ten campsites, a backpacker lodge with 9 cheaper doubles and 3 dorms further up the hill (backpackers/campers can use hotel facilities). Swimming pool, bar, restaurant, pool tables, volleyball court, TV lounge, nightly seafood braais. A good all-round option on the Wild Coast and can organize plenty of activities.

D-F The Coffee Shack, on the beach next to the river estuary, T047-575 2048, www.coffee shack.co.za. Daily shuttle to Shell Ultra City in Mthatha to hook up with the mainline buses and Baz Bus. Popular party place set right on the beach. Mix of dorms and doubles, some en suite, in thatched rondavels. Camping, good kitchen facilities. **Bablaza** pub which gets very noisy at night, offers great seafood, African suppers and big breakfasts. Plenty of activities on offer, free surfing lessons. Great spot for a couple of wild days by the beach. Recommended.

E-F Bomvu Paradise, on the main beach, T047-575 2073, www.bomvubackpackers. com. Another party lodge set in tropical gardens with decks and hammocks. There are dorms, double rooms and campsites, and a restaurant and a bar. Be wary of the space cakes. An alternative place, with yoga lessons, drum sessions, monthly full-moon parties, Xhosa song and dance performances, and a strong emphasis on surfing. Again will pick up from buses in Mthatha.

Mthatha *p425*

It is far preferable to stay in Coffee Bay or Port St Johns and visit Mthatha when passing. There is no backpacker accommodation here and the centre is not particularly safe both during the day and at night.

B-C Garden Court Mthatha 3 km north on the N2, T047-537 0181, www.southersun.com. Part of the **Holiday Inn** chain. Bland block but really the only option in town. 117 a/c rooms, TV, Wi-Fi, pool, restaurant serving reasonable buffets, bar, slot machines and secure parking. Comfortable but unremarkable.

Port St Johns *p425*

Backpackers will find plenty of accommo-dation and things to do here, and the principle upmarket resort offers excellent facilities.

A Umngazi River Bungalows and Spa, about 25 km west of the town, off the R61 back towards Mthatha, T047-564 1115, www.umn gazi.co.za. Thatched luxury bungalows facing the estuary surrounded by mangrove forest. Restaurant, bar (dine in the wine cellar), shop and pool. Wide range of watersports, including sunset cruises up the river and night fishing. Conference centre, beauty spa, fly-in packages. Award-winning resort, good value for families, full-board rates. Check out the website for off-season 3 night specials.

B Lily's Lodge, Second Beach T047-564 1229, www.lilylodge.info. 30 simple but adequate rooms in brick chalets with DSTV, a/c, nestled among trees full of birds and monkeys, a short stroll to the beach. Rates include break-fast and dinner, so good value and excellent country-style food and seafood, and a varied selection of wine. The owner's husband is Irish, so Jameson Irish coffees are on offer and there's a St Patrick's Day party here each year.

C The Spotted Grunter Resort, off the R61, 3 km from the town centre by the river, T047-564 1279, www.spottedgrunter.co.za. A small, peaceful resort with attractive timber cabins with TV, kitchenette and braais, sleeping 4-6. Set in beautiful gardens with swimming pool on a bank of the Umzimvuba River, full of avocado and lychee trees where the rare Cape parrot feeds. If you don't want to cook, all meals are available from the **Angler's Arms**. A good location for a few relaxing days, and the owners can organize fishing (it's named after a fish). Recommended.

C-D Outspan Inn, Main Rd, T047-564 1057, www.outspaninn.co.za. A local favourite with 10 double B&B rooms, plus 4 self-catering units set in sub-tropical gardens full of birds at the mouth of the Umzimvuba River. Restaurant, pub, TV room and swimming pool. Reception also act as an unofficial local information centre.

D-F Ikaya Le Intlabati, Second Beach, T047-564 1266, www.portstjohns.com/houseon thebeach. A fine, small guesthouse-cum-backpackers, one of the last places at the end of the dirt road on Second Beach. The building is surrounded by tropical indigenous bush and the gardens extend down to the beach.

A mix of singles, doubles and triples, 1 cottage sleeping 4 and camping. Self-catering or meals, pre-book a pickup from Mthatha. Next door is a hand-dyed clothing workshop – **Jakotz Clothing**. Worth a visit if you're spending some time in PSJ. Secure parking.

D-F Jungle Monkey and Island Backpackers, 340-1 Berea Rd, First Beach, T047-564 1517, www.junglemonkey.co.za. A mixture of accommodation here, including double en suite wooden log cabins, doubles, triples and safari tents with shared bathrooms, dorms and camping. There's a bar, restaurant with pizza oven, TV room, bright murals and rambling garden with hammocks and swings, pool with wooden deck. Arranges plenty of activities, including a 5-km cliff top walk through Xhosa villages.

E-F The Kraal, Mpande, head out from Port St Johns on the R61, after 20 km turn left for 20 km, which takes you back to the coast; alternatively the turn off is 80 km from Mthatha, T082-871 4964, www.thekraal-backpackers.co.za. The last 20 km to the Kraal is on a bad dirt road, but is well worth the trip. Set on an isolated hill above a beach and lagoon, the lodge is made up of 3 traditional Xhosa rondavels with dirt floors, no electricity and 'eco-loos'. Accommodation is in dorms, or there is space for camping. Communal kitchen (bring all food with you), or pre-book the superb meals like crayfish or T-bone steaks. Hot showers and wonderful views over the sea. The Kraal built the local school which often needs volunteer teachers, call them if you're interested. A genuine retreat and perfect for experiencing village life in the old Transkei. Recommended.

Silaka Nature Reserve *p427*
Reservations are made through Eastern Cape Parks, T043-742 4450, www.ecparks.co.za. 18 simple self-catering, thatched **bungalows** (**B-D**) with 1 or 2 bedrooms, sleeping 2-6, with fully-equipped kitchen, bathroom, arranged on 3 terraces on the hillside with good ocean views, an easy stroll to the beach. You will have to book in advance to stay here.

Mkambati Nature Reserve *p427*
A Wild Coast Sun, accessed from the R61 north of the reserve, near Port Edward, T039-305 9111, www.sun-international.com. This modern, brash, luxury hotel is outside the reserve on the northern boundary. 245 rooms, pool, casino, cabaret, cinema, championship golf course, beach and watersports. Undeniably good location with miles of sweeping beach. Once part of the Transkei and only 90 mins' drive from Durban, this used to be the place gamblers from KwaZulu Natal would come when gaming was only legal in the homelands.

D Gwe Gwe Rondavels reservations through Eastern Cape Parks, T043-735 4400, www.ecparks.co.za. 6 very simple rondavels sleeping 2, with basic self-catering facilities but are in a good position on a grassy mound overlooking the beach. There are also 2 larger houses in the reserve, sleeping groups of 10 or 20, more suited to groups of fishermen.

🍴 Eating

Most eating along the Wild Coast is in hotels and resorts, where non-overnight guests are more than welcome. There is the usual range of chicken and burger chain restaurants in Mthatha and Gcuwa (Butterworth) but not much else. Most of the petrol stations along the N2 have restaurants such as **Wimpy** attached. If you are self-catering along the coast, the supermarkets in East London or in Port Shepstone in KwaZulu Natal are the best places to stock up on provisions.

Chintsa *p422*
🍴 **Michaela's**, Steenbras Drive, Chintsa East, T043-738 5139, www.michaelas.co.za. Wed-Sun 1130-1430, 1830-2130, Mon 1130-1430 only. This is a remarkable restaurant perched on the top of Chintsa's biggest sand dune, reached by a short funicular train ride. If you are not fit, call ahead to check this is operating. The thatched restaurant has 2 levels with large windows and outside decks overlooking

the ocean, the seafood is excellent as are the salads that make good use of seasonal fruits and vegetables. The gut-busting Sun lunch buffet is recommended, booking is essential.

Port St Johns p425

Gecko Moon, First Beach, T047-564 1221. Open 1100-2000. Excellent German cook specializes in seafood menus, plus good wood-fired pizza. Outside tables are in a sub-tropical garden, also sells locally made crafts.

Wood'n'Spoon, Second Beach, T047-564 8202. Simple daytime restaurant with a kitchen in an old container and rustic outdoor tables set under banana-leaf thatch. Serves breakfasts and light meals. Try their cheese fondue or hamburgers.

▲ Activities and tours

Chintsa p422

African Heartland Journeys, Buccaneer's Backpackers, see Sleeping, page 428, T043-734 3012, www.africanheartland.co.za. Sensitively-run camping tours by 4WD, bike and canoe that go right into the heartland of the Wild Coast to places you could never get to otherwise. Accommodation is in Xhosa villages, which is an excellent way to see how people live without roads, electricity or cars. Highly recommended.

North to Port Edward and Durban p427

Amadiba Adventures, trails start at the office at the Mzamba Craft Village, 6 km south of Port Edward opposite the **Wild Coast Sun**, T/F039-305 6455, www.amadibaadventures.co.za. Part of a government tourism develop-ment programme funded by the European Union, where coastal communities run and own the tourism initiatives. Accommodation is in mobile camps with eco-toilets and hot bush showers, and prices include 3 meals per day. There are plenty of activities available, such as hiking and swimming beneath waterfalls, and excellent 4- to 6-day horse or hiking trails up the coast and inland. Local

guides are very knowledgeable about the area and much of the tour involves contact with local people. All proceeds go back into the local community. Excellent reports and it is an organization worthy of support.

⊖ Transport

Mthatha p425

From East London the **Baz Bus**, T021-439 2323, www.bazbus.com, runs along the N2, stopping at **Chintsa** and **Mthatha** before continuing on to **Port Shepstone** in KwaZulu Natal. It runs the same route in reverse. For both the 100-km or so journeys to the **Coffee Bay** and **Port St Johns**, the hostels will collect backpackers from the **Baz Bus** at the Shell Ultra City on the N2 outside Mthatha for a small fee and by prior arrangement. Hotels may also pick up guests by prior arrangement. Minibus taxis run to both resorts and leave from Circus Triangle in town. It is not advisable to hitch these routes. Avoid driving here after dark, as there have been violent incidents.

Bus

For **Baz Bus**, see above. Greyhound, Inter-cape and Translux buses all stick to the N2 and Mthatha is on the Cape Town–Durban route. **Cape Town** (18½ hrs) via **Nelson Mandela Bay** (**Port Elizabeth**) (7 hrs) and **East London** (3 hrs). **Durban** (6 hrs) via **Port Shepstone** (4½ hrs).

Bus companies All bus tickets can be booked online at www.computicket.com. Greyhound, www.greyhound.co.za; Intercape, www.intercape.co.za; Translux, www.translux.co.za. For more information, see Getting around, page 41.

⊕ Directory

Mthatha p425

Medical services St Mary's Private Hospital, 30 Durham St, T047-531 2911, offers 24-hr service.

Contents

Footprint features

Border crossings

KwaZulu Natal

At a glance

◉ **Getting around** Buses and Baz
Bus on major routes, car hire,
tours start and finish in Durban.

◉ **Time required** Minimum
1-2 weeks to cover in depth.

◑ **Weather** Good all year around,
though humid Jun-Aug.

✖ **When not to go** Christmas
and Easter school holidays.

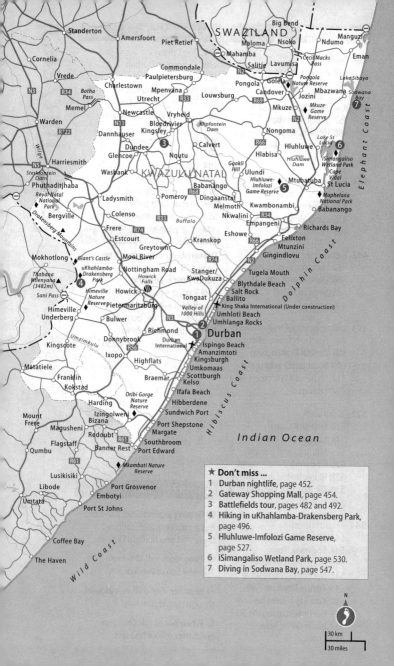

SWAZILAND

Standerton • Amersfoort • Piet Retief Big Bend Maloma Nsoko Manguzi
Cornelia Paulpietersburg Mahamba Salitje Lavumisa Ndumo Eman
Vrede Commondale Pongola Golela Candover Jozini Mbazwana Sodwana Bay
Charlestown Mpenvana Louwsburg Pongola Nature Reserve Lake Sibaya
Memel Utrecht Vryheid Klipfontein Dam Mkuze Mkuze Game Reserve
Warden Newcastle Bloedrivier Kingsley Nongoma Hluhluwe Lake St Lucia
Dannhauser Dundee Nqutu Calvert Hlabisa iSimangaliso Wetland Park
Harriesmith Glencoe Washbank KWAZULU/NATAL Gqokli Hill Ulundi Cape Vidal
Phuthaditjhaba Ladysmith Pomeroy Dingaanstat Hluhluwe-Imfolozi Game Reserve St Lucia
Royal Natal National Park Colenso Buffalo Melmoth Kwambonambi Maphelana National Park
Bergville Frere Nkwalini Empangeni Babanango
Mokhotlong Estcourt Kranskop Eshowe Richards Bay
Giant's Castle Greytown Felixton Mtunzini Gingindlovu
Thabana Ntlenyana Mooi River Stanger/KwaDukuza Tugela Mouth Dolphin Coast
uKhahlamba-Drakensberg Park Nottingham Road Howick Falls Blythdale Beach Salt Rock Ballito
Himeville Nature Reserve Howick King Shaka International (Under construction)
Sani Pass Pietermaritzburg Tongaat Umhloti Beach Umhlanga Rocks
Himeville Underberg Bulwer Valley of 1000 Hills Durban
Kingscote Donnybrook Richmond Durban International Ispingo Beach
Matatiele Ixopo Highflats Amanzimtoti Kingsburgh
Franklin Braemar Umkomaas Scottburgh Kelso
Kokstad Harding Ifafa Beach Hibberdene Sundwich Port
Mount Frere Izingolweni Bizana Oribi Gorge Nature Reserve Port Shepstone Margate
Magusheni Redoubt Southbroom Port Edward
Flagstaff Banner Rest Mkambati Nature Reserve
Qumbu Lusikisiki Libode Port Grosvenor
Umtata Embotyi Port St Johns
Coffee Bay
The Haven Wild Coast

Indian Ocean

Hibiscus Coast

Elephant Coast

★ Don't miss ...
1 Durban nightlife, page 452.
2 Gateway Shopping Mall, page 454.
3 Battlefields tour, pages 482 and 492.
4 Hiking in uKhahlamba-Drakensberg Park, page 496.
5 Hluhluwe-Imfolozi Game Reserve, page 527.
6 iSimangaliso Wetland Park, page 530.
7 Diving in Sodwana Bay, page 547.

N

30 km
30 miles

KwaZulu Natal manages to squash the country's greatest diversity into a wedge of land between the towering Drakensberg Mountains and the long sweep of sub-tropical coastline. Here, visitors can go on safari, hike through dramatic wilderness, surf the country's best beaches and experience South Africa's strongest African culture. The mountains in the uKhahlamba-Drakensberg Park soar to over 3000 m, offering the country's finest hiking on an extensive network of remote trails. Zululand, rich in history and evocative landscapes, draws visitors both for its traditional Zulu lifestyles, and the superb game reserves, some of the finest in South Africa. Hluhluwe-Imfolozi Game Reserve is the best known and has become famous for its rhino conservation programme, which has brought the rhino back from the brink of extinction. Maputaland, lying to the north of Zululand, is an extraordinary area of undisturbed African wilderness, with remote game parks and pristine coastlines, far off the usual tourist trail. The variety of wildlife experiences on offer here is on a par with Kruger – but without the crowds. The landscape of the central region, dotted with small industrial towns and rolling farmland, makes up in history what it lacks in scenic drama. This area, better known as the Battlefields, still bears the scars of the Zulu Wars: the Zulu-Boer War, the Anglo-Zulu War and the Boer War. There are dozens of battlefield sites, but the most evocative are those at Isandlwana, Rorke's Drift and Blood River. For a more light-hearted alternative, KwaZulu Natal's beaches are some of the most beautiful in the country. While those around Durban and to the south are heavily developed, the coastline extending from the north towards Maputaland is relatively wild, with long empty sweeps of white sand backed by thick tropical dune forests – an excellent place for interesting wildlife encounters.

Getting around

Travel within KwaZulu Natal is uncomplicated; the main areas of interest are connected by either the N2 or the N3. The **N2** runs along most of the coast from Port Shepstone in the south, through to Durban, Zululand and Maputaland in the north, before heading inland north to Mpumalanga, past Swaziland. The **N3** heads inland from Durban towards Pietermaritzburg, skirting the Battlefield Route to the east and the uKhahlamba-Drakensberg National Park in the west, eventually reaching Gauteng. The **Baz Bus** is convenient for exploring the province as it runs all the way along the coast as far as Mkuzi before heading inland to Swaziland. A second service runs from Durban towards Gauteng through the Drakensberg. All the main centres are linked by mainline bus services, so KwaZulu Natal can quite feasibly be visited by local transport, though you may want to consider a hire car for some of the national parks and game reserves. To the north, the roads in Maputaland are gradually being surfaced but there are still vast tracts of wilderness which are best explored in a 4WD. The most accessible reserve is Sodwana Bay where the colourful tropical reefs have become South Africa's most popular diving destination. The battlefield sites in the centre of the province are isolated and best experienced on a guided historical tour (see page 492).

Tourist information

Tourism KwaZulu-Natal ① *T031-366 7500, www.zulu.org.za, Mon-Fri 0800-1630, Sat 0900-1400, Sun 0900-1300*, also known as the Kingdom of the Zulu, is the regional tourist office and is based at **Tourist Junction** in Durban (see page 439). This is an excellent office with a huge range of information on the province, as well as an attractive curio shop.

   KZN Wildlife ① *PO Box 13053, Cascades 3202, Pietermaritzburg, T033-845 1000, www.kznwildlife.com,* is the central reservations office for all the accommodation within the various nature reserves and conservation areas throughout the KwaZulu Natal. This includes many of the Drakensberg resorts, as well as excellent wildlife reserves such as Ithala and Hluhluwe-Imfolozi. All the parks' offices are open October to March 0800-1900 and April to September 0800-1800. Reservations can be made six months in advance and some of the popular camps are fully booked during the local school holidays. Credit card and online bookings are accepted. Note that accommodation in huts must be booked through KZN Wildlife, whereas campsites are booked directly through the campsite manager or reception by phone. (Do not confuse KZN Wildlife with SANParks (see page 48), SANParks is responsible for parks such as Kruger, Tsitsikamma and Addo Elephant National Park.)

Durban

→ Colour map 5, B2. Phone code: 031.
The sprawling conurbation of Durban is Africa's largest port and although its appeal is not immediately apparent – few original buildings survive and it can feel hectic and overcrowded – it boasts wide beaches, an extensive beachfront and a steamy tropical climate. The city also has one of the country's most interesting cultural mixes – it is home to substantial Zulu and white communities and South Africa's largest Indian population. Away from the Central Business District (CBD) are attractive suburbs, where tropical foliage spills from ornate balconies and the fast pace of city life is all but forgotten. ▶▶ *For listings, see pages 449-456.*

Ins and outs
Getting there Even though it has status, no international flights fly direct into **Durban International Airport** ① T031-451 6758, www.acsa.co.za, but instead come via Johannesburg. There are, however, numerous and regular domestic flights. Car hire desks can be found in the terminal building and outside in the car park. There is a **tourist information office** ① T031-408 1000, daily 0630-2100, in the domestic arrivals hall, and several mobile phone rental shops. The airport is 16 km from the city centre and transport into Durban

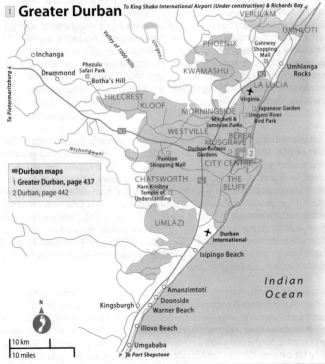

24 hours in Durban

Head down to the Golden Mile in the early morning; except for the few early-rising surf fanatics and muscular lifeguards limbering up, you will have the wide promenade, sandy beaches and crashing waves to yourself, before the crowds, holiday-resort tackiness and humidity set in. Breakfast at one of the small cafés where the surfers congregate to swap wave stories.

Explore the Indian shopping district off Grey Street, an exotic, cross-cultural, shopping experience, where the tangy aroma of eastern spices mingles with the colourful fabrics, trinkets and jewellery in the courtyard bazaars. When entering the Juma Masjid Mosque on Grey Street, the largest in the southern hemisphere, make sure you remove your shoes. Relish the cool tranquillity here before heading back on to Durban's hectic streets. Enjoy an African shopping experience at Victoria Market, where curios and souvenirs can be haggled over, and sample a famous Durban bunny chow at one the traditional food stalls.

Afterwards, catch the bird show at Umgeni River Bird Park, the only one of its kind in the world. Some of South Africa's largest and rarest birds, including the blue crane, are on display in this innovative show.

Sink a couple of cold Castle lagers and watch the sun go down on the deck of the **Bat Café** in the small craft harbour. If you're lucky you may catch some township jazz here before heading to one of Durban's top Indian restaurants to sample a fine Durban curry. The best are the **Jewel of India**, with cushions and low tables where you can kick off your shoes and relax, and **Ulundi**, where days of colonial Natal are echoed through turbaned waiters and rattan furniture.

Florida Road in Morningside and Musgrave Road in Musgrave are Durban's current hip and happening café-lined streets. Take your pick of fashionable late-night bars, pubs, open-air restaurants and live music venues, all conveniently located along these two suburban streets.

takes about 30 minutes. Many hotels and backpacker hostels offer free airport collection/transfer service. Alternatively, there are several private companies providing airport transfer services departing from the departure terminal such as **Airport Shuttle** ⓘ *T031-465 1606, www.airportshuttle.co.za*. Note the new **King Shaka International Airport** is presently being built at La Mercy, 35 km north of Durban and is scheduled to be operational by mid-2010, when it will replace the current airport which will be decommissioned. It is expected that operations at the airport will be transferred to King Shaka overnight. For progress, visit the Airport Company of South Africa's website, www.acsa.co.za. Behind Durban railway station on Masabalala Yengwa Road (M12) is the **Motorcoach Terminal** for major long-distance coaches run by **Translux**, **Intercape** and **Greyhound**. » *For more detailed information, see Transport, page 455.*

Getting around Durban has developed into South Africa's largest sea port and is also one of its main tourist centres. The approach to Durban passes through coastal tourist resorts, industrial areas, townships and eventually reaches the Central Business District (CBD). The extensive beachfront and the most important landmarks are within easy walking distance in the city centre, but the CBD is now a pretty rough and ready district and you'd be advised to take a taxi between the sites. Confusingly, the street names in the CBD were changed in

2008 and presently signs feature the old and new names. **Mynah**, T031-307 3503, is a frequent local bus service that runs between the city centre, the beachfront and Berea and Morningside, R3; it's very useful if you want to get to town from the suburbs, or from the north or south of the city centre. Timetables are free and can be obtained from the city centre bus terminal, opposite the Workshop Shopping Mall on Commercial Road.

Tourist information Durban Africa ① *Tourist Junction, Station Building, 160 Monty Naicker Rd, T031-304 4934, www.durban.kzn.org.za, www.bookabedahead.co.za, Mon-Fri 0800-1630, Sat 0900-1400, Sun 0900-1300,* is the city tourist information service, which is very helpful and produces a range of brochures, including accommodation, restaurant and events guides. It also offers hotel and tour bookings, coach and rail bookings, foreign exchange, a curio shop, a café and runs extremely good city tours.

Safety Safety has been a long-standing issue in downtown Durban. Although safety standards plummeted in the late 1990s, a number of initiatives in recent years, such as an increased police presence, the installation of CCTV cameras and upgrading of local housing, has improved the situation a great deal. Nevertheless, it's sensible to keep your wits about you – stick to busy areas, don't carry valuables and avoid looking like a tourist. Most importantly, avoid the CBD at night unless you take a taxi. The suburbs by contrast are relatively safe.

Background

The area around the bay was once covered with mangroves and inhabited by pelicans, flamingos and hippos. The earliest inhabitants were members of the Lala tribe who fished in the estuary, and hunted and grew crops in the fertile tropical forests along the coast. The first Europeans to land here were Portuguese explorers en route to the east. On 25 December 1497, Vasco da Gama sighted land and called it Natal, though this was probably off the coast of present-day Eastern Cape. The Portuguese cartographer Manuel Perestrello mapped the coast of Natal in 1576, but it was nearly 200 years after the earliest European sighting that the first trading ships arrived. In 1684 the *Francis* began a new era when she sailed to Natal to buy ivory.

After the relative success of the first trading expedition, the Dutch East India Company planned to open a trading post here (after buying land off Chief Inyangesi for 1000 guilders worth of beads, copper rings and iron). But after a few technical hitches involving the estuary's sandbars, trade was never really developed and in 1730 the Dutch established an alternative trading station at Delagoa Bay.

The first British traders arrived in 1823 on the *Salisbury*, spurred on by news of Shaka, the powerful chief of the Zulus and his Empire. Lieutenant Francis and George Farewell arrived in the Bay of Natal and were blown over the sandbars in a storm. They returned in May 1824, with Henry Francis Fynn and a group of other adventurers, and set up their first camp in what is now known as Farewell Square. Henry Fynn was the first European trader to make contact with Shaka. Fynn and the other adventurers claimed (falsely) to be envoys of King George and were well received. Fynn became a favourite of the royal household after he helped Shaka recover from a stab wound sustained during a battle. In thanks Shaka granted Fynn a huge tract of land, over 9000 sq km.

Fynn and his young colleague Nathaniel Issacs ran this area as their own personal fief-dom, taking many Zulu wives and fathering dozens of children. Fynn declared himself King of Natal and wielded power in the same brutal manner as his infamous neighbour, Shaka.

Even though Fynn and his men broke many Zulu laws, including the prohibition on all but the king from trading in ivory, they were treated with great respect by Shaka (though the chiefs they bought the ivory from were invariably executed).

The area remained undeveloped, however, with just a few dozen European settlers, and the British refused to annex the region. It was not until the establishment of the Voortrekker republic of Natalia in 1838 that the British felt their interests to be under threat. The capital of Natalia was in Pietermaritzburg, but settlements had also been established at Weenen and Durban, giving the Voortrekkers access to the sea. The possibility of a viable independent Voortrekker republic wasn't acceptable to the Cape Colony and an expeditionary force was sent from the Cape in 1842. Although they were besieged by the Voortrekkers on their arrival, by June of that year the parliament in Pietermaritzburg had accepted British rule. The Cape Colony annexed Natal in 1844, and the security given by becoming part of the Cape Colony encouraged many new settlers in search of land to come to Durban.

The development of the sugarcane industry in the 1860s encouraged the growth of Durban as a port and gave the city one of its most unique characteristics. Initially the sugarcane industry suffered from a lack of cheap labour, so the planters imported a large number of indentured labourers from India, who lived in conditions not dissimilar to slavery. After working off their five-year indenture contracts some returned home, but a number remained in Natal. Many continued farming and eventually came to dominate the local fruit and vegetable market. Others established small businesses and gradually built up important trade connections with India. These ex-indentured labourers were joined by a number of more affluent traders, mainly from Gujarat, who arrived direct from India to set up a business.

With the development of the Golden Mile in the 1970s, Durban was promoted as a seaside resort for white holidaymakers, particularly for families from Gauteng. During Apartheid, the extensive beach was split according to colour – black people were permitted to walk the length of the whole beach but, on the whites-only Addington Beach, they were not allowed to sit down or go into the sea. The late 1980s, however, saw a huge influx of workers from Zululand, transforming the fabric of the city. With the end of Apartheid came another influx: that of black holidaymakers, which gave the city the tag of 'Soweto-on-Sea' – a phrase used by both whites and blacks. However, divisions still remain: far fewer white people holiday in Durban, while the city centre has taken on a distinctly African feel.

Sights

The main areas of interest to tourists are the **city centre** around Farewell Square, the **Indian district** around Queen and Grey streets, and the beachfront **Golden Mile**. The best way of seeing the major sights in the city centre is on one of the guided tours run by the tourist office.

City centre

The small area surrounding City Hall between Dr A B Xuma Street and Anton Lembede Street in central Durban is one of the city's more interesting spots. The colonial buildings and gardens offer a striking contrast between Durban's past and the present. High-rise office blocks tower over the remains of Durban's colonial history, where pastel-coloured art deco buildings are dwarfed by mirrored skyscrapers. The city centre's eclectic mixture of architectural styles is the responsibility of Lord Holford, the town planner who developed the city centre during the 1970s. Lord Holford was originally from South Africa but became one of England's most notorious town planners when he created many of the soulless city centres built in England during the 1960s. He returned to South Africa to help redesign city centres as part of the Apartheid programme; his work destroyed the bustling Indian atmosphere of the city centre when thousands of Indians were moved out. The original plans for the new centre involved the demolition of the City Hall and the old railway station, but vociferous protests by conservationists prevented this.

Francis Farewell Square is the hub of this area and is named after the first British settler who built his home here out of wattle and daub in 1824. Today the square has a busy street market, but at night it resembles, rather incongruously, a Victorian cemetery as this is where most of Durban's commemorative statues have been placed. There is a cenotaph to those who died in both world wars, a memorial to the dead of the Boer War and statues of Queen Victoria, in commemoration of her diamond jubilee, and Natal's first two prime ministers.

The **City Hall**, on Anton Lembede Street, faces directly onto the Francis Farewell Square. This is one of Durban's most impressive buildings and reflects the town's municipal might at the turn of the 20th century. The neo-baroque building was completed in 1910 and in its day was one of the British Empire's finest city halls in the southern hemisphere. The main entrance is on Farewell Square and the hall inside is decorated with an interesting collection of portraits of Durban's mayors. What is particularly appealing about the building are the palms lining the street outside. You will also find the Natural Science Museum and Durban Art Gallery here.

The **Natural Science Museum** ① *T031-311 2256, Mon-Fri 0830-1600, Sat 0830-1200, Sun 1100-1600, free entry, gift shop and coffee shop*, has a grand colonial entrance adorned with palm trees. Inside is an assortment of scientific displays, including a huge gallery of stuffed African mammals. More interestingly, the museum also houses an extremely rare Dodo skeleton and South Africa's only Egyptian mummy. The **KwaZuzulwazi Science Centre** has an excellent series of displays dedicated to the Zulu culture.

The **Durban Art Gallery** ① *T031-311 2265, Mon-Sat 0830-1600, Sun 1100-1600, free*, on the upper floor of City Hall, has a superb collection of work by South African artists dating from the beginning of this century. This was one of the first galleries in South Africa to collect black art, and it remains an important cultural centre. It also hosts regularly changing exhibitions of contemporary art and handicrafts, and the **Durban RedEye arts festival** takes place here several times a year.

The Playhouse is directly opposite the Anton Lembede Street entrance to the City Hall. It was built in 1935 and was originally used as a bioscope, which seated 1900 people. The lounge bar became popular with visiting sailors during the 1970s and was notorious for its heavy drinking sessions and occasional fights. The cinema was eventually forced to close after a fire and has now been restored and converted into an arts complex with five theatres (see Entertainment, page 453).

St Paul's Church was originally built in 1853, and was rebuilt in 1906 after a fire. The church is purely British in architectural style and inside there are commemorative plaques to Durban's early settlers. The chapel of St Nicholas on the left side of the aisle was part of the Mission to Seamen between 1899 and 1989. Reverend Wade, who was rector of the church between 1952 and 1961, was the father of tennis one-hit-wonder Virginia Wade, who won the ladies singles title at Wimbledon in 1977.

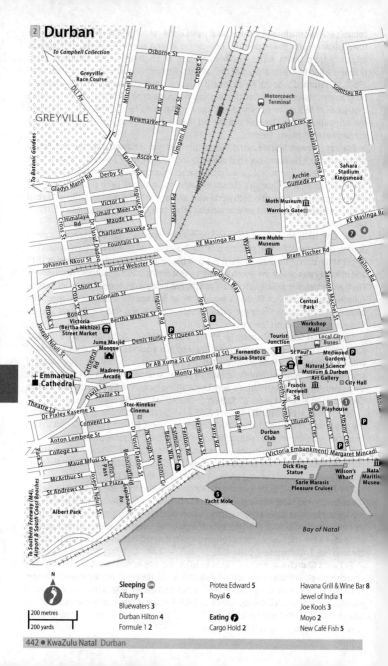

2 Durban

To Campbell Collection

Osborne St

Greyville Race Course

Fynn St

Crabbe St

Motorcoach Terminal

Somtseu Rd

Mitchel Rd

1st Av

May's St

Newmarket St

Jeff Taylor Cres

GREYVILLE

Dll Av

Umgeni Rd

To Botanic Gardens

Ascot St

Epsom Rd

Archie Gumede Pl

Masabalala Yengwa Av

Sahara Stadium Kingsmead

Derby St

Gladys Manzi Rd

Victor La

Ismail C Meer Rd

Maude La

Charlotte Maxeke St

Fountain La

Ingcuce Rd

Mansel Rd

Moth Museum

Warrior's Gate

KE Masinga Rd

Himalaya Rd

Cross Rd

Dr Yusuf Dadoo St

KE Masinga Rd

Kwa Muhle Museum

Wyatt Rd

Bram Fischer Rd

KE Masinga Rd

Walnut Rd

Johannes Nkosi St

David Webster St

Short St

Dr Goonam St

Soldiers Way

Samora Machel St

Bond St

Brook St

Bertha Mkhize St

Ingcuce Rd

Joe Slovo St

Joseph Nduli St

Victoria (Bertha Mkhize) Street Market

Juma Masjid Mosque

Denis Hurley St (Queen St)

Central Park

Workshop Mall

Local City Buses

Tourist Junction

Cathedral Rd

Dr AB Xuma St (Commercial St)

Madressa Arcade

Monty Naicker Rd

Fernando Pessoa Statue

St Paul's

Medwood Gardens

Natural Science Museum & Durban Art Gallery

City Hall

Emmanuel Cathedral

Davis La

Saville St

Dorothy Nyembe St

Francis Farewell Sq

Theatre La

Dr Pixley Kaseme St

Ster-Kinekor Cinema

Beach Wlk

Playhouse

Convent La

Anton Lembede St

Bay Terr

Ulundi

Aliwal St

Albany Cres

College La

Maud Mfusi St

McArthur St

St Andrews St

Joseph Nduli St

Dr Yusuf Dadoo St

IN Singh St

Tello's Pass

Le Plaza

Bonningfield

Esplanade

Masonic Gr

Salmon Cres

Fenton Rd

Hermitage St

Parry Rd

Beach St

Bay Terr

Durban Club

(Victoria Embankment) Margaret Mincadi

Dick King Statue

Sarie Marais Pleasure Cruises

Wilson's Wharf

Natal Maritime Museum

To Southern Freeway (M4), Airport & South Coast Beaches

Albert Park

Yacht Mole

Bay of Natal

N

200 metres
200 yards

Sleeping
Albany 1
Bluewaters 3
Durban Hilton 4
Formule 1 2
Protea Edward 5
Royal 6

Eating
Cargo Hold 2
Havana Grill & Wine Bar 8
Jewel of India 1
Joe Kools 3
Moyo 2
New Café Fish 5

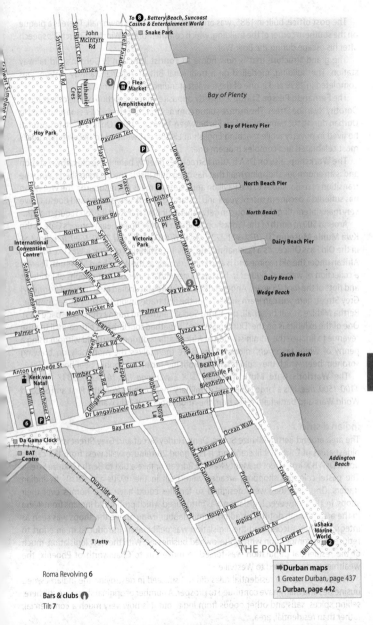

To 8, Battery Beach, Suncoast
Casino & Entertainment World

■ Snake Park

Bay of Plenty

Bay of Plenty Pier

North Beach Pier

North Beach

Dairy Beach Pier

Dairy Beach

Wedge Beach

South Beach

Addington
Beach

Flea
Market

Amphitheatre

Hoy Park

International
Convention
Centre

Victoria
Park

Kerk van
Natal

Da Gama Clock

BAT
Centre

uShaka
Marine
World

THE POINT

Sol Harris Cres

John
McIntyre
Rd

Sylvester Ntuli Rd

Somtseu Rd

Nathaniel
Isaac
Cres

Shell Parade

Molyneux Rd

Pavilion Terr

Playfair Rd

Travers Pl

Gresham
Pl

Brews Rd

North La

Morrison Rd

Sylvester Ntuli Rd

West La

John Milne Rd

Hunter La

East La

Milne St

South La

Monty Naicker Rd

Florence Nzama St

Stalwart Simelane St

Palmer St

Palmer St

Kearsney Rd

Peck Rd

Farewell St

Anton Lembede St

Mills St

Kitchener St

Timber St

Creek St

Roy Rd

Gillian St

Mazeppa St

Gull St

Pickering St

Dr Langalibalele Dube St

Bay Terr

Robin La

Norge

Quayside Rd

T Jetty

Frobisher
Pl

Foster
Pl

OR Tambo Par (Marine Par)

Lower Marine Par

Sea View St

Tyzack St

Gillespie St

Brighton Pl

Beatty Pl

Grenville Pl

Blenheim Pl

Rochester St Sturdee Pl

Rutherford St

Ocean Walk

Mahatma Gandhi Rd

Shearer Rd

Masonic Rd

Shepstone Pl

Prince St

Hospital Rd

Ripley Ter

South Beach Av

Crieff Pl

Bell St

Erskine Terr

Roma Revolving 6

Bars & clubs

Tilt 7

➡ **Durban maps**
1 Greater Durban, page 437
2 Durban, page 442

The **post office**, built in 1885, was originally Durban's first town hall. There is a plaque on the southern corner of the building, which commemorates Winston Churchill's speech after his escape during the Boer War.

The grand structure that is now home to **Tourist Junction** is Durban's old railway station. The building, modelled on a traditional British Victorian railway station, was completed in 1899 and is one of the few left standing in South Africa.

The **Fernando Pessoa Statue** is directly opposite Tourist Junction on the other side of Dorothy Nyembe Street. The bronze statue commemorates Fernando Pessoa who lived in Durban during the early years of his life between 1896 and 1906. On his return to Portugal he lived in poverty while teaching English in Lisbon but went on to become Portugal's most celebrated and complex modern poet.

The Workshop, also on Dr A B Xuma Street, lies directly behind the old railway station and is an enormous shopping mall that has been built inside the old train sheds. With the transition of major shops to the Pavilion and Gateway malls in the suburbs, the Workshop has suffered a decline in recent years and is starting to look very shabby and doesn't have very many interesting shops. You can get authentic Indian snacks at the food court though.

Around 500 m north of the Workshop, on Bram Fischer Road, near Warrior's Gate, is the **Kwa Muhle Museum** ① T031-311 2223, Mon-Fri, 0800-1600, Sat 0900-1600, free, housed in the Old Pass Office. It's a fascinating and moving exhibition of what it was like to be an African under the old regime and is also known locally as the **Apartheid Museum**. There is a collection of waxwork figures in hostels along with a series of photographs of incidents and riots of the past 25 years. Another display features the Indian merchants of (formerly) Grey Street; here you can learn more about the first trade union, the Grey Street mosque, Bertha Mkhize Street beer hall, the Bantu Social Centre and bunny chow (see page 453). One of the exhibits is on the 'Durban System', a method for Durban's city council to raise revenue to finance the administration of African affairs during Apartheid without using a penny of white taxpayers' money: they gave themselves the monopoly on brewing sorghum beer, which they sold for a fine profit in African-only public beer houses.

The **Warrior's Gate Moth Museum** ① K E Masinga Rd, T031-307 3337, Tue-Sun 1100-1500, free, has a large collection of military memorabilia from the First and Second World Wars and battlefield relics from the Anglo-Boer and Zulu wars.

Indian district

The area around Bertha Mkhize Street, Denis Hurley Street and Grey Street is one of the oldest areas of Durban still standing. It is a good 20-minute walk west from the centre down Dr A B Xuma Street or Monty Naicker Rdreet, or take a taxi to Bertha Mkhize Street. The pastel-coloured shopping arcades were built in the 1920s and 1930s by Indian traders. Originally they were designed so families could have their homes over their shops. In 1973, however, legislation was introduced which prohibited Indians from living in the area, though not from trading. Family labour living above the shops was seen as integral to their success and the legislation was deliberately introduced in an effort to reduce their competition with white-owned businesses. With the new legislation, much of the residential population was forced to move out to Chatsworth or Phoenix; the wealthier traders moved to Westville.

Thankfully the new residential rules did not succeed in destroying the Indian-owned businesses and many have continued to prosper. A number of original shops are still here, selling spices, saris and other goods from India, but it is now very much a commercial, rather than residential, area.

Victoria (effectively now **Bertha Mkhize**) **Street Market** ① *T031-306 4021, Mon-Sat 0600-1800, Sun 1000-1600*, is on the corner of Denis Hurley Street and Bertha Mkhize Street. The original market was destroyed in 1973 by fire and has been replaced by a modern market. The new concrete building is rather dingy, but there are over 170 stalls inside selling curios, leather goods, fabrics, copper and spices. The main attraction of the stalls here are the spices and dried beans imported from India. Upstairs are a variety of food stalls serving up delicious snacks such as bunny chow, samosas and Durban curries. It gets extremely busy, so beware of pickpockets and don't take anything valuable with you.

The entrance to the **Madressa Arcade** is on Grey Street. The bazaar-like arcade was built in 1927 and houses shops selling luggage, CDs and Indian fabrics.

The **Juma Masjid Mosque** ① *corner of Denis Hurley St and Grey St, T031-306 0026, open to all Mon-Fri 0900-1600 but not during prayer times*, was also built in 1927 and claims to be the largest mosque in the southern hemisphere, despite the fact that Muslims are a minority in Durban, which is largely Hindu. It sports gilt-domed minarets and a peaceful marble hall. The dress code must be adhered to: no shorts for men and women should wear long skirts or trousers and cover their shoulders; leave your shoes at the door.

Margaret Mncadi Avenue (Victoria Embankment)

The Victoria Embankment was originally built in 1897 and was a grand and desirable residential area facing a beautiful stretch of beach. Very little of this remains today, and at first glance the Embankment seems like any other busy road lined with skyscrapers. There are still a few sights worth seeking out, though. At the eastern end of the Embankment is the ornate **Da Gama Clock**. A good example of late-Victorian design, this large cast-iron clock was erected to commemorate the 400th anniversary of Vasco da Gama's discovery of the sea route to India in 1487.

A short walk further on at the junction of Dorothy Nyembe Street and the Victoria Embankment is the **Dick King Statue** which commemorates Dick King's epic 10-day ride to Grahamstown in 1842 whilst Durban was under siege. The **Durban Club** is on the opposite side of the embankment and was built in 1904. This is one of the few original buildings left on the Victoria Embankment, a grand edifice which gives an inkling of what the Victoria Embankment once looked like.

Wilson's Wharf is a modern development overlooking the harbour, home to a couple of cafés, a fish market and three boats which house the **Natal Maritime Museum** ① *entrance is on the docks opposite the junction of Samora Machel St and the Margaret Mncadi Av, T031-311 2230, Mon-Sat 0830-1545, Sun 1100-1545, small entry fee*. Visitors can walk through the minesweeper, the *SAS Durban*, and the two tugs, the *Ulundi* and the *JR More*.

Just beyond the Maritime Museum is the excellent non-profit making **BAT (Bartle Arts Trust) Centre** ① *on the harbour front, T031-332 0451, www.batcentre.co.za*. This is a popular arts centre with a concert hall and a bar and restaurant, as well as several little shops selling excellent contemporary Zulu weavings, wood-cut prints and hand made shoes.

Beachfront

The most popular seafront area extends along the length of Marine Parade (now O R Tambo Parade). Traditionally known as the **Golden Mile**, it's a favourite with South African holidaymakers. The beachfront is lined with high-rise hotels, gardens and a promenade; behind is a built-up urban area which had become distinctly insalubrious. Developments over the last few years, however, have upgraded housing, brought in investment and improved safety here, although it's still best avoided at night. There's a police station on the promenade and a high police presence.

The beaches, all of which are impressive stretches of long, golden sand, are divided into areas designated for surfing, boogy boarding and swimming. All are protected with shark nets and lifeguards are on patrol daily 0800-1700. At the northern end of the Lower Marine (O R Tambo) Parade is a **flea market**, a hive of activity at weekends, with stalls selling Indian snacks and curios.

The promenade along Lower Marine (O R Tambo) Parade and Snell Parade has numerous tourist attractions. Running from north to south, the entertainment starts with the flea market and the **Snake Park** ① *T031-563 6395, 0900-1630, small entry fee*. The park has a large collection of snakes from around the world with daily snake-handling demonstrations several times daily and feedings at weekends. Nearby are several stands where extravagantly dressed rickshaw drivers wait for tourists. The options are either a quick and painless photograph with the driver, or a photograph and ride up and down Marine (O R Tambo) Parade, usually costing around R20.

The leading attraction here, however, is **uShaka Marine World** ① *1 Bell St, T031-328 8000, www.ushakamarineworld.co.za, 0900-1800, Wet 'n' Wild closed Mon-Tue Apr-Oct, Wet 'n' Wild R79, children (under 16) R62, SeaWorld R104, children (under 16) R70, combined ticket R152, children (under 16) R100; free entry to Village Walk; Phantom Ship R45, children (under 16) R30 – this ticket is redeemed against your bill if eating at the Cargo Hold restaurant (see Eating, page 451).* To get here drive down Mahatma Gandhi Road (formerly Point Road) from the city centre and it's on the beach at The Point (see below). This enormous waterpark is the largest in Africa, and has the fourth largest aquarium in the world. The park is split into three areas: SeaWorld is an impressive underground aquarium; Wet 'n' Wild has a huge choice of impressive waterslides and rides; and Village Walk is a retail village that is filled with shops and restaurants. The highlight in SeaWorld is the phantom ship, where visitors walk through glass tunnels surrounded by ragged-tooth sharks and game fish. Each corridor has a different theme, and there is a range of presentations in pools surrounding the ship throughout the day. There's also a dolphinarium, a seal pool, dive tank and a snorkel reef. Another free zone is the uShaka Beach, which hosts a variety of activities such as beach volleyball and surfing, and has 24-hour security.

A new waterfront housing and leisure development to be known as The Point Waterfront (www.durbanpoint.co.za) is currently under construction at the entrance of the harbour at the end of Mahatma Gandhi (Point) Road. However, even though construction started in 2005, to date it's just a clutch of half-finished (or largely unsold) luxury flats and unfinished roads, and on our visit development had all but ground to a halt. This may be because of the current economic climate, or perhaps because the area around Point Road has long been known for its criminal element and so the development has failed to attract buyers.

Battery Beach

Heading 1 km north of Snell Parade and the Golden Mile, Battery Beach is perhaps the most attractive of Durban's beaches, with good swimming and fewer crowds. It's also the location of the **Suncoast Casino and Entertainment World**, with slot machines, cinemas, a selection of bars, takeaway joints, themed restaurants and a car park for 2000 vehicles. There's a boardwalk linking the complex to the beach where you can sunbathe or rollerblade on the sundeck.

Durban suburbs

This residential district, to the west of the city centre, is one of Durban's oldest and most attractive. Fine whitewashed mansions and Victorian bungalows line the quiet streets, and this is one of the best places to head for restaurants and nightlife. On John Zikhali Road, in Upper Berea, are the **Durban Botanic Gardens** ⓘ *T031-309 1271, www.durban botanicgardens.org.za, daily 0730-1715, until 1745 in summer, free entry, a free tour leaves from the information centre on the last Sun of every month at 0930.* The gardens were founded in 1849, making them, supposedly, the oldest botanical gardens in Africa, and they cover almost 15 ha. There are some impressive avenues of palms crossing the park, an ornamental lake, an orchid house and an information centre. The tea garden, open 0930-1615, is a pleasant place to relax. The KwaZulu Natal Philharmonic Orchestra and other musical groups perform by the lake on Sunday afternoons during summer.

Three other smaller parks are **Mitchell Park** ⓘ *corner of Innes and Ferndale roads, Morningside, T031-303 2275, free but a small entry fee to the aviaries and animal enclosures,* which are public gardens with an open-air café, aviaries and a few small animals and reptiles in cages; the adjoining **Jameson Park** ⓘ *350 Montpelier Rd, Morningside, T031-312 2318, free,* which has extensive rose gardens (proving that roses can grow in a sub-tropical climate) and a good view of Durban from the top; and the **Japanese Gardens** ⓘ *Prospect Hall Rd, Durban North, take the off-ramp as soon as you have crossed the Umgeni River bridge, T031-563 1333, free,* which are good for birdwatching and where there are some pleasant paths through the gardens with their many water features, bridges and gazebos. Species include paradise and black flycatchers, various weavers, Egyptian Geese and in summer various species of swallow and martin can be skimming over the lawns and water.

The **Campbell Collection** ⓘ *220 Gladys Mazibuko Rd, Berea, T031-207 3432, main house open to the public by appointment only Mon-Fri 0830-1630, free entry,* is a museum and African library in a Cape Dutch house built in 1914, which still has most of its original decorations. There are some fine examples of Cape furniture and early South African oil paintings, displays of African sculpture, weapons, musical instruments and a rare collection of paintings by Barbara Tyrrell. Most of the paintings are of Africans dressed in traditional clothes from the 19th century; the paintings form part of a unique record of what people wore before contact with European settlers.

Reached from the N2 south of the centre, the **Hare Krishna Temple of Understanding** ⓘ *south of the centre on Ambassador Rd, T031-4033 328, daily, free entry,* opened as an ashram in 1969, but the futuristic marble temple set in extensive ornamental gardens was only opened to the public in 1975. There is a good vegetarian restaurant here.

Umgeni River Bird Park
ⓘ *Riverside Rd, turn left off the M4 just north of the city centre, T031-579 4600, www.umgeniriverbirdpark.co.za. Daily 0900-1700, R30, children (under 12) R25, there's also the Cockatoo Cafe.*

On the opposite side of the Umgeni River is the Umgeni River Bird Park, which has over 3000 exotic and indigenous birds, from flamingos to macaws and plenty of pathways through the aviaries. There is an impressive free flight show (1100 and 1400), where large birds such as owls, raptures and vultures fly over the heads of the audience to perches at the top of the open-air auditorium and a presenter tells you a bit about the various species.

Durban's motorway network opens up a range of day trips within driving distance of the city centre, although good public transport connections are limited to the south coast, Pietermaritzburg and Umhlanga.

To the north, inland along the N3, is the Valley of 1000 Hills, Pietermaritzburg, the Natal Midlands and the Battlefields. To the south on the N2 are the surfing beaches and tourist resorts heading to Port Shepstone and Margate. To the north along the N2 lies Umhlanga and the coastal resorts of the north coast, whilst just inland from the N2 is the historical Zulu town of Eshowe.

Valley of 1000 Hills

The Valley of 1000 Hills, a peaceful area named after the dozens of hills which fold down towards the Umgeni River, is an easy 35-km drive from Durban. Follow the N3 north out of the city and leave at the Westville/Pavilion Mall exit. Join the old Pietermaritzburg road (R103) and drive through the suburbs of Kloof and Hillcrest. Here you will pick up signs for the Valley of 1000 Hills Meander which runs through the villages of Botha's Hill, Drummond, Monteseel and Inchanga. The **Comrades Marathon**, a gruelling 90 km between Pieter-maritzburg and Durban, follows this route in June. For information contact **1000 Hills Tourism** ① *Old Main Rd, Botha's Hill, T031-777 1874, www.1000hills.kzn.org.za, Mon-Sat 0900-1600.*

Between Durban and Pietermaritzburg the landscape quickly climbs some 700 m over a series of rolling hills characteristic of the suburbs around the two cities. From Botha's Rest, there are many viewpoints on the R103 from where you can see the valley unfold. The fertile hills are dotted with villages, farms and encroaching townships closer to Durban. The valley has historically been a Zulu stronghold and, in the early 19th century, it became a refuge for dispossessed Zulus who had lost their farmland through battle further north.

The R103 runs along the lip of the valley; tourism has gone into overdrive along this route, with a variety of craft shops, restaurants, B&Bs, guesthouses, farm stalls and several Zulu cultural villages. The most popular of these is **PheZulu Safari Park** ① *5 Old Main Rd, Botha's Hill, T031-777 1000, www.phezulusafaripark.co.za, Zulu shows daily 1000, 1130, 1400, 1530, R90, additional 1 hr game drives R120.* There are commanding views of the valley from here, a reptile farm, a small game park with zebra and antelope, curio shops, and the **Croctilians** restaurant which specializes in croc steaks. The main attraction here is the Zulu show, where visitors are taken into traditional beehive-shaped huts and Zulu beliefs, rituals and artefacts are explained. There follows an impressive dancing display.

The Umgeni Steam Railway's **1000 Hills Choo-Choo** ① *T082-353 6003 (mob), www.umgenisteamrailway.co.za, 2 daily departures on the 2nd and last Sun of each month, 0845 and 1230, tickets from Kloof Station, R130, children (2-13) R100 return,* is a vintage 1912 steam train that runs along a line built 1877-1880. On departure days there are two round trips, between Kloof Station and Inchanga, and it's a leisurely way to enjoy the scenery.

◗ *The Valley of 1000 Hills was supposedly named by the writer Mark Twain on a visit to South Africa at the end of the 19th century.*

⊚ Durban listings

Hotel and guesthouse prices

L over R2550 **AL** R1871-2550 **A** R1271-1870
B R851-1270 **C** R641-850 **D** R301-640
E R131-300 **F** under R130

Restaurant prices

ⅢⅠ over R260 ⅢⅠ R131-260 Ⅰ under R130

See pages 46-53 for further information.

⊜ Sleeping

Central Durban and the beachfront have a
wide selection of accommodation, although
safety issues have caused a decline in tourist
numbers in recent years. Safer, more attractive
and with a wider range of restaurants are the
suburbs of Morningside and Berea. Contact
the **Accommodation Reservation Service**,
Tourist Junction, 160 Monty Naicker Rd,
T031-304 3868, www.bookabedahead.co.za.

The **Baz Bus** collects and drops off from
all backpacker hostels daily.

City centre *p440, map p442*

A Durban Hilton, 12-14 Walnut St, next to
the International Conference Centre, T031-
336 8100, www1.hilton.com. All the trappings
you'd expect from a modern 5-star 'name'
city hotel. Popular with conference delegates.
327 rooms, restaurant, bar, gym, pool, shop.

A Royal Hotel, 267 Anton Lembede St, T031-
333 6000, www.theroyal.co.za. The hotel
originally built on this site in 1842 was made
of wattle and daub; it now has luxurious 5-star
service, 251 rooms, a/c, DSTV, pleasant decor,
attractive outdoor pool, and 6 restaurants
including an excellent Indian one, a grill and
a theatre supper club (see Eating, page 451).

C Albany, 225 Anton Lembede St, T031-304
4381, www.albanyhotel.co.za. Classic art deco
hotel in a big pink block, 72 simple, functional
rooms, en suite, a/c, M-Net TV, rooms have
views over gardens. Restaurant, 2 bars, central
location opposite City Hall and Playhouse, but
this is now a rather run down area.

D Formule 1, Masabalala Yengwa Av, next to
the railway station and long-distance coach
station, T031-301 1551, www.formule1.co.za.

Modern, clean, budget rooms for up to 3, ideal
for late arrivals but nothing to keep you there
other than sleeping. Book to guarantee a room
as there are few budget options in the centre.

Beachfront *p445, map p442*

B Bluewaters, 175 Snell Parade, North Beach
T31-327 7000, www.bluewatershotel.co.za.
250 rooms, standard modern beachfront
hotel, rooms have DSTV, a/c, plus excellent
views of the beach. Restaurant, indoor pool,
cocktail bar, hairdressing salon, avoid if there
is a large conference on.

B Protea Hotel Edward, 149 Marine Park,
T031-337 3681, www.proteahotels.com. Large
luxury hotel on the Golden Mile, with 100 a/c
rooms with M-Net and minibar, 2 restaurants,
bar, pool and deck, secure covered parking,
one of the most luxurious beachfront hotels.

Durban suburbs *p447*

The suburbs are far more appealing than the
centre, both for their attractive, historical architecture and the choice of restaurants and bars,
all within safe walking distance of each other.

A Quarters, 101 Florida Rd, Morningside,
T031-303 5246, www.quarters.co.za. 4 historic
homes have been converted to create this
boutique hotel. Refreshingly modern feel, 25
rooms, cool white walls and dark red fabrics,
black and white photos on the walls. Excellent
brasserie, shaded courtyard, modern bar. Some
rooms have a small veranda overlooking palm-
shaded gardens, but some are slightly
cramped and set on a busy corner. Good
location close to restaurants.

A Riverside Hotel & Spa, Northway, T031-
563 0600, www.riversidehotel.co.za. Large
modern hotel overlooking the river, 169
spacious rooms, a/c, DSTV, dark wood furniture,
beauty and wellness spa. Friendly service and a
great restaurant (see Eating, page 452) and
popular bar, pool, secure parking. Some noise
from traffic, popular with tour groups.

A The Westville, 124 Jan Hofmeyr Rd, Westville T031-266 6326, www.thewestville.co.za.

Luxury hotel aimed at business travellers and tour groups, 42 a/c rooms, TV, **Sage** restaurant (famed for good Mediterranean cuisine), pool, squash courts, big Irish-themed sports bar.
B 164, 164 St Thomas Rd, Musgrave, T031-201 4493, www.164.co.za. Stylish boutique hotel in the centre of Musgrave. Luxurious rooms with polished wooden floors, fashionable decor, simple colour palette, Victorian bathrooms, DSTV. Secure parking, pool set in gardens, delicious cooked-to-order breakfasts, attractive bar with ocean liner decor. Low-key, friendly service, excellent value for what is one of the best guesthouses in Durban. Recommended.
B Anstey's Guest House, 477 Marine Drive, Bluff, T031-467 9692, www.ansteysguest house.co.za. The Bluff is the section to the south of Durban that sticks out to sea on the opposite side of the entrance to the port. Small but comfortable rooms with pine and wicker furnishings, DSTV, a/c, thatched bar and lapa, pool, good location close to the beach, but overpriced.
B Beside Still Waters, 30 Braemar Av, La Lucia, T031-572 7797, www.besidestill waters.co.za. 14 a/c self-catering units with DSTV and Wi-Fi, in a lovely tract of tropical gardens with fish ponds and a swimming pool, very friendly management, breakfast and dinner available, stylish bright decor. Recommended by readers.
C Bali on the Ridge, 268 South Ridge Rd, Glenwood, T031-261 9574, www.baliridge.co.za. Close to University of Natal, spectacular views of city and harbour, 8 rooms, elegant Bali furniture, attractive polished wooden floors, stylish a/c rooms, TV, bar fridge, pool.
C Ridgeview Lodge, 17 Loudoun Rd, Berea, T031-202 9777, www.ridgeview.co.za. 7 double rooms each with a/c, bathrooms, TV, phone with email connection and private patios. An elegant house with excellent guest facilities. Secluded, lush gardens with pool and good views. Close to restaurants and shops. Airport transfer can be arranged.
C Rosetta House, 126 Rosetta Rd, Morning-side, T031-303 6180, www.rosettahouse.com.

4 luxury a/c double rooms, cool tiled or wood floors, country inn-style furnishings, TV, 3 have separate entrances and patios. Secure parking, a fine old Edwardian town house set in tranquil gardens. Good value and close to the restaurants on Florida Rd.
C-E On the Beach, 17 Promenade, Glenashley, T031-562 1591, www.durban backpackers.com. Great location on the beach, north of the city centre and with easy access to the Gateway Mall. Smart set-up with mix of guesthouse-type en suite doubles with TV and self-catering dorms. Most rooms have floor-to-ceiling glass windows with ocean views. Prices include breakfast. Lively bar, home-cooked meals, comprehensive travel centre, pool, internet, DSTV, secure parking. To get here follow the M4 through Durban North; after Virginia Airport take the Aubery Dr exit to the beach. Recommended.
D Elephant House, 745 Ridge Rd, Berea, T031-208 9580, elephanthouse@mweb.co.za. The building housing this small B&B is said to be one of the oldest in Durban, and got its name from once having come under attack from elephants. Peaceful and friendly, 2 doubles, a/c, en suite, TV. Guest lounge, laundry and attractive, quiet tropical gardens. Meals on request.
D Triple Five, 555 Essenwood Rd, Berea, T031-209 6787, www.triplefive.co.za. Two 2-bed a/c separate apartments, extremely comfortable, with well-equipped kitchens, lounges, balconies and DSTV. Garden with jacuzzi, dining area, B&B or self-catering, secure off-street parking.
E-F Hippo Hide, 2 Jesmond Rd, Berea, T031-207 4366, www.hippohide.co.za. A small, upmarket backpacker place set in a pretty tropical garden, double rooms, some en suite with TV, one en suite dorm with attached self-catering kitchen, relaxed atmosphere, rock pool, outside bar and pleasant deck, close to shopping centres and restaurants on Musgrove Rd. Good information desk which can help with tours and bookings.
E-F Tekweni Backpackers, 169 Ninth Av, Morningside, T031-303 1433, www.tekweni

backpackers.co.za. One of the liveliest, most popular hostels in Durban, 2 km from the beach, bus station and town. Dorms and double rooms, small pool and bar out front, space for a couple of tents, laundry facilities, internet access. Often in a party mood, quieter doubles next door.

🍴 Eating

A wide choice of restaurants, bars and cinemas can be found in the Gateway Shopping Mall, see page 454.

City centre p440, map p442

₩₩₩ New Café Fish, Yacht Mole, Margaret Mncadi Av, T031-305 5062. Open 1200-1500, 1830-2200. Set right on the water with yachts moored within arms reach, upstairs bar is great for a sundowner, a basket of calamari and view of the working harbour. Downstairs is a more formal restaurant, seafood a speciality, very popular, outdoor deck in summer.

₩₩₩ Royal Grill, Royal Hotel, 267 Anton Lembede St, T031-333 6000. Mon-Sat 1830-2300. One of 6 restaurants in this upmarket hotel, and the hotel's 70-year-old flagship restaurant, serving excellent steaks in an opulent setting with chandeliers, grand piano, soaring ceilings and potted palms. An elegant, colonial dining experience. Save room for something from the dessert trolley.

₩₩₩ Ulundi, Royal Hotel, 267 Anton Lembede St, T031-333 6000. Open 1200-1430, 1800-2230, closed Sat lunch. Also based in the Royal Hotel, this is regarded as one of the best Indian restaurants in town. Top-end curries with a feel of colonial Natal, turbaned waiters, rattan furniture, ceiling fans, tandoori grills and traditional Durban curries. Good choice for vegetarians.

₩₩ Roma Revolving, John Ross House, Margaret Mncadi Av, T031-368 2275, www.roma.co.za. Mon-Sat 1200-1430, 1800-2230. Old-fashioned and kitsch concept, this long-running Italian restaurant is set on the 32nd floor, with a revolving floor offering excellent city views. Italian dishes, seafood and pasta, heavily laden dessert trolley, good value 3-course set meals, unparalleled views

Beachfront p445, map p442

₩₩₩ Cargo Hold, uShaka Marine World, T031-328 8065, www.ushakamarineworld.co.za. 1200-1500, 1800-2230. Great location, popular with families, spread over 3 floors in the phantom ship, with a glass wall looking into the shark tank, with ragged tooth sharks sidling by as you eat. Impressive menu, including good seafood, steaks, warm salads and Mediterranean starters. Reservations essential.

₩₩₩ Jewel of India, Holiday Inn Elangeni, 63 Snell Parade, T031-337 8168. Open 1200-1500, 1800-2200. Large restaurant with traditional Indian decor, serving tasty North Indian dishes served with tandoori breads, each dish is cooked from scratch and the waiters are knowledgeable about the menu and make recommendations.

₩₩₩ Moyo, uShaka Marine World, T031-332 0606, www.moyo.co.za. 1100-2230. The successful Moyo chain has now opened in Durban (other branches in Johannesburg and Stellenbosh) with good ocean views from the pier at uShaka Marine World, a pan-African menu with dishes from Morocco tagines to Mozambique curries and traditional South African potjies, live music, Xhosa face painting, fantastic atmosphere and professional service.

₩₩ Havana Grill & Wine Bar, Suncoast Casino, North Beach, T031-337 1305, www.havana grill.co.za. 1200-1430, 1800-late. Great veranda with views of the Golden Mile and Cuban inspired decor and menu, this offers a variety of dishes and is well known for its aged steaks – try the rib-eye in mustard sauce – seafood and tapas. There are several other quality restaurants at the casino plus a food court for snacks.

₩ Joe Kools, North Beach, T031-332 9698, www.joecools.co.za. Tue-Sun 1100-late. Superb views of North Beach, large restaurant and pub with a set of wooden decks over-looking the sand. Standard pub fare, range of burgers, pizza, pasta, calamari, fish and chips and club sandwiches. Perfect for people-watching, turns into a lively bar at night.

Durban suburbs *p447, map p437*
Durban's most popular nighttime hubs are Florida Rd in Morningside and Musgrave Rd in Berea, both lined with bars and restaurants.
♥♥♥ **9th Avenue Bistro & Bar**, Avonmore Centre, 9th Av, Morningside, T031-312 9134. Open Tue-Fri 1200-1430, Mon-Sat 1800-2200. Classic bistro atmosphere with a smart, traditional setting, award-winning wine list, good oxtail and roast duck, and seared tuna and lobster bisque. Plenty of loyal local regulars.
♥♥♥ **Sage at Christina's**, The Westville, see Sleeping, page 449. Tue-Sat, 0800-2200. Linked to a chef's training school, offering a weekly changing menu. Excellent standard of French cuisine in the evenings, international, themed buffets at lunch, teas and fancy cakes in the afternoon, and superb build-your-own breakfasts. Elegant chrome and white decor.
♥♥ **Bangkok Wok**, 116 Florida Rd, Berea, T031-303 8250, www.bangkokwok.co.za. 1200-late. Popular and ever-expanding Thai chain restaurant with a number of branches around Durban, including the Gateway Mall, Lighthouse Mall in Umhlanga and Wilson's Wharf, with a bustling ambience and standard but good chicken and prawn dishes, spring rolls and satay served up swiftly by Thai chefs.
♥♥ **Bean Bag Bohemia**, 18 Windermere Rd, Morningside, T031-309 6019. Open 1000-2400. Hugely popular set-up, with a vibey bar on the ground floor and smarter tatty-chic restaurant upstairs, in an old converted Durban town house. Quirky decor, great Mediterranean-based menu, mezze platters, pasta and steak. Popular cocktail evenings on Wed. Recommended.
♥♥ **Café 1999**, corner of Silverton and Vasue roads, Berea, T031-202 3406. Mon-Fri 1230-1430, Mon-Sat 1830-1030. Sheltered outdoor eating area and relaxed, stylish interior. Modern European food, excellent salads, Italian-style mains, great coffees and cakes, too. Young, well-dressed crowd.
♥♥ **Indian Connection**, 485 Windermere Rd, Mornigside,T031-312 1440. Open 1100-1500,

1730-1030. Traditional suburban home, which has been converted into a modern, stylish Indian restaurant. Refreshingly free of the usual curry house decor, the interior is white with wooden floors. Mix of north and south Indian dishes, choice of tandooris, tikkas and biriyanis, plus local coconut prawn curries, friendly service and a trendy, urban crowd.
♥♥ **Thunder Road Rock Diner**, 136 Florida Rd, Morningside, T031-303 3440, www.thunder roaddiner.co.za. 1000-late. Themed American rock 'n' roll restaurant with a menu of salads, smoked meats, seafood and no fewer than 10 types of excellent nachos. Run by music industry people, it's best known for promoting local musicians on the small stage.
♥♥-♥ **Blue Zoo Restaurant and Tea Garden**, in Mitchell Park, Musgrave Rd, T031-312 9134. Mon-Sun 0800-1700, Tue-Sat 1800-2230. Pleasant spot in picturesque park with out-side tables, simple and cheap build-your-own breakfasts, sandwiches, salads, and light meals, more sophisticated dishes on the dinner menu like steaks, seafood and curries.
♥ **Riverside Café**, Riverside Hotel & Spa, see Sleeping, page 449. Open 0600-2300. Informal setting on a terrace around the pool with good leisurely breakfasts and light meals like tortilla wraps, sandwiches and salads, and a more sophisticated menu (♥♥♥) of seafood and grills in the evening. The adjoining cocktail bar is popular for after work drinks on a Fri when there's live music and a happy hour 1700-1800.

⊙ Bars and clubs

Durban *p437, maps p437 and p442*
Bean Bag Bohemia, 18 Windermere Rd, Morningside, T031-309 6019. The trendy bar is one of the area's most popular. Great cocktail menu, including a long list of martinis, popular cocktail nights on Wed. Arty, stylish crowd.
Café Vacca Matta, Suncoast Casino and Entertainment World, T031-368 6535, www.vaccamatta.co.za. Wed-Sat 1900-late, Sun 1500-late. This super-sleek bar and club

Bunny chow

One of the more popular and delicious takeaway meals in Durban is bunny chow: a quarter, half or whole loaf of bread with the middle scooped out and filled with curry. The scooped-out bread is then used instead of a spoon to soak up the sauce. There are lots of theories about where it got its name but it's generally thought the dish was originally created for Indian caddies, known as bunnies, at the Royal Durban Golf Course in the 1940s. They were unable to get off from work for long enough to nip into Grey Street for a curry at lunchtime, so the story goes that they got their friends to go and buy the curry for them and that it was brought back to the golf course in hollowed-out loaves of bread because there were no disposable food containers at the time. There's quite an art to eating a bunny; after eating the scooped out piece of bread, you tear pieces off of the side of the loaf and dip them into the curry. The trick is to avoid tearing off pieces of loaf which are below the current gravy line otherwise you end up with a steaming-hot mass in your lap. You should also check whether your bunny chow was made from the end of a loaf or whether it is a *funny bunny* made from the middle and without a crust at the bottom.

has enormous interiors, ultra-chic decor, lounge areas and bar-dancers. Strictly over 25s and smart dress code, varied music including house, hip-hop and R&B.

Joe Kools, North Beach, TT031-332 9698, www.joecools.co.za, Tue-Sun 0100-late. Right on beach opposite one of the most popular surf sites, terraces with live DJs at night, very popular bar with the surfing fraternity.

Society, 178 Florida Rd, Morningside, T031-312 3213, Tue-Sat 1200-late. Converted historical house, formal restaurant downstairs and ultra-stylish lounge bar upstairs, popular with well-heeled fashion types. Good cocktails, sushi and Asian tapas, good for a bout of posing.

Tilt, 11 Walnut Rd, next to the Hilton Hotel, T031-306 9356, www.clubtilt.co.za, Fri-Sat 2100-late. Stylish club on two floors in an old Victorian house, sunken dance floor, 2 bars, white cube-shaped seating, mixed music, check the website for special events.

⊙ Entertainment

Durban *p437, maps p437 and p442*
Cinema
The following are multi-screen cinemas.
Nu Metro, www.numetro.co.za, at Suncoast

Entertainment World, Snell Parade, and the Pavilion Mall in Westville.

Ster-Kinekor, www.sterkinekor.co.za, Musgrave Centre, Musgrave Rd, Berea and the Gateway Mall, Umhlanga Rocks.

Theatre

Catalina Theatre, Wilson's Wharf, Margaret Mncadi Av, T031-305 6889, www.catalina theatre.co.za. 175-seater venue for comedy, theatre and music with new productions every 2-3 weeks.

The Playhouse, 231 Anton Lembede St, T031-369 9596, www.playhousecompany.com. Performances in 5 auditoriums: the Opera, Loft, Drama, Studio and Cellar Supper Theatre. Eclectic range from Shakespeare to modern dance and contemporary political satire.

The Royal Backstage, Royal Hotel, 267 Anton Lembede St, T031-333 6000, www.theroyal. co.za. A cabaret venue and supper theatre with 3-course meals. Wed-Sat from 1900.

○ Shopping

Durban *p437, maps p437 and p442*
African Art Centre, 94 Florida Rd, Morningside, T031-312 3804,

www.afriart.org.za. One of the best places in Durban to buy Zulu beadwork, baskets and ceramics, at slightly marked-up prices, but excellent quality. The shop is a non-profit making outlet for rural craftspeople.

Antiques and Bygones, 437 Windermere Rd, Morningside, T031-303 8880, www.antiques andbygones.co.za. Sells a range of silver jewellery and European antiques.

BAT Centre, Margaret Mncadi Av, T031-332 0451, www.batcentre.co.za. Superb arts and crafts shops selling contemporary Zulu art and jewellery to traditional wood cut prints or handmade shoes.

Matombo Art Gallery, Tourist Junction, T031-304 9963. Good quality but expensive stone sculptures from Zimbabwe.

Victoria Street Market, corner of Queen and Bertha Mkhize Streets, T031-306 4021. This modern, rather dingy market is crammed with over 170 stalls selling African curios, leather goods, fabric, copper and spices. The highlight is the Indian spices and dried beans.

Village Walk, uShaka Marine World, 1 Bell St, T031-328 000, www.ushakamarine world.co.za. The shopping arm of this huge marine park, with a wide range of shops, including chain stores and independent boutiques, surf shops and fast-food outlets.

Suburban shopping malls

Gateway, north out of town in Umhlanga Rocks, T031-566 2332, www.gateway world.co.za. This vast complex is supposedly the largest mall in the southern hemisphere – easily believable once you step inside. With a huge variety of shops and restaurants, 18-screen cinema, IMAX theatre, impressive climbing and abseiling wall, an artificial surf wave and the world's only man-made double point break (for those who understand surf jargon), plus a championship skateboard park, you can easily spend a day here.

Musgrave Centre, 115 Musgrave Rd, Berea, T031-201 5129. Over 110 shops with a mix of trendy boutiques and national chain stores. A craft and curio market is held on level 5 of the car park on Sun 0900-1600.

Pavillion, accessed from the N3, Westville, T031-265 0558, www.thepav.co.za. 320 shops and restaurants, and a multi-screen cinema. It's always busy – an estimated 1.7 million people visit this mall each month.

▲▲ Activities and tours

Durban p437, maps p437 and p442
Boat trips
Durban Charter Boat Association, at the Durban Marina next to Cafe Fish, Margaret Mncadi Av, T031-301 1115, www.charter boats.co.za. Offers a wide range of boats, for small speed boat diving trips and deep-sea shark fishing to luxury booze cruises.

Sarie Marasis Pleasure Cruises, T031-305 4022, at the Durban Marina, www.sariemaraiscruises.co.za. A good way to get a grip on the size and workings of Durban Harbour is to go on a harbour cruise, which depart whenever there is the demand from the jetty, R80, children R40, phone ahead.

Cricket
Sahara Stadium Kingsmead, T031-332 9703, information and tickets from www.sacrickettickets.co.za. Home to the KwaZulu Natal provincial cricket team, Kingsmead is a modern stadium with large grandstands. All Durban's big matches are played at this popular venue and it recently hosted the 2009 Indian Premier League. The weather for matches is generally good but being close to the sea there is always a chance of rain or poor visibility.

Diving
Operators dive from Durban or can arrange trips to other sites such as Sodwana Bay or the Aliwal Shoal. Visibility is at its best during the winter months.

Meridian Dive Centre, T031-573 2190, www.scubadivesouthafrica.co.za. PADI courses and single dives.

Football

Named after a former leader of the Communist party during Apartheid, Durban's new 70,000 seat Moses Mabhida Stadium is on its way to completion in readiness for the 2010 FIFA World Cup™, and the 2 distinctive 100 m tall white arches over the top, now feature on the city's skyline. It has been built at the existing King's Park Sporting Precinct, where there's also a smaller soccer stadium.

Golf

Windsor Park Municipal Golf Course, next to the Umgeni River just north of Durban, T031-312 2245. 18 holes, phone for teeing-off times for visitors as competitions are held here, equipment can be hired here by the day or by the week. A number of newer golf courses are further north or south along the coast.

Horse racing

Race meetings are held at one of Durban's racecourses operated by the Golden Circle Turf Club: **Greyville**, 150 Avondale Rd, Greyville, T031-314 1500; and **Clairwood Park**, 89 Barrier Lane, Merewent, T031-4691020, www.goldcircle.co.za. Each has regular stands and an indoor buffet restaurant overlooking the course for which you will need to dress up a bit. Night racing is held at Greyville only. Check the website for racing calendars.

Surfing

There are several designated surfing and boogie-boarding beaches along the seafront, and a number of surf shops on the South Beach promenade have boards for hire. **Surf Zone**, Ocean Sports Centre, North Beach, T031-368 5818. Rents surf- and body boards by the hr (R40), ½-day (R70) or full-day (R100), and organizes surf lessons from R180 per hr.

Tour operators

Catchet Tours, T031-205 7502, www.cachet tours.co.za. Good range of ½- and full-day tours including Durban city, Valley of the 1000 Hills, overnight trips to St Lucia and the Drakensberg.

Durban Africa, Tourist Junction, T031-304 4934. The tourist office runs walking tours Mon-Fri, from R100, children (under 12) R70. The 3-hr tours must be booked a day in advance and are a good, safe way of getting to know the city. There's a choice of an Oriental/Indian or a history theme.
Jikeleza Tours, T031-702 1189, www.jikeleza tours.co.za. Township tour starting at the Kwa-Muhle Museum to explain the nature of Apartheid, before visiting the Umlazi or Nanda township. Also evening trips with local guides for drinks at the township shebeens, plus wider city tours.
Strelitzia Tours, T031-267 2252, www.strelitziatours.com. A comprehensive range of tours in the province 1-3 days with regular departures. City tours and day trips to townships and Valley of 1000 hills.
Tekweni Ecotours, T031-332 0575, www.tekwenicotours.co.za. Budget tour operator offering a huge range of tours. Regular tours to Hluhluwe-Umfolozi and St Lucia game parks, scuba-diving trips, tailor-made bird trips, and city, Valley of 1000 Hills and township day tours. There are also a number of cultural day and overnight trips to Zululand. Consistently good reports.

● Transport

Durban p437, maps p437 and p442
Air
Comair/British Airways has daily flights to and from **Johannesburg**. South African Airways (SAA) has a number of daily flights to **Cape Town** and **Johannesburg**, as well as to other principal South African cities. **Mango** has daily flights between Durban and **Cape Town** and **Johannesburg**. Kulula flies to **Johannesburg**, **Port Elizabeth** and **Cape Town**. 1Time flies to **Johannesburg** and **Cape Town**.
   Airline offices Tickets can be booked online at www.computicket.com. 1Time, www.1time.aero. British Airways Comair, www.britishairways.com. Kulula, www.kulula.com. Mango, ww5.flymango.com.

South African Airways (SAA), reservations T0861-359722 (in South Africa), T011-978 5313 (from overseas), ww2.flysaa. com. For further details, see Essentials, page 40.

Bus
Greyhound, Intercape and Translux run buses to **Cape Town** via Mthatha, East London, Port Elizabeth, Knysna and Swellendam, or via Harrismith, Bloemfontein and Beaufort West; **Tshwane (Pretoria)** and **Johannesburg** on the N3 or via **Richards Bay** and the N2.

Margate Mini Coach, T039-312 1406, after hours T082-455 9736 (mob), www.margate.co.za/minicoach.htm, departs Durban Station, advance booking essential, to the **Wild Coast Sun** in the Eastern Cape (see page 431), 3 hrs 15 mins. There are up to 3 services in each direction via **Durban Airport, Scottburgh, Hibberdene, Port Shepstone, Margate**; R170 for one-way trip.

Underberg Express, bookings T0861-114 924, www.underbergexpress.co.za, runs between **Sani Pass, Himeville, Underberg, Howick, Pietermaritzburg, Durban**, and **Durban International Airport**, every day. It departs from Sani Lodge at 0730 and arrives at Durban International Airport at 1200, from where it leaves again at 1300 and arrives back again at Sani Lodge at 1730. The full one-way fare is R220.

Baz Bus, T021-439 2323, www.bazbus. com, to **Port Elizabeth**, and **Johannesburg** and **Tshwane (Pretoria)**, via Northern Drakensberg, or via Zululand and Swaziland.

Bus companies All bus tickets can be booked online at www.computicket.com. Greyhound, www.greyhound.co.za; Intercape, www.intercape.co.za; and Translux, www.translux.co.za. For more information, see Getting around, page 41.

Car hire
For main companies, visit the websites or call the toll-free numbers listed on page 43. Avis, airport, T031-408 1777, www.avis.co.za; Budget, airport T031-408 1888, www.budget.co.za; Hertz, airport, T031-469 4247, www.

hertz.com; **Tempest**, airport T031-469 0660, www.tempestcarhire.co.za.

Taxi
Taxis must be booked in advance, or any restaurant and hotel can phone for one: **Mozzie Cabs**, T031-263 0467; **Zippy Cabs**, T031-202 7067.

Train
Trains for Durban arrive at the **Durban Station**, Masabalala Yengwa Rd. Central reservations, **Shosholoza Meyl**, T0860-00888 (in South Africa), T011-774 4555 (from overseas), www.shosholozameyl.co.za, timetables and fares are published on the website. The country's longest route, from Durban to **Cape Town** (36 hrs), leaves weekly on Wed, and runs via **Bloemfontein** and **Kimberley**. The route to **Johannesburg** (13 hrs), via **Pietermaritzburg** (2 hrs) and **Ladysmith** (6 hrs), leaves Sun, Mon and Wed-Fri.

❶ Directory

Durban p437, maps p437 and p442
Banks Banks and ATMs are found in all the malls. ABSA, has a branch at the airport that opens 30 mins before the first flight and closes 30 mins after the last flight. **American Express**, Pavilion Mall, T031-265 1455/6; 213 Musgrave Rd, T031-202 8733, Mon-Fri 0800-1700, Sat 0830-1200. **Consulates** Mozambique, 5th floor, 320 Dr Pixley KaSeme St, T031-304 0200. **Emergencies** Police Tourism Unit, T031-368 2207; Sea Rescue, T082-911. **Internet** Number of outlets in the malls and most of the hotels and hostels offer internet. **Medical services** Entabeni Private Hospital, 148 South Ridge Rd, Berea, T031-204 1300; North Beach Medical Centre, 37 Sol Harris Cres, T031-332 6060; The Travel Doctor, 45 Bram Fischer Rd, International Convention Centre, T031-360 1122, www.traveldoctor.co.za, vaccination centre, and good place for anti-malarials. **Pharmacies** Emergency pharmacy T031-207 3946.

KwaZulu Natal coast

The stretch of coast directly north of Durban is a mix of built-up holiday resort and city suburbs. To the south, the coastal resorts have more of a holiday feel. Much of this stretch has undergone considerable development and is extremely popular with domestic tourists.

▸▸ *For listings, see pages 465-470.*

South of Durban ⬤🅿🏕🅐 ▸▸ *pp465-470.*

The landscape south of Durban includes a fertile subtropical region stretching from the southern tip of the Drakensberg Mountain Range to the Indian Ocean. The Umzimkulu, the Umkomaas and the Elands rivers wind their way from the Drakensberg escarpment through the rolling hills of KwaZulu Natal to the sea. This was one of the first areas to be settled by the British during the 19th century and continuous agricultural development has left its mark on the landscape. Some of South Africa's largest pine and eucalyptus plantations extend for mile after mile around Harding, while, nearer to the coast, sugarcane and banana plantations dominate the scenery. A strip of subtropical forest runs down the coast bordering onto the beach. Excellent roads also make the Strelitzia and Hibiscus coastlines among South Africa's most popular holiday destinations.

Dolphin watching and scuba-diving on the Aliwal Shoal and on the reefs south of Port Shepstone thrill an ever-growing number of enthusiasts. A wide range of sporting facilities, including numerous golf courses and tennis courts, are available at the resorts. The main attractions inland are the nature reserves at Oribi Gorge and Umtamvuna.

Amanzimtoti → *Colour map 5, B2.*

The Srtrelitzia Coast is one of the more built-up areas south of Durban. Driving down the N2, the road passes Durban's international airport and goes through an extensive industrial belt. Amanzimtoti, or 'toti', only 22 km south of Durban, is effectively a suburb, a huge built-up holiday resort with little to keep you in town. The Zulu name translates as 'sweet waters', as described by Shaka. Thousands of locals spend their annual holiday here, swimming, soaking up the sun and partying. A wide range of holiday accommodation is available among the high-rise flats and holiday homes facing the beach. **Inyoni Rocks** and **Pipeline Beach** are the two main beaches for swimmers and sunbathers, behind which is a busy main road. On the outskirts of town is a large chemical factory and an explosives factory. However, the lagoons beyond Amanzimtoti have been spared the relentless pace of development and these havens of tropical vegetation are sanctuaries for the coast's prolific birdlife.

Kingsburgh to Scottburgh → *Colour map 5, B1.*

Between Amanzimtoti and Umgababa are a series of coastal resorts and beaches known collectively as Kingsburgh. The 8-km stretch is known for its good beaches and is popular with surfers and jet-skiers. Travelling down the coast from Amanzimtoti, the first beach you reach is **Doonside**; across the Little Manzimtoti River is **Warner Beach**. **Winkelspruit** is one of the more developed parts of the area. Across the Lovu River is **Illovo** beach, which is backed by a lagoon at the mouth of the river. **Karridene** is at the mouth of another river, the Msimbazi. **Umkomaas** is the last resort in this area, next to the **Empisini Nature Reserve**, where a small dam has been built on the river which attracts an interesting variety of birdlife. The reserve can be reached by taking the Umkomaas and Widenham exit off the N2.

Scottburgh → *Colour map 5, B1.*

Scottburgh, 58 km south of Durban, is one of the busiest resorts on the Strelitzia coast. The popular beach by the estuary of the Mpambanyoni is protected by shark nets. The beaches are connected by a miniature seafront railway. There is a **tourist office** ① *library centre, Scott St, T039-976 1364, www.scottburgh.co.za, Mon-Fri 0900-1630.*

The **Aliwal Shoal** lies just north of Scottburgh, and after Sodwana Bay is one of South Africa's most popular diving areas (see page 469). The shoal is a haven for marine life and has good dives on wrecks and the reef. The caves attract ragged-tooth sharks each winter.

Hibiscus Coast ⊜❼⊛▲ → *pp465-470.*

There is less industrial development along this coast, which stretches from Scottburgh to Port Edward, but the overall impression as you drive down the coast is of a long line of caravan parks and holiday homes, set in a lush subtropical strip of forest. The ocean is the highlight here. During the warm winter months billions of sardines travel close to the beaches, attracting dolphins, sharks, game fish and birds, and the ocean teams with life.

Vernon Crookes Nature Reserve

① *Sunrise to sunset, R10, children R5.*

From the N2, the R612 heads inland towards Ixopo. After passing Umzinto (8 km), there is a signpost to the Vernon Crookes Nature Reserve. The road passes through eucalyptus and sugarcane plantations as it heads towards a landscape of grassland and thornveld, which supports 56 species of mammals.

This is one of the best reserves to see blue wildebeest, eland, impala, nyala, oribi, reedbuck and zebra near to the south coast. The wide range of habitats support over 300 species of bird. The best time of year to see the reserve's wild flowers is during the spring in September and October, when there are some magnificent displays of orchids, lobelias and watsonias. A network of dirt roads crosses the park and there are picnic sites and viewpoints.

Umzumbe Village

This small, pleasant village 100 km south of Durban has a great backpackers' place to chill out at by the sea. It's also a good spot for dolphin watching and scuba-diving. From Durban, turn off the N2 at Hibberdene and follow the R102. Turn right at the sign for Umzumbe Fairview Mission and look out for the sign after about 1 km. It's also on the Baz Bus route.

Port Shepstone → *128 km from Durban. Colour map 5, C1.*

Located at the mouth of the Umzimkulu River, Port Shepstone is the largest town on the south coast and is more of an industrial centre than a tourist resort. **Hibiscus Coast Tourism** ① *16 Bissett St, T039-682 7944, www.hibiscuscoast.kzn.org.za, Mon-Fri 0900-1700, Sat-Sun in season.*

South of Port Shepstone

The towns and villages on this southernmost stretch of coast are the last of the chain of resorts that feel like seaside holiday camps before the R620 enters the Wild Coast (see page 419). Hiking in Umtamvuna Nature Reserve, diving on Protea Banks and the reefs off Shelly Beach, and whale and dolphin watching are the highlights of this region.

Shelly Beach is 5 km south of Port Shepstone on the R620. It is quite a large suburb with one of the region's biggest shopping malls and has a wide variety of shops, restaurants and a cinema. The beach here is a popular launch site for fishing and diving charter companies.

Uvongo, 12 km south of Port Shepstone, is built on cliffs looking out to sea and is one of the more pleasant resorts on the south coast. The beach, protected by shark nets, is safe for swimming and surfing. The waterfall at the nearby **Uvongo River Nature Reserve**, open from sunrise to sunset, is a pleasant place for a picnic. The 23-m-high waterfall tumbling over cliffs into the beachside lagoon is the reserve's main feature. At the rear of the beach are some steps to a viewpoint overlooking the falls.

South Coast

Margate → Colour map 5, C1.
Originally a palm-fringed stretch of sand, the town began to be developed in 1919 and is now a highly developed family resort, popular with holidaymakers from Gauteng. The beach is excellent and was awarded the Blue Flag a few years ago. From the junction with the South Coast Toll Road, the link road immediately enters the tourist zone passing the mini-golf and holiday homes on the way into town. In the centre, high-rise flats are crammed in towards the beachfront, which can get very crowded during the school holidays. Contact the **Hibiscus Coast Publicity Association** ① *Panorama Parade, Margate Beachfront, T039-312 2322, www.hibiscuscoast.kzn.org.za, Mon-Fri 0830-1630, weekends in season*, for further information.

Ramsgate is 2 km south of Margate and is now practically a suburb, but the beach here is a little quieter and has shark nets so is popular for surfing. It has a tidal pool for swimming and some pedalos and canoes available for hire.

Southbroom
Southbroom is a popular resort with subtropical trees coming down to the beach. It consists mainly of private holiday homes belonging to wealthy Gautengers and can feel deserted out of season. There is safe swimming in a tidal pool just down the coast at Marina Beach, a beautiful 5-km stretch of sand and rolling dunes.

The **Riverbend Crocodile Farm and Art Gallery** ① *Old National Rd, T039-316 6204, www.crocodilecrazy.co.za, daily 0900-1630, feeding time Sun 1500, small entry fee*, breeds around 200 Nile crocodiles. There is also a snake house, with snake handling demos every day at 1430. On Tuesday and Thursday (by appointment only) you can visit a large banana packing shed on the farm. It also has a tea garden, restaurant, farm stall and art gallery.

Mpenjati Nature Reserve ① *sunrise to sunset, R10, children (under 12) R5*, is 12 km south of Southbroom and is popular with windsurfers, canoeists and fishermen. The reserve covers a small area of coastal forest and wetlands along the edge of the lagoon and is good for spotting wetland and woodland birds including a resident pair of breeding fish eagles. There are some leisurely walking trails along the Mpenjati River and around the lagoon, with two picnic spots.

Port Edward → Colour map 5, C1.
This small tourist resort has a large palm-fringed beach backing onto tropical forest. There are shark nets here, and good swimming and surfing. It is a convenient place to stay when visiting Umthamvuna Nature Reserve.

Umtamvuna Nature Reserve
① *8 km north of Port Edward towards Izingolweni, T039-313 2383, sunrise to sunset, R10, children (under 12) R5.*
This is the southernmost and one of the lesser visited reserves in KwaZulu Natal, but has some of the finest hiking in the region. The sheer walls of lichen-covered rock, dropping down into thick rainforest at the bottom of the gorge, are the centre of this dramatic landscape. There is no big game here but the reserve is known for its displays of wild flowers in the spring and its colony of Cape vultures. It's also regarded as one of the world's top plant spots with over 330 species of woody plants and 80 herbaceous plants, of which 30 are endemic to South Africa. One shrub, *Raspalia trigyna*, is very rare and only found in this reserve. It is usually fairly easy to spot bushbuck, blue and common duiker, and the ubiquitous chacma baboons. Shy Cape clawless otters inhabit the reserve but the most visitors ever see of them are the white calcareous droppings found along river banks. There are two entrances to the reserve: the first turning, off the Izingolweni road, leads to the southern gate; the second turning, 5 km further on, leads to the northern gate. A simple map, bird checklist and some ecology information leaflets are available at the entrance.

Towards the Wild Coast
The Wild Coast lies to the south of Port Edward, on the other side of the former border over the River Umtamvuna. This used to be part of the former homeland of Transkei but since the abolishment of the homelands it is now part of Eastern Cape (see page 419). The contrast between the former homeland and KwaZulu Natal could hardly be more marked – crossing the old border is like crossing into another, much poorer, country. Road conditions deteriorate immediately and this is not a good route for access to the Wild Coast unless you have a 4WD. The alternative route to the Wild Coast is along the N2 via Kokstad and Mthatha to Port St Johns on a tarred road. It is dangerous to drive at night because of the goats, cattle and stray dogs that wander across the roads.

West from Port Shepstone
The road heading inland from Port Shepstone to the Oribi Gorge Nature Reserve passes through an extensive agricultural area of sugarcane fields, eucalyptus plantations and cattle pastures, crowded with Zulu huts and smallholdings. The contrast between the outlying farmland and the untouched African bush in the gorge is striking. There are two

routes to Oribi Gorge (21 km). The fastest route is to follow the N2; just past Oribi Flats East there is a signpost to the park on the right-hand side of the road. The alternative route is slightly longer and involves turning off the N2 onto a minor road 7 km outside of Port Shepstone. This road leads to Oribi Flats (21 km) and to the **Oribi Gorge Hotel**. The road passes through some rugged scenery along the Umzimkulweni River Valley.

Oribi Gorge Nature Reserve → Colour map 5, B1.

ⓘ *21 km west of Port Shepstone via the N2, T039-679 1644, www.kznwildlife.com. Daily 0630-1930, R10, children (under 12) R5.*

Established in 1950 to protect this area of thick woodland and towering cliffs where the Umzimkulu and Umzimkulweni rivers meet, the Oribi Gorge Nature Reserve is 24 km long and 5 km wide. The views from the top of the sandstone cliffs, some of which are up to 280 m high, look out over the forest, which clings to the sides of the ravines below. The cliffs provide nesting sites for birds of prey, and the forest, home to the African python, is so thick that although leopard live here they are never seen. One of their prey, the Samango monkey, can sometimes be seen in small groups. Favouring dense, evergreen jungle, the Samango has a dark brown face and longish hair. Birdlife here is prolific, with over 250 species present, including Knysna louries, narina trogons, trumpeter hornbills and five kingfisher species. Ironically, oribi are not common and are very rarely seen.

Samango Falls, **Hoopoe Falls** and **Lehr's Falls** are the most spectacular waterfalls in the gorge and are best seen after heavy rain when vast quantities of water come crashing down into the ravines below. There are several clearly marked hikes, from 1 km to 9 km. A series of tracks lead to viewpoints over the gorge. There are stunning views from **Oribi Heads**, **Horseshoe Rock**, **Camel Rock** and the **Overhanging Rock**.

A tarred road winds down 4 km from the hutted camp to a picnic spot next to the bridge crossing the Umzimkulweni River. There are some impressive views of the gorge. The Umzimkulweni River is not safe to swim in as it is infected with bilharzia but there is a pleasant swimming pool in the camp. The camp shop sells wildlife books, souvenirs, charcoal, firewood and a limited range of food. Fresh meat, vegetables and cheese are available from a farm shop just by the entrance to the reserve. The nearest petrol station is 4 km away in Paddock.

Don't leave valuables in your car when you walk to the edge of the gorge as cases of petty theft have been reported.

North of Durban (Dolphin Coast) ☺☻☺▲☺ ►► pp465-470.

The area north of Durban, between Umhlanga and Tugela Mouth, is known as the Dolphin Coast, thanks to the bottlenose dolphins that frolic in the waves year-round. It is also known as the Sugar Coast, thanks to the rolling sugar plantations backing the sea. Like the coastline to the south of Durban it is possible to miss many of the sights and small coastal settlements if you remain on the N2 highway. The inland towns of Verulam, Tongaat and Stanger/KwaDukuza, tucked between vast rolling sugar plantations, have large resident Indian populations and are processing centres for the area's industry, with few attractions for tourists.

The old coast road, however, runs parallel to the sea passing through the beach resorts of Umhlanga Rocks, Ballito and Salt Rock, attracting vast crowds of holidaying South Africans in summer. After Umhlanga Rocks, most of the resorts are far smaller than those found on the south coast and appeal to more upmarket holidaymakers, but the area is developing quickly. Nevertheless, it feels more relaxed and far less developed than the south coast, with crowds thinning out the further you get from Durban. The beaches are beautifully wild stretches of soft sand, pounded by impressive waves (but remember to check if they're protected by shark nets before going for a dip). Away from the water, locals flock to the impressive golf courses, although a quieter choice are the numerous tropical nature reserves; seldom overrun with visitors, these well-run protected areas provide some fine birdwatching opportunities.

Umhlanga Rocks → *Colour map 5, B2.*

Umhlanga Rocks Tourism ① *Chartwell Drive, T031-561 4257, www.umhlanga-rocks.com, Mon-Fri 0800-1630, Sat 0900-1200,* arranges accommodation and provides advice on visiting the nature reserves. It also has maps and brochures.

The upmarket holiday resort of Umhlanga Rocks is a short drive north of Durban – these days it is virtually a suburb of the city, although its sprawl of concrete highrises makes it feel more like a Spanish costa. The main attraction here away from the beach is **Gateway**, South Africa's premier shopping mall, allegedly the largest in the southern hemisphere (see page 454).

Umhlanga Rocks beach is a beautiful stretch of wave-lashed sand, although day visitors have little chance of seeing it, thanks to the belt of highrises stretching along its length. Access to the water is almost exclusively through resort complexes and hotels, and there's no beachfront area. Nevertheless, South Africans flock to the hotels and condominiums, and the area has a buzzing atmosphere in high season. **Umhlanga Lagoon** lies just to the north of town, where there are beautiful expanses of wetland, forest and an unspoilt, open beach yet to be concreted by the developers.

The town's name means 'Place of Reeds' in Zulu, after the reeds that are washed down the river to the north and onto the pristine beaches. The area was once covered with dune forest; today, only small pockets of original vegetation have been preserved in surrounding nature reserves. In the 19th century, the land was part of a large sugar estate, Natal Estates Ltd, owned by Sir Marshall Campbell. The estate was managed from Mount Edgecombe in the interior; a track was built from here to the coast and local farmers began to lease small plots on the beach and build holiday cottages. The first cottage was built in 1869 and was known as the Oyster Box, today the **Oyster Box Hotel**, which is presently being refurbished.

A popular local landmark is the **Umhlanga Lighthouse**. The distinct red and white circular concrete tower stands 21 m above the beach and acts as a fixed point to help ships waiting to dock in Durban harbour confirm their exact position in the outer anchorage. The lighthouse tower has stood here since November 1954, occupying the centre point on the beach, right in front of the Oyster Box Hotel. The lighthouse has never had a keeper; instead it was operated by the owner of the Oyster Box Hotel from controls in the hotel office, though now its fully automated.

The **KZN Sharks Board** ① *Herrwood Drive, T031-566 0400, www.shark.co.za, display hall and curio shop Mon-Fri 0800-1600, tour and video Tue-Thu 0900 and 1400, Sun 1400, R25, children (4-12) R12,* set inland from the resort, studies the life cycles of the sharks that inhabit the sea off the coast of KwaZulu Natal and investigates how best to protect bathers with various forms of netting. Umhlanga Rocks became the first beach to erect shark nets in 1962, following a series of attacks along the whole coast in December 1957. Today the Sharks Board is responsible for looking after more than 400 nets, which protect nearly 50 beaches. Tours at the Sharks Board begin with a 25-minute multimedia video

Dolphin Coast

To St Lucia & Hluhluwe
Enselini Nature Reserve
Richards Bay
R34
Empangeni
R34
To Melmoth & Ulundi
N2
Umhlatuzi Lagoon
Umlalazi
Mtunzini
Umlalazi Nature Reserve
To Ulundi, Eshowe & Vryheid
Umlalazi
R68
Gingindlovu
aMatikulu
R102
Mandini
Tugela Mouth
Harold Johnson Nature Reserve
Tugela
Fort Pearson
Darnall
Shakaland
Zinkwazi Beach
R74
Shaka's Memorial
Stanger
KwaDukuza
Blythdale Beach
To Greytown & Ladysmith
To Pietermaritzburg
Salt Rock
R102
Shaka's Rock
R614
Ballito
Tongaat
King Shaka International Airport (Under construction)
Umhloti
Verulam
Umhloti Beach
N2
Sharks Board
Umhlanga Rocks
Gateway Shopping Mall
N
Virginia Airport
Durban
10 km
10 miles
To South Coast

show on the biology of sharks and their role as top predators in the marine food chain. This is followed by a stomach-churning shark dissection. The display hall has a variety of replicas of sharks, fish and rays, including that of an 892-kg shark. It is also possible to accompany researchers on the **Sharks Board boat** ⓘ *T082-403 9206 (booking essential), R250 per person, no children under 6, min 6 people, max 12 people, 2 hrs*, as they conduct daily servicing of the shark nets off Durban's Golden Mile. The boat goes from Wilson's Wharf back in Durban at 0630. You won't necessarily see sharks in the nets, but you have a good chance of spotting dolphins and sea birds and there are good views back across to Durban. The ride out beyond the harbour walls can be bumpy.

Hawaan Nature Reserve is 4 km north of Umhlanga Rocks at the end of Newlands Drive. During the 1920s, William Alfred Campbell, son of Sir Marshall who had founded the sugar estates, used to stage a hunt every year in this unique forest environment. It was not until 1980 that 60 ha were protected as part of the nature reserve. Within the reserve there are 4 km of leisurely guided walks through an unusual area of mature coastal forest. The trails are not open to the public but you can join the 0800 Saturday morning **guided walk** ⓘ *T031-566 4018*. The area is rich in birdlife and you can also see bushbuck, duiker and vervet monkeys.

Ballito and around → Colour map 5, B2.

The N2 north of Umhlanga Rocks passes by the construction site of the new King Shaka Airport and an access road is being built from the N2, before reaching Ballito. This small-scale, largely low-rise resort of Ballito is far more attractive than Umhlanga, with easy access to the long beach and attractive accommodation nestled in lush vegetation stretching up the hillside. At the entrance of town, just off the coast road, is the **Dolphin Coast Publicity Association**

ⓘ *T032-946 1997, www.thedolphincoast.co.za, Mon-Fri 0830-1700, Sat 0900-1300*, a useful stop-off with information on the Dolphin Coast area. Most visitors to Ballito are South African holidaymakers, who settle in for a bucket-and-spade holiday every summer. If you're passing through, it's a pleasant enough spot for a day or two by the beach, but stick to the southern, less developed end.

North of Ballito, **Salt Rock** is named after a rock where the Zulus used to collect salt and is similar to Ballito, while nearby **Shaka's Rock**, also developing fast, is named after the cliff from which Shaka is said to have thrown his enemies to their foamy deaths. There is good snorkelling at Tiffany's Reef and Sheffield Reef, but neither resort holds much appeal other than for those after a sand and sea holiday.

Tongaat, Verulam and Stanger/KwaDukuza

Inland from Umhlanga Rocks, the R102 passes through the towns of Verulam, Tongaat and Stanger/KwaDukuza, which collectively form the heart of KwaZulu Natal's sugar processing industry. The descendants of the indentured labourers, who were brought here from India in the 1860s, give the region a distinct Indian atmosphere and, although the towns are now predominantly industrial centres, the Hindu temples and Indian markets are interesting. Accommodation is available but the coastal beach resorts are more pleasant places to stay.

In Tongaat, the **Juggernath Puri Temple** is 23 m high and can be seen from miles away. There are no windows in the tower, but inside, as the eye adjusts to the darkness, the Vishnu statue gradually becomes visible. **Shri Gopalal Temple** is just outside of Verulam on the road to the Packo food factory. The temple was opened by Gandhi in 1912, and catered for wealthier and more educated Gujurati immigrants. **Subramanyar Alayam Temple** is set in a beautiful tropical garden just north of town as you reach the railway bridge. A good time to experience the atmosphere of the temple is at weekends when many weddings are held. It is customary to remove your shoes before entering the temple buildings.

Stanger/KwaDukuza is a busy commercial centre surrounded by sugar plantations. It is currently undergoing a name change to KwaDukuza, which was the original settlement here founded by Shaka as his capital. At its height there were up to 2000 beehive huts surrounding Shaka's royal kraal. Shaka was murdered here by his half-brothers Dingaan and Umhlangana on 22 September 1828 and a monument was erected in his memory in 1932, allegedly on the site of his grave. For further information on Shaka, see page 848.

🌙 *Albert Luthuli, who won the Nobel Peace Prize in 1960, was restricted to living in Stanger as punishment for his political activities with the ANC. He died here in 1967.*

Harold Johnson Nature Reserve

ⓘ *T031-486 1574, www.kznwildlife.com. Daily 0600-1800, R10, children (under 12) R5.*
Just over 20 km north of Stanger/KwaDukuza on the N2, a signposted dirt track leads through sugar plantations up to the entrance of this 100-ha reserve, where there is a parking area and a picnic site. In the reserve are the remains of **Fort Pearson**, which was used as a base from which British troops invaded Zululand in 1879. The **Ultimatum Tree**, the other attraction here, was where Shepstone read out the ultimatum to Cetshwayo's *izindunas* (warriors) giving them 20 days to disband their armies, pay fines in cattle and conform to the coronation vows that Shepstone had imposed. These demands and others were totally unreasonable to the Zulus but non-compliance with the ultimatum was used by the colonial authorities as an excuse for war.

In the reserve, wildlife includes red and grey duiker, bushbuck, impala, vervet monkey and over 110 species of butterfly, which can be sought out on 7 km of walking trails.

The **Muthi Trail** gives an interesting insight into the medicinal uses of various traditional plants used by the Zulu people; a booklet can be bought at the entrance. At the picnic site there's a small cultural **museum** portraying traditional Zulu dress and culture.

⦿ KwaZulu Natal coast listings

For Sleeping and Eating price codes and other relevant information, see pages 46-53.

⦿ Sleeping

If you are looking for upmarket quality accommodation, then the north coast has a better choice. The south coast has been a popular holiday destination for many years and as such features some older and somewhat soulless self-catering blocks of apartments or faded hotels.

Kingsburgh *p457*

E-F Angle Rock Backpackers, 5 Ellcock Rd, Warner Beach, T031-916 7007, www.angle rock.co.za. Smart backpackers' place in a great beachside location, with octagonal-shaped dorms and double rooms. Also has camping, excellent kitchen, laundry facilities, snooker table, pool in a private garden full of palm trees and a great tropical feel. Owners organize diving at the Aliwal Shoal, free use of surfboards and fishing rods, recommended as the place to stay south of Durban, call in advance for pickups from Durban stations and airport.

Scottburgh *p458*

B Cutty Sark, beachfront, T039-976 1230, www.cuttysark.co.za. Modern, slightly dated hotel in a lovely beachside location, with 55 rooms, TV, 2 restaurants, rates include breakfast and dinner, bar, swimming pool, tennis and squash courts, gym, in 6 ha of well-kept tropical gardens. Horse riding on the beach and diving can be arranged from here. Popular family hotel.
C Blue Marlin Resort, 180 Scott St, T039-978 3361, www.bluemarlin.co.za. Large resort on a hill overlooking the beach. Pool, gardens, games room, 2 bars, inclusive of buffet meals so very good value, 120 spacious and

functional rooms, weekly specials for senior citizens so, as you can imagine, activities lean towards bingo, bowls and bridge.

Camping

Scottburgh Caravan Park, seafront, T039-976 0291, www.scottburghcaravanpark.co.za. Giant camping and caravan park, over 300 sites stretching along 1 km of beach, designed to cater for families during school holidays. The park has several swimming pools and has good sports facilities. Gets very busy during school holidays, a great setting out of season.

Umzumbe Village *p458*

E-F Mantis & Moon, Station Rd, T039-684 6256, www.mantisandmoon.net. Rustic backpackers set in lush jungle, with dorms, doubles and camping dotted between wild banana trees, also has newer tree house, with double rooms. Pool table, candle-lit bar, great music, home-cooked food, free use of surf boards, courtyard with a wild garden, outdoor hot tub, rooftop deck. Recommended.

Port Shepstone *p458*

B Kapenta Bay, 11-12 Princess Elizabeth Drive, T039-682 5528, www.kapentabay.co.za. 50 units, all 3 room self-catering suites with 2 bathrooms, bland modern block over-looking the beach, large swimming pool, restaurant, secure parking, typical resort set-up and popular conference venue.
D-F Pepper Pots, 60 Commercial Rd, T039-695 0852, pepperpots@telkomsa.net. Family-run set-up, smaller and less sprawling as the usual beachside resorts, with self-catering chalets, backpackers dorm, caravan and campsites, bar, restaurant, TV lounge, walking distance to the beach.

South of Port Shepstone *p458*

C Ayton Manor, 2.5 km inland from Shelly Beach, after driving under the N2, take the first right, T039-685 0777, www.aytonmanor. co.za. B&B and self-catering guest lodge with 6 rooms and 2 family suites set in a fine country house on a sugar estate, rather over-the-top decor (frills, heavy curtains), private balconies and separate entrances, TV, fridge, microwave, bar, pool, dinners on request, children will like the working farmyard and fishing on the farm dam can be arranged.

D Lavender Lodge, 228 Wilma Rd, Shelly Beach, T039-315 5376, www.lavenderlodge sc.co.za. Neat set-up 5 min's drive from the beach, with 5 B&B or 1 self-catering room with kitchenette, interesting abstract decor – think gothic statues and candelabras. Lovely gardens, pool, leisurely breakfasts are taken on the patio.

Margate *p459*

B Margate Hotel, 71 Marine Drive, T039-312 1410, www.margate.co.za/margatehotel.htm. 69 a/c standard rooms with TV, **Keg** pub and restaurant, swimming pool, tennis, comfortable but run-of-the-mill family hotel set in mature gardens overlooking the beach. Discounts in low season.

B Wailana Beach Lodge, 436 Ashmead Rd, T039-314 4606, www.wailana.co.za. Luxury guesthouse located 1 km to both Ramsgate and Margate centres, easy walking distance to all amenities, nice gardens with hammocks and pool, B&B. 5 stylish rooms, with TV, fan, lovely private sun decks with ocean views, evening meals on request, much friendlier than the standard holiday flats.

C Beach Lodge Hotel, Marine Drive, T039-312 1483, www.beachlodge.org.za. 35 a/c rooms, TV, plus modern self-catering units, all with well-equipped kitchens, dining area, TV, DVD player. Restaurant serving buffet breakfast, bar, large swimming pool, secure parking, Dutch spoken. Faded resort but affordable.

C-D Dumela Holiday Resort, St Patrick's Rd, T039-317 3301, www.dumelamargate.co.za. Simple self-catering cabanas overlooking

Margate's Blue Flag beach, 2 bed, 2 bath, kitchen, balcony with braai, DSTV, café and takeaway, pool, thatched bar. Good value for groups/families up to 6, especially in low season.

Southbroom *p459*

B Nature's Cottage, Churchill Rd, T039-316 8533, www.naturescottage.co.za. Charming log buildings encircled by large verandas and raised decks with cane furniture, set in a patch of indigenous forest and competition-winning gardens. 3 guest rooms, 2 self-catering cottages, 1 of which is built on stilts, a/c, TV, DVD and CD player, 2 swimming pools, hammocks. No under 13s. Recommended.

Port Edward *p460*

A Estuary Country Hotel, 1 km before Port Edward on the N2, clearly signposted, T039-313 2675, www.estuaryhotel.co.za. 24 a/c rooms in a restored Cape Dutch manor house, most with balcony overlooking the estuary, TV, bar, pool, health and beauty spa, close to a safe swimming beach. The **Fish Eagle Restaurant** is open to non-residents, run by an Austrian family it offers an interesting and varied South African and European menu. Recommended.

D Ku-Boboyi River Lodge and Backpackers, 4 km north of Port Edward in Leisure Beach on the R61, T039-319 1371, www.kuboboyi. co.za. A bright hilltop lodge with good views over the ocean and beach, with singles, doubles, triples with en suites or shared bathrooms, decorated in an African theme. Plenty of space for camping, pool, sunny veranda, B&B. The owner, Eric, is a chef and cooks exceptionally good value gourmet meals each night.

Oribi Gorge Nature Reserve *p461*

B Oribi Gorge Hotel, 22 km from Port Shepstone and 11 km from the N2, clearly signposted, T039-687 0253, www.oribigorge. co.za. Small family hotel with 18 comfortable rooms, restaurant, snooker table, gym, country pub, curio shop, and swimming pool, set in a

1870s colonial building encircled by a veranda. The restaurant serves burgers, steaks, pies and pub food, and there is a pleasant beer garden under the trees. The gorge can be seen from viewpoints on farmland adjoining the hotel, which is only 17 km from the hutted camp. A number of activities can be arranged from here with **Wild 5 Adventures** (see page 470).

D-E Oribi Gorge Camp, reservations through **KZN Wildlife**, T033-845 1000, www.kznwildlife.com. Accommodation here is very basic and even KZN Wildlife admits it's in need of major repair, but nevertheless its very cheap and in a lovely setting. The camp has 6 huts with 2 beds in each, equipped with braai, fridge, kettle, toaster, crockery and cutlery but no cooker, a 6-bed chalet with the same equipment plus a cooker, and a 10-bed chalet with 2 bathrooms and again with a cooker but this is the most run-down, plus 4 rustic tent sites. Bring all food and drinks with you. There's also a communal braai area, with lounge with satellite TV and a swimming pool with sundeck for use by guests and campers.

Umhlanga Rocks p462

In addition to hotels and B&Bs, there is a large selection of holiday apartments, most of which are rented out by the week. During the off season it may be possible to organize shorter lets in the middle of the week. **Umhlanga & Coastal Letting**, at the Caltex service station on Lighthouse Rd, T031-561 5838, www.get coastal.co.za, offers short and long term lets as well as time share. Contact well in advance if you are planning on renting a family-size apartment during any local school holidays.

L Beverly Hills Hotel, Lighthouse Rd, T031-561 2211, www.southernsun.com. 90 rooms with ocean views in a smart luxury hotel overlooking the beach. A/c, TV, the suites have butlers, choice of top-end restaurants including the **Sugar Club** and **Elements** cocktail bar, swimming pool, fitness centre, tennis and squash courts, afternoon tea served daily.

L The Oyster Box Hotel, Lighthouse Rd, T031-561 2233, www.oysterbox.co.za. This was the area's 1st hotel and dates back to the 1940s. It was always popular with British travellers visiting the colonies and is in a spectacular setting behind the dunes, the beach and the lighthouse. It's presently undergoing an extensive refurbishment but should be open by the time you read this. It will feature 78 rooms, 6 garden suites with private plunge pools, a spa, 2 restaurants, an oyster bar, 2 heated pools, a cinema and a gym.

AL Teremok Marine, 49 Marine Drive, T031-561 5848, www.teremok.co.za. A boutique lodge set in a tropical garden, contemporary and stylish decor and design, 8 luxury suites with a/c, stand-alone baths, rain showers, home entertainment systems, Wi-Fi, spacious lounge, pool, wellness spa, lovely breakfast room with picture windows opening on to a giant milkwood tree. Recommended.

B Cathy's Place, 18 Stanley Grace Cres, T031-561 3286, www.cathysplace.co.za. Homely B&B run by the affable Irish Cathy, with en suite doubles and singles in modern bungalow and 1 self-catering family cottage in the garden. TV, swimming pool, 5 mins' walk from the beach and shops, can arrange airport pickups.

C Honey Pot 11 Hilken Drive, T031-561 3795, www.honeypot.co.za. Set in a restored farm manager's house surrounded by mango and avocado trees, 5 smart B&B rooms with private entrances and patios, Mnet TV, fridge, bar, communal lounge in the old ox wagon shed, swimming pool. Child and dog friendly.

D Jessica's, 35 Portland Drive, T031-561 3369, www.jessicaskzn.co.za. Close to the beach and shops, 3 self-catering comfortable cottages in the tropical garden sleeping 2-4, with TV, overlooking the pool and small garden, breakfast and dinner on request.

Ballito and around p463

L Zimbali Lodge, just off the coast road, south of Ballito, T032-538 1007, www.zimbali.org.

Luxurious lodge set in the grounds of a country club and golf course, stretching along the coast. Golf carts ferry guests around the estate, between the sport facilities, spa, restaurants and opulent rooms, with polished wooden floors, huge beds, balconies and all mod cons. All set in beautiful tropical forest. Stunning pool area and direct access to the beach.

A Boathouse, 33 Compensation Beach Rd, Ballito, T032-946 0300, www.boathouse.co.za. Luxury guesthouse on the beach, 22 beautifully decorated rooms, the floor-to-ceiling windows have a boat rail with life rings attached, TV, phone, a/c, the bar is a great place to have a sundowner and spot dolphins, lovely pool on a wooden deck. Recommended.

B Salt Rock, Basil Hluett Drive, Salt Rock, T032-525 5025, www.saltrockbeach.co.za. A big block overlooking the beach but a friendly hotel and recently refurbished in a beautiful location, restaurant, bar and swimming pool, all rooms are sea facing and have DSTV, fridge. Caravan and camping park attached (**E**).

C Saffron House, 15 Robbins Rd, Salt Rock, T/F084-525 8707 www.thesaffronhouse.co.za. Comfortable and friendly guesthouse with 5 double rooms, TV, Wi-Fi, separate entrances and private patios, tropical garden, swimming pool, 5 mins' walk to the beach, secure parking, dinner on request.

D-E Dolphin Holiday Resort, Ballito, T032-946 2187, www.dolphinholidayresort.co.za. Pleasant caravan park with shady campsites and 10 self-catering log cabins sleeping 2-6, pool, games room, kiosk, trampolines for kids and volley ball court. You can't see the sea from here but it's only a couple of mins' walk to the beach.

Harold Johnson Nature Reserve p464
There are 6 shady sites for tents or caravans (**F**) with a tap, braai pit and ablution block. Come fully prepared as there are no other facilities. Reservations are made directly with the campsite office, T032-486 1574.

Eating

Amanzimtoti p457
¶ **Butcher Boys**, 417 Kingsway, T031-903 7390. 1200-1500, 1800-2200. Lively pub atmosphere and wide range of food served, including steaks with a selection of sauces, seafood, chicken and burgers. Children's menu. Good setting in an old house with sea views.
¶ **Clearwaters Spur**, 97 Beach Rd, T031-903 8813. Busy Western-style saloon bar with enormous steaks, roast chicken and beer.

South of Port Shepstone p458
¶¶¶ **Stephward Estate**, 17 Peter St, Uvongo, T039-315 5926, www.stephward.co.za. Part of a guesthouse with a tea garden open daily for light lunches and cakes, and upmarket restaurant serving à la carte dinners in the elegant dining room or al fresco on Wed, Fri and Sat evening, booking essential. The menu changes, but expect duck and seafood.

Margate p459
¶ **The Bistro**, 2450 Marine Drive, Ramsgate, T039-314 4128, www.thebistro.co.za. 1200-1500, 1800-2200, closed Sun lunch out of season. Friendly restaurant serving traditional cuisine, such as a good rack of lamb, roast duck, as well as grilled seafood and curries, comprehensive wine list, bright pink decor and comfortable bar.
¶ **La Capannina**, 206 Marine Drive, Ramsgate, T039-317 1078. Tue 1800-2100, Wed-Sat 1200-1400. Well-established authentic Italian restaurant with an Italian chef. Full range of pizza and pasta, and known for slow its tasty traditional soups, roast lamb and tripe stew, plus good fried prawns, a favourite with locals, and with a bustling trattoria-style atmosphere.
¶ **Larry's**, corner of O'Connor Dr and Panorama, beachfront, Margate, T039-317 2277, 0900-late. Pizza restaurant with a long menu, some salads and pasta choices, breakfasts, roast dinners at Sun lunch, and specials like chicken and prawn curry or liver and onions, with seating on a busy terrace overlooking the beach.

¶ **Just So Chinese**, Uplands Rd, Margate, T039-312 2165. Good-quality and cheap Cantonese food with a broad range of noodle dishes and good spring onion chicken and lemon kingklip, tatty decor but swift service.

¶ **The Waffle House**, Marine Drive, Ramsgate, T039-314 9424. Open 0900-1700. Sweet and savoury authentic Belgium waffles on a terrace next to Ramsgate Lagoon, breakfast waffles until 1100, beer and wine by the glass or good milkshakes, next door is the Gaze Gallery exhibiting the work of local artists.

Umhlanga Rocks *p462*

¶¶¶ **Razzmatazz**, Cabana Beach Hotel, 10 Lagoon Drive, T031-561 5847. Open 1230-1530, 1830-2200. Five-star prices in a 5-star hotel serving excellent food, unusual game and seafood dishes, such as lemongrass-steamed langoustines or venison with blueberries and baby onions, and a great setting on an outdoor deck overlooking the ocean.

¶¶¶ **Sugar Club**, Beverly Hills Hotel, Lighthouse Rd, T031-561 2211. Open 0700-2300. Pricey but lovely colonial theme restaurant with ocean views, terrace and downstairs cocktail bar, 2-, 3- or 4-course options at lunch, dinner is à la carte, seafood platters, curries, steaks, breakfast buffets open to non-hotel guests. The long wine list includes French champagne. Leave room for the decadent and rich desserts.

¶¶ **Al Firenze**, 21 Ray Paul Drive, La Lucia, T031-572 5559. Tue-Sun 1100-2230. Home-made pasta, wood-fired pizzas, seafood, specials could include quail, rabbit, duck or oxtail, and there's a comprehensive wine list. There's a lively terrace or else takeaways are available.

¶¶ **Cottonfields**, 2 Lagoon Drive, T031-561 2744, www.cottonfieldsrestaurant.co.za. 1200-late. Popular bistro and bar, freshly cooked seafood and meat dishes cooked in *potjiekos*, traditional cast-iron pots, large-screen TVs to watch sport, occasional live bands and karaoke, and DJs on Sat night.

¶¶ **Lord Prawn**, Umhlanga Plaza, T031-561 1133. Open 1130-1430, 1730-2200.

Recommended for its good-value seafood dishes, including surf 'n' turf combos, fish and chips, 1 kg of prawns, and very good Durban prawn curries. Cheerful maritime decor with an informal atmosphere.

Ballito and around *p463*

¶¶¶ **Mariner's**, Valenti Centre, Compensation Beach Rd, T032-946 1858. Tue-Sun 1200-1430, Mon-Sun 1830-2200. A tiny but elegant restaurant with smartly dressed tables and white linen, serving excellent but pricey seafood, with good prawn curries and fresh linefish.

¶ **Food Matters**, The Well, Albertina Way, T032-946 1527. Mon-Sat 0800-1700. A light airy café-deli serving gourmet breakfasts like scrambled eggs with truffle shavings, and buffet lunches of salads, grilled vegetables, and wholesome breads, plus afternoon teas with delicious cakes. Small wine selection of baby bottles to go with lunch.

⊙ Entertainment

Margate *p459*
Funworld, Marine Drive, T039-312 0741. Cinema, bowling, pool tables, arcade games.

⊙ Shopping

Umhlanga Rocks *p462*
The enormous **Gateway** shopping mall lies uphill from the coast in Umhlanga (see page 454). The other malls in the area are far smaller and more manageable, such as **Granada Centre**, on Chartwell Dr and **La Lucia Mall**, on Armstrong Rd. In town, there is a small selection of craft and souvenir shops.

▲ Activities and tours

Scottburgh *p458*
Aliwal Dive Centre, 2 Moodie St, Umkosaas, T039-973 2233, www.aliwalshoal.co.za. PADI 5-star dive centre, courses, snorkelling and

whale- and dolphin-watching trips. Good-value accommodation for divers above dive centre with dorms, en suite doubles and meals.

Margate *p459*
As the main tourist centre on the south coast, Margate is a good place to organize activities. Fishing is allowed off the pier and off Margate Rocks and there are plenty of tackle shops in town. Designated surfing and boogie-boarding areas are on Main Beach and at Lucien Point. Boards can be hired from shops in town. Main Beach is shark-protected and therefore the safest and most popular for swimming.
African Dive Adventures, T039-317 1483, www.africandiveadventures.co.za. Wide range of dive courses, specializes in shark dives. Dives at the Protea Banks where schools of hammerhead and Zambezi sharks are regularly seen.
Margate Country Club, T039-312 0571, www.margategolf.co.za. Tue-Sat 0800-1700, Sun 1400-1700. Attractive 18-hole golf course surrounded by palms and banana trees, visitors welcome, green fees R250.

Oribi Gorge Nature Reserve *p461*
As well as having hiking trails, Oribi Gorge is also the ideal location for adventure sports.
Wild 5 Adventures, Oribi Gorge Hotel (see page 466), T039-687 0253, www.oribigorge.co.za. Offers whitewater rafting (R450) in conventional rafts or large inner tubes on the Umzimkulu River, and abseiling (R250) from Lehr's Waterfall, the last 66 m being a free abseil during which you can feel the spray of the falls on your back. Also has the Wild Swing (R350), a 75-m freefall and a 100-m outward swing over the falls, and the Wild Slide (R200), a 120-m steel cable slide over Lehr's.

Umhlanga Rocks *p462*
Diving
2 interesting wreck dives are at the *T-Barge* and the *Fontao*. Both are at 20 m deep with good visibility. The boats were sunk to create artificial reefs and provide habitats for tropical fish.
36 Degrees, at ski boat launch ramp on main beach in Umhlanga Rocks, T082-553 2834

(mob), www.36degrees.co.za. PADI and NAUI, equipment hire and sales, courses, single dives, 2-hr dolphin-watching boat trips, and exciting speed boat trips.

Golf
Zimbali Country Course, just off coast road, south of Ballito, T032-538 1041, www.zimbali.co.za. An 18-hole championship course designed by Tom Weiskopf, lovely clubhouse with a broad wooden deck overlooking the course, green fees for visitors R220-400.

⊖ Transport

South of Durban *p457, map p459*
Bus
Baz Bus runs between **Durban** and **Port Elizabeth**, in 1 day before continuing on to **Cape Town** the next day, dropping off at the backpackers' hotels along the south coast. Greyhound and Translux run between **Durban** and **Cape Town** and stop in resorts along N2. **Margate Mini Coach**, reservations T039-312 1406, after hours T082-455 9736 (mob), www.margate.co.za/minicoach.htm, runs between **Durban** and the **Wild Coast Sun** in the Eastern Cape (see page 431). There are up to 3 daily services in each direction via Durban Airport, Scottburgh, Hibberdene, Port Shepstone and Margate.
Bus companies All bus tickets can be booked online at www.computicket.com. Baz Bus, T021-439 2323, www.bazbus.com; Greyhound, www.greyhound.co.za; and Translux, www.translux.co.za. For more information, see Getting around, page 41.

North of Durban *p461, map p463*
Bus
Greyhound, has a regular service between **Durban** and **Tshwane** (**Pretoria**) via Richards Bay, Vryheid, Piet Retief and Evander.

Taxi
Dolphin Coast Taxis, T032-525 9449.

Pietermaritzburg and the Natal Midlands

→ *Colour map 5, B1. Altitude: 647 m.*

This attractive city, the capital of the Colony of Natal in the late 19th century, was named after the Voortrekker leaders Gert Maritz and Piet Reteif, who settled here in 1838 after the Battle of Blood River; today it is the legislative capital of KwaZulu Natal. It markets itself as a distinctly English city and, despite its largely African population and bustling street life, its red-brick buildings do give it a strikingly similar look to a provincial English town centre. An important trading centre for the local farming industry, Pietermaritzburg is also home to the University of Natal and a number of technical colleges, giving it a young, studenty feel during term time, with a decent selection of nightlife. ►► *For listings, see pages 478-481.*

Ins and outs

Getting there Pietermaritzburg is only 80 km from Durban on the N3 and can easily be visited in a day. **Durban International Airport** (see page 437) is 45 minutes' drive from Pietermaritzburg. **Peitermaritzburg/Msunduzi Airport** is 6 km from the centre of town and has daily domestic flights to Johannesburg operated by **SA Airlink**. The **railway station** is on the corner of Church and Pine streets. This is a rough part of town, so arrange to be collected in advance if you're arriving by train. Long-distance buses stop here on the route between Durban and Johannesburg. Pietermaritzburg lies on the Durban–Johannesburg **Baz Bus** route, via the Northern Drakensberg; **Underberg Express** runs regular shuttles to the Southern Drakensberg on its route from Durban.

Best time to visit The climate is subtropical with heavy rainfall December to February. The rest of the year tends to be warm and dry and makes a change from the humidity in Durban.

Tourist information **Pietermaritzburg Tourism** ⓘ *Publicity House, 177 Chief Albert Luthuli (Commercial) Rd, T033-345 1348, www.pmbtourism.co.za, Mon-Fri 0800-1700, Sat 0800-1300,* is conveniently situated and has a comprehensive range of maps and leaflets, as well as an accommodation and mainline bus booking service. Staff are helpful, friendly and keen to promote their city. The original building was completed in 1884 and used to be the local police station. Pietermaritzburg is also the location of the central **KZN Wildlife** ⓘ *T033-845 1000, www.kznwildlife.com,* office. To get here, follow Commercial Street out of town towards Hilton, and follow signs for the Cascades shopping mall. The KZN offices are next to the mall in the Queen Elizabeth Park Nature Reserve.

Background

Pietermaritzburg was founded as the capital of Natalia in 1838. Originally, the town was laid out in the same way as Cape Dutch towns, with thatched houses, wide streets, large gardens and irrigation channels running down the streets. The small rural capital was a trading centre for farmers and game hunters, and later became a stopover for wagon trains heading for the interior.

The republic of Natalia only lasted a few years; the British arrived in 1843 and established a garrison here, and the safety provided by the garrison encouraged other settlers to arrive from Britain and Germany. Pietermaritzburg became a prosperous Victorian town and many of its most attractive buildings date from this period. The administrative buildings of the Colony of Natal are in the city centre, but it is the quiet side streets, lined with fine Victorian houses built by wealthy merchants, which make the town so pretty. Here, the mix of bungalows and two-storey red-brick houses retain their original verandas, decorated with cast-iron lattice work, hardwood windows and brass fittings, all shaded by huge, arching jacaranda trees.

Pietermaritzburg ⊖🅿🅒🔺🅔🅒 » pp478-481. Colour map 5, B1

The city centre has Pietermaritzburg's most imposing Victorian buildings, civic gardens and war memorials. The old buildings are not all open to the public but it is possible to walk around most of the sites in a morning. Dominating the centre is the grand **City Hall**, which looms on the corner of Chief Albert Luthuli (Commercial) Road and Church Street. Built on the site of the Volksraadsaal (people's council) in 1900, it is supposedly the largest all-brick building in the southern hemisphere and is decorated with stained-glass windows.

Tatham Art Gallery
ⓘ *60 Chief Albert Luthuli (Commercial) Rd, T033-342 2801, www.tatham.org.za. Mon-Fri 0800-1700, free.*
Opposite the City Hall is a similarly imposing red-brick structure, completed in 1879 and used as a post office until 1906, when it became the site of the Supreme Court. Renovation work started during the late 1980s and, in 1990, it was inaugurated as the new home for the Tatham Art Gallery.

Inside is a fairly ramshackle selection of modern and Victorian art; the original collections are of French and British Victorian art, and although the landscapes are fairly pleasant there is nothing particularly striking about them. But the gallery does have some interesting and unusual works, including a Stanley Spencer landscape called *Near Nareta, Bosnia*, and paintings by Degas, Renoir, Braque and Picasso. There is a large, highly ornate ormolu late-Victorian clock at the top of the stairs on the first floor which is worth seeing. During chiming, a screen is raised to reveal a clockwork blacksmith and some bellringers moving in time with the chimes. The **South African Gallery** is perhaps the most interesting, with a collection of contemporary art including beadwork of Zulu and Xhosa origins. These eclectic works are a refreshing change from the worthy but somewhat staid collections of Victoriana. There is a tea room on the first floor, overlooking the gardens.

Voortrekker Museum
ⓘ *351 Langalibalele (Longmarket) St, T033-394 6834, www.voortrekkermuseum.co.za. Mon-Fri 0900-1600, Sat 0900-1300, R5, children (under 16) R2.*
This museum is on the site of the original Church of the Vow and has a collection of period farm machinery, furniture and Voortrekker relics, as well as some more up-to-date exhibits. There is an interesting display that ponders the subject of Kruger's war chest, which disappeared en route to Lorenço Marques (known today as Maputo – the capital of Mozambique) and has never been recovered. Another item to look out for is a pair of enormous Voortrekker trousers. The former Longmarket Street Girls' School building has been incorporated into the site, and now houses more culturally significant exhibitions on Zulu heritage, including a reproduction of a traditional Zulu home, filled with household goods. There is also a display on the life of Prince Imperial of France, Louis Napoleon, who stayed in Pietermaritzburg before being killed by a Zulu ambush near Ulundi during the Anglo-Boer war. His death in South Africa ended the Bonaparte dynasty. In the garden is a replica of a Hindu Shiva temple.

Welverdient House, the thatched house opposite the Voortrekker Museum, was moved from Edendale, a farm outside the city, in 1981. It used to be the house of Andries Pretorius, the victor at the battle of Blood River, and gives a good idea of the spartan conditions in which the early Voortrekkers lived.

Supreme Court Gardens

The Supreme Court Gardens are opposite the City Hall on the corner of Church and Commercial streets and are the site of several war memorials. The **Memorial Arch** is flanked by two field guns captured from the Germans by South African forces in Southwest Africa in 1915. The **Zulu War Memorial** has a cannon next to it which was cast in Scotland in 1812 and used to be fired to let the citizens of Pietermaritzburg know that the mail had arrived. The **statue of Gandhi**, commemorating the centenary of his arrival in South Africa (1893), is just below the gardens on Church Street, and across the street is the old **Colonial Building**, built in 1899, decorated with Natal's coat of arms, featuring a wildebeest and Pietermaritzburg's coat of arms, featuring an elephant. From the Gandhi statue continue down Church Street on the same side and you'll reach the **Presbyterian Church** built in 1852, the first British church in Pietermaritzburg.

The Lanes

The Lanes are a network of alleyways between Langalibalele (Longmarket) and Church streets. They were originally the site of Pietermaritzburg's legal and financial centre and used to be private rights of way to the small offices behind the Supreme Court. Today, they are lined with small shops, cafés and administrative buildings dating from the turn of the 20th century. From Church Street, enter the Lanes on Timber Street where you can see **Harwin's Arcade**. The arcade was built in 1904 and has a skylight running through it, illuminating the second-hand bookshops.

Timber Street leads into Langalibalele (Longmarket) Street; turn left here and return to Chief Albert Luthuli (Commercial) Road. This route passes the impressive **General Post Office**, opened in 1903, and the offices of the *Natal Witness*, South Africa's oldest newspaper established in 1846. The **Old Legislative Assembly** and the **Old Legislative Council** are on the left-hand side. On the right is Witness Lane which leads to the Natal Museum.

Natal Museum

① *237 Jabu Ndlova (Loop) St, T033-345 1404, www.nmsa.org.za. Mon-Fri 0815-1630, Sat 1000-1600, Sun 1100-1500, R5, children (under 16) R2.*

The Natal Museum has a more diverse collection than many other South African museums. The natural history gallery has a considerable collection of stuffed creatures that date from the foundation of the museum. The last wild elephant shot in Natal in 1911 is on display, as are two specimens of the black and white rhino. The first treasure chest of the Colony of Natal can be found here; it is an old iron chest that used to travel around the colony by wagon and was used to collect the Native Hut Tax. The colony's finances were at times so desperate that the chest held less than a pound.

Upstairs is the relatively new **Origins** gallery, with anthropology displays including a fascinating section on the Ashanti people of the Gold Coast. There is a wooden stool decorated with strips of gold, a sacred object which was demanded by the British as a token of surrender. The collection of brass weights is particularly beautiful; they were used for weighing gold and were moulded from natural objects such as snails, ground nuts and grasshoppers. There are also a number of archaeological displays, with examples of San rock art in a reconstructed cave, and recreations of Stone Age life. The final gallery focuses on Portuguese shipwrecks.

South of the Lanes

At the other end of Langalibalele (Longmarket) Street is **St Peter's Church**, a museum with displays of European stained glass. The church was built in 1857 after Colenso split with the Church of England. Bishop Colenso is buried in front of the altar. From here, turn left into Peter Kerchhoff (Chapel) Street, then right into Jabu Ndlova (Loop) Street. At No 11 is the **Macrorie House Museum** ⓘ *T033-394 2161, Mon 1100-1600, Tue-Thu 0900-1300, closed Fri-Sun, small entry fee*, where Bishop Macrorie lived from 1870 to 1892. The house is decorated with period furniture and houses a collection of Victorian costumes.

Pietermaritzburg

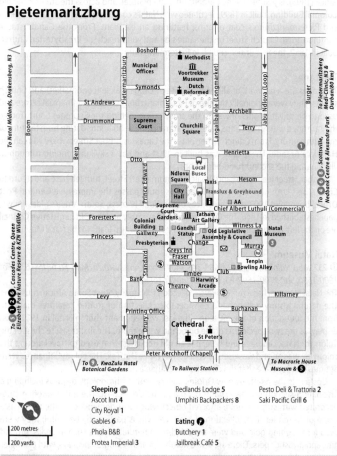

Sleeping 🛏️
Ascot Inn 4
City Royal 1
Gables 6
Phola B&B
Protea Imperial 3

Redlands Lodge 5
Umphiti Backpackers 8

Eating 🍴
Butchery 1
Jailbreak Café 5

Pesto Deli & Trattoria 2
Saki Pacific Grill 6

200 metres
200 yards

Beyond the city centre

Butterflies for Africa ① *Willowton Rd, T033-387 1356, www.butterflies.co.za, Tue-Fri 0900-1630, Sat 0930-1530, Sun 1030-1530, R24,* is clearly signposted from the N3 towards Durban. It incorporates a large enclosed butterfly house, a butterfly garden and nursery with a maze, a craft and coffee shop, an art gallery and museum, and audio-visual presentations on the life of a butterfly. There's a new monkey house, with examples of small monkeys and a walk-through path.

Alexandra Park lies to the south of the city centre and can be reached by following Chief Albert Luthuli (Commercial) Road past the Voortrekker Cemetery. The park was founded in 1863 and has large public gardens with a beautiful old cricket pavilion built in 1898. Two other interesting features here are the Victorian bandstand and a cast-iron water trough for horses. An open-air art show is held here every May.

World's View lies to the west of town and you can get to it by following the Old Howick Road (R103), past the Country Club golf course and into World's View Road. A plaque at World's View, next to the Voortrekker Road, marks the route taken by the early Voortrekkers. The short trails follow the path of an old railway line and pass through pine and wattle plantations where it is possible to see interesting birdlife and some small buck. There are magnificent views of Pietermaritzburg from the top of the hill.

KwaZulu Natal Botanical Gardens ① *2 Swartkops Rd, Mayors Walk, T033-344 3585, www.sanbi.org, daily 0800-1730, restaurant Tue-Sun, R12, children (under 16) R6,* were founded in 1870 and following a fine Victorian tradition have a collection of plants from all over the world. The most interesting feature is the **Zulu Muthi Garden**, created with the help of local healers and including a traditional beehive-shaped healer's hut. This is a 'living display' to inform visitors about traditional plant-use and associated conservation issues but is also designed as a centre where healers can attend courses on the sustainable use of traditional medicine plants. It is ideal for a leisurely stroll or afternoon tea next to the ornamental lake.

Queen Elizabeth Park Nature Reserve ① *off the Howick road on the outskirts of Pietermaritzburg, free,* is small but has a network of short walking trails from which you can see blesbock, impala and zebra. The flora here is particularly interesting; the park has been a wild flower reserve since 1960 and has stunning displays of colour in the spring. The headquarters of **KZN Wildlife** (see page 471) are located within the park.

Natal Midlands ⊖⊙⊘⊝ ➤➤ *pp478-481. Colour map 5, B1.*

The Midlands cover the region between Greytown and Richmond, Pietermaritzburg and Estcourt. The many rivers flowing off the Drakensberg escarpment have created a well-watered, fertile landscape that originally supported a large population of Zulu cattle herders and farmers in the lowlands. San migrated between here and the Drakensberg, following the herds of eland according to the changes of the seasons. Later the fertile territory attracted first the Voortrekkers and then British immigrants in the 1850s, all of whom fought for control of the land.

Today, the farms here cultivate wattle for tanning and paper pulp, and there are large horse-breeding studs, cattle and sheep ranches. The N3 bisects the Midlands and the majority of traffic passes through on its way between Gauteng and Durban. However, by taking the alternative R103, the Midlands towns and countryside can be explored by following the Midlands Meander route, a tourist initiative highlighting the multitude of craft outlets, country restaurants and rural retreats, popular with South African tourists.

Mahatma Gandhi in South Africa

Gandhi was asked by a journalist when he was on a visit to Europe what he thought of Western civilization. He paused and then replied: "It would be very nice, wouldn't it". The answer illustrated just one facet of his extraordinarily complex character. A Westernized, English-educated lawyer, who practised law in South Africa from 1893 to 1914, he preached the general acceptance of some of the doctrines he had grown to respect in his childhood, which stemmed from deep Indian traditions – notably *ahimsa*, or non-violence. From 1921 he gave up his Western style of dress and adopted the hand-spun *dhoti* worn by poor Indian villagers, giving rise to Churchill's jibe that he was a 'naked fakir' (holy man). Yet, if he was a thorn in the British side, he was also fiercely critical of many aspects of traditional Hindu society. He preached against the iniquities of the caste system, which still dominated life for the overwhelming majority of Hindus. Through the 1920s much of his work was based on writing for the weekly newspaper *Young India*, which became *The Harijan* in 1932. The change in name symbolized his commitment to improving the status of the outcastes, Harijan (person of God) being coined to replace the term outcaste. Often despised by British in India, he succeeded in gaining the reluctant respect and ultimately outright admiration of many.

Gandhi arrived in South Africa in 1893 but soon became involved in South African politics after being a victim of racial prejudice himself when he was forcibly removed from a whites-only train carriage in Pietermaritzburg. He founded the Natal Indian Congress in 1894 to fight for the freedom of the indentured Indian labourers that were working in the docks, sugar plantations and railways. He moved to a farm just outside Durban with his family and followers in 1903, to produce a resistance magazine called *Indian Opinion*, and his fame as an opponent to the rising racial prejudice saw him negotiating with General Jan Smuts in person. Thousands of indentured workers went on strike when the government passed a law to ban Indians entering the Transvaal in 1907, which led to the Indian Relief Bill in 1914 that finally emancipated the Indians. With the fight over, Gandhi returned to England in July 1914 and never saw South Africa again.

His death at the hands of an extreme Hindu chauvinist in January 1948 was a final testimony to the ambiguity of his achievements: successfully contributing so much to India's Independence, yet failing to resolve some of the bitter communal legacies, which he gave his life to overcome.

Ins and outs

There is an excellent map and brochure available in the region's tourist information offices promoting a series of routes for visiting the Midlands by car. The 'meander' is reminiscent of a Sunday afternoon drive through English countryside and is one of South Africa's local tourism success stories. Over 400 places are marked on the map and include a selection of B&Bs, craft shops and restaurants. The antique shops, potteries and weavers are good places to buy gifts. Information is available from **Midlands Meander Association** ① T033-330 7260, www.midlandsmeander.co.za.

Howick → Colour map 5, B1.

The small and quiet town of Howick has grown up around what was originally a fording point across the Umgeni River on the wagon route to the interior. The original settlement was named by the colonial secretary Earl Grey after his English home of Howick in Northumberland. More recently, Howick was the location where Nelson Mandela was arrested in 1962 before being sent to jail for 27 years. The actual spot where the police arrested him is just outside of town on the R103, on a road heading towards Tweedie Junction. He was disguised as a driver for a white friend and it is thought the police stopped the car because of a tip off. There is a memorial, unveiled by Mandela himself in 1996, marking this otherwise unassuming spot in a field next to the road.

The 95-m-high **Howick Falls** are popular with South African tourists, who stop off here for a break while travelling on the N3. In 1951 they were proclaimed a national monument. To the Zulu people the waterfall is known as kwaNogqaza, 'the place of the tall one'. There is a path to the bottom of the falls but beware of the slippery rocks. Above the falls is an open-air café.

The **Howick Museum** ① *T033-330 6124, Tue-Fri 0930-1530, Sat-Sun 1000-1300, small entry fee*, is just next to the falls and has a display of Victorian furniture and farm machinery. There is also an interesting collection of military badges. Next door is the Old Agricultural Hall, now home to an excellent craft and curio shop, **Craft Southern Africa**, T033-330 5859. The hall was built in 1899 and is well worth a look.

Midmar Dam Nature Reserve
① *From Howick the R617 crosses the N3 and passes Midmar Dam Nature Reserve (7 km) en route to Bulwer (90 km) and Underberg (120 km), T033-330 2067, www.kznwildlife.com, reserve open 24 hrs, office 0800-1600, R20, after 1200 R13.*
This attractive dam is a hugely popular holiday resort with numerous sporting facilities on offer, including power boating, jet-skiing, windsurfing and yachting. Sunset cruises can be organized with advance notice. There is a small shop open at weekends and peak periods where bikes, windsurfs and canoes can be hired. Day visitors are permitted. The Midmar Mile swimming contest is held here every February and attracts around 10,000 entrants. It's now the world's largest inland swimming race.

Towards Estcourt
The fastest route north from Howick to Mooi River (37 km), Estcourt (60 km), Spioenkop (92 km) and the Free State is on the N3. An alternative scenic route is to take the R103 through Nottingham Road (29 km) to Mooi River (48 km).

The Nottingham Regiment gave their name to the small farming settlement of **Nottingham Road** after being stationed near here in the 1870s. This is a quiet, rural area, known for its trout fishing and holiday farms. The **Nottingham Road Brewery Company** ① *Old Main Rd, Rawdons Estate, T033-266 6044, www.rawdons.co.za, tastings and shop daily 0800-1700*, is a rustic brewery with enticingly named beers that are hand-brewed using spring water: Tiddly Toad Lager, Pie-eyed Possum Pilsner, Pickled Pig Porter. From Nottingham Road, the R27 heads west towards the Drakensberg reserves at Kamberg (48 km; see page 509) and Lotheni (70 km; see page 512). This road is a rough dirt track which can become impassable after rain; check on road conditions before starting out.

Further northwest, the **Mooi River** flows through a small farming community en route from the Drakensberg Mountains to the Tugela River. The area around Mooi River is well known for stud farming; it's smaller than the Cape but has produced a higher proportion of winners. The Drakensberg reserves at Kamberg (42 km) and Giant's Castle (see page 506) are well signposted from here.

Estcourt → *Colour map 5, B1.*

Estcourt is a thriving industrial town, site of South Africa's largest sausage factory and a Nestlé factory, both of which can be visited on a factory tour, if you're that way inclined. Factories aside, there's no reason to stop in Estcourt other than to stock up if you're on the way to self-catering accommodation in the Drakensberg.

Bushman's River Tourism ① *Old Civic Building, Upper Harding St, T/F033-352 6253, Mon-Fri 0900-1600,* is an excellent tourist office, stacked full of brochures from all over the country. Well worth a stop if you are passing through town, it also has internet facilities and a craft shop. **Greyhound** and **Translux** buses stop outside.

Fort Durnford ① *T033-352 3000, daily 0900-1200, 1300-1600, R5,* has interesting displays on military history, a good section on fossils and, rather oddly, one of Africa's most complete bird egg collections, donated by a local collector. In the grounds you can look around a reconstructed Amangwane Zulu kraal. The fort itself was built in 1874 in order to protect local residents from feared Zulu attacks. It was named after Major Anthony Durnford who commanded the Natal Carbineers and was killed during the heroic last stand at Isandlwana.

⊙ Pietermaritzburg and the Natal Midlands listings

For Sleeping and Eating price codes and other relevant information, see pages 46-53.

⊜ Sleeping

Pietermaritzburg *p471, map p474*
There are lots more B&Bs in town; check with the tourist office for details.
B City Royal, 301 Burger St, T033-394 7072, www.cityroyalhotel.co.za. 44 rooms, with a/c and TV, some with kitchenettes, set in a modern, run-of-the-mill town hotel, but its recently had a smart refurbishment. Restaurant serving traditional food and good value buffets on Fri and Sat nights and Sun lunchtime, sports bar, plus an open-air terrace for drinks. Secure parking.
B Protea Hotel Imperial, 224 Jabu Ndlova (Loop) St, T033-342 6551, www.proteahotels. com. Historical building with 70 comfortable rooms with DSTV, a/c, room service, secure parking, restaurant and bar (restaurant is recommended for its game dishes). It's the oldest hotel in town and recently refurbished, but feels a little impersonal. The Imperial Crown Prince of France, Louis Napoleon, stayed here during the Anglo-Boer War.
B Redlands Lodge and Hotel, 1 George Mcfarlane Lane (off the Old Hilton Rd), T033-394 3333, www.redlandshotel.co.za.

A luxury hotel set in a slightly surreal gated development, in a quiet suburb. Country-style pastel-coloured rooms with private balconies, DSTV, internet, bar and mediocre restaurant, pool. Popular with business people. Comfortable with friendly service, but feels isolated.
C Ascot Inn, 210 Woodhouse Rd, Scottsville, T033-386 2226, www.ascot-inn.co.za. B&B or self-catering cottages set in a large garden with 2 swimming pools. Simple, cosy decor and friendly bar and grill restaurant on site. Has become a popular conference venue.
C Gables, 216 Woodhouse Rd, Scottsville, T033-346 0792, www.thegables.co.za. Comfortable B&B or self-catering units in converted stables of a former racehorse stud, with rooms set around a small garden. All units have TV. Small restaurant and bar with set meals each night.
D Phola B&B, 6 Cheviot Way, Blackridge, T033-344 3346, http://pholabnb.co.za. Small, quiet B&B in the suburbs near the botanical gardens with good views over the city. 3 rooms with DSTV, bright orange and white decor, healthy breakfasts, dinner on request, swimming pool.
E-F Umphiti Backpackers, 317 Bulwer St, T033-394 3490, www.umphiti.co.za. Backpacker's hostel housed in a Victorian

home bang in the centre of town, with a pleasant veranda and small, lush garden with pool. Lounge with DVDs, very good meals available, accommodation in dorms and doubles and space for camping. Adventure tours can be arranged, including good value 3-day tours to Lesotho. Baz Bus stop. Recommended.

Howick *p476*
A-B Shafton Grange, 12 km from Howick towards Rietvlei, T033-330 2386, www.shaftongrange.co.za. A fine old farmhouse built in 1852, with 6 rooms, some with Victorian baths and wash-stands, lounge, country meals, swimming pool. The attraction here is horse riding or polo on the 52-ha farm, there are 21 stables and people from Johannesburg bring their horses here on holiday. Trout fishing can also be arranged and there are lots of walks on the farm, which has a number of antelope.
B Old Halliwell Country Inn, 10 km north of Howick on Curry's Post Rd, T033-330 2602, http://oldhalliwell.co.za. A traditional English-style country hotel and restaurant built in 1830 as a wagon stop. Each of the 15 double rooms have fireplaces, some have jacuzzis, underfloor heating and private patios. Cosy pub and restaurant, and swimming pool set in lovely gardens with rolling lawns.
B Penny Lane Guest House, 11 km from Howick on the R103 towards Lidgetton, T033-234 4332, www.pennylane.co.za. 10 spacious rooms, decor varies from twee to tasteful, fan-cooled and heaters for the winter months. The guest lounge has a log fire, DSTV and a bar with a rustic African feel, traditional meals served. Swimming pool and tennis court.
C Howick Falls Hotel, 2 Main St, T033-330 2809, www.howickfallshotel.co.za. 18 rooms in one of Howick's oldest buildings, built in 1872. Former guests include Mark Twain and Cecil Rhodes. It's full of atmosphere and the rooms have been renovated and now feature a/c, DSTV, some family units with 2 bedrooms and sharing a bathroom, bar, lounge, a café

for light meals and a restaurant for quality dinners – expect the likes of seared tuna or Thai green curry.

Midmar Dam Nature Reserve *p477*
B-D Midmar Camp, KZN Wildlife, T033-845 1000, www.kznwildlife.com. Range of rustic cabins, en suite self-catering units, chalets and campsites, some set on the shoreline, including a 6-bed chalet equipped for the disabled, shared ablution blocks for units without bathrooms. The campsites (**F**) get very crowded during the school holidays, and again have shared ablution blocks, and some have electricity.

Towards Estcourt *p477*
AL Fordoun's, Nottingham Rd, T033-266 6217, www.fordoun.com. Luxury country retreat, with 17 spacious and stylish rooms, overlooking a farm dam and rolling lawns. Excellent and intimate restaurant and an award-winning spa with indoor pool, flotation pool in the old silo tower and treatments using both international products and some created by a traditional African healer. Can organize fly-fishing in the area.
A-B The Bend, 14 km from Nottingham Rd towards Kamburg on the R103, T033-266 6441, www.thebend.co.za. Smart lodge set in a nature reserve with a variety of lodge rooms and cottages, spacious with attractive decor and antique furniture, country meals, indoor swimming pool, horse riding and hiking, 5 km of the Mooi River runs through this reserve, trout fishing on 6 dams. Has its own chapel for country weddings.
B Rawdons, Old Main Rd (R103), T033-263 6044, www.rawdons.co.za. A luxurious, thatched English-style country hotel in a 195-ha estate, with 25 double rooms, with light and airy decor, TV and heating, restaurant, swimming pool, bowls, tennis, 7 trout dams for fishing, also location of the **Nottingham Road Brewery** (see page 477).
C Thatchings, 12 km from Nottingham Rd on the Curry Post Rd on the other side of the N3, T033-266 6275, www.thatchings.co.za.

Rural guesthouse set in a huge garden, 7 rooms with TV, country-style decor, fresh flowers, á la carte evening meals, bar with snooker table, golf course nearby as well as trout fishing on the farm.

C-E Sierra Ranch, on the R622 or Old Greytown Rd, 16 km from Mooi River, T033-263 1073, www.sierraranch.co.za. Huge Western-themed resort with restaurant and swimming pool. Offers a wide range of sporting activities, including tennis, bowls, river tubing, horse-riding. Accommodation is in chalets, rondavels, doubles or the bunkhouse.

Estcourt p478

B Blue Haze Country Lodge, 6 km from Estcourt on the Giant's Castle road, T036-352 5772, www.bluehaze.co.za. Thatched lodge located on the way to the Battlefields and mountains, overlooking a peaceful lake, with 23 comfortable garden suites, swimming pool fringed by palms, cosy pub serving meals. Game trails, horse riding and river rafting can be organized.

🍴 Eating

Pietermaritzburg p471, map p474

The Butchery, 101 Roberts Rd, Wembley, T033-342 5239, www.thebutchery.co.za. 1200-late. Informal family steakhouse and bar with friendly staff, steaks can be cut to order, and come with a variety of vegetables and sauces, plus other meaty dishes, pasta and seafood, and for the not so hungry a good selection of stuffed baked potatoes. Good choice of wine, which is displayed in a giant wine rack along 1 wall.

Pesto Deli & Trattoria, 5 Roberts Rd, Wembley, T033-342 2778. Open 1200-late. Pizza, pasta, fish dishes and decent wine list, plus tasty Italian desserts like tiramsu. The ambience is laid back with traditional red and white checked tablecloths and staff in jeans and T-shirts.

Saki Pacific Grill, 137 Victoria Rd, T033-342 6999, www.saki.co.za. 1200-late.

Asian-themed restaurant in the Victoria Centre mall, informal atmosphere at long wooden tables, family orientated, a wide selection of affordable Thai, Indian, Japanese and Chinese food, something for everyone, Singapore and Indian beer to drink and, of course, saki.

Jailbreak Café, corner of Burger St and Pine St, T033-394 5342. Mon-Fri 0800-1630, Sat 0800-1400. Located in the old prison that is a national monument, slightly musty but friendly café and tea garden, breakfasts, cakes, lunches, surrounded by number of excellent African craft shops, which are open 0800-1600.

Howick p476

Harry Jack's House, 118 Main St, T033-330 5036, www.harryjacks.co.za. Tue-Sun 0900-late. Set in a lovingly restored former blacksmiths built in 1900 with wooden floors and sash windows, this has an astonishingly long menu of starters, grills, pastas, seafood and desserts, and most of the main courses can be ordered in half or full portions. You can also make up your own brunch and there's a children's menu.

🎭 Entertainment

Pietermaritzburg p471, map p474

Club Lanes, Club Lane, T033-342 8220. Offers 10-pin bowling.

Numetro, Cascades Centre near the new Grey's Hospital. 8-screen cinema.

▲ Activities and tours

Pietermaritzburg p471, map p474

Meet us in Africa, T033-239 4607, www.meetusinafrica.co.za. Interesting tours for older travellers to some of the lesser visited nature reserves near Pietermaritzburg, plus flower trips to Drakensberg. Informative company run by Carolyn and Derek McDonald who are specialist field guides and can arrange birding and flower tours to the Drakensberg.

Umphiti Adventure Tours, Umphiti Backpackers, see Sleeping, page 478. Good value 3-day trips to Lesotho, plus day tours to the battlefields, Howick Falls and the Valley of a 1000 Hills.

☉ Transport

Pietermaritzburg *p471, map p474*
Air
Durban International Airport is a 45-min drive from Pietermaritzburg.

Bus
Baz Bus stops in Pietermaritzburg 3 times a week. **Greyhound**, **Intercape** and **Translux** stop in Pietermaritzburg on the route between **Durban**, and **Johannesburg** and **Tshwane (Pretoria)**. Underberg Express, T0861-114924, www.underbergexpress. co.za, has a daily service to **Underberg**, **Himeville**, and **Sani Pass**, useful if you wish to get close to the Drakensberg Mountains without your own transport, and in the other direction **Howick**, and **Durban**. Check their website for time-tables and fares. The bus picks up and drops off at the Protea Hotel Imperial mid-morning.

Bus companies All bus tickets can be booked online at www.computicket.com. Baz Bus, T021-439 2323, www.bazbus.com; **Greyhound**, www.greyhound.co.za;

Intercape, www.intercape.co.za; and **Translux**, www.translux.co.za. For more information, see Getting around, page 41.

Car hire
Budget, Protea Hotel Imperial, T033-342 8433, www.budget.co.za.

Taxi
Yellow Cabs, T033-397 1910.

Train
The railway station is on the corner of Church and Pine streets. Central reservations, **Shosholoza Meyl**, T0860-00888 (in South Africa), T011-774 4555 (from overseas), www.shosholozameyl.co.za, timetables and fares are published on the website. Trains running between Durban and Johannesburg stop here Wed-Fri, Sun-Mon.

Estcourt *p478*
Greyhound stops in Estcourt between **Durban**, **Johannesburg** and **Pretoria**.

❶ Directory

Pietermaritzburg *p471, map p474*
Banks Most of the major banks can be found along Church St and in the shopping malls. **Internet** Hive Media Café, Nedbank Centre, 50 Durban Rd, Scottsville, T033-342 8988. **Medical services** Medi-Clinic, 90 Payne St, T033-845 3911.

Battlefields Route

The vast, open landscapes of northern KwaZulu Natal are as evocative as one would hope, with rolling plains and savannah grasslands stretching to the horizons and studded with flat-topped acacias, mysterious rock formations and granite koppies. This landscape forms the stage upon which three major wars have been fought, and the battlefields of the clashes between Boers, Britons and Zulus can all be visited. Don't expect self-explanatory sights, however – many of the battlefields are marked by little more than small commemorative plaques, and you'll need a good guide to really bring the history of the region to life. This area also provides an eye-opening glimpse into the lives of rural Zulus, the roads passing numerous traditional subsistence kraals, with their thatched rondavals, herds of goats and waving children. The poverty of these remote areas can be striking after the affluence of the coastal resorts.

The best way to appreciate the history of the battles is to go on an organized tour; with a decent guide it can be very moving. The major sites can be visited in a day. Two of the best museums are the Siege Museum in Ladysmith and the Talana Museum in Dundee. Of the wars fought between the Voortrekkers and the Zulus, the most interesting battlefield site is Blood River, east of Dundee. Two of the most interesting historical sites of the Anglo-Zulu War are Isandlwana and Rorke's Drift; the latter has a good museum, making it the best site to visit without a guide. The most interesting Boer War sites to visit are Talana, the Siege of Ladysmith and Spioenkop. ⟫ For more information visit www.battlefields.kzn.org.za. For listings, see pages 490-492.

Ladysmith and around ⟫ pp490-492. Colour map 4, A6.

Ladysmith is a quiet rural town surrounded by cattle and sheep ranches, with little more than a run-down shopping complex, a handful of Victorian buildings and the Siege Museum – a good place from which to start a visit to the Battlefields Route. In recent years, the town centre has undergone something of a transformation, and today has a vibrant African feel to it, although it remains an unattractive place to stay. The siege aside, Ladysmith is perhaps best known as being home to Ladysmith Black Mambazo band, the phenomenally popular South Africa band. The region lying to the south of Ladysmith is where many of the Boer War Battlefields are located. The Siege Museum in Ladysmith will help to arrange tours or provide a detailed map of the battlesites.

 One of Ladysmith's first industries was a lard factory set up by two Scotsmen who culled the region's vast herds of zebra and melted down their fat.

Ins and outs

Getting there Ladysmith is on the N11 and is well connected to the highway network. The N11 heads north to Newcastle (100 km), Volksrust (153 km) and into Mpumalanga. Some 26 km south of Ladysmith, the N11 connects with the N3, which in turn leads north into the Free State and south to Durban. The N11 also connects at this junction with the R616 leading to the Northern Drakensberg.

Tourist information **Ladysmith Tourist Information Office** ⓘ *Siege Museum, Murchison St, T036-637 2992, www.ladysmith.kzn.org.za, Mon-Fri 0900-1600, Sat 0900-1300*, has a good selection of maps and leaflets on the battlefields. The bureau is also very helpful with accommodation suggestions and advising on battlefield tours.

The siege of Ladysmith

The siege of the British in Ladysmith by Boer forces lasted from early in the Anglo-Boer War, October 1899, until February 1900, 118 days in total. The British forces in northern Natal, under General White, had been forced to withdraw into Ladysmith after a series of defeats at the hands of Boers from both the Free State and Transvaal. The Boer forces had taken up positions in a six-mile radius around the town but made few attempts to defeat decisively the 10,000 remaining British troops.

The Boers, under the command of Piet Joubert (ably assisted by his tactically minded wife), did make one major assault on the British defences at Bester's Ridge on 6 January 1900. The British were, however, able to repulse the Boer attack, although it succeeded in placing a further strain on their already stretched resources.

The Boer forces decided to concentrate on starving out the British or shelling them into submission while they held off any British attempts to relieve the town from the south by securing defensive positions in the hills overlooking the Tugela River.

For the besieged British troops the defence of Ladysmith required patience and organization rather than heroics. In December 1899 General White had been ordered to try to break-out and join up with the British forces under Buller attempting an advance through Colenso – but details of when the advance was to take place were never relayed to him and the first he knew of the attack was when he heard the artillery fire. After the losses sustained in the defence of Bester's Ridge in January 1900, White was unable to offer any support to General Buller's forces in their attempts to relieve Ladysmith and all his troops could do was sit tight and survive the bombardment as best they possibly could.

Conditions for the town's inhabitants, whether military or civilian, were harsh. Food and other provisions were in short supply and what was available became exceptionally expensive. Tins of condensed milk, for example, could fetch up to a pound and bottles of whisky seven pounds. One source of comfort for the civilians and wounded was that the Boer commanders allowed them to set up a camp and hospital at Intombi, some four miles southeast of the town, so that they were spared the heavy artillery bombardment of the town centre. News of Buller's numerous blunders at Colenso, Spion Kop and other battles along the Tugela did nothing for morale, however, and many inhabitants felt it was only a matter of time before they had to give in to the Boers.

In February 1900 Buller's substantial army at last had some success in assaults on the Boer positions along the Tugela. On 27 February the British succeeded in taking Pieter's Railway and Terrace Hills overlooking the railway crossing of the Tugela at Colenso and the Boer forces surrounding Ladysmith rapidly lost morale. As news of the decisive defeat of General Conje's forces in the northern Cape filtered through to the Boer military lines, their resolve snapped and they fell back towards Elandslaagte, many in fact returning home, leaving the path clear for Buller's troops to at last relieve the beleaguered troops and citizens at Ladysmith.

Background

The Voortrekkers first arrived in 1847 and established a small republican settlement on the banks of the Klip River. However, it was only a matter of months before the area fell under the British sphere of influence. British settlers began to arrive during the 1850s to farm in the area. Ladysmith grew in importance as a trading centre because it was on the trail connecting the diamond and gold mines of the interior, Kimberley and Barberton, with Port Natal on the coast. Ladysmith is most famous for being besieged by General Piet Joubert for 118 days during the Boer War (see box, page 483). The British garrison of 12,500 men was cut off from the outside world for the duration of the siege.

Sights

Ladysmith's historical monuments are on the main square by the town hall on Murchison Street. The **town hall**, on the corner of Murchison and Queen streets, is a classic Victorian municipal building which was completed in 1893. During the siege, it was converted into a hospital until the clock tower was hit by a six-inch shell. The town hall was repaired in 1901. There is a small **museum** ① *Mon-Fri 0900-1600*, with a gallery of photographs illustrating Ladysmith's history up to the present day. The **Siege Museum** ① *Murchison St, T036-637 2992, Mon-Fri 0900-1600, Sat 0900-1300, R11, children (under 14) R5*, is next to the town hall. This is a fascinating museum, with one of the country's largest collections of South African military memorabilia, including reconstructions of scenes from the Siege of Ladysmith and the Boer War. There are displays of weapons, uniforms and household goods that were used during the siege, with explanations in English, Afrikaans and Zulu.

There are four field guns on Murchison Street just outside the museum: **Castor** and **Pollux** are the two guns sent from Cape Town at the outbreak of the Boer War for the defence of the town; **Long Tom** is a replica of the Creussot Fortress Guns, which were used by the Transvaal Republic to bombard Ladysmith from the surrounding hills.

Ladysmith

Sleeping
Bonnie Highlands 4
Bullers Rest Lodge 1
Naunton Guest House 5

Peaches & Cream 2
Royal 3

Eating ⑦
Santa Catalina Spur 1

Ladysmith Black Mambazo

Ladysmith Black Mambazo is one of the best-known South African musical groups of all time, outselling both the Beatles and Michael Jackson in their homeland. Over the years their music has been traditionally based on *isicathamiya* music and dance born in the gold mines of Johannesburg at the turn of the 20th century. The word itself does not have a literal translation; it is derived from the Zulu verb *cathama*, which means walk softly, or tread carefully. Back then, blacks went to the mines from all over southern Africa as migrant workers, leaving their homes and families for 11 months a year. Poorly housed in overcrowded hostels, they would entertain themselves after a six-day week by singing songs into the early hours every Sunday morning, with dance steps that were choreographed softly so as not to disturb the hostel security guards.

As a child, founding member Joseph Shabalala worked as a simple herd boy in the Ladysmith area. In 1961 he formed the group Ladysmith Black Mambazo, meaning the black axe of Ladysmith. At their first concert in Soweto the band was an immediate hit and each member received the princely sum of R5.28.

Internationally, Ladysmith Black Mambazo were relatively unknown until Paul Simon 'discovered' the band on a visit to Johannesburg in the mid-1980s. They collaborated with him on his album *Graceland*, released in 1986, which sold millions of copies worldwide and brought them instant fame. Joseph gave Paul Simon the Zulu nickname *Vulindlela*, 'he who has opened the gate'. To date, the band has rather astonishingly been going strong for over 45 years. For more information visit www.mambazo.com.

The Boers destroyed the original gun at Haenertsburg when Kitchener's Fighting Scouts threatened to capture it. The last gun is a German **Feldkanonne**, which was captured in German Southwest Africa and sent back as a war trophy.

Walking south down Murchison Street will take you past two historical hotels which are still in use. The **Royal Hotel** was built before the siege during the gold and diamond rushes of the interior. During the siege it was used by the press corps as a base. The **Crown Hotel** is the site of Ladysmith's first hotel, built of wattle and daub. The earliest battlefield tours, on horseback, could be booked here in 1904. Further down Murchison Street, on the corner with Princess Street, is the **Old Toll House** where wagon drivers paid a toll before entering town.

A refreshingly non-historical site is the **Cultural Centre** ① *Old Railway Institute Building, 316 Murchison St, T036-635 4231, Mon-Fri 0900-1600, small entry fee*. There is a collection of cultural and natural history exhibits, a township shack and a tribute to the Drakensberg Boys' Choir. There is also a hall dedicated to Ladysmith Black Mambazo, the world-renowned group that became South Africa's most successful band (see box, above). The music-filled hall contains the footprints of the members of the band eternalized in concrete, and life-size cut outs of the band on a mock-up stage. The curio shops sells the band's CDs. Further along Murchison Street is the **Central Mosque**, which was completed in 1922, and has a beautiful fountain and courtyard surrounded by palm trees.

Colenso

An easy excursion from Ladysmith, the town was named after John William Colenso, the Anglican Bishop of Natal from 1853 to 1883. The first advance by British troops trying to break the siege at Ladysmith was foiled here by General Louis Botha in a battle fought along the Tugela River. It was to be a further two months before Ladysmith was relieved. The small **RE Stevenson Museum** ① *Sir George St, T036-637 2992, open on request, ask at the police station next door for the key*, concentrates on the Battle of Colenso, with exhibits of weapons, medals and photographs. There are also two vintage steam engines and a steam tractor. The building itself was erected in 1879 as a toll house.

Weenen Game Reserve
① *20 km south of Colenso on the R74. From Durban take the N3 to the Estcourt junction and follow the R74 to the reserve, 25 km. From Ladysmith follow the R74 to Colenso and then on to Weenen, T036-354 7013, www.kznwildlife.com, Oct-Mar 0500-1900, Apr-Sep 0600-1800, R20, children (under 12) R10, car R20.*

The 6500-ha reserve is the core area of the much larger **Thukela Biosphere Reserve**. The reserve has been hailed as a conservation success as it has succeeded in converting heavily eroded farmland into an area where the flora and fauna indigenous to the Natal Midlands have been re-established. The vegetation is mostly grassland, interspersed with acacia woodland. One of the great attractions are the black and white rhino. More common species include giraffe, red hartebeest, eland, zebra, kudu, ostrich and common reedbuck. This is a good reserve for birdwatchers; more than 250 species have been recorded including korhaans, blue crane and the scimitarbilled woodhoopoe. Thukela has short walking trails, picnic sites, a 47-km network of game viewing dirt roads, 4WD trails and the Isipho Hide, which can be rented at night for game viewing.

Dundee and around ⊖❼❷❶▲ ▸▸ *pp490-492. Colour map 5, A1.*

The R602 leaves the N11 26 km north of Ladysmith and shortly passes the village of **Elandslaagte**, where there is a signpost leading to the site of the Battle of Elandslaagte. On 21 October 1899, British forces abandoned the village and the railway station. They had kept it open to enable the Dundee garrison to retreat to Ladysmith. The R602 continues to Dundee through a vast treeless plain with plateaux rising up in the distance. The small mining and farming town of **Glencoe**, just before Dundee, is named after the town in the Highlands of Scotland, from where some of the first miners originated.

   The modern town of Dundee grew up around the coal mining deposits which were first exploited here on a large scale in the 1880s. The town centre unfortunately fell victim to South Africa's town planners, and is today a rather dull grid of modern streets lined with sleepy shops. Although it provides a convenient base from which to explore the battlefield sites at **Isandlwana**, **Rorke's Drift** and **Blood River**, it might be preferable to stay at one of the more remote lodges away from town.

Ins and outs
Tourist information **Tourism Dundee** ① *Civic Gardens, Victoria St, T034-212 2121, www.tourdundee.co.za, Mon-Fri 0900-1630*, is a helpful office with information on accommodation and excellent advice on how best to view the battlefields depending upon your time, budget and level of interest. Ask about personal tour guides.

Sights
The **MOTH Museum** ① *corner of Beaconsfield and Wilson streets, open by appointment through the tourist office*, is one of the best private collections of military memorabilia in South Africa and includes pieces from the Anglo-Zulu War. The museum can usually only

be visited on an organized tour. MOTH stands for Memorable Order of Tin Hats and refers to the British ex-servicemen of the Anglo-Boer War.

The **Talana Museum** ① *1 km north of town on the R33, T034-212 2654, www.talana.co.za, Mon-Fri 0800-1630, Sat and Sun 1000-1630, R15, children (under 16) R2*, has been built on the site of the Battle of Talana Hill, which took place on 20 October 1899 and was the first major battle of the Boer War. British forces had been sent to Dundee to protect the coal field from the advancing Boers. General Lucas Meyer, moving down from the Transvaal, took the hill and began bombarding the British. The counter attack succeeded in forcing the Boers off the hill but only at great cost to the British, who lost 255 soldiers including their commanding officer General Penn Symons. A self-guided trail visits the remains of two British forts and the Boer gun emplacements, passing a cairn where General Penn Symons was wounded.

The main building is a modern museum with good displays on the Zulu Wars and the Anglo-Boer War. The industrial section includes the **Consol Glass Museum**, which has an extensive display of glass products, which were once produced here, illustrating the changes in taste from highly decorative Victorian vases to the crisp designer products of today. The **Chamber of Mines Coal Museum** has re-created scenes of early mining in Dundee with many of the original tools on display. The **Miner's Rest** restaurant and curio shop is housed in a typical miner's cottage of the 1920s in the gardens behind the new building.

Many outlying buildings are original. The **Peter Smith Cottage** has been restored and decorated with period furniture, while the workshop and stables outside have a collection of original blacksmith's tools and several wagons. **Talana House** has historical displays on the lifestyles of the Zulus and the early settlers in Dundee, with interesting bead collections. Both these buildings were used as dressing stations during the Battle of Talana Hill.

Battlefield excursions

The battlefield sites around Dundee can easily be visited on day trips. The major sites are clearly signposted and can be reached from Dundee or Ulundi. However, the sites themselves are often little more than a war memorial in a windswept field; they are isolated and accessed along dirt roads. Allow enough time to return in daylight as the bad roads and wandering cattle make it dangerous to drive at night. The best way to appreciate

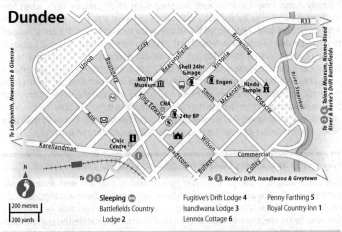

Dundee

Sleeping
Battlefields Country Lodge **2**

Fugitive's Drift Lodge **4**
Isandlwana Lodge **3**
Lennox Cottage **6**

Penny Farthing **5**
Royal Country Inn **1**

the sites and the epic events that took place in this region is to take a guided tour with a qualified historian. ➤➤ *For further details, see Activities and tours, page 492.*

Ncome-Blood River ⓘ *48 km from Dundee, T034-271 8121, www.ncomemuseum.co.za, 0900-1600, free*, is the site of a replica *laager* that commemorates the dreadful battle between the Zulus and the Boers on 16 December 1838 (see box, opposite). The 64 wagons are made of bronze and include replica bronze spades, lamps and buckets, all slightly larger than life size, and there is a small museum, the **Ncome Museum**. There is also a café selling historical leaflets. To get to the site, take the R33 northeast as far as Dejagersdrif, where there is a turning on the right leading to Blood River. The last section of the journey is on a dirt road.

Isandlwana ⓘ *80 km southeast of Dundee, T034-271 8165, Mon-Fri 0800-1600, Sat-Sun 0900-1600, R15, children (under 16) R2*, is where the 24th Regiment were defeated by 25,000 Zulu warriors on 22 January 1879. This is the most epic of the great Zulu War stories, where the Zulus sat silently in a valley watching a small British regiment (which thought the Zulus were elsewhere), waiting for the signal to attack. A British patrol stumbled across them, upon which the impis leapt to their feet and stormed over the lip of the hill, descending upon the small regiment in the characteristic 'horns of the buffalo' manoeuvre. Within two hours, 1329 of the 1700 British soldiers were dead. Today, it is an atmospheric spot, with white-painted cairns marking the places where British soldiers were buried, and a self-guided trail taking in the memorials, starting with the relatively new memorial to the Zulu dead, a giant bronze replica of a Zulu victory necklace. To get here, take the R68 west, passing through Vant's Drift and Nqutu; the dirt road leading to Isandlwana is clearly signposted south of Nqutu.

Rorke's Drift ⓘ *42 km from southeast of Dundee, T034-642 1687, daily 0900-1600, R15, children (under 16) R2*, is clearly signposted off the R68 between Dundee and Nqutu. Made famous by Michael Caine and his memorable performance in the movie *Zulu*, this site was a Swedish Mission next to a ford over the Buffalo River. In 1879, the mission consisted of two small stone buildings, a house and a storeroom, which was also used as a church, and these were commandeered by the British at the start of the war and converted into a hospital and a supply depot. Only 110 men were stationed there on 23 January 1879, when two survivors of Isandlwana arrived warning about an imminent attack. Four thousand Zulus arrived 1½ hours later and launched the assault on the mission station. The British refused to surrender, and succeeded in defending the mission from behind a makeshift barricade of grain bags and biscuit boxes. The ferocious attack was resisted for 12 hours before the Zulu impis withdrew, losing around 400 men; 17 British officers were killed. The mission station has been converted into a fascinating little **museum** which illustrates scenes from the battle and outlines the lives of the men who were awarded the Victoria Cross. Just beyond the museum there is a cemetery and a memorial to those who died.

🌙 *The defence of Rorke's Drift is one of the epic tales of British military history. No fewer than 11 Victoria Crosses were awarded here, the most ever awarded at a single battle.*

Newcastle and around ⊜❼⊕ ➤➤ *pp490-492. Colour map 5, A1.*

This major industrial town is supported by surrounding coal and steel mines. It was established in 1864 by a Dr Sutherland from Newcastle in England who was trapped on the swollen banks of the Ncandu River during his honeymoon. To pass time he planned a township for the site, named streets after the then government, and filed his plan on return

Blood River

The year 1838 had been a difficult one for the Voortrekkers in Natal. In February their leader Piet Retief was beaten to death at the Zulu king Dingane's kraal and shortly afterwards about 500 members of a Voortrekker party at Bloukrans River were killed in a Zulu ambush. The majority of the dead were in fact 'coloured' servants but subsequent generations of Boers honoured the defeat by naming the site *Weenen* – meaning 'weeping'. Voortrekker attempts at reprisals against the Zulus similarly failed and in a battle near the Buffalo River Piet Uys, another Voortrekker leader, was killed. It was only with the arrival later in the year of Andries Pretorius and a party of 60 experienced commandos that Voortrekker fortunes began to take a turn for the better.

On 9 December Pretorius set out with 468 men and three cannon to confront Dingane's army. Before setting out he reportedly stood on a gun carriage and made the famous vow that if God gave them victory "we would note the date of victory to make it known even to our latest posterity in order that it might be celebrated to the honour of God". Many historians doubt if the vow was ever really made; certainly it was not commemorated until many years after the event. Nevertheless the vow has taken on an important place in Afrikaner traditions.

On 15 December Pretorius' scouts reported a heavy Zulu presence nearby and he ordered the column to move their wagons into the tried and tested Voortrekker defensive *laager*. The method involved lashing all the wagons together into a ring and protecting all cattle, horses and stores in the centre. This allowed trekkers to hide in and under the wagons and fire out at any approaching attackers. Pretorius had formed his *laager* on the banks of the Ncome River with a deep gully to the rear and an open plain to the front. He placed the three cannon at points along the perimeter of the *laager* to give them a clear line of fire across the open ground. Early in the morning of 16 December the Zulu army, estimated at about 10,000, began its attack.

Wave upon wave of Zulu soldiers charged the *laager* but their short spears, so effective in hand to hand combat, were useless against the trekkers' rifles and the grapeshot from the cannons. Finally the Zulu attack faltered and Pretorius sent out a party of mounted commandos to pursue the shattered Zulus. The trekkers were merciless and shot every Zulu in sight, including more than 400 hiding in a small ravine. No prisoners were taken and around 3000 people were killed. No trekkers had been killed and only three were injured – including Pretorius who was stabbed in the hand. So many Zulu soldiers were shot whilst trying to flee back across the Ncome River the waters ran red – hence the name Blood River.

---

to Pietermaritzburg. There is little in this modern town to attract tourists, although the nearby mountain range, rising to over 2000 m, is popular with South African hikers.

Ins and outs

Newcastle is well connected by road and rail and local taxis will take hikers out to the farms that organize private hiking trails. **Tourism Newcastle** ① *Town Hall, Scott St, T034-315 3318, www.tourismnewcastle.co.za, Mon-Fri 0900-1600, Sat 0930-1530*, has a useful range of brochures and information on hiking and birdwatching.

Sights

Fort Amiel ① *Memel Rd, Mon-Fri 1000-1600, free*, was built in 1876 and used for military operations until 1902. It was built by a detachment of the Staffordshire Volunteers (80th regiment) and named after their commander Major Charles Frederick Amiel. It was used as a hospital during both Anglo-Boer wars. After the original plans for the fort were found in a London museum in 1985 the fort was completely rebuilt. The museum has displays on the Boer War and has an interesting section on Rider Haggard, world-famous writer of novels such as *King Solomon's Mines, She, Jess* among others. A Boer War cemetery is just outside.

Majuba Battlefield is 43 km from Newcastle on the N11 to Volksrust. The site is signposted from the highway. A 2-km dirt road leads to the battlefield where there is a caravan park, a youth hostel and a small museum. Majuba is the site where the British were defeated by the Boers in 1881. There is a short trail (45 minutes) heading up Majuba Mountain from where there are spectacular views of Volksrust, Newcastle and the surrounding countryside. The N11 continues north from here into Volksrust and Mpumalanga Province.

⊚ Battlefields Route listings

For Sleeping and Eating price codes and other relevant information, see pages 46-53.

⊜ Sleeping

If you've got a thirst for the history of the Battlefields, and the cash, then there are no better places to stay than **Isandlwana Lodge** or **Fugitive's Drift Lodge**, which both offer outstanding tours.

Ladysmith and around *p482, map p484*
B Bullers Rest Lodge, 61 Cove Cres, T036-637 6154, www.bullersrestlodge.co.za. B&B accommodation in a family-run lodge, set in a thatched house with fine views of the mountains with double and single rooms. The **Boer War Pub** on site has a fine collection of battlefield artefacts. Located near the site of the Naval Gun Shield. Recommended.
C Royal Hotel, 140 Murchison St, T036-637 2176, www.royalhotel.co.za. Busy central hotel with an interesting history, but the 71 en suite rooms are well overdue for a facelift. TV, a/c, the good **Tipsy Trooper** pub and restaurant, and the town's major meeting place, MacKathini's sports bar, with a pool table.
D Bonnie Highlands, 10 Tozer St, T036-637 8390. A fine old town house built in the 1920s with good views of the surrounding area and 5 homely rooms set along a shady veranda. Evening meals on request. The peaceful

gardens with pool are the perfect place to relax after a day exploring the Battlefields.
D Naunton Guest House, 4 km from town centre off the Newcastle Rd (N11), T036-631 3307, www.nauntons.co.za. 6 double rooms in a farmhouse with crisp white linen, DSTV, a/c and coffee and tea trays, cosy pub with pool table, evening meals available on request, pool. A pleasant alternative to suburban B&Bs.
D Peaches & Cream, 4 Berea Rd, T036-631 0954, pc.bb@mweb.co.za. Centrally located old-fashioned B&B in a colonial home, family-run, with 8 en suite rooms with DSTV, electric blankets and a/c, shady veranda and balcony, small pool set in manicured gardens, dinner served on request, friendly management.

Weenen Game Reserve *p486*
D Cottage, reservations T036-354 7013, www.kznwildlife.com. 5-bed self-catering cottage, 2 bedrooms, fully equipped modern bungalow. Also 12 pitches for caravans and tents (**F**) near the entrance, 7 with electricity points, shared ablution block. There's also a game-viewing hide overlooking a waterhole.

Dundee and around *p486, map p487*
L Fugitive's Drift Lodge, approximately 50 km south of Dundee towards Grey-town on the R33, T034-642 1843, www.fugitives drift.com. Home to the Rattray family, this

lodge offers traditional accommodation and excellent guided tours. Bedrooms are stylish and comfortable, and have private verandas. There are also rooms in an annex cottage. The lounge and dining room is filled with Battlefields memorabilia. Very sadly, the Battlefields finest historian David Rattray died in 2007 but prodigies Rob Caskie, George Irwin and Joseph Ndima now take tours, and like David Rattray, are superb storytellers bringing the history alive. The original Battlefields experience. Recommended.

L Isandlwana Lodge, Islandlwana, 74 km southeast of Dundee, accessed off the R68, T034-271 8301, www.isandlwana.co.za. Superbly constructed luxury lodge with awesome views over Isandlwana and the rolling grasslands. The stunning wood, thatch and stone double-storey building sensitively blends in with the landscape and is built into the rock that the Zulu commander stood on at the start of the Isandlwana battle. 13 tastefully decorated rooms, with huge beds, stylish mirrors and fashionable stone bathrooms, plus private balconies with views over the battle site. The smart dining room, also with brilliant views, has Zulu chefs. Rob Gerrard is the resident historian, offering excellent battlefield tours – his storytelling will provide a startlingly moving insight to the battles (R400 per person). Rates include all meals. Recommended.

B Penny Farthing, 14 km south of Dundee on the R33 towards Greytown, the farm is 2 km off the road on the right, T034-642 1925, www.pennyf.co.za. This farm has a choice of 1 room in a restored old fort with its own lounge and fireplace, or 5 rooms in the colonial sandstone farmhouse, decorated with antiques with French doors leading to the garden. Meals are taken communally at the 16 seater table and battlefield tours are with resident guide Foy Vermaak, a descendent of a Voortrekker family who fought in the Zulu and Anglo-Boer wars. Reservations essential.

C Lennox Cottage, a few kilometres out of town off the R68 towards Nqutu, T034-218 2201, www.battlefieldsaccommodation. co.za. A comfortable spacious guesthouse on a dairy farm with 10 rooms, a pool, tennis court, snooker room, and some wildlife on the farm including eland and giraffe. Owned by former Springbok rugby player Dirk Froneman. All meals available on request.

C Royal Country Inn, 61 Victoria St, T034-212 2147, www.royalcountryinn.com. 24 a/c en suite double rooms and 5 cheaper rooms with shared bathrooms in a mock-Tudor building over 100 years old, with well-preserved pressed-iron ceilings and wrought-iron fittings, opening onto a peaceful garden. Decent meals served in the à la carte restaurant, a bar decorated with Zulu and Boer War memorabilia, and a tea garden.

C-D Battlefields Country Lodge, over-looking Talana Hill battlefield site, T034-218 1641, www.battlefieldslodge.co.za. 33 rooms in quiet, comfortable double storey circular thatched bungalows, plus 10 cheaper budget rooms in a long block, **Warriors Arms** pub where 3-course country evening meals are served. Organizes battlefield tours in English, French or German, or alternatively take a tour with a Zulu guide for a different perspective.

Newcastle and around p488

Many of the farms offering hiking trails have camping facilities and overnight huts.

C Haggard's Hilldrop, 15 Hilldrop Rd, 3 km out of town, T034-315 2098, www.haggards hilldrop.co.za. Beautiful house which used to be the home of Sir Rider Haggard, whose novel *Jess* (1887) was based on his experiences at Hilldrop. The house is now a national monument set in 3 ha of indigenous forest and gardens. 29 rooms, stylish decor, some rooms under thatch, TV, pub, log fires, large pool, evening meals on request. Ask for the forest rooms, which have private balconies and separate entrances. Recommended.

D The Cannon, Allen St, T034-315 2307, www.thecannon.co.za. 22 en suite doubles, motel-style set-up, all rooms have phone, a/c, TV, room service, basic decor. Attached to **The**

Cannon pub and restaurant, very popular with locals, and next door to a gym.

D Majuba Lodge, 27 Victoria St, T034-315 5011, www.majubalodge.co.za. Self-catering chalets, fully equipped, DSTV, kitchen facilities, set around main building where meals are served, pool, gym, golf driving range, friendly set-up, but avoid if a big conference is going on.

🍴 Eating

Ladysmith and around *p482, map p484*
🍴-🍴 **Royal Hotel**, 140 Murchison St, T036-637 2176. Open 0700-1000, 1200-1400, 1800-2100. An old-fashioned carvery restaurant, serving a selection of steaks, pub lunches, and with the occasional large, good-value buffet dinner. Friendly, laid-back staff.
🍴 **Santa Catalina Spur**, Oval Shopping Centre, T036-631 1260. Usual family chain restaurant serving reliable if uninspiring steak, ribs and chicken, and there is a salad bar.

Dundee and around *p486, map p487*
🍴 **Royal Country Inn**, see Sleeping, page 491. 1200-1400, 1600-2200. The best place to eat in town is at the main hotel, with 2 dining rooms, tables outside in a courtyard and the **Garrulous Griffin Pub**, named after the 24th Welsh Regiment who fought at Rorkes Drift.

Newcastle and around *p488*
🍴 **The Cannon**, see Sleeping, page 491. 1200-late. Bar and restaurant attached to a hotel, large menu and portions, children's menu, playground, outside terrace, very popular with local families and there's a good-value Sun lunch.

🛍 Shopping

Dundee and around *p486, map p487*
ELC Craft Centre, Rorke's Drift Museum. Mon-Fri 0800-1730, Sat and Sun 1000-1600. Sells locally produced Zulu crafts: baskets, ceramics, dyed cloth and replica spears.

⛰ Activities and tours

Battlefield tours can be organized at tourist offices in Ladysmith, page 482, and at the Talana Museum in Dundee. Tours cost R700-900 for a full-day guided tour in your own car.

Dundee and around *p486, map p487*
Battlefield tours
Mike Nel, T034-212 2601, mike@dundee kzn.co.za, battlefields and Zulu culture tours.
Paul Garner, T034-212 1931, garner@xsinet. co.za. Enjoyable tales of the San paintings found in the area.
PMB Heritage Tours, T034-212 4040, www.battleguide.co.za. One of the leading operators on the **Battlefields Route**, Evan Jones is a member of the British Guild of Battlefield Guides, tours are tailor-made. Recommended.
Rob Gerrard, based at Isandlwana Lodge, see Sleeping, page 491. Excellent tours of Isandlwana, Rorke's Drift and walks between the 2, known as the Fugitive's Trail, providing a nail-biting account of the area's history. Recommended.

🚌 Transport

Ladysmith and around *p482, map p484*
Train
Central reservations, **Shosholoza Meyl**, T0860-00888 (in South Africa), T011-774 4555 (from overseas), www.shosholozameyl.co.za, timetables and fares on website. Trains from **Johannesburg** and **Tshwane (Pretoria)** most days, en route to **Durban**.

Newcastle and around *p488*
Train
To **Durban** and **Johannesburg**, see above.

🛈 Directory

Ladysmith and around *p482, map p484*
Medical services La Verna Private Hospital, 1 Convent Rd, T036-631 0065.

uKhahlamba-Drakensberg Park

The Drakensberg Mountains, which rise to 3000 m and extend 180 km along the western edge of KwaZulu Natal, form the backbone of the uKhahlamba-Drakensberg Park, and determine the border with Lesotho. This formidable mountain range is one of South Africa's most staggeringly beautiful destinations, and in 2001 it was awarded the status of a World Heritage Site by UNESCO, both for its diverse flora and fauna and its impressive San rock paintings. The greater uKhahlamba-Drakensberg Park extends from the Royal Natal National Park in the north to Sehlabathebe National Park, part of Lesotho, in the south. The protected area is 180 km long and up to 20 km wide. Almost the entire range falls within protected reserves managed by KZN Wildlife (see page 436). Despite going through a series of name changes over the years, this conservation body has looked after the region's natural heritage for decades and succeeded in striking a balance between protecting the fragile resources and giving visitors an opportunity to appreciate all the mountains have to offer. There are numerous points from which to explore the Berg, ranging from fully equipped holiday resorts and luxury hotels to campsites, mountain huts and isolated caves.
▶▶ *For listings, see pages 514-522.*

Ins and outs → *Colour map 4, B6.*

Getting there **Baz Bus** ① *T021-439 2323, www.bazbus.com*, runs through the Drakensberg three times a week en route between Johannesburg and Durban, stopping at Oliviershoek Pass and Winterton. In the southern Drakensberg **Underberg Express** ① *T0861-114924, www.underbergexpress.co.za*, run to and from Underberg/Sani Pass and Pietermaritzburg and Durban.

Getting around There is little in the way of public transport, so the best way of exploring the area is by car. The most popular resorts are within two to three hours' drive of Johannesburg, Tshwane (Pretoria) or Durban, accessed from the N3 and then a network of minor roads heading west into the mountains. The popular sights and resorts are well signposted. Those in the far south are best approached via Underberg on the R617 from Pietermaritzburg, or the R626 from Kokstad. The Central Drakensberg resorts, and the reserves around Monk's Cowl and Cathedral Peak, are signposted from Winterton and Bergville, off the N3, along the R74 and then onto the R600. The Northern Drakensberg resorts can be reached by taking the N3 as far as the Northern Berg turning. From here the R74 goes through Winterton and Bergville, and on to the Royal Natal National Park. The Battlefields Route lies to the northeast (see page 482). ▶▶ *For further details, see Transport, page 522.*

Best time to visit The weather in the Drakensberg can be divided into two main seasons: summer and winter. Although the weather tends to be pleasant all year round, the altitude and the mountain climate shouldn't be underestimated. Climatic conditions can change rapidly and snow, fog, rain and thunderstorms can develop within minutes, enveloping hikers on exposed hillsides.

Winter (May to August) is the driest time of the year and also the coolest. There will always be some rain during the winter months which, when it's cold enough, will occasionally fall as snow. Daytime temperatures can be as high as 15°C, while at night temperatures will often fall below 0°C. Despite the risk of snow, this the best season for hiking.

Summer (November to February) is the wettest time. The mornings tend to be warm and bright, but as the heat builds up clouds begin to collect in the afternoon. The violence of the thunderstorms when they break is quite spectacular, usually accompanied by short bursts of torrential rain. Daytime temperatures average around 20°C and the nights are generally mild with temperatures not falling much below 10°C. The summer is a less popular season for hiking, although then the landscape is greener and the wildlife more abundant.

Tourist information There are a number of information offices in the area. The **Drakensberg Tourism Association** ① *Municipal Building, Thatham Rd, Bergville, T036-448 1557, www.drakensberg.org.za Mon-Fri 0900-1700*, provides information on the whole region. The **Central Drakensberg Information Centre** ① *Thokozisa, on the R600, 13 km west of Winterton, T036-488 1207, www.cdic.co.za, daily 0900-1700*, is an arts, crafts and tourist centre, which has a coffee shop and restaurant, and stocks useful maps and brochures. It can also help arrange accommodation.

Safety There have been a number of carjacking incidents in the Drakensberg. Beware when driving down isolated roads and always take local advice.

Entry fees An entry fee, which includes a community levy and an emergency rescue levy, is payable each time you enter a protected area administered by **KZN Wildlife**. This fee is included in the cost of accommodation within the parks so only day visitors pay an entry fee at the gate. Current rates for day visitors are R20-30, children R10-20 depending on the park, and in some cases there's a fee for a car of about R25.

Background
San
The earliest human inhabitants of the Drakensberg were the San who lived here as hunter-gatherers. Evidence of their time here is the rock art which can be seen in numerous caves and rock shelters throughout the range. It is thought that groups of San would gather at certain points in the year at these sites to exchange goods, arrange marriages and carry out shamanic ceremonies.

For the rest of the year they dispersed into smaller family groups moving slowly in search of food. The women gathered edible plants and looked after children while the men hunted. Part of the reason for the success of their lifestyle was its relative simplicity. The few goods that they needed could be made from local materials – hides for clothing, bones, flint and wood for tools, and hunting poison from crushed insects and plants.

Anthropological studies of modern hunter gatherers in Australia and the Amazon estimate that they only spend about 20 hours a week collecting enough food to survive. Considering the relative abundance of food, it is thought likely that the Drakensberg San had a similar working week, dedicating much of the rest of their time to rock painting, singing and dancing.

The San came under increasing pressure towards the middle of the 19th century as new settlers established themselves on their land. Opportunities for hunting decreased as European immigrants shot such large numbers of game, and gradually the San were forced to adapt. They were driven further and further into the mountains, and eventually abandoned their stone tools and hunting poisons in favour of horses and guns and became cattle rustlers. Their raids on farms in Natal were so successful that the raiders were often hunted down and shot.

Attitudes of Europeans towards the San during 19th century couldn't be more different from the rather romantic view in which they are held today. They were seen, at best, as pests, were often shot on sight and were captured and forced into slavery. The last records of San being seen in the Drakensberg date from 1878 just before the Natal government began auctioning plots of land at the base of the mountains themselves.

🌙 *Originally the Nguni people called the mountains uKhalamba (Barrier of Spears), an apt description of the escarpment that rises sharply from the rolling hills of Natal.*

Colonial The first Europeans to see the Drakensberg were a group of Portuguese sailors whose ship was wrecked on the Transkei coast in 1593. They had decided to head inland on their way back to Lourenço Marques and reported having seen snow-covered mountains in the distance.

Almost 250 years later the first hunters, missionaries and farmers began to arrive. The Voortrekkers arrived from the north, moving down into Natal through what was later to be called Oliviershoek Pass while the settlers from the Eastern Cape moved up from the south. As the land gradually fell under their control, the Drakensberg's natural resources were subject to the settler's rapacious exploitation. The timber and sheep farming industries were particularly successful in the short term, but their effects on the delicate ecosystem of the Drakensberg were eventually to lead to the creation of the national park.

Modern The first area of the park to receive protection was the Giant's Castle Game Reserve in 1903. Over the years more land was acquired and given protected status.

One of the main reasons for creating a national park here is that the Drakensberg escarpment is the source of many of the rivers which flow through Natal. The Tugela, the Mkhomazi and the Mzimkhulu are three of the most important sources of water in Natal. During the 1950s, damage caused by deforestation and overgrazing was proved to be affecting the water supply. The indigenous vegetation of the Drakensberg was shown to play an essential role in holding water from torrential seasonal rain and preventing flash floods. The root systems in the soil release the water gradually throughout the year providing Natal with a regular water supply. The park now protects a unique area of Afro-montane and Afro-alpine vegetation and access to this delicate ecosystem is restricted in order to prevent further damage. In 2001 UNESCO named the park a World Heritage Site, in recognition of its universal environmental value to mankind. Presently, the Maloti-Drakensberg Transfrontier Conservation Area initiative is underway. This links the Sehlaba-Thebe National Park in Lesotho and the uKhahlamba-Drakensberg Park, which covers 8113 sq km in total. The main objectives of the project are to conserve the globally significant biodiversity in the Maloti and the Drakensberg Mountains.

Landscape

The Drakensberg are divided into two areas known as the High Berg and the Little Berg. The **High Berg**, covering the area which rises steeply up to the plateau, is the more interesting of the two with its spectacular scenery of high peaks and cliffs. The top of the escarpment averages an altitude of around 3000 m and forms the western boundary of the park along the watershed between Natal and Lesotho. The **Little Berg** lies at lower altitude and consists of the spurs of sandstone which stretch out towards the plains of Natal. The landscape here is of rolling hills and grassland divided by forested ravines. The Little Berg is the most popular area for hiking and many of the KZN Wildlife resorts are located here.

Wildlife and vegetation

The different wildlife habitats in the Drakensberg vary according to altitude, which can range from the subtropical at around 1000 m to the Afro-alpine at over 3000 m. The wealth of plantlife in the Drakensberg is quite staggering: over 1500 plant species have been identified here, among which 350 are endemic. By far the best time of year to see the veldt is during the spring, when the grass is green and lush and many of the orchids, irises and lilies are in flower. Plants on the high plateau are hardy, small alpine plants consisting mostly of grasses, shrubs and succulents.

The **wildlife** is not as easy to spot as in some of South Africa's other wildlife reserves. Numbers are relatively low, and viewing wildlife is more the preserve of enthusiastic naturalists rather than casual observers. The large mammals you might see include eland, baboon, and some of the small antelope such as klipspringer and duiker. Red hartebeest, blesbok, bushbuck and oribi are present but are seen less often as they only inhabit certain areas. Leopard, lynx, serval, aardvark, aardwolf and porcupine are thought to be present but are almost never seen, even by park staff or regular hikers.

Birdlife in the Drakensberg is particularly rich, as it is possible to visit several different ecosystems within a relatively small area. Over 300 species have been recorded here, most of which live below 2000 m. The best time to see the birds is during the summer when they are courting and nesting. This is their most active time of year and their most colourful, as the birds will be in their breeding plumage.

The rarest birds live at higher altitudes on the summit plateau, and include the orange-breasted rockjumper, the Drakensberg siskin, the bald ibis, the Cape vulture and the lammergeyer. Conditions are so harsh in this environment that only 54 species have been recorded here. The environment in the Little Berg is less extreme and many species of bird common to other parts of KwaZulu Natal can be seen here.

Hiking

Trails vary between short, well-marked strolls to challenging hikes at high altitude, lasting several days. The majority of visitors to the Drakensberg prefer to complete a number of day hikes and stay overnight in KZN Wildlife camps.

Experienced hikers have compared some of the longer trails to hiking in the Himalayas, where several days are spent in isolated wilderness areas at altitudes of up to 3000 m. Some of the longer hiking trails can last up to 10 days crossing through isolated and challenging mountain passes such as the Mnweni and Ifidi, which are among the wildest and most beautiful trails along the Northern Berg. Planning ahead is essential for longer hikes as overnight caves and mountain huts have to be booked in advance. It is recommended that all overnight hikers read KZN Wildlife's brochure *It's Tough at the Top – Hiking Safely in the Drakensberg*.

Permits Permits are necessary on all longer walks and are available from camp offices for a small fee. Maximum group size is 12 people and the minimum size is three. Hikers intending to stay overnight in the mountains must fill in the **Mountain Rescue Register**, carry detailed maps and be equipped to deal with extreme weather. Mountain registers are located at all the trail heads and should be filled in even for short day walks.

Hazards The most common problems to watch out for are the effects of intense sunlight at high altitudes. Sunstroke and dehydration are best avoided by wearing a sun hat, using a high protection factor suncream and by carrying enough water. It's worth considering

Drakensberg snakes

There are only two deadly poisonous snakes in the Drakensberg, the puff adder and the *rinkhals* or ring-necked spitting cobra. Both are extremely rare and mostly live at lower altitudes in the low-lying farmlands and, as they are both brightly coloured, are fairly easy to see. At higher altitudes, the Berg adder, which is poisonous but not life-threatening, is more common and is endemic to the area. Several other species of non-poisonous snake occur in the Berg, although again they are rarely encountered. The largest of these is the brown water snake, which frequents river banks and can grow to over 2 m in length.

Most snakes will be terrified at your approach and will try to make a quick getaway. If you are walking in single file, this gives them an almost 360° choice of route. Both the puff adder and Berg adder adopt a defensive coiled posture if they feel they cannot escape in time, while the cobra will rear up and flatten its hood. The adders can strike at an alarming speed, straightening one or more of their coils in the process and thus extending their reach. Never approach a coiled snake. As terrifying as it sounds, if you get almost to within striking distance of an adder or cobra, it's best to freeze. Neither snake really wants to bite you; they prefer to keep their venom for catching food, and in any case have poor vision and are best at detecting movement. In the unfortunate event of a snake bite get to a hospital as soon as possible (for further advice see Health, page 60).

going on a guided hike, as registered guides will be well versed in mountain safety. Contact any of the tourist offices in the Drakensberg region who will be able to arrange a guided hike.

Equipment and supplies See page 24 for a full list of recommended hiking equipment. Note that **camping stoves** are essential for overnight hikes as fires are not allowed in the park. Petrol is available for multi-fuel stoves from some of the larger resorts. **Camping gas** and other fuels should be bought in advance from a camping shop in a large urban centre such as Durban or Pietermaritzburg. It is better to buy meths from a pharmacy than a supermarket, as it is much better quality.

Resort shops and the local stores up in the mountains have a limited selection of tinned **food**. It's best to bring lightweight dry food from Durban or Johannesburg. Fresh produce can be bought in the towns en route to the mountains.

Some hikers choose not to carry a tent if they have booked accommodation in caves or mountain huts. However, these are not always marked accurately on maps and they can be difficult to find, so it's sensible to have a tent as a backup in case you get caught out at nightfall. On overnight hikes a **trowel** or a spade is necessary for digging toilets to prevent litter and pollution. Dig a hole at least 30 m away from streams and make sure everything is properly buried.

The most exciting Drakensberg hikes are the ones up to the summit plateau. The **clothing** you carry with you should protect you from the weather you are likely to encounter over 3000 m. An anorak made from waterproof breathable fabrics like Goretex will be useful all year round, while in winter layers of thermal underwear, fleece, a woolly hat and gloves should prepare you for sub-zero temperatures. Even on short day hikes in the Little Berg a waterproof jacket and a sweater are invaluable.

Border crossing: South Africa–Lesotho

Drakensberg escarpment
The border between South Africa and Lesotho follows the watershed along the top edge of the Drakensberg escarpment. It is essential to carry your passport with you at all times.

Maps A map, a compass and a good knowledge of map reading are essential for hiking in the Drakensberg. KZN Wildlife produce a series of six comprehensive 1:50,000 maps, which usefully also cover the Lesotho side of the mountains. Contact KZN Wildlife in advance.

Activities and tours
Hiking, horse riding and mountaineering are the traditional Drakensberg sports but newer activities like mountain biking and hang-gliding are becoming very popular. Many of the larger resort hotels also offer a wide range of sporting facilities such as tennis, squash, golf and swimming. ▸▸ *For further details, see Activities and tours, page 520.*

Staying in the park
There is a huge choice in the area, including within KZN Wildlife accommodation and in private establishments on the fringes of the park. KZN Wildlife offers a wide range of facilities, from luxury lodges and chalets through to campsites, mountain huts and caves. All of the KZN Wildlife camps are basically self-catering and although there are some camp shops which sell food, the choice is limited. It is far better to come prepared and buy your food beforehand in the nearest large town.

The area bordering the national park is increasingly being developed for tourism and a number of self-contained holiday resorts and timeshares have sprung up. These tend to offer numerous sporting and entertainment facilities but they are sometimes rather distant from the Drakensberg Mountains themselves. There is also a good selection of B&Bs, which can offer better value.

Reservations for **KZN Wildlife** ① *T033-845 1000, www.kznwildlife.com.* Bookings can be made by telephone or online; camping reservations must be made directly with the officer in charge of the campsite, see individual areas for details.

Northern Drakensberg ●●●● ▸▸ *pp514-522.*

The scenery of the Northern Berg is exceptional in its grandeur, and is perhaps the most photographed section of the range. The Royal Natal National Park is the most popular of all the resorts in the Drakensberg, and although there are some good hikes outside the park, they don't really compare with the sheer majesty of those within its boundaries.

Ins and outs
From Royal Natal National Park the R74 heads east to Bergville (41 km) and Winterton (62 km). The R615 heads north off the R74, 14 km from the park gates. After 11 km it reaches the top of Oliviershoek Pass from where it is a further 37 km to Harrismith.

Royal Natal National Park

The highlight of a visit to the park is the first view of the massive rock walls that form the **Amphitheatre**. The **Eastern Buttress** (3009 m) is the southernmost peak of the 4-km of cliff face, which arcs northwards towards the **Sentinel** (3165 m) forming an impressive barrier. On the plateau directly behind the Amphitheatre is **Mont-aux-Sources** (3299 m) named by French missionaries in 1836. This mountain is the source of five rivers: the **Elands** which flows into the Vaal; the **Khudeda** and the **Singu** leading into the Orange/Gariep River in the Free State; and the **Tugela** and the **Bilanjil** which lead into Natal.

The most impressive of these is the Tugela which plunges over the edge of the Amphitheatre wall, dropping around 800 m through a series of five falls. The gorge created by the waters of the Tugela is a steep-sided tangle of boulders and trees which at a point near the Devil's Tooth Gully has bored straight through the sandstone to form what appears to be a tunnel around 40 m long.

The national park was established in 1916 when farms around the Amphitheatre were bought by the government to protect the land. Tourism started around this time and the park has been popular since then. Queen Elizabeth II visited the park in 1947, five years before she became queen; since then, the national park and the (now closed) hotel are prefixed by the word 'Royal' in memory of this visit.

1 Royal Natal National Park

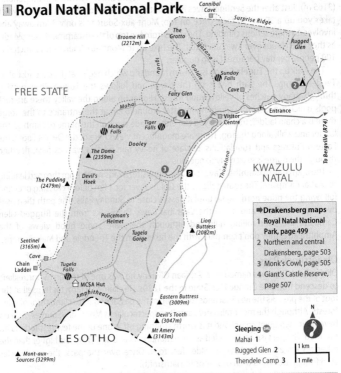

➡ **Drakensberg maps**
1 Royal Natal National Park, page 499
2 Northern and central Drakensberg, page 503
3 Monk's Cowl, page 505
4 Giant's Castle Reserve, page 507

Sleeping 😴
Mahai 1
Rugged Glen 2
Thendele Camp 3

1 km
1 mile

Ins and outs The park can be reached on tarred roads from Harrismith (60 km) or Bergville (40 km). The route is well signposted from the N3. Note that the number of day visitors is controlled to prevent overcrowding in the park; however, this only tends to be a problem at weekends and on holidays. The **visitor centre** ① *T036-438 6303, daily 0800-1630, R30, children (under 12) R20*, has a gift shop that sells a good selection of books, T-shirts, a very limited range of tinned goods, curios, alcoholic and soft drinks, maps and sometimes fresh trout. Petrol is also available here.

Hiking There are over 130 km of walking trails around the Royal Natal National Park, many of which are easy half-day strolls. Even the hikes that don't climb up to the top of the escarpment wind through beautiful countryside of grassland dotted with patches of yellowwood forest and proteas set against the stunning backdrop of the Amphitheatre. The visitor centre sells hiking maps and a leaflet describing the many possible walks around the park. Permits are also available here. Soil erosion has increasingly become a problem as more and more hikers visit the park. In an attempt to control erosion some paths may be closed to hikers.

The 20-km hike up to **Mont-aux-Sources** (3299 m) can be completed in a strenuous day's walk. The path starts at **Mahai Campsite** and heads steadily uphill following the course of the Mahai River. The path climbs steeply around the eastern flank of the Sentinel (3165 m). Just after the Sentinel Caves is the notorious chain ladder, built in 1930, which takes you up a 30-m cliff face. Once on top, Mont-aux-Sources is only 3 km away and involves no more serious climbing. The views from the top of the escarpment are splendid as they stretch out over KwaZulu Natal. The hike up to Mont-aux-Sources is restricted to 100 people per day because it is so popular.

The walk up the **Tugela Gorge** is a 14-km round trip which begins at the car park below Tendele Camp. The path heads up the gorge and follows the Tugela River passing through shady patches of yellowwood forest. Higher up along the valley there are rock pools which are ideal for swimming in. After around 6 km at the entrance to the gorge there is a chain ladder; from here you can either wade through the gorge or climb up the ladder and walk along the top. There are magnificent views here of the Devil's Tooth, the Eastern Buttress and Tugela Falls. Beware of heavy rain on this walk as flash flooding through the gorge is extremely dangerous.

The 8-km trail to **Cannibal Cave** (see box, opposite) heads north from the road leading to **Mahai Campsite**. The route follows the Goldie River for 1 km before crossing over and following the ridge north again until it passes close to Sunday Falls. The path then rises over Surprise Ridge and on to the Cannibal Cave. The walks from the **Rugged Glen Campsite** are over rolling hills and although there are some good views of the Amphitheatre, they don't compare with the hikes from the Thendele and Mahai camps.

Oliviershoek Pass

Oliviershoek Pass was named after Adriaan Olivier who was one of the first Voortrekkers to descend from the Orange Free State in the 1830s. He claimed a farm for himself at the foot of the pass. As the R615 ascends to the top of the pass it begins to climb through pine forests. Although the mountains here aren't as spectacular as Mont-aux-Sources, they do have their own quiet charm and it is worth stopping off at one of the few restaurants on this road. The pass isn't as crowded as the national park and at 1730 m it is higher than the other resorts and does have a wilder feel to it. Once over the pass, the road circles Sterkfontein Dam and then descends to Harrismith.

Cannibal Cave

This large cave overlooking a quiet valley is accessible on foot either from Mahai Campsite or Rugged Glen. The remains of some San paintings can still be seen.

During the Zulu wars, refugees escaped into the mountains and lived in the caves. Times were so turbulent that people were unable to plant crops and, as game became scarcer, the refugees were forced to eat passing travellers or even their own children. Rumour has it that the bodies were hung from the cave roof to keep them fresh.

The cannibals lived here for around 20 years, eventually becoming such a threat that they were hunted and killed by the Zulus.

Bergville → *Colour map 4, A6.*

This quiet country town is in the centre of a maize and dairy farming area. Most visitors will either be passing through en route to the resorts in the Northern Drakensberg or be heading northeast towards Ladysmith and the Battlefields. The main reason for stopping is to visit the helpful **Drakensberg Tourism Association** (see page 494).

Central Drakensberg ⊜❼❹❺❻ ➤ *pp514-522.*

The Giant's Castle Nature Reserve is the most spectacular of the Central Berg resorts. It has two camps: Giant's Castle and Injisuthi. Here, the basalt cliff faces rise up to 3000 m and stretch out to the north and south for over 30 km. Further north, the road to Monk's Cowl, with its string of resorts, curio villages and golf courses, is one of the most heavily developed areas of the Drakensberg. While you may see more tourists in this region, the scenery is no less spectacular and access is easier than in other areas of the park. This is also home to the internationally famous Drakensberg Boys' Choir.

Ins and outs Two roads from Winterton lead towards the central Drakensberg resorts: heading north the R74 goes via Bergville, 22 km, to the **Royal Natal National Park**, 62 km. Two kilometres south of Winterton on the R600 there is a signposted turning to **Cathedral Peak**, 43 km. The R600 continues on to **Monk's Cowl** (Champagne Valley), 35 km. To reach **Injisuthi**, take the turning to Loskop off the R600, before reaching Loskop there is a dirt road on the right. Follow the signposts to Injisuthi from here. Heading southeast, the R74 crosses the N3 to **Estcourt**, 43 km.

Winterton → *Colour map 4, A/B6.*

This village is an important centre for dairy farms as well as being the last place to stock up on supplies for visitors to Cathedral Peak or Monk's Cowl. It's worth stopping here for a look around its pleasant tree-lined streets and small museum, and to gather some local information. The petrol station and the supermarket are on the junction of the R74 with the road leading into the centre of village. Nearby in Thokosiza is the **Central Drakensberg Information Centre**, a major arts, crafts and tourist centre, see page 494.

Spioenkop Dam Nature Reserve → *Colour map 4, A6.*

ⓘ *14 km north of Winterton on the R600. Office T036-488 1578. Oct-Mar 0600-1900, Apr-Sep 0600-1800, R20.*

This 6000-ha game park is a popular tourist resort for boating and fishing. Almost all the game here has been reintroduced and there is a good chance of seeing white rhino and buffalo. With this in mind visitors must be careful when walking in the open around their campsite. Other animals you can expect to see include giraffe, kudu, mountain reedbuck, waterbuck, blesbok, impala, zebra, eland, duiker and steenbok. The area is particularly rich in birdlife and more than 270 species have been recorded here. Anglers can fish the reservoir from the dam or from the shore.

The **Battle of Spion Kop**, 24 January 1890, was yet another embarrassing defeat for the British at the hands of the Boers and had a marked impact upon British public opinion. In order to relieve the beleaguered British troops at Ladysmith (see page 483), General Warren attempted a direct assault on the Rangeworthy Hills to dislodge the Boer positions. He decided to occupy the highest peak on the ridge – Spion Kop. However, this meant that the shallow British defences were exposed to Boer gunfire from all sides and soon suffered heavy losses. A brigade under General Lyttelton came to Warren's assistance but General Buller disastrously reversed the decision, ordering all British forces to retreat down from Spion Kop and back across the Tugela. Some 1750 British troops were either killed, wounded or captured at Spion Kop compared to about 300 Boers. The famous battlefield overlooks the dam and is clearly visible from the reserve. It can be reached on one of the self-guided trails.

> *In 1906 Liverpool Football Club named the home stands at Anfield 'Spionkop' in memory of those who died here during the Boer War. The stands are still called 'the Kop' to this day.*

Cathedral Peak → *Colour map 4, B6.*

① *T036-488 8000. Reception, shop and information office daily 0700-1900. R25, children (under 12) R13, or R50/25 with a visit to the Rock Art Centre, vehicles to Mike's Pass R50. Signposted from Bergville and Winterton. The road is tarred and is usually passable even after rain.*

Cathedral Peak is the main point of access to some of the wildest areas of the central Drakensberg, and provides some of the most spectacular scenery for hikers. Driving into the area, the road passes traditional Zulu villages and dips through leafy valleys, with the views gradually opening up as you get closer to the park. The park itself is ringed by dramatic peaks with views of the Cathedral Spur and Cathedral Peak (3004 m), the Inner and Outer Horns (3005 m) and the Bell (2930 m). An alternative to hiking round the peaks is to drive up Mike's Pass, suitable for saloon cars (although it says 4WD only), from where there are spectacular views of the Little Berg (R35 per car).

The sheltered valleys in this area are thought to have been one of the last refuges of the San in the Drakensberg. This is one of the best places to see a large number of San cave paintings found in the Drankensberg; the Rock Art Centre at Didimi makes a good starting point. Leopard's Cave and Poacher's Cave in the Ndedema Gorge have especially good galleries of paintings.

An earlier name for Cathedral Peak was Zikhali's Horn, named after Zikhali who escaped to Swaziland after his father was killed by Dingaan. During the years that he and his tribe spent in Swaziland they assimilated many aspects of Swazi culture. Swazi influences can still be seen today in the way that traditional huts are built in this region.

Hiking The Cathedral Peak area is growing in popularity with hikers. There is a good network of paths heading up the Mlambonja Valley to the escarpment from where there are trails heading south to Monk's Cowl and Injisuthi or heading north to Royal Natal

National Park. The campsite at Mike's Pass or the **Cathedral Peak Hotel** are good bases from which to set out exploring the area on a series of day walks. Maps are available in the information office and show a number of walks departing from the hotel. For keen hikers there are designated caves and mountain huts on the longer trails. The 10-km hike to the top of **Cathedral Peak** (3004 m) is one of the most exciting and strenuous hikes in this part of the Drakensberg, and the views from the top of the Drakensberg stretching out to the north and south are unforgettable.

Cave paintings An excellent introduction to San rock art in the area is just past the entrance to the park, at the **Rock Art Centre** ⓘ *Didima Camp, T036-488 8025, 0800-1300, 1400-1600, coffee shop and craft centre.* The stylish thatched building holds a series of displays interpreting the art found in the surrounding mountains. A key thread in the museum is the eland, a vital aspect in San mythology and culture, with some life-size replicas in the

2 Northern & central Drakensberg

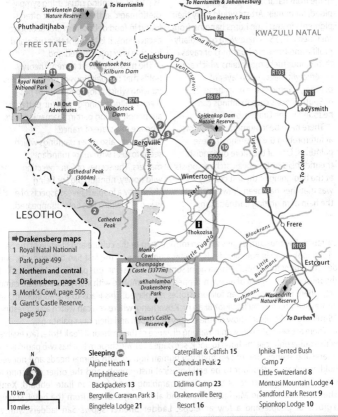

⇒Drakensberg maps
1 Royal Natal National Park, page 499
2 Northern and central Drakensberg, page 503
3 Monk's Cowl, page 505
4 Giant's Castle Reserve, page 507

Sleeping
Alpine Heath **1**
Amphitheatre Backpackers **13**
Bergville Caravan Park **3**
Bingelela Lodge **21**
Caterpillar & Catfish **15**
Cathedral Peak **2**
Cavern **11**
Didima Camp **23**
Drakensville Berg Resort **16**
Iphika Tented Bush Camp **7**
Little Switzerland **8**
Montusi Mountain Lodge **4**
Sandford Park Resort **9**
Spionkop Lodge **10**

Cave paintings

The sandstone caves of the Drakensberg are one of the best places in the world to see rock art. Most of the surviving paintings are on the walls of rock shelters. There are traces of paintings on exposed rocks but they have been heavily weathered. The paintings tend to be quite recent and are probably only 200 to 300 years old, but they do form part of a long-standing tradition. The earliest cave paintings in Southern Africa date from 28,000 years ago.

The pigments used by the San were made from natural ochre mixed with blood, fat or milk. Artists would carry their pigments in antelope horns hanging from their belts. The San here were particularly prolific and there are hundreds of caves throughout these mountains which are covered with layer upon layer of paintings. Some of the most beautiful of South Africa's cave paintings can be found in the Drakensberg.

There have been numerous attempts at interpreting the meaning of these paintings. One of the more outlandish theories held by European archaeologists at the beginning of the last century was that they had been drawn with the help of migrating Carthaginians.

Other more recent theories hold that the paintings are either little more than well-executed graffitos illustrating scenes from daily life or that they were used in sympathetic magic.

The most recent research has drawn from ethnographic records from the end of the last century and interviews with the remaining San people in this century. The eland features largely in San mythology and is one of the most frequently painted subjects. It seems unlikely that the eland were painted as part of a hunting ritual using sympathetic magic as the eland is not often found in food debris from archaeological excavations. It is thought that the eland in some way represented god.

The most prevalent current theory holds that the paintings of human figures dancing which show people with nose bleeds hallucinating geometric patterns, are people taking part in shamanic rituals who are in a state of trance.

There are also other paintings which seem to deal with more mundane matters. The scenes of San collecting wild honey, hunting pigs or being chased by a leopard reveal aspects of a way of life which has now disappeared.

entrance. The museum begins with an introduction to the culture and lifestyle of the San, with a look at archaeological finds, quotes from some of the last San descendants, and descriptions of the symbolic meaning of some of the most famous paintings. At the back of the museum is a replica of an open-topped cave, complete with starry sky and fake camp fire, where recordings of San folklore stories are played. This leads to the auditorium, an impressive structure built to look like a rock overhang, where you can watch an interesting 15-minute audio-visual show on the history of the San and their cave paintings.

There are several caves within walking distance of the **Cathedral Peak Hotel** (accessible with a guide only; call the hotel to book, see page 515). **Mushroom Hill** has two particularly interesting scenes, one of two mythical human figures with animal heads and hooves holding what are thought to be early musical instruments, and the other depicting a more lighthearted scene of some San scrambling away from an irate leopard. **Xeni Shelter**, 2 km beyond Mushroom Rock and also easily reached from the hotel, shows a group of people and a few antelope. **Ladder Shelter** shows San ladders with a small picture of a man climbing up the rock face. **Junction Shelter** has a number of interesting scenes of men crossing on a rope bridge, a baboon hunt and some human figures dancing. **Eland Cave** is a large cave with many splendid paintings; more mysteriously, a San hunting kit was found here in the 1920s, which can now be seen at the Rock Art Centre. See also box, opposite.

Monk's Cowl → Colour map 4, B6.

ⓘ *T036-468 1103. Park gates Oct-Mar 0700-2000, Apr-Sep 0600-1800. Camp office daily 0800-1230, 1400-1630. R35, children (under 12) R18. The nearest shop to Monk's Cowl is opposite the Champagne Sports Resort (9 km).*

The road to Monk's Cowl passes through one of the most developed areas of the Drakensberg. Looking down from Monk's Cowl the view of KwaZulu Natal is dotted with hotels, golf courses and timeshare developments and the area is locally dubbed 'Champagne Valley'. However, **Champagne Castle**, **Monk's Cowl** and **Cathkin Peak** are still impressive features in this landscape and several interesting long-distance hikes begin from here.

The **Drakensberg Boys' Choir School** is on the right of the R600 towards Monk's Cowl and is one of the most beautiful locations for a school in the whole of South Africa.

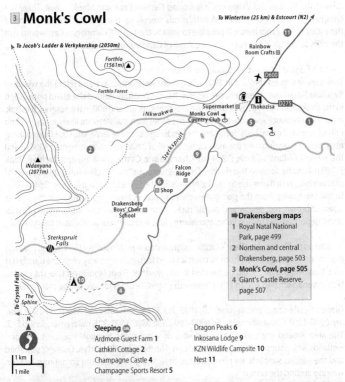

3 Monk's Cowl

To Winterton (25 km) & Estcourt (N2)

To Jacob's Ladder & Verkykerskop (2050m)

Forthlo (1561m) ▲

Rainbow Room Crafts ▥

Forthlo Forest

iNkwakwa

Supermarket ▥
Monks Cowl Country Club ⛳

Thokozisa

D600

D275

▲ iNdanyana (2071m)

Sterkspruit

Falcon Ridge

⑨

⑥ ▥ Shop

Drakensberg Boys' Choir School ▥

Sterkspruit Falls ⋙

To Crystal Falls

The Sphinx

Ⓐ ⑩

④

N

1 km
1 mile

➡ Drakensberg maps
1 Royal Natal National Park, page 499
2 Northern and central Drakensberg, page 503
3 Monk's Cowl, page 505
4 Giant's Castle Reserve, page 507

Sleeping ⬤
Ardmore Guest Farm **1**
Cathkin Cottage **2**
Champagne Castle **4**
Champagne Sports Resort **5**

Dragon Peaks **6**
Inkosana Lodge **9**
KZN Wildlife Campsite **10**
Nest **11**

The school is highly accredited in its own right, but is most famous for the choir that has performed all over the world over the last three decades. Boys aged between nine and 15 have performed in front of the Pope and 25,000 people at the Vatican City, sung with the Vienna Boys' Choir in Austria, and have been proclaimed top choir three times at the World Festival of Choirs. The choir has even received a special award at Disney's Magic Kingdom. Most audiences expect only classical choral renditions but the boys sing anything from Beethoven to Freddy Mercury. ▶ *For further details, see Entertainment, page 520.*

Just before the **Champagne Castle Hotel**, turn off the R600 to reach **Falcon Ridge** ① *T082-774 6398 (mob), bird shows Sat-Thu 1030*, a rehabilitation centre for rescued birds of prey, mostly injured through flying into power lines. The daily show is a big attraction, and you can don a glove and have your photo taken with a large raptor.

Hiking The short hikes around Monk's Cowl get busy as so many tourists visit here for the day. A map is available from the office and the paths are clear and well signposted. Places to visit include **Nandi's Falls** (5 km), **Sterkspruit Falls** (2 km), and **The Sphinx** (3 km). The paths cross areas of proteas and some woodland.

The hike up to **Champagne Castle** (3377 m) is a 20-km, two-day hike which involves a steady slog uphill, but no climbing skills are needed. From the camp, the trail rises up and follows the Mhlawazini Valley circling around Cathkin Peak and Monk's Cowl. There is a campsite just below Gray's Pass. A path winds steeply up the pass for 2 km to the top of the escarpment. From here it is possible to walk to the top of Champagne Castle or to visit the cliffs at Vulture's Retreat where a colony of Cape vultures breed.

Giant's Castle Reserve → *Colour map 4, B6.*
This reserve was established in 1903 when there were only 200 eland left in the whole of KwaZulu Natal. Over the years, the reserve has successfully helped the eland population in the Drakensberg to recover and at present there are around 600 in the reserve. Blesbok, mountain reedbuck and oribi are some of the other mammals you are likely to see. Rolling hills of sourveld grasslands dominate the landscape of the reserve, with the Drakensberg escarpment towering over the main camp. A wall of basalt cliffs rise up to over 3000 m and the peaks of **Giant's Castle** (3314 m), **Champagne Castle** (3248 m) and **Cathkin Peak** (3149 m) can be seen on the skyline. The grasslands below the cliffs roll out in a series of massive hills, which give rise to the Bushman's River and the Little Tugela River. On the drive to the main camp from the park gates, the road passes through a cutting which exposes layers of brown, red, yellow and purple rock. These are the **Molteno Beds**, layers of sandstone deposited 200 million years ago where plant and dinosaur fossils have been found.

Ins and outs The road to Giant's Castle is signposted from Mooi River (64 km) and Estcourt (65 km) on the N3. The road from Estcourt is tarred for most of the way while the mostly dirt road from Mooi River should be avoided in wet weather. From Mooi River take the road to Ncibidwana Store, 46 km, and then follow the signs. Petrol is for sale by the main gate.

Giant's Castle camp and around ① *T036-353 3718. Park gates Oct-Mar 0500-1900, Apr-Sep 0600-1800. Camp office Mon-Fri 0800-1800, Sun 0800-1600, R25, children (under 12) R13.* The area around the camp has a network of short paths through riverine forest and wetlands which supports many species of bird. The malachite kingfisher, Gurney's sugarbird and the various sunbirds are often spotted here and grey duiker can sometimes be seen walking around the camp.

There are numerous interconnected hikes crossing the reserve. The shorter walks explore the forests and river valleys within a few kilometres of the camp, whilst the longer ones take up to three days and can reach areas as far afield as Injisuthi. A comprehensive leaflet detailing the hiking choices is available from the camp office.

The **Main Cave** is half an hour's walk from the camp and has a large wall covered in paintings and a simple display on the archaeology of the cave and the San who lived there. The cave must be visited with a guide; book at the main office, T036-353 3718.

The 7-km hike up to **World's View** (1842 m) follows a path north along a ridge overlooking the Bushman's River. The climb up to the top is not too strenuous and the views looking over Wildebeest Plateau to Giant's Castle and Cathkin Peak are well worth the effort. The best time to see the peaks of the mountains is early in the morning as clouds tend to descend in the afternoon.

The more challenging walks to **Langalibalele Pass**, 12 km, **Bannerman Pass**, 20 km, and **Giant's Castle** involve a long uphill struggle to reach the top of the escarpment.

④ Giant's Castle Reserve

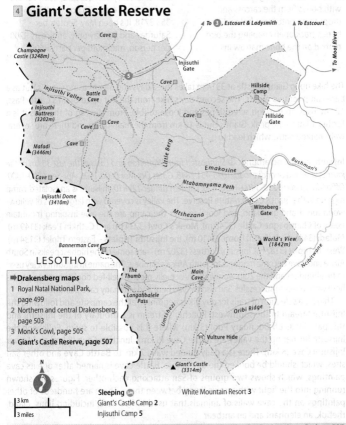

⇨ **Drakensberg maps**
1 Royal Natal National Park, page 499
2 Northern and central Drakensberg, page 503
3 Monk's Cowl, page 505
4 Giant's Castle Reserve, page 507

Sleeping
Giant's Castle Camp 2
Injisuthi Camp 5

White Mountain Resort 3

Lammergeyers

Lammergeyers are one of the world's rarest vultures, living mainly in isolated high mountain areas in the Pyrenees, the Atlas Mountains of Morocco and the Middle East. However, there are around 200 pairs of lammergeyers in the Drakensberg and Lesotho, and a visit to the hide at Giant's Castle is one of the best ways to see them.

They live on a diet of dried bones, waiting for a carcass to be cleaned by other vultures before they will start to feed. The lammergeyer flies off with bones from the carcass and drops them onto rocks below. The bones crack open enabling the bird to feed on the bone marrow inside.

The lammergeyer is a rare and endangered species, under threat from local farmers, who leave poisoned carcasses out in the wild to kill jackals. The carcasses attract vultures who, in turn, are poisoned.

The **lammergeyer hide** is a popular attraction and advance booking is necessary. Up to six people are driven up to the hide in the early morning but must make their own way back to the camp on foot. In addition to the lammergeyer you can expect to see the lanner falcon, jackal buzzard, Cape vulture and the black eagle. To book, call T036-353 3718. It's open May-September Saturday and Sunday only, and costs R200 per person, minimum per party R600.

The hike up to Giant's Castle at 3314 m takes three days and means using Giant's Hut as a base camp for two nights. The second day's hike from the hut up to Giant's Castle Pass, 12 km, rises up through scree slopes and loose rubble. From the top of the pass it is a further 1 km to the peak. Giant's Hut is 10 km from the main camp and there are several well-marked paths which lead to it.

Injisuthi camp and around ① *Signposted from Winterton and Loskop, the last 30 km of the journey are on a poor dirt road, T036-431 7848. Gates Oct-Mar 0500-1900, Apr-Sep 0600-1800. Office daily 0800-1230, 1400-1630. R20, children (under 12) R10.* Injisuthi is an isolated camp high up in the Giant's Castle Nature Reserve. The valley is covered with large areas of yellow-wood forest and grassland, and looming over the camp are the awe-inspiring mountain peaks of **Champagne Castle** (3248 m), **Monk's Cowl** (3234 m) and **Cathkin Peak** (3149 m). **Mafadi** (3446 m), **Injisuthi Dome** (3410 m), the **Injisuthi Triplets** – Eastern Triplet (3134 m), Western Triplet (3187 m), Injisuthi Buttress (3202 m) – are some of the highest peaks in South Africa and have become magnets to South Africa's climbers. The game in Injisuthi Valley used to be abundant and the Zulu word *Injisuthi* actually means 'well-fed dog' as hunting parties here were often so successful. San also thrived here and left many cave paintings.

There is a selection of trails for day hikes beginning at the campsite and following the Injisuthi Stream to the southwest. Poacher's Stream is a tributary of the Injisuthi and this path leads off Boundary Pool (3 km) where it is possible to swim. Following the Injisuthi further up the valley are Battle Cave (5 km), Junction Cave (8 km) and Lower Injisuthi Cave (8 km). There is a daily guided walk, 7 km, to **Battle Cave** and other San sites, which should be booked the day before. Battle Cave is named after one its cave paintings, which shows two groups of San attacking each other. Figures are shown running into the fight with arrows flying between them. There are hundreds of other paintings on the cave walls of animals that used to live here, including lions, eland, rhebok, an elephant and an antbear.

Giant's Castle is a three-day hike from Injisuthi following the contour path south. The trail can be exhausting but it does pass through spectacular mountain scenery including Popple Peak. Reservations for sleeping at Lower Injisuthi Cave and Bannerman Hut have to be made beforehand.

Kamberg Nature Reserve

ⓘ *48 km from Nottingham Rd travelling via Rosetta; the route is well signposted and only the last 19 km are on dirt roads. If travelling from Mooi River (42 km) on the N3, take the turning to Rosetta, T033-263 7312. Gates Oct-Mar 0500-1900, Apr-Sep 0600-1800. Office daily 0800-1130, 1400-1530. All visitors must report to the office on arrival. R28, children (under 12) R15.*

The reserve was established on farmland in 1951. The scenery is not as spectacular as at some of the other resorts, however, the Clarens Sandstone around Kamberg does have its own special appeal, and there is some good San rock art within the reserve. The reserve is at relatively low altitude, the highest point being **Gladstone's Nose** at 2265 m, and is therefore known for its birdlife with over 200 species recorded here.

Kamberg is probably best known for its trout fishing; there is a hatchery open to the public and several dams stocked with brown and rainbow trout which can be fished all year round. The Mooi River can only be fished during the season between September and April. Food and petrol are not for sale at the camp. The nearest shops and petrol station are 42 km away in Rosetta.

The trails around Kamberg are quite leisurely and involve no steep climbs. The **Mooi River Trail**, 4 km, has been designed with wheelchair access in mind, and is a relaxing stroll past willows and eucalyptus trees along the banks of the Mooi River. Longer trails, such as the hike up to **Emeweni Falls**, are detailed in a booklet available in the camp office.

There are several rock art sites in the reserve, but the two main sites worth visiting for the variety and quality of the paintings are Game Pass Shelter and The Kranses. The sheer number of paintings at **Game Pass Shelter** (about a 7-km walk from Kamberg) is impressive. Among the many scenes on the rock wall is one of a human with hooves instead of feet holding the tail of a dying eland. This is thought to have shamanic meaning and to be connected to a trance-like state. Just outside the shelter there are some fossilized dinosaur footprints. An impressive **San Rock Art Interpretation Centre** ⓘ *T033-263 7312, daily 0800, 1100, 1230 and 1330, R40 per person, book in advance*, provides visitors with an insight into the lifestyle of the San hunter-gatherers. There's an audio-visual presentation followed by a guided walk to the Game Pass Shelter that takes about 2½ hours. The centre also has a small restaurant.

The walk to the **Kranses** group of caves is a 12-km round trip. Apart from these there are also several other interesting caves to visit. The Kranses has a long sheltered rock wall covered in paintings of eland. Among these are some smaller scenes showing a group of people, some of whom are carrying shields. It is known that the San didn't use shields so they must be paintings of cattle herders, possibly the Amazizi, who moved up into the Drakensberg and lived peacefully with the San.

Southern Drakensberg ●⦾⊛⦿● ≫ *pp514-522.*

The southern section of the Drakensberg is the least visited part of the mountain range, although the scenery here is no less spectacular, and offers some excellent walks – particularly around Cobham. The area is best known for the Sani Pass, a spectacular track crossing over to the mountains to Lesotho, reaching 3000 m at its highest point. The main towns in the south are Underberg and Himeville – both are convenient stop-off points for stocking up on supplies.

Ins and outs Underberg is the main access point to the Southern Drakensberg resorts. Both Underberg and Himeville are sleepy farming villages but have shops, and are convenient stop-offs for provisions en route to the KZN Wildlife camps or the Sani Pass. Despite its relative isolation, **Underberg Express** offers transport to/from Underberg and Sani Pass, which helps make this beautiful area of the Drakensberg accessible for budget travellers.

Southern Berg Escape ① *7 Clock Tower Centre, Main Rd, Underberg, T033-701 1471, www.sanisaunter.com, Mon-Fri 0800-1600*, produces a leaflet with information on activities and accommodation in the Southern Drakensberg, and can book accommodation.

Always make sure you have warm clothing as conditions can change very quickly in this area. Try and hike in groups of three or more people.

Towards Underberg
Bulwer is a small village in the foothills of the Drakensberg set among pine plantations. There is little of interest for tourists here but it is one of the few centres for paragliding and hang-gliding in the Drakensberg. ▶ *For further details, see Activities and tours, page 520.*

Underberg → *Colour map 4, B6.*
This small market town was founded in 1886 and is still very much the main service centre for this part of the Drakensberg. The junction with the road to Himeville is where the banks, supermarkets and the tourist information office can all be found.

Himeville → *Colour map 4, B6.*
Founded in 1893, Himeville is a small prosperous village reminiscent of England. Arbuckle Street runs through the village centre where there is a supermarket, post office, museum, hotel and petrol station. **Himeville Arms** is the main hotel; its distinctive Tudor architecture wouldn't be out of place in an English village. Opposite, there is a small **museum** ① *T033-702 1184, Tue-Sun 0930-1230, free but donations accepted,* in the old fort and prison. It is an early sandstone building with exhibits on settler history and one of the better displays on San.

Himeville Nature Reserve ① *0600-1800, free,* is set on the outskirts of Himeville, where there are two dams surrounded by grassland, and it takes about 30 minutes to stroll around. The 105-ha protected area is a home for waterbirds and the occasional blesbok and black wildebeest; look out for three different species of crane which have been bred here in captivity.

Cobham
① *T033-702 0831. Park gates Oct-Mar 0500-1900, Apr-Sep 0600-1800. Office daily 0730-1300, 1400-1630. R25, children (under 12) R13. There is a curio shop at Cobham; otherwise plan on being totally self sufficient. The nearest shops and supermarkets are in Underberg.*
On the road between Underberg and Himeville, a signposted turning leads down a dirt road (D7) to Cobham (14 km). This is a fascinating wilderness area and is an ideal base for many exciting hikes. The land rising up towards the escarpment has been gouged with steep-sided gorges filled with thick yellowwood forest. The view above the cliffs of the escarpment is of the Giant's Cup, lying between Hodgson's Peaks, and the Drakensberg stretching out to the north and south. The Mzimkulu River rises here and flows to

Port Shepstone. This area is relatively undisturbed by human activity and the clean waters of the high Drakensberg streams are a sanctuary for Cape clawless otters and spotted-necked otters. People rarely see them, as they are very shy animals, but they tend to be active at dusk and dawn. White droppings on riverbanks are a sign of their presence; the distinctive colour comes from the calcium of the crab shells that make up a large proportion of their diet.

Hiking   There are five hikes of various lengths in the reserve, most of which leave from the campsite, including the **Gxalingenwa River Trail, Ouhout Trail, Troutbeck Loop, Emerald Stream Trail** and the **Pholela River Trail.** The camp office has full information on all hikes available. Most notable is the Giant's Cup Hiking Trail, a 60-km five-day trail.

Note that hiking permits for the Sani Pass area (see below), including the Giant's Cup Hiking Trail, are available from Cobham. Caves should also be reserved here. For your own safety, a mountain rescue register must be filled in. Nights at Cobham are cold all year round, so it is a good idea to bring some warm clothing.

Sani Pass → *Colour map 4, B6.*

The road from Himeville to Sani Pass (15 km) rises steadily through rolling hills covered in grassland and patches of pine plantation until it passes the **Sani Top Chalet** and the 3000 m peaks on the escarpment come into view. **Hodgson's Peaks,** at 3256 m and 3229 m, the **Twelve Apostles** and **Sani Pass,** at 2874 m, are at their most beautiful after snow. Flora and fauna have adapted to this harsh environment and some of the Drakensberg's rarest species can be found here. The road is one of the most dramatic in Africa and is the only route leading into Lesotho on its eastern border with South Africa.

Sani Pass was originally used by traders transporting goods by mule into Basutoland. A trading post was opened in the 1920s at Good Hope Farm at the bottom of the pass, which was the closest store to Mokhotlong in Lesotho. Then the Sani Pass was little more than a bridle path, but it was upgraded to a road in 1955 after the first 4WD Land Rover managed to complete the ascent. Maize and trade goods, including a fair number of guns, were taken up, while wool and hides were taken down. Trade still continues on this route, although these days most traders supplying shops in Lesotho have their own 4WDs and prefer to drive to the larger warehouses in Pietermaritzburg to stock up on goods. The Good Hope trading post closed in 1990 but the remains of the buildings can still be seen at the bottom of the pass. The provincial government of KwaZulu Natal has recently decided to have the Sani Pass road tarred, and the project should be completed in the next couple of years. Some of the flat part of the road from Himeville has already been tarred. It might be a loss for adventure tourism as it's a thrilling ride up by 4WD, but for the poor rural people of Lesotho, economically completely dependent on South Africa, it would definitely mean progress. ▸▸ *See also box, page 512.*

Tours and hikes   The pass is a popular attraction with tourists, and organized trips to the top of the pass and over the border to Lesotho are available from Underberg, the **Sani Pass Hotel** and **Sani Lodge.** Travellers are taken up by Land Rover; the road is terrifyingly steep and winding but the views are outstanding. The tours are a good way to discover local history and wildlife and include a visit to a Basotho village to see sheep shearing, maize cultivation or beer making. A picnic lunch in the Black Mountains or lunch at the **Sani Top Chalet** is included; don't miss a glass of warming mulled wine at the pub at the Sani Top Chalet – at 2874 m it is the highest pub in Africa.

ZOLL DOUANE — Border crossing: South Africa–Lesotho

Sani Pass

Until the road is tarred (should be completed by end of 2010) access to the pass is restricted to 4WD vehicles, motorbikes, mountain bikes and pedestrians. In spite of its isolation you should expect full border formalities at Sani Pass. The South African border is at the bottom and the Lesotho post is at the top and both are normally quick and easy. These are likely to be moved closer together when the road is tarred. The road is so rough that saloon cars are not allowed past the border post. If you are hiking, the walk between the two border posts takes about three hours.

Border opening hours South African border post daily 0800-1600; Lesotho border post daily 0700-1700.

Customs and immigration Interestingly, there are no customs and immigration officials at this border and all formalities are conducted by the police. This could be due in some part to the high incidence of *dagga* (marijuana) smuggling. Some overnight hikers on the KZN Wildlife trails have reported coming across Lesotho smugglers with great bags of *dagga* hiding in the mountains so they can cross into South Africa undetected by night.

Sleeping See page 518.

Hiking permits for the Sani Pass area are available from Cobham (see page 510). For your own safety, a mountain rescue register must be filled in. The most rewarding hike in this area is the day hike up to the top of Sani Pass at 2874 m. There is a car park at the South African border post from where it is a further 14-km hike to the top. The trail is quite straightforward and just involves following the road. A number of shorter walks visit **Gxalingwena, Kaula** and **Ikanti Shelter**. These cave-like dwellings are home to a number of San rock paintings. New regulations stipulate that for the protection of the paintings, they must only be visited with a registered guide. These can be arranged from the **Sani Pass Hotel** or **Sani Lodge**, where survey maps are also available for a deposit of R50.

Mkhomazi Wilderness Area ● ↦ *Colour map 4, B6.*

Vergelegen
ⓘ *T033-702 0712, entry fee R25, children (under 12) R13, overnight hiking permits R40.*

Vergelegen is one of the most remote reserves in the Drakensberg National Park and as such receives fewer visitors than most other reserves. Thaba Ntlenyana on the Lesotho side of the border is the highest mountain in southern Africa at 3482 m and can be seen from the top of the escarpment in the reserve. The rugged mountain terrain here makes this an ideal base from which to explore the mountains on some of the most inaccessible and demanding hiking trails in the Drakensberg. Permits are needed for hikes which leave from Vergelegen. Hikers can register at the camp office. **Note** Facilities such as petrol or basic food supplies are not available at Vergelegen; visitors should be completely self-sufficient.

Lotheni
ⓘ *T033-702 0540. Park gates Oct-Mar, 0500-1900, Apr-Sep, 0600-1800. Office daily 0800-1230, 1400-1630. R25, children (under 12) R13.*

The reserve can be reached either from Himeville or from Nottingham Road; both access routes are along rough dirt tracks which can become impassable during heavy rains. The most popular route is the signposted dirt track from Himeville which heads north for 45 km towards **Lotheni Store** and the reserve. The Nottingham Road track heads southeast for 60 km to **Lotheni Store**, from where there is a signposted turning for the last 10 km to the reserve. There is a camp shop here which sells hiking maps and permits; otherwise the nearest shop is **Lotheni Store**, 14 km from the entrance to the camp. Petrol is not available here.

The landscape at Lotheni is mainly rolling grassland rising up towards the High Berg and Redi Peak at 3298 m. The grassland is interspersed with patches of protea woodland, tree ferns and the rare Berg bamboo. The demand for timber in the first half of this century resulted in most of the indigenous woodland being cut down leaving large areas of grassland. The land was then used for grazing and as farmland until the 1950s when it was bought by the **KwaZulu Natal Parks Board**.

Streams cutting down through the rock have formed narrow wooded gorges, which have been stocked with brown trout. The trout season lasts from September to April and during these months accommodation at weekends can be fully booked. Spring is also a popular time for visitors who come to see the magnificent wild flowers. There are three leisurely day hikes and two overnight trails in the reserve, for which maps can be bought in the camp shop. During hot weather it is worth remembering that it is safe to swim in the Lotheni River when it is not in flood. There are some natural pools a short walk from the camp although the water flowing straight off the mountains can be icy.

Garden Castle

① *Entrances at Drakensberg Garden (34 km from Underberg) and Bushmen's Nek (45 km from Underberg), both signposted off the R626, T033-7011823. Park gates Oct-Mar 0500-1900, Apr-Sep 0600-1800. Office daily 0800-1300, 1400-1600. R25, children (under 12) R13. Overnight hiking fee R40. There are plenty of huts and caves to spend the night in, but no fires are allowed anywhere within the Garden Castle Reserve.*

Garden Castle is the southernmost reserve in the Drakensberg Park, a wild area with few visitors, home to eland, grey rhebok and reedbuck. The landscape consists mostly of grassland with patches of proteas and tree ferns. There are many tarns in this part of the Drakensberg where waterbirds and wildlife can be seen. There are magnificent views up into the mountains on a clear day, with the mountain peaks of **Walker** (3322 m), **Wilson** (3342 m) and the **Rhino** (3051 m), towering over the reserve.

Overnight hikers must complete the Mountain Rescue Register before starting their hike and make sure they sign in on return. The office has a small shop which sells basic supplies, permits and hiking maps, otherwise the nearest shops are in Underberg. Petrol is not available here.

The highest peaks in this area, which can be hiked in a day via a strenuous 11-km trail, are **Mashai Pass** (peak 3313 m) and **Rhino Peak** (3051 m). **Engagement Cave** and **Sleeping Beauty Cave** are only 4 km from the KWS office and are easily visited in a morning. There are many options for day hikes around Bushman's Nek to various caves.

For Sleeping and Eating price codes and other relevant information, see pages 46-53.

⊖ Sleeping

Royal Natal National Park *p499, map p499*

While the prices for the private resorts may seem high, remember many consist of family units sleeping at least 4, and some, even if they are standard doubles, include all meals.
A-C Thendele Camp, camp office open daily 0800-1600, advance bookings on T033-845 1000, www.kznwildlife.com. Stunning location with unrivalled views of the Amphitheatre from a cluster of chalets, cottages and a lodge sleeping 4-12. The cottages and lodge have cooks who prepare food supplied by the guests, while the chalets are self-catering with fully equipped kitchens, coal fire, private terrace and braai overlooking the Amphitheatre. The camp's setting makes it one of the most popular in the entire Drakensberg, so must be booked months in advance. A curio shop sells books, T-shirts and souvenirs.

Camping
Mahai, T036-4386 310. The spacious campsite has pleasant lawns and is bordered by large pine trees and a stream. 120 sites, most with power points, 5 modern ablution blocks, washing machines, good views of the Drakensberg and footpaths leading straight up into the hills make this campsite very popular (it can be crowded and noisy at weekends).
Rugged Glen, T036-438 6303. Small site to the north of the park, with 20 sites shaded by pine trees and a central ablution block, some with power points. There are no other facilities here.

Oliviershoek Pass *p500, map p503*
AL Alpine Heath, below Oliviershoek Pass, follow signs along the R74 (Cavern Berg Rd), T036-438 6484, www.alpineheath.co.za. A fully self-contained and well-established resort, with a large conference village, and offering a range of activities, 100 self-catering chalets with 3-bedrooms, lounge, 2 bathrooms, and private patio, TV. Facilities include 2 pools, gym, sauna, tennis, squash, restaurant.
AL Montusi Mountain Lodge, follow signs along R74 towards Royal Natal National Park, T036-438 6243, www.montusi.co.za. Attractive series of luxury chalets, with large bedrooms and plush sitting rooms with large TVs, fridge, private terrace with staggering views towards the Amphitheatre. Chalets are surrounded by lawns. Good restaurant and small bar. The owners run daily guided walks to the Royal Natal Park, including San rock art walks. Fly-fishing, horse riding, pool, cycling, flying trapeze on attached grounds. It's not as family orientated as other resorts.
A The Cavern, 10 km, follow the signs heading off the R74 towards the Royal Natal National Park, T036-438 6270, www.cavern.co.za. Large complex set among gardens and woodland offering accommodation in 55 luxury thatched cottages. Wide range of activities including horse riding, bowls, swimming and a weekend disco. Rates include all meals and guided hikes. A superb location, with well-kept mature gardens and an overall friendly and welcoming atmosphere; good choice for families.
B Little Switzerland, look out for the signposted turning off the R74 next to the petrol station, just below Oliviershoek Pass, T036-438 6220, www.lsh.co.za. 66 thatched cottages and self-catering chalets set in a 2000-ha reserve, this large resort has many sporting facilities, including riding, fishing, canoeing, tennis and swimming. Recent additions include indoor heated pool, health and beauty centre, and gym. Geared towards South African families.
B-C Drakensville Berg Resort, from Oliviershoek Pass, the turning is on the left towards Jagersrust, T036-438 6287, www.drakensville.co.za. A large all-purpose holiday camp with 70 self-catering chalets for couples, plus family units and more upmarket B&B rooms. Sports include waterskiing, fishing, riding, tennis, squash and mini-golf. There's

also a camping and caravan park set under big shady trees.

C Caterpillar & Catfish, at the top of Olivier-shoek Pass, T036-438 6130, www.cookhouse.co.za. A pine-panelled mountain lodge in a restored trading post, tucked under large pine trees with great views. Decorated with African antiques, stripped pine and handmade furniture, 9 comfortable and stylish rooms, huge buffet breakfasts, guided hikes to some fascinating rock art, fishing in a well-stocked trout dam. Beautifully decorated piano bar and restaurant specializing in trout and fusion cooking. Popular with groups from Gauteng for Sun lunch. Recommended.

E-F Amphitheatre Backpackers, 21 km northwest of Bergville on the R74, T036-438 6675, www.amphibackpackers.co.za. Excellent backpackers, the main building is a converted sandstone house with log fires, dorms, doubles and camping, hearty home-cooked meals, packed lunches to take with you on over 30 hikes in the area. If you don't have your own transport, this is a perfect introduction to the mountains. Daily guided hikes to the top of the amphitheatre and day trips into Lesotho. On the **Baz Bus** route. Recommended.

Bergville *p501, map p503*
B Sandford Park Resort, R616 to Ladysmith, T036-448 1001, www.sandford.co.za. One of the finest lodges in the region, this resort has grown up around a hotel dating back to 1852. There are 50 charming rooms, some in separate rondavels, with tasteful furnishings. Neat gardens around the house, large pool, horse riding, hiking and canoeing, and a popular restaurant and bar. Rates are for dinner, B&B. Good base from which to explore both the Drakensberg and the battlefields.

C Bingelela Lodge, a short drive out of town towards Woodstock Dam, T036-448 1336, www.bingelela.co.za. 12 units in comfortable, rustic, thatched cottages, honeymoon suite with spa bath, pool, à la carte restaurant, friendly pub serving good South African cuisine.

E-F Bergville Caravan Park, on the R74 just south of town, T036-448 1273, www.berg

villeaccommodation.co.za. There are 10 self-catering bungalows sleeping 2-4, 2 rondavels sleeping 2 and a campsite next to the Tugela River. In low season and Mon-Fri the resort offers big discounts on accommodation, the river is popular for canoeing and there's a pool.

Spioenkop Dam Nature Reserve *p501*
A Spionkop Lodge, on the R600 between Winterton and Ladysmith, T036-488 1404, www.spionkop.co.za. This delightful country lodge makes an excellent base from which to explore the surroundings. 8 comfortable double rooms, fully inclusive, and 2 family self-catering cottages, on a farm close to Spioenkop. Owner Raymond Heron is a vivid story teller and excellent guide to the area. Can also arrange canoe rides on the nearby Tugela River, birdwatching trips to Spioenkop Dam and horse riding (including Battlefield tours on horseback). Recommended.

D Iphika Tented Bush Camp, KZN Wildlife, T033-845 1000, www.kznwildlife.com. Can sleep up to 4 in 2 large 2-bed tents and also has a stone and thatch lounge area with fireplace and kitchen. It is set on the slopes of Spioenkop Mountain overlooking a small waterhole and it is possible to go on game walks from here; Spioenkop battlefield is a short walk away, up a steep slope. Visitors need to bring their own food and drink. The closest shops are in Winterton, 14 km away.

Camping
Next to the dam are 30 sites with power points, slipways for launching of boats, popular with anglers. Reservations direct with the officer, T036-488 1578.

Cathedral Peak *p502, map p503*
A Cathedral Peak Hotel, at the end of the road past the entry gates, T036-488 1888, www.cathedralpeak.co.za. An all-round resort, popular for weddings in its own stone chapel, traditionally used as a base by hikers and climbers because of its stunning location close to the high peaks of the Drakensberg. 90 luxurious double rooms, several

restaurants and bars, 3 swimming pools, 9-hole floodlit golf course, horse riding, squash, jogging and mountain bike trail, 10-m climbing tower, gym, beauty spa and tennis. It is one of South Africa's most popular destinations and booking in advance is essential all year. Rates include meals.

B-C Didima Camp, on the road leading into Cathedral Peak, just before **Cathedral Peak Hotel**, KZN Wildlife, T033-845 1000, www.kznwildlife.com. The camp is themed around the art of the San people and the thatched chalets have been designed to look like caves. 63 self-catering units sleeping 2, built back to back so can be converted into 4-bed units using a connecting door, one 6-bed chalet and a honeymoon suite. All have satellite TV and fireplace, and there's a restaurant, bar and small shop. Conference centre/wedding chapel has a full height glass wall framing a view of Cathedral Peak. Also here is the **Rock Art Centre** (see page 503).

Camping

There are 21 campsites opposite the information office. This is a secluded campsite up in the mountains with a quiet, tranquil feel. Simple facilities: there is only an ablution block for campers. The campsite is popular so it's advisable to book up to a month in advance. Camp gates are open daily 0600-1800, and until 2100 on Fri. There are also at least 15 caves near here in which hikers can camp, book these well in advance. Reservations through the officer in charge, T036-488 8000.

Monk's Cowl p505, map p505

All the accommodation listed below is outside the park and signposted off the R600. The distances shown are from each hotel to the entrance to Monk's Cowl.

AL Champagne Sports Resort, 9 km, T036-468 8000, www.champagnesportsresort.com. Large sporty resort with beautiful views, attracting weekenders from Gauteng and Durban. 62 newly refurbished rooms with bright furnishings, stylish bathrooms and private balconies. Impressive 18-hole golf

course, large buffet restaurant, sports bar, 4 pools, tennis, squash, horse riding, gym and beauty salon. Also has timeshare bungalows. Pleasant, typically South African family resort. Rates include breakfast and dinner.

A Champagne Castle, 2 km, T036-468 1063, www.champagnecastle.co.za. Traditional Drakensberg resort in a spectacular mountain setting, with 47 luxurious rooms (rates include all meals), some self-catering cottages, set in the main lodge and annexes with thatched roofs, surrounded by attractive leafy grounds. Restaurant, horse riding, tennis, swimming pool, spa.

A The Nest, 13 km, T036-468 1068, www.the nest.co.za. 55 guestrooms in thatched rondavels with private verandas and mountain views, bright furnishings and wood furniture. Restaurant, bar, guest lounges, pool, bowls, horse riding. Rates include all meals and after-noon tea. Good base for exploring the area.

B Ardmore Guest Farm, 12 km, T036-468 1314, www.ardmore.co.za. Superb views with lovely gardens overlooking a dam. Mix of B&B, full board or self-catering in 8 en suite rooms. Popular with anglers for the dam fishing, where you can also canoe. Good local reputation for home-cooked meals, 4-course dinners are taken at a long table with hosts and other guests, also known for its ceramic art studio – worth a visit, with a tea garden on site. Recommended by several readers.

C Cathkin Cottage, 13 km, after the **Drakens berg Sun** hotel, turn right into Yellowwood Drive, T036-468 1513, www.cathkincottage. co.za. Simple double rooms and family units with en suite facilities and private entrances. Some rooms have fridge and TV, small pool and pretty garden. Good breakfasts served and provides picnic lunches for hiking and several trails start from the cottage.

C-D Dragon Peaks, 4 km, T036-468 1031, www.dragonpeaks.com. Mix of B&B and self-catering chalets with TV, plus a camp and caravan site. Popular restaurant with outdoor lapa area. Good facilities for families, including 2 swimming pools, tennis, and horse riding, plus a wide range of organized entertainment. There is a small supermarket here with an ATM and a petrol pump. It has a rather unique thatched wedding venue on an island in the middle of a dam.

D-F Inkosana Lodge, 7 km, easy access via a good surfaced road, T036-468 1202, www.inkosana.co.za. Simple lodge with fine views towards the mountains, set in a large garden with a pool, with 4 small dorms, double rooms, some en suite, rondavels and camping. Large dining area with hearty home-made meals on request or kitchen available for self-catering. Can give lots of advice on hiking and can arrange other activities in the valley like horse riding.

Camping

KZN Wildlife Campsite, literally at the end of the road. Reservations for this campsite should be made through the officer in charge, T036-468 1103. This is a delightful campsite in a stunning spot with views back across the valley. There are 38 pitches, some with power points, and an ablution block bordered with indigenous trees and shrubs next to the camp office. At the office is a tea garden, open 0800-1600 for light meals that also provide hiker's picnics in backpacks with cutlery, and a slot for a bottle of champagne, and sundowner snack-packs to eat later in the evening. Order both these the day before (T036-468 1103).

Giant's Castle Reserve *p506, map p507*

A-C Giant's Castle camp, KZN Wildlife, T033-845 1000, www.kznwildlife.com. Revamped camp, 44 chalets with between 2 and 6 beds, lounge, dining area and fully equipped kitchen. Shop sells a wide range of books and curios but only a limited selection of dried and frozen food. The camp is popular all year and tends to be full at weekends. **Izimbali** restaurant and pub if you don't want to self-cater. Swimming in summer is permitted in the Bushmen's River below the camp.

B-D White Mountain Resort, on the road to Giant's Castle from Estcourt, T036-353 3437, www.whitemountain.co.za. Family holiday

camp, full-board rooms, self-catering chalets sleeping 2-6, camping and caravan sites, pool, bar, restaurant. The resort is self-contained and offers a wide range of organized activities, but is a long distance from the higher parts of the Drakensberg. There is a small supermarket and petrol is also available.

C-F Injisuthi camp, KZN Wildlife, T033-845 1000, www.kznwildlife.com. Sixteen 6-bed chalets, fully equipped for self-catering, with gas stove and fridge, no plug points. Also basic 8-bed dormitory cabins. Electricity 1730-2200 only. Coffee bar, TV room, there is no shop here so visitors need to bring all supplies with them.

Mountain huts

There are 4 mountain huts about 4-5 hrs walk from Giant's Castle camp: **Giant's Hut, Centenary Hut** and **Bannerman Hut** sleep 8 people each, and **Meander Hut** sleeps 4. All the huts are at an altitude of around 2000 m and can get very cold at night. Bunks and mattresses are provided. Reservations KZN Wildlife, T033-845 1000, www.kznwildlife.com.

Camping

There are 20 sites at Injisuthi camp that can accommodate 120 people, three 2-bed pre-erected tents, and shared ablution blocks. Reservations direct, T036-431 7848. **Lower Injisuthi Cave, Upper Injisuthi Cave** and **Grindstone Cave**, can all be used by hikers for overnight stops but should be reserved in advance. No fires allowed, very basic facilities. Come well equipped. Reservations T036-431 7848.

Kamberg Nature Reserve *p509*

It is possible to camp on overnight hikes but you need to be fully equipped.
C Main Camp, KZN Wildlife, T033-845 1000, www.kznwildlife.com. 7 self-catering chalets with 2-6 beds. Kitchenettes and a communal lounge area.
C Stillerus Rustic Cottage, 8 km from the main camp, KZN Wildlife, T033-845 1000, www.kznwildlife.com. 1 cottage with 8 beds,

for a minimum of 6. Self-catering and fully equipped with a gas stove, a fridge and gas lighting. Bring your own bedding.

Underberg p510

B-C Elgin, Bushman's Nek Valley, 7 km from Underberg towards Swartberg, T033-701 1918, www.elginholidayfarm.co.za. 4 luxurious suites set in wings attached to a farmhouse, with DSTV fridge, attractive decor and bright white linen, and dinner on request. Also has a self-catering log cabin sleeping 10, all set on a working farm, with organic dairy and vegetables for sale.
C Rocky Mountain Lodge, off the Swartberg Rd, T033-701 1676, www.rockylodge.com. 1 self-catering log cabin sleeping up to 12, and a stone cottage with 4 double rooms sleeping 8, both with cosy log fires and spacious lounges. Magnificently positioned on a mountain plateau, with beautiful views and a peaceful setting overlooking the Mzimkulu River, and this area is quite special in winter when it snows. B&B is also an option.

Himeville p510

B Moorcroft Manor Country House, 2 km from Himeville on the Sani Pass Rd, T033-702 1967, www.moorcroft.co.za. Rural retreat with 8 spacious rooms, some with Victorian baths, decorated with antiques, good restaurant with bar and outside terrace, mountain views, provides picnic lunches for hikers, rents out tackle for fly-fishing and can organize the day trip up the Sani Pass.
C-E Himeville Arms, Arbuckle St, T033-702 1305, www.himevillehotel.co.za. Old-fashioned, 100-year-old hotel. Rooms can be rather gloomy in summer, but are cosy in winter with well-stocked log fires. Cheaper backpacker beds in shared rooms. Good lunch-time bar menu in the excellent **Arms Pub** with home-brewed real ale, 2 restaurants and pool.

Cobham p510

Reservations for campsites, trail huts and caves should be made through the Cobham officer in charge, T033-702 0831. The camp-

site here is very basic with an open area for setting up tents and you need to be totally self-sufficient. Basic toilets and hot showers and campers may swim in the river below the campsite if it's not too cold.

Sani Pass p511

A Sani Pass Hotel, Sani Pass Rd, 22 km from Underberg, T033-702 1320, www.sanipass hotel.co.za. A large resort hotel in a beautiful location offering accommodation either in the hotel building or in luxury cottages in the gardens, and rates include breakfast and dinner. Facilities and activities include squash, fly-fishing, tennis, bowls, horse riding, there's a 9-hole golf course, spa and swimming pool, and tours are on offer up Sani Pass by 4WD or quad bike.
B Sani Top Chalet, top of the pass, next to the Lesotho border post, T033-702 1158, T082-715 1131 (mob), www.sanitopchalet.co.za. A combination of double rooms in the main building or in stone en suite rondavels out back, plus backpacker rooms (**E**) with dorms and shared bathrooms and a kitchen in a converted store in the nearby village, bedding provided but bring towels. You can camp but you'll need thermals. The hotel has a licensed pub (the highest in Africa) and restaurant warmed by roaring wood fires, overlooking the dramatic road below. Fantastic hikes and pony trekking to some awe-inspiring viewpoints along the escarpment. When it does snow it is possible to hire skis from the hotel.
D-F Sani Lodge, 19 km from Underberg on the Sani Pass road, T033-702 0330, www.sani lodge.co.za. If you are coming from Pieter-maritzburg, travel with Underberg Express, see page 456 for details, who drop off here. There is a mixture of dorms, double rooms, 2 en suite rondavels, 2 en suite family cottages, and plenty of space to pitch a tent. Large kitchen, comfortable lounge with open fire for the winter months when it can get very cold, and a veranda with a superb uninterrupted view of the Drakensberg escarpment. Run by Russell and Simone who are experts on hiking in Lesotho and organize

several tours and guided hikes, including an excellent Sani Pass tour by 4WD.

Mkhomazi Wilderness Area p512

Reservations for all accommodation are made through **KZN Wildlife**, T033-845 1000, www.kznwildlife.com.

B-D Lotheni, 2 self-catering cottages with 6 beds, and 12 self-catering bungalows, with 2 or 3 beds. All the accommodation is fully equipped; there are 2 freezers in the camp kitchen which can be used by guests. Electricity 1700-2200 only.

D Simes Rustic Cottage, sleeps 10, although the minimum charge is for 6 people. The small dam nearby has been stocked with brown trout and is exclusively for the use of visitors staying at the cottage. The cottage has a gas supply but visitors are expected to bring their own bedding, gas lamps and torches.

Camping

The 10 campsites at **Lotheni**, T033-702 0540, are a secluded 2 km from the hutted camp and it's a beautiful spot. The only facility is an ablution block with hot and cold water. It is possible to camp overnight within the **Verlegen** Reserve on long-distance hikes.

Garden Castle p513

There are 3 rustic huts on the Giant's Cup Hiking Trail. Each can accommodate up to 30 people. During the winter months hikers are strongly advised to stay in these huts as there can be heavy snowfalls and very cold conditions. There are 10 camping sites and an ablution block near to the park entrance as well as 12 caves in the park available to hikers. Campsites, caves and huts (**E-F**) should be booked in advance through the camp office T033-701 1823.

A-D Penwarn Country Lodge, close to Bushman's Nek, 25 km from Underberg, T033-701 1417, www.penwarn.com. Luxury lodge with 4 comfortable rooms opening up to a wooden deck with broad views over a lake and the mountains, rates include breakfast and dinner, or cheaper simple self-

catering log cabins. This peaceful mountain farm offers a wide range of activities: canoeing, fly-fishing, mountain and quad-biking, horse riding, including rounding up cattle on horseback, and hiking. Excellent food served in a colonial-style restaurant, and a homely atmosphere during the winter months.

🍴 Eating

All the large mountain resorts have restaurants and bars on site. Much of the other accommodation is self catering; as a result there is little need for restaurants in the region.

Winterton p501

🍴 **Thokosiza Centre**, on the R100, 13 km west of Winterton, T036-488 1273. Coffee shop and restaurant in this cultural/craft/tourist centre, popular spot for a light lunch or mid-afternoon tea, with pleasant wooden tables on a shady deck. Closed evenings.

Underberg p510

🍴 **Lemon Tree Bistro**, White Cottage Shopping Centre, T033-701 1589. Open 0830-1645, Fri-Sat 1800-2045. Well worth a stop for light lunches. Coffee, good produce in the deli and winery during the day, also open Fri and Sat evening, with a bistro-style menu, phone ahead.

Himeville p510

🍴🍴-🍴 **Moorcroft Manor Country House**, see Sleeping, page 518. Open 0730-2130. Restaurant within the luxury lodge of the same name, stylish dining room with beautiful terrace, breakfasts, light lunches like ploughman's platter or gourmet steak sandwiches, upmarket menu with a French feel for dinner. Bookings are essential.

🍴🍴-🍴 **Himeville Arms Hotel**, Arbuckle St, T033-702 1305, www.himevillehotel.co.za. The **Himeville Arms** (1100-late) is a local pub with lots of character (and characters) with cosy wooden interior and crackling fire selling pub grub. The **Torridon Restaurant**

(1230-1500, 1830-2100) serves country cuisine including good steaks, fresh local trout and some traditional sticky desserts and again there's a fire to sit next to with a nightcap.

⊙ Entertainment

Monk's Cowl p505, map p505
Drakensberg Boys' Choir, T036-468 1012, www.dbchoir.info. During term-time, the choir performs on Wed at 1530 in the school's impressive auditorium. Booking essential.

⊛ Festivals and events

Underberg p510
Easter weekend Splashy Fen Festival, www.splashyfen.co.za. A popular music festival held on Splashy Fen Farm. Over the years it has increased in size and now attracts a broad range of modern musicians as well as South Africa's folk crowd.

◯ Shopping

Bergville p501
There are several supermarkets in town to stock up in before heading into the reserves. The shops at the campsites stock only the most basic supplies. Outside the centre, look out for farms selling fresh produce.
Tevreden Cheese, take the R74 out of the village towards the Northern Berg, take a left turn after approximately 7 km, T036-448 1840. Open 1000-1500. Cheesemaking farm with tastings, a good spot to stock up before a hike.

Winterton p501
There are several craft shops along the R600 to Champagne Valley and Monk's Cowl.
KwaZulu Weavers, 12 km west of Winterton on the R600, T036-488 1098, www.kwazulu weavers.com. Colourful handwoven rugs made from wool and mohair. Attached is a popular handmade candle shop.

Rainbow Room, off the R600 just after the Nest Hotel, heading towards Monk's Cowl, T036-468 1801. An unusual selection of handmade crafts; unfortunately, the larger pieces are a bit too big to take home for overseas visitors but they can arrange shipping. Run by Inger.
Thokozisa, on the R600, 13 km west of Winterton, T036-488 1207. A one-stop tourist centre (the **Central Drakensberg Information Centre** is here) with shops selling arts and crafts and wines, and a coffee shop.

Cathedral Peak p502, map p503
The shop at Mike's Pass sells a limited range of basic groceries, otherwise the nearest supermarket is at Winterton. Petrol can be bought at the **Cathedral Peak Hotel**.

Giant's Castle Reserve p506, p507
Petrol is for sale by the main gate. There's a farm shop next to the park gates selling fresh and smoked trout, otherwise the nearest supermarket is in Estcourt.

Underberg p510
There are a number of craft shops and a coffee shop in the **White Cottage Shopping Centre**, a rather twee mini shopping mall.

▲ Activities and tours

uKhahlamba-Drakensberg Park p493, maps p499, 503, p505 and p507
Adventure activities
All Out Adventures, near the entrance to the **Alpine Heath resort**, T036-438 6242, www.all outadventures.co.za. 0900-1630, closed Tue out of season. Fun activities for young and old; a flying trapeze (R100 for 3 flights), a bungee bounce (R60), where you're put in a bungee harness and then bounce very high from a trampoline, a big swing (R150) from the top of a pine tree, a zip liner slide (R100), and a canopy cable tour (R350) to various platforms in the trees. Also organize paintballing and quad-biking. Coffee shop serves light lunches.

Climbing

Contact Gavin Raubenheimer at **Peak High**, T033-343 3168, www.peakhigh.co.za, for details of guided climbs in the Drakensberg, and about the possibility of ice climbing the **Lotheni Falls**, which are usually frozen from mid-Jun to mid-Aug. Strictly for experienced mountaineers only, with full equipment, including an ice pick.

Mountain Club of South Africa, www.kzn. mcsa.org.za. A useful source of information for experienced rock climbers.

Fishing

Trout were introduced into the rivers of the Drakensberg around 1900 and over the years fly-fishing has become popular. Fishing licences are available from some of the offices at the camps, and some rent out rods and tackle. Enquire with **KZN Wildlife**, T033-845 1000, www.kznwildlife.com.

Golf

Green fees are very reasonable; call in advance to check on availability of equipment hire. There are courses at the **Amphitheatre Golf Club**, T036-438 6308, 9 holes, is in Royal Natal National Park; **Cathedral Peak Hotel**, T036-488 1888, www.cathedralpeak.co.za, 9 holes; **Monk's Cowl Country Club**, T036-468 1300, www.monkscowl.co.za, 9 holes; and **Champagne Sports Resort**, T036-468 8000, www.champagnesportsresort.com, 18 holes. In good weather, the backdrop is spectacular.

Hang-gliding and paragliding

Wildsky Adventures, Bulwer, 50 km west of Pietermaritzburg, T082-748 8637, www.wildsky.co.za. Courses or one-off tandem glides. Also offers other activities, including abseiling, horse riding or fishing, and has simple accommodation in log cabins available to those who are undertaking paragliding courses.

Helicopter flights

There is an airfield opposite the **Champagne Sports Resort** (see page 516) from where you can take short helicopter flights over the mountains. Bookings can be made at the **Cathedral Peak Hotel**, or the **Champagne Sports Resort**, or call **Westline Aviation**, T036-468 1104. A 20-min scenic flight should cost R650 per person.

Horse riding

The full length of the Berg is negotiable on horseback, by way of trails and bridleways. Riding is available in the KZN Wildlife parks of Rugged Glen and Spioenkop and can be arranged at the parks offices (R110 per hr). The rides are very popular during the holiday period and it is best to book in advance at the stables. Some resorts also offer horse riding.

Khotso Horse Trails, Bergvlei Farm, 10 km from Underberg towards Drakensberg Gardens, T033-701 1502, www.khotsotrails. co.za. Mountain rides for beginners and advanced riders, specialist adventure rides (some to Lesotho, see page 814) and cattle round-ups. Accommodation in dorms in a log cabin with shared kitchen and bathroom or in self-catering thatched chalets.

Mountain biking

Mountain biking has become hugely popular in recent years. 3 areas of the Drakensberg have designated biking trails: Cathedral Peak, Champagne Valley and Underberg. There are 70 km of dirt roads in the Cathedral Peak area which can be used by mountain bikers. The routes are by no means extreme but they pass through some spectacular scenery. The views from the top of Mike's Pass are as exhilarating as the 5-km ride back down.

The route from Underberg to Sani Pass and back is one of South Africa's epic mountain bike rides. The 20-km climb up to the Lesotho border is a challenging ascent along a trail cut out of the rock. The altitude at the highest point of the trail is around 2800 m from where there are spectacular views over the sheer cliffs and gorges of the Mkhomazana Valley. There are also a number of more sedate rides around Underberg itself.

A 75-km Mountain Bike Challenge is held at Giant's Castle annually on the last Sun in Apr. Check www.ultimatemtb.org.za for further details.

Tour operators
Based in Underberg, **Major Adventures**, T033-701 1628, www.majoradventures.com; **Sani Pass Tours**, T033-701 1064, www.sani tours.co.za; and **Thaba Tours**, T033-701 2888, www.thabatours.co.za, all offer daily 4WD day trips to the top of Sani Pass for about R450 per person with a stop for (optional) lunch at the Sani Top Chalet.
Drakensberg Adventures, Sani Pass Lodge, T033-702 0330, www.sanilodge.co.za. Great selection of tours in area, including an overnight trip into Lesotho. Russell is a formidable guide for the Sani Pass excursion and local hikes. On offer are 4WD tours, hikes to San rock art, horse riding and visits to local Zulu families where you can spend the night. Guided climbs of Thabana Ntlenyana (Africa's second tallest mountain) also organized.
Traverse Line, 30 Tower St, Cirencester, Gloucestershire GL7 1EF, UK, T+44-(0)1285 650 906, www.traverseline.co.uk. Specializes in trekking and walking tours in the Drakensberg. Also organizes safaris.

⊖ Transport

Northern Drakensberg *p498, map p503*
Baz Bus, T021-439 2323, www.bazbus.com, runs from Ampitheatre Backpackers, Olivier-shoek Pass to **Johannesburg** and **Durban**.

Central Drakensberg *p501, map p503*
Baz Bus, T021-439 2323, www.bazbus. com, runs in both directions between **Johannesburg** and **Durban**, drops-off and picks-up outside of the First National Bank, Winterton.

Southern Drakensberg *p509*
Underberg Express, bookings T0861-114924, www.underbergexpress.co.za, runs between **Sani Pass**, **Himeville**, **Underberg**, **Howick**, **Pietermaritzburg**, **Durban**, and **Durban International Airport**, every day. It departs from Sani Lodge at 0730 and arrives at Durban International Airport at 1200, from where it leaves again at 1300 and arrives back again at Sani Lodge at 1730. The full one-way fare is R220. You also have the option to get on or off in Pietermaritzburg to connect with the **Baz Bus** and other mainline buses heading towards Johannesburg. Check the website for full timetables and fares.

❶ Directory

Bergville *p501, map p503*
Banks First National Bank, South St.
Emergencies Mountain Rescue Service T031-307 7744, T084-629 1647. **Medical services** Bergville Medical Centre, T036-448 2507.

Zululand

Zululand, homeland of Shaka and one of the most evocative regions of South Africa, will forever be associated with the classic movie starring Michael Caine as the redoubtable British officer fighting Zulu warriors. Today, this region – extending from the northern bank of the Tugela River up to Mkhuze and Maputaland – is rather more peaceful and offers long, unspoilt beaches, excellent game reserves and a chance to experience traditional Zulu culture. Gone are the vast herds of migrating elephant, wildebeest and springbok, victim in part to the many battles fought over this wealthy province. Despite being one of the more traditional areas of South Africa, it has thriving industrial cities and vast areas of sugarcane and eucalyptus plantations. However, game reserves at St Lucia and Hluhluwe-Umfolozi are still natural magnets for tourists and around six per cent of KwaZulu Natal is managed by KZN Wildlife as conservation areas. ▶▶ *For listings, see pages 537-543.*

Elephant Coast ● ▶▶ *pp537-543.*

Ins and outs

The route into the Zulu heartland follows the N2 north from Stanger/KwaDukuza to the village of Gingindlovu. From here the R68 goes inland to Eshowe (26 km), Ulundi and the Battlefield sites (see page 482), while the N2 continues up the coast to Mtunzini, Empangeni, Richards Bay, Hluhluwe-Umfolozi, St Lucia and Maputaland. This is the most popular area of Zululand, and was recently renamed the Elephant Coast – thanks to the reintroduction of elephant in sections of the iSimangaliso Wetland Park. There are a number of game farms in the area offering luxury accommodation, while scuba-diving and deep-sea fishing are available in the coastal resorts. The region has a subtropical climate; it is hot and humid from December to March and warm and dry from April to November. ▶▶ *For more information on the region visit www.zululand.kzn.org.za.*

Gingindlovu and around → *Colour map 5, B2.*

Gingindlovu was originally a military kraal established by Cetshwayo after the Battle of Ndondakusuka where he defeated his half-brother Mbulazi and gained control of the Zulu Kingdom. Today Gingindlovu is a small commercial centre surrounded by farmland and sugarcane plantations.

Six kilometres from Gingindhlovu on the coast is the entrance to **Amatigulu Nature Reserve** ① *T032-453 0155, www.kznwildlife.com, open sunrise to sunset, R10, children (under 12) R5.* The reserve is 100 km from Durban and covers approximately 2000 ha of forested dunes overlooking the sea and is a beautiful place to combine game watching with a beach holiday. Unlike the other small reserves in this area, Amatigulu does have some big game since giraffe, zebra and waterbuck have been reintroduced; it is the one of the few places to see animals grazing close to the sea. Bush baby and large-spotted genet are frequently seen around the camp at night and the Nyoni River attracts the elusive African finfoot and other unusual waterbirds. There are game drives and walking trails but the most interesting way to see the reserve is by canoeing up the Amatigulu River; canoes can be hired from the camp office. A newer addition in the reserve is a whale-watching tower built on the dunes.

● *Gingindlovu means 'the swallower of the elephant', although the British used to call it 'Gin-Gin-I-love-you'.*

ⓘ *The northern KwaZulu Natal coast is a low-risk malarial area.*

Eshowe is a historical inland town named after the sound of a breeze passing through bushes. Situated on a hill, the town has pleasant views over Dlinza forest and is an administrative centre for the surrounding sugarcane growing region. Although there's little in town for visitors, this makes a good base for taking a cultural tour of Zululand. The historical origins of Eshowe are based around a kraal called Eziqwaqweni, which was established here by Cetshwayo. In 1860 the Norwegian missionary, Reverend Oftebro, was allowed to open a mission station here which was occupied by the British in 1879 while they planned an attack on Ulundi. The Zulus briefly gained the upper hand here when they laid siege to the garrison for 10 weeks. Eshowe was relieved by Lord Chelmsford in April 1879, but not before the Zulus had managed to burn the mission station down.

Dlinza Forest ⓘ *T035-474 4029, www.zbr.co.za/boardwalk, Sep-Apr daily 0600-1800, May-Aug daily 0800-1700, R25, children (5-18) R5, includes guide,* is next to the municipal caravan park. It is a 250-ha area of dense hardwood forest, ferns and creepers where Shaka supposedly hid his wives and children during attacks. There are two short walking trails here through orchids, wild plum and milkwood trees, and knarled vines that are clearly labelled, which in turn attract a number of birds and butterflies. Dhlinza is great for birdwatchers, with 65 species recorded in the forest, including the endangered spotted thrush and Delegorgue's pigeon. A recent addition, and the first of its kind in South Africa, is a 125-m wheelchair-accessible aerial timber boardwalk, which takes you through the treeline to the 20-m viewing platform that overlooks the canopy of the forest.

On Fort Nongqai Road is the **Zululand Historical Museum** ⓘ *T035-474 2281, daily 0900-1600, R20, children (under 16) R10, tearoom.* Fort Nongqai was built in 1883 and served as a residence for the Natal Native Police who acted as bodyguards for Sir Melmoth Osborn, the Resident for British Zululand. It is a square fort with high towers on each corner. The museum has displays on John Dunn and his 49 wives and on the Bambata rebellion, as well as a number of Zulu items. John Dunn was the first European settler in what is now KwaZulu Natal. He became an honorary chief and was granted land by the Zulus, ruled at the time by Cetshwayo. His 49 wives gave him 117 children. Given this statistic, not surprisingly the surname Dunn is still very common in this region.

Vukani Collection Museum ⓘ *T035-474 5274, Mon-Fri 0900-1600, Sun 1000-1500, small donation, tearoom,* is housed in a purpose-built centre in the grounds of Fort Nongqayi. While there are antique items on display, this is actually an exhibition of the Vukani Association – a body of over 1000 Zulu craftspeople run and owned by the crafters themselves to manage the pricing and quality of their products. It is quite probably the largest display of Zulu art in existence with some 3000 to 4000 pieces on display. Some of the exhibits are by award-winning artists and include carvings, pottery, colourful basketry and the famous Zulu beadwork.

North of Eshowe

From Eshowe the R66 heads north through the **Nkwalini Valley** to **Melmoth** (52 km). **Shakaland** ⓘ *signposted off the R66, 14 km north of Eshowe, T035-460 0912, www.shaka land.com, 3-hr tours at 1100 and 1200, R265, children (6-11) half price, under 6s free,* is a very popular Zulu theme park with daily cultural shows, which include Zulu dancing and tours of a traditional village where tribal customs such as spearmaking, the beer ceremony and Sangoma rituals are explained. This is a reconstruction of a 19th-century village but it doesn't give a very authentic insight into how the Zulu people live today. However, the food isn't bad and a lunch in the **Shisa Nyama Restaurant** is included.

The **Protea Simunye Zulu Lodge** is about 30 km out of Eshowe; look out for a left turning, marked with a wagon wheel and a large 'S', on to the D256. This road will take you to another popular Zululand stop, a lodge hosted by the Biyela clan, offering a marginally more authentic introduction to Zulu culture. Follow the gravel road for 12 km until you reach an old trading store. This is the assembly point for guests before they are

Zululand game reserves

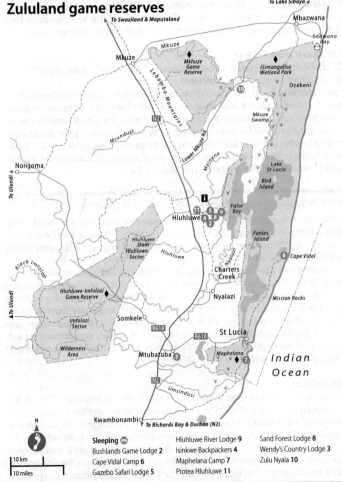

To Lake Sibaya
To Swaziland & Maputaland
Mbazwana
Sodwana Bay
Mkuze
Mkhuze Game Reserve
iSimangaliso Wetland Park
Ozabeni
Lebombo Mountains
N2
Lower Mkuze Rd
Mkuze Swamp
Msunduzi
Nongoma
Mzinene
Lake St Lucia
Bird Island
To Ulundi
False Bay
Hluhluwe
Fanies Island
Cape Vidal
Hluhluwe Dam Hluhluwe Sector
Hluhluwe
Charters Creek
Nyalazi
Mission Rocks
Black Imfolozi
To Ulundi
Hluhluwe-Imfolozi Game Reserve
Imfolozi Sector
Somkele
R618
R618
St Lucia
Wilderness Area
Mtubatuba
Maphelana
Indian Ocean
N2
Umsindusi
Kwambonambi
To Richards Bay & Durban (N2)

N
10 km
10 miles

Sleeping
Bushlands Game Lodge **2**
Cape Vidal Camp **6**
Gazebo Safari Lodge **5**

Hluhluwe River Lodge **9**
Isinkwe Backpackers **4**
Maphelana Camp **7**
Protea Hluhluwe **11**

Sand Forest Lodge **8**
Wendy's Country Lodge **3**
Zulu Nyala **10**

taken down to the lodge on horseback, ox wagon or donkey cart (for accommodation, see page 537). West of Melmouth, Central Zululand is famous for its rich cultural heritage. The museums and battlefield sites are the main attractions and are the best way to gain an insight into the region's history. ➤ For further details, see pages 482-492.

Note The R66 north of Eshowe is notorious for having one of the highest rates of carjacking in KwaZulu Natal province.

Mtunzini and around 🌐 ➤ pp537-543. Colour map 5, B2.

Mtunzini means 'the shady place' and is a pleasant town at the mouth of the Umlalazi River facing the lagoon, 18 km from Gingindhlovu, set in an area of coastal forest and mangrove swamps. John Dunn, who had become a Zulu chief in his own right and was one of Cetshwayo's advisors, lived here with his 49 wives and 117 children.

Umlalazi Nature Reserve

ⓘ 132 km north of Durban, 1 km east of Mtunzini, T035-340 1836, www.kznwildlife.com, daily 0500-2200, R10, children (under12) R5.

Signposted from the N2, this is a small nature reserve but it is popular with South African tourists and, when full, can accommodate at least 300 people, who come here for fishing, windsurfing and the beaches. There are no shark nets. The natural ambience of the 1028-ha reserve is best felt when it is less crowded and it is easier to appreciate the long tropical beaches and walks along the banks of the lagoon and mangrove swamps. There's good fishing in the lagoon and Mlalazi River but crocodiles and sharks are present. Other wildlife includes red, grey and blue duiker, and bushbuck.

Empangeni and around 🌐🔵🔵🔵🔵 ➤ pp537-543. Colour map 5, A2.

Empangeni is named after the Zulu word of *pangaed* meaning grabbed – due to many people being taken by crocs on the banks of the Mpangeni River, on which the town is situated. King Shaka grew up in this area before the Norwegian Missionary Society mission station opened in 1851.

The town has developed into a busy industrial centre and has been pulping wood since the first eucalyptus plantations were established in 1905. While many visitors pass through on their way between St Lucia and the Battlefields, there is nothing to merit a stop. Nor is there any reason to follow the R34 east from Empangeni, crossing the N2, towards Richards Bay (18 km), although those using Richards Bay airport might pass through this flat plantation landscape, loomed over by clusters of pylons and the ugly chimneys of industrial complexes. The N2, meanwhile, allows a quick escape north to St Lucia (80 km), and Hluhluwe-Umfolozi (106 km).

Ins and outs

This area is undergoing a series of name changes. Officially Empangeni and Richards Bay, 18 km away (as well as Esikhawini, Vulindlela, Felixton, Nseleni and Ngwelezane, and the rural areas under Amakhosi Dube, Mkhwanazi, Khoza, Mbuyazi and Zungu), have now joined together as one municipal area, referred to jointly as the city of **uMhlathuze**. It will be some time before this change is reflected on maps or signposts and in reality they are still some distance from one another, so, for the purposes of this guide, the old names are used, despite the fact that the towns share many of the same facilities.

Game reserves

West of Empangeni and north of the small village of Heatonville, **Thula Thula Private Game Reserve** ⓘ *T035-792 8322, www.thulathula.com*, makes for an excellent stopover for those who have missed the larger parks further north. Day visitors are welcome for game drives and either breakfast, lunch or dinner from R425 (check out the website for options). To get there, take the R34 for 8 km before turning onto the road to Heatonville, which is a further 10 km. Thula Thula is signposted down a gravel road from Heatonville. The reserve is a large private game reserve in the Enselini Valley, originally part of King Shaka's hunting ground. It was converted from farmland in 1964, and the present owners offer exclusive accommodation, game drives and bush walks through rolling, acacia-covered thornveld. Some of the larger mammals you can expect to see are white rhino, elephant, cheetah, giraffe, kudu, nyala and other antelopes and, if you're lucky, a leopard.

Enselini Nature Reserve ⓘ *17 km north of Empangeni on the N2, T035-792 0034, sunrise to sunset, free*, is a small, 293-ha reserve on the banks of the Enselini River, run by KZN Wildlife. The **Nkonikini Trail**, 7 km, passes along raised platforms over the swamp and through grasslands where game has been reintroduced. Here you can see hippo, crocodile, giraffe, nyala, waterbuck, wildebeest and zebra. The shorter **Mvuvu Trail** passes through similar terrain. This is an interesting reserve to visit and a good chance to break the monotony of driving through the vast plantations that line the N2. At the reception centre there is a picnic site, where maps and information leaflets are available.

Richards Bay → Colour map 5, B2.

Richards Bay, a modern rash of a town, focuses entirely on its enormous industrial port, soon to be the largest in southern Africa. The port exports mineral ores and coal, and massive tankers arrive here to discharge oil for Gauteng through the oil pipeline; this is the first port of call for ships coming from Asia and Suez. Characterized by a series of vast industrial plants and featureless highways (albeit skirting around a pretty series of canals and a lagoon), the only reason for coming here is to use the small airport (see page 543), and then hire a car to speed up the coast to the parks.

Hluhluwe-Imfolozi Game Reserve ⊖⚫⚫⚫▲ ▸▸ pp537-543. Colour map 5, A2.

This is one of Africa's oldest game reserves and one of the few parks in KwaZulu Natal where you can see the Big Five. What were traditionally two reserves have been joined into one national park. Hluhluwe is named after the umHluhluwe or 'thorny rope', a climber which is found in the forests of this area. The aerial roots hanging from the sycamore figs where the Black Umfolozi and the White Umfolozi rivers meet give the area its name. Imfolozi is named after 'uMfula walosi' or the 'river of fibres'. The park has a variety of landscapes – thick forests, dry bushveld and open savannah – that are home to a number of species of game, including healthy populations of rhino and the rare nyala. What is unusual about the park is the hilly terrain, which provides a great vantage point for game viewing.

Ins and outs

Getting there Hluhluwe-Imfolozi is 280 km north of Durban just off the N2. There is a turning at Mtubatuba leading west on the R618 (50 km) to the **Imfolozi sector** ⓘ *Oct-Mar 0500-1900, Apr-Sep 0600-1800, office daily 0800-1230, 1400-1630, conservation levy (per day) R120, children (3-12) R45, under 3s free*, and a turning opposite the exit to Hluhluwe

Saving the rhino

The biggest conservation success story for Hluhluwe-Imfolozi is the white rhino, brought back from the brink of extinction. It is estimated that in the late 1800s when the reserve was proclaimed, the entire world population of southern white rhinos was only 20, all of them living in this area. Southern Africa is the genetic home for the white rhino and all populations in the world have their origins here.

The rhino's early protection from hunting allowed numbers to grow to such an extent that, since the 1950s, surplus rhino have been transferred to other areas as part of the internationally famous 'Operation Rhino'. As a result,

the population of white rhino in South Africa has grown from around 500 in the 1950s to 6000 today, and the global population is put at about 13,000.

Hluhluwe-Imfolozi is now focusing on saving the black rhino, whose numbers in Africa over the last decade have dwindled from 14,000 to a mere 1550. KZN Wildlife is currently working with the World Wildlife Fund (WWF) on the Black Rhino Range Expansion Project, which identifies and helps to stock suitable conservation areas with surplus black rhinos from KZN Wildlife reserves. At least a quarter of the world's population of black and white rhino are found in Hluhluwe-Imfolozi.

village, which leads (14 km) to the northern Memorial Gate entrance to the **Hluhluwe sector** ① *same hours and levies as above, camp reception at Hilltop daily 0700-1930.* This is an easy park to visit on a day trip if you are staying in the Maputaland or St Lucia regions.

Best time to visit The best time to see the park is between March and November. The park's vegetation is lush during the summer months, when the weather is hot and humid, but this makes it more difficult to see the game. During the winter months the climate is cool and dry and you might even need a sweater in the evenings. Animals congregate at the waterholes and rivers at this time of year and the lack of vegetation makes it easier to see them.

Background

The confluence of the Black and White Umfolozi rivers is where Zulu King Shaka dug his hunting pits. Once a year game was driven into the area and would fall into the pits, where it was speared by young warriors eager to prove their courage. Consequently, Hluhluwe-Umfolozi was established as a protected area as long ago as 1895. Since then the park has suffered a number of setbacks, such as temporary de-proclamation and the massive slaughter of thousands of game animals in a campaign to eliminate tsetse fly. Aerial spraying of the chemical DDT eventually eliminated the tsetse fly but at great cost to the environment. In 1947 the newly formed **Natal Parks, Game and Fish Preservation Board** took control of the park and reintroduced locally extinct species such as lion, elephant, rhino and giraffe.

Wildlife

This is one of the best reserves in KwaZulu Natal for seeing wildlife, and one of the finest in the world for seeing rhino; see also box above. The varied landscapes of Hluhluwe-Imfolozi provide a wide range of habitats which support large numbers of big game. The Big Five are present and there are large populations of three rarely seen animals: the white rhino, the black rhino and the nyala. Despite the thriving hippo populations in nearby St Lucia, there are fewer than 20 hippo in this park because the rivers flow too fast. Over 300 species of bird, including the rare bateleur eagle, have been recorded in Hluhluwe-Imfolozi; bird lists are available from the camp offices.

Hluhluwe is the northern sector of the reserve and has a hilly and wooded landscape; elephant are often seen in the area around the Hluhluwe Dam, where the thick forests are inhabited by the rare samango monkey. There are some areas of savanna in this sector where white rhino and giraffe can be seen feeding.

Imfolozi, in the south, is characterized by thornveld and semi-desert; the grasslands here support large populations of impala, kudu, waterbuck, giraffe, blue wildebeest and zebra. Predators are rarely seen but cheetah, lion, leopard and wild dog are all present.

An extensive network of dirt roads crosses the reserve which can easily be negotiated in a saloon car. There are hides at Mphafa waterhole and Thiyeni waterhole but much of the best game viewing can be done from a car. Good areas for viewing game are the Sontuli Loop, the corridor linking Imfolozi to Hluhluwe and the areas around the Hluhluwe River.

Wilderness trails
One of the most exciting ways to see wildlife here is on foot. Although this experience is not always as spectacular as viewing from a car, it tends to be more intense; there is little

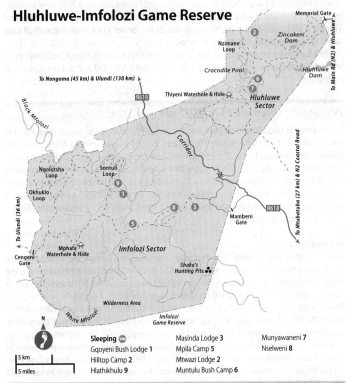

Hluhluwe-Imfolozi Game Reserve

Sleeping
Gqoyeni Bush Lodge 1
Hilltop Camp 2
Hlathikhulu 9
Masinda Lodge 3
Mpila Camp 5
Mtwazi Lodge 2
Muntulu Bush Camp 6
Munyawaneni 7
Nselweni 8

that can compare with the excitement of tracking rhino through the wilderness. **Guided walks** must be booked well in advance at the camp offices, which run through the wilderness in the southern section of the park. The area used to be part of traditional royal Zulu hunting grounds and is now totally undisturbed by man – there are no roads and access is only allowed on foot; you must be accompanied by a game ranger. Three **wilderness trails** cross the wilderness area, with guided walks running from mid-March to December. They are limited to a maximum of eight people and are extremely popular, so should be booked well in advance. Food, drinks, water bottles, cutlery and cooking equipment, bedding, towels, day packs, backpacks and donkey bags are all provided by KZN Wildlife. The trails cover about 15 km per day and cost from R2015 to R3265 per person for up to three nights (accommodation is in tented camps in the wilderness area). There are also three self-guided walks in the Imfolozi sector. Reservations for all accommodation and wilderness trails within the park can be made up to six months in advance through **KZN Wildlife** ① *T033-845 1000, www.kznwildlife.com.*

Hluhluwe → *Colour map 5, A3.*

Hluhluwe is a small village in an area surrounded by large luxury game farms. It is a good base to explore the region as it is within easy reach of many of the local game parks and is only 15 km from St Lucia's False Bay. An international game auction is held here annually by KZN Wildlife. There are a couple of craft villages in the area; **Dumazulu Traditional Village**, a short drive from Hluhluwe, is one of the better ones, with displays of Zulu dancing, spear making and basket weaving.

The **Hluhluwe Tourism Association** ① *next to the Engen garage, Main St, T035-562 0353, www.elephantcoasttourism.com, Mon-Fri 0800-1700, Sat 0900-1300,* acts as a booking agent for the area.

iSimangaliso Wetland Park ◎❶❷◭❶ ›› *pp537-543. Colour map 5, A3.*

The **Greater St Lucia Wetland Park** was declared a World Heritage Site in 1999, the first place in South Africa to be awarded this status. In 2008 it went under a name change to iSimangaliso Wetland Park – iSimangaliso is isiZulu for 'miracle'. The protected area is the largest estuarine lake system in Africa, with a variety of flora and fauna which compares favourably with the Okavango Delta or Kruger National Park. The birdlife is outstanding, with a staggering 420 species recorded here. But despite drawing a huge number of visitors throughout the year, the town remains small and low-key, with an appealingly languid, tropical atmosphere.

Ins and outs

Getting there and around The area now known as the iSimangaliso Wetland Park consists of a number of formerly separate nature reserves and state forests. These are still referred to locally under a bewildering array of old and new names, but the greater area is considered to be South Africa's third largest park. The entire 328,000-ha reserve starts south of the St Lucia Estuary and stretches north to the border with Mozambique, and is about 280 km in length. The terrestrial section of the park varies from 1 km to 24 km wide, and the marine section extends 5 km out to sea, protecting 155 km of coastline.

In the southern region, accessible from St Lucia, the park falls into three main areas: **St Lucia Public Resort and Estuary National Park**, which is a good area to see crocodile, hippo, impala, waterbuck, wildebeest and zebra; the coastline up to **Cape Vidal**, 32 km north of St Lucia, with the beautiful Cape beach; and the **western shore** of the lake, which is much quieter than the other two and affords the opportunity to explore the lake by boat.

The iSimangaliso Wetland Park also encompasses **Maphelana** to the south (see page 534), accessed from Kwambonambi, and all the coastal parks to the north, from Sodwana Bay to Kosi Bay Nature Reserve on the border of Mozambique. ▸▸ *For further details, see Maputaland, page 544.*

Best time to visit Each season in the wetlands has its own attraction. From November to February there tends to be more rain, making the vegetation greener. June to August is the best time for birdwatching, as this is the breeding season. The best months for walking are March to November when it is less hot and humid. The school holidays are always a popular time for South African tourists to visit and accommodation at these times should be booked well in advance.

Tourist information For information about the iSimangaliso Wetland Park, visit the St Lucia office of **KZN Wildlife** ① *Pelikan Rd, near Eden Park campsite, T035-590 1340, www.kznwildlife.com, daily 0800-1630.* It has a small selection of brochures and can help with accommodation and trail information; reservations should be made well in advance, though (see below). Information can also be found at www.isimangaliso.co.za.

Staying in the park Reservations for self-catering accommodation and wilderness trails within the park can be made up to 12 months in advance through **KZN Wildlife Reservations** ① *T033-845 1000, www.kznwildlife.com.* There are only limited supplies available in the camp shops so it is essential to bring your own food. The nearest supermarket is in St Lucia, unless you are staying at Charters Creek or one the camps around False Bay, in which case the nearest shops are in Hluhluwe.

Safety When hiking around the lake, watch out for hippos – they kill more people than any other mammal in Africa. If you come across one on land, retreat and, if possible, try and climb a tree. Also keep an eye out for snakes and crocodiles; avoid the water's edge. When swimming in the sea, stay well away from the estuary, which is inhabited by crocodiles and Zambezi sharks. Note that most self-guided trails in the area have been closed following the reintroduction of elephant. St Lucia is a malarial area and prophylactics should be taken.

Background

The land now occupied by the park has had human inhabitants since the Early Iron Age. Archaeological excavations have uncovered the remains of settlements and middens, and large areas of forest and dunes are thought to have been cleared to provide charcoal for iron smelting. St Lucia was named by the Portuguese explorer Manuel Perestrello in 1575, although European influence in the area was minimal until the 1850s. Up to that time the area was inhabited by a relatively large population of Thongas and Zulus who herded cattle and cultivated the land.

Professional hunters began visiting the lake in the 1850s in search of ivory, hides and horns which were at one point the Colony of Natal's main source of income. So successful were these hunters that within 50 years the last elephant in this region had been shot. Amongst the big game hunters here were William Baldwin, Robert Briggs Struthers, 'Elephant' White and John Dunn who recorded having shot 23 seacows in one morning

St Lucia

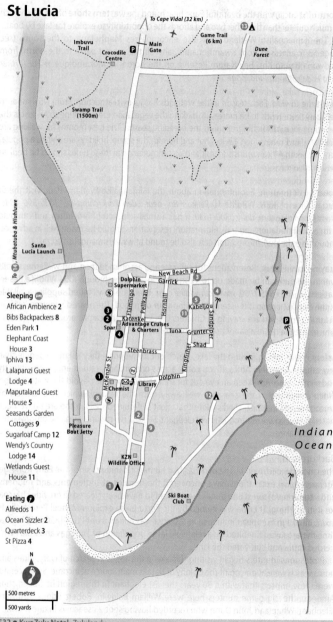

To Cape Vidal (32 km)

Imbuvu Trail

Crocodile Centre

Main Gate

Game Trail (6 km)

Dune Forest

P

Swamp Trail (1500m)

To Mtubatuba & Hluhluwe

Santa Lucia Launch

New Beach Rd

Garrick

Dolphin Supermarket

Flamingo

Pelikaan

Hornbill

Kabeljou

Katenke

Advantage Cruises & Charters

Sandpiper

Tuna

Grunter

Spar

Steenbrass

Kingfisher

Shad

McKenzie St

Dolphin

Pol

Chemist

Library

P

Pleasure Boat Jetty

KZN Wildlife Office

Ski Boat Club

Indian Ocean

Sleeping
African Ambience 2
Bibs Backpackers 8
Eden Park 1
Elephant Coast House 3
Iphiva 13
Lalapanzi Guest Lodge 4
Maputaland Guest House 5
Seasands Garden Cottages 9
Sugarloaf Camp 12
Wendy's Country Lodge 14
Wetlands Guest House 11

Eating
Alfredos 1
Ocean Sizzler 2
Quarterdeck 3
St Pizza 4

N

500 metres
500 yards

and a total of 203 seacows in the following three months. Hunting parties would kill hundreds of elephants, crocodiles and hippos on each expedition.

During the 1880s the British government annexed St Lucia in a move which would foil the Boers from the New Republic in their search for access to the sea. It was after this that land was distributed to settlers and that missions were founded at Mount Tabor, Cape Vidal and Ozabeni.

St Lucia Lake, along with Hluhluwe-Umfolozi, was one of the first game reserves to be established in Africa in 1895. Further moves to protect wildlife also took place in 1944 with the addition of False Bay Park to the protected areas, and in 1975 South Africa signed the international RAMSAR Convention to protect wetlands. It was then that the Greater St Lucia Wetland region was declared. More recently, land was recovered by the park in 1987 when the Eastern Shores State Forest was returned to the Natal Parks Board. Conservation measures have continued in the last decade, and many conservation initiatives were introduced when St Lucia won World Heritage status in 1999. One of the most important of these was the controversial national ban on beach driving in February 2002, enraging many South African 4WD owners. Species have also been reintroduced, including cheetah and elephant.

In spite of these measures to protect St Lucia, the survival of the lake system has been under constant threat since the turn of the 20th century. One of the most intractable problems has been the effect of agriculture on the lake's water supply: land reclamation, drainage canals, the diversion of the Umfolozi River and the damming of the Hluhluwe River for irrigation have all contributed to the silting up of the lake. In the 1960s salinity levels increased to such an extent during a series of droughts that the water in the lake system was twice as salty as sea water, killing numerous plants, fish and crocodiles. A further problem was that of the vast pine plantations in the region that were first planted in 1954. The thirsty pines consumed a huge amount of water, but an ambitious reclamation plan was put in place in 1999. As of July 2005, the pine tracts have been removed, and it is hoped that indigenous trees will once again flourish in the area, attracting more wildlife. However, a continuing drought has dramatically reduced the level of water in some areas, notably Charter's Creek, False Bay and Fanies Island. The three KZN Wildlife camps in these places are no longer open to the public and boat trips cannot be operated on the low water. Recently the drought has become so severe, that by October 2007 the St Lucia rivermouth had become completely silted up, closing off access to the sea.

Wildlife

On the land Fringing the park's 155-km coastline are vegetated sand dunes exceeding 180 m in height and estimated to be over 30,000 years old. These are the second highest vegetated dunes in the world, after Fraser Island in Australia.

The Mkhuze, Mzinene, Hluhluwe and Nyalazi rivers flow into the northern end of the lake system. The lakes are shallow and interspersed with islands and reedbeds and reach a maximum of 3 m in depth although large areas are only up to 1-m deep. A narrow channel connects the lakes to the estuary and the sea, and the lake's shores are bounded by papyrus, reeds, mangrove and forest swamps. The other inland areas in the park are grasslands with zones of thornveld, coastal and dune forest. Depending on where you are in the park, there are chances of seeing elephant, buffalo, kudu, waterbuck, rare black rhinos and leopards.

From November to March, giant leatherback and loggerhead turtles nest on the park's beaches up to 10 times each season. They are protected by KZN Wildlife who monitor them and protect them from predators such as honey badgers and jackals.

In the water Lake St Lucia is a nursery and feeding ground for fish and crustaceans. As salinity changes in the water from fresh to salt water, so do the corresponding ecosystems. Fresh water attracts tilapia, catfish and ducks while saltier water attracts pelicans and herons. Zambezi and black-tipped sharks come into the estuary to breed. Although game is being reintroduced to the area, the animals that are most often seen are the large populations of common reedbuck, hippopotamus and Nile crocodile. There are an estimated 2000 crocs in the entire lake system, and it is thought to be the only place in the world where sharks and crocodiles share the same water.

In the air The birdlife is the main attraction here, and the fish eagle, easily spotted, has become the unofficial symbol of the area. Other species often seen around the water include kingfishers and weaverbirds, and large numbers of unusual migrant birds can also be spotted. Southern African waterbirds migrate depending on regional droughts between Bangweulu and Kafue in Zambia, the Okavango Delta in Botswana, the Zambezi Delta in Mozambique and the wetlands of Maputaland and St Lucia. The St Lucia waters are high in nutrients and support large populations of pinkbacked and white pelicans, greater and lesser flamingos, ducks, spoonbills and ibises.

The pelicans arrive every autumn to feed on migrating mullet in the Narrows, north of St Lucia Village. Around 6000 pelicans nest at the northern end of the lake where visitors can see their courtship displays.

Maphelana → Colour map 5, A3.

ⓘ Head east from Kwambonambe to the Kwambonambi Lighthouse, from where it is a further 50 km to Maphelana along a narrow sand track. Oct-Mar 0600-1900, Apr-Sep 0600-1800; office daily 0800-1230, 1400-1630, T035-5901407. R20 per person. 4WDs are recommended for the track to Maphelana but vehicles with high road clearance can also get through in dry weather.

Maphelana National Park was established in 1897, but was later handed over to the Department of Forestry. After the campaign waged by the Wildlife Society of Southern Africa, the threat of strip-mining the titanium-rich dunes was averted. It is now the southernmost part of the iSimangaliso Wetland Park. The Maphelana Camp is tucked away in a sheltered bay on the south bank of the Umfolozi River and is popular with fishermen who can launch their speedboats here. There is a safe beach for swimming and licences are available to collect mussels, oysters and crayfish. Swimming or wading in the Umfolozi River is prohibited as there are too many crocodiles.

St Lucia → Colour map 5, A3.

The holiday resort of St Lucia lies to the south of the lake and is surrounded by the iSimangaliso Wetland Park. St Lucia is the largest seaside holiday destination on this part of the coast and is particularly popular during the South African school holidays. Although it can get very busy around Christmas, it remains a sleepy provincial town off season, making a pleasant base from which to explore both the wetlands and the nearby wildlife parks.

Many visitors come for a day trip, to explore the narrow reaches of the estuary leading up to the lake. Boats leave regularly from the jetty at the far end of McKenzie Street, usually seating around 20 people and taking a two-hour tour upriver. These provide an excellent introduction to the wetlands, with chances of seeing large pods of hippo and crocodile, and prolific birdlife.

Ins and outs The end of the R618 leads directly into the centre of the resort on McKenzie Street, which is lined with supermarkets, banks, restaurants, handicraft shops and boat charter companies. Continuing down past the end of McKenzie Street, the road leads to the large KZN Wildlife office to the left, and the jetty from which river cruises leave to the right. Passengers using the **Baz Bus** can be dropped off at **Bib's Backpackers** on Mackenzie Street.

The best source is **Advantage Cruises and Charters** ⓘ *McKenzie St, close to the Spar, T035-590 1259, www.advantagetours.co.za, daily 0700-1900,* a booking agent for all local activities and accommodation. St Lucia is the main tourist centre in this part of Zululand and is a good base to stock up on supplies before staying in self-catering accommodation either in the iSimangaliso Wetland Park or in game reserves at Hluhluwe-Imfolozi and Mkuzi. Information and an accommodation booking service can be found at www.stluciasouthafrica.co.za. For information on the iSimangaliso Wetland Park, see page 531.

Beaches

The beaches lying to the east of St Lucia are large swathes of pristine white sand backed by dune forest, which stretch all the way to Cape Vidal. Visitors swim here at their own risk as there are dangerous currents, no shark nets and no lifeguards. Swimming is prohibited in the estuary and within 100 m of the river mouth as the strong unpredictable currents, sharks and crocodiles make it too dangerous.

St Lucia Public Resort and Estuary national parks

These areas directly surround St Lucia village. There is a 12-km network of self-guided trails, which start in the area near the Crocodile Centre (see below). As the trails extend from the Indian Ocean to the estuary they cross several different habitats such as dune forest, grasslands, mangroves and swamps. The trail leading from the Crocodile Centre to the estuary takes you to some good hippo-viewing spots. The grasslands to the north of the village are a source of ncema grass, traditionally used by Zulus to make sleeping and sitting mats. The cutting season starts on 1 May when thousands of people come for the annual harvest.

The **Crocodile Centre** ⓘ *T035-590 1386, Mon-Fri 0800-1600, Sat 0830-1700, Sun 0900-1600, crocodile feeding Sat 1500, R30, children (under 12) R15,* is next to the entrance gate to Cape Vidal, where a small display highlights the important role crocodiles play in the ecosystem of the park. The Nile, long snouted and dwarf crocodiles that are kept here in pens, are all endangered in the wild and are part of an international breeding programme to protect them. KZN Wildlife routinely releases Nile crocodiles back into Lake St Lucia. The curio shop here is one of the best in St Lucia with a good selection of books and leaflets on the area. The tea garden serves light lunches.

Cape Vidal

ⓘ *32 km north of St Lucia, T035-590 9012. Gates Oct-Mar 0500-1900, Apr-Sep 0600-1800; office daily 0800-1230, 1400-1630. R30, under 12s R15, R35 per vehicle. Only 100 vehicles per day are allowed past the gate at Cape Vidal; the park speed limit is 40 kph. Beach driving is not allowed.* Cape Vidal makes an easy and pleasant day trip from St Lucia. A road heads north from the park gates (near the crocodile centre), passing through an area that was until recently pine forest but is now returning to indigenous wilderness. Elephants were recently reintroduced here, and the area is also home to kudu and cheetah.

Mission Rocks is 16 km from St Lucia, signposted off the dirt road. Snorkelling and scuba-diving are allowed here but there are no facilities so it is essential to bring your own equipment. The rock pools here are full of life and are best seen at low tide.

Cape Vidal is an area of vegetated dunes along what must be one of the most spectacular beaches in KwaZulu Natal. The sand is pure white and the Indian Ocean is warm and inviting; the rocks just off the beach are teeming with tropical fish and the shallow water is safe to snorkel in. Thanks to the daily limit of cars into the reserve, the beach is never crowded even at the busiest of times. The camp has facilities for launching powerboats and is popular for game fishing, but as Cape Vidal marks the beginning of a marine reserve that stretches north to the Mozambique border, anglers require permits and many fish are on a tag and release system.

Exploring the park

Mount Tabor is the starting point for the three-day **Mziki Trail** ① *T033-845 1000, T035-590 002 (local office), www.kznwildlife.com, advance booking essential*, operated by KZN Wildlife. Hikers sleep at the self-catering **Mount Tabor base camp**, which is reached by foot from Mission Rocks (2 km), and go out on three full-day hikes accompanied by armed game guides. Each day, a different loop is completed: the 10-km **South Coast Loop** passes through dune forest before reaching the sea at Rangers Rocks. From here the trail returns along the coastline to Mission Rocks before heading back to Mount Tabor through dune forest. Kudu are often seen on this trail. The 10-km **Mfazana Pan Loop** crosses the road to Cape Vidal and heads for the hides at Mfazana Pan, from where it turns north through grassland to the shore of Lake St Lucia. At 18 km, the **North Coast Loop** is the longest day hike. It heads north along Mount Tabor Ridge to Bokkie Valley and then returns along the coast past Bat's Cave and on to Mount Tabor. **Note** Ticks and mosquitoes can be a problem on the trail.

Western shores

There are three reserves on the western shores of Lake St Lucia. However, a continuing drought has dramatically reduced the level of water in this area, and these reserves have been closed to visitors for some time. The KZN Wildlife camps are no longer open to the public and boat trips cannot be operated on the low water. Check with the KZN Wildlife office in St Lucia for updates. Access is via the N2 north of St Lucia. **Charter's Creek** is 20 km north of Mtubatuba on the N2; take the signposted turning 18 km to Charter's Creek, the last 6 km are on a dirt road. For **Fanies Island**, follow the signs to Charter's Creek from the N2; before reaching Charter's Creek, take the signposted turning north for 13 km. For **False Bay**, take the turning from the N2 to Hluhluwe village; the road continues 15 km to the park.

For Sleeping and Eating price codes and other relevant information, see pages 46-53.

● Sleeping

Gingindhlovu and around *p523*

E Amatigulu Tented Camp, Amatigulu Nature Reserve, KZN Wildlife, T033-845 1000, www.kznwildlife.com. 6 2-bed tents are connected by wooden walkways. They have proper beds on raised wooden platforms overlooking the sea, a shared ablution block, dining area and fully equipped kitchen with gas stoves, fridge and freezer; there is no shop here so bring all your own food and supplies.

Eshowe and inland *p524*

AL Protea Shakaland, T035-460 0912, www.shakaland.com. If you are staying the night the Shaka experience continues in the adjacent **Protea** hotel, where Zulu dancers escort you to your beehive-shaped hut. The evenings are spent sampling the local brew *tshwala* around the campfire while being entertained with dancing and story telling. The huts are huge and have all mod cons.

A Protea Simunye Zulu Lodge, T035-450 0103, www.proteahotels.com. You must be at the trading post by 1530, from where you travel for 1 hr on horseback, donkey cart or ox wagon (disabled guests can request a 4WD transfer). The lodge is simple and traditional with rooms in thatched stone huts and open-air rock baths lit by candles and oil lamps. In the evening, music, singing and dancing is performed by local people. Rates include all meals, guides and demonstrations.

C Kwabhekithunga/Stewarts Farm, 36 km from Eshowe on the R34 towards Empangeni, T035-460 0929, www.stewartsfarm.com. Rather than having been built especially for tourists like many similar Zulu 'experiences' in the area, this village is the real home of Chief Mbhangucuza Fakude, his 4 brothers and their extended families. Accommodation is in Zulu beehive-shaped huts, all en suite, with bright and colourful interiors and electricity. Bar and swimming pool on site. Visitors are treated to a 'cultural experience' – Zulu dancing and singing, and a taste of Zulu food and home-brewed beer. Pre-booking is essential. Recommended for a feel of real Zulu life.

D George Hotel, 116 Main St, Eshowe, T035-474 1300, www.eshowe.co.za. Friendly country style hotel with 30 rooms with TV, in a historical building adjacent to the Dlinza Forest (see page 524). **Quarters Restaurant**, **Happy George Pub**, which serves home brewed Zulu Blond ale, and a swimming pool. Runs excellent tours (see Activities and tours, page 542) and there's a Zulu singing and dancing display each evening.

E-F Zululand Backpackers, 38 Main St, T035-474 4919, www.eshowe.com. At the back of the **George Hotel**. Dorms, kitchen, showers, double rooms, camping possible, M-Net TV, pool table, internet, swimming pool, close to shops and banks, Baz Bus stop. Has an excellent reputation for organizing local tours, such as visits to traditional Zulu weddings, mountain bikes available for hire. Recommended.

Mtunzini and around *p526*

B Umlalazi Nature Reserve, KZN Wildlife, T033-845 1000, www.kznwildlife.com. The camp has 13 self-catering 5-bedroom log cabins with DSTV, and 50 camping and caravan sites, all with braais, coin operated washing machines, swimming pool. Located in coastal dune forest a short walk to the beach.

B-C Mtunzini Forest Lodge, off Valley Drive, T035-368 5642, www.goodersonvacations. com/mtunzinilodge.html. 22 self-catering beach chalets set in attractive dune forest right by the beach, sleeping up to 6 people in rustic log cabins. Swimming pool, thatched lapa with pool table and TV. Meals available in the **Sundowner Pub & Grill** (closed Mon).

C Trade Winds, 12 Hely Hutchinson Rd, T035-340 2266, www.tradewindscountry inn.co.za. Well-established, small town hotel with 19 neat rooms, a/c, DSTV, modern furnishings, swimming pool and à la carte restaurant with a pleasant wooden terrace surrounded by palms.

D Highfield Country Home, 7 km from town off the N2, however, you must get to it from Mtunzini on the old Durban road, T035-340 1731, www.mtunzini.co.za/highfield.htm. 5 double rooms with traditional Victorian bathrooms, TV room, B&B or you can self-cater in the kitchen, 3-course dinners on request, pool, set in a beautiful farmhouse in 4 ha of parklands with sea views.

E-F Xaxaza Caravan Park, at the top of town, T035-340 1843, www.xaxaza.caravan parks.com. Standard caravan park with decent facilities, including simple self-catering cabins, need to bring own bedding. Electrical points, clean ablutions, shop, games room and pool, a significant distance from the beach.

Empangeni and around *p526*

There is little accommodation in the town itself, and it doesn't make a very pleasant stop over; head along the R34 inland instead.

L1 Thula Thula, Thula Thula Private Game Reserve, T035-792 8322, www.thulathula. com. Family-run exclusive safari lodge with 8 luxury thatched chalets and 8 safari tents decorated in an ethnic style, set on rolling lawns and surrounded by forests ringing with bird calls. Rates are inclusive of meals and game drives, and the excellent French food is served in an outside boma, with tables set around a fire. Guests can also relax in the large, thatched bar area, overlooking the pool. Recommended.

Richards Bay *p527*

C The Ridge – Jacks Corner, 1 Jack's Corner, T035-753 4312, www.jackscorner.co.za. Good choice if you're passing through Richards Bay, this upmarket guesthouse has 14 tasteful rooms set around a pool, with views of the ocean and harbour. Restaurant and bar.

Hluhluwe-Imfolozi Game Reserve
p527, map *p529*

All reservations through **KZN Wildlife**, T033-845 1000, www.kznwildlife.com.

A-C Hilltop Camp, Hluhluwe sector. The main camp was refurbished a few years ago and offers 4 types of accommodation. At the top end are 20 **2-bed chalets** (**A**) with 2 bedrooms, 2 bathrooms and fully equipped kitchen; slightly cheaper are the 7 **2-bed chalets** (**B**), with fully equipped kitchen, and the 20 2-bed rest huts (not self-catering) with fridge and kettle. The cheapest options are the 20, **2-bed rest huts** (**C**) with communal kitchen and ablution block. This is the largest and most accessible of the camps and has a fabulous hilltop location, with sweeping views over much of the park and parts of Swaziland. Although this doesn't have the exclusivity of the smaller bush camps, the central lounge, restaurant, bar, pool and veranda are welcome at the end of the day. Game drives and guided walks can be arranged here.

A-D Mpila Camp, centrally situated in the heart of Imfolozim sector. Commands magnificent views over the wilderness area to the east and the Msasaneni Hills to the west. 2 self-contained 3-bed cottages (**A**) sleeping 7 (cook on hand to prepare food supplied by guests); 6 self-catering 2-bed chalets (**B**), sleeping up to 5, with fully equipped kitchen; tented camp with 9 units of walk-in en suite tents (**B**), self-catering with a communal kitchen and dining area; and 12, 1-bed self-catering thatched cottages (**D**), sleeping 4 with a communal kitchen and ablutions. The shop stocks curios and cold drinks but no food, there's a petrol station.

Private lodges and camps

The private lodges and camps are only available for single group bookings. Codes refer to minimum charge.

L2 Gqoyeni Bush Lodge, Imfolozi sector. 8-bed bush lodge with 4 thatched cottages, each with 2 bedrooms, on stilts connected by raised wooden walkways to the living area with lounge, dining area and kitchen, the camp has its own viewing platform overlooking the Mfolozi River where there are good chances of seeing crocodiles, lions and elephants in the summer. Bring own food but in residence are a cook and a game guard for bush walks.

L2 Hlathikhulu, Imfolozi sector. 8-bed bush camp, rustic decor, lovely setting overlooking the Black Mfolozi. Four 2-bed chalets, a central lounging area and kitchen linked by wooden boardwalks, cook (bring own food) and game guard for bush walks.

L2 Muntulu Bush Camp, Hluhluwe sector. Four 2-bed units in this rustic bush lodge, linked by wooden walkway to a central lounge and dining area, all overlooking the Hluhluwe River, verandas, cook (bring own food) and game guard for bush walks

L2 Munyawaneni, Hluhluwe sector. 8-bed bush lodge on the banks of the Hluhluwe River in a good area for seeing the elephant and nyala that come to drink at the secluded waterhole that can be seen from each of the 4 rooms. Boardwalks link the units to a central lounge and kitchen, cook (bring own food) and game guard for bush walks.

AL Masinda Lodge, Imfolozi sector. Luxury 6-bed self-catering lodge, with lounge and dining room with Zulu decor. Beautiful setting with good views of the bush, cook (bring own food) and game guard for bush walks.

A Mtwazi Lodge, Hluhluwe sector. Original thatched house which was home to the park's first warden, with 3 double bedrooms, comfortable lounge, dining room, cook (bring food) and a game guard for walks.

A Nselweni, Imfolozi sector. A wonderfully atmospheric reed and thatch bush lodge raised on stilts just above the floodplain of Mfolozi River, with four 2-bed units, shared ablutions, lounge, dining area, cook (bring own food) and game guard for bush walks.

Hluhluwe *p530*

L Hluhluwe River Lodge, 15 km from Hluhluwe village off the road to False Bay Park, T035-562 0246, www.hluhluwe.co.za.

8 double A-frame thatched chalets with great views and swimming pool. Also has 2 family chalets and 2 luxury honeymoon chalets, with open bath area and private viewing deck. Central lodge houses a dining area, bar, lounge, curio shop and library. Rates are fully inclusive of meals and a game drive. Recommended.

AL Gazebo Safari Lodge, a short drive from Hluhluwe village, off the road to False Bay, T035-562 1066, www.gazebo.co.za. 12 doubles and 1 family room, stylishly decorated with TV, a/c, verandas with stunning views of the bush. Restaurant, bar, lounge, beautiful swimming pool and deck, boma area where meals are served in summer, game drives to nearby reserves. Rates include breakfast, dinner and 1 game drive on the property.

AL Zulu Nyala, 15 km on the Mzinene Rd, T035-562 0177, www.zulunyala.com. Set within a private game reserve, 53 twin a/c rooms, restaurant, 2 bars, curio shop, pool, tennis, clay-pigeon shooting. Also 10 luxury 'Hemmingway'-style tents in the extensive gardens. Also on this reserve is the **Heritage Hotel**, set in a lovely 1940s colonial home.

A Protea Hotel Hluhluwe, 104 Bush Rd, T035-562 4000, www.hluhluwehotel.co.za. 75 a/c rooms, TV, tennis, swimming pool and volleyball, smart modern hotel decorated with African motifs, 2 restaurants serving an à la carte menu or a buffet, occasional performances of Zulu dancing in the evenings around the pool. Can organize safaris to the local parks.

B Bushlands Game Lodge, T035-562 0144, www.goodersonvacations.com/bushlands.html. 20 luxurious a/c self-catering wooden cabins sleeping 6 with rich decor set in lush gardens overlooking the swimming pool. Boardwalks lit by flaming lanterns in the evening link the cabins to the central eating boma and lounge. If not self-catering, meals in the restaurant must be pre-booked.

C Sand Forest Lodge, 10 km from Hluhluwe village off False Bay Rd, T035-562 2509, www.sandforest.co.za. A quality game farm within an ancient sand forest, with 1 or 2 bed a/c self-catering cottages, with verandas overlooking a neat lawn with acacia trees. Plus there's a variety of simpler self-catering log cabins on stilts in the forest with separate kitchen. Central bar, swimming pool and thatched lapa. Game walks and drives with resident guide plus visits to Zulu villages. Good value and peaceful setup.

D-F Isinkwe Backpackers, look out for the 'Bushlands' turning on the N2, 40 km north of the St Lucia/Mtubatuba turning, the lodge is a further 2 km down this road, T035-562 2258, www.isinkwe.co.za. The Baz Bus stops here. A neat hostel with 40 beds in dorms, double rooms and camping. Swimming pool and a bar area for star gazing. Rustic set-up, has done much to create employment for local people. Great home-made meals served up most nights, or self-catering in the kitchen. Laundry. Well-organized day trips in a 4WD to all the local sights and transfers to Sodwana Bay.

Maphelana p534

C Maphelana Camp, KZN Wildlife, T033-845 1000, www.kznwildlife.com. Ten 5-bed log cabins, self-catering, with kitchen, bathroom, dining room and lounge. The cabins are set on a large forested dune with views over a large beach and the sea.

Camping

Maphelana Camp, campsite reservations T035-590 1407. Offers 45 sites, ablution blocks. Electricity is restricted to generator times. Basic supplies are available at the campsite; petrol is not available.

St Lucia p534, map p532

Accommodation is cheap by international standards, however, there is almost always a shortage of beds so book well in advance.

B Seasands Garden Cottages, 135 Hornbill St, T035-590 1082, www.seasands.co.za. Fairly large hotel, offering a mix of B&B rooms and self-catering cottages set in tropical gardens. Attracts groups and some conferences, but

remains a popular choice. Restaurant, swimming pool and extensive gardens.

C African Ambience, 124 Pelikaan St, T035-590 1212, www.africanambience.com. Delightful modern guesthouse in a quiet thatched house a few blocks from the centre. Bright and airy TV-free rooms have chunky wooden furniture and ethnic fabrics, with huge beds and attractive bathrooms. Downstairs rooms have private terraces and there is a garden with a swimming pool and fish ponds. An excellent, peaceful choice. Recommended.

C Elephant Coast House, corner of Garrick and Kingfisher streets, T035-590 1888, www.elephantcoastbnb.co.za. 5 spacious rooms with balconies overlooking a large garden (where hippos sometimes come to graze) with a small fenced-off terrace and pool. Rooms are large and sunny, with tiled floors and vaguely ethnic decor. Friendly service, big breakfasts served in the large dining area, TV lounge, secure parking. Recommended.

C Lalapanzi Guest Lodge, 7 Sandpiper St, T035-590 1167, www.lalapanzi.co.za. 6 large B&B double rooms with a/c, en suite facilities and fridge full of cool drinks. TV lounge, swimming pool, lush tropical garden full of birds, secure off-street parking.

C Wendy's Country Lodge, Riverview, just off the R618 in Mtubatuba, 10 km west of St Lucia, T035-550 0407, www.wendybnb.co.za. Well outside town, but in an excellent location for access both to St Lucia and Hluhluwe-Imfolozi. Family-run guesthouse surrounded by tropical gardens, with spacious double rooms filled with quirky and antique furniture, and Victorian-style bathrooms. Good food served in the little restaurant. Range of activities organized, from game drives and fishing to tours of the wetlands. Very friendly and welcoming. Recommended.

C Wetlands Guest House, 20 Kingfisher St, T/F035-590 1098, www.stluciawetlands.com. Family-run B&B set in a quiet street close to the centre. 6 large a/c rooms, 1 family unit with high ceilings and wood floors, which help keep things cool in the summer.

Guest lounge with bar and TV. Self-catering flat also available. Large swimming pool with child protection fence.

D Maputaland Guest House, 1 Kabeljou St, T/F035-590 1041, www.maputaland.com. 5 rooms, TV lounge, B&B, swimming pool set in a large tropical garden in a quiet suburb away from the main drag. Wide selection of wildlife tours organized from here. German speaking. Recommended.

D-F Bibs Backpackers, 310 McKenzie St, T035-590 1056, www.bibs.co.za. Small dorms, double rooms with DSTV and a/c, en suite chalets with kitchenette sleeping 2 or 4. Great kitchen and self-catering area, Spar shop next door for supplies, evening meals on request, braai area, rock swimming pool, relaxing gardens with hammock and bar area, Zulu dancing on Sat nights, internet access. Well-organized guided day trips to Hluhluwe and other local sights. On the Baz Bus route.

Camping

There are 3 **KZN Wildlife** campsites on the edge of town, reservations T035-590 1340. Each has a shop selling a wide range of guides and curios, and a restaurant.
Eden Park, in a small forest to the south of town. 20 sites, ablution block.
Iphiva, near the Crocodile Centre. 88 sites, ablution blocks and laundry facilities.
Sugarloaf Camp, close to the beach and estuary. 92 sites, swimming pool, ablution blocks, laundry facilities.

Cape Vidal *p535*

The small shop at Cape Vidal has a couple of narrow shelves stocked with food. Petrol and firewood are also on sale in the camp. If you are staying overnight stock up in St Lucia.

B-D Cape Vidal Camp, KZN Wildlife, T033-845 1000, www.kznwildlife.com. 5- to 20-bed log cabins, all are self-catering with fully equipped kitchens, dining rooms, terraces and bathrooms. These represent great value for a group. All the cabins are set under trees on the dunes 200 m from the beach.

Camping

Cape Vidal Camp, T035-590 9012. 50 sites set among the pines. Shared ablution blocks, power points and an area for cleaning fish. It gets overcrowded with fishermen here during high season. The minimum charge of R320 per day is expensive by local standards and there are better options closer to St Lucia.

🍴 Eating

Decent restaurants in this area are limited to the hotels. If you find yourself in St Lucia there is a wider choice.

Richards Bay *p527*

♙♙ **The Grill Fish**, Tuzi Gazi Waterfront, T035-788 0110. Offers views of the harbour and quality seafood, including excellent grills and a decent wine list.

Hluhluwe-Imfolozi Game Reserve
p527, map p529

♙♙-♙ **Hilltop Camp**, see Sleeping, page 538. Open until 2100. A good restaurant serving full English breakfasts, buffet meals, light snacks and braais. The tables on the shady outdoor terrace are in a superb setting overlooking the reserve. The game burgers are highly recommended.

St Lucia *p534, map p532*

♙♙ **Alfredos**, McKenzie St, T035-590 1150. Mon-Sat 1200-1500, 1830-late. Good Italian food at this affordable and cheerful set-up, run by an Italian chef, with a good range of pasta, seafood and veal dishes, and tables inside and out. Fun, easy-going atmosphere.
♙♙ **The Ocean Sizzler**, 37 McKenzie St, T035-590 1554. Open 1200-late. Hugely popular local restaurant serving steaks, seafood and a couple of Greek specials to tables spilling out onto the pavement. There's also a good wine and cocktail list.
♙♙ **Quarterdeck**, McKenzie St, T035-590 1116. Open 1100-late. Great wooden deck overlooking the road, with a large (more beery)

interior. Good selection of fresh grilled seafood, as well as burgers and salads. Popular cocktail bar downstairs.

¶ St Pizza, 13 McKenzie St, T035-590 1048. Open 1130-2200. Ever-expanding pizza joint with wooden tables strung out on a large deck overlooking the street. As well as good thin-crust pizzas, the seafood specials are filling. Wide choice of wines and beers, and a good atmosphere in the evenings.

O Shopping

Richards Bay p527
There are a number of shopping malls in the centre of town, the largest of which is the **Boardwalk**, where facilities include banks, chemists, supermarkets, restaurants, a wide range of shops and a cinema.

Hluhluwe-Imfolozi Game Reserve
p527, map p529
In the Imfolozi sector there are souvenir shops selling at Masinda and Mpila Camps, gifts and books on natural history. Otherwise there are no shops in the reserve so it is necessary to bring all your own food and other supplies; the nearest shop is in Mtubatuba. Petrol is sold at Mpila Camp.

In the Hluhluwe sector there is a curio shop at **Hilltop Camp** and a small supermarket, but it only has limited basic supplies. Petrol and oil are on sale.

Hluhluwe p530
Ilala Weavers, Thembalethu Craft Village, T035-562 0630, www.ilala.co.za. A quality handicraft shop selling traditional basketwork and beadwork, decorated with geometric patterns. There's a café and children's play ground. By contrast it's also a good spot for birdwatching and there's an identification bird board.

St Lucia p534, map p532
There is a large, modern **Spar** on the main street – McKenzie St – which sells a good

range of supplies. In season, women often peddle fresh tropical fruit from stalls along this street.

Cape Vidal p535
There is a small shop selling a good range of wildlife identification books, T-shirts, souvenirs and limited supplies of food.

▲▲ Activities and tours

Eshowe and inland p524
Tour operators
Zululand Eco-adventures, based at the **George Hotel** and **Zululand Backpackers**, T035-474 4919, www.eshowe.com. Run by Graham Chennells, a registered guide involved in community projects for many years. Unusual cultural tours of the surrounding countryside moving from village to village, no shows are visited, see contemporary traditional life as it is. Interesting projects include the **Eshowe Skills Centre**, a papermaking project, and the **Rotary Classroom Project** (the building of 2000 classrooms in the region). Graham is the former mayor of Eshowe who has intimate knowledge of the Zulu people. Highly recommended for more of an insight into Zulu traditions than the usual all-singing all-dancing tourist traps.

Hluhluwe-Imfolozi Game Reserve
p527, map p529
Day and night drives, R250, children (under 12) R15, which last about 2 hrs, and 2-3 hr game walks, R200 (no children under 13), can be booked through the camp office. Remember if you're staying at the private lodges, you'll have your own game guard for wildlife activities.
Zululand Adventures, T035-550 0243, www.zululand-adventures.com. Morning and afternoon game drives run by the cheery Gavin to Hluhluwe-Imfolozi Game Reserve, including a bush breakfast or a steak braai and sundowners. Good on history of the park and very knowledgeable and enthusiastic

about the area. Also offers day-long fishing trips off the coast.

Hluhluwe p530

Dinizulu Safaris, T035-562 0025, www.dinizulu.co.za. An established family outfit with excellent knowledge of Zululand and its parks, full- and ½-day guided game drives in 4WD open vehicles to Hluhluwe-Imfolozi and Mkhuze game reserves.

Isinkwe Tours & Safaris, Isinkwe Backpackers, see page 540. Tours in open-top 4WDs to Hluhluwe-Imfolozi, St Lucia and Mkhuze, including breakfast and braai lunch. Good value.

St Lucia p534, map p532

Advantage Charters, T035-590 1259, www.advantagetours.co.za. A wide choice of boat rides, including 2-hr estuary trips, from R150. Whale-watching trips run Jun-Nov when humpback, mink and occasional southern right whales travel along the coast heading for the warmer breeding waters of Mozambique. Trips cost about R700, 40% of which is refundable if no whales are spotted after 2 hrs at sea. This is the only licensed whale-watching operator in St Lucia and is permitted to get within 50 m of the whales. If you don't have a car, this is a good-value tour operator for day trips to Cape Vidal and deep-sea fishing.

Santa Lucia, T035-590 1340, www.kznwildlife.com. 80-seater double-storey launch with a bar departs from the jetty next to the bridge at 0830, 1030 and 1430, R130, under 12s R65. The tour lasts for 1½ hrs and travels up the estuary past thick banks of vegetation as far as the Narrows. There is a good chance of seeing hippo and waterfowl. Migrating mullet are often seen leaping out of the water during the autumn when they move from the lake into the sea.

⊖ Transport

Empangeni and around p526

Greyhound coaches leave from the museum in Turnbull St, to **Durban**, **Johannesburg** and **Tshwane (Pretoria)**.

Bus companies Greyhound, www.greyhound.co.za.

Richards Bay p527
Air

There is a small airport located at the northern edge of town, around 5 km from the centre. SAA, T011-978 1111, www.flysaa.com, operates daily flights to **Johannesburg**.

Bus

Greyhound has regular coaches to **Durban**, **Tshwane (Pretoria)** and **Johannesburg**.

Car hire

All offices are located at the airport: **Avis**, T035-789 6549; **Budget**, T035-786 0986; **Hertz**, T035-786 1201; **Tempest**, T035-786 0448.

❶ Directory

Richards Bay p527

Banks Nedbank and Standard Bank are both found on Bullion Blvd.
Medical services The Bay Hospital, is at Krugerrand CBD, T035-780 6111.

St Lucia p534, map p532

Banks First National Bank, and Standard Bank, are on McKenzie St.

Maputaland

Named after the Maputa River, which flows through southern Mozambique, Maputaland covers an area of 9000 sq km stretching north from Lake St Lucia to the Mozambique border and east from the Indian Ocean to the Lebombo Mountains. One of South Africa's least developed regions, Maputaland has preserved a traditional African atmosphere. The land is unsuitable for intensive modern agriculture, and small farmsteads and fishing communities dot the landscape.

The climate varies from being tropical in the north to subtropical in the south, and this has created a fascinatingly diverse range of ecosystems, from the forested Lebombo Mountains at 700 m to the low-lying expanses of the coastal plain. Maputaland's features include Lake Sibaya – South Africa's largest freshwater lake – as well as mangrove swamps, coral reefs, dune forest, riverine forest and savannah. And seeing Maputaland's last wild elephants from a Land Rover in Tembe or diving on the reefs at Sodwana Bay are among South Africa's ultimate wilderness experiences. ▶ *For listings, see pages 553-556.*

Ins and outs

Getting there Maputaland is well connected by road on the N2 highway. By car it is only a three-hour drive from Durban or six hours from Johannesburg. Leave the N2 at the Hluhluwe exit, and follow the Lower Mkuzi Road (R22), which runs along the southern boundary of Mkhuze Game Reserve and passes a number of luxury private game lodges. This tarred road continues on to Mbazwana and Sodwana Bay (90 km), see page 547, and then on to Kosi Bay (see page 550) and the border with Mozambique at Ponta Do Ouro (see box, page 549).

From Mkhuze there is a dirt road heading south parallel to the N2 which leads to the turning to Mkhuze Game Reserve (20 km). There is also an alternative northern route on dirt roads from Mkhuze to Sodwana Bay (120 km), passing through Ubombo, Tshongwe and Mbazwana. The drive to Mkhuze passes through sisal plantations before entering a beautiful rustic area. The road winds through gently rounded hills dotted with aloes and acacias. Donkeys and cows graze on the meadows at the side of the road and wander about freely. The road is in good condition but after rain it is crossed by numerous streams. Mkhuze has a supermarket, bank and petrol station.

A further 10 km along the N2 from Mkhuze is the exit for **Jozini** (the N2 continues north towards Lavumisa, 40 km, on the frontier with Swaziland). Jozini is the last place of any size before the reserves in northern Maputaland; it is a good idea to fill up on petrol and buy any last minute supplies while you are here. The tarred road east from Jozini crosses the Lebombo Mountains and the Maputaland coastal plain and is an alternative to the R22 if you are coming from the north.

Passengers using the **Baz Bus** ① *T021-439 2323, www.bazbus.com,* are dropped off and picked up at the **Ghost Mountain Inn** (see Sleeping, page 553). ▶ *For further details, see Transport, page 556.*

Mkhuze Game Reserve ● ▶ *pp553-556.*

① *Clearly signposted from the N2, 335 km from Durban and 145 km from Richards Bay, T035-573 9004, www.kznwildlife.com. Oct-Mar 0500-1900, Apr-Sep 0600-1800, office daily 0800-1630, R35, children (under 12) R18, plus R35 per vehicle.*

The reserve, established in 1912 and covering an area of 40,000 ha, has a flat and dry landscape of open grasslands, dense forests, coastal dunes and pans. The area to the north is tropical whereas the southern part of the reserve is more temperate. The protected area conserves a representative cross-section of the Maputaland ecosystem. Mkhuze is not visited as often as Hluhluwe-Imfolozi (see page 527) as there are not as many rhino, but it offers opportunities to go on guided bush walks and see some of Maputaland's more unusual animals.

There is some frozen food for sale in the curio shop and a selection of books on natural history and postcards. It's also a good place to pick up some informative leaflets on birds, trees, walks and drives. There's petrol for sale at the entrance gate. Reservations for camping should be made here.

Maputaland game reserves

Maputaland turtles

Five species of turtle can be found off the Maputaland coast but the loggerhead and the leatherback turtles are the only ones to breed here. The turtles arrive between October and February, migrating vast distances from as far afield as Madagascar, Kenya and the Cape. There are two theories as to how the turtles return to the beaches where they were born after spending at least 15 years at sea. One proposes that the turtles are guided by the earth's magnetic fields, while the other holds that they use their sense of smell to find the right beach.

After mating offshore the female turtles, who can weigh up to 900 kg, struggle through the surf and up the beach to lay their eggs. Egg laying takes place at night and after digging a hole in the beach the female will lay around 100 eggs. She then covers the nest with sand and returns to the sea.

Incubation takes around 60 days, the tiny turtles then hatch together and dig their way to the surface. Few hatchlings live to become adults and the threat of being eaten by predators begins immediately with ghost crabs and jackals waiting to catch them before they can reach the sea. About one turtle in every 500 will survive.

The Maputaland Marine Reserve has played a vital role in rescuing the loggerhead and the leatherback from extinction. The beaches along this coast are an important breeding area and years of protection have finally resulted in increasing the numbers of turtles returning each year to breed.

Some of the lodges north of Sodwana Bay offer turtle-watching tips. In St Lucia, KZN Wildlife has granted a single concession to **Shaka Barker Tours**, 4 Hornbill St, T035-590 1162, www.shakabarker.co.za, who run night time trips to see the turtles laying at Leven Point, which is normally a restricted area between November and February. It's not uncommon to see crocodiles and snakes, as well as turtles, on the beach. This is a very special wildlife experience conducted in an eco-friendly way and highly recommended. The tour departs at 1830 and returns at 0300 the following morning. A minimum of two people are required and advance booking is essential. The cost is R2100, which includes supper and night drives in search of genets, leopard, bush babies, chameleons and hippos.

Wildlife

Mkhuze is an excellent place to see some of Maputaland's big game. Elephant, giraffe, blue wildebeest, eland, kudu, black and white rhino, cheetah, leopard and hyena are all present in the reserve. It is also one of the best places to see the shy nyala antelope – nearly 8000 live here. As part of the Mozambique coastal plain, Mkhuze attracts many tropical birds often seen further north. Over 450 species have been recorded here, representing 7% of the world's total number of species. Look out for Neergard's sunbird, the yellowspotted nicator and the African broadbill. Many aquatic birds visit the pans here during the summer when you can see woolly necked storks, herons, flamingos, pink-backed and white pelicans, ibises, spoonbills and jacanas from the hides overlooking the pans. You may also spot hippo and crocodile.

Exploring the reserve

A 100-km network of roads crosses the reserve, passing through areas of thick bush, which are not ideal for game viewing; the grasslands, however, are more open and animals are easier to see. The best game-viewing areas are the **Loop Road**, the **Nsumo Pan** and the **airstrip**.

There are four game-viewing hides next to the Kubube, Kumasinga, Kwamalibala and Kumahlala pans. The viewing here is excellent and you can watch the game coming down to drink. There are car parks nearby where you can leave your car and walk to the hides.

Sodwana Bay ⊙▲▲⊖ ▸▸ pp553-556. Colour map 5, A3.

ⓘ *Gates open 24 hrs, T035-571 0051, www.kznwildlife.com, R20, children (under 12) R15.*
Sodwana's is South Africa's premier scuba-diving destination – and is the site of the world's southernmost tropical reefs. Eighty per cent of South Africa's 1200 species of fish can be found in the waters off Sodwana; ragged-toothed and whale sharks, humpback whales, black marlin and turtles are some of the major attractions. Diving has become so popular here that over 100,000 dives a year are made on these reefs.

Ins and outs

Getting there Sodwana Bay is 350 km from Durban and is well signposted from the N2, approaching from the south on the N2 take the Ngwenya/Sodwana Bay exit. The road is tarred and goes through **Mbazwana** en route to Sodwana Bay (80 km). This small village has mushroomed in recent years. There is a colourful market selling fruit and handicrafts, as well as a petrol station and ATM. It is 15 km from here to Sodwana Bay along a tar road.

From the N2 in the north take the turning to Jozini and Mbazwana. Follow the dirt road to Sodwana Bay (120 km), passing through Ubombo, Tshongwe and Mbazwana, which can be tackled without a 4WD.

Best time to visit Sodwana is popular with visitors all year round. Divers prefer April to September, whereas fishermen tend to congregate here in November and December. December and January are the best times to see the turtles laying their eggs. Sodwana gets very crowded during the school holidays when the accommodation is fully booked months in advance.

Diving

The coral reefs at Sodwana lie just offshore and teem with colourful tropical fish. Among some of the more unusual sightings are the loggerhead, leatherback and hawksbill turtles, honeycomb moray eels, dolphins, whale sharks, stingrays, humpback whales and black marlins. **Two Mile Reef** is very popular with divers. It is 1.5 km long and nearly 1 km wide, with depths ranging from 9 m to 34 m. There are numerous dive sites to explore here and anemones, triggerfish, sponges and fan-shaped gorgoniums can be seen in this area of overhangs and caves. The dives at **Five Mile Reef** and **Seven Mile Reef** are at around 22 m, and both are renowned for their corals. Access to Five Mile Reef is limited, but it is worth trying to get on a dive to see this protected area with its delicate miniature Staghorn Coral Gardens. **Nine Mile Reef** is only open for a limited number of dives and is well known for its soft corals. There are some large caves which can shelter pyjama sharks. Depths range from 5 m to 24 m. ▸▸ *For more detailed dive facts and recommendations, see the colour section, page 22.*

The closest snorkelling site to Sodwana is on **Quarter Mile Reef**, 500 m off Jesser Point. Further south are **Algae Reef** (5 km) and **Adams Reef** (10 km). These are shallow rocky reefs with good visibility inhabited by tiny tropical fish.

North from Mbazwana 🖥 ➍ *pp553-556.*

Lake Sibaya → *Colour map 2, C6.*
ⓘ *This is an endemic low-risk malaria area.*
North of **Mbazwana** the R22 has been newly tarred all the way to the Mozambique border at Ponta do Ouro (see box, opposite) and provides access to the remote northern coastal reserves. An alternative dirt track heads from Mbazwana towards the coast to **Manzengwenya** but this route can only be negotiated with a 4WD. Lake Sibaya, 20 km north of Sodwana, is the largest freshwater lake in South Africa and was previously connected to the sea. The lake is now surrounded by swampy reed beds and patches of forest, which provide varied habitats for the many species of birds which can be found here. A long strip of thickly forested dunes runs between the Indian Ocean and the lake. Tropical birdlife is Lake Sibaya's main attraction and kingfishers, cormorants and fish eagles are often seen, as are the lake's hippos and crocodiles.

Lala Neck, Rocktail Bay and Black Rock
Continuing north past the forest station of **Manzengwenya** there is a dirt track running parallel to the coast, which leads to three secluded beaches: **Lala Neck** (8 km), **Rocktail Bay** (12 km) and **Black Rock** (20 km). These are renowned for being among the ultimate game fishing sites in South Africa. **Lala Neck** and **Black Rock** have clear waters that offer spectacular opportunities for snorkelling and diving, with good chances of seeing turtles and sharks as well as hundreds of colourful tropical fish. There are no facilities here other than one upmarket place to stay.

Ndumo Game Reserve 🖥 ➍ *pp553-556. Colour map 2, C6.*
ⓘ *T035-591 0098, www.kznwildlife.com, park gates Apr-Sep 0600-1800, Oct-Mar 0500-1900; office daily 0800-1200, 1300-1600. R40, children (under 12) R20, plus R35 per vehicle. Shop sells beer, wine, soft drinks but no food.*
Ndumo is a low-lying and humid tropical floodplain renowned for its magnificent birdlife and large numbers of crocodiles and hippos. This is one of the wildest and most beautiful reserves in South Africa and its verdant wetlands have been compared with the Okavango Delta. The area had been heavily hunted since the 1850s. Early hunters left records of having seen large herds of game here, but within 50 years a huge proportion of them had been shot. One of the species which has recovered well is the nyala which was hunted here by Courtney Selous. He visited this region at the turn of the last century to capture nyala for London Zoo.

Ins and outs
Getting there and around From Jozini the road heads directly north to Ndumo. The reserve is 14 km beyond the village of Ndumo on a rough dirt road and lies along the border of Mozambique. The roads are in good condition and visitors can drive around the reserve in their own cars or travel by Land Rover with a guide. There are five game viewing hides to stop at and a leaflet is available for a self-guided car trail.

Wildlife
The reserve was initially established in 1924 to protect the hippos which lived here. As human activity has decreased the animal population of the park has increased dramatically.

Border crossing: South Africa–Mozambique

Ponta do Ouro
The R22 is tarred all the way to the border but on the Mozambique side it is soft sand and a 4WD is required. However, there is the option of parking a vehicle safely at the border and pre-arrange for the Mozambique lodges south of Maputo to come and pick you up.

Border opening hours The border post is small but open daily 0800-1700.
Customs and immigration Mozambique visas are available, payable in South African rand or US dollars.

Some species have been reintroduced and the varied flora of the reserve, which includes numerous pans and reedbeds interspersed with patches of riverine forest and mixed woodland, provides habitats for many different species.

The pans at Banzi and Nyamithi are fascinating areas to experience the atmosphere of an African tropical swamp. There are many waterbirds to look out for on the pans including some rare tropical species at the southern limit of their habitats. Thousands of birds congregate here in the evenings and it is possible to see flocks of flamingos, geese, pelicans and storks.

Buffalo are occasionally seen in the swampy areas of the reserve, but nyala, hippo and crocodiles are present in large numbers. The vegetation in the rest of the reserve is quite thick and makes game viewing difficult. Black and white rhino, leopard and suni antelope thrive in these thickets but they are very rarely seen. A good way to see Ndumo is on one of the tours organized by the reserve. It is possible to go on five different guided walks with a game ranger.

Tembe Elephant Park ☺ ➤➤ pp553-556. Colour map 2, C6.

ⓘ *72 km from Jozini, camp privately run (see Sleeping page 554), www.kznwildlife.com. Park gates Apr-Sep 0600-1800, Oct-Mar 0500-1900; office daily 0700-1600. R35, children (under 12) R18, plus R35 vehicle.*

The reserve was established in 1983 to protect this area's elephant population, which had declined to just 130. They used to migrate over the border into Mozambique but suffered greatly at the hands of poachers; scars left by poachers can still be seen on some of the older elephants. This herd is reckoned to be the only indigenous elephants in KwaZulu Natal. The 30,000-ha protected area at Tembe is a vast impenetrable wilderness of sand forest, thick bush and the Muzi Swamp. This is a very special place to visit, but you will need to plan well in advance, given the strict access controls.

Ins and outs
Getting there Tembe lies on the border with Mozambique between Ndumo Game Reserve and Kosi Bay. It is 72 km from Jozini and although the road is tarred as far as the entrance to the park, the roads inside are so rough that only 4WDs are allowed in. If you are staying at the luxury lodge (the only accommodation within the park), you can leave your car at the gate and arrange for a 4WD transfer.

Elephants crossing

Ndumo Game Reserve and Tembe Elephant Park are now part of the Ndumo-Tembe-Futi Transfrontier Conservation Area (commonly known as the Futi Corridor). This will eventually conserve 79,500 ha of elephant habitat and link the two parks with Maputo Special Reserve, also known as Maputo Elephant Reserve, over the border in Mozambique. In 1986 the South African Defence Force erected an electrified fence between South Africa and Mozambique due to the civil war across the border. This blocked a natural elephant migration path. By removing fences in the transfrontier conservation area, the elephants' range has expanded. The approximate number of elephants in this area is 1350-1500 in Tembe, 600 in Ndumo, and 250 in Maputo Special Reserve.

Wildlife

In addition to overnight visitors staying in the lodge, only a further five groups of day visitors in a 4WD are allowed into the park each day. Each group is accompanied by a park ranger and there are good chances of seeing Tembe's abundant game and birdlife. Some of the more common species to be seen include giraffe, elephant (see box, above), waterbuck, zebra, nyala and buffalo. Lion have been introduced to the park, now making it home to the Big Five. If you are lucky you may see the small, shy, suni antelope and a leopard. There are two hides in the reserve: one at Ponweni by Muzi swamp, this overlooks an elephant crossing point; the second overlooks Mahlasela Pan. There is also a self-guided walk within the Ngobazane enclosure area.

Kosi Bay Nature Reserve ⊜ ⧽ pp553-556. Colour map 2, C6.

ⓘ 96 km from Jozini, T035-592 0236, www.kznwildlfe.com. Gates open Apr-Sep 0600-2000, Oct-Mar 0500-2000; office daily 0700-1600. R20, children (under 12) R10, R15 per vehicle.

Kosi Bay is one of South Africa's favourite wilderness destinations. The protected area is over 25 km long and consists of four lakes separated from the sea by a long strip of forest-covered dunes. Lakes Amanzimnyama, Nhlange, Mpungwini and Sifungwe are part of a fascinating tropical wetland environment. Lake Amanzimnyama is a freshwater lake with darkened water due to decomposing plants. The shores of the lakes are bordered with reedbeds, ferns, swamp figs and umdoni trees. Five species of mangrove thrive in the estuary. Kosi Bay is home to South Africa's only remaining estuarine hunter-gatherer tribe, the Tembe-Thonga, whose traditional fishing traps you can see across the estuary.

Ins and outs

Getting there and around From Jozini head north as if going to Ndumo but stay on the road through the villages of Sihangwana and Ngwanase, from where the entrance gate to Kosi is around 10 km to the north. Alternatively, take the R22 north from Mbazwana and Sodwana Bay. There is a rough dirt road leading to the park and access to Kosi Mouth itself is through deep sand for which a 4WD is needed. The nearest petrol station and supermarket are at Kwangwanase.

Best time to visit The tropical climate here can be debilitatingly hot and humid. The best time to visit is August and September, the coolest months when it tends not to be as humid.

Border crossing: South Africa–Swaziland

Golela–Lavumisa

Just after the Pongola Nature Reserve is Golela and the border with Swaziland. From here it is possible to head north into Swaziland through **Lavumisa**. This is not a very interesting place and most people pass straight through. The alternative route into Swaziland is to head west into Mpumalanga along the N2 towards **Piet Retief**.

Border opening hours Daily 0700-2200.

Customs and immigration You will need a valid passport.

Facilities Fuel and snacks are available here and there is a basic hotel.

Public transport Continuing on into Swaziland is relatively easy as this is one of the busiest crossings into Swaziland, with many local buses plying the route between Lavumisa and Manzini.

Vehicle formalities If you are driving a hired car, make sure you get a letter from your car hire firm confirming that you may take the car out of South Africa.

Wildlife

The lakes are inhabited by hippos and crocodiles, which can be seen basking in the sun around Lake Amanzimnyama. There are no large mammals here but you are likely to see samango and vervet monkeys. The tropical climate is a boon to reptiles and two species of monitor lizard, the Rock and the Nile, are often seen. Many of the snakes which live here are poisonous. The gaboon adder, boomslang, green mamba and forest cobras are all found here.

Many aquatic birds are attracted to the lakes and over 200 species have been spotted here. Rarities include the palmnut vulture and Pel's fishing owl.

The research station at Bhanga Nek has been tagging turtles and protecting nesting sites since 1963. Leatherback and loggerhead turtles arrive on these beaches after lengthy journeys from as far away as Madagascar and the Cape.

Exploring the reserve

A four-day trail, recently taken over by the local community, can be booked on T035-592 0234. The trail is 34 km long and is probably the best way to see the Kosi Bay Nature Reserve. Hikers are accompanied by a guide who leads the group through the entire ecosystem. The distances covered every day are quite short, so this gives ample time to relax and enjoy the atmosphere of the lakes. The trail is very popular and can be fully booked up to six months in advance, a maximum of 10 people are allowed on each trail. More information can be found at www.kznwildlife.com.

Northwest along the N2 ● ›› pp553-556.

Returning to the N2 via Jozini, the highway heads northwest towards Pongola and Swaziland (see box, above). The Pongola Dam can be seen lying to the east with the Lebombo Mountains in the background. The entrance to the Pongola Nature Reserve is clearly signposted off the N2.

Pongola Nature Reserve → *Colour map 2, C5.*

ⓘ *The reserve is accessed from the right of the N2 approximately 25 km before the town of Pongola. Take the Golela turn-off to Swaziland for 10 km. At Golela take the road turning right and follow this road to the main entrance gate, T034-4351012, www.kznwildlife.com. Park gates open summer 0500-1900, winter 0600-1800, R20, children (under 16) R10, plus R20 per vehicle.*

This large area of bush surrounding the dam has been declared a biosphere reserve and large game was reintroduced some years ago. These include white rhino, elephant, giraffe, blue wildebeest and zebra that now live alongside resident nyala, kudu, impala, suni antelope, reedbuck and warthog. The dam itself has significant populations of hippo and crocodile, and the elusive tiger fish that lures fishermen every year for the annual tiger-fishing competition. The landscape is rolling grasslands interspersed with acacias and patches of thick bush. There is a beautiful stretch of lush riverine woodland along the Pongola River and the dam itself attracts thousands of aquatic birds during the winter months (probably the best time to visit as the tracks within the reserve become impassable after rain in the summer months). Interestingly, this was the site of the first game reserve in Africa, proclaimed by Paul Kruger in 1894, which comprised 17,400 ha of farmland between Swaziland, the Lebombo Mountains and the Pongola River. The Anglo-Boer War doomed the existence of the reserve but the Pongola Nature Reserve was reinstated in 1964.

Ithala Game Reserve ● ▶▶ *pp553-556. Colour map 5, A2.*

ⓘ *74 km east of Pongola, 400 km north of Durban and 500 km from Johannesburg, T034-983 2540, www.kznwildlife.com. Park gates Oct-Mar 0500-1900, Apr-Sep 0600-1800; reception office is at Ntshondwe Camp, daily 0700-1930; R35, children (under 12) R18, plus R30 per vehicle.*

The R69 heads west off the N2 at Candova. The gravel road goes as far as Magudu. From there the R69 is tarred leading to the Ithala Game Reserve. This section of the R69 is a fascinating drive through rural Zululand, passing through low-lying grasslands and cattle-ranching country. In November and December, after the rains, the countryside is green and lush and rich in birdlife. Many private game reserves and farms have opened over recent years, stocking their land with game bought at the annual game auctions that occur in the area. Ithala reserve was established in 1972 after the Natal Parks Board began buying farms on the land lying between the top of the escarpment at Louwsburg and the Pongola River Valley. After years of overgrazing the land had seriously deteriorated and very little wildlife remained. In the last 30 years Ithala has been transformed into one of KwaZulu Natal's most spectacular reserves.

Ins and outs

Getting there From Durban, travel north on the N2 as far as Pongola. From here take the R66 and then the R69 for 73 km and the park entrance is near the village of Louwsburg. From Gauteng the easiest route is via the N2 to Pongola, though the park can also be approached via Vryheid from the Battlefield region.

Getting around There is a network of dirt roads looping around the reserve, which offer good game viewing by car. Large herds of grazers are often seen on the grasslands. Near the airstrip look out for white rhino and tsessebe and particularly cheetah, which favour grass airstrips because of their openness. There are also some self-guided walking trails passing through forest.

Best time to visit The climate is warm all year round but it can get cold in the evenings from May to August when there are occasional frosts. Most of the rain falls in the summer months of November, December and January.

Safety The rivers at Thalu and Mbiso camps are not infected with bilharzia and are safe for swimming.

Wildlife and vegetation

The reserve's landscapes are mostly large areas of low-lying grasslands at 400 m rising up through steep-sided forested valleys to granite cliffs at 1450 m. The streams in these mountains flow down into the Pongola River. The steep terrain has created several different ecosystems from deep narrow valleys and boulder outcrops to cliff faces, with an interesting diversity of wildlife. Twenty new species have been reintroduced into the reserve including a herd of young elephant and the only herd of tsessebe in Natal. Animals commonly seen include eland, giraffe, kudu, blue wildebeest and zebra. The following animals are also present here but are rarely seen: cheetah, white rhino, elephant, klipspringer, leopard, nyala and black rhino. For visitors wanting to see the park on foot, guided day hikes (as well as self-guided trails) can be booked at reception (see details, above).

Some 320 species of bird have been recorded here, including black eagle, bathawk, bald ibis, martial eagle and brown-necked parrot. Some interesting plants to look out for in season are the flowering aloes trees, unmistakable in June and July when they come into bloom. Their large orange flowers are an important source of nectar at this time of year and they attract birds and insects.

◉ Maputaland listings

For Sleeping and Eating price codes and other relevant information, see pages 46-53.

◉ Sleeping

Mkhuze Game Reserve *p544*
The prices for the following are for the whole lodge or cottage; when split among a group, they are quite good value. Reservations: KZN Wildlife, T033-845 1000, www.kznwild life.com. Camping is booked directly, T035-573 0001.
AL Nhlonhlela. This luxury 8-bed bush lodge looks out over the fever trees and Nhlonhlela Pan. There is a central lounge and kitchen where a cook will prepare your meals and there's a game guard for guided bush walks.
A Ghost Mountain Inn, T035-573 1025/7, www.ghostmountaininn.co.za. Next to the northern entrance to Mkhuze, with 52 rooms, a/c, stylish decor, TV, restaurant serving excellent food, spa and 2 swimming pools.

Good-value safari packages and Zulu cultural experiences with knowlegable guides and this is a good option if you don't want to self-cater. Look out for specials on the website that include activities and spa treatments. Recommended.
A-D Mantuma. The main camp with a variety of cottages, including 2 7-bed cottages with 3 bedrooms, 2 bathrooms and fully equipped kitchen; 5 4-bed en suite bungalows with 2 bedrooms and fully equipped kitchen; 4 3-bed en suite chalets with fully equipped kitchen; ten 2-bed and three 3-bed tents raised on a wooden deck with en suite bathrooms and communal open-plan kitchen; six 3-bed rest huts with communal kitchen and ablution block. This is the largest camp, the buildings are set among natural gardens and are not fenced off from the reserve so game does sometimes wander through. There is also a pool and a shop; game drives and guided walks can be arranged.

Camping

The campsite is 1 km from the main gate, 9 km from Mantuma, and can accommodate 60 people. Ablution blocks with hot and cold water.

Sodwana Bay *p547*

The supermarket sells petrol and oil, and stocks bread, tinned food and beach gear. Freezer drawers are available for hire and should be booked in advance, but at R50 for 24 hrs they are expensive.

B Sodwana Bay Camp, KZN Wildlife, T033-845 1000, www.kznwildlife.com. Ten 8-bed and ten 5-bed self-catering fully equipped log cabins, some recently renovated.

B Sodwana Bay Lodge, T035-571 6010, www.sodwanadiving.co.za. Accommodation is in 20 twin-bedded reed and thatch huts on stilts overlooking woodland, restaurant serving seafood (what else) bar, pool, game-fishing trips available. The lodge offers a number of all-inclusive diving package deals plus a full range of PADI courses, with a fully equipped dive shop and learning pool.

E-F Gwalagwala. A large campsite with 413 basic sites in the main section which can become very crowded, plus 33 luxury sites with their own water and electricity supplies. Camping is booked directly T035-571 0051/3.

North from Mbazwana *p548*
Private lodges and camps

L3 Thonga Beach Lodge, on the coast 6 km from Lake Sibaya, T035-475 6000, www.isibindiafrica.co.za. New super-luxury lodge with 24 spacious a/c thatched suites with stone bathrooms, reed walls, large open windows, built on stilts in the forest, each very private, bar and restaurant with ocean views, rates inclusive of meals. Activities include turtle tracking, kayaking on Lake Sibaya, diving and snorkelling. The lodge is set in one of the most isolated stretches of the Coastal Forest Reserve and is the ideal place for a tropical beach holiday. It lies on the strip of forested dunes between Lake Sibaya and the sea, and a path connecting

the camp to the beach passes through thick tropical forest rich in birdlife. Lying just offshore is a fascinating area of rarely visited coral reefs and rock pools, but it's only possible to visit here in a 4WD. Guests can leave their 2WD cars at a cashew nut factory approx 40 km north of Mbazwana and the lodge will collect them by 4WD.

L2 Rocktail Bay Lodge, 12 km north of Manzengwenya along a dirt track running parallel with the beach, www.rocktailbay. com. A luxury bush camp with 11 A-frame chalets set on stilts among dunes and coastal forest a few hundred metres from the beach and the Indian Ocean. A wide range of activities available, including birdwatching, diving, snorkelling, swimming, fishing and 4WD trips to nearby beaches and Lake Sibaya. The highlight of a stay here is a night-time search for egg-laying turtles on the beach just below the lodge. Access is by 4WD only. Same arrangement as above for pickups at the cashew nut factory. Reservations through **Wilderness Safaris**, Johannesburg, T011-883 0747, www.wilderness-safaris.com.

Ndumo Game Reserve *p548*

D Ndumo Camp, KZN Wildlife, T033-845 1000, www.kznwildlife.com. Seven 2-bed rest huts, with a/c and private verandas. Lovely setting overlooking the Pongola floodplain, surrounded by tropical vegetation. Well-equipped kitchen, swimming pool. Cook on hand to prepare meals (but guests must bring their own food). Game drives and walks can be arranged from here.

Camping

8 sites near the hutted camp, with kitchen and ablution block, T035-591 0058.

Tembe Elephant Park *p549*

L1 Tembe Elephant Lodge, T031-267 0144, www.tembe.co.za. The bush camp consists of 9 upmarket tents raised on wooden platforms tucked away in secluded areas. There are hot showers with glass walls that look out over the bush, small pool with thatched roof and relaxing veranda. Rates include meals and game drives, which are also available to day visitors by prior arrangement.

Kosi Bay Nature Reserve p550

L3 Kosi Forest Lodge, reservations T035-592 9239, www.isibindiafrica.co.za. Luxury all-inclusive safari camp within the reserve. 16-bed lodge, with individual reed and thatch suites, beautiful hardwood floors, open-air bathrooms, very secluded – popular with honeymooners. Excellent restaurant, bar, swimming pool. Beautiful setting, range of activities on offer including turtle-watching trips, canoeing and diving. Non-4WD drivers can park cars at the Total garage in Kwa-Ngwanase and prearrange a 4WD pickup by the lodge.

A-C Kosi Bay Lodge, 500 m from the lake, 500 m from the bay itself outside the reserve, T035-592 9561, www.kosibaylodge.co.za. Restaurant, swimming pool, pub, self-catering also an option, in A-frame chalets with communal ablution block or 2-bed reed en suite huts. The lodge runs trips to the eastern shore of the lake from where you can hike 5 km to the beautiful beaches. One of the cheaper options in the region. Normal cars can reach here, only the last 3 km are dirt road. Rates drop cpnsiderably in low season.

B-D Kosi Bay Camp, KZN Wildlife, T033-845 1000, www.kznwildlife.com. There are 3 thatched cabins here with either 6, 5 or 2 beds. All are fully equipped for self-catering.

Camping

15 pitches with electricity points and an ablution block among the trees near Lake Nhlange, T035-592 0236.

Northwest along the N2 p551

B-C Pongola Country Lodge, 14 Jan Mielie St, Pongola, T034-413 1352, www.pongola countrylodge.co.za. Hardly a country lodge as it's next to an industrial area in the village but pleasant enough inside, with 62 individually decorated rooms, some on the small side, hence they're much cheaper. DSTV, a/c,

phone, parking outside of the rooms, pool, extensive gardens, 2 restaurants, bar. You might catch some Zulu dancing if a tour group is staying.

D-F Pongola Caravan Park, 219 Hans Meyer St, PO Box 539, Pongola, T034-413 1789, http://pongolacaravanpark.co.za. 9 self-catering chalets, TV, a/c, shady and grassed caravan and camping sites with electric points, spotless ablution block, mini-golf course, small kiosk with basic supplies, large swimming pool, well-managed spot.

Camping

Pongola Nature Reserve, T034-435 1012. 20 basic sites next to the dam, ablution block, cold water only.

Private lodges and camps

L3 Mkuze Falls Private Game Reserve, near the village of Mahlangasi, access off the R66, T034-414 1018, www.mkuzefalls.com. Super luxury in 8 thatched chalets with private plunge pool and open-air showers, 1 safari suite, or 5 en suite tents with a/c, mosquito nets. All accommodation has fantastic views of the waterfall on the Mkhuze River, personal attentive service, all-inclusive with meals and game drives. The reserve is home to the Big Five. Rates drop May-Jul.

L1 Pakamisa Private Game Reserve, off the R66, 15 km southwest of Pongola, T034-413 3559, www.pakamisa.co.za. 2500-ha estate that is home to several species of antelope, giraffe and zebra, with 8 spacious luxury rooms designed in a Spanish villa-style with private balconies, terrace restaurant overlooking the Pakamisa Mountains, dinners 'out bush' can be arranged, horse riding, game drives and walks, clay pigeon shooting, swimming pool. Rates are all inclusive.

L1 White Elephant Lodge, next to the dam Pongola Nature Reserve, T034-413 2489, www.whiteelephant.co.za. A luxurious, all-inclusive 5-star game lodge. The 8 elegant safari tents have a colonial theme and en suite open-air baths and 7 cheaper thatch and reed chalets. Lots of activities on offer, including game drives, guided mountain biking, boat cruises, tiger fishing, rhino walks and short flights in a 6-seater plane. Rates include brunch (after game drives), afternoon tea and dinner.

Ithala Game Reserve *p552*
Reservations through **KZN Wildlife**, T033-845 1000, www.kznwildlife.com.
AL Ntshondwe Lodge. Sleeps 6 in 3 luxurious en suite double bedrooms, small plunge pool, viewing deck, self-catering but with a cook. Ingeniously camouflaged in a jumble of boulders and flowering plants and trees. Game drives and walks are available.
C-D Ntshondwe Camp. Offers 42 self-catering chalets, 2-bed and 4-bed, with fully equipped kitchens, a lounge and dining room. There's a shop, restaurant serving meals and takeaways, bar and a pool. The camp shop sells limited tinned and dried food, wildlife books and charcoal, and petrol is on sale next to the main gates. The nearest shop is in Louwsburg (5 km).

Bush camps
The camps are all self-catering but are supplied with bedding and have a fully equipped kitchen; the lodges are thatched and built from natural materials. The camps are set by themselves in the bush and guests can game watch from the comfort of their verandas in front of the huts or go on a game walk accompanied by a guard. Price codes refer to the price of minimum rates although the bush camps are only available for single group bookings.
AL Mhlangeni. Sleeps 10 in 2 lodges, and is set in a rocky area overlooking the Ncence River well away from the busiest areas of the park and is renowned for its game viewing. A central open-plan lounge and kitchen with its own sundeck provide wonderful views.
A Mbizo. Sleeps 8 in 2 lodges with a shared lounge, kitchen and viewing deck. Overlooks the rapids on the Mbizo River.

B Thalu. 4-bed camp with kitchen, lounge and viewing deck on the banks of the Thalu River.

Camping
Main camp, T034-983 2540. Ablution block with 1 toilet and cold showers only. Maximum 20, tents only, caravans not permitted. Animals can be seen wandering around and it's a great place for wilderness camping.

▲ Activities and tours

Sodwana Bay *p547*
Coral Divers, T033-345 6531, www.coral divers.co.za. Consistently recommended. PADI courses from open water to dive master and include dorm/tent accommodation, equipment but no meals or park entry fees. Open water courses start from R2995. It has its own backpacker resort at Sodwana, with bar, restaurant, deck, pool, TV room and internet access, and will pick you up from Hluhluwe for an extra R195.
Ghost Mountain Inn, T035-573 1025, www.ghostmountaininn.co.za. Offers a range of all-inclusive safari tours in the area, ranging from 1-5 days.

⊖ Transport

North from Mbazwana *p548*
This is a relatively remote part of the coast and until recently it was only accessible to people with 4WDs. Now many roads have been tarred, it's possible to get to the coastal reserves in a normal car, or at least get part way there, park, and arrange 4WD transfers to the lodges. See individual listings for details.

Bus
The **Baz Bus**, T021-439 2323, www.bazbus. com, drops passengers off at the Isinkwe Backpackers near **Hluhluwe** on its way north to **Swaziland**.

Contents

Footprint features

Gauteng

At a glance

⊖ **Getting around** Buses and Baz Bus on major routes, car hire, tours start and finish in Johannesburg.

◉ **Time required** 2-4 days.

☀ **Weather** Cold, dry and sunny in winter, summer thunder showers.

✗ **When not to go** Good all year.

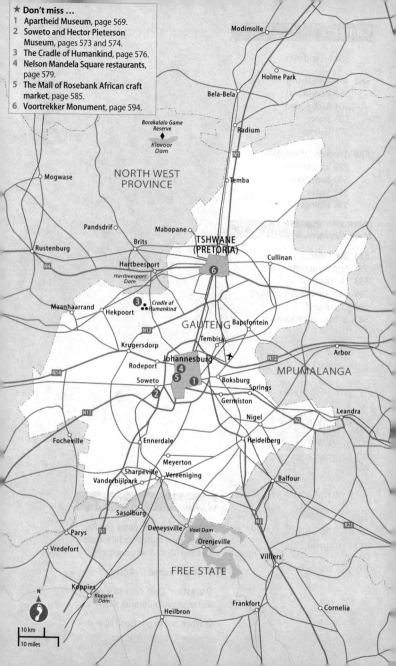

Modimolle

Holme Park

Bela-Bela

Radium

NORTH WEST PROVINCE

Temba

Mogwase

Borakalalo Game Reserve

♦ *Klovoor Dam*

Pandsdrif

Mabopane

Brits

TSHWANE (PRETORIA) ⑥

Cullinan

Rustenburg

Hartbeesport

Hartbeesport Dam

Maanhaarrand

③ *Cradle of Humankind*

Hekpoort

GAUTENG

Bapsfonten

Krugersdorp

Tembisa

Rodeport

Johannesburg

④⑤ ①

Boksburg

MPUMALANGA

Arbor

Soweto ②

Springs

Germiston

Nigel

Leandra

Focheville

Ennerdale

Heidelberg

Meyerton

Sharpeville

Vereeniging

Balfour

Vanderbijlpark

Sasolburg

Parys

Deneysville

Vaal Dam

Orenjeville

Villiers

Vredefort

FREE STATE

N ↑

Koppies

Koppies Dam

Frankfort

Cornelia

Heilbron

10 km
10 miles

Loud, brash and rich, Johannesburg has long been both the bane and lifeblood of South Africa. Since its sudden birth in 1886 when a hapless Aussie discovered gold on the Highveld, it has dominated the country, morphing from a rough frontier town into a financial metropolis with a good deal of debauchery still imbedded in its fabric. Built on a high plateau surrounded by the world's richest gold mines, Johannesburg dominates Gauteng. The high-rise city centre is surrounded by some 600 suburbs: to the north lie the realms of the wealthy and white, while in the southwest is the vast township of Soweto. Although the city has suffered from much-publicized high crime rates, it is now dusting off its dodgy reputation and drawing back visitors for the first time in over a decade. Crime-busting regeneration programmes have seen areas like run-down Newtown transformed and filled with restaurants and shops, while recent additions include some of South Africa's finest cutting-edge museums, including the Apartheid Museum. The northern suburbs are an enclave of posh boutiques, good restaurants and sophisticated nightlife, while Soweto now attracts more tourists than Kruger National Park.

Fifty kilometres to the north is the recently renamed capital of the state, Tshwane (Pretoria). Although connected by an almost unbroken ribbon of development, the two cities couldn't be more different. Tshwane (Pretoria) is staid and conservative, with wide streets lined with jacaranda trees which bloom a ladylike purple in spring. The centre feels peaceful and orderly, with attractive sandstone buildings and large, tidy parks. Tshwane (Pretoria) has long been a centre of Afrikanerdom, best summed up by the sombre Voortrekker Monument. But its conservative feel has mellowed of late, with a lively student population and the influx of a multilingual diplomatic community.

Neither Johannesburg nor Tshwane (Pretoria) merit more than a couple of days' exploration; if you're on a tight schedule, a day or two will cover the major sights and give you time to explore the excellent shopping and dining opportunities, some of the best in Africa. However, it is the area's history and its excellent museums which give a real feel for the country's troubled past – and for the shape of its future.

Arriving by air

OR Tambo International Airport ⓘ *Kempton Park, T011-921 5262, www.acsa.co.za*, is 24 km from the city centre and 35 km from the northern suburbs on the R24, roughly halfway between Johannesburg and Tshwane (Pretoria). Both cities can be reached by car in 30 minutes. The airport has been undergoing steady redevelopment in recent years in-line with requirements for the 2010 FIFA World Cup™, and is now a slick complex and the most important hub for air travel in the southern hemisphere. Already, it is capable of receiving the new A380 planes. The airport had a name change in 2006 to honour late anti-Apartheid activist Oliver Reginald Tambo.

To check the status of a flight, check the website or send an SMS to T38648 with the flight number, in reply to which you'll receive up-to-date flight details.

Facilities for international passengers include food courts, some decent shops and several banks. **Master Currency** and **American Express** branches are open 0530-2130 and there are a number of ATMs. In international arrivals, there is a cell phone and South African SIM card hire counter and a post office. Note that the airport post office can put post on the next flight to Europe for a small fee, in addition to the cost of postage. This is as close to overnight delivery you can get apart from sending via a courier service. There is also a branch of **Postnet** on the shopping level of the domestic terminal. The duty-free shops in international departures are extensive and the terminal now resembles a typical South African shopping mall. **Excess Baggage**, in the Parkade Centre (see below), T011-3901 8044, can provide 24-hour secure luggage storage. Wi-Fi is available in international departures and there are internet cafés in all terminals.

Opposite the two terminals is the **Parkade Centre**, a multi-storey car park and site of all car hire offices (see Transport, page 587) and shuttle bus companies. **Magic Bus** ⓘ *T011-394 6902, www.magicbus.co.za*, and **Airport Link** ⓘ *T011-792 2017, www.airportlink.co.za*, drop off at the major hotels in Johannesburg and Tshwane (Pretoria). Metered taxis can be found outside the main terminal building but tend to be more expensive than the shuttle services and drivers often do not know the way without direction to the lesser known hotels or guesthouses. Be sure to use an approved Airports Company South Africa (ACSA) taxi and ignore the touts. The taxis have the ACSA logo on them.

All the hotels located within the environs of the airport offer a free pickup shuttle service, and a drop-off service for a nominal fee. Opposite the main terminal building are a series of hotel bus stops where the hotel shuttles come and go, but at quieter times of the day you may need to phone the hotel to tell them you are waiting. Some backpacker hostels also offer pickups, so phone ahead to check.

The station for the Gautrain (see box, page 563) at the airport has been completed and the high speed rail service will be running from the airport to both Tshwane (Pretoria) and Johannesburg in time for the 2010 FIFA World Cup™. It will take less than 15 minutes to get to Sandton.

Arriving at night

Although OR Tambo International Airport is open 24 hours, the last arrivals are at about midnight and the first departures are from 0530 and most flights from Europe arrive in the early morning. If you do happen to arrive at night, you will find the airport perfectly safe, some restaurants and shops stay open late and banking hours are until 2130. There are also ATMs. Shuttle buses will collect you at any time though it is worth arranging this in advance, as the shuttle desks at the airport close at night. The same is true for the car hire companies. There are several hotels within a few kilometres of the airport that will collect you for free if you phone ahead.

> Johannesburg Airport is served by almost 60 airlines, more than 17 million passengers pass through each year, and it employs 18,000 people. With a growth rate in passenger traffic of 10% per annum, it has overtaken Cairo and Dubai airports.

Best time to visit

The area on which Johannesburg and Tshwane (Pretoria) are located is known as the Highveld, a high plateau with an average altitude of over 1500 m. The weather here can be extreme. Summer, from October to March, can get very hot, with most of the yearly rainfall, characterized by spectacular electric storms. Temperatures drop in winter, and during June and July frosts are common. Johannesburg also suffers from unpleasant yellow-tinged hazes before the arrival of the first rains in summer, when strong winds blow loose particles from the mine workings into the atmosphere.

Tourist information

The **Gauteng Tourism Authority** ① *1 Central Pl, corner of Jeppe and Henry Nxumalo streets, Newtown, T011-639 1600, www.gauteng.net,* is responsible for information for the whole province. It has a small selection of maps and brochures, and the staff are very helpful and will advise you on sites and attractions. **Johannesburg Tourism Company** ① *Grosvenor Corner, 195 Jan Smuts Av, Parktown, T011-214 0700, www.joburgtourism.co.za,* is a rather odd set-up, with limited information in the walk-in office but a good website. The **City Council** ① *www.joburg.org.za,* also has tourist information on its excellent website, which covers every aspect of the city. For information on Tshwane (Pretoria) contact the **Tshwane Tourism Information Bureau** ① *Old Nederlandsche Bank Building, Church Sq, T012-358 1430, www.tshwane.gov.za.*

Johannesburg

→ *Colour map 2, C2. Phone code: 011.*

Johannesburg is the largest financial, commercial and industrial centre in South Africa. Barely over 100 years old, the discovery of gold transformed this deserted heartland into a vast urban sprawl and made it one of the wealthiest cities in the world. The gold rush brought in settlers from all over the world creating a multiracial and cosmopolitan city, but Apartheid changed all that. Forced relocations altered the fabric of Johannesburg, creating deep divisions in society that are still evident today. Despite Apartheid's demise, Johannesburg is still mostly segregated, albeit no longer by legal requisite. The city centre and neighbouring suburbs, such as Hillbrow,

1 Greater Johannesburg

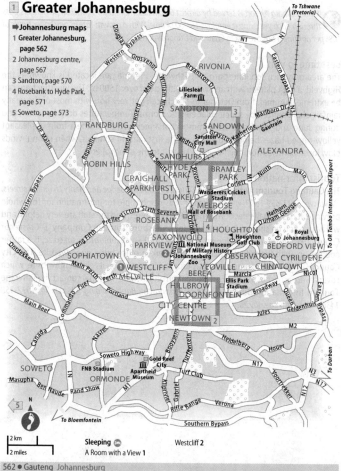

➡ Johannesburg maps
1 Greater Johannesburg,
   page 562
2 Johannesburg centre,
   page 567
3 Sandton, page 570
4 Rosebank to Hyde Park,
   page 571
5 Soweto, page 573

Sleeping 😴
A Room with a View **1**

Westcliff **2**

The Gautrain

The Gautrain Rapid Rail Link is an 80-km high-speed railway network that will link Tshwane (Pretoria) with Johannesburg, with a branch line from Sandton to OR Tambo International Airport. It should be completed in early 2010 and it is hoped it will relieve chronic commuter road traffic on the M1, which in the mornings and late afternoons resembles a car park, and is also part of the transport plans for the 2010 FIFA World Cup™. The trains will be capable of travelling up to 160 kph and part of the line will be underground. It will take 40 minutes to go between Johannesburg and Tshwane (Pretoria), and 15 minutes from Sandton to the airport. It is expected that Sandton Station will have a check-in facility for air passengers. The Gautrain Bus Link will connect the stations to destinations within a 15 km radius. For progress visit www.gautrain.co.za.

are largely home to the urban black population, a condensed area of overcrowded high-rise flats where poverty and crime is rife. Soweto is a vast, sprawling township of government housing and informal settlements, home to the majority of Johannesburg's black commuters. Most white residents, on the other hand, live in the leafy and affluent northern suburbs.

But things are changing. Soweto has become a city in its own right, with new affluent suburbs and a fast-growing middle class, while a breed of wealthy, successful black people – known locally as 'Buppies' (Black Upwardly-mobile People) – have moved into what were until recently the reserves of rich whites. The notorious city centre, meanwhile, is undergoing extensive regeneration programmes, with streets being cleaned up and closed-circuit cameras deterring casual criminals. But while crime rates have dropped considerably, safety remains an issue, with most visitors, like most well-off locals, confining themselves to the safe suburbs and numerous shopping malls. ▶▶ *For listings, see pages 577-588.*

Ins and outs

Getting there

For information on Johannesburg International Airport, see page 560. The **railway station** and the **main bus terminal** are at the Park City Transit Centre. ▶▶ *See Transport, page 587.*

Getting around

Although public transport is improving in Johannesburg, it is still advisable to stick to private transport, hire cars and metered taxis. Locals rely mainly on minibus taxis, thousands of which ply the centre throughout the day, but these are not recommended for visitors due to high accident rates and issues of crime. The new council **metrobuses** ⓘ *Joburg Connect Call Centre, T011-375 5555 (option 8), www.joburg.org.za,* are a far safer option, running along 80 routes in and around the city from 0600 to 1900. Routes and timetables can be found on the city's website. Tickets run on zones; the central zone starts from the bus terminus in Gandhi Square (formerly Vaderbijl Square) at the corner of Main and Rissik streets where there is an information office. A single tickets costs from R6.50. If you hire a car, plan your route before setting out and always carry a map – the system of one-way streets and snaking highways can be utterly bewildering.

Orientation

The once-prosperous central business district is today a hectic muddle of abandoned office blocks, market stalls and concrete flyovers. Crime remains a problem here and most businesses have moved out to the safer northern suburbs, although recent regeneration projects are starting to draw back investment. A visit to the city centre is well worthwhile for an insight into how Johannesburg has developed over the decades, although it is recommended that you go on an organized tour.

Johannesburg's affluent suburbs are in the northern part of the city. Clustered around the main freeway to Tshwane (Pretoria), the M1, they feel far removed from the hectic bustle of the centre. These are the safest areas in town and home to most of the city's tourist accommodation.

The largest of Johannesburg's suburbs feels very different. The infamous township of Soweto lies southwest of the city, named because of its location – South West Township. Soweto is linked to the city by a number of freeways that carry hundreds of thousands of commuters to the city centre and northern suburbs each day. Adjoining Soweto to the south, are smaller townships where other communities were relocated during Apartheid; coloured people were forced to move to **Eldorado Park**, and Indians were moved to **Lenasia**.

Tourist information

Gauteng Tourism Authority ⓘ *1 Central Pl, corner of Jeppe and Henry Nxumalo streets, Newtown, T011-639 1600, www.gauteng.net, Mon-Fri 0800-1700*, is the main source of information in the city centre. There are also kiosks in the Mall of Rosebank at the **African Craft Market** ⓘ *T011-327 2000, daily 0900-1800*, **Sandton City Mall** ⓘ *T011-784 9596, daily 0900-1800* and **OR Tambo International Airport** ⓘ *T011-390 3614, daily 0600-2200*. All have a selection of maps and brochures and can help with accommodation. **Johannesburg Tourism Company** ⓘ *Grosvenor Corner, 195 Jan Smuts Av, Parktown, T011-214 0700, www.joburgtourism.co.za, Mon-Fri 0800-1700, Sat 0900-1300*, has limited information but an excellent website.

🌙 *Johannesburg is a city full of trees, there are over six million on pavements, in parks and private residences. The city resembles a rainforest on pictures taken from satellites, making it one of the greenest urban areas in the world.*

Background

The city centre of Johannesburg is surrounded by some 600 suburbs covering approximately 500 sq km. The population of the municipal city of Johannesburg is roughly 3.8 million. Although it is almost impossible to estimate the population of Soweto due to the constant arrival of people from rural areas and illegal immigrants looking for work, the population of greater Johannesburg, including Soweto and the suburbs on the East Rand (from Germiston in the west to Springs in the east, where the towns are effectively now part of the city) is put at just over ten million.

Much of Johannesburg's fabric was formed by the actions of the Apartheid regime from the mid-1950s. The thriving multi-racial conurbation (see page 568) was changed dramatically with the advent of the Group Areas Act, which forcibly relocated the city's black population from the centre to specially built townships outside town, such as Soweto. The most infamous forced removal was the bulldozing of an area to the west of Johannesburg called Sophiatown. This was an area of slum housing near to the city centre and was home to a diverse population of Africans, coloureds and 'poor whites'. During the

24 hours in Johannesburg

Start the day with a sumptuous breakfast at **Fourno's Bakery**. It's a great place to watch Jo'burg's high-fliers conduct power breakfasts over fashionable coffees.

Set off on a mind-expanding morning tour of **Soweto**, South Africa's oldest and most famous township. Drop in at Mandela's former home which is now a museum; drink a cool Castle lager in a *shebeen*; and visit the memorials and museums dedicated to the struggle against Apartheid.

Lunch at **The Mall of Rosebank** before hitting the shops. Jo'burger's love their shopping malls and Rosebank has an excellent **African Craft Market** and a lively rooftop flea market on a Sunday.

In the afternoon drive out to the **Lion Park**, where you can get close to lions and play with some cubs, then go to the **Lesedi Cultural Village**. After the two-hour tour of four authentic African villages recreated from the Xhosa, Zulu, Pedi and Sotho tribes, enjoy traditional dancing from over 60 performers around a large fire and dinner of game meat such as impala or crocodile.

Crack open a good bottle of South African wine at the stylish **Blues Room** in Sandton, one of the best jazz and blues venues in Gauteng, before heading to **Melville**, Jo'burg's happening nightlife district – two streets of bars, restaurants and late night lounges where people go to be seen.

1940s and 1950s there was a huge outburst of a new African urban culture in Sophiatown, based mainly on the influence of American jazz musicians. This cultural explosion attracted bohemian whites and a huge number of African writers, journalists and politicians. To the Apartheid planners, the area stood for everything they opposed. In the mid-1950s the entire population was removed and the bulldozers were sent in. A new white suburb was built over the ruins and, in a gesture that was crass even by the standards of Apartheid, they named the new suburb Triomf – Afrikaans for 'triumph'. In 2006, the name was changed back to Sophiatown.

Since the mid-1980s this forced movement of Africans from the city centre to the townships has been reversed. The breakdown of influx controls led to the rapid growth of the African population of Johannesburg city centre, especially in Hillbrow, which has one of Africa's highest population densities. Since the end of Apartheid this trend has continued and has been bolstered by the arrival of new immigrants from outside South Africa's borders. Tens of thousands of Nigerians, Congolese and Zimbabweans have flooded, often illegally, into the centre, suburbs and townships. The population has mushroomed in the last decade, with a growth of around 23% since 1996.

The inner city has suffered from soaring crime rates in the last two decades, although much is being done to reverse the trend. While the mid-1990s saw much of central Johannesburg being deserted, with business and offices moving out to the northern suburbs, and the city being tagged as the murder capital of the world, the local government has clamped down in recent years. Massive raids on apartment blocks in Hillbrow have ousted thousands of illegal immigrants. An extensive network of CCTV cameras (which are now installed on every street corner), a huge new Metro police force (which has the ability to respond to a crime in 60 seconds) and numerous regeneration projects have made the centre far safer. Improved border security arrangements with neighbouring countries have blocked the traffic in stolen cars to other African countries, and the rate of carjackings has been reduced considerably. According to one study street crime in general has dropped dramatically, and you're just as likely to be a victim of violent crime in the Cape as in Johannesburg. The first of the regenerated areas was Newtown, where the streets were pedestrianized and the Mary Fitzgerald Square upgraded; the area is now filled with restaurants and shops and is attracting businesses back to the centre, including the new Gauteng tourism office. This is acting as a model for other parts of town, and it's hoped that the centre will once again become as safe as it once was. During the preparation for the 2010 FIFA World Cup™, the city enlisted the advice of former mayor of New York Rudolph Giuliani to assist in combating crime. He after all, turned New York, formerly the crime capital of the world, into a globally accepted safe city.

Improved security is drawing back visitors, but it's still sensible to take common sense precautions. Johannesburg is still not yet a city which can be casually explored on foot, and the best way of seeing the sights is on a guided tour.

Sights

City centre

The **Newtown** area, www.newtown.co.za, once the cultural heart of Johannesburg, has once again, after years of deterioration, become a popular spot with locals. A huge regeneration project, which saw the introduction of CCTV, a police presence and the revamping of Mary Fitzgerald Square into a smart cobbled square, has transformed the area. Shops and cafés have moved in, and this is the site of the new **Gauteng Tourism Authority** office, see page 564. Unlike the rest of the city centre, it is safe to wander around the square and the facilities lining it, including the Market Theatre, Museum Africa and Newtown Park. There is safe parking on the eastern part of Mary Fitzgerald Square, just in front of the Museum Africa, and behind at the back of the Market Theatre. Newtown can now be accessed from Braamfontein in the north by the new Nelson Mandela Bridge that spans over 40 railway lines.

The **Museum Africa** ① *Old Market Building, 121 Bree St, T011-833 5624, Tue-Sun 0900-1700, free*, is one of the city's major museums, but despite its reputation it is rather run down and disappointing. Nevertheless, it is currently undergoing a bit of a revamp and intends in the future to display more cultural exhibits. Housed in the city's former fruit and vegetable market, it attempts to explain the black experience of living in Johannesburg. There are displays on the struggle for democracy and on life in the goldmines and the townships, with mock-ups of an informal settlement. On the second floor is a gallery dedicated to San rock art and the most popular gallery is called 'Tried for Treason', with some interesting original editions of newspapers dating from treason trials in the 1960s, although the displays pale in comparison to those of the Apartheid Museum (see page 569). Perhaps most rewarding is the ground floor gallery, with changing temporary exhibitions, including some excellent photography shows. There is a small café and gift shop by the entrance.

The **Market Theatre Complex**, next to Museum Africa, is the main hub of the area's regeneration. As well as the theatre, there is the **Market Theatre Mall** (a series of small craft shops), and a couple of popular restaurants and bars, with stalls strung along the street selling Zulu beadwork, jewellery and crafts. At weekends, the market expands into Mary Fitzgerald Square, which also holds special events and occasional live music. In one corner is a giant TV screen that shows important sports matches. The theatre itself is one of the best and most established in Gauteng (see page 584).

The **KwaZulu Muti Museum of Man and Science** ① *corner of Diagonal (14) and President St, T011-836 4470, Mon-Fri 0730-1700, Sat 0730-1300*, isn't actually a museum but a *muti* shop, which has been on this site since 1897. *Muti* is a form of witchcraft practised exclusively by witch doctors, and this shop is crammed with products used in traditional herbal medicine and magic. The ingredients on sale include leaves, seeds and bark, as well as more specialized items like monkey skulls, dried crocodiles and ostrich feet.

South African Breweries' (SAB) **World of Beer** ① *15 President St, T011-836 4900, www.worldofbeer.co.za, Tue-Sat 1000-1800, R25 including 2 complimentary beers, pub lunches available 1100-1600*, will appeal to anyone who enjoys the golden nectar. SAB dominate the African beer industry and control many local breweries throughout southern and eastern Africa and now owns Miller Lite in the US. Their flagship lager, Castle, is probably now the most popular beer between Cape Town and Cairo. The 90-minute tour covers the brewing process, a greenhouse that nurtures ingredients, and a variety

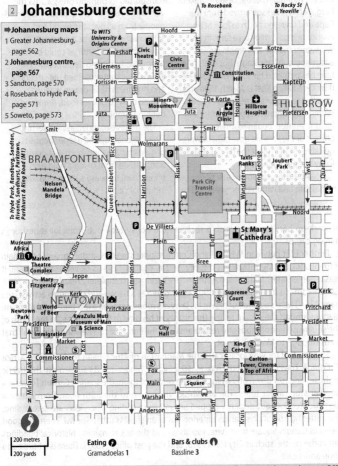

2 Johannesburg centre

➡ Johannesburg maps
1 Greater Johannesburg, page 562
2 **Johannesburg centre, page 567**
3 Sandton, page 570
4 Rosebank to Hyde Park, page 571
5 Soweto, page 573

200 metres
200 yards

Eating 🍴
Gramadoelas 1

Bars & clubs 🍸
Bassline 3

City of gold

The high plateau on which Johannesburg was built was originally an arid place inhabited by a few Boer farmers grazing cattle and cultivating maize and wheat. This harsh and isolated landscape was transformed after the discovery of gold in 1886. During the 1880s, prospectors began arriving in the Eastern Transvaal attracted by reports of gold in Barberton and the mountains of the Eastern Drakensberg. George Harrison arrived from the Cape and travelled north to look at an abandoned gold mine on a farm in the Witwatersrand. He was employed to build a farmhouse at Langlaagte but in his free time he continued his search for gold. He discovered Main Reef in March 1886 and travelled to Pretoria to register his claim. Within weeks hordes of prospectors and fortune hunters began to arrive and officials of the Pretoria government were quickly sent to inspect the diggings and to lay out plans for a town.

Johannesburg expanded at a phenomenal rate and within three years had become the largest town in the eastern Transvaal. Confidence in Johannesburg's future was so great that traders in other regions of South Africa dismantled their wood and corrugated-iron buildings and transported the component parts to reassemble them in the new boom town. *The Star* newspaper relocated to Johannesburg from Grahamstown and transported its printing press across the veld by ox wagon. The gold rush attracted people from all over the world and Johannesburg became a cosmopolitan town where vast fortunes could be made overnight. Gambling dens, brothels and riotous canteens lined the streets and hundreds of ox-drawn wagons arrived daily to deliver food, drink and building supplies.

The mines expanded as new technologies opened up the deeper deposits of gold and Johannesburg was gradually transformed from being a gold rush boom town to being a large modern industrial city.

---

of mock-up bars from a township *shebeen* to a honky-tonk pub from Johannesburg's mining camps.

Further east between Marshall and Commissioner streets, Gandhi Square is the main terminus for the Metrobuses in the city centre. Built in 1893 as Government Square, it was renamed after Mahatma Gandhi in 1999 and was completely refurbished in 2002. Gandhi came to Johannesburg in 1902 and worked as a lawyer and civil rights activist (see page 476). There's a statue of him in his lawyer's robes, carrying a law book, and there are plaques around the square telling the history of his time in South Africa. To the south of the square is a line of shops and restaurants and the entrance to a new shopping mall that leads through to Marshall Street.

To get a feel for why locals call it the Manhattan of Africa, head to the **Top of Africa** ⓘ *Carlton Tower, daily 0900-1700, R7.50, children (under 12) R3.50*. Amidst the hectic highrises and run-down office blocks in the centre of town, the soaring Carlton Tower is a popular stop-off for tours. The lift whisks visitors up to the 50th floor, from where a glass-fronted lookout deck is wrapped around the building. The views are astounding, the glittering grid of skyscrapers tapering out to an endless urban sprawl. There are good views of Gandhi Square from here, too, as well as the few remaining historical buildings left in the centre, such as City Hall (1915) and the post office (1897). There is a little curio shop and a café.

Constitution Hill ① *1 Kotze St, Braamfontein, T011-381 3100, www.constitutionhill. org.za, Mon-Fri 0900-1700, Sat 1000-1500, R22, children (under 16) R15, the complex is completely wheelchair accessible*, is the site of the notorious Old Fort Prison Complex (to the north of the centre). Opened in 2004, this is one of Johannesburg's newest tourist attractions and, in a similar way to the Apartheid Museum, it uses multimedia tools to display its exhibits. Known as Number Four, the old prison, which only closed in the 1980s, was known for holding hundreds of blacks in appalling overcrowded conditions; most had been arrested for not carrying their pass books. Illustrious prisoners include Nelson Mandela, Mahatma Gandhi and many of the leading anti-Apartheid activists. You can wander around the complex yourself or there are regular tours, which include a video about Mandela's time here, a tour of the women's gaol and a photo exhibition of ex-inmates and wardens. You can still see graffiti on the backs of the cell doors and the giant pots that prisoners ate simple porridge from. South Africa's Constitutional Court has recently been built here and some of the bricks from the old prison were used in the new court to demonstrate the injustice of the past being used towards justice in the future. The site is seen as an important symbol of the changes that the country has witnessed since 1994, and it's another of the city's excellent contemporary museums.

Not far from Constitution Hill at the top of Rissik Street, is the Miner's Monument. The bronze statue of three giant miners in shorts, hard hats and gum boots holding a giant drill was erected by the Chamber of Mines in 1964. The Civic Theatre is just to the north of here (see page 584).

Outside the city centre

Apartheid Museum ① *next to Gold Reef City, T011-390 4700, www.apartheidmuseum.org, Tue-Sun 1000-1700, entry R30, children (under 16) R15.* Twenty years ago, few people would have believed that a museum about Apartheid could ever exist. Today, this is the most critically acclaimed museum in the country and an excellent insight to what South Africa – past and present – is all about. This extraordinarily powerful museum was officially opened by Nelson Mandela in April 2002 and is the city's leading tourist attraction. The museum is divided into 'spaces' which follow the birth of Apartheid to the present day. When paying your entry fee you are issued with a random white or non-white ticket that takes you through two different entry points to symbolize segregation. The building itself has an innovative design to reflect the cold subject of Apartheid – harsh concrete, raw brick, steel bars and barbed wire.

The museum begins with a 15-minute video, taking you briefly through Voortrekker history to the Afrikaner government of 1948 which implemented Apartheid. The 'spaces' are dedicated to the rise of nationalism in 1948, pass laws, segregation, the first response from townships such as Sharpeville and Langa, the forced removals and the implementation of the Group Areas Act. From here, exhibits cover the rise of Black Consciousness, the student uprisings in Soweto in 1976, and political prisoners and executions.

The reforms during the 1980s and 1990s are well documented, including President FW DeKlerk's un-banning of political parties, Mandela's release, the 1994 election, sanction lifting, and the new constitution. One of the most interesting 'spaces' is the House of Bondage, named after a book of photographs published in 1967 by Ernest Cole and banned in South Africa at the time. A white photographer, he managed to class himself as coloured in order to go into the townships and take the pictures. The black and white photographs are both tragic and beautiful. The exhibitions effectively use multimedia, such as television screens, recorded interviews and news footage, all providing a startlingly clear picture of the harshness and tragedy of the Apartheid years. Allow at least three or four hours for a visit.

The **Johannesburg Zoo** ⓘ *Jan Smuts Av, Parktown, T011-646 2000, www.jhbzoo.org.za, daily 0830-1730, last ticket 1600, R38, children (3-12) R22*, has over 400 different species of bird and animal set in an area of parkland and gardens. Covering 54 ha of spacious enclosures surrounded by moats and trees, the zoo is home to over 2000 animals from 355 species. The only polar bears in Africa can be found in the zoo. The ponds attract free-ranging aquatic birds, which come here to breed. All the enclosures have been upgraded and the night tours to see the nocturnal animals are fun, ending with marshmallows and hot chocolate around a bonfire. There is a small restaurant here for light meals and drinks.

Near the Johannesburg Zoo is the **South African National Museum of Military History** ⓘ *20 Erlswold Way, Saxonwold, T011-646 5513, www.militarymuseum.co.za, daily 0900-1630, R20*, which has exhibits on the role South African forces played in the Second World War, including artillery pieces, aircraft and tanks. There is a more up-to-date section illustrating the war in Angola with displays of modern armaments, including captured Soviet tanks and French Mirage fighter planes. CASSPIRS, the armoured personnel carriers used by security forces in the townships during black uprisings against Apartheid are on display.

3 Sandton

Johannesburg maps
1 Greater Johannesburg, page 562
2 Johannesburg centre, page 567
3 Sandton, page 570
4 Rosebank to Hyde Park, page 571
5 Soweto, page 573

500 metres
500 yards

Sleeping
Michelangelo 1
Quatermain Inn 3
Sandton Hilton 2
Tladi Lodge 4

Eating
Browns of Rivonia 4
Bukhara 3
Butcher Shop & Grill 2
Linger Longer 8
Pappas on the Square 5
Piatto Mediterranean
Kitchen 6
Sheikh's Palace 7

Bars & clubs
Blues Room 1

To Sandton

3

To 6 & Randberg

HYDE PARK

ILLOVO

Hyde La

Magaliesig

11

6th

Hyde Park
Mall

CRAIGHALL

Morsim

4th

Tweedale

Rivona

Melville

Illovo
Square
Mall

8

Central

2nd

3rd

Upfill

Harries

Illovo
Square
Mall

Curzon

Rullin

Hyde
Square Mall

North

8

Jan Smuts

North

4

Dunkeld
West Mall

Bompas

Kent

Oxford

Chaplin

Otto

Wanderer's
Cricket
Stadium

WANDERERS

PARKHURST

Hume

Pirie

Christopherson

Winston

Hurlingham

Fricker

Corlett

Northumberland

Smits

Bompas

Kent

Hume

Cradock

2

Sports
Club

Eastwood

Christopherson

Smits

Gautrain

Oxford

North

To 2 Melrose Arch, M1 & Pretoria

12th Av

Eastwood

Rosebank

DUNKELD

Reform

St Andrew

Arran

Bute

Melville

18 17 16

Jan Smuts

Keyes

Barh

Victoria

Greenacres

To 2
m

12th Av East

Jellicoe

Tyrwhitt

3 7 9 14 15 16

8th Av

Jellicoe

Library

The Firs

MELROSE

Avenue

Wingfield

PARKTOWN
NORTH

2nd Av

7th Av

Biermann
Mall

1 6 5

10

Mall of Rosebank &
African Craft Market

Rosebank
(Gautrain)

Rosebank
Mews Mall

Tottenham

Jameson

Melrose

Cecil

To 13

6th
Av

Tyrwhitt

Rosebank
Clinic

Keyes

Sturdee

Bath

ROSEBANK

Oxford

9th St

To Houghton
& Hillbrow

5th Av

Walters

Keyes

Sturdee

Bath

Baker

Shopping
Mall &
Cinema

Arnold

Torquay

Sussex

Bolton

Selby

Ashford

To 4 Parktown
M1 & City Centre

To Hillbrow & City Centre

➡ Johannesburg maps

N

200 metres
200 yards

Sleeping
Backpackers Ritz 8
Grace 1
Melrose Arch 3
Protea Wanderers 2
Saxon 6
Sunnyside Park 4

Eating
Benkei 8
Cranks 1

Fourno's Bakery 4
Grillhouse 5
Melville Grill 7
Moyo 2
Nino's 6
Osteria Tre Nonni 14
Primi Piatti 10
Soi 9
Willoughby & Co 11
Wombles 3

Bars & clubs
Catz Pyjamas 12
Cool Runnings 13
Jolly Roger 15
Ratz 17
Roxy's Rhythm Bar 18
Xai Xai 16

Origins Centre ⓘ *Wits University, Braamfontein, can be accessed from both Bertha St and Yale Rd on the east and west of the university respectively, T011-717 4700, www. origins.org.za, daily 0900-1700, R60, children (under 12) R35, audio guides in several languages included in the entry fee*, is another of Johannesburg's excellent new attractions which was opened in 2006 by President Mbeki. Wits's Rock Art Research Institute has over the last few decades been very much involved in the archaeological sites to the northwest of the city in the Cradle of Humankind (see page 576) and all the guides at the centre are required to complete a course with the institute. The museum covers archaeological and genetic materials relating to the origins of humankind. There are displays of tools made by early man that show how they were made, as well as their spiritual significance. There are also examples of South Africa's ancient rock paintings and engravings, and their supposed meanings, with a large part of the display dedicated to the beliefs of the San (Bushmen), which the centre claims to be the planet's oldest inhabitants. There's a film of the San retreating into their spiritual world through trance which is both vivid and a little disturbing. The final exhibit focuses on how genetic testing can contribute to understanding our ancestry and visitors can add their own DNA to a world database. There's a café and good shop selling books and DVDs and crafts.

Gold Reef City ⓘ *Northern Parkway, Ormonde, T011-248 6800, www.goldreefcity.co.za, Tue-Sun 0930-1700, Story of Jozi, R180, children (under 6) R140 (excludes mine tour), theme park rides, R120, family combination tickets available, casino open 24 hrs*, is built on the site of one of Johannesburg's gold mining areas, but today has developed into a garish theme park with rides, amusement arcades and a gaudy casino. Of greater interest is the Story of Jozi tour, which takes you around the original miners' cottages, and includes a gold-pouring demonstration and the tour of the gold mine. The tour drops to a depth of about 220 m, taking you down No 14 Shaft, one of the richest deposits of gold in its day.

Opened in 2008 as a museum, **Liliesleaf Farm** ⓘ *7 George Av, Rivonia, T011-803 7882, www.liliesleaf.co.za, 0800-1800, R95*, is where in the 1960s the most prominent leaders of South Africa's struggle from the then banned ANC and Communist Party sought shelter and attended meetings. These included Nelson Mandela, Govan Mbeki and Walter Sisulu among many others. Although today it's surrounded by Johannesburg's northern suburbs, it was once an isolated rural spot and the farm was actually bought by the Communist party and fronted by 'white owners', Arthur Goldreich, a member of the Communist Party, and his family. On 11 July 1963, a meeting was held by Umkhonto we Sizwe or the MK (meaning 'spear of the nation' and the ANC's armed wing) to discuss Operation Mayibuye, a plot to overthrow the apartheid government. However, the police has been tipped off that Walter Sisulu was at the farm and it was raided, and Sisulu and just about the entire leadership of the MK were arrested (Mandela had been arrested six months earlier in KwaZulu Natal). This led to what became known as the Rivonia Trials in late 1963, and the subsequent imprisonment of the ANC's leaders. Today you can walk around the farm, where there are exhibits in the main house and outbuildings, and watch a short film.

Northern suburbs

The hills to the north of the city centre are criss-crossed by wide avenues, lined with posh shopping malls and large houses with well-tended gardens. Here, homes are surrounded by high walls, topped with razor wire and guarded by dogs and armed response units. **Rosebank**, a few kilometres north of the city, and **Sandton**, further north off the M1 to Tshwane (Pretoria), are the most popular areas. To the east of Rosebank are the fashionable suburbs of **Melville**, one of the few places in Johannesburg with a street restaurant and bar scene, as well as **Parkhurst** and **Parktown**.

Soweto

ⓘ *It's recommended you only visit Soweto on a guided tour, see Activities and tours, page 586.*

The most popular excursion from Johannesburg is to the (in)famous township of Soweto, lying 13 km southwest of Johannesburg city centre. Soweto has mushroomed into a city in its own right, it covers 135 sq km and is home to around one million people. Short for South West Township, people first moved here in 1904 from Sophiatown where there was an outbreak of plague. The township increased in size dramatically in the 1950s and 1960s when black peoples were forced to relocate from the city centre into designated areas outside the city. Since then, the population has soared, bolstered by immigrants from rural areas, as well as from Nigeria, Mozambique, Zimbabwe and other African countries.

Despite its reputation, Soweto feels remarkably ordinary. Large areas are given over to tidy rows of affluent suburban houses. Like in any other South African city, there are districts and suburbs and shopping centres. The streets are well maintained, there are banks and golf courses and the giant FNB Soccer City, which is currently going under an overhaul for the 2010 FIFA World Cup™. Yellow commuter trains trundle to Johannesburg and Mercedes cruise between smart homes with well-tended gardens and satellite dishes. Soweto allegedly has the highest concentration of millionaires in the country and one of the most successful BMW dealerships, and in 2007, one of Johannesburg's largest shopping malls, **Maponya Mall**, opened on Old Potchefstroom Road. The flip-side however, much like in any other city in the country, is that there are also still areas of squatter camps and informal housing, where unemployment is as high as 90% and people have to share amenities like taps and toilets. The government is constantly trying to improve the situation by building two-room rudimentary houses to replace the shacks,

5 **Soweto**

➡ **Johannesburg maps**
1 Greater Johannesburg, page 562
2 Johannesburg centre, page 567
3 Sandton, page 570
4 Rosebank to Hyde Park, page 571
5 Soweto, page 573

Eating 🍴
Wandie's 1

but efforts are hampered by the thousands of people who flood into Soweto every month, fleeing rural poverty and desperate for jobs.

Most tours of Soweto take in a handful of important historical sites. The **Soweto Tourism Information office (STIC)** ① *T011-945 3111, www.sowetotourism.com*, is located in the Walter Sisulu Square of Independence (www.waltersisulusquare.co.za) in Kliptown. This square is at the site where the Freedom Charter, calling for equality for all, was presented by the ANC to a mass gathering of people in 1955. The square, which used to be called Freedom Square, was renamed after one of the delegates, Walter Sisulu, when he died in 2003. The authorities broke up the illegal gathering but the charter was adopted as a guiding document, and it remains the cornerstone of ANC policy to this day and is seen by many as the foundation of South Africa's 1996 Constitution. Back in 1955 it was just a dusty patch of land, but since 2003 it has been redeveloped as a tourist attraction and is now an attractive paved square housing a number of monuments. These include the 10 Pillars of the Freedom Charter; 10 giant slabs of concrete representing the clauses of the Freedom Charter, and the red-brick conical Freedom Charter Monument.

The **Baragwanath Hospital**, which claims to be the largest hospital in the world, with over 5000 beds and 20,000 employees is usually the first sight to be pointed out on a tour of Soweto. It is estimated that half of Soweto's residents were born here and it also attracts unfortunate attention for its large proportion of AIDS patients and victims of street violence. All tours take in the excellent **Hector Pieterson Museum** ① *Khumalo and Pela streets, Orlando West, T011-536 2253, Mon-Sat 1000-1700, Sun 1000-1600, R15, children (under 16) R5.* This modern museum stands two blocks away from where 13-year-old Hector Pierterson was shot dead by riot police during a school demonstration on 16 June 1976. The children had been demonstrating about the use of Afrikaans as the dominant language in education, before the police opened fire and killed more than 170 students. This event, captured on camera in an image that shocked the world, sparked the final 10-year battle against Apartheid causing townships across the country to rise up in bitter revolt. (The incident is now known as the Soweto Uprising and the 16 June is a public holiday, Youth Day.) Outside the museum is a memorial to Hector, marked by the iconic image of his body being carried by a friend with Hector's wailing 17-year-old sister running alongside. The photograph was taken by journalist Sam Nzima who said at the time, "I saw a child fall down. Under a shower of bullets I rushed forward and went for the picture. It had been a peaceful march, the children were told to disperse, they started singing Nkosi Sikelele. The police were ordered to shoot." Nkosi Sikelele is now South Africa's National Anthem. The inscription on the monument reads 'To honour the youth who gave their lives in the struggle for democracy and freedom'. Each slab of slate in it represents a child that died needlessly on that fateful day and the water feature is symbolic of children's tears. Inside, this incredibly moving and powerful museum is similar to the Apartheid Museum, in that it uses multimedia exhibits, films, newspapers, personal accounts and photographs to piece together what happened on and around that date. One of the tour guides is Antoinette Sithole – Hector's sister who was in the photograph. There is an excellent museum bookshop with dozens of interesting books on South Africa.

Mandela House Museum ① *8115 Vilakazi St, Orlando West, T011-936 7754, www.mandelahouse.co.za, Mon-Sat 0930-1700, R60, South African residents R40, children (under 16) R20.* A short walk from the Hector Pieterson Museum is Nelson Mandela's house, where he lived before he was incarcerated. He moved into the diminutive three-roomed house in 1946 with his first wife, Evelyn Mase, and in 1958 brought his second wife, Winnie, to live with him. Mandela insisted on moving back to the house on his release from prison in 1990. He said in Long Walk to Freedom: "It was only then that I knew in my heart that I had left prison." But eventually its small size and the difficulty of keeping it secure put too much of a strain on him and he moved out of the township to a larger house in Houghton. It was opened as a museum by Winnie in 1997 and for many years displayed an odd collection of Mandela's personal effects like his shoes and his furry bedspread, but it's now in the hands of the Soweto Heritage Trust who refurbished it in 2008. It has now been transformed into what it would have looked like in the 1950s – bare concrete floors and a corrugated tin roof and it displays information about his time in the house. There's also a visitor's centre. Further down the road is the home of Archbishop Desmond Tutu, hidden behind high walls. **Vilakazi Street** is the only street in the world to have been home to two Nobel Peace Prize winners, Nelson Mandela and Desmond Tutu.

Also worth visiting is **Regina Mundi**, to the southwest, off Potchesfstroom Street, the largest church in Soweto, and an important site of demonstrations in the 1980s. You can still see bullet holes in the ceiling, a lasting testament to shots fired by police. Old photos of government attacks are pasted outside, and, if you're lucky, you'll catch the choir practising inside.

Finally, Soweto's newest attractions are, oddly, the two 100-m-high **Orlando cooling towers** off Old Potchefstroom Road. They have long been a landmark and are part of a now-disused power station that was built in the 1950s to provide central Johannesburg with electricity (even though Soweto didn't get electricity until 1986). In 2003, the First National Bank (FNB) sponsored the painting of the towers. One is painted in the FNB's logo with 'How can we help?' on one side and 'Proudly South African' on another, and the second tower is painted in a fantastic vivid mural of life in Soweto, with cartoon characters of musicians, children playing, a woman selling her wares on a stall, minibus taxis, a metrorail train, and of course a figure of a smiling and waving Nelson Mandela in one of his trademark African print shirts. The area around the cooling towers is now earmarked for development for housing, and the power station itself is to become a retail and entertainment centre in the future. For now, the real reason to come to the cooling towers is **Orlando Towers Adventure Centre** (see Activities and tours, page 585), which opened mid-2008. They have built a lift on one of the towers, a viewing platform on top and now offer bungee jumping and swings inside (a world first), power swings and zip liners run between the towers.

Around Johannesburg

Lesedi Cultural Village ⓘ *on the R512, 12 km north of Lanseria Airport, T012-205 1394, www.lesedi.com, tours at 1130 and 1630, R360 per person including lunch or dinner, or R220 excluding lunch or dinner, children (6-12) ½-price, (under 5) free,* is an easy day-trip from Johannesburg or Tshwane (Pretoria). Four African villages have been recreated from the Xhosa, Zulu, Pedi, and Sotho tribes and there are two tours daily (each lasting three hours). These include an audio-visual presentation on all aspects of tribal life of the 11 ethnic groups that live in South Africa, as well as music, singing and traditional dancing from over 60 performers around a large fire in an amphitheatre. The morning tour concludes with lunch, and the afternoon tour finishes with dinner of game meat such as impala or crocodile. Lesedi is the Sotho word for 'light'. For those who wish to extend the experience, there is mid-range accommodation in traditional bomas or rondavels decorated with Ndebele crafts.

The **Lion Park** ⓘ *30-min drive from Johannesburg on the Old Tshwane (Pretoria)– Krugersdorp road, T011-691 9905, www.lion-park.com, Mon-Fri 0830-1700, Sat-Sun 0830-1800, R100, children (4-12) R70, restaurant and curio shop,* en route to Lesedi (see above), is worth a stop for the excellent photo opportunities. There are over 80 lions in the park, including many cubs and a rare pride of white lions. Although they are bred in captivity, they are well cared for and have ample room in the drive-through enclosures. The lions are accustomed to vehicles and don't think twice about strolling right up to a car. Keep windows at least half closed. Other animals kept here include hyenas, cheetah and a variety of antelope and you can climb a tower to feed giraffes. Walks and close encounters with cubs are on offer.

Approximately 40 km to the northwest of Johannesburg is a region dubbed the **Cradle of Humankind** ① *www.cradleofhumankind.co.za*, thanks to thousands of humanoid and animal fossils being unearthed over recent decades. It holds some of the world's most important archaeological sites, revealing over 40% of all hominid fossils ever discovered and rivals Tanzania's Olduvai Gorge in significance. The 470 sq km area was declared a UNESCO World Heritage Site in 1999.

Maropeng ① *7 km from the Sterkfontein Caves (see below) on the R24, T014-577 9000, www.maropeng.co.za, 0900-1700, last boat ride 1600, R95, children (4-14) R55, combination tickets with Sterkfontein Caves R150, children (4-14) R90*, meaning 'returning to the place of origin' in the setswana language, is an interactive museum that tells the story of the creation of our world and the evolution of man over a four billion-year period. Opened by President Mbeki in 2005, it's another of Johannesburg's excellent new cutting-edge museums that uses computer wizardry and multimedia displays. The entrance has been built as a grassy burial mound, while the exit is a sleek structure of modern glass and concrete and the journey from one to the other takes the visitor from the birth of planet earth to where we are today. The first experience is a boat ride through a tunnel of erupting volcanoes, icebergs, an eye of a storm and swirling gases that made up the planet. It's rather magical and the sounds and temperatures are lifelike, but be warned that it may frighten very small children. Once off the boat the series of exhibits start from how the earth was formed, early life forms and the emergence of man, and go through to cover topics on how man has changed the environment, such as population explosion, use of the earth's resources and global appetite. Towards the end is a large display of photographs of people's faces from all over the world and a mesmerizing series of images of man's achievements are flashed on a giant screen, covering everything from man inventing the wheel to landing on the moon. Allow at least two to three hours for the experience and there are three restaurants on site.

Although the dolomite hill holding the **Sterkfontein Caves** ① *off the N14 from Randburg towards Hartbeetspoort Dam, T014-577 9000, www.maropeng.co.za, 0900-1700, guided tours run every 30 mins, last tour 1600, R95, children (4-14) R55, combination tickets with Maropeng R150, children (4-14) R90*, was discovered in the late 19th century, it was not until 1936 that the most important find was made, the first adult skull of the ape-man Australopithecus africanus – 'Mrs Ples' for short. The skull is estimated to be over 2.6 million years old, and was found by Dr Robert Broom. Even older hominid remains have been found here since. The caves consist of six chambers connected by passages. Tours begin in the impressive multimedia visitor centre, which includes comprehensive exhibitions on our ancestors, with displays of life-sized hominid replicas and a large amphitheatre. Tours then pass through the six caves, taking in the archaeological sites. There is a craft market and a choice of restaurants on site. **Note** Wear comfortable shoes and be prepared for a lot of stairs.

The **Walter Sisulu Botanical Gardens** ① *30-min drive from the city centre on the banks of the Emmarentia Dam in Roodepoort, take the Beyers Naude exit off the N1 and follow the R564, T011-958 1750, www.sanbi.org, daily 0800-1700, exit closes 1800, R23, children (6-16)*

R13, restaurant, are a pleasant place to visit for a quiet stroll away from the bustle of the city. The gardens are planted with oaks, cherry trees and a mixture of exotic and indigenous plants. The nursery, with over 2500 species of succulents, is a fascinating area and the nearby ponds attract birds, including yellowbilled ducks, Egyptian geese and crested grebes. The only pair of nesting black eagles in urban Johannesburg can be seen on the rock face near the waterfall.

◉ Johannesburg listings

Hotel and guesthouse prices

L over R2550	AL R1871-2550	A R1271-1870	
B R851-1270	C R641-850	D R301-640	
E R131-300	F under R130		

Restaurant prices

₩₩₩ over R260   ₩₩ R131-260   ₩ under R130
See pages 46-53 for further information.

◉ Sleeping

Most of the city's best hotels are in the safe areas of Sandton, Rosebank, Parkhurst and Melville. Accommodation tends to be pricey; there's a wide selection of luxury hotels, but little in the lower price bracket other than the odd hostel. Alternatively, there are mid-range options from the City Lodge Group and there are dozens of **City Lodges**, **Road Lodges** and **Town Lodges** all over Johannesburg; www.citylodge.co.za. These are all identical, purpose-built, modern, functional blocks with comfortable rooms TV and internet and car parks in the **C-D** range. They hardly need individual descriptions. Check out the website for locations, and if you can't get a room at your first choice the staff at each will try and get you into the nearest one.

Township B&Bs are mushrooming in Soweto and many have opened their doors near to the sights in Orlando West. Visit the website of the **Soweto Bed & Breakfast Association**, www.sowetobedandbreakfast.co.za. Most are spare double rooms in people's houses where you are likely to become friendly with the hosts.

Near the airport

There are several airport hotels within a few kilometres, all providing free pickups. The closest are:

A Airport Sun Intercontinental, T011-961 5400, www.southernsun.com. This smart 5-star hotel is conveniently located directly opposite the terminal buildings. You can push your trolley from the airport into your room, there's flight arrival and departure TV information throughout the hotel. Gym and beauty salon available for passengers on long waits between flights. The other Southern Sun hotels within walking distance of the airport are the **Southern Sun OR Tambo International Airport (B)** and the **Garden Court OR Tambo International Airport (B)**.
B City Lodge, Sandvale Rd, Edenvale, T011-392 1750, www.citylodge.co.za. Modern, well-run hotel for the business traveller. Restaurant, pool, 4 km from the airport. There are also the slightly cheaper **Road Lodge** and **Town Lodge** within striking distance of the airport in Germiston. All offer airport pickups.
C-D Africa Centre, 65 Sunny Rd, Lakefield-Benoni, T011-894 4857, www.africacentre lodge.co.za. A well run set-up only 15 mins' drive from the airport with modern double, single and family/group triple or quad rooms, shared kitchen, meals available, garden with pool, sauna and jacuzzi, Wi-Fi, travel services and free airport pick-up.
D-E Purple Palms Travel Lodge, 1 Boom-pieper Av, Birch Acres, Kempton Park, T011-393 4393, www.purplepalms.co.za. Owned by the same couple as **North South Backpackers** in Tshwane (Pretoria), this lodge is 10 km from the airport and offers free airport shuttles, as well as free shuttles to North South and is a Baz Bus stop. Dorms, doubles and twin rooms, bar area, swimming pool, lapa area, kitchen and meals available. Well run with a good travel centre.

E-F Airport Backpackers, 3 Mohawk St, Rhodesfield, Kempton Park, T011-394 0485, www.airportbackpackers.co.za. Only 2 km from the airport close to the end of the runway, so planes fly low overhead. Dorms, double rooms and camping. Internet, swimming pool, free airport pickup and drop-off, free basic breakfast. **Festival Mall** nearby, but little else to do in area.

Northern suburbs *p572, maps p570 and p571*

L Melrose Arch, Melrose Arch, T011-214 6666, www.africanpridehotels.com. A trendy addition to the northern suburbs, with stylish rooms, lots of chrome, bare-brick walls and flat-screen TVs, mood-enhancing lighting, designer furniture. Smart bar and superb **March Restaurant** for gourmet food. Overlooks the attractive square in the Melrose Arch gated development, and its many upmarket shops and restaurants are just a safe stroll away.

L The Michelangelo, 135 West St, Nelson Mandela Sq, T011-282 7000, www.legacyhotels.co.za. 242 super-luxury rooms, including a variety of giant suites, residents' lounge, restaurants, bar, heated swimming pool, fitness centre. One of the best luxury options of Sandton, which has contributed to the area becoming one of the smartest centres of Johannesburg. Plenty of restaurants and shops in the lovely Nelson Mandela Sq.

L Saxon, 36 Saxon Rd, Sandhurst, T011-292 6000, www.thesaxon.com. Voted the 'World's Leading Boutique Hotel' every year since it opened in 2000. 26 suites including one named after Nelson Mandela, who spent 7 months here working on his book *Long Walk to Freedom*. Set in 2 ha of beautifully tended grounds, gigantic heated swimming pools, state-of-the-art gym, spa, restaurant, 2 wine cellars. Stunning but expensive by South African standards, the cheapest suite is R6400.

L-AL Westcliff, 67 Jan Smuts Av, Westcliff, near **Johannesburg Zoo**, T011-481 6000, www.westcliff.co.za. A bright pink Mediterranean-style hillside village on a 3-ha estate, with 106 a/c rooms and 14 suites, 2 heated swimming pools, flood-lit tennis court with resident coach, gym, health spa, old-fashioned charm in the cigar bar and restaurant, great views of the northern suburbs and zoo.

AL The Grace, 54 Bath Av, Rosebank, T011-280 7200, www.africansunhotels.com. Beautiful luxury hotel right next to **The Mall of Rosebank** (with a convenient sky bridge connecting to it). Large rooms spread over 9 floors, some with great city views, decorated in country-style fabrics, with pretty pale-green colour themes, dark wood and colonial prints on the walls. Excellent restaurant, popular for brunch, serving contemporary South African cuisine, plus good extras such as complimentary tea and cakes in the

afternoon. Business centre with free internet access, spa, stunning rooftop pool and efficient friendly service. Recommended.

AL Sandton Hilton, 138 Rivonia Rd, Sandton, T011-322 1888, www1.hilton.com. Big business hotel with 329 luxury rooms, including the latest Hilton feature – a separate executive floor with its own lounge-cum-club room where business folk can breakfast and snack throughout the day. 2 restaurants, bar, health club, swimming pool, tennis court, extensive conference facilities, all set in a beautiful landscaped garden, close to smart shopping malls in Sandton.

A Quatermain Inn, 137 West Rd South, Morningside, Sandton, T011-290 0900, www.quatermain.co.za. Home-from-home in the heart of Sandton, 114 spacious luxury rooms set in manicured indigenous gardens with oak trees and swimming pool, comfortable lounge, gym and bar.

B A Room with a View, 1 Tolip St, corner of 4th Av, Melville, T011-482 5435, www.aroomwithaview.co.za. As the name would suggest, beautiful views over leafy Melville from this delightful hotel. 12 rooms in 2 buildings; those in the newer building, designed to look like an Italian villa, have bare-brick walls, soaring ceilings and stylish, colourful furnishings, as well as huge beds, slate-tiled bathrooms and private balconies. Those in the older house have carved wooden bed frames and polished wooden floors. Legendary breakfasts, pleasant pool and very friendly service. Highly recommended.

B Protea Wanderers, corner of Corlett Dr and Rudd Rd, Illovo, T011-770 5500, www.proteahotels.com. Directly opposite Wanderers Cricket Stadium. Quality modern hotel, but lacking in character. 230 rooms have individual office station with faux African and sporting motifs, and sound proofing. Pleasant pool area except for the traffic noise from the busy road below.

B Sunnyside Park, Prince of Wales Terr, Parktown, T011-640 0400, www.thesunnyside.co.za. 154 rooms, restaurant, pub,

swimming pool, converted Victorian mansion declared a national monument, with new annexes set in picturesque gardens; an unusual find and close to the city. Decent restaurant. Pleasant old-fashioned atmosphere but not great service.

B Tladi Lodge, 1 David St, Sandton, T011-784 9240, www.tladilodge.co.za. Attractive and spacious 10 rooms and 2 suites with contemporary furnishings, under-floor heating, set in low thatched buildings in extensive gardens, pool, red-brick terraces, a peaceful spot with easy access to Sandton and an alternative to the big hotels.

D-F Backpackers Ritz, 1A North Rd, Dunkeld West, T011-325 7125, www.backpackers-ritz.co.za. One of Johannesburg's best-established long-running hostels. Large house in a secure neighbourhood with garden and swimming pool. Dorms, double rooms, travel desk, Soweto and city tours, internet access, individual safes plus long-term baggage storage, helpful place to start your visit. Meals available. Close to shops and entertainment at Hyde Park and Rosebank, all in a safe suburb, 30 mins from airport, free pickup, call before leaving home. Recommended.

🍴 Eating

Johannesburg p562, maps p567, p570 and p571

Many of Johannesburg's restaurants and bars are within the confines of a shopping mall. However, thanks to good architecture, in the most part you will not be aware that you are eating in a mall. This is especially true of the 14 restaurants lining Nelson Mandela Sq, which is an atmospheric place to eat out with twinkly lights in the trees and a large statue of a smiling Mandela over the outside tables. Another mall hotspot is the square at Melrose Arch off Corlett Dr in Melrose not far from the Wanderer's Cricket Stadium. This is currently the place to be seen in the evening. The best area in town for lively streetside restaurants and bars is the suburb of **Melville**, in the northern suburbs off the M1. The streets around 7th St are lined with popular bars, fashionable restaurants and kooky cafés. Most appealing is the fact that it's safe to park and wander around here, even at night. Other smaller streetside restaurant districts include the Gleneagles roundabout in Greenside, 4th Av in Parkhurst and 7th Av in Parktown North.

₦₦₦ Benkei, Ilovo Square, 3 Rivonia Rd, Ilovo, T011-268 6622. Open 1200-2300. Popular Japanese spot and considered by some as the best sushi in Johannesburg, this offers platters of tempura and sushi, traditional stir-fries, and unusual items like eel and deep fried salmon skins. There's formal seating, a sushi bar and a teppanyaki grill.

₦₦₦ Browns of Rivonia, 21 Wessels St, Rivonia, T011-803 7533, www.browns.co.za. Sun-Fri 1200-1500, Mon-Sat 1800-2230. Meals served in the courtyard of an old farm house, expensive but extensive menu includes roast lamb, salmon timbale, mustard sirloin and crêpes and you can choose your own cheese from the cheese room. Impressive wine list with some 30,000 bottles in the cellar and live jazz on Sat night.

₦₦₦ Bukhara, Nelson Mandela Sq, Sandton City, T011-883 5555, www.bukhara.com. 1200-1500, 1800-2300. Inarguably the best Indian food in the city, this elegant restaurant at the entrance of the **Michelangelo Hotel** has a broad range of aromatic and flavoursome North Indian dishes, all cooked from scratch, and you can watch the chefs in the glass-fronted kitchen.

₦₦₦ Carnivore, 69 Drift Blvd, Muldersdrift, 30 mins' drive (approx 30 km) from Johannesburg centre on the N14, some hotels and backpackers arrange transport out here, T011-957 3132. Open 1200-1600, 1800-2400. This has become something of an institution and is the ultimate 'African' eating experience. Rustic decor, zebra-skin chairs and a large central fire pit characterizes the interior. Meals consist of eat-as-much-as-you-can, with slabs of game carved off Masaai spears onto cast-iron plates. There's a choice of at least 10 different types of meat every

day, which usually includes ostrich, crocodile, warthog as well as beef and pork. If vegetarians can bear it, they actually have a good choice, including *aviyal*, a mix of vegetables cooked in spicy coconut sauce.

₦₦₦ Gramadoelas, Market Theatre Complex, Bree St, Newtown, T011-838 6960, www.gramadoelas.co.za. Tue-Sat 1200-1500, Mon-Sat 1800-2200. One of the best places to get a full overview of southern African dishes is at this long-standing favourite, set in the renovated Market Theatre Complex. The faux-ramshackle decor adds to the atmosphere, and there are tables outside in summer. Starters include fried *mopani* worms served in peri-peri sauce, and to follow you can try *sosaties* (spicy kebabs), *bobotie* (sweet and spicy ground beef pie), or a range of dishes from further afield such as Morocco or Ethiopia. A delicious desert is the sticky malva pudding, or *melktert* (milk tart). This is also the place to try home-brewed sorghum beer or *mageu* (fermented milk).

₦₦₦ Grillhouse, The Firs, Oxford Rd, Rosebank, T011-880 3945. Popular for its melt-in-the-mouth fillets and succulent sauces. Exposed brick and green leather furniture, excellent service and a lively atmosphere. Opposite and under the same ownership is **Katzy's** late night piano bar and cigar lounge, which has live music most nights. Vast selection of Cognacs and malt whiskies. You would never know you're in a shopping mall.

₦₦₦ Linger Longer, 58 Wierda Rd, Wierda Valley, Sandton, T011-884 0465. Mon-Fri lunch and dinner, Sat dinner only. One of Johannesburg's top restaurants and something of an institution – it's been going for 45 years – serving an imaginative mix of old-fashioned and contemporary cooking, from lobster bisque to Asian roast duck. Attractive homely setting.

₦₦₦ Melville Grill, corner of 3rd Av and 7th St, Melville, T011-726 2890, www.melvillegrill. com. Mon-Sat lunch and dinner. Slick, upmarket steakhouse with an interior of low lighting and wooden floors, white tablecloths and red walls. Different cuts and prices are

Jo'burg's Chinatown

Johannesburg's Chinatown is a vibey strip of neon-lit Chinese supermarkets and restaurants in a less than salubrious part of the city located on Derrick Avenue, Cyrildene, just east of Observatory. To get there you'll need to rely on a good-natured taxi driver or someone who knows Jo'burg well. From the northern suburbs it involves a drive through Hillbrow and along the notorious Rockey Street, before it turns into Observatory Street and follows through to Cyrildene. Once at Chinatown, there are car guards and vehicles are looked after safely for a tip. On each side of Derrick Street are restaurants, dumpling shops, noodle bars, teashops, Chinese greengrocers and general dealers, herbalists, beauty salons and DVD-rental shops. Walk up and down until you find a restaurant that takes your liking or one that's not already full. Most are small eateries with formica-top tables,

plastic chairs, fluorescent lights, take away counters, unbelievably kitsch decorations on the walls, and sometimes dead ducklings hanging in the window. Some only seat several people at a time whereas others have the luxury of four or five tables. Regional dishes include Szechuan, Shanghai, Hong Kong and Taiwanese; and there's sushi, Mongolian and Korean for good measure. The food is delicious and you won't get more authentic Chinese dishes elsewhere in South Africa. Few menus are written in English, and it's best to order a selection of dishes to share. Drink Chinese beer or tea, or bring your own wine. The most delightful aspect of this eating experience is the bill: hardly any of the staff speak English and they simply write the total down on the paper tablecloth or a napkin, only cash is accepted and it's ridiculously cheap. Arrive early, most kitchens close at 2100.

chalked up on the walls, and the menu includes details such as how long a cut was aged and whether the meat is free range. Simple salad starters and a couple of fish and poultry choices, followed by warm chocolate brownies. Good, unpretentious service. Recommended.

¶¶¶ **Moyo**, Melrose Sq Melrose Arch, T0861-006696, www.moyo.co.za. The original branch of the popular chain of upmarket African-themed restaurants appearing around South Africa. This outlet is in chi-chi Melrose Arch, and is spread over 3 floors, with rustic, candle-lit ethno-fashionable decor, and pan-African cuisine, including good Moroccan tagines. Live music in the evenings. There is also a branch in Zoo Lake Park near the zoo.

¶¶¶ **Osteria Tre Nonni**, 9 Grafton Av, Craighall, T011-327 0095, www.osteriatrenonni.co.za. Tue-Sun 1200-1500, Tue-Sat 1800-2200. Expensive but sophisticated north Italian cuisine, home-made pasta, fresh seafood,

best tiger prawns in the city, rich creamy sauces, reservations recommended.

¶¶ **Butcher Shop & Grill**, Nelson Mandela Sq, Sandton City Mall, T011-784 8676/7. Mon-Sat 1200-2245, Sun 1200-2145. This award-winning steakhouse is a top-quality restaurant and shouldn't be missed by meat-lovers. The Butcher Shop is famous for its aged steaks, and although there are a few outlets around the country now, this is the original and gets through 5 tons of steak each week. The menu is, obviously, focused on steak and other grills: when available, there's a specially aged T-bone which is cut to order. There's also a selection of seafood, and a good range of starters and desserts, but almost nothing for vegetarians other than a couple of salads.

¶¶ **Cranks,** Shop 162, **Rosebank Mall**, next to the African Craft Market, T011-880 3442. Open 1200-late. Delicious Vietnamese and Thai dishes are served in this eccentric Asian eatery, well situated in the popular Mall of

Rosebank. The decor is in itself worth a visit, with Barbie and Ken dolls dangling from the ceiling in compromising positions. Freshly prepared Thai, including green chicken curry and pad thai, and some spicy Vietnamese dishes. Asian beer plus Thai schnapps and soothing herbal teas. Live blues performed Sat and Sun.

Ⅶ Pappas on the Square, Nelson Mandela Sq, **Sandton City Mall**, T011-884 9991. Open 0930-2330. Authentic Greek themed restaurant with plate breaking, Greek wine and a fun atmosphere, the chef once cooked for Christina Onassis. Share a mezze or try the *kleftiko* (lamb shank). One of the many restaurants overlooking the square.

Ⅶ Primi Piatti, Upper Level, The Zone, **The Mall of Rosebank**, T011-447 0300; Melrose Sq, Melrose Arch, T011-684 1648, www.primi-world.com. Stylish Italian chain found in 9 locations, though the hippest are at Rosebank and Melrose Arch, with colourful, industrial-style decor and lively staff. Huge portions of imaginative pasta, excellent wood-fired pizzas and big salads. **Primi Studio**, attached, is a lounge bar with big comfy sofas and music, perfect for relaxing after a meal.

Ⅶ Sheikh's Palace, corner of Ninth Av and Rivonia Rd, Sandton, T011-807 4119, www.sheikspalace.co.za. 1100-late. Very authentic Lebanese restaurant with belly dancers in the evening and hubbly bubbly pipes, serving great lamb dishes and mixed grills, plus interesting and varied mezze selections which are ideal to share.

Ⅶ Soi, corner of 7th and 3rd Av, Melville, T011-726 5775. Open 1200-1415, 1800-2200. Excellent Thai and Vietnamese cuisine in this low-lit restaurant. Wide selection of curries, pad thai noodles and interesting dishes like 'angry duck' – perfect for those with fiery tastes. Fashionable, friendly serving staff, stylish, understated decor and a chatty crowd make this one of the best places on the Melville drag. Recommended.

Ⅶ Wandie's, 618 Makhalamele St, Dube, Soweto, T011-982 2796, www.wandies. co.za. 1100-2200. The affable Wandie Ndala

significantly contributed to tourism in Soweto when he opened this restaurant in 1991 and today more than 100 tourists visit a day as part of Soweto tours. Traditional township food like chicken, oxtail and mutton stews, pap (mealie porridge), rice and dumplings is served buffet style and sociable eating is at long tables.

Ⅶ Willoughby & Co, **Hyde Park Mall**, Jan Smuts Av, Hyde Park T011-325 5107. Mon 1130-1500, Tue-Sat 1130-2200. Pick out fish from the chilled cabinets and have it cooked in a variety of ways, or choose the reliably good sushi, prawns and calamari from the à la carte menu. Popular with the 'ladies who lunch' in this glitzy mall.

Ⅶ Wombles, 17 3rd St, Parktown North, T011-880 2470, www.wombles.co.za. Mon-Fri 1200-1500, Mon-Sat 1830-2200. Wombles has been going for nearly 25 years – first in Zimbabwe, then in Australia and now in Johannesburg, and has fast gained an excellent reputation for its matured steaks. The setting is attractive colonial style, with dark wood tables, high-backed chairs and white linen table cloths. It's a simple menu, with traditional starters like grilled mushrooms or chicken liver salad, followed by a choice of cuts and sauces. There's also a fair choice of poultry, fish and even a couple of vegetarian dishes. Service is friendly and relaxed.

Ⅶ-Ⅰ Piatto Mediterranean Kitchen, Nelson Mandela Sq, **Sandton City Mall**, T011-784 2510, www.piatto.co.za. Mon-Fri 1030-2300, Sat-Sun 0930-2300. Another popular restaurant with tables in the square, offering a long menu of pastas, pizzas, wraps, crunchy salads, and decadent desserts like warm chocolate parcels or Italian kisses. There's a cheap kid's menu. More expensive mains include seafood and grills.

Cafés
Fourno's Bakery, Dunkeld West Centre, Jan Smuts Av, T011-325 2110, www.fournos.co.za. Mon-Fri 0700-1800, Sat-Sun 0700-1400. Cheap eats with a number of branches around the city. The bakers work through the night to provide a huge range of fresh

pastries, cakes, croissants, quiches and pies. Big breakfasts, coffee, simple lunches, very popular at the weekend.

Nino's, 22 Cradock Av, Rosebank, T011-447 4758, www.ninos.co.za. 0700-1800. Branch of this popular café with a large, open, street-side eating area, reasonably priced coffee and build-your-own panini sandwich bar, opposite the **Rosebank Craft Market**. A good place to start the day with a fat 3-egg omelette.

⟁ Bars and clubs

Johannesburg *p562, maps p567, p570 and p571*
Entertainment listings are published in the weekly *Mail and Guardian*, with a 'Gig of the Week' review and online listings can be found at www.theguide.co.za and www.tonight.co.za.

Bassline, 10 Henry Nxumalo St, Newtown, T011-838 9145, www.bassline.co.za. Established and popular South African jazz venue set in Newtown's old red-brick Music Hall. Has a capacity of 1000 and regularly hosts South Africa's top jazz, hip-hop and kwaito artists. Tickets through Computicket, www.computicket.com. Cover charge varies. Outside is a lovely statue of a soulful bare-footed singer leaning into a microphone. You can sit on the seat next to her for a photo.

Blues Room, Village Walk, Sandton, T011-784 5527, www.bluesroom.co.za. Tue-Sat 1900-late. One of the best jazz and blues venues in Gauteng, this is a stylish basement bar and restaurant, catering to music lovers who are after a decent meal. There's live music every night and the pace picks up later on when diners take to the floor for a dance.

Catz Pyjamas, corner of 3rd and Main streets, Melville, T011-726 8596, www.catzpyjamas. co.za. Jo'burg's original 24-hr bistro and cocktail bar, rather shabby these days but with a funky atmosphere and reasonable food. It's open throughout the day but the atmosphere really only picks up late in the

evening, carrying on until the early hours. There's occasional live music and comedy.

Cool Runnings, 27a, 4th Av, Melville, T011-482 4786. Sun-Thu 1100-0200, Fri-Sat 1100-0400. The popular Jamaican-themed chain of bars/clubs comes into its own at this Melville branch, which is one of the most popular bars around. There's loud music every night, when a young crowd gathers to work its way through the extensive cocktail list. There are occasional drumming sessions held in the bar.

Jolly Roger, 10, 4th Av, Parkhurst, T011-442 3954. Open 1200-late. Landmark pub on the main stretch in popular Parkhurst, with an excellent balcony perfect for watching the area's stylish locals swan up and down 4th Av. Good draught beer and pizza specials, plus live music at weekends.

Monsoon Lagoon, Emperor's Palace Casino, Jones Rd, next to the airport, T011-928 1000, www.monsoonlagoon.co.za. Wed-Sat 2100-late, R40-70. One of Jo'burg's biggest and brashest clubs is this huge special events venue, regularly hosting TV and fashion parties. It's an upmarket mainstream club (over 23s only) covering several floors with a number of dance floors, bars and lounges. It's lavish and totally over the top – great for a big night out.

Ratz, 7th St, Melville, T011-726 2019, www.ratzbar.co.za, 1700-late. Friendly drinking hole with a couple of sofas and high tables dotted around in front of the wooden bar. Gets packed on Fri nights and serves decent cocktails, but is more of a low-key beer joint for students.

Roxy's Rhythm Bar, 20 Main Rd, Melville, T011-726 6019, www.clubroxy.co.za. Mon-Sat 2000-late. Melville's most established club has been in existence for 20 years and is popular with a younger crowd for the varied up-to-date music from deep funk to hip-hop. Live music most nights and this is where many of Gauteng's rock groups get their first break.

Xai Xai, 9b 7th St, Melville. Super-trendy lounge bar with a Mozambique theme. Great cocktails, low-level sofas, good-looking punters and chilled music make this a relaxing and stylish setting for a few pre-dinner drinks.

✪ Entertainment

Johannesburg *p562, maps p567, p570 and p571*

Computicket, T011-340 8000, www.compu ticket.com. A central booking agency for tickets to the cinema, theatre, concerts, sports events and bus tickets. You can book online or there are kiosks in most of the large shopping malls and Checkers supermarkets. If you're heading to one of the downtown theatres, its best to travel by taxi and pre-order one for after the show. The Market Theatre area is safe, but don't wander away from Mary Fitzgerald Sq.

Cinema

All the latest Hollywood, European and home-grown releases can be seen at multi-screen cinemas in shopping malls and casinos. Check local newspapers for listings. They are run by **Nu Metro**, T011-325 4257, www.numetro.co.za, or **Ster-Kinekor**, T011-445 7700, www.sterkinekor.co.za.

Theatre

Civic Theatre, Loveday St, Braamfontein, T011-877 6800, www.showbusiness.co.za. Modern theatre complex with 3 auditoriums, frequent performances of South African plays, visiting international musicals, ballets and classical orchestras.
Gold Reef City, Northern Parkway, Ormonde, T011-248 5168, www.goldreefcity.co.za. The 300-seat **Globe Theatre** shows cabaret and comedy, while the new much larger 1100-seat **Lyric Theatre** shows pop concerts and tribute band acts.
Market Theatre, 56 Margaret Mcingana St, Newtown, T011-832 1614, www.market theatre.co.za. 3 auditoriums, famous for its community theatre and controversial political plays during the 1980s. The recommended Gramadoelas restaurant is here.
Montecasino, corner of William Nicol Drive and Witkoppen Rd, Fourways, T011-511 1818, www.montecasinotheatre.co.za. 3 theatres in the casino and entertainment complex, one

of which was specifically built to stage South Africa's version of the **Lion King** musical and can seat over 1800.
Old Mutual Theatre on the Square, Nelson Mandela Sq, Sandton City Mall, T011-883 8606. Drama, comedy and on Fri at 1230 a lunchtime classical concert.

◎ Shopping

Johannesburg *p562, maps p567, p570 and p571*
African art

African Craft Market of Rosebank, Cradock Av, Rosebank, T011-880 2906, www.craft. co.za. 0900-1800. The former street traders of this area have now been housed in one ethnic-inspired building in the centre of the popular Mall of Rosebank. Curios from all over Africa are for sale at over 140 stalls. Credit cards are accepted and shipping can be arranged. It's a lively spot, with street performers and musicians.
Art Africa, 62 Tyrone Av, Parkview, T011-486 2052. Mon-Fri 0900-1800, Sat 0900-1500. Great place to pick up inexpensive gifts, strong emphasis on recycled art products. Some of the most interesting pieces include flowers made from recycled plastic and baskets woven from telephone wire. There are some genuinely rare antiques from across Africa.
Kim Sacks Gallery, 153 Jan Smuts Av, Park-wood, T011-447 5804. Mon-Sat 0800-1700. A selection of quality ethnic art from all over Africa is on show in this gallery, housed in a lovely old home and regarded as one of the top galleries in the city. There is a good range of contemporary South African pieces, including prints, beadwork, sculptures, beadwork, and ceramics.

Camera equipment

Kameraz, Rosebank Mews, Oxford Rd, Rose-bank, T011-880 2885, www.kameraz.co.za. Mon-Fri 0800-1700, Sat 0800-1400. One of the largest dealers in new and second-hand camera equipment in Gauteng. New and used accessories and lenses, and specialists in insurance claims. On the first Sun of every even month they hold a flea market of second-hand equipment, and on the first Sun of every odd month, an exhibition and sale of work from local photographers.

Camping and hiking equipment
Cape Union Mart, Hyde Park Mall, Jan Smuts Av, T011-325 5038, www.capeunionmart. co.za, and 14 other branches in Johannesburg's various shopping malls, plus one at the airport. Excellent shop selling outdoor equipment, clothing, backpacks, mosquito nets, and a great range of walking shoes.

Gold
Scoin Shop, U24a, Sandton City Mall, T011-784 8551, www.sagoldcoin.com. Mon-Fri 0830-1630. Krugerrands, South Africa's famous gold coins, can be bought here as an investment or souvenir. It also produces collector's coins such as the Mandela Medallion.

Shopping malls
Johannesburg has an abundance of vast, modern shopping malls filled with shops, restaurants, cinemas and bars. There are over 25 malls around the city, some of which are so enormous and extravagant that they are worth visiting in their own right. In most, the shops open 0900-1800, while the restaurants and cinemas stay open until 2200 or 2300.
Hyde Park, Jan Smuts Av, Hyde Park, T011-325 4340, www.hydeparkshopping.co.za. Luxury shopping aimed at ladies who lunch. Also has cinemas, and the excellent **Exclusive Books** has an outlet here.
The Mall of Rosebank, corner of Cradock and Baker streets, Rosebank, T011-788 5530, www.themallofrosebank.co.za. One of the more pleasant malls with a large open-air plaza lined with cafés, ideal for sitting in the sun and watching people go by. The flea market on the roof of the car park every Sun

sells crafts and snacks. Also home to the excellent **African Craft Market** (see box, page 565). At the time of writing the mall's layout was changing to incorporate the new line and station for the Gautrain, which is currently under construction underground beneath Oxford Rd.
Sandton City Mall and Nelson Mandela Square, corner of Sandton Dr and Rivonia Rd (attached by a walkway and sky bridge), T011-883 2011, www.sandton-city.co.za; T011-217 6000, www.nelsonmandelasquare.com. Massive double-storey mall featuring all of South Africa's chain stores, cinemas, African art galleries and hyper-markets. The opulent Nelson Mandela Sq has international exclusive stores and fashionable restaurants around an attractive piazza-style square, which is now home to a formidable 6-m bronze statue of the great man himself. His shoes are 1 m across and children can sit on them.

▲▲ Activities and tours

Johannesburg p562, maps p567, p570 and p571
Bungee jumping
Orlando Towers Adventure Centre, Dynamo St, Orlando, Soweto, T012-345 5114, www.orlandotowers.co.za, Wed, Fri, Sat, Sun 0900-1700. Quite bizarrely you can now bungee or rap jump from Soweto's famous painted cooling towers (see page 575). There are a number of exhilarating swings inside and outside the towers to choose from R360 or you can go up in the newly constructed lift 100 m to the viewing platform at the top for R60. This is not for the faint-hearted – the lift is open air and the last 3 m to the top is by a sort of suspended stairway as the top of the tower curves outwards. Nevertheless the views of Soweto are unbeatable. This is the brainchild of Bob Woods, a rope access specialist and he is now planning to build an aerial bridge between the towers and then erect a bungee jump from the bridge.

Cricket

Wanderers' Stadium, Corlett Drive, Illovo, T011-340 1500 information T011-340 1509 tickets, www.wanderers.co.za. This is one of South Africa's premier cricket grounds and regular international matches are played in season.

Football

FNB Stadium, Nasvec Rd, Ormonde. More popularly called Soccer City, it is the largest of Johannesburg's stadiums and home of the South African Football Association. This will be the venue of the opening ceremony, the opening match and the final of the 2010 FIFA World Cup™ (see colour section, pages 28-29) and the whole of Soweto is euphoric these will be played on their doorstep. It is currently undergoing a complete upgrade and will reopen in 2010 when it will seat 94,000.

Golf

There are over 40 golf courses around Johannesburg and several of South Africa's top courses are open to visitors midweek.
Glendower Club, Marais Rd, Bedfordview, T011-453 1013, www.glendower.co.za. Beautiful location in a bird sanctuary, tough course with 85 bunkers, 20 mins from city.
Houghton Golf Club, 2nd Av, Lower Houghton, T011-792 2349, www.hough ton.co.za. Historically one of the country's top courses but at the time of writing this was closed for redevelopment.
Wanderers Golf Club, Rudd Rd, Illovo, T011-447 3311, www.wanderersgolfclub.co.za. One of the oldest courses in South Africa, quite challenging, hosts the South African PGA Championship, next to the cricket ground, just north of Rosebank.

Rugby

Ellis Park, Staib St, Doornfontein, T011-402 8644, www.ellispark.co.za. Also known as Coca-Cola Park, after its sponsors, this is South Africa's premier rugby venue and matches are played regularly during the season. The stadium seats 62,000 spectators and it can be a rowdy day out, with fans bringing their braais and beers with them. It's also home to Orlando Pirates soccer club, and will be a venue for the 2010 FIFA World Cup™.

Tour operators

There are dozens of tour operators in Johannesburg that offer a range of ½- and full-day tours. Most use minibuses, have registered guides and pick up from hotels. Expect to pay in the region of R400-450 for a ½-day tour.
A Taste of Africa, www.tasteofafrica.co.za. A full range of day tours, including all the museums and interactive Soweto tours. Use minibus taxis as transport. Recommended.
African Time Out, T011-477 4612, www.africantimeout.com. Day tours around the city and further afield, including Maropeng and Sterkfontein Caves.
Jimmy's Face to Face Tours, T011-331 6109, www.face2face.co.za. One of the original Soweto tour operators, with a focus on climbing out of the minibuses and meeting local people. Good for exploring on foot.
JMT Tours, T011-980 6038, www.jmttours.co.za. ½-day Soweto tours, trips to Lesedi, Sun City, and longer trips to Kruger.
Karabo Tours, based at the Backpackers Ritz, see Sleeping, page 579. Will pick up from all northern suburb hotels. Affordable in-depth Soweto tours, plus historic Tshwane (Pretoria) tours, Gold Reef City, Lion Park and comprehensive Johannesburg city tours.
Lords Travel & Tours, T011-791 5494, www.lordstravel.co.za. Range of set and tailor-made city tours to Soweto, Sterk-fontein Caves, Botanical Gardens, Lion Park and Lesedi; further afield packages to Pilanesberg and Sun City and Kruger.

⊖ Transport

Johannesburg *p562, maps p567, p570 and p571*

Air

OR Tambo International Airport is southern African's biggest transport hub and one of the largest airports in the world, with numerous daily flights connecting to all major cities domestically and internationally.

South African Airways (SAA) has countless daily flights run in conjunction with its subsidiary, SA Airlink, covering the entire country. Comair/British Airways has several daily flights to all major cities.

Mango has daily flights from Johannesburg to **Cape Town** and **Durban**; Kulula flies to **Cape Town**, **Durban**, **George** and **Port Elizabeth**; 1Time flies to **Cape Town**, **Durban**, **George**, **Port Elizabeth** and **East London**.

Airlines 1Time, www.1time.aero; Air Botswana, www.airbotswana.co.bw; Air France, www.airfrance.com; Air Malawi, www.airmalawi.com; Air Namibia, www.airnamibia.com.na; Air Zimbabwe, www.airzimbabwe.com; Cathay Pacific, www.cathaypacific.com; Comair/British Airways, www.britishairways.com; Delta Airlines, www.delta.com; Egypt Air, www.egyptair.com; Emirates, www.emirates.com; Ethiopian Airlines, www.ethiopianairlines.com; Kenya Airways, www.kenya-airways.com; KLM, www.klm.com; Kulula, www.kulula.com; Lufthansa, www.lufthansa.com; Mango, ww5.flymango.com; Malaysia Airlines, www.malaysiaairlines.com; Singapore Airlines, T011-880 8560; South African Airways (SAA), central reservations T011-978 1111, www.flysaa.com. Virgin Atlantic, www.virgin-atlantic.com. For further details, see Essentials, page 40.

Bus

Local Magic Bus, T011-394 6902, www.magicbus.co.za and Airport Link Shuttle, T011-792 2017, www.airportlink.co.za,

run shuttle services to the major hotels in Johannesburg and Tshwane (Pretoria).

Long distance Translux, Intercape, Greyhound, and all the smaller bus companies depart from and arrive at the Park City Transit Centre in central Johannesburg, which is also where the railway station is and the terminus for the new Gautrain. The surrounding area has long had a bad reputation for muggings. Although crime levels have dropped in the area, be extra vigilant in and around the terminal and don't go wandering outside with a backpack. Many of the buses depart and arrive late at night or early in the morning, so make sure you have pre-arranged a pickup with your hotel or one of the shuttle companies (see above) or take a metered taxi.

All the bus companies listed below have frequent departures between Johannesburg and Tshwane (Pretoria) throughout the day (1 hr). You can pre-book this short journey, but it is never a problem to get a standby ticket; expect to pay around R60.

The 3 main coach companies cover routes from Johannesburg across the country and some services go as far as Malawi. Full timetables can be found on the websites. Tickets can be booked at www.computicket.com.

The Baz Bus, reservations T021-4392323, www.bazbus.com, is the best option for backpackers. See Essentials, page 42 for full details of the service.

Bus companies All bus tickets can be booked online at www.computicket.com. Baz Bus, reservations T021-439 2323, www.bazbus.com; Greyhound, www.greyhound.co.za; Intercape, www.intercape.co.za; Translux, www.translux.co.za. For more information, see Getting around, page 41.

Car hire

Phone toll-free numbers for nearest branch. Avis, T0861-113 748 (in South Africa), T011-923 3660 (from overseas), www.avis.co.za;

Budget, T0861-016622 (in South Africa) T011-398 0123 (from overseas), www.budget. co.za; Europcar, T0801-131000 (in South Africa), T011-574 1000 (from overseas), www.europcar.co.za; Hertz, T0861-600136 (in South Africa), T011-021-935 4800 (from overseas), www.hertz.co.za.

Taxi
Most of the malls have taxi ranks outside. Maxi Taxi Cabs, T011-648 1212; Rose Taxis, T011-403 9625/403 0000, www.rosetaxis.com.

Train
Local Metrorail trains run between Johannesburg and Tshwane (Pretoria) every 30 mins, but are best avoided due to problems with crime.

The Gautrain, www.gautrain.co.za, a new high-speed rail link between Johannesburg and Tshwane (Pretoria) via the airport and Midrand is currently being built and should be completed by 2010. The journey time between the 2 cities will be 40 mins, and trains will run every 12 mins during peak hours and every 20 mins off peak. They will run from 0530 to 2030. Fares are expected to be around R30 between the 2 cities.

Long distance The railway station is in the Park City Transit Centre. Passenger trains are run by Shosholoza Meyl, T086-000 888 (in South Africa), T011-774 4555 (from overseas), www.shosholozameyl. co.za, which is part of South Africa's national railway company Spoornet. Even though rail travel is relatively slow, the train service is popular and seats should be reserved well in advance. There are services to **East London**, **Musina**, **Komatipoort**, **Cape Town** via **Bloemfontien**, **Durban** and **Port Elizabeth**.

Johannesburg p562, maps p567, p570 and p571

❻ Directory

Banks American Express, Sandton City Mall, T011-294 4444; 33 Bath Av, Rosebank, T011-880 8382; Hyde Park Mall, T011-325 4424. **Master Currency**, has several branches at the airport, T011-390 2725, and a branch at Sandton City, T011-883 0881. All the banks have branches in the larger shopping malls. **Embassies and consulates** Although there are some consulates in Johannesburg, for any passport or consular queries, you'll have to go to the embassies in Tshwane (Pretoria), see page 600. **Immigration** Dept of Home Affairs, President St, T011-836 3228, www.home-affairs.gov.za. Mon-Fri 0730-1600. Visa extensions cost R425 and take 5 working days. You will need to produce an onward ticket and proof of funds. **Internet** All the shopping malls have internet cafés; you will also be able to access the internet in most hostels and hotels and increasingly free Wi-Fi is available in coffee shops and other public places including the airport. **Medical services** Netcare 911, there are 32 private Netcare hospitals in Gauteng, for 24-hr medical services and ambulances T082-911, to locate a hospital T011-301 0000. Netcare Travel Clinic, Morningside Close Office Park, 222 Rivonia Rd, Morningside, Sandton, T011-802 0059, www.travelclinic.co.za, Mon-Fri 0730-1800, Sat 0830-1300, useful stop to update vaccinations and pick up anti-malarials; Rosebank Clinic (private), 14 Sturdee Av, Rosebank, T011-328 0500; Sandton Medi-Clini c (private), corner of Peter Pl and Hendrik Verwoerd Drive, Bryanston, T011-709 2000, www.sandtonmc.co.za. **Post office** Main post office, T012-401 7902 customer services, www.sapo.co.za (there's a store locater on the website). Again found in all shopping malls.

Tshwane (Pretoria)

→ *Colour map 2, B2. Phone code: 012. Altitude: 1363 m.*

The name Pretoria was given to the new settlement by Marthinus Wessel Pretorius, in memory of his father, Andries Pretorius, who had led the Voortrekkers in the bloody massacre of the Zulus at Blood River. Today it is the administrative capital of South Africa and the third largest city in the country. Despite being almost joined to Johannesburg 56 km to the south by a band of green-belt towns, the atmosphere of each city couldn't be more different. While Johannesburg was built on gold and industry, Pretoria's was founded on the Voortrekker period of South Africa's turbulent past and retains a rather stern, bureaucratic atmosphere – albeit softened by a large student population. In 2000, it underwent a name change to Tshwane, which after many years has finally caught on, is now in common use and is reflected on maps and signposts. While it is safer than Johannesburg, downtown Tshwane (Pretoria), like most major cities in South Africa, has gone through a transformation in recent years. With the demise of Apartheid, black South Africans are again permitted to live and work freely within the city centre, and it has much more of an African feel about it. ▸▸ *For listings, see pages 596-600.*

Ins and outs

Getting there

The centre of Tshwane (Pretoria) is 45 km from OR Tambo International Airport. The easiest way to travel to/from the airport is to use the airport shuttle. There is a Metro commuter train between Tshwane (Pretoria) and Johannesburg but high crime levels means you should avoid it. **Intercape**, **Greyhound** and **Translux** have several daily departures between the two cities. The high-speed **Gautrain** is under construction and will link Tshwane (Pretoria), Johannesburg and the airport. There will also be a branch line from the main railway station in the city centre to the suburb of Hatfield. ▸▸ *See Transport, page 599.*

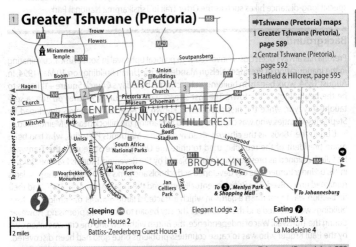

1 Greater Tshwane (Pretoria)

➡ Tshwane (Pretoria) maps
1 Greater Tshwane (Pretoria), page 589
2 Central Tshwane (Pretoria), page 592
3 Hatfield & Hillcrest, page 595

Sleeping
Alpine House 2
Battiss-Zeederberg Guest House 1

Elegant Lodge 2

Eating
Cynthia's 3
La Madeleine 4

Getting around

Most of Tshwane (Pretoria)'s sights lie in the surrounding hills. While there is a good local bus service, it does not connect between the various monuments in the city's suburbs. The easiest way to see the city sights is either on a guided tour or with a hire car. During the day, taking a municipal bus that runs between the centre and suburbs is a safe and cheap way of getting about town. **Church Street** is Tshwane (Pretoria)'s main through road, running from east to west, and at 26 km long is considered to be one of the world's longest streets. From the city centre it leads east to **Arcadia** where many of the embassies and the Union Buildings are located. To the south of here is **Sunnyside**, which until recently was home to most hotels and nightlife. However, the area has suffered a decline in recent years, with increasing crime rates. Many restaurants, hotels and backpacker hostels have relocated to the safer suburbs of **Hatfield** and **Brooklyn** a few kilometres further east where the colleges, universities and sports stadiums are located. Both are attractive suburbs, dotted with parks and gardens, and streets lined with Tshwane (Pretoria)'s distinctive jacaranda trees.

Best time to visit

Tshwane (Pretoria) has a pleasant climate with warm to hot summers and mild sunny winters. In winter the daily temperature averages 19°C, the days are still and the skies are clear. In the evening it can get cool. The average annual rainfall is 741 mm, mostly falling between November and March. The best time to visit is during the spring when the city is transformed by 60,000 flowering jacaranda trees, covering the parks and gardens in a mauve blanket.

Tourist information

The **Tshwane Tourism Information Bureau** ⓘ *Church Sq, T012-358 1430, www.tshwane. gov.za, Mon-Fri 0800-1600*, is in the Old Netherlands Bank Building. While there isn't the usual desk and helpful staff found in most local tourist offices, this bureau does produce a couple of useful maps, highlighting the major sights. The Tshwane (Pretoria) office of **South Africa National Parks (SANParks)** ⓘ *643 Leyds St, Muckleneuk, reservations T012-426 5000, www.sanparks.org*, is the head office and handles all bookings for accommodation and special long-distance hikes such as the Otter Trail in Tsitsikamma National Park.

Background

Pretoria has always been closely involved with political upheaval in South Africa, culminating in the inauguration of President Nelson Mandela at the Union Buildings on 10 May 1994. In August 1854, work began on building a church right by today's Church Square – this was to be the beginnings of the town. The first streets were laid out by Andries du Toit, a self-taught surveyor, while the first suburb was known as Arcadia, which was developed by Stephanus Meintjes who was commemorated by naming the hillock nearby, Meintjeskop.

During the 1860s, as the city was steadily growing, Marthinus Pretorius, who had been made president of the republic, tried to unite the Orange Free State with the Transvaal. He failed, resigned as president and was replaced by the Reverand Thomas François Burgers in 1870. Under Burgers, the city developed and schools and parks were built, but the problems remained unresolved. The British eventually annexed the Transvaal in April 1877, and their first action was to establish a garrison which attracted a large number of immigrants. New buildings were erected and the fortunes of the city began to look more promising. However, during the Transvaal War of Independence, the British withdrew and the city was taken over by the Paul Kruger who was to cause countless problems once gold had been discovered.

At the end of the Anglo-Boer War, Pretoria was named as the capital of the British colony, and as such it continued to prosper so that when the Union of South Africa was created in 1910, Pretoria was made the administrative capital of the new state. Shortly afterwards, the Union Buildings were constructed to house the new government. The growth of the town was now closely related to the expanding civil service and its status as an important city was assured. The city has remained a centre for government and today most overseas diplomats are based there. The city is also headquarters of the defence forces and home to the University of South Africa (UNISA). Today it has over 125,000 students throughout the world and is regarded as one of the largest correspondence universities in the world.

The metropolitan council has reorganized itself to unite the previously segregated areas under one administration. The greater area is now called Tshwane, meaning 'we are the same'. Like Johannesburg, Tshwane (Pretoria) has large townships to the northwest and northeast of the city. The municipality covers 1600 sq km and the population is estimated at 2.2 million.

Sights

Tshwane (Pretoria)'s sights are spread between the city centre, the Church Square area and the suburbs, and can easily be seen in a day. Most popular is the controversial Voortrekker Monument, although there are also a couple of decent museums and historical buildings worth visiting. The other major attractions are the glitzy distractions of Sun City, a couple of hours' drive away and often visited as a day trip. Johannesburg and its outlying attractions such as Soweto (see page 573) and Walter Sisulu Botanical Gardens (see page 576) are dealt with in the Johannesburg section but are easily accessed from Tshwane (Pretoria).

City centre

The oldest buildings in Tshwane (Pretoria) are clustered around Church Square, once a Voortrekker marketplace. Today, it is the heart of the city and is a popular meeting spot for locals, with suited businessmen stopping on the grass for lunch and hawkers selling roasted mealies to passersby. A rather unattractive statue of a grim-faced, grizzled Paul Kruger stands in the middle, surrounded by fluttering flocks of pigeons and flanked with important late 19th-century banks and government offices. The most interesting of these is the **Palace of Justice**, where Nelson Mandela and other leaders of the ANC were tried during the notorious Treason Trials of 1963-1964. On the southwest side is the Raadsall, or parliament, and the Old Netherlands Bank building, which now houses the tourist office.

The **Transvaal Museum** ① *Paul Kruger St, T012-322 7632, daily 0800-1600, R10, children (under 16) R8*, is a typically dusty natural history museum that was founded in 1892 and moved into its current premises in 1912. The museum serves as a research and documentation centre for the fauna of southern Africa, and is one of the leading centres for zoological research in the country. The displays, focusing on geology and stuffed animals, are spread over a series of halls, including the Austin Roberts Bird Hall, which showcases the varied birdlife of southern Africa, and a collection of semi-precious stones. More interesting, perhaps, is the fact that the world-renowned hominid fossil, 'Mrs Ples' (*Australopithecus africanus transvaalensis*), is kept here, although sadly the public doesn't have access to her. Opposite the museum is **City Hall**, dating from 1935, a grand building fronted by broad square, with a fountain and a statue of Andries Pretorius on horseback.

The **Treaty of Vereeniging** ending the Anglo-Boer War (1899-1902) was signed in **Melrose House** ① *275 Jacob Maré St, T012-322 2805, www.melrosehouse.co.za, Tue-Sun 1000-1700, R8, children (under 16) R5, small café in the converted stables*, on 31 May 1902,

2 Central Tshwane (Pretoria)

➡ Tshwane (Pretoria) maps
1 Greater Tshwane (Pretoria), page 589
2 Central Tshwane (Pretoria), page 592
3 Hatfield & Hillcrest, page 595

National Zoological Gardens of South Africa

To ① & Union Buildings

To Miriamman Temple

To Kruger House Museum

Boom
De Waal
Bloed
Turtel
Ford
Brown
Strubben
Shepherd
Paul Kruger
Bosman
Andries
Van der Walt
Prinsloo
Proes
Du Toit
Palace of Justice
Vermeulen
Groote Kerk
Palace
Church Square
First National
Ned Bank
Queen
Sammy Marks Square
Airport Shuttle
Reserve Bank
Church
Bureau
Standard
Lilian Ngoyi Square
Taxis
State Theatre
Raadsaal
Taxis
Nelson Mandela Dr
ABSA
Yolkstem
Schoeman
ABSA
Cinema
St Albans's Cathedral
VD By
Skinner
Skinner
To ② & Pretoria Art Museum
To Sunnyside, Arcadia, Muckleneuk & Mpumalanga (Kruger National Park)
To ② ③ Sunnyside & Arcadia
Visagie
City Hall
Pretorius Square
Transvaal Museum
Burgers Park
Minnaar
Minnaar
Nelson Mandela
Van Boeschoten
Paul Kruger
Burgers Park
Jacob Maré
Hoop
Christina
Melrose House
Scheiding
Rissik
Gerard Moerdyk
Taxis
Greyhound, Translux & Intercape
Loop
Rhodes
Berea Park
Joubert
Walker
To ⑤
Gautrain
Railway

N
200 metres
200 yards

Sleeping 🛏
224 **4**
Arcadia **3**

Court Classique **2**
That's It **5**
Whistletree Lodge **1**

Eating 🍴
Café Riche **1**
Oriental Palace **2**

592 • Gauteng Tshwane (Pretoria)

between the British High Command and Boer Republican Forces. The house was originally built in 1886 for George Heys, who made his fortune from trade and a stagecoach service to the Transvaal. It is regarded as one of the finest examples of Victorian domestic architecture in South Africa; marble columns, stained-glass windows and mosaic floors all help create a feeling of serene style and wealth. The house was restored after being bombed by right-wingers in 1990. Today the grounds are used for classical concerts.

Kruger House Museum ① *60 Church St West, T012-326 9172, daily 0830-1700, R16, children (under 16) R10*, where President Kruger lived between 1884-1901, is now a museum that displays a fairly diverting collection of his possessions, as well as objects relating to the Anglo-Boer War. At the back of the house is the state coach and his private railway carriage.

The **National Zoological Gardens of South Africa** ① *corner of Paul Kruger and Boom streets, entrance on Boom St, T012-328 3265, www.zoo.ac.za, 0800-1730, R45, children (2-15) R30, last ticket 1630, café,* formerly Pretoria Zoo, covers 80 ha, with 6 km of walkways and just over 3100 species. Heavily involved in research and conservation, it is South Africa's largest and best-designed zoo. It is home to the only koala bear to be born in Africa. Golf buggies are available to get around and there's an aerial cableway and tractor rides for kids.

Difficult to miss if you are walking about in the centre of town, the sprawling **Lilian Ngoyi Square** was known until 2006 as Strijdom Square and used to be dominated by a massive bust of JG Strijdom, covered by a curved concrete roof. The roof, considered something of an architectural feat, collapsed on 31 May 2001, 40 years to the day from when it was built. Strijdom was prime minister between 1954 and 1958 when the government started to place heavy restrictions on the ANC and banned the Communist Party – his statue doesn't seem to be missed much today. In 1956, Lilian Ngoyi led a march of 20,000 women from the square to the Union Buildings to demonstrate against obligatory carrying of pass books. The square was renamed after her on Women's Day 2006, the 50th anniversary of the march. It is flanked by the tall ABSA Bank building and the State Theatre, and remains a popular meeting place at lunchtime.

Burgers Park ① *between Van der Walt and Andries streets, winter 0600-1800, summer 0600-2200*, is the most central of Tshwane (Pretoria)'s parks. It was first laid out as a botanical garden in the early 1870s, and is today a popular meeting place where visitors relax in the shade of rubber trees, palms and jacarandas. The 'florarium' houses a collection of exotic plants in contrasting environments, from subtropical flowers to succulents from the Karoo and Kalahari regions. Elsewhere in the garden is a statue of remembrance for the officers of the South African Scottish Regiment who were killed during the First World War.

Sunnyside and Arcadia

Pretoria Art Museum ① *Arcadia Park, T021-344 1807, Tue-Sun 1000-1700, guided tours, www.pretoriaartmuseum.co.za, R6, children (under 16) R4,* houses a fine collection of South African art as well as a selection of run-of-the-mill 17th-century Dutch paintings. The collection includes works by Pierneef, Frans Oerder and Anton van Wouw. It also houses interesting temporary exhibitions, including photography. Teas and light meals are available.

This magnificent red sandstone complex of the **Union Buildings** ① *Church St, Arcadia, T012-300 5200*, sits proudly on top of Meintjeskop overlooking the city centre. This is the administrative headquarters of the South African President, most famous for being the site of Nelson Mandela's speech after his inauguration as president on 10 May 1994, when the grounds in front of the building where packed with thousands of well-wishers. The building, designed by Herbert Baker, who also designed St George's Cathedral and Rhodes Memorial in Cape Town, was completed in 1913. Baker went on to help Edwin

Lutyens in the planning of New Delhi, India. (The Union Buildings in Pretoria influenced his designs for the new Government Secretariat and the Imperial Legislative Assembly). The formal gardens below the buildings are pleasant to walk around, but the best reason for coming here is for the city view. Look out for the statues of South Africa's famous generals: Botha, on horseback, Hertzog and Smuts. Also found on the hill is the Pretoria War Memorial, Delville Wood Memorial and the Garden of Remembrance.

Tshwane (Pretoria)'s suburbs

Miriammen Temple ① *follow the N4, Proes St, from the city centre for 2 km, turn right into 7 St, daily all day*, is a pleasant reminder of the importance of the Indian population in South Africa. The temple is one of the oldest (1905) buildings in Tshwane (Pretoria). The imposing *gopuram*, or tower, is a 12.5-m-high layered structure of brightly painted gods, goddesses and demons interspersed with white layers of stones. The temple is devoted to Miriammen, the Hindu goddess of infectious diseases such as smallpox. You are free to enter most areas but remember to remove your shoes.

South of the city is the looming granite hulk of the **Voortrekker Monument** ① *south of the city, just off the R28, T012-326 6770, www.voortrekkermon.org.za, winter daily 0800-1700, summer daily 0800-1800, R32, children (under 16) R10, R13 car*, a controversial Afrikaner memorial. The monument, a 40-m cube, was completed in 1949 after 11 years of work. It is a sombre and unattractive structure, a windowless block dominating the landscape, but one of particular significance to Afrikaners. It was built to commemorate the Great Trek of the 1830s, when the Afrikaners struck inland from the Cape with just their ox wagons and little idea of the trials that lay ahead of them. Inside is the cavernous Hall of Heroes, guarded by a carved head of a buffalo above the entrance (thought to be the most dangerous animal in Africa). Around the walls 27 marble friezes depict both the trek and scenes from the Zulu wars, including a seriously suspect portrayal of the Battle of Blood River (see page 849), where the Afrikaners are shown as brave soldiers and the Zulus as cowardly savages. The monument was, until recently, the site of a huge annual celebration on 16 December, the date of the battle (known as the Day of the Covenant). At exactly midday on this date a ray of sunlight falls onto a large slab of stone in the centre of the basement (rather like a tomb), spotlighting the carved words: "Ons Vir Jou, Suid Afrika" (We are for you, South Africa). The fact that this date celebrated the bloody massacre of Zulus proved, unsurprisingly, hugely controversial, and after the end of Apartheid, this national holiday was renamed the Day of Reconciliation. Today, the celebrations are very low key indeed. For impressive views of the surrounding countryside and the city, take the lift to the viewing area around the roof. In the basement are some displays of life during the Great Trek. Outside, the surrounding wall recreates the circular laager of 64 ox-wagons that can be seen at the battlefield site.

Located significantly on a hill opposite the Voortrekker Monument, **Freedom Park** ① *entrance off Potgieter St, across from the Central Prison, T012-470 7400, www.freedom park.co.za, free 1½-hr tours daily at 0900, 1200 and 1500, must be pre-booked, fill in the form on the website*, is a work in progress and is currently being built to commemorate the country's political history and to celebrate its cultural and natural heritage. Its mission is to be a testament to the truth and reconciliation process that occurred at the end of Apartheid. For now, tours start with an explanation of the purpose of the park and a viewing of the eternal flame, before heading to the amphitheatre and an impressive structure at the summit of the park built to resemble a graceful spiral of reeds to symbolize the re-growth of South Africa. The tour then visits a giant wall, where the thousands of names of those who lost their lives in the eight conflicts that shaped the history of South

Africa are being inscribed. These include the Boer wars, world wars and the struggle against Apartheid. Each of South Africa's nine provinces have also donated a boulder of historical value to the park – the boulder representing Gauteng for example, comes from the township Mamelodi, in the east of Tshwane (Pretoria), where in 1985 the South African Security Forces killed 13 people during a peaceful protest march against rent increases. Once completed the 52-ha site will also comprise a museum and garden of remembrance, with statues and sculptures to honour ordinary South Africans who contributed to the country's development. So far the impressive design and architecture using lots of slate and granite is sleek and modern, and there are neat pathways linking the sights and tranquil ornamental water features. Like the Voortrekker Monument, there are tremendous views over the city from here.

3 Hatfield & Hillcrest

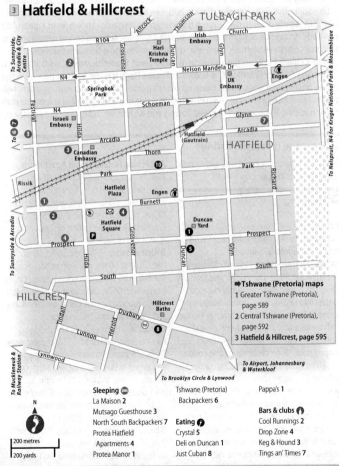

➡Tshwane (Pretoria) maps
1 Greater Tshwane (Pretoria), page 589
2 Central Tshwane (Pretoria), page 592
3 Hatfield & Hillcrest, page 595

200 metres
200 yards

N

Sleeping 🛏
La Maison **2**
Mutsago Guesthouse **3**
North South Backpackers **7**
Protea Hatfield
 Apartments **4**
Protea Manor **1**

Tshwane (Pretoria)
 Backpackers **6**

Eating 🍴
Crystal **5**
Deli on Duncan **1**
Just Cuban **8**

Pappa's **1**

Bars & clubs 🍸
Cool Runnings **2**
Drop Zone **4**
Keg & Hound **3**
Tings an' Times **7**

You can walk around the battlements and enjoy the excellent views from **Klapperkop Fort** ① *off the R28 on Johan Rissik Drive, T012-346 7703, daily 0800-1700, small entry fee*, but the rest of the fort is closed to the public. A separate building houses a **museum** of South Africa's military history, there is an old steam locomotive in the car park and a couple of tanks in the grounds. The fort was built to guard the southern entrance to the town, but no resistance was put up when the British entered the town in May 1900.

Tshwane (Pretoria), known as the Garden City, is well known for its parks and gardens and the city takes much pride in its magnificent open space. To the east of the centre towards the N1, **Springbok Park**, between Schoeman Street and Nelson Mandela Drive in Hatfield, has a much more informal layout. This park was declared a national monument in 1979. It was first planted in 1905 when WH Lanham was planning the suburb of Hatfield. A stream flows through the grounds and there are some fine trees from different regions of the country.

Like Springbok Park, **Venning Park** is between Schoeman Street and Nelson Mandela Drive, but slightly closer to the centre. It is a neatly planned garden known for its immaculate rose beds. An avenue of palm trees ends beside a pleasant tea garden and restaurant; the park is close to the diplomatic enclave and many families come here at weekends.

Jan Celliers Park, on the corner of Wenning and Broderick streets, west of Queen Wilhelmina Road in Groenkloof, is known as **Protea Park**. It is the furthest park from the centre, on a natural slope and is made up of rock gardens, trees and a water garden; two ponds are linked by a series of 14 small waterfalls. Aside from being a relaxing spot, the park is worth visiting if you are keen on wild flowers and wish to see indigenous flora close up.

◉ Tshwane (Pretoria) listings

For Sleeping and Eating price codes and other relevant information, see pages 46-53.

◉ Sleeping

Tshwane *p589, maps p589, p592 and p595*
Most of the best accommodation is found in Tshwane (Pretoria)'s suburbs.
AL Whistletree Lodge, 1267 Whistletree Dr, Queenswood, T012-333 9915/6, www.whistletree.co.za. Award-winning guesthouse close to the Union Buildings. 12 rooms elegantly decorated, private balconies, attractive lounge with traditional, sumptuous furniture and high ceilings, landscaped gardens, heart-shaped pool, tennis court, sauna and cocktail bar. Dinner and snacks. No children under 12.
A Court Classique, corner of Schoeman and Beckett streets, Arcadia, T012-344 4420, www.courtclassique.co.za. Practical, spacious suites with kitchenettes, aimed at families or business travellers. Set around landscaped patios with water features, swimming pool, restaurant, bar and conference centre.

A-B Protea Hotel Hatfield Apartments, 1080 Prospect St, Hatfield, T012-362 6105, www.proteahotels.com. Functional option with 28 suites (1- or 2-bed), with kitchenette TV, a/c, pleasant decor, pool area and bar. Great location in the throng of shops and restaurants of Hatfield.
B Alpine House, 552 Atterbury Rd, Menlo Park, T012-811 0169, www.alpinehouse.co.za. 5 self-catering units, open-plan kitchen, private lounge with DSTV, undercover parking, stylish furniture, contemporary decor, wooden floors and framed artwork. B&B available.
B Arcadia, 515 Proes St, T012-326 9311, www.arcadiahotel.co.za. 139 a/c rooms with TV, quality city centre hotel, well-managed and aimed at business travellers and tour groups. Restaurant, bar, coffee shop, lounge, gym, undercover parking, part of the Arcadia shopping complex, close to embassies and a short walk to the Union Buildings.
B Elegant Lodge, 83 Atterbury Rd, Menlo Park, T012-346 6460, www.elegantlodge.co.za. Attractive business hotel with easy

access to the N1 and Menlyn Park Mall. 16 a/c rooms, comfortable furnishings, TV, internet, small pleasant restaurant, escape the traffic on the main road in the pretty courtyards.

B La Maison, 235 Hilda St, Hatfield, T012-430 4341, www.lamaison.co.za. 6 large bedrooms with old-fashioned decor, in a grand white Victorian mansion, close to many diplomatic missions, restaurant is highly regarded and serves 4 course silver service dinners, lush gardens, swimming pool, roof-top terrace.

B Protea Hotel Manor, corner Feastival and Burnett Sts, Hatfield, T012-362 7077, www.proteahotels.com. Another quality Protea offering. Newly refurbished in modern, crisp decor, with 122 rooms, restaurant, bar and swimming pool. In a good location in the middle of Hatfield and within walking distance to Loftus Stadium.

B-C Mutsago Guesthouse, 327 Festival St, Hatfield, T012-430 7193, www.mutsago.co.za. Smart 2-storey home surrounded by lush tropical gardens, good-sized pool with deck chairs set around it. 14 rooms with an African theme, murals painted on the walls depicting Zulu homesteads, African-print fabrics on the beds, TV and minibar.

C Battiss-Zeederberg Guest House, 3 Fook Island, 92 20th St, Menlo Park, T/F012-460 7318, http://battiss.co.za. Guesthouse set in original home of artist Walter Battiss, and much of his character is still evident – his murals remain on the walls and the floors as a reminder of his love for San paintings. 4 double rooms with lofty ceilings, shiny wood floors and large French windows open on to a leafy courtyard. En suite, TV, fan, kitchenette. You'll need a car to get into town, but it's a short drive from the N1 and Menlyn Park shopping mall. See Greater Tshwane map, page 589).

D Hotel 224, corner of Schoeman and Leyds St, T012-440 5281, www.hotel224.com. Huge concrete block with 224 single and a/c doubles, rooms are dated and on the small side but cheap, DSTV, video channel, restaurant, bar, secure parking, short walk from Union Buildings.

D-F North South Backpackers, 355 Glynn St, Hatfield, T012-362 0989, www.northsouth backpackers.com. Clean and airy lodge with well-tended gardens and spotless pool within a few mins' walk of the shops and restaurants at Hatfield Sq. Doubles and dorms, bar with fireplace, pool table, helpful with booking tours. Will pick up from Johannesburg airport if arranged in advance.

D That's It, 5 Brecher St, Clydesdale, T012-344 3404, www.thatsit.co.za. Neat B&B set in a family home in a quiet suburb, with 5 simple and pleasant rooms, whitewashed walls and blue-and-white fabrics, thatched lapa in the tropical gardens, swimming pool, TV lounge. Useful location if you need to apply for visas at one of the nearby embassies.

D-F Tshwane (Pretoria) Backpackers, 425 Farenden Rd, Clydesdale, T012-343 9754, www.pretoriabackpackers.net. The oldest backpacker hostel in town, with 2 houses around the corner from each other, 2 small dorms, several very comfortable doubles in garden huts or in the main house, 1 family unit sleeping 4. Stylishly decorated with a guesthouse feel, lovely tropical gardens with fish ponds and gazebos, pool and travel desk. Organize local tours of Tshwane (Pretoria), Sun City/Pilanesberg, Lesedi Cultural Village. Will collect from Johannesburg airport. Staff will accompany guests to football and rugby matches at Loftus Stadium. Recommended.

🍴 Eating

Tshwane *p589, maps p589, p592 and p595*
In a city as spread out as Tshwane (Pretoria), restaurants tend to be found in or near the large shopping malls (see page 599). The centre has plenty of sandwich bars and fast-food outlets, but few places to eat at night. In the evening, head to **Hatfield** and **Brooklyn**.

TTT Crystal, 525 Duncan St, Hatfield, T012-362 8888, www.crystalrestaurant.co.za, Mon-Thu 1000-2200, Fri-Sat 1000-2330. This is an upmarket French and Lebanese restaurant, and as the name suggests is decorated in crystal including the napkin rings and a magnificent chandelier, and offers French

Crystal champagne. It has a good selection of mezzes and grills, the likes of foie gras and tender fillet steaks are on the French menu.

¶¶¶ **Cynthia's**, Maroelana Centre, near Tshwane (Pretoria) Country Club, Maroelana Centre, in the southern suburbs off the N1, T012-460 3220, www.cynthias.co.za. Mon-Fri 1200-1500, 1800-2200, Sat 1800-2200, Sun 1200-1500. Popular restaurant, sophisticated glass and wood decor with art and mirrors on the walls. Traditional meat dishes such as fillets with gourmet toppings and chateaubriand, some seafood and game. Extensive wine list.

¶¶¶ **La Madeleine**, 122 Priory Rd, Lynnwood Ridge (from the N1 go east on the M6, then left into Camelia Av and left again into Priory Rd), T012-361 3667. Tue-Sat 1900-2200. Long-standing top restaurant, running for over 30 years, with a pleasant, airy setting, classical French cuisine. Dishes include Provençal lamb and confit of duck, award-winning wine list. Reservations recommended.

¶¶ **Just Cuban**, 129 Duxbury Rd, Hillcrest, T012-362 1800, www.justcuban.co.za. 0900-late. Located in a converted old post office, this has a formal restaurant, a cocktail bar and an upstairs cigar lounge, with contemporary earthy decor. Cuban fare such as *espetadas*, plus seafood platters, steaks and good crunchy salads.

¶¶ **Oriental Palace**, Colosseum Hotel, 410 Schoeman St, Arcadia, T012-322 2195. Open 1130-1430, 1800-2200. Authentic Indian restaurant, chefs from Pakistan and north India prepare genuine curries, good tikka and tandoori, delicious and cheap dhal, tandoori breads and kulfi. Everything halaal, no alcohol.

¶ **Pappa's**, corner of Duncan and Prospect streets, Hatfield, T012-362 2224. Mon-Sat 0800-2200, Sun 0800-1500. In a converted historical building, Duncan Yard, with its quirky shops, art galleries and cobbled alleyways, makes a good lunch stop and offers gourmets burgers, Mediterranean fare and decadent desserts.

Cafés and delis

Café Riche, Church Sq (southwest corner), T012-328 3173. Open 0600-2400. Restored historical building, feels like a Parisian café,

great views over the square. Breakfasts, light meals and late night dinners, thought to be the oldest café in town. Atmospheric.

The Deli on Duncan, corner of Duncan and Prospect streets, Hatfield, T012-362 4054. Tue-Sat 0800-1700. Quaint old fashioned deli serving generous breakfasts, and light lunches such as quiche or pies and salad and delicious home baked cheesecake and cupcakes.

❶ Bars and clubs

Tshwane *p589, maps p589, p592 and p595*
Again, by far the best areas to head for in the evening and at weekends are Hatfield and Brooklyn, both to the east of the town centre. Ask the taxi to take you to Hatfield Sq, from where there are dozen or so places to explore within a short walk of each other.

Cool Runnings, Burnett St, Hatfield, T012-362 0100. Open 1100-late. One of the chain of bar-cum-restaurants that attract a young studenty crowd. Loud and raucous evenings, live reggae music on Sun. Always busy at the weekend, garish cocktails and imported beers.

Drop Zone, 141 Burnett St, Hatfield Sq, T012-362 6528, www.clubdropzone.co.za, Mon-Sat 2000-late. Popular nightclub, with DJs and dance music, Afrikaans music on Mon and rock 'n' roll on Tue, over 21s, more popular with young professionals than the usual student crowd, happy hour daily 2000-2100.

Hillside Tavern, 320 Hillside Rd, Lynnwood, T012-348 1402. Closed Sat lunch. Pub and steak restaurant, substantial bar with wide choice of beers and ciders, revamped to look like a traditional English country pub.

Keg & Hound, 1077 Arcadia St, Hatfield. Good choice of imported beers, plus a snack menu. Popular pub atmosphere among the local university students, late nights at the weekend.

Tings an' Times, 21 Arcadia St, Arcadia, T012-430 3176, www.tings.co.za. Mon-Sat 1200-0130. Popular for live music, can get very crowded, best to arrive mid-evening to secure a table. Great cocktails, Middle Eastern and vegetarian meals, including filled pittas.

☻ Entertainment

Tshwane *p589, maps p589, p592 and p595*
Computicket, T083-915 8000, www.compu
ticket.com. Advance booking for all events,
kiosks in Hatfield Plaza and Menlyn Park malls.

Cinema
Drive-in, on the roof of **Menlyn Park** shopping
mall, T012-348 8766, www.menlynpark.co.za.
Shows 2 movies Mon-Sat at 1930 and 2130,
R65 per car, and 1 movie on Sun 1930, R30 per
car. If you don't have your own car, you can
hire a renovated Chevy or Chrysler convertible.
IMAX, Menlyn Park, T012-368 1186, www.
imax.co.za. Giant screen with wrap-around
sound, showing wildlife and landscape films.
NuMetro, Menlyn Park, T012-368 1301. Has
15 screens; **Hatfield Plaza**, T012-362 5898,
www.numetro.co.za.

○ Shopping

Tshwane *p589, maps p589, p592 and p595*
Most of Tshwane (Pretoria)'s shopping is
limited to its large shopping malls: the best
are **Brooklyn Mall**, 338 Bronkhorst St, New
Muckleneuk, T012-346 1063, www.brooklyn
mall.co.za; **Hatfield Plaza**, 1122 Burnett St,
Hatfield, T012-362 5842, www.hatfieldplaza.
com; and **Menlyn Park**, Atterbury Rd, Menlo
Park, clearly seen from the N1, T012-348
8766, www.menlynpark.co.za. The latter is
Tshwane (Pretoria)'s premier mall for 'shopper-
tainment', with 300 shops and restaurants,
a 15-screen cinema, IMAX, bowling alley, and
drive-in cinema. Its architectural focal point is
its tent-like roof that can be seen from far away.

⛰ Activities and tours

Tshwane *p589, maps p589, p592 and p595*
Cricket
Supersport Stadium, formerly Centurion
Park, 23 km from the centre of town, off the
R21 to Johannesburg, enquiries T012-663

1005, www.titans.co.za, tickets www.compu
ticket.com. The ground where international
matches are played and home to the Nashua
Titans cricket team. A modern circular stadium
dominated by a huge single grandstand.
The rest of the boundary is made up of grass
banks which are great for picnics and braais.

Rugby
Tshwane (Pretoria) is the home town of the
Vodacom Bulls, T012-344 4011, www.the
bulls.co.za. Tickets from www.computicket.com.
Loftus Versfeld Rugby Stadium, Kirkness St,
Sunnyside. The main stadium; also the venue
for the 2010 FIFA World Cup™ and concerts.

Tour operators
Apart from city tours, the most popular day
trips are to Sun City, Pilanesberg National Park
and the Gold Mines. Expect to pay R350-450
per person for a ½-day tour of the city, which
takes in sights such as the Voortrekker
Monument and Union Buildings. Operators in
Johannesburg (see page 585) offer city tours of
Tshwane (Pretoria) and can pick up from
accommodation in Tshwane (Pretoria).
Ulysses, T012-663 4941, www.ulysses.co.za.
Daily city tours and trips to Pilanesberg,
Sun City and Cullinan Diamond Mine.

☻ Transport

Tshwane *p589, maps p589, p592 and p595*
From Tshwane (Pretoria) it is 500 km to the
Zimbabwe border (**Beitbridge**), 474 km to
Bloemfontein, 1492 km to **Cape Town**,
688 km to **Durban**, 1060 km to **East London**,
1078 km to **Harare** (Zimbabwe), 53 km to
Johannesburg, 530 km to **Kimberley**, 1406 km
to **Knysna**, and 1133 km to **Port Elizabeth**.

Air
See page 587 for OR Tambo International
Airport. **Magic Bus**, T011-548 0822, www.magic
bus.co.za, and **Airport Link Shuttle**, T011-792
2017, www.airportlink.co.za, drop off at major
hotels in Johannesburg and Tshwane (Pretoria).

Bus

Local Municipal buses run between the city centre and suburbs. Timetables are available in chemists and from the information office in Church Sq, T012-308 0839. **Translux, Greyhound**, and **Intercape** buses run between Tshwane (Pretoria) and Johannesburg (1 hr), with several departures daily. They can be pre-booked but seats are always available; expect to pay around R60 standby. You can then connect with other buses or trains at Johannesburg's Park City Transit Centre.

Long distance The bus stand is to the left of the railway station (as you face it) in the 1928 Building. **Translux, Intercape** and **Greyhound** have offices here. There are departures to all over the country, though on some southern routes, you have to change in Johannesburg. Timetables can be found on the websites and tickets can be booked at www.computicket.com. **Baz Bus** is the only budget transport that will pick up/drop off at hostels in Tshwane (Pretoria). See page 42.

Bus companies All bus tickets can be booked online at www.computicket.com. Baz Bus, T021-4392323, www.bazbus.com; Greyhound, www.greyhound.co.za; Intercape, www.intercape.co.za; Translux, www.translux.co.za. For more information, see Getting around, page 41.

Car hire

Phone the toll-free numbers for nearest branch. **Avis**, T0861-113748 (in South Africa), T011-923 3660 (from overseas), www.avis. co.za; **Budget**, T0861-016622 (in South Africa) T011-398 0123 (from overseas), www.budget. co.za; **Europcar**, T0801-131000 (in South Africa), T011-574 1000 (from overseas), www.europcar.co.za; **Hertz**, T0861-600136 (in South Africa), T011-021-935 4800 (from overseas), www.hertz.co.za.

Taxi

In front of the railway station, on Prinsloo opposite the tourist office, and on Church St by Lilian Ngoyi Sq. **Rixi Taxi**, T012-325 8072.

Train

Local The Gautrain is being built at the railway station. There's also a station in Hatfield.

Long distance Tshwane (Pretoria) is on the **Johannesburg–Musina** route. All other long-distance trains depart from Johannesburg. The booking office is to the right in the main station building. **Central Reservations**, T086-000 8888, www.spoornet.co.za.

⊕ Directory

Tshwane *p589, maps p589, p592 and p595*
Banks American Express, 306 Brooklyn Mall, Bronkhorst St, T012-346 3580. All banks have outlets in shopping malls with foreign exchange or ATMs. **Embassies and consulates** Australia, 282 Orient St, Arcadia, T012-423 6000, www.southafrica.embassy.gov.au. Botswana, 24 Amos St, Colbyn, T012-4309640. Canada, 1103 Arcadia St, Hatfield, T012-4223000, www.canada.co.za. Ireland, 1059 Schoeman St, Arcadia, T012-342 5062, www.embassy ireland.org.za. Lesotho, 391 Anderson St, Menlo Park, T012-460 7648. Mozambique, 75 Hamilton St, Arcadia, T012-321 2288, www.embamoc. co.za. Namibia, 191 Blackwood St, Arcadia, T012-481 9100, www.namibia.org.za. Swaziland, 71 Government Av, Arcadia, T012-344 1910, www.swazihighcom.co.za. UK, 255 Hill St, Arcadia, T012-4217500, http://ukin southafrica.fco.gov.uk. USA, 887 Pretorius St, Arcadia, T012-341 4000, http://southafrica. usembassy.gov. Zambia, 57 Ziervoel Rd, Arcadia, T012-326 1847, www.zambiapretoria.net. Zimbabwe, 78 Merton St, Arcadia, T012-342 5125. **Immigration** Dept of Home Affairs, corner of Maggs and Petroleum streets, Waltloo, T012-810 8911, www.dha.gov.za, Mon-Fri 0730-1600. Visa extensions take 5 working days. Onward ticket and proof of funds needed. **Medical services** Wilgers Hospital, Denneboom Rd, Lynnewood Ridge, T012-807 0019; Zuid-Afrikaans Hospital, (private) 255 Bourke St, Muckleneuk, T012-243 0300. **Vaccinations** Netcare Travel Clinic, 213 Middelberg St, Muckleneuk, T012-4216805, www.travelclinic.co.za.

Contents

Footprint features

Border crossings

South Africa–Mozambique

At a glance

🌐 **Getting around** Buses and Baz
Bus to Nelspruit, car hire, tours start
and finish in Johannesburg.

⬤ **Time required** 4-6 days for
Kruger and Panorama region.

🌤 **Weather** Chilly but sunny in
winter, some humidity and
showers in summer.

✖ **When not to go** Christmas
and Easter South African
school holidays.

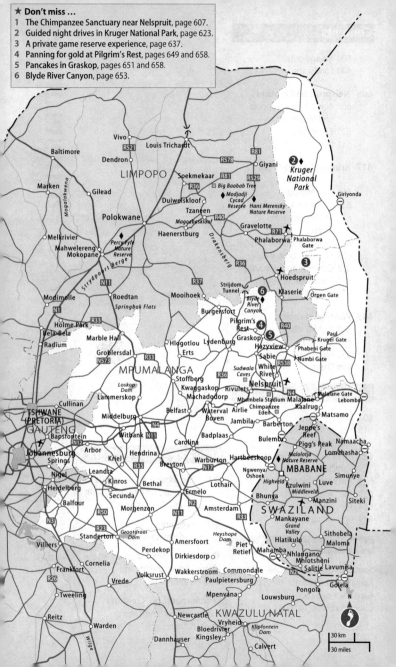

Mpumalanga, the 'place of the rising sun', is one of South Africa's most popular tourist destinations, thanks almost entirely to the magnificent Kruger National Park. Despite being completely geared towards tourism – and receiving a staggering one million visitors every year – there are few places in Africa offering such excellent game viewing. It's a vast area, roughly the same size as Wales and with a bewildering variety of habitats. While it's entirely possible to see the Big Five in one afternoon, a longer stay allows visitors to fully appreciate the wilderness of the park – and to escape to its less-visited corners. Fringing the national park are large private reserves where game wanders unrestricted by fences; also here are some of the world's most luxurious safari lodges.

The rest of the province is understandably eclipsed by Kruger, but the area west of the park is well worth a detour. The forests and waterfalls of the Eastern Drakensberg make a pleasant change from the heat of the Lowveld. This mountainous area is dotted with quiet agricultural towns, clustered along the top of the spectacular Blyde River Canyon, the third largest in the world, and a handful of viewpoints open up stunning vistas to the Lowveld shimmering to the horizon. Further into the mountains is the historical gold-mining town of Pilgrim's Rest, a string of restored miners' cottages nestling in a quiet valley. The gold-rush story continues in the Victorian town of Barberton, set in the hills close to Swaziland.

Getting there

Kruger Mpumalanga International Airport (KMIA) ① *airport enquiries, T013-753 7500, www.kmiairport.co.za*, is 25 km from the centre of Nelspruit towards Kruger off the R538, 10 km from the Maputo corridor (N4) and a short drive from Kruger's Numbi and Malalane gates. The airport is served by national airlines as well as a number of small private charter companies flying visitors into the private game reserves. With prior arrangement **City Bug** ① *T013-753 3392, www.citybug.co.za*, will take you from the airport to Nelspruit or any of the lodges in the Lowveld region around Kruger. There are also a number of car rental desks at the airport. ▸▸ *For further details, see Ins and outs, page 605, and Transport, page 615.*

Getting around

The two main areas of interest in Mpumalanga are the Kruger National Park and the eastern Drakensberg, or Panorama Region, famous for the Blyde River Canyon. The public transport network doesn't link the towns and sights effectively, so the best way to visit the more isolated beauty spots is to hire a car, and it's possible to do a leisurely circuit in two or three days. For budget travellers, the **Baz Bus** picks up and drops off at backpacker hostels in Nelspruit. From here it is possible to arrange pickups by other hostels and there are many tour operators to choose from who run inexpensive two- to three-day tours combining Kruger and the Panorama region. Alternatively, a number of affordable tours run from Johannesburg, see page 585.

Malaria

Visitors to this region must take a malaria prophylactic. Look at a map and imagine a straight line running from Nelspruit in the south directly north to the border with Zimbabwe in the Northern Province. Anywhere to the right or east of this line is an endemic malarial area. Kruger National Park is regarded as a low to medium risk, especially during and just after the rainy season when there is a lot of free-standing water. Advice is available from the very useful Kruger malaria hotline, T082-234 1800 (mob). Also visit the Malaria Research Programme of South Africa's website, www.malaria.org.za.

Tourist information

Mpumalanga Tourism Authority ① *T013-752 7001, www.mpumalanga.com, Mon-Fri 0800-1630*, is the regional office. It is located next door to the Mpumalanga Parks Board. They publish a useful regional guide and have numerous leaflets on the surrounding area, and they can make bookings and give advice on Kruger. To get there, head 5 km west of Nelspruit on the N4 (turn off at the Shell Halls Gateway service station). There is also a desk at the Kruger Mpumalanga International Airport, T013-750 2136.

Landscape

The **Lowveld** is the strip of land which extends eastwards from the foot of the Drakensberg escarpment to the border with Mozambique. It begins below the foothills of Swaziland and stretches as far north as the Blyde River Canyon and the border with the Limpopo Province. Most of the region is a low-lying humid plain, crossed by many small rivers and broken up with ridges of hills, none of which rise above 600 m.

Kruger National Park is a classic Lowveld region with its rolling savannah plains, acacia trees and herds of slowly moving game. There is superb game viewing to the west of Kruger, which is where most of the luxury private game reserves can be found. These lodges are administered separately, but now form part of what is termed as the Greater Kruger National Park thanks to the removal of fences between private reserves and the park itself.

There are several irrigation schemes along the rivers which flow eastwards off the escarpment into Kruger. The actual land under cultivation isn't large, but this is an important area for growing tropical fruit. The plantations, a major source of employment, produce bananas, avocados, mangoes, lychees and citrus fruits. Throughout the year, stalls line the roads in the area selling off fresh produce.

Nelspruit and around

→ *Colour map 2, B5. Phone code: 013. Altitude: 716 m.*
Nelspruit developed around the railway when the line between Pretoria and Lourenço Marques (now Maputo) was completed in 1891. Briefly the capital of the Transvaal Republic after Paul Kruger abandoned Pretoria in 1900 during the Boer War, Nelspruit is now the industrial centre of the Lowveld and a processing point for the fruit, tobacco and beef farms of the surrounding region. The town has a sleepy, tropical feel with broad, modern streets lined with acacias, bougainvillea and jacaranda trees. Although there's little to keep you here, most visitors to the region pass through at some point. ▸▸ *For listings, see pages 611-616. For places north of Nelspruit, see pages 645-660.*

Ins and outs
Getting there Nelspruit has good transport links, with an important international airport and good train and bus links. There are great facilities here for tourists planning trips to Swaziland, the Panorama region and Kruger National Park, as well as across the border to Mozambique (there is a daily train service between Tshwane (Pretoria)/Johannesburg and Komatipoort, the border post with Mozambique). The **Baz Bus** runs from Johannesburg, Tshwane (Pretoria) and Swaziland. **Greyhound**, **Intercape** and **Translux** all operate services from Johannesburg and Tshwane (Pretoria) to Maputo in Mozambique, which stop in Nelspruit. ▸▸ *For details, see Transport, page 615.*

Getting around Nelspruit has excellent road links to Mpumalanga's major tourist attractions. The nearest entrance gates to Kruger are less than 80 km away on the N4 (east), and the R40 through White River (north), and a day trip to see the southern sector of the park is quite feasible. The gold rush town of Barberton is 43 km to the south on the R40, and a visit here could be combined with a day trip over the border to Swaziland. The mountain villages of Sabie and Graskop are equally accessible and make a pleasant change from the heat of the Lowveld. All these places have an excellent range of accommodation and there is little reason to stay in the centre of town. The shopping centres in town are convenient for stocking up on food and equipment before setting off to stay in self-catering accommodation in Kruger.

Orientation Nelspruit has grown rapidly in recent years and it has a prosperous air with a new sprawl of well-off suburbs surrounding the city centre. New business parks and a number of shopping malls have been built in the area, especially along the road to White River. As a consequence, Nelspruit has extended its municipality by joining with neighbouring White River and Hazyview to form the Mbombela Municipal Region (meaning, appropriately, 'a lot of people put together in a small space'). Mbombela is now the provincial capital of Mpumalanga Province. The new Mbombela Stadium is 8 km northwest of Nelspruit (follow the N4 out of town) for the 2010 FIFA World Cup™. The signature feature is the 18 tall roof supports that resemble giraffes.

Tourist information **Lowveld Tourism Association** ① *Crossing Centre, at the junction of the N4 and the R40, just west of the centre, T013-755 1988, www.lowveldtourism.com, Mon-Fri 0800-1700, Sat 0800-1500,* is the main tourist office for the entire region. It can organize car hire, safaris, game drives and accommodation in Kruger.

From Gauteng to Nelspruit
The journey east along the N4 from Gauteng crosses a bland, sprawling area of cattle ranching country, broken up by industrial towns like Witbank and Middleberg. There's little to break the monotony of the drive, other than a couple of looming coal-fired power stations. At **Machadodorp** the views improve; the road starts to drop into the Elands River Valley and the vista opens up over the Lowveld, passing through the towns of **Waterval**

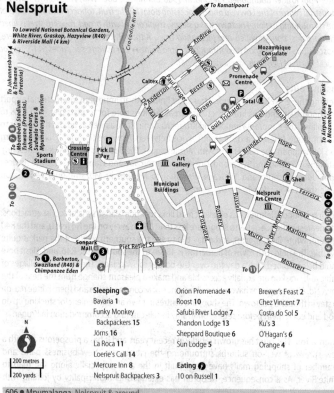

Nelspruit

To Komatipoort

To Lowveld National Botanical Gardens, White River, Graskop, Hazyview (R40) & Riverside Mall (4 km)

To Johannesburg & Tshwane (Pretoria)

To Johannesburg & Tshwane (Pretoria), Johannesburg, Suvuela Cave & Mpumalanga Tourism

To Mbombela Stadium, Tshwane (Pretoria), Johannesburg, Suvuela Cave & Mpumalanga Tourism

Crocodile River

Andrew
Moortrekker
Mozambique Consulate
Brown
Caltex
Paul Kruger
Bester
Promenade Centre
Anderson
De Waal
Brown
Total
Louis Trichardt
Bell
Henshall
To Airport, Kruger Park & Mozambique

Crossing Centre
Sports Stadium
Pick n'Pay
Art Gallery
Hope
Brandels
Streak
Jones
Shell
Ferreira

N4

Municipal Buildings
Nelspruit Art Centre
Russell
Rothery
H Potgieter
Ehmke
Marloth

Sonpark Mall
Piet Retief St
Van der Merwe
Murry
Monstert

To ①, Barberton, Swaziland (R40) & Chimpanzee Eden

To ⑪

N

200 metres
200 yards

Sleeping	Orion Promenade 4	Brewer's Feast 2
Bavaria 1	Roost 10	Chez Vincent 7
Funky Monkey	Safubi River Lodge 7	Costa do Sol 5
Backpackers 15	Shandon Lodge 13	Ku's 3
Jörns 16	Sheppard Boutique 6	O'Hagan's 6
La Roca 11	Sun Lodge 5	Orange 4
Loerie's Call 14		
Mercure Inn 8	**Eating**	
Nelspruit Backpackers 3	10 on Russell 1	

Boven and **Waterval Onder**. This is a beautiful stretch of road with high cliffs on either side. Dotted along the valley are a number of country hotels and motels which catch the holiday traffic en route to Kruger Park and Mozambique.

Lowveld National Botanical Gardens

ⓘ *1 km north of Nelspruit on the R40, T013-752 5531, www.sanbi.org. Sep-May 0800-1800, Apr-Aug 0800-1700, R17, children (under 16) R7, also has a restaurant.*

The Lowveld National Botanical Gardens are relatively small but have a very important and rare collection of plants, and there are a number of trails you can follow. The visitor centre has interesting information on the flora and fauna of the area, as well as an attached nursery and bookshop. If you turn left after entering the gardens you will see a boardwalk which takes you through a 3-ha **Tropical Rainforest**. At the far end of the path is an open area of marshland which is good birdwatching country. A fair amount of this developed part of the gardens is wheelchair accessible.

At the other end of the gardens is the **Cycad Collection**, the largest of its kind in Africa, and the **Riverside Trail** – a 1-km walk along the banks of the Crocodile River, with a bridge linking the two sides. The well-illustrated guide that accompanies the trail identifies over 130 plants and shrubs that were once typical of a wilderness around Nelspruit. This is also home to the rare and shy African finfoot, but you will have to walk very quietly to have any chance of spotting this bird. The trail takes about an hour but is steep and uneven in parts.

Sudwala Caves

ⓘ *36 km northwest of Nelspruit, follow the N4 westwards, turn onto the R539 (towards Sabie) after 30 km and follow the signs for the caves, T013-733 4152, www.sudwalacaves.co.za. A 90-min tour departs every 30 mins 0830-1630, R50, children (5-15) R25, under 5s free.*

The entrance to the caves is on a forested hillside in the Houtbosloop Valley. Only the first 2.5 km of the cave system has been explored and it is thought that the passages could lead much further into the mountains. A tour explores the first 600 m of the cave system, where the stalactites and stalagmites are lit by coloured spotlights. The rock formations have been given biblical names, such as Lot's wife, Devil's pulpit and the weeping Madonna. One of the most interesting formations is the Gong, which resonates through the cave chambers when struck. Keen cavers can organize a special visit to the Crystal Chamber on the first Saturday of each month, which takes five hours and must be booked in advance; no children and some of the spaces are very tight.

Chimpanzee Eden

ⓘ *16 km south of Nelspruit off the R40 towards Barberton, T013-745 7406, www.jane goodall.co.za. A 1½ hr tour departs at 1000, 1200 and 1400, feeding times 1000 and 1400, R170, children (under 12) R50.*

Jane Goodall Institute's Chimpanzee Eden (also known as Chimp Eden) is set on 1000 ha, part of the Umholti Nature Reserve. The nature reserve is naturally home to species including giraffe, zebra and various antelope. Chimp Eden is a equal partnership between the Cussons family who own the reserve, and the Jane Goodall Institute, which is committed to the rescue and care of chimps in need of refuge. It's the first and only chimp sanctuary in South Africa and at present is home to 29 chimps who live in spacious semi-wild enclosures with plenty of trees. Although chimps do not naturally live in South Africa, the enclosure is made up of vegetation similar to that of the chimp's indigenous homes. Many of them have arrived here as a result of being rescued from the bushmeat trade or

Border crossing: South Africa–Mozambique

Komatipoort/Lebombo–Ressano Garcia

The South African border post is at Lebombo, 3 km out of town. There is a viewpoint on a hill by the border from where one can look into Mozambique, striking for the rolls of barbed wire that stretch along either side of the border to prevent people crossing illegally. There is a new toll road between Nelspruit and Maputo; the journey between the two cities takes around 2½ hours. Komatipoort is 96 km from Maputo.

Border opening hours Daily 0600-2200.

Customs and immigration Most visitors require visas for Mozambique; these are issued at the border, US$25 or the equivalent in rand. South African's do not need a visa.

Vehicle formalities Note that most hire car firms do not allow vehicles into Mozambique. If you are in your own vehicle, you will need a carnet de passages and will need to purchase third-party insurance at the border.

as pets from other parts of Africa. Interestingly, a few were rescued from Luanda in Angola where they use tame chimps as attractions in nightclubs. There's a visitors' centre, which tells the stories of the individual chimps, a pleasant café called **Junglicious** and tours that take you to shaded observation platforms around the enclosure from where you can watch the chimps socialize, play and swing through the branches. Each has a distinctive personality and they put on quite a comical performance for visitors, children will love it.

Towards Komatipoort and Mozambique ●●●● ➤ *pp611-616.*

The N4 heads east from Nelspruit to Komatipoort (104 km), past the villages of Kaapmuiden, Malalane and Hectorspruit. The road follows the Crocodile River Valley through an area of fruit plantations at the bottom edge of Kruger National Park. This valley is one of the hottest areas of South Africa with year-round temperatures averaging 25-30°C.

Malalane → *Colour map 2, B5. Phone code: 013.*

A dusty town with a sprawling shopping centre, Malalane is the hub of a sugarcane- and fruit-growing area. There's not much to the town itself but thanks to its proximity to Kruger there are a number of excellent game lodges along the Crocodile River around this region. The R570 continues north through the village to the entrance to Kruger Park at Malalane Gate. If you are self-catering in Kruger, Malalane has a Pick n' Pay and Spar.

The Matsamo/Jeppes Reef border crossing into **Swaziland** (open 0800-2000), is 38 km south of Malalane on the R570.

Komatipoort → *Colour map 2, B5. Phone code: 013. Altitude: 137 m. 104 km from Nelspruit.*

Komatipoort is the last town in South Africa before the main road enters Mozambique at Lebombo. In the early days, it was just a campsite by the river crossing but as soon as the railway arrived in 1890, it quickly developed into a permanent settlement. Travelling from Lourenço Marques (today Maputo), this was the only place where the railway could pass through the Lebombo Mountains. The Nkhomati Accord was signed here in March 1984 between Samora Machel, President of Mozambique and PW Botha, Prime Minister of South Africa. The accord intended to promote peace and co-operation between the two countries but met with limited success as Mozambique, along with the rest of Africa, was still a staunch

Footprint Mini Atlas
South Africa

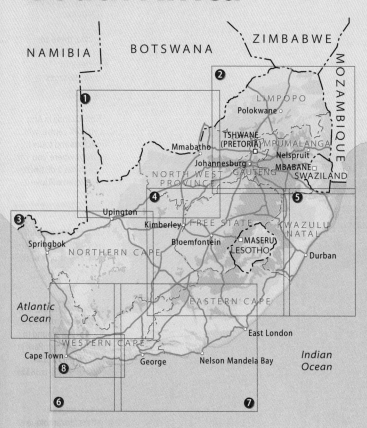

NAMIBIA   BOTSWANA   ZIMBABWE

MOZAMBIQUE

①

②

LIMPOPO

Polokwane ○

Mmabatho

TSHWANE
(PRETORIA) □ MPUMALANGA

Nelspruit

Johannesburg ○

■ MBABANE □

GAUTENG   SWAZILAND

NORTH WEST
PROVINCE

④

⑤

③

Upington ○

KWAZULU
NATAL

Kimberley ○ FREE STATE

Springbok ○

Bloemfontein ○

■ MASERU
LESOTHO

NORTHERN CAPE

Durban ○

Atlantic
Ocean

EASTERN CAPE

East London ○

WESTERN CAPE

Cape Town ○

George ○

Nelson Mandela Bay

Indian
Ocean

⑧

⑥

⑦

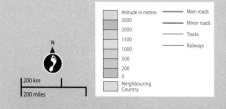

Altitude in metres		Main roads
3000		Minor roads
2000		Tracks
1500		Railways
1000		
500		
200		
0		
	Neighbouring Country	

N

200 km
200 miles

Map 1

BOTSWANA

A

B

C

Kgalagadi
Transfrontier
Park ◆

Nossob ○

Kgalagadi
Transfrontier
Park ◆

Nossob

⊖ Mata Mata

Auob

Twee Rivieren ○—○ Two Riviers

Rietfontein ⊖

Hakskeenpan

Andriesvale ○

Askham ○—○ Staansaam ○

Cramond ○

Obobogorap ○

Noenieput ○

Makapong ○

Molopo

Vorstershoo ○

Tshabong ○

McCarthy's Rest ○

R380

Severn ○

Middelputs ○

Molopo

Aansluit ○

Van Zylsrus ○

R31

Black
Rock ○

Sonstraal ○

Hotazel ○

Tswalu Kalahari ◆
Reserve

Gordonia

Koranneberg

Kalahari

Kathi

Olifantshoek ○

3↓

To Keetmanshoop
⊖ Nakop

Ariamsvlei ⊖

1

N8

Green Kalahari

R360

Spitskop ◆
Nature Reserve

Lutzputz

2

N14

3

Postmasbu

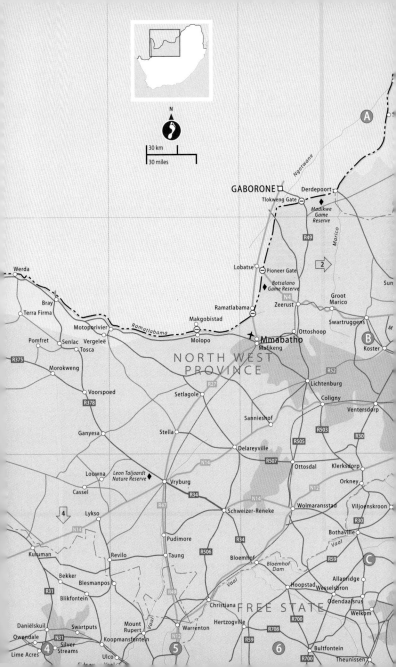

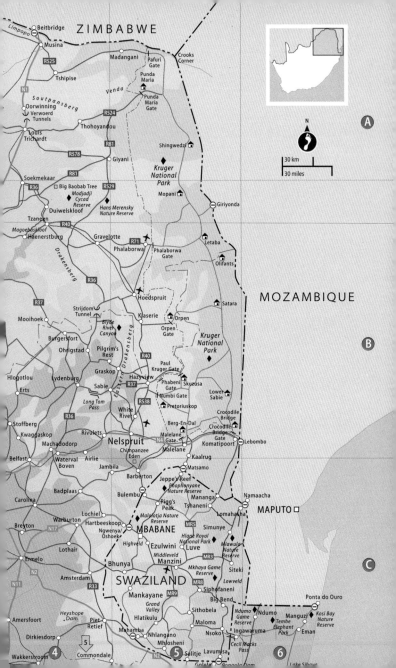

Map 3

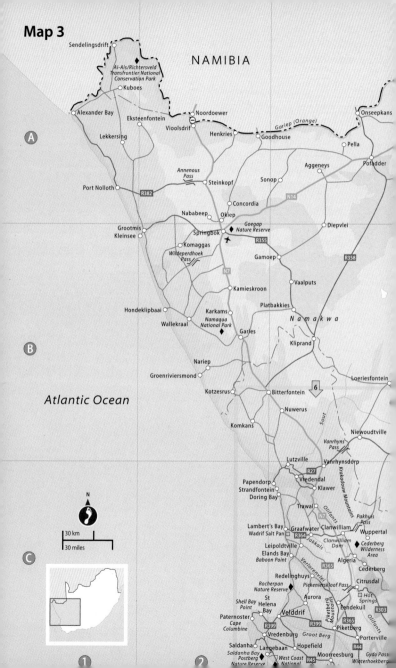

NAMIBIA

Sendelingsdrift
Ai-Ais/Richtersveld Transfrontier National Conservation Park
Kuboes
Alexander Bay
Eksteenfontein
Noordoewer
Viooolsdrif
Henkries
Gariep (Orange)
Onseepkans

Lekkersing
Goodhouse
Pella

A

Annenous Pass
Steinkopf
Sonop
Aggeneys
Pofadder

Port Nolloth
R382
Concordia
N14

Nababeep
Okiep
Diepvlei

Grootmis
Kleinsee
Springbok
Goegap Nature Reserve
R355

Komaggas
Wildeperdhoek Pass
N7
Gamoep
R358

Kamieskroon
Vaalputs

B

Hondeklipbaai
Platbakkies
Namakwa

Wallekraal
Karkams
Namaqua National Park
Garies

Kliprand

Nariep
Loeriesfontein

Groenriviersmond
Kotzesrus
Bitterfontein
6

Atlantic Ocean
Nuwerus
Sout
Niewoudtville

Komkans
Vanrhyns Pass

Lutzville
Vanrhynsdorp

N
30 km
30 miles

Papendorp
Strandfontein
Doring Bay
Vredendal
R27
Klawer
Krakadouw Mountains

Trawal
N7
Olifants
Pakhuis Pass

C

Lambert's Bay
Wadrif Salt Pan
Graafwater
R364
Clanwilliam
Wuppertal

Leipoldtville
Clanwilliam Dam
Cederberg Wilderness Area

Elands Bay
Baboon Point
R365
Algeria
Cederberg

Redelinghuys
Rocherpan Nature Reserve
Piekenierskloof Pass
Citrusdal
Hot Springs

Shell Bay Point
St Helena Bay
Aurora
Piketberg Mountains
R303

Paternoster
Cape Columbine
Velddrif
Groot Berg
Piketberg
Porterville
R44

Saldanha
Langebaan
R399
Vredenburg
R399
Hopefield
Moorreesburg
R365
Gydo Pass
Winterhoekberg

Saldanha Bay
Postberg
Nature Reserve
West Coast National
R45

1
2

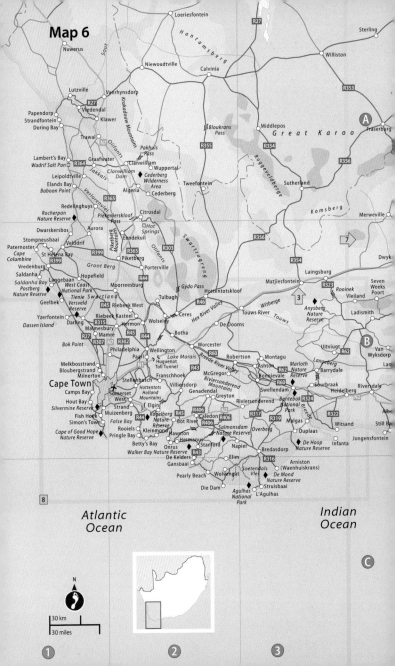

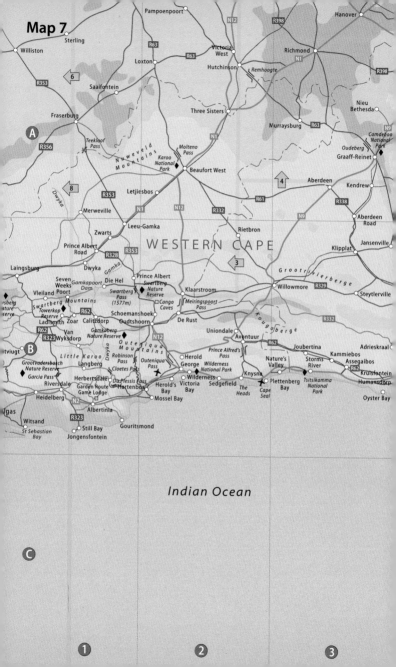

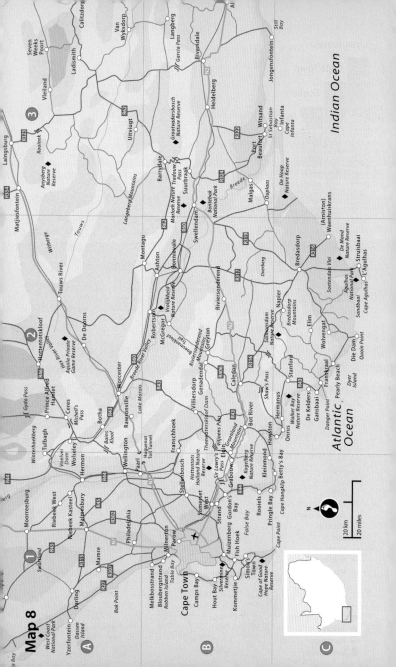

South Africa distance chart

Bloemfontein										
1004	**Cape Town**									
634	1753	**Durban**								
584	1079	674	**East London**							
773	438	1319	645	**George**						
398	1402	588	982	1171	**Johannesburg**					
177	962	811	780	762	472	**Kimberley**				
677	769	984	310	335	1075	743	**Nelson Mandela Bay**			
757	1762	707	1226	1530	355	827	1434	**Nelspruit**		
727	1736	929	1323	1499	331	798	1393	315	**Polokwane**	
456	1460	646	1040	1229	58	530	322	273	1133	**Tshwane (Pretoria)**

Distances in kilometres   1 kilometre = 0.62 miles

Map symbols

□	Capital city
○	Other city, town
⁓⁓	International border
⁓⁓	Regional border
⊖	Customs
◯	Contours (approx)
▲	Mountain, volcano
⌐	Mountain pass
⌐	Escarpment
⌐	Glacier
▦	Salt flat
⊙	Rocks
⩊	Seasonal marshland
⠿	Beach, sandbank
⩍	Waterfall
⌒	Reef
═══	Motorway
───	Main road
───	Minor road
≍≍≍	Track
⋮⋮⋮	Footpath
─┼─	Railway
⊹■	Railway with station
✈	Airport
⊟	Bus station
Ⓜ	Metro station

- - - -	Cable car
⊞⊞⊞	Funicular
⚓	Ferry
▭▭▭	Pedestrianized street
⊃ ⊂	Tunnel
→	One way-street
⋮⋮⋮⋮⋮	Steps
⊐⊏	Bridge
▴▴▴	Fortified wall
▱	Park, garden, stadium
⊙	Sleeping
❶	Eating
❽	Bars & clubs
▨	Building
■	Sight
✝	Cathedral, church
⛩	Chinese temple
⛩	Hindu temple
⚶	Meru
☪	Mosque
⛄	Stupa
✡	Synagogue
⊞	Tourist office
⛫	Museum
✉	Post office
℗	Police

Ⓢ	Bank
@	Internet
♪	Telephone
☎	Market
⊞	Medical services
Ⓟ	Parking
ⓟ	Petrol
⚘	Golf
∴	Archaeological site
♦	National park, wildlife reserve
✿	Viewing point
⋀	Campsite
⌂	Refuge, lodge
⛫	Castle, fort
⚲	Diving
ⴷⴷ	Deciduous, coniferous, palm trees
⌂	Hide
⚘	Vineyard, winery
⚗	Distillery
⚓	Shipwreck
✕	Historic battlefield
Ⓐ	Detail map
Ⓐ	Related map

Index

opponent to the Apartheid regime and supported sanctions. Not far from here on the Komati flats is the **Machel Memorial**, which is a national monument marking the site where President Samora Machel died in a plane crash in 1986. Joaquim Chissano succeeded him and his widow, Graca Machel, went on to marry Nelson Mandela a few years later.

Today, the town is an important marshalling yard for the railways and a popular centre for supplies for visitors to Kruger National Park (**Crocodile Gate** is only 9 km away). Lying at the foot of the Lebombo Mountains at the confluence of the Komati and Crocodile rivers and little over 60 km from the Indian Ocean, the climate here is tropical and humid, with high summer temperatures and rainfall. Fortunately, the streets are shaded by poinciana and jacaranda trees, which provide essential shade. There are supermarkets in the town centre along Rissik Street.

)) *Mahatma Gandhi was imprisoned in Komatipoort in 1907, before escaping to the coast (see box, Mahatma Gandhi in South Africa, page 476).*

Barberton ⬤🅑🅞🅞🅖 ▶▶ pp611-616. Colour map 2, C5.

→ *Phone code: 013.*

This quiet colonial town, 43 km from Nelspruit, is a pleasant place to spend a day or two, and offers a surprising amount to do and see, including a couple of community projects and several museums. The Swaziland border is only 43 km away. It has an interesting gold mining past and, unlike the gold mining town of Pilgrim's Rest near Sabie, which is completely devoted to tourism, the old corrugated-iron roofed mining buildings in Barberton are very much part of the working commercial town. **Lone Tree Hill**, on the outskirts of Barberton, is one of the most popular hang-gliding centres in South Africa. It is set in the De Kaap Valley where some of the oldest sedimentary rock formations in the world have been found (4200 million years). The Makhonjwa Mountains around Barberton are covered in grasslands and woods and are an extension of the southern Drakensberg.

The road into Barberton passes the Emjindini township before entering the quiet, wealthy, garden suburbs on the edge of town. An old, abandoned mining centre, suitably named Eureka City, is tucked up in the hills at the back of the working Sheba mine (visits can be arranged in a 4WD). The main sights in town are all within walking distance and the hiking trails start from the edge of town.

Ins and outs

Tourist information **Barberton Information Bureau** ① *Market Sq, T013-712 2880, www.barberton.co.za, Mon-Fri 0800-1300, 1400-1630, Sat 0830-1200*, is a friendly and helpful office with good information on tours and accommodation in the area.

Background

The De Kaap Valley was originally known as the 'Valley of Death' due to the many prospectors who had died here of malaria. Barberton is famous for being the site of one of South Africa's first large-scale gold rushes. Pioneer Reef was discovered in 1883 by 'French Bob' and by 1886 over 4000 claims were being worked in the valley. Barberton became a wild frontier town of corrugated-iron shacks, gambling dens and whisky bars.

The town soon developed into a wealthy hub. South Africa's first gold stock exchange opened here in 1887 and many of Barberton's most attractive colonial buildings were erected during the gold rush. Unfortunately, the gold rush only lasted a few years – the stock market crashed after too many speculators were sold shares in bogus companies and investors lost fortunes in the Transvaal and Britain. By the outbreak of the Boer War, Barberton had been virtually abandoned by the miners who had moved on to Witwatersrand. However, in recent years the industry has been revived and four gold mines operate within the area: Sheba, Fairview, New Consort, and Agnes, providing employment for much of the local community.

Sights

The historical sites within the town have been clearly mapped out by Barberton's tourism initiative as the **Heritage Walk**, and are all within walking distance of Market Square. Pick up a map at the tourist office. The walk starts from the Barberton Museum and ends at the Steam Locomotive. The sights have been listed below in order of the walk. Only Belhaven House Museum and Stopforth House Museum have an entry fee, R10 per person, but you only need pay once to cover entrance at both.

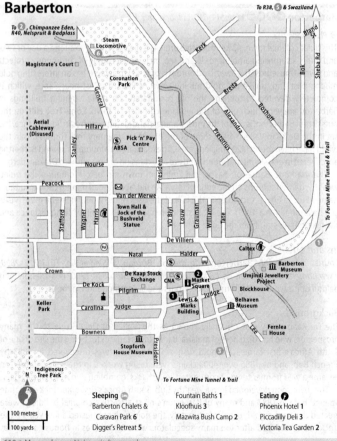

Barberton

To R38, ⑤ & Swaziland

To ②, Chimpanzee Eden, R40, Nelspruit & Badplass

Steam Locomotive ⑥

Magistrate's Court □

Coronation Park

Kerk

Breda

Boshoff

Brand St

Bok

Sheba Rd

Aerial Cableway (Disused)

Hillary

Stanley

Pick 'n' Pay Centre
$ ABSA

President

Pretorius

Alexandra

❸

To Fortuna Mine Tunnel & Trail

Nourse

Peacock

Stafford

Wagner

Harris

✉ Van der Merwe

Town Hall & Jock of the Bushveld Statue □

VD Biyl

Louw

Grauman

Williams

Tate

De Villiers

Natal

(Pol)

Halder

Caltex ⛽

❶

Crown

De Kock

De Kaap Stock Exchange

$ CNA

❷ ℹ Market Square

Barberton Museum 🏛

Umjindi Jewellery Project

Blockhouse

Pilgrim

Carolina

Judge

Keller Park

Bowness

❶ Lewis & Marks Building

Judge

Belhaven Museum 🏛

Lee

Fernlea House

Stopforth House Museum 🏛

President

❸

Indigenous Tree Park

N

To Fortuna Mine Tunnel & Trail

👣

100 metres
100 yards

Sleeping 🛏
Barberton Chalets & Caravan Park 6
Digger's Retreat 5

Fountain Baths 1
Kloofhuis 3
Mazwita Bush Camp 2

Eating 🍴
Phoenix Hotel 1
Piccadilly Deli 3
Victoria Tea Garden 2

Barberton Museum ① *36 Pilgrim St, T013-712 4280, daily 0900-1600*, is the town's local history museum with displays on geology, mining and cultural history of the area, including some displays on Swazi history. **The Blockhouse** ① *on the corner of Lee Rd and Judge St*, is a small fort built in 1901 during the Boer War as part of the defence of Barberton. It is made from wood and corrugated iron and is one of the earliest examples of its kind. **Belhaven Museum** ① *Lee Rd, daily 1000-1200, 1400-1500*, is a large, early Edwardian mansion built in 1904 and set in mature gardens. The interior is decorated with period furniture and gives an interesting insight into the comfortable lifestyles of Barberton's middle class. **Fernlea House** ① *Lee Rd, Mon-Fri 0900-1300, 1400-1600*, was built in the 1890s from wood and iron. The house is in a beautiful setting at the bottom of a wooded valley on the edge of Barberton. It is decorated with period furniture and has displays on Barberton's famous botanists.

The walk passes **Rimer's Creek**, the site where, on 24 June 1884, David Wilson the mining commissioner, broke a bottle of gin over a rock to christen the new town of Barberton. At the time, Rimer's Creek was a popular recreational spot for the townsfolk, particularly on Wednesdays when it was frequented by the barmaids of the town.

To the west, **Stopforth House** ① *18 Bowness St, daily 1000-1200, 1400-1500*, belonged to James Stopforth, a baker and a general dealer, and was built in 1886. The Stopforth family lived here until 1983.

The **De Kaap Stock Exchange** on Pilgrim Street was built in 1887. All that remains of the original structure is the façade, which has been declared a national monument. The **Lewis and Marks Building**, also on Pilgrim Street and completed in 1887, was Barberton's first two-storey building and housed the **Bank of Africa**. In later years, the iron veranda was removed and a third storey added. Close by, **Market Square**, is a quiet place shaded by trees with whitewashed colonial buildings on all four sides.

Heading north, the walk continues to President Square and the town hall. In front is a statue of **Jock of the Bushveld**, the faithful dog of Percy Fitzpatrick during his days as a transport rider. The **steam locomotive** on General Street, by the entrance to the caravan park, dates to 1899 and used to run between Barberton and Kaapmuiden.

An **aerial cableway** crosses town and is clearly visible climbing the mountains that border Swaziland. It was built in 1938 to transport asbestos 20 km over mountainous terrain from the Havelock mine in Swaziland to the railhead in Barberton. Until 2002 it was still in use taking coal, transported to Barberton from Witbank, back to Swaziland on the return journey to fuel the mine. Today, it hangs rather forlornly over Barberton.

There are two other short local walking trails starting from the centre of town; the **Rose Creek Walk** and the **Fortuna Trail** (2 km). The Fortuna Trail starts on Crown Street and passes through a 500-m tunnel, which is part of an old mine. There is no lighting inside the tunnel so bring a torch.

◉ Nelspruit and around listings

For Sleeping and Eating price codes and other relevant information, see pages 46-53.

Nelspruit *p605, map p606*

A Sheppard Boutique Hotel, 23 Sheppard Drive, T013-752 3394, www.sheppard boutique.co.za. A relative newcomer and the only luxury offering in town, with tastefully decorated suites with large beds, antique furnishings, stylish prints, and low-key lighting. Elegant, old-fashioned lounge and

◉ Sleeping

Being so tantalizingly close to Kruger, it makes little sense to stay in town, but nevertheless there's a surprisingly good range of accommodation in Nelspruit.

dining room serving good South African cuisine. Swimming pool and tennis courts.

B La Roca, 56 van Wyk St, T013-752 6628, www.laroca.co.za. Recently refurbished guesthouse with 9 rooms, each with a private balcony or patio with views across the Lowveld, stylish decor and stone bathrooms, TV, bar fridge, ceiling fans, lounge, lovely swimming pool surrounded by boulders, thatched pool bar and dining lapa, dinner on request, will collect from town centre and airport. Recommended.

B Mercure Inn, corner of Graniet St and N4, T013-741 4222, www.mercure.com. Part of a successful quality French chain, with 104 luxury self-catering, single-storey units, TV, a/c, airport transfers, large conference facilities. Spacious lounge and bar, attractive pool area (harps on a bit about having the largest pool in Nelspruit). Good deals on the website if booking online.

B Orion Hotel Promenade, Louis Trichardt St, T013-753 3000, www.oriongroup.co.za. A smart hotel in what used to be Nelspruit's town hall, complete with a clock tower. 72 a/c rooms with DSTV, non-smoking rooms available. Restaurant, bar, terrace overlooking a small pool, tastefully designed interior, secure parking, but suffers from a lack of recreational space. Many of the mainline buses stop here.

C Jörns, 62 Hunter St, T013-744 1894, www.jorns.co.za. Large guesthouse run by a German who is a registered guide so can organize local tours. 9 comfortable rooms, all en suite and some with corner bath in the bedroom. Lounge, bar, swimming pool with beautiful views over the Lowveld, koi fishpond in the tropical garden.

C The Loerie's Call, 2 Du Preez St, T013-744 1251, www.loeriescall.co.za. Boutique-style guesthouse with 10 spacious double rooms with a/c, DSTV, CD players, minibar, all set in a modern building, with private terraces from where there are views across the Crocodile River Valley. Non-smoking room, TV, laundry service, B&B, swimming pool, gardens.

C Safubi River Lodge, 45 Graniet St, 2 km from the city centre, T013-741 3253,

www.safubi.co.za. Self-catering upmarket apartments, with 1-3 bedrooms, fully equipped kitchen, bathroom, lounge, DSTV, secure parking, braai in the garden, set in 16 ha of bushveld on the banks of the Gladdespruit River. Also a 40-site camping and caravan park. Large, peaceful and secure, with swimming pool and communal kitchens. Coffee shop serving breakfast and light meals.

C Shandon Lodge, 1 Saturn St, a distance from the town centre, follow Ferreira St out of town, T013-744 9934, www.shandon.co.za. Fine colonial-style house on a hilltop suburb, 5 mins' drive from town. Each room opens up onto a shaded veranda running around the house, with views over the small pool and terrace overlooking the countryside. 7 large double rooms with country-style decor, separate seating area, M-Net TV, and tea and coffee facilities with home-made biscuits. Pleasant bar, meals on request, huge breakfasts served in the cool dining room. Friendly, family-run with lots of advice on the area. No children under 12. Recommended.

D Bavaria, 45 Zebrina Cres, T013-741 1703 http://bavariaguestlodge.co.za. Homely guesthouse set in a converted home surrounded by tropical gardens, in a quiet suburb just west of town. 9 en suite rooms with bright, African-themed decor, all rooms have M-Net TV, tea and coffee facilities and work stations. Breakfasts served in bright breakfast room overlooking garden and pool, and there's a cosy bar.

D The Roost, 21c Koraalboom St, T013-741 1419, www.roostguestlodge.co.za. Spacious old house with 8 smart double rooms and en suite bathrooms, TV, M-Net, overhead fans, swimming pool, set apart from the main house, conference facilities, secure parking, plenty of atmosphere. Recommended.

D-F Sun Lodge, 7 de Villiers St, T013-741 2253, www.sunlodge.co.za. Garden chalet plus double room in main house, dorms, pool set in colourful lush gardens, close to shops and restaurants. On the Baz Bus route.

E-F Funky Monkey Backpackers, 102 van Wyk St, T013-7441310, www.funkymonkeys.

co.za. Dorms, doubles and camping, with rooms spread through a spacious house adorned with bright artwork. Swimming pool, pool table and bar. Can organize trips to Kruger and Blyde River Canyon. Baz Bus stop.
E-F Nelspruit Backpackers, 9 Andries Pretorius St, T013-741 2237. Mix of dorms and double rooms in a good location next to a nature reserve. Kitchen, laundry, bar, pool table, swimming pool, close to restaurants and pubs in the Sunpark Centre. Free pickup service from town, on the Baz Bus route. Excellent base from which to explore the area and can organize day trips to Blyde River Canyon and Kruger.

Malalane p608

L Serenity Forest Eco Reserve, T013-790 2000, www.serenitylodge.co.za. While most of the lodges in this region are on the fringes of Kruger and the Crocodile River, this lodge is in an unusual location in a patch of rainforest high up in the hills in the opposite direction, 12 km off the R570 toward the Jeppe's Reef border with Swaziland. 2 camps of luxury thatched chalets overlooking the trees, with private verandas overlooking the butterfly-filled forest, all linked by walkways in the trees, unusual sunken bar and spa. Hiking and 4WD trails through forest, no children under 14, rates include dinner and afternoon tea. Beautiful spot that combines visits to Kruger with somewhere a little different to stay. Recommended.
B Thanda-Nani Game Lodge, the turning is 11 km east of Malalane, clearly signposted on the left of the N4, T013-792 4543, www.thandanani.com. 6500-ha private luxury game farm with 10 a/c stylish double rooms set in thatched rondavels. Lounge and dining area set under an open thatched area, rates include breakfast and dinner, attractive pool, game drives with chance of seeing range of wildlife including black and white rhino and a fairly tame herd of zebra that wander through the grounds and can be fed with carrots. Enjoyable and good-value variation on the full-on Kruger experience.

D Selati 103 Guest Cottages, 103 Selati Cres, 2 km before the Malalane Gate on the same road, T013-790 0978, www.selati103.co.za. 9 garden cottages, self-catering or B&B and dinner on request, colourful decor, TV, large swimming pool, comfortable option before entering Kruger.

Komatipoort p608

C Tree's Too, 11 Furley St, T013-790 8262, www.treestoo.com. 8 large, a/c double or family rooms under thatch, all with separate entrances and set in lush tropical gardens under palm trees. Lounge, pleasant pool area, small restaurant serving breakfast and dinner on request, or can provide picnic breakfasts for those making an early start into Kruger.

Barberton p609, map p610

B Mazwita Bush Camp, 17 km from Barberton on the R40 towards Nelspruit, T082-604 1190, www.mazwita.co.za. 4 spacious and stylishly decorated thatched chalets with private patios, linked by board-walks in a pretty tract of indigenous forest. Bar and lapa with African decor for dining, overlooking a waterhole that attracts various antelope. A peaceful country retreat.
D Barberton Chalets & Caravan Park, General St, T013-712 3323, www.barbertonchalets.co.za. 26 self-catering chalets sleeping up to 6, serviced daily. Caravan spots and campsite set in the neatly maintained shady gardens with a swimming pool, children's playground, tea garden, shop and launderette.
D Digger's Retreat, 11 km out of town, signposted just off the R38 to Kaapmuiden, T013- 719 9681, www.diggersretreat hotel.com. Country hotel dating to the 1930s with 18 simple but comfortable rooms in the main building or in thatched rondavels in the lush garden. A grassy campsite, à la carte restaurant with a long menu, **Old Gold Rush** pub with themed decor, and a large swimming pool.
D Fountain Baths, 48 Pilgrim St, T013-712 2707. Mix of B&B double rooms and self-catering units sleeping 2-4, dinner on request.

Simple decor with wooden floors, garden with swimming pool, peaceful setting edging on to the hills. The house was originally built in 1884 as a bath house for miners.
D Kloofhuis, 1 Kloof St, T013-712 4268. Central location just behind **Belhaven House**, a short walk from the tourist office. A fine Victorian home with wrap-around veranda and 4 double and twin rooms, en suite or shared bathroom. Homely setting, floral decor, relaxing place to stay.

⊘ Eating

Nelspruit *p605, map p606*
The centre of town gets very quiet at night, with just a handful of restaurants open for evening meals. Most places are in the suburbs.
ⓗⓗ Chez Vincent, 56 Ferreira St, T013-744 1146. Fri-Sat 1800-2030. Weekend dinner venue in an informal restaurant with modern paintings on the wall and a bistro-style French menu (the chef comes from Toulouse). Good calamari, prawns, beef fillet and interesting vegetable side dishes, and a small but well-selected wine list.
ⓗⓗ-ⓗ Orange Restaurant, 4 Du Preez St, T013-744 9507, www.orangerestaurant.co.za. Mon-Sat 1200-1500, 1800-2200, Sat 0900-1100 for brunch. Provincial French-style cuisine in intimate surroundings with contemporary decor, broad deck with good views over Nelspruit and excellent wine list. Menu changes seasonally but expect the likes of duck, salmon, venison or rack of lamb. You can also opt for a build-your-own salad at lunchtime and a 6-course set gourmet menu at dinner. Recommended.
ⓗ 10 on Russell, 10 Russell St, T013-755 2376, http://10onrussell.co.za. Mon-Sat 1130-1430, 1800-2230. Sophisticated restaurant set in an historical building, decorated with oil paintings and flowers, with a small but creative menu of dishes like an avocado, biltong and feta tower for starters and smoked trout pie and beef fillet rolled

in coconut and stuffed with sun-dried tomatoes for mains.
ⓗ Costa do Sol, ABSA Sq, Paul Kruger St, T013-752 6382, www.nelspruitrestaurants. co.za. Mon-Sat 1100-2200. Well-established restaurant set in a mall, specializing in Mozambique seafood that arrives fresh from the coast daily. Italian and Portuguese dishes, pizzas and pastas, seafood platters; best known for their giant prawns. Good wine list that includes some Portuguese wines.
ⓣ Brewer's Feast, on the corner of the N4, T013-741 4674. Cheap and cheerful roadside restaurant open all day and well into the night serving truck drivers and passing tourists, budget takeaway meals. Huge menu, and bargain breakfasts.
ⓣ Ku's, Sonpark Mall, corner of General Dan Pienaar and Piet Retief streets, T013-741 3989. Economically priced Chinese dishes, takeaway service, close to some of the backpackers and other budget accommodation, and O'Hagan's pub, so popular for a cheap night out.
ⓣ O'Hagan's, Sonpark Mall, corner of General Dan Pienaar and Piet Retief streets, T013-741 3580. Open 1100-late. Good-value English-style pub/restaurant chain, with a varied menu of pub grub like bangers and mash, shepherd's pie, burgers, lasagne, etc and large portions, a wide selection of imported beers, open-air terrace and music.

Malalane *p608*
ⓗ Crocafellas, 150 m before Malalane Gate into Kruger, T013-790 3415. Open 0800-1700, Thu-Sat until 2000. A thatched boma overlooking a small lake with 7 crocodiles; you can watch them from the wooden deck, 500 g T-bones are a speciality as is peri-peri Mozambique chicken and seafood, also has a curio shop, popular with tour groups.

Komatipoort *p608*
This small town is well known for its seafood, which arrives daily from Mozambique.
ⓗ The Border Country Inn, on the N4, 1 km before the border, T013-793 7328. Open

0700-2100. A very old-fashioned and dated hotel, which is not recommended for its rooms, but the restaurant has pleasant outdoor setting on a leafy terrace under thatch (watch the mosquitoes at night), serving excellent prawns and calamari and there's some alternative African dishes on the menu, from Kenya and Zimbabwe, for example.

♜ **Tambarina**, 77 Rissik St, T013-793 7057. Open 1200-2100. A fun restaurant decorated in bright colours with a lovely courtyard shaded by mango trees and serving good Portuguese cuisine and seafood. If you can't make it to the coast, the meals here are the next best thing. Guests from Crocodile Bridge camp in Kruger Park often dine here, bookings essential.

Barberton p609, map p610

♜ **Phoenix Hotel**, 20 Pilgrim St, T013-712 4211, www.thephoenixhotel.co.za. Open 0800-2200. Historical town hotel dating from the gold rush; apparently Paul Kruger was entertained here after meetings with the miners. The hotel was so popular in its day that on occasions guests had to sleep on or under the billiards table. Today the accommodation is rather dated and not recommended, but the à la carte restaurant is adequate and **Jocks Tavern** is a lively bar that serves good pub lunches and there's a pleasant beer garden.

♜ **Piccadilly Deli**, cnr Van der Merwe and Sheba roads, T013-712 7224. Open 0900-1700. A deli selling home-made goodies and local produce, with outside tables on a wooden deck for breakfast and lunch and specials chalked up on blackboards. Expect the likes of quiches, lasagne, Mexican wraps and filled paninis. Good place to buy cheeses, hams, olives, pickles and fresh bread.

♜ **Victoria Tea Garden**, Market Sq, Crown St, T013-712 4985. Mon-Fri 0800-1700, Sat 0800-1300. Charming open-air café under a white gazebo serving toasted sandwiches, juice and light snacks, close to the tourist office, so a good place to start the Heritage Walk around town.

○ Shopping

Nelspruit p605, map p606
Crossing Centre, at the junction of the N4 and the R40, just west of the centre. A variety of shops and banks, including a **Woolworths** food shop and a **Clicks** pharmacy.
Riverside Mall, 5 km out of town on the White River road. A wider selection than the Crossing Centre and boasts it's the largest shopping centre in Mpumalanga, with a variety of shops, restaurants and a **Nu Metro** 8-screen cinema. Next door is the **Emnotweni Casino**.

Barberton p609, map p610
Umjindi Jewellery Project, Pilgrim St, next to the **museum**. An initiative by the municipality to teach young people from disadvantaged communities jewellery design and manufacture.

▲▲ Activities and tours

Nelspruit p605, map p606
Funky Safaris, Funky Monkey Backpackers, see Sleeping, page 612. Will pick up from any hotel in Nelspruit. 2-day and 1-night Kruger tour, from R2100 per person, longer tours available, free night's stay at the backpackers if you book a Funky safari.
Place of Rock, T013-751 5319, www.placeof rock.co.za. Wide range of day and overnight trips to Kruger, the Panorama region and elsewhere, for a variety of budgets.
Vula Tours, T031-741 2826, www.vulatours. co.za. Affordable day trips to Kruger, the Panorama region and Sudwala Caves.

⊖ Transport

Nelspruit p605, map p606
Air
Flights arrive and depart from **Kruger Mpumalanga International Airport** terminal building, 25 km from Nelspruit towards Kruger's Numbi Gate, off the R538.

SAA has flights to **Johannesburg**, **Cape Town** and **Durban**.

Airline offices SAA, T011-978 1111, www.flysaa.com.

Bus
Baz Bus has services towards **Johannesburg**, **Tshwane (Pretoria)** and **Swaziland**. Greyhound has buses to **Pretoria**, **Johannesburg**, **Durban** and **Maputo** in Mozambique. Translux runs buses to **Tshwane (Pretoria)**, **Johannesburg** and **Maputo**.

Bus companies All bus tickets can be booked online at www.computicket.com. Baz Bus, T021-439 2323, www.bazbus.com; Greyhound, www.greyhound.co.za; Translux, www.translux.co.za. For more information, see Getting around, page 41.

Car hire
All offices are at the **Kruger Mpumalanga International Airport** terminal building, 25 km from Nelspruit: **Avis**, T013-750 1015, www.avis.co.za; **Budget**, T013-751 1774, www.budget.co.za; **Hertz**, T013-750 9150, www.hertz.co.za; **Imperial**, T013-750 1855, www.imperialcarrental.co.za.

Taxi
City Bug, T013-753 3392, www.citybug.co.za, taxi service and does intercity transfers on request and picks up from Kruger airport.

Train
The Komati Express between **Tshwane (Pretoria)/Johannesburg** and **Komatipoort** (border post with Mozambique) stops daily in Nelspruit, and the station is at the end of Henshall St. Central reservations, Shosholoza Meyl, T0860-00888 (in South Africa), T011-774 4555 (from overseas), www.shosholozameyl.co.za, timetables and fares are published on the website.

Komatipoort p608
Bus
The buses between **Tshwane (Pretoria)/Johannesburg** and **Maputo** stop at the border post.

Train
The Komati Express is the daily service running between **Tshwane (Pretoria)/Johannesburg** and **Komatipoort**, see Nelspruit, above for contact details. The train connects with a shuttle minibus service to the border. There is a railway from the border to **Maputo** but it is currently only used for freight. Minibuses can be found on the Mozambique side of the border for Maputo.

Barberton p609, map p610
There is no public transport to Barberton. Without a car, the only (expensive) option is take a taxi from Nelspruit.

● Directory

Nelspruit p605, map p606
Banks American Express, Riverside Mall, T013-757 0400. There are branches of all other banks in the Riverside Mall and the Crossing Centre. **Consulates** Mozambique Consulate, 43 Brown St, T013-752 7396, Mon-Fri 0830-1500. You can apply for visas here but it's much easier to get them at the border for US$25 or equivalent. South African passport-holders no longer need visas. **Internet** Alpha Internet Café, Riverside Mall. **Medical services** Chemist, after hours, T013-752 5721; Medi Clinic, 1 Louise St, T013-759 0500, www.nelspruitmc.co.za.

Komatipoort p608
Banks First National, Rissik St, open for foreign exchange. FX Bureau de Change, at the Komati Oasis service station just before the border, T031-790 7457, Mon-Sat 0700-1700, Sun 0700-1300.

Kruger National Park

→ *Colour map 2, B5.*

Kruger Park is the king of South African game parks and one of the best game-viewing areas in all of Africa. The figures speak for themselves: 507 bird species, 114 reptiles, 49 fish, 34 amphibians, 147 mammal and over 23,000 plant species have been recorded here. The region itself is enormous, extending from the Crocodile River in the south to the Limpopo in the north, from the wooded foothills of the eastern escarpment to the humid plains of the Lowveld. It certainly fulfils most visitors' fantasies of seeing magnificent herds of game roaming across acacia-studded stretches of savannah and, of course, is home to the Big Five. The park is 60 km wide and over 350 km long, conserving 21,497 sq km, an area the size of Wales or Israel. Despite its size, it is very well developed, with a good network covering 2600 km of roads and numerous camps, making a Kruger safari relatively hassle free.

Don't expect to have the park to yourself, however. Kruger receives over one million visitors a year and the park camps cater for up to 5000 visitors a day. Nevertheless, despite the huge number of people passing through, Kruger has managed to maintain its wild atmosphere. Only 5% of the park is affected by the activities of the visitors and only a few areas in the south come close to the overcrowding seen in East Africa's game parks.

While much of the park is designed for self-driving and self-catering, it is possible to stay in an ever-expanding choice of top-end private reserves, which are popular with first-time visitors as all game drives are led by rangers, so you can leave the animal-spotting to the experts. The fences that once split Kruger from the private reserves have now come down, so game can roam freely between the park and private concessions. Moreover, the fences between the countries bordering South Africa have also come down in the last few years: the demolition of fences between Kruger and Mozambique's Limpopo National Park and Zimbabwe's Gonarezhou have created the Great Limpopo Transfrontier Park (www.greatlimpopopark.com) – a conservation area straddling a staggering 35,000 sq km. ►► *For private game reserves along the park's western boundary, see pages 637-639. For listings, see pages 639-644.*

Ins and outs

Getting there and around

Air **South African Airways** (SAA) flies between Johannesburg and Kruger Mpumalanga International Airport, Phalaborwa Airport and Eastgate Airport. **Kruger Mpumalanga International Airport** is the largest airport in the area, located 22 km from Nelspruit. **Phalaborwa Airport** is just outside the park and within easy reach of many of the entry gates, while the **Eastgate Airport**, at Hoedspruit, is close to Orpen Gate. Some of the luxury game lodges also have their own landing strips for chartered flights.

Road Most people arrive in Kruger by road, either on a tour or in their own vehicle. There are nine entry gates and numerous options of approach. Which area you end up staying in will depend to a large extent on where you are coming from. Petrol is available at all the camps during office hours, and the mark-up on litre prices is not as unreasonable as you'd expect (although note that credit cards aren't accepted). There is a speed limit of 50 kph on the surfaced roads in the park. **Kruger Emergency Road Services** is based at Skukuza, T013-735 4152. The service is not equipped to do any major repairs, but if you break down within the park they will tow you to the nearest garage outside the park.

Orientation Given its huge size, many visitors to Kruger concentrate on one area of the park on each visit. Unless you are staying for more than a couple of nights, it is impossible to combine effective game viewing and visit all the areas. For the purposes of this guide, the park has been divided into three areas: Southern, Central and Northern, with a description of each of the different camps within these areas.

Best time to visit

Each season has its advantages. The park looks its best after the summer rains when the new shoots and lush vegetation provide a surplus of food for the grazers. Migratory birds are attracted and display their colourful breeding plumage, and this is a good time to see courtship rituals and nesting. The animals look their best thanks to their good diet, and mammals give birth to their young. The disadvantages of summer are that the thick foliage and tall grasses make it harder to spot animals and daytime temperatures can rise to a sweltering 40°C; afternoon rains are also common.

The winter months are good for game viewing because the dry weather forces animals to congregate around waterholes and there is less foliage for them to hide in. However, the animals tend not to be in their best condition. The winter months of June, July and August are more comfortable with daytime temperatures of around 30°C, but nights can be surprisingly cold with temperatures at times dropping to 0°C. This is a good time of year to visit the northern areas of the park which can be unbearably hot in the summer.

Kruger is at its most crowded during the South African school holidays. Accommodation within the park will be completely full and the heavy traffic on the roads can detract from the wilderness experience.

Cost

Conservation fees are R160, children (2-11) R80, under 2's free. South Africans get a substantial discount. If you're planning to stay for several days it may be worth investing in a Wild Card (see page 25).

Malaria

The park is in an endemic malaria area. Take anti-malarial medication and use insect repellent. Malaria hotline, T082-234 1800.

Arriving

Most of the camps are at least an hour's drive from the nearest entrance gate so always make sure you arrive in time to get to the camp. At the park gate, your reservation will usually be checked before you are allowed in, especially during the busy periods when all the accommodation, including campsites, gets booked up. You could be fined if you arrive at the camp gate after it has closed. Camp receptions are open daily April to June 0800-1800; March, September and October 0800-1830; November to February 0800-1900.

Background

The first area of what was to become Kruger National Park was officially protected in 1898 by President Kruger when he established the Sabie River Game Reserve. This consisted of what is now the southern sector of Kruger, the area between the Crocodile and the Sabie rivers. The early inhabitants were San and the Baphalaborwa tribes, who had little impact on the region's wildlife but did leave their mark in cave paintings throughout the area.

Kruger National Park opening times

National Park gates		Camp gates	
January	0530-1830	January	0430-1830
February	0530-1830	February	0530-1830
March	0530-1800	March	0530-1800
April	0600-1800	April	0600-1800
May-July	0630-1730	May-July	0630-1730
August	0600-1800	August	0600-1800
September	0600-1800	September	0600-1800
October	0530-1800	October	0530-1800
November	0530-1830	November	0430-1830
December	0530-1830	December	0430-1830

The game reserve was established to protect wildlife from the threat of 'biltong hunters' who were visiting the Lowveld in ever increasing numbers during the dry season. Hunters had already slaughtered vast herds of animals throughout South Africa and this was an early attempt to preserve an undisturbed wilderness. A single police sergeant at Komatipoort was given the daunting task of protecting the entire area from poachers.

It was re-proclaimed by the British in 1903, increasing the size of the park with both the Shingwedzi Game Reserve, the area between the Letaba and the Luvuvhu rivers, and the 5000 sq km of unworked ranches between the Sabi and the Letaba rivers. The new area under protection covered roughly the same area as Kruger does today. However, numerous factions threatened the survival of the park: hunters wanted access to the park, soldiers returning from the First World War expected land for sheep farming; prospectors looking for gold, coal and copper wanted mining rights; and South Africa's vets were campaigning for a mass slaughter of wildlife to prevent the possible spread of tsetse fly.

The seeds of creating a self-financing national park open to visitors were unwittingly sown by South African Railways when they opened a new tour running from Pretoria to Lorenço Marques (today Maputo) which stopped in the reserve for game rangers to take visitors into the bush. The first tourists arrived in 1923 and the visits became such a popular feature of the holiday that park visits were used as publicity by the railways. Public support for a national park empowered the conservationist lobby and public access was finally allowed in 1926.

The first cars arrived in 1927 and were able to travel by road through Sabi Bridge between the Olifants and Crocodile rivers. Visitors were expected to fend for themselves and made their own thorn bush camps to stay in. The animals reacted well to visitors in cars as long as they stayed inside them, but night driving was stopped almost immediately as too many animals were being killed. The first camp was built for tourists at Pretoriuskop after the chaos of the early years when tourists had been known to spend the night in trees hiding from predators.

By 1946, 38,000 tourists a year were visiting Kruger and in 1947 Princess Elizabeth and Princess Margaret visited the park on their royal tour of South Africa where they stayed in the first luxury lodges. The publicity surrounding the tour ensured that a visit to Kruger became a fixture on every tourist's trip to South Africa. By 1955 over 100,000 people were visiting each year.

Major James Stevenson-Hamilton

James Stevenson-Hamilton, Kruger's first game warden, was appointed at the end of the Boer War. He established his headquarters of Sabie Bridge at the end of the railway on the branch line from Komatipoort to the Sabie River. He began his work with two other rangers and spent years patrolling the reserve on horseback and on foot. His main duties were to encourage a healthy game population and to rid the park of poachers. However, his deep love of the African bush inspired him to campaign to increase the size of the park and to ensure the continued protection of the wildlife within its borders. His philosophy was that man's attempts to manage the park only interfered with natural processes. He believed that all the creatures within the park deserved to live regardless of temporary effects and that the balance of nature would always be preserved. James was known as Skukuza, a Shangaan name meaning either "he who sweeps clean" or "he who turns everything upside down", by his staff at Kruger National Park. He retired in 1946 after working in Kruger for 44 years.

The land area available to the park's wildlife has increased considerably in the last two decades. In 1994 the game fences between the private reserves on Kruger's western border were taken down, allowing animals to roam freely in an extra 2000 sq km of bush. Even more significantly, 2001 saw the removal of the fences between the international borders, creating the Greater Limpopo Transfrontier Conservation Area. This now incorporates Parque Nacional do Limpopo in Mozambique and Gonarezhou National Park in Zimbabwe, forming one of the largest conservation areas in Africa. The Mozambique section of the park can now be accessed from the Giriyondo border gate (see border box, page 622).

Staying in the park

Kruger has 12 main rest camps, five bushveld camps, two bush lodges and five satellite camps, owned and managed by **South African National Parks (SANParks)**, head office in Tshwane (Pretoria). Although there is a choice in the type of accommodation available, all the room rates are very reasonable. There are also a handful of private luxury lodges within Kruger run by concessionaires and not SANParks, such as **Tinga Private Lodge** and **Jock Safari Lodge**. The SANParks website, www.sanparks.org, has excellent information on all the lodges within Kruger. If you're looking for luxury, the private game reserves adjoining Kruger offer some of the finest camps in Africa. ▶▶ *For private reserves outside the park, see pages 637–640.*

Reservations

The direct line for each camp is included with the description of the camp. This number can only be used for making a last-minute booking, up to 48 hours prior to arrival. All other bookings should be made through **SANParks** ① *T012-428 9111, www.sanparks.org*. Once you are in the park it is always worth calling a day ahead or in the early morning to see if there have been any cancellations. The camp receptions will also be able to change your reservations to another camp if there is availability.

As with the conservation fees, children (2-11) pay child rates for accommodation and under 2s are free. Price codes listed in the camp descriptions refer to the minimum price per accommodation unit – meaning, for example, a cottage that sleeps 6 people, can take a minimum of 4, so it is these prices that are listed. Expect to pay a little more if you are filling a unit. Disabled travellers should check out the comprehensive, Information for People with Disabilities pages on the SANParks website, www.sanparks.org. It has information about which camps have accommodation units equipped for wheelchair users, as well as disabled facilities in every other region of the park such as public toilets and picnic sites.

Main rest camps
The majority of overnight visitors stay in one of the 12 main rest camps in the park at **Berg-en-Dal**, **Crocodile Bridge**, **Lower Sabie**, **Pretoriuskop**, **Skukuza**, **Letaba**, **Mopani**, **Olifants**, **Orpen**, **Satara**, **Shingwedzi** and **Punda Maria**. Most of the accommodation is in the form of chalets or cottages, which can sleep between two and 12. If you are self-catering, you'll have the choice between a separate fully equipped kitchen, a kitchenette or the use of a communal kitchen. The units with just a kitchenette do not have any cutlery or crockery. All accommodation comes with a refrigerator, bedding and towels. If in doubt, always check when booking exactly what you will be getting. More precise details of the choices are listed under the separate entry for each of the camps.

Some of the older camps feel a little outdated, but the grounds are universally clean and well kept. The facilities vary from one camp to the next but in most cases they include a shop selling basic self-catering supplies, a petrol pump, a restaurant or cafeteria, launderette, toilets and hot showers, braai areas with seating, public telephones and an office with information on the other camps. During the school holidays, the atmosphere in the larger camps can feel like holiday camps, and you can easily forget you are in the middle of a game reserve.

Campsites
Although most of the main rest camps have a separate area for caravans, tents and camper vans, there are two separate campsites at **Maroela** and **Balule**. The only facilities here are washblocks and communal kitchen facilities – there are no power points. Camping costs R1150 (with an electric point), R135 (without) per site for two people, and R48 per extra adult and R24 per extra child, up to a maximum of six people per site.

Bush lodges
Bush lodges offer secluded luxury accommodation and are smaller and more remote than public camps, without facilities such as shops, restaurants or petrol stations. These camps are ideal for a large group of friends, since the whole camp has to be taken with each booking. The two bush lodges are **Boulders**, which sleeps 12, and **Roodewal**, sleeping 16. Reservations should be made well in advance, as they offer exceptionally good value if the maximum number of people stay in the camp. The camps are located away from the main rest camps but are close enough for visits to the shops for supplies. Although they are privately owned, all bookings are dealt with by SANParks.

Bushveld camps
The five bushveld camps at **Biyamiti**, **Shimuwini**, **Talamati**, **Bateleur** and **Sirheni** are smaller and offer more of a wilderness experience than the main camps, but they also have far fewer facilities. Staying in these camps is one of the best ways to experience Kruger, but it does involve a degree of advanced planning. The chalets are all self-catering with fully equipped kitchens; bedding and towels are provided, and each chalet can sleep up to four people.

Border crossing: South Africa–Mozambique

Giriyondo border gate

The Mozambique section of the park can now be accessed from the Giriyondo border gate, situated 45 km northeast of Letaba on the eastern boundary of Kruger Park. There is a limit of 250 cars per day and they must be 4WD vehicles or have reasonable ground clearance as the roads on the Mozambique side are still being developed.

Border opening times October-March 0800-1600 and April-September 0800-1500.

Customs and immigration Entry is R50 per person plus R50 per vehicle. South African passport holders do not need a visa; foreign visitors can get visas at the border.

Facilities On the Mozambique side facilities remain very basic, although there have been a few new initiatives including a self-drive 4WD eco-trail, the **Machampane wilderness trail** (with a new luxury bush lodge) and **Massingir hiking trail**, for hikers willing to carry their food in and rubbish out. In addition to this there is a national parks campsite 50 km from the border post. Bookings for the trails and camp can be made through SANParks, www.sanparks.org, or Transfrontier Trails do Limpopo, www.dolimpopo.co.za. This website has full details of activities and access on the Mozambique side.

Eating

The camp restaurants are open daily for breakfast (0700-0900), lunch (1200-1400) and dinner (1800-2100). Some of the camps also have a bar. At small camps, or when there are fewer guests, you will be asked to order your evening meal in advance.

Shopping

Camp shops are open daily April to June 0800-1800; March, September and October 0800-1830; and November to February 0800-1900. The closer you are to Skukuza (the largest camp), the fresher the produce stocked in camp shops. Most shops stock firewood and braai lighters, bread, frozen meat, tinned vegetables, jams, biscuits, beer, wines, spirits, cool drinks, books and a few curio items. If you don't have a cool box in your car and you are self-catering, it is still possible to buy all you need for a meal from the shops each day.

Other facilities

Some of the camps have swimming pools for residents, a good option if you choose to base yourself at a camp for several days in summer and want to relax during the midday heat. Camping areas have laundry blocks and hot, clean showers. The communal kitchens have power points, instant boiling water machines, electric rings and a sink. It is your responsibility to clean up after yourself. Always secure rubbish to minimize the risk of baboons raiding the bins. There is a bank with ATM and an internet café at Skukuza.

Wildlife, activities and tours

Wildlife management

Although Kruger appears impressively wild, many aspects of the ecosystem are carefully monitored and controlled by the park authorities. Windpumps, for example, have been built at waterholes in dry areas so that game congregates in large numbers, and a number of species have been reintroduced. White rhinos were first reintroduced in 1961; the programme has been so successful that there are now over 2000 in the park. Black rhino were reintroduced in 1971, 40 years after they had last been seen here. Other animals which have been re-established include tsessebe and roan.

Game viewing

Kruger is, of course, home to the Big Five: lion, elephant, buffalo, black rhino and leopard. The highest concentrations and variety of game are around **Lower Sabie**, **Satara** and **Skukuza**. The best times for game viewing are after dawn and just before dusk, as animals tend to rest during the heat of the day.

There is a network of tarred and dirt roads linking the camps and looping through the best game-viewing areas. They are only open to the public during daylight hours and are subject to speed limits, which are monitored by radar. Game viewing takes time and it is best to drive below 20 kph to maximize your chances of spotting animals. Although there is a temptation to head for the most isolated dirt tracks and to neglect the tarred roads, this can be a mistake as cars are quieter on tarred roads and the animals living near them are more used to traffic. The run-off from tarred roads also makes the vegetation greener and attracts more animals. Driving around Kruger can be very tiring, so it's a good idea to visit one of the get-out points (marked on park maps) and to spend time game viewing at a waterhole.

Kruger shops sell a wide choice of identification guides. Their own publications, including the map, travel guide and the comprehensive *Find it* guide are an excellent introduction to the geology, history, vegetation and wildlife of Kruger.

Game drives

A guided tour with a game ranger can increase your chance of game spotting and provides a deeper understanding of the wilderness. Most camps offer guided day and night drives. Both are very popular and should be booked in advance at camp reception as soon as you arrive. A drive costs from R140-210 per person, depending on the camp and time of day. Night drives are an added attraction as private vehicles are not allowed outside the camps after sundown. These usually depart around 1700. Make sure you have warm clothing as temperatures drop in the evenings. The drives finish in time for guests to have an evening meal at the camp restaurant. Some camps also offer a late drive after dinner, departing at 2030 and lasting for up to three hours.

Guided walks and mountain biking

A number of camps offer two- or three-hour walks in the morning or afternoon accompanied by an armed game ranger from around R310 per person. Groups are kept small – up to eight people – and the rangers are trained in field guiding. These provide an excellent way of getting close to smaller animals and are a thrilling way of exploring the bush.

Wilderness trails

The seven wilderness trails offer three-day guided walking safaris. Seeing the park on foot is the most exciting way to experience the wilderness, and places on hiking trails are booked up months in advance. A maximum of eight people go on each trail and they are accompanied by an armed ranger. Hikers spend every night at the same rustic bush camp and go out on day walks. Food, water bottles, sleeping bags, rucksacks and cutlery are all provided.

The wilderness trails last for two days and three nights, and cost R3120 per person, no children under 12. For reservations contact **South African National Parks (SANParks)** offices; bookings can be made up to a year ahead and places fill up quickly. The best time of year for hiking is March to July when the weather is dry and daytime temperatures are cooler.

The 'Magnificent Seven'

The herds of elephant that roam around Kruger, migrating from east to west, are one of the park's biggest attractions. The population was estimated at 12,000 in 2007, having grown substantially from the 986 elephants found during an aerial census of 1959.

Elephants have voracious appetites and will eat bark, fruit, leaves and roots. Their habits have played an important role in the creation of the African landscape. However, too many elephants feeding in a restricted area can cause serious damage to trees and shrubs.

The air-conditioned **Letaba Elephant Hall** at Letaba camp in central Kruger has an amazing exhibition devoted to elephants. A small theatre shows wildlife videos and a large hall has displays related to the life cycle of the elephant.

The most impressive section of the museum, however focuses on the 'Magnificent Seven'. These were Kruger's finest elephants who became famous for their exceptionally large tusks. The skulls and tusks are on display, accompanied by a photo of the elephant and a map showing each animal's range.

Bushman Wilderness Trail This is a good area for seeing white rhino and wild dogs, and the walks also visit nearby San paintings. The camp is in an area of mountain bushveld, southwest of Kruger in an isolated valley surrounded by koppies. Hikers stay in thatched bush huts. Hikers check in at Berg-en-Dal, which is an hour's drive by Land Rover from the camp.

Napi Wilderness Trail Passes through various habitats following the banks of the Biyamiti River through thick riverine bush and crossing mixed woodlands. This is a good area for black and white rhinos, duiker, jackal, kudu and giraffe. Hikers check in at Pretoriuskop.

Metsi-Metsi Wilderness Trail The camp is in an area of mountain bushveld near the N'waswitsontso River. The trail also visits areas of marula savannah where many plains animals are seen. Hikers check in at Skukuza.

Nyalaland Wilderness Trail Passes through a vast expanse of mopane scrub, dotted with baobabs, aloes and koppies. The wildlife here is unique to this sector of the park and nyala are often seen. The birdlife here is spectacular. The hutted camp is shaded by kuduberry trees next to the Madzaringwe Stream. Hikers check in at Punda Maria.

Olifants Wilderness Trail Crosses through a region of classic African plains. It is excellent for seeing large herds of buffalo, wildebeest and zebra. The hutted camp overlooks the Olifants River and is 1½ hours by Land Rover to Letaba. Hikers check in at Letaba.

Sweni Wilderness Trail Southeast of Satara overlooking the Sweni River and crossing knobthorn and marula savannah where large herds of buffalo, wildebeest and zebra can be seen. Interesting species are cheetah, lion, kudu, sable and steenbok. Hikers check in at Satara.

Wolhuter Wilderness Trail Passes through Lowveld savannah, where it is possible to see lions, cheetah, black and white rhino, roan, sable and wild dog. The trail is named after the park ranger Harry Wolhuter, who killed a lion with his knife in 1903. The bush camp has wooden huts and is near the Mlambane River. Hikers check in at Berg-en-Dal.

The Olifants River Back-pack Trails

This is run from April to October and is different to the wilderness trails in that hikers cover the 42 km over four days and three nights but camp in a different place each night, and the guide picks out a suitable spot. As such, hikers have to carry packs with tents and sleeping gear, and all their own cooking equipment and food, which they cook themselves. Hikers also take turns carrying a fold up shelter used as cover for when going to the toilet. Orientation (and pack-checking) is at Olifants, before hikers are transferred by vehicle to the western edge of the park where the Olifants River enters Kruger, and then trace the river back to the rest camp again over four days. This is a tough hike – 10-15 km a day carrying heavy packs – hikers need to be fit and show a medical certificate of good health. Don't be deceived by the short distances, as the Olifant's River Valley features hills, deep gullies and dense thickets. Bookings are made per trail and it costs R14,030 for four days for eight people.

Tours

Organized tours of Kruger are widely available throughout South Africa and can be booked in all major cities. The variety of tours on offer can be baffling, so it is a good idea to shop around. Prices vary according to the quality of accommodation, the length of the tour, additional destinations, and whether you travel by minibus, open-air game vehicle or air-conditioned coach. There are dozens of companies offering tours; the tourist offices at Nelspruit (see pages 604 and 606) have a list of operators, and there are more Johannesburg operators on page 585. ▸▸ *See Activities and tours, page 644.*

Camps in southern Kruger

The greatest concentrations of game and most of Kruger's large camps are in the southern section of Kruger and many visitors only ever see this section of the park. The landscape here is far more varied than the rest of the park and therefore supports a wider range of animals.

Ins and outs

The entrance gates at **Crocodile Bridge** and **Malalane** are on the southern boundary of the park and are clearly signposted from the N4 running between Nelspruit and Komatipoort. The entrance gates at Numbi, Paul Kruger and **Phabeni** are on the southwestern boundary. **Numbi Gate** is signposted off the R538 between Nelspruit and Hazyview; **Paul Kruger Gate** is on the R536 from Hazyview.

Berg-En-Dal

ⓘ *12 km to Malalane Gate, T013-735 6106 for last-minute reservations (maximum 48 hrs before arrival).*

This large, modern camp has a rather austere, institutional feel to it. It is set in a hilly landscape, wooded with acacias, marulas and jackalberry overlooking the Matjulu Dam. Facilities include a swimming pool, in-camp trail, environmental centre showing wildlife films, petrol station, camp shop, restaurant, telephones and launderette; open to day visitors. The camp accommodates 300 guests when full and offers day walks, and day and night game drives. The 23 **cottages** (A) at this camp are slightly larger than at the other camps and sleep six to eight people. There are also 69 three-bed **bungalows** (C) and 74 camping and caravan sites with ablution blocks and kitchen units.

Biyamiti

ⓘ 26 km to Crocodile Gate, 45 km to Malalane, T013-735 6171 for reservations (maximum 48 hrs before arrival).

This bushveld camp is in the far south of Kruger on the banks of the Mbiyamiti River set in an area of crocodile thorn thicket. The camp sleeps 70 people in 15 one- or two-bed **cottages** (B-C) with kitchen. Day walks and night drives can be booked at reception.

Crocodile Bridge

ⓘ 34 km to Lower Sabie, 175 km to Orpen, 125 km to Pretoriuskop, 127 km to Satara, 77 km to Skukuza, T013-735 6012 for reservations (maximum 48 hrs before arrival).

This small camp is next to the park's southern gate set in acacia woodland. There is a hippo pool on the dirt road to Malalane where elephant and other animals come to drink. The camp has 20 two- or three-bed self-catering **chalets** (C), eight **safari tents** (D), and 15 camping and caravan sites with ablution block and kitchen units. Facilities include a petrol station, camp shop, café, telephones and launderette. Night drives and game walks can be booked at reception; day drives are open to people staying outside the park.

Lower Sabie

ⓘ 113 km to Berg-en-Dal, 141 km to Orpen, 53 km to Paul Kruger Gate, 213 km to Phalaborwa, 90 km to Pretoriuskop, 342 km to Punda Maria, 93 km to Satara, 43 km to Skukuza, T013-735 6056 for last-minute reservations (maximum 48 hrs before arrival).

The region around Lower Sabie is part of a classic African savannah landscape, with grasslands, umbrella thorn and round-leaf teak stretching off into the distance. This is one of the best regions for seeing game, particularly rhino. Game is attracted here by water at the Mlondosi and Nhlanganzwani dams and the camp overlooks the Sabie River. The accommodation is impersonal but the camp itself is fairly peaceful. Facilities include the **Ingwe Restaurant**, a bar, shop, petrol station, launderette, phones and a swimming pool. Day walks and night drives can be booked at reception.

   Accommodation is provided in large four-, five- or seven-bed **cottages** (A-B) with two bathrooms and a kitchen; two- or three-bed **chalets** (C) with bathroom, fridge and hot-plate; two-bed **rondavels** (C) with bathroom and fridge; two-bed **huts** (D), with bathroom and fridge; small, two-bed **cottages** (C) with a/c, fridge, veranda, ablution block; one-bed **safari tents** (D) with ablution block; one-bed **huts** (E) with a/c, fridge and ablution block; plus camping and caravan sites, with ablution blocks and kitchen facilities.

Malalane

ⓘ Check in at Berg-en-Dal.

Malalane is a luxury satellite camp to Berg-en-Dal, set in a rugged area of mountain bushveld on the banks of the Crocodile River on the southern boundary of the park. It has five luxury three- and four-bed **cottages** (C), with bathroom and solar-powered communal kitchen unit, plus camping and caravan sites with ablution block and kitchen unit.

Pretoriuskop

ⓘ Near Numbi Gate, 92 km to Berg-en-Dal, 125 km to Crocodile Bridge, 90 km to Lower Sabie, 184 km to Orpen, 140 km to Satara, 49 km to Skukuza, T013-735 5128 for last-minute reservations (maximum 48 hrs before arrival).

This is the oldest camp in Kruger and is also the third largest, with a fairly institutional feel. The game drives around Pretoriuskop pass through marula woodland and tall grassland, with good game-viewing areas to the north along the Sabie River and to the south along the Voortrekker Road, which follows the original wagon route through the veld. Rhino are often seen close to Numbi Gate. More animals congregate in this area in the summer than in the winter but it is always a rewarding area for game. Facilities include a restaurant, cafeteria, swimming pool made out of natural rock, petrol station, shop and launderette; day walks and night drives can be booked at reception. It is also possible to join a night drive at Numbi Gate if you are staying outside the park in the Hazyview Area.

There are 142 sleeping units: six-, eight- and nine-bed guest **cottages (A)**, with two bathrooms and a kitchen; four-bed **cottages (B)** with one bathroom and a kitchen; two- to four-bed **bungalows (D)** with bathroom, fridge and hot plate; two-, three-, five- and six-bed **huts (E)** with a/c, fridge and ablution block, plus 45 camping and caravan sites with ablution blocks and kitchen units.

1 Kruger National Park southern sector

➡ **Kruger Park maps**
1 **Kruger Park southern sector, page 627**
2 Kruger Park central sector, page 629
3 Kruger Park northern sector, page 633

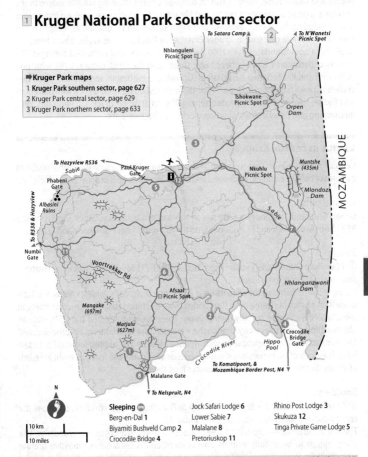

Sleeping	Jock Safari Lodge 6	Rhino Post Lodge 3
Berg-en-Dal 1	Lower Sabie 7	Skukuza 12
Biyamiti Bushveld Camp 2	Malalane 8	Tinga Private Game Lodge 5
Crocodile Bridge 4	Pretoriuskop 11	

Skukuza

ⓘ *72 km to Berg-en-Dal, 77 km to Crocodile Bridge, 43 km to Lower Sabie, 137 km to Orpen, 213 km to Phalaborwa, 49 km to Pretoriuskop, 342 km to Punda Maria, 93 km to Satara, T013-735 4152 for last-minute reservations (maximum 48 hrs before arrival).*

Located on the south bank of the Sabie River, Skukuza is Kruger's largest camp and the administrative centre of the park. The camp has grown to such an extent that it resembles a small town and you can forget that you're in by a national park. Despite its size, Skukuza is at the centre of Kruger's prime game-viewing area and is a good base for game drives. The road heading northeast towards Satara has high concentrations of game and is said have one of the densest concentrations of lion in Africa – and the densest population of cars in Kruger.

Facilities here cater to almost every need and include a supermarket, petrol station, car wash, two restaurants, bank, post office, telephones, internet café, two swimming pools, doctor and launderette. There is also an open-air cinema showing wildlife videos in the evenings, a good information centre and library, and a small nursery selling indigenous plants including baobabs. Day walks and night drives can be booked at reception and there's a nine-hole golf course. **Kruger Emergency Road Services** is also based here.

Skukuza accommodates over 1000 people in four-, six- and eight-bed **cottages (A)**, with two bathrooms and kitchen; two-, three- and four-bed **cottages (B)** with one bathroom and kitchen; two-bed **chalets (C)** with one bathroom and kitchen; three-bed **chalets (C)** with bathroom, fridge and hot-plate; three-bed **bungalows (C)**, with bathroom and fridge; two- and four-bed **safari tents (D)** with ablution block, kitchen units, plus 80 camping and caravan sites, ablution blocks and kitchen units.

Camps in central Kruger

Central Kruger is quieter than the south, with large areas of flat mopane woodland inhabited by herds of buffalo, elephant, wildebeest and zebra. Olifants camp is in a spectacular location.

Ins and outs

Orpen Gate and **Phalaborwa Gate** are on the western boundary. Orpen Gate is on the R531 from Acornhoek and Phalaborwa is on the R71 route from Polokwane and Tzaneen.

Balule

ⓘ *11 km from Olifants where visitors must check in, T013-735 6606 for last-minute reservations (maximum 48 hrs before arrival).*

Balule is on the banks of the Olifants River and is one of Kruger's wildest camps. It is little more than a patch of cleared bush surrounded by an electrified chain-link fence; visitors can see animals wandering by only metres away. There are six three-bed **huts (D)**, with an ablution block but no electricity, though there are gas stoves and lanterns are provided, and 15 basic caravan and camping sites, with ablution block and braai sites; firewood is on sale here. The smell of barbecued meat attracts hyenas who patrol the fence all night in search of scraps (but don't under any circumstances feed them).

Boulders

ⓘ *54 km to Letaba, 31 km to Mopani, 54 km to Phalaborwa Gate; check in at Mopani, the camp must be booked as a single unit, maximum 12.*

This unfenced private camp is in an area of acacia, knobthorn and mopane woodland. The camp blends in beautifully with its environment and is set amongst massive granite

2 Kruger National Park central sector

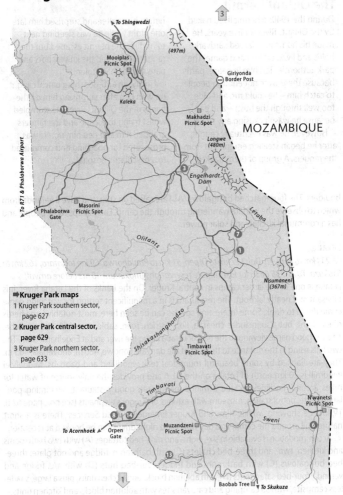

To Shingwedzi

⑤ Mooiplas Picnic Spot

②

Kaleka

(497m)

Giriyonda Border Post ⊖

Makhadzi Picnic Spot

⑪

MOZAMBIQUE

Longwe (480m)

③ Engelhardt Dam

To R71 & Phalaborwa Airport

Masorini Picnic Spot

Phalaborwa Gate

Olifants

Letaba

⑦

①

Nisumaneni (367m)

➡ **Kruger Park maps**
1 Kruger Park southern sector, page 627
2 **Kruger Park central sector, page 629**
3 Kruger Park northern sector, page 633

Shisakashanghondzo

Timbavati Picnic Spot

Timbavati

④
⑧ ⑭

To Acornhoek ▲ Orpen Gate

Muzandzeni Picnic Spot

⑬

Sweni

N'wanetsi Picnic Spot

⑥

Baobab Tree ⊓ *To Skukuza*

①

N

⬇

|10 km|
|10 miles|

Sleeping 🛏
Balule **1**
Boulders **2**
Letaba **3**
Maroela **4**
Mopani **5**
Olifants **7**

Orpen **8**
Satara **10**
Shimuwini Bushveld Camp **11**
Singita Lebombo **6**
Singita Sweni **6**

Talamati Bushveld Camp **13**
Tamboti **14**

The Olifant hermit

During the 1940s a hermit lived naked by the Olifants River for five years. He made his home in enlarged aardvark holes and lived off fruit and game. The park authorities left him in peace, partly because there were not enough people to catch him – he could run and hide too well through the bush – and partly because he wasn't causing any trouble.

However, he was eventually caught, after he began stealing equipment from the rangers. A group of them tracked him to his shelter and surprised him late one night while he was sleeping next to his fire. The hermit escaped but the rangers recovered the knives, pots and pans that he had stolen.

Finally, an anti-poaching patrol caught up with him after surprising him on the banks of the Olifants River. He stumbled whilst trying to escape and the rangers grabbed him and tied him up. He was prosecuted for poaching and committed to a psychiatric hospital.

boulders. The four thatched **bungalows (AL)** are raised on stilts and have a veranda from which to observe the wildlife wandering through the camp. Each sleeps three people and has a communal kitchen and solar power.

Letaba

ⓘ *234 km to Berg-en-Dal, 117 km to Orpen, 51 km to Phalaborwa, 69 km to Satara, 162 km to Skukuza, T013-735 6636 for last-minute reservations (maximum 48 hrs before arrival).*

Letaba is one of the larger camps in central Kruger. On the banks of the Letaba River, it is pleasant and neatly laid-out. The restaurant is in a magnificent setting for watching game come down to drink. Some interesting species can be seen here, most notably large herds of elephant, but also includes cheetah, lion, ostrich, roan, sable, steenbok and tsessebe. There is good game viewing to the east of Letaba along the river and at Engelhardt Dam. The two hills rising in the distance to the east of the dam are Longwe, 480 m, and Mhla, 465 m. They are flanked by some beautiful round-leaf teak woodland and baobabs. Middelvlei windmill is 20 km north of Letaba on the H1-6 and provides the only source of water for miles around. Facilities include a mini supermarket, good restaurant, swimming pool, launderette, petrol station, museum with exhibits on Kruger's elephants (see box, page 624), TV lounge showing wildlife films and Kruger Emergency Road Services. There is a short nature trail around the camp, and day walks and night drives can be booked at reception.

Accommodation is available in six-, eight- and nine-bed **cottages (A)** with two bath rooms and kitchen; two- and three-bed **chalets (C)** with bathroom, fridge and hot plate; three-bed **bungalows (C)** with bathroom and fridge; four-bed **huts (D)** with a/c, fridge and veranda; four-bed **safari tents (D)** with ablution blocks and kitchen units, plus a large, shade-less campsite, with 35 camping and caravan sites with ablution blocks and kitchen units.

Maroela and Tamboti satellite camps

ⓘ *Check in at Orpen Gate, 4 km.*

These are both satellite camps to Orpen. Maroela large camp ground is on the south bank of the Timbavati River, and has 20 camping and caravan sites, ablution blocks and kitchen units. There are no other facilities here, but there is a shop at Orpen Gate where you check in and where you can also arrange day walks and night drives. Not far from Maroela, **Tamboti (C-D)** is a tented camp on the banks of the Timbavati River, offering 35 furnished safari tents for two to four people, either fully equipped or sharing communal kitchen, ablutions and eating boma. This is the ideal spot for people looking for a complete bush experience without having to bring all the equipment. There is no restaurant or shop.

Mopani
ⓘ *281 km to Berg-en-Dal, 47 km to Letaba, 86 km to Olifants, 74 km to Phalaborwa Gate, 258 km to Punda Maria, 209 km to Skukuza, T013-735 6535 for last-minute reservations (maximum 48 hrs before arrival).*
This is one of Kruger's largest public camps set on a rocky hill overlooking the Pioneer Dam. It is only a few kilometres south of the Tropic of Capricorn, set on a seemingly endless plain of mopane shrub. The accommodation at Mopani has been made from natural materials and is more pleasant and spacious than some of the older camps. Choose from an eight-bed **cottage** (**AL**); six-bed **cottages** (**B**) with kitchen, or two- and three-bed **bungalows** (**C**) with kitchen. Facilities include swimming pool, nature trail, petrol station, shop, restaurant, bar overlooking the dam, cafeteria and launderette; game walks and night drives can be booked at reception.

Olifants
ⓘ *219 km to Berg-en-Dal, 147 km to Lower Sabie, 102 km to Orpen, 158 km to Paul Kruger Gate, 83 km to Phalaborwa Gate, 212 km to Punda Maria, 147 km to Skukuza, T013-735 6606 for last-minute reservations (maximum 48 hrs before arrival).*
This peaceful camp is in a spectacular setting high on a hill overlooking fever trees and wild figs lining the banks of the Olifants River. The game drives in the immediate area pass through flat mopane woodland in the north and a hilly area of rocks and woodland in the south where klipspringer are often seen. Olifants is one of Kruger's most attractive camps, blending into the surrounding woodland. Facilities include a restaurant, shop, information centre, wildlife films, petrol, launderette, open to day visitors; night drives can be booked through reception. A thatched veranda perched on the edge of the camp looks down into the river valley and is a superb place for game viewing. The thatched accommodation, shaded by large old sycamores and sausage trees, encompasses eight-bed **cottages** (**AL**); four-bed **cottages** (**B**) with kitchen; two-bed **chalets** (**C**) with kitchen or bathroom, fridge and hot plate and three- or two-bed **bungalows** (**D**) with bathroom and fridge.

Orpen
ⓘ *Just beyond Orpen Gate, T013-735 6355 for last-minute reservations (maximum 48 hrs before arrival).*
Orpen is a small camp past the entrance gate on the western central plains, set amongst acacias, marulas and aloes. The road passing along the Timbavati River offers a chance of seeing game, and the area around the camp is known as a good place to see leopard, lion and cheetah. There are six-bed **cottages** (**B**) with bathroom and kitchen, and three-bed **bungalows** (**C**) with bathroom and kitchen. Facilities include a petrol station and camp shop, and day walks and night drives can be booked at reception.

Satara
ⓘ *15 km from Berg-en-Dal, 127 km from Crocodile Bridge, 69 km from Letaba, 93 km from Lower Sabie, 48 km from Orpen, 104 km from Paul Kruger Gate, 140 km from Pretoriuskop, 245 km from Punda Maria, 93 km from Skukuza, T013-735 6306 for reservations (maximum 48 hrs before arrival).*

Satara, Kruger's second-largest camp looks rather like a motorway service station in the middle of the bush, although the institutional atmosphere of the accommodation is softened by its trees and lawns. Satara is set in the flat grasslands of the eastern region, which attract large herds of wildebeest, buffalo, kudu, impala, zebra and elephant. There is good game viewing on the road to Orpen.

Accommodation is available in guest **cottages (AL-A)** sleeping six, eight or nine, with one or two bathrooms and kitchen; two- or three-bed **bungalows (C)** with bathroom and kitchen; two- or three-bed **bungalows (D)** with bathroom and communal kitchen; and on 87 camping and caravan sites, with ablution blocks, kitchen units. Facilities include petrol station, car wash, Kruger Emergency Road Service, camp shop, cafeteria, restaurant, launderette and swimming pool, day walks and night drives can be booked at reception.

Shimuwini

ⓘ *66 km to Letaba, 118 km to Olifants, 52 km to Phalaborwa, T013-735 6683 for reservations (maximum 48 hrs before arrival).*

This bushveld camp is set in a region of bushwillow and mopane woodland, with less of a concentration of wildlife, compared to the south of Kruger. However, this is still an interesting wilderness area with a good variety of wildlife. The private access road leading to Shimuwini follows the Letaba River where elephant can sometimes be seen bathing and the riverine forest around the camp is good for birdwatching.

The camp overlooks the Shimuwini Dam. Visitors to the camp have private access to the dam, which is surrounded by giant sycamore trees. There is a hide here from which to see crocodiles, hippo, waterbuck and waterbirds. The camp consists of a row of four- and six-bed thatched **cottages (B)** with kitchen and veranda, some have additional outside showers, shaded by appleleaf trees and acacias. The camp can accommodate up to 70 visitors and offers day and night game drives.

Talamati

ⓘ *30 km to Orpen Gate, T013-735 6343 for reservations (maximum 48 hrs before arrival).*

This rustic bushveld camp is set on the banks of the Nwaswitsonto River, which is normally dry. The grassland and acacia woodland along the western boundary attract kudu, giraffe, sable and white rhino. Klipspringer can be seen on the rocky outcrops. There are two hides in the camp for game viewing and birdwatching. The camp accommodates 80 visitors in two-, four- and six-bed **cottages (B)**, with bathroom and kitchen, and offers day/night game drives.

Camps in northern Kruger

This is a dry and remote region that is rarely visited by tourists. As there is no year-round water supply, there isn't the same density of animals as in the south of Kruger, but the area does support animals unique to this part of Kruger, including Sharpe's grysbok, tsessebe, sable and nyala.

The **Luvuvhu River** offers some of the best wildlife viewing in the area. The river banks are lined with ironwood, ebony and sycamore fig – huge pythons thrive in the thick forests, and some of the largest crocodiles in Kruger can be seen in the Luvuvhu River. The bridge over the Luvuvhu is an excellent spot for birdwatchers after heavy rains. Many birds are attracted to the fruit trees, and some of the more unusual species which can be seen here are the Cape parrot, Basra reed warbler, tropical boubou and yellow-bellied sunbird. There are also two interesting raptors here, Ayre's eagle and Dickinson's kestrel.

A good location is the picnic site at Mooiplaas between Letaba and Shingwedzi, which overlooks a waterhole on the Tsende River where game can be seen.

Close to the Luvuvhu River, in the northern corner of Kruger Park, is the late Iron Age site of **Thulamela**. This is an important archaeological site that has forced people to reconsider their understanding and interpretation of the local regional history. Sidney Miller was responsible for the excavation project, which was sponsored by the Gold Fields

③ **Kruger National Park northern sector**

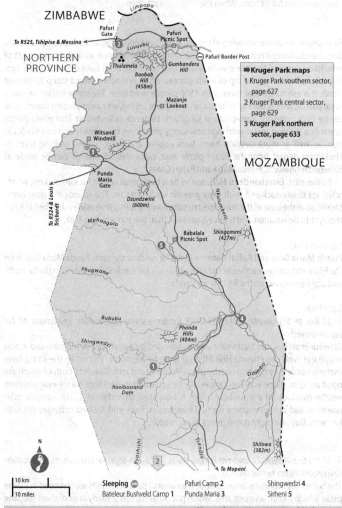

ZIMBABWE

Limpopo

Pafuri Gate

To R525, Tshipise & Messina

Pafuri Picnic Spot

Luvuvhu

NORTHERN PROVINCE

Pafuri Border Post

Thulamela

Gumbandeni Hill

Baobab Hill (458m)

Mazanje Lookout

Witsand Windmill

Punda Maria Gate

MOZAMBIQUE

Dzundzwini (600m)

To R524 & Louis Trichardt

Mphongolo

Nkulumbeni

Babalala Picnic Spot

Shingomeni (427m)

⑤

Phugwane

Bububu

Phonda Hills (404m)

Shingwedzi

Dzombo

Rooibosrand Dam

Shilowa (382m)

Byashishi

Tendze

To Mopani

N

10 km
10 miles

Sleeping
Bateleur Bushveld Camp 1

Pafuri Camp 2
Punda Maria 3

Shingwedzi 4
Sirheni 5

The railway lions

The entrance gate to Sabi Sand at Newington used to be the site of a layby on the Selati railway line, and the graves of the construction workers who died of malaria or were killed by wild animals can still be seen here. This area is known for its lions. When the railway was still running, the threat to passengers waiting for trains was so serious that they were provided with ladders by the railway company so that they could climb to safety in the trees, where the lions couldn't reach them.

Foundation. Aside from clearing all the vegetation and collecting items such as spearheads, pots, beads, bracelets and harpoons, the team embarked upon an ambitious project of rebuilding some of the stone walls, which had originally been built over 400 years ago. The whole site lies on the top of a sub-plateau which is reached after a steep 25-minute climb. It is estimated that more than 1500 people lived here. The stone enclosure was a royal palace, which, during its heyday in the Khami period, was an important commercial centre of a powerful agro-pastoral kingdom. Evidence collected at Thulamela points towards a thriving metal-working community producing spearheads and hoe blades in iron, as well as more delicate items from copper and gold. Guided walking tours to Thulamela depart from the Pafuri picnic spot twice daily. Bookings can be made at Sirheni, Shingwedzi, Punda Maria and Pafuri Gates.

To the east, **Gumbandevu Hill** used to be a traditional centre for rain makers, where offerings of livestock and snuff were given in return for rain. The sounds of a goat being sacrificed at the base of the hill helped to summon the spirits that made rain. The hill is still thought to be haunted and is always greener than the surrounding area.

Ins and outs

Punda Maria Gate and **Pafuri Gate** are in the far north of the park. Punda Maria Gate is on the R524 and can be reached from Makhado/Louis Trichardt. Pafuri Gate is in the far north and can be reached on the R525 from Venda.

Bateleur

ⓘ *37 km to Shingwedzi, T013-735 6843 for last-minute reservations (maximum 48 hrs before arrival).*

Bateleur is an isolated bushveld camp surrounded by a vast area of mopane and acacia woodland with the Phonda Hills (400 m) lying to the north. Visitors to the camp have exclusive access to the two nearby dams, Rooibosrand and Silverfish, both of which are good areas for game watching, especially for sable and nyala. There is a viewing platform nearby overlooking a waterhole which is best seen after the rains. The camp is solar powered and accommodates up to 34 visitors in four- and six-bed **cottages** (B) with kitchens. Day and night game drives are available.

Shingwedzi

ⓘ *37 km to Bateleur, 71 km from Punda Maria, T013-735 6806 for last-minute reservations (maximum 48 hrs before arrival).*

This is the most northerly large camp in the national park. Brick units are arranged in a large circle, looking in on an open area, which has no grass, just a shady area of short mopane trees. The best game viewing in this area is around Kanniedood Dam and the riverine forest along the banks of the Shingwedzi. Many animals from the surrounding areas come here for water. There is a bird hide south of the camp on the S134 overlooking the river.

Accommodation comprises one four-bed **cottage** (AL) with kitchen; two-bed **chalets** (B-C) with bathroom and fridge or kitchen; two-bed **bungalows** (C) with bathroom and kitchen; three-bed **huts** (D), with fridge, veranda, ablution blocks and kitchen facilities. Facilities include a restaurant, cafeteria, shop, petrol, information centre, swimming pool and launderette. Night drives and guided walks can be booked at reception. The restaurant has a pleasant outside terrace where you can sit during the day and look out over the Shingwedzi River. The campsite is well away from the cottages and chalets. It has plenty of space, but there is limited shade and virtually no grass.

Punda Maria
ⓘ *8 km from the Punda Maria Gate, 415 km from Berg-en-Dal, 176 km from Letaba, 130 km from Mopani, 201 km from Phalaborwa Gate, 71 km from Shingwedzi, 342 km from Skukuza, T013-735 6873 for last-minute reservations (maximum 48 hrs before arrival).*

This peaceful camp, hidden by dense woodland, is the northernmost large public camp in Kruger and by far the most pleasant. It is situated in a unique area of sandveld dotted with baobabs, white seringa and pod mahogany. There are spectacular views of the surrounding landscapes from the top of Dzundzwini (600 m) and good game viewing near the camp on the Mahonie Loop and up by the Witsand windmill. Look out for nyala and kudu. The game drive north to Pafuri passes through mopane shrubveld inhabited by roan, sable and tsessebe. The bridge over the Luvuvhu River is a top place for birdwatchers, where many species of bird are attracted to the fruit trees along the banks of the river. This is the only area in the park where you can see and enjoy Mopani Forest. The short Paradise Flycatcher nature trail loops around the camp.

Accommodation is available in four-bed **cottages** (B) with kitchen; two-bed **chalets** (C) with kitchen – some of the chalets date from the 1930s but are still adequately comfortable; two-bed **bungalows** (D) with bathroom, fridge, ablution block and communal kitchen, plus a camping and caravan park, with ablution block, braai sites and communal kitchen. Note that this is a small camp and is often fully booked at weekends. Facilities include restaurant, bar, shop and petrol, and day walks and night drives can be booked at reception. The food in the restaurant is better than other camps, but meals must be ordered in advance.

☾ *Punda Maria was named after the zebra that Captain JJ Coetzer saw when he first arrived here; he mistakenly believed 'punda maria' to be the Swahili word for zebra. In fact, it's 'punda milia', but the first name has stuck.*

Sirheni
ⓘ *28 km to Shingwezi, 48 km to Punda Maria, T013-735 6860 for reservations (maximum 48 hrs before arrival).*

This is a bushveld camp overlooking Sirheni Dam, surrounded by mopane and acacia woodland. This region is better known for birdwatching than game viewing and, although game is present, it is not found in the same concentrations as in southern Kruger. The road approaching the camp from the south on the S66 passes through the alluvial plains and riverine forest of the Mphongolo River, inhabited by leopard, nyala and waterbuck. It is signposted off the H1-7. The camp accommodates up to 80 visitors in four- and six-bed **cottages** (B) with kitchen, and offers day and night bush drives.

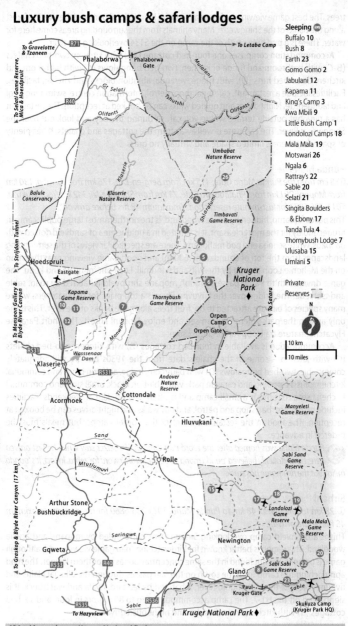

Luxury bush camps & safari lodges

10 km
10 miles

Private game reserves 💿 ⏩ pp639-640.

The reserves fringing the western border of Kruger offer some of the most exclusive game viewing in the world. Here you have the chance of seeing the Big Five and exploring the natural environment of Kruger from the comfort of a private 4WD, with the promise of luxury accommodation and superb cuisine at the end of your game drive. Each lodge has its own secluded setting, providing an enjoyable 'in the wild' experience. But the biggest advantage of staying in the private reserves are the excellent game guides, who provide a fantastic introduction to the bush – usually with far better game-spotting skills, too, which means you'll see much more than if you were self-driving.

Ins and outs

Access to the lodges is straightforward. Guests are collected from either **Phalaborwa Airport**, **Eastgate Airport** at Hoedspruit, or **Kruger Mpumalanga International Airport** near Nelspruit (scheduled flights or charter flights are usually included in packages) and driven by safari vehicle to the lodge. Alternatively, a charter by light aircraft will take you directly to those lodges that have a private airstrip, or you can drive yourself – it takes around six hours from Johannesburg.

Reserves

There are now numerous private reserves, each holding countless game lodges. The best-known private reserves include **Klaserie**, **Timbavati**, **Thornybush**, **Mala Mala** and **Sabi Sabi**, which together form the largest private game area in the world. The first three are in Limpopo, but are included here together with the Mpumalanga reserves. Within these reserves are several smaller reserves, which have been incorporated into a single wilderness area; some still retain their original name which can be a bit confusing. For example, **Idube Game Reserve** and **Londolozi Game Reserve** are now both part of the much larger Sabi Sand Game Reserve. In the last 20 years, the fences between all these reserves have been removed, including, most significantly, the western Kruger National Park fence. This development has helped, in part, to restore natural east-west migration routes and has created an area that is most often dubbed as the **Greater Kruger National Park**. Despite a confusing range of names for reserves and camps, they all now fall into this greater area.

Game viewing

Game viewing is, of course, the main activity in all the lodges. Days normally begin with an early-morning game drive, returning in mid- to late-morning for breakfast. Guests can then either choose to go on a game walk or relax by the pool before lunch. When the worst of the day's heat has passed, the vehicles set off on another game drive, returning for dinner. Optional night drives are usually also available.

Game viewing can vary from lodge to lodge, depending on how many vehicles patrol an area and, of course, how much effort the rangers put into showing visitors around. Nevertheless, game viewing is always dependent on luck, and staying in a five-star private game lodge does not mean that you will be guaranteed better animal sightings than if you were travelling around Kruger in a hire car and staying in a SANParks campsite. The benefits, however, are that you will have a personal and knowledgeable guide, and you're unlikely to come across many other tourists.

Lodges

Most guests spend between two and three days at a lodge to get the most out of game viewing. Prices vary considerably, and can range from fairly expensive, old-fashioned lodges, to full-on luxury living, with extravagant accommodation, sumptuous cuisine and a variety of extras such as butler service. Most lodges are fairly luxurious, however, and in between outings you can appreciate the full extent of your surroundings: most camps have platforms overlooking a waterhole or a river, there are usually comfortable lounge areas, libraries of books and magazines about wildlife, and most lodges have swimming pools. Recent additions to some camps include gyms, spas and conference facilities.

Special deals are often available, and it is worth looking out for fly-drive packages and discounts out of peak season. The daily cost of staying at a lodge vary from R5000 to R10000 for two people sharing, though rates can soar to over R20,000; prices include all meals, game walks and game drives. Reservations should be made well in advance because the most popular lodges get fully booked very quickly. ▸▸ *See Sleeping, page 639.*

Timbavati Game Reserve

Timbavati extends from Orpen to the region just south of the Olifants River. As well as large herds of elephant, giraffe, blue wildebeest, zebra and impala, this area is known for its white lions, although these have largely become assimilated in to the larger lion population. Open savannah, riverine forest, acacia, marula and mopane woodlands support a tremendous variety of wildlife, including 350 species of bird. The reserve was created in the 1950s from a group of privately owned farms where hunting was banned. Game, such as cheetah, sable and white rhino, was reintroduced to re-establish populations which were originally present in this area. You can get to the lodges in the northern part of the reserve via the turning 7 km south of Hoedspruit off the R40. The nearest airport is **Eastgate**, although many of the lodges have private airstrips. Camps in the southern areas are accessed by the turning 9 km north of Klaserie at Kapama, off the R40. ▸▸ *There are 13 luxury lodges and camps dotted about the reserve, www.timbavati.co.za.*

Kapama Private Game Reserve

Kapama Private Game Reserve is one with the easiest to access as it's right next to **Eastgate** airport near Hoedspruit in Limpopo Province. The reserve covers approximately 13,000 ha of prime big game territory, with three luxury lodges within its borders. A highlight here are the elephant-back safaris offered at **Camp Jabulani**, the first operation of its kind in South Africa, following a successful programme at Victoria Falls in Zimbabwe. Twelve fully trained African elephants arrived at Kapama in early 2002, after being relocated from Zimbabwe. Guests are seated on canvas-covered saddles positioned behind an experienced elephant handler. From this vantage point, they are able to view game from a close proximity as the elephants move silently and in a single file through the bush. The reserve also offers game drives, clay pigeon shooting, bush walks, birdwatching from a bird hide on the banks of a large dam, sundowner cruises, traditional dancing, hot-air ballooning and quad-biking. All the activities are exclusively for the guests at the luxury lodges within the reserve. ▸▸ *There are five luxury lodges in the reserve, www.kapama.co.za.*

Thornybush Nature Reserve

Thornybush started life as a private farm sharing a border with Timbavati. It was converted into a private game reserve of 11,500 ha and is now part of the Greater Kruger National Park. There are eight game lodges here. The main entrance is 9 km north of

Klaserie off the R40; look out for the signs for Kapama and the Hoedspruit Cheetah project. The nearest airport is **Eastgate** at Hoedspruit. ▸▸ *There are seven luxury lodges in the reserve, www.thornybush.co.za.*

Mala Mala Game Reserve

Mala Mala was one of the first private reserves to identify and cater for the top end of the luxury market. Guests have exclusive access to over 50 km of riverfront along the Sand River, offering some of the best game viewing in South Africa thanks to the fact that this is a perennial river. Seeing the Big Five is a central part of the Mala Mala experience and guests get a certificate to authenticate their sightings. The camps in the south of the reserve are approached from the R536, the Hazyview to Skukuza road. For the lodges to the north, turn off the R40 about 15 km north of Hazyview. It is at least a further 50 km to the accommodation. ▸▸ *There are three luxury lodges in the reserve, www.malamala.com.*

Sabi Sabi Game Reserve

Sabi Sabi Private Game Reserve is a relatively small area of land in the extreme south of the block of contiguous reserves which stretch all the way from the Olifants River to the Sabie River. To get there, follow the R536 from Hazyview to Skukuza, turn off at Glano. Although it is now part of the Greater Kruger National Park, the collection of private lodges and camps in Sabi Sabi couldn't be more different than the Skukuza camp across the Sabie River. Sabi Sabi has an excellent reputation by virtue of being the only private reserve on the perennial Sabie River. ▸▸ *Sabi Sabi is home to four of the most fashionable lodges, www.sabisabi.com.*

Sabi Sand Game Reserve

Sabi Sand has the highest density of lodges and game-viewing vehicles and is slightly more crowded than Timbavati or Thornybush. However, the Sand River has water all year round, which does attract large numbers of game. The reserve was established in 1934 by the owners of farms in this area but the first lodge wasn't opened to the public until 1962. Some of the most famous private concessions are within Sabi Sand, including Londolozi and Ulusaba. The game-viewing experience here is intended to give visitors a deeper understanding of the wilderness and don't just concentrate on the Big Five. To reach the reserve, turn off the R40 about 15 km north of Hazyview; this is the same road for Mala Mala Game Reserve. It is at least a further 50 km to the accommodation. ▸▸ *There are no fewer than 17 lodges in the reserve, www.sabisand.co.za.*

Kruger National Park listings

Private game reserves

L4	over R7650	L2	R3831-4680
L3	R4861-7650	L1	R2250-3830

Restaurant prices

TTT over R260 TT R131-260 T under R130

See pages 46-53 for further information.

Sleeping

For SANParks accommodation within the different sections of Kruger, see pages 620 and 625-635. There are far too many lodges in the private game reserves to list in full, but below is a selection – be sure to shop around while choosing where to stay. Most reserves have good websites.

Kruger Park concessions *p620, map p627*

Several concessions have been granted to private camps within the boundaries of the Kruger National Park. The safari experience at these is similar to the private reserves and rates include game drives, bush walks and all meals and, if you don't have your own vehicle, transfers from the nearest airport can be arranged. Singita Lebombo and Singita Sweni are part of Singita (see above) and are close to one another on the banks of the Sweni River near the border with Mozambique, 64 km from Orpen Gate.

L4 Jock Safari Lodge, southeast of the park, 35 km from Malalane Gate, T041-407 1000, www.jocksafarilodge.com. The camp is in an area of mixed woodland between Malalane and Skukuza. This used to be a national park camp and was the first to be turned over to private hands. The 15 cottages have been refurbished to the highest standard and are decorated with prints of the original illustrations from the novel, *Jock of the Bushveld*. Each has its own private viewing deck and outside showers overlooking the Mitomeni and Biyamiti rivers. Rock swimming pool and spa.

L4 Singita Lebombo, on the banks of the Sweni River near the Mozambique border, 64 km from Orpen Gate. A modern and stylish lodge with gym and spa built of glass, steel and stone. Fashionable alternative to the usual colonial or ethnic themes. 15 suites, linked by walkways, with sleek decks, designer furniture, infinity pool with white loungers and bar area.

L4 Singita Sweni, near Singita Lebombo. Smallest of the Singita lodges, with just 6 suites built on stilts tucked away in the trees with views over the bush, stylish dining room with floor-to-ceiling windows and views over the river. Decor is dark wood, ethnic fabrics and earthenware with splashes of bright lime.

L4 Tinga Private Game Lodge, 8 km from Paul Kruger Gate, T013-735 8400, www.tinga. co.za. 2 luxurious lodges close together set under jackelberry trees overlooking the game-rich Sabie River, each with 9 vast suites with plunge pools, double showers, enormous baths, separate lounges, DSTV, DVD players, huge windows with uninterrupted views of the bush, superb food and a wellness centre, library and lounge, walks on offer to a nearby hippo pool as well as the regular game drives.

L3 Rhino Post Lodge and Rhino Walking Safaris, a 12,000-ha concession 10 km northeast of Skukuza, T011-467 1886, www.rws.co.za. 8 elegant suites on the banks of the Mutlumuvi River, free-standing baths and outdoor showers, swimming pool with deck overlooking a water hole. As well as game drives, offers multi-day walking safaris accompanied by an armed guard, utilizing both the lodge and simple bush camps.

L2 Pafuri Camp, close to the Pafuri Gate, Wilderness Safaris, reservations T011-257 5111, www.pafuri.com. Not as luxurious as some of the others, this camp is in a concession in the extreme north of Kruger between the Limpopo and Luvuvhu rivers and is excellent for birdwatching, the area was proclaimed a RAMSAR site in 2007. It sits under giant ebony trees and overlooks the Luvuvhu River, and has 20 tents on raised platforms under thatch, some sleep families of 4. Outdoor shower, game viewing deck, eating boma, plunge pool, children's activities (over 6 years old) to learn about the bush.

Timbavati Game Reserve *p638, map p636*
L4 King's Camp, T013-755 4408, www.kings camp.com. An exclusive camp with 1 luxury, a/c thatched suites, with minibar, Victorian claw and foot baths and outdoor showers, lounge-dining room, bar, swimming pool, gym, spa, game-viewing platform and deck overlooking a very active waterhole. After a night drive guests enjoy dinner in the boma, wine cellar, or out bush under canvas.

L4 Tanda Tula, T015-793 3191, www.tanda tula.co.za. Set in an area of thick acacia woodland, is not ideal country for seeing the Big Five but you will see some of the more unusual animals. The accommodation consists of 12 thatched luxury East African safari tents furnished with wicker furniture and Victorian bathrooms. The bar on the veranda overlooks the swimming pool and a waterhole. In the evenings, weather permitting, barbecued dinners are held in the dried-up river bed in front of the camp.

L3 Motswari, T011-463 1990, www.mot swari.co.za. One of the smaller luxury camps, located in the northern region of Timbavati, with exclusive access to a large area. Game viewing can be from a jeep, on foot or at hides overlooking waterholes. Lodge facilities include a traditional open-air boma, a spacious lounge and bar overlooking a beautiful dam, an art gallery exhibiting original wildlife art, a fully equipped conference room and a refreshing swimming pool. It has 15 luxury bungalows with a/c and overhead fans, and magnificent bush and river views from the beds.

L3 Ngala, T011-809 4300, www.andbeyond. com. Ngala is a long-running favourite amongst the area's luxury lodges. The lodge is on the Timbavati Flood Plain, a region known for its herds of elephant and prides of lion. Visitors in this part of the reserve experience 2 contrasting ecosystems; the open savannah grasslands, and the magnificent mopane woodlands. The range of habitat means that the birdlife in this area is particularly interesting and varied. The 20 a/c thatched cottages and tents, filled with antique furnishings, and the luxury Safari Suite with its own lounge, dining area, swimming pool, and private Land Rover, are all set in an area of mopane woodland overlooking a waterhole. Meals are served on the open decking area overlooking the waterhole, or in a lantern-lit lapa area. The food here is particularly good, and the game rangers very knowledgeable. Recommended.

L3 Umlani Bush Camp, T021-785 5547, www.umlani.com. Reed and thatch double or family rondavels with open-air showers, in a Lowveld area where kudu, nyala, giraffe, elephant, lion and white rhino can be seen. Game drives are run during the day and in the evenings but the emphasis is on the game walks. There is a treehouse overlooking a waterhole which is good for birdwatching. No electricity and the whole camp is lit atmospherically by candles and oil lamps.

L1 Gomo Gomo Game Lodge, T013-752 3954, www.gomogomo.co.za. A relatively simple bush camp, one of the less expensive

options around, were the emphasis is very much on the bush and the wildlife, rather than the luxury and the food and drink. A friendly camp where guests enjoy traditional South African fare under the open sky. There are 8 brick and thatched double and family rondavels, the gardens are an interesting collection of aloes and other indigenous plants and have a swimming pool. Game drives and bush walks included.

Kapama Game Reserve *p638, map p636*
L4 Camp Jabulani, see page 638, T012-460 5605, www.campjabulani.com. Opulent accommodation and elephant-back safaris. 7 stylish suites, with private decks and splash pools, butler service, open showers, fireplaces, fashionable fusion food spread over several courses and a spa. Rates are inclusive of everything except spa treatments.

L2 Buffalo Camp, T012-368 0600, www.kapama.co.za. Built on the theme of an East African safari camp of bygone days, 8 luxury canvas tents, each sleeping 2 guests, set on stilts in the upper reaches of tall trees, overlooking a seasonal river. Each tent is interconnected to other tents by wooden walkways high above a sandy river bed. Dining is in an outside boma around a fire, and there's a pool, wellness centre with lap pool, gym and spa.

L2 Kapama Lodge, T012-368 0600, www.kapama.co.za, 20 luxurious thatched chalets set in indigenous gardens. Winding timber walkways link the reception area, conference room, lounge, library and dining room. The tea deck is a relaxing venue for watching an abundance of birds in the balmy evening, while the lounge offers a warm, cosy welcome on cool winter evenings. A good option for families and offers extra activities for small children while parents go on game drives. Shares the same wellness centre (above).

Thornybush Nature Reserve *p638, map p636*
L4 Thornybush Game Lodge, T011-253 6500, www.thornybush.co.za. The largest lodge in the reserve but you can still enjoy

a relaxing and private time in the bush here. 18 a/c rooms and 2 family suites with outdoor showers, the bar and the boma are a popular feature beside the Monwana River. Discuss with the camp rangers how you would most like to enjoy your game viewing; night drives, bush walks and morning drives are all possible and there are children's activities, swimming pool and spa.

L1 Kwa Mbili Game Lodge, T015-793 2773, www.kwambili.com. A pleasant small lodge that offers comparatively inexpensive accommodation. Game drives in open vehicles or bush walks are on offer, all in the company of experienced game rangers and trackers. The lodge has a choice of thatched chalets or safari tents, all with en suite bathrooms and simple decor. Meals are served around a camp fire or on the open veranda where there is also a bar and a lounge area, plus a swimming pool.

Mala Mala Game Reserve *p639, map p636*
There are 3 camps to choose from, each with its own character. There is a safari programme for children under 12 at **Mala Mala Main Camp** but no under 12s at **Sable Camp**; and no under 16s at **Rattray's**. Reservations: T011-442 2267, www.malamala.com.

L4 Mala Mala Main Camp. Accommodation consists of 18 ochre-coloured thatched rondavels, extremely spacious, each with his and hers bathrooms, a/c, heating, and minibar, 1 room for wheelchair users. Lounge area is decorated with elephant tusks, hunting rifles, spears and African memorabilia. The whole camp is set in a shady wood beside the river; good meals served. Swimming pool.

L4 Rattray's. Original farmhouse dating from the 1920s when the area was a cattle ranch belonging to Harry Kirkman. Kirkman was one of Kruger's first game rangers and the house is decorated with early photos, hunting rifles and old maps of the Transvaal. Appealing colonial atmosphere, 8 luxury suites each with private veranda and plunge pool, antique furnishings, satellite TV and internet access. Swimming pool, gym and massage room.

L4 Sable Camp, in the southern corner of the reserve, away from the **Main Camp**. The most intimate of the 3 camps, with just 5 luxury suites, and one 2-bedroom suite, colonial theme, beautiful setting overlooking the Sabie River. Deck and swimming pool with views, meals served outdoors. Excellent game viewing from here – the camp is very close to Kruger Park headquarters at Skukuza.

Sabi Sabi Game Reserve *p639, map p636*
The 4 lodges have won multiple 'Best Game Lodge in Southern Africa' awards. Rates as high as R15,000 per person per night. Reservations: T011-4477172, www.sabisabi.com.

L4 Bush Lodge, overlooking a water hole amongst trees on the banks of the Msuthlu River. 20 a/c thatched chalets and 5 luxury suites, ethnic decor, swimming pool, spa, meals served in open-air boma. The main building is decorated with African art and sculptures made from uprooted trees.

L4 Earth Lodge, set on the banks of the Sabie River. This innovative lodge feels like an ultra-trendy boutique hotel set deep in the African bush. The design cuts into the earth, which means that the lodge is virtually invisible, with smooth stone and grass-covered roofs blending into the surroundings. 13 suites with stylish decor of muted colours and natural materials, private plunge pool, glass-fronted bathrooms and butler. Bar area made up of the roots of trees, luxury spa, and meals are served in an open-air boma cut into the ground.

L4 Little Bush Camp. Small camp that can be booked exclusively by a group, with 6 thatched suites decorated with contemporary African art, outdoor showers, private viewing decks, the camp is linked by boardwalks, meals are taken outside under the arms of giant trees, guests can use spa facilities at the **Bush Lodge**.

L4 Selati Lodge. 8 stone and thatch chalets, colonial and steam train theme, antiques and 4-poster beds. The camp is lit with oil lamps at night, but there's electricity for ceiling fans and a/c. Meals served on a deck next to the pool or in a boma or farmhouse-style kitchen.

Sabi Sand Game Reserve *p639, map p636*
Several of the private concerns have more
than 1 camp, providing you with a choice
in style as well as price. The camps have
been grouped under their collective names.

Londolozi

Along with Mala Mala, Londolozi is one of
the best-known and most exclusive luxury
game lodges in the region. The highlight of
a game drive here is the opportunity to see
leopards (in Londolozi these normally elusive
creatures are used to game-viewing vehicles).
There is an emphasis on finding the Big Five,
but the rangers here are also willing to spend
time searching for other animals. Londolozi
operates 5 camps along the banks of the Sand
River. The Life Centre offers a spa, yoga and
gym to guests of all the lodges. Reservations,
T011-280 6640, www.londolozi.co.za.

L4 Founders Camp. 6 chalets and 1 suite
secluded in dense riverine forest. The a/c
chalets with their wooden decks feature a
personal bar and the suite has a stone-laid
outdoor shower. Charming and intimate,
the dining area at Founders Camp overlooks
the Sand River, with a walkway leading to
a thatched viewing deck where guests can
relax while game and bird viewing. The
boma is adjacent to the camp's swimming
pool. There is a covered sitting area, with a
well-stocked drinks cabinet.

L4 Granite Suites. Very private and ideal
for honeymooners, with just 3 thatched
spacious suites built on stilts on a granite
rise overlooking the river, each with private,
plunge pools, rim-flow heated swimming
pool and broad viewing decks lit by lanterns
in the evening, contemporary silver and grey
decor. No under 16s but a family can book
it exclusively.

L4 Pioneer Camp. Sitting on a gentle rise
in the landscape with elevated views of the
reserve and breathtaking river views, the
camp consists of just 3 suites furnished in
classic safari style. The suites have a fireplace,
all have a personal bar, and bathrooms with
baths and indoor and outdoor showers. The

intimate guest area provides a unique interactive experience with the kitchen, sitting
and dining areas all being open-plan. The
camp has a swimming pool and boma
where evening meals are enjoyed
under the stars. No children under 16.

L4 Tree Camp. One of the best game lodges
in Africa, with 6 thatched chalets each with
private viewing platforms high in the trees
above the Sand River, and plunge pools. The
furniture is made from old railway sleepers of
polished hardwoods and the beds are made
from leather, giving the camp a luxurious but
ethnic feel. It is set amongst the rocks in a
patch of riverine forest and has a platform on
stilts over the river. No children under 16.

L4 Varty Camp. 10 luxurious chalets on the
site of an old hunting camp built in 1926. All
have private plunge pools and wooden decks,
earthy decor. Bathrooms have capacious tubs
with uninterrupted views of the surrounding
bush. The camp has a well-stocked wine cellar,
a library (with internet), historical photographs
of the reserve, a spacious deck which
incorporates an ancient ebony tree with views
of the Sand River, and there is a large
swimming pool. Guests from the other camps
can use the gym and massage room here too.

Ulusaba

Owned by Sir Richard Branson, Ulusaba
has 2 camps, the **Safari Lodge** and the more
expensive **Rock Lodge**. Both are hugely
expensive but super luxurious and offer
game drives and bush walks, pampering
in the Aroma Boma beauty spa, many of
the suites have a private splash pools,
and dining at both is either outside or in
thatched bomas. Rates start from R12,000
per couple per night. Reservations: T011-
325 4405, www.ulusaba.virgin.com.

L4 Rock Lodge, in an extraordinary setting
on a koppie 200 m above the reserve.
10 spacious a/c rooms with colourful furnishings. The views are spectacular and there
are pathways lead down the rock face to a
veranda, from where you can see the animals
coming to drink at the Ulusaba dam. There

is a rock pool surrounded by a sundeck, and meals are served on the deck.

L4 Safari Lodge. 10 thatched chalets built on elevated wooden platforms shaded by wild fig trees. Some of them can only be reached by rope swing bridges. Each chalet has an outside shower, and there is also a rock pool above the river where guests can swim. This is a 15 min walk from **Rock Lodge** along a raised wooden walkway.

Singita

This luxury operator runs 4 lodges that are generally regarded as some of the finest and most expensive in South Africa (they have won the Condé Nast Traveller Best Hotel award for several years running (rates are over R19,000 per couple per night). The company has also won the Fair Trade in Tourism stamp. No children under 10, unless the lodges are booked exclusively. Reservations: T021-683 3424, www.singita.com.

L4 Singita Boulders. Impressive lodge built of curving thatch and stone moulded into the rock. Set on the banks of the Sand River. 12 luxurious suites, stone theme, natural decor and cool, neutral colours, beautiful views from the beds and plunge pools. Spa, sun deck, swimming pool, attractive lounge, meals served on deck.

L4 Singita Ebony. 12 suites nestling in the shade of jackleberry trees on the banks of the Sand River, with stunning decor, of a mix of antiques and splashes of vibrant colour, open-plan bathrooms, plunge pools and private decks. Super-stylish lounge area, excellent meals served outdoors on deck. Gym and spa.

▲ Activities and tours

Tour operators

Intrepid Bundu Safaris, T011-675 0767, www.intrepidbundu.com. Budget 4-day backpacker camping tours of Kruger from Johannesburg; they have their own simple camp in the park from where is possible to go game walking.

Spurwing, T011-957 2222, www.spurwing tourism.com. 3-5 day safaris to Kruger and the Panorama region using mid-range lodges outside of, but near, the park gates, and includes game drives in the park using 4WDs, and more expensive safaris utilizing the top-end lodges.

Transfrontier Walking Safaris, T015-793 3816, www.transfrontiers.com. Offers 4- or 5-day walking safaris in the private reserves accessed from Hoedspruit and is popular with budget travellers. Rates include transfers to and from Johannesburg and Tshwane (Pretoria), though you can arrange to meet them in Hoedspruit, The 5-day safari (R6670) starts on Mon and the 4-day safari (R5145) starts on Fri, there's a maximum of 8 people so early booking is advised. Accommodation is in 2 simple bush camps with pre-erected walk in tents with twin beds, and communal ablution facilities, and daily walks leave from these. Each camp has an honesty bar and a dining tent, and costs include all meals. No children under 16 and you need to be reasonably fit. Highly recommended for a peaceful, authentic and informative bush experience well away from the crowds.

Viva Safaris, T011-476 8842, www.viva safaris.com. 3- to 5-day budget safaris from Johannesburg to its own mid-range lodges in Balule Nature Reserve, which borders the park north of Hoedspruit. Range of accommodation, including some simple but unique treehouses, game drives into the park, and all meals. Rates for a 3-day and 2-night safari start from R5000 per person and children get discounts.

Wildlife Safaris, Randburg 2125, Johannesburg, T011-791 4238, www.wildlifesafaris. com. 3- to 5-day safaris from Johannesburg with mid-range prices and accommodation in the larger Kruger Park rest camps, and includes lunches and dinners in the rest camps' restaurants. Again prices start from R5000 for the 3-day trip.

Panorama region

The road north of Nelspruit gradually climbs up into the eastern Drakensberg, generally referred to as the Panorama region. The region is dotted with small towns, popular with local tourists who come for the craft shops and restaurants, but the main reason for a visit is the spectacular Blyde River Canyon, the third largest canyon in the world. The mountains provide blessed relief from the heat on the plains of the Lowveld. ➤➤ *For listings, see pages 654-660.*

White River → *Colour map 2, B5. Phone code: 013. Altitude: 800 m.*

This small country town is at the centre of a citrus fruit-growing area; fresh local produce includes macadamia nuts, pecans, cashews, avocados, lychees and mangoes. The first settlers here were Boer cattle ranchers who arrived in the 1880s, at the end of the Anglo-Boer War a settlement was created to accommodate a new farming community made up of newly demobilized soldiers. There's little in the town itself, although the Motor Museum and Orange Winery attract a fair share of South Africa tourists. **Lowveld Tourist information** ① *T013-750 1073, www.lowveldtourism.com, Mon-Fri 0900-1700, Sat 0900-1500* has a small helpful office on the Hazyview road, at Casterbridge Farm (see below), which can give local advice and make reservations for lodges in Kruger.

The **Casterbridge Farm** ① *2 km from town on the Hazyview road, T013-750 1540, www.casterbridge.co.za, Mon-Fri 0900-1630, Sat-Sun 0900-1600, restaurant hours vary*, is a very attractive old farmstead that has been converted into a shopping centre for arts and crafts, and there's a good bookshop selling new and second-hand books and an internet café. There are also a number of restaurants, a little cinema, the Barnyard Theatre for local productions, and a farmer's market every Saturday morning. Children will enjoy the **Farmyard Petting Zoo** ① *Tue-Sun, 0900-1730, adults free, children (under 12) R15*, which has the likes of bunnies, ponies and goats, as well as a bouncy castle and baby quad bikes. There's also a pleasant garden café, which serves breakfast, light meals and cream teas, and a plant nursery.

The **White River Local History and Motor Museum** ① *Casterbridge Farm, 2 km from town on the Hazyview road, T013-750 2196, daily 0900-1630, R20, children (under 12) R10*, has small displays on local history, but more impressive is the collection of over 60 vintage cars on three floors of exhibition space. They are owned by a private collector, though it's still quite astonishing to see such a comprehensive collection of beautifully restored classic cars in such a backwater location. Among the oldest vehicles to be displayed are those built in 1911, not too long after the introduction of the automobile or 'horseless carriage' as it was then known. Of interest is the 1924 7-seater Packhard Phaeton with a giant 8-cylinder engine, bought new by Lord Delamere and discovered on his Kenyan estate in the 1970s, and a 1936 Jaguar SS100, which is one of only 314 ever built. There are several interesting racing cars, including the Fatman, an MG single-seater racing car built in Durban in 1954, and a replica of Ayrton Senna's 99T Honda Formula 1 car. One of the most remarkable cars on display is a 1912 Willy's Overland, which was purchased by a Mr Brandt in 1924. Legend has it that he parked his beloved car in a room in his house and, presumably in an eccentric effort to preserve it, bricked up all the doors and the windows. Many years later, after his death, Mr Brandt's grandson unearthed the vehicle and it was restored in 1997.

In the heart of the Nutcracker Valley, a short distance from White River, **Rottcher Wineries** ① *T013-751 3884, Mon-Fri 0800-1700, Sat and Sun 0800-1500; tours 1000 and 1400*, incorporates a nuttery, macadamia nut farm and nut factory, as well as the orange winery, which produces a range of orange liquors. For children there is a riding school offering pony and horse rides each day.

Hazyview → *Colour map 2, B5. Phone code: 013. 58 km from Nelspruit.*

Hazyview lies on the banks of the Sabie River in the hot Lowveld country on the south-western border of Kruger, surrounded by banana plantations. The town is a convenient

Panorama region

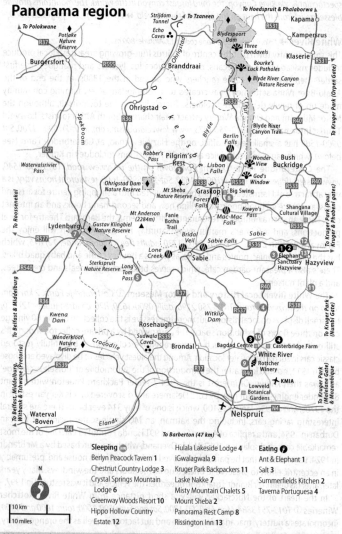

Sleeping
Berlyn Peacock Tavern 1
Chestnut Country Lodge 3
Crystal Springs Mountain Lodge 6
Greenway Woods Resort 10
Hippo Hollow Country Estate 12

Hulala Lakeside Lodge 4
iGwalagwala 9
Kruger Park Backpackers 11
Laske Nakke 7
Misty Mountain Chalets 5
Mount Sheba 2
Panorama Rest Camp 8
Rissington Inn 13

Eating
Ant & Elephant 1
Salt 3
Summerfields Kitchen 2
Taverna Portuguesa 4

stop on the way to Kruger, and is only 16 km to Numbi Gate and 10 km to Phabeni Gate. There is a wide range of accommodation from caravan parks to luxury private game reserves, useful if you'd rather not stay in the park itself. Information is available from **Big 5 Reservations** ① *Perry's Bridge Trading Post, Main Rd, T013-737 8191, www.big5 country.co.za, Mon-Sat 0800-1700, Sun 0800-1300*, which acts as an agent for a range of tour operators and safari lodges in the region.

Elephant Sanctuary Hazyview ① *on the R536, 5km from Hazyview towards Sabie, T013-737 6609, www.elephantsanctuary.co.za, 0800-1700, elephant walks R450, children (4-14) R225, walks and elephant-back riding R750, children (8-14) R375*, is run by the same outfit that established the elephant sanctuaries on the Garden Route (see page 323) and Hartbeespoort Dam (see page 703). It recently opened here with two elephants, though they may add to this number. Pre-booking is advised as activities start at certain times. The **Trunk-in-Hand** experience is a 1½-hour interaction with the elephants, including a walk through the bush holding on to their trunks, an informative talk on African elephants and an optional 20-minute elephant ride. Visitors can also brush down the elephants and accompany them to their stables at the end of the day. Check out the website for the programmes and times.

The Shangana family that lives in the **Shangana Cultural Village** ① *on the R535, 5km from Hazyview towards Graskop, T013-737 5805, www.shangana.co.za, 0900-1600, tea garden, 1-hr tour, R90, tour and lunch R195, evening festival R310, children (under 12) ½-price*, are descendents of Chief Shoshangana, an important tribal leader in the early 19th century. This is not a typical 'tribal village' experience as the family are keen to preserve their traditional lifestyles. One hour tours take place throughout the day and follow a path from the Marula Market (a cut-above-the-rest curio market) to the village, and a guide explains traditional practices such as farming, food preparation, hut building and clothing, and there is plenty opportunity to interact with the family members. On the midday tour a traditional lunch is included, and in the evening a festival dinner is served and the history of the Shanganas is presented by singers and dancers, which begins with drumming and a procession of flaming torches. The food is quite delicious; crocodile in groundnut sauce, baked vegetables, salads, venison and oxtail stews and fresh fruit.

Sabie → *Colour map 2, B4/5. Phone code: 013. Altitude: 1020 m.*

Once a gold-mining town, Sabie has little left to show of its glistening age and is now a prosaic timber-processing centre. Nevertheless, it has a pretty setting, ringed by mountains, pine and eucalyptus plantations, and it attracts a fair number of visitors who flock to its main road, lined with pleasant craft and coffee shops.

Prospectors first found gold in the region during the 1870s, but it wasn't until 1895 that gold was discovered at Sabie. The land here belonged to a big game hunter named Glynn who found the gold while on a picnic at Lower Sabie Falls. Glynn and his friends began shooting at a row of empty bottles on an outcrop of rock – the bullets chipped away at the rock revealing flecks of sparkling gold. This led to an influx of fortune hunters who came and camped on the banks of the Sabie River. In the process, many indigenous forests were chopped down to meet the demand for mine props and firewood. Fortunately, the far-sighted mine manager, Joseph Brook Shires, realized that man-made forests were necessary and planted the first trees in 1876. Planting continued into the next century, creating forestry jobs during the 1930s depression.

Today, Sabie lies in one of the largest man-made forests in the world. Driving around this region, the roads pass through endless tracts of neat rows of trees – impressive, but only a very few remaining patches of indigenous forest remain. Tourist information is available from **Sabie Information** ① *Sabie Market Sq, T013-764 1177, www.sabie.co.za, Mon-Fro 0800-1630, Sat 0900-1300.*

The **Forestry Museum** ① *Ford St, T013-764 1058, www.komatiecotourism.co.za, Mon-Fri 0800-1630, Sat 0800-1200, R5, children (under 14) R2,* has displays on the development of South Africa's plantations and the timber industry, including an interesting cross-section of a 250-year-old yellowwood tree, which highlights aspects of South African history on its rings. The museum is also home to a satellite office of **Komatiland Forestry**, T013-764 1392, which has information on hiking and mountain bike trails in the region, and you can download information and maps for several trails in the forests around Sabie from the website.

Mac Mac Falls and **Mac Mac Pools** ① *11 km from Sabie on the road to Graskop, R5 per person,* are 65 m high. Over 1000 miners rushed to the falls in 1873 after gold was discovered above them. Originally there was a single fall, but in their eagerness to get to gold, some miners tried to divert the waterfall's flow and an over-enthusiastic application of dynamite created the second fall. The name of Mac Mac Falls originates from the large numbers of Scottish miners who came here. The tourist office has leaflets on day hikes which visit these and other local waterfalls: **Bonnet Falls**, **Maria Shires Falls** and **Forest Falls**. These are signposted off the road to Graskop. There is a turning before Graskop onto the R533 to Pilgrim's Rest.

.**Lydenburg** → *Colour map 2, B4. Phone code: 013. Altitude: 1469 m.*

This quiet agricultural and mining town is a typically unexceptional town in the central region of Mpumalanga. The descent from **Long Tom Pass** west to Lydenburg opens up vistas of rolling grasslands, cattle ranches and wheat-growing country stretching out into the distance. Approaching from the south, the town is often described as the

Sabie

To Mac Mac Falls, Graskop (R532) & Pilgrim's Rest

Sabie River

Sabie Falls

Power

Lydenburg

Maliveld

To Trout Farm & Lone Creek Falls

Main St

Ford

Lea

Simmons

Michael

Quick Spar

Church

Pol

Forestry Museum

Glynn

CNA

10th

6th

Town Hall & Library

7th La

9th La

6th

To 5 & Hazyview

Louis Trichardt

R536

4th La

Mac-Mac

Maliveld

3rd La

To White River

R537

Caltex

Main Rd

1st La

2nd La

Potgieter

Nelson

Andrew

R532

To 1 & Lydenburg via Long Tom Pass (R532)

N

200 metres
200 yards

Sleeping
Hillwatering Country House 5

Jock Sabie Lodge 2
Misty Mountain Chalets 1
Villa Ticino 4
Woodsman, Restaurant & Woodsman Centre 6

Eating
Wild Fig Tree 1

Lydenburg Heads

The Lydenburg Heads are a collection of seven clay heads that date back to AD 590. They are unique pieces in the history of South African art and some of the earliest sculptures of the human form. The clay heads have only ever been found in this region and it is thought that they may have been used in initiation ceremonies.

The heads were first discovered in 1957 by Ludwig von Bezig on a farm near Lydenburg. Ludwig was 10 years old when he found the pieces of pottery but it wasn't until five years later that he became interested in archaeology. He returned to the farm several times between 1962 and 1966, where he found the pieces of the broken heads. When they were reconstructed he had seven heads of different sizes, one of which had the snout of an animal.

The heads on display in the Lydenburg Museum are replicas of the originals, now in the South African Museum in Cape Town.

gateway to the Lowveld. On the other side of Long Tom Pass you are over the escarpment formed by the Drakensberg, which marks the boundary between the Highveld and the Lowveld. Information is available from **Lydenburg Information Centre** ① *at the museum T013-235 2213, www.lydenburg.org*. **Note** Beware of fog at the top of Long Tom Pass and, in the winter months, remember that the pass is sometimes blocked by snow.

Lydenburg Museum ① *1 km from town on the R37, T013-235 2213, www.lydenburg museum.org.za, Mon-Fri 0800-1300, 1400-1600, Sat and Sun 0800-1700, small entry fee*, is fascinating, with well-presented displays on the history of the Lydenburg region from the Stone Age to the present. It is famous for being the first home of the **Lydenburg Heads** (see box, above), and has displays illustrating South African history before the arrival of the Voortrekkers. This is the best local museum in the region, and superior to most local history museums in the country. The museum also distils its own *mampoer* – a local brew similar to brandy or schnapps – ask for a taster.

Several short hiking trails lead from the museum into the adjoining 2200-ha **Gustav Klingbiel Nature Reserve**, where you have the opportunity to view some small antelope and a vulture's restaurant. Staff at the museum can direct you to some Iron Age sites and the remains of some early trenches from the Boer War. You can also pick up a birdlist from the museum and some 256 species have been recorded in the reserve including the rare African finfoot.

Pilgrim's Rest ●●②☺ ►► *pp654-660. Colour map 2, B4.*

Pilgrim's Rest, a tiny mining town dating from the late 19th century, has been totally reconstructed as a living museum to preserve a fascinating part of South Africa's cultural heritage. It's a pretty spot: lining the main street, a row of miners' cottages with their corrugated-iron roofs and wooden walls nestles in a lush, leafy and utterly quiet valley. It's easy to imagine how it must have once looked, with a magistrate's court, church, local newspaper and schoolhouse. However, it's all almost too perfect, and the artificial atmosphere is exacerbated by the coachloads of tourists that pitch up throughout the day. Many of the reconstructed cottages today house gift shops and cafés, and a large craft market is held at the entrance to the village. The best time to see Pilgrim's Rest is early in the morning or in the late afternoon after the day-trippers have gone and the locals creep back onto the streets and into the bars. Although most of the buildings are strung out along one long street, the settlement has a very clear division between Uptown and Downtown, but both now attract tourists.

Background

The history of Pilgrim's Rest is a fascinating tale of gold fever in southern Africa during the late 19th century, as prospectors opened up new areas in search of a fortune. The town was named by one of the first prospectors, William Trafford, because he believed that his wandering days in search of gold had finally ended and yelled out "the pilgrim is at rest!". The first gold was found by Alec 'Wheelbarrow' Patterson, in a fertile valley then known as Lone Peach Tree Creek, in September 1873. Once Trafford announced that he had also found gold, the newspapers quickly spread the word and by the end of the year more than 1500 prospectors had pitched their tents along the creek. Life was far from easy for these fortune seekers, who slept on grass mattresses in makeshift tents, often sick with malaria and exposure, in a place where lawlessness and violence was rife.

Although some of the best finds were made in 1875, the region continued to produce gold until 1972, when the last mine was closed. In 1881, a financier, David Benjamin, formed the Transvaal Gold Exploration and Land Company, which effectively ran the gold fields until they were closed. Although there were poor years there were also some bountiful periods: in the 1890s a particularly rich reef – the Theta Reef – was discovered, which yielded more than five million ounces of gold over a period of 50 years. In 1986 Pilgrim's Rest was declared a National Monument and restoration of the old mining buildings began.

Pilgrim's Rest

To ③ ④ , Robber's Pass & Lydenburg

To Blyde River Canyon & Alanglade Period House Museum

Blyde

DOWNTOWN

Transvaal Gold Mining Estates

Main

Bypass

Historic Cemetery

Pilgrim's Creek

Pilgrim's Rest Museum

Old PO

Town Hall

UPTOWN

R533

Diggings Site Museum

To Graskop (16 km)

200 metres
200 yards

Sleeping
Crystal Springs
Mountain Lodge 3
District Six
Miners' Cottages 1

Mount Sheba 4
Royal 2

Eating
Jubilee Potters
& Coffee Shop 2
Pilgrim's Pantry 3
Scott's Café 4
The Vine 5

Sights

Historical displays and exhibits on gold-panning techniques can be found at the **Pilgrim's Rest Tourist Information Centre and Museum** ① *Main St, T013-768 1060, www.pilgrims-rest.co.za, daily 0900-1245, 1345-1630.* There are three other small village museums, housed in old miner's cottages, within walking distance.

The **Diggings Site Museum** ① *daily tours 1000, 1100, 1200, 1400 and 1500 with gold-panning demonstration, R10, children (under 16) R5, tickets from the tourist office*, is at the top of Uptown where the coaches park. A visit here helps visitors gain an insight into the lives of the diggers and prospectors during the gold rush at the end of the 19th century, before the first gold mining company took control of the town. Gold panning is demonstrated and visitors can have a go themselves.

The **Alanglade Period House Museum** ① *guided tours only and need at least 30 mins' notice, daily 1100 and 1400, R20, tickets from the tourist office*, is north of the village on the Mpumalanga escarpment. Built in 1915, the house is typically early 20th century and was the official mine manager's residence for Pilgrim's Rest up until 1972. Today it is furnished with Edwardian, art nouveau and art deco pieces.

Robber's Pass

Robber's Pass is 9 km from Pilgrim's Rest on the R533 and rises 650 m in only 9 km. Gold bullion and mail from Pilgrim's Rest was taken to the commercial banks in Lydenburg by coach twice a week via the pass north of town. The first major robbery took place here when two masked gunmen on horseback held up the stagecoach and made off with £10,000 worth of gold bullion. The second robbery in 1912 was not as successful. The armed robber was Tommy Dennison, a local barber, who carried out the crime and returned to Pilgrim's Rest to celebrate. He was soon arrested and spent five years in jail in Pretoria. On his release he returned and went into business at the Highwayman's Garage.

Graskop ●●●●● ►► pp654-660. Colour map 2, B5.

→ *Phone code: 013.*

This small town lies just south of the Blyde River Canyon, but despite having a large selection of holiday accommodation, restaurants and craft shops, it remains surprisingly quiet and makes a peaceful base from which to explore the region. Miners arrived here during the 1880s and established a camp, but modern Graskop is surrounded by forestry plantations and is an important centre of the timber industry. Today Graskop attracts fame as being home of the South African stuffed pancake – the famous **Harrie's** restaurant started it all, and the stuffed sweet and savoury pancakes are renowned throughout the country. Local residents have capitalized on this reputation, and there is now a line of pancake houses along the main street.

Information is available in the private **information office** ① *Louis Trichardt St, T013-767 1866, www.graskop.co.za, daily 0800-1700.*

Graskop is 1000 m higher than the Lowveld at the bottom of the escarpment and temperatures here are normally up to 8°C cooler; night-time temperatures in winter often go below 0°C and even in summer a sweater can be useful. This is also one of the wettest regions in South Africa but most of the rain falls during torrential thunderstorms in the summer months. This is the best time of year to see the waterfalls; the force of the water crashing into the pools below is spectacular.

Around Graskop

The road east goes over **Kowyn's Pass** a few kilometres from Graskop. Before descending towards the Lowveld it passes **Graskop Gorge**, where adrenaline junkies try out the **Big Swing** (see Activities and tours, page 659), and there are views looking up to **God's Window** (see page 653). This is a fruit-growing area of mangoes and lychees, which are sold at stalls on the side of the road in season.

Jock of the Bushveld Trail is an 8-km circular trail starting from within **Graskop Holiday Resort**. Along the trail you will pass a magnificent 500-year-old bearded yellowwood tree, as well as several eroded sandstone formations mentioned in the story of *Jock of the Bushveld*; the walk can be completed in three hours.

Berlin Falls and **Lisbon Falls** are further north on the R532 heading straight out of Graskop. Berlin Falls are 45 m high, and the water cascades into a circular pool surrounded by forest. At 92 m, Lisbon Falls are the highest in the area, and the river is separated into three streams as it plunges into the pool below.

Blyde River Canyon ⊙ ▸▸ pp654-660. Colour map 2, B5.

The Blyde River Canyon is the third largest in the world after the Grand Canyon in the USA and Fish River Canyon in Namibia. It is the product of the Blyde River, which tumbles down from the Drakensberg escarpment to the Lowveld over a series of waterfalls and cascades that spill into the **Blydespoort Dam** at the bottom. Blyde means 'river of joy', and the river was so named after Hendrik Potgieter and his party returned safely from Delagoa Bay (Mozambique) in 1844. Voortrekkers, who had stayed behind at their camp, first named the river Treur River ('river of mourning'), under the mistaken impression that the party had been killed, so when Pogieter returned, they had to rename it.

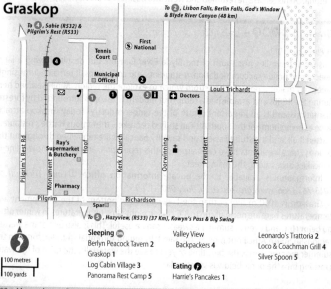

Graskop

To ②, Lisbon Falls, Berlin Falls, God's Window & Blyde River Canyon (48 km)

To ④, Sabie (R532) & Pilgrim's Rest (R533)

Tennis Court

First National ⑤

Municipal Offices ②

Louis Trichardt

Doctors

Ray's Supermarket & Butchery

Pharmacy

Pilgrim

Richardson

Spar

To ⑤, Hazyview, (R533) (37 Km), Kowyn's Pass & Big Swing

N

100 metres
100 yards

Sleeping 🛏
Berlyn Peacock Tavern 2
Graskop 1
Log Cabin Village 3
Panorama Rest Camp 5

Valley View
Backpackers 4

Eating 🍴
Harrie's Pancakes 1

Leonardo's Trattoria 2
Loco & Coachman Grill 4
Silver Spoon 5

The winding canyon is 26 km in length and is joined by the similarly spectacular 11 km **Ohrigstad Canyon** near Swadini. The 27,000 ha **Blyde River Canyon Nature Reserve** extends from God's Window down to the far side of the Blyde River dam. The canyon drops down 750 m, and for most of its length it is inaccessible. There are no roads crossing the reserve or linking the top and bottom of the canyon, but there are some short walking trails, and a number of view points snake off the along the R532 and overlook the Canyon and Lowveld beyond. Do take the time to drive down to the viewpoints, as you can't see much of the spectacular canyon if you stick to the R532.

Viewpoints

The most famous of the viewpoints is **God's Window**, right on the edge of the escarpment overlooking an almost sheer 300-m drop into the tangle of forest below. The views through the heat haze stretch over the Lowveld as far as Kruger. At the top of the hill there is a tiny patch of rainforest, which survives in the micro-climate on the very tip of the ridge. At 1730 m, **Wonder View** is the highest viewpoint accessible from the road and **Pinnacle Rock** is a 30-m-high quartzite 'needle' that rises dramatically out of the fern-clad ravine. From here it is possible to see the tops of the eight waterfalls that take the Blyde River down 450 m in a series of cascades to the dam.

The most developed viewpoint is at **Bourke's Luck Potholes**, an unusual series of rock formation resembling Swiss cheese. The smooth rock has been moulded and formed by the swirling action of whirlpools where the Treur and the Blyde rivers meet, creating spectacular dips, hollows and holes. The name 'Bourke's Luck' comes from Tom Bourke, a prospector who worked a claim here in the vain belief that he would find gold. There is a **visitor centre and kiosk** ⓘ *daily 0700-1700, R20, children (under 16) R10, serving snacks and light meals.* The visitor centre includes an eco-awareness exhibition outlining the geological history of the area. From here, a wood walkway winds around and over the potholes. A short drive further north, the viewpoint at the **Three Rondavels** is by far the most dramatic. At the car park by the walkway is a small craft market and some toilets. From here, a walkway leads out onto the lip of the canyon, with the vast cleft in the rock opening out in front of you, and **Blydespoort Dam** shimmering intensely blue at the bottom. The Three Rondavels easily recognized as the three circular rocky peaks opposite, capped with grass and vegetation and looking distinctly like thatched African rondavel huts.

North into Limpopo

The R532 continues north from the top of the canyon until it joins the R36 and the road descends through the **Strijdom Tunnel** and north to Hoedspruit and Phalaborwa. **Echo Caves** ⓘ *T013-238 0015, www.echocaves.co.za, daily 0830-1630, guided tours R50, children (under12) R20,* are on the R36 continuing south to **Ohrigstad**. The caves extend 2 km into the mountain and are known for the echoes produced when the stalactites are tapped. Many human bones have been found inside, proving that at one time they were inhabited. A tour takes 45 minutes, and there are lights and rails throughout the caves, although you may have to crawl to get to the further reaches of the caves, such as the spectacular Crystal Palace cave.

You could easily spend a few days exploring the lower section of the **Blyde River Canyon Nature Reserve** around the dam on the Limpopo side of the Strijdom Tunnel. Once you have passed through the tunnel the road quickly descends and you will immediately notice the rise in temperature. You can either continue to Hoedspruit and into Kruger Park via Phalaborwa or Orpen Gates, or take the R36 to Tzaneen, where another region awaits you. ▸▸ *For details, see the Limpopo chapter, pages 661-690.*

For Sleeping and Eating price codes and other relevant information, see pages 46-53.

◉ Sleeping

White River *p645*

AL Hulala Lakeside Lodge, 22 km from White River on the R40 towards Hazyview, T013-764 1893, www.hulala.co.za. Situated on a peninsula in a lake that gives the feeling of being on an island, this lodge has 25 luxury suites, private lounge, fireplace, TV, secluded patios overlooking the garden or lake, fine dining in the restaurant, a pool and 2 bars. Choice of canoes, rowing boats, specially adapted boats for anglers, or the nightly sundowner cruise. A romantic setting, recommended for couples. The completely secluded honeymoon suite has its own pool.

B Balcony Manor, 51 Frank Townsend St, T013-751 2024, www.balcony.co.za. 4 rooms set in a fine old 2-storey house with an elegant upstairs balcony, a mix of modern fittings with antique furnishings, old fashioned and comfortable. Each room has its own character, mature gardens, swimming pool, very ornate.

B Greenway Woods Resort, 7 km north of town on the R40, T013-751 1094, www.greenway.co.za. 35 modern self-catering chalets set in the beautiful countryside focussed on a championship golf course, with swimming pool. Each chalet has 3 bedrooms, 2 bathrooms, a/c and DSTV. It's a popular conference venue, there's an open fireplace in the lounge, swimming pool, mountain bikes for hire, African themed restaurant and bar. Prices depend on how many people share a chalet.

C iGwalagwala, 5 km to the south of town off the R40, T013-750 1723, www.igwalagwala.co.za. 5 garden suites, each with own entrance and private terrace, simple decor with cool tiled floors, 2 self-catering units, large swimming pool. Good breakfasts and dinners on request. *iGwalagwala* means purple-crested loerie; these are sometimes spotted in the beautiful mature gardens.

C Karula, Old Plaston Rd, 1 km from town centre, T013-751 2277, www.karulahotel.co.za. 46 double rooms with en suite bathroom, TV, restaurant, bar, swimming pool, tennis, billiard room. A slightly dated, old-fashioned hotel but nevertheless it is popular and has an excellent local reputation. Rates include good set traditional 3-course dinners.

C Linga Longa, Karee Cres, T013-751 1942, www.lingalongabb.co.za. 10 elegantly and individually decorated bedrooms with private entrances and fan or a/c, DSTV, bar fridge, lovely verandas, pool and jacuzzi in tropical gardens, generous breakfasts and other meals on request.

Hazyview *p646*

A Rissington Inn, 2 km from Hazyview on the R40 White River road, T013-737 7700, www.rissington.co.za. 17 comfortable cottages, some with outside showers, Victorian baths and private verandas overlooking the countryside. Neat gardens, views of the river, swimming pool. Best known for its good à la carte restaurant that is also open to non-guests, pub and outside eating on the veranda, great breakfasts and brunch, good vegetarian dishes. Recommended.

A-B Hippo Hollow Country Estate, 3 km from Hazyview off the R40 en route to Paul Kruger Gate, T013-737 6628, www.hippohollow.co.za. A selection of 37 thatched cottages with private balconies overlooking the Sabie River populated with hippos. Stylish, understated decor, large bathrooms, each has a gas braai and kitchenette. Also has 54 en suite hotel rooms, good restaurant, bar, curio shop, 2 swimming pools. Watch the hippos on the lawn at night. Kruger game drives can be arranged for those without a car.

B Chestnut Country Lodge, 11 km out of Hazyview off the R40 to White River and Nelspruit, T013-737 8195, www.chestnutlodge.co.za. A comfortable rural retreat with 13 individually designed rooms with simple

decor, TV, each with a private patio, all set on a 48-ha farm. Restaurant serving 3-course evening meals, swimming pool with deck where sun-downers are served, homely lounge with reference library bar. 15 mins' drive from Numbi Gate. Off-season deals.
E-F Kruger Park Backpackers, junction of R40 and the road leading to Numbi Gate, T013-737 7224, www.krugerparkbackpackers.co.za. Dorms and doubles set in Zulu huts with en suite bathrooms, painted in bright tribal designs. Lounge, bar, pool table, swimming pool, meals using home-grown organic produce, camping available. Kruger and Drakensberg tours are organized from here. Will collect Baz Bus passengers from Nelspruit at no extra charge if you book one of their tours.

Sabie *p647, map p648*
B Misty Mountain Chalets, 24 km from Sabie, at Long Tom Pass on the R532, T013-764 3377, www.mistymountain.co.za. 27 self-catering or B&B chalets sleeping 2-6 in a beautiful mountain setting, all linked to a cosy pub and restaurant, veranda with small infinity pool and stunning views, the endangered blue swallow nests on the site.
C Jock Sabie Lodge, off Main St, T013-764 2178, www.jock.co.za. 2.5 ha of attractive lawns with wide choice of accommodation, including self-catering log cabins with 2 bedrooms, 11 en suite hotel rooms, backpackers dorm (**E**) sleeping 40. Restaurant and bar selling cheap pub grub, pool, wheelchair friendly, very popular with South African families.
C-D Villa Ticino, Louis Trichardt St, T013-764 2598, www.villaticino.co.za. German-owned guesthouse with 6 double rooms with en suite bathrooms, B&B, plain decor but comfortable, TV lounge, swimming pool, non-smoking, no children under 14, pleasant gardens with a superb view across the valley and forests, central, next door to **Wild Fig Tree** restaurant.
D Hillwatering Country House, 50 Marula St, T013-764 1421, www.hillwatering.co.za.

Country house set in a beautiful garden on the outskirts of Sabie, 5 en suite rooms with private terraces and mountain views, simple, homely decor, breakfast is served outside in summer, or packed as a picnic if on an early start into Kruger, other meals on request.
D The Woodsman, next door to restaurant and bookshop of the same name, 94 Main St, T013-764 2204, www.thewoodsman.co.za. 12 suites set in an uninspiring block, but very comfortable inside with dark wood furniture, TV, tea- and coffee-making facilities, and excellent value. Restaurant and pub serving Greek Cypriot dishes, with pleasant deck overlooking the valley, underground parking, walking distance to restaurants and shops.

Lydenburg *p648*
D Laske Nakke, 2 km on the Dullstroom road, T013-235 2886, www.laskenakke.co.za. Self-catering chalets or budget en suite B&B rooms, camping and caravan park, 2 pools, bar, simple restaurant. Don't be put off by the sad-looking concrete blocks, the good-value rooms are fine inside.

Pilgrim's Rest *p649, map p650*
A Mount Sheba, 19 km from Pilgrim's Rest off the R533, T013-768 1241, www.forever sa.co.za. Set in the Mount Sheba Nature Reserve. 25 double-storey chalets with kitchen, lounge with fireplace and DSTV, **Owl & Trout** pub, **Chandelier** restaurant, a luxury retreat high up in the hills, excellent birdwatching, swimming pool, tennis and squash courts and can organize trout fishing. Rates include dinner and breakfast. Cheaper rates in the low season.
B-C Crystal Springs Mountain Lodge, high up in the hills off the R533 north of Pilgrim's Rest, T013-768 5000, www.grc-resorts.co.za. A holiday resort with a large number of luxurious self-catering chalets set in 5000 ha of mountain bushveld, plus larger lodges sleeping up to 8. Popular **Pointer's Rest** restaurant, bush boma braais, a full range of sporting activities, including hiking, tennis, squash, birdwatching, health spa, gym,

game drives, indoor and outdoor heated swimming pools. An all-round resort in a convenient location to explore the region, rates drop considerably off-season but it can be very cold here in winter.

C The Royal, Main St, Uppertown, T013-768 1100, www.royal-hotel.co.za. The original Royal Hotel is over 100 years old and dates from the time of the gold rush; it has been thoroughly restored with period-style corrugated-iron roof and wooden walls. 50 rooms set around courtyards, decorated with reproduction antique furniture and floral fabrics, open-plan bathrooms and claw-foot baths, very rickety brass beds. Also has rooms in cottages spread around the village. Great restaurant serving excellent traditional buffets, popular with tour groups, also has the historical **Church Bar** filled with Victorian memorabilia.

D District Six Miners' Cottages, on the hill above Pilgrim's Rest, book through the tourist office, T013-768 1060, www.pilgrims-rest. co.za. 7 self-catering cottages with 4 or 6 beds that were built in 1920 and are decorated in the original style, with brass bedsteads and period furniture. The best-value budget accommodation in the area, book in advance.

Graskop *p651, map p652*

B-C Graskop Hotel, Hoof St, T/F013-767 1244, www.graskophotel.co.za. An excellent recently renovated hotel in the centre of town, with a range of rooms at different prices, decorated with an attractive mixture of modern and African furniture (from the shop next door). Contemporary feel, the 'artist's' rooms have funky splashes of colour and modern art on the walls. Great main restaurant, worth making a detour to eat here, bar with large fireplace, swimming pool in the gardens.

C Berlyn Peacock Tavern, Berlin Waterfalls, T031-767 1085, www.peacocktavern.co.za. A fine old house in the country with 5 double rooms, although rather fussy frilly decor, with private verandas, non-smoking room, dining room, bar, comfortable lounge, swimming

pool, nearby hikes and horse riding, emphasis is on peace and privacy, no young children.

D Log Cabin Village, Louis Trichardt St, T013-767 1974, www.logcabin.co.za. 8 wooden self-catering cabins with 1 or 2 bedrooms, comfortably furnished, TV, well-equipped kitchen, small private garden with swimming pool, situated on the main road right in the middle of town. Good for families, and must be booked in advance during local school holidays.

D Panorama Rest Camp, on the road to Kowyn's Pass, T013-767 1091, http://panorama viewchalets.co.za. Holiday resort overlooking the Blyde River Canyon. Has a selection of very basic self-catering chalets and camping sites with a kitchen block, kiosk selling provisions, TV and pool room, the highlight here is the amazing rock swimming pool perched on the edge of the escarpment.

E-F Valley View Backpackers, 47 De Lange St, T013-767 1112, www.yebo-afrika.nl. Located on the west of the village, this backpacker place offers good dorms, comfortable doubles in self-catering rondavels and apartments, plus space for camping. Also arranges a wide variety of activities in the area and has mountain bike rentals. Kitchen, TV room with DVD player.

Blyde River Canyon *p652, map p646*
There is a wide range of accommodation around Hoedspruit in Limpopo. For further details, see page 687.

D-E Forever Resorts Blyde Canyon, T013-769 8005, www.foreversa.co.za. Huge family resort in a great setting, with 93 self-catering chalets, campsite, restaurant, shop selling provisions, bar, swimming pool, golf course, view points. This is a very popular family resort that gets packed during school holidays.

🍴 Eating

White River *p645*
🍴 **Injabula Boma**, Greenway Woods Resort, T013-751 1094, www.greenway.co.za.

1800-late. African-themed restaurant set in a luxury hotel in a lovely setting, with a price tag to match. Good range of traditional dishes such as oxtail, potjies, game meat and South African desserts like melk tart and a comprehensive wine list, but is often booked out for functions.

♥♥♥ **Salt**, in the Bagdad Centre across the road from **Casterbridge Farm**, T013-751 1555. Wed-Sat 1200-1430, Mon-Sat 1800-2130, Sun 1200-2030. Modern open-plan restaurant, some tables outside beneath bougainvillea, the chefs work in an open kitchen. Excellent, if unpretentious, fusion food: blue cheese, Cajun chicken and liquorice salad. The apricot glazed duck is delicious and there are some rich and tempting desserts.

♥♥ **Taverna Portuguesa**, Casterbridge Farm, 2 km out of town towards Hazyview, T013-750 2302. Tue-Sun 0900-late, no dinner on Sun. Mixed menu in pleasant, atmospheric converted farm building, located in a smartly renovated series of courtyards on Casterbridge Farm (see page 645). Good daily specials on the blackboard; try the excellent Mozambique prawns, peri-peri chicken or the good sized steaks.

Hazyview p646
Most restaurants are located in the hotels.
♥♥ **Ant & Elephant**, 6 km from Hazyview on the R536 to Sabie, T013-737 8172. Mon-Sat 0700-2100. Worth stopping just to enjoy the wonderful gardens among mango and lychee plantations. Good breakfasts, and a sophisticated evening menu of T-bone steaks, seafood chowder, venison and good pan-fried calamari and prawns.

♥♥ **Summerfields Kitchen**, 4 km on the R536 to Sabie, next to the Elephant Sanctuary, T013-737 6500, www.summerfields.co.za. Tue-Sun 0900-late, no dinner on Sun. Gourmet restaurant open for breakfast, light lunches and formal dinners. Perfectly presented dishes with all the trimmings, expect the likes of tiger prawn curry or lamb cutlets with rosemary mash and crème brûlée and pavlova for dessert. Eat at old wooden

kitchen tables and the ones outside are surrounded by rose bushes.

Sabie p647, map p648
♥♥ **The Wild Fig Tree**, Main St, T013-764 2239. Open 0800-2100. Quality restaurant serving light lunches and more ambitious meals in the evening. Choice of cool interior or shaded veranda. Fresh trout, guinea fowl, crocodile, warthog and some delicious home-made desserts, good choice for vegetarians. Attached curio shop full of overpriced but good-quality items.

♥♥ **The Woodsman**, 94 Main St, T013-764 2015, www.thewoodsman.co.za. 0900-late. Smart restaurant and bar on the outskirts of town attached to a B&B and craft centre, emphasis on Greek food and wine, try the *stifadho* (a rich stew made from beef, onions, red wine and spices), local trout and steaks also available, sit outside on the terrace for a few beers in the evening.

Lydenburg p648
♥ **Vroutjies Coffee Shop**, corner of Voortrekker and Rensburg streets, T013-235 3016. Mon-Sat 0700-1700. Coffee shop in a historic building, a refuelling stop on the way through town for sandwiches, cakes, break-fasts, burgers, quiches and baked potatoes with fillings.

Pilgrim's Rest p649, map p650
♥♥♥-♥♥ **Mount Sheba**, 19 km from Pilgrim's Rest off the R533, T013-768 1241, www.foreversa.co.za. 0700-1000, 1200-1500, 1800-2200. Upmarket restaurant serving light meals at lunchtime and a more sophisticated set table d'hôte menu for dinner, with the likes of flavoursome linefish and steaks, hearty country stews, and finished off with decadent desserts and cheese. Nice ambience in old-world charm dining room with candle-light and a crackling fire.

♥♥ **The Vine**, Main St, Downtown, T013-768 1080. Open 1100-2100. Old world pub-cum-restaurant with small **Ladies Bar**, very popular and typical of the town, filled with tour groups during the day. Hearty steaks and other typical local fare such as bobotie, ostrich-neck *potje*, and oxtail and samp.

¥ Jubilee Potters & Coffee Shop, Main St, Downtown, T013-768 1151. Open 0900-1900, early closing Tue. Burgers and salads along with coffee, cakes and Blyde River trout.

¥ Pilgrim's Pantry, Main St, Downtown, T013-768 1129. Open 0800-1700. Local baker, also acts as a coffee shop and handicraft shop. The pancakes make for a pleasant light lunch, there are also home-made jams, mustards, and pickles.

¥ Scott's Café, Main St, Uppertown, T013-768 1061. Open 0900-1800. Salads and hot dishes, quality country cooking using local fruit and vegetables, afternoon teas with scones and fresh cream, also an art gallery.

Graskop *p651, map p652*
Most restaurants only open for lunch off season.

¥¥ Leonardo's Trattoria, Louis Trichardt St, T013-767 1078. Mon-Sat 0900-2100, Sun 1000-1500. Family-run Italian restaurant on the main drag, serving standard pizzas and wide selection of pasta dishes, average quality meals but one of the few places open in the evening.

¥ Harrie's Pancakes, Louis Trichardt St, T013-767 1273. Open 0800-1730. Wide selection of pancakes, with sweet and savoury fillings, including a good chicken and mushroom or spicy butternut, and a mouth-watering banana and caramel. Also serves salads and other snacks. This is the original pancake house that somehow established a countrywide reputation; consequently pancake houses have opened up all over town.

¥ Loco & Coachman Grill, in the old converted railway station, T013-767 1961. Open 1200-late. Popular pub decorated with railway memorabilia, busy wooden bar, beer garden with kid's playground, cosy dining rooms, and a good-value menu of pub grub like eisbein, spare ribs, burgers, steak and chicken and chips, and some seafood.

¥ The Silver Spoon, corner of Louis Trichardt and Church streets, T013-761 1039, www.silver spoon.org. 0700-1900. More pancakes, also has huge burgers, salads and famous Black Forest gateau that's made from a German recipe. Hosts art shows and there's a pleasant deck overlooking the street or a cosy interior with a roaring fire in winter.

⊛ Festivals and events

Pilgrim's Rest *p649, map p650*
Sep The South African Gold Panning Championships, www.sagoldpanning.co.za. Held annually in Pilgrim's Rest and attract about 700 participants. Anyone can enter, including small children, and there's also a parade, a wheelbarrow race, and a pub crawl up and down the main street.

O Shopping

Throughout the Panorama region are curio markets in the car parks of the waterfalls and viewpoints.

White River *p645*
Bagdad Centre, across the road from **Casterbridge Farm**. 0830-1800, restaurants vary. A small shopping centre selling African handicrafts, furniture, safari clothes and books, and home to trendy **Salt** restaurant (see Eating, page 657). Nursery sells bonsais grown from indigenous trees. Delicatessen sells home-made jams, cheeses, chocolates, fresh trout, soups, pies and ready-made frozen meals – good place to stock up on provisions en route to self-catering accommodation in Kruger. The indigenous African butterfly sanctuary is worth a look.

Casterbridge Farm, 2 km from White River on the R40 to Hazyview, T013-750 1540, www.casterbridge.co.za. Mon-Fri 0900-1630, Sat-Sun 0900-1600, restaurant hours vary (see also page 645). Upmarket group of boutiques set in converted farm buildings, selling railway sleeper furniture, leather goods, art, ceramics and hand-blown glass. There's also a bookshop and a home-made chocolate shop.

Hazyview *p646*
Marula Market, Shangana Cultural Village (see page 647), 5 mins from Hazyview on the R535 to Graskop. 0900-1700, tea garden open until 1600. Traditional market with a good range of curios, including clay pots, wooden sculptures and contemporary metalwork.
Perry's Bridge Trading Post, Main St. This group of shops include the Trading post curio shop with some good-value African crafts as well as maps, books and gifts. There's also an internet café here.

Sabie *p647, map p648*
The Bookcase, Woodsman Centre, Main St, T013-764 2014. One of the best second-hand bookshops in South Africa, full of collectors' items. The African section is particularly good with turn-of-the-20th-century volumes on the great explorers and once-controversial titles from the 1950s and 1960s on the rise of Apartheid. A number of books that were banned in South Africa during the Apartheid years have resurfaced in this shop.
Mphozeni, Woodsman Centre, Main St. Large selection of African arts and crafts, jewellery and fabrics.

Graskop *p651, map p652*
Africa Silks, Louis Trichardt St, T013-767 1655. Fine selection of hand-woven silk products, including hand-dyed scarves, clothes, cushion covers and bedspreads. Also has outlets in Pilgrim's Rest and Hoedspruit.

▲ Activities and tours

Panorama region *p645, map p646*
For a the most comprehensive choice of adventure activities in the Panorama region, contact **Big 5 Reservations**, in Hazyview, T013-737 8191, www.big5country.com. See also page 647.

Adrenalin activities
Big Swing & Foefie Slide, Graskop Gorge, R533 just out of Graskop, T013-767 1621, www.bigswing.co.za. 0900-1700, weather permitting. R300 or R450 tandem, which includes the Foefie Slide, or slide on its own R60. Similar to a bungee jump, but with more of an outward swing on the descent. The free fall is 68 m and lasts 3 seconds. Once the bungee cord has reached its optimum length, you are lowered down into the rainforest at the bottom of the gorge, before a 10-min walk back to the top. The 131-m Foefie Slide goes across the gorge at a height of 80 m.

Mountain biking
Increasingly popular in the forests around Sabie, and several self-guided trails have been marked out by the forestry department, **SAFCOL**, including challenging ascents and downhill runs over loose shale and eroded gullies. Information can be found at the **Forestry Museum** (see page 648), T013-764 1058, www.komatiecotourism.co.za, and you can download information and maps from the website.
The Bike Doc, Valley View Backpackers, 47 De Lange St, Graskop, T013-767 1112, www.yebo-afrika.nl. Rents mountain bikes for R1175 for a full day of cycling in the forests around Graskop and Sabie with maps, permits, spare tubes, helmets and basic first-aid kits. Guided trips can also be arranged.

Scenic flights
The Blyde River Canyon region and the Sabie Valley look even more impressive from the air. **Helicopter** trips from 45 mins to 2½ hrs fly right into the canyon and dip down to the various waterfalls in the region. It's an exhilarating experience but prices are steep, from R2360 per person for a minimum of 4 people, and R3650 per person for a minimum of 2. Early morning (1-hr) **balloon rides** float wherever the wind may be going over the Sabie Valley, R2400 per person, and

microlight flights from Hazyview take in Graskop, God's Window, and the Sabie River, from R950 per person. Reservations and details from **Big 5 Reservations** (see above and page 647).

Whitewater rafting

The tamest rafting routes are on the lower Blyde River – 3 km of mild rapids – or the Sabie River – 3-hr trips through well-wooded banks. A day on the Olifants River takes you over Grade II-III rapids and the odd Grade IV rapid that can be avoided if you walk around. Arguably the best river action in South Africa is at the northern section of the Blyde River, 8 km of intense rapids with the occasional Grade V, which can also be walked around. A 5-km ferry trip on the Blydepoort Dam is usually included on this day trip. Expect to pay in the region of R450 for a 4-hr trip. For adrenaline junkies, day or multi-day trips on Blyde River and Olifants River offer a combination of exciting rapids and gentle paddles through some spectacular scenery, overnight in either riverside bush camps, local accommodation or a combination of both. Check that operators are members of the **South African River Association** (SARA). Tourist offices can supply further information, or again reservations and details available from **Big 5 Reservations** (see page 647).
Hardy Ventures, T013-751 1693, www.hardy venture.com. A wide choice of whitewater rafting and canoeing trips on a choice of 3 rivers, suited to all ages and experience.
Induna Adventures, T015-737 8308, www.indunaadventures.com. Olifants and Sabie River rafting, including overnight trips staying at a camp on the banks of the Olifants River.

⊖ Transport

Panorama region *p645, map p646*
White River is 20 km from **Nelspruit** on the R40. The entrance to Kruger Park at **Numbi Gate** (35 km), is signposted off the R538 heading north towards **Hazyview** (40 km); the entrance at Paul Kruger Gate is on the R536. The R40 continues north into Limpopo Province to **Acornhoek** (56 km), **Orpen Gate** (100 km), and the private game reserves on Kruger's western boundary. The R536 climbs up from the Lowveld around Hazyview onto the edge of the Drakensberg escarpment at Sabie. **Sabie** is 34 km west of Hazyview on the R536. **Graskop** is 24 km west of Hazyview on the R535. **Lydenburg** lies 66 km from the N4 on an important route that takes traffic from the Highveld down to the Lowveld.

❶ Directory

Hazyview *p646*
Internet Perry's Bridge Trading Post, Main St.

Sabie *p647, map p648*
Banks First National Bank, Main St.
Medical services Hospital, T013-764 1222, although in the event of a medical emergency, if possible it's best to go to the private Medi Clinic in Nelspruit (see page 616).

Graskop *p651, map p652*
Banks First National Bank, Church St.
Medical services Chemist, T013-767 1055, open all hours.

Contents

Footprint features

Border crossings

Limpopo

At a glance

⊖ **Getting around** Buses only
on N1, car hire.

◉ **Time required** 3-6 days; can
be visited from Kruger.

☼ **Weather** Good all year round,
hot Dec and Jan.

✗ **When not to go** Good all year.

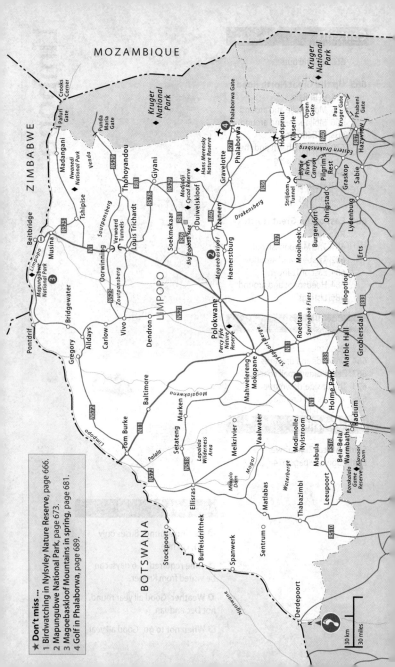

★ Don't miss ...
1 Birdwatching in Nylsvley Nature Reserve, page 666.
2 Mapungubwe National Park, page 673.
3 Magoebaskloof Mountains in spring, page 681.
4 Golf in Phalaborwa, page 689.

MOZAMBIQUE

ZIMBABWE

Kruger National Park

BOTSWANA

LIMPOPO

30 km
30 miles

Few foreign visitors see much of Limpopo, formerly the Northern Province, unless travelling to the northern reaches of Kruger National Park which makes up a chunk of the eastern side of the province (and is covered in the Mpumalanga chapter). Many, however, pass through Limpopo on the Great North Road, the thoroughfare linking South Africa with the rest of the continent via its neighbours: Zimbabwe and Botswana. The importance of this route has defined development in the region but the province offers plenty more than the service stations and dusty towns dotting the highway. As well as Kruger, Limpopo has over 50 nature reserves and countless private game farms that sustain intricate African ecosystems. While much of the countryside is dry bushveld, the mountains around Louis Trichardt and Tzaneen are green and lush, forming some of the most important agricultural districts in South Africa. The Drakensberg Escarpment is a beautiful forested area and, within the Magoebaskloof range, there are spectacular waterfalls and patches of indigenous forest, providing excellent hiking territory. Further south is a region promoted as the 'Valley of the Olifants', an area rich in wildlife and with an interesting history. To the north, the landscape opens up into dry plains dotted with tubby boabab trees, home to the fascinating Venda people, famous for their wood carvings.

Onwards and upwards

Due to a new permit ruling that a South African bus company may not offer passenger services within South Africa on the same route they operate across borders, all intermediate stops on the Johannesburg/Tshwane (Pretoria) to Harare or Bulawayo route (Polokwane, Louis Trichardt, Musina, etc) have been cancelled. There is now a non-stop direct service between the starting cities in South Africa and Zimbabwe. **Greyhound** is the only operator (www.greyhound.co.za). It runs a daily service between Johannesburg/Tshwane (Pretoria) and Harare (14½ hours) and Bulawayo (12 hours 15 minutes), in each direction.

Ins and outs

Getting around

The mainline buses no longer serve the towns in Limpopo Province (see box, above), so the only option is to explore by car. Although there are some long distances, driving is easy and the main roads are well served with petrol stations and roadside restaurants. On leaving Tshwane (Pretoria), the N1 passes through the **Springbok Flats**, a featureless plain between Bela-Bela and Mokopane. Before the road reaches the provincial capital, **Polokwane**, it runs parallel to the Waterberg plateau, an area which in recent years has seen the development of many private game reserves for hunting and game viewing. The route to the east of Polokwane on the R71 will take you through the green and fertile **Magoebaskloof Mountains**, before continuing on to either Phalaborwa and central Kruger, or the Lowveld region of the Limpopo Province. Continuing north of Polokwane on the N1, the country is flat, typical bushveld country where the principal activity is cattle ranching, but as you approach **Louis Trichardt** the impressive **Soutpansberg Mountains** dominate the horizon and straddle the N1.

From Louis Trichardt most visitors will be faced with the choice of two routes: to turn off the N1 and head east through **Venda** to the northern camps in Kruger; or to continue over the mountains to **Musina** and **Zimbabwe**. The Great North Road cuts through Wyllie's Port and the two Hendrik Verwoerd tunnels in order to cross the Soutpansberg. On the northern side of the mountains the landscape quickly changes; much of the country is in rain shadow from the Soutpansberg and the temperatures are significantly warmer. As you approach Musina, look out for groups of the distinctive baobab tree, a popular sight in these parts. From Musina it is only 12 km to the border at Beitbridge. ▸▸ *For further details, see Transport, pages 680 and 690.*

Tourist information

The **Limpopo Tourism Board** ① *corner of Grobler and Church streets, Polokwane, T015-290 7300, www.golimpopo.com*, is responsible for promoting tourism in the whole province. It produces a good brochure, map and guides to accommodation and activities. The tourist board also produces a self-drive route booklet, which includes the popular **African Ivory Route** ① *T015-295 3025, www.africanivoryroute.co.za*, a 4WD driving and camping route, which covers most of the Limpopo Province from the far north of Kruger National Park to the remote game farms towards the Botswana border.

Up the Great North Road

The N1, sometimes referred to as the Great North Road, is the only direct route linking South Africa with Zimbabwe and, in effect, the rest of Africa. Between Tshwane (Pretoria) and the Zimbabwe border, the road passes through four regional centres, which are linked by (slow) train but not by bus anymore (see box, opposite). As such, you really need a car to explore the towns, which have few attractions in any case, or more likely, the countryside on either side of the N1 to fully appreciate Limpopo Province. ▶▶ *For listings, see pages 676-680.*

Bela-Bela ⬤🟡🟢 ▶▶ *pp676-680. Colour map 2, B2.*

→ *Phone code: 014.*

This resort town only exists because of the natural hot springs 'discovered' in the 1860s by Jan Grobler and Carl van Heerden whilst hunting in the region. Previously known as Warmbaths, the new name comes from the Tswana *Biela bela*, 'the water that boils on its own'. The 50°C springs bubble out of the earth at about 22,000 litres per hour and are rich in sodium chloride, calcium carbonate and are also slightly radioactive. Less than an hour's drive from Tshwane (Pretoria), a staggering two million people visit Bela-Bela each year. The mild climate during the winter months ensures an average of 286 sunny days a year. The principal springs now lie engulfed within the massive **Forever Resort** (see page 676), where visitors can enrol in a variety of treatments at the spa.

Sights

There is very little of interest in town and no point in stopping unless you're here to take the waters. If you stay overnight, the most popular attraction is the **Carousel Entertainment World**, 56 km from Bela-Bela on the N1 (free shuttle bus from town at weekends), a 24-hour gambling and entertainment complex on a bleak section of the highway. Otherwise, the **Thaba Kwena Crocodile Farm** ① *T014-736 5059, daily 0900-1600, feeding Sat 1500, R15,* has over 20,000 crocs. **Bela-Bela Tourism Association** ① *corner of Old Pretoria and Voortrekker streets, Waterfront, T014-736 3694, www.belabelatourism.co.za, Mon-Fri 0800-1700, Sat-Sun 0900-1200,* is a useful municipal office that can book local accommodation. Ask about the choice of game farms in the area, offering game drives and meals. There are also a number of shops and restaurants in the Waterfront development and a petting farm for kids.

Modimolle and around ⬤🟡 ▶▶ *pp676-680. Colour map 2, B2.*

→ *Phone code: 014.*

Formerly called Nylstroom, Modimolle, meaning 'place of the spirits', is the commercial centre of the Waterberg region with a small centre shaded by jacaranda and poinciana trees. Grapes, watermelons and peaches are the principal sources of income, and stalls sell boxes of fruit at the roadside after the harvests. A grape festival is held here in January. The NTK is the largest agricultural cooperative society in the Limpopo Province, where you can see nuts being sorted and peanut butter being made.

Sights

The main attraction in the area is **Nylsvley Nature Reserve**, one of the finest birdwatching spots in South Africa. Being a quiet rural centre, Modimolle itself has little in the way of sites, although it does boast a surprising number of distinguished previous residents, including Gerhard Moerdijik, the architect that designed the Voortrekker Monument in Tshwane (Pretoria), and South Africa's fifth prime minister (1954-1958), JG Strijdom, who lived here while he was a member of parliament for the Waterberg constituency. His house, **Strijdom House** ① *Church St, Tue-Sat 0900-1300, 1400-1700, Sun 1400-1700*, is a national monument and a museum about his life. The **Hervormde Kerk** on Calvyn Street, is also a national monument, built in 1889.

Nylsvley Nature Reserve
① *20 km out of town towards Naboomspruit. Daily 0600-1800, R10, children (6-12) R5, information can be found on the* Friends of Nylsvley *website, www.nylsvley.co.za.*
The Nyl River rises in the hills near Modimolle and eventually spills into the Limpopo. For much of its journey, the river meanders back and forth, forming a marshy floodplain that is the largest and best conserved in South Africa. The floodplain reaches 6 km in width and extends for nearly 70 km between Middlefontein and Moordriftan. It is an important wetland ecosystem, which attracts up to 80,000 breeding birds during the rains. Consequently, this is a hugely popular birdwatching destination; it's not unheard of to see 200 of the 420 recorded species on a single day. It's home to the biggest concentration of water birds in the southern hemisphere, with species numbering just over 100, and 37 red-data species, including the critically endangered bittern. Up to 80,000 wetland birds are attracted to the area at any one time. The reserve is listed as a RAMSAR site, an internationally important habitat for waterfowl. A birdwatching festival and bird census are held here each year. Visitors are allowed to walk or ride bikes on tracks through the reserve and there are a number of bird hides, from which you may also spot eland, tsessbe, kudu, waterbuck, reedbuck, zebra, and giraffe. Even if birdwatching isn't your thing, this is a beautiful environment.

Mokopane and around ⊝🅕🅖⊜ ›› *pp676-680. Colour map 2, B3.*

→ *Phone code: 015.*
Mokopane is a busy centre for the surrounding agricultural area. Peanuts, cotton, wheat and oranges are major crops; the Zebediela Citrus Estate, 55 km to the southeast, is the largest citrus farm in the country and was handed back to its original owners, the Bjatladi community, in 2003. It is a modern town with few attractions, although it does have an interesting past. In 1854 the local chief, Makapan, hid in caves in the Makapan Valley with his people to escape from the Voortrekker commandos. During the siege, which lasted from 25 October to 21 November, the Boer leader Piet Potgieter was killed by the warriors of Makapan; over 1500 of the warriors and their families died from starvation during the siege. After these events, the local town changed its name from Vredenburg to Pieter Potgietersrus and, in 1935, to Potgietersrus. In 2002 it was renamed Mokopane after the Ndebele chief.

Sights
If you find yourself in the area with time to spare then the **Arend Dieperink Museum** ① *Voortrekker Rd, T015-491 2244, Mon-Fri 0800-1630, small entry fee*, is a cut above the average provincial collection. It has displays on the Sotho and the early settlers of the Transvaal, as well as dinosaur fossils and a reproduction of the *Australopithecus africanus* skull found in the **Makapan's Caves**, which are 15 km north of the town.

Zebra-drawn mail coach

A weekly mail-coach service between Pretoria and Pietersburg was introduced by the Zeederberg Coach Company in 1890 and was later extended north into Rhodesia (Zimbabwe). The coaches seated 12 passengers inside and two on top, together with the driver, co-driver and luggage. Trips by coach could be hazardous and drivers had to negotiate mountain passes, swollen rivers, muddy tracks, and attacks by wild animals and highwaymen. In order to deal with the problem of the tsetse fly, which causes sleeping sickness in horses, the company trained a team of zebras to pull the coaches on the eastern leg of the run through Limpopo. Although the training was fairly successful, the zebras lacked the stamina of horses and the practice was later discontinued.

Around Mokopane

The **Mokopane Biodiversity Conservation Centre** ① *1 km north of town on the N1 to Polokwane, T015-491 4314, www.zoo.ac.za, Mon-Fri 0800-1600, Sat and Sun 0800-1800, R15, children (under 16) R8*, is part of the National Zoological Gardens of Pretoria and breeds rare species such as cheetah, roan antelope, black rhino and pygmy hippo from West Africa. These are then taken to Pretoria in order to expand the national zoo's breeding programmes. It is a member of the World Zoo Organisation, which focuses on the breeding of exotic, indigenous and endangered wildlife. A network of roads run

Mokopane

To Percy Fyfe Nature Reserve, Makapan's Caves (19 km) & Polokwane

To Marken & Ana Trees

To Tshwane (Pretoria) (R101/N1)

N

400 metres
400 yards

Sleeping 🛏
Lutea Guest House 2
Oasis Lodge 1
Protea Park 3

Eating 🍴
KFC 2
Nando's 3
Spur 4

throughout the 1500-ha area of bushveld but dense vegetation makes game viewing difficult. At the entrance is a pleasant picnic area and small aviary. Guided tours and game drives can be organized from reception.

Fifteen kilometres northwest of Mokopane on the R518 to Marken are the **Ana Trees**, a clump of apiesdoring trees *Acacia albida* under which David Livingstone camped on one of his journeys. The biggest tree has a circumference of 6 m; they are considered a botanical rarity in this area.

Percy Fyfe Nature Reserve is an important reserve about 35 km northeast of Mokopane. Percy Fyfe was a local farmer who, in 1933, bought a few head of blesbok from the Orange Free State to try and introduce the species to the region. After he donated the farm to the state in 1954 it has been used as a sanctuary to breed threatened antelope. Roan, sable and tsessebe have all been successfully bred here and then reintroduced to parts of the Waterberg range. Addo buffalo have recently been introduced. There is a simple campsite here for overnight visitors.

Polokwane ⬤🄵🄷🄶🄲🄲 ›› *pp676-680. Colour map 2, B3.*

→ *Phone code: 015. Altitude: 1312 m.*

Formerly known as Pietersburg, the capital of Limpopo Province is a sprawling, low-rise town built on a grid system. It was founded in 1884 by Voortrekker Commandant-General Pieter Joubert as the main agricultural and industrial centre for the thinly populated province. The town is located in a shallow hollow surrounded by level grass plains, a rather dull setting, but making a practical base nevertheless. Polokwane offers alternative routes to Kruger: one via Louis Trichardt to the northernmost entrance at Punda Maria, and the other through the beautiful Magoebaskloof to Phalaborwa.

Ins and outs

Tourist information The **Limpopo Tourism Board** ⓘ *corner of Grobler and Kerk streets, T015-290 7300, www.golimpopo.com, Mon-Fri 0800-1630,* is responsible for promoting tourism in the province and has a useful brochure. Little information on the city though.

Best time to visit The town enjoys a very pleasant climate; the summer temperatures are moderated by the altitude and in winter the average temperature is 20°C. Rainfall varies between 400-600 mm and falls during the summer months.

City centre

As the regional capital, the city has grown rapidly in recent years and is by far the largest centre between Tshwane (Pretoria) and Harare (in Zimbabwe). If you have spent a few days in the surrounding countryside it can come as quite a shock as you drive into the busy centre

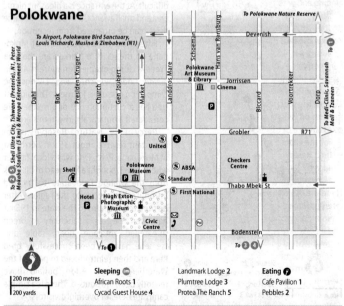

Polokwane

Sleeping	
African Roots **1**	Landmark Lodge **2**
Cycad Guest House **4**	Plumtree Lodge **3**
	Protea The Ranch **5**

Eating
Cafe Pavilion **1**
Pebbles **2**

200 metres
200 yards

with its wide tree-lined roads, traffic jams and tall buildings. New on the skyline, 5 km south of the city and accessed from the N1, is the Peter Mokaba Stadium for the 2010 FIFA World Cup™, named after a former ANC leader of the ANC Youth League who came from Polokwane.

The first stop for most visitors is likely to be the 'Irish House', home to the **Polokwane Museum** ⓘ *corner of Thabo Mbeki and Market streets, T015-290 2183, Mon-Fri 0800-1600, Sat 0900-1200, Sun 1500-1700, free.* The history of the building is as interesting as the collection it houses. The building is a prefabricated steel structure from Germany which was imported by Aug Julius Möschke after his shop had been destroyed by a fire in 1906. It is a classic example of late Victorian architecture with wrought-iron decorations topped by a fine clock tower and weather vane. During the First World War, Möschke was interned and on his return to Pietersburg he found his business to be bankrupt and was forced to sell the shop to James Albert Jones in 1920. It was Jones who named the building the Irish House and over the years it grew into a very successful local fashion shop, which imported the latest quality materials from Europe. The museum itself traces the history of the region from the Stone Age to modern times; it is a well-presented display in a spacious and airy building.

On the other side of Thabo Mbeki Street from the Irish House, in the gardens which form the civic square, you will find the **Hugh Exton Photographic Museum** ⓘ *T015-290 2186, Mon-Fri 0900-1530, Sun 1100-1300, free*, housed in the town's first Dutch Reformed Church, dating from 1890. This is a superb collection of prints and over 23,000 glass negatives, tracing the first 50 years of Pietersburg – few towns have such a record of their past. Hugh Exton was a local photographer who had a studio in Pietersburg. North of the Civic Centre on Jorrissen Street is the library, which houses the **Polokwane Art Museum** ⓘ *T015-290 2177, Mon-Fri 0900-1600, Sat 0900-1200, free*, a fine collection of South African modern art and sculptures from Jacobus Botes's collection. Although lacking in funding and with poor labelling, the collection is interesting.

Around Polokwane

Polokwane Bird Sanctuary ⓘ *T015-290 2331, daily 0700-1700, R12, entry on foot only*, is an award-winning sanctuary set around a couple of lakes in the acacia bush. There are numerous hides all around the lakes for spotting the more than 280 bird species that have been recorded here. These include a resident breeding pair of African fish eagles, as well as African goshawks and African harrier-hawks, and the shallow waters attract a number of waders. The sanctuary is 4 km north of town along Market Street, on the R521 to Dendron; the turn-off is on the right-hand side just after crossing the Sand River, and is diagonally across from a petrol station.

For the chance to see larger wildlife, and just on the edge of town, visit **Polokwane Nature Reserve** ⓘ *T015-290 2331, daily 0700-1630, R20, car R15*, one of the largest municipal game reserves in South Africa. You can walk or drive around the 3200-ha reserve and view 21 species of game, including white rhino, tsessebe and sable antelope. There are several hides and view points along the streams, which flow through the reserve. Game drives can be arranged and night drives run on Friday evenings during the summer; phone for details. There is also a 20-km trail, with overnight accommodation. Bird species include grey-backed camaroptera, yellow-bellied greenbul, terrestrial brownbul, yellow-breasted apalis and many other warbler species, which can be seen in the summer.

One of the most significant modern-day landmarks in this region is the **Zion City** at Moria, 30 km from Polokwane on the R71 towards Haenertsburg. Although there is nothing much for the visitor to see here, this is the seat of the Zion Christian Church, an entirely black denomination that has the largest following of any denomination in southern Africa.

During Easter weekend each year, up to one million followers congregate here from all over South Africa and Zimbabwe for mass worship, when they traditionally wear white robes. It's extraordinary to see such staggering numbers of people in the Polokwane region.

Routes east and north of Polokwane

If you are not heading for Zimbabwe or the northern camps in Kruger National Park, an interesting alternative route out of Polokwane is to take the R71 to **Tzaneen** (95 km) and **Phalaborwa** (see page 684). Once in Tzaneen it is possible to take the R40 south through the game farm region of the Lowveld to either the **Blyde River Canyon** in Mpumalanga (see page 652) or central Kruger's Orpen Gate (see page 631).

The N1, meanwhile, continues north to **Louis Trichardt**. This section of the road has been upgraded to a dual carriageway, although the onward stretch from Louis Trichardt to the Zimbabwe border is still single carriageway. About 61 km from Polokwane the N1 crosses the **Tropic of Capricorn**.

Louis Trichardt and the Soutpansberg ⊜❼▲⊜❻ ➤ pp676-680.
Colour map 2, A4.

➔ *Phone code: 015. Altitude: 984 m.*

Along with other towns in Limpopo Province, Louis Trichardt was renamed **Makhado** in 2003, after the Venda King Makhado who ruled in the region from the mid-1800s until his death in 1887. However, there was local rejection to the new name, and it was claimed less than 1% of the town's population had been consulted on the change. It wasn't just Afrikaaner people that complained; many Shangaan people regard Makhado as an oppressor. A residents' association applied to Pretoria's High Court in 2005 to have the name overturned. They were rejected but rather astonishingly appealed in South Africa's Supreme Court and won, and the name was changed back to Louis Trichardt in 2007.

It's another important agricultural centre, where tea, coffee, timber and sub-tropical fruits are the main crops. The world-renowned Elim Hospital is 25 km southeast of Louis Trichardt on the Gyani Road. There's not much to see in town itself – it's a sleepy backwater that trucks rumble through on the N1 – but to the north and west is the sandstone **Soutpansberg** mountain range, which stretches for about 130 km and reaches 1753 m at its highest point, known as Lejume. It takes its name from the salt-pan and brine spring at the western end of the range. These hills have played an important role in the early history of the region and now offer good wilderness hikes. Dotted along the high plateau are traditional Venda villages.

Many of the valleys and lakes in the Soutpansberg are considered sacred – the best known of these are the Phiphidi Falls and Guvhukuvhu Pool, Lwamomdo Hill, Lake Fundudzi and the Thathe Vondo Forest. These sights are difficult to find and you should enlist the services of a registered guide if you wish to visit them. This will also help ensure that you approach and treat the sights sensitively. A self-drive route, taking in the area's arts and crafts highlights, begins in Louis Trichardt – information is available from the **Soutpansberg Tourist Office** ⓘ *corner of Songozwi St and the N1, T015-516 0040, www.tourismsoutpansberg.co.za, Mon-Fri 0900-1700, Sat 0800-1300.*

Background

The town was named after Louis Trichardt, the Voortrekker leader who set up camp near here in May 1836. He had travelled up to the Soutpansberg with another group of Voortrekkers under Hans Van Rensburg. After arguments between the two groups, Hans Van Rensburg led his people east in search of a route to Lourenço Marques (today's Maputo in Mozambique). They disappeared into the wilderness and were never heard from again. Louis Trichardt remained in the area for a year before following Hans Van Rensburg east. This was one of the classic journeys of the Voortrekkers, taking seven months to reach Lourenço Marques. It took them two and a half months to get down the Drakensberg escarpment and by the end of their trek, 27 of the original 53 Boers had died. Louis Trichardt and his wife survived the journey but both died of malaria soon after. After his death other Voortrekkers settled in the area as ivory hunters but left after Chief Makhado and his vhaVenda people defeated them in 1867. Only in 1898 did the Zuid-Afrikaansche Republiek take control of the region.

Manavhela Ben Lavin Nature Reserve
ⓘ *T015-516 4534. Daily 0600-1900, R30. To get there, follow the N1, 8 km south of the town, and look out for the Fort Edward Rd, the reserve is 5 km along this road.*
The Manavhela Ben Lavin Nature Reserve is a protected area of indigenous woodland with 18 km of walking trails, mountain biking trails and hides. The reserve is a good place for bird-watching and has giraffes, wildebeest and other game indigenous to the area. There are also some interesting archaeological sites, which have been dated to around AD 1250. Hikers and bikers are provided with a booklet that helps interpret the environment. There are some new overnight huts along the hiking trail (see Sleeping page 678), which are fully furnished. When exploring the park on foot always remember to look out for wild animals.

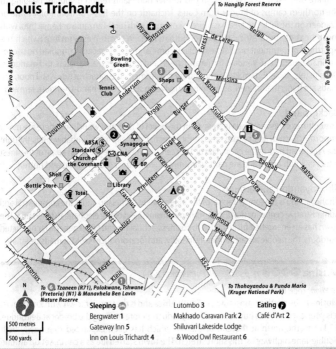

Louis Trichardt

Sleeping	Lutombo 3	Eating
Bergwater 1	Makhado Caravan Park 2	Café d'Art 2
Gateway Inn 5	Shiluvari Lakeside Lodge	
Inn on Louis Trichardt 4	& Wood Owl Restaurant 6	

To 6 Tzaneen (R71), Polokwane, Tshwane (Pretoria) (N1) & Manavhela Ben Lavin Nature Reserve

To Thohoyandou & Punda Maria (Kruger National Park)

500 metres
500 yards

Hanglip Forest Reserve

ⓘ *3 km west of town, signposted off the N1, R10.*

The Hanglip Forest Reserve is an area of indigenous forest around the base of the Hanglip, a wall of rock rising 1719 m. The top of the cliffs are some of the highest points of the Soutpansberg. From the picnic site is a 20 minute circular trail which is excellent for bird-watching in the forest. The **Soutpansberg Hike** is a 21-km, three-day walk with overnight accommodation in huts. Although this is a circular route all hikers must walk in the same direction and only 30 people are allowed on the trail at any one time. For further details contact **Komatiland Forestry**, a subsidiary of the **Department of Forestry (SAFCOL)** ⓘ *Nelspruit, T013-754 2724, www.komatiecotourism.co.za*, which has information on the trail, and issues permits. Listen out for scaly throated honeyguides at the picnic site.

Beyond Louis Trichardt

The N1 continues to the north winding through wooded valleys. After 21 km the highway passes through the Soutpansberg, via the **Verwoerd Tunnels**. The R524 heads east from town through **Thohoyandou**, the former capital of the Venda homeland, to Punda Maria Camp (140 km), one of the most northerly camps in **Kruger National Park** (see page 617).

Venda ➤➤ *Colour map 2, A4/5.*

You are only likely to pass through this former homeland region if you are heading to the northern camps of Kruger from Louis Trichardt on the R524 or from Polokwane or Tzaneen on the R81. The area has more in common with rural Tanzania or Kenya than with most areas of South Africa. Unlike Bophuthatswana in North West Province, which the Apartheid government proclaimed a black homeland simply because they had no use for the inadequate land, Venda is fertile and green and produces tea, bananas and mangoes. Despite this, and efforts made by the current government, the infrastructure is still poor, the roads are badly maintained, and families survive on subsistence hand-to-mouth farming.

Background

The culture of the vhaVenda is steeped in the belief of the spirit world, and there are many important sacred, and private, sites in the region. Originally from Zimbabwe, it is thought they migrated here at the beginning of 18th century. They are regarded as some of the finest artists in South Africa, and are particularly renowned for their drum making and pottery.

Thohoyandou and around

Thohoyandou is the former capital of the independent homeland and is the commercial and administrative centre for the district. Its name means 'head of the elephant' in tshiVenda. The town has an energetic African feel to it: business, schooling and life in general is conducted outdoors, the people are astoundingly friendly, and local produce is sold at roadside stalls.

Musina ⬤🅿️⬤🅲 ➤➤ *pp676-680. Colour map 2, A4.*

→ *Phone code: 015.*

Musina is the northernmost town in South Africa and is the frontier town with Zimbabwe. It is your last chance to buy South African products before crossing the border at Beitbridge, 12 km to the north at the end of the N1, which has been expanded to a newly built double-lane highway on this short stretch. The town started life as a camp, set up around

The upside-down tree

The baobab tree (*Adansonia digitata*) is the undisputed king of the African savannah and grows throughout east and southern Africa. The trees reach to about 25 m in height, with trunk diameters of up to 10 m, and live for thousands of years. They are noted for storing water inside their swollen trunk, with the capacity to hold up to 120,000 litres of water to endure harsh drought conditions. This giant tree, with its enormous girth and unmistakable appearance, is surrounded by legend. One story suggests that the tree's root-like branches are a result of the gods, in a frivolous mood, planting the tree upside down. Another legend has it that if you drink water in which you have soaked baobab seeds, you can wade across a crocodile-infested river and get to the other side unharmed. However, few people seem willing to test this theory.

the copper mines that opened in 1905, though these closed down decades ago. The main street is lined with shops, banks, petrol stations and fast-food outlets all catering to the steady stream of traffic to and from the border. It's not an especially attractive town, and is increasingly being dwarfed by large hastily built townships that are home to Zimbabweans who have managed to cross the border. There's also a large, more formal, refugee camp on the town's former showgrounds that is reputedly home to about 15,000 Zimbabweans. Be aware, because of poor sanitation at this camp, there was a severe outbreak of cholera in Musina in 2009. Although there's little of interest in town, you will pass through Musina en route to Venda to the east, Mapungubwe National Park to the west and there is also a good road across to the northern camps of Kruger via Tshipise.

Mapungubwe National Park → *Colour map 2, A3.*
ⓘ *Gates 0600-1800, office 0800-1600, T015-534 0102, www.sanparks.org, R88, children (under 12) R44.*

Mapungubwe is the country's youngest and northernmost national park, developed on the South African side of the confluence of the Shashe and Limpopo rivers. At the confluence itself is a picnic site with a view over the point where South Africa, Zimbabwe and Botswana meet. The park forms part of what has become the Greater Mapungubwe Transfrontier Conservation Area, covering the corner of the province which borders Zimbabwe and Botswana with the Tuli Block in Botswana and communal land in Zimbabwe. It protects important San rock art sites, but is best known for **Mapungubwe Hill**, which researchers believe was the site of the first capital of the ancient kingdom of Great Zimbabwe between AD 900 and 1300. Gold and silver artefacts have been unearthed here, including the famous Golden Rhino, as well as items of Arab, Chinese, Indonesian and Indian origin – indicated important trading routes – many of which are on display at the University of Pretoria. Mapungubwe is the earliest evidence of Africa's Iron Age and was awarded World Heritage status in 2003. The park now covers 28,000 ha of arid bush and tufted grassveld dotted with acacia thorn and giant baobab trees. It's home to a variety of wildlife, including black and white rhino, elephant, kudu, zebra, eland, waterbuck, gemsbok, giraffe and baboon. Although predators such as lion, cheetah, hyena and leopard are present, they are rarely sighted. Pythons and black mambas, on the other hand, are common. Birders can tick off 400 species, including kori bustard, tropical boubou and Pel's fishing owl. There are four camps within the park, all accessible by normal car.

Border crossing: South Africa–Zimbabwe

Beitbridge

In view of the current political climate in Zimbabwe, it is recommended that all visitors refer to the British Foreign and Commonwealth Office website, www.fco.org, for up-to-date travel advice before attempting to enter Zimbabwe. Do not state your occupation to Zimbabwe custom officials as that of journalist or any other media-related job.

Border opening hours 24 hours. Considering the problems in Zimbabwe (see box, page 675) formalities at the border can be very slow. It also gets very hot here during the summer, and quite coversely freezing very early in the morning in winter (when buses pull in to the border).

Customs and immigration Visa requirements for Zimbabwe change frequently but most nationals do need a visa and they can be issued at the border post. Costs vary from US$30 to US$55 depending on nationality. Entry visas are valid for a maximum of 90 days. South Africans do not require visas.

Facilities There is a duty-free shop on the South African side, selling a limited range of cigarettes and spirits, and a VAT refund office (see page 56), but expect a long wait.

Public transport Expect to pay no more than R15 for a ride from Musina to the border post in a minibus taxi. Once you have negotiated the South African side, you will either have to walk or hitch across the bridge over the Limpopo River. Minibus taxis to **Bulawayo**, **Masvingo** and **Harare** can be found waiting on the other side of Zimbabwe immigration, but due to the lack of fuel in Zimbabwe, these services cannot be relied on. The better option is to take the through service with Greyhound (www.greyhound.co.za) between Johannesburg/Tshwane (Pretoria) and Bulawayo (12 hours) or Harare (14½ hours). However, there are often long delays at the border, as all Zimbabwean bus passengers are searched thoroughly and there can be lengthy vehicle queues on both sides.

Vehicle formalities At present, most hired cars from South Africa are not allowed into Zimbabwe. For those that are, **third-party insurance** is required by law for all vehicles entering Zimbabwe. Short-term policies can be bought at the border. You will also need to pay a carbon tax, a road tax and a toll fee to drive over the bridge. All payments can be made in Rand or US$ cash. Visitors from overseas must have an English translation of their **licence** plus a photograph. Tourists in private vehicles must also have a **vehicle registration certificate** and will normally be granted a temporary **import permit** free of charge, provided the vehicle is licensed in its home country and has the appropriate number plates. People travelling in their own vehicle on a **carnet** must get it stamped when exiting South Africa and entering Zimbabwe, as Zimbabwe is not part of the South African Development Community (SADC), the shared customs agreement that covers vehicles in South Africa, Lesotho, Swaziland, Namibia and Botswana.

Be wary of petty thieves, especially on the Zimbabwe side. Lock everything up and make sure anything on the outside of the vehicle is tied down. Do not under any circumstances accept help from touts in the car park who offer to sell relevant forms or 'look after' your car; all forms are available free of charge inside the border control building, and official uniformed security guards patrol the car park.

Africa's Rio Grande

The Limpopo River marks the 300-km border between South Africa and Zimbabwe, and Beitbridge is the only border post. For a decade now, the river has been likened to the Rio Grande, the river that marks the border between the US and Mexico, over which thousands of Mexicans try to cross illegally in search of a better life in the US. Similarly, because of the ongoing dire political and economic situation in Zimbabwe, several thousand Zimbabwean people attempt to cross this border every week, in hope of better facilities or a future in South Africa. Some cross legally and legitimately through Beitbridge to shop in South Africa, and return again with much-needed provisions. For the most part though, for many years, most crossed the (crocodile-infested) Limpopo River illegally, and then needed to get through the three walls of fortified fencing on the South African side. If they didn't get stopped, and sent back to Zimbabwe, many made it down to Gauteng to live in relative anonymity in the townships, (though these are routinely raided for illegal immigrants). In reality, this still happens, and the holes in the fence have become a notorious escape route for many Zimbabweans on a plight to escape poverty and unemployment. However in early 2009,

the situation was eased when South Africa relented and scrapped visas for Zimbabweans. Their policy now is to accept the mass migration into South Africa rather than prevent it, and the government takes the view that the people from Zimbabwe looking for a better economic fortune in South Africa are economic migrants, not political asylum seekers, who will return to Zimbabwe once they have earned enough money to return home (and support their families). This decision makes the paperwork between the two countries less confusing, and in turn it is hoped that this will also boost Zimbabwe's economy thanks to an increased influx of foreign currency from returning migrant workers. There is a refugee camp and reception centre in Musina, monitored by the UN Refugee Agency, which provides special new six-month permits for Zimbabweans allowing them to live and work in South Africa, to gain access to public health care and education, and to cross the border at Bietbridge both legally and freely. No one knows for sure how many Zimbabweans have come into South Africa since the crisis began, but estimates have been as high as three million. Zimbabweans are now living and working all over South Africa, even as far south as Cape Town.

Ins and outs

Getting there and around The park is 68 km due west from Musina on the R572. It can also be reached from the east via the R521, an alternative route from Polokwane. Facilities are still being developed in the park, but at present a series of rough roads pass through a variety of terrains, offering a range of wildlife viewing opportunities. Of these, 35 km are suitable for normal cars while another 100 km are open to 4WDs, so make sure you pick up a map at reception. There are a handful of hides overlooking pans and dams, and an interpretive centre at the main entrance gate. One of the highlights of the park is its hiking trails: **Vhembe Trails** operates much like the wilderness trails in Kruger, with guests venturing out on guided day hikes from a main base camp. There are also a couple of 4WD routes going through rugged hilly terrain, including the **Tshugulu Eco Route** which covers 45 km, with a game hide en route.

Park information This is a malarial area, so take prophylactics. There are, as yet, no shops or petrol available in the park, so stock up in Musina before you visit.

Best time to visit This region gets on average just 10 days of rain a year and summer temperatures can reach 45°C.

⦿ Up the Great North Road listings

For Sleeping and Eating price codes and other relevant information, see pages 46-53.

⦿ Sleeping

Bela-Bela *p665*
L1 Mabula Game Lodge, 35 km west of Bela-Bela off the Thabazimbi–Rooiberg Rd, T014-734 7000, www.mabula.com. 53 luxury full-board double rooms in chalets or upmarket tents, with restaurant, swimming pool, squash, tennis, gym, sauna, bush walks, game drives, horseback trails. Luxury lodge on a private game reserve in the Waterberg Mountains, which is home to rhino and lion among other species, with excellent facilities, recommended for a longer break.
A-E Forever Resorts Warmbaths, T014-736 8500, www.foreversa.co.za. This resort contains the main Bela-Bela springs and is so vast that guests are required to wear plastic identity bracelets at all times. The caravan and camping park alone extends for a couple of kilometres to the edge of the town. Chalets and log cabins (**C**), 124 in total, surround 3 man-made dams, and there's a standard 45-room hotel (**A-B**) at the entrance gate. A selection of restaurants and bars, mineral pools, spa and hydro with a full range of beauty treatments, horse riding, squash, tennis, cable water ski circuit, water slides, go-karts, quad bikes, fishing. Advance booking is essential. Day visitors permitted until 1700.
C Villa Palmeira, 9 Knoppiesdoring Av, T014-736 2558, www.villapalmeira.co.za. 13 a/c, en suite rooms in this comfortable guesthouse in a quiet suburb 2 km from the springs. DSTV, internet, set in a thatched villa surrounded by well-tended sub-tropical gardens. B&B, other meals on request, pool, thatched lapa, braai.

Modimolle and around *p665*
B Shangri-La, Eerstebewood Rd (R101), midway between Bela-Bela and Modimolle, T014-718 1600, www.shangri-la.co.za. On a bushveld farm, part of Protea group. Geared towards conferences, but with decent accommodation in 42 thatched cottages, with en suite bathrooms, spacious and tastefully decorated. Pool, restaurant, bar, tennis courts, all set in lush gardens. Views of the Waterberg.

Camping
Nylsvley Nature Reserve, T015-290 7336. Simple campsite with 80 spaces in a beautiful setting within the nature reserve. Bring everything, including drinking water and firewood.

Mokopane *p666, map p667*
B Protea Hotel Park, 1 Beitel St, T015-491 3101, www.thepark.co.za. 125 a/c double rooms with en suite bathroom, non-smoking rooms, TV MNet, lounge, restaurant, bar, laundry, swimming pool set in garden in the middle of the complex with a few decorative palms. Regular quality Protea hotel.
C Oasis Lodge, 1 Thabo Mbeki Drive, T015-491 4124, www.oasishotel.co.za. Plain double rooms with en suite bathroom, a/c, cool tiled floors, DSTV, conference facilities, Wi-Fi, restaurant for simple buffet meals, shady garden, overpriced for what you get though.
D Lutea Guest House, 66 Rabe St, T072-071 5499, www.lutea.co.za. Small, quiet guesthouse with neat en suite rooms. Ceiling fans, TV, internet access for own laptops, fridge, private entrances and patios with braais.

Polokwane *p668, map p668*
Don't go out of your way to stay here. With 1 or 2 exceptions, accommodation is aimed

at the business traveller and, while perfectly functional, is also unremarkable.

A Protea Hotel The Ranch, 25 km southwest of Polokwane on the N1, T015-290 5000, www.theranch.co.za. Set on a 1000 ha ranch, which is home to antelope, zebra, wildebeest and giraffe, and a pride of semi-tame lion, this luxury country retreat offers over 100 smartly furnished rooms of differing sizes, with a/c, internet and DSTV, 2 restaurants, bar and pool. Lots of activities, including horse riding and mountain biking, but the highlight here is the morning walk with some lion cubs.

B African Roots, 58a Devenish St, T015-297 0113, www.africanroots.info. Attractive converted farmhouse dating from 1928 with wrap-around veranda, owned by artists so the rooms have an interesting mix of antique furnishings and contemporary art. 21 en suite a/c garden rooms, lounge and bar, deck overlooking swimming pool. Recommended.

B Landmark Lodge, next to the N1 Shell Ultra City just south of town, T015-255 8100, www.proteahotels.com. 80 a/c functional rooms, aimed at business travellers. TV, pool, bar, restaurant, buffet breakfast, Wi-Fi. Standard business hotel but conveniently located.

C Plumtree Lodge, 138 Marshall St, T015-295 6153/4, www.plumtree.co.za. 14 double rooms in a modern house, with en suite bath or shower, separate lounge area with sofas, a desk and TV, motel-style parking. Palm-shaded pool surrounded by sun loungers, breakfast is served in a bright dining room. The staff are friendly and helpful. Gets booked up quickly.

D Cycad Guest House, corner of Schoeman and Suid streets, T015-291 2123, www.cycad guesthouse.co.za. Red-brick block of modern a/c rooms with neat decor, DSTV, internet, fridge, secure parking and conference facilities. Business orientated. Cheaper rates at weekend.

Camping

D-E Polokwane Game Reserve, 5 km out of town along Dorp St, T015-290 2331. Reserve with 60 sites for caravans and tents, 12 rondavels, self-catering, clean ablution block, electric points, laundry.

Louis Trichardt and the Soutpansberg *p670, map p671*

A Shiluvari Lakeside Lodge, off the R578, 4.5 km northeast of Elim, T015-556 3406, www.shiluvari.com. A peaceful country lodge located in the Albasini Conservancy, 23 km from Louis Trichardt, with 60 ha of grounds, ideal for birdwatching, fishing and hiking. Spacious thatched double rooms and chalets overlooking a dam, attractive decor, cool tiled floors, mosquito nets over beds, separate seating area with wicker furniture, and some have kitchenettes. Full-board rates available, **Wood Owl** restaurant and pub with fireplace is well regarded, swimming pool, Fair Trade curio shop. Boat trips organized during the day and at sunset on the dam. Recommended.

B Gateway Inn, 6 Koraalboom St, T015-516 1266, www.thegatewayinn.co.za. 15 smart a/c rooms in a modern purpose-built guest-house. Swimming pool with shaded terrace, restaurant for à la carte meals and cosy pub for light meals, fairly inventive food for a small town, and non-guests can eat here.

C Inn on Louis Trichardt, 11 km north of Louis Trichardt on the N1, T015-517 7020, www.inn-on-louistrichardt.co.za. The tranquil setting makes this guesthouse a popular choice, great views of the Soutpansberg Mountains from its 18 thatched rondavels, dotted around tended gardens, with enormous beds, en suite bathrooms, TV and phone. Swimming pool in the garden, rates include dinner and breakfast served on the terrace restaurant so rates are good value, also has a bar and tea rooms. Recommended.

D Bergwater Hotel, 5 Rissik St, T015-516 0262, bergho2@mweb.co.za. A whitewashed double-storey building overlooking a pond on edge of town. Standard small town hotel with 36 en suite rooms, a/c, DSTV, à la carte restaurant favoured by the locals, 2 bars, lounge, pool and conference facilities.

D Lutombo, 141 Anderson St, T015-516 0850, www.lutombo.co.za. 3 homely rooms with en suite. Non-smoking, TV lounge, all meals available on request, tropical gardens, pool, undercover parking. Good value B&B.

D-F Manavhela Ben Lavin Nature Reserve, T015-516 4534. Range of thatched self-catering chalets and huts, plus 30 campsites, caravan park, electric points and lighting, plenty of shade, spotless ablution block. Also has permanent tents that sleep 4, with en suite bathrooms and attached kitchen.

Camping

Makhado Caravan Park, middle of town next to the Indigenous Tree Park, T015-519 3025, www.makhado.caravanparks.com. Excellent caravan site which has won national prizes. 120 sites with electric points, hot water, plenty of shade, in a lovely setting next to a meandering stream with 2 dams. Mosquitoes can be a problem. Walking distance from restaurants and pubs, peaceful most of the year but can get very busy in school holidays.

Musina p672
B Musina Lodge, 9-13 Limpopo Av, T015-534 3352, www.musina-lodge.co.za. Good standard, 13 spacious rooms set in tropical gardens with an enormous baobab tree and swimming pool, a/c, DVD players and TV, internet, modern interiors, private terraces, cosy bar and good restaurant.
B-D Forever Resorts Tshipise, 37 km from Musina, 105 km from Kruger's Pafuri Gate on the R508 or R525, T015-539 0634, www.foreversa.co.za. Family resort conveniently situated en route to Kruger. Tennis, swimming pools, horse riding, hiking, mini-golf, hot springs, laundry, shops and restaurants on site. 96 a/c self-catering rondavels sleeping up to 6, and cheaper hotel rooms sleeping 2, TV, braai area, large camping and caravan park with shared ablutions. Summer temperatures are regularly over 40° C.
D Bushmen Inn, 43 Irwin St, T015-534 0243, www.bushmen.co.za. 7 non-smoking a/c B&B rooms in a modern house or in garden units next to the swimming pool, with fridge, DSTV, thatched lapa in the neat tropical garden, dinner on request.
D-F Baobab Caravan Park, on the left as you approach town from Louis Trichardt,

T015-534 3504. Tent and caravan sites, some self-catering chalets, electric points, laundry, well-grassed and shaded. A greatly improved site since the management passed from the municipality into private hands.

Mapungubwe National Park p673
Reservations through SANParks, T012-428 9111, www.sanparks.org. For bookings under 48 hrs prior to arrival and camping, T015-534 2014. The SANParks accommodation here is fairly new, so the furnishings and fabrics are still fresh and there's good kitchen equipment. Some units are equipped for wheelchair-users.
AL Tshugulu Lodge, in the western corner of the park. Exclusive lodge with 6 twin/double bedrooms sleeping 12, which must be booked as 1 unit (minimum number of guests is 4). A/c, kitchen and swimming pool.
AL Vhembe Wilderness Camp, eastern section of the park. This has been built on a small ridge within a valley and is within walking distance of the Limpopo River and Mapungubwe Hill. 4 wooden en suite cabins sleeping 2, and communal kitchen and solar power. Rates include morning game walks and night drives with a guide. If interested in the history of the area this is your best bet.
B-C Leokwe Camp, in the eastern side of the park among sandstone hills. In a particularly good region for birdwatching. 18 stone and thatch cottages sleeping up to 4, with a/c and open-plan kitchen. There's a swimming pool, sundeck and communal braai area.
D Limpopo Forest Camp, in the northwest of the park in riverine forest close to the Limpopo River. 8 permanent en suite safari tents sleeping 2-4 under reed roofs, communal kitchen and swimming pool. Nearby is the campsite, which has 10 pitches, shared ablutions and is well-shaded.

❶ Eating

Hotels are your best bet for eating. The small towns in Limpopo offer little more than chain steak restaurants with identical menus.

Bela-Bela *p665*

🍴 **O'Hagans**, in the Waterfront development close to the tourist office, T014-736 5068. Open 1200-late. Successful nationwide chain with attractive setting in the Waterfront development. Outdoor tables, interior filled with mock Irish touches, menu is Irish-style pub fare. Small choice, steaks and schnitzels, steak and ale pie, and sausages and mash. Good range of local and imported beers.

🍴 **Tocoma Spur**, Aventura Resort, T014-736 6436. Open 0900-2200 Family steakhouse chain found in most small towns in South Africa. Steaks, burgers and average salad bar.

Modimolle and around *p665*

🍴 **Die Koffiekan**, in the same shopping centre as the OK Supermarket off Nelson Mandela Dr. Mon-Sat 0900-1700, Sun 0900-11400. Daytime coffee shop with outside tables, set in pretty rose gardens with a children's playground and bird aviary with parrots and toucans, and small animals wandering around like ducks and rabbits. Country-style breakfasts, light lunches and tea and cake.

Mokopane *p666, map p667*

The restaurant scene here is limited to the standard chain outlets: **KFC**, **Nando's**, and **Spur**, all on Thabo Mbeki Dr. Otherwise head to the restaurant in the **Protea Hotel Park**.

Polokwane *p668, map p668*

Even though it's the largest town in Limpopo, eating out is limited to the standard chain restaurants, most of which are in **Savannah Mall** on Grobler St, away from the centre.

🍴 **Basil's**, Protea Hotel The Ranch, see Sleeping, page 677. Fine dining in a sophisticated country setting with a wooden deck overlooking the gardens. The inventive menu features gnocchi with clams and farm mushrooms, fillet steak stuffed with oysters, or Nile perch in roast pepper sauce. Sun buffet lunches are legendary. Booking essential.

🍴 **Cafe Pavilion**, 1171 Church St, a 5 min drive from the centre, T015-291 5359. Mon-Sat 0900-2130, Sun 0900-1500. In a garden nursery, well known for its good value buffets of stews, curries, salads, vegetables and baked puddings, or you can choose from the à la carte menu. Warm interior with Indonesian touches, broad outside deck and a children's playground and petting farm where they can feed the rabbits with carrots.

🍴-🍴 **Pebbles**, 32 Grobler St, T015-295 6999. Mon-Fri 0900-2130, Sat-Sun 0900-1400. Old converted house with a cosy bar and tables on the veranda, offering breakfasts, sandwiches and light meals, coffee and cakes and a more sophisticated menu in the evening with the likes of steak stuffed with mussels and fresh trout. Good choice for vegetarians and a varied wine list.

Louis Trichardt and the Soutpansberg *p670, map p671*

🍴 **Wood Owl**, Shiluvari Lakeside Lodge, see Sleeping, page 677. Open 1200-1500, 1830-2030. Excellent local reputation, with smart à la carte menu, using local produce such as Venda maize bread and beef. Delicious specials, beef with mustard mash or sweet potato soup, good choice of desserts and the decor is from the attached Fair Trade shop.

🍴 **Café d'Art**, 129 Krogh St, T015-516 5760. Open 1000-2100. Central family-run restaurant in attractive old house and serving traditional South African food, including good T-bone steaks, light lunches such as soup or quiche, great desserts or afternoon tea and cakes. All the baking is done on the premises.

Musina *p672*

The only restaurants in town are either in the hotels or are the standard chains, such as **Buffalo Ridge Spur**, Main St, which serves the usual choice of ribs, steaks and fried chicken.

❼ Entertainment

Polokwane *p668, map p668*

Meropa Entertainment World, Roodepoort Rd, off the N1 5 km southwest of the city, T015-290 5400, www.suninternational.com.

Like many other places in South Africa, this is a standard casino complex built on the edge of the city, which as well as the gaming floor has 4 restaurants, bars and a 102-bed hotel (Town Lodge, D). It's worth a detour for the excellent craft market, located in 4 authentic African huts, and next door, the bird and butterfly park will appeal to children.

▲ Activities and tours

Louis Trichardt and the Soutpansberg *p670, map p671*
Kuvona Cultural Tours, T015-556 3512, www.kuvona.com. Tours to the tribal sacred sites, traditional ceremonies and villages in the Soutpansberg and Venda. Promotes community development through tourism.
Saddles Horse Trails, Lalapanzi Hotel, 28 km south of Louis Trichardt on the N1, T072-516 5455. Horse trails in the Soutpansberg Mountain, suitable for novices, overnight at bush camps, swim bareback with the horses.

⊖ Transport

Bela-Bela *p665*
Train
Trains run between **Johannesburg** and **Musina** (11 hrs) via Polokwane and Louis Trichardt. Central reservations, Shosholoza Meyl, T0860-00888 (in South Africa), T011-774 4555 (from overseas), www.shosholoza meyl.co.za, timetables and fares are published on the website.

Mokopane *p666, map p667*
Train
Trains run between **Johannesburg** and **Musina** via Polokwane and Louis Trichardt. See Bela-Bela transport for contact details.

Polokwane *p668, map p668*
Air
Gateway Airport is 5 km north of the city centre off the N1, information T015-288

0122. **SAA**, T011-978 1111, www.flysaa.com, operate daily flights (50 mins) between Polokwane and **Johannesburg**.

Car hire
The following companies are located at Gateway Airport. **Budget** T015-288 0169, www.budget.co.za; **Europcar** T015-288 0097, www.europcar.co.za; **Hertz** T015-288 9900, www.hertz.co.za.

Train
Trains to **Johannesburg** and **Musina**. See Bela-Bela transport for contact details.

Louis Trichardt and the Soutpansberg *p670, map p671*
Train
Trains to **Musina** and **Johannesburg**. See Bela-Bela transport for contact details.

Musina *p672*
Train
Trains to **Johannesburg** via Louis Trichardt, Polokwane and Mokopane. See Bela-Bela transport for contact details.

⊙ Directory

Polokwane *p668, map p668*
Internet Hotels and at the Savannah Centre. **Medical services** Medi-Clinic, corner of Thabo Mbeki and Burger streets, T015-290 3600, www.limpopomc.co.za.

Louis Trichardt and the Soutpansberg *p670, map p671*
Banks ABSA and Standard, Krogh St.

Musina *p672*
Banks First National, Main Rd; Standard, corner of Main Rd and Emery St. **Bureau de change**, Main Rd next to the Post Office, T015-534 3412, daily 0700-1700. There are also bureaux de changes at the service station just before the Zimbabwe border.

East of the Great North Road

→ Colour map 2, A4.
While the area north towards Zimbabwe seems largely flat and featureless, venturing off the main north-south route leads to more varied landscapes and interesting sights. This is especially true of the region around the agricultural centre of Tzaneen, surrounded by tea plantations, lush mountains and fruit farms. Turning off the N1 at Polokwane onto the R71 towards Tzaneen, the landscape changes dramatically after around 30 km, from dusty scrubland dotted with acacias and untidy villages, to forest-covered hills. This craggy range, swathed in indigenous forests and peppered with waterfalls and dams, is known as the Magoebaskloof. ▸▸ *For listings, see pages 686-690.*

Ins and outs

Getting there and around The best way of exploring the area is by car; there is no public transport in the region. **SAA** flies between Johannesburg and **Phalaborwa Kruger Park Gateway Airport**, T015-781 5823, on the edge of Phalaborwa, 2 km from the entrance to Kruger National Park. ▸▸ *For further details, see Transport, page 690.*

The Magoebaskloof ◔◑◒✿ ▸▸ *pp686-690. Colour map 2, B4.*

→ Phone code: 015.
One of the best times of the year to explore this mountainous area is in spring, when the tropical valleys burst into a riot of colour. The area is best known for its cherry blossoms, and a small cherry blossom festival takes place here every year. The valleys are also famed for their orchids (over 200 species have been recorded here), and during December and January you can see bright pink and mauve 'pride of India' trees. Many of the country hotels in the area get fully booked at this time of year, as this is the most popular time for walking. Birdlife is prolific and includes knysna and purple-crested louries, several species of eagle, and the rare black-fronted bush shrike. The lower slopes are cultivated with tea and banana plantations and gum tree forests, creating the effect of a rolling green patchwork quilt.

Before the region was peacefully settled, it witnessed a bloody feud between the Transvaal government and the Tlou tribe of the chief Makgoba. In 1894 the followers of Makgoba retreated into the forests refusing to pay government taxes. The European soldiers were unable to dislodge the force and it took a group of Swazi warriors, working for the government, to defeat Makgoba. The warriors beheaded Makgoba to prove to the government that they had killed him, and the mountains were named after him.

Towards Tzaneen

The small village of **Haenertsburg** is the principal centre at the western end of the mountains. It's named after Carl Ferdinand Haenert who was born near Erfurt in Germany. He came to South Africa in 1857 to hunt, but fell in love with the area and never returned to Germany. In 1880 he found a small amount of gold in the hills, which led to a small gold rush and the proclamation and the founding of the village in 1887. There are a handful of tea gardens and craft shops in town, and Market Square is dominated by a display of over 400 species of trees from each of the five continents laid out in five rings, much like the Olympic Games logo. Information and accommodation bookings are available from **Magoebaskloof Tourism** ① *Rissik St, behind the Atholl Arms, T015-276 4972, www.magoebaskloof.com,*

Mon-Fri 0800-1700, Sat and Sun 0830-1200. From Haenertsburg you are faced with the choice of two possible routes to Tzaneen. The R71 continues past Ebenezer Dam and winds through the beautiful, forested **Magoebaskloof Valley**; the other option is to follow the R528 along the less scenic George's Valley.

Magoebaskloof Hiking Trail

The Magoebaskloof Hiking Trail has a variety of sections, ranging from two- to five-day hikes, with six huts for overnighting. The trail is considered tough and should only be attempted by seasoned hikers. Permits must be obtained from **Komatiland Forestry** ⓘ *T013-754 2724, www.komatiecotourism.co.za*, a subsidiary of the Forestry Department (SAFCOL), as each section has restrictions on the minimum and a maximum number of hikers. The website has detailed trail information, with information of overnight huts.

Tzaneen and around ⬤🅰🅱❯❯ *pp686-690. Colour map 2, A/B4.*

→ *Phone code: 015.*

Tzaneen lies at the centre of a prosperous agricultural region on the eastern side of the Magoebaskloof Mountains. After the scrubby dryness of surrounding areas, this region seems gloriously green and fertile, with verdant banana plantations and sweet-smelling orange groves creating a tropical setting. Although the town itself is little more than a busy grid of chain stores and petrol stations ringed by quiet suburbs, the abundance of the area's soil is apparent in the numerous stalls selling tropical fruits – this is, in fact, South Africa's biggest producer of avocados, mangoes and tomatoes. **Limpopo Tourism and Parks Board** ⓘ *T051-307 3582, www.golimpopo.com, Mon-Fri 0800-1700*, is on the R71, on the right-hand side as you approach town from the Phalaborwa and Kruger National Park. It's a very helpful office with a wealth of information on the area.

Background

Although now the largest town in Limpopo after Polokwane, Tzaneen is relatively young. It only became a permanent settlement when the Selati Railway arrived in 1912. There are several versions of how the town was named but one theory suggests Tzaneen comes from the old Bantu word, *Tsaneng*, used to refer to the people in this area. The change in spelling is explained by German settlers transcribing the sound 'ts' as 'tz' when they wrote it down.

Sights

Do not be deceived by its unassuming appearance, the **Tzaneen Museum** ⓘ *Agatha St, T015-307 2425, Mon-Fri 0900-1600 (donate generously for the upkeep of the building)*, is one of the best provincial museums in South Africa and deserves far greater recognition and resources. The displays are a private collection of ethnological artefacts put together by Jurgen Witt. Crammed into three small rooms is an impressive and absorbing selection of pottery, carvings, drums and beadwork from the regional Tsonga and Venda peoples. The enthusiastic staff lead visitors around the displays, explaining certain items and providing a fascinating overview of this priceless muddle of a collection.

Modjadji Cycad Reserve → *Colour map 2, A4.*

ⓘ *32 km north of Tzaneen on the R36, daily 0830-1600, R20 per car.*

Modjadj Cycad Reserve is the home of the Rain Queen, the hereditary female monarch of the Lobedu people, who has reigned since the 16th century. The last queen, the sixth

Queen Makobo, died of AIDS in June 2005 at the age of 27. Traditionally the Rain Queen never marries, and her sexual partners are chosen by the Royal Council so that all of her children will have blue blood. Because Makobo's daughter, who was only born in 2005, was fathered by a commoner, the traditionalists are not likely to accept her as the rightful heiress to the Rain Queen crown. Consequently, there are worries that the 400-year-old Rain Queen dynasty may be coming to an end. No new Rain Queen has been chosen since Makobo died. That aside, the position of Rain Queen remains of huge importance in the area. Legend maintains that she has the power to produce rain, which is traditionally very important in this fertile region. Her powers seem to have had considerable success: the 12,000 cycads in the reserve stand at over 13 m high (normal growth in other areas is around 5-8 m tall). This particular species of fern, *Encephalartos transvenosus*, is thought to be billions of years old and has been protected for four centuries by the Modjadji Rain Queen. The reserve at the top of a steep hill protects these plants and surrounds the royal village. There are a few trails within the reserve, a picnic site and an information centre.

Magoebaskloof & Tzaneen

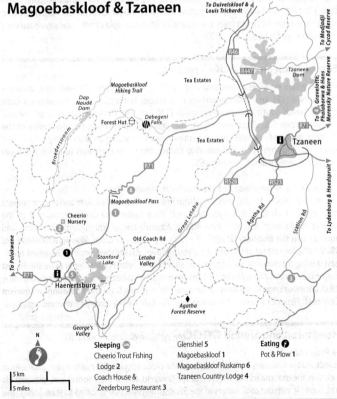

Sleeping 🛏️
Cheerio Trout Fishing Lodge 2
Coach House & Zeederburg Restaurant 3

Glenshiel 5
Magoebaskloof 1
Magoebaskloof Ruskamp 6
Tzaneen Country Lodge 4

Eating 🍴
Pot & Plow 1

Hans Merensky Nature Reserve → *Colour map 2, A4.*

ⓘ *68 km east of Tzaneen, on the R529 towards Giyani, T015-288 9000, R10, children (under 12) R2.*

Hans Merensky Nature Reserve is on the southern banks of the Great Letaba River and was founded in 1954 to protect various species of Lowveld antelope, in particular roan and sable. The natural vegetation is described as mopane Lowveld and there is a chance of viewing giraffe, bushbuck, zebra, impala, duiker, impala, tsessebe and blue wildebeest. There are leopard but they remain elusive. There are four species of poisonous snake in the reserve: puff adder, Mozambique spitting cobra, black mamba and boomslang. There's a 32-km network of roads. Most people visit here while staying at the **Eiland Spa and Eco Park** (see Sleeping, page 687), which is in the reserve.

Sunland Nursery

ⓘ *68 km north of Tzaneen, just off the R526, signposted off the main road, T015-309 9039, www.bigbaobab.co.za. R10, children (under 16) free.*

The Sunland Nursery is home to what claims to be the world's largest boabab tree, with an impressive 46.8 m circumference. It is said to be over 6000 years old, and the owners have built a bar into the hollow areas in part of the trunk and reputedly it can hold 60 people, and a wine cellar has been built in a second hollow. A couple of self-catering chalets and quad bikes are for hire.

East of Tzaneen ⊜⦿▲⊖⦿ ›› *pp686-690.*

There are two possible routes east and south of Tzaneen: the R71 leads to Gravelotte, Phalaborwa (111 km) and the entrance to Kruger National Park at Phalaborwa Gate; the R36 heads south towards Hoedspruit (120 km), the Drakensberg escarpment and Kruger's Orpen Gate. Both routes pass through the region known as the **Valley of the Olifants**, an area filled with private game reserves providing an attractively wild drive if you're passing through. If not entering Kruger, the route continues to the **Blyde River Canyon** in Mpumalanga, see page 652.

Phalaborwa → *Colour map 2, B5. Phone code: 015. Altitude: 450 m.*

This quiet Afrikaner town is only 2 km from Kruger's Phalaborwa Gate and is a convenient base from which to visit Kruger, although it's a rather dull choice compared to the reserves and camps nearby. South Africa's Amarula cream liqueur is distilled here, and you can visit the **distillery** ⓘ *T015-781 7766, www.amarula.com, Mon-Fri 0900-1600, Sat 0900-1200,* for tasting and tours. It's a young town, established since 1958, when open-cast mining for minerals and copper began here. The mine is considered to be the widest man-made hole in Africa at almost 2 km wide and 890 m deep. It currently produces some 28,000 tons of copper ore daily. Information is available from the **Phalaborwa Tourism Centre** ⓘ *Hendrick van Eck St, near the Spar, T015-769 5090, www.phalaborwa.org.za.*

Hoedspruit and around ⊜⦿⦿⊖ ›› *pp686-690. Colour map 2, B5.*

→ *Phone code: 015.*

Hoedspruit is Afrikaans for 'hat creek', and the place acquired its name when, after a long trek over the mountains into the heat of the Lowveld, one of the Voortrekkers removed his hat, threw it into the cool waters of the Sandspruit River and decided to stay. Today, the town has barely expanded beyond its string of shops, banks and petrol station, and remains a sleepy outpost surrounded by game-rich country, loomed over by the Drakensberg escarpment. At the very south of Limpopo in the Lowveld region, Hoedspruit is close to both the private game reserves around Kruger (see page 637), and the Panorama region of Mpumalanga (see pages 645-660). There is little of interest to keep you in town itself; the main attractions and accommodation options are along the R531 towards Blyde River Canyon.

Bombyx Mori Silk Farm
ⓘ *23 km south of Hoedspruit on the R531, T015-795 5682, www.silkcompany.co.za. Mon-Sat 0900-1600, Sun in summer 1100-1400; 5 daily tours on the hour, R30, children (under 16) R15.*
Skilled women weavers from the local community show visitors the intricate methods of commercial silk farming and weaving at this farm. The cultivated silk, a soft creamy colour, is produced from the cocoons of the Bombyx Mori silkworm, and the farm shop sells a wide range of products: silk scarves, blankets, silk-filled duvets and cushions, **The Cotton Club** restaurant (see Eating, page 689) is a fine venue for lunch or afternoon tea.

Hoedspruit Endangered Species Centre
ⓘ *23 km south of Hoedspruit on the R531, T015-793 1633, www.wildlifecentre.co.za. 0800-1700, 2-hr tours depart hourly 0800-1600, R120, children (under 12) R50, elephant riding R1100, no children under 12. Curio shop and tea garden.*
This project conducts essential research on endangered species, in particular cheetah. There are daily standard tours lasting two hours, which begin with an informative video about the plight of endangered species, before viewing cheetah, African wild dog, ground hornbills, and the 'vulture restaurant', where wild vultures come to feed. Around 80 cheetah can be seen. The extended tour, which runs twice daily for three hours, also includes a visit to a breeding and rehabilitation camp for rhino and the rare Barbary lion. Booking is advised for both tours as many local school groups visit the centre. The new activity here is elephant riding, and there are 13 elephants at Camp Jabulani (see page 638) on the adjacent Kapama Game Reserve.

Moholoholo Rehabilitation Centre
ⓘ *T015-795 5236, www.moholoholo.co.za. Tours Mon-Sat 0930 and 1500, Sun 1500, they leave promptly so get to the gate in plenty of time, R95, children (7-13) R45, under 7s free.*
Moholoholo is a rehabilitation centre for abandoned, injured and poisoned wildlife. Animals are brought here from all over South Africa and, once healthy enough, are reintroduced into their natural environment. Some of the big cats however, cannot be rereleased back into the wild, so the centre is now home to them. There are a number of big birds such as raptors and vultures, many of which are injured from flying into power lines. Another important function of the centre is breeding and they have successfully bred and released into the wild the endangered crowned eagle, serval and many other species.

Khamai Reptile Park
ⓘ *33 km south of Hoedspruit on the R531, T015-795 5203. Daily 0800-1700. R25.*
This impressive reptile park was established 25 years ago by Donald Strydom, one of Africa's leading snake specialists, as a refuge and platform for understanding reptiles. There are numerous enclosures holding a wide variety of snakes, lizards, tortoises and crocodiles, and Donald's staff provide a good understanding of how many snakes are needlessly killed by farmers in South Africa. For an extra fee you can have a photo taken

with a python wrapped over your shoulders. The park also offers a free service to cure people of their phobias of snakes and spiders.

◉ East of the Great North Road listings

For Sleeping and Eating price codes and other relevant information, see pages 46-53.

● Sleeping

The Magoebaskloof *p681, map p683*
There is a range of accommodation options in the 2 valleys; if you are not staying in the more expensive hotels they are still worth visiting for lunch or afternoon tea.
A Glenshiel, 2 km from Haenertsburg on the R71, T015-276 4335, www.glenshiel.co.za. 15 luxury suites in a country lodge, each with an open fireplace and TV. The lodge is well known for its excellent cuisine. Tennis, swimming pool, trout fishing, delightful gardens, walking trails, good service. Worth trying to bargain on the price out of season.
B Magoebaskloof Hotel, off the R71, approximately 26 km from Tzaneen, T015-276 5400, www.magoebaskloof.co.za. Recently rebuilt leisure hotel with range of self-catering units, double rooms and family rooms, all with en suite bathroom, disabled access, and some with fabulous valley views. À la carte restaurant and café, pub showing big-screen sport, squash, swimming and the **Samango monkey project**, with viewing platforms to watch the monkeys in their natural habitat. Popular with weekending groups from Gauteng. Wide choice of walks available from here.
C-D Cheerio Trout Fishing Lodge, at the **Cheerio Nursery** off the R71, T015-276 1804, www.cheerio.co.za. Self-catering chalets or B&B in pretty rondavels, sleeping 2-5. Swimming pool and tennis court. Perfect setting with fine views across the valley. Trout fishing offered in 3 dams. The nursery is the site of the annual cherry blossom festival.
D Magoebaskloof Ruskamp, 25 km from Tzaneen on the R71, T015-305 4142, www.magoebaskloofruskamp.co.za.

Long-established good value resort with a cluster of 27 rondavels perched high up on the R71 where it climbs over a winding pass; gets a bit chilly at night. Self-catering or smaller B&B units, TV, heater, pool, sub-tropical gardens, good restaurant with fantastic terrace overlooking the valley, but availability on the menu a bit hit-and-miss depending on how many people are staying.

Tzaneen and around *p682, map p683*
Most accommodation options are around Tzaneen, on the road from Phalaborwa.
AL Coach House, 15 km from Tzaneen, T015-306 8000, www.coachhouse.co.za. Hidden away in the forests south of Tzaneen, close to the Agatha Forest Reserve, delightful country hotel with mountain views and colourful gardens with a swimming pool and stunning beauty spa (see page 17). 39 cosy bedrooms with en suite bathrooms, DSTV, and little touches like mohair blankets on the beds and home-made biscuits and fruit laid out each day. Some have log fires. Much of the fresh produce served in the restaurant is grown within the grounds, and it is possible to hire mountain bikes or walk on marked trails in the forest straight from the hotel. Excellent restaurant and they have a dedicated kitchen for making nougat, biscuits and brittle (www.nougat.co.za).
A Tzaneen Country Lodge, 17 km from Tzaneen on the R71 from Phalaborwa, T015-304 3290, www.tznlodge.co.za. 45 a/c elegant rooms with DSTV, bar, large, pretty gardens, the **Earth Spa** that offers treatment/accommodation packages, farmyard with animals that kids can stroke, outside restaurant that serves pub lunches and good pancakes, plus fancier evening meals. Popular wedding venue. If not staying, their Sun buffet lunch is worth dropping in for.

Hans Merensky Nature Reserve *p684*
C-D Eiland Spa & Eco Park, 68 km east of Tzaneen T015-386 8000, www.eiland.co.za. A huge resort with 103 self-catering a/c thatched rondavels with TV, sleeping 2-6. 250-stand caravan and camping park with electric points, restaurant, bar, swimming pool, sauna, mineral pools, horse riding, water park, beauty spa, gym, mini-golf and tennis. Full-on family resort with entertainment programs, aimed at the local market and overrun in school holidays.

Phalaborwa *p684*
Being so close to Kruger, this town has a wide range of accommodation options, although it's still preferable to stay closer to the wildlife in the park.
A Hans Merensky Estate, just out of town, at the Kruger end, off Koper Rd, T015-781 3931, www.hansmerensky.com. Marketed as a golf and wildlife resort, with 30 self-catering a/c chalets in a long, low, thatched building overlooking a golf course where game from Kruger casually wanders around. 14 hotel rooms surrounding the swimming pool. Clubhouse has a restaurant and bar and new additions are a gym and spa. Offers game drives into Kruger.
B Sefapane Lodge, corner of Copper and Essenhout streets, T015-780 6700, www.sefapane.co.za. 19 upmarket, thatched, 2-bed self-catering chalets, and cheaper 1- and 2-bed rondavels, set in a large indigenous garden. Braai boma, restaurant, swimming pool with a sunken bar. They have a 'meet and greet' desk at the airport, fly-in packages available, day trips to Kruger and other regional tours. If you don't have a car this is a good mid-range option. Also offers beach time in Mozambique, check out the website for packages.
B Tulani Safari Lodge, on the R40 to Mica, T015-781 5414, www.tulanisafarilodge.co.za. Set in the **Balule Nature Reserve** on the western border of Kruger. 24 chalets with mix of ethnic and modern decor, a/c, restaurant, bar, swimming pool, tennis,

hiking trails, open bush drives into Kruger. Rates include breakfast and dinner.
C-D Raintree Cottage, 1 Essenhout St, T015-781 0995, www.raintreecottage.co.za. 8 a/c en suite rooms with private entrances, attractive Victorian-style decor and TV. Rates are B&B, evening meals and picnic baskets to take into Kruger on request. Pool, close to park gates, friendly hosts.
D Daan & Zena, 15 Birkenhead St, T015-781 6049, www.daanzena.co.za. 21 funky units spread over 3 houses, individually decorated en suite double rooms, self-catering units and budget rooms with communal kitchen, all decorated with wacky furniture and bright colours. M-Net TV, a/c and tea- and coffee-making facilities. Swimming pool, colourful lounge, secure parking. Friendly set-up. Recommended.
D Ingwe Park, 3 km out of town on the Tzaneen road, T015-781 3776, www.ingwepark.com. This relaxed and fun bush lodge is set in a restored old miners' camp with comfortable, self-contained bungalows, each with TV and kitchen. There are cheaper backpacker rooms with shared ablutions and kitchen under a thatched lapa. Swimming pool, hiking and day tours into Kruger, meals on request.
D-F Elephant Walk, 30 Anna Scheepers Av, T015-781 5860, www.accommodationphalaborwa.com. A welcome backpacker place close to Kruger Park which also offers good-value game-viewing trips into Kruger Park and some interesting cultural tours to rural villages and townships. Choice of 10-bed dorm, 4 attractive en suite B&B double rooms, or camping in the shady garden with separate ablution block. Fully equipped kitchen, laundry, meals on request, braai, pool.

Hoedspruit and around *p684*
The accommodation listed below is at the bottom of Blyde River Canyon close to Hoedspruit. For accommodation at the top of the canyon, refer to the Mpumalanga chapter, page 656. All are situated within 1 hr's drive of Kruger's Orpen Gate.

A-D Moholoholo Mountain View Camp, from Hoedspruit, turn off the R531 towards the bottom of the Blyde River Canyon Nature Reserve, opposite **Blyde River Canyon Lodge**, T/F015-795 5684, www.moholoholo.co.za. A 4000-ha private reserve with wild lion, rhino and hippo and a range of accommodation to suit most budgets. 19 simple, reed-wall, self-catering chalets, dining boma overlooking a waterhole, or 10 upmarket thatched chalets where the price includes all meals and game activities. Game walks with a ranger, night drives, an educational bush experience.

B Blyde River Canyon Lodge, 28 km from Hoedspruit, turn off the R531 towards the bottom of the Blyde River Canyon Nature Reserve and **Aventura Swadini**, T015-795 5305, www.blyderivercanyonlodge.com. A very intimate and individual lodge, with 6 double thatched rooms with verandas, bar, pool and excellent cuisine. The building is constructed from natural materials on beautiful grounds, which the owners have gone to great lengths to keep totally indigenous. Zebra, warthog, and a blue wildebeest wander across the lawns and through the car park. Recommended.

C Blue Cottages Country House, 37 km from Hoedspruit on the R527 towards Blyde River Canyon, T015-795 5114, www.country house.co.za. 5 bungalows and 2 suites, set in a beautiful bush garden, swimming pool, each unit is decorated with unique pieces of artwork and African antiques from the attached **Monsoon Gallery**. Home-cooked breakfast included and 3-course dinner on request, served on the verandas. An enchanting overnight stop on the way to Kruger, recommended.

C-D Forever Resorts Swadini, at the very base of Blyde River Canyon off the R531, adjacent to the **Blyde River Nature Reserve** and dam, T015-795 5141, www.foreversa. co.za. Award-winning resort in a stunning location. 78 chalets, 180 camping/caravan stands, shops, restaurants, swimming pools, tennis, mini-golf, lots of hikes and a pleasant drive to viewpoints in the reserve, boat rides

on the dam. As the crow flies, there is another Forever Resort, **Blyde Canyon** only a few kilometres away at the top of the canyon (see page 656 in the Mpumalanga chapter), but they are actually over 100 km apart by road.

🍴 Eating

The Magoebaskloof *p681, map p683*

🍴 **Iron Crown Pub and Grill**, in front of the tourist office in Haenertsburg on Rissik St, T015-276 4755. Tue-Sat 1000-late, Sun 0900-1500. Friendly, atmospheric pub, big-screen TV for sports, hearty country fare, good steaks and sauces, schnitzels and fish and chips, Sun set lunch.

🍴 **Picasso's**, a prominent wood cabin just off the main road through Haenertsburg, T015-276 4724. Closes at 1630. Comfortable restaurant and curio shop with a good choice of light meals. The pancakes are a speciality, but also on offer are more substantial dishes like beef stew or chicken casserole. Great local grilled trout, too. Resident African grey parrot. Internet access.

🍴 **Pot & Plow**, 8 km out of town on the R41. Mon-Sat 1200-2130, Sun 1200-1600. Popular roadside restaurant and bar, good for lunch, decent home-made pies and tasty salads, and well known locally for its excellent pizzas and good value Sun roasts, also sells a few curios and home-made preserves.

Tzaneen and around *p682, map p683*
The town features the usual steakhouse chains such as **Spur** and **Steers**. The best restaurants are in the country hotels, and during the day there are a number of roadside tea gardens, which serve snack lunches.

🍴🍴 **Zeederburg**, Coach House, 15 km from town, T015-306 8000, www.coachhouse.co.za. 1230-1400, 1930-2100. One of the finest restaurants in the region set in this top-class lodge. Colonial decor, professional service, a menu using good local produce, including smoked trout, avocados, mangos and macadamia nuts, delicious mains, plus some decent veggie options. Huge wine list, laden dessert trolley and famous for their home-made nougat.

♥-♥ Ashley's Cafe, 30 Agatha St, T015-307 7270. Mon-Sat 0730-2100, Sun lunch only. Best restaurant in town, offering great breakfasts, coffees, salads and sandwiches at lunchtime, and larger meals in the evenings, including a good pepper-crusted fillet steak, plus a decent cocktail menu. Pleasant balcony overlooking gardens.

Phalaborwa p684
♥ Buffalo's Pub & Grill, 1 Lekkerbreek St, T015-781 0829. Mon-Sat 1200-2200. A carnivore's hangout with a long menu of steaks and sauces and specials like fillet stuffed with mushrooms or mussels, but poor choice for vegetarians who also may not like the game trophies on the wall. Popular bar and wooden deck.

♥ Sefepane Lodge, Copper Rd, T015-780 6700. Open 0700-2100. Smart lodge restaurant with indoor ethnic dining room and pleasant outdoor boma lit by lanterns and candles. Good South African fare such as lamb *potjies* or bobotie, plus venison specials such as springbok. The boma is popular with tour groups when buffets served.

Hoedspruit and around p684
♥♥♥ Mad Dogz Café, on the R527, east of the junction of the R527 and R36, T015-795 5425, by the entrance for the **Blue Cottages** on the main road. 0730-1630. The food here is some of the best you'll find in the region, and this makes for a great lunchtime stop-off en route to Kruger National Park. Big, wholesome breakfasts, excellent lunches using fusion dishes, Creole chicken, spicy Thai beef and Cape Malay bobotie. The setting is lovely, with brightly painted tables clustered under thatched roofs, surrounded by lush tropical vegetation. Recommended.

♥♥ The Trading Post, 26 km from Hoedspruit via Klaserie on the R531, T015-795 5219. Open 0800-late. An attractive and unusual restaurant and pub owned by a friendly ex-game ranger and his French wife. A happy combination of the traditional South African way of cooking and the French social way of eating. Each table has an built-in gas braai, and you cook your meat to your liking. Game platters including strips of warthog and crocodile meat are available, as are ready-prepared meat dishes, salads, and pizzas.

♥ The Cotton Club, 23 km from Hoedspruit on the R531, at the Bombyz Mori Silk Farm, T015-795 5682. Open 0830-1630. Set in an attractive thatched building in landscaped gardens where a family of warthog trot around, serves light meals such as sandwiches, salads and quiches, main courses include ostrich kebabs, pies and burgers, or opt for tea and cake in the afternoon.

⊛ Festivals and events

The Magoebaskloof p681, map p683
Sep The **Spring Cherry and Azalea Blossom Festival**, **Craft Fair** and **Orchid Exhibition** take place around Haenertsburg. Flowers transform entire valleys into blankets of colour.

O Shopping

Hoedspruit and around p684
Monsoon Gallery, next door to the **Mad Dogz Café** (see Eating, left), www.monsoon gallery.com. Tasteful gallery selling fine African art, jewellery, cloth and antiques, plus some contemporary pieces. All the packing and shipping can be arranged from here. There is also a shop here selling items produced at the **Bombyx Mori Silk Farm** (see page 685).

▲ Activities and tours

Phalaborwa p684
Golf
Hans Merensky Country Club, T015-781 3931, www.hansmerensky.com. Based around

an 18-hole PGA championship golf course. Golfers negotiate wildlife on the greens while they play; watch out for the hippos on the 17th hole. Also has accommodation. Call in advance. The best times for a round to see animals is early morning or late afternoon.

Tour operators
Jumbo River Safaris, T015-781 6168. Organizes a fun 3-hr boat trip on the Olifants River for ever-popular sundowners. Always a good chance of seeing game and colourful water birds. Arranges longer Kruger safaris.

⊖ Transport

Phalaborwa *p684*
Air
Phalaborwa Kruger Park Gateway Airport, 2 km from town centre and entrance to Kruger Phalaborwa Gate, T015-781 5823, has a fabulous design. The baggage reclaim is under a thatched roof, the seats in the waiting area are rocks and the drinking fountain spouts from a tree stump. SAA, T011-978 1111, www.flysaa.com, operates daily flights between Phalaborwa and **Johannesburg** (1 hr).

Car hire
At the airport: Avis T015-781 3169; **Budget** T015-781 5404, www.budget.co.za; **Europcar** T015-781 0376, www.europcar.co.za.

Hoedspruit and around *p684*
Air
Eastgate Airport is 7 km from Hoedspruit on the road to the Timbavati Game Reserve, T015-793 3681, www.eastgateairport.co.za. SAA, T011-978 1111, www.flysaa.com, operates daily flights between Eastgate and **Johannesburg** (1 hr 10 min). It is also used by charter companies for guests of the luxury lodges in private reserves.

Car hire
Avis, airport, T015-793 2014, www.avis.co.za.

➊ Directory

Tzaneen and around *p682, map p683*
Medical services Medi Clinic, Wolkberg Av, T015-306 8500, www.tzaneenmc.co.za.

Phalaborwa *p684*
Medical services Hospital, Grosvenor Cres, T015-785 3511.

Contents

Footprint features

Border crossings

South Africa–Botswana,
Pioneer Gate, Tlokweng Gate,
Ramatlabama and Makgobistad,
see page 699

North West Province

At a glance

⊜ **Getting around** Buses on major routes, car hire, tours start and finish in Johannesburg.

◉ **Time required** 2-5 days for major sights.

☀ **Weather** Mostly dry, sunny and hot, chilly nights in winter.

✖ **When not to go** Avoid Sun City on public holidays.

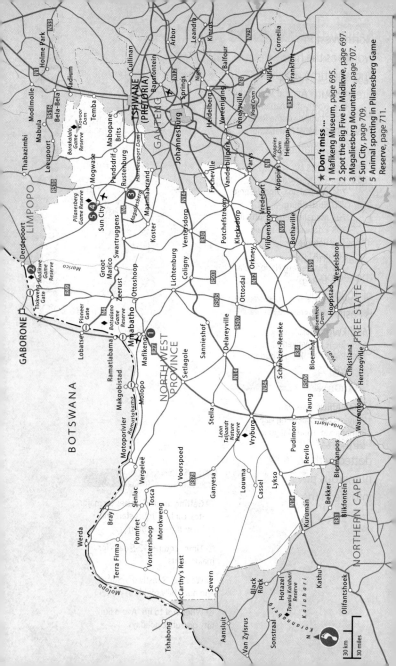

★ **Don't miss ...**

1 Mafikeng Museum, page 695.
2 Spot the Big Five in Madikwe, page 697.
3 Magaliesberg Mountains, page 707.
4 Sun City, page 709.
5 Animal spotting in Pilanesberg Game Reserve, page 711.

North West Province is known first and foremost (for better or worse) as the home of Sun City, a huge entertainment complex and one-time gambling haven which was once the most visited site in South Africa. It remains hugely popular, and is the most likely reason for visitors to venture into this dry and stark state.

Much of North West Province is visually unremarkable, made up of flat Kalahari grasslands and dotted with lonely farming communities which were some of the most important agricultural centres in the 19th century. This was once the Western Transvaal, one of the areas where the Voortrekkers settled at the end of the Great Trek, and towns such as Mafikeng and Rustenburg have a fascinating history.

Gambling and history aside, the best reason for visiting is the region's excellent game parks, all at a malaria-free altitude of 1000-2000 m. The well-publicized Pilanesberg Game Reserve is easily accessible, lying incongruously close to Sun City, while Madikwe Game Reserve is one of the finest parks in the country, offering excellent accommodation and the chance of seeing the Big Five just a few hours from Johannesburg and Tshwane (Pretoria).

A more low-key attraction and a big draw for locals are the Magaliesberg Mountains, less than one hour's drive from Tshwane (Pretoria). Although made up by a fairly bland series of bush-covered hills, they are filled with wild hiking trails and dotted with comfortable holiday resorts. Further west are numerous private game farms, which provide an insight into life in the bushveld on the edge of the Kalahari.

Ins and outs

Getting around

The North West Province can only really be visited by car. Public transport is virtually non-existent and very few mainline buses run services to this region. Driving, however, isn't a terribly pleasant experience and involves covering long distances through isolated farmland. Plan journeys so you arrive at your destination before dark as goats, cows, stray dogs and antelope are a hazard on the roads at night, and be careful not to fall asleep at the wheel. It's a good idea to fill up with petrol where you can, as there are some big distances between service stations. Carry a mobile phone in case of breakdown, the emergency number is T112.

Tourist information

North West Parks and Tourism Board ⓘ *Heritage House, Cookes Lake, 30/31 Nelson Mandela Drive, Mafikeng, T018-397 1500, Mon-Fri 0800-1640, www.tourismnorthwest.co.za*, is responsible for promoting tourism throughout the province. Contact them in advance for maps and useful brochures they have on the little-known parks.

Western region

The western region of the province is a largely empty expanse of rough scrub given over to huge game farms and remote hamlets. This empty corner of South Africa holds little of interest, and the arrival of visitors can stir up quite a bit of interest amongst the sleepy inhabitants of the ancient farming communities dotted around the region. Most visitors to the area are actually just passing through en route to Botswana, where things liven up again over the border. The largest settlement of note is scruffy Mmabatho, a modern and featureless town, and neighbouring Mafikeng, which despite having a chequered history doesn't warrant much distraction. The highlight of this region is undoubtedly the Madikwe Game Reserve, one of South Africa's best-kept secrets. ►► *For listings, see pages 700-702.*

Mafikeng and Mmabatho ⊖❶❷❸❹ ►► *pp700-702. Colour map 1, B6.*

Mmabatho is a modern town created in 1977. Before the free elections were held in South Africa and the new political boundaries came into effect, **Mafikeng** was in the old Western Transvaal and Mmabatho was the capital of the homeland known as Bophuthatswana and was the site of several government buildings. When the North West Province was created, it was decided to keep Mmabatho on as the regional capital. However, there has been a gradual shift of power back to the principal town in the region, Rustenburg. Mmabatho remains a rather garish concrete sprawl, and although the majority of government offices are still here there remains an air of artificiality and incompleteness. Dusty open ground between isolated buildings waits for the city to grow around it, and the poverty of the former homeland of Bophuthatswana remains evident. The whole town is dominated by a sports stadium of Olympic proportions that seats 70,000, which is in itself quite an impressive architectural specimen. Its other claim to fame, rather bizarrely, is that of being home to a state-of-the-art recording studio where the soundtrack to *The Lion King* was recorded. But the most likely reason for visiting here is to have a quick look around the historic town of Mafikeng, another hot and dusty commercial centre on the Highveld, but one with an interesting early history, and plenty of buildings that help tell its story. Having said that, neither town warrant a specific journey, and they act mainly as stop-off points to the Ramatlabama border of Botswana, 25 km away.

Ins and outs → *Phone code: 018. Altitude: 1278 m.*

Getting around There are regular minibus taxis running between Mafikeng railway station and Mega City shopping centre in Mmabatho.

Tourist information There are several sources of tourist information in the two towns. For local and regional information call at the **North West Parks and Tourism Board** ① *Heritage House, Cookes Lake, 30/31 Nelson Mandela Drive, Mafikeng, T018-397 1500, Mon-Fri 0800-1640, www.tourismnorthwest.co.za.* The **Mafikeng Museum** (see below) is also a useful source.

Background

Mafikeng was founded as a British administrative centre in 1885, when Sir Charles Warren was sent with a military force to occupy and bring peace to this frontier territory. Only 20 km away was the Goshen Republic, an independent state created by a group of European mercenaries who had been given farms by the local Rolong tribe. The name of the new settlement came from the Tswana *maFikeng*, 'place of boulders'. The surrounding territory became known as British Bechuanaland, with Mafikeng as the centre for the local farmers, traders and hunters. At the time this was still very much frontier territory, occupied by a rough crowd and policed by the tough Bechuanaland Border Police.

On 14 October 1899, a Boer force under the command of General JP Snyman besieged the town, and so started the period of events that was to put the town on the map. The Siege of Mafeking lasted 217 days until 17 May 1900, when the town was relieved by a combined force of Rhodesian troops from the north and Imperial troops from the south. At the time, the siege captured the imagination of the British public in England – the Anglo-Boer War was the first war to be reported in such detail, with pictures, cartoons and newspaper articles. It was during the siege that the British commander, Colonel RSS Baden-Powell, made his name and conceived the idea for the Boy Scout movement (see box, page 696).

Baden-Powell proved himself to be very competent in organizing the defences, but in later years was criticized for his treatment of the black troops. One of his well-documented ideas was to place life-size dummies in observation posts around the town. The Boer commander, General Cronje believed that he was pinning down a large British force planned for the invasion of the Western Transvaal. Mafikeng was, in fact, an insignificant centre but it became an important focal point and when the siege had been lifted, the Boer resolve seemed to weaken and the towns of Ladysmith and Kimberley were relieved soon after.

After the war, Mafikeng returned to the life of a sleepy border town. Up until 1965 it was the centre for the British administration of the Bechuanaland Protectorate. This was a fairly unusual set-up where the government for one state, Bechuanaland, was in fact located in a foreign country, South Africa. In 1965 the government moved to Gaborone and on 30 September 1966 Botswana became an independent republic, led by Sir Seretse Khama. Today the town is the centre for the local cattle industry. Although the relics from the Boer War are interesting, the town does not attract many tourists and is well off the beaten track.

Sights

The **Mafikeng Museum** ① *corner of Martin and Robinson streets, Mafikeng, T018-3816102, Mon-Fri 0800-1600, Sat 0900-1230, free.* Housed in the old town hall built in 1902, this has an excellent series of displays relating to the Siege of Mafeking, as well as some informative

Siege of Mafikeng

During the long days of the seven-month Siege of Mafikeng (which lasted from 13 October 1899 to 17 May 1900), the English schoolboys in this colonial town started to become undisciplined – especially when their school closed because of the daily bombardment of the town by artillery shells. The commander of the town's British forces, Colonel Baden-Powell, whose small force was having difficulty defending the town, had an idea. He organized boys, aged between nine and 15 years, into a disciplined Siege Cadet Corps and put them to non-combat use. Their tasks included carrying supplies and messages between the front line and command posts, delivering post within the town, assisting the aged, and acting as observers for the regular soldiers. They were given uniforms and bicycles, and sport and military drills all played a part in fostering self-discipline and responsibility. Despite the dangers there was only one casualty during the siege among the cadets, that of nine-year-old Frankie Brown, who was killed by an exploding shell; his grave can be seen in Mafikeng cemetery. Baden-Powell went on to found the Boy Scout movement at Brownsea in southern England in 1907. He said of the boys of Mafikeng, "These lads proved by their achievements that, if trusted, boys can be relied upon to act as men when needed."

The impact of the war between Britons and Boers on the majority of the southern African population is also often forgotten. Neither side made much use of African soldiers directly, though a great many were employed (or forced to work) as porters, transport handlers and messengers. Nevertheless, they were inevitably caught up in the war and a great many were killed, either directly or as a result of disease or starvation, and many more had their livelihoods destroyed.

exhibits which trace the history of the region along with the culture of the indigenous peoples. **Mafikeng Cemetery** contains the graves of British servicemen, the Town Guard and South African troops. The most prominent grave is that of Andrew Beauchamp-Proctor, South Africa's most highly decorated First World War airman. **Kanon Kopje** is the site of a fort on the southern banks of the Molopo River built during a conflict between the Goshen Republic and the Barolong Boo Tshidi. The fort has been restored along with some cannon and guns and there are panoramic views out over Mafikeng.

The **Mafikeng Game Reserve** ① *T018-3815611, Sep-Apr 0730-1900, May-Aug 0730-1800, R25, children (2-12) R15, car R5*, lies at the edge of town, and the entrance is on Jacaranda Drive. The reserve, covering 4600 ha of open Kalahari grassland and acacia thorn scrub, contains large populations of plains game, buffalo, and giraffe and is a good place to try and see white rhino. Birdlife is good too, especially along the Molopo River. There are various tracks through the reserve, dotted with picnic sites, and the main circuit takes only two hours to drive around.

North of Mmabatho ◉ ⇢ *pp700-702.*

Botsalano Game Reserve → *Colour map 1, B6.*

① *Follow the R52 Ramatlabama border road north from Mmabatho for 30 km (the park is signposted), T018-386 8900, www.tourismnorthwest.co.za/botsalano. Apr-Aug 0800-1700, Sep-Mar 0600-1800, R25, children (2-12) R15, car R5. Hunting is still permitted in the reserve and between Apr and Aug it may well be closed.*

Like many of the game reserves in the North West Province, this is a little-known park in beautiful countryside, stocked with a good range of wild animals. The 5800-ha reserve is set in typical Kalahari country – open grasslands with patches of acacia and karee woodlands. It is well known locally for its successful breeding of white rhino. You can also hope to see gemsbok, eland, springbok, steenbok, giraffe, jackal, hartebeest, zebra, kudu, duiker, warthog and impala. There is an extensive road network and several waterholes and dams, which are ideal spots for game viewing.

Zeerust → Colour map 1, B6. Altitude: 1187 m.

Zeerust is a small centre for the local sheep and cattle industry, with little of interest in the town, although it does serve as a useful overnight stop between Gauteng and Gaborone. In the mid-1800s a church was built on the farm of Casper Coetzee, who died before its completion. The church was named Coetzee-Rust (Coetzee's Rest), which was later shortened to Zeerust. The commercial centre is along **Church Street**, where you will find banks to change money, supermarkets and snack bars at the 24-hour petrol stations.

Madikwe Game Reserve ☺ ⟩⟩ pp700-702. Colour map 1, A6.

Madikwe is the fourth largest game reserve in South Africa. Although the reserve lies entirely within South Africa, it is only 35 km from the Botswana capital, Gaborone. The northern limits of the park are marked by the international border, while the southern limits coincide with the Dwarsberg Mountains. Most of the park sits between the main road to Botswana and the Marico River to the east. Covering over 60,000 ha, it has the second largest elephant population and it lies in a malaria-free zone. At present the park is not open to day visitors, but they are allowed into the reserve if they pre-book through one of the lodges for a game drive, which usually includes lunch. For overnight visitors, Madikwe offers excellent accommodation and activities. There are now 22 lodges within the reserve.

Ins and outs

Getting there If you are driving from Gauteng, take the N4 west through Magalies, Swartruggens. At Zeerust turn right onto the R49 following signs to Gaborone. After about 100 km, just before the border crossing, turn right onto a sand road for 12 km to the Tau Gate. There are other gates at Derdepoort and Abjaterskop. Visitors should establish entry points before arrival; gates are opened by arrangement for pre-booked visitors. Entrance fees are included in the rates for the lodges, and for day visitors R50, children (under 12) R20. **Madikwe Charters** ① T011-805 4888, www.madikwecharter.com, flies daily to and from the reserve and Johannesburg (50 minutes). The lodges pick up from the Madikwe airstrip. ⟩⟩ For more information visit www.madikwe-game-reserve.co.za.

Best time to visit Most of the rain falls during the summer between November and March. Up to 600 mm is expected in the south, but as you move across the plains northwards, the annual rainfall averages about 100 mm less. In summer it can get very hot during the day – this is not ideal weather for walking. During winter it is dry but gets very cold at night.

Wildlife

One of the great features of the reserve is its diverse geology which has resulted in a broad mix of habitats suitable for a wide range of animals. In the northern part of the reserve the land is a level savannah plain. Running across the middle of the park and, in effect, dividing it in two, is the **Tweedepoort Escarpment**. Above the escarpment is an undulating plateau covered with dense vegetation, a marked contrast to the grasslands below. At the southern edge is a more extensive range of rocky mountains, the **Dwarsberg Range**. These are similar in appearance to the Magaliesberg but have been severely eroded over the years, the highest point being only 1228 m. The final distinct environment is provided by the perennial **Marico River** along the eastern boundary, where an aquatic and well-vegetated environment exists.

When the area was being prepared for inclusion within a game reserve, only a few of the indigenous species had survived the years of hunting and farming, as well as an outbreak of *rinderpest*. Back in 1836 the hunter William Cornwallis came across the first known sable in the Marico Valley and wrote of large herds of elephant and prides of lion frightening the local farmers. In 1991, Operation Phoenix was launched – one of the largest game translocation programmes in the world. By 1996 more than 10,000 animals from 28 species had been successfully released into the reserve.

Animals now present in the park include elephant, zebra, lion, buffalo, white rhino, spotted hyena, wild dog, steenbok, duiker, kudu, leopard and cheetah. Visitors are able to view these animals during game drives or on morning walks with a guide and experienced tracker. A special feature of the reserve is the introduction of community projects, which allow local communities to benefit from, and contribute to, the ecological management of the reserve. Another project in the planning is the development of the Heritage Park

Madikwe Game Reserve

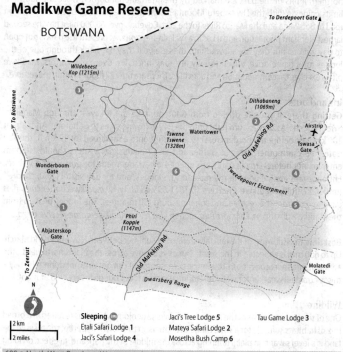

BOTSWANA

To Derdepoort Gate

Wildebeest
Kop (1215m)
3

To Botswana

Dithabaneng
(1069m)
2

Tswene
Tswene   Watertower
(1328m)

Airstrip

Tswasa
Gate

Old Mafeking Rd

Wonderboom
Gate

6

4

Tweedepoort Escarpment

5

Phiri
Koppie
(1147m)

Abjaterskop
Gate

1

Old Mafeking Rd

To Zeerust

Molatedi
Gate

N

Dwarsberg Range

2 km
2 miles

Sleeping 🛏
Etali Safari Lodge **1**
Jaci's Safari Lodge **4**

Jaci's Tree Lodge **5**
Mateya Safari Lodge **2**
Mosetlha Bush Camp **6**

Tau Game Lodge **3**

Border crossing: South Africa–Botswana

Pioneer Gate, Tlokweng Gate, Ramatlabama and Makgobistad

The most commonly used border crossings between the North West Province and Botswana is **Pioneer Gate** (24 hours), 56 km northwest of Zeerust, the route most of the haulage trucks take along on the N4 between Tshwane (Pretoria) and Gaborone, and part of the Great Kalahari Highway that stretches all the way to Walvis Bay in Namibia. **Tlokweng Gate** (6000-2200), next to Madikwe Game Reserve and 101 km north of Zeerust on the R49, is an alternative crossing and links with Botswana's main A1 highway between Gaborone and Francistown. The **Ramatlabama** (0600-2000) border post is on the R503, 26 km north of Mafikeng, which is more convenient if coming from the Cape or interior of South Africa. Around 70 km west of Mafikeng is the **Makgobistad** border post which, despite being more remote on a minor road, is open 24 hours so is an alternative to Ramatlabama if crossing at night.

Customs and immigration All the borders are easy to cross and formalities at customs and immigration are quick and courteous.

Facilities There are bureaux de change at the border where you can change rand into Botswana pula, as well as small duty-free shops (mostly booze and cigarettes) and a VAT refund desk (see page 56).

Public transport Intercape buses use the Pioneer Gate border post on the service between Tshwane (Pretoria) and Gaborone – the Botswana capital is only 102 km north of the border.

Vehicle formalities If you are in a hire car, ensure that you have documentation from the car rental company that allows you to take a car out of South Africa. Botswana is part of the Southern Africa Development Community (SADC) customs agreement so if you are in your own car travelling on a carnet, you do not need to produce your carnet here and won't need to until you reach Zimbabwe or Zambia which are outside SADC. You simply fill out the car's details in a book. On the Botswana side you will have to pay for temporary third-party insurance but this costs very little.

---

conservation corridor that will join Madikwe with Pilanesberg (as the crow flies, about 75 km apart). This proposed conservation estate will allow greater migration for the animals, creating a prime ecotourism destination. It's expected to take many years to achieve, as although the land inbetween the two parks is effectively empty, it is privately owned and used for marginal cattle-grazing, though the initiative has the support of the local people.

South of Mmabatho ►► *Colour map 1, B5.*

After leaving Mafikeng, the R27 leads southwest across a large expanse of unremarkable savannah broken only by the occasional stands of acacia trees. For most of the year this is a hot and dusty region, in desperate need of rain. Most of the country is given over to farming cattle, maize and groundnuts and it's often referred to as the 'Texas of South Africa' given its featureless plains and agricultural economy. **Stella**, 181 km from Mafikeng, is the largest settlement between Mafikeng and Vryburg. This is a typical, quiet farming centre where nothing much seems to be going on when you drive through. However, every October the town wakes up for the national **Cattle and Beef Festival**, which attracts farmers from all over the country.

No matter which direction you approach from, the size of Vryburg often takes visitors by surprise, appearing as it does in the middle of a vast area of flat dry savannah. This is an important cattle centre where an auction is held every Friday. From Vryburg, the N14 continues 126 km to Kuruman in the Northern Cape (see page 755).

Background

The early history of Vryburg is interesting in so far as it provides a vivid picture of life along the frontier of the British empire. Before the arrival of any organized form of authority in the region, there was a protracted war between the Tlapin people of Chief Mankwarane and the Koranna Khoikhoi, led by David Massouw. In an effort to win the conflict, Massouw offered farms to a collection of European mercenaries as their share of the loot and eventually 416 farms were given away. Shortly afterwards, in August 1883, the ex-mercenaries proclaimed their block of farms to be a new (short-lived) independent republic, which would be known as Stellaland. The capital of this new republic was Vryburg, the 'town of freedom'.

Sights

Leon Taljaardt Nature Reserve ① *Apr-Aug 0700-1500, Sep-Mar 0700-1800, free,* 5 km from the town centre, to the left off the Botswana road, is the municipal game reserve. It's a small, pleasant reserve with a mix of plains game, including black and blue wildebeest, eland, gemsbok, impala, red hartebeest, Burchell's and mountain zebra and waterbuck.

◉ Central region listings

For Sleeping and Eating price codes and other relevant information, see pages 46-53.

● Sleeping

Mafikeng and Mmabatho *p694*

B Mmabatho Palms, Nelson Mandela Drive, Mmabatho, T018-389 1839, www.peermont. com. Modern hotel complex with several restaurants, swimming pool, 18-hole golf course and casino. It was once an important gambling centre when gaming was illegal in the rest of South Africa, but now looks some-what out of place next to the dusty townships.
B Protea Hotel Mafikeng, 80 Nelson Mandela Drive, Mafikeng, T018-381 0400, www.proteahotels.com. Newly built and another quality Protea hotel. 99 a/c rooms with DSTV and pleasant modern decor, swimming pool, bar, good restaurant with generous buffet breakfast, professional service.
C Buffalo Park Lodge, 59 Molopo St, corner of Botha and Molopo streets, Mafikeng, T018-

381 2159, www.buffalolodge.co.za. Modern guesthouse with 20 simply decorated rooms, mix of en suite double and twin rooms, all with DSTV. Swimming pool, very popular bar and restaurant, home-cooked meals and good Sun lunch.
C Ferns Country House, 12 Cook St, Mafikeng, T018-381 5971, www.restinations. co.za/ferns. A modern quality guesthouse with 24 double rooms. Pleasant decor, a/c, en suite bath or shower, TV, guest lounge, bar, laundry service, swimming pool, secure parking. Good value. The smart restaurant is probably one of the better places to eat in town.
D Getaway Lodge, corner Tillard and Baden Powell streets, Mafikeng, T018-381 6717, www.travellodge.co.za. Friendly guesthouse in a good, central location, with 33 en suite rooms with TV, fridge, good reasonably priced restaurant and relaxing gardens with swimming pool. Very welcoming staff who can advise on what to do in the area.

Also run 2 other similar lodges in Mafikeng, which jointly offer conference facilities.

Botsalano Game Reserve *p696*
Reservations T018-381 5611, www.tourismnorthwest.co.za/botsalano.
E Mogobe Tented Camp. 4 tents with 2 beds in each, bedding supplied, shared ablutions and fully equipped kitchen. The camp is in a typical shady thicket overlooking Mogobe Dam, in a central position.

Camping
Next to the main entrance gate, open camp-site and picnic area with basic amenities.

Zeerust *p697*
D-E Kranz Hotel, on the N4, 1.5 km to the east of Zeerust, T018-642 2008, www.kranz hotel.co.za. Mix of guestrooms and rondavels set in gardens, this is good value and the most comfortable and friendly option in town. 19 a/c rooms with en suite bathrooms and DSTV, and cheaper accommodation in 10 simple rondavels with showers and braais round the back. Camping and caravan site. Restaurant, bar serving home-distilled peach schnapps, lounge, swimming pool, gardens, secure parking, rates include breakfast.

Madikwe Game Reserve *p697, map p698*
Private lodges and camps
Madikwe is a low-density tourism facility and the luxury lodges are built as far away as possible from each other. There are at present 22 lodges run under various concessions; below are a selection. Rates include all meals and game activities. A full list of lodges can be found at www.madikwe-game-reserve.co.za. Each will provide details about access into the reserve by air or road.
L4 Etali Safari Lodge, reservations T012-346 0124, www.etalisafari.co.za. 8 luxury a/c thatched chalets joined by wooden board-walks, rooms are a blend of contemporary earth colours and crisp white linen, each with a deck and outdoor jacuzzi. The main lodge

has a pool, outdoor gym, there's pampering in the Wellness Centre or beauty therapists will give guests a massage on their private sun deck after a day of game driving. Outside eating around a fire, cuisine is African and Asian using organic vegetables.
L4 Jaci's Safari Lodge and **Jaci's Tree Lodge**, T014-778 9900, www.madikwe.com. Both lodges regularly win awards. The **Safari Lodge** has 8 large thatched suites with gauze walls, double-poster beds, handcrafted stone baths, outside shower, private plunge pool, viewing deck, personal safari guide for all game drives, walks and information. The **Tree Lodge** comprises 8 treehouses on stilts up to 4 m from the ground, built in the arms of giant leadwood or tambotie trees, outdoor jungle shower and stone bath, private decks, linked by raised boardwalks, central outside boma for eating set on a circular candlelit table around a fire.
L4 Mateya Safari Lodge, T014-778 9200, www.mateyasafari.com. 5 enormous, super-luxurious, thatched suites, en suite bathrooms and open-air showers, each with its own pool and deck with views of the plains and a waterhole below. The lodge is decorated with a valuable African art collection with pieces from as far away as Cameroon and Ghana, the library has 3500 books, the wine cellar has 7000 bottles, and there are 40 staff to look after the whims of only 10 guests.
L3 Tau Game Lodge, reservations T011-131 44350, www.taugamelodge.co.za. 30 luxury chalets with en suite bathrooms, private wooden view/sun deck and swimming pool. Not as luxurious and a bit more crowded than some of the lodges but very comfortable nevertheless. The chalets are arranged in an arc looking out onto a large seasonal waterhole, allowing good game viewing. Also has a spa and a kid's club that organizes children's game experiences..
L1 Mosetlha Bushcamp, reservations T011-444 9345, www.thebushcamp.com. Good-value alternative to the luxury camps. Offers rustic accommodation in an unfenced camp without electricity, with 9 simple, raised

wooden cabins with oil lamps, shared outdoor safari showers, bush food cooked over an open fire. The camp is in the middle of the park close to the Tswene Tswene Hills, game drives or guided walks are available twice a day, the guides are exceptionally good. Friendly and well run.

Vryburg p700

D Lockerbie Lodge, corner of Vry and Van Neikerk streets, T053-927 2302, www.locker bielodge.co.za. 15 rooms, 5 of which are family self-catering units. Comfortable with TV and heating, swimming pool and motel-style parking. The original part of the lodge was built in 1890.

D Villa Lin-Zane, 4 km out of town on the N14 towards Tshwane (Pretoria), T053-927 2654, www.villalinzane.com. Simple B&B with 4 doubles and 1 family room, a/c and private entrances, tea trays, rustic wooden furniture, spacious gardens, pool and braai. Can organize braai packs with side dishes for supper.

🍴 Eating

Mafikeng and Mmabatho p694
Apart from the obligatory **Spur** (♈), found in most of South Africa's small towns, there are very few eating options in either town. Unusually, however, most of the hotels and guesthouses have their own decent, à la carte restaurants, which are reasonably priced and open to non-residents. These are where local people go out to eat.

Vryburg p700

Chain steakhouses and little else; vegetarians may struggle to find something to eat.

🛍 Shopping

Mafikeng and Mmabatho p694
Despite being in a remote corner of the country, Mafikeng and Mmabatho surprisingly feature all the major South African chain stores as its popular with shoppers from Botswana who make the most of the favourable exchange rate and VAT refunds. **Mega City** is a modern shopping centre close to the parliament buildings in Mmabatho. It has a 4-screen cinema and outside the main entrance is a small selection of Botswana curio sellers with some marula, mopane and ebony carvings. **The Crossing** is on the corner of Nelson Mandela and Sekame drives in Mafikeng and features a large branch of Pick 'n Pay and a Woolworths.

⊖ Transport

Mafikeng and Mmabatho p694
It's 217 km to **Gaborone**, 287 km to **Johannesburg**, 320 km to **Kimberley**, 200 km to **Rustenburg**, 156 km to **Vryburg**, 70 km to **Zeerust**. Although you can fly to Mafikeng, once there public transport is almost nonexistent and there are no buses or trains; you will need a car to explore this region.

Air

Mafikeng/Mmabatho International Airport is 15 km north of the city centre. Follow Dr. Albert Lithuli Dr from Nelson Mandela Dr (N18), the turn-off is 4 km southwest of Mafikeng centre, information T018-385 1130. SAA, T011-978 1111, www.flysaa.com, operate daily flights (1 hr) to **Johannesburg**. No interational flights but the airport has international status for cargo.

Car hire

Avis, at the airport, T018-385 1114, www.avis. co.za; **Tempest**, 46 Carrington Rd, Mafikeng, T018-381 4070, www.tempestcarhire.co.za.

Vryburg p700

It's 250 km to **Botswana** (Bray), 420 km to **Johannesburg**, 212 km to **Kimberley**, 156 km to **Mafikeng**, 400 km to **Upington**.

Eastern region

The eastern region of the province gets the lion's share of visitors, thanks to the extravagant attractions of Sun City and the excellent Pilanesberg Game Reserve, where stocks of game readily stand to attention for camera-toting safari enthusiasts. Surrounding the historic town of Rustenburg are the gently rolling Magaliesberg Mountains, which, thanks to their proximity to the urban sprawl of Tshwane (Pretoria) and Johannesburg, are a popular weekend retreat offering a number of good country hotels and nature reserves. It's a scenic region for sports and outdoor pursuits and the mountains are ideal for hiking. ►► *For listings, see pages 712-716.*

Pretoria to Botswana

The N4, which heads westwards from Tshwane (Pretoria), is a toll road and therefore avoided by most local traffic, which sticks to an alternative route via the R27. The N4 has been upgraded and most of the tract between Gauteng and Botswana is well maintained tar broken up by frequent toll gates. This road is part of the Trans-Kalahari Highway which links Tshwane (Pretoria) with Walvis Bay in Namibia.

Hartbeespoort Dam → *Colour map 2, C2. Altitude: 1200 m.*

The proximity of Johannesburg and Tshwane (Pretoria) (35 km) has made this dam in the Magaliesberg Mountains a popular watersports resort and weekend retreat. Around the shoreline are marinas and large private homes overlooking the lake. For information contact the **Hartbeespoort Dam Information Shop** ① *Dam Doryn crossroads next to the curio market, T012-253 1567, www.hartbeespoortdam.com, Tue-Sun 1000-1700.*

The dam was built in 1923 in a narrow gorge where the Crocodile River cuts through the Magaliesberg Mountains. There are two major canals which conduct water away from the dam into a series of smaller canals that irrigate the farmlands around Brits. The old main road from Tshwane (Pretoria) runs through the village of **Schoemansville** on the north shore of the lake before crossing the dam wall and continuing to Rustenburg and Sun City. There is a **Snake and Animal Park** ① *T012-253 1162, www.hartbeespoortsnake animalpark.co.za, daily, 0800-1730, R50, children (3-12) R20, tea garden,* which remains a popular attraction for visiting families from Gauteng, but alongside the collection of reptiles are chimpanzees, panthers and Bengal tigers, making it unpleasant and zoo-like. Boat trips on the dam leave hourly and there are seal demonstrations at 1200 and 1500 on Saturday and Sunday. Also here is the **Hartbeespoort Dam Cableway** ① *on the R513 towards Tshwane (Pretoria), T012-253 1706, Mon-Fri 1000-1530, Sat and Sun 1000-1700, R30,* a 2.3-km link to one of the highest points of the Magaliesberg Mountains, and the **De Wildt Cheetah Centre** ① *on the R513, T012-504 1921, www.dewildt.org.za, R145, children (6-12) R70, under 6s free, extra fee for a photograph with a cheetah (when available), 2-hr tours Tue-Sat at 1000 and 1400, booking ahead is essential,* an important breeding centre famous for being the first such place where a cheetah was successfully born in captivity. Other species include wild dog, brown hyena and vultures. The tour begins with a talk about the centre and the genetics of cheetahs, followed by a game drive around the spacious enclosures. There is also a set lunch, but this must be booked in advance.

Once over the dam wall from Schoemansville, the road reaches the Dam Doryn cross-roads where the tourist office, the Welwitschia Country Market (see page 715) and a large curio market are located. From here, 2 km along the R104 is the **Elephant Sanctuary**

Hartbeespoort Dam ① *T012-258 0423, www.elephantsanctuary.co.za, daily programmes start at 0800, 1000 and 1400, starting from R375, children (3-14) R195,* which is a sister operation of the elephant sanctuaries on the Garden Route (see page 323) and in Hazyview (see page 647). Guests can interact with the five tame elephants and ride them. Check the website for programmes, some include lunch or dinner. There's luxury accommodation (**L**) and overnight guests can 'brush down' the elephants first thing in the morning.

Brits → *Colour map 2, B2.*

Brits is a medium-sized industrial centre surrounded by highly productive farmlands irrigated from the Hartbeespoort Dam. It is also, incidentally, the sole producer in Africa of optical fibres. However, most visitors steam past Brits on their way west and are only likely to pass through town if heading north to the little-known Borakalalo Game Reserve (see below), one of several excellent reserves tucked away in the province.

Borakalalo Game Reserve ◉ ▸▸ *pp712-716. Colour map 2, B2.*

① *T012-252 0131, www.borakalalo.co.za, Apr-Aug 0600-1900, Sep-Mar 0500-2000, R25, children (2-12) R15, car R10.*

This is a pleasant nature reserve north of Tshwane (Pretoria), primarily known for the excellent fishing in the Klipvoor Dam (permits issued at the gate). The reserve surrounds the dam and the area on the northern shore has been restocked with a variety of wild animals, so visitors have a choice of hiking, game viewing or fishing. There is a small shop at the main gate.

Ins and outs

Getting there From Brits, take the R512 and then the right turning signposted Lethlabile. After Lethlabile follow the signs for Jericho. At Jericho take a right at the T-junction and then the first left signposted Legonyane. The reserve is signposted along this road. There is no petrol available here, so fill up in advance.

Best time to visit The reserve receives most of its rain during the summer months, October to April; the summer temperatures range from a very hot 37°C to an average 20°C in the evening. During winter it can get very cold at night.

Wildlife

At 13,000 ha this was, for a time, the second largest national park in the former Bophuthatswana. It is closer to Tshwane (Pretoria) than Pilanesberg Game Reserve, yet it receives far fewer visitors. Since the reserve was proclaimed in 1984, there has been a complete restocking programme in order to replace the animals that once roamed the plains: white rhino, buffalo, giraffe, zebra, eland, hippo, buffalo, nyala, leopard, crocodile, jackal, tsessebe, gemsbok and roan antelope. There are over 350 species of bird in the park – enough to keep any keen ornithologist happy. Several sturdy hides have been built where you can enjoy viewing the wildlife without being stuck inside a car.

The Moretele River flows through the park which encompasses the 800-ha **Klipvoor Dam**. The dam contains carp, bream and barbel. To the southwest of the dam is the game-viewing area, where 50 km of gravel roads have been cut through the open savannah woodland. There is also another small dam, **Sefudi Dam**, where animals may be seen drinking.

Royal baFokeng Kingdom

Located on the mineral-rich Merensky Reef, which is the world's richest platinum deposit, the 800-year-old baFokeng Kingdom spreads over 45 farms, or around 70,000 ha, to the northwest of Rustenberg. The people number around 300,000 and the administrative capital is Phokeng.

A branch of the Sotho-Tswana people, the name baFokeng means 'people of the dew' and is thought to refer to the good climate for agriculture, probably the reason they originally settled here. In 1999, the baFokeng people won a benchmark legal battle for compensation from the platinum companies mining their land. They now receive annual royalties and have been given substantial shares in Impala Platinum Holdings and SA Chrome and Alloys. In the last decade the baFokeng have used this income to build schools, civic buildings, roads, clinics and the **Royal Bafokeng Stadium** (a venue for the 2010 FIFA World Cup™). Much of this development has been spearheaded by the peoples' king, Kgosi Leruo Molotlegi, who holds a degree in architecture and urban planning and is a member of the Mineral Rights Association of Indigenous People of South Africa.

Hiking trails

One of the most rewarding experiences is to go on a self-guided walk through the riverine forest along the banks of the Moretele River, these vary from 1-4 km. Guides are available for the longer walks, which are usually made in the early morning and last up to three hours.

Rustenburg ⊖❶❷❶ ▸▸ pp712-716. Colour map 2, B1.

→ *Phone code: 014. Altitude: 1160 m.*

Rustenburg, or 'castle of rest', is one of the oldest towns in the region and was an important centre under the Transvaal Republic. Today, much of its old charm has disappeared and it is little more than a scruffy, sprawling crossroads between Gauteng, Sun City and Pilanesburg. Nevertheless, its proximity to Johannesburg and Tshwane (Pretoria) on the one hand, and the Magaliesberg Mountains and the Kgaswane Mountain Reserve on the other, means that the country hotels outside of town are often full and it's a good idea to book in advance. The Royal Bafokeng Stadium, a venue for 2010 FIFA World Cup South Africa ™, is on the R565, 12 km northwest of Rustenburg in Phokeng and is named after the baFokeng people in the area (see box, above). It's the only South African stadium hosting the tournament that is not in a city, Phokeng itself is little more than an overgrown village. Nevertheless, it's a much used venue and South Africans refer to it as the 'Stadium in the Village'. The nearest accommodation is in Rustenburg or Sun City.

Ins and outs

Getting around There is little in the way of public transport and a hire car is essential for exploring the area. If you're heading to Sun City, Pilanesberg or Madikwe, go straight through.

Tourist information Rustenburg Tourism Information and Development Centre ⓘ *corner of Nelson Mandela Drive and Kloof St, T014-597 0904, outskirts of town, visible when approaching from the Tshwane side on the N4, Mon-Fri 0800-1630, Sat 0800-1200,* is staffed by a friendly and enthusiastic team (take accommodation recommendations with a pinch of salt). The office has some useful maps and leaflets for the **Magalies Meander** ⓘ *www.magaliesmeander.co.za,*

Rustenburg, the Magaliesberg & Sun City

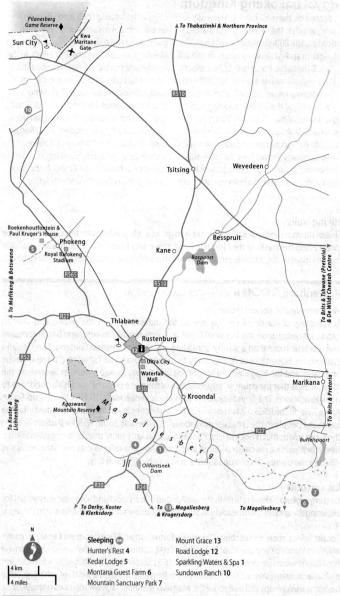

Pilanesberg Game Reserve

Sun City

Kwa Maritane Gate

▲ To Thabazimbi & Northern Province

R510

Tsitsing

Wevedeen

Boekenhoutfontein & Paul Kruger's House

Phokeng

Royal Bafokeng Stadium

R565

Besspruit

Kane

Bospoort Dam

R510

To Mafikeng & Botswana

To Brits & Tshwane (Pretoria) & De Wildt Cheetah Centre

R27

Thlabane

R52

Rustenburg

Ultra City

Waterfall Mall

R30

Kroondal

Marikana

To Koster & Lichtenburg

Kgaswane Mountain Reserve

Magaliesberg

R27

To Brits & Pretoria

R24

Olifantsnek Dam

Buffelspoort

R30

To Derby, Koster & Klerksdorp

To 13, Magaliesberg & Krugersdorp

To Magaliesberg

N

4 km

4 miles

Sleeping
Hunter's Rest 4
Kedar Lodge 5
Montana Guest Farm 6
Mountain Sanctuary Park 7

Mount Grace 13
Road Lodge 12
Sparkling Waters & Spa 1
Sundown Ranch 10

a self-drive route through the mountains. It's a satellite office for the **North West Parks and Tourism Board** so they can provide information on the whole region.

Background
The first white settlers were a group of burghers who had followed the Voortrekker leader Andries Pretorius from the Cape. Among the first Voortrekkers to start farming on the northern slopes of the fertile Magaliesberg in the mid-1800s were AH Potgieter and Casper Kruger, the father of the future president of the Transvaal, Paul Kruger.

During the short existence of the Boer Republic, Rustenburg was the capital before the government moved to Pretoria. On 16 March 1852, it was the scene of the reconciliation between Andries Pretorius and Hendrik Potgieter, two of the leaders of the splintered Voortrekkers' Great Trek. This was an important step within the republic, as Pretorius had gone to the Orange Free State and Potgieter to the Eastern Transvaal and Mozambique. Reconciling their differences helped unify the two states as a strong force against the British.

Sights
Despite being the third oldest town in the region and an important historic settling point for the Voortrekkers, there is little of historical interest within Rustenburg. Two exceptions are **Hervormde Church Square**, which was the site of the reconciliation between Andries Pretorius and Hendrik Potgieter, and the **Statue of a Voortrekker Girl** in Plein Street opposite the Hervormde Church. The candle represents the introduction of Christianity to the area.

Around Rustenburg
Paul Kruger Country House Museum ⓘ *18 km northwest of Rustenburg, off the R565 towards Sun City, look out for a left turning just after Phokeng, T014-573 3218, www.rali.co.za, daily 1000-1600, R30, children (under 12) R15,* is at Boekenhoutfontein, the farm where Paul Kruger lived as a farmer before he became the president of the Transvaal Republic from 1883 until the end of the Anglo-Boer War. Four buildings have been preserved and restored as museums to the life of Paul Kruger and the earliest farmers in the Transvaal. The oldest building is a cottage built in 1841 by the first owner of Boekenhoutfontein, a single-storey building with a thatched roof and stone patio out front. When Paul Kruger moved here in 1863, he built a new thatched homestead for his family, known as the 'Pioneer House'. To its right stands the main homestead, a double-storey stone house built in 1872 in typical Eastern-Cape style. It contains many of Kruger's possessions along with an assortment of period furniture from other homes. The fourth house, built for Kruger's son Pieter, dates from 1892.

Of the original 500-ha farm, 32 ha have been kept as part of the museum. The gardens have been partially restored and visitors are free to stroll around looking at the birds and plants; picnic areas have been laid out. The old **Rustenburg Museum** has moved here and has a small but interesting collection of local historical items. The statue of Paul Kruger, which used to stand in front of the information office in Rustenburg, has also been moved to Boekenhoutfontein. Sculpted in bronze by a French artist, Jean Archand, the statue was discovered in Paris in 1919 by General Louis Botha and General Jan Smuts. It is of the president sitting grumpily in his armchair during his last days in exile in France.

Magaliesberg Mountains ⊕▲↠ *pp712-716. Colour map 2, C1.*

The Magaliesberg are a range of flat-topped quartzite mountains, which extend roughly from Tshwane (Pretoria) to just beyond Rustenburg. In 1977 the area was declared a Natural

Heritage Site, and the entire area is one of the most visited in South Africa. Much of the mountains have been parcelled off into private resorts, but there remain some pockets of indigenous landscapes, notably in the Pilanesberg Park and Kgaswane Mountain Reserve.

Ins and outs
Getting around To explore the Magaliesberg take the R30 shortly before entering Rustenburg from Tshwane (Pretoria). This road leads up into the mountains to **Olifantsnek**, a gap created by the Hex River. There are plenty of hotels and resorts along this road.

Background
When the first white hunters came to the region they named the hills the 'Cashan Mountains', a corruption of Khashane, the name of the local chief. They were renamed by the Voortrekkers who called the range after another local leader, Mohale, which they misspelt as Magalie.

The region witnessed a number of bloody battles during the 19th century. The first major conflicts were between Mzilikazi, leader of the Ndebele, and the local peoples when he arrived here from modern-day KwaZulu Natal. A few decades later, the mountains were the scene of several important battles during the Anglo-Boer War. One of these was the Battle of Nooitgedacht on 13 December 1900, in which the British forces suffered their heaviest defeat since their arrival in July 1900. Three hundred men were killed and a similar number taken prisoner, and the Boers managed to seize 70 full wagons, 200 tents, ammunition, 300 mules, some cattle and over 400 horses. The gorge where the battle took place is just off the R560 close to Hekpoort.

Wildlife and vegetation
The range is about 160 km long, reaching 1852 m at its highest point – which is actually no more than 400 m above the surrounding countryside. The difference in elevation is, however, sufficient to ensure that the hills receive a relatively high rainfall and are far greener than the plains, with some remaining stands of forest. Most of the wild animals that once lived in the hills have long since been hunted out. An exception can be found on the ledges on the south-facing cliff faces, which are important nesting sites for the endangered Cape vulture. The north-facing slopes are no more than a gentle climb, cut by mountain streams and leafy gorges. The range forms the natural divide between the cool Highveld to the south and the warm bushveld to the north.

Kgaswane Mountain Reserve ☺ ▶▶ pp712-716. Colour map 2, B/C1.
ⓘ T014-533 2050, www.tourismnorthwest.co.za/kgaswane. Sep-Mar 0530-1900, Apr-Aug 0600-1830, R20, children (2-12) R10, car R10.
This popular mountain reserve stretches along the summit and the northern slopes of the Magaliesberg range, 400 m above Rustenburg, providing excellent hiking territory. The reserve is an important recreational area for visitors from Johannesburg and Tshwane (Pretoria), just over 100 km away, and school buses are a regular sight. Because it is so close to the large cities, the number of visitors is tightly controlled and anyone wishing to camp or enjoy the longer hiking trails needs to book well in advance.

Ins and outs
From the centre of Rustenburg, follow Wolmarans Street (from the junction with Van Staden by the municipal offices) through the residential suburbs to the very end where it then

curves to the left and becomes Boekenhout Road. Follow this road out of town until you come to a T-junction, turn left (the right is signposted to the **Ananda Hotel**). Shortly after passing Rustenburg Kloof, just before the entrance gates to the **Orion Safari Lodge**, is a right turn to the main gates of the reserve. The reserve is not clearly signposted in town.

Wildlife
The land was originally part of Rietvallei farm, which belonged to President Paul Kruger. The reserve was proclaimed in 1967 after the council had been given the land by one of Kruger's descendants. In 1981 the nature reserve was extended to include an adjoining farm to the east and today the total area protected is 4257 ha. From the top of the reserve you can see the flat bushveld to the south, while the ridge of the mountains disappears east towards the Hartbeespoort Dam and Tshwane (Pretoria).

Some of the species of antelope found here include grey duiker, klipspringer, mountain reedbuck, impala, oribi, waterbuck, steenbuck, kudu, sable and red hartebeest. Jackal, leopard, hyena and caracal are also known to live in the mountains. There are also raptors which live high up along the rocky cliff faces. Scops owl, martial eagles and black eagles can be viewed along with an important breeding colony of the endangered Cape vulture.

Hiking
There are currently three marked hiking trails in the reserve. Two are open for day visitors; the third requires spending a couple of nights in the reserve. For information on the trails, www.tourismnorthwest.co.za/kgaswane. Detailed maps are available at the reserve office.

Sun City ⊜⊜ ›› pp712-716. Colour map 2, B1.
Tucked between dusty plains and rolling bushveld is the surreal highrise, neon-lit resort of Sun City, one of the most-visited sights in the country. Much like Las Vegas in the US, the resort was built around gambling and today comprises a vast complex of four hotels, linked by a skytrain, and extravagant recreational facilities, including a fake sandy lagoon and a constructed tropical rainforest. The result is both staggeringly impressive and laughably tacky – all good fun if you take it with a pinch of salt.

Ins and outs
Getting there If arriving by air via Pilanesberg International Airport, 10 km from Sun City, T014-552 1261, www.acsa.co.za, there's a free shuttle service to Sun City. By car, follow Nelson Mandela Street straight out of Rustenburg, past the golf course to your left, and then take the right turning on the R565, signposted Phokeng and Sun City. Shortly before Sun City is a left turn for Pilanesberg Game Reserve. The entrance to Sun City is just after a large shopping mall by the staff housing complex. There is an entrance fee for day visitors, R70 per person, part of which is redeemable in tokens to spend inside at the casino and slots; Valley of the Waves R80, children (under 13) R40. The **Welcome Centre** ① *T014-557 1544, www.suncity.co.za, daily 0800-2000*, is in the middle of the complex and is a good place to start and pick up a map. The free skytrain runs throughout the complex, and shuttle buses run to and from the car park. Day visitors can join an hour's tour of **The Palace of the Lost City** (see below) for R60, between 1130 and 1600, booked at the Welcome Centre.

The complex has four hotels, numerous restaurants and fast-food outlets, two golf courses, a water park, a man-made rainforest, a crocodile park, an aviary, a lake offering watersports, a cultural centre, casino and the Superbowl, a large entertainment hall.

Background

The first part of the complex was opened in 1979, when the central features were the **Sun City Hotel** and a golf course designed by Gary Player. Much of the appeal of Sun City was its gambling licence: the hotel was in Bophuthatswana where gambling was legal. Wealthy whites travelled to what were then the designated black homelands to gamble, and like many other casino resorts from the Apartheid era, the contrasts between the luxury of the resorts and the impoverished areas around them were (and, to some extent, still are) stark.

In the same year, Pilanesberg Game Reserve opened. A year later the second phase was complete – the 284-room **Sun City Cabanas** opened, aimed at families. In 1980 the famous **Sun City Million Dollar Golf Challenge** was founded, and over the years this has attracted most of the world's top golfers. In 1984 the third hotel was opened, the five-star **Cascades**, surrounded by waterfalls, streams and a tract of forest. In 1992 came the icing on the cake: the **Lost City** and the **Valley of the Waves** (see Sights and activities, below).

With the change in gambling laws, visitor numbers dropped sharply in the 1990s, but these have crept up again as the focus has switched from gambling to family entertainment, golf and conferences. Although far removed from the culture and landscapes that draw most tourists to South Africa, Sun City's glitz and garishness is fascinating and worth a day's visit.

Sights and activities

The complex focuses on the newest and most excessive addition to the Sun City stable, the **Palace of the Lost City**, a magnificent hotel completed in 1992. The vaguely Moorish construction is characterized by soaring dome-capped towers ringed by prancing statues of antelope; you can only actually reach the hotel if you're staying there, but regular tours are held for day visitors. Below the hotel is the **Valley of the Waves**, reached by a bridge that trembles and spouts steam during mock earthquakes (every 30 minutes). This stunning artificial sandy lagoon, complete with desert island and palm-lined soft white sand, has a wave machine capable of creating metre-high waves. Day visitors have to pay extra to enter the Valley of the Waves, accessed from the entertainments centre, but this doesn't seem to put anyone off – the beach gets completely packed at weekends, with noisy music pumping out of loudspeakers and every large wave bringing forth a yell of jubilation from the crowds. Smaller swimming pools dotted around the lagoon are quieter.

A welcome retreat lies around the hotel and lagoon, the impressive 25-ha **man-made forest**. Remarkably lush and quiet, the forest was originally made up of 1.6 million plants, trees and shrubs, and the rainforest component includes three layers with creepers and orchids growing in the canopy. Although the moulded cement rocks and perfectly pruned paths give it a distinctly Disney feel, the plants have attracted prolific birdlife and the walking trails, lasting up to 1½ hours, allow a real sense of isolation from the resort.

Elsewhere, an abundance of activities are available to guests. There are two 18-hole golf courses, including the Gary Player course, home to the annual **Nedbank Golf Challenge**, one of the world's great championships with prizes valuing over US$4 million. At **Waterworld**, guests can try parasailing, waterskiing and jetskiing. There is a horse-riding centre, tennis, mini-golf, squash, a gym and spa, mountain biking trails, jogging routes, 10-pin bowling and swimming pools (the more peaceful of which are located in the hotels).

Close to the entrance is **Kwena Gardens Crocodile Sanctuary** with over 7000 crocs, including the three biggest captive Nile crocodiles in the world. Nearby is the **Cultural Village**, where guests are shown around mock-ups of villages of eight tribal groups, with dancing and singing, and a Shebeen serving pan-African cuisine. There's also an aviary, a bird of prey centre, cinemas, a casino, a hall filled with slot machines, and countless restaurants and bars.

ⓘ *T014-555 1600, www.pilanesberg-game-reserve.co.za, Nov-Feb 0530-1900, Mar-Apr 0600-1830, May-Aug 0630-1800, Sep-Oct 0600-1830, R45, children (under 14) R20, car R20.*
This is the fourth largest national park in South Africa, and was created in 1979 to complement the luxury development being built at Sun City. The two have been closely linked ever since.

Ins and outs
Follow directions for Sun City and take the R565 from Rustenburg. Alternatively, follow the R510 from Rustenburg and after 51 km take a left turn, follow this road for a further 5 km past a couple of factories and take a right turn by the petrol station. The entrance to **Pilanesberg Game Reserve** and **Manyane Camp** is just on the left. Tshwane (Pretoria) is about 140 km from the park. It can be visited as a long day trip from Tshwane (Pretoria) or Johannesburg, but most visitors stay at least one night in the region and combine a trip to Pilanesberg with Sun City. Visitors to Sun City can book on one of the numerous two-hour game drives that leave the Welcome Centre throughout the day.

Background and sights
The area earmarked for the park in the 1970s was home to a large number of Tswana people who were either coerced into leaving or forcibly removed – a hugely controversial move, but one that was not reported at the time. On a more positive note, the area's

Pilanesberg Game Reserve

Sleeping 🛏️
Bakgatla Resort 1
Bakubung Lodge 2
Kwa Maritane 3
Manyane Resort 4
Tshukudu Game Lodge 5

reintroduction of game has been heralded as a huge success. This complex and ambitious project was known as Operation Genesis. The animals came from all over southern Africa: elephant and buffalo from Addo Elephant National Park, black and white rhino from the Natal Parks Board, eland from Namibia, Burchell's zebra and waterbuck from the Transvaal and red hartebeest from the Northern Cape and Namibia. As a transition zone between the Kalahari sandveld and the bushveld, it was also the natural habitat for a number of rare species already in existence, including brown hyena, Cape hunting dog and sable antelope. As you drive around the 55,000-ha reserve you now have a good chance of seeing all the large animals, including rhino, elephant, lion, cheetah, buffalo and the occasional leopard. More than 8000 animals have now been successfully introduced.

The park encompasses the caldera of an extinct volcano, which is geographically similar to the Ngorongoro Conservation Area in Tanzania. The crater is surrounded by three concentric rings of hills and in the centre is a lake, **Mankwe Dam**, where you can see crocodile and hippo. The hills are broken up with wooded valleys, which gradually give way to open savannah grasslands. This variety of habitat is ideal for wild animals and it is a rewarding birdwatching environment where over 340 species have been recorded, some of which are extremely rare. A number of walk-in viewing hides have been constructed. Excellent tar and gravel roads traverse the park, and maps and game checklists are available at each of the four gates: Manyane, Bakgatla, Bakubung and Kwa Maritane – the last one being the closest to Sun City.

◉ Eastern region listings

For Sleeping and Eating price codes and other relevant information, see pages 46-53.

● Sleeping

Hartbeespoort Dam *p703*

B Villa Paradiso Country Lodge, 4 km from Schoemansville on the R513 towards Tshwane (Pretoria), T012-253 1847, www.villaparadiso. co.za. 30 smart modern well-equipped rooms with DSTV and balconies or patios with views over the dam or mountains. Cosy little The Rouge, restaurant with bright red walls, and black and white photos and cocktail bar.

B-C Berg & Dam, 90 Scott St, Schoemansville, T012-253 0522, www.bergdam.co.za. 3 modern guesthouses, with a choice of B&B, self-catering or semi-self-catering (ie rooms with microwaves and kettles). All come with TV, en suite, a/c and heating. Pretty gardens, secure parking, meals on request, welcoming staff. Great choice but very popular, often booked months in advance. Recommended.

C-E The Ring Oxwagon Inn, on the R511, 4 km north of the N4, T012-259 1506, www. thering.co.za. 6 chalets attached to historical,

restored and furnished ox-wagons, sleeping up to 6 (double beds in the wagons), en suite bathroom, homely restaurant, pool, cheaper beds available in a backpackers' dorm built in an old double-decker bus, situated high up in the hills with nice views and hiking trails.

D Squires on the Dam, 1 Scott St, opposite the snake and animal park, T012-253 1001, www.squiresonthedam.co.za. A simple set of 8 rooms attached to the Squires on the Dam restaurant. Plain, but comfortable en suite motel rooms with Mnet TV.

Borakalalo Game Reserve *p704*

For reservations contact T012-252 0131, www.borakalalo.co.za.

D Moretele Camp. 2 camps of semi-permanent tents with basic furnishings, including gas lamps and fridge. Self-catering facilities and shared ablution blocks. Bring everything you need with you, including towels and all eating and cooking utensils.

D Phudufudu Safari Camp, set in a secluded corner, shaded by large trees. Tented camp, 10 upmarket tents, fully self-catering. Shared ablution block, central dining area and lounge overlooking a small waterhole. Fully equipped kitchen with freezer and utensils, plunge pool.

Camping

A basic, rustic camp beside the dam, primarily used by anglers. Camping sites have braai area and a water tap, the central washblock is made from reeds, there's hot water and clean washing and toilet facilities. No electricity or fridges.

Rustenburg *p705, map p706*

Most hotels are located beyond the built-up area towards the Magaliesberg Mountains. In town, the choice is fairly dire. The fine country resort hotels in the Magaliesberg range are far more attractive, or the (albeit pricey) hotels in Sun City and Pilanesberg Game Reserve.

A-B Kedar Lodge, 20 km from Rustenburg towards Sun City on the R565, T014-573 3218, www.rali.co.za. A peaceful group of cottages next to the historic farm of President Kruger, with 62 en suite double rooms with DSTV, the de luxe ones feature open log fires, plunge pools, and rustic stone outdoor showers. Zebra and ostrich within the grounds, small restaurant and bar, new addition is a beauty spa. Fishing trips can be organized from here.

C Sundown Ranch, 33 km from Rustenburg centre, on the R565, T014-573 1000, www.sundownlionpark.com. 10 km from Sun City and Pilanesberg Game Reserve. 101 double hotel rooms set within 1600 ha of grounds, 2 restaurants, swimming pool in a palm courtyard, outdoor bar, tennis courts, squash, bowls, horse trails and a lion park, where visitors can play with lion cubs. Dated decor but cheaper than the hotels in Sun City.

D Bergsig Lodge, 9 Fourth Av, T014-597 4844, www.bergsiglodge.co.za. Friendly B&B with handful of double rooms and a couple of singles with en suite facilities. Ceiling fans, TV lounge, M-Net, separate entrance, braai area, swimming pool and well-kept garden with shady corners. Central location, secure parking. Dinner available. Well-run and good value.

D Road Lodge, on the N4, corner Howick and Magaliesberg roads, T014-537 3088, www.roadlodge.co.za. Standard functional modern block favoured by business travellers. 90 rooms, TV, same price for 1-3 people, breakfast available in the lobby.

Magaliesberg Mountains *p707, map p706*

L Mount Grace, approaching Magaliesberg village on the R24 towards Johannesburg, T014-577 5600, www.africanpridehotels.com. 121 luxury rooms in thatched cottages set in 10 ha of beautiful gardens with lakes and waterfalls. Heated swimming pool, tennis, library, excellent food, guests are driven around in a golf buggy. Sumptuous spa (see page 16), with hydro pools. Most treatments, such as massages, scrubs, hand and foot grooming, are conducted outside beneath olive trees. Spa and restaurant open to non-guests. No children under 12. Recommended.

A Hunter's Rest, 14 km from Rustenburg on the R30, T014-537 8300, www.hunters rest.co.za. 91 spacious rooms with private patio; a bit of a hike from the furthest room to the restaurant. Bar saves a good range of imported beers and has an English pub feel, large swimming pool, well-kept garden, curio shop. Huge range of activities, including tennis, sauna, squash, fitness centre, horse riding and 9-hole golf course. Good for families.

B Sparkling Waters Hotel & Spa, 10 km off the R24, T014-535 0019, www.sparkling waters.co.za. Pleasant country retreat in a clutch of thatched buildings, with 56 spacious a/c rooms and plenty of family-friendly activities, including tennis, swimming pools, a sand pit and games room. Good restaurant, rates include breakfast and dinner. The spa is quite special with an indoor pool, hydro-therapy rooms, gym and outdoor jacuzzi.

D Montana Guest Farm, 15 km on good dirt road south off the R104, clearly signposted, T014-534 0113, www.montanagf.co.za. 8 self-catering chalets, some with thatched roofs. Well-equipped kitchens, surrounded by the woodlands of the Magaliesberg, pool, pub and games room. No restaurant, bring your own food. Small and friendly with some excellent local hikes.

D Mountain Sanctuary Park, a private nature reserve in the mountains 35 km from Rustenburg, T014-534 0114, www.mountain-sanctuary.co.za. Simple rest camp, visitor numbers are controlled and there are strict regulations to preserve and maintain this mountain wilderness, so early booking is advised even for day visits. Self-catering chalets, fully equipped and furnished (but bring your own towels, soap and food), and a shady campsite with a thatched lapa and freezer facilities. Stunning pool built from natural stone on the lip of the valley, offering fantastic views. Guests have access to over 1000 ha of hiking country. Horse trails offered.

Kgaswane Mountain Reserve *p708*
E Hiking Huts, reservations T014-533 2050. Offers 4 huts sleeping 4. Between the 2 bedrooms is a communal seating and dining area. Meals have to be cooked by wood fire over a braai, cooking pots, buckets to collect water and 2 lamps are provided. There is also a veld toilet close by. During the winter months you'll need a sleeping bag.

Sun City *p709, map p706*
The whole complex is part of the **Sun International Group**, central reservations T011-780 7800, www.suninternational.com. The rooms aren't cheap and a double starts from around R2000 at the **Cabanas** and R5000 at the **Palace of the Lost City**, but are of a very high standard. The hotels listed below must be booked through central reservations. Off-season packages are sometimes available.
L The Cascades. Has the best of both worlds: it has 5-star amenities but is neither over the top nor overrun with families. The 242 a/c rooms have been renovated in muted colours, with dark wood furniture and olive and beige fabrics. M-Net TV, minibar, stylish bathrooms, 24-hr room service. All rooms face the forest and pools with waterfalls and streams. The **Peninsula** is a smart international restaurant with a weekend buffet. The **Santorini** is a Greek and seafood restaurant overlooking the pool and there are 2 bars.

L The Palace of the Lost City, is the central point of the complex. Both impossibly kitsch and beautifully lavish. 338 a/c rooms spread across a string of airy courtyards, each over-looking fountains and sculptures of game. The entrance is marked by a super-sized sculpture of cheetahs hunting, surrounded by lakes and fountains. The lobby is a palatial hall lined with vast columns, leading to a variety of restaurants and elegant bars. It's all totally over the top, and has attracted so many goggling visitors that only guests are now allowed entry, unless you're on a pre-paid tour (organized through the **Welcome Centre**). Villa del Palazzo, with its classic northern Italian cuisine, is an excellent restaurant over-looking the pools; **Crystal Court** has gourmet cuisine, live piano music and is surrounded by jungle (smart dress code). Elsewhere there are 3 bars and a poolside snack bar; a selection of shops, a beauty spa and a heated pool.
L Sun City. The original hotel was refurbished in 2007 and now offers 341 a/c rooms over-looking the swimming pool and lush lawns. There's plenty of choice on the restaurant front: **Setta Bello**, à la carte; **The Calabash**, carvery and salad bar; **Sun Terrace**, fast food during the day, formal restaurant at night; and **The Orchid**, which offers an Asian inspired menu. There are also 4 cocktail bars.
AL Sun City Cabanas. 144 standard cabanas for 2 people; 236 family cabanas which can accommodate 4, all with a/c and TV. Cottages set in neat gardens close to a lake and **Water-world**, with a kid's petting farm and adventure playground. Best-value option available, and has families firmly in mind. **Palm Terrace** is an informal buffet restaurant with a supervised kid's play area; **Pool Bar** serves snacks.

Pilanesberg Game Reserve *p711, map p711*
These 2 are run by **Golden Leopard Resorts**, T014-555 1000, www.goldenleopard.co.za.
AL-B Manyane Resort, 300 m from Manyane Gate. Sixty 2- to 6-bed self-catering thatched chalets with kitchen, lounge, bathroom, braai and a couple of swimming pools among the

chalets. Behind the chalets is a caravan and campsite with electric points, clean wash-blocks and shady trees. Breakfast is included in the rates for the chalets and there's a central restaurant block open for all meals. Bar, central swimming pool, children's play area. The camp is in open savannah grasslands with a few trees dotted about. Can get very busy during school holidays. There is a day visitors' complex with a shop, picnic area, swimming pool, a couple of walk-in aviaries, a 4WD track, walking trails, and mini-golf.

AL-D Bakgatla Resort, at the northwest of the park close to the Bakgatla Gate. 58 self-catering chalets, sleeping maximum, all a/c and are fitted with a kitchen, en suite bath-room, lounge area plus a private patio and braai area. At the centre of the complex is a large swimming pool, picnic site and kiosk. Rates include breakfast and if guests don't want to self-cater there's a restaurant offering buffet meals. There are also 5 cheaper en suite safari tents (not self-catering) (**D**) and a limited number of caravan and campsites. The camp-sites have a central kiosk and a small bar.

Private lodges and camps

Several camps within the reserve, operated by different concessionaries. Advance booking is essential. The following 3 lodges are part of **Legacy Hotels Group**, reservations T011-806 6888, www.legacyhotels.co.za. **Bakubung** and **Kwa Maritane** also have time-share self-catering chalets that may be available to international visitors so it's worth enquiring.

L4 Tshukudu Game Lodge, in the middle of the park on the slope of a steep rock outcrop, www.tshukudu.co.za. 6 chalets built into the rock with slate floors, wicker furniture, a fire-place, beds on an elevated platform, sunken double bath with a view, lounge area with bar fridge, and books and magazines. Chalets linked to the main lodge by a steep, winding stone staircase (not for the elderly or less mobile) and from the top you have clear views of the park and a floodlit waterhole. Restaurant, bar, pool. Rates include meals, game drives and transfers. No children under 12.

L1 Bakubung Lodge, on the southwest edge of the park, 10 km from Sun City, www.baku bung.co.za. Large complex with 76 a/c rooms with patios or balconies. Rates from R3400 for a double include breakfast and dinner. There's a restaurant, bar, curio shop, tennis court and swimming pool but game drives and hikes are extra. Superb views of the surrounding bush and a waterhole with resident hippos. Free shuttle to Sun City every couple of hours.

L1 Kwa Maritane, near the gate of the same name, in the south of the park, www.kwa maritane.co.za. A smart bush lodge with 90 a/c rooms, each with a TV, high thatched ceilings, and a private veranda. Restaurant, and rates from R3400 include breakfast and dinner. Nearby waterhole with underground hide reached via a 180-m tunnel from the lodge. Game drives and guided walks are extra. 2 swimming pools, floodlit tennis courts, table tennis, sauna and gym. Free shuttle to Sun City.

🍴 Eating

Rustenburg *p705, map p706*
There is little choice in the town centre and most restaurants are in the shopping centre area of the **Waterfall Mall** on the edge of town on the R30; here there's a predictable range of pasta, steak and fast-food joints. Otherwise, there are some fine restaurants in the Magaliesburg Mountain resorts and hotels and of course top-class dining at Sun City.

🛍 Shopping

Hartbeespoort Dam *p703*
At the junction after crossing the Hartbees-poort Dam on the R514 from Schoemansville is an enormous open-air curio market and the **Welwitschia Country Market**, T083-302 8085, www.countrymarket.co.za, Tue-Sun 0900-1700. Over 40 shops, in prefabricated sheds arranged in lanes, sell crafts, clothes, snacks, furniture, toys and all manner of other things aimed at day trippers from the cities. There are also

2 open-air restaurants and a mini kids' fairground and live (Afrikaans) music at weekends.

▲ Activities and tours

Magaliesberg Mountains *p707, map p706*
Most resorts are equipped with a range of sports facilities. Pick up a map for **Magalies Meander**, www.magaliesmeander.co.za, or the **Crocodile Ramble**, www.theramble.co.za, at the tourist office in Rustenburg. Both maps list craft shops, accommodation, sports and restaurants in the region.

Balloon rides
Bill Harrop's Original Balloon Safaris, T011-705 3201, www.balloon.co.za. 1-hr flights over Magaliesberg followed by champagne breakfast, R2515, minimum 2 people.

Hiking
Hiking remains the most popular pastime in the region and each resort has their own hiking trails (some lead further up into the mountains). Maps and permits from resorts.

Pilanesberg Game Reserve *p711, map p711*
Balloon rides
Air Trackers, desk at **Welcome Centre**, Sun City, T014-552 5020, www.airtrackers.co.za. 1-hr safari flights from the centre of the reserve, price includes transfers, a glass of bubbly and game drive to, and breakfast at, one of the lodges. R3200 per person.

Safaris
You'll get most out of the park by going on a guided tour, as rangers are in constant contact and monitor movements of the Big Five.
Game Trackers, desk at **Welcome Centre**, Sun City, T014-552 5020, www.gametrac.co.za. If visiting Sun City on a day or overnight trip, 2½-hr guided tours leave from **Welcome Centre**, R350, children (10-16) R200, (under 10) R130. 2-hr night drives, R370, children

(10-16) R230, (under 10) R140. Also organize a number of other activities, including quad-biking, archery and clay-pigeon shooting.
Mankwe Safaris, Pilanesberg's Manyane Gate, T014-555 7056, www.mankwesafaris.co.za. 2½-hr game drives in the morning, afternoon and at night, R295, children (under 10) R150.
Pilanesberg Elephant Back Safaris, pick ups and booking at **Welcome Centre**, T014-552 5020, www.pilanesbergelephantback.co.za. The 5 elephants can carry 2 riders, plus the guide and there's a baby elephant. Silently travelling through the bush on an elephant is a unique game-viewing experience. The ride takes about 1 hr but the whole excursion lasts 2-3 hrs, and includes interaction with the elephants; R1440, no children under 5.

⊖ Transport

Rustenburg *p705, map p706*
48 km to **Sun City** via R27 and R565, 200 km to **Mafikeng**, 130 km to **Zeerust**, 105 km to **Tshwane**, 112 km to **Johannesburg**.

Sun City *p709, map p706*
Air
Pilanesberg International Airport, 10 km from Sun City, close to Kwa Maritane Gate, T014-552 1261, www.acsa.co.za. Upgraded a few years ago to an international airport for flights from neighbouring countries. Currently no scheduled flights, but there are charter flights from **Johannesburg** and **Cape Town**.

Car hire
All have desks at the airport. **Avis**, T014-557 1000, www.avis.co.za; **Budget**, T014-552 1497, www.budget.co.za; **Europcar**, T014-574 1000, www.europcar.co.za.

❶ Directory

Rustenburg *p705, map p706*
Medical services Peglerae (private) Hospital 173 Beyers Naude Dr, T014-597 7200.

Contents

Footprint features

At a glance

⊖ **Getting around** Buses only on the N1, car hire.

◉ **Time required** 3-5 days for major sights.

☽ **Weather** Hot summers, cool winters with snow on the highlands.

✖ **When not to go** Good all year round.

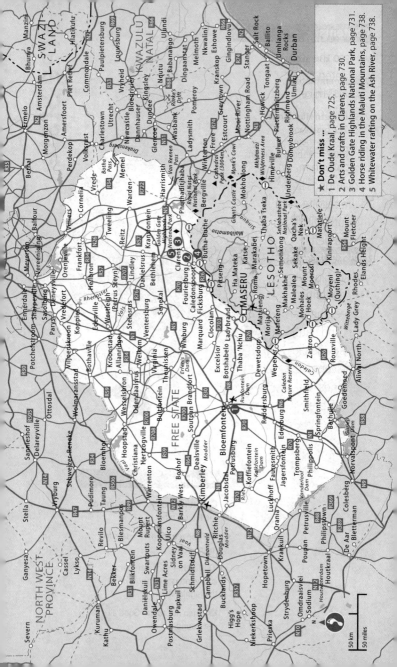

★ Don't miss...
1 De Oude Kraal, page 725.
2 Arts and crafts in Clarens, page 730.
3 Golden Gate Highlands National Park, page 731.
4 Horse riding in the Maluti Mountains, page 738.
5 Whitewater rafting on the Ash River, page 738.

Between the Vaal River to the north and the Gariep (Orange) River to the south lies an undulating plateau and sparsely populated prairie land known as Free State. In the latter half of the 19th century the region was an independent Boer Republic governed by the Voortrekkers who had left the British Cape Colony in the 1830s. During this brief period of independence, Bloemfontein developed into a fine modern capital with many grand sandstone buildings. But the discovery of diamonds at Jagersfontein and Kimberley, along with gold in the second independent Boer Republic of the time, led to the outbreak of the Anglo-Boer War on 11 October 1899, a fact that has left its mark on the province.

While there is not much to see in the arid farmlands to the west of Bloemfontein, the Maluti Mountains in the eastern Free State hold many surprises. The scenery is spectacular as it rises to meet the lands of Lesotho, scattered with dams, mountain rivers and nature reserves, and connected by pretty rural villages with a wide range of accommodation choices and activities. At the centre of this area lies the spectacular Golden Gate Highlands National Park, where, even during the summer months, the hills can sometimes be covered with snow.

Getting there and around

Bloemfontein is one of South Africa's most central transport hubs for buses, flights and trains, so you will not have any trouble getting to the Free State's capital. Getting around this part of South Africa is another matter, however, and you will need a car to explore it properly. The general flow of traffic is between the Cape and Johannesburg along the N1 but there are several contrasting routes you can take from Bloemfontein.

The **N1 north** takes you across the veld to Johannesburg; most of the countryside is flat and scattered with ugly mine dumps. There is little to stop for between here and Gauteng. The **N1 south** passes by the early settler towns of the **Xhariep** region before entering the **Great Karoo**. There is a long way to go before you reach the first fertile valleys of the Cape. The **N8** to the east goes to the higher lands of Lesotho and what are known as the **Eastern Highlands**. The countryside here is the most spectacular in Free State and this is the main road to Maseru (140 km), the capital of Lesotho. **Thaba 'Nchu** is a huge township that used not to be signposted from the main road during Apartheid; the lands around here were once part of the quasi-independent homeland known as Bophuthatswana, but it is all Free State today. Finally a short trip to the west along the N8 takes you to the mining town of **Kimberley**; further west the road skirts the fringes of the Kalahari en route to Namibia.

Bloemfontein

→ *Colour map 4, B3. Phone code: 051. Altitude: 1392 m.*

With one million residents, the provincial capital of the Free State is the sixth biggest city in South Africa and the country's judicial capital; the Court of Appeal sits here. The city is located on the Highveld plains surrounded by a group of flat-topped hillocks. It has warm, wet summers and cold, dry winters. The surrounding countryside is very fertile and an important farming region, maize being the principal crop. The city centre is an interesting mix of modern tower blocks built during the 1960s and 1970s with the State's mineral wealth, and a core of fine sandstone buildings dating from the late 19th century, when Bloemfontein was the capital of the small independent Orange Free State Republic. Its location right in the centre of South Africa, makes it an important transport centre, and a popular overnight spot for motorists driving between Gauteng and the Cape. Like much of the Free State it has yet to figure on the tourist map, though fans of Lord of the Rings should note that JRR Tolkien was born here in 1892, moving to England when he was four years old. Despite its interesting history, modern Bloemfontein has few visitor attractions, although it is a pleasant enough place to spend a couple of days. ▶▶ *For listings, see pages 725-728.*

Ins and outs

Getting there **Bloemfontein Airport** ① *T051-407 2240, www.acsa.co.za*, is 10 km east of the city centre, off the N8, the Thaba Nchu road. Taxis are available for transfers. Three different long-distance trains stop in Bloemfontein each week, it is thus possible to travel to all the major towns in South Africa. While the train is very comfortable it is much slower than the bus, for example the journey from Cape Town takes 20 hours by train, but only 11 hours by bus. Check timings carefully if you plan on changing bus or train in Bloemfontein. Buses starting their journey from here tend to leave at a convenient hour, but those stopping to pick up and drop off can pass through in the middle of the night or very early in the morning. **Greyhound**, **Intercape** and **Translux** buses depart from, and stop at, the Tourist Centre on Park Road. ▶▶ *For further details, see Transport, page 728.*

Tourist information The **Tourist Centre** ① *60 Park Rd, T051-405 8489, www.bloem fontein.co.za, Mon-Fri 0800-1615, Sat 0800-1200,* is helpful and the staff are knowledgeable and keen to promote Bloemfontein as a tourist destination. **Motheo District Municipality Tourism** ① *next to the Tourist Centre, T051-447 1362, www.motheo.co.za, Mon-Fri 0730-1600,* has a range of leaflets covering most of the province including the Xhariep. It has a good selection of information on the Free State, is a strong supporter of cultural and community-based tourism projects and arranges township tours.

Background

There are several theories about the name Bloemfontein, but the accepted version is that the wife of Johannes Nicolaas Brits, one of the first settlers in the area who started to farm here in 1840, planted some flowers around the fountain which was used by everyone travelling across the central plains.

In 1846 the Governor of the Cape Colony, Sir Peregrine Maitland, made a treaty with the Griqua chief, Adam Kok, whereby the land between the Riet and Modder rivers was opened to European settlement. Major Henry Warden, the British resident in Griqua territory, was instructed to move to the location to co-ordinate the new settlers. He chose Bloemfontein farm and Brits received £37.10 in compensation, followed by £50 a few years later and a farm in Harrismith, which he also named Bloemfontein.

In 1848 Sir Harry Smith visited the new settlement and proclaimed the territory between the Orange and Vaal rivers as British, calling it the Orange River Sovereignty, with Bloemfontein as its capital. Queen's Fort was built and the town slowly started to take shape. By 1853, Church Square and Market Square (now Hoffman Square) had been laid out. However, the surrounding countryside was still full of wild animals, which meant that travellers and farmers were in danger of attacks from lions, leopards and wild dogs. The British Government had decided the territory was hardly fit for habitation and not worth the trouble of maintaining. In 1854 the Bloemfontein Convention was signed, giving independence to the land between the Orange and Vaal rivers, and the British soldiers marched out of the town.

Josias Hoffman was the first President of the Republic of the Orange Free State and a *volksraad* (people's council) was elected to sit in the simple *raadsaal* (council chamber). This first council chamber can still be seen in St George's Street. President Johannes Brand followed him in 1863, under whom the town enjoyed 25 years of stable and prosperous independence when some fine government buildings were built. In 1890 the railway link with the Cape was finally completed and the town prospered further, though in 1904 there was a disastrous flood that cut the city in half and destroyed many buildings.

The discovery of diamonds at Jagersfontein and Kimberley along with gold, quickly led to the British wanting to re-establish control over these two regions. The Anglo-Boer War broke out and President Steyn of the Orange Free State sided with the South African Republic. When the British forces approached the town in March 1900 the Boer forces retreated to save the citizens and historic buildings. After the war was over, Bloemfontein became the capital of the Orange River Colony. In 1910, with the creation of the Union of South Africa, Bloemfontein aspired to be the country's capital; as it was it became the judicial capital, and remains so today.

Sights

ⓘ *The Tourist Centre produces a useful map showing 'The Rose Walk through Bloemfontein', which covers the major historical sites and takes about 1½ hrs.*

Most buildings of note are within easy walking distance of each other along President Brand Street. Many of these grand sandstone buildings date from the second half of the 19th century when Bloemfontein was the capital of the small – in terms of population – Orange Free State Republic. (It is not possible to go inside all of them because some are still in use today.) On the corner of President Brand and Charles streets is the **Appeal Court** ⓘ *T051-447 2631, by appointment only.* Although Bloemfontein was designated as the

Bloemfontein

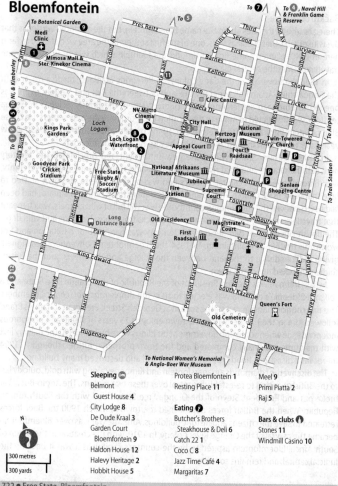

Sleeping		Protea Bloemfontein 1	Meel 9
Belmont		Resting Place 11	Primi Piatta 2
Guest House 4			Raj 5
City Lodge 8		**Eating**	
De Oude Kraal 3		Butcher's Brothers	**Bars & clubs**
Garden Court		Steakhouse & Deli 6	Stones 11
Bloemfontein 9		Catch 22 1	Windmill Casino 10
Haldon House 12		Coco C 8	
Halevy Heritage 2		Jazz Time Café 4	
Hobbit House 5		Margaritas 7	

seat of the Appeal Court with the advent of the Union in 1910, this building was only completed in 1929. It was built in a free-Roman style with corrugated Italian tiles on the roof and window ledges. Above the main entrance the helmet of Faith and the torches of Truth are portrayed.

Standing opposite is the neoclassical, Doric-columned **Fourth Raadsaal** (Council Chamber) ① *T051-447 8899, by appointment only*, with its domed tower. This was the last home of the *volksraad* (council) in the days of the independent republic and is now the seat of the Provincial Council. The impressive building was designed by L Canning and was completed in 1893. Inside, the original coat of arms of the Free State carved out of wood hangs behind the seat of the chairman, and the busts of six presidents are arranged around the chamber walls.

East of of here is the **National Museum** ① *36 Aliwal St, T051-447 9609, www.nas mus.co.za, Mon-Fri 0800-1700, Sat 1000-1700, Sun 1200-1730, R5, children (under 16) R2*. It has the usual collection of natural history exhibits, including a number of interesting dinosaur skeletons and a live snake park, as well as rooms dedicated to Bloemfontein's history and a mock-up early-19th-century street with dummies of various traders and families. The museum also has a café.

On the corner of President Brand and Maitland streets is the **Old Government Building**, now the **National Afrikaans Literature Museum** ① *Mon-Fri 0800-1215, 1300-1600, Sat 0900-1200, T051-405 4711*, an important collection of Afrikaans literature, and original manuscripts by leading poets and novelists. The original single-storey building had a high clock tower and was built by Richard Wocke in 1875 to house a government office. A second storey was added and then in 1906 an extension designed by Herbert Baker was built at the back. Baker created the present form after a serious fire in 1908.

On President Brand Street is the **Jubileum** building. It was built in the late 1920s by boys from a local orphanage to provide a venue for reading and refreshments for young Afrikaners. A variety of entertainments were staged here, including concerts and art exhibitions, as well as political rallies.

Opposite the fire station is the **Supreme Court** ① *corner of President Brand and Fontein streets, T051-447 8837, by appointment only*. This seat of the Provincial Law Court was built in 1909 at a cost of £60,000. It is a stately and vast court building where many famous cases have been tried in recent years.

Across the river is the **Old Presidency** ① *corner of President Brand and St George's streets, T051-448 0949, Tue-Fri 1000-1200, 1300-1600, Sat-Sun 1300-1700, free*. This was home to the last three state presidents before the British invasion, and it occupies the site where Brits erected his original farm buildings and where Major Warden built his first residence in 1846. It has now been converted into a concert hall and a museum depicting the lives of the presidents. The original stables at the back have been converted into a coffee shop.

Just around the corner is the **First Raadsaal** (Council Chamber) ① *St George's St, Mon-Fri 1015-1500, Sat-Sun 1400-1700, R5, children (under 16) R2*, a typical pioneers' building with a thatched roof, beaten dung floor and long white mud walls. It was opened in 1849 as the Government Schoolhouse, but was also used as a church and council chamber. After the creation of the Orange Free State Republic, the inauguration ceremonies for the first two presidents, Josias Hoffman and Jacobus Boshof, were held here. The *volksraad*, or people's council, met here until 1856, hence the name First Raadsaal. In 1877 the building was given to the town to be used as a museum. Today it features exhibits about the Free State's history and has a collection of old wagons and other forms of early pioneer transport.

On Church Street, the **Twin-towered Church**, which was fully restored in 1985, is on the site of the first small church built in 1849. Inaugurated in 1880, the church played a major role as the venue for the inauguration ceremonies for the last three state presidents, JH Brand, FW Reitz and MT Steyn. In 1935 the western tower collapsed and the other tower was removed, only for residents then to complain that the absence of spires spoilt the church's appearance; so in 1942 the two spires were re-erected.

In **Hertzog Square**, outside the City Hall, is a memorial and statue of General Hertzog. He became Prime Minister of South Africa in 1929 and again in 1934. A founder member of the Afrikaans-supporting, right-wing National Party in 1914, he introduced much of the legislation against non-whites.

The **National Women's Memorial** and **Anglo-Boer War Museum** ⓘ *Monument Rd, T051-447 0079, www.anglo-boer.co.za, Mon-Fri 0800-1630, Sat 1000-1700, Sun 1400-1700, R5, children (under 16) R2*, are 2 km south of the city centre. The memorial is an obelisk, 36.5 m high, built of sandstone from Kroonstad and resting at the foot of two *koppies* on the outskirts of Bloemfontein on Monument Road. On each side of the column is a bronze bas-relief depicting scenes from the suffering of women and children during the Anglo-Boer War. The monument was unveiled on 16 December 1913 to commemorate the 26,370 women and children who died in concentration camps as a result of the Anglo-Boer War. (In a niche at the foot of the memorial are the ashes of Emily Hobhouse, a British woman who campaigned against the harsh conditions in the concentration camps.) The museum tells the story of the Anglo-Boer War, with extensive background information on the discovery of gold on the Witwatersrand and displays of the British and Boer campaigns.

Naval Hill was once outside the city, but is now almost completely engulfed by the expanding suburbs. The panoramic views of the city are worth the drive. At the top of this hill are the **Franklin Game Reserve**, the **Observatory Theatre** and a **White Horse**. The White Horse was laid out by soldiers during the Anglo-Boer War as a landmark for returning horsemen. There are eland, hartebeest and springbok in the reserve, and it is not uncommon to get very close to giraffe in the car park of the Observatory Theatre where they seek shade.

South of the centre is the **Queen's Fort**, or **Military Museum** ⓘ *Church St, T051-447 5478, Mon-Fri 0800-1600, free*. Following his victory over the Boers at the battle of Boomplaats, Sir Harry Smith decided to build a new fort on a more strategically situated hill, named after Queen Victoria. For the first 30 years of the Free State Republic it was left to fall into a state of disrepair. In 1879, Captain FW Albrecht was appointed to oversee the complete rebuilding of the fort and mounted four iron nine-pounder guns. During the Second Anglo-Boer War it was occupied by British troops and at the end of the war it was given to the South African Constabulary. After housing a military headquarters the building is now a museum.

Free State National Botanical Garden ⓘ *Rayton Rd, off Dan Pienaar Drive, R702, T051-436 3612, www.sanbi.org, daily 0800-1800, R12, children (under 16) R8*, covers 70 ha on the outskirts of Bloemfontein and spans a valley between picturesque dolerite koppies. Its natural vegetation comprises tall grassland and woodland, dominated by magnificent wild olive and karee trees and is home to about 400 species of plants. From November to March most of the plants in the garden are in full leaf; from March to June the colourful autumn shades dominate. There are pleasant walks through the gardens and up to the koppies and there's a birdhide, restaurant and visitor centre. Two new demonstration gardens have been developed; one on plants with medicinal properties, and the other to show water-wise gardening techniques.

Township tours

Township tours are playing an increasingly important role in the South African tourism industry, creating jobs for local communities. While Bloemfontein has important 'white' historical sites, the nearby townships also have significance relating to the birth of the ANC and the legacy of the struggle. To see how life is lived in these places is interesting in its own right, and tours visit cultural and art centres, *shebeens* (pubs), dance demonstrations, traditional restaurants, jazz clubs and the various historical sites. There are three major townships outside Bloemfontein.

Within the city limits, **Mangaung** was where the ANC was founded in 1912. **Botshabelo**, meaning 'place of refugees', is 60 km from Bloemfontein on the N8. Estimated to be the second largest in the country after Soweto, it was established when blacks were forcibly removed from the Orange Free State towns. The vision of Tshwane (Pretoria) during the Apartheid era was to develop Botshabelo into a so called 'Golden City' for the Sotho and Xhosa people, and rapid Apartheid planning at the time made it the fastest-growing urban centre in South Africa. Beyond Botshabelo, 65 km from Bloemfontein, **Thaba 'Nchu** was originally settled by Voortrekkers and later by Chief Moroka, the founder of the Barolong tribe and an important member of the early ANC. There is a rich Tswana culture here, particularly in the villages, which are still governed by chiefs and traditional courts.

▸▸ For further details, see City and township tours, page 727.

◉ Bloemfontein listings

For Sleeping and Eating price codes and other relevant information, see pages 46-53.

● Sleeping

Bloemfontein *p720, map p722*
As Bloemfontein is an overnight stop for traffic between Jo'burg and Cape Town, there is a vast range of accommodation here. Look out for signs as you drive into town from the N1. The tourist centre has a full list.

A-B De Oude Kraal, 35 km out of town, off the N1 to Cape Town, T051-564 0733, www.oudekraal.co.za. 8 spacious garden rooms and 6 suites with additional spa baths and fireplaces. Very stylish furnishings and interiors, superb and atmospheric restaurant decorated with antiques and art (see Eating, page 726), and activities including farm walks and horse riding. Recommended as a peaceful country retreat with gourmet food.

B Garden Court Bloemfontein, corner of Nelson Mandela Dr and Melville Drive, T051-444 1253, www.southernsun.com. A Holiday Inn which has been rebranded. 147 a/c rooms, smoking and non-smoking, set around an open courtyard. Restaurant, bar, pool, disabled facilities and secure parking.

B Halevy Heritage Hotel, corner of Mark-graaff and Charles streets, T051-403 0600, www.halevyheritage.com. Very stylish, historic building dating from 1893, now completely refurbished with Victorian and Edwardian decor. 21 elegant rooms with DSTV and a/c, 2 bars, quality restaurant, tea room open from 1100-1800 and cosy courtyard.

B Hobbit House, 19 President Steyn Av, T051-447 0663, www.hobbit.co.za. 12 double en suite rooms with fluffy towels and duck-down duvets in a superior renovated boutique hotel dating from 1925 and obviously named after Tolkien's creation, full of period furnishings. Bar fashioned out of a tree, gourmet food in the restaurant served on china and silverware. After a day exploring the city on foot, the neat garden and swimming pool are a welcome sight. A special touch is a glass of sherry and chocolate at bedtime. Recommended.

B Protea Hotel Bloemfontein, 202 Nelson Mandela Drive, T051-444 4321, www.protea hotels.com. 94 a/c rooms, smoking and non-smoking, set around an open courtyard.

Restaurant, bar, swimming pool, disabled facilities, secure parking, comfortable if not predictable hotel on the outskirts of the city.
C Belmont Guest House, 4 Sixth St, T051-448 8168, www.belmontguesthouse.co.za. A smart modern guesthouse in a quiet suburb north of the city centre. 9 rooms, with a/c, DSTV, comfortable communal lounge with leather sofas, kitchen for guests' use, breakfast extra and dinner on request.
C City Lodge, corner of Nelson Mandela St and Parfitt Av, T051-444 2974, www.citylodge.co.za. 151 rooms with a/c, DSTV and Wi-Fi. Good-value town hotel geared to business travellers, option of non-smoking. Coffee shop, evening bar, extra for breakfast which is served in lobby lounge, small pool, mini-gym. Rooms suffer from traffic noise when windows open.
D Glen Country Lodge, 20 km north of Bloemfontein on the N1, T051-861 2042, www.glencountrylodge.co.za. An alternative to city accommodation for drivers, 12 thatched chalets with bathrooms and kitchenettes, nestled amongst acacia trees, breakfast and dinner on request, swimming pool, lovely spot in the bush with sweeping lawns.
D Haldon House, Japie Spesery Lane, Kwaggafontein, 3 km west of the city, T051-523 3607, www.haldon.co.za. 8 en suite double rooms with TV, most have a separate entrance. This is a fine house set in a mature estate with a swimming pool and a large shady veranda. Evening meals can be arranged. Short drive from city centre. Recommended.
D The Resting Place, 50 Scholtz St, T051-522 5008. A total of 23 units set around the garden or pool, doubles and family rooms, some with DSTV, microwave, a/c, safe, jet bath and Turkish bath, also self-catering chalets. Breakfast on request. Spacious, central and secure, children and wheelchair friendly.

❶ Eating

There are more than 20 restaurants and cafés in the **Loch Logan Waterfront**, see Shopping, below.

Bloemfontein *p720, map p722*
ᵼᵼᵼ Coco C, Loch Logan Waterfront, T051-447 8523, www.cococ.co.za. Daily 1200-1500, Mon-Sat 1800-late. With stunning black, white and bright red decor, crystal chandeliers and inspired by the movie Chocolat, this offers a very unusual and temping menu of dishes infused in cocoa oil or served with chocolate. Some, like the butternut soup with white chocolate or the duck breast with cocoa sauce, work very well, while others are a bit over ambitious with mixed flavours. Predictably, the desserts are superb.
ᵼᵼᵼ De Oude Kraal, see Sleeping, page 725. Open 0730-2130. Something a bit special, so despite its remote location, booking is essential. Famous for its typical South African food, such as *boerekos*; formal 6-course dinners; fine wines and cigars. In a wonderful setting in a restored farmhouse, this restaurant is a favourite of South Africa's *Eat Out* magazine.
ᵼᵼᵼ-ᵼᵼ The Raj, Windmill Casino, corner of Jan Pierewiet Rd and the N1, T051-421 0034, www.therajrestaurant.com. 1200-1500, 1730-2230. Upmarket Indian restaurant with chefs from North India. Authentic cuisine, informed waiting staff and a nice ambience with gold and orange decor and candlelight. Starters include lamb samosas with chutney, followed by vindaloos, kormas and biriyanis, and try the dumplings in rose syrup for dessert.
ᵼᵼ Butcher's Brothers Steakhouse and Deli, Loch Logan Waterfront, T051-430 1253, http://butcherbrothers.co.za. Mon-Sat 1100-2200, Sun 1100-1500. Quality steakhouse with excellent cuts of beef, and some interesting sauces and toppings. Also available to take home from the deli, along with olives and home-made pasta. Excellent though expensive wine list, quick service.
ᵼᵼ Catch 22, Mimosa Mall, T051-444 6877, www.catch22.co.za. 1030-2300. Good and fresh seafood, despite the distance from the sea; try the seafood paella or casserole, or snails in garlic sauce. Also serves sushi, and for meat eaters Mozambique-style spicy

chicken and beef dishes. Pleasant jaunty nautical decor and friendly staff.

♥♥ **Jazz Time Café**, Loch Logan Waterfront, T051-430 5727, www.jazztimecafe.co.za. 1100-2400. Huge cocktail bar, outside terrace, excellent music, including jazz, blues and big band. Hubble-bubble pipes, extensive menu, of breakfasts, light meals, grills, seafood and desserts, a great place for an evening out.

♥♥ **Margaritas**, Bays Village, 59 Milner Rd, Bayswater, T051-436 3729. Tue-Fri 1200-1430, 1830-2230, Sat 1830-2230, Sun 1200-1430. A good choice of fresh seafood and steaks, try the well-matured rump with creamy biltong and brandy sauce or the sole with mussel sauce. Extensive wine list, or snacks at the English pub-style bar.

♥♥ **Primi Piatta**, Loch Logan Waterfront, T051-448 7662, www.primi-world.com. 0900-2200. Modern funky decor, walls lined with coloured bottles and an open kitchen. Leans towards Italian but has a long menu of breakfasts. Daily specials, pizza, pasta and snacks. Good service, staff in orange overalls.

♥ **Meel**, 87 Kellner St, Westdene, T051-448 8836. Open 0800-1700. Lovely all white decor with old bevelled mirrors, this is a great spot for breakfast or lunch and it's well known for its home-made natural wheat bread, which you can also take away. Lunchtime dishes are set out on the feast table; pastas, veggie bakes, roasts and soup, and are priced by weight.

🕐 Bars and clubs

Bloemfontein *p720, map p722*
The high number of students mean there's a large club scene. As in any city, clubs go in and out of favour quickly and often change names or move location. For the latest ask the waiters at the Jazz Time Café (see above).
Stones, 150 Zastron St, T051-448 6484, http://stones.co.za. Mon-Sat 1900-0400. Large-scale club with sophisticated sound system and lighting, large screen TVs for sports, a full range of cocktails and shooters, and a youthful crowd.

Windmill Casino, corner of Jan Pierewiet Rd and the N1, T051-410 2000. Casino open 24 hrs, restaurants vary. This new tacky venue features slots and gaming tables, a sports bar, ten-pin bowling and several restaurants.

🛍 Shopping

Bloemfontein *p720, map p722*
Loch Logan Waterfront, 1st Av, www.loch loganwaterfront.co.za. An attractive shopping mall next to a lake and dam in Kings Park. Some of Bloemfontein's trendiest restaurants and bars are scattered along the boardwalk on the water's edge and there is a 6-screen cinema. It's recently been extended to incorporate most of South Africa's chain stores, including **Kloppers**, a large department store. An arts and crafts market is held here on the 1st Sat of every month.
Mimosa Mall, corner of Nelson Mandela and Parfitt streets, www.mimosamall.co.za. A standard South African mall with the usual facilities, including banks, food court, 4-screen Ster-Kinekor cinema, 2 internet cafés and an American Express office.

🅰 Activities and tours

Bloemfontein *p720, map p722*
Cricket
International cricket matches are played at the **Goodyear Park Stadium**, which is part of the complex of excellent sports facilities to the west of the city centre close to the tourist office. It's currently called **OUTsurance Oval** after its sponsors, but it is mostly referred to by its old name. The cricket ground is a fun, small stadium, which has yet to be spoilt by towering modern stands. Here fans can still lounge around or cook up a braai on grass banks as the game unfolds in front of them, a cool beer in hand. Tickets available through Computicket, www.computicket. com; www.cricket.co.za for fixtures.

Football and rugby

Free State Stadium, is next door to the cricket ground in Kings Park, and is a neat modern stadium where international football and rugby matches are played. It has been upgraded for the 2010 FIFA World Cup™ when it will accommodate 45,000. It's also known as the **Vodacom Stadium** after its sponsors and is home to the Free State Cheetahs rugby team, www.vodacom cheetahs.co.za. Tickets through **Computicket**, www.computicket.com.

City and township tours

A full-day tour visits all 3 townships; a ½-day tour visits 1 or 2, which can be combined with a ½-day city tour. Contact **Motheo District Municipality Tourism** (see page 721).

⊖ Transport

Bloemfontein *p720, map p722*
It's 1000 km to **Cape Town**; 415 km to **Johannesburg**; 186 km to **Kimberley**; 157 km to **Maseru**.

Air

Airport information, T051-407 2240, www.ac sa.co.za. **Mango** has flights between **Cape Town** and Bloemfontein; SAA has flights to **Johannesburg**, **Cape Town**, **Durban** and **Port Elizabeth**.

Airline offices All air tickets can be booked online at www.computicket.com. Mango, ww5.flymango.com. South African Airways (SAA), central reservations T0861-359 722 (in South Africa), T011-978 5313 (from overseas), www.flysaa.com. For further details, see Essentials, page 40.

Bus

Intercape, Greyhound and Translux have offices in the tourist centre on Park Rd where the buses stop. They run daily services to just about all the other large cities, including **Cape Town**, **Durban**, **Johannesburg** and **Port Elizabeth**.

Bus companies All bus tickets can be booked online at www.computicket.com. Greyhound, www.greyhound.co.za; Intercape, www.intercape.co.za; and Translux, www.translux.co.za. For more information, see Getting around, page 41.

Car hire

Avis, airport, T051-433 2331, and Gysie Pienaar Motors, 123 Nelson Mandela St, T051-447 6185, www.avis.co.za; Budget, airport, T051-433 2931, www.budget.co.za; Europcar, airport T051-574 1000, www.europ car.co.za; Hertz, airport, T051-400 2100, www.hertz.co.za.

Taxi

Silver Leaf Taxis, at the tourist centre T051-430 2005, for airport transfers.

Train

Part of the original station building from 1890 still remains. Information T051-408 2941. Central reservations, Shosholoza Meyl, T0860-00888 (in South Africa), T011-774 4555 (from overseas), www.shosholoza meyl.co.za, timetables and fares are published on the website. Bloemfontein is connected to most major cities, there are services to **Port Elizabeth**, **Johannesburg**, **East London**, **Kimberley** and **Cape Town**.

⊕ Directory

Bloemfontein *p720, map p722*
Banks All the main branches are within the Mimosa Mall, corner of Nelson Mandela and Parfitt streets. **Medical services** Chemist and Medi-Clinic, corner of Parfitt and Keller streets, T051-404 6666, www.bloemfonteinmc.co.za.

Eastern Highlands

The countryside neighbouring the Lesotho border, dominated by sandstone outcrops and eroded river valleys, is the most dramatic and interesting in the Free State. The hills once provided shelter for the early San hunters who lived in the region and there are some fine examples of cave paintings as a record of this past. (You will need guidance from the local tourist offices to find and see the art.) The region looks its best in the spring when the cherry orchards are in blossom. During winter there can be heavy snowfalls in the mountains. The highlands are perfect hiking country and ideal for pony trekking, and there are some great accommodation options on farms and in secluded valleys. Running parallel to the Lesotho border, the R26 passes through all the towns of note in this region. ▸▸ *For listings, see pages 733-738.*

Ladybrand ●●▸▸ pp733-738. Colour map 4, B4.

→ *Phone code: 051.*

A pleasant country town surrounded by a sandstone ridge full of San paintings and hidden caves, Ladybrand is the closest South African town to the Lesotho capital, Maseru (15 km). Along with Ficksburg, the town was founded in 1867 after the war between the Boers and the Basothos, to help guarantee peace in the Conquered Territory. It was named after Lady Catharina Brand, the mother of President Brand of the Orange Free State Republic. Sandstone from this area was used to build the Union Building in Tshwane (Pretoria). The small **Catharina Brand Museum** ⓘ *17 Church St, T051-914 0654, Tue-Fri 0900-1200, 1400-1600, Sat 0900-1200*, has an interesting feature on the **Lesotho Highlands Water Project** (see page 805), as well as some exhibits on Bushmen and early administration of the Lesotho border.

Ins and outs

Tourist information The **Maloti Route Tourism Office** ⓘ *Catharina Brand Museum, T051-924 5131, www.malotiroute.co.za, Mon-Fri 0800-1700*, is an enthusiastic office, well worth going out of your way for if you are planning to travel in any of these regions. The Maloti Route covers the Free State's Eastern Highlands, parts of the Eastern Cape and Lesotho, and this tourism office can provide an excellent booklet and map.

Sights

There are two major **San rock painting** sites nearby that can be visited with a guide from the tourist office. One of 12 San art national monuments in the country, it is thought that they are the most concentrated San paintings in South Africa, ranging from 250 to 5000 years old.

Ficksburg ●●▸▸ pp733-738. Colour map 4, A/B5.

→ *Phone code: 051. Altitude: 1629 m.*

Named after Commandant-General Johan Fick, a hero of the Basotho wars, the town was founded in 1867 to occupy what was known as the Conquered Territory after the Basotho war. Its role was to prevent cattle rustlers coming over from Lesotho and to strengthen general control over the area. Interestingly, cattle rustling still occasionally occurs in this region. A cherry festival, is held here during the third week of November each year, when you can indulge in cherry liqueur, maraschino, schnapps, and brandied cherries in syrup. These days the small town has important trade links with Lesotho, but otherwise it is only worth visiting for basic supplies and for the **tourist office** ① *96 McCabe St, T051-933 2130, www.ficksburg.org.za, Mon-Fri 0900-1200, 1300-1500,* which has an exhibition on the **Lesotho Highlands Water Project** (see also page 805). A small **museum** ① *Mon-Fri 1000-1200, 1400-1600,* commemorates the (not very interesting) life of General Fick.

Rustler's Valley was a popular destination to the north of Ficksburg in the foothills of the Witteberge Mountains, which had become famous as one of South Africa's premier festival sites. Unfortunately, a fire destroyed the lodge and the whole valley in September 2007. It remains to be seen if the site will be resurrected in the future.

Fouriesburg to Clarens ● ⇥ pp733-738. Colour map 5, A5.

→ Phone code: 058.

Fouriesburg is a small, untidy town 12 km from the **Caledonspoort** border post with Lesotho. Founded in 1892, it was named after Christoffel Fourie, the local farmer who originally owned the land. For a few months during the **Anglo-Boer War**, the town was the last seat of the Orange Free State's republican government and a stronghold of the Boer forces. As a consequence it was almost destroyed by the British army.

About 2 km south of Fouriesburg is the **Meiringskloof Nature Park** ① *T058-223 0067, www.meiringskloof.co.za, R10, children (4-16) R5, car R20.* Within the park are overnight chalets, a campsite and short walks among the cliffs where there is a large open cave, 'holkrans', once used as a hide-out during the Anglo-Boer War. For visitors with a head for heights there is a chain ladder, which goes up a steep cliff face to a dam supplying water to Fouriesburg.

North of Fouriesburg

Travelling north from Fouriesburg there is a choice of two routes; 45 km direct to Bethlehem on the R26, or a much more interesting route, the R711 to Clarens, which also provides the opportunity to visit the Golden Gate Highlands National Park (see page 731).

Surrender Hill is 7 km before Clarens on the R711. The name reminds the Boers of their most devastating defeat during the Anglo-Boer War, when on 29 July 1900, 4314 Free State soldiers under General Prinsloo were cornered in the mountains and surrendered to the British. Most were sent to India as prisoners of war.

Clarens ●●●▲ ⇥ pp733-738. Colour map 4, A5.

→ Phone code: 058.

This village was named after the Swiss resort on the shore of Lake Geneva where President Paul Kruger died in 1904. The settlement was only laid out in 1912 and has no historical past to explore, but the relaxed feel of the place makes it the ideal spot to use as a base to explore the highlands. Tourism has taken over in this tiny, pretty village and a number of galleries, craft shops and tea rooms surround a grassed square with a few sandstone buildings and large trees. The grasslands which dominate the sandstone slopes are known for their large variety of wild flowers in the summer months. It is the closest village to the Golden Gate Highlands National Park when approaching from the west. The natural beauty of the area has attracted a number of artists to the region.

There are five quite well-preserved **cave paintings** on a farm called Schaapplaats, 20 minutes' walk from town. To visit these paintings, call in at the local tourist office, **Clarens Destinations** ① *Market St, T058-256 1542, www.clarenstourism.co.za, daily 0900-1300, 1400-1700,* who will phone ahead to let the farm owners know you are coming. Clarens is a small community and the staff in this office are helpful, local booking agents for accommodation and activities, and know all the local artists and craftspeople. It's worth a stop if you are considering buying quality pieces.

Around Clarens

From Clarens, head towards Golden Gate Highlands National Park, to **Basotho Cultural Village** ① *10 km before the park gate on the right, T058-721 0300, Mon-Fri 0800-1630, Sat-Sun 0900-1700, entry and 30-min guided tour R50, children (6-15) R30, under 6s free.* It is a worthwhile stop and offers an insight into the lives of the Basotho people who have similar traditions to those people living over the border in Lesotho. Guided tours take you around a scattering of bomas and huts, where traditional craft-making is demonstrated, local beer can be sampled and a lively band and dancers provide entertainment. The village also has tea gardens, a curio shop and an art gallery.

On the Bethlehem road, 8 km from Clarens, there's a viewpoint over the Ash River outfall, a new surge of water created by the Lesotho Highlands Water Project.

Golden Gate Highlands National Park ●▲▶ *pp733-738. Colour map 4, A5.*

A small (11,600-ha) national park on the edge of the Drakensberg and Maluti Mountains, the Golden Gate Highlands National Park is set in an area of massive sandstone rock formations. The eroded valleys have produced some spectacular shapes, with caves, cliffs and green grasslands against a backdrop of golden rocks. This is a particularly special place at sunset when the colours of the rocks are at their most intense. The Caledon River rises in these mountains. It is a popular park given its proximity to Johannesburg (three hours by car). The principal attractions are the hiking opportunities, the climbing and the spectacular rock formations. The Rhebok Hiking Trail is also in the park, see below.

Ins and outs

Getting there The common approach is the main road from Clarens (15 km), which is surfaced all the way through the park. As you enter the park and approach the offices the road passes through a narrow valley with giant cliffs which give the name 'Golden Gate'. The sun shining on the oxides in the sandstone produces a brilliant golden hue to the cliff face.

Tourist information A public road runs through the middle of the park so day visitors do not have to pay an entrance fee. Overnight visitors, R78, children R36. All enquiries can be dealt with at the **Glen Reenan Camp reception** ① *T058-255 0000.* Fuel is available at Glen Reenen, 0700-1730. **Glen Reenen Shop** ① *daily winter 0730-1700, summer 0700-1730,* stocks limited groceries, beer and wine, firewood and a few fresh items, maps and curios.

Climate The typical climate is cool rainy summers and cold winters with a high chance of snow. There is heavy snowfall on the high peaks while the valleys and surrounds remain untouched. Do not hike without suitable protective clothing in the winter. The park receives over 800 mm of rain annually so it is lush and green nearly all year.

Bread basket

About 90% of the Free State is used for agriculture with about two million hectares under cultivation for crops. Of these, about 100,000 are irrigated. The Free State is aptly referred to as the 'bread basket' of South Africa, producing about 40% of the total maize production of South Africa, 50% of wheat, 80% of sorghum, 33% of potatoes, 18% of red meat, 30% of groundnuts and 15% of wool. Around 11,500 commercial farmers are farming on some 50,000 farms in the province. The other big earner is mining and the Free State produces about one third of South Africa's gold. It also has large deposits of coal, and produces approximately 80% of South Africa's bentonite (a sort of clay that used in the building trade). The mining industry is also the biggest net supplier of jobs in the province, employing approximately 22% of the labour force.

Wildlife

You are unlikely to see many wild animals from the car, but once you get into the wooded valleys and the quiet hills you may well see black wildebeest, Burchell's zebra, mountain reedbuck, blesbok, eland and grey rhebok. The larger raptors favour the high rocky cliffs; look out for the bearded vulture, jackal buzzard, bald ibis and black eagle.

Rhebok Hiking Trail

ⓘ *The trail has to be booked in advance through one of the SANParks offices or online at www.sanparks.org, bookings open 13 months in advance.*

This popular two-day hike covers a total distance of 30 km. The path starts from the campsite at Glen Reenen and it is about 16 km to the overnight Rhebok Hut; look out for the San cave near the start of the trail. On the second day you will cover 14 km, but this includes the ascent of Generaalskop (2837 m). This is the highest point in the Free State and has views to match. On hot sunny days, the waterfall and Langtoon Dam are welcome sights near the end of the second day. The trail ends back at Glen Reenen, so you can look forward to hot showers at the end of some strenuous walking. Do not walk alone, a minimum of four people is ideal in this terrain. There are plenty of shorter day walks that have been marked out; some will take you to a peak top and back, others enable you to explore wooded kloofs. Keep an eye out for game at all times. ⇥ *For horse riding and other activities in the area, see page 737.*

Bethlehem ⊜❶❷❸ ⇥ *pp733-738. Colour map 4, A5.*

→ *Phone code: 058.*

The town was founded in 1864 on a farm known as Pretoriuskloof. It is the principal town of the Eastern Free State, an important wheat-growing area and one of South Africa's biggest exporters of roses. It is also where South Africa's national hot-air balloon race is held in May each year. A prominent local church minister, FP Naude, gave the settlement its name, reflecting the fact that the first settlers found that wheat flourished in the fertile Jordan Valley. It is a large town with a good range of restaurants and accommodation, but there is little here for the visitor apart from some fine examples of early sandstone buildings. The Dihlabeng Municipality **tourist office** ⓘ *9 Muller St, T058-303 5732, www. dihlabeng.org.za, Mon-Sat 0830-1300, 1400-1600,* has a good range of brochures, including a map of the **Sandstone Walking Tour** ① *1½ hrs*, which takes you around the old buildings.

The **Museum of Cultural History** ① *in the former Nazareth Mission Church at the top end of Muller St, T058-303 3477, Fri 1000-1230, 1430-1700*, has a collection depicting the region's local history, with an early steam locomotive in the grounds.

Harrismith ⚫🔵⚫⚫ ➤➤ pp733-738. Colour map 4, A6.

→ *Phone code: 058.*

Most visitors pass Harrismith on the N3 en route to Durban. The town is dominated by a long flat mountain, the **Platberg**, 2377 m. Each year on 10 October a race is run up the mountain and along the top for 5 km before returning to the town. The origin of the race is very much part of local history. At the end of the Anglo-Boer War a Major John Belcher from the British Army referred to the mountain as 'that little hill of yours'. He was immediately bet he could not run to the top in less than an hour. He duly won the bet, and the race, along with a trophy, was born.

The town was named after the British Governor Sir Harry Smith and nearby Ladysmith is named after his Spanish wife. The growth of the settlement was influenced by the discovery of diamonds at Barkly West and Kimberley in the 1860s, and gold on the Witwatersrand in 1886. Before the railway was built from the coast, at least 50 wagons a day used to stop over in the town.

Today it is still a popular stop for travellers between Gauteng and Durban, either overnight or for a break in one of the many service stations off the N3. Information is available from the **tourist office** ① *Southey St, T058-622 3525, Mon-Fri 0800-1630, Sat 0930-1230.*

Around Harrismith
Sterkfontein Dam Nature Reserve, set in the foothills of the Drakensberg, 23 km from Harrismith, covers an area of more than 7000 ha with a 104-km shoreline and is one of the largest in South Africa. Most visitors come here for watersports and fishing. Hiking is possible and there are good opportunities for viewing raptors, and an interesting vulture 'restaurant' that attracts Cape and bearded vultures. The entrance is off the R74 between Harrismith and Bergville. For those staying overnight at the reserve's resort, day trips can easily be made from here to the Northern Drakensberg (see page 498).

⊙ Eastern Highlands listings

For Sleeping and Eating price codes and other relevant information, see pages 46-53.

⊖ Sleeping

Ladybrand *p729*
C Cranberry Cottage, 37 Beeton St, T051-924 2290, www.cranberrycottage.co.za. Smart award-winning B&B in a restored Victorian country house with additional rooms in the original ticket office and waiting rooms of Ladybrand Railway Station, decorated with railway memorabilia and antiques. 31 en suite double rooms with DSTV and kettles, some with fireplaces, swimming pool, gym and beauty spa. Gourmet dinners are served on the patio or in the candlelit dining room. If you're not staying, the **Duck Pond** restaurant is still worth a visit on the way through the village. Recommended.
C-D My Housy, 17a Prinsloo St, T051-924 1010, www.myhousy.co.za. A well-run B&B with 7 double and 1 family room with en

suite bathrooms, TV, heaters for winter and private entrances, peaceful garden, all individually decorated thanks to one of the owners being an artist. Very stylish breakfasts, think stacked omelettes garnished with asparagus spears and flower petals.

D Oldenburg Lodge, signposted off the R46, 14 km north of Ladybrand, T051-924 5857, www.oldenburglodge.com. Set on a private nature reserve, which is home to a number of antelope, black wildebeest and giraffe, this has B&B double/twin rooms in the old farmhouse plus garden chalets sleeping 4. Restaurant, bar, simple country furnishings and swimming pool. You can also camp at a grassy site with ablutions and braais. Can organize game drives, horse riding, visits to rock art, mountain biking and fishing. A good all-round affordable rural retreat.

Ficksburg p729

Apart from the dreary **Highland Hotel**, which isn't recommended, there's a limited choice in town, but there are a couple of good rural retreats.

B Franshoek Polo Lodge, Km 9 Fouriesburg Rd, turn left onto a dirt road, the S385 for 18 km, T/F051-933 2828, www.franshoek.co.za. A comfortable rural lodge with 10 rooms, some with wrought-iron beds. Thatched restaurant with cosy log fires. Plenty of emphasis on outdoor pursuits, including polo, rock climbing, abseiling, trout fishing, swimming pool. Limited numbers, intimate atmosphere, rates include breakfast and dinner. There's also a self-catering thatched cottage on the farm sleeping up to 8.

D Bella Rosa, 21 Bloem St, T/F051-933 2623, bellarosa@telkomsa.net. 11 elegant suites make up this quality B&B set in a sandstone Victorian town house. Start the day with a delicious breakfast, overlooking the mature gardens. A quiet and comfortable home decorated with antiques, pub and wine cellar with roaring fire, dinner on request, no young children.

D Green Acorn, 7 Fontein St, T051-933 2746, www.greenacorn.co.za. Comfortable guest-

house centrally situated in Ficksburg, quiet and tranquil. 10 rooms with private entrances in the house and in pretty garden cottages, light and airy furnishings.

D Hoekfontein Oxwagon Camp, 10 km to the south of Ficksburg on the R26 is a turning onto a gravel road, follow signs for 15 km, T/F051-933 3915, oxwagon@telkomsa.net. Accommodation in original ox wagons arranged in a semi-circle around a central eating and lounge boma. Double beds in the wagons themselves under white starched canvas roofs, shared ablution block and self-catering kitchen, also some en suite rondavels. Tractor rides, visits to San rock art and abseiling on the neighbouring cliffs. Recommended.

Fouriesburg to Clarens p730

C Fouriesburg Country Inn, 17 Reitz St, T058-223 0207, www.fouriesburgcountry inn.co.za. 22 rooms, the only hotel in town, the façades have been taken from the old railway buildings. A comfortable, quiet overnight stop, with small rooms opening onto sheltered veranda overlooking the church. A pleasant touch is being able to go into the original sandstone wine cellar and choose your wine before dinner. Restaurant offers a selection of mixed grills and salads, and rates include breakfast and dinner.

D-F Meiringskloof Nature Park, 2 km south of Fouriesburg, follow Fleck St out of town, T058-223 0067, www.meiringskloof.co.za. Simple self-catering stone chalets and basic campsite with braai pits and power points, in a beautiful kloof surrounded by sandstone cliffs with open caves, thick indigenous bush and abundant bird life. Swimming pool, horse riding, 4WD trails, a number of short hikes and kiosk selling basic groceries. Popular with families.

D-F Shumba Valley Farm, 9 km south of Fouriesburg towards Ficksburg, turn off at the S293 for 3 km, T058-223 0277, www.shumbavalleyfarm.co.za. A mixture of accommodation in B&B en suite rooms, self-catering caravans or cottages, some in converted stables, or camping. Cosy lounge and pub. Farm retreat with lots of activities, quad-biking, hiking, clay pigeon shooting and excellent horse trails from 1 hr for beginners to 5-day excursions into the mountains for experienced riders sleeping out under the stars with the horses.

Clarens p730
The tourist office will fax or email a complete list of accommodation.

B Protea Hotel Clarens, corner of Main and Van de Merwe streets, T058-256 1212, www.proteahotels.com. A very striking modern sandstone, glass and steel building. 70 smart rooms with all mod cons and DSTV, 2 equipped for disabled travellers, lovely bar with picture windows and great views of the Maluti Mountains, excellent restaurant with broad terrace. Another quality offering from Protea, and the design here – inside and out – is very impressive. Recommended.

B-C Cranford Inn, 19 Larola St, T/F058-256 1358. Modern red-brick hotel with 24 comfortable and recently refurbished rooms, private patios, fresh flowers, mini-bars, DSTV, hot-water bottles and heating. Restaurant and bar with spacious veranda and lawns. Rates are higher at the weekends.

C Maluti Mountain Lodge, Steil St, T058-256 1422, www.malutilodge.co.za. 20 en suite double rooms, 4 family rondavels, with heating and M-Net TV, set in neat gardens. Good country cooking, fun atmosphere in the **Duck & Hound** pub and a drink on the balcony is a nice way to end the day. Also has a swimming pool.

C-F Bokpoort, signposted 5 km out of Clarens on road to Golden Gate, T/F058-256 1181, www.bokpoort.co.za. A 3-km dirt road winds up into the hills onto a ridge where the farms and stables are laid out. There are 8 B&B chalets, two 8-bed hikers' huts and camping. The shower block has plenty of hot water when the wood fires are burning, and there's a simple dining room and bar. Well known for their excellent horse-riding safaris from 2 hrs to 10 days in the Maluti Mountains, when

you are treated to some superb countryside and real South African breakfasts. A 2-day ride takes you to the snowline in winter. Recommended for keen riders.

D Patcham Place, 262 Church St, T058-256 1017, www.clarenstourism.co.za/patcham place. 5 double or twin rooms with en suite facilities in a timber cottage. Good mountain views, TV, each has a private balcony and separate entrance. Electric blankets and heaters serve as a reminder as to how cold it can get in this area during winter.

D The Thistle Stop, 58 Le Roux St, T/F058-258 1003. A neat town house B&B, lounge area where tea, coffee and rusks are available, also a family self-catering cottage sleeping 4. Electric blankets and heaters are available in the winter months.

Golden Gate Highlands National Park p731
All accommodation is booked through SAN-Parks, T012-428 9111, www.sanparks.org.

B Brandwag Hotel, beside the main road that runs through the park, T058-255 1000. Refurbished large hotel with rooms for up to 4, with bathroom and TV; in the grounds are 4-bed chalets, with bathroom, kitchenette, fridge, TV and braai facilities. The restaurant has excellent views, bar serves pub lunches, kiosk does takeaways. Professional set-up and from your room you have an unimpeded view of the mountains, but unfortunately no effort was made to blend the complex into the otherwise uninterrupted scenery and it really shouldn't have been built in 1965 in such a naturally beautiful spot.

B Highlands Mountain Retreat, 7 km from Glen Reenen off the Oribi Loop road (2200 m above sea level), SANParks, T058-255 0012. This new camp set high up in the mountains with stunning views. Has 8 double and family log cabins with kitchen, braai, TV and fire-place (pretty essential most nights), some with disabled access. Check in is at Glen Reenen where you will be given a map and directions. The last kilometre to the camp is quite steep, but manageable in a normal car.

C-D Glen Reenen Camp, beside the main road that runs through the park, it is always worth calling the park reception on T058-255 0000 to check for late availability. Reception hours, winter 0730-1700, summer 0700-1730. If you arrive outside these hours the night-watchman can give keys to pre-booked guests but cannot check you in without a prior booking. There are 2 types of self-catering hut, each has shower, fridge and cooking utensils. 1 type has a TV, 2 single beds and a double bed in the loft, the other has 3 single beds in 1 room. Some have fireplaces. All have been recently refurbished and the old staff houses have been turned into ten 2-bed units. Across the road is the campsite, which has plenty of shade and is beside a mountain stream, it has a kitchen and electric points in the shower block. Peaceful setting in a narrow, steep-sided valley. Be warned it can get far too cold for camping in the winter. Some recognized hikes start from here; you can pick up a map at the shop. Swimming pool.
E Rhebok Hut, overnight hut on the Rhebok Hiking Trail. 3 bedrooms with 6 bunks and mattresses, coal stove, paraffin cooker, basic utensils in the kitchen, cold showers and toilets. Bring a sleeping bag and food.

Bethlehem p732
C Fisant, Bokmakierie and Hoephoep Guest House, 8-10 Thoi Oosthuyse St, T058-303 7144, www.fisant.co.za. Smart modern houses on the outskirts of town. 7 double rooms and 9 family units with en suite bathroom, some with kitchenettes for self-catering, non-smoking room available. Buffet breakfasts, TV, laundry, garden, undercover parking, German spoken, well run and good value.
D Bread House, 14 President Vorster St, T058-303 4329, www.breadhouse.co.za. 6 modern double rooms with en suite bathroom, DSTV, underfloor heating, electric blankets, homely guest lounge with fireplace, braai area, swimming pool. Excellent value. Generous breakfasts including home-made bread.
D Die Nes, 3 van Raalte St, T058-303 4073, www.dienesguesthouse.co.za. 8 double

and twin en suite rooms with, bar fridge and TV. A smart B&B decorated in strong primary colours, bright, fresh and hospitable. Lower rates at the weekend.
D Park Hotel, 23 Muller St, T/F058-303 5191. 15 double rooms, 27 single rooms, all a/c and with TV, cheaper family and double rooms in old block, the new part is built around a leafy atrium. Restaurant, bar, swimming pool, secure parking, one of the best in town.

Harrismith and around p733
C Shady Pines, 67 Stuart St, T058-622 3020, www.shadypines.co.za. Comfortable and hospitable guesthouse in a restored house built in 1880. Wooden floors, some 4-poster beds, white linen, spacious gardens, 7 en suite rooms and 2 self-catering units, home-cooked meals available, tiny chapel in the grounds for weddings.
C-D Harrismith Inn, McKechnie Rd, T058-622 1011, www.africanskyhotels.com. 119 a/c en suite modern rooms in a 2-storey block surrounding a swimming pool. Restaurant offering buffet meals and **Harry's Bar**. Business orientated but a comfortable overnight stop.
D Eagle Mountain Game Lodge, 21 km northeast of Harrismith on the R722 to Verkykerskop, T058-6230 235, www.eagle mountain.co.za. 5 simple self-catering log cabins and chalets sleeping up to 6, tent sites and caravan stands, all with plenty of privacy. On a private 1000-ha reserve with the usual collection of antelope roaming freely among the rondavels. No other facilities.

⊙ Eating

Ladybrand p729
⊙ **The Duck Pond**, Cranberry Cottage, 37 Beeton St, T051-924 2290, www.cran berrycottage.co.za. If you're not staying at this guesthouse, phone ahead to book dinner. 3-course set meals, generous portions, country cooking, some game and duck dishes, extensive wine list.

Ficksburg p729

The Bottling Co, Piet Retief St, T051-933 2404. Mon-Sat 1200-1400, 1700-2200. Pub and restaurant in an old sandstone house with good choice of beer in the homely dark wood bar, and standard but filling steak, chicken and fish dishes and has some historical photos of Ficksburg on the walls.

Clarens p730

Clementine's, 731 Church St, T058-256 1616. Tue-Sun 1200-2200. This little red and green corrugated-iron building is a bit of a Clarens landmark, and unusually for South Africa it serves locally brewed stout, ale and cider. Small but good menu of comfort food like slow-cooked oxtail stews and curries, and traditional desserts like rhubarb crumble. Look-out for rainbow trout on the specials board.

Artist's Café, Windmill Centre, Main Rd, T058-256 1404. Open 0800-1700. Great spot for milkshakes, pies, cakes, waffles, pastries, light meals and sandwiches made from fresh bread. Jungle gym in the garden for kids, sociable shady outside bench seating.

Café Moulin, Windmill Centre, Main St, T082-690 1382. Mon-Sat 0800-2100, Sun 0800-1600. Country cooking, light meals, salads and quiches, ploughman's platters with home-made bread and preserves, chicken pies. Sun lunch is their Harvest Table buffet which is priced by weight. BYO.

Bethlehem p732

O'Hagans, 8 Theron St, T058-303 0919. Open 1100-late. Good-value pub/restaurant chain, English pub decor, varied menu of pub grub like bangers and mash, shepherd's pie, burgers, lasagne, etc, and large portions.

Park Grill, Park Hotel, see Sleeping page 736. Open 0700-2130. Extensive menu, including good healthy stir-frys and steaks and sauces, but slow service and gloomy dark wood interior.

Harrismith and around p733

Eating out in Harrismith is limited though during the day there are plenty of takeaways

and cafés at the many petrol stations in town and along the N2. This is about the midway lunchtime spot on the drive between Johannesburg and Durban.

Harrismith Inn, McKechnie Rd, T058-622 1011, www.africanskyhotels.com. 0700-2200. Standard hotel restaurant, mediocre decor but decent service and a good variety of food. Buffets for breakfast and dinner, when there's also a carvery and an à la carte menu for light meals. **Sir Harry's Bar** has a pool table.

O Shopping

Clarens p730

For a small village Clarens has no fewer than 18 galleries and craft shops, so its just a case of browsing. For sale are local handicrafts and jewellery, various paintings by local artists, antiques, ceramics and decorations, and furniture from as far away as Malaysia. As Clarens is a popular day tripping destination, all are open at the weekends.

Art & Wine Gallery on Main, Main St, T058-256 1298, www.artandwine.co.za. Sells wines from Stellenbosch and exhibits paintings, sculptures, ceramics and glassware.

Clarens Meander Shops, next to the Caltex garage as you approach town. Has several craft shops and galleries, a farm stall selling home-made treats, ATMs and a café. There's also an information office for the **Lesotho Highlands Water Project**, www.lhwp.org.ls.

Windmill Centre, Main St, www.windmill centre.co.za. Set in a number of sandstone restored farm outbuildings, there are a number of galleries, a deli and some cafés, which are listed under Eating, above.

▲ Activities and tours

Clarens p730
Golf

Clarens Golf and Trout Estate, on the road to Golden Gate, T058-256 1270, www.the clarens.co.za. A new 18-hole golf and trout fishing estate laid out in the lee of the Maluti Mountains, with breathtaking views and a fairway surrounded by trout dams. Part of residential country estate but visitors welcome.

Horse riding
Bokpoort, see Sleeping, page 735. The most exciting horse trails in the region. Standard route lasts for 2 days, with a night at a deserted homestead in the Maluti Mountains. The larger the group the better the value. Shorter rides also available and the Basotho ponies are suitable for young children.

Quad-biking
Sethuthuthu Tours, T058-256 1569, or book at the tourist office. Quad-bike tours from 1 hr to a full day, on guided trails connecting local farms. Not for the thrill seeker as the pace is quite slow, but there are some great views over the Free State and Maluti Mountains.

Whitewater rafting
Outrageous Adventures, T083-485 9654, www.outrageousadventures.co.za. Since the opening of the Katse Dam in Lesotho, part of the mammoth Lesotho Highlands Water Project to increase the feed of many of South Africa's rivers, **Clarens Ash River** has experienced a surge of extra water from the new Trans Caledon Transfer Tunnel. The water exits the tunnel at 54 cu m per second and a series of rapids has developed on the river; some Grade III-IV. This company offers full-day whitewater rafting trips, including lunch, drinks and transfers to and from Clarens. This is now considered one of the best runs in the country.

Golden Gate Highlands National Park *p731*
Horse riding
There are stables outside the park at Gladstone, 3 km from the Glen Reenan towards Clarens,

T058-225 0951. Although the owners will tell you that anyone can go on these rides they are not suitable for the totally inexperienced, as the horses will occasionally break into a gallop. There are plenty of horses and it is not necessary to book, just turn up around 1000. However, to be certain of a ride, phone ahead. Rides cost about R70 per hr.

Transport

Bethlehem *p732*
Bus
Translux and Greyhound buses stop at the Wimpy on Church St. Bethlehem is on the **Bloemfontein–Durban** route. For **Johannesburg** and **Cape Town** there are connections in Bloemfontein.

Bus companies All bus tickets can be booked online at www.computicket.com. Greyhound, www.greyhound.co.za; and Translux, www.translux.co.za. For more information, see Getting around, page 41.

Train
There is a weekly service between **Cape Town** and **Durban** that stops in Bethlehem. Central reservations, **Shosholoza Meyl**, T0860-00888 (in South Africa), T011-774 4555 (from overseas), www.shosholoza meyl.co.za, timetables and fares are published on the website.

Harrismith and around *p733*
Translux, Intercape and Greyhound buses stop at the Truck Stop on the junction road with N2. The **Johannesburg–Durban** route.

Bus companies All bus tickets can be booked online at www.computicket.com. Greyhound, www.greyhound.co.za; Intercape, www.intercape.co.za; and Translux, www.translux.co.za. For more information, see Getting around, page 41.

Contents

Footprint features

Border crossings

South Africa–Namibia/Botswana,
Kgalagadi Transfrontier Park, see
page 764

South Africa–Namibia, Vioolsdrif,
see page 778

Northern Cape

At a glance

⊜ **Getting around** Buses only
on N7 and N14, car hire, tours
from Cape Town during spring
flower season.

⊙ **Time required** 3-5 days for
major sites, 1 week for Kgalagadi
Transfrontier Park.

☼ **Weather** Mostly dry, sunny
and hot.

✕ **When not to go** Desert regions
get very cold on winter nights.

BOTSWANA

NAMIBIA

NORTH WEST
PROVINCE

Nossob

② Kgalagadi Transfrontier Park

Vorstershoop

Setlagole

Mata Matar

Twee Rivieren

Van Zylsrus

Rietfontein

Askham

Sonstraal

Black Rock
Hotazel

Vryburg

Lykso

R41

Kalahari

Noenieput

Tswalu Kalahari
Reserve

Kathu

Kuruman

Ariamsvlei

Nakop

Spitskop
Nature
Reserve

NORTHERN
CAPE

N14

④ Ai-Ais/Richtersveld Transfrontier
National Conservation Park

N8

Witsand Nature
Reserve

Upington

Barkly West

Kuboes

Augrabies Falls
National Park

Keimoes

③

Kakamas

Cannon Island
(Kanoneiland)

Kimberley

①

Vioolsdrif

Pella

Alexander Bay

Magersfontein

Mokala
National Park

Steinkopf

Pofadder

Kenhardt

N8

Petrusburg

Port
Nolloth

Goegap
Nature Reserve

N10

Copperton

Prieska

Krankuil

Springbok

Gamoep

Grootvloer

Verneuk Pan

Van Wyksuki

Sodium

Kamieskroon

⑤

Namaqua
National Park

Brandvlei

Vosburg

Britstown

Colesberg

Nariep

Kliprand

Sakrivier

Carnarvon

De Aar

N12

N1

N7

Niewoudtville

Williston

Loxton

Richmond

*Atlantic
Ocean*

Vanrhynsdorp

Doring Bay

Middlepos

Fraserburg

Three
Sisters

N9

Graaff-
Reinet

Lambert's Bay

Beaufort West

Aberdeen

N12

Velddrif

Porterville

Dwyka

Rietbron

WESTERN CAPE

Willowmore

Saldanha

Hottentotskloof

Die Hel

N2

Yzerfontein

Ceres

Touws River

Calitzdorp

Herold

N2

Cape Town

Stellenbosch

Riviersonderend

Mossel Bay

Betty's Bay

Napier

Albertinia

Struisbaai

*Indian
Ocean*

N

100 km

100 miles

The Northern Cape is South Africa's largest province, although it is home to fewer than a million people. It is also one of the most beautiful areas of the country but, compared to other provinces, it remains tourist-free. Much of this has to do with the sheer harshness of the area: this is where the rock-strewn semi-desert of Namakwa (Namaqualand) merges with the rolling red dunes of the Kalahari, where cruel heat pounds the parched wilderness for much of the year. But it is this sun-bleached emptiness and inaccessibility that gives the area its stark beauty, endless shimmering plains and hazy saltpans providing it with a real sense of isolation.

The state can be divided into three distinct regions: Namakwa in the west; the Kalahari to the north of the Gariep River; and the Karoo to the south. Despite the pervasive arid conditions, it is an area of excellent game viewing, with the magnificent Kgalagadi Transfrontier Park offering one of the finest national park experiences in Africa. In spring, Namakwa becomes the main attraction, as the valleys are transformed into carpets of vibrant colour as desert flowers explode from the earth with the first rains. The Gariep River – formerly the Orange – runs through much of the state; it was recently been given its Nama name, meaning 'great river'. It thunders over the surreal Augrabies Falls, the fifth largest in the world, and offers superb whitewater rafting. Lastly, this is diamond country, and the key town of Kimberley has a rich history and a number of sights, not least the colossal diamond mines themselves.

Getting around

The Northern Cape is not well served by public transport and long-distance buses only run along the N7, the route from Cape Town to Namibia. To explore the remote settlements of the Kalahari, Namakwa (Namaqualand) or the Kgalagadi Transfrontier Park, you'll need a car and should be prepared for some challenging driving. Distances are vast, fuel needs careful attention and you need to plan your journey carefully to reach your destination before dark, as animals on the road make driving at night dangerous. Breakdowns can be a problem in remote regions, so it's useful to carry a mobile phone, and, in some areas, a 4WD is advised.

4WD driving is hugely popular in South Africa but 4WD companies are loathe to rent their vehicles to complete novices. Consider doing a one-day 4WD course in your home country before your arrival in South Africa. Alternatively, if you don't want to self-drive there are tours on offer from the regional centres.

Best time to visit

Although summer can be oppressively hot, winter has pleasant daytime temperatures but frost at night; the best times to visit are the more moderate seasons of spring or autumn.

Tourist information

Northern Cape Tourism Authority ① *15 Dalham Rd, Belgravia, Kimberley, T053-833 1434, www.northerncape.org.za*, is responsible for regional information and produces some excellent literature which they can post you.

Kimberley

→ *Colour map 4, A2. Phone code: 053.*

Kimberley, the capital of the Northern Cape, has a fascinating history and it is en route to some of the most beautiful and unspoilt wild country in South Africa – yet it is rarely visited by tourists. It is known first and foremost for its diamonds, and the flat land surrounding the town is pockmarked with mines. No longer the fortune-seeker's frontier town, Kimberley is today a bustling centre with a surprising number of interesting sights. The climate is one of hot summers, with sporadic raging thunderstorms accounting for most of the annual rainfall. The winters are warm but with cold nights and morning frosts. ▶ *For listings, see pages 751-754.*

Ins and outs

Getting there **Kimberley Airport** ① *T053-830 7101, www.acsa.co.za*, is 10 km south of the centre off the N8. Taxis meet incoming flights. There are daily flights to Cape Town and Johannesburg with **SAA**. Mainline trains stop in Kimberley daily on the Tshwane (Pretoria)/Johannesburg–Cape Town route. **Greyhound**, **Intercape** and **Translux** buses to Cape Town, Tshwane (Pretoria) and Johannesburg start and finish their journey outside the Tourist Information Centre in Bultfontein Street. All through services stop at the Shell Ultra City on the Transvaal Road (N12) in the northern suburbs. ▶ *For further details, see Transport, page 754.*

Getting around A subtle reminder of Kimberley's past is the irregular street pattern, reflecting the mud tracks that once criss-crossed between the tented camps and diamond diggings.

Tourist information **Diamond Fields Tourist Information Centre** ⓘ *corner of Bultfontein and Lyndhurst streets, T053-832 7298, www.kimberley.co.za, Mon-Fri 0800-1700, Sat 0800-1300,* has a list of local SATOUR registered guides for tours of the town, the surrounding region and the Kimberley Mine Museum. Staff can also organize a night-time ghost tour, which includes a visit to the spot where a former librarian committed suicide. It is reputed that his ghost is responsible for regularly rearranging the books in the Africana Library. For self-guided walks, pick up one of the useful maps of the Belgravia Historical Walk and the Great Kimberley North Walk, which take in most of the sights. For regional information, visit the **Northern Cape Tourism Authority** (see Tourist information, page 742).

Background

The early history of Kimberley is also the tale of the discovery of diamonds, a definitive turning point in the history of the country. The first significant find was in 1866 on a farm called De Kalk, owned by Daniel Jacobs, near modern-day Hopetown. Jacobs' children gave a stone to their neighbour, Schalk van Niekerk. He in turn gave it to a trader, John O'Reilly, and asked him to find out the value of the stone. The stone ended up in Grahamstown in the hands of Dr Guyborn Atherstone, who found it to be a diamond of 21.25 carats, worth R1000 and later named *Eureka*. In 1869 Schalk van Niekerk bartered for a larger stone from a Griqua shepherd; news soon spread of this stone and public interest began to grow. It came to be known as *The Star of Africa* and, in 1974 was sold in Geneva for over half a million US dollars.

In 1869 the search for diamonds was divided between two areas: the wet diggings along the Vaal River and the dry diggings on two farms 40 km south. The Vaal River diggings attracted most prospectors, as the summer heat and drought made conditions very tough on farms at Bultfontein and Dorstfontein. In December 1870 the future of the region was determined when the children of Adriaan van Wyk found diamonds near their farm, Dorstfontein. The area was immediately overrun by diamond-diggers and their equipment, including a party from Colesberg led by Fletwood Rawstone, known as the Red Caps. One night a servant appeared at his master's tent with a handful of diamonds. He had found them on the slopes of a hill on the nearby farm of Vooruitzicht, owned by the brothers Diederick and Nicolaas Johannes de Beer. The hill was named Colesberg Kopje and, within just a few months, 50,000 diggers had turned the hill into a hole. Living conditions were very tough and supplies expensive. In 1873 the name 'New Rush' was changed to Kimberley in honour of the Earl of Kimberley, British Secretary of State for the Colonies. A twin town grew up around the Bultfontein and Du Toit's pan mines, called Beaconsfield, after Benjamin Disraeli, the Earl of Beaconsfield. In 1912 the two towns amalgamated to become a city.

As the mines delved deeper, it became clear that individual claims would have to merge; there was simply no way of keeping them separate. At one point, there were 1600 separate claims at the Kimberley mine (now known as the Big Hole; see page 745). In addition to the problems of mining logistics, the price of diamonds started falling because of over production. It was at this point that Cecil John Rhodes (see page 746) and his partner, Charles Dunell Rudd, entered the scene. Together they began buying up claims in the De Beers mine and, in 1880, they founded the De Beers Mining Company. As Rhodes and Rudd expanded their operation, they came up against a man with similar ideas, Barney Barnato. The ensuing infamous power struggle was only resolved when Rhodes gave Barnato a colossal pay-off for his Kimberley Central Mining Company. The Big Hole stopped producing diamonds in 1914 but three mines remain productive today: Dutoitspan, Bultfontein and Wesselton.

Sights

Most of Kimberley's attractions are connected to the diamond industry. Although there are some elegant Victorian buildings in town, there is far less evidence of the diamond wealth here than one might expect. Indeed, Kimberley was little more than a rough frontier settlement for much of its history, with most of the diamond wealth returning to the more civilized and comfortable surroundings of the Cape. Nevertheless, it is thought that in the 1890s more millionaires met together under the roof of the **Kimberley Club** ① *T053-832 4224, www.kimberleyclub.co.za, now a luxury hotel (see Sleeping, page 751),* than anywhere else in the world. Past members include Cecil Rhodes and Ernest and Harry Oppenheimer. The club still stands in Du Toitspan Road close to the Africana Library, and the 1891 building is now a national monument. Also on Du Toitspan Road is a **statue of Cecil Rhodes** astride his horse with a map of Africa on his lap, while just south of here, opposite the Civic Centre, are the **Oppenheimer Memorial Gardens** and the **Diggers Fountain**. This is a memorial to Sir Ernest Oppenheimer, mining magnet and erstwhile Mayor of Kimberley, featuring a fountain and a statue of five miners holding up a sieve, surrounded by a rose garden.

The suburb of **Belgravia** (see page 748) has a fine collection of Victorian houses but the rest of the centre has dull modern shops and office blocks. (The Kimberley Mine Museum

Kimberley

| 300 metres |
| 300 yards |

N

Sleeping 🛏
Carrington Lodge 12

Cecil John Rhodes
Guest House 2
Edgerton House 11
Estate 4
Garden Court
Kimberley 6

Greatbatch Guest House
& Backpackers 1
Gum Tree Lodge 9
Kimberley Club 5
Milner House 7
Protea Diamond Lodge 3

Eating 🍴
George & Dragon 1
Halfway House 5
Old Diggers Inn 7
Star of the West 4
Umberto's 6

Big Hole: big statistics

The Big Hole is the largest hand-dug hole on earth, with a surface area of 17 ha and perimeter of 1.6 km. Before consolidation of diggings, 50,000 men dug here night and day, and for several kilometres around Kimberley you could hear the dull noise of tapping and machinery. The diggers reached 400 m down before it became impossible to mine as a group of individuals. In 1889 De Beers sunk the first shaft, extending the hole to a depth of 800 m. By August 1914, when the mine was closed, the shafts were 1100 m deep.

It is estimated that between 22 and 28 million tonnes of earth were removed to create the Big Hole. All this labour resulted in the recovery of 14.5 million carats: only 2722 kg of diamonds or less than three metric tonnes. Today, water fills the hole to a depth of over 600 m.

has some early pictures of the city centre, see below.) Today, the town's skyline is dominated by the **Telkom Tower** and the De Beers headquarters, an ugly tinted-glass building. More interesting is the equally unattractive **Harry Oppenheimer House**, near the Civic Centre. This is the main diamond sorting centre in South Africa, which was designed to allow in optimum natural light by which to judge the stones.

The pale yellow and white, Corinthian-style **City Hall** was built in 1899. From here, you can catch a **tram** ⓘ *daily 0900-1600, on the hour every hour, R7*, to the Kimberley Mine Museum. Trams played an important role in the history of public transport in Kimberley. The first passenger tramway, pulled by mule, was opened in June 1887 to bring labour from the Beaconsfield township to Kimberley. Today, the restored model in Kimberley, dating from the early 1900s, is the only working tram in South Africa.

Africana Library

ⓘ *Du Toitspan Rd, T053-830 6247. Mon-Fri 0800-1245, 1330-1630.*

The Africana Library is a major research centre and a rewarding place to visit for those with a particular interest in local history. There is a wealth of archive material on the diamond industry, missionary work in the region and early SeTswana books. Two of its most famous books are Dr Moffat's copy of his 1829 translation of the Old Testament into SeTswana, the first bible to be printed in Africa, and a first edition of Schedel's *Nuremburg Chronicle*, 1493.

William Humphreys Art Gallery

ⓘ *Jan Smuts Blvd, in the Civic Centre complex, T053-831 1724, www.whag.co.za. Mon-Fri 0800-1645, Sat 1000-1645, Sun 1400-1645, R5, children (under 16) R2.*

This gallery houses one of the most important art collections in South Africa, with fine examples of 16th- and 17th-century art by British and Flemish Old Masters. More interesting is the newer collection of contemporary South African art. There are works by South African impressionists, an excellent graphics and prints display and a few individual treasures, such as the Irma Stern portraits. Also of interest is the rock engravings collection, tracing ancient San engravings dating back to 12,000 BC with photographs and actual examples.

Kimberley Mine Museum and the Big Hole

ⓘ *Entrance on Tucker St, T053-830 4417, www.thebighole.co.za. 0800-1700; 1-hr guided tours run throughout the day, last tour 1600, R70, children (4-17) R40, under 4s free, family of four package R180. All facilities are wheelchair friendly, there are shops and restaurants.*

Cecil John Rhodes

Cecil Rhodes was perhaps the ultimate British imperialist and he played a central role in the history of southern Africa in the years after the discovery of diamonds at Kimberley.

He was born in the English town of Bishops Stortford in 1853 and was sent to Natal at the age of 17 to work on his brother's farm and to recuperate from bouts of tuberculosis. He was not, however, suited to farming life and soon set off for the new diamond sites at Kimberley. From humble beginnings he began to prosper, slowly buying up shares in diamond-buying concerns and through other schemes related to the diggings. With the money he earned from these businesses, he went back to England in 1872 to study for a degree at Oxford. The contacts he made while at Oxford put him in an advantageous position in Kimberley and he was able to utilize British capital in his programme of gaining control of all the diamond mining activities. In 1880 Rhodes founded the De Beers Diamond Mining Company and continued to expand his commercial interests.

When diamonds were first discovered, plots were sold cheaply to the first digger to lay claim to the site but, very quickly, and especially as the diggings became deeper, one or two individuals and companies managed to buy up all the shares and monopolize the buying and selling of diamonds. By the end of the 1880s, there were only really two players left in the game: Cecil Rhodes and Barney Barnato. In 1888, with the backing of British capital, Rhodes eventually bought out Barnato – with one cheque for the sum of £5,338,650.

As befits a grand imperialist, Rhodes combined his hugely successful business career with a career in politics. He was first elected to the Cape parliament, as member for Barkly West, in 1880, and soon gained a reputation as an ardent supporter of British interests in South Africa and the expansion of British rule to the whole of southern Africa. In 1890 he became the colony's Prime Minister and continued to advocate British imperial expansion into remaining African-controlled areas, such as Pondoland. This expansionism was driven partly by jingoistic pride in Britain but mainly by his commercial ambitions.

Despite Rhodes' commercial genius he had made a serious miscalculation when

Sitting alongside the Big Hole, this fascinating museum underwent a major R52 million revamp and extension in 2006. Guided tours take in all the components and begin with a short film that tells the full Kimberley diamond story.

The **Old Mining Town** is made up of a collection of 40 original and model buildings dating from the late 19th century that have been arranged to form a muddle of streets, with sound effects such as singing or snatches of conversation playing inside the shops. Each shop or office is furnished with items dating from the early days of Kimberley, and the overall result is very effective. There are a number of professions on show, including Dr JM Osborne's dental surgery, R Bodley & Son Undertakers, Barney Barnato's Boxing Academy, EHW Awty, a well-known watchmaker, the Standard Bank and A Ciring, the Pawnbroker – the window display includes objects that have never been redeemed. One of the most impressive items is the original De Beers Directors' Private Pullman Railway Coach, a very plush carriage complete with a dining table, laid with silverware and cut-glass decanters, and luxurious leather chairs. Another highlight is Sir Davis Harris' ballroom, an ingenious structure built in 1901. It is constructed entirely out of corrugated gold was first discovered on the Witwatersrand. Taking the advice of an American prospector who told him that the gold was not even worth getting off a horse for, Rhodes decided to sit out the initial rush to buy up the best goldfields. By the time the true worth of the new reef was apparent, Rhodes was too late to make an economic killing, though he did become involved with deep-level mining activities. Frustrated by missing a golden opportunity, Rhodes began to look to the lands further to the north, beyond the Limpopo River. Gold had been mined in these areas for centuries in small-scale mines. In 1888 Rhodes sent his Kimberley business partner, Charles Dunell Rudd, to secure from Lobengula, the leader of the Ndebele, mineral rights in the area they controlled. Armed with the mineral concession, he was able to secure agreement from London to set up a 'charter company' (the South Africa Company), which would not only prospect for minerals in the area but also be granted ownership of all the land and run all the administration. In 1890 Rhodes sent out a 'Pioneer Column' to lay claim to the area. Their dreams of huge gold reserves proved illusory but the country was still rich in minerals and many of the pioneers indulged in the settlers' favourite activity of land speculation.

With the failure to find a second Witwatersrand, Rhodes turned his attention back to his investments in the Transvaal. Rhodes' annoyance with President Kruger's constraints on non-Boer residents led him to make one of his worst political mistakes in backing the ill-fated Jameson Raid. This failed attempt to topple Kruger's government led to a serious breach in relations between Rhodes and Afrikaners in the Cape. He was forced to resign as Prime Minister and take a less public role in the Charter Company in Rhodesia.

At the outbreak of the Anglo-Boer War, Rhodes was staying at his house in Kimberley, where he remained throughout the siege (see page 749). His health was poor throughout much of his life and the harsh conditions during the siege did not help. He died in his Muizenberg cottage outside Cape Town in 1902; his body was transported by train and gun carriage to be buried in the Matopo Hills in present-day Zimbabwe.

iron, with stamped steel walls made to look like smart wallpaper, fake skirting boards and metal stucco on the ceilings.

The new and very impressive 90 m-long viewing platform over the **Big Hole** (see also page 745) looks a bit like half a suspension bridge, and it sticks out over the rim of the hole so you can look down and see the murky green lake at the bottom. It is an astounding sight when you remember that only a fraction of the hole lies above the water level, and that every piece of earth and rock was removed by hand. The viewing platform is 30 x 30 ft in size – the exact size of a 19th-century mining claim.

The **Underground Mine Experience** is a mock-up of a 19th-century mine shaft, where visitors can experience the heat and dust and hear trembling dynamite blasts. Inside the **Exhibition Centre** are examples of the first machines used in the diamond-mining industry, and early photographs of the diggings as the Big Hole gradually started to take shape, providing a vivid impression of life during the heady days of the boom. In the art gallery is a set of De Beers-commissioned watercolours depicting Victorian life in Kimberley. Equipment used to process diamonds can be seen in the Pulsator Building, where you can try your hand at sorting and selecting diamonds. The **Real Diamond Display** is more of a bank vault than a hall, and contains a collection of uncut stones, including the *616 diamond* (at 616 carats, it's the world's largest octahedron uncut diamond), and *Eureka*, the first diamond found on the banks of the Orange River in 1864 by curious children.

Belgravia
Just to the east of the city centre is the residential suburb of Belgravia where many of the wealthy mines people built grand Victorian houses. There is a 2-km historical walk through the suburb, which takes you past most of the old buildings, and a map is available from the tourist office. The majority can only be appreciated from the outside, as they remain in private hands, but the best of the buildings open to the public are **Rudd House** ① *5-7 Loch Rd*, and **Dunluce** ① *10 Lodge Rd*. Both are national monuments and have been fully restored. They are kept closed for security reasons but they can be viewed on weekdays by prior arrangement with the McGregor Museum (see below). The first owner of Dunluce was Gustav Bonus of Dunluce, who instructed the architect to design a house fit for a member of the Diamond Syndicate. He was not disappointed; when the house was completed in 1897 it perfectly reflected the prosperity of the period. Unfortunately, it was badly damaged during the Siege of Kimberley in 1899 by a shell from the Boers' infamous 'Long Tom' gun.

Also in Belgravia is the **Duggan-Cronin Gallery** ① *T053-839 2700, Mon-Sat 1000-1300, 1400-1700, Sun 1400-1700, donation*, set back on Edgerton Road. The basis of this collection is a series of 8000 ethnographic photographs taken between 1919 and 1939 by Alfred Martin Duggan-Cronin, a De Beers' nightwatchman with an interest in photography.

McGregor Museum
① *2 Edgerton Rd, entrance from Atlas St, T053-842 0099, www.museumsnc.co.za. Mon-Sat 0900-1700, Sun 1400-1700, R12, children (under 16) R6, café and museum shop.*
The history of this building is worth mentioning in addition to the collection inside. The original house was built by Rhodes to serve as a hotel and a health spa, since the pure dry climate of Kimberley was thought to be healthy. During the siege of Kimberley, Rhodes lived in two rooms on the ground floor. These now form part of the museum and are furnished as he had them; note the austere surroundings preferred by Rhodes. During the next period of use, the building was converted into the very elegant **Hotel Belgrave**. One of the rooms upstairs has been furnished as it would have been in the 1920s. As the diamond industry fell into decline, the wealthy customers disappeared and the hotel was forced to close. In 1933 it was taken over by the Sisters of the Holy Family and turned into a school and convent. Forty years later the McGregor Museum moved its displays and offices here.

The collection is a mix of objects depicting the history of Kimberley and the northern region, and standard displays of natural history. While the latter are of little interest, the displays relating to Kimberley are reasonably absorbing.

Galeshewe
① *For tours of Galeshewe, contact the tourist office.*
Kimberley was the first town in South Africa to establish 'locations' for housing non-white mine labourers on its outskirts. The resulting township, rose significantly in importance during the struggle against Apartheid, and was second only to Soweto as a centre of political activism. It was home to **Robert Sobukwe**, the leader of the Pan African Congress (PAC), who spent the last days of his life under house arrest in Galeshewe, following his imprisonment on Robben Island.

Siege of Kimberley

During the Anglo-Boer War, Kimberley was besieged by some 4000 Boer soldiers between 15 October 1899 and 16 February 1900. Hemmed inside the town were 500 British troops under Colonel Kekewich and about 50,000 civilians including the town's most famous resident, Cecil Rhodes, whose capture was a particularly enticing prospect for the Boers. However, they never broke through carefully mounted British defences, as the surrounding countryside made an attack difficult.

The Boers, therefore, had to content themselves with trying to starve the town into surrender. Nevertheless, the extensive stores owned by De Beers Diamond Mining Company meant that the town did not suffer from food shortages to the same extent as Ladysmith or Mafeking, and Kekewich prudently passed a military law that all food prices were to remain at pre-siege levels. The town's inhabitants did suffer, though, and inevitably the African population suffered the most. There were widespread reports of scurvy and high rates of infant mortality. By the end horse meat was the main item on many menus.

Rhodes, nearing the end of his life, put the resources of De Beers into defending the town. This included manufacturing ammunition in the mine's workshops and, most impressively, a big gun, nicknamed 'Long Cecil', that could return fire on the Boer siege guns. The main mine tower was invaluable as a lookout post. The system undoubtedly saved many lives – though the shelling did take a heavy toll.

Relations between Colonel Kekewich and Rhodes were very poor. Rhodes wanted the town relieved and could not understand why a large British army located just 20 miles away at Modder River was unable to break through and relieve them. To the ire of Kekewich he managed to get out to the South African and British press increasingly critical statements about the performance of the British military. In February 1900 Rhodes threatened to call a public meeting, at which Kekewich was convinced he would call for Kimberley to surrender, unless they were given specific information about plans to relieve the town. Kekewich was determined that the meeting should not take place so, instead, Rhodes and 12 other leading citizens demanded that Kekewich send a message to the British Commander-in-Chief, General Roberts, calling for their immediate relief. When Kekewich refused, the two of them almost resorted to a fist fight.

Relief was not far off, however. General Roberts' arrival at Modder River with reinforcements had revitalized the British efforts. A bold plan of attack was developed. The British cavalry completely outflanked General Cronje's Boer forces, unblocking the main advance and allowing Roberts to relieve Kimberley. With this attack the whole impetus of the war turned against the Boers. On 16 February Kimberley was at last relieved and Cecil Rhodes (and many London stockbrokers) could celebrate.

Pioneers of Aviation Museum

ⓘ *General van der Spuy Drive, 4 km from the airport, T053-839 2700. Mon-Sat 0900-1300, 1400-1700 Sun 1400-1700, R5, children (under 16) R2.*

On the site of South Africa's first flying school, this museum comprises a reconstructed hangar and a replica of the biplane used in the early days of flight training. The flying school was set up here in 1913 and graduates were the first pilots of the newly formed South African Aviation Corps, which in turn saw its first action over Walvis Bay in May 1915.

Around Kimberley

Kamfers Dam

Kamfers Dam is 5 km out of town on the N12 towards Johannesburg, partially hidden from the road by the raised railway line. This is a natural heritage site and an important area for greater and lesser flamingos; drive past the dam and look out for the carpet of pink created by the flamingos. Sadly, the waters are under threat from continual agricultural pollution, and it has been predicted that the flamingos may soon disappear from here. Look out for a gravel track leading from the road under the railway line, where there is a small parking area.

Magersfontein Battlefield Museum → *Colour map 4, B2.*

ⓘ *32 km from Kimberley; follow the road to Bloemfontein and follow signs for Modder River, T053-833 7115. 0800-1645, R10, children (5-16) R5. Tea room.*

On 11 December 1899 one of the most famous battles of the Anglo-Boer War took place here. The British force, commanded by Lieutenant-General Lord Methuen, was defeated by a Boer force under General Piet Cronje while trying to aid a besieged Kimberley (see page 749). This was the first appearance of trench warfare and the first major defeat suffered by the British: in the first encounter 239 British soldiers were killed and 663 wounded. The Boer trenches can still be seen from the hilltop and in the museum you can experience what it was like in a trench mock-up. There are nine memorials commemorating the dead, including a Celtic cross in memory of the Highland Regiment, a granite memorial to the Scandinavians who fought with the Boers, and a marble cross in memory of the Guards Brigade.

Mokala National Park

ⓘ *Roughly 80 km southwest of Kimberley; take the N12 towards Cape Town and after 57 km, at the Heuningneskloof Crossing, turn right, then drive 21 km along a gravel road to the park turn-off, T053-204 0158, www.sanparks.org. Gate and office, Sep-Apr 0600-1900, May-Aug 0700-1800, R72, children (under 12) R36.*

South Africa's newest national park was proclaimed in June 2007. The name means 'camel thorn' in Setswana and aptly describes the 19,611 ha region of dry savannah dotted with acacia trees. It also features a number of rocky outcrops and a Mokala was created as a home for animals relocated from the former Vaalbos National Park closer to Kimberley, which was de-proclaimed after a successful land claim made by local people. Some 863 animals were moved, including five white rhinos and 141 buffalo, and other species such as giraffe, red hartebeest, blue wildebeest, tsessebe, gemsbok, zebra, springbok and eland. SANParks are expected to use the park for breeding projects for roan and sable antelope.

A 70-km network of good gravel roads for game viewing has been laid out and you can arrange guided game walks and night drives with reception. SANParks are considering introducing horse riding and mountain biking, given that there are no predators. As everything is new, there's excellent accommodation here (see Sleeping, page 752).

Routes west from Kimberley

Wildebeest Kuil Rock Art Centre

ⓘ *16 km from Kimberley on the R31 towards Barkly West, T053-833 7069, www.wildebeest kuil.itgo.com, Mon-Fri 1000-1700, Sat and Sun 1100-1600, R15, children (under) 16) R5.*

This is a community tourism initiative offering guided tours to open-air sites displaying glacial geological rock formations, which have been covered in ancient San rock engravings, thought to be 1500 years old. There is a visitor centre with shop and tearoom, an auditorium showing a short film about the rock art and an 800-m walking trail. You can meet the local community of Xun and Khwe San people who were granted 1200 ha of land under the Land Reform Programme. The communities share this land, from where they produce traditional and progressive arts and crafts, which are for sale in the shop.

Barkly West → *Colour map 4, A2. Phone code: 053.*
The R31 passes through Barkly West, 32 km from Kimberley en route to Kuruman. The first site of the diamond rush in South Africa, the town is named after Sir Henry Barkly, Governor of the Cape when diamonds were discovered here. This is also the town Cecil Rhodes represented when he was first elected to the Cape parliament.

Today, the town is tatty and run down, and you may still see prospectors using manual methods to work their claims along the **Vaal River**. In 1869, the first diamond-digging area, known as **Klipdrift**, drew thousands of prospectors to the river. The following year the diggers at Canteen Kopje took the unexpected step of establishing the independent Republic of Klipdrift. In 1871 the Cape government decided to annex the territory to keep it out of the hands of the Transvaal government. On the north bank of the Vaal River is the steel-girdered **Barkly Bridge**, which was the first bridge to span the river in 1885.

Wonderwerk Cave
ⓘ *Signposted 45 km before Kuruman, T082-832 7226, book in advance and then stop at the homestead to collect a key, 0830-1300, 1400-1700, R7, children (5-16) R4. Allow 1 hr for a visit. Small display centre and toilets, and there are 3 simple self-catering chalets.*
Wonderwerk Cave is an important archaeological site on a private farm, set back from the road in the Kuruman Hills. The main attraction is some rock paintings and the evidence of early human habitation. The display contains interesting material on the prehistory of the region. The cave has been extensively examined by the Mcgregor Museum in Kimberley; most of the floor has been divided into squares for research purposes and archaeologists are often at work here. In 2008, stone tools were found thought to date to two million years. It stretches back 140 m into the hillside, with a level path leading into it. The rock paintings are near the entrance. The great-grandparents of the current owners (and their 11 children) lived in the cave when they first settled in the region and started farming.

◉ Kimberley listings

For Sleeping and Eating price codes and other relevant information, see pages 46-53.

● Sleeping
All the hotels can organize transfers by taxi from the airport.

Kimberley *p742, map p744*
B Edgerton House, 5 Edgerton Rd, T053-831 1150, www.edgertonhouse.co.za. Historic house built in 1901 with pressed ceilings, wooden floors, fireplaces, plenty of antiques, 11 a/c double rooms with en suite bathroom,

some with free-standing tubs and gold-plated fittings, TV, all meals available, swimming pool, gardens, secure parking. A relatively large guesthouse with home comforts. Nelson Mandela has stayed here.
B Kimberley Club, Du Toitspan Rd, T053-832 4224, www.kimberleyclub.co.za. Founded in 1881 by Cecil Rhodes, this beautiful building is now Kimberley's most atmospheric place to stay with gleaming wooden floors, stained-glass windows, chandeliers, fine antique furniture and oil paintings. The comfortable rooms have old-fashioned writing desks,

wing-back chairs and some have Victorian baths. Modern amenities include a/c, internet and DSTV. Superb restaurant in the elegant original club dining room.

B-C Carrington Lodge, 60 Carrington Rd, T053-831 6448, www.carringtonlodge.co.za. A comfortable guesthouse with 15 en suite rooms with DSTV, ceiling fans and minibar opening up to the colonial-style veranda. Spacious gardens with pool, hearty cooked breakfasts and dinner on request served in the pretty dining room. Central, secure parking.

C Cecil John Rhodes Guest House, 138 Du Toitspan Rd, T053-830 2500, www.ceciljohn rhodes.co.za. Luxurious old-style guesthouse set in converted house built in 1895 that is a national monument. 7 comfortable rooms, en suite bathrooms, a/c, DSTV, shady tea garden, friendly management, attached tea garden, dinner on request. Recommended.

C The Estate Private Hotel, 7 Lodge Rd, T053-832 2668, www.theestate.co.za. Luxury hotel set in a house built for Sir Ernest Oppenheimer's wife as a wedding present in 1907. Offers 7 a/c rooms, grand furnishings such as gilt mirrors and wing-back chairs, gardens with pool, superb **Butler's** restaurant offering gourmet food (see Eating), close to sights.

C Garden Court Kimberley, 120 Du Toitspan Rd, T053-833 1751, www.southernsun.com. Bland but comfortable hotel with 135 a/c rooms in a concrete block, some with disabled access. Restaurant is an attached franchise **Spur** steakhouse. Bar, swimming pool, sauna.

C Milner House, 31 Milner St, T053-831 6405, www.milnerhouse.co.za. Well-run guesthouse in a good location in Belgravia. 6 luxurious double rooms with fans, en suite bathroom, TV, bar, swimming pool, large gardens, log fires in the winter evenings, good breakfasts, internet access, an excellent B&B.

C Protea Hotel Diamond Lodge, 124 Du Toitspan Rd, T053-831 1281, www.protea hotels.com. 34 large a/c modern rooms, with 2 double beds, minibar, Mnet TV, restaurant, bar and swimming pool. Good value, but all the rooms are on the 1st and 2nd floors and there are no lifts.

D-F Greatbatch Guest House and Backpackers, 3 Edgerton Rd, T053-832 1113. Backpackers set-up in an original mining mansion built by Daniel Greatbatch, who was the architect of many of Kimberley's historic homes. Good central location in Belgravia and on the historic walk route, a mixture of doubles, self-catering flats, with or without bathrooms but all with DSTV, kettle and microwave, and 2 dorms sleeping 10 in each, pool, central thatched lapa, bar with pool table, kitchen for self-catering or you can order meals. Communal areas are decorated with antiques and mining memorabilia.

D-F Gum Tree Lodge, Old Bloemfontein Rd (R64), 4 km from town, T053-832 8577, www.gumtreelodge.com. Large complex on 5 ha, with 150 beds in dorms and doubles with communal kitchen, some self-contained flats, lounge, **Old Diggers** restaurant and bar next door, shop, TV room, pool. A fair option for budget travellers and families, quiet but inconvenient for the sights.

Mokala National Park *p750*

There are 3 brand new high-quality camps in the park (and more rustic ones are planned for the future) and a campsite. Reservations through **SANParks** in Tshwane (Pretoria), T012-428 9111, www.sanparks.org, Mon-Fri. For late bookings (under 48 hrs) and camping contact the park direct, T053-204 0158. Wheelchair-bound visitors are accommodated in all the camps, enquire with SANParks.

B Mosu Lodge. 16 en suite rooms with ceiling fans, crisp white linen and quality wooden furniture set in attractive stone buildings with neat thatched roofs. Pool, restaurant with bar, very comfortable and well-furnished lounge and entertainment area with fireplace, and outdoor fire-pit.

C Mofele Lodge. More rustic than Mosu, with 9 en suite rooms with ceiling fans, sleeping up to 5. Bar, lounge and entertainment area with fireplace. Although there is a restaurant, this is presently only open to conference groups. Visitors eat at Mosu, which is only a short drive away.

D Lilydale Lodge. 12 self-catering units sleeping up to 5, with a/c, veranda and braai. Overlooking the Riet River in the north of the park, where canoeing and fly fishing can be arranged and the birdlife is especially good.

Camping
Haak-en-Steek. Simple unfenced site with 10 pitches, ablutions, lapa and braai but no kitchen facilities. A lovely spot overlooking a large waterhole where rhino and buffalo are regular visitors. There's also 1 self-catering family cottage (**C**) here.

🍴 Eating

Kimberley *p742, map p744*
Kimberley is better served by pubs and bars than restaurants. There are the usual fast-food outlets by the taxi stand behind the City Hall, including **King Pie**, **Steer's** and **Captain Do Regos**. There are also the standard chain steak restaurants, and a number of bars and restaurants in the **Flamingo Casino** complex just out of town on the N12 towards Johannesburg (see right).
♔♔♔ Butler's, **The Estate Private Hotel**, see Sleeping, page 752, T053-833 1038. Open 1600-2200. Gourmet, formal and intimate restaurant with sweeping drapes, starched white linen and silverware. Inventive menu that mixes flavours such as springbok carpaccio with rose petal ice cream or mussels with biltong and peppadew sauce. Reservations essential.
♔♔ George & Dragon, 187 Du Toitspan Rd, T053-833 2075. Open 1100-late. Popular English-style pub serving decent meals and beer on tap, varied menu from steaks to their famous foot-long pies. Part of a chain that is slightly more upmarket than most bars. Good for lunch and stays open until 0200 if the demand is there.
♔♔ Halfway House, Du Toitspan Rd, T053-831 6324. Mon-Sat 1030-0200. Historical pub with bizarre drive-in section, claiming to be where Cecil Rhodes used to ride in to sip a quick

beer while still on his horse. Good atmosphere, late opening, simple pub meals, can get very busy at weekends.
♔♔ Star of the West, North Circular Rd, T053-832 6463. Open 1000-late. The oldest pub in South Africa, dating from 1873. It was originally a corrugated-iron shack were thirsty miners paid tuppence for a beer and a halfpenny for a glass of wine. Bit of a tourist trap but characterful, with a long wooden bar. Tram to the Mine Museum stops outside across the road (on request). Enjoy a cool beer and a pub lunch before visiting the Big Hole.
♔♔ Umberto's, 229 Du Toitspan Rd, T053-832 5741, www.umbertos.co.za. Mon-Sat 1200-1430, 1800-late. Excellent Italian restaurant just next to the **Halfway House**. Superb pizza and home-made pasta dishes, meat and fish a little more expensive, traditional red and white checked tablecloths and friendly service. Recommended.
♔ Old Diggers Inn, next to the **Gum Tree Lodge**, T053-832 8577. Open 0900-2200. Large restaurant frequented by backpackers staying next door. Good-value meals, hearty portions, busy bar, beer on tap, also does takeaways.

🎭 Entertainment

Kimberley *p742, map p744*
Flamingo Casino, 5 km northeast on N12, T053-830 2600, www.suninternational.com. Like many others in South Africa, this is a standard casino complex built on the edge of the city. Gaming floor has a restaurant and bars including the large **129 Show Bar**, which hosts South African bands and comedians, and a 90-bed **Road Lodge** hotel. Adjacent to Kimberley Golf Club (see below).

⛰ Activities and tours

Kimberley *p742, map p744*
Birdwatching
Kimberley is less known for its birds than its Big Hole but there are a number of sites

around town excellent for birdwatching. There are flamingos on Kamfers Dam (see page 750), and 50 pairs of African white-backed vultures can be spotted on the De Beers' Dronfield Farm 2 km north of the city. During summer European bee-eaters breed in the suburb of West End, and saltpans and rivers in the region support populations of waterbirds and raptors.

Cricket
International matches are played at **De Beers Diamond Oval**, Dickenson Av, Cassandra, enquiries T053-833 2601, tickets www.compu ticket.com. Watching a game here makes a pleasant change from the large stadiums found in the cities. The atmosphere is very relaxed and if you're lucky you may meet the players in the club bar. During the domestic season, Kimberley is home to Griqualand West.

Golf
Kimberley Golf Club, 5 km northeast of the city on the N12, T053-841 0484, www.kimberley golfclub.co.za. The course was first laid out in 1890 when dynamite from the mine was used to clear stones for the fairways. In 2001 it was extensively upgraded when they built the adjoining **Flamingo Casino**. Visitors welcome.

Tour operators
Diamond Tours Unlimited, T083-265 7795, www.diamondtours.co.za. ½- and full-day tours of local diamond-mining sites including Barkly West, 35 km northwest of Kimberley, where old prospectors still pan by hand.

⊖ Transport

Kimberley *p742, map p744*
Johannesburg is 485 km, **Cape Town** 979 km, **Kuruman** 238 km and **Upington** 401 km.

Air
Kimberley Airport is 10 km south of the centre, T053-830 7101, www.acsa.co.za. SAA, T011-978 1111, www.flysaa.com, operates daily flights between Kimberley and **Johannesburg**.

Bus
Buses depart from outside the Tourist Information Centre on Bultfontein Rd. There are daily services to **Cape Town** (13 hrs), **Johannesburg** and **Tshwane** (**Pretoria**) (6½ hrs). The latter 2 services also stop at the Shell Ultra City on N12, 6 km from the centre.

Bus companies All bus tickets can be booked online at www.computicket.com. **Greyhound**, www.greyhound.co.za; **Intercape**, www.intercape.co.za; and **Translux**, www.translux.co.za. For more information, see Getting around, page 41.

Car hire
All companies are based at the airport and are open all day Mon-Fri, but only when flights arrive Sat-Sun. If you plan taking a vehicle to cross the border to Namibia make sure you mention this. **Avis**, T053-851 1082; www.avis.co.za; **Budget**, T053-851 1182, www.budget.co.za; **Hertz**, T053-830 2200, www.hertz.co.za; **Tempest**, T053-851 1516, www.tempestcarhire.co.za.

Taxi
AA Taxis, T053-861 4015. The main taxi rank is behind the City Hall.

Train
Station is on Florence St. Central reservations, **Shosholoza Meyl**, T0860-00888, T011-774 4555 (from overseas), www.shosholoza meyl.co.za. Check website for timetables and fares. There are daily trains to **Cape Town** and **Johannesburg/Tshwane** (**Pretoria**).

⊙ Directory

Kimberley *p742, map p744*
Banks ABSA, 69 Du Toitspan Rd; Standard Bank, 10 Old Main St. **Internet** At the hotels and backpackers; Small World Net Café, 42 Sidney St, T053-831 3484. **Medical services** Medi-Clinic Private Hospital, 177 Du Toitspan Rd, T053-838 1111, www.kimberleymc.co.za.

The Kalahari

The Kalahari, like all great deserts, evokes images of vast lapis skies, shimmering horizons and cruel heat. The name Kalahari is derived from Kgalagadi, the San term for 'place without water'. It is at once enthralling and intimidating, begging to be explored but overwhelming in its sheer size and harshness. The landscape is semi-desert – rolling red sand dunes, salt pans, dry river beds and endless scrub – stretching from the Gariep (Orange) River to northern Botswana and west into Namibia. Despite the arid conditions, the Kalahari supports some of the best game viewing in South Africa, in the magnificent Kgalagadi Transfrontier Park. But the main draw of the Kalahari is its vast open spaces and the true wilderness of the desert; even today, travelling here evokes a real sense of adventure. For more information on the Kalahari visit www.roaringkalahari.co.za. ➤➤ *For listings, see pages 765-770.*

Ins and outs

Getting around Kuruman is the principal town in this part of the Kalahari. If you plan to travel north from here, make sure you stock up on all supplies and check the condition of your car, especially water, oil and fuel levels. The R31 north is one of only two routes to the Kgalagadi Transfrontier Park. The only other road into the park is from Upington. Each route involves stretches on gravel, although much of the road between Upington and Askam is now tarred. Note that driving on loose gravel and sand can be dangerous and these are not the best conditions in which to break down. Do not be tempted to drive too fast if the roads are empty and straight. If you have an accident you could be waiting a long time for help.

Climate As a desert, the Kalahari region is known for its extreme temperatures. Rainfall in the region is only 50 mm annually and usually arrives in dramatic but brief thunderstorms during summer. Temperatures in the northern Kalahari and along the Gariep (Orange) River often reach above 40°C during the summer, while, on winter nights, they can drop as low as 6°C – a consideration if camping.

Kuruman ⊜🅿🅰🅱🅲 ➤➤ *pp765-770. Colour map 1, C4.*

→ *Phone code: 053.*

This isolated northern town has two reasons for being on the tourist map: the Moffat family and their mission station; and a natural spring known as The Eye. Neither take up much time and the town itself is scruffy and unappealing, so half a day here should be more than enough on your way through. However, Kuruman is an important regional centre, so it's a good place to stock up on fuel and supplies.

Ins and outs

The **tourist office** ⓘ *Voortrekker St, T053-712 1001, www.kurumankalahari.co.za, Mon-Fri, 0930-1300, 1400-1600*, is in an old cottage next to The Eye. This is, in fact, the old Drostdy House, once home to the local magistrate. Part of the building is given over to a tea room that serves light lunches and tea and coffee throughout the day. Birdwatchers can pick up a map and an identification list for the northern Kalahari Raptor Route. More than 50 species, 35 of which are resident, have been recorded in the region.

The Eye

ⓘ *Main St, daylight hours, R7, children (under 12) R5.*

The Eye, or 'die oog' in Afrikaans, is an amazing spring which has continuously produced almost 20 million litres of fresh water per day, with little variance between the wet and the dry season. It was the presence of this water and the resultant river that made settlement possible in this area. The site was proclaimed a national monument in 1992. There is little to see of the spring, save for a wet, moss-covered rock, but the gardens around the clear pond are a popular and attractive picnic spot – the pond is full of large goldfish, fattened by breadcrumbs. The enormous willow trees were planted by the first magistrate in 1881. Unfortunately, the grounds are not quite as peaceful as they might appear: there is a constant background noise of buried pumping equipment. The gardens around town rely on the spring water, which is fed into two 7-km-long irrigation channels, giving Kuruman the feel of an oasis during the dry season when the surrounding farmlands are burnt brown.

There is an 11-km **hiking trail** that starts at The Eye, crosses the golf course, goes through some local villages and ends at another small natural spring to the west of Kuruman. Ask the tourist office for a map.

Moffat Mission

ⓘ *5 km north of town, Moffat Lane. Follow Voortrekker St out of town past the police station, T053-712 1352, no public transport, 0800-1700. Allow at least 2 hrs, R10, children (under 12) R5.*

Under the guidance of Robert Moffat (see page 758), the Kuruman Mission Station became one of the best-known missions in Africa. Today it is run by the United Congregational Church of Southern Africa, and the complex is an atmospheric and fascinating place. This was the first house that Livingstone lived in when he came to Africa.

The first building you come to is the **stable**, with a few portraits on the walls and an early wagon used by the mission. Turning left out of the stable, you find yourself walking parallel to a **furrow** that Moffat had dug to bring water from The Eye, 5 km away (see above). Across the furrow is a small garden created by Mary Moffat; it was here that explorer David Livingstone proposed to the Moffats' daughter, after she had nursed him back to health following an attack by a lion. Opposite the garden is the **Moffat Homestead**, built in 1824 and fully restored in the 1980s. Inside, the main room has a few objects on display but, overall, it is disappointing. The kitchen has been turned into a tea room and curio shop. Just beyond the homestead is the original **Mission Church**, for many years the largest building in the interior of South Africa. Despite having only nine converts when he designed the T-shaped church, Moffat planned for it to seat 800 people. The stone walls stood for seven years before timber of sufficient length could be found for the roof. Moffat found the trees on one of his journeys 350 km away in the Marico Valley. The building still has a thatch roof, dung floor and wooden pews, and the acoustics are surprisingly good.

The final building of note is the **school classroom**; inside are the original wooden school benches and desks. The room is now home to the original press Moffat used to print the Tswana Bible, the first bible to be printed in Africa. The press was also used to print school books and publications for the church.

Northwest from Kuruman ● ➤ pp765-770.

Hotazel → *Phone code: 053.*

Travelling on the R31 from Kuruman allows you to explore more of the Kalahari region. This is a good road but it is only surfaced as far north as Hotazel, 61 km from Kuruman.

This is nothing more than searingly hot dorp but is an important manganese ore-mining centre. Oddly enough, **Hotazel Recreation Club** has tennis and squash courts, golf, even bowls, built for the miners but they can be used by visitors for a small fee, and it's not a bad idea to stop for a swim after a hot drive. From Hotazel, the gravel R31 continues through Sonstraal and on to Van Zylsrus, 105 km from Hotazel.

Tswalu Kalahari Reserve
ⓘ *Off the R31 between Hotazel and Sonstraal, www.tswalu.com.*
Tswalu is a magnificent 100,000-ha reserve created by the late Stephen Boler (British multi-millionaire and former share-holder of Manchester City). Over US$7 million was spent in establishing the enterprise, reputedly South Africa's largest private reserve. Today it is owned by the Oppenheimer family.

At the foot of the Korannaberg mountains, this is a region of stunning red sand dunes and typical savannah dotted with acacia trees. The park has been well stocked with wildlife, including lion, cheetah, buffalo, three types of zebra, red hartebeest, blue and black wildebeest, giraffe, gemsbok, kudu, impala and wild dog. A breeding programme for the rare desert black rhino has been set up and, from just eight that were introduced from Namibia in 1995, the population now stands at 19. The head count for large game has risen from 5000 to 14,000 in the last decade, so conservation in this region has been incredibly successful. You can explore the reserve on game walks, by 4WD or on horseback. The only places to stay are in the two five-star lodges. Generally, guests arrive by the reserve's private plane from Johannesburg or Cape Town. ⏭ *For further details, see Sleeping, page 765.*

Van Zylsrus to Kgalagadi Transfrontier Park
Van Zylsrus is a typical Kalahari town: one dusty street is lined with a few shops and a tea garden, fittingly called **The Oasis**, but other than that there is little of interest. From Van Zylsrus the road follows the dry course of the Kuruman River for 143 km as far as **Askham**. At this point the route combines with the tarred R360 road from Upington, and just one (gravel) road leads a further 75 km to the gates of the Kgalagadi Transfrontier Park. After a long and dusty drive, the national park camp at **Twee Rivieren** is a welcome sight, especially the swimming pool. The total distance from Kuruman to the park gates is 385 km and from Upington 255 km. These are undeniably tiring journeys but allow you to experience the vast southern fringes of the Kalahari Desert. Obviously your approach to the park rather depends on where you've from, but if you do need to choose, the R360 from Upington is better (given that it's tarred most of the way), whereas the gravel road from Van Zylsrus as far as Askham is badly corrugated. There is also the option of arranging hire car or an organized safari in Upington.

Southwest from Kuruman ⏺ ⏭ *pp765-770.*

Kathu → *Colour map 1, C3. Phone code: 053.*
Just off the main road (N14), this modern settlement is 51 km southwest of Kuruman and has grown up entirely around the mining industry, first started in 1972. This is the location of **Sishen Iron Ore Mine** ⓘ *guided tours are usually held on the first Sat of the month, contact T083-660 5336*, a massive scar in the earth and the largest single pit opencast mine in the world. It's roughly 12 km long and 1.5 km wide, and over 28 million tonnes of iron ore is extracted each year, employing 3200 people. Everything associated with the

Robert Moffat

Robert Moffat is known in southern Africa for two reasons, first for translating the Bible into Tswana and secondly for his association with David Livingstone, the great Victorian explorer of the region. Moffat was born at Ormiston in Scotland into a poor family; he left school at the age of 11 and then worked as a gardener for 10 years – hardly a background to prepare him for 50 years of scholarly work in remotest Africa. After a brief theological training he was accepted by the London Missionary Society on 30 September 1816. His first posting was to Namaqualand where he immediately made a name for himself by converting an outlaw called Jager Afrikaner. In 1819 he married Mary Smith, his employer's daughter, in St George's Church in Cape Town. The first days of their marriage were spent in a wagon crossing the Karoo to Kuruman.

In 1824 Moffat persuaded the missionaries to move to the present site, which he considered far more suitable due to an abundant water supply, and fertile level land ideal for farming. It took four years to build the Moffat Homestead and a house for his colleague, Robert Hamilton. Fine materials were used and neat gardens were laid out. They wanted to show what Christianity could do. The homestead is still standing today and is the oldest building north of the Orange River.

An important part of a missionary's work was teaching. And it was when Moffat was confronted with a class "of Batswanas, Hottentots, two Bushmen and two Mantatees", that he realized the problem of language. The next 40 years of his life were dominated by translation and printing. He was the first person to print the language of the Matabele people, on his press in Kuruman, and so laid the foundations for their modern education system. His greatest feat was the translation of the Bible into Tswana. In 1857 he printed 1000 copies despite a whole range of problems. He then had to teach the Tswana people to read their own language. It was both the first time the Bible had been printed anywhere in Africa, and the first time it had been produced in a previously unwritten African tongue.

It was beyond the capacity of the Kuruman press to print the New Testament, and Moffat could find no one in South Africa to help, so the couple had no choice but to return to England, only to find out that they were famous. This helped them to raise vital funds and to get the printing done but, after three years away, they both yearned for Africa. The Moffats worked in Kuruman until 1870, when the Missionary Society persuaded them to return to England. Mary died within six months of their return but Robert Moffat continued to work for the LMS. He died 13 years later on 9 August 1883. In 1983 a bronze bust of Moffat was moved from Brixton, London, to Kuruman to mark the centenary of his death.

mine is giant – the trucks that move the ore look oversized, and can carry over 170 metric tons. The mine is connected to Saldanha ore terminal on the west coast by a single railway line which you can see in the vicinity of Elands Bay and Velddrif (see page 196). For a small fee visitors are welcome at the mine's **Sishen Golf & Country Club** ① T053-723 3288, www.sishengolfclub.co.za, which has an 18-hole golf course, a clubhouse and bar, a swimming pool, and squash and tennis courts.

→ *Phone code: 054.*

Despite Upington's attractive setting on the banks of the Gariep (Orange) River, it is a bland and modern town with searing summer temperatures and little in the way of sights. It is, however, the largest town in the region, making it a welcome stop for those who've been off the beaten track for a while. It is a major service centre, with all the usual South African shops and high-street chains, and is an excellent place to restock. As a major entry point to the Kalahari, Upington is also a good spot to organize trips to the Kgalagadi Transfrontier Park and Augrabies Falls National Park, and it is also en route, via the **Ariamsvlei/Nakop border crossing**, to the Fish River Canyon in Namibia to the west on the N8.

Ins and outs

Getting there Recently upgraded, **Upington Airport** ① *T054-337 7900, www.acsa.co.za*, is 6 km north of the town off the N10. Taxis meet arriving flights. There are daily flights from Cape Town and Johannesburg, and buses from Cape Town via Clanwilliam, and from Johannesburg and Tshwane (Pretoria). There is a train station but no South African passenger trains stop here and it's only used for freight. However, Namibia's railway company, **Transnamib Starline Passenger Services**, runs a service from Upington in South Africa to Windhoek twice a week. » *For further details, see Transport, page 769.*

Tourist information **Upington Tourist Office** ① *Kalahari Oranje Museum, Schröder St, T054-332 6064, www.upington.co.za, www.upington.com, www.greenkalahari.co.za, Mon-Fri 0900-1230, 1400-1700, Sat 0900-1200,* has a good selection of brochures on the Kalahari area.

Background

The origin of the town is rather more disreputable than one might expect. In the mid-19th century the northern reaches of the Cape Colony were home to a colourful variety of outlaws and rustlers; there were no settlements, making it impossible for the police to track people into the uncharted wilderness. By 1879 the Cape government had had enough and founded a small settlement on the Gariep (Orange) River to try and exercise some control over the area. In 1884 Sir Thomas Upington, the new Prime Minister of the colony, visited the settlement, which was renamed in his honour.

The fortunes of the new settlement and the subsequent development of the district, can be attributed to the pioneering work of two men, the Reverend Christiaan Schröder and Johann 'Japie' Lutz. Together they built the first irrigation canal, constructed a pump on the river and started a pontoon ferry. After the Anglo-Boer War, Lutz built canals at Kakamas, Marchand and Onseepkans. These irrigated areas now produce cotton, lucerne, vegetables, grapes and sultanas. Today the **SA Dried Fruit Cooperative** and the **Gariep (Orange) River Wine Cellars Cooperative** are responsible for handling most of the agricultural produce in the region. Another famous resident was Scotty Smith, a legendary rogue and Robin Hood of the Northern Cape, who stole and gave to the poor. He died in Upington in 1918 during a flu epidemic and his grave is in the local cemetery.

Sights

The main building of the **Kalahari Oranje Museum** ① *Schröder St, overlooking the road bridge, T054-332 6064, 0900-1230, 1400-1700, Sat 0900-1200, free,* is the restored manse where the Reverend Schröder lived in the 1870s. This houses a collection of Victorian furniture and household objects. Look out for item No 20, a fine old compendium of games. The doorways are all very low on account of the Reverend Schröder being somewhat vertically challenged. Inside the church are some odd bits and pieces from Upington's past. They are poorly displayed, although worth seeking out are the photographs of Augrabies Falls in 1957 when they were dry. The building also houses the town tourist office. Outside is a statue of a bronze donkey working a horsemill.

Around Upington

Upington is the nearest town to **Augrabies Falls National Park**, a visit to which is possible in a day trip (see page 772). The highlight of the Northern Cape, the **Kgalagadi Transfrontier Park** is also relatively near, lying 255 km to the north (see page 761), but you'll definitely need a few days to fully appreciate the park.

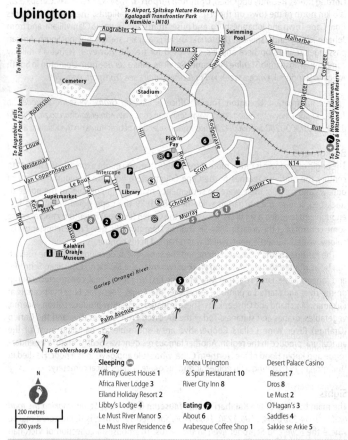

Upington

Sleeping
Affinity Guest House 1
Africa River Lodge 3
Eiland Holiday Resort 2
Libby's Lodge 4
Le Must River Manor 5
Le Must River Residence 6

Protea Upington
  & Spur Restaurant 10
River City Inn 8

Eating
About 6
Arabesque Coffee Shop 1

Desert Palace Casino
  Resort 7
Dros 8
Le Must 2
O'Hagan's 3
Saddles 4
Sakkie se Arkie 5

More than 1000 ha of grapes and 8000 ha of sultanas are cultivated along the Gariep (Orange) River. Upington is a convenient centre for trying some of the wines produced on the vineyards in the region by the **Gariep (Orange) River Wine Cellars Cooperative** ① *T054-337 8800, www.orangeriverwines.com*. You can visit the cooperative shop in Upington's industrial area; ask at the town tourist office for more information. The grapes originate from several hundred wineries along the Gariep (Orange) River and produce an extensive range of wines, from dry whites to dessert wines. Also, an estimated one million tons of table (eating) grapes are exported from the region annually.

Witsand Nature Reserve ① *220 km from Upington, take the N10 and turn off on to the N8 at Groblershoop towards Kimberley, after 59 km turn off north on to the gravel road to the reserve (signposted) for 45 km, information and bookings T053-313 1061, www.witsand kalahari.co.za, gate hours daily 0800-1800, R40, children (under 16) R20*, is a popular day or overnight trip from Upington, and is a beautiful area of desert landscape. The highlight is a collection of white sand dunes set incongruously on the typical red sand of the Kalahari. The dunes are up to 60 m high and stretch for 9 km, making them an impressive sight. The reserve is also home to the well-known 'Brulsand', the phenomenon of roaring sand dunes, thought to be caused by shifting sand lacking the usual red coating of iron oxide, plus the dry air. There is a comfortable resort (see Sleeping, page 766), visitors can walk freely around the reserve, and there is a 4WD trail. However, it gets very hot in summer, when it's best to avoid hiking. There is also a bird hide dug into the ground, allowing an eye-level view of a waterhole; if you're lucky you might spot the pygmy falcon, Africa's smallest raptor. Dune boarding is a new activity here, and boards as well as bicycles can be hired from the information centre.

The 5000-ha **Spitskop Nature Reserve** ① *about 13 km north of Upington off the R360, en route to the Kgalagadi Transfrontier Park, information and bookings, T054-332 1336, www.spitskopmonate.co.za*, makes for a pleasant day or overnight trip at the resort (see Sleeping, page 766) and acts as a good introduction to the flora and fauna that lie further north. Here you can view a variety of wildlife commonly found throughout the Kalahari region, including springbok, eland, zebra and gemsbok. In the centre of the reserve is a *koppie* with an observation platform and telescope. There are hiking trails throughout the reserve, the staff at reception will point you in the right direction, or you can explore the reserve in your own car and there is 37 km of gravel roads.

Kgalagadi Transfrontier Park ● ›› *pp765-770. Colour map 1, B1.*

① *Twee Rivieren is the only entrance on the South African side, T054-561 2000, www.sanparks.org. Gate/office/shop hours vary: Jan and Feb 0600-1930, Mar 0630-1900, Apr and Aug 0700-1830, May 0700-1800, Jun and Jul 0730-1800, Sep 0630-1830, Oct 0600-1900, Nov-Dec 0530-1930. Daily conservation entrance fee R160, children (under 12) R80, also covers your vehicle (South Africans pay reduced rates).*

Although probably one of the least visited national parks in the country, the Kgalagadi Transfrontier Park has some of the finest game viewing in Africa. It is remote and relatively undeveloped, with uncomfortably high summer temperatures, but few begrudge the hot dusty roads once they've glimpsed their first lion. The roads follow the scrubby valleys of two seasonal rivers, the Auob and Nossob, and cut across red sand dunes typical of the Kalahari.

Ins and outs

Getting there From Upington, the first 190 km is an excellent tarred road followed by 61 km of badly corrugated gravel; allow at least 3½ hours to the park gates. Petrol is available at Noenieput and Andriesvale. From Kuruman, it is 385 km to the park gates, via Hotazel, Sonstraal and Van Zylsrus (see page 757).

Best time to visit This is an arid region with less than 200 m of rainfall a year, falling between the summer months of January and April. In the summer it gets very hot and you should carry at least 10 litres of drinking water in your vehicle. The best months are February to May, but most of the accommodation is fully booked during this time, especially at weekends and around Easter. Camping is usually possible, although the main camp, Twee Rivieren, is likely to be very busy. Camping in winter requires warm sleeping bags as temperatures fall below zero. Always check the availability of rooms in advance – this is the end of the road and even space for tents gets fully booked. If you plan to visit during the main season, pre-book your accommodation before your arrival in South Africa.

Park information Kgalagadi is free from malaria. The three main rest camps – **Twee Rivieren**, **Nossob** and **Mata-Mata** – have shops which stock basic groceries including meat, eggs, cheese, milk, bread, soft drinks, beer and wine but none stock fresh vegetables. Twee Rivieren also has a restaurant and swimming pool. Petrol and diesel are available at all the camps; electricity is provided by generators (220v) and is available in the early morning and evening (1700-2300). From each camp guided day walks and night drives are available and can be booked at reception. There are also six unfenced wilderness camps: **Gharagab**, **Kielie Krankie**, **Urikaruus**, **Kalahari Tented Camp**, **Bitterpan** and **Grootkolk**, none of which have shops or other facilities.

Due to the remoteness of the region a close record is kept of your movements and you have to sign in and out of every camp. There is a curfew on returning to the camps in the evening; if you do not make it back to the gates on time, you will be fined. When driving here you have to remember that distances are vast and you may well be delayed considerably by game viewing so some careful planning on driving times is needed. Note, too, that some tracks are one-way only (see map below). Without stops, it takes 2½ hours to drive between Twee Riveren and Mata-Mata (and Kalahari Tented Camp which is 3 km from Mata-Mata); Twee Riveren to Nossob, 3½ hours; Twee Riveren to Grootkolk, six hours; Twee Riveren to Kieliekrankie, 1½ hours; Twee Riveren to Urikaruus, two hours; Nossob to Grootkolk, 2½ hours; Nossob to Bitterpan, 2½ hours; Nossob to Gharagab, four hours; Nossob to Bitterpan, 2½ hours; Bitterpan to Mata-Mata, two hours.

Although the park authorities do allow saloon vehicles into the park, they also point out that they can be uncomfortable on the gravel roads and prone to flat tyres. If you don't have a 4WD, be sure that your car is in good condition and can deal with several days on gravel. Although Twee Rivieren has a car workshop, there is no system in place to cope with breakdowns. In the event of a breakdown, stay in the car and wait for passing cars to assist you. You will have to get back to Twee Rivieren, from where a mechanic can drive out to your car. Never leave the gravel roads; it is illegal to drive off road and it's easy to get stuck in the soft sand. The nearest place to rent a 4WD is in Upington and many operators also hire out camping equipment. Note that all routes on the Botswana side of the park are strictly 4WD and must be travelled in a convoy of at least two vehicles. Except for Twee Riveren, remember there is no mobile phone reception in the park in the event of an emergency.

Background

The area was proclaimed a national park on 3 July 1931 as part of a progressive initiative to combat the problem of poachers. Known until a few years ago as the Kalahari Gemsbok

National Park, the area was adjacent to the Gemsbok National Park in Botswana. On 7 April 1999 the two parks were formally merged into a single ecological unit, now known as the Kgalagadi Transfrontier Park.

The first camp for tourists was built in 1940 near the confluence of the Auob and Nossob rivers. Most of the game viewing is along these riverbeds where the vegetation is concentrated. Thanks to the aridity of the region, vegetation remains sparse and mostly close to the ground, which is why game viewing is so good here. The rivers rarely flow but rainwater collects in the bed under the sand, which is sufficient for grasses and plants to survive. Both rivers were once thundering waterways, evident in the great width of their valleys in some areas. Between the two rivers stretch mighty red sand dunes, aligned from north to south and covered in yellow grass following good rains. These are fossil dunes, and their red tint is produced by an iron oxide coating on the white grains of sand.

Kgalagadi Transfrontier Park

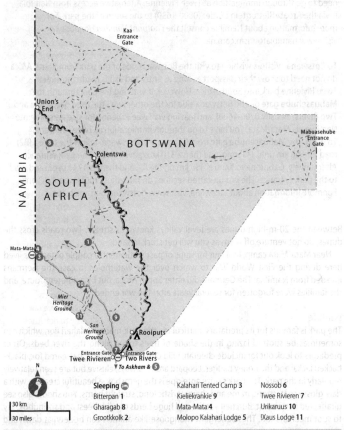

Sleeping 🛏		
Bitterpan 1	Kalahari Tented Camp 3	Nossob 6
Gharagab 8	Kieliekrankie 9	Twee Rivieren 7
Grootkolk 2	Mata-Mata 4	Urikaruus 10
	Molopo Kalahari Lodge 5	!Xaus Lodge 11

Border crossings: South Africa–Namibia and Botswana

Kgalagadi Transfrontier Park

To Namibia There is now direct access from Namibia, through the **Mata-Mata** border gate which opened in October 2007. The gate is 120 km northwest of Twee Rivierine and 203 km southeast of Gochas in Namibia on the C15 and is open 0800-1630 (T054-561 2000). Visitors entering the park from Namibia and returning to Namibia through the Mata-Mata gate are not required to show their passports. However, if visitors from Namibia enter the park through the Mata-Mata gate and exit into South Africa through the Twee Rivierine gate, will need to go through immigration procedures at Twee Rivierine. Likewise, if visitors enter the park from the South African side and plan to exit through the Mata-Mata gate into Namibia, they too need to go through immigration at Twee Rivierine. Alternative access from Namibia is via the **Aroab/Rietfontein** border (0800-1630) to the south of the park. For more information about Namibia consult the *Footprint Namibia Handbook* or visit www.namibiatourism.com.na.

To Botswana Visitors wishing to visit the Botswana side of the park from South Africa do not need to show their passport as long as entry and exit is made through the Twee Rivierine back into South Africa. However, if entering the park through the **Mabuasehube** gate on the Botswana side (or the other two little used gates; **Kaa** and **Two Rivers**; all daily 0700-1600), and leaving via Twee Rivierine (or vice versa) or into Namibia via Mata-Mata, you have to go through immigration at Twee Rivierine. To get to the **Mabuasehube** gate from Gaborone in Botswana, follow the tarred (B2) road for 550 km until Tsabong, and then a 310 km gravel road to the park entrance. Alternatively, Gaborone to Kang is 450 km on the B2, and then its 171 km of sand road to the park entrance. The last un-tarred sections on both these routes are 4WD only. For more information about Botswana, visit www.botswanatourism.co.bw.

Between the 20-m-high dunes are level valleys known as streets. Two roads cross the dunes; do not venture off them as you will get stuck in sand.

Near Mata-Mata camp, look out for signs of past settlement; a couple of families lived here during the First World War to watch over the waterholes in case the Germans invaded from Namibia. The Germans did enter South Africa, but by a different route, and the families were forgotten for several years after the war ended.

Wildlife

The park is famous for its predators, particularly the dark-maned Kalahari lion which can sometimes be spotted lazing in the shade of trees found along the river beds. Other predators to look out for include cheetah, wild dog, spotted hyena, bat-eared fox, black-backed jackal and the honey badger. Leopard are, as always, elusive but are seen relatively regularly in the park. The park's prize antelope is the gemsbok, a beautiful creature with a dark glossy coat, strong frame and characteristic long, straight horns. You should also see giraffe, red hartebeest, Burchell's zebra and huge herds of wildebeest and springbok. Try to spot meerkats too. These energetic mongoose-like animals can be seen at dawn and dusk scurrying round their burrows in search of food. Look out for the windmills which pump the boreholes – these waterholes are usually frequented by some form of wildlife.

The birdlife, too, is impressive. Over 200 species have been recorded in the park. The best viewing months are between February and May, especially if the rains have been good. The park is known for its variety of raptors, which prey upon the smaller mammals. Look out for tawny eagle, martial eagle, chanting goshawk, white-backed vulture and eagle owl. Other birds include Burchell's courser, Namaqua sandgrouse, the Kalahari robin and the pink-billed lark. You also frequently see pairs of secretary birds strutting along the dry riverbeds.

◉ The Kalahari listings

For Sleeping and Eating price codes and other relevant information, see pages 46-53.

◉ Sleeping

Kuruman *p755*
B Oude Werf Lodge, Winkel St, T053-712 0117, www.oudewerf-lodge.co.za. 22 comfortable a/c en suite rooms, 1 sleeping 4, with DSTV and minibar. Well-stocked bar, à la carte restaurant with tables outside under acacia trees, motel-style parking. Friendly.
Č Eldorado Motel, Main St, T053-712 2191, www.eldoradohotel.co.za. Bland 1960s roadside motel on the outskirts, but with 72 a/c newly refurbished rooms with DSTV, in 4 blocks around pool. Good facilities including a bar and beer garden, and good restaurant with pictures of African animals and birds.
D Riverfield, 12 Seodin Rd, T053-712 0003, www.riverfield.co.za. Modern house set in large well-kept gardens, with 12 en suite doubles or family rooms, TV, lounge, braai area, pool, self-service bar, good breakfasts.

Tswalu Kalahari Reserve *p757*
Private lodges and camps
L4 The Motse, T053-781 9234, www.tswalu. com. Part of the **Relais & Chateaux** luxury hotel group. Luxury lodge, 8 beautifully appointed stone cottages with private decks, outdoor showers with views of the Kalahari, swimming pool, library. Excellent service and meals, beauty spa, swimming pool. Rates include all meals, game drives, bush walks, children's activities and horse riding. Hot-air ballooning over the Kalahari is extra. Air transfers from

Cape Town or Johannesburg can be arranged in the private jet. At over R13,000 per couple per night this is a serious extravagance but a wonderful experience. **Turkuni**. Equally luxurious house, with its own staff. Available for groups of up to 10 for R30,000.

Southwest from Kuruman *p757*
D Red Sands Country Lodge, 15 km from Kuruman, along the N14 towards Upington, T082-801 4414, www.redsands.co.za. Located on a private game farm in the hills above town, it is home to several species of antelope. Selection of B&B double rooms, fully equipped self-catering chalets, and camping and caravan sites with braais and electric points. Pool with slide, thatched restaurant serving country cuisine with an outdoor deck.

Upington *p759, map p760*
B Protea Hotel Upington, 24 Schröder St, T054-337 8400, www.proteahotels.com. A well-run hotel, with 56 spacious a/c rooms, some with river views, and 4 family self-catering rooms, which are good value, all with DSTV and modern furnishings. Pool at back in secluded grounds overlooking the river, attached is a standard steak restaurant, the **Totem Creek Spur** and there's a bar. Ask about weekend specials. If heading for the national parks ask here about 4WD hire.
B-C Le Must River Residence and **Le Must River Manor**, 14 Butler St and 12 Murray Av, T054-332 3971, www.lemustupington.com. 2 elegant guesthouses set in mock Cape Dutch buildings overlooking the river. 18 en suite doubles, TV, heating and a/c. The houses are

filled with South African art and antiques and a large selection of books and music. The **Residence** is a 5-star guesthouse, while the **Manor** is a 3-star. Recommended.

C Africa River Lodge, T054-331 1846, www.africariverlodge.co.za. 10 indvidually decorated en suite rooms and 2 self-catering family cottages arranged around attractive lawns under palms. Antiques, fresh flowers, some 4-poster beds, meals on request, pool. Relaxing and peaceful riverside spot.

D Affinity Guest House, 4 Butler St, T054-331 2101, www.affinityguesthouse.co.za. 25 en suite rooms in a bright pink building, all with a/c, DSTV and fridge. Secure parking, swimming pool, good views of the river from the spacious garden, can arrange boat cruises. Good value. Recommended.

D Libby's Lodge, 140 Schröder St, T054-332 2661, www.upington.co.za/libbys_lodge. Peaceful B&B in the suburbs, with 7 a/c en suite rooms with private garden verandas and 3 family self-catering flats sleeping 3-5. TV, swimming pool, braai, covered parking.

D River City Inn, Scott and Park streets, T054-331 1971, www.upingtonhotels.co.za. A newish mid-range hotel in the centre of town popular with business travellers, with 29 a/c rooms, TV, bar and braai area, small gym, breakfast area but no restaurant.

D-E Eiland Holiday Resort, on a large island opposite town, T/F054-334 0286, www.kharahais.gov.za/eiland. Good location, a mix of 58 self-catering chalets and rondavels, good value for 4 people, campsite has plenty of large trees and grass and electric points. Clean, swimming pool, restaurant, shop, telephones, a well-run municipal resort. Has what is claimed to be the longest palm avenue (1041 m) in the southern hemisphere. The 200 palms were planted in 1935 and the avenue is a national monument. Sundowner cruises on the river depart from here when there is sufficient demand. Recommended.

Around Upington p760

B Witsand Nature Reserve, see page 761, T053-313 1061, www.witsandkalahari.co.za.

10 comfortable self-catering, en suite chalets with 3 bedrooms sleeping 6, and 7 cheaper bungalows sleeping 2-4 with communal ablution block and field kitchen. All a/c, safari decor, 1 chalet has disabled facilities. Small shop, 2 pools, breakfast and dinner on request. Also a **campsite** with basic facilities, ablution block and electricity points.

C-E Monate Lodge, Spitskop Nature Reserve, see page 761, T054-332 1336, www.spitskop monate.com. 6 self-catering, a/c **chalets** with 3 beds, patios and braais, a/c and heating. 43 **campsites** with electricity, pool and braais.

Kgalagadi Transfrontier Park p761, map p763

There are 3 main camps in the park: **Twee Rivieren**, the main camp at the entrance gate; **Mata-Mata**, a more remote camp on the Namibian border; and **Nossob**, on the Botswana border. At each main camp there is a mix of self-catering cottages plus a campsite with washing and braai facilities. There are no electric points in the campsites, but lighting is provided by generator until 2300. Check in is from 1200 but all rooms must be vacated by 0900. Reservations through **SANParks** in Tshwane (Pretoria), T012-428 9111, www.sanparks.org, Mon-Fri. For late bookings (under 48 hrs) and camping contact the park direct, T054-561 2000. Wheelchair-bound visitors are accommodated in nearly all camps; enquire with SANParks.

6 new, upmarket wilderness camps have opened. Unlike the main camps, these are not fenced but a ranger is on duty at all times. For this reason, in all but 1, children under 12 are not permitted. If the park is full there are several options just outside (see below).

On the Botswana side there are campsites at Polentswa, Rooiputs and Two Rivers. Bookings are made through the **Botswana Parks Authority**, PO Box 131, Gaborone, T+267(0)3-918 0774, dwnp@gov.bw.

L2 !Xaus Lodge, 94 km from Twee Rivierene, central reservations T021-426 5111, www. xauslodge.co.za. This is a new initiative between SANParks and the local Khomani

(San Bushmen) and Mier communities that live on the fringes of the park. 12 upmarket en suite thatched chalets, perched on stilts decorated with Bushmen art, overlooking the Klein Skrij Pan and a waterhole, splash pool. A typical day begins with an early-morning walk in the sand dunes with a Bushman tracker to follow animal spoor, a visit to the cultural village where Bushmen women make traditional beads and tell spiritual stories, an afternoon game drive, followed by dinner, including traditional dishes, in the thatched boma. They have telescopes for star-gazing. An interactive experience that the Bushmen benefit from financially. Excellent reports.

Twee Rivieren
The biggest of the camps with 31 units. Accommodation and administrative buildings. Shop sells groceries, meat, bread, wine, beer and souvenirs. Takeaway selling snacks, a bar with TV, a pool and an overpriced (and frankly awful) restaurant. Self-catering is a far better option. Night drives and guided walks can be arranged at the information centre.
B Chalets. Self-contained thatched cottages with a/c, sleeping 6, shower, fully equipped kitchen, no oven but hot plate and braai area.
D Cottages. Sleep 3 (2 adults and 1 child on a sleeper bed) or 4; 1 has wheelchair access, kitchenette and a/c.

Camping Dusty campsite but with good prefabricated shade, some trees, plus good ablutions including a laundry but no cooking facilities other than braais. Swimming pool. Can be very busy with noisy families.

Mata-Mata
118 km from the entrance gate, allow at least 2½ hrs travelling time. This road is one of the most beautiful in the park with some of the best game-viewing opportunities. Has a small shop selling groceries and firewood. Electricity from 0500 for a few hours, and 1700-2300.
B Chalets. Self-contained chalets sleeping up to 6 in 2 bedrooms, with extra beds in dining room, shower, kitchen, oven plate, braai area.

D Huts. 1 double room, shower, kitchen, hot plate and braai area.

Camping Sandy plots in front of the chalets, little shade but fantastic setting, good ablution facilities, braai areas.

Nossob
152 km from the entrance gate, allow at least 3½ hrs travelling time; the first sign of camp is a pair of white gates and a few battered trees beside the white buildings. This is the most remote camp, with the least facilities, and probably provides the best opportunity for hearing lions roar at night. Has recently been refurbished and there is now a predator information centre where you can organize guided game walks and night drives, plus a pool, shop and a generator provides electricity morning and evening.
B Guesthouse. 2 units with connecting door, sleeping 8 or 2 groups of 4. Each has 2 bedrooms, bathroom, dining room, lounge, fully equipped kitchen, enclosed veranda, good value for a group.
C Cottages. Sleep 4 or 6, 2 bedrooms, 2 bathrooms, dining room, kitchen (stove and fridge).
D Chalets. Sleep 2 or 4 in 1 or 2 bedrooms, bathroom, kitchen with hotplate and fridge.

Camping Campsite with ablution bock and braai pits. Overlooks a broad section of the riverbed and a waterhole.

Wilderness camps
All have strictly 4WD access and you need to take your own drinking water and firewood.
C Bitterpan, in the dunes, about 3 hrs from Nossob, where you check in. Stilted huts sleeping 2, with en suite bathroom, built with natural materials. Walkways link the 4 huts to a communal kitchen/entertainment/braai area. There is also a 6-m-high tower allowing excellent views out over the dunes. Electricity is solar powered.
C Gharagab, 164 km north of Nossob. 4 log cabins sleeping 2, en suite bathroom, kitchen,

braai, solar power, good views of the Kalahari dunes from the wooden decks.

C Grootkkolk, 100 km north of Nossob. Set in red sand dunes. The most basic, with 4 simple en suite chalets sleeping 2, built out of sandbags and canvas. Communal bathroom and kitchen with fridge and hotplates, plus a braai. Solar-power.

C Kalahari Tented Camp, 3 km from Mata-Mata. 15 fully equipped spacious tents with kitchen and bathroom, sleeping 2-4, swimming pool, overlooks a waterhole in the Auob riverbed. This is the only Wilderness Camp where children under 12 are permitted.

C Kieliekrankie, 50 km north of Twee Rivieren. 4 dune cabins, with 2 single beds, shower, kitchen, fridge, braai, solar power.

C Urikaruus, 72 km north of Twee Rivieren. Units sleeping 2, built on stilts, kitchen, fridge, shower, braai, solar power.

Outside the park
During peak season park accommodation is fully booked for weeks on end. There are several other accommodation options en route to Twee Rivieren, but these are also likely to be booked up at peak times.

C-D Askham Post Office Guest House, on the R360 in Askham, T054-511 0040, http://postofficeguesthouse.com. Restored post office offering 3 en suite rooms and a family chalet sleeping 6 with country-style decor, communal kitchen. Meals on request, TV lounge, pretty garden patio. Pre-arrange to take firewood and braai packs to the park.

C-D Kalahari Trails Nature Reserve, 10 km east of Askham on the R31 to Van Zylsrus, T054-511 0140, www.kalahari-trails.co.za. Simple guesthouse rooms sleeping 2-3, some en suite; a self-catering chalet sleeping 6; permanent tents under thatch for 2; campsites with shade. All is self-catering in the large shared fully equipped kitchen, dining room, lounge with fireplace, shop selling meat and firewood. Offers guided game drives and bush walks.

C-D Molopo Kalahari Lodge, 15 km from Askham, on the gravel road to the park

(50 km), T054-511 0008, www.molopolodge.co.za. Well-run lodge on the edge of the park, with 50 en suite rondavels, and campsite set in dusty grounds. Large restaurant, bar, TV lounge, pool. Rates are very reasonable and children under 6 go free. The last stop before the park, own petrol station and limited supplies of oil, tyres and tubes, plus a liquor store that sells ice, and you can pre-arrange braai packs to take to the park. Recommended.

D Kalahari Sands Guest House, on the R360 in Askham, T054-511 0021, www.kalahari sandsguesthouse.com. 7 simple self-catering double and family chalets, with modern decor, bright white linen, cool tiled floors, TV, a/c. 16 camping sites with reed shelters, lights, taps and electric points, and a rustic pool.

❶ Eating

Kuruman *p755*
Eating is limited in Kuruman, though there are branches of **Spur**, **Wimpy** and **KFC** on Main St. The food is good at both the **Red Sands Country Lodge**, 15 km from town, or the **Eldorado Motel**, in town, so if you are staying at these, stay put for dinner. For those self-catering, **Pick 'n Pay** supermarket is on Beare St and **Spar** is on Main St.

Upington *p759, map p760*
All South African small towns have the standard and unimaginative steakhouse chain restaurants; Upington must feature every single one of them. **Saddles** is on Market St and **Spur** is in the Protea Hotel Upington. For coffee try the **Pick 'n Pay** shopping mall and, for a late night drink, try **Scotty's Bar**, also at the Protea Hotel.

ⁿⁿⁿ About, T054-332 4329, Mon-Sat 1830-2200. Elegant and stylish dining with crisp white linen and high back chairs, but with a relaxed atmosphere. Very good contemporary cuisine and beautifully presented, with frequently changing menu and handpicked boutique wines. Probably the best place in town for seafood.

⫴⫴⫴ Le Must, 11 Schröder St, T054-332 3971. Daily 1800-2200, Sun-Fri also 1200-1500. By far the best restaurant in town and one of the best in the Northern Cape – Mandela, Mbeki and FW De Klerk have eaten here. Book ahead. Not to be confused with **Le Must** accommodation – the 2 are now under separate management despite the same name. Sophisticated decor, tables overlooking the riverbank, well-prepared dishes, good service, interesting local wine list priced with overseas visitors in mind. If you've been out in the desert for a few days, this is the place to treat yourself. Intriguing items on the menu include springbok shank or fillet with prune sauce. It's a must! Recommended.

⫴⫴ Desert Palace Casino Resort, Upington Golf Course, 7 km on the Kuruman road N14, T054-338 4100, www.desertpalace. co.za. 1000-0200. New casino complex with a passable Italian-themed restaurant and bar serving pizza and pasta, as well as a bar, gaming tables and 145 slot machines.

⫴⫴ Dros, Pick 'n Pay Centre, Le Roux St, T054-331 3331. Open 0900-2200. Another chain with mock wine cellar decor but relatively good and varied food. Steaks, grills and pizza. Aimed at families.

⫴ Arabesque Coffee Shop, 24 Scott St, T054-331 3412. Mon-Tue 0800-1700, Wed-Sat 0800-late. Brightly decorated café with internet and small garden. Serves breakfast, tea, cake, smoothies and shakes, and simple meals in the evening like lasagne. In good weather, braais.

⫴ O'Hagan's, 20 Schröder St, T054-331 2005. Open 1100-late. Irish theme pub and restaurant, usual steak, pasta and pies, big portions and good selection of beers. Unusually for this chain, and probably because this is pure red meat eating country, it also does tasty and flavoursome *pojkie* stews.

⫴ Sakkie se Arkie, on an attractive double-storey pontoon departing from the **Eiland Holiday Resort**, T082-564 5447 (mob). Sun-downer cruise with a braai. If you're not staying at the resort, enquire at reception.

▲▲ Activities and tours

Kuruman *p755*
Golf
Kuruman Country Club, T053-732 1242. A 9-hole course. Also tennis, squash and bowls.

Upington *p759, map p760*
Tour operators
Trips into the Kalahari are not cheap, as 4WDs are essential and all equipment and provisions (including water) have to be taken. This needs a lot of organization, but the rewards are well worth it. Expect to pay R3500 per person for a 2-night/3-day guided camping tour. These operators can also organize tours to the the Ai-Ais/Richtersveld Transfrontier National Park. **Kalahari Safaris**, 3 Oranje St, T054-332 5653, www.kalaharisafaris.co.za. Budget tours, including 3- to 5-day trips to the Kgalagadi Transfrontier Park; 1-day trip to Augrabies Falls; rafting on the Gariep (Orange) River; and trips to Witsand and Spitskop nature reserves. Pieter knows and loves the area, making him a great guide. Consistently recommended. **Kalahari Tours & Travel**, T054-338 0375, www.kalahari-tours.co.za. Well-organized and established local operator organizing a range of tours into the Kgalagadi Transfrontier Park, as well as to Augrabies and Namakwa.

⊖ Transport

Kuruman *p755*
238 km to **Kimberley**, 263 km to **Upington**.

Bus
Intercape buses daily from Leach petrol station (main road) for **Johannesburg** and **Tshwane** (**Pretoria**) (7½ hrs), and **Upington** (3 hrs).

Upington *p759, map p760*
It's 804 km to **Johannesburg**, 894 km to **Cape Town**, 401 km to **Kimberley**, 263 km to **Kuruman**, 374 km to **Springbok**, 120 km to **Augrabies Falls National Park**, 80 km to **Kakamas**, 50 km to **Keimoes**.

Air

Upington Airport has the longest runway in the Southern Hemisphere, which (although it never has) is capable of landing a space shuttle. It is, however, used by **South African Airways** and the South African Air Force to train pilots in the handling of large aircraft. It was built in 1968 to accommodate the new jumbo jets on international flights from South Africa to Europe. Concorde was tested here in 1976.

SAA, T011-978 1111, www.flysaa.com, has 1 flight a day between Upington and **Cape Town** and 2 flights a day between Upington and **Johannesburg**. The Cape Town flight arrives in the late afternoon, but the services from Johannesburg are useful as they arrive in Upington early in the morning, so if time is short and you wish to visit the magnificent Kgalagadi Tranfrontier Park, you can fly in, arrange for your hire car to meet you and be in the park by the end of the day.

Bus

Intercape buses depart from their office in Lutz St, which is a short walk from the Protea hotels. Buses run daily to **Cape Town** (10 hrs), via **Springbok** (5 hrs) and **Clanwilliam** (7 hrs); to **Johannesburg** and **Tshwane** (**Pretoria**) (10 hrs) via **Kuruman** (3 hrs), and to **Windhoek** in Namibia (12 hrs).

Bus companies All bus tickets can be booked online at www.computicket.com. Intercape, www.intercape.co.za. For more information, see Getting around, page 41.

Car and 4WD hire

Car hire at the airport: Avis, T054-332 4746/7, www.avis.co.za; Hertz, T054-337 3613 and 56 Le Roux St, T054-3373600; www.hertz.co.za.

There are several local 4WD companies catering specifically for the wilderness regions of the Northern Cape, some also hire camping equipment such as rooftop tents, fridges and cooking and eating equipment. Expect to pay about R700-900 per day, although some packages have additional kilometre costs, which can make it very expensive; it's definitely worth shopping

around. However, saying that, by splitting the costs between a family or group of 4, and camping, this can be an affordable way to explore the park. Ask about emergency back-up. Some firms will allow you to take the vehicle into Botswana and Namibia, too. Try **Desert 4x4**, 26 Swartmodder Av, T054-332 1560, www.desert4x4.co.za; **Kalahari 4x4**, 66 Scott St, T054-332 3098, www.kalahari4x4hire.co.za; or **Kgalagadi 4x4**, T054-3377133, www.kgalagadi4x4.com.

Train

There is a service of sorts between Upington and **Windhoek** in Namibia run by Transnamib Starline Passenger Services, T+264 (0)61-298 2032, www.transnamib.com.na. However, as Namibia's trains are primarily used for freight, it is slow going with many stops. However, compartments are comfortable with airline-like seats, videos and vending machines for drinks and snacks. There are often delays but, in theory, the service departs Upington on Thu and Sun at 0500 and arrives in Windhoek the following morning at 0700. In the other direction the train departs Windhoek on Wed and Sat at 1940 and arrives in Upington the following day at 2130 with a lengthy stop at Keetman-shoop en route. (Intercape Mainliner bus takes 12 hrs to do the same route, compared with 24 hrs by train.)

Directory

Kuruman *p755*
Banks First National and ABSA Bank, Beare St; **Standard Bank**, Voortrekker St. **Medical services** Hospital, Main St, T053-712 8100. **Post office** School St.

Upington *p759, map p760*
Banks First National and ABSA have branches in Schröder St, close to the hotels. **Internet** Café de Net, in the Pick 'n Pay Centre. **Medical services** Upington Medi-Clinic, corner 4th Av and Du Toit St, T054-338 8900, www.upingtonmc.co.za.

West towards Namakwa and Springbok

Driving along the N14 across the Northern Cape between Upington and Springbok, stop for a moment and look out over the endless horizons and stillness of the desert. Here one gets a real sense of how large South Africa is, pausing in countryside that has barely changed in thousands of years. Although stark and deserted, the emptiness has a certain beauty. The first part of the journey is particularly striking as the road follows the Gariep (Orange) River, with its band of lush vegetation along either bank. The highlight in this region is a visit to the dramatic waterfall in Augrabies Falls National Park. Once in Springbok, you will have arrived in Namakwa (Namaqualand), the name given to the arid northwest corner of the Northern Cape, starting in the south at the Doorn River bridge near Klawer and extending north to the Namibian border. The area is best known for its magnificent wild flowers, which transform the barren, rocky countryside every spring. The regional centre is Springbok, the most viable base for exploring the area. ▶▶ *For listings, see pages 780-784.*

Cannon Island (Kanoneiland) → *Colour map 3, A5. Phone code: 054.*

Between Upington and Keimoes there is a choice of two roads along the banks of the Gariep (Orange) River. The main road follows the northern bank, but if you take the southern road you can stop off at Cannon Island (Kanoneiland). This is the largest island on the river, 14 km long and 3 km at its widest point. These days, 1700 ha out of a total area of 2500 ha are irrigated. Before the Cape government had managed to establish control over the region, the island was a stronghold for Korana tribes who harassed the early sheep farmers. The island was named after a terrible incident when the Korana tried to fire a cannon made from the hollowed-out trunk of a quiver tree – when the smoke cleared, six of them lay dead amongst the debris.

Keimoes → *Colour map 3, A5. Phone code: 054.*

Keimoes is the local farming centre at the junction with the R27, the main road south across the Karoo to Calvinia. This is the quickest route to Cape Town but it means missing out Namakwa. The name in Afrikaans means 'mouse nest' so presumably the settlement once had a problem with mice. Look out for the Persian waterwheel in the centre of town, still in use on an irrigation canal. A short 4-km drive from the centre takes you to **Tierberg Nature Reserve**, a municipal reserve covering some 160 ha which is notable for aloes and succulents. Most of the flowers are in bloom between August and September.

Kakamas → *Colour map 3, A4. Phone code: 054.*

The second most important farming centre along this stretch of the Gariep (Orange) River is Kakamas. The settlement was founded in 1893 by the Cape Parliament, as a centre for the Dutch Reformed Church to establish a colony for poor farmers who had lost everything following periods of drought and an outbreak of *rinderpest*. For tourist information contact **Kalahari Gateway Hotel** ① *19 Voortrekker Rd, T054-431 0838, www.kalaharigateway.co.za.*

Most of the town is strung out along the main road which runs parallel to the southern canal. The canal is one of several fed by the **Neus Weir**, which irrigate the surrounding vineyards and fruit farms. The weir is 936 m long and was the first cylindrical weir with a smooth overflow to be built in South Africa. Driving along Voortrekker Road in the town centre, look out for the set of fine, giant **waterwheels**. These nine wheels were built by a local farmer, Piet Burger, to help lift water from the canals into his fields. They are still in use today and are considerably more economical to operate than modern lifting methods such as pumps. Along the route of the northern irrigation canal are a couple of **water tunnels**. One tunnel is 97 m long; the second is an incredible 172 m, and both are 2 m high and 3-4 m wide. They were built in 1889-1901 by Cornish tin miners.

Augrabies Falls National Park ⊜🖾▲ » *pp780-784. Colour map 3, A4.*

ⓘ *T054-452 9200, www.sanparks.org. Gates 0700-1830, office 0700-1900, R88, children (under 12) R44.*

The remote location of the Augrabies Falls Park has saved it from mass development, and it remains one of the highlights of the north. The main reason for coming here is to see the huge waterfall, although the surrounding landscape is equally impressive: a bizarre moonscape of moulded rock formations, surrounded by shimmering semi-desert. There is good hiking here, and the Gariep (Orange) River above and below the falls has some excellent whitewater rafting. » *For further details, see Activities and tours, page 784.*

Ins and outs

Getting there There is only one route into the park, the R359. From Upington, take the N14 and turn off at Alheit. From Springbok, there is a left turning before you reach Alheit. All are clearly signposted. The park is 120 km from Upington and 304 km from Springbok.

Best time to visit March to October is the best time to visit. This area has a typical arid climate, with very hot summer days. Rain falls in autumn and, in winter, conditions are ideal for walking, although it gets very cold at night.

Tourist information There is a large shop stocking a selection of groceries, including meat and a few fresh vegetables, plus beer and wine; open office hours. In the same building there is a restaurant with views of the falls. Petrol is available by the entrance and there are pay phones (card only) by the reception desk.

Landscape and wildlife

The park was created in 1966 to protect the waterfall and conserve the surrounding area, a unique ecosystem of riverine and desert environments. The landscape is typical of the arid north, seemingly barren but rich in wild plants and with a growing population of small mammals. It was extended in 1973 but not without some controversy. Around the small settlement of Riemvasmak to the northeast of the park, the residents were forcibly removed as part of Apartheid's Group Areas Act and to extend the park. The community was displaced, with the Xhosa resettled in Cape Town and the Nama people sent to South West Africa (now Namibia). However 74,000 ha of land to the northeast of the park was returned to the community in 1995 and many people have now returned to the area to live.

The impressive **waterfall** is the sixth largest in the world. Above the falls, the Gariep (Orange) River passes over a series of impressive cataracts, dropping about 100 m. From here the main channel passes over a 56-m drop into a narrow gorge of steep, smooth rock, the water churning below. There are a number of viewpoints along the southern side of the gorge. Thanks to the slippery surface of the rock and the number of over-curious visitors who slid to their deaths, the edge of the gorge is today lined with a small fence. Following heavy rains, a number of smaller waterfalls drop into the main gorge along the sides of the main falls – a tremendous sight, but fairly rare.

Walking along the cliffs above the river, you pass a number of unusual plants that have adapted to the harsh desert environment. Some of the more notable trees include the quiver tree, camel thorn, tree fuschia and the wild olive; there are some informative displays by reception. There is also a fair range of wildlife, including klipspringer, eland, kudu, gemsbok and springbok, although these all tend to be elusive. You are more likely to see ground squirrels foraging between the rocks. A good time of day to visit is around sunset, when the swallows flitting through the gorge are slowly replaced by small bats that stream from cracks in the rock faces surrounding the falls.

Hiking

There is a popular three-day, 40-km hiking trail, the **Klipspringer Trail**, which is open 1 April to 30 September but is often booked up during local school holidays (see Sleeping, page 781, for details of overnight huts). There are also several one-hour hikes which you don't have to book, each leading to a scenic point close to the camp. The walk to **Arrow Point** is perhaps the best, with superb views downstream. You need to wear shoes with a good grip, but the walk does not involve any climbing. Note that there are some dangerous spots at the edge of the gorge. Take care when approaching it, especially if you are with small children.

Game drives

There are several short game drives from the campsite; ask at reception for a map. The gravel roads take you to Echo Corner, Oranjekom, Ararat and Moon Rock. The only game you're likely to see is klipspringer and eland, but the birdlife is very rewarding, as is the unusual desert plantlife. The park also organizes guided night drives in an open 4WD, which may be a better way of learning about the flora and fauna found in the park. These can be booked at reception.

Augrabies Falls National Park

North bank of the river - closed to the public

Eagles Nest

Klipspringer Hiking Trail

Gariep (Orange) River

Gate

Dry Spring

Canoe & boat launch

Gate

seasonal channel

Mist Falls

Arrow Point

Augrabies Falls (56m)

Twin Falls

Klipspringer Hiking Trail

Moon Rock

R359

To Upington & Pofadder

N

1 km
1 mile

Sleeping 🛌
Augrabies Falls 1

Fish Eagle 2
Mountain 3

Eating 🍴
Shibula 1

Pofadder and around → *Colour map 3, A3. Phone code: 054.*

Back on the N14, the road to Springbok runs through the dusty town of Pofadder, which is a small *dorp* (village) lying on a particularly arid stretch of road; were it not for a small natural spring it would never have come into being. There is little more here than a cluster of ramshackle houses, a petrol station, a general store and bottle shop. It is only worth a mention as it is one of the most remote settlements in the country and is the butt of much South African humour. For those South Africans who admit they have been to Pofadder, it's as good as saying that they have been to the ends of the earth. Pofadder is not actually named after the venomous snake, but after Klaas Pofadder, a cattle rustler, who based himself here during the 1860s.

To the north of here is the settlement of **Pella**, founded by the London Missionary Society in 1814, and named after the village which provided refuge for Christians in Macedonia. In 1878 the running of the station was taken over by the Catholic church. Of particular interest is the original **mission church** which has been consecrated as a cathedral. It was designed and built by Father LM Simon and Father Leo Wolf – neither had any experience or knowledge of building, so they used an encyclopaedia for reference. The cathedral comes as a welcome cool refuge, standing in a neat walled garden fringed with date palms. Back on the N14, it's another 165 km from Pofadder to Springbok across the featureless plains.

Springbok and around ⊖❶❷❸❹❺ ➤➤ *pp780-784. Colour map 3, B2.*

→ *Phone code: 027.*

The capital of Namakwa (Small Copper Mountains) is set in a narrow valley surrounded by the Klein Koperberge (Small Copper Mountains) and hemmed in by koppies littered with rough butter-coloured rocks. It is a modern town with little of interest within its confines, but it has an important position, straddling the N7, and is a good base from which to explore the countryside north to the Namibian border and west to the Atlantic coast. The town is quiet for most of the year but is totally transformed when the spring wild flowers start to bloom.

Namakwa Tourism Information ⓘ *Voortrekker St, on the left as you enter town, T027-712 8035, www.namakwa-dm.gov.za, Mon-Fri 0800-1615, during the flower season also Sat-Sun 0830-1600,* is the main office for the Namakwa region. The staff are very knowledgeable and have a good selection of pamphlets and maps on the region, but the office sometimes closes completely out of season.

Sights

In the past, the fortunes of the town were closely linked with the copper industry. In 1852 the first copper mine started production; this was the first commercial mining operation of any type in South Africa. Despite several other discoveries further north, Springbok was able to develop into an important regional centre because of its abundant supply of drinking water from a spring, a rare and valuable commodity in the region before dams and pipelines were built. There is a small town **museum** ⓘ *Van der Stel St, T027-718 8100 Mon, Wed and Fri 0830-1530, free,* outlining local history, housed in what was once a synagogue.

Goegap Nature Reserve → *Colour map 3, B2.*

ⓘ *From the centre of Springbok, pass under the N7 and turn right; just before the airport, take a left turn; it is 15 km to the gates, T027-718 9906. 0800-1600, R15, children (under 16) free. Visitor centre and café.*

Named after the Nama word for waterhole, this popular little reserve has a well known aloe collection, a couple of mountain-bike trails and a 4WD route. The local O'Okiep Copper Company donated the area to the government in 1960 to establish a reserve to help protect the wild flowers of the region. The park has since been added to, including the opening of the **Hester Malan Wild Flower Garden** in 1966, which displays over 100 different species of aloes and succulents, and sells plants and seeds; it's a beautiful spot in August and September. The reserve is a mix of granite koppies and dry valleys, with a good cross-section of typical Namakwa vegetation. Although the area looks parched and barren, it supports a surprisingly varied ecology – 581 plant species have been recorded in the reserve. Like much of the area, the park becomes carpeted with wild flowers after the rains, making it very popular during spring.

Visitors can drive a 17-km loop which wends into the hills, offering opportunities to see game and birdlife – the most common species are gemsbok, mountain zebra, springbok, klipspringer, duiker and steenbok. The longer 4WD route can only be visited by booking a trip through the reserve office. The route travels through more remote and dramatic corners of the reserve and lasts for three hours. There are also two hiking trails, 6 km and 12 km long, and when the flowers are in full bloom the walks allow visitors to gain some height, providing excellent views of the colourful carpets below. During the summer temperatures soar; it is unwise to go walking in these conditions.

Springbok

Sleeping 🛏	Old Mill Lodge 3	Eating 🍴
Annie's Cottage 1	Springbok 5	Titbits 6
Masonic 2	Springbok Caravan Park 8	
Okiep Country 7	Springbok Lodge 6	

Springbok to Namibia ●❸❷❶ ⇢ pp780-784. Colour map 3, A1.

→ Phone code: 027.

The N7 continues directly north of Springbok for 118 km to the border with Namibia. The unremarkable and untidy settlement of **Okiep**, 8 km north of Springbok, lays claim to having once been the world's richest copper mine, before production ceased in 1918. From the late 1880s miners from the tin mines in Cornwall arrived to help establish the mines and share their expert knowledge. Today the Cornish pump house, containing a steam engine that used to pump water from the mine, and the smokestack next to it, are evidence of the only Cornish mining techniques found in the southern hemisphere. The N7 continues north to **Steinkopf** which marks the junction with the R382 that goes to Port Nolloth, Alexander Bay and the Ai-Ais/Richtersveld Transfrontier National Conservation Park (see below).

Port Nolloth → Colour map 3, A1. Phone code: 027.

Port Nolloth is an odd little town on the windswept west coast. It is an important fishing centre but, more interestingly, it is renowned for attracting fortune-seekers who trade (often illegally) in diamonds. The town was established as a harbour and railway junction for the copper industry in 1854, but it proved too shallow for the bulk-ore carriers and the trade moved north to Alexander Bay. These days it has developed into a small holiday centre – the only one on this stretch of the coast – with crayfishing and diamonds supplementing local income. The town is split into two sections, Port Nolloth being the business and fishing sector, and **McDougall's Bay**, 4 km to the south, the holiday resort. The local fishing fleets are not permitted to fish off the coast at McDougall's Bay, which is reserved for angling and crayfish diving for visitors. The beaches have a wild, windswept beauty to them, although the long stretches of sun-bleached sand can appear rather bleak at times and it often gets misty along the coast. Don't be deceived by the calm sea; it's very cold all year round.

Alexander Bay → Colour map 3, A1. Phone code: 027.

The diamond industry becomes more apparent further north in Alexander Bay, by the Namibian border. Diamonds were first found here in 1925, and today the town is run by the mining company Alexkor Ltd. Alexander Bay was closed to visitors until a few years ago; today visitors go on diamond mine tours, although most come for easy access to the Ai-Ais/Richtersveld Transfrontier National Park (see below). The Gariep (Orange) River estuary has RAMSAR status as an important wetland; more than 200 bird species have been recorded.

If you wish to explore the diamond region, contact **Alexkor Ltd** ⓘ *Alexander Bay, T027-831 1330, www.alexkor.co.za, www.coastofdiamonds.co.za.* Tours run on Friday 0800-1230; book a week in advance as you need to supply copies of your passport; no children under 16. The price depends on the size of the group. The tour starts at the town museum and goes into the mining region to visit the workshops and mining blocks, and the harbour area, as well as an oyster farm and seal colony. The **museum** ⓘ *Mon-Fri 1000-1400,* has exhibits on the history of the region's diamond industry and a video of the mine. Alexkor also runs the **tourist information office** ⓘ *in the museum, T027-831 1330, www.diamondcoast.co.za.*

Ai-Ais/Richtersveld Transfrontier National Conservation Park
●▲▲ ⇢ pp780-784. Colour map 3, A1.

The magnificent Ai-Ais/Richtersveld Transfrontier National Park covers some of the most remote and starkly beautiful scenery in Namakwa. The park is isolated and inaccessible

Transfrontier conservation area

Since 2003, the Richtersveld National Park in South Africa, and Fish River Canyon, Ai-Ais Hot Springs and the Hunsberg Conservation Area in Namibia, are all part of the Ai-Ais/Richtersveld Transfrontier Conservation Park. This is the first such park between Namibia and South Africa. The ultimate aim is to link the Ai-Ais/Richtersveld Transfrontier Conservation Park with the newly proclaimed Sperrgebiet National Park along Namibia's coast and then to the Lona National Park in Angola.

The park currently covers 6045 sq km and spans some of the most spectacular desert scenery in southern Africa. The park is managed jointly by SANParks and the Namibian Ministry of Environment and Tourism, is and sponsored by the Peace Parks Foundation (www.peaceparks.org), which promotes sustainable development, conservation and political stability across the region.

By taking down fences, original migration routes for the game are re-established and park authorities from neighbouring countries are encouraged to work as a team. Other transfrontier parks include the Kgalagadi Transfrontier Park, between South Africa and Botswana, and the Great Limpopo Transfrontier Park between South Africa, Zimbabwe and Mozambique where the fences along Kruger National Park and the international borders have been removed. There are others in the pipeline throughout southern Africa.

and the terrain is rough – much of it can only be reached by 4WD. Richtersveld was proclaimed a national park in 1991. The northern boundary was the Gariep (Orange) River and the international border with Namibia. However, after much negotiation, the Richtersveld is now part of a transfrontier park, joining it with Namibia's Ai-Ais Hot Springs and Fish River Canyon over the border.

The park encompasses a mountainous desert, seemingly barren but full of sturdy succulents, many of them endemic. These, coupled with the surreal rugged terrain, are the principal attractions of the park. Some of the most visible plants include the kokerboom (quiver) and halfmens trees, while hidden in the mountains are hundreds of different succulents. None of the larger mammals are able to survive in such a hostile environment, but you may come across klipspringer, grey rhebok, steenbok, duiker and mountain zebra; consider yourself very fortunate if you see leopard, jackal, brown hyena or caracal. Swimming and fishing (with a permit) are allowed in the Gariep (Orange) River, but you always need to be wary of the current.

Ins and outs

Getting there The easiest route is to drive north from Springbok on the N7 to Steinkopf (49 km). Take the Port Nolloth turning and follow the R382 to the coast via Annenous Pass. In Port Nolloth take the coast road north towards Alexander Bay. The park is signposted from Alexander Bay. It is a further 93 km of gravel along the Gariep (Orange) River, curving back inland to the park's office at Sendelingsdrift (see below). Those coming from Namibia can take the road from Vioolsdrift, via Kotzehoop, through spectacular scenery to Eksteenfontein and then on to Sendelingsdrift. If you don't want to drive yourself, you can organize guided 4WD tours through **Kalahari Safaris** or **Kalahari Tours & Travel** in Upington Activities, see page 769, or **Kalahari Outventures** at Augrabies Falls, see page 784.

Border crossing: South Africa–Namibia

Vioolsdrif

The N7 continues to the Vioolsdrif border with Namibia where there is a bridge over the Gariep (Orange) River. This is the major border between South Africa and Namibia.

Customs and immigration The border crossing (open 24 hours) is pretty straightforward and, although there is a lot of traffic, formalities at customs and immigration are quick and courteous.

Facilities There is a VAT refund desk at the border (see page 56). It is worth noting that the Namibian dollar is interchangeable with the South African Rand and both are accepted throughout Namibia, so you do not need to change money.

Vehicle formalities Vehicles are likely to be searched. You are not permitted to take firewood across the border. If you are in a hire car, ensure that you have documentation from the rental company that allows you to take a car out of South Africa. Namibia is part of the Southern Africa Development Community (SADC) customs agreement so if you are in your own car travelling on a carnet, you do not need to get it signed here, and you won't need to until you reach Zimbabwe or Zambia which are outside the SADC. You simply fill out the car's details in a book. On the Namibia side you will have to pay for temporary third-party insurance but this costs very little.

Into Namibia Noordoewer is the first town in Namibia, 1 km beyond the border, and has a petrol station, a small shop and one hotel: the Orange River Lodge, which has a bar and restaurant; you can also camp here. Beyond Noordoewer, it is 350 km to the next major town – **Keetmanshoop**. If you want to explore the Ai-Ais Hot Springs and Fish River Canyon before you get here then you need to stock up on provisions in South Africa; the Spar in Springbok is the best bet.

Getting around None of the routes within the reserve are suitable for normal cars; a 4WD is essential. Due to its remoteness, it is not possible to visit the park on a day trip and it is recommended that you don't go alone, so try to group up with other vehicles. Those in single vehicles have to sign an agreement to report back to the office on departure. Petrol and diesel is available at reception at Sendelingsdrift, though not unleaded. The nearest unleaded fuel available is in Alexander Bay. Visitors must arrive at the Sendelingsdrift office before 1600 to pay park entry and to reach the designated campsites before dark. Keep clear of all 'no entry' signs, most of which denote mining and security areas. At Sendelingsdrift, a pontoon has been established to ferry people and vehicles across the Gariep (Orange) River to the Namibian side of the park (0800-1615). This has capacity for two fully loaded double-cab 4WD vehicles. If you are exiting the park in Namibia, then immigration is done at Sendelingsdrift.

Best time to visit Visits in the spring and autumn avoid the climatic extremes. The region receives virtually no rainfall in the east, while the western margin is frequently covered by coastal fog known as the *malmokkie*. In summer the daytime temperatures can exceed 50°C, so this is definitely a time to avoid the area. Three hiking trails are open from 1 April to 30 September: **Vensterval Trail** (four days, three nights); **Lelieshoek-Oemsberg Trail** (three days, two nights) and the **Kodaspiek Trail** (two days, one night). Conditions are tough and for experienced hikers only. It is also possible to walk a little in the vicinity of the campsites.

Namakwa flowers

Namaqualand, now referred to as Namakwa, the 'land of the Nama people', is a scorched area of semi-desert which, for much of the year, holds little more than shimmering dust and rock-strewn mountains. However, following the spring rains the ground explodes in a riot of colour, literally carpeting the region with wild flowers. The Namakwa flowers have become a major tourist attraction and, in spring, the still valleys and sleepy towns are transformed into busy visitor hubs.

Nevertheless, the very nature of the attraction – the flowers appear in different locations from year to year – prevents the flower-viewing industry from getting too over the top. Under normal conditions, rains are expected in July and August; the further north you travel, the less rain the land receives. The occurrence and distribution of the wild flowers is determined by the interaction between temperature, light, and the timing and intensity of rainfall. As climatic factors vary from year to year, so too does the composition of the vegetation. A late frost or intense sandstorm can cause a sudden end to the flower season in an area, while in the mountains, some blooms last until the end of October.

Over 4000 species have been discovered, the most common of which is the **orange and black gousblom**, a large daisy. These flowers look their best when they occupy a valley floor, forming a stunning carpet of orange. On the mountainsides or rocky hills you will see **mesembryanthemums**, commonly known as vygies or sour figs. Their blossoms can be pink, scarlet, blue or yellow. Closer to Springbok are **quiver trees** (*Aloe dichotoma*), the tree from which the San made their quivers. This is a slow-growing plant which reaches a height of 7 m when fully grown. Another interesting plant to look out for is the **halfmens** (*Pachypodium namaquanum*), a strange-looking succulent which has a long spine with a clump of leaves at the top; some specimens are thought to be several hundred years old. These are usually seen along the Gariep (Orange) River and on isolated granite koppies.

Tourist information The **park office** ① *Sendelingsdrift, 330 km from Springbok, T027-8311 506, www.sanparks.org, gate hours 0700-1800, office hours 0800-1600, R110, children (under 12) R55 per day*, strictly controls visitor numbers; always call in advance. There is a small general store (weekdays only), selling cool drinks and basic provisions. The nearest shops are at Kuboes and Alexander Bay. Petrol and diesel are also available in the latter. Fresh drinking water is only available at Sendelingsdrift; make sure you have containers which can hold up to 20 litres. The park authorities advise visitors to bring gas stoves for cooking, rather than camp-fires, as there can be strong winds at the end of the day. All rubbish must be removed from the park so ensure you have rubbish bags. There is no mobile phone reception in the park, but if you have international roaming you can call from a few spots around Sendelingsdrift, which picks up reception from Namibia.

Springbok to Cape Town ● ▶▶ *pp780-784.*

As you travel south from Springbok, the N7 winds through rugged granite scenery. There are no settlements of note until you reach Van Rhynsdorp. After 66 km the road passes the small settlement of **Kamieskroon**, with only a petrol station, a shop, a few houses and a couple of places to stay. During the spring many stop in this area to admire the wild flowers.

Continuing south on the N7 there is little of interest until you are past Van Rhynsdorp and enter the **Olifants River Valley**. From here you can explore the West Coast fishing villages (see page 190) or the beautiful Cederberg Mountains (see page 207). Cape Town (495 km) can easily be reached in a single day.

Namaqua National Park → *Colour map 3, B2.*

ⓘ *T027-672 1948, 0800-1700 during the flower season (usually Aug-Sep) when the park can get very crowded; the best time is 1030-1600, R40, children (under 12) R20. Outside the flower season, there is little to see. The information centre has a shop, tea room and toilets (only open in season).*

Formerly known as the Skilpad Wildflower Reserve, the 1000-ha Namaqua National Park has some of the best flower displays in the region. Lying to the west of the N7 highway between Garies and Kharkams, it covers the area between the Spoeg and Groen rivers, allowing for the protection of the Atlantic seaboard marine ecosystems as well as the associated estuaries.

Its fine flowers have much to do with the park's location, which is set on the first ridge of hills in from the coast, a fact that ensures it receives the very first rains of the season. Even in poor years, the displays here are better than in most areas. Visitors can expect to see various bulb species: namely, *babianas, lapeirousias* and *romuleas*, plus duikerwortel (*Grielum humifusum*) and orange mountain daisies (*Ursinia cakilefolia*). See also box, page 779.

Access is via a gravel road, heading north and then west from the **Kamieskroon Hotel**. The entrance is 17 km from the N7. From here, a 5-km gravel road winds in a loop around the hill, which, during the flower season, is a carpet of orange. Visitors can either walk around the park or ride a mountain bike. There is also a slight chance of seeing some wildlife: klipspringer, steenbok, duiker and black-backed jackal. The park is home to the world's smallest tortoise, the Namaqua Speckled Padloper.

◉ West towards Namakwa and Springbok listings

For Sleeping and Eating price codes and other relevant information, see pages 46-53.

● Sleeping

Kakamas *p771*
C Kalahari Gateway Hotel, Voortrekker St, T054-431 0838, www.kalaharigateway.co.za. 25 a/c rooms, 4 self-catering units, restaurant, 2 bars, swimming pool in pleasant palm setting, comfortable, good-value hotel. Very enthusiastic about the region and can advise on local activities.
C Vergelegen, from Upington the farm is located just before Kakamas before crossing the Gariep River, T054-431 0976, www.augrabiesfalls.co.za. 10 comfortable rooms with a/c and heating, some have

internet access. Swimming pool, superb restaurant that has been rated by the South African magazine *Eat Out*, try the unusual biltong and peppadew soup, also has a farm stall and tea garden so well worth a stop even if not staying. During harvest they can organize tours to a local grape packing shed.

Augrabies Falls National Park *p772, map p773*
Reservations through **SANParks**, Tshwane, T012-428 9111, www.sanparks.org, Mon-Fri. Bookings can also be made in person at offices in Cape Town and Durban (see page 48). For camping and reservations under 48 hrs, contact reception directly, T054-452 9200.

Next to the falls

Check-in is from 1200, but all rooms must be vacated by 0900. The cottages and campsite are well spaced out and private. There are 3 small swimming pools, ideal for hot summer days when temperatures can rise above 40°C. The campsite is located at the far end of the complex from the office. In between are a mix of 2-, 3- and 4-bed cottages. These are self-catering, but many guests choose to eat in the restaurant in the evening. Overall the park's accommodation here is good, and while the campsite can get crowded, it is in a beautiful setting. The shop and restaurant are in the main reception centre.

C Cottages. All 59 cottages have a/c and fully equipped kitchen. Clean, comfortable units with views towards gorge, typical parks style, good value for 4 people, 3 units are adapted for wheelchair use.

Camping Not all 40 pitches have electricity, grass patches are preserved for recreational use, which means you have to pitch your tent in the dust. The best shady spots get occupied quickly. The kitchen block has electric hot plates, a laundry and an ironing room.

Klipspringer Trail

E Fish Eagle and **Mountain** are both overnight stone huts. Each sleeps 12 and is fitted with bunks, mattresses, toilets, drinking water, firewood and simple cooking utensils. There are no showers or lamps. Hikers must carry their own food, eating utensils, sleeping bag and torches/candles. Numbers are limited so it is always advisable to book in advance. The trail is closed mid-Oct to end Mar due to high temperatures.

Pofadder and around p774

D Pofadder Hotel, Voortrekker St, T/F054-933 0063, www.pofadderhotel.co.za. Squat, orange building on the main street, 23 basic rooms, restaurant with hot buffet in the evening, lively bar, swimming pool, secure parking, the only hotel in town. Also has 5 newly built a/c self-catering

chalets sleeping 4. Can organize quad bike trips.

Springbok and around p774, map p775

At present there are insufficient hotel rooms to cope with the peak seasonal demand. During spring, Aug-Oct, you should reserve well in advance. If you are unable to find a room, try to join a tour to the region; there are plenty advertised in Cape Town.

AL-D Naries Namakwa Retreat, 27 km west of Springbok on the R355 (which has been newly tarred), reservations T021-930 4564, www.naries.co.za. An isolated and peaceful country retreat with accommodation in 3 Namakwa Mountain Suites in stunning domed units designed to look like giant boulders (**AL**); 5 en suite rooms in the main manor house (**B**), dinner and breakfast included in rates for both; or a self-catering unit sleeping 4 (**D**). In all, decor is in stylish muted browns and creams, and there's a swimming pool and superb gourmet cuisine.

A Annie's Cottage, 4 King St, T/F027-712 1451, www.springbokinfo.com. Finely restored old farmhouse with immaculate polished floors and comfortable furnishings. 11 en suite double rooms, 1 in the attic and 2 with kitchenettes, DSTV and internet. Neat and mature gardens with 40-year-old jacaranda trees, swimming pool, secure off-street parking. Annie can also organize stays on farms in the surrounding area. Recommended.

B Old Mill Lodge, 69 Van Riebeeck St, T027-718 1705, www.oldmilllodge.com. 11 a/c stylish individually decorated en suite rooms with queen-size bed, duck-down duvets, electric blankets, TV, bar, lounge and braai area, a comfortable B&B option.

C Masonic Hotel, 3 Van Riebeeck St, T027-712 1505, www.namaqualandflowers.co.za. 26 a/c en suite rooms with TV. Restaurant, bar, homely rooms, plenty of character, retains much of the original 1940s decor, helpful and friendly management. Some of the rooms are next door in a renovated Victorian cottage.

C Springbok Hotel, 87 van Riebeeck St, T027-712 1161, www.namaqualandflowers.

co.za. The main hotel in town, an old building but comfortable and in a central setting, 28 a/c rooms. Bar with pool table, à la carte restaurant, which serves buffet dinners during flower season. Popular with coach groups.

C-D Springbok Lodge, Voortrekker St, T027-712 1321, www.springboklodge.com. 45 rooms of various formats, most of the houses in neighbouring streets are outbuildings belonging to the lodge, look out for the deep yellow paintwork, some are double rooms, others are self-catering flats. A bizarre local institution run by Jopie Kotze, who spends his day at reception watching all the goings-on of his mini empire. The reception area is also an information centre, newsagent and curio shop, with an interesting semi-precious stone display and some old photographs on historic Springbok. In the middle of all this is the restaurant (see Eating, page 783). This popular lodge has a prime central location and is good value when compared with the larger hotels.

F Springbok Caravan Park, 2 km from town centre, on the opposite side of the N7, on the left off the road to Goegap Nature Reserve, T027-718 1584. Small, with 1 chalet and 2 caravans. Limited shade, few power points, coin-operated washing machine, kitchen, swimming pool, small shop.

Springbok to Namibia *p776*
D Bedrock Lodge, 2 Beach Rd, Port Nolloth, T027-851 8865, www.bedrocklodge.co.za. An attractive collection of simple restored fisherman's cottages with tin roofs and corrugated-iron walls, yellowwood floors, cottage-style decor, MNet TV, fully equipped for self-catering for 2-6.

D Okiep Country Hotel, 120 km south of the border with Namibia and 8 km north of Springbok on the N7, T027-744 1000, www.okiep.co.za. Pleasant en suite rooms with DSTV, parking, good country cooking in restaurant and bar, and a swimming pool. Cheaper self-catering units are in another building across the road. A good overnight stop en route to Namibia.

D-F McDougall's Bay Caravan Park, 4 km south of Port Nolloth, T027-8511 110. A delightful clutch of self-catering cottages and chalets right on the beachfront, and some sheltered sites for camping and caravans. Beautiful clean beach to walk along. This area is well known for lobster and crayfish, so enjoy a delicious seafood braai while staying here.

E-F Port Nolloth Backpackers, Dougal St, Port Nolloth, T079-886 69960, www.port nolloth.net. Plain but adequate doubles or dorms in a beachside cabin decorated with fishing nets in McDougall's Bay. Offers cooked or health breakfasts, meat or seafood braais (crayfish in season) and *pojkies* for dinner. TV lounge, patio, and has canoes, bikes and snorkelling equipment for hire and can arrange fishing trips.

Camping Fiddler's Creek, just before the border, by the police station, is a track to the left that follows the banks of the Gariep (Orange) River, 12 km from Viooolsdrift border, T027-761 8953, www.bushwhacked.co.za. Beautiful shady camping on the river, hot/cold showers in reed huts, tents and sleeping bags can be hired, boma for buffet meals, great little rustic bar next to the river. Also the home of **Bush whacked**, a tour operator offering full-, ½-day or overnight canoeing trips on the Gariep, a very relaxing way to explore the scenery. A very popular New Year's Eve party is held here each year, attracting revellers and bands from Cape Town, followed by canoeing on New Year's Day. Similar set-ups on the Namibian side of the river – see *Footprint Namibia*. Recommended.

Ai-Ais/Richtersveld Transfrontier National Conservation Park *p776*
Reservations through **SANParks**, T012-428 9111, www.sanparks.org, or through the offices in Cape Town and Durban (see page 48). For late availability and camping contact reception direct, T027-831 1506.

D Sendelingsdrift Restcamp. New rest camp at park gate with 10 chalets, 4-bed and 6-bed units, with a/c, fridge and stoves. Porches have views over the Gariep (Orange) River. 12 campsites with shared ablutions (cold showers). Pool. **D Tatasberg and Ganakouriep Wilderness Camps.** The former is near the river and the latter is in the south of the park. Both have four 2-bed self-catering units. Hot showers, lighting, fridges, gas stoves and a there's a caretaker. Bring your own drinking water.

Camping There are 4 designated sites in the park: **Potjiespram, De Hoop, Richtersberg** (all close to the river) and **Kokerboomkloof** to the southeast of the park. Do not sleep on the bare ground, as there are many scorpions in the park and heavy dew in the mornings. Kokerboomkloof only has toilets, each of the other sites has toilets and cold showers. You must bring everything you might need with you, including containers to carry drinking and cooking water. 4WDs and all necessary camping equipment can be hired in Upington (see Activities and tours, page 769) but it is strongly advised that you have experience in driving 4WDs (see Ins and outs, page 742).

Springbok to Cape Town *p779*
D Kamieskroon Hotel, Kamieskroon, T027-672 1614, www.kamieskroonhotel.com. Well-run family hotel and handy for the Namaqua National Park which is just 17 km away, with 24 rooms, a caravan and camping park and 5 self-catering apartments. Rates include breakfast and dinner, tasty country meals. Good source of information and has an excellent reputation for its photographic courses during the flower season.

❶ Eating

Augrabies Falls National Park *p772, map p773*
❦ **Shibula**, at the park entrance. 1200-1400, 1800-2200. A surprisingly smart dining room given the location, with a choice of pricey continental dishes. Last orders are at 2030. Next to the restaurant is the cosy **Gariep**

ladies bar, while downstairs is a cafeteria for drinks and light meals during the day.

Springbok and around *p774, map p775*
There are few options in Springbok and most visitors and locals eat in the hotels. The elegant dining room in the **Masonic Hotel** is probably the best bet. There are a few fast-food options along Voortrekker St and by the petrol stations.
❦ **Springbok Lodge**, see Sleeping, page 782. Open 0700-2200. Part of the reception area and the curio shop is the hotel restaurant. Interesting photos of the region on the walls, popular – most residents seem to eat here. Good selection and generous portions but bland food and slow service.
❦ **Titbits**, Voortrekker St, T027-718 1455. Mon-Sat 0800-2200. A friendly pizzeria with excellent stone-baked pizzas, also a range of other dishes such as pasta and steaks, and generous breakfasts. Breezy outdoor seating overlooking the main road.

Port Nolloth *p776*
❦ **Anita's Tavern**, Coastal Rd, next door to FNB, T084-726 7090. Mon-Sat 1200-2130. Set in a cosy rustic fisherman's beachside cabin with a fireplace, this offers cheap and simple seafood like creamy garlic mussels, linefish or grilled calamari, plus some meat dishes and traditional desserts like malva pudding with custard. There's a small but sufficient choice of wine.

❻ Shopping

Springbok and around *p774, map p775*
Springbok has all of South Africa's main high street shops and supermarkets. Most within walking distance of the car park below the small koppie in the centre of town. **CNA Books**, Van der Stel St, stock glossy coffee-table books showing the flowers at their best. If you are self-catering or heading towards Namibia, the large **Spar**, on the outskirts of town is probably the biggest and best supermarket in the Northern Cape and a good stop for provisions, charcoal and ice. Remember,

there are no shops for a long distance on the Namibian side of the border. Overland trucks do a big shop here before entering Namibia.

Port Nolloth *p776*
There's a fish shop and a small branch of **Spar**, if you need more provisions en route to Ai-Ais/Richtersveld Transfrontier National Park.

▲▲ Activities and tours

Augrabies Falls National Park *p772, map p773*
Canoeing and rafting
An excellent way of experiencing the gorge at Augrabies is by rafting its rapids. The most popular stretch is the Augrabies Rush, an 8-km section of Grade II-III rapids pulling out 300 m above the falls. Longer 2- to 5-day trails involve rafting some excellent rapids as well as calmer stretches in 2-man inflatables. The park also organizes the Gariep 3-in-1 Adventure, which involves descending into the gorge, canoeing for 3 km and then hiking the 4 km out of the gorge. The final 11 km to the rest camp is completed by mountain bike. The river is still relatively uncommercial, which means that you're unlikely to see anyone on the longer trails. Contact **Kalahari Outventures**, T082-476 8213, www.kalahari.co.za, prices start around R320 for the 3-hr Augrabies Rush. The centre also offers rafting and back-road tours to the **Kgalagadi Transfrontier Park**. Recommended. Check website for options.

Ai-Ais/Richtersveld Transfrontier National Conservation Park *p776*
Canoeing and rafting
Many Cape Town companies offer multi-day canoe trips on the Gariep (Orange) River through the Ai-Ais/Richtersveld Transfrontier National Park in 2-man inflatable or fibreglass canoes. This is a wonderful experience. The trips pass amazing rock formations and each night is spent on the riverbank under the stars, with meals cooked over an open fire.

Rapids are Grades II-III. A guide boat carries all equipment but you will need a sleeping bag, sleeping mat, torch, cutlery, a plate and a cup. You will also need your passport as some nights are spent on the Namibian side. Prices start from about a not unreasonable R2000 for a 4-day catered trip.
Amanzi Trails, Cape Town, T021-559 1573, www.amanzitrails.co.za. 4- to 5-day trips either catered or self-catering. You just need to bring food and drink for the self-catering option as they provide equipment such as cool boxes, kettles and braai grids.
Umkulu, Cape Town, T021-853 7952, www.umkulu.co.za. 60-80 km, 4- to 6-day fully-catered rafting and canoeing trips, with return transport from Cape Town included or meet them at their Vioolsdrift base camp, which has secure parking, lock-up storage, showers and a bar. The guides have years of experience and come highly recommended.
Wildthing Adventures, Cape Town, T021-556 1917, www.wildthing.co.za. 4- to 5-day trips, fully catered, except drinks.

⊖ Transport

Springbok and around *p774, map p775*
It's 1274 km to **Johannesburg**, 554 km to **Cape Town**, 374 km to **Upington**, 401 km to **Lamberts Bay**, 256 km to **Van Rhynsdorp**, 239 km to **Ai-Ais** (Namibia), 941 km to **Windhoek** (Namibia).

Air
There is a small airfield close to Goegap Nature Reserve but it is only used by charter airlines en route to Namibia.

⊙ Directory

Springbok and around *p774, map p775*
Banks ABSA, Van der Stel St; Standard, Voortrekker St.

Contents

Footprint features

At a glance

⊖ **Getting around** Poor local buses, car hire.

◉ **Time required** 3-7 days, longer if hiking.

☼ **Weather** Best in Oct and Nov and Mar-May.

✕ **When not to go** Roads deteriorate in wet summers and snowy winters.

★ **Don't miss ...**
1 Thaba Bosiu, page 794.
2 Maletsunyane Falls, page 795.
3 The road to Katse Dam, page 804.
4 Morija Arts and Cultural Festival, page 809.
5 Pony trekking from Malealea Lodge, page 813.

Lesotho, the 'Kingdom in the Sky', is a tiny, proudly independent country completely surrounded by South Africa. Its nickname is apt – not one of its 30,000 sq km lies below 1000 m and many of its peaks reach as high as 3480 m. It is dominated by the Maluti Mountains, which cover three-quarters of the country, with the dramatic Drakensberg escarpment forming the eastern side and the border with KwaZulu Natal. This region of lofty landscapes has been declared the Maluti Drakensberg Transfrontier Park. To the west the land flattens out somewhat into what is known as the Lowlands. Here are most of the kingdom's towns, the small capital of Maseru, the richest agricultural land, and it is where the majority of the population lives.

Lesotho's mountain scenery is markedly different from any of South Africa's landscapes: the mountains are more rugged, the lower slopes drier and the villages maintain a traditional subsistence lifestyle. Tourism is still in its infancy here, and heading even a little off the beaten track will allow a fascinating insight into time-honoured Lesotho customs. Herder boys roam the mountains and farmers travel on horseback, wrapped in traditional blankets. The country's lack of fences also provides excellent hiking conditions, while trekking with mountain ponies opens up some of the most remote areas of the country.

Maseru

→ *Colour map 4, B4.*

Maseru must be one of the world's sleepiest capital cities – though, in comparison with the rest of the country, life here seems almost frantic. The city centre straggles along the Clarendon River, with most of the shops, offices, hotels and restaurants strung along one long central street, called Kingsway. Even this main road is surprisingly quiet, however, with the languid pace of life broken only by beeping minibus taxis. Although largely modern and unremarkable with very few sights, it is a pleasant enough place for a wander and a good spot to soak up the vibrant feel of an African town. The Basotho people are outstandingly friendly, and it's not uncommon for people to approach you in the street simply to ask how you are and where you come from. During the day safety isn't an issue, but it's best to avoid wandering around after dark, particularly around the eastern end of Kingsway. Approaching from the rural farmland on the South African side, the city centre appears unexpectedly and even the

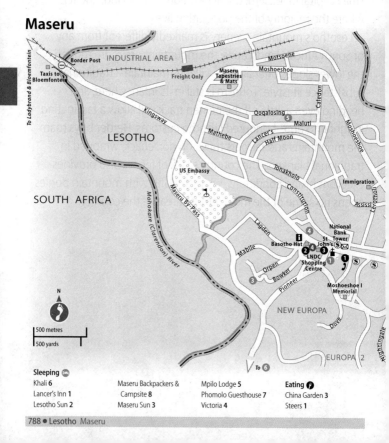

Maseru

Sleeping
Khali **6**
Lancer's Inn **1**
Lesotho Sun **2**

Maseru Backpackers & Campsite **8**
Maseru Sun **3**

Mpilo Lodge **5**
Phomolo Guesthouse **7**
Victoria **4**

Eating
China Garden **3**
Steers **1**

newer tower blocks look pretty behind the numerous trees of the more affluent suburbs above the river. In the other direction, the city sprawls for miles of poorer, often unplanned, suburbs.
➤➤ *For listings, see pages 790-793.*

Ins and outs

Getting there
Moshoeshoe I International Airport ① *T2235 0777*, is 21 km south of Maseru along the Main South Road. By road, the nearest border crossing with South Africa is Maseru Bridge (24-hr), which is just outside the city centre at the end of Kingsway. There are buses or taxis to most centres in Lesotho. Long-distance buses depart from the bus station about 500 m along the Main South Road from Cathedral Circle. The main bus and taxi station is on and around Market Street one block from Cathedral Circle, where buses for the towns in the Lowveld depart and from where minibus taxis depart randomly to all centres in the country. ➤➤ *For further details, see Transport, page 792.*

Getting around
The city is easily navigated on foot but if you're in a car, there is parking outside the shopping centres, in a guarded car park behind the Besotho Hat building, and in front of the tourist office. A fairly constant stream of minibus taxis moves up and down Kingsway from Cathedral Circle down to the border post. The two main roads out of Maseru start at the Cathedral Circle; Main Road North (A1) and Main South Road (A2).

Tourist information
The **Tourist Information Centre** ① *Basotho Shield building, central Kingsway (opposite the Basotho Hat building; both are hard to miss thanks to their huge thatched roofs), T2231 2427, www.ltdc.org.ls, Mon-Fri 0800-1630, Sat 0830-1300,* is extremely helpful and welcoming, with a wide range of leaflets on accommodation, national parks and tour operators. They also produce a useful official brochure, with information and addresses on sights and accommodation. The staff can assist with advice on road conditions and the best routes around the country. If you are crossing into the country through Maseru Bridge, drop in at the **Maloti Tourist Office** in Ladybrand which also covers Lesotho in its juris-diction. (See Free State chapter, page 729, for details.)

The Regal 2

Bars & clubs 🎵
Good Times Cafe 4

Note Lesotho phone numbers are given as they should be dialled within Lesotho; South African numbers as they should be dialled within South Africa. Other numbers are shown with their international code. See also page 69.

Background

Maseru was founded in 1869 when Lesotho's second colonial leader, Commandant JH Bowker, sited his headquarters at this strategically important site overlooking a good fording point on the Clarendon. Shortly afterwards the first traders were also established on the site now occupied by the Lancer's Inn. In the early years the city grew only very slowly and up to independence in 1966 the city centre underwent few changes. The main street was only tarred when King George VI visited in 1947 (when it was also renamed Kingsway) and by the mid-1960s there were still no buildings over two storeys.

Since the 1960s the city has grown rapidly, both in terms of population and urban development. Along central Kingsway there are modern office and shopping buildings holding the same high street shops as you'll find in urban South Africa.

Sights

There are very few sights worth visiting. There is nothing of architectural significance, though a couple of buildings are interesting for historical reasons. In front of **Lancer's Inn**, on Central Kingsway, is **St John's Church**. Built in 1912 the small church's interior has a number of inscriptions to some of Maseru's more important past residents.

Behind the Lesotho **National Bank Tower** is a park with a statue of **Moshoeshoe I**, the founder of the Basotho nation. It was unveiled in 1976 to mark 10 years of independence. To the north of Kingsway and along Constitution and Parliament roads there are many of the main government departments, mostly in colonial sandstone one-storey buildings.

The **parliament** building is at the far end of Parliament Road and is a fairly impressive modern structure in well-maintained grounds. This is due to move premises when the new parliament is completed in mid-2010 on the hill behind the Lesotho Sun, which is being funded by the Chinese.

◉ Maseru listings

For Sleeping and Eating price codes and other relevant information, see pages 46-53.

● Sleeping

For a capital city, Maseru has very few hotels (although this is gradually improving), or indeed eating and drinking venues. The first 2 Sun International properties are the most luxurious hotels in the country; but saying that they were built in the 1970s and today are a little drab and old-fashioned. Don't expect the same standards as South Africa. **A Lesotho Sun**, off Nightingale Rd, behind Queen Elizabeth Hospital, T2231 3111,

www.suninternational.com. Most luxurious hotel in Lesotho, on a hilltop setting overlooking town. Large, modern, with 192 a/c rooms with satellite TV, great city views, 2 popular bars, an attached casino, 2 good restaurants, gym, massage room, outdoor swimming pool with a pleasant terrace, and a shopping arcade with internet café. Transfers to and from the airport available. **A Maseru Sun**, 12 Orpen Rd, T2231 2434, www.suninternational.com. The other luxury choice in town, also part of the Sun International Chain, smaller than the **Lesotho Sun**, but modern with 115 a/c rooms, all with

DSTV and good standard decor. Restaurant, café, 2 bars, gym, sauna, swimming pool, tennis courts, small casino with slot machines.

C Hotel Khali, Manong Rd, in quiet suburb of Hillside, south of the prison, T2232 6326. Large rambling place with 50 simple en suite rooms in concrete blocks with TV, reasonable à la carte restaurant, bar and thatched garden bar, breakfast is included in the rate (which is unusual for Lesotho). Friendly staff and can organize airport pick-ups.

C Hotel Victoria, central Kingsway, T2231 3687. In a modern, plain multi-storey tower in the centre of town, with comfortable, contemporary rooms with a/c and TV. Popular, if slightly dreary, restaurant serving international dishes, bar. Attracts business travellers. Downside is this area is a red light district at night.

C Lancer's Inn, central Kingsway, T2231 2114, www.lancersinn.co.ls. Historical hotel in centre of town, with 21 rooms, some self-catering, and cosy en suite rondavels in the garden. 2 popular bars, gym, decent restaurant, bakery, bottle store, swimming pool, relaxed atmosphere. The best mid-range option in town.

C-D Phomolo Guest House, 9 km from town on the road to Moshoeshoe I International Airport, T2231 0755, www.phomologuesthouse.co.ls. Immaculate modern guesthouse with two 2-bed self-catering flats and 4 B&B rooms, with modern furnishings, bright white linen, Wi-Fi, DSTV, braai in the garden, off-street parking and breakfast on request. Will pick up from airport with prior notice.

D Mpilo Lodge, Maluti Rd, off Kingsway, T2231 7800, mpilo@ilesotho.com. Family-run guesthouse on the western outskirts of town, a low-key alternative, with 15 spacious en suite rooms, satellite TV and telephones, simple tiled floors and vaguely African theme. Restaurant and bar with views over the golf course and mountains.

D-F Maseru Backpackers & Campsite, 3 km from the centre on Airport Rd (this road refers to the old airport), T223 25166, www.durham-lesotholink.org.uk. A well overdue budget option in the city, this is the centre for the Durham Lesotho Link, a church initiative between Durham in the UK and Lesotho, which supports community and youth educational programmes and environmental projects. In a scenic setting next to a small dam, simple accommodation in dorms (guests can use the kitchen); in 1 family en suite self-catering rondavel with terrace and braai (they plan to build more); or 20 grassy campsites with neat ablution block, campers can also use the kitchen. All meals on request. Organize canoeing on the dam.

🍴 Eating

South African chains are springing up around town, including a **Steers**, opposite the post office. There are street vendors along Kingsway and around the taxi station during the day selling the staple Basotho meal of stiff maize porridge (pap) and stew, or roasted maize.

🍴🍴🍴 **Lehaha Grill**, Lesotho Sun, see Sleeping, page 790. Open 1830-2330. The main à la carte restaurant in the basement of the hotel, popular with Maseru's richer residents. Rather grand, if slightly faded decor, but very friendly service and decent meals, including Lesotho trout and traditional stewed oxtail, and a good choice of South African wine. Reservations necessary at weekends and public holidays. Recommended.

🍴 **China Dragon**, Lesotho Sun, see Sleeping, page 790. Open 1830-2230. Authentic Chinese restaurant with red and white decor, long menu with a good choice for vegetarians. The buffet on Sat night is good value.

🍴 **Rendezvous**, Lancer's Inn, see left. Open 0900-2000. Popular restaurant, with chandeliers and a vaguely African theme, serving standard international cuisine, including African and French dishes. Some outside seating in the beer garden. King Letsie III regularly dines here.

🍴 **China Garden**, LNDC Shopping Centre, T2231 3915. Mon-Sat. Reasonable Chinese food, catering in part for the city's burgeoning Chinese population. Central location, service is notoriously slow but the food isn't bad, cheaper takeaways available. Popular early evening bar attached.

† **The Regal**, next door to the **Basotho Hat craft shop**, T2231 3930. Open 1200-2200. Vaguely oriental decor in this international restaurant, serving good-value lunches (chicken with chips or pap, plus toasted sandwiches) and (British-style) Indian curries and grills in the evenings. Very friendly service. Excellent coffee served all day.

① Bars and clubs

The few bars are attached to big hotels or to restaurants. The small public bar at **Lancer's Inn** is often referred to as the alternative Parliament; it is frequented by a regular clientele of (male) civil servants, teachers and lecturers from the National University. The lounge bar has a more relaxed atmosphere, especially for women, and there are a couple of pool tables; ignore the sign that says the bar is for hotel residents only – everybody else does. The terrace of the 1st-floor bar at the **Hotel Victoria** is ideal for watching the world go by on Kingsway. The casino at the **Lesotho Sun Hotel** is popular with guests, and the basement bar is a busy meeting spot for well-heeled locals.

Good Times Café, LNDC Shopping Centre, T2231 7705. Mon-Sat, 1200-late. The only non-hotel bar that also serves food (†). Surprisingly modern decor for Maseru with chrome and suede sofas and a big screen TV for sports. Busy at weekends, but weeknights are very quiet, more popular for lunch.

① Shopping

Central Maseru has various outlets of South African chain stores and supermarkets, including **Shoprite**, in the LNDC Shopping Centre on Kingsway, and another branch in the Sanlam Mall near the Cathedral Circle, which are useful stops if you are self-catering. The main hotels all have craft or curio shops

but these tend to be overpriced. The best craft shop is the **Basotho Hat**, opposite the tourist office, T2232 2523, Mon-Sat 0800-1700, although even here the selection of local crafts is basic. The best buys include mohair blankets, woven baskets and the traditional wicker Basotho hats. In industrial area to the north of town on Raboshabane Rd is the **Maseru Tapestries and Mats** workshop, T2231 1773, which is operated by a group of women weavers who produce colourful mohair tapestries of animal and village scenes as well as geometric patterns. Mohair, woollen, sheepskin and leather products can be bought from a handful of other workshops around Maseru – look out for signs by the road as you drive out of town. One of these is **Seithati Weavers**, 7 km out of town on Main South Rd, T2231 3975, www.villageweavers.co.ls. This cooperative of 14 women makes a range of mohair, rugs, tapestries, bags and shawls; you can watch them at work in the workshop or browse in the shop. One of their tapestries depicting Basotho village life decorates the lobby of the Lesotho Sun Hotel.

▲ Activities and tours

Tourist Information Centre recommend local guides to take you to areas of scenic, historic or artistic interest around Maseru, although most of these areas are easily explored alone. **Sun International** hotels also organize tours.

⊕ Transport

Air
SAA, central reservations T011-978 1111, www.flysaa.com, operates the route between Moshoeshoe I International Airport and Johannesburg's **OR Tambo International Airport**. 4 flights a day (1 hr 10 mins).

Bus
Long-distance buses, run by **Lesotho Freight and Bus Services**, T2231 3535, running to

Thaba Tseka (7 hrs), Semonkong (6 hrs), Linakaneng (9 hrs), Mokhotlong (8 hrs) and Qacha's Nek (11 hrs) depart from the main bus terminal about 500 m along the Main South Rd from Cathedral Circle. The longer journeys depart at 0630.

If you just miss the bus to Semonkong, it is worth catching a taxi to **Roma**, which will inevitably overtake the slow-moving buses.

Car hire

Avis, Moshoeshoe I International Airport, T2235 0328, www.avis.co.za; **Budget**, Maseru Sun Hotel, T2231 6344, www.budget.co.za, can arrange pickup and drop-off at airport.

In reality most visitors to Lesotho hire cars in South Africa. Ensure that you get the right paperwork to take a car across the border and that the engine size/type of car is suitable for your chosen route. You'll need a 4WD to drive on un-tarred roads, and even if you are sticking to the tarred roads, a saloon car with a high engine size is recommended as there are some steep hills, and high clearance is worth considering too.

Taxis

There have been reports of pick-pocketing and muggings around the Cathedral Circle and bus and taxi terminals. Guard your valuables and avoid the area after dark.

Local Minibus taxis depart from the maze of streets around Market St just north of the Cathedral Circle. There is a regular stream of minibus taxis up and down Kingsway from Cathedral Circle down to the Border Post. Minibus taxis will take you off their set route for a negotiable price as long as they do not have other passengers. For conventional taxis try **Moonlight Telephone Taxis**, T2231 2695, or **Luxury Telephone Taxis**, T2232 6211.

Long distance Most going south depart the **New Taxi Rank**, Moshoeshoe Rd behind the Shoprite Supermarket, about 300 m north of Cathedral Circle, while those heading east and north go from the **Old Taxi Rank**, 200 m to the east of here.

Taxis towards **Bloemfontein** and **Ficksburg** in South Africa leave from the South African side of Maseru Bridge border post.

Directory

Banks Lesotho Bank, Nedbank and Standard Bank, central Kingsway, Mon-Fri 0830-1530, Sat 0830-1200. The best and quickest place for foreign exchange is the Standard Bank, Lesotho Bank Tower, which also has an ATM. **Embassies and consulates** South Africa (High Commission), 10th floor, Lesotho Bank Centre, Kingsway, T2231 5758; **USA**, 254 Kingsway, T2231 2666, http://maseru.usembassy.gov. Most other countries deal with Lesotho from their embassies in South Africa. **Emergencies** Police, Constitution Rd, T2231 7262, T124. **Internet** Data Kare, in the LNDC Shopping Centre, Kingsway, daily 0800-2100; **Leo Internet Services**, by the Basotho Hat, Mon-Fri 0800-1700. There are also business centres in the Sun International hotels. **Medical services** Maseru Private Hospital, Ha Thetsane, 7 km south of the city, T2231 3260; **Queen Elizabeth Hospital**, Kingsway, T2231 2501. Both reasonably well equipped and staffed, but patients with serious illness or injuries will be transported to a South African hospital. There are pharmacies in the shopping centres but no after-hours pharmacy; in an emergency you will have to go to a hospital. **Post office** New Post Office Building, Kingsway opposite Steers, Mon-Fri 0800-1630, Sat 0800-1200. **Telephone** You can send and receive faxes at the main post office. Local and international calls can be made from the phone boxes outside or from the public phone shop in the LNDC Shopping Centre. The main hotels will make international connections but these are expensive. Mobile phones work well in Maseru, but don't expect much coverage away from the capital although services are improving all the time. Local SIM and top up cards are available to buy everywhere.

Maseru to Semonkong

There are three main routes out of Maseru: the well-maintained Main North Road that runs along Lesotho's narrow lowland strip; the Main South Road through the farming towns of the wider lowland strip; and the road from Maseru branching off to Semonkong in the central mountains or Thaba Tseka in the east (see page 804). Beyond Roma, the road climbs into the eastern side of the Thabo Pusoa Mountains, part of the Lesotho Highlands, and ends at Semonkong. This dramatic drive passes through beautiful mountain scenery and a string of traditional Lesotho villages, with very different lifestyles from those of Maseru's city streets.

▶▶ *For listings, see pages 796-797.*

Thaba Bosiu → Colour map 4, B4.

Thaba Bosiu, 25 km outside Maseru, was the mountain stronghold of the founder of the Basotho nation, Chief Moshoeshoe. It is an isolated and steep-sided mountain with a large flat plateau at the top. From this secure defensive position Moshoeshoe was able to launch raids against his neighbours before retreating to safety. He, and many other important Basotho (including King Moshoeshoe II who died in 1996 in a car accident), are buried at the mountain's summit. There are remnants of Moshoeshoe's village and his restored two-roomed house. Also here on a protruding rock is a chiselled out footprint left by Maleleka, one of Moshoeshoe's sons. The story goes that he was forbidden to marry the girl he loved because she was below his rank, so lamenting the loss of his loved one, he carved the footprint as an epitaph before throwing himself off the mountain to his death. Thaba Bosiu means 'mountain at night' and legend has it that what is a hill during the day becomes a mountain at night. Today regarded as a national monument, it has earned recognition as a UNESCO World Heritage Site for its importance to the Lesotho people.

If you are arriving from Roma or the Semonkong road, taxis and the twice-daily bus from Semonkong will drop you off at the junction with the Thaba Bosiu Road, from where it is fairly easy to pick up a connecting taxi. There are a number of pathways up the mountain but visitors usually use the steep Rafutho's Pass. The defensive wall built by Moshoeshoe's men when they first arrived at the mountain can still be seen. The views are lovely, and nearby is **Qiloane**, a strangely nipple-shaped mountain, the shape of which is supposed to have inspired the Basotho Hat.

Tour guides can be found at the car park and small visitor centre between 0800-1700, T5888 3504, at the base of the mountain; most are fairly knowledgeable and will give visitors a fascinating (if not always completely accurate) account of the role of the Thaba Bosiu stronghold and much of Lesotho's early history. The tours usually take about two hours in total and the price will depend on your skills of negotiation. There is talk of a cultural village being developed at the site.

Roma → Colour map 4, B5.

Roma is 31 km east of Maseru along the road to Semonkong. It is the last place to buy fuel if you are driving to Semonkong, a further 85 km away. It is the principal centre of the Roman Catholic Church in Lesotho, hence the Italian sounding name, and was founded in 1862 when Mosheshwe granted the land to Father Joseph Gerard, a French pioneer missionary. It is the site of the National University of Lesotho and a large number of churches, presbyteries and schools. The town itself is little more than a few houses scattered around these institutions in a pretty, wooded valley at the foothills of the Maluti. The University was founded in 1945 by the Catholic Church. It became part of the combined university of Botswana, Lesotho and Swaziland in the 1960s until that institution collapsed and it was brought under the sole control of the Lesotho Ministry of Education. The entrance to the University is on the left as you enter the town from Maseru. Few of the University buildings are of any historical interest but the campus is green and well maintained and visitors are welcome to wander around.

 Pope John Paul II visited Roma in 1988 to posthumously beatify Father Joseph Gerard, who died in Roma in 1914.

Semonkong and around ⊜❼▲⊜ ▶▶ pp796-797. Colour map 4, B5.

From Roma to Semonkong (85 km) the road climbs into the central mountains and the scenery becomes more dramatic, passing through tiny villages and past Lesotho horsemen in their gum boots and blankets. The tar road turns to gravel at **Moitsupeli**, 19 km beyond Roma, after which it continues to climb through **Ramabanta** (access point for the excellent **Trading Post Adventures** lodge) and into the Thabo Putsoa Mountains, peaking at 2000 m. Under normal conditions, the journey from Maseru to Semonkong (120 km) is about four hours and is manageable in a 2WD, though a 4WD is vital in winter or if it's wet. Alternatively, there are two daily buses that takes about six hours and leave Maseru at 1000 and 1400. **Semonkong** is at the end of the road and is a small town that historically had a reputation for being a secret hideout of outlaws.

Maletsunyane Falls

Semonkong is of interest mainly because of the nearby **Maletsunyane Falls** which are the highest single drop falls in southern Africa. They are also referred to as the **Semonkong Falls**, Semonkong means 'place of smoke', or the **Lebinhan Falls** after Father François Le Binhan, the first European to see them in 1881. They can be visited on a hike or pony trek from **Semonkong Lodge** or on a pony trek from **Malealea Lodge**. Though the volume of water is usually small, the falls are very impressive and drop 192 m (twice the drop of the Victoria Falls, though a fraction of the width) into a huge gorge that winds through the mountains for many kilometres. Part of the attraction is that there are absolutely no tourist facilities around the falls. They are about 4 km south of Semonkong; it is possible to drive part of the way but the walk from Semonkong is easy. They are best seen during the late rainy season when they are full. At the end of very dry periods they are often reduced to little more than a trickle and occasionally in winter they freeze, forming spectacular ice pinnacles.

Ketane Falls

Very few people have seen the pristine Ketane Falls which drop 122 m as they are in one of the highest and most remote regions of Lesotho, midway between Semonkong and Malealea (see page 809). From Semonkong it's possible to reach them in a day's hike or to drive (by 4WD only) to the tiny village of Ha Bati, 5 km from the falls, and hike the rest of the way. From both Semonkong and Malealea lodges the option is to get to the falls by horseback, overnight from Semonkong and four days from Malealea. This is stunning mountain scenery and you are unlikely to see other people, except for the occasional herd boy.

◉ Maseru to Semongkong listings

For Sleeping and Eating price codes and other relevant information, see pages 46-53.

● Sleeping

Thaba Bosiu p794

D Mmelesi Lodge, near the bottom of the main path, T5250 0007, www.mmelesi.co.ls. This has a good restaurant and a rather plush bar, which is a popular venue at weekends for the people from Maseru who come for lunch, when there's traditional dancing and singing. 27 comfortable en suite rondavels with TV set in pretty gardens at the back. Heaters provided in winter. Avoid if there is a conference on, but at other times is a pleasant place to stay. Can organize pony trekking and guided hiking.

Roma p794

C-E Trading Post Guest House, signposted off the main street, T2234 0202, www.trading post.co.za. Offers a mix of luxury rondavels and more basic backpacker accommodation in an original sandstone trading post building built in 1903, and camping in the well-tended gardens. Breakfast is available and other meals by prior arrangement, self-catering facilities, small pool. Also owns the excellent **Trading Post** in Ramabanta (see below). Ashley and Jennifer Thorn are experts on the area and can organize short pony treks to the surrounding hills above Roma. Recommended.

Semonkong and around p795

Like Malealea (see page 813) the 2 options below offer the authentic Lesotho visitor experience; pony trekking (and numerous other activities), the opportunity to meet the rural people, and to enjoy the beautiful mountain scenery.

C-E Trading Post Adventures, signposted from the centre of the village of Ramabanta, 45 km from Roma, and about 40 km before Semonkong, T2234 0202, www.tradingpost. co.za. Stunning location in a trading post dating from 1939, with wide-reaching mountain views. Luxurious and stylishly decorated rondavels, or more basic en suite rooms in the old stables. Delicious meals served in the candlelit dining room. Huge range of activities on offer (see Activities and tours, page 797), including short walks, pony treks, 4WD routes, dirt-bike tracks and overnight stays in a nearby village. Run by the affable and hugely knowledgeable Rosemary.

D-F Semonkong Lodge, Semonkong, T2700 6037, T62021021 (mob), www.placeofsmoke. co.ls. This popular lodge offers a handful of thatched en suite huts, with African decor and log fires, plus simpler rooms in the house. There's also a dorm and camping space. Excellent meals served in the restaurant, bar, well-equipped communal kitchen, braai fire pits and gas braai, plenty of hot water (unless pipes freeze in which case boiling water is provided from the kitchen), pool table. There is broad range of outdoor activities on offer (see Activities and tours, page 797). They offer a free shuttle to/from Maseru every Tue and Sat. If you are driving yourself, allow at least 3 hrs to cover the 130 km from Maseru.

🍴 Eating

Roma p794

If you are self-catering you need to bring everything with you from Maseru, but basic commodities are available from the trading stores in the village.

Trading Post Guest House, see Sleeping, page 796. Provides breakfast, and with prior arrangement other meals for overnight guests. Non-guests can also organize meals here if you contact them in advance.

Semonkong and around p795

There is a restaurant and bar in both the **Trading Post Adventures** and **Semonkong Lodge**, and a couple of bars near the main bus stop Semonkong that serve up alcohol and basic meals. If you're self-catering, buy food in Maseru.

⛰ Activities and tours

Thaba Bosiu p794

The main hotels in Maseru organize frequent ½-day trips to the mountain, though it is just as easy and cheaper to go under your own steam.

Semonkong and around p795

Semonkong Lodge, see Sleeping, page 796. Offers pony trekking excursions from 3 hrs to 5 days. Expect to pay in the region of R350 for a short ride and M700 per overnight ride. Overnight rides are quite strenuous and involve 6-7 hrs riding each day but they can be attempted by novices. Accommodation is in Basotho huts with cooking equipment. Pack horses are also available for hire to hikers. A recent initiative is the world's highest commercial abseil, a 204-m drop down Maletsunyane Falls. This costs M850 and takes place over 2 days with training on 25-m cliffs the first day, followed by the spectacular drop at the falls the following morning. Another activity to make time for is on the last Sat of the month, the local people

stage a horse race in Semonkong. It's great fun to watch, draws quite a crowd and people bet on their favourite steeds. Contact the lodge for specific dates.

Trading Post Adventures, see Sleeping, page 796. Offers a wide range of activities from short self-guided walks, crossing the valley and passing through villages, to longer pony treks with a local Basotho guide. 4WD trails have been established in the wilder reaches of the mountains. Overnight stays in villages can be arranged, as well as fly-fishing for trout and singing performances from local children.

🚌 Transport

Thaba Bosiu p794
Taxi
There are frequent minibus taxis to **Maseru** along a good tarred road.

Roma p794
Bus
The buses between **Maseru** and **Semonkong** pass through Roma in the afternoon.

Taxi
Taxis to **Maseru** leave throughout the day, but stop at sunset.

Semonkong and around p795
Bus
The gravel road to Semonkong is fairly good except for the last 10 km or so. There are 2 daily buses to **Maseru**, which leave at 1000 and 1400, and the journey takes about 6 hrs. If you miss the daily bus at Semonkong, ask about lifts at the bar next to the bus stop.

ⓘ Directory

Roma p794
Banks Lesotho Bank, opposite the main University entrance. Will make foreign transactions, open Mon-Fri 0900-1300.

North from Maseru

The main route north out of Maseru is along the well-maintained Main North Road that runs along Lesotho's narrow lowland strip. The countryside on either side of the route is fairly heavily populated, dotted with affluent villages and banded by terraced fields, with good views across to the mountains. Commonly referred to as the 'Roof of Africa', these northern mountains are the highest and harshest in southern Africa. The high mountain peaks have a stark beauty – desolate and empty bar the odd herd boy during summer, and cloaked in snow every winter. There is one main road that runs across the area, from Butha-Buthe to Sani Pass, known for being the highest road in all of Africa. Upgraded to tar, the 200-km stretch between Butha-Buthe and Mokhotlong has opened up the entire region to visitors, but remember, in winter this road may well be blocked by snow. ▶▶ For listings, see pages 800-803.

Teyateyaneng → *Colour map 4, B5.*

The ramshackle town of Teyateyaneng, 'TY' as it is referred to, is 45 km north of Maseru and was founded as an administrative centre by the British in 1886. Teyateyaneng, meaning 'the place of quick sands', takes its name from the quicksand in the river that runs past the town occasionally sucking in hapless cattle. TY is well known as a handicraft centre and this is the main reason most people visit. Traditional Sesotho goods tend to be cheaper here than in Maseru and there are well-established centres that are run to ensure that profits return to the artists and not middlemen (see Shopping, page 802). Having said that, don't expect slick shops or smart complexes; goods are sold in run-down cement blocks by the roadside.

Ha Maketa

A half-hour's drive or minibus ride southeast from Teyateyaneng on a good tarred road brings you to the village of Ha Maketa. The reason to come here and a worthy distraction off the Main North Road is the **Kome Caves**, a collection of cave dwellings under an overhang of rock where people have lived since the 19th century. The seven residences, rounded mud-built domes with semi-circular doorways, have been recently restored and declared a National Monument. Were they covered in grass, they would not be too dissimilar to the Hobbit houses of Hobberton. There's a small visitor centre and you can park in the village. For a small fee local children will take you along the path for the half hour walk. The people that live here are accustomed to visitors and if you are friendly you may be invited inside.

Leribe (Hlotse) → *Colour map 4, B5.*

Back on the Main North Road, Hlotse is the administrative centre of Leribe district (and is often also known simply as Leribe). Founded in 1876, it was an important town in the 1880 Gun War. Still to be seen today are the remains of a British fort and a primitive statue of a kneeling British soldier. The Anglican Church dates from 1877 and is the oldest building in town. About 8 km north on the old Butha-Buthe road, in the Subeng stream about 400 m downstream from the bridge, are three- and five-toed dinosaur tracks estimated to be 108-200 million years old. Ask for directions in the village.

Butha-Buthe ●●●●● ▶▶ *pp800-803. Colour map 4, A5.*

Butha-Buthe is the northernmost town in the lowlands, and not too far from the **Caledon-spoort border post**, which is open daily 0600-2200. This is the last place to get fuel before

Oxbow, 68 km away. From here you can either continue north into South Africa or turn east onto the mountain road. Butha-Buthe gets its name (meaning 'place of lying down' or 'place of security') from the mountain that dominates the town; and it is here that Moshoeshoe had his first mountain stronghold. Towering above the town, this is the main attraction. The walk to the top is fairly strenuous but is worth it for the views across the town and surrounding countryside. The town itself is a busy centre with a number of supermarkets where people from the highlands come every few weeks to stock up on provisions. A large suburb known as Likileng has been constructed to provide accommodation for the workforce engaged on the tunnelling and hydropower components of the Lesotho Highlands Water Project.

From Butha-Buthe the mountain road begins in earnest and this is the original 'Roof of Africa' motor rally route that takes place annually at the beginning of summer. About 25 km from Butha-Buthe is the small **'Muela Dam**, and a short 7-km tar road leads up to a lookout point on the right of the Main North Road. This is another component of the Lesotho Highlands Water Project, and although you can't see it, the newly opened underground 'Muela Hydroelectric Power Station now provides the majority of Lesotho with power. Water is transferred to 'Muela from Katse Dam by way of a 45-km-long tunnel which has a diameter of 4 km. It then flows though 'Muela's power station before emptying into a second tunnel 37 km through the mountains to the Ash River near Clarens in South Africa's Free State. The Ash is a tributary of the Vaal River that leads to Vaal Dam in Gauteng, which provides all the thirsty province's water. There's a **visitor centre** ① *T2248 1212, www.lhwp.org.ls, 0830-1630, free tours go to the underground power station at 0900 and 1400*, at 'Muela and there are plans to turn some of the construction buildings into a lodge.

Another 5 km beyond 'Muela is the **Liphofung Cave Cultural and Historical Site** ① *T2291 3206, www.lhwp.org.ls, daily 0830-1630, M15, children (under 16) M5*. This cultural centre is another Lesotho Highlands Water Project initiative and includes three traditional Basotho huts, a small museum displaying some traditional agricultural tools and musical instruments, and a pathway and boardwalk leading to some San rock paintings dotted under and around a large overhang of rock. More significant for the Basotho, it was once a hideout of the young Moshoeshoe I. Local guides accompany visitors and explain the significance of the art. They also point out an unusual plant, the spiral aloe, which is the national plant of Lesotho. Its leaves twirl clockwise if the plant is male, and anticlockwise if it's female. The curio shop sells high standard local handicrafts and you can camp here or stay overnight in a couple of basic rondavels.

Moteng Pass
Travelling northeast, spending much of the journey over 2500 m, this tightly twisting road climbs up gradients of over 35% to the scenic **Moteng Pass** (2840 m) 68 km before Oxbow. The summit offers excellent views of the authentic Basotho homesteads in the valley below. In winter it can be quite a hazardous drive because of ice on the steep section as it ascends towards Oxbow, and in the extreme the pass can be blocked by snow.

Oxbow → *Colour map 4, A5.*
Oxbow has the last petrol until Mokhotlong and is also the centre of the Lesotho ski industry – as you'd expect, the industry isn't exactly booming, but there's a fairly new 1 km ski slope and a beginners area 11 km beyond Oxbow in a valley below the Mahlasela Pass (3220 m), which has a T-bar ski lift, a smaller rope lift and a snow-making machine. Operations are run by Afri-Ski (see page 801), and the ski season generally runs from the beginning of June to the end of August, though the lodge is open all year round and offers other activities such

as hiking. This Austrian-run outfit has built comfortable self-catering chalets at the site and there's a shop for renting equipment. They can also arrange tuition.

Tlaeeng Pass

The road between Oxbow and Mokhotlong (114 km; approximately three hours) snakes and twists higher until almost at the halfway point it reaches the **Tlaeeng Pass**. The summit of the highest road in Africa is 3275 m above sea level. As you can imagine, the views here are truly outstanding, and the drive offers undulating mountain scenery and clean crisp air. About 40 km after the pass the road starts to climb down towards Mokhotlong. Although tarred, the cold weather has taken its toll on this high stretch of the road and the ice has cracked it in parts causing pot holes so drive carefully.

Mokhotlong → *Colour map 4, B6. Population: 75,000.*

Mokhotlong Town or Camp is one of Lesotho's remotest towns and is the administrative and economic centre of the northern mountain area. The town's name means 'the place of the bald ibis', and these birds can still be seen along the river and in the surrounding valleys. The town was established as a police post in 1905 and grew as a trading centre supplied by pack ponies coming over the Drakensberg from KwaZulu Natal. Until 1947 when radio contact was established with Maseru, it had no connections with the rest of the country and until the 1950s it had no road connection with the outside world. Despite the arrival of the tarred road, in winter, Mokhotlong can still be cut off for many weeks by snow.

There is little of great interest in the town itself, but it retains something of an isolated outpost atmosphere. Sheep and goats are still shorn by hand in the surrounding sheds. An interesting sight is the Basotho in their striking blankets, hitching their horses outside and entering the modern bank. This is also the logical place from which to start exploring the remote valleys and high mountains of this area. The main supply stores are either near the bank or next to the airfield. There is a petrol station opposite the bank.

Sani Pass → *Colour map 4, B6.*

About 5 km south of Mokhotlong is the turn off to Sani Pass (60 km), which is a rough gravel road that should only be attempted by 4WD and can be blocked by snow in winter. It is a torturously steep, cork-screwing road and is the only pass from the northern mountains into South Africa. The views across the mountains of KwaZulu Natal are awe inspiring. Sani Pass was originally a bridle track for pack horses and was opened to vehicles in the 1950s. It is presently being tarred on the South African side. About 12 km from Sani Pass is the highest mountain in southern Africa, Thabana-Ntlenyana (3482 m). The name means 'pretty little mountain', hardly a fitting name for the second tallest mountain in Africa after Kilimanjaro. There are some beautiful walks in this rugged area; for details of hikes see page 511 and for details of approaching the Sani Pass from the South African side see page 511.

◉ North from Maseru listings

For Sleeping and Eating price codes and other relevant information, see pages 46-53.

especially in winter in the event that you maybe snowed in for an extra day or 2.

⊜ Sleeping

None of the places listed take credit cards. Ensure you have enough cash to pay,

Teyateyaneng *p798*
D Blue Mountain Inn, signposted from Main North Rd, T2250 0362. An ugly block

just outside the centre with 43 fairly basic but comfortable rooms with TV. Simple bar and restaurant (serving pizza) and pleasant gardens. Friendly staff and secure parking.

D Ka-Pitseng Guest House, signposted from Main North Rd 2 km before 'TY', T2234 7766, www.molengoane-kapitseng.co.ls. A brick building with 13 simple rooms with TV, set in pleasant gardens with thatched tables and chairs, children's playground and swimming pool. Bar and restaurant serving authentic Basotho cuisine, as well as staples like chicken and chips. Although it doesn't have facilities, it is accessible by wheelchair.

D Palace Hotel, 15 km south of TY and 25 km north of Maseru on Main North Rd, T5886 4905. A modern motel popular as a conference location for businesses from Maseru, but in a pleasant rural setting with neat gardens with swimming pool. Rooms have big beds, decent bathrooms, TV, phone and communal balconies (ensure doors are locked at all times). The restaurant and bar serves the usual meat and chicken with chips, rice or pap, and there's a nightclub next door that gets very noisy at the weekends.

Leribe (Hlotse) p798

D Leribe, town centre, T2240 0559. Dilapidated exterior but pleasant enough inside, with 33 en suite rooms with TV, in either a motel-style terrace or rondavels in the pretty garden, 2 bars (busy at weekends). Restaurant serves standard grills, steak and trout.

Camping

The **Anglican Mission** will sometimes allow visitors to camp in their grounds, no charge but leave a donation.

Butha-Buthe p798

D Crocodile Inn, in the southern suburbs of town, signposted from main road, T2246 0223. Local hangout (more for its heaving 2 bars than its rooms), with 29 run-down but clean rooms with en suite bathrooms and TV. Restaurant serves standard Basotho food. Pool table, secure parking, camping allowed.

Oxbow p799

A-C Afri-Ski, 11 km from Oxbow before the Mahlasela Pass, T058-303 6831 (South Africa), www.afriski.net. A range of new Alpine-style, double storey wooden self-catering chalets sleeping 2, 4 or 8, plus 10 comfortable en suite B&B rooms, with contemporary decor, fireplaces and heating, all set on the hillside near the ski slope. There's a good restaurant and bar with a pool table, and the après ski is just as popular as the skiing in season. Skis and snowboards can be hired from the shop.

B New Oxbow Lodge, T051-933 2247 (South Africa), www.oxbow.co.za. 35 cosy en suite heated chalets, either in doubles or family rooms, set in a mix of Alpine and thatched Lesotho buildings. Licensed restaurant, great bar overlooking the river, log fires in the lounge. Pony trekking, and trout fishing arranged, and it's 11 km from the ski slope, popular especially when there is snow which attracts curious South Africans, so make reservations in advance. Rates include breakfast and dinner and they can provide lunch boxes. The little shop sells among other things, gloves, beanie hats and thermal underwear.

Mokhotlong p800

D Senqu Hotel, on left-hand side of road as you enter town from the west, T2292 0330. Standard small-town hotel with 10 pokey but clean en suite rooms, better are the 8 new rooms in brick blocks with tin roofs, which have heating and DSTV. Restaurant with the usual meat, bar and public lounge. Nothing special, but the best bet in town.

D-F Molumong Guest House, 20 km from Mokhotlong on the Thaba Tseka Rd, T033-344 3074 (South Africa), www.molumong.net. An old colonial trading post homestead built in 1926, high on the mountainside affording great views. Dorms and doubles with bedding in rondavels with shared bathrooms, plus plenty of space to camp, no electricity, gas and candles are used, basic supplies available, a bottle store is close by and wholesome meals are on offer. There is no signpost to the lodge from the road, but 'Molumong' is painted on the roof. Confusingly, it is not in Molumong village, but in upper Rafalotsane village. Pony trekking can be arranged with the affable Jakob from 1 hr to 3 days.

Sani Pass p800
There are several options on the South African side at the bottom of the pass, including **Sani Pass Hotel** and **Sani Lodge**, see page 518. **B-F Sani Top Chalet**, top of the pass, next to the Lesotho border post, T033-702 1305 or T082-715 1131 (mob), www.sanitopchalet. co.za. The lodge offers a 4WD shuttle service up the pass from South Africa, and you can leave your car at 1 of the hotels at the bottom of the pass or at the South African border post. A combination of double rooms (**B**) in the main building or in stone en suite rondavels out back, plus backpacker rooms (**E**) with bunks, shared bathrooms and a small kitchen in a converted store in the nearby village. You can camp but you'll need thermals. The hotel has a licensed pub (the highest in Africa) and dining room warmed by roaring wood fires, overlooking the dramatic road below. Room rates include breakfast and dinner, and if backpackers and campers want these, inform the lodge in advance. Fantastic hiking and pony trekking to some awesome view-points along the escarpment.

❶ Eating

Teyateyaneng p798
The **Blue Mountain Inn** has a decent standard restaurant and bar, and there are numerous (very) basic cafés and bars around the main road junction of the Main North Rd.

Leribe (Hlotse) p798
There's little to be found other than a handful of basic cafés serving pap and stew.

Butha-Buthe p798
There are a number of small, cheap eateries on the main road near the bus stop or you can get a basic meal at the **Crocodile Inn**.

Mokhotlong p800
The **Senqu Hotel** has a reasonable restaurant with a fairly varied menu. There are a number of small eating and drinking houses and street vendors along the main street, selling mutton stew and pap or the delicious local brown bread with a hot sauce. The **Sunshine Bar**, is the busiest in town thanks to its satellite TV, which draws in highland horsemen in droves.

⭘ Shopping

Teyateyaneng p798
Elelloang Basali Weavers, on the right, 3 km north of town, T2250 1520. Open 0900-1700. Meaning 'be aware women', this is a women's weaving cooperative which was founded in 1997, and produces wall hangings, handbags, table mats and rugs.
Helang Basali Handicrafts, Main North Rd to the south of town centre, T2250 1546. Open 0830-1630. A women's cooperative run by a local mission, selling reasonably priced rugs, blankets, tapestries and other handicrafts from a run-down shop next to the road. They are best known for their soft hand-woven mohair scarves. A short walk away at the mission is the workshop, where you're welcome to watch the ladies at work.
Setsoto Design, opposite **Blue Mountain Inn**, T5808 6312, www.setsotodesign.com. 0800-1700. Lesotho's oldest and finest weaving company where visitors can watch women weaving. A great selection of wall hangings and carpets, all hand-woven with homespun mohair, are for sale in the show room. As well as standard village life scenes, there are some contemporary abstract designs.

Leribe (Hlotse) p798
Leribe Craft Centre, on Main North Rd at the turn off to Katse Dam, T2240 0323. Open 0830-1700. A handicraft cooperative run by the Anglican Church for physically disabled and deaf women, selling mohair blankets, ponchos, scarves, baskets, hats, beadwork and unique Basotho dolls.

⊖ Transport

There's a daily bus run by the **Lesotho Freight and Bus Services** from **Maseru** to **Mokhotlong** that departs Maseru at 0630 and takes about 8 hrs and stops in all the towns on the Main North Rd as well as **Oxbow**.

Teyateyaneng *p798*

There are frequent taxis, leaving from near the main junction along the Main North Rd. If you are going to **Leribe** (**Hlotse**) it is usually necessary to change taxis at the junction for Maputsoe where most turn off the Main North Rd for the Ficksburg border crossing. There are plenty of petrol stations in the town centre.

Leribe (Hlotse) *p798*
Taxi

Taxis to **Butha-Buthe** leave throughout the day from the south end of the main street. Taxis towards **Teyateyaneng** and **Maseru** leave from the same area, though passengers usually have to change at **Maputsoe** (where the approach road to the Ficksburg border crossing turns off from the Main North Rd).

Butha-Buthe *p798*
Bus

The bus towards **Oxbow** and **Mokhotlong** leaves from the far side of the petrol station near the main junction and usually gets to Butha-Buthe from Maseru about 0900. This is a steep road so your nerves need to be up to it.

Taxi

Taxis heading towards **Leribe Maseru** and the **Caledonspoort** border leave from the end of the main street. Taxis to **Ficksburg** and **Fouriesburg** can be found on the South African side of the border.

Oxbow *p799*
Bus and taxi

The daily bus and 2-3 taxis a day operate between **Butha-Buthe** and **Mokhotlong**, and stop at Oxbow.

Mokhotlong *p800*
Bus

There is a daily bus to **Maseru** and the lowland towns, departing about 0800 from outside the **Pep** store on the main street.

Car

The road from Mokhotlong to **Sani Pass** (60 km) is very poor and should only be attempted by 4WDs. It is a spectacular road that winds over the Black Mountain Pass (3240 m) then down to the Sani Flats and Sani Top village.

Hitchhiking

Drivers on the road from Mokhotlong to **Sani Pass** are good about giving lifts and most traders in Mokhotlong do their shopping in South Africa, so during the week there is plenty of traffic. In Mokhotlong it may be worth going to some of the stores the day before you plan to make the journey, to see if you can organize a ride.

Taxi

There are only taxis over **Sani Pass** if the weather and the state of the road is good enough, so travellers without their own transport will have to hitch a lift. A couple of taxis go to **Butha-Buthe**. They are much faster than the bus.

ⓘ Directory

Teyateyaneng *p798*
Banks The main banks have branches in the town centre, near the Blue Mountain Inn.

Mokhotlong *p800*
Banks Lesotho Bank on the north side of the main street, slow foreign exchange transactions. **Emergencies** The Lesotho Mounted Police is at the east end of the main street, near the large radio mast. **Post office** Next to the police station and LTC Office. **Telephone** Local and international calls can be made from the LTC Office.

Central mountains

The central mountain areas are the most accessible highland regions from Maseru. The new dams built here as part of the Lesotho Highlands Water Project have created excellent tar roads, opening up the region to tourists. This is the best area to visit for a glimpse of mountain life if you lack the time to travel in the more challenging areas to the north and the less accessible areas to the south. ▶▶ *For listings, see pages 807-808.*

Mohale Dam

The Mohale Dam, part of the Lesotho Highlands Water Project (see box, page 805), is accessed along the A3. The irregular-shaped lake made by the dam is stunning and the drive is beautiful, passing through untouched swathes of mountains east of the usual tourist route. The road passes through the small town of Nazareth and dips down before climbing up to Bushmen's Pass at 2263 m, offering beautiful views towards the highlands. From here, you dip down into a series of winding valleys, dotted with homesteads, to a police check point. Do not under any circumstances pass the 'Stop' sign here without permission: the bored officers have been known to root for bribes for the tiniest breach of the rules. Also look out for the rather aggressive herd boys, who run into the road to try and sell lumps of quartz and cutting from rare aloes (it is illegal to buy the latter). The road then continues up to the wonderfully named **God Help Me Pass**, at 2281 m and on over **Blue Mountain Pass**, when you'll catch your first glimpse of the impressive dam, mirroring the peaks around it. At the village of Likalaneng there's a small **visitor centre** ① *T2293 6217, 0800-1700, M5, children (under 16) M2*, from where you can organize a tour of the 165-m-tall dam wall. A lodge recently opened with expansive views of the dam. It offers daily boat cruises (see Sleeping, page 807). From here, the road turns to gravel and continues over the mountains to Thaba-Tseka, which peaks at the steep Mokhoabong Pass (2860 m).

Thaba Tseka → *Colour map 4, B5.*

This town was established in 1980 as the administrative centre for a new mountain district. There has been a large number of aid projects established in and around Thaba Tseka and there are, therefore, a disproportionate number of government and aid organization offices in the town. There are three roads into Thaba Tseka: from Leribe (Hlotse) via the Katse Dam (tarred as far as the dam followed by good gravel); a gravel road from Mokhotlong; and a decent gravel road from Maseru, tarred for about the first 50 km out of Maseru. This last one is a beautiful route, crossing the lowlands before ascending the first range of the Maluti Mountains via Bushman's Pass (2268 m). It is commonly known as the Mountain Road because it was the first road into the mountains that could be negotiated by saloon car.

There is little of interest in the town itself, although it is a place through which most visitors to the central mountains will pass. The advent of the Lesotho Highlands Water Project has had considerable impact on Thaba Tseka. Apart from a good gravel road linkage, the project sponsored a skills training centre to enable inhabitants to acquire expertise that would help them find jobs with project contractors.

Katse Dam ●● ▶▶ *p807-808. Colour map 4, B5.*

The new road from Leribe (Hlotse) to the Katse Dam (121 km) is an impressive feat of engineering. The drive from Hlotse to the visitors' centre at Katse Dam takes about three

Lesotho Highlands Water Project

Water is a resource that Lesotho has in abundance. Mean annual rainfall is 600 mm in the lowlands but is as high as 1000 mm along the mountain ranges, which dominate the country. The high peaks are also covered in frost for up to 250 days a year and in winter are covered in snow. The massive Lesotho Highlands Water Project, one of the biggest of its kind in the world, is currently under construction with final completion expected in the 2020s. The project has received major funding from South Africa, which maintains a large degree of control over its administration, although eventually it will provide the whole of Lesotho with electricity. The hydro-electrical power plant at Muela has been up and running since 2003 and supplies electricity to the lowlands.

The first phase of the project, completed in 1997, was the construction at Katse of a huge dam which pumps water into the South African river system to help meet the demand of thirsty mines and industry in Gauteng. The second phase, the construction of the Mohole Dam further upstream, was completed in 2003; by early 2006 it had filled up, and has now doubled the water supply to South Africa. The water makes its way to South Africa via a sophisticated transfer tunnel that feeds the Ash River in South Africa's Free State, and goes on to feed the Vaal River system in Gauteng. The water is icy cold and very clean, with good chemical properties and low sediment content – Lesotho's rivers, and subsequently the new dams (or perhaps more correctly reservoirs) – are fed by snow and rain at altitude. Consequently, the water is barely contaminated. Studies of the Vaal River ecosystem in Gauteng undertaken in the years since the Lesotho Highlands Water Project has been feeding South Africa's rivers, have shown that the quality of water has improved significantly.

The **Lesotho Highlands Development Authority** (LHDA) has stressed tourism development as a major part of the project. It has established new national reserves, including Ts'ehlanyane National Park and the Bokong Nature Reserve, both north of the Katse Dam. As a result of the new roads and infrastructure put in place for the construction of the dams, the previously difficult-to-access central mountain area of Lesotho has opened up and new lodges and facilities are being established. The dams themselves, surrounded by stunning mountain vistas, have become tourist attractions in their own right. For more information and updates, visit www.lhwp.org.ls.

to four hours but allow more time for stops at the top of the mountain passes to take in the sweeping views. What used to be the roughest track in the country is now smooth tar, though there are some very steep ascents and sheer drops to the side of the road. Bearded vultures and other unusual montane birds can often be seen from the pass summits and this region is also home to the ice rat, a rodent that is endemic to Lesotho and only lives above 2000 m. The highest point is the **Mafika-Lisiu Pass** (3090 m), where there is a car park and viewpoint and the visitors' centre for the **Bokong Nature Reserve** (see below).

From the pass, the road drops down to the northern end of the Katse Dam and passes the **Intake Tower**, which marks the beginning of the tunnel that takes water through to 'Muela Dam and then ultimately Gauteng. It then crosses the impressive 465 m long and 85 m high **Malibamatso Bridge** at the northern end of the dam before climbing again to 2600 m over the **Laitsoka Pass** and 2500 m over the **Nkaobee Pass** before dropping to below the dam wall where the growing settlement of Katse is located. The dam wall itself is the highest in Africa, and the second largest after Lake Volta Akosombo Dam in Ghana. It is an impressive structure and can hold over two billion cubic litres of water. The dam wall was built with over two million cubic metres of concrete, and is 185 m high and 60 m thick. It curves inward to such an extent that when looking down from the top, the bottom of the dam wall is invisible, and when looking up at from the bottom it appears to be leaning towards you – an odd experience. The catchment area for the reservoir is 1876 sq km when it's full, and the flooded valleys extend for 45 km.

As you enter Katse you will see the modern yellow building with a blue roof of the Lesotho Highlands Water Project **visitor centre** ① *T2291 0377, Mon-Fri 0800-1200, 1300-1600, Sat-Sun 0800-1200, M5, children (under 16) M2*, from where popular free tours into the dam wall take place at 0900 and 1400. The centre also has displays on the dam's construction, with a video and models of how water will be moved around when all five dams are completed in the 2020s. Nearby is the **Katse Alpine Botanical Gardens** ① *T2291 00311, M5, children (under 16) M2*, which was created to replant some of the indigenous flora that was disrupted in the construction of the dam, especially orchids and the spiral aloe, the latter being Lesotho's national flower. There are three water features, a medicinal plant garden, an area of succulents and a short wild flower walking trail.

Bokong Nature Reserve → *Colour map 4, B5.*
① *T2291 3206, www.lhwp.org.ls, sunrise to sunset, M5, children (under 16) M3.*
Bokong Nature Reserve covers 1970 ha and straddles the main road from Hlotse to Katse Dam at the 3000 m high Mafika Lisiu Pass. It claims to be one of the highest nature reserves in Africa and there are some outstanding views across the highlands. There is an **information centre** ① *daily 0800-1700*, perched on the edge of a 100-m cliff, which features exhibits on the ecology of the highlands, information on the 39 km overnight hiking trail to Ts'ehlanyane National Park and the network of shorter trails, and pony trekking. At this alpine altitude the reserve is of course not exactly full of animals, other than colonies of the ice rat, the occasional hardy rhebuck and a number of raptors including the bearded vulture. However, the scenery is tremendous, with extensive wetlands at the source of the Bokong River and vast heath covered plateaus. In winter the Lepaqoa Waterfall freezes into a column of ice.

Ts'ehlanyane National Park
① *T2291 3206, www.lhwp.org.ls. 24 hrs. M15, children (under 16) M5, car M5.*
Ts'ehlanyane National Park covers some 5600 ha, and lies at the junction of the Ts'ehlanyane and the Holomo rivers on the western range of the Maluti mountains. Its name lends itself to the small yellow flowers that appear along the riverbanks in spring, and it owes its origin to the access road to the Hlotse tunnel as part of the Lesotho Highlands Water Project. To get there take the gravel road which leaves the Main North Road 3 km south of Butha-Buthe. The 32-km road parallels the Hlotse River along a very picturesque valley until it reaches the park entrance. It can be bumpy in places but is accessed by a saloon car, although not in snow. In the park are extensive tracts of woodlands and it's full of rivers and streams bordered by bamboo and montane fynbos. Again there are very few animals, although 10 eland were relocated here in 2008 from KwaZulu Natal and have adapted well, but it's a haven for butterflies and birds. The latter include the bearded vulture, rock kestrel and ground woodpecker. Developments in the park include picnic areas, overnight trails with accommodation huts, walks and trails of varying length and pony rides (M25 per hour). There's basic accommodation at the visitor's centre and a new luxury lodge (see below).

For Sleeping and Eating price codes and other relevant information, see pages 46-53.

◉ Sleeping

Mohale Dam *p804*

B Mohale Lodge, Likalaneng, T2293 6432, www.oriongroup.co.za. Comfortable mid-range option managed by the Orion hotel group, which used to be accommodation for the construction workers of the dam. 69 en suite a/c rooms in red brick blocks with good views of the dam, or self-catering flats sleeping 6-10, with swimming pool, tennis and squash courts, à la carte restaurant, bar. Good option for eating if you've driving past too. Can arrange pony trekking and offers boat cruises on the dam.

D-F Marakabei Lodge, a few kilometres beyond Likalaneng at the settlement of Miaakabei, T6306 2650. Attractive country lodge with 6 rustic double en suite thatched rondavels, a dorm with 10 beds and camping. Shared bathroom with hot water. Meals available, bar with TV, self-catering kitchen, all set in pretty gardens on the Senqunyane River. May be able to loan out fishing tackle.

Thaba Tseka *p804*

D Mountain Star Hotel, T2290 0415. Scruffy and unappealing hotel with simple en suite rooms with TV and phone, popular with local businessmen. Friendly service and the only option in town, also has restaurant and bar.

Katse Dam *p804*

C Katse Lodge, Katse village, T2291 0202, www.oriongroup.co.za. Managed by the Orion hotel group, this is a sprawling ex-construction worker settlement in stone-clad buildings with red tin roofs that has been transformed into tourist accommodation, with 40 basic en suite rooms with stunning views over the dam (watching sunrise from the lodge is quite a special experience). Good restaurant, pool, tennis and squash courts.

Camping

Enquire at the Lesotho Highlands Water Project visitor centre about where to camp.

Ts'ehlanyane National Park *p806*

AL Maliba Lodge, just inside the park gate, reservations T031-266 1344 (Durban), www.maliba-lodge.com. A new luxury lodge that has received great reports so far. Run by a friendly Zimbabwean couple and has stunning mountain views. Group of thatched buildings with African contemporary decor, which house a comfortable lounge, restaurant and bar. The 5 very spacious suites are linked by pathways and have lavish bathrooms with big baths and flat screen satellite TV. The cuisine is of a very high standard and rates include all meals. Pony trekking and swimming in mountain streams can be arranged. Recommended and a fine addition to the area's limited accommodation options.

D-F Ts'ehlanyane National Park Bush Camp, next to the visitor's centre at the entrance gate, T2291 3206, www.lhwp.org.ls. Very simple stone and thatch rondavals sleeping 4 in bunks with Lesotho blankets, or in twin bedded safari tents. You can also camp. There's a communal ablution block, taps and a basic thatched braai area but you will need to bring everything with you. Bear in mind it gets very cold at night up here.

◉ Eating

Thaba Tseka *p804*

A couple of basic options and numerous small, cheap eating and drinking places in the older section of town, north of the stream.

◉ Transport

Thaba Tseka *p804*

There are no roads from Thaba Tseka to **Semonkong** though it's possible to hike.

Bus

There are 3 daily **Lesotho Freight and Bus Services** buses to **Maseru** leaving at 0830, 0900 and 0930 from the main bus terminal, which take 7 hrs. These stop in **Likalaneng** for the **Mohale Dam**.

Taxi

Minibus taxis run to **Katse Dam**, from where there are buses and taxis to **Leribe** (**Hlotse**). There is no public transport to **Mokhotlong** and this is a very difficult road, which should only be attempted with a 4WD and in good weather. Another basic gravel road (4WD only) runs south to **Selabathebe National Park**.

Katse Dam *p804*

The tar stops here but the road that continues to **Thaba Tseka** (45 km) is good gravel. While most of this route is tarred, to do this circuit in your own vehicle, it is recommended you have a vehicle with high clearance. The untarred stretch between Thaba Tseka and **Marakabei** is difficult going over the steep Mokhoabong Pass (2860 m).

Bus and taxi

From Katse there are taxis to **Thaba Tseka**, from where there are buses and taxis to **Maseru** that follow the mountain road. There are also buses and taxis from Katse to **Leribe** (**Hlotse**) where again you can hook up with a bus to **Maseru** via Main North Rd.

South from Maseru

The main route south from Maseru runs along the southern lowland strip. This is one of the main farming regions, but it tends to be a drier area than further north. There are a number of important urban centres along the route connected by tar roads, so it's easy to get around, although none of them could be considered tourist attractions.

The southern mountain area is dominated by the Senqu River Valley that winds through the area. The majestic river meanders through rugged mountain scenery and past steep cliffs but the water level has been reduced considerably as all the dams of the Lesotho Highlands Water Project are being completed. The mountain road from Moyeni (Quthing) in the Lowveld is tarred until Qacha's Nek, and passes through beautiful highland terrain. Although steep in places, it can, in fine weather, be managed in an ordinary vehicle, but you'll need a 4WD to get to the Sehlabathebe National Park. ▶▶ *For listings, see pages 812-816.*

Morija/Matsieng → *Colour map 4, B4.*

Morija is the site of Lesotho's oldest church and a well-run museum. The French Protestant missionaries who established the church named the town after Mount Moriah in Palestine. Lesotho's first printing press was established here and the village is still an important centre for culture, theology and printing. Books in more than 50 languages have been printed here for export to other African countries. The **Morija Museum** ⓘ *T2236 0308, www.morijafest.com/museum, Mon-Fri 0800-1700, Sun 1200-1700, R10, children (under 16) M3,* has a number of important historic and prehistoric exhibits and a well organized archive of personal and church papers. There is a large fossil collection and a good display on the dinosaur relics found throughout the country, and there are some of Moshoeshoe's personal belongings on display, including his china tea set. It's all a bit jumbled but the staff are very helpful and the museum is presently looking for funding to extend the premises. Outside are some old transport ox and horse wagons used by Lesotho's early traders. There is a delightful tea shop in the grounds serving tea, cold drinks, and snacks, and nearby a thatched craft shop selling pottery and textiles. The annual **Morija Arts and Cultural Festival** (contact the museum or visit www.morijafest.com for information) takes place here in the first week of April, and includes concerts, traditional dance, choirs, food and craft fairs. This is the only event of its kind in Lesotho's so it's worth making an effort to get here if you are in the country at the time.

About 7 km from Morija is the royal family's country home, **Matsieng**. The royal court met at Matsieng more or less throughout the colonial period and, in theory, all decisions taken by the colonial authorities in Maseru had to be agreed to by the monarch. Though the village is of great historical interest there is not a great deal to see or anywhere to stay.

Malealea → *Colour map 4, B4.*

South from Morija the road continues to Mafeteng. About 10 km south of Morija the B40 turns off the Main South Road to the left and follows through to Malealea about 32 km away. In the spring the sides of the road are covered in flowering mountain plants. Apart from the last 7 km, the road is tarred and fine for a normal car, though take care going over the Gates of Paradise in wet weather, which is 6 km before the lodge. This is an escarpment that opens out to a broad panorama over the plains below where there's a plaque on the rock to the right of the road that says 'Wayfarer pause and look upon a gateway to Paradise' – words uttered by Mervyn Bosworth-Smith, the founder of the Malealea trading post in the early 1900s. Today it's a popular pony trekking and hiking centre in the foothills of the Thaba Putsoa range, 85 km south of Maseru, and is probably the best place to stay to experience what Lesotho is all about. Here there are San rock paintings, isolated waterfalls, rock pools and peaceful hikes and treks in the surrounding mountains.

Mafeteng → Colour map 4, B4.

Mafeteng is 36 km south on the Main South Road from Morija. The name means 'the place of the passers by'. It is the main commercial and administrative centre for the southern lowlands. The town is a 15-minute drive from **Van Rooyens border post** (open 0600-2200) so this will be the first place you get to if crossing from Wepner in South Africa's Free State. There are pleasant views from the town across the lowlands towards the Thaba-Putsoa range of mountains. The town suffered considerably during Lesotho's 1998 riots. The **British War Memorial**, erected in memory of members of the Cape Mounted Rifles who died during the Gun War of 1880, is located near St John's Primary School on the road from Mafeteng towards the Van Rooyens border post. The town has a large clothing factory that manufactures for Gap.

Mohales Hoek → Colour map 4, B4.

This is a pleasant town named after King Moeshoeshoe's younger half-brother. There are San cave paintings in the cliffs beside the Main South Road as you enter town from the north, but they are difficult to get to. There are also paintings in various caves about 10 km from the Main South Road up the Maphutseng Valley. Although there is nothing to see in town, the most interesting story behind this region are the **Cannibal Caves**, 2 km south near the Agricultural Training Farm. Found throughout Lesotho, they are a reminder of *lifaqane*, 'the terrible time', when in the 1820s roving bands of warriors fleeing the Zulu attackers prevented farmers from growing crops, and people resorted to cannibalism to survive. The Makhaleng Bridge border crossing is close to Mohales Hoek.

Moyeni (Quthing) ●❼❽❾ ▸▸ pp812-816. Colour map 4, B5.

Moyeni ('place of the wind') is the administrative centre of Quthing district (the town itself is often also called Quthing – 'Qu' means river in San). It was established as an administrative centre by the British in 1877 but was abandoned three years later during the Gun War, and later rebuilt. It's a ramshackle town that straddles one main street running uphill from the Main South Road and the transport hub and a petrol station can be found at the bottom end. The town is in the far south of the lowlands at the point where the Senqu (Orange) River leaves the mountains and winds out across the flatter central South African plateau.

Sights

There are a couple of good sets of **dinosaur footprints** on the riverbank on the northern outskirts of Moyeni. There are also some dinosaur footprints further up the **Qomoqomong Valley**, though they are hard to find without a guide. The Qomoqomong Valley is also the home to some **San cave paintings**; follow the small road east out of Moyeni towards the village of Qomoqomong (where the road ends), the caves are in the hills to the southwest. However they are faded, and unfortunately vandalised, so aren't really worth the effort of getting there. More interesting is the **Masitise Cave House** ① T8979 4167, www.morija fest.com/masitise, Mon-Fri 0900-1630, donation, about 5 km to the west of Moyeni near Masitise Primary School. The cave house, which was renovated and turned into a small museum, has five rooms and was home to the Reverand DF Ellenberger and his family who established a mission in the area in the late 19th century. This is now a national monument, and there are displays of objects from that time in the house.

Southern mountains ◉❶❷❸◉ ▸▸ pp812-816.

Mount Moorosi → Colour map 4, B5.

About 40 km beyond Moyeni (Quthing) towards Qacha's Nek is Mount Moorosi and the village of the same name, which lies at the foot of Thaba Mokotjemela (2358 m). This is an important historical site. In the mid-19th century it was the home of the Chief of the Baphuthi clan (Moorosi), who carried out numerous raids against white settlers in nearby areas. After the British made Moyeni the district capital in 1877, they tried to subdue Moorosi by taking his son captive, but Moorosi resisted and managed to free his son. The British then spent over two years trying to eliminate the threat of Moorosi, eventually succeeding in capturing his mountain stronghold and massacring him and about 500 of his followers, including many children. Near to the village is **Letsie Lake**, a reeded wetlands area that attracts waterbirds. A wildlife conservation project has been set up here involving the local people in the protection of the bearded vulture.

Qacha's Nek → Colour map 4, B5.

This border town at the southeastern corner of Lesotho is on the only road pass from the southern mountain area into South Africa's Eastern Cape. Its location means that, unlike most of the country, there are residents from a number of southern African ethnic groups and visitors are as likely to hear isiXhosa being spoken in the street as Sesotho. Until 1970, Qacha's Nek had no direct road communication with the rest of Lesotho, and depended on the town of Matatiele in the Eastern Cape for supplies. This linkage was particularly important, given that Matatiele had a rail link by which migrant workers could travel to the South African mines. Qacha, meaning 'hideaway', was the name of a local 19th-century chief who was apparently able to disappear into the mountains for months at a time. The British established an administrative centre at the location in 1888 in an attempt to maintain control of this region which had a reputation for lawlessness. This is one of the few regions of Lesotho that is heavily forested and of particular interest are the giant California redwood trees, which exceed 25 m and are over 60 years old. This region also gets the most rain in Lesotho, about 900 mm per year, and summer temperatures only reach an average of 17 °C and it's often foggy. Interestingly, the government hospital here is used exclusively to treat tuberculosis patients.

Sehlabathebe National Park ◉ ▸▸ pp812-816. Colour map 4, B6.

This national park is isolated, inaccessible and rugged – but these are the main reasons for coming here. The park is situated in the far east of Lesotho on the border with South Africa and has more than 6500 ha of sub-alpine grasslands, with an average elevation of 2400 m. It has some breathtaking landscape with sandstone overhangs and rock features, mountain streams, natural pools, waterfalls, and 65 San rock art sites, some of which are accessible by foot or pony. It is part of the 300 km long Maloti Drakensberg Transfrontier Conservation Area, a joint environmental management initiative between Lesotho and South Africa joining the Sehlabathebe and the uKhahlamba-Drakensberg national parks. Facilities are limited and the park is only really popular with South Africa 4WD owners and trout fishermen.

Sotho: what's in a name?

Lesotho is one of the few countries in Africa in which the vast majority of people belong to the same ethnic ('tribal') group: the Basotho. Many people in South Africa will talk about 'the Sotho' but in Lesotho you will rarely hear the phrase; rather people will use the word 'Basotho', meaning 'the Sotho people'. The singular of Basotho is Mosotho, Sesotho is the language spoken by the Basotho and Lesotho means the place, or home, of the Basotho. Today there are as many Basotho living in South Africa as in Lesotho.

There is little large game within the park, except for the occasional hardy eland or baboon but there is plenty of birdlife, including the rare bearded vulture and black eagle. There is excellent trout fishing and the park is also home to the water lily of the Sehlabathebe and the tiny Maluti minnow, a flower and fish both thought to be extinct for many years. The park was gazetted in 1970; the prime minister of the time, Leabua Jonathan, loved trout fishing, which may explain the park's existence. The park lodge used to be called Jonathan's Lodge, and when he stayed all the other guests had to leave. There are stables here and guided pony treks and hikes can be arranged.

Ins and outs

Getting there There are two routes into the park: one via Sehlabathebe village and one across the border from South Africa. Access to Sehlabathebe village is either from Qacha's Nek about 100 km to the southwest, or from Thaba Tseka about 120 km to the northwest. Both roads are difficult and a 4WD is essential, but the route from Thaba Tseka is especially challenging. The route from South Africa is possible on foot or horse only; the path crosses the border at **Nkonkoana Gate** (open 0800-1600) and then heads down to the South African border post at **Bushman's Nek** which is 38 km from Underberg in KwaZulu Natal. Sehlabathebe Lodge is a 10 km walk or ride from Bushman's Nek. There are no border facilities here on the Lesotho side but there is a small office on the South African side, next to which is a basic campsite and a hikers hut run by KZN Wildlife. You can also walk here from Sani Top Chalet (see page 802) on a 40-km, three-day hike, but you'll have to have a good map and be completely self-sufficient.

◉ South from Maseru listings

For Sleeping and Eating price codes and other relevant information, see pages 46-53.

◉ Sleeping

Morija *p809*

C-E Morija Guesthouse, perched on a hill at the top of the village behind the museum, T6306 5093, www.morijaguesthouses.com. Attractive sandstone and thatch house with outstanding views of the Maluti Mountains (on a clear day you can see for 45 km), and a veranda and pretty gardens. The main house sleeps 16 in 5 bedrooms with shared bathroom, kitchen and lounge with fireplace, while several smaller, ethnic-themed rondavels in the garden sleep 2. Meals on request. The lodge can organize pony trekking and overnight stays in local villages and several easy hikes start here, too. Often used by school or church groups so book in advance. Stunning spot. Recommended.

Malealea p809

D-F Malealea Lodge, reservations South Africa, T051-436 6766, T082-552 4215 (mob), www.malealea.com. A collection of en suite rooms; comfortable thatched Basotho huts; en suite rooms in the old farmhouse; and dorms in forest huts, built around old trading post established in 1905. Communal kitchens for self-catering or great meals served on request. Camping allowed in grounds, honesty bar, general store, beautiful setting. Owners Mick, Di and Glenn are active in supporting community projects in the area. Introduced pony trekking for tourists here, lasting from 1 hr to 6 days. They also offer hiking, and visits to villages. Recommended for an all-round Lesotho experience.

Mafeteng p810

D Golden Hotel, to the right of the road as it enters the town from Maseru, T2270 0566. Plain brick block in neat gardens with comfortable but small en suite rooms and friendly staff. Lounge with DSTV, bar with pool table, restaurant serving standard meat dishes and surprisingly good pizzas.
D Mafeteng Hotel, town centre, T5885 5555. Offers 27 en suite rooms or cottages with satellite TV. Swimming pool set around the odd looking main building, which resembles an air traffic control tower. Restaurant and 3 bars. The whole set-up is run-down and shabby and can get noisy at weekends when the bars and the Las Vegas disco in the hotel grounds fill up and go on until 0400.

Mohales Hoek p810

C Hotel Mount Maluti, north of the town centre, T2278 5224, www.hotelmount maluti.co.za. One of the oldest hotels in Lesotho, with 34 en suite rooms with TV and heating. Colourful, if rather dark, most with patios on to the garden. Camping, the restaurant has a good vegetarian choice (rare in Lesotho), bars, tennis courts, swimming pool, nice gardens, one of the country's better small town hotels, run by Danny and Anne who are very helpful in organizing activities. Often booked out for conferences so reservations recommended.

Moyeni (Quthing) p810

There are a couple of run-down hotels in town, where things barely function, so you're better off staying in Mohales Hoek and visiting here on a day trip.

Mount Moorosi p811

D-E Moorosi Chalets, 2 km towards Qacha's Nek, follow the (good) signposted road on the right for 4 km. This is a joint community initiative between **Malealea Lodge** (reservations above) and the Quthing Wildlife Development Trust, offering a clutch of peaceful thatched rondavels, and a self-catering house in the scenic Quthing River Valley, at the bottom of Mount Moorosi. You can also camp and there's a neat ablution block with hot showers. No electricity but gas water geysers and fridge and paraffin lights are provided. Guided hikes can be arranged.

Qacha's Nek p811

D Nthatuoa Hotel, near the airfield, T2295 0260. A little faded with an intermittent water supply but has a variety of tidy en suite rooms set in a series of blocks of varying size and price. Good restaurant with high ceilings and ancient chandeliers, bar. Rates include an excellent breakfast. Can arrange pony treks or trout fishing. Camping in grounds.
D-F Letloepe Lodge, 4 km before border, T2295 0383, www.letloepelodge.co.ls. String of neat thatched rondavels housing en suite rooms with electric blankets, some with small kitchenettes and TV. Dorms, camping, restaurant serving basic meals, neat grounds with car park, run by the friendly Moletsane family who can organize pony trekking and boat trips on the Senqu River, easily the better of the 2 places to stay.
F St Joseph's Mission, in wooded valley, north of town centre. Visitors may camp in the grounds or stay in an outbuilding.

Sehlabathebe National Park *p811*

The park is undergoing changes as part of the Maloti Drakensberg Transfrontier Conservation Area and there are plans to build 15 new self-contained, self-catering chalets to be run by a private operator.

D-F Khotso Horse Trails, Bergvlei Farm, 10 km from Underberg towards Drakensberg Gardens, in South Africa, T033-701 1502, www.khotsotrails.co.za. On a working horse and cattle farm. Presently this is the best way to explore the park and they have backpackers accommodation in dorms, and self-catering log cabins and rondavels. Bar serving good meals. 3-day pony trekking into Sehlabathebe is on offer crossing the border at Bushmen's Nek, and overnight accommodation is in Basotho huts with hot water, All meals are included, rates from R950 per day/night. The climb by horseback from South Africa into the park is over 1000 m.

E-F Sehlabathebe Lodge, approximately 10 km from the entrance gate and visitor centre, reservations Ministry of Tourism, Environment and Culture, Post Office Building, Maseru, T2231 1767, www.maloti.org.ls. The original 14-bed lodge is unlikely to be open when you read this, as accommodation in the park has been put out to tender to find an investor (see above).

Camping

Camping is allowed anywhere but you have to buy a permit from the park office. There is no food available and very little in Sehlabathebe village, so bring your own supplies. Payment can only be made in cash.

🍴 Eating

Mafeteng *p810*

Other than the restaurants in the **Mafeteng** and **Golden** hotels, there are a large number of street vendors in the town centre and some cafés in the area just to the south. There is a popular open-air restaurant and a KFC near the minibus taxi terminal.

Mohales Hoek *p810*

There are few places to eat other than the **Hotel Mount Maluti** restaurant. There are a couple of cafés and street vendors on Mafoso Rd.

Moyeni (Quthing) *p810*

There are numerous street vendors and cafés around the minibus taxi terminal in lower Moyeni. There are a number of popular and noisy bars in lower Moyeni.

Mount Moroosi *p811*

You can get takeaways at the **Mitchell Brothers' Trading Store,** which serves as the village's main petrol station and general store.

Qacha's Nek *p811*

The **Nthatuoa Hotel** dining room has a varied menu and a good reputation. There are a number of smaller cafés selling cheap and filling meals near bus and minitaxi terminal.

🔺 Activities and tours

Malealea *p809*

Malealea Lodge, see Sleeping, page 813. Mike and Di Jones, who were born in Lesotho, can organize pony treks (no experience necessary), hikes or 4WD tours to all the local sites from 1 hr to 6 days. These include day treks to the Botsoela Waterfalls, and Pitseng Gorge and rock pools, plus overnight treks to the Ribaneng (2 days), Ketane (4 days) and Maletsunyane waterfalls (4 days), the 3 highest in Lesotho. Expect to pay in the region of M360 per person per day on the overnight pony trekking trips and M160 for a 2 to 3-hr trek, slightly less on the guided hikes.

The horses and huts used for overnight accommodation on the trails are hired from local Basotho, who also act as guides. The huts are equipped with mattresses, gas cooker, cooking and eating utensils and a bucket of water. Remember to bring a torch and candles. Mike and Di can also arrange informal performances by the village youth choir, accompanied by home-made instruments, and visits to local villages. All activities can be arranged as soon as you get to the lodge.

⊖ Transport

Morija p809
Bus and taxi
Frequent buses and taxis to **Maseru**, **Mafeteng** and **Mohale's Hoek**.

Malealea p809
Bus
There is a daily mid-morning bus between Malealea and **Mafeteng**. If travelling from **Maseru**, you can intercept the bus at Motsekuoa where the B40 turns off from the Main South Rd (about 10 km south of Morija) and you should catch it if you get there before noon.

Taxi
Some taxis go all the way from **Mafeteng** to Malealea Lodge.

Mafeteng p810
Bus and taxi
There are buses and taxis to **Maseru** via **Morija**, and to **Mohales Hoek** and **Moyeni**. This is also the place to pick up public transport to **Malealea Lodge**, and there is a daily bus that leaves mid morning and the occasional taxi.

Mohales Hoek p810
Bus
If travelling from Mohales Hoek to **Malealea**, you can catch one of the taxis going along the road marked B40 on most maps (though not on signposts).

Taxi
Taxis leave from either side of Mafoso Rd. People hitchhiking south may find it easier to get a lift if they first get a taxi about 4 km out

of town to the turn off to the **Makhaleen Bridge** border post. The road over the border is now tarred but on the South African side the road to Zastron in Free State reverts to a good gravel road.

Moyeni (Quthing) p810
Bus and taxi
Frequent buses and taxis towards **Maseru** via **Mohales Hoek** leave from near the petrol station in lower Moyeni. There is 1 bus a day to **Qacha's Nek** that leaves at around 0630 and takes about 8 hrs, and frequent taxis to the nearby border post **Tele Bridge** 21 km away.

Mount Moorosi p811
Car
This is the last place to get fuel before Qacha's Nek, 130 km. The road towards Qacha's Nek is now tarred and is passable in a saloon car (but check locally in wet weather as it's steep in places).

Taxi
There are fairly frequent taxis running the route between **Moyeni** and Mount Moorosi, and the daily bus between **Maseru** and **Qacha's Nek** passes through the town.

Qacha's Nek p811
Visitors without their own transport wanting to cross into South Africa will have to walk across the border and then hitchhike. It's 87 km to Kokstad and the N2 from here.

Bus
Daily bus to **Maseru** that takes 10 hrs.

Car
The drive to Qacha's Nek **border post** is steep and winding, but can be accessed in a saloon car (check locally if the weather is wet).

Taxi
Daily taxis between Qacha's Nek and **Moyeni** depart from outside the Shell petrol station.

➊ Directory

Mafeteng *p810*
Banks Standard Bank and the Lesotho Bank have branches in the town centre.

Mohales Hoek *p810*
Banks Lesotho Bank, Maluti Ring Rd, near the post office; **Standard Bank**, Mafoso Rd.

Moyeni (Quthing) *p810*
Banks There is a branch of **Lesotho Bank** in upper Moyeni.

Qacha's Nek *p811*
Banks There is a branch of **Lesotho Bank** on the western outskirts of town.

Swaziland

Contents

Footprint features

Border crossings

Swaziland–South Africa,
Lavumisa–Golela, see page 834

Swaziland–Mozambique,
Lomahasha–Namaacha, see page 835
Mahamba, see page 835

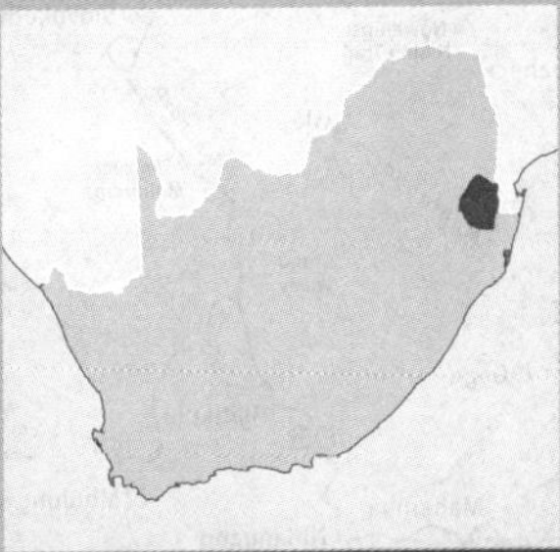

At a glance

Getting around Baz Bus, car hire, poor local buses.

Time required 3-5 days.

Weather Mostly warm and sunny, summer thunderstorms.

When not to go Good all year.

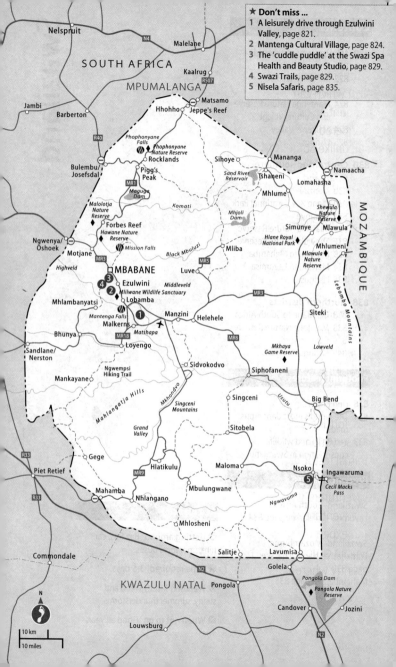

★ **Don't miss ...**

1 A leisurely drive through Ezulwini Valley, page 821.

2 Mantenga Cultural Village, page 824.

3 The 'cuddle puddle' at the Swazi Spa Health and Beauty Studio, page 829.

4 Swazi Trails, page 829.

5 Nisela Safaris, page 835.

With an area of just over 17,000 sq km (less than the Kruger National Park), Swaziland may be the smallest country in the southern hemisphere but it has myriad African landscapes, all of which can be seen from the top of Mlembe (1862 m), a mountain on the country's western border. Swaziland was plundered by European gold prospectors in the 19th century but, unlike South Africa, huge fortunes were never really made here and even throughout the colonial period, the government was more or less left in the hands of the royal family. Following independence in 1968, Swaziland has remained one of only three monarchies left in Africa, and is the only absolute monarchy on the continent.

On the whole, Swaziland is an accessible country to visit; it has moderate temperatures all year round, you can travel between the Highveld and the Lowveld in a day, and none of the major sights are more than a two-hour drive away. The tourist industry developed during the Apartheid years, when South African tourists left their puritanical regime to visit Swaziland's casinos and nightclubs. Unfortunately, as a consequence, the country developed a reputation for seedy sex and gambling holidays, but since the change of government in South Africa, this market has, fortunately, plummeted. Thanks to a handful of pioneering conservationists, effective anti-poaching initiatives and substantial animal restocking, Swaziland's game parks have improved dramatically in recent years. It's also a good destination for adventurers, with an effective backpackers' set-up and a number of adventure activities on offer. The Swazi people are friendly and expert craft makers, producing a wealth of high-quality African curios. Compared to South Africa, Swaziland is a country where tribal values, craftsmanship and royal loyalty have withstood the test of encroaching modernization.

Mbabane and around

→ *Colour map 2, C5. Altitude: 1250 m.*

Swaziland's capital Mbabane (pronounced 'M-buh-ban') is a small modern town built on the site of a trading station on the busy route between Mozambique and the Transvaal. After the Boer War the British established their administrative headquarters here and the town grew up around them. The first government building was erected on Allister Miller (now Gwamile) Street, which today is the site of the Mbabane Branch of the Swaziland Building Society. The town derives its name from Chief Mbabane Kunene, who was ruler over the area when the British arrived. Mbabane was proclaimed the capital of Swaziland in 1903, although records show that it was declared an urban area only in 1912. Despite being set among attractive mountain scenery of the Dlangeni Hills at an altitude of 1200 m, over the last few decades, development has been in the form of a disorganized collection of unattractive concrete blocks and a snarled traffic system, broken up by modern shopping malls. Mbabane was declared a city by King Mswati III in 1992, but with a population of just under 100,000, it remains small, and the main business district is spread over a small grid of busy streets in the centre of town.
▶▶ *For listings, see pages 825-829.*

Ins and outs

Getting there and around The most popular route into Swaziland is through the Oshoek/Ngwenya border post, which is only 20 km west of Mbabane. In South Africa, this border is about 350 km from Johannesburg along the N17. From Mbabane there are buses to all major centres in Swaziland, though they may only run a couple of times a day on each route – arrive early at the bus station. Minibus taxis run regular short routes, but the vehicles are generally of a poor standard, making them dangerous. Do not use them. The **Baz Bus** (see page 42) includes Swaziland on its route between Durban and Johannesburg and Tshwane (Pretoria) and drops off and picks up at the backpacker hostels. ▶▶ *For further details, see Transport page 829.*

Mbabane

Sleeping
City Inn 1
Kapola Guest House 3
Kent Rock B&B 4
Mountain Inn 2
Veki's Guesthouse 5

Eating
Finesse 6
La Casserole 3
Phoenix Spur 1
Plaza Tandoori 2
Steers 4

Tourist information The **Swaziland Information Office** ① *Swazi Plaza, T404 2531, www.welcometoswaziland.com, Mon-Fri 0800-1700, Sat 0830-1230,* is an extremely helpful office with a wide range of information on hotels, nature reserves and tour operators. It also produces a useful map and annual brochure, covering the whole country.

The world's most dangerous road?

The road to Manzini and the Ezulwini Valley from Mbabane has to be one of the world's most dramatic roads. It is very straight and alarmingly steep. Before the completion of a double-lane highway, which involved whole sides of the mountain being blasted away, this road was little more than a narrow track going straight down a cliff face. All other traffic had to get out of the way if the royal family's motorcade was going up or down between Mbabane and the Royal Palace in the Ezulwini Valley. It once made a listing in the Guinness Book of World Records as having the highest car accident rate in the world. The father of Ted Reilly (the man who was instrumental in reintroducing wildlife into Swaziland's parks), owned the first car in Swaziland, a Model T Ford. This road was so steep for the rudimentary car that the only way he could get back up to the top was in reverse.

Sights

Mbabane is a cluster of concrete shopping malls at the bottom of a hill, surrounded by ring roads and the highway that leads to the nearby Ezulwini Valley. There isn't much to do here and it's the valley itself that holds the best of the Swazi attractions, but the **Swazi market** near the central roundabout is worth a quick look for its excellent display of fresh produce. Piled in high pyramids on wooden stalls are mangoes, tomatoes, cabbages, pineapples and avocados. You can engage in some good-humoured bartering with the Swazi women. There are also a few curios, although you'll get better value in the rural areas where these items are made. Mbabane also has a selection of South African chain supermarkets, which are useful for stocking up.

Ezulwini Valley ⊖⊘⊙⊙▲⇥ *pp825-829. Colour map 2, C5.*

Clearly signposted from Mbabane, the Ezulwini Valley (the Valley of Heaven) is the centre of Swaziland's tourist industry. The tourist route follows the old main road through Ezulwini. Take the fly-off at the bottom of Malagwane Hill. In the daytime there are superb views as you leave the Highveld and drop into the middleveld. The valley itself has no real centre, but every few hundred metres you will pass a smart hotel, craft shop or restaurant. The 30-km-long valley ends at Lobamba, the Royal Village of the King.

Lobamba

At the eastern end of the Ezulwini Valley before the airport is the royal village of Lobamba, set amongst typical open bush countryside. This is where the present king, King Mswati III, lives and from where he rules Swaziland with his Queen Mother or Ndlovukazi, meaning 'she-elephant'. Every August the king gets to add to his growing stable of wives at the **Umhlanga (Reed) Dance** when virgins perform in front of the 'she-elephant' and present her with tall reeds which are used to act as windbreakers around her house. It is also the time that the King may pick out his next wife (which doesn't happen every year) – but is an honour she cannot refuse. The custom has attracted increasing criticism over the years, notably in 2003 when the King's choice was not supported by the bride's family. Nevertheless, it is an astounding event, where thousands of young women from across the country congregate and dance bare-breasted in front of a congregation of royalty, subjects and curious tourists. The King currently has 14 wives and 23 children. A Swazi King's first two wives are chosen for him by a royal council, and within the (somewhat complicated) royal decrees, these two have special functions in rituals and their sons can never claim kingship, so the King's eldest son is quite often not the heir. The first wife must be a member of the Matsebula clan, the second of the Motsa clan. According to tradition, he only marries his subsequent fiancées, which he chooses at the Reed Dance after they have fallen pregnant; proving they can bear heirs. Until then, they are termed *liphovela*, meaning 'brides'.

All of the royal buildings are closed to the public, but the **Somhlolo National Stadium** is the venue for major celebrations, including sports events, musical shows and royal events such as the annual independence celebrations and the Reed Dance. On no account try to take any photographs of the Lozitha Palace or the Embo State Palace. The parliament buildings are open to visitors but the effort to gain admittance is not worth the tour.

Of much greater interest is the **National Museum** and the **King Sobhuza II Memorial Park** ⓘ *T416 1516, Mon-Fri 0800-1300, 1400-1545, Sat-Sun 1000-1300, 1400-1545, E20, children (under 16) E10, memorial park E10, children (under 16) E3, combination entry E25, children (under 16) E15*, which has some excellent displays relating to Swazi life throughout history, with old photographs, traditional dress and Stone Age implements. If you wish to find out more ask for a guided tour, well worth it for an insight into local life and customs. Opposite the museum is the King Sobhuza II Memorial Park, which has a small museum depicting his life. The showroom houses his three rather splendid royal black limousines. His statue stands under a domed cover with open arches and an immaculate white tiled floor.

Mlilwane Wildlife Sanctuary 🌐 ▸▸ *pp825-829.*

ⓘ *T528 3992, www.biggameparks.org, gate hours 24-hr, reception 0830-1900, E25 per person, which covers the whole length of your stay within the sanctuary.*
Mlilwane is one of the most popular of Swaziland's nature reserves and covers 4560 ha of varied landscape of Highveld and Lowveld along a section of the Ezulwini Valley. It is a

Ezulwini Valley to Manzini

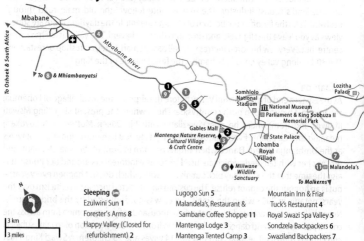

Sleeping 🛏		
Ezulwini Sun **1**	Lugogo Sun **5**	Mountain Inn & Friar
Forester's Arms **8**	Malandela's, Restaurant &	Tuck's Restaurant **4**
Happy Valley (Closed for	Sambane Coffee Shoppe **11**	Royal Swazi Spa Valley **5**
refurbishment) **2**	Mantenga Lodge **3**	Sondzela Backpackers **6**
	Mantenga Tented Camp **3**	Swaziland Backpackers **7**

peaceful and beautiful reserve, allowing a wide range of activities, from self-guided walking to mountain biking, with a good chance of getting very close to wildlife. It is possible to see a wide variety of bird and animal species, including: hippo, giraffe, crocodile, eland, zebra, blue wildebeest, kudu, nyala, klipspringer, waterbuck, impala, steenbuck, duiker, warthog, suni antelope, oribi, many species of birds, especially waterfowl, and if you are lucky, possibly the purple-crested lourie, the brilliantly coloured national bird of Swaziland.

Background

James Weighton Reilly (nicknamed Mickey), Ted Reilly's father, settled at Mlilwane in 1906 and built the main homestead, which today is part of the accommodation in the reserve. He mined tin on the farm and for many years was the largest employer of industrial labour in Swaziland. He married Billie Wallis in 1920, who was for a long time the only white woman between Mbabane and Manzini, and Ted Reilly was born in 1938. The Reilly family witnessed the rapid disappearance of Swaziland's game and the last wild animal was seen at Mlilwane in 1959. This had a profound impact on young Ted Reilly. Coupled with this, his father's (now defunct) tin mining operation, meant that the hydraulic sluicing used to mine the tin with high pressure water jets had caused massive damage to the landscape leaving it scarred with ravines. Ted Reilly decided to regenerate the land back to its natural state, and turn over the Mlilwane farm to provide a wildlife sanctuary. In 1963 the rest camp opened and in 1969 Mlilwane was gazetted as a wildlife sanctuary (see also box, page 833).

Ins and outs

Getting there The reserve is signposted just past the Caltex service station at Lobamba. Turn right and travel 4 km to Sangweni Gate at eSitjeni. Gates are open 24 hours allowing guests staying in the reserve to visit the nightlife, casinos and restaurants in the Ezulwini Valley. The Interpretorium in the rest camp and the Sangwen Gate complex has interesting information on nature conservation in Swaziland, including anti-poaching efforts.

To Usuthu & Mankayane

Timbali Lodge &
Boma Restaurant 9
Tum's George 13

Eating
Calabash 1
Quartermain's Pub 2
Village Café 4
Woodlands 3

Sights

There are over 100 km of dirt roads, with some marked for 4WD vehicles only. As there are no predators in the park, the wildlife is quite relaxed, enabling close viewing. Alternatives for exploring the sanctuary include guided horse rides, open 4WD game drives, guided mountain-bike rides, and an extensive system of self-guided walking trails, including the Macobane, Sondzela, Hippo and Mhlambanyatsi Trails. The 8-km **Macobane Trail** offers an easy gradient and particularly spectacular views of the Ezulwini Valley as it winds its way along the contours of an old aqueduct on the Nyonyane Mountain (1136 m). All activities can be booked through the activity centre at the main camp. For all activities a minimum of two people is necessary.

① 1 km south of the Ezulwini Valley road, clearly signposted, T416 1151, www.sntc.org.sz. Day visits between 0800-1700, E150 per person, dance shows 1115 and 1515, buffet breakfast E95, buffet lunch E120, evening visits from 1800, E350 per person (including buffet dinner and dance show). See also Sleeping, page 827, for accommodation.

Close to the Mantenga Lodge is an area of outstanding beauty and mature patches of forest between the main road and the Mantenga Falls. The Little Usutu River flows through the 725-ha reserve and the well-known waterfalls are about a 2-km walk away. Despite Mantenga's small size, it is home to a number of medium-sized mammals, including vervet monkey, baboon, bushpig, porcupine, rock dassie, bushbaby, kudu, nyala, klipspringer and grey and red duiker. Birdlife abounds, including the endangered bald ibis. Picnic spots and walking trails have been marked out and you can drive as far as the waterfall. The **Cultural Village** is just beyond the gate of the reserve and every aspect of this 'show' village is based upon traditional methods and materials. This is exactly how a medium-sized Swazi homestead would have looked 100 years ago. There are 16 beehive-shaped huts built from local materials, laid out in a plan that can be seen throughout rural Swaziland. The huts form a semicircle partly surrounded by a cattle kraal. The focal point is a larger hut, the 'great hut', and the kraal. This is a polygamous homestead – each wife has her own circle of huts for cooking, making beer and sleeping in. Slightly separate are the huts for unmarried mature boys and girls and for married sons.

The whole complex is brought to life by traditional dance performances and songs as the guides show visitors around. You will also see food being prepared, clothes and household objects being made. Meals are served at the **Village Café** (see Eating, page 828).

Mantenga Craft Centre

① At the entrance of the Mantenga Nature Reserve and Cultural Village, you don't need to pay entry fee into the reserve to visit, T416 1136. Daily 0830-1700.

Swaziland is an excellent place to buy curios, with a wider selection and lower prices than in South Africa. The Mantenga Foundation was formed in 1974 to retail the finished works of local artists in the Mantenga Craft Centre. From the outset, the project has been managed on the basis of long-term self-sufficiency. The centre stocks an excellent range of jewellery, crafts, clothes, gold and silver, screen prints, leather goods, ceramics, rugs and carvings. There is also a coffee shop and snack bar and a small tourist information desk with a selection of brochures. **Swazi Trails** are also based here, see page 829.

Malkerns Valley ⬤⬤⬤⬤ ⏩ pp825-829.

About 5 km beyond the National Museum is a right turning for Malkerns, M18. This makes for an enjoyable circuit from Mbabane which can easily be covered on a day trip, although most people stay overnight in Mlilwane Wildlife Sanctuary (see page 826). This is the ideal place to discover a more typical Swazi lifestyle than along the Ezulwini Valley.

Malandela's

① 1 km from the junction towards Malkerns T528 3448, www.malandelas.com. Shops 0900-1700, restaurant 1100-1500, 1800-late. For accommodation, see page 827.

This delightful stylish complex of roadside shops and farmstalls is well worth stopping for. It includes **Malandela**'s restaurant (see page 828), with superb views of the mountains from the deck and an adjoining pub; an internet café; the **House on Fire** live music venue (see page 828); and there is a small patch of newly established botanical gardens planted with indigenous species. The shops offer an excellent choice of both modern and traditional crafts. Among them **Swazi Candles** ① T528 3219, www.swazicandles.com, is one of the best known shops in the country, producing interesting candles in a variety of designs and colours. You can watch the candle-making process in the workshop. **Baobab Batik** ① T528 3982, www.baobab-batik.com, supports over 30 local artists and offers brightly coloured batiks (and not one is the same), which are also fashioned into clothes, cushion covers, table linen and other products. **Gone Rural** ① T550 4932, www.goneruralswazi.com, sells stylish, contemporary woven goods in bright colours and supports rural women; again, you can watch them in the workshop.

Bhunya and around

The road west from Malkerns towards Bhunya (26 km) is tarred, and for part of the route it follows the Great Usutu River, passing rolling farmlands and pineapple plantations; be careful of groups of schoolchildren and cattle straying into the road. As the road climbs up into the highlands, the forest closes in and it can get quite cool out of the sunlight. The factory town of Bhunya is the centre of the local timber industry – the local pulp mill is responsible for much of the local pollution. From Bhunya there is a choice of two routes. The road to the South African border (32 km) at **Sandlane/Nerston** (daily 0800-1800) crosses the Lusutfu River and then climbs steeply for 2 km into the coniferous plantations. This is the **Usutu Forest** a man-made (mostly pine) plantation which extends for over 65,000 ha. The second road out of Bhunya heads north towards **Mhlambanyatsi** and Mbabane.

Mbabane and around listings

For Sleeping and Eating price codes and other relevant information, see pages 46-53.

● Sleeping

Mbabane *p820, map p820*
There is little reason to stay in the city centre when the Ezulwini Valley is such a short drive away, but there are some places if you are arriving late from the border.
B Mountain Inn, 4 km out of town on the road to Ezulwini Valley, T404 2781, www. mountaininn.sz. 60 smart, comfortable rooms with en suite bathrooms, telephone and TV. Swimming pool, neat lawns, Friar Tuck à la carte restaurant, balconies have commanding views over the mountains and valley. Excursions and mountain bike hire.
C Kent Rock B&B, 230 Somhlolo Rd, which is the extension of Gwamile St to the north of the centre, T404 4826, www.visitswazi.com/kentrock. Set in a lush garden with a decent

sized pool, this comfortable family home has 3 nicely decorated en suite B&B doubles, with breakfast included and dinner on request, and 2 self-catering units sleeping 2-4. Can arrange gym visits or spa treatments at the Serendipity Wellness Centre next door.
C-D City Inn, Gwamile St, city centre, T404 2406, www.cityinn.sz. 24 large rooms, with en suite bathroom, some a/c, DSTV and laundry service. **Pablo's** restaurant and **Caribbean Coffee Shop** plus a bar. Simple town hotel and recently refurbished, the rooms in the new block are considerably better than those in the old part.
D Kapola Guest House, Malagwane Hill, T404 8266; phone Annette for directions, 6 km in a suburb west of town off the MR3 towards the Ezulwini Valley. 5 en suite rooms, comfortable decor, TV lounge, breakfast buffet, peaceful thatched balcony overlooking lovely forest scenery, secure parking, dinner on request. The fence outside is decorated with little flags.

D Veki's Guesthouse, 223 Gilfillan St, T404 8485, www.swazilodgings.com/vekis. 7 comfortable rooms within a 5-min walk from the centre of town, with DSTV. You can make use of the kitchen and braai, or good value home-cooked meals are on offer. Also rents self-catering apartments and cottages in some of Mbabane's suburbs, which are aimed at long-stay business people but they will consider short stays.

Ezulwini Valley *p821, map p822*

The valley's most famous hotel, the **Happy Valley Motel**, which was also home to the **Why Not Disco**, and **If Not Go-Go Bar**, which entertained guests for more than 30 years, is presently closed for a complete structural revamp and refurbishment. It may reopen before the end of 2010.

L Royal Swazi Spa Valley, T416 5000, www.suninternational.com. 149 a/c rooms with TV, bar, restaurant, gym, sauna, spa, pool, bowls, squash, tennis, horse riding, 18-hole golf course, casino and **Planter's** colonial-themed restaurant. All room have magnificent views of the valley and mountains. The most luxurious hotel in Swaziland, an amazing contrast to life in the rest of the country.

AL Ezulwini Sun, T416 6000, www.suninter national.com. 60 a/c rooms, TV, **Valley Blues** restaurant, coffee shop, swimming pool, sauna, tennis, horse riding, volleyball and casino next door. Ghastly Caribbean decor.

AL Lugogo Sun, in the grounds of the **Royal Swazi**, T416 4000, www.suninternational. com. 202 a/c rooms, **Ilanga restaurant**, bar, a large establishment aimed at families, caters for conferences and large tour groups. 'Pub night' on Wed has a live band – popular with expats and locals from all over the country.

B-C Timbali Lodge & Boma Restaurant, Old Main Rd, T416 1156, www.timbalilodge.co.sz. 23 nicely decorated en suite rooms, with a/c, minibar and DSTV, some with spa baths, and 5 well-equipped self-catering family cottages. Pool, dinner is served in a huge thatched boma, and is either buffet, braai or a variety of *potjies*, and there's often Swazi dancing.

C Mantenga Lodge, next to the **Mantenga Craft Centre**, T416 1049, www.mantenga lodge.com. 38 en suite double rooms with satellite TV, à la carte restaurant with wide outdoor terrace, lively bar, swimming pool and sauna. Hidden amongst the trees this is a pleasant country hotel on the edge of Mantenga Nature Reserve, with easy access to the Mlilwane Wildlife Sanctuary.

Mlilwane Wildlife Sanctuary *p822, map p822*

Reservations for all through **Big Game Parks**, T528 3944/3, www.biggameparks.org.

A Reilly's Rock Hilltop Lodge, or 'kaGogo', 3 km from the Main Camp. This is an exclusive 6-room period guesthouse and 3-room cottage, both brimming with antiques and local history, en suite facilities, set in a lush tract of botanical gardens with fabulous views of the game sanctuary. Rates include entry, dinner, bed and breakfast. No children under 13. This is the original home of Ted Reilly's father and the main house dates back to 1906. Recommended.

D Main Camp. A mixture of stone cottages, thatched rondavels and traditional domed Swazi thatched huts known as the Beehive Village, many are en suite, or there's a neat ablution block, camping ground under the shade of eucalyptus trees with self-catering facilities. Note that if you are self-catering you need to watch your food – the local warthogs don't think twice about foraging in tents or kitchen huts. The **Hippo Haunt** restaurant has a lovely deck overlooking a hippo pool. Warthogs, ostriches and impalas frequently wander through the grounds. Swimming pool. Traditional dancing team, made up of park staff, performs on a nightly basis in The iNkhundla, a boma in the Main Camp.

E-F Sondzela Backpackers, 15 mins' walk from the main camp. Excellent backpackers in a stunning setting overlooking the Nyonyane Mountains, in the centre of the reserve. Spotless dorms, twins and doubles in the large main house, plus very comfortable and spacious thatched rondavels sleeping up to 4, with shared ablutions. Camping, tents and bedding can be hired, pool, volleyball court, bar with pool table. Great meals served around a roaring fire, shop selling basic food, ATM. Travel desk can arrange a wide choice of local tours, making this a great choice for people without their own transport. **Baz Bus** stop. Excellent value, good fun and in a beautiful setting – one of the best budget options in the country. Highly recommended.

Mantenga Nature Reserve *p824*
D Mantenga Tented Camp, T416 1151, www.sntc.org.sz. 20 simple en suite tents on stilts under thatched roofs climbing up the mountain, some with views of the river. Game is present, sandy paths lead to the **Village Restaurant** in the reserve and breakfast is included in the rates.

Malkerns Valley *p824*
A-B Forester's Arms, 12 km out of Bhunya, T467 4177, www.forestersarms.co.za. Delightful hotel set in the cool Great Usuthu highlands with a number of pretty waterfalls and surrounded by forest in its own colourful garden. 30 en suite rooms, colourful decor, restaurant which serves excellent meals (see Eating, page 828), and occasional Swazi dancing performed in the evenings. Swimming pool, sauna, trout and bass fishing in the local dams, tennis and squash courts, hiking, horse riding from their own stables, mountain bikes for hire. Rates include dinner and bed and breakfast. A fine country retreat.
C Malandela's, Malkerns Rd, T528 3448, www.malandelas.com. Part of the excellent Malandela's complex (see page 824). Excellent restaurant, pub, shops and the House on Fire venue, set in quiet gardens, with a pool. This restored farmhouse has 8 stylish en suite double rooms and 2 family units, Afro-chic decor, family run, friendly staff, great addition to the area. Recommended.
E Swaziland Backpackers, near the turn-off to Malkerns Rd, T528 2038, swazilandbackpackers@realnet.co.sz. Dorms, doubles, camping, internet and laundry facilities.

The main house has a comfy lounge, pretty gardens with pool, jacuzzi and hammocks, communal kitchen for self-catering or meals are provided with advance notice. Range of tours on offer, including free hikes in the area. The **Baz Bus** stays overnight here on the route between Durban and Johannesburg.

🍴 Eating

Mbabane *p820, map p820*
Mbabane features the usual South African steak chain restaurants. **Steers**, is in New Mall, and the **Phoenix Spur**, is in The Mall,
Finesse, New Mall, T404 5936. Mon-Sat 1100-late. French-owned à la carte restaurant with a seasonal menu, excellent seafood such as lobster with vanilla sauce or oriental prawns and Mozambique chicken. Dishes are beautifully presented. Lovely shady outside tables among potted plants.
Friar Tuck's, Mountain Inn, T404 2781. Open 1200-1400, 1900-2200. Good quality hotel restaurant in a somewhat dark vaulted cellar, but also has pleasant outside tables on the patio overlooking the pool. Great views, filling buffet lunches, an à la carte evening menu and traditional British-style puddings.
La Casserole, Omni Centre, Gwamile St, T404 6426. Open 0900-late. Smart restaurant serving German and international cuisine, fully licenced, pizza oven, afternoon teas, outside patio, relaxed, charming atmosphere.
Plaza Tandoori, Swazi Mall, T404 7559. Open 1000-2200. Cheap and cheerful, this offers great value curries, other Asian dishes like stir-fry chicken and egg fried rice, as well as burgers and some grills. Rapid service, outside terrace and does takeaways.

Ezulwini Valley *p821, map p822*
All the valley's hotels have a good choice of eating and are open to passing trade. There are 5 restaurants in the Royal Swazi Spa Valley alone.
Calabash, close to **Timbali Lodge**, T416 1187, www.restaurant-calabash.com. 1200-

1500, 1730-late. Delicious German, Swiss and Austrian meals like eisbein, schnitzel and veal, plus seafood and good choice for vegetarians. Becks beer on draught, lovely wooden wine cellar where you can choose a bottle, a very popular venue and one of Swaziland's top à la carte restaurants, booking advised.

Village Café, Mantenga Nature Reserve. Open all day for buffet breakfast, lunch and dinner, which are part of the cultural village experience, but also serves à la carte light meals and teas and coffees. Specializing in dishes such as stroganoff made from game meat and peri-peri chicken livers, there's a late bar, and it's a great place for a sundowner on the wooden deck. Also has weekly braais on a Sun starting from 1000 at the waterfalls.

Woodlands, near Royal Swazi Valley Spa, T416 3466. Open 1100-late. Smart addition to the valley, airy dining room serving good international cuisine. Romantically lit with lanterns at night, broad outside deck with mountain views, popular Sun buffets.

Quartermain's Pub, Gables Mall, T416 3023. Mon-Sat 1000-late, Sun 0900-late. Pub and restaurant in the confines of a mall but with a beer garden where there's live music on a Sat afternoon. Typical pub decor, pub grub like spare ribs, steak or fish and chips, popular with locals on a Fri evening. Wi-Fi.

Malkerns Valley p824

Forester's Arms, 12 km out of Bhunya, T467 4177, www.forestersarms.co.za. 0800-2200. Catering mostly for tour groups, this fine hotel offers light lunches and expansive buffet dinners with home-made bread, stir-frys, spit roasts and some gooey desserts. Caters well for vegetarians, cosy pub with log fire, it's less than 40 km away from the Nerston/Sandlane border so people from South Africa come here for famous Sun lunch.

Malandela's, T528 3115, www.malandelas.com. 1100-1500, 1800-late. Excellent restaurant in a stylish setting, surrounded by gardens, pleasant shady deck, great menu, fusion food mixing African and European dishes. Also has a popular pub with draft beer

and DSTV for sports. Is attached to the **House on Fire** live music venue.

Sambane Coffee Shoppe, Swazi Candles, Malandela's, T528 3219. Open 0900-1700. Lovely bright café with murals of lizards and butterflies on the walls. Outside are white trestle tables. Serves breakfasts, light lunches, afternoon teas and speciality coffees. Fully licensed, unusual treats like chilli chocolate fudge cake, which administers a bit of a kick. Very popular with locals for Sun brunch.

● Entertainment

Ezulwini Valley p821, map p822
The **Royal Swazi Spa Valley**, see Sleeping, page 826, has a number of upmarket bars, and casino with bar that's open until 0400 if there is the demand.

Malkerns Valley p824
House on Fire, Malkerns Rd, T528 2100, www.house-on-fire.com. Excellent venue, which has quickly become the country's leading spot for live performance. Open air, extravagant, funky decor including colourful, mirrored mosaics, surreal statues, moulded seating area around a circular stage. Check the website for events, including rock music, live jazz, dance and theatre. Also holds occasional art exhibitions.

○ Shopping

Mbabane p820, map p820
Crafts and curios
African Fantasy, The Mall in Mbabane; the Mantenga Craft Centre; and The Gables, Ezulwini Valley, T404 0205, www.african fantasy.de. A wide selection of Swazi curios, including sculptures, pottery, textiles, paintings, jewellery, candles and T-shirts.
Swazi Market, Msunduza Rd, end of Gwamile St. A range of curios from all over Swaziland, although you will have to haggle for the best bargains. The fruit and vegetable market is

here too and is an excellent place to buy fresh guavas, mangoes and other tropical fruits.

Shopping malls

Swazi Plaza, The Mall and New Mall, are all within walking distance of each other on OK Link Rd. They are large, covered, modern malls with department stores, banks, pharmacies, travel agents, cafés and restaurants. There's a Shoprite at Swazi Plaza and a Spar at the Mall.

Ezulwini Valley *p821, map p822*

The main road passing through the valley is lined with craft stalls selling a good range of handmade curios. See also page 824 for details of the Mantenga Craft Centre and page 825 for craft shops in the Malkerns Valley. The Gables Mall on the main road near the turn-off to the Mantenga Nature Reserve, is a mall with cafés, ATMs and a branch of Pick n' Pay.

▲ Activities and tours

Ezulwini Valley *p821, map p822*

Swazi Spa Health and Beauty Studio, T416 1164. Open 1000-1800. A hugely popular resort, mainly for the intriguingly named 'cuddle puddle', a pool fed by a hot natural mineral spring. Housed in dome-shaped buildings modelled on a Swazi village, there are 2 large saunas, 2 indoor hot mineral pools, cold plunge pools, a whirl and bubble bath and an aromatherapy steam-tube. Gym and massages.

Tour operators

Swazi Trails, Mantenga Craft Centre, T416 2180; T011-704 1975 (South Africa), www.swazitrails.co.sz. A leading countrywide tour operator specializing in Swaziland culture, wildlife and adventure tours, including caving, whitewater rafting and hiking. The new activity is quad-biking on an 8-km trail in the Ezulwini Valley. All guides are local Swazis with excellent local knowledge. Swazi Trails also manages an excellent community tourism initiative and part of the fee you pay goes to the local Mphaphati community.

⊖ Transport

Mbabane *p820, map p820*
Bus

The South African Baz Bus, T021-439 2323, www.bazbus.com, includes Swaziland on its route 3 times a week. The bus overnights in Swaziland at Swaziland Backpackers and arrives in the Ezulwini Valley from Durban at about 1830, then departs to Johannesburg next morning at 0730. In the other direction it arrives from Johannesburg/Tshwane (Pretoria) about 1730, and departs towards Durban at 0730 the next day. To see anything of Swaziland, and because the bus runs 3 times a week, this means you'll have to spend 3 nights in Swaziland to hook up with the next bus.

Car hire

Avis and Europcar have desks at Matsapha Airport near Manzini (see page 837). Europcar, T404 0459, www.europcar.co.za, also has a branch at the Engen petrol station on By Pass Rd. However, in reality and given its size, most visitors to Swaziland arrive in cars hired in South Africa. Ensure you have a covering letter from the company you hired the car from, remember to mention this when you hire it.

❶ Directory

Mbabane *p820, map p820*

Embassies and consulates Most countries deal with consular services for Swaziland through their embassies or high commissions in Tshwane (Pretoria) (see page 600). **Mozambique**, Highland View Princess Drive Rd, T404 3700, issues visas for Mozambique but it's far easier to get them at the border. **South Africa**, 2nd floor, New Mall, Dr Sishayi Rd, T404 4651. **US**, 2350 Mbabane Pl, T404 2445, www.swaziland.usembassy.gov. **Emergencies** T999. **Medical services** Mbabane Clinic (private), St Michael St, T404 2423; **Mbabane Government Hospital**, Usutu Rd, T404 2111.

Central and southern Swaziland

The central and southern regions of Swaziland are home to the country's now-healthy populations of big game, including rhino, elephant, lion and cheetah. Big Game Parks manage the Hlane Royal National Park and Mkhaya Game Reserve where game drives and other activities are on offer. Meanwhile there's good hiking in the Lebombo Mountains in the smaller private nature reserves. ▸▸ *For listings, see pages 835-837.*

Manzini ◉❻❷◉ ▸▸ *pp835-837. Colour map 2, C5.*

Manzini and its outlying districts comprise of Swaziland's largest urban population. The town is an industrial centre with a brewery, a meat-processing plant and electronics factories that attract commuter labourers from outlying areas. The industrial atmosphere is not particularly pleasant and there is little of interest for the visitor. The **market** ⓘ *corner of Mhlakuvane St and Mancishane Rd, daily except Sun*, is worth a browse. This is one of the busiest local markets in Swaziland, selling fresh fruit and vegetables, clothes, a good selection of curios and freshly cooked snacks. The **Bhunu Mall** on Ngwane Street and **The Hub** on Mhlakuzane Street are Manzini's newest shopping centres. **Tiger-City** on Villiers Street is a small complex where the cinema and a couple of restaurants are located.

Background

The first trading station was opened here in 1885 and was originally run from a tent. The plot was later sold on to Alfred Bremer who built a hotel and a shop. Manzini was originally known as Bremersdorp after Alfred Bremer, but it was renamed Manzini after the Boers burnt the settlement to the ground during the Anglo-Boer War. The administrative centre then moved to Mbabane. In 1894, while Swaziland was being administrated by a temporary government composed of representatives of the Transvaal, the British government and the king, the headquarters were in the local hotel.

Hlane Royal National Park ◉ ▸▸ *pp835-837. Colour map 2, C5.*

ⓘ *T383 8100, www.biggameparks.org. Park gates close at sunset, notify in advance if you think your arrival will be after dark. E25 per person.*

Formerly a royal hunting ground, Hlane was declared a protected area in 1967 by King Sobhuza II. Covering 30,000 ha, this is the kingdom's largest protected area. Following heavy poaching in the 1960s, the park has been restocked by **Big Game Parks**, with wildlife from neighbouring countries as well as species propagated at Mkhaya Game Reserve. A number of predators have been reintroduced and the park now has healthy numbers of lion, cheetah and leopard. Other game includes elephant, white rhino, herds of wildebeest, and zebra, kudu, steenbuck, bushbuck, giraffe, impala, hyena and jackal. In the past, poaching was such a serious problem that the rhino had to have their horns removed for their own protection. Hlane supports the densest population of raptors in the kingdom, with vultures in particular being very visible at kills and waterholes. The nesting density for the white-backed vulture is the highest in the whole of Africa, and the most southerly nesting colony of marabou stork is found here. Birdlife in and around the two camps is prolific.

Ins and outs

Getting there The park is 67 km from Manzini towards Simunye, where the main road bisects the park. Turn left into the Ngongoni Gate, where all arrivals must report.

Sights

The western area of the park is linked with a network of roads which the visitor can use for game viewing. The area around the **Black Mbuluzi River** attracts animals during the dry winter season. Close to Ndlovu camp is an **Endangered Species area**, where elephant and rhino have been concentrated for security reasons. The **Mahlindza waterhole**, with its hippo, crocodile and waterbird population, is one of the most peaceful picnic sites in the country. There are two camps in the park (see page 835). A wide range of activities are offer in the park include guided walks (2½ hours; E90), guided mountain biking (E95 per hour), and two-hour game drives (day or night; E190). There is also the option to pick up a guide to accompany you in your own car to a nearby Swazi village (E60 per person; minimum four), which is 20 km from the park gates, where you will meet the people, take a tour of the village, watch dancing and possibly sample some home-made beer. These can all be booked at the park office, or through Big Game Parks, and are available to day visitors between 1000-1600, who can park their cars at the gate and buy lunch at the Ndlovu Camp.

Simunye ⊜🕜 ⟩⟩ pp835-837. Colour map 2, C5.

Simunye is a small town that is quite unusual in that the centre lies behind the boom gate of the Royal Swazi Sugar Corporation that owns the surrounding sugar plantations. There are two sugar mills here and between April and November, look out for the cane-cutters in the fields who also burn the cane as they cut it; it is quite a sight to see the (carefully controlled) flames licking through the plantations. There is nothing much here but it is a stop-off en route to Hlane, Mlawula and the border with Mozambique at Lomahasha/Namaacha. The **Simunye Country Club** offers a fine buffet lunch and there's a petrol station and small Spar supermarket. The main road to Simunye coming north skirts Hlane Game Sanctuary and there are amusing if sobering signposts warning cyclists and pedestrians to beware of lion and elephant.

Mlawula Nature Reserve ⊜ ⟩⟩ pp835-837. Colour map 2, C5.

ⓘ T416 1151, www.sntc.org.sz. Gate open sunrise-sunset, E25, children (under 16) E12.
Mlawula is signposted after Simunye and Hlane. The nature reserve covers an area extending from the Lebombo Mountains down to the Lowveld and is part of the greater Lubombo Conservancy. The Siphiso Valley and the Mbuluzi Gorge are good areas for game viewing on hiking trails or game drives.

Ins and outs

Best time to visit Summers are hot and humid with high rainfall, the winters are warm and dry although they can be cold at night with the occasional frost. The best time for birdwatching is between September and October.

Sights

This is a region of amazing and varied scenery ranging from Lebombo Mountain forest to dry thorn savanna and coastal thickets. The reserve is criss-crossed with 54 km of rough roads for self-guided tours. Over 1000 species of plant have been identified here although this region is best known for its birdlife: 350 species have been recorded including African fin foot, crested guinea fowl and yellow spotted nicator, and facilities include the vulture feeding area and the bird hide. The **Mbuluzi Gorge** is an excellent area for birdwatching but the road is not always in good condition.

The game likely to be seen in the reserve includes kudu, oribi, mountain reedbuck, samango monkeys, and Sharpe's grysbok, but sadly there are no longer any rhino. Early traces of *homo sapiens* dating back 100,000 years have been found in the riverbeds of the Mbuluzi and Mlawula rivers, good places to spot crocodiles. Many of the animals which are protected here are particularly difficult to spot and include rare species of reptile and amphibian. The interesting plantlife includes the rare Lebombo ironwood and the *Encephalartos umeluziensis*, a cycad that only grows in the deep mountain valleys of the reserve. Visitors to the reserve are encouraged to hike on the network of trails, which pass through beautiful gorges, pools, waterfalls and rapids with views over Mozambique from the top of the escarpment. There is a leaflet on the trails and the reserve itself, which is available from the camp shop, where you can also pick up a guide to go with you.

Shewula Nature Reserve ⬤ ►► *pp835-837*.

ⓘ *T605 1160, www.shewulacamp.com.*

The community-owned Shewula Nature Reserve just north of Mlawula is also part of the Lebombo Conservancy, straddling the 500-m-high Lebombo Mountains on the border with Mozambique and covering an escarpment of ancient ironwood mountain forest stretching down the Mbuluzi River. The views from the **Shewula Mountain Camp**, which is literally perched on top of a mountain, are incredible – on a clear day the high-rise blocks of Maputo can be seen to the east, and there is an uninterrupted 100-km view across Swaziland.

Ins and outs

The Shewula turning is 10 km south of the Lomahasha/Namaacha border with Mozambique. The camp is a further 30-minute drive from here. Apart from during heavy rains (December to February) it is accessible by ordinary saloon cars. When the road is too muddy, it is possible to leave your vehicle at the chief's office in the village, and be transported in a 4WD.

Sights

The Shewula community is a friendly agricultural people, and their traditional thatch and stone houses are dotted neatly among fields of maize cotton and vegetables. They encourage visitors not only to enjoy the incredible view, but gain an insight into traditional Swazi lifestyles. Proceeds from tourism here go back into the community in the way of HIV/Aids programme funding as well as managing the reserve. Overnight visitors can enjoy a number of interactive activities like village walks when you can take part in chores, kick a soccer ball around with the kids, taste the local home-made beer or visit the school. Traditional singing and dancing and visits to a traditional doctor can be arranged, as can donkey cart rides and guided mountain biking (you can hire bikes). Prices for these activities vary from R30-100 per person, and they provide a real experience of Swazi rural life, coupled with the fantastic view.

Ted Reilly and wildlife conservation in Swaziland

Like the rest of Africa, Swaziland used to teem with game before the Europeans arrived in the mid-1800s with guns, modern farming methods and medical knowledge. Morality went downhill, the human population flourished and the need for space meant that the wildlife was doomed. This was followed by other problems. The cattle plague, *rinderpest*, reached Swaziland by 1896, wiping out not only cattle but many antelope which led to the death by starvation of many predators. During the 1930s the so-called 'wildebeest scourge' led to one of the most shocking episodes in the history of wildlife conservation. A great number of wildebeest entered Swaziland following a migratory route, as they had for centuries. Their invasion of farmland led to them being declared vermin and they were exterminated by any possible means. Whole herds were wiped out by machine guns and drinking water was poisoned, the latter undoubtedly causing the deaths of many other animals and birds. By 1960, most of Swaziland's remaining game had been decimated by uncontrolled hunting, poaching and by rapid commercial and agricultural development. The preservation of the few wild animals that survived, and the reintroduction of species that had become extinct, was largely due to the efforts of two men – the late King Sobhuza II and Ted Reilly, founder of Mlilwane Wildlife Sanctuary. In 1963, Reilly turned the family farm in the Ezulwini Valley into a game reserve, planted indigenous trees, created wetland habitat, and began a game restocking programme. Meanwhile the king asked Reilly to help stamp out poaching in the royal reserve of Hlane, and for three decades Reilly embarked on a near-military campaign to eradicate poaching in Swaziland. In 1967, Sobhuza declared Hlane a protected national park and it was restocked with wildlife from neighbouring countries. The Reilly family then donated Mlilwane to a non-profit-making trust in 1969 and it has since grown to 10 times it original size. All of Swazi's parks are now home to substantial numbers of game and at least some of the country again looks like it did 150 years ago. Without Ted Reilly and King Sobhuza II, the Swaziland game reserves would simply not exist. Today the Reilly family still live at Mlilwane where they manage Big Game Parks.

Manzini to Mahamba ⬤ ⏩ *pp835-837*.

Grand Valley

The drive down through Grand Valley passes through beautiful mountain scenery with cliff faces rising above the Mkhondvo River and forests on either side of the road. The MR9 passes through the village of **Hlatikulu** before reaching Nhlangano. The weather here is often misty with drizzle, which for many is a welcome relief after the hot and humid plains.

Nhlangano → *Colour map 2, C5*.

Nhlangano means 'meeting place' and was named to commemorate when King Sobhuza II met King George VI here in 1947. This used to be a popular resort with South African tourists who crossed the border to gamble and watch films which were banned at home. While the casino resort is still here (see Sleeping, page 836), since gaming became legal in South Africa the number of South African visitors has fallen sharply. There is a small

Border crossing: Swaziland–South Africa

Lavumisa–Golela
Lavumisa–Golela is a busy border post which most travellers pass through on their way to Big Bend or into KwaZulu Natal. There is one main street lined with snack bars and petrol stations.
Border opening hours 0700-2200.
Public transport The bus station is on the main street and buses regularly leave for Big Bend, Manzini and Mbabane.

Mahamba
The MR9 continues south to the border at Mahamba, daily 0700-2200. The routes into South Africa from here lead to Piet Retief in Mpumalanga.

shopping centre in town and a market. Buses depart from the station next to the mall, to Manzini, Mahamba and Lavumisa.

Manzini to Lavumisa ⊕⊕ ▶▶ pp835-837.

Mkhaya Game Reserve → Colour map 2, C5.
ⓘ Access by prior reservation only, T528 3943, www.biggameparks.org.
This small reserve, one of the best places in southern Africa to see black rhino, is Swaziland's most exclusive reserve, set in an area of acacia Lowveld southeast of Manzini. Mkhaya was established as a game reserve in 1979 to protect the Nguni breed of long-horned cattle from extinction that today graze among the zebra and wildebeest, but it has expanded over the years to include other endangered species such as black rhino, roan and sable antelope, tsessebe, white rhino and elephant. In 1995 the park received six black rhino from South Africa, a project funded, rather oddly, by the Taiwanese Government, and during 1997 the first two baby elephant to be born in Swaziland in 100 years were born at Mkhaya. At present the only large cat you might see is the leopard. The birdlife here is interesting and there are chances of seeing a good number of raptors, including bateleur, booted, martial and tawny eagles. The summers here are very hot and humid with potentially heavy thunderstorms, while in winter the climate is warm during the day and cool at night.

Ins and outs Travelling from Mbabane and Ezulwini Valley go through Manzini; 8 km after Manzini take a right turn and continue towards Big Bend. The reserve is signposted to the left after about 44 km. If you are approaching from Durban via the Lavumisa border follow the road to Big Bend and then Siphofaneni. The turning is on the right, 22 km after Big Bend. All visitors are met at the locked gates by a ranger. This is a private reserve and guests must arrange to arrive at either 1000 and 1600 when the rangers will pick you up. Cars are parked at the gate. Mkhaya is a private reserve and it can be visited by prior reservation as an overnight visitor staying at the tented safari camp. Open-top Land Rover game drives are the main activity, with the opportunity to take guided bush walks, all promising close contact with a variety of big game. Rates include all activities. Day visitors can pre-arrange to meet guides at the gate at 1000 for game drives and lunch and are returned to their cars at 1600.

Border crossing: Swaziland–Mozambique

Lomahasha–Namaacha

This is the only border crossing between Swaziland and Mozambique, and is 98 km northeast of Manzini and 75 km from Maputo on a newly tarred road. While you can use Rand in southern Mozambique, this is not the case for Emalangeni, so ensure you change all your Emalangeni into Rand before leaving Swaziland.

Border opening hours 0700-2000.

Customs and immigration Most visitors require visas for Mozambique; these are issued at the border, US$25 or equivalent in rand. South African passport holders do not require a visa.

Big Bend → *Colour map 2, C5.*

Big Bend is named after the loop of the Lusutfu River that passes by the town. The land around Big Bend is covered in sugar plantations and the Ubombo Ranches sugarmill in town is the area's main processing centre. The terrain here is very similar to South Africa's northern KwaZulu Natal, which is only 50 km to the south. The town is a quiet, neatly laid out settlement with a small shopping centre and craft centre, **Emoya Crafts**, which sells crafts from all over Swaziland – ethnic clothing, glassware, candles, cotton rugs, place mats, tablecloths, batiks, baskets and ethnic jewellery.

Nisela Safaris

ⓘ *T303 0318, www.niselasafaris.co.za. Day visitors E10 per person, for game drives and walks there needs to be a minimum of 6 people.*

Nisela Safaris is a private game lodge development nestled at the foot of the Lebombo Mountains, near the village of Nsoko, 30 km south from Big Bend on the road to the Lavumisa border, which is a further 20 km. This is a small private reserve where game including lion, wilderbeest, giraffe and zebra have been introduced; existing populations of nyala, red and grey duiker, jackal, bushbuck, reedbuck and steenbok are also present. Day visitors can pre-book game drives and there are also a number of hand-reared lion cubs to visit near the entrance gate where there is also a reptile park, coffee shop and curio stall.

Central and southern Swaziland

For Sleeping and Eating price codes and other relevant information, see pages 46-53.

 Sleeping

Manzini *p830*

There's no real reason to stay in Manzani but drop by to eat if you're passing at lunchtime as there are a number of good options here, see Eating, page 837.

B Tum's George Hotel, corner of Ngwane and Du Toit streets, T505 8991 www.tgh.sz.

53 a/c comfortable rooms with DSTV, conference facilities, large pool with sociable pool bar, gym, steam room and secure parking.

Hlane Royal National Park *p830*

Reservations: T528 3943, www.biggame parks.org. Traditional dance performances, open-air bar and restaurant at Ndlovu but in Bhubesi visitors must be fully self-sufficient.

C-D Bhubesi Camp. 6 self-catering stone cottages, 2 bedrooms, bathroom, kitchenette, bedding and towels, electricity, a beautiful setting overlooking the Umbuluzana River.

D Ndlovu Camp. 14 en suite rondavels sleeping 2 and 7 en suite thatched family cottages sleeping up to 8. Bedding, towels, cutlery and crockery provided, hot outside showers. No electricity, paraffin lanterns provide light, fridges are gas powered and cooking is over an open fire, a camp assistant will help with this and he keeps the fire going all day, you just need to bring food, or eat at the camp restaurant. Next to a waterhole just near the main gate to the park. A small shop sells some provisions and curios; game activities can be organized. There are few simple camping sites nearby, with an ablution block at Ndlovu Camp.

Simunye *p831*

C-D Simunye Country Club, once through the boom gate turn right (15-min drive to Mozambique, and 30 mins to South African borders), T313 4758, www.visitswazi.com/simunyeclub. Owned by the Royal Swazi Sugar Corporation, this has a variety of cheap single rooms, and self-catering houses and flats. Pool, very good restaurant, 3 bars, one serving pizza and filled wraps, TV lounge. Tennis, squash and gym available for a nominal fee. Accommodation is nothing special but facilities are good.

Mlawula Nature Reserve *p831*
Reservations: National Trust Commission, T383 8885, www.sntc.org.sz.

C Mapehlephele Cottage. Has recently been upgraded to sleep 8, with 2 upper (baboon-proof) sleeping porches with a double bed on each, plus 2 twin rooms inside, bathroom, lounge with fireplace, braai, kitchen, gas hot water, oven and fridge. No electricity but paraffin lights are provided.

Camping
Sara Bush Camp. 4 tents sleeping 2, each with braai area, communal lounge and kitchen with gas stove and fridge, bring all your own food, no electricity but paraffin

lamps are provided. The highlight here is the position of the tents, perched on the edge of a sheer cliff with outstanding views. The outside bathrooms have a boiler heated by fire and a galvanized bath tub hidden in a cleft of rock on the cliff edge.

Siphiso Campsite. Camping and caravan sites with taps and braais on the banks of the usually dry Sipisi stream with an ablution block and cooking facilities, firewood available.

Shewula Nature Reserve *p832*
E-F Shewula Mountain Camp, T605 1160, www.shewulacamp.com. Beautiful hilltop setting, community-owned, 7 stone and thatch huts sleeping up to 5 with bedding, camping ground, shared ablution block and kitchen. No electricity, but there are gas stoves and fridge, paraffin lamps, hot showers. Traditional meals can be ordered, and are prepared by local families and you can join them to help cook. Activities include guided nature walks, swimming in the river and cultural tours around the villages.

Manzini to Mahamba *p833*
A-B Nhlangano Casino Royale 4 km out of Nhlangano on the road to Mhlosheni, T207 8211, www.nhlanganocasino.com. 47 chalet-style rooms with smart decor in earthy tones, DSTV and a/c. Recently refurbished after a fire, restaurant, bar, casino with gaming tables and 40 slots, pool, tennis courts, golf course, all set in 7 ha of lush grounds. High standard of facilities but mostly attracts gamblers and conference groups from South Africa.

C Phumula Guesthouse, 10 km before the Mahamba border post, T207 9099, www.phumulaguesthouse.co.za. Farm guesthouse not far from Nhlangano with 11 comfortable rooms in modern garden units. DSTV, ceiling fans and electric blankets. Some have patios. Bass fishing can be arranged in the farm dam, 3-course candlelit dinners on request.

Mkhaya Game Reserve *p834*
Access by prior reservation only, T528 3943, www.biggameparks.org. Rates include entry,

3 meals and 3 guided game-viewing trips. No children under 7.

L Stone Camp. 12 luxury self-contained stone and thatched cottages sleeping 3-5, shaded by hardwood forest and linked by walkways lit by paraffin lights at night. Thatched dining boma where buffet meals are served with South African wines, staff perform traditional dances around the campfire after dinner. Small animals like warthog and springbok can be seen around the camp. One of Swaziland's most comfortable game-viewing experiences.

Big Bend *p835*
C Lebombo Villa, on a hill to the south of town, T343 4329, www.swazilive.com/thele bombovilla. Neat B&B in an attractive salmon-coloured house with pool and garden full of palms, TV lounge with DSTV and snooker table, bar. The 10 rooms have a/c, modern decor and white linen. Some open up to the balcony.

Nisela Safaris *p835*
Reservations: T303 0318, www.niselasafaris.co.za.
D Bhubesi Camp, 16 km into the bush on a dirt road, usually accessible by 2WD but may not be in the wet. 7 a/c rondavels sleeping 4 with mezzanine floor and spacious bathrooms and five 4-bed rustic self-catering chalets.
D LaMatata Guest House, 5 km from the entrance to the reserve at Nsoko. 10 en suite rooms in a very pleasant colonial house. B&B, a/c, ceiling fans and attractive lawns surrounding the house.
E Msipi Camp, near the reserve entrance. The pool, bar and restaurant here is used by guests of all the facilities. 10 traditional Swazi grass huts with twin beds, shared ablution block and kitchen. There's also a campsite.

🍴 Eating

Manzini *p830*
There's very little choice for eating out, except for simple chicken and chip-type places in the shopping malls. There's a KFC and a Debonaire's Pizza on Ngwane St.
♛ Tum's George Hotel, corner of Ngwane and Du Toit streets, T505 8991 www.tgh.sz. 0730-2200. Buffets and set menus in the main dining room, à la carte menu in **St Georges Pub & Lounge**, generous Sun lunch by the pool, and a coffee shop. They also run the oddly named **Egg Yolk Sports Bar** next door.

Simunye *p831*
♛-♛ Simunye Country Club, T313 4758, www.visitswazi.com/simunyeclub. 0730-2200. A popular family restaurant, with an à la carte menu and buffet/carvery lunches and dinners on weekdays and at Sun lunch. Lighter meals like toasted sandwiches and pizza, occasional braai evenings and outside seating on the terrace. Surprisingly good food for such an out-of-the-way place but then they do cater for the King's birthday every year.

⊖ Transport

Manzini *p830*
Air
Matsapha International Airport, T518 6192, also known as Manzini International Airport, is 8 km from Manzini. Buses and minibus taxis go to Manzini and Mbabane and regular taxis meet the flights. **SAA** reservations South Africa, T011-978 1111, ww2.flysaa.co.za, has 4 daily flights to and from **Jo'burg** (1hr 5mins).

Bus
Buses and minibus taxis leave from the bus station on Louw St to **Mbabane**, **Big Bend**, **Lavumisa**, **Nhlangano** and **Mahamba**.

Car hire
There are offices at the airport for **Avis**, T518 6266, www.avis.co.za; and **Europcar**, T518 4396, www.europcar.co.za.

Big Bend *p835*
Buses to **Manzini**, **Mbabane** and **Lavumisa**.

Northern districts

The only settlement of note between Mbabane and South Africa is Motjane, where the MR1 branches north to Malolotja Nature Reserve and Pigg's Peak. There are a couple of good places to stay in this region. ▶ *For listings, see page 840.*

Mbabane to South Africa ●● ▶ p840.

Motjana and around

Motjane is a good centre for curio items. **Ngwenya Glass** ① *5 km before the border, T442 4053, www.ngwenyaglass.co.sz, 0830-1730*, and its attached coffee shop are a popular stop-off for coach parties. All the items for sale are made from 100% recycled glass, and you can watch glass blowers do their thing. A kilometre or so on the road behind the glass factory is **Endlotane Studios** ① *T442 4940, www.endlotane.net, 0900-1700*, which sells a varied collection of crafts from mohair tapestries to rugs, wall hangings, paintings, woodcrafts and pottery.

The border with South Africa is west of Motjane at **Ngwenya/Oshoek** ① *23 km from Mbabane, daily 0700-2200*. **Tourist information** ① *T442 4206*, is available here. Close to the border post are numerous curio stalls, worth a glance if you are leaving Swaziland. Buses to the capital and the rest of the country depart from Ngwenya.

The road north from Motjane is the MR1; 9 km along this road is the small **Hawane Nature Reserve** and dam. As the surfaced road heads north it passes through the small settlement of **Forbes Reef**. A general store is the centre of activity here, hidden close by are the remains of a long-abandoned gold mine.

Hawane Nature Reserve

① *T416 1151, www.sntc.org.sz. Open sunrise to sunset, free.*
Established in 1978, this small nature reserve protects an area of wetlands along the Mbuluzi river. When the Hawane Dam was built in 1988, the reserve was extended to protect the area's water supply. The main reason for coming here is for the excellent birdwatching, with many rare species being attracted by the river and dam. Look out for the endangered red hot poker plant, which can be found here. There is a good birdwatching trail set out in the park. Other activities include horseback trails, available from the **Hawane Resort** (see page 840).

Malolotja Nature Reserve ● ▶ p840. Colour map 2, C5.

① *T416 1151, www.sntc.org.sz, sunrise to sunset, R28, children (4-16) R14, under 4s free.*
Malolotja is a wild region of mountains and forest along the northwestern border with Mpumalanga, offering the country's finest hiking with challenging landscapes and altitudes rising from 615 m to 1800 m. Mgwayiza, Ngwenya (1829 m) and Silotfwane (1680 m) are three of Swaziland's highest peaks and local hikes cross deep forested ravines, high plateaux and grasslands dotted with waterfalls. Archaeological remains show that this region has been inhabited for thousands of years and the site of the world's oldest mine, thought to be 43,000 years old, is within the park. The diggings were used to excavate red and black earth, possibly for use as pigments.

Ins and outs

Getting there From the MR3 there is a turning at Motjane on to the MR1 heading north to Pigg's Peak. The turning into the reserve, easily identified by the collection of curio sellers (look out for the fine soapstone sculptures), is 7 km from this junction. Be wary of traffic along MR1; there are a few precipitous drops and buses tend to drive in the middle of the road.

Best time to visit The weather can change suddenly with rain and fog closing in without warning. The summers here are hot and humid with heavy rains. Winter is warm and dry but the nights can be bitterly cold with occasional frost.

Wildlife

There is a chance of seeing blesbok, klipspringer, oribi, zebra and both blue and black wildebeest, and surplus game from other reserves is gradually being introduced. Rare plants here include aloes, Barberton and Kaapasche Hoop cycads, proteas, orchids and fever trees. The small herbarium at the main camp has a good collection of unusual plants. Malolotja is an excellent area for birdwatching, and over 280 species have been recorded here. There is a breeding colony of the rare bald ibis at the **Malolotja Falls**, which drop an impressive 90 m into the Nkomati River. This is also a site for breeding blue swallows and the blue crane. There is a 25-km network of gravel roads for self-guided game drives but the best way to see the park is on foot by going on one of the many hiking trails. The longest is 7 km and leads up to the 95-m Malolotja Falls. Maps for the overnight hiking trails, information brochures and wildlife lists are all available from the Malolotja camp office, and many guided activities are on offer (see Sleeping, page 840).

Further north ⊙ ⇢ *p840*.

Pigg's Peak → *Colour map 2, C5.*

The MR1 continues north and on the right is the new Maguga Dam, some 12 km south of Pigg's Peak. A joint venture with South Africa, the Komati River was damned in 2002 and has now formed a picturesque lake surrounded by green hills. There's an alternative Maguga Dam loop road to Pigg's Peak that veers off 26 km north of Motjane, which offers view points. Pigg's Peak is a small, straggling town was named after William Pigg, a French gold prospector who came here in 1884. There was a working gold mine here until 1954, although no great fortunes were ever recovered. There's nothing here to warrant a stop, other than to stock up on cool drinks and petrol. From Pigg's Peak, the MR20 dirt road, heads west to the border post at **Bulembu/Josefsdal** (daily 0800-1600). Beyond here it's a short 39-km drive on the R40 to Barberton (see page 609).

Phophonyane Nature Reserve

Look out for a signpost for Phophonyane Lodge and Reserve about 15 km after Pigg's Peak. This is one of the most beautiful and relatively unspoilt patches of Swazi countryside, including dense riverine forest, home to small mammals such as duiker, bushbuck and the clawless otter. A number of 4WD and walking trails have been set out, including to the **Phophonyane Falls** – some of the best known falls in Swaziland. An artificial swimming pool has been created in the rocks just below the lower Phophonyane Falls. There is another scenic route north on a tarred road through Rocklands and Hhohho to the border post at **Matsamo/Jeppe's Reef** (daily 0800-2000). From here it's 43 km on the R570 to the N4, and a couple of kilometres beyond to the Kruger National Park's Malalane Gate (see page 608).

For Sleeping and Eating price codes and other relevant information, see pages 46-53.

🛏 Sleeping

Mbabane to South Africa *p838*

B-E Hawane Resort, 9 km from Ngwenya/ Oshoek border post and 2 km south of Malolotja Nature Reserve, T442 4744, www. hawane.co.sz. 23 luxury chalets, intriguing mix of traditional Swazi and contemporary architecture, stylish decor with splashes of bright colour. Also 22 backpacker beds arranged in twin units in a converted barn. Excellent restaurant serving fusion cuisine in a stylish open-plan dining room. Also has a bright lounge area, a bush spa, swimming pool, sauna and outside bar. Loads of activities can be arranged, including horse riding, archery, kayaking and guided hiking. An excellent set-up for all budgets.

E-F Sobantu Guest Farm, 26 km north of Motjane look out for the turning to Maguga Dam, the farm is 6 km on this dirt road, T605 3954, www.swaziplace.com/sobantu. Backpacker place with basic doubles, dorms and camping space. Nice farmland views, bar, kitchen (you can buy organic vegetables), or meals provided, short hikes through the farm or borrow the mountain bike, swimming in the dam or nearby rock pools. Will pick up from Pigg's Peak or Mbabane, and existing guests can hop on to go and check email or get cash.

Malolotja Nature Reserve *p838*

C Malolotja Cabins and Campsite cabins. Although a Swaziland National Trust Commission reserve, accommodation is managed by **Hawane Resort** (see above). 13 self-catering cabins with fireplaces sleeping up to 6, fully equipped kitchen, communal thatched lapa with braai, set in a beautiful mountain location. Activities include breakfast and sundowner drives, game drives, guided hiking to the Malolotja Falls, bird walks, village trips and fishing.

Camping

The main site has room for 15 tents or caravans, an ablution block, communal cooking area and firewood. Along the hiking trails are very basic campsites but you need to be totally self-sufficient, and as no fires are allowed outside the main campsite, a portable cooker is essential.

Pigg's Peak *p839*

B Orion Pigg's Peak, 10 km northeast of Pigg's Peak, T437 1104, www.oriongroup. co.za. 103 rooms set in a vast unattractive block but in a beautiful setting, with DSTV and great views of the forested Phophonyane Valley from every balcony. Restaurant, bar, pool with pool bar, tennis, squash, bowls, gym, sauna and casino. This is another resort built when gaming was illegal in South Africa, attracting gamblers from over the border, but thanks to its commanding highland location, it's remained popular.

Phophonyane Nature Reserve *p839*

B Phophonyane Lodge, 3km off the MR1, T437 1429, www.phophonyane.co.sz. Designed for peace and privacy, 23 guests sleep in luxury cottages and tented camps, perched on stilts with fabulous private balconies. Some are self-catering. Good restaurant, bar on a balcony overlooking the river. There are several tranquil nature trails marked out in the reserve. Recommended.

🍴 Eating

Mbabane to South Africa *p838*

Hotel restaurants are open to passing trade and Ngwenya Glass has a coffee shop.

♥ Maguga View Point, on Maguga Dam loop road, T675 8611. Open 0800-1800. Daytime restaurant popular with tour groups, with sunny spacious wooden decks and great views over the picturesque dam. Breakfasts all day, paninis, pancakes, spare ribs, grilled hake or southern fried chicken. Craft shop.

Contents

Footprint features

Background

History

South Africa

Early humans in South Africa

South Africa is actually home to some of the oldest fossil human remains in the world. Three million-year-old fossil remains of an early human-like species *Australopithecus africanus*, have been discovered at a number of sites on the Highveld. The exact way in which the evolution of the early human-like species into modern human took place is a matter of considerable debate amongst archaeologists. Whatever the exact timing and process of this evolution, by one million years ago a species that looked and behaved very much like modern humans, called *Homo erectus*, ranged far and wide across Asia, Africa and Europe. Within the last 100,000 years some of these groups seem to have developed still further into *Homo sapiens*, or modern humans. According to some archaeologists the earliest fossil remains anywhere in the world of modern man come from Klasies River mouth in Eastern Cape and Border Cave on the KwaZulu Natal border. They are dated as being more than 50,000 years old.

As elsewhere in the world, early humans in southern Africa were hunter-gatherers. They had stone tools to help with basic tasks. At first these tended to be large and multi-purpose but over time they became increasingly specialized and usually smaller. Early humans tended to live in small nomadic groups and their activities were largely dependent upon the particular environment they occupied. It is often assumed that the life of hunter-gatherers is necessarily harsh with very little leisure time, but anthropological studies of present-day hunter-gatherers indicates that this is probably not the case.

The Khoi and the San The fossil evidence of early humans in present-day South Africa confirms that the Apartheid myth of an unpopulated land is indeed simply fiction. However, Apartheid historians were too sophisticated in telling their particular stories to be put off by the presence of a few fossils. The argument was not so much that the land was totally empty when Europeans arrived but that it was not populated by the ancestors of the present-day African population of South Africa. The fossil remains, according to this argument, were of the ancestors of a totally separate race of people who were killed by the ancestors of the present-day African population as they migrated south.

Physical anthropologists working early in the 20th century believed that all humans fell into a small number of distinct race groups that had evolved independently from early human-like species. The Khoi and San people of southern Africa, called Hottentots or Bushmen by European settlers, were believed to have been one of these totally distinct race groups and to be the direct descendants of the early humans whose fossils are found across South Africa. More recent scientific studies, especially studies of the gene pools of present-day populations, indicate that this was not the case. While Khoi and San people may look racially distinct from other African peoples, they share many of the same genes (as do Europeans with Africans and so on). However, the perception that Khoi and San people were very different from other human groups and stuck in some sort of stone-age past where little ever changed, has lived on. While Khoi and San technologies had remained relatively unsophisticated, political units small and populations sparse, it is wrong to think that when Europeans first arrived at the tip of Africa they some-how encountered primitive stone-age people. These communities had changed and adapted over time and had long established trading contacts with other groups in southern Africa.

Up until about 20,000 years ago, the ancestors of the Khoi and San people were all hunter-gatherers living in small egalitarian communities of about 20 to 30 people. They were nomadic and moved with the herds of wild game as they undertook seasonal migrations. Their tools were made out of stone, water was stored in ostrich egg shells rather than pottery and they lived in caves or simple tents. As they were nomadic they had few personal possessions and there was no concept of personal possession of land or wealth. They spoke a series of similar languages distinctive for the large number of clicks and whistling noises included in their speech.

Given their lifestyle, few of their remains have been discovered by archaeologists, with one notable exception: their famous and beautiful **cave paintings**. These are found throughout southern Africa and usually depict hunting expeditions or the trance dances through which the San believed they could communicate with their dead ancestors. These paintings were at first monochrome but over time some artists began to experiment with colour. The contents also changed over time with later paintings showing domesticated animals, especially cattle and, after the arrival of Europeans, people holding guns.

Around 20,000 years ago some of these hunter-gatherer communities underwent a huge and relatively rapid change that was to have far reaching effects on their lifestyles. At this time a number of groups, probably sited in present-day northern Botswana, acquired domesticated livestock. The first livestock they had were fat-tailed sheep. These were probably originally domesticated in North Africa and the Middle East and the southern African hunter-gatherers traded for them with the Sudanic tribes who then occupied much of eastern Africa. Later they were able to acquire cattle from Bantu groups who migrated from the forest margins of West Africa into East and southern Africa.

The arrival of domesticated livestock radically altered the social relations within hunter-gatherer communities. With livestock came the concept of ownership of property and it was possible for one or two individuals to amass wealth and prestige. The people who acquired cattle also became more politically powerful and formed into larger groups under one or two chiefs. These groups, who became known as the Khoi, migrated south from present-day Botswana and occupied the coast zone of the Cape region from the Fish River right round to Namibia. The interior was occupied by San hunter-gatherers who maintained the smaller social units and a more egalitarian society. There was a large degree of interchange between these two peoples. The San hunters often raided the livestock herds of the Khoi, especially if these herds had displaced the wild animals upon which they relied and there is some evidence that the Khoi had San working for them as servants. There was also probably a large flow of people backwards and forwards between the two categories – if San acquired livestock they could become Khoi and if Khoi fell on hard times and lost all their cattle they could end up as San.

Arrival of the Bantu speakers There was also contact between the Khoi and San and other African peoples living in southern Africa. Apartheid history was right when it taught that these other African peoples had migrated into southern Africa from the north but got the dates wrong by some 1000 years. These newer arrivals, the ancestors of the vast majority of South Africa's present-day population, spoke a group of languages known as the Bantu group of languages. The people themselves are sometimes called Bantu people but this word is now associated with the racist institutions of the 1960s that used the name.

Bantu-speaking peoples began migrating into present-day South Africa about the period AD 500, bringing with them new technologies, especially iron smelting and new domesticated livestock. The migration was not one big trek southwards but a whole series of small movements by groups of individuals setting off in search of new pastures and looking to establish new villages. Where they came into contact with San and Khoi groups occupying good pasture they tended to displace them, pushing them into the more marginal desert and mountain areas. Some groups occupied the Highveld areas whilst others spread out along the fertile coastal strip that was later to become KwaZulu Natal and the Eastern Cape. The peoples who settled along the coastal strip were known as **Nguni** and were the ancestors of the present-day Zulu and Xhosa people, whilst those who settled on the Highveld were eventually to become the Sotho, Tswana and other related people. When the Bantu speakers came up against organized and established coastal Khoi groups in the area between the Fish and Sundays rivers, in present-day Eastern Cape, and the drier interior Karoo and Kalahari areas on the Highveld, the migration came to a halt.

Like the Khoi these newer arrivals were essentially herders and cattle were the mainstay of their economy. But they were also keen agriculturists and raised crops of millet, sorghum and other cereals and vegetables. In good rainfall years any surplus was exchanged for cattle with other people not so fortunate and in bad years cattle could in turn be exchanged for cereals. The Bantu-speaking peoples tended to form larger and more politically organized groups with clear hierarchical structures. In the dry interior they tended to form large villages around regular water supplies, whilst on the better-watered coastal strip they tended to live in more isolated homesteads. Iron smelting was an important activity and iron goods were traded over long-distance exchange networks. In present-day Zimbabwe some Bantu-speaking peoples were especially successful with smelting gold and this was traded with Arabs along the east African coast and later with Europeans.

There is a good deal of trading contact between the Bantu speakers and the Khoi. The Khoi were particularly keen to get hold of iron which they used in their tools, as well as *dagga* (marijuana), which they enjoyed eating or drinking in tea and which did not grow well in the dry Cape. Both Khoi, San and Bantu speakers only started smoking *dagga* after being introduced to pipes by Europeans. This large degree of contact is reflected in the fact that some Bantu speakers incorporated the Khoi-San clicks into their language – today these clicks can be heard in both Xhosa and Zulu. There was also a degree, small but significant, of intermarrying between the Khoi and Bantu-speakers, the Xhosa in particular.

Arrival of the Europeans

Dutch, Khoi and slave society at the Cape The first Europeans to make contact with these three different social groups in southern Africa were Portuguese sailors attempting to find routes to the spice islands of Asia. For many years the Portuguese had been pushing further and further south along Africa's western coastline and in 1487 a ship captained by Bartholomew Diaz made it around the Cape of Good Hope and sailed up the eastern coast of southern Africa as far as Algoa Bay. Ten years later another Portuguese sailor, Vasco da Gama, rounded the Cape and continued up the continent's eastern coast before heading further east, eventually to India. Over the next 200 years increasing numbers of Portuguese traders and their Dutch and British competitors began to make the journey to the east via the Cape of Good Hope. Though they occasionally stopped for fresh water and supplies in some of the more sheltered Cape bays and river mouths, the

Portuguese usually tried to give a wide berth to the territory that is now South Africa. Apart from the treacherous coastline they also often encountered a hostile reception from the local inhabitants. Instead the Portuguese had trading and supply posts in present-day Angola and Mozambique where they were able to both resupply their ships on the way to their eastern empire and capture slaves to send to their American colonies.

The Dutch were the first European trading power to set up a permanent settlement in South Africa. In 1652 the powerful **Dutch East India Company** built a fort and established a supply station under the command of Jan Van Riebeeck on a site that later became Cape Town. The idea was that this was to be simply a point where passing Dutch ships could drop in to get fresh supplies and to rest sick members of their crew. The company did not envisage the settlement growing into a larger community and at first, every inhabitant was a company servant. This situation soon altered, however, when the company decided that it would allow a group of servants who had worked out their contracts to settle close by as independent farmers and supply the post with their produce. Prior to this decision all fresh supplies had been either delivered by sea or brought from the Khoi groups living in and around the Cape Peninsula. These independent settlers were known as burghers and their number was soon increased by the freeing of more servants and the arrival of new settlers from Holland and, after 1685, Huguenots fleeing French anti-protestant legislation.

With the advent of free burghers, the size of the settlement began to increase and some farmers moved out into outlying districts. This brought them into increased conflict with Khoi herders. There were a series of small skirmishes which the Dutch, with their superior weapons, easily won and the Khoi found themselves displaced from more and more land and their herds of cattle diminished. Under these circumstances some began to work for the burghers on their farms, theoretically as free labourers but in effect as little more than slaves. In this early expansion and subjection of the Khoi the seeds of a whole long history of dispossession of the established population of South Africa are apparent. As the settler farming areas expanded they came into contact with San groups whom they systematically slaughtered in revenge for their raids on settler livestock. European and Asian diseases, especially smallpox, also killed many more San and Khoi and by the end of the 18th century they had almost all been either absorbed into the settler economy as servants, pushed into the most marginal mountain and desert areas, such as the Kalahari, or exterminated.

As the settlers moved further to the east and north they encountered environments less conducive to settled agriculture and more suited to pastoralism. Many settlers adopted a life as semi-nomadic trekboers living exclusively by trading their livestock and the products of hunting with the settled colonists in the Western Cape. As they moved east they also began to come into contact with Bantu-speaking Africans, in particular the Xhosa in what is now the Eastern Cape. Trading relations were established between the settlers and Xhosa, and some Xhosa also came to work on settler farms in return for guns and other European imports. As well as trade, however, the settlers and Xhosa also interacted through warfare. Cattle raiding was especially common and some historians argue that settlers also indulged in widespread slave raiding (see mfecane section, page 848, for more details). These battles were, however, inconclusive and a fluid and unstable boundary between the trekboers and Xhosa persisted for many years.

The other factor that began to alter the original function of the settlement was the arrival, in 1658, of a group of slaves captured from the Portuguese in Angola. The company had originally intended that there would be no slaves at the settlement but the company servants and free burghers soon became accustomed to avoiding the hardest and most menial manual tasks and demanded that they be supplied with more slaves. Unlike in the Americas most of these slaves did not come from West Africa but from Asia and Madagascar. They tended not to be owned in large numbers on huge plantations but in small groups, often less than 10, by individual farmers. The balance between the slave and free population of the Cape remained much more even than in West Indian and South American colonies.

There was, however, always a big gender imbalance in both the settler and slave populations, with far more men than women. Sexual encounters between slave owners and their female slaves, or Khoi servants, were frequent and a number of slave owners married freed slaves. Apartheid history taught that the present-day coloured population are the descendants of slaves and passing sailors, but even a cursory reading of the contemporary Dutch and other European reports of the settlement show that it it is probably more accurate to see the present-day Afrikaner and coloured population as having the same ancestry. Another fact about the present-day coloured population that is seldom recognized is that they are frequently the direct descendants of original Khoi inhabitants of the area. This is especially so in the Eastern and Northern Cape, where there was never a large slave population and certainly no sailors.

A number of slaves managed to escape from their captivity and joined up with still-independent groups of Khoi and miscellaneous European and mixed-race adventurers beyond the frontiers of the Dutch colony. Here they formed new and unusual political groupings and often existed by raiding both European settlers and African groups in the interior. The best-known of these bands were the so-called **Griquas**. With European horses and guns they became an important political force in the South African interior right through until the mid-19th century.

Arrival of the British During the 18th century Dutch economic and political power began to wane. Just as the Dutch had superseded the Portuguese they were themselves challenged by the rising power of the British. In 1795 the British sailed into False Bay and annexed the Dutch colony (The Battle of Muizenberg). The British were concerned that the French, with whom they were fighting in Europe, would take over the strategic port. In a general peace settlement of 1803 the colony was returned to the Dutch but in 1806 the British reconquered the territory and their sovereignty was finally accepted by other European powers in the peace settlement of 1816.

The British were only really interested in the Cape as a staging post and strategic port to protect trade with their new Asian empire. The colony was not profitable and neither the British government nor business took much interest in the new possession. There were, however, two important events in the early years of British rule that were to have crucial impacts on the subsequent history of South Africa.

The first factor was the British authorities' concern over persistent and inconclusive fighting along the colony's eastern frontier with the Xhosa. Some Xhosa groups had taken advantage of the instability in the colony to re-establish themselves to the west of the Fish River. The British decided that the only way to stop the persistent battles was to push the Xhosa back across the Fish River and establish a secure and clear frontier. During the first years of their rule they cleared the Xhosa occupying this area and tried to ban trekboers from having any contact with them. It was decided that what was needed was a group of permanent settlers on new farms in the area from which the Xhosa had been cleared in order to keep them apart from the trekboers.

In 1820 the British parliament agreed to release £50,000 to transport settlers from Britain to occupy this area. The money was used to send out 4000 settlers, with an additional 1000 paying their own passage to the region. These people became known as the **1820 Settlers** and formed the nucleus of the subsequent British settler community. Though the British authorities had intended that they should become farmers and hence occupy the disputed territory, most of the settlers were from urban artisan backgrounds and few had the skills or inclination necessary to become successful cultivators in the difficult and unfamiliar environment of the Eastern Cape. Most of them quickly gravitated towards the small towns, especially Port Elizabeth and Grahamstown, where they used their previous experience to become traders or skilled artisans. Their presence introduced an important new element to the equation, not least cultural, and 1820 Settler attitudes towards things such as the freedom of the press and towards the proper role of government played an important part in shaping 19th-century Cape settler society.

It soon became apparent that the British attempts to create a permanent border between the Xhosa and settlers had failed and cattle raiding backwards and forwards across the border continued. The Xhosa tried on numerous occasions to reclaim their land, occupied now by the settlers, but these attempts always failed, despite many initial successes. The **Frontier Wars** between Xhosa and settler continued for the next half century with Xhosa independence and land occupation being progressively eroded until their remaining areas (which became known as Transkei), were eventually incorporated into the Cape Colony.

The other fundamental change that British rule brought about was the **ending of the slave trade** and then the total banning of slavery. The peripheral role of South Africa in the British colonial empire and the dispersed nature of its slave population meant that it was seldom considered in debates about slavery, which instead concentrated on the massive slave plantations of the West Indies. Nevertheless, when the British parliament eventually decided to call an end to the institution that many felt was both inhumane and, more importantly, not beneficial to the empire's economy, it was also banned in South Africa. In 1834 slaves throughout the British Empire were officially emancipated, though they were to remain with their owners as apprentices until 1838. Slave owners were also offered compensation of one third of the value of their slaves. Though emancipation provided some slaves with new opportunities, in reality many of them continued to live very similar lives, carrying out the same heavy manual labour, under extremely harsh conditions, on the same Cape farms.

Nevertheless, many of the original Dutch settlers were extremely unhappy about the emancipation of slaves. To make things worse the British government, after extensive lobbying by British missionaries working in South Africa, also prevented them from introducing legislation aimed at tying both freed slaves and Khoi servants to individual farms as indentured labourers. The Dutch settlers had already been annoyed by the way their extremely loose system of administration had been reformed by the British, making it more difficult for individual farmers to impose their own law on their particular district. Many trekboers in the eastern districts also felt that the British were not quick enough in coming to their support when they had cattle raided by Xhosa groups to the east. Now they were not only losing a large proportion of their 'property' (slaves) but were being prevented from making sure they had a captive (cheap) labour supply. Though they were offered compensation at one third of the value of their slaves this had to be claimed in London. Many slave owners, therefore, sold their compensation rights to agents at usually about one fifth of the slave's value.

In response to these complaints a number of Dutch settlers decided that they would set out with their families and servants in search of new land beyond the British colonial boundaries. Between 1835 and 1840 around 5000 people left the Cape colony and headed east in a movement that later became known as the **Great Trek**. It tended to be the trekboers from the eastern areas, who had fewer possessions and little investment in established farms who took part in this movement. The settlers taking part in the trek became known as Voortrekkers and their experiences beyond the colonial frontiers became fertile ground for 20th-century Afrikaner nationalism. One thing not often celebrated in the national myths that grew up around the Great Trek is that accompanying the treks were a large number of Khoi servants and a small number of freed slaves still economically and socially bound to their masters/patrons.

African States and the mfecane

The area the Voortrekkers were entering into was the home of numerous Bantu-speaking African chiefdoms, but at the very time they made their appearance on the scene these political groupings were undergoing unprecedented political upheaval. The causes and indeed the very nature of this upheaval is a matter of considerable debate amongst historians and for once this is not a debate between Apartheid historians and their opponents. Rather, the debate is between those who believe that the turmoil was caused by wholly internal African political manoeuvrers and those who believe that external parties, especially slave raiders from Mozambique and the Cape, were to blame. Inevitably, the truth is probably somewhere between the two. External factors, such as the presence of European traders interested in products such as ivory, may have lead to increased competition amongst African chiefdoms for lucrative resources, but the dynamics of the upheaval probably had more to do with internal African state formation. On balance, the evidence used by those who argue for a basically internal dynamic to the process seems to be stronger than those arguing the opposite.

Prior to the early 19th century, African political units tended to be small and loyalty fluid. If there was disagreement within a chiefdom one section would simply set off and establish a new village in a new area. In the early 19th century, however, new larger and more strictly organized African political groupings (something closer to European nations), were formed. The epicentre of this new process of state formation was between the Tugela and Pongola rivers in present-day northern KwaZulu Natal and involved one of the best-known pre-colonial African personalities: **Shaka Zulu**.

Before the rise of Shaka, the Zulu clan had been just one of a large number of small political groups amongst the northern Nguni people in the coastal strip below the Drakensberg escarpment. At the time of Shaka's birth there were two powerful chiefdoms in the area, the Ndwandwe and the Mthethwa, who clashed repeatedly and with unprecedented ferocity. Shaka, an illegitimate son of the head of the Zulu clan, joined the army of the Mthethwa and proved to be a highly successful warrior and quickly rose through the ranks. When his father died and with the support of the chief of the Mthethwa, he managed to overcome all his half-brothers' claims to lead the Zulu clan. With Shaka as their chief, the Zulus were transformed into a very powerful political and military force. When the chief of the Mthethwa was killed by the Ndwandwe, Shaka was able to reunite the larger chieftainship under his Zulu clan. Unlike previous chiefs who had been willing to make loose alliances with other groups, Shaka ensured that everyone who came under his leadership expressed loyalty to the Zulu alone. He vigorously enforced a rule that his followers had to follow only Zulu cultural and religious practices and speak only the Zulu dialect.

By the process of incorporating surrounding smaller groups Shaka quickly forged a very powerful Zulu state. He took on and decisively beat the Ndwandwe and then set about raiding all surrounding chiefdoms for cattle and grain. His *impis*, organized regiments of full-time soldiers, were a new innovation amongst the Bantu speakers, as was their method of attack, which involved using short spears that were thrown or thrust from close quarters.

During the 1820s the Zulu *impis* became increasingly predatory, whilst at home Shaka's reign became even more autocratic and his punishment of any sign of opposition truly terrible. This lead to an era of unprecedented disruption, fighting and suffering known in the Nguni areas as the *mfecane* and on the Highveld as the *difaqane*.

Shaka's reign of terror eventually came to an end in 1828 when he was assassinated by Dingane, one of his half brothers. Dingane continued many of the same domestic and external policies as Shaka, though with less vigour and skill but the Zulu chiefdom maintained its position as the most powerful African state in southern Africa until its eventual defeat by the British Imperial forces in 1879.

The *mfecane* had caused havoc across southeastern Africa. People's crops and cattle had been destroyed and starvation was widespread. The population of the southern Highveld was decimated and survivors existed mainly in small, frightened bands. A number of larger political groups had arisen out of the chaos, such as the Zulu, the Ndebele, the Sotho, the Swazi and the Pedi, all of whom to some extent regarded large portions of Highveld as either belonging to them or falling within their sphere of influence but none of them really occupied the area. This was the arena into which the Voortrekkers made their unexpected arrival in the late 1830s.

European expansion

The Voortrekkers were by no means a unified movement. In fact there were numerous splits and some of the leaders were not on speaking terms. In the early years there were a number of small autonomous communities established by the Voortrekkers, but these often failed because of a poor location or challenges from nearby African states. Over time, however, two separate republics were established, the Orange Free State and the Transvaal. In the 1850s the British recognized these two states' sovereignty over most of the South African Highveld to the east of the Orange River. However, this was not exactly the location to establish their republics that the Voortrekkers had hoped for.

After leaving the Cape Colony one of the groups of Voortrekkers turned south and crossed the Drakensberg in search of a site for the new republic with access to the sea. In so doing they entered into the Zulu kingdom's domain. The Zulu king did not trust these new arrivals, especially as he had heard they had inflicted a defeat on the Ndebele and the Zulu killed the Voortrekkers leader when he came to negotiate a deal to be given land. A few months later, in the Battle of Blood River, the Voortrekkers extracted a terrible revenge and carved out a space for themselves south of the Tugela River. Their plans for a new republic with access to the sea were scuppered, however, when the British set up a new colony based at a site that became Durban and created the colony of Natal.

The Natal colony was not willing to challenge the might of the Zulu kingdom to the north of the Tugela until 1879, so for many years the two separate entities existed side-by-side. During this time the Zulu kingdom was an inward-looking entity and the Natal colonists were unable to attract many Zulu labourers to work on the sugar plantations they established in the area. They therefore turned to India as a source of labour following the lead of West Indian plantation owners who had imported indentured Indian servants as a replacement labour force for the newly emancipated slaves. These indentured Indian labourers were followed by free Indian merchants and together the two groups make up the ancestry of the present-day Indian population based in Natal.

On the Highveld the Boer Republics also appropriated land from African polities. The Sotho lost much of their territory in a long series of wars with the Orange Free State and eventually turned to the British for protection. A similar chain of events led to the declaration of the Bechuanaland Protectorate (present-day Botswana). Through the 19th century the Boer Republics on the Highveld gradually defeated all the independent African states, the last one, the Venda, fell in 1898. The defeated African populations usually managed to maintain access to at least some land. These areas were later exclusively reserved for African occupation after it was realized that if all the land was appropriated the colonies and republics would have to find space for large numbers of African people.

Whilst Voortrekkers may have lodged claims to certain farms they invariably contained resident African populations. More often than not the Boers were happy to leave the African population in place and simply collect rent, either in the form of produce or labour. Later on in the century this created tensions when some landowners wanted to set up proper productive farms and had trouble getting enough labour. They often looked across at the neighbours' farms and saw a potential labour force simply getting on with its own peasant farming activities. They therefore lobbied for legislation outlawing what they described as kaffir farming. This was to become a more important issue after the 1870s when an unexpected event was to transform the South African economy and produce a new market for agricultural goods.

Mineral revolution

Despite the machinations on and beyond their frontiers the two colonies remained very much a backwater of the British empire. Wool exports from the Karoo and wine from the Western Cape created some commercial interest but other colonial possession held greater promise. This was all to change in 1867 when alluvial diamonds were discovered near the confluence of the Harts and Vaal rivers. The flurry of interest and activity that this discovery created were just petering out when a larger outcrop of diamonds were found at a dry digging nearby. By 1872, 20,000 Europeans and a larger number of Africans and coloureds had converged on the site that soon revealed itself as the world's richest diamond pipe and grew to become the world's diamond capital, Kimberley. At first there were numerous small individual plots at the mines but these soon became concentrated into the hands of one or two companies who bought up the claims from small entities. Eventually total control of the mines rested in the hands of Cecil Rhodes' DeBeers Consolidated Mines.

In 1886 there was a further mineral discovery in South Africa; this time it was gold on the Witwatersrand in the Transvaal Republic. Miners from across the world rushed to the new reef and capitalists were quick to make sure they got a slice of the pie. The deep level and relatively poor grade of the ore meant that it was only large capitalist organizations that could secure the investment necessary to succeed and, just as at Kimberley, mine ownership was quickly consolidated into a few hands. The main town on the Rand, Johannesburg, grew rapidly from nothing to about 75,000 white residents and many more Africans by the turn of the 20th century.

These mineral discoveries fundamentally altered South African society. It was at the mines that many of the features that dominated life in 20th-century South Africa first came into existence, in particular the pass laws, the migrant labour system, the compounds and the colour bar. The deep-level diggings and the complicated process of extraction from poor gold ores meant that production expenses were high and, as the gold price was fixed internationally, the one way mining companies could ensure high profits was to hold down or reduce labour costs. The diamond mines at Kimberley provided the model of how this was to be done.

At first all labour at Kimberley was able to demand a high wage, but as the number of companies were rationalized there were fewer and fewer opportunities. White labourers began to realize that they were losing out to cheaper African labourers and pressurized the government to reduce this competition. Whilst government was unwilling to institute too overtly racist legislation, they did introduce a pass law that required all Africans present in the town to carry a pass signed either by a magistrate or a mine owner showing that they had legitimate employment. This legislation was aimed at preventing large numbers of Africans arriving at Kimberley in hope of jobs and hence pushing down wage rates.

The mines' owners, however, wanted to keep wages as low as possible and therefore to substitute more expensive white labour with cheaper African labour. The solution to this problem lay in the migrant labour system, where only male Africans came to the mines leaving their families at home on the reserves. The DeBeers mining company had quickly introduced a system whereby all African labour had to live in a single compound above the mine from which they were prohibited to leave for the duration of their contract. The official reason was that this was to prevent diamond thefts, but there were also many other advantages for the employers. As the compounds were only to house single male African labourers the company did not have to pay adequate wages to support the miner's family, who usually remained in the reserves and farmed to meet their own subsistence needs. Furthermore the mine owners could be assured of economies of scales in buying in provisions and therefore were able to feed African labourers on the site. If Africans had to buy their own food they would have needed higher wages. At first DeBeers wanted to introduce a compound system for white labourers, but because they had a political voice they were able to resist these plans.

For white labour the migrant labour system meant that they were being squeezed out of the job market by cheaper African labour. The mining companies were always nervous that white and African labour would unite, especially as many of the white labourers were experienced trade union activists. Over time there developed a sort of tacit agreement between white labour and capitalists that in exchange for the political support of labour, the capitalists would introduce a colour bar that reserved the more skilled and better paid jobs for whites only. At times this arrangement broke down, especially in the years after the First World War, but on the whole white labour never rocked the boat.

While capitalists on the Rand were able to develop a labour system that ensured wages were kept low, they were not always able to secure African labour in the quantities they required. They were, therefore, always pressurizing the respective governments to introduce policies to push more African men out of the reserves. They also went to great lengths to get labour from wherever it was available, including beyond the borders of South Africa as far away as Malawi. The mine owners decided to co-operate with one another to keep wages low and formed a Witwatersrand Native Labour Association that was to look after all recruitment of African labour. When mine owners experienced a particular shortage of labour early in the 20th century, they recruited 63,000 Chinese labourers on fixed contracts who undermined the wage levels demanded by Africans. Once the wage rate had been forced down, the Chinese labourers were simply repatriated.

One reason the capitalists felt that Africans were not entering the labour market in the numbers they required was the success that African peasant farmers were having at this time. African farmers were the first to react to the new markets created by the mines at Kimberley and on the Rand and, using new farming techniques learnt from missionaries, they increased their grain output tremendously. Many of the successful African peasant farmers lived in the reserves, but others had managed to buy or rent land outside these areas. White farmers were not usually able to cope with the competition these new African peasants presented and lobbied government for support. This was forthcoming in the form of subsidies, soft loans and technical advice and after the turn of the last century these African peasant farmers began to lose out against their white competitors. In 1913 legislation was introduced that made it impossible for Africans to buy or rent land in many 'white' areas. The depression of the 1930s was the final nail in the coffin for many peasant farmers and after that date very few struggled on. Today it seems hard to believe that there was once a highly successful African peasant class, outperforming their white neighbours, and that it was deliberately ruined by government action. The success of African farmers at this time was ignored by all school history textbooks during the Apartheid era and even today few South Africans, black or white, know that African farmers were at one time much more successful than their white competitors.

Anglo-Boer War

When diamonds were discovered at Kimberley it was not quite clear who had sovereignty over the area, with a Tswana chiefdom, the Orange Free State, the Transvaal Republic and the Griquas all claiming the area. Britain pressurized the rival claimants to undergo a process of arbitration under their direction. At the arbitration it was decided that the Griqua's claim was strongest, but the British immediately offered the Griqua leader substantial compensation if he agreed that the territory should be administered by the British. Not surprisingly, the Orange Free State, which had the strongest claim out of the two republics, was annoyed by this sleight of hand, especially as the British soon incorporated the area into the Cape Colony, but there was little they could do about it.

The Rand, on the other hand, was clearly within the Transvaal Republic. The British had annexed the Transvaal in 1877 but after a brief Boer uprising they handed control back. They must have regretted the decision when gold was discovered just five years later. The government of the Republic was primarily concerned with looking after the interests of its richer Boers, the vast majority of whom were farmers. They were a little unsure about how to treat the new mining economy. On the one hand the extra revenue from taxing the operations was clearly to be welcomed, whilst on the other they were nervous about the implications of having a large number of new immigrants, known by them as uitlanders, or foreigners, in their midst. They therefore introduced legislation restricting the franchise to white adult male naturalized citizens who had lived in the Republic for at least 14 years.

While most uitlanders were too busy trying to make their fortune to worry about politics, they did complain about the inefficiency of the Transvaal government in meeting the conditions necessary for an efficient capitalist system. British Imperialist forces were keen to get their hands on the Republic and in 1895 tried to manipulate uitlander dissatisfaction in a plot to overthrow the Transvaal government. In 1895, with the backing of the Colonial Office in London, Cecil Rhodes, then Prime Minister of the Cape Colony, tried to organize a committee of leading uitlanders to seize control of Johannesburg and declare a new government. Rhodes also arranged for a column of British police, under the control of his old friend Leander Starr Jameson, based in the Bechuanaland Protectorate, to come to their assistance. The plot, later known as the Jameson Raid, was a fiasco. The uitlander committee in Johannesburg bickered amongst themselves and did not command any mass following. Realizing this, Rhodes called off the proposed intervention by Jameson's force, but Jameson ignored his command and entered the Transvaal. When the committee learnt of this, they did belatedly declare that they had taken over Johannesburg but even in the process of doing so they entered into negotiations with the Transvaal Republic and came to an agreement. Jameson's column, therefore, had no crisis in which to intervene and were simply met and arrested by a Transvaal commando. This embarrassing incident marked the end of Rhodes' political career and helped to alienate British and Afrikaners across South Africa.

Despite the failures of the Jameson Raid the British were still keen to gain control of the Transvaal. Just four years after, Britain mounted a far better equipped, more sustained and ultimately successful bid to gain control of the whole of South Africa; the Anglo-Boer (or South African) War of 1899 to 1902. There is some disagreement among historians about the underlying cause of the war. Afrikaner Nationalist historians tend to view it simply as an example of British Imperial expressionism. Some historians of the British Empire, on the other hand, argue that it was more to do with British strategic concerns; they were worried that the Transvaal Republic could inspire Afrikaners in the Cape to rebel against the British who would, therefore, lose control of ports such as Simon's Town which were vital for protecting her sea routes. Most historians, however, see gold as being the key. The British were, not surprisingly, keen to control the world's largest supply of gold and make sure their investment in the mines was profitable.

During the late 1890s the Colonial Office in London and the British High Commissioner in the Cape both lobbied for direct British military intervention to overthrow the Transvaal and the Orange Free State Republics. The situation grew more and more tense and in September 1899 Britain sent a large party of British soldiers to reinforce their troops. Sensing that Britain was about to invade the Transvaal, the Orange Free State decided to strike before the reinforcements arrived and on 11 October 1899 declared war on Britain in an attempt to preserve their independence. Deciding that attack was the best form of defence, they invaded both the Cape and Natal colonies.

At first the Boer Republics had great success and achieved victories in both northern Natal and the northeastern Cape. They drove back British forces and laid siege to Ladysmith, Kimberley and Mafikeng. They were, however, unable to advance much further in either colony and the general uprising of Afrikaners in the Cape that they had hoped for never materialized. Initially they held off British attempts to relieve the three towns, but with the arrival of huge numbers of British troops the fortunes changed. During 1900 the British set off on a triumphant and unstoppable advance on Pretoria and Paul Kruger, the president of the Transvaal Republic, escaped into exile via the Portuguese colony of Mozambique.

British victory seemed secure, but a number of die-hard Boers had other ideas. For the next two years they indulged in a continuous and, for the British, exceptionally frustrating, guerrilla war. The British were unable to capture the small bands of highly skilled Boer commandos so set about instituting a scorched earth policy to deny the guerrillas any help from local populations. Large numbers of Boers from areas with a guerrilla presence were placed in concentration camps to prevent them from supplying the commandos in the field with provisions. Though it was by no means a deliberate policy of the British, poor administration meant that food and medical supplies in the camps often ran out and many Boers, including many women and children, died of disease or starvation. Memories of the British scorched earth policy were often revived by Afrikaner politicians throughout the 20th century, though they conveniently forgot that the Boers tended to use very similar techniques in their battles against African chiefdoms. Also forgotten is the British policy of rounding up any African workers on Boer farms and placing them in similar concentration camps during the war.

Peace and Union The British scorched earth policy and the sheer hopelessness of their situation eventually lead many Boers to abandon the fight and return to their farms. The remaining guerrilla bands, who became known as the bitterenders, eventually surrendered to the British under the Treaty of Vereening in April 1902. The British were keen to ensure that the two defeated Boer republics were fully incorporated into a unified South Africa and therefore agreed a number of concessions for the defeated army. One of the key issues that the British were willing to concede was that any discussion of political rights for Africans be delayed until some unspecified future date.

The British hoped that after the war they would be able to substantially Anglicize the country by enforcing English as an official language and encouraging mass immigration from Britain. This policy proved to be a failure but they were successful in encouraging the four territories to agree to Union just seven years after the end of the war. One of the key sticking points in discussions over Union was the issue of African voting rights. In the Cape Africans and coloureds had the right to vote as long as they owned above a set value in property. While this excluded most Africans it did give at least some an opportunity to vote and therefore a political voice, however weak. Natal also had a property qualification but the figure was set so high for Africans that only a handful ever managed to vote. The other two Boer republics had never allowed Africans any political rights whatsoever. During the discussions over Union, which only Natal had reservations about, it was decided that the issue of voter representation for Africans would be side-stepped by entrenching a constitutional clause maintaining the pre-Union franchise arrangements in each of the four territories. With this issue solved and agreement on things such as dual official languages (English and Dutch), all sides agreed on the **Act of Union**, which was passed by the British Houses of Parliament in 1909 and the Union of South Africa came into being in 1910.

The rise of nationalism
First stirrings of African nationalism The Act of Union, and particularly the entrenchment of the Boer republics' voting arrangements, felt like a powerful slap in the face for very many Africans. Most Africans had supported the British during the Anglo-Boer War and had assumed that their loyalty would be recognized in the post-war settlement. Though Africans in the Cape had their voting rights entrenched in the Constitution they feared that the Cape government's willingness (with British backing) to placate the two northern former republics was a very bad omen. This proved all too correct; in 1935 they had their voting rights removed by an Act which amended the Constitution.

In the early 20th century African political opposition to racist policies tended to be exceptionally moderate. During the 19th century there had been small but steady growth of the African educated middle class. They were mostly educated in mission schools, were committed Christians and employed as teachers or government clerks. They tended to look to London for support and were especially concerned about preserving their voting rights. Not surprisingly, these early African political leaders were dismayed by the proposals for Union and sent a delegation to London to try to urge the British House of Commons to amend the Act. Despite receiving some support from Labour politicians they failed in this venture. In 1912 a group of African leaders called for a national convention for all African political groups in the country. This gathering in Bloemfontein marked the formation of a more organized phase in African opposition to racist legislation and lead to the South African Native National Congress, later renamed the **African National Congress**.

Despite the formation of a national opposition organization, African protest still tended to be extremely moderate. Many African leaders placed a special emphasis on education as a means to achieving political recognition. Many still believed in the old Cape liberal ideology of 'equal rights for all civilized men' and went to great lengths to prove just how civilized they were. London remained the mecca for these early leaders and the most common form of protest was appeals to the Imperial authorities.

Over the next few decades, however, there were also a number of shorter lived, more radical, opposition movements. The most successful of these was the Industrial and Commercial Union (ICU) established by the very colourful figure, Clements Kadalie. The ICU spread rapidly through South Africa in the 1920s and was especially successful amongst farm workers. It demanded fairer wages for African workers and full political rights for all. The organization of the ICU left much to be desired, however, and just as quickly as it grew it subsided.

After the First World War a few white communists also made attempts to forge links between the White Union movements and African workers. Though there were many influential Africans who came up through these Communist Party links the movement was never able to reach out to a wide range of Africans, especially Africans in the rural areas. The Party also suffered from numerous internal splits, often caused by contradictory statements coming from the international Communist leadership and from continual harassment from the police. White Unionists also resisted the attempts to form a non-racial movement and in 1922 the South African Labour Party, which represented the interests of white working-class voters, entered into an election pact with the Afrikaner nationalists in the National Party.

While the 1920s had seen a great deal of protest from African peoples, especially from the ICU, the 1930s were a period of relative quiet. The international depression also affected the South African economy and many Africans found themselves unemployed or on low wages. To make matters worse the early years of the decade also saw one of the worst ever droughts, ruining the residual African farming economy in the reserves. Under these circumstances political protest seemed to be secondary to the tough job of simply surviving. During the Second World War, however, there was an upswing of African protest culminating in a series of protest movements amongst squatters outside Johannesburg and a massive African mineworkers strike. After the war African protest entered a more radical phase as younger leaders came to the forefront.

Rise of Afrikaner nationalism It is a common misconception that Afrikaner nationalist sentiments existed right from the arrival of Van Riebeeck and that the 'Afrikaner spirit' somehow grew out of the harsh conditions of the frontier. This is a misconception that has often been fuelled by Afrikaner nationalists' versions of history. The reality is very different and, whilst Afrikaners have used the imagery of the Great Trek to help create a sense of nationalism, it was by no means an event in which all Afrikaners took part.

Class divisions were strong among both the descendants of the original settlers who remained in the Cape and those who migrated to the north. The established richer Western Cape farmers looked down both on the people who migrated to the new Republics and their poorer neighbours. Because of these deep-rooted divisions it is not really correct to talk about Afrikaners as a single category prior to the 20th century, when there were potent political forces that led to increased collective nationalism. It is, therefore, somewhat of an anachronism to talk about *Afrikaners*, which simply means African in Dutch, prior to the 20th century. In the Western Cape it is possible to see an earlier sense of Afrikaner nationalism, but this might more accurately be called a Dutch settler identity, whilst in the two Republics the sense of nationalism was firmly tied up with an extremely local (agricultural) identity, hence the use of the term Boer, which simply means farmer in Dutch.

In the 19th century the Afrikaans language, later to become a potent symbol of Afrikaner nationalism, was regarded by the more elite settlers as a bit of an embarrassment. Because the language had developed out of a mixture of Dutch and the various languages spoken by the Khoi and slaves, it was regarded as a rather low form of dialect and its association with coloured servants was apparently the common description of a language known as kitchen Dutch. There had been one attempt to raise the profile of Afrikaans in the 1870s but it had not spread much beyond the movement's base in Paarl. During the negotiations over Union, Boer leaders were not arguing for Afrikaans to be a dual official language, they were arguing for Dutch. At the very time these negotiations were taking place, however, there was a second attempt to gain respectability for the Afrikaans language. The political climate was much more conducive to the movement and it quickly spread throughout the Cape and the two former Boer Republics.

The ravages of the war and the development of mechanized agriculture meant that many poorer Afrikaner tenant farmers were being forced off the land in the early decades of this century. They migrated to the new towns in search of work, but had few skills to offer and often ended up poor and unemployed. Their plight, often labelled 'the poor white problem', was a continual worry for Afrikaner politicians. They were especially fearful that their marginal position in the new towns was pushing them into closer contact with the growing band of African urban poor. The 'poor white problem' was a key motivation behind the deepening of segregationist policies in the urban areas, designed to keep black and white apart. During the first half of the century the nitty-gritty of segregation tended to be largely left up to local authorities to implement, with central government simply providing the legislative framework for local regulations. Nevertheless, in almost every town residential segregation and pass laws strictly regulated the daily lives of Africans.

The 'poor white problem' was also an important force behind the development of Afrikaner nationalism. As poorer Afrikaners moved to the towns they became immersed in a very different working-class culture to the one they had experienced in the countryside. The Afrikaner leaders realized that if these new urban residents became part of this new urban culture they may well lose much of their separate Afrikaner identity and the Afrikaner politicians would find their support base undermined. They therefore decided that they needed to create a stronger sense of Afrikaner nationalism that would incorporate all Afrikaners, rich and poor. Historical events, such as the Great Trek, were deliberately resurrected and celebrated, the Afrikaans language was encouraged and, crucially, the Afrikaner leaders developed exclusively Afrikaner economic institutions that deliberately helped Afrikaner small businesses.

Afrikaner politics

Despite the deliberate fostering of Afrikaner nationalism the Afrikaner leadership was constantly fighting amongst itself and political parties frequently split and reformed. One of the key issues of disagreement was over the relationship between the new Union and the British Empire. After Union the British asked an ex-Boer General, Louis Botha to form the first government. He, and his close ally and successor General Jan Smuts, both strongly believed that the Afrikaners should strive to have good relations with the Imperial government and unite English and Dutch/Afrikaans-speaking white South Africans. Their **South Africa Party**, built on a coalition between the Transvaal and Cape ruling parties easily won the first election, but another important ex-Boer General, Hertzog, felt that they were too keen on maintaining good relations with the British government and formed a rival **National Party**. At first the National Party only had support in Hertzog's home province, the Orange Free State, but later he was joined by DF Malan, an ardent anti-British Afrikaner from the Cape province.

The First World War caused a further and more vicious split in Afrikaner ranks. A number of important generals resisted Botha's strong support for Britain in the war and his commitment to send South African troops to Europe. Their attempted coup failed and Botha quickly put the rebellion down, but the issue resurfaced again and again over the next few decades. A strike by white miners in 1922, which grew into a mini revolt as workers seized power in Johannesburg, was dealt with in a similar fashion by Botha's successor, Smuts. This time, however, white workers were able to gain a measure of revenge: in 1924 their support was crucial in electing a coalition Labour/Nationalist government.

Under Hertzog, Afrikaner nationalist sentiment was given an important boost by the replacement of Dutch by Afrikaans as one of the two official languages. In 1934 there even seemed a chance of forging a united Afrikaner leadership when Hertzog and Smuts joined together under a new United Party banner during the crisis caused by the great depression. This, however, was not to be, as Malan led a breakaway group to form a new 'Purified' National Party. The decision whether or not to join the Second World War caused a further split and Hertzog resigned as Prime Minister to join Malan in opposition, in so doing creating yet another version of the National Party – this time the Herenigde (Reunited) National Party. Smuts, the ardent supporter of close ties with Britain, became the new Prime Minister and took South Africa into the war. He won an election in 1943 on the back of a wave of pro-British feeling and his international reputation grew and grew. After the war, however, he found his popularity at home waning. The economic boom caused by the war had lead to massive African urban migration and the National Party was able to use this to stir up fear amongst white, especially Afrikaner, voters. In 1948 they voted in Malan's Nationalists on an election platform promising a new ideology of Apartheid.

The Apartheid programme

What exactly was meant by Apartheid was not clear in 1948; and the full programme of legislation was only really finalized in the mid-1950s. In fact, the real beauty of the concept in 1948 was that it meant different things to different sections of the white voting population. The word simply means 'apart', and as such can be seen as simply a refinement of segregationist ideas that had dominated in the first half of the century. Despite the image of Apartheid created by many populairst historians and journalists, it was by no means or exclusively Afrikaner ideology. Indeed the roots of the idea can be traced back to English-speaking liberals in the early years of the century.

There was a distinct group of white South Africans who were very concerned about the plight of Africans and saw the solution as being total separation of the two races. They believed that rapid urbanization was destroying the basis of African culture and that they needed to be protected from the evils of white urban civilization. This ideology was tied up with ideas of both paternalism – that whites should be like parents to child-like Africans – and ideas of Social Darwinism, that different races were at different points along an evolutionary scale. In the middle decades of the century these ideas began to be considered by a group of Afrikaner intellectuals who saw the total separation of the races as being the only way in which whites could maintain political power over South Africa. They began to argue that if Africans were allowed to take part in the white capitalist economy they could rightly expect to be given political rights, so the solution was to keep them in a totally separate political and economic sphere where they could exercise their own rights.

This political philosophy was obviously not at all popular amongst white factory owners and farmers who relied upon cheap African labour to run their business. To these people Apartheid should be simply a way of maintaining a cheap supply of African labour with few employment or political rights that would allow the demand of higher wages. There was, therefore, a clear conflict between the ideology of Apartheid as expressed by Afrikaner intellectuals and the wishes of the average Afrikaner voter. During the early 1950s this conflict was solved by the nationalists stating that their long-term aim was the total separation of races, but in the meantime they had to be practical and recognize the economic reality that white industry relied upon African labour.

Apartheid became in essence a way of ensuring a continual supply of cheap African labour whilst denying Africans any political rights. Legislation such as the Group Areas Act tightened previous segregation regulations and the government set about a massive national campaign to remove Africans from urban areas or squatter camps close to urban centres. Africans living in vibrant urban communities such as Sophiatown in Johannesburg found their homes bulldozed as they were ordered out. Those without passes were returned to the reserves, now restyled as homelands, whilst those with rights to reside in urban areas were removed to distant townships such as Soweto. Segregation of all amenities was also tightened and there became no areas of African life where the state did not intervene. In the countryside, Africans who had retained access to land either as freeholders or tenant farmers, in areas that were labelled 'black spots', were also forcibly removed to the homelands.

African opposition Africans did not take these new assaults lying down, and the 1950s saw an unprecedented display of African political opposition to the white state. The **ANC** was revitalized and radicalized by the rise of a group of young militant activists, including **Nelson Mandela**, who had joined the ANC's Youth League in the 1940s. The organization saw that their attempts to appear moderate had not done them any favours and they could clearly not rely upon Britain to look after their interests. In 1952 the ANC launched a **Defiance Campaign** that used Gandhian tactics of peaceful resistance to the new Apartheid legislation. The ANC, in alliance with Indians, coloureds and a few radical whites, took the lead in deliberately breaking racist laws and offering themselves up for arrest. These peaceful protests were often met with violence from the police and many ANC members were harshly treated after arrest. Though the campaign failed, the ANC's membership mushroomed in its aftermath.

The National Party met this increased opposition with new legislation that firstly banned the South African Communist Party and then increased restrictions on the ANC and other political organizations. The banning of the Communist Party meant that many Communists now looked to the ANC as their main political organization. Some within the ANC were worried about the increased prominence of communists within the organization, especially as they tended to have very strong links with white communists, many of whom joined a newly formed white organization called the Congress of Democrats. These people were also concerned about the developing alliances with Indian and coloured organizations and wanted to maintain the ANC as an exclusively African organization.

Uniting under the slogan "Africa for the Africans", they formed a splinter group within the ANC and finally broke off to form a rival **Pan African Congress** (PAC) under Robert Sobukwe.

Apartheid policies also made themselves felt in the homelands where the government introduced 'betterment' policies designed to shore up the faltering subsistence economy in the areas which provided food for the families of migrant workers and for the workers themselves when unemployed. The plans consisted of regulations to consolidate small plots of land and setting aside areas for farming and areas for grazing. A crucial element of the plans was the compulsory culling of African cattle when there were deemed to be too many head of livestock on grazing land. This was really the first time that the white state had intervened in the daily lives of Africans living in the reserves and many resented the fact that there was now no area of their life free from the control of the racist authorities. The compulsory culling regulations were especially resented and when the government tried to implement them there was violent resistance in a number of areas. These outbreaks were inevitably dealt with extremely harshly.

A number of urban areas also experienced bouts of violence, with African protesters displaying their frustration through rioting. In response to the growing protest the government moved to break the ANC-led alliance and put 156 of its leaders on trial for treason. The mammoth trial lasted from 1956 to 1960, eventually resulting in their acquittal. Despite the acquittal it was important in diverting the accuseds' energy away from organizing opposition. Furthermore, by the time the trial was over it had also been overtaken by other events.

In late 1959 the newly formed PAC decided to launch a massive anti-pass law campaign. The pass laws were one of the most hated Apartheid policies as they strictly controlled African mobility and were also used by the police as an excuse to stop and search any African. Their campaign was to start on 21 March 1960, in order to pre-empt an ANC led campaign due to start on 31 March 1960. The PAC called on all African men to leave their passes at home and present themselves for arrest at the nearest police station. They believed that the prison system would be swamped and the pass laws would have to be revoked. One of the main areas of PAC activity on the morning of 21 March was the southern Transvaal. At Evaton and Vanderbijlpark police stations large crowds were dispersed by police baton charges and low flying jets, but at Sharpville the crowd stayed put when they were buzzed by the jets. At 1315 there was a small scuffle and a small section of the wire fence surrounding the police station was knocked over. The police later claimed they were under extreme danger and were being stoned but this is denied by almost all eyewitness accounts. What is clear, however, is that the police suddenly opened fire on the crowd with machine guns. The terrified crowd ran for cover but the police continued to fire on the fleeing protesters. Most of the 69 dead and 180 wounded were shot in the back.

Moves towards armed resistance The Sharpville Massacre marked a turning point in African political opposition to Apartheid. As news of the killings spread around the country Africans rioted and refused to go to work. In Cape Town there was a series of huge marches from the townships into the city centre which created panic amongst the white residents and police. The march leaders were, however, insistent that they passed off peacefully and had negotiations with the local police chief to ensure this was the case. They were rewarded with arrest, and the Cape Town townships also erupted into rioting. A nationwide state of emergency was declared and the police arrested thousands of political activists from across the country. Strikers were beaten and township food supplies cut off to force people back to work. Both the ANC and PAC were banned and many of their leaders thrown in prison under new security legislation that meant they could be held without being charged. Over the next few months the unprecedented harshness of the police action broke the back of the widespread resistance. It also convinced many ANC and PAC members that non-violent action meant nothing if it was met by police brutality.

The leadership of both the PAC and ANC were concerned that they were about to lose control of their rank-and-file members unless they modified their position on the use of violence. The ANC leadership decided that it would establish an organized armed wing, named Umkhonto we Sizwe (Spear of the Nation), to carry out sabotage attacks on economic targets and not to threaten human lives. During an 18-month period from December 1961 the organization carried out a total of 200 attacks on targets such as post offices, government buildings, electricity sub-stations and railway lines. Despite the official policy on not putting human lives at risk a number of Umkhonto we Sizwe activists did attack policemen and collaborators. The organization was effectively neutralized by the security police in July 1963 when its headquarters at Lilliesleaf Farm in Rivonia were discovered and a number of crucial documents were unearthed. The majority of the organization's leadership, including Nelson Mandela, Walter Sisulu and Govan Mbeki, were arrested and sentenced to life imprisonment.

The PAC leadership had more ambitious and less well-organized plans for armed struggle. The PAC's armed wing, Poqo (meaning 'standing alone'), attempted to organize a general armed uprising to overthrow the white government once and for all. The leadership had little control over the individual cells and was unable to coordinate the armed attacks. One cell did organize an attack by some 250 men armed with makeshift weapons on the police station and prison in Paarl, but the attack failed against a police force armed with guns, and instead they attacked nearby houses, killing two people. There was also an isolated attack which killed five unarmed whites asleep in a car in the Transkei. Plans for a general uprising were effectively crushed when Potlako Leballo, one of the organization's founders and then resident in the British colony of Lesotho, stupidly boasted of the plans. As a result the PAC headquarters were raided by the British authorities and Poqo membership lists were handed over to the South Africans. Hundreds of people were arrested in a huge police operation and the PAC was effectively smashed. Despite its short-lived publicity and success, the organization was unable to reorganize effectively in exile and it was never again able to compete with the ANC for the leadership of South Africa's disposed African population.

1960s: the darkest days   With the ANC and PAC banned and their leaders either in prison or exile, political opposition by Africans to the Apartheid state was muted in the 1960s. The 'separate development' policies of the nationalists began to be applied with more rigour and economic opportunities for Africans became even more constrained. The winds of change may have been sweeping across the rest of Africa but for most South Africans the 1960s represented the darkest days.

The newly declared Republic appeared confident and strong and the National Party was able to gain support from all sections of the white electorate, English-speaking as well as Afrikaans. The economy boomed and quickly recovered from the financial crash in the aftermath of Sharpville. International capital was attracted back by exceptionally good rates of return on investment and by the promise of cheap and non-unionized African labour. Germany and France were particularly keen on grabbing a piece of the pie and began to invest heavily in South African industry for the first time. In response to this new investment the South African economy rapidly diversified and actively sought out new export markets. The South African government played an active role in the economic boom and channelled investment into state-run enterprises including, significantly, the arms industry. The National Party also set about promoting Afrikaners within the civil service and state-run industry. Over this period the economic divide between English and Afrikaans-speaking white South Africans significantly narrowed.

The economic divide between white and black, however, widened. Whilst wages in manufacturing for whites increased, Africans found theirs held down. With organized opposition smashed, the government set about fully implementing its Apartheid policies. Forced removals increased as the government set about dividing the country into clear white, Indian, coloured and African zones. The official policy was that all Africans should live within the homelands though the presence of large townships like Soweto made this policy look unlikely. Nevertheless, Africans living in cities such as Pretoria with homeland areas within daily commuting distance (in reality huge distances), found themselves removed to new townships within the homeland. On occasions the government also altered the borders of homelands so that townships on the outskirts of cities were absorbed into a new administrative structure. Forced removals and natural population growth meant that the populations of the homelands increased rapidly and though these areas were officially rural, their population densities were closer to urban areas.

Apart from the insidious change of name there were important differences between the previous reserve system and the homelands. The Apartheid government attempted to allocate each and every African to one of eight tribes and then allocated them to a homeland. This proved very difficult, partly because many Africans, especially those who were long-term residents in urban areas, did not identify themselves as belonging to a particular tribe and partly because, as the history of pre-colonial African groups discussed above indicates, tribal identity was often fluid and somewhat confused. Many people resisted attempts to define them as belonging to one of eight hard and fast categories and the government tacitly admitted this problem when it increased the number of possible tribes to which people could be allocated to 10.

Under the Apartheid system all Africans were supposed to express their political rights through the homeland administration. The government established totally separate bureaucracies in each homeland and then began a process of encouraging the areas to become increasingly autonomous. A number of African leaders saw that they could gain power and economic wealth through the new system and actively collaborated with the Apartheid state.

During the 1970s the South African government encouraged the homeland administrations to become independent states. They argued that this was a process that would allow Africans to enjoy full political rights in their own area. The first homeland to accept independence was Transkei in 1976 and over the next five years Ciskei, Bophuthatswana and Venda followed suit. Transkei was at least a more or less unified block of land with a long coastline, but the other three were divided into numerous small blocks totally surrounded by South Africa. Their independence was never recognized by any country other than the Republic of South Africa: and they even refused to recognize each other's independence. The borders of Bophuthatswana were so complicated that neither South Africa's nor the homeland government were ever quite sure exactly where they were. Indeed, just before independence the borders had to be altered when it was discovered that the South African embassy to Bophuthatswana was not actually inside the homeland. Though homeland independence was a farce it had great significance for the South Africans labelled as belonging to that particular tribe. They were now considered foreigners in the land of their birth.

The developing Apartheid programme had not just material effects on the African population but also psychological. In the late 1950s and early 1960s many African people felt that the overthrow of the racist white state was imminent. But the Apartheid state had managed to break African opposition and for almost a decade renewed resistance seemed impossible. The effects on many Africans' morale was not surprisingly extremely bad.

Union and student opposition In the early 1970s South Africa entered a new era of opposition to Apartheid, but this time not led by organized political groups such as the ANC and PAC but by the trade unions. During the 1960s there had been very little labour unrest; only about 2000 workers went on strike each year. Then in early 1973 there was suddenly a huge rise in strike activity and in the first three months of the year there were 160 strikes involving something like 61,000 workers. The epicentre for the strike activity was Durban but they quickly spread to other areas such as East London and then on to the Rand. These strikes were unusually successful in gaining the workers' demands; almost always this was for increased wages to reflect the recent sharp rises in the inflation rate. One reason they were surprisingly successful was that the workers refused to elect leaders to enter into negotiations with their employers; rather they simply published their demands and then went on strike for short periods, usually staying in the vicinity of the factory. This meant that the employers had no target on which to aim reprisals and the police could not be called in to arrest strike leaders.

The early 1970s also saw the rise of a more vocal African student protest movement. This was spearheaded by the **South Africa Students Organization** (SASO), which had broken away from the white-dominated National Union of South African Students in 1968, under the leadership of Steve Biko. SASO had a Black Consciousness ideology which stressed the need for all black people in South Africa, Africans, Indians and coloureds, to free themselves from the mental oppression that taught them white people were somehow innately superior to blacks. SASO took this message out into the country at large and played particular attention to spreading the ideology amongst school pupils.

With the example of the striking workers before them and a Black Consciousness message in their minds, school pupils began to rebel against an education system designed to make them fit only for unskilled and semi-skilled occupations. The immediate issue around which they organized their protest was the new rules enforcing the Afrikaans language as a medium of instruction. On the 16 June 1976 a Soweto school pupils' committee organized a mass march to deliver their complaints to the local authorities. This peaceful march was met with a violent response and the police shot two of the pupils. At first the pupils fled but then many turned and started throwing stones at the police. They then went on a rampage throughout the township destroying every symbol of their oppression that they could get to, including the government-run beer halls which many pupils felt bought off their fathers' opposition to state oppression with cheap beer. The **Soweto Uprising**, as the incident soon became known, marked an important turning point in the history of opposition to Apartheid: from 16 June 1976 onwards there was constant and violent unrest across South Africa, lead by school pupils but gaining widespread support.

Rioting erupted around the country when news of the Soweto Uprising spread. The government was hard pressed to stop the unrest spreading beyond the townships but in a nationwide clampdown they eventually managed to quieten some of the protest. The

SASO and school pupil leaders found themselves under arrest or harassed by the police. Many of the young people involved in the uprising escaped across the border.

ANC re-enters the scene Though the ANC had not been involved in the organization of the school pupils' protest, their underground cells, which had been carefully and quietly organizing in the early 1970s, it did help channel escaping pupils towards the guerrilla training camps they had set up in countries like Tanzania, Algeria and the newly independent Angola. The ANC benefited greatly from this new arrival of activists and managed effectively to amalgamate them into their organization. The ANC had made better use of their time in exile than the PAC, who suffered from poor organization and internal splits. Many of the pupils were ideologically closer to the PAC but they nevertheless ended up in ANC camps. In recent years these camps have been revealed to have often been pretty brutal places and people who disagreed with the camps' leaders were sometimes dealt with extremely harshly.

Despite the government crackdown, protests continued and a generalized culture of resistance was fostered. The ANC made use of this new climate of opposition to begin to reinfiltrate South Africa. In the late 1970s they began a new campaign of sabotage, but now there was less care to avoid civilian casualties and the ANC released a statement saying they were at war with the Apartheid state and, whilst their attacks were aimed at Apartheid and economic targets, they could not promise that civilians would not be caught up in the struggle. A number of Unkhonto cells seemed to ignore these commands and bombs were set off in shopping centres and similar locations.

The ANC quickly regained legitimacy amongst Africans, many of whom had been disillusioned with the organization during its long dormant period. Black Consciousness organizations, smashed apart by the police after the Soweto Uprising, lost support to the ANC, though it could be argued that the movement had achieved its aim of increasing African pride. In August 1983 there was a large gathering of 575 community, church and similar non-governmental organizations which resulted in the formation of the United Democratic Front (UDF), which spearheaded protest throughout the 1980s. The government argued that the organization was simply a front for the ANC. This was an exaggeration but it is true that the UDF did have strong links with the ANC and that they regarded it as the government in exile and the imprisoned Mandela as the legitimate president of the country.

'Total onslaught' and destabilization The Apartheid state was not only coming under attack from internal protest but from international criticism of the Pretoria regime. The ANC in exile had managed to foster anti-Apartheid groups in Europe and North America that began to put pressure on their governments to institute economic sanctions against South Africa. Most Commonwealth governments supported these sanctions and also instituted sporting and cultural sanctions on South Africa. The anti-Apartheid movement also started campaigns detailing the working conditions inside branches of multi-national companies in South Africa and asking individuals to boycott companies with large investments in South Africa. Despite the resistance of Margaret Thatcher and Ronald Reagan, during the 1980s these campaigns began to take effect and a number of important companies withdrew from South Africa.

This international isolation of Pretoria added to their gradual geopolitical isolation in southern Africa during the 1970s. Up until the mid-1970s South Africa had been surrounded either by states run by white settler régimes or by small states that rarely criticized their actions. However, independence for Angola and Mozambique in 1976 and Zimbabwe in 1980 changed all that. Now South Africa had hostile, left-wing neighbours right on its doorstep, and even the previously compliant weaker states, such as Lesotho, began actively to oppose the Apartheid state. White South Africa felt increasingly vulnerable and the government argued that they were now facing a 'total onslaught' led by communists that were intent on bringing them down.

The Apartheid government reacted to this 'total onslaught' with a careful mixture of economic, diplomatic and military foreign policy designed to neutralize the threat. The exact mix of the different elements varied in each country and over time. In Angola, for example, intervention was in the form of a direct military invasion designed to overthrow the communist government. When the invasion faltered they concentrated on supplying an armed opposition movement and therefore helped to fuel a bloody civil war that has gone on more or less ever since. In Mozambique they also intervened militarily, but this time through another opposition organization that had originally been set up by Ian Smith's settler régime in Rhodesia/Zimbabwe. They encouraged their clients in Mozambique to blow up railways and pipelines running from Zimbabwe to their nearest ports. With these out of action, Zimbabwe and other landlocked central African states were forced to continue trading with South Africa in order to get access to the sea. This, in turn, gave the South Africans an important economic hold over the countries to the north.

Across the region South African guerrilla troops carried out occasional raids designed both to knock out ANC camps and to keep their neighbours in political and economic turmoil and therefore as less effective opponents. South Africa's proxy war with the rest of the region caused a huge amount of suffering to very many people, especially in Mozambique and Angola. Though these states did receive some international support the international media tended to concentrate more on events unfurling in the South African townships than on these regional events.

Reform or revolution?

In the mid-1980s South Africa's townships, simmering since the Soweto Uprising, exploded into violence. The primary target of the violence were Africans who had taken jobs as administrators in the 'homelands' or townships and African policemen. Many had their families killed and their houses burnt down and a new and horrendous form of execution was invented, called 'necklacing'. This involved placing a car tyre full of petrol over the victim's torso and then setting fire to it. The police reacted violently to unrest in the townships and shot, arrested and beat many protesters. Bus boycotts, strikes and 'stay aways', were frequent and often met with violence by the police.

Violence became endemic to the townships and there was a fine line between political violence and general crime. Many of the young ANC supporting comrades decided that they should take the law into their own hands and kangaroo courts were frequent occurrences. Older Africans sometimes found it hard to take orders from the youngsters and inter-generational battles broke out on a number of occasions, most violently at Crossroads squatter camp on the outskirts of Cape Town. The violence was fanned by massive new flows of illegal migrants into the towns. The government was unable to cope with the new influx of people and eventually was forced into the withdrawal of the hated pass laws. The growth of squatter camps was spectacular and no sooner had the government removed squatters from one site than they appeared somewhere else. During the 1970s wage increases in established industry had been generous, partly reflecting the move towards a more capital intensive economy and partly a result of the strikes. The downside of this was massive and endemic unemployment, especially among the young. A whole generation of young people missed all their formal education because of their involvement in 'the struggle' and their chances of employment were extremely remote. Inevitably this fuelled the violence and crime.

The worst violence took place in the townships surrounding Pietermaritzburg and Durban. These areas were within the KwaZulu 'homeland' run by Gatsha Buthelezi. Originally Buthelezi had been an ANC supporter and had even received the organization's (reserved) blessing in the establishment of a Zulu cultural organization called Inkatha. The organization, however, began to act much more like a political party and ran the KwaZulu 'homeland' administration. When ANC supporters began to challenge the 'homelands' authority this lead to violent clashes as the two organizations vied for control of the townships. This conflict has continued until the present and has involved numerous atrocities committed by both sides.

By the late 1980s the South African state had more or less lost control of large portions of the townships. The unrest and international sanctions were hitting the economy hard and South African businesses were feeling the pinch. While the state security apparatus was strengthened and numerous crackdowns were attempted, the government, fearing revolution, also undertook a programme of reform.

To some extent this programme had begun in the 1970s but it was accelerated in the early 1980s under the presidency of **PW Botha**. One strand of the reform process was to pull coloureds and Indians into the political process under a new tri-cameral parliament. Under a new constitution there were to be three houses in the parliament, one for white voters, one for coloureds and one for Indians. Most coloureds and Indians saw this move as an attempt to drive a wedge between them and the African population and refused to vote for the new parliament. The National Party's reform policy also lead to a new split in Afrikaner ranks and the creation of a new, more right-wing, Conservative Party. Over the 1980s the new Party was to attract more and more Afrikaner support and the National Party became increasingly reliant upon English-speaking supporters.

Botha also set about dismantling some of the segregationist policies, in particular the 'petty Apartheid' legislation that divided up facilities such as beaches. These did very little to assuage the unrest in the townships and were probably more to do with creating an international impression of reform to hold off further sanctions. Under these circumstances the National Party began to do the unthinkable and sat down to negotiate with the ANC. Business leaders were the first South African establishment figures to talk with the ANC in exile, in September 1985. With sanctions and unrest big business was being squeezed hard and Apartheid was no longer making them good profits as it had in the 1960s. The business leaders were therefore keen for a political settlement, but were obviously nervous about the intentions of an ANC strongly influenced by communist ideology. South African ministers and eventually Botha himself met with Mandela, offering him his freedom if he repudiated the use of violence as a weapon in the fight against Apartheid. Mandela refused the offer and for a time it seemed further reform was impossible.

The late 1980s, however, saw a crucial shift in the global political scene that opened up an important window to allow a negotiated settlement. The unexpected collapse of the Soviet block suddenly made Botha's image of a 'total onslaught' seem meaningless and the ANC was no longer seen by whites as a front for Soviet-backed communist expansion into South Africa. These changes coincided with a change in leadership of the National Party and the replacement of Botha with **FW de Klerk**. Even though de Klerk had been regarded as a conservative he soon made it clear he was embarking on a bold new policy. The ANC was unbanned, Mandela and other political leaders were released and the process of negotiating a settlement got underway.

Lesotho

As the history of Lesotho is so tied up in that of South Africa, you should also refer to pages 842-865.

The rise of the Basotho state

The roots of modern-day Lesotho were in an era of intense political upheaval known to the Basotho as the *difaqane* (and the Zulu and Xhosa as the *mfecane*). The exact causes of the *difaqane* are a subject of considerable debate (see page 849) but what is clear is that out of this intense upheaval a new and powerful Basotho state was forged under the influential ruler Moshoeshoe. Before this time there had not been such a thing as a Basotho state, but simply a set of clans speaking similar dialects and with similar cultural practices. These clans formed constantly shifting sets of loose alliances and rivalries and their fortunes tended to wax and wane over time.

During the early 19th century these clans came under attack from highly organized and militarily ruthless Zulu and Ndebele armies (*impis*). Instead of uniting against these new enemies most clans ended up attacking their neighbours in an attempt to raid back cattle and grain lost to the *impis*. Moshoeshoe, chief of the insignificant Koena clan, however, had a more sophisticated approach. He carefully sued for peace with all the more powerful clans or marauding *impis* with whom he came into contact and would send them tribute gifts of cattle. At the same time he attacked and stole the cattle of weaker clans and then invited them to join with him in a new alliance. Using this strategy, Moshoeshoe was able to build up the power and influence of the Koena clan, especially after moving his headquarters to the strong defensive position at Thaba Boisiu. Soon his influence spread over the whole of the southern Highveld with his chiefdom centred on the fertile Clarendon Valley. Unlike Shaka and Dingane, kings of the Zulu, Moshoeshoe did not insist that all his followers give up their previous clan identity and indeed his new Basotho state was more an alliance of a number of different clans than a united and centralized kingdom.

Wars with the Free State

During the 1830s, two new forces entered into the Basotho sphere from the south and west: Voortrekkers leaving the Cape Colony in search of new territory (see page 849); and missionaries looking for converts. These groups offered both threats and opportunities for the new Basotho state. The first missionaries to arrive in Lesotho were French Protestants. Moshoeshoe was keen to have them in Lesotho, partially because he wanted to learn more about the powerful Europeans impinging more and more on his state and partially to help him gain access to European guns. Their presence also presented a threat, however, as the converts' loyalty could sometimes be divided.

A more obvious threat came from the Voortrekkers. They wanted land and, unlike other new African arrivals, were unwilling to show allegiance to a Basotho state. With their guns and wagons they were a powerful military force and over the next 30 years slowly gained more and more control over areas formerly belonging to the Basotho. By the end of the 1860s the Basotho had lost half of their best arable land in the Clarendon Valley to the new Voortrekker Free State republic. But despite this major setback the Voortrekkers also provided the Basotho with an opportunity. Most were unable or unwilling to survive by farming, instead relying on hunting, trading and land speculating as their economic mainstay. They, therefore, had to buy food, especially grain, and the

Chief Moshoeshoe and Thaba Bosiu

Chief Moshoeshoe, often regarded as the founder of the Basotho nation, was born in about 1786 at Menkhoaneng in the north of present-day Lesotho. Though he was later to become one of the most powerful chiefs in southern Africa, he was by birth no more than a village headman. According to oral tradition, however, even as a young man he had dreams of becoming a great chief. Fearing that his short temper and over-weening ambition would lead him into trouble, Moshoeshoe's father sent him for instruction from the famous chief Mohlomi. Mohlomi impressed on the young Moshoeshoe the need for a ruler to gain loyalty from his followers not just through violence but by ensuring they were materially reliant upon his protection.

Moshoeshoe learnt his lessons well and realized that control of large numbers of cattle was the key to political power. With many cattle he could afford the brideprice needed to marry many wives (eventually over 40) and therefore bind other lineages and clans to his own, and by lending some of his cattle to his supporters he was able to make them materially reliant upon his power. So Moshoeshoe set about building up his herds by both careful management and raiding his neighbours. His reputation soon grew and with his followers he broke away from his previous clan to establish a new chieftainship on Butha-Buthe.

Through a careful strategic balance of making alliances with stronger chiefs and attacking weaker ones (and raiding their cattle), Moshoeshoe soon built up his power base. He never went into any battle he could risk losing and often managed to buy off enemies with gifts of cattle – sometimes raiding the same herds back if his rival fell upon hard times. Nevertheless the interior of South Africa in the early 19th century was a violent and complex political world and Moshoeshoe came under increasing military pressure from nearby chiefs. Realizing Butha-Buthe was not easy to defend Moshoeshoe sent out his brother to find a new stronghold. He returned with news of a larger flat-topped mountain with plenty of water resources two days' journey to the south.

In June 1824 Moshoeshoe and his followers set off on the dangerous trek to their new headquarters. Despite coming under attack during the move and losing Moshoeshoe's grandfather to a band of cannibals, he and his followers managed to secure themselves in their new stronghold. From this new position Moshoeshoe was able to extend his power and controlled the whole of the Clarendon Valley and a large number of followers.

Later in his reign he came under intense pressure from the new Boer republics and lost much of his kingdom, eventually turning to the British for protection. Nevertheless, this remarkable leader had managed to build a powerful and unified kingdom during a time of intense strife and continual conflict out of an initial handful of followers. He died at Thaba Bosiu in 1870.

Basotho were able to provide them with it. Using new techniques, often learnt from the missionaries, and the new grain crop maize, brought by Europeans from the Americas, the Basotho developed a thriving agricultural economy. They soon began to trade not just with the Voortrekkers but also further afield, especially with the eastern districts of the Cape Colony. In exchange for grain the Basotho bought new European goods, especially guns.

Moshoeshoe realized, however, that their booming economy did not make them immune to attack from the Free State and he decided to turn to the British for help. At first the British refused to become involved but over time they began to realize that it was in their interests to have peace between the Boers and Basotho. In 1868, with Voortrekker commandos laying siege to Thaba Bosiu and burning acres of the Basotho's maize, the British declared Lesotho a British Protectorate. At a peace convention the following year the boundaries of Lesotho, or 'Basutoland' as the British named the area, were firmly established. The Basotho had lost huge swathes of their territory to the Free State but British protection did allow them to maintain a degree of political independence. This was more or less the last big political manoeuvre by Moshoeshoe, who died just two years later.

British Protection and the Gun War

At first the sole concern of the British was to maintain peace along the new boundaries, but that changed when administration was handed over from direct British rule to rule by the Cape Colony. The Cape Colony began to intervene in a more direct way in the government of the country. Chiefs found their powers reduced and everybody found themselves subject to a new hut tax. Not surprisingly, many Basotho were unhappy about these new arrangements. There were also tensions between the new Paramount Chief Letsie and his two brothers and also between the main Koena lineage and other clans who had been integrated into the Basotho state. One of these clans, the Phuti in southern Lesotho, refused to recognize the authority of the local Cape magistrate. When the magistrate tried to arrest the son of the Phuti's chief, Moorosi, open conflict broke out. To the disgust of many Basotho, Letsie sided with the Cape Colony and assisted in putting down the rebellion. In November 1879 after months of fighting the Cape forces finally stormed Moorosi's stronghold, slaughtering him and many of his people.

The following year there was another, more serious, outbreak of fighting. The immediate cause was the attempts by the Cape Colony to enforce a general policy of disarming all Basotho. For most Basotho, already unhappy about the way they were being administered and worried about rumours that the south of the country would be opened to white settlement, this was too much. The so-called Gun War of 1880-1881 saw the Cape forces verging on the brink of outright defeat and there were numerous bloody battles. Not all chiefs agreed with the war, however, and Letsie himself never publicly supported the attacks on the Cape authorities. Fighting broke out, especially in the north, between elements in favour of the war and those against it. Peace only returned when the British agreed to suspend the policy of enforced disarmament and agree that administration should be taken away from the Cape Colony and returned to rule from London.

Colonial era

The return to British rule also saw a return to the much less interventionist policy, and the country was basically administered through the chiefs, not white magistrates. The British continued with the policy right through until the 1930s and there were few significant political developments. Economically and socially, however, the country changed drastically. The early years of British rule saw the agricultural economy continue to thrive, especially as the new diamond mines at Kimberley gave the Basotho a new and profitable market to serve. Over time, however, these markets became less and less lucrative. The arrival of railways meant that Basotho farmers had to compete with cheap imported grain from places like the USA and Canada. And as time went on, white farmers were also providing more and more competition, especially after they began to receive vast quantities of state subsidies and other assistance. The agricultural economy began to falter and during the first decades of the 20th century the country no longer managed to produce enough food for export and indeed became a major importer. Part of the problem was also the migrant labour system that the Basotho found themselves tied into. Basotho men began to travel to the mines to earn wages to buy European goods and to pay taxes, but as the agricultural economy faltered it became more important for simple survival. This created a vicious cycle, as more Basotho men went to the mines there were fewer of them to help their wives with agriculture which, as a consequence, became less productive.

The early decades of the 20th century also saw the growth of a small but important educated class within Lesotho. They resented the continued political power of the chiefs and, through their Progressive Association, lobbied the British to introduce a more democratic system of administration. Another more radical political organization also began to make a mark. Known as *Lekhotla la Bafo* (Council of Commoners) this group was highly critical of both the British and of the chiefs, who they claimed were corrupt, and conniving with the British to impoverish the Basotho nation. While criticizing the chiefs for their individual actions they strongly supported the institution of chieftainship and advocated a return to pre-colonial systems of government.

One of the key reasons the British never bothered to intervene (and certainly not invest any money) in Lesotho was their belief that the country would at some stage be incorporated into the rest of South Africa. Over time, however, this eventuality became less and less likely, especially with the enactment of increasingly racist segregation legislation in South Africa. The British colonial authorities realized that transferring the country's administration to South Africa would not only encounter stiff opposition in Lesotho but also from the increasing number of people in Britain criticizing the South African government. From the mid-1930s and especially after 1945 the British colonial authorities, therefore, began to take a more active interest in the internal affairs of Lesotho, and even began to invest some capital into development schemes for the country.

The Progressive Association lobbied the British hard for the introduction of a more democratic government, believing that they, the educated elite, should be the country's natural leaders not the chiefs. Starting in the late 1930s, the British started to reform the system of government. These reforms at first had the effect of increasing the power of a few of the most important chiefs, to the detriment of some of the less important ones. This was one of the major causes of an outbreak of 'medicine murders' in which people were killed in order to use parts of their bodies in 'medicines' believed to bring power or protection. A number of the most important chiefs were implicated in these murders, which were seen by many as further proof that the chiefs were incapable of running the country. From the mid-1950s onwards new reforms led to a decrease in all chiefs' political powers and the gradual handing over of the national administration to the developing political parties.

The first of these new political parties was the Basutoland Congress Party (BCP). The BCP had many of its roots in the *Lekhotla la Bafo* organization and strong links with the ANC in South Africa, especially with the 'Africanist' wing of the ANC who later split to form the PAC (see pages 859 and 872). Not unlike *Lekhotla la Bafo*, which withered away as the BCP grew, the BCP did not call for a return to 'traditional' Basotho political systems but for a new democratic and independent nation. One of the key elements of its platform was strong criticism of the racist South African regime. This stance was opposed by some more conservative elements within the organization and they split to form a rival Basutoland National Party (BNP). The BNP was more traditional in outlook and received substantial support from the Catholic Church. The first elections in the country were held in 1960 to elect members to District Councils who then sent representatives to the National Council. These elections returned BCP candidates around the country, but the turnout was extremely low and women had still not been granted suffrage.

The British colonial authorities entered into wide-ranging discussions with the members of the National Council about writing a new national constitution under which the country would be granted its independence. After numerous wranglings a new constitution, based on the Westminster model, was produced. There would be a directly elected lower house from which the prime minister and cabinet would be chosen and an appointed upper house (Senate) consisting of the most important chiefs. The Senate's powers were limited to delaying legislation. Much to the dismay of the new and young incumbent, Moshoeshoe II, the monarch was to be no more than a ceremonial Head of State. Under this new constitutional framework elections were held in 1965 to form the government to take Lesotho to independence. To the surprise of many these were won by a tiny majority by the BNP. Their leader, Leabua Jonathan, therefore became the country's first Prime Minister and on 4 October 1966 Lesotho became an independent country.

Independence

Most Basotho had high expectations for this new system of government; expectation which the BNP proved incapable of fulfilling. The civil service was dominated by BCP members and the BNP was unwilling to work with them and instead relied on many expatriate workers, including a number from South Africa. The BNP's inability to deliver once in power helped the BCP regroup and in the 1970 elections they won a clear majority, maintaining their urban powerbase and managing to gain widespread support in the mountains as well. To the surprise of just about everyone Leabua Jonathan refused to hand over power, declared a state of emergency and arrested hundreds of BCP supporters. At first it looked as if he would have to come to an agreement with the BCP especially when Britain suspended all aid to Lesotho but as the crisis dragged on and Britain and other countries resumed their aid programmes the BNP's position became stronger.

Under pressure from Britain the BCP split, with some moderates entering into a new national assembly appointed by Jonathan to write a new constitution and others turning to more radical methods. An attempted counter-coup by elements of the BCP in January 1974 was a fiasco and the BNP tightened their grip on power. BCP civil servants were purged and activists arrested or sent into exile. Jonathan concentrated more and more power into his hands and developed many of the state security policies of other dictators. His attitude towards South Africa, however, shifted somewhat unexpectedly. From having been an advocate of close and cordial relations with the Apartheid regime he began to be more and more outspoken in his opposition. He developed close links with the ANC, who were offered support within Lesotho. This stance in turn brought him into confrontation with South Africa and led to attempts by South Africa to destabilize his regime. On the other hand the changed stance gave him increased legitimacy in the eyes of the international community and the government benefited from a generous influx of development aid.

The BCP, meanwhile, tried to build on its links with the PAC and some of their members received guerrilla training at camps in Libya. Elements within the South African security apparatus actively courted members of the BCP and offered them assistance in their attempts to wage a guerrilla war against Jonathan's regime. Some BCP members seemed willing to drink from this poison chalice and during much of the 1980s the country suffered a very low-level guerrilla war. Some members of the military were very unhappy with the situation and in 1986 the South Africans managed to toppled Jonathan's government.

At first the new government was a coalition between the military and Moshoeshoe II. Though they promised to hold new elections, things moved very slowly and if anything the new regime was more corrupt than the previous one. Relations soon broke down between the military and Moshoeshoe II, who went into exile. In the early 1990s the military government began to make arrangements for new elections, with the process being spurred on by outbreaks of rioting and by the negotiation process across the border in South Africa. These long-awaited elections finally took place in March 1993 and the BCP won a huge majority and every single seat in the national Parliament. Twenty-three years after being denied his position the leader of the BCP, Ntsu Mokhehle, at last became Prime Minister.

Swaziland

The precolonial history of Swaziland started with the Dlamini clan in the late 16th century when they migrated south settling in the region around what is now Delagoa Bay. Around two centuries later, in 1750, Ngwane III migrated to what is now Swaziland. The land was a well-watered mountain area with fertile soils and good pastures for raising cattle. The mountainous territory also offered good protection from Zulu raids.

By the 19th century, Swaziland had become a major power in the region controlling a much larger area than it does today. Europeans arrived in 1836, and called the place Swaziland after the leader at the time Mswasi II. After gold was discovered at Pigg's Peak and Forbes' Reef, large numbers foreigners were attracted to the area and pressure for land concessions increased. The 'concession rush' occurred during the reign of Mbandeni when speculators believed there was about to be a great boom in Swaziland. Five hundred concessions were eventually granted on which the king received a payment. When the gold rush ended without any great results most of the concessionaires left the country.

The Transvaal administered Swaziland from 1894 to 1903. After the Anglo Boer War the British took control of the country leaving the traditional forms of government in the hands of the royal family. One of the major problems was that most of the land had been granted to foreigners in concessions. The Swazis believed that the concessions were only temporary but a government commission recognized the concessions as valid as long as the rents continued to be paid. In 1907 a third of the land under concession was expropriated to give the Swazis somewhere to live. Sobhuza II, the grandson of Mbandeni, became king in 1921 and spent his resources on regaining the land for the Swazi nation. Over 60% of the land has now been bought back from the concession holders.

Political activity in modern Swaziland began in the 1960s with the formation of the Swaziland Progressive Party by younger educated Swazis. The party later split into three factions of which the Ngwane National Liberatory Congress (NNLC) became the most influential. Swazi royalists formed the Imbokodvo National Movement in 1964. They formed an alliance with the European Advisory Council which had been established to look after the interests of European farmers and miners. The elections held before independence in 1964 were won by Imbokodvo who controlled all the seats.

Modern southern Africa

South Africa

Politics

Constitution South Africa's first democratic constitution was passed by the Constitutional Assembly in May 1996, the 1994 elections being held under an interim version. After ratification by the Supreme Court most of it passed into law, while some elements were returned to the Constitutional Assembly for reconsideration. The Constitutional Assembly is made up of both Houses of Parliament sitting together and constitutional provision needs to be passed by a two-thirds majority. The bi-cameral Parliament consists of a directly elected lower house (the National Assembly) and an upper house (the Senate) appointed by provincial assemblies. The National Assembly is elected via a system of proportional representation. The President is elected by members of the National Assembly and chooses his cabinet from those members.

Parliament sits in Cape Town and government ministries are in Pretoria. This geographical division dates from the Act of Union in 1910 as a way of balancing power between the two former British colonies and the two former Boer republics. Significant powers are devolved to the nine provincial administrations. Provincial assemblies are also elected via proportional representation and in turn they elect members to the Senate who are specifically charged with looking after provincial interests against the power of central Government.

Provincial governments have significant scope over things such as regional planning, investment policies, social services and education. Provincial leaders are, therefore, powerful political figures and a number of politicians of national standing have decided to serve as provincial representatives rather than seek election to Parliament.

1994 elections

The African National Congress (ANC), together with its alliance partners, the South African Communist Party (SACP) and the Congress of South African Trade Unions (Cosatu) won the national vote in South Africa's first democratic elections in April 1994 by a huge majority. They gained 63% of the total vote giving them 252 seats in the National Assembly. The only other parties to win significant numbers of votes were the National Party (NP) (20.5%) and Inkharta Freedom Party (IFP) (10.8%). The ANC's victory was based upon widespread support from the majority African population throughout the country. The only area in which its support amongst Africans was threatened was in KwaZulu Natal where the IFP received significant support from rural Zulu speakers. The IFP were unable to convert their popularity in their political heartland to any other parts of the country. The NP received widespread support from the white population and, more surprisingly, from a majority of coloured voters in the Western Cape.

Four other parties managed to secure seats, though with tiny proportions of the total vote. The Freedom Front (FF), an alliance of right-wing Afrikaner Nationalists, won nine seats with a 2.3% share of the vote, coming mainly from working-class Afrikaners fearful of the new political dispensation. The Democratic Party (DP), traditionally the party of liberal English-speaking white South Africans, were unable to expand their attraction and won a paltry 1.7% of the vote. The Pan African Congress (PAC) fared particularly badly; an organization which in the 1950s had seriously challenged the ANC's position as the most popular political organization amongst the African population received only 1.2% of the national vote, giving them just five seats. The remaining two seats were won by a newly formed political organization called the African Christian Democratic Party (ACDP) which called for the enactment of policies in line with the gospels.

In line with the interim Constitution, the leader of the ANC, Nelson Mandela, was duly elected President and set about choosing his cabinet. The constitution stated that any party who gained more than 20% of the vote was eligible to have its leader instated as a Deputy President. Mandela, therefore had two deputy presidents, Thabo Mbeki from the ANC and FW de Klerk, the leader of the NP. The selection of Thabo Mbeki as Deputy President effectively marked him as Mandela's likely successor. All other parties were invited to join the ANC in a Government of National Unity (GNU). Despite the continued antagonism between the ANC and IFP, Mongosuthu Buthelezi was given the important post of Minister of Home Affairs. A number of cabinet posts were also filled by delegates from the NP. The only party to stay out of the GNU were the DP who felt they could have more of an impact as the official opposition.

The elections for provincial assemblies resulted in the ANC winning control of seven out of the nine provinces. In a number of provinces they won huge majorities: 80% of the vote in the Free State, 83% in Mpumalanga, 85% in the Eastern Cape, 87% in North West Province, and a staggering 95% in Northern Province. Though many of these areas are associated with hardline Afrikaner nationalism it has to be born in mind that the vast majority of the population in these areas are poor, rural Africans who solidly support the ANC.

In the more populous provinces of Gauteng and KwaZulu Natal, the ANC fared less well. In KwaZulu Natal the ANC were beaten into second place by the IFP who won just over half of the votes. In Gauteng the ANC still won an impressive overall majority of 58%, but they lost seats to the NP (24%) who gained the support of the urban middle-class whites and to smaller parties such as the FF and DP. Three seats in Gauteng also went to the IFP: their only seats outside KwaZulu Natal.

In the Western and Northern Cape the NP did better than many people had expected. Their 40% in the Northern Cape was still substantially behind the ANC's 50% but in the Western Cape they managed to gain 55% to the ANC's 33%. In both these provinces the NP vote was based upon widespread support amongst coloured voters who feared an ANC government would put the interests of Africans ahead of their own. The irony of the only NP election victory being built on the back of coloured voters is quintessentially South African.

Politics since the 1994 election

The GNU's first task was to set about ratifying the interim constitution. Debate on some issues was intense. Labour rights proved to be a bone of contention between the NP and ANC while the ANC and IFP frequently clashed over the division of power between central government and the provinces. Despite their official position as part of the GNU and Buthelezi's cabinet seat the IFP boycotted much of the debate on the constitution on the grounds that the ANC had gone back on a pre-election promise to allow international mediation on the issue of KwaZulu Natal ceding from the rest of the country. Nevertheless by May 1996 all the clauses of the new constitution had been agreed and the Constitutional Assembly voted to ratify the new constitution. With the new constitution in place, De Klerk announced his retirement from politics and the NP ministers selected in 1994 left the cabinet in June 1996 and were replaced by members of the ANC. No new Deputy President was selected; effectively increasing the power of Thabo Mbeki. The IFP remained within the GNU.

In the aftermath of the election the most pressing political problem was the continuation of violence in KwaZulu Natal between supporters of the ANC and supporters of the IFP. Unprovoked attacks, revenge killings and political intrigue all continued to haunt the townships and villages of the province. Peace talks between the leaderships of the provincial parties and high-level discussions between Mandela and Buthelezi were frequently called off and when they did take place made no impact on the rate of violence. Local elections for new unitary local government structures took place throughout the country in mid-1995 but were frequently delayed in KwaZulu Natal because of the violence and allegations over fraudulent electoral rolls. The elections did eventually take place, about one year after the rest of the country and marked the beginnings of the end violence in the province.

Mandela commanded huge popular support amongst the African population and won the backing of many of South Africa's white population as well. Mbeki lacked the same mass popularity, but was seen as having aa good grasp of the major issues and was credited with being a key player in bringing peace to KwaZulu Natal. Mandela's punishing international schedule meant that Mbeki was left with many of the domestic political chores, especially dealing with the ANC's internal problems. His position as Mandela's successor left him vulnerable to accusations of manipulating internal ANC politics to strengthen his position over some of his colleagues. This was particularly the case with the easing out of Cyril Ramaphosa, who had led the ANC negotiating team during initial negotiations with the NP. Prior to the election he was seen by many as Mandela's likely successor and his decision to leave politics and join a commercial company was seen as evidence that his leadership ambitions had been frustrated.

The ANC had its fair share of internal wranglings. In 1995 the most serious of these was over the role of Winnie Mandela (or since her divorce, Winnie Madikizela-Mandela). In mid-1995, she experienced a spectacular fall from grace. She was sacked from her cabinet position in 1995, and was divorced by Nelson Mandela the following year. She faced a series of charges and convictions, including for her role in the kidnapping and murder of a 14-year-old anti-Apartheid activist; she received a six-year prison sentence, which was reduced to a fine. Later, in 2003 she was found guilty of 43 counts of fraud and 25 of theft. Although she again managed to walk away from a prison sentence, she resigned from her positions as a Member of Parliament and President of the ANC Women's League.

The NP had very little success in repositioning itself as a non-racial centrist party. In the late 1990s, its efforts to change its image were not helped by the continual unearthing of more and more horror stories from the Apartheid years. Particularly damaging to the NP were the stories about covert actions taking place right up to the evening of the 1994 elections, a time when the party had supposedly thrown off its old ways and embraced democracy. The Steyn Report into the actions of the Third Force included many disturbing allegations, including reports that SADF operatives initiated the spate of train massacres that took place on the Witwatersrand in the run up to the 1994 election. Other allegations in the report included reports that the SADF used chemical bombs against Frelimo troops in Mozambique in the late 1980s and that they stockpiled weapons in game reserves in countries as far away as Kenya. In 1997, the NP renamed itself the New National Party; a move perhaps to distance itself from the past, and merged with the Democratic Party (DP). However, by 2000 members of the former National Party had broken away from the alliance and the remaining members of the alliance became the Democratic Alliance (DA) and were the official opposition in parliament. The NP had effectively disintegrated; officially-so in 2005 when its federal council dissolved the party.

Other reports of atrocities during Apartheid came out of the hearings of the Truth and Reconciliation Commission (TRC) chaired by Desmond Tutu. This was a court-like body which invited anyone who felt that they were a victim of Apartheid's violence to come forward and be heard. Perpetrators of violence could also give testimony and request amnesty from prosecution. The TRC was set up in terms of the Promotion of National Unity and Reconciliation Act, passed in 1995, and brought forth many witnesses giving testimony about the secret and immoral acts committed by both the Apartheid government, and the liberation groups including the armed wing of the ANC. In late 1998, the commission presented its final report, which condemned both sides for committing human rights abuses.

In June 1999 Nelson Mandela passed the mantle of power as president of the ANC over to his long time deputy Thabo Mbeki. In the national elections the ANC won a large victory despite a widespread feeling that they had still to deliver on promises they made when they first came to power in 1994; particularly on service delivery – housing and basic amenities – which remains a contentious issue to this day. Nevertheless, the elections were seen as a great triumph for the country on a continent which has so rarely witnessed fair and peaceful democratic elections, and Mbeki became the second democratically elected (black) president.

However, Mbeki was always going to find Mandela a hard act to follow. Although he surrounded himself with a cabinet of loyal supporters, he was generally regarded as an efficient if not dynamic party leader.

Perhaps his greatest success was pushing South Africa to expand its scope of activity in regional and international affairs. Infused with a vision for an African Renaissance, during his term, South Africa was a driving force behind restructuring the Southern African Development Community (SADC), the establishment of the new African Union, and developed the New Partnership for Africa's Development (Nepad). In the last decade, South Africa has also been involved in efforts to solve a number of conflicts and political crises on the continent, such as the long-running war in the DRC and instability in Burundi. However, South Africa also courted controversy by declaring the contentious 2002 Zimbabwean elections free and fair, but Mbeki ultimately decided, along with the leaders of Australia and Nigeria, to recommend Zimbabwe's suspension from the Commonwealth. Nevertheless, the government's continued refusal to openly criticize Robert Mugabe's regime – preferring instead to stick to 'quiet diplomacy' – has attracted condemnation.

Mbeki's views on AIDS cast a shadow over the first four years of his presidency. Going against the weight of medical opinion, he questioned the link between HIV and AIDS, and the effectiveness of anti-retroviral drugs. The Department of Health's refusal to provide anti-AIDS drugs to pregnant women and rape survivors angered AIDS activists and drew widespread criticism of the government. However, the Treatment Action Campaign won a High Court case against the Department of Health in 2001, forcing it to provide the anti-retroviral drug Nevirapine to all HIV-positive pregnant women. In November 2003, the cabinet voted to provide anti-retroviral drug across the board.

The 1999 election was again won by the ANC who received 66.3% of the vote. It did not dramatically alter South Africa's political landscape, except for some growth in support for the Democratic Party (DP); later to become the Democratic Alliance (DA) in 2000, which got 9.6% of the vote. The DP's line on crime and tough talk from its leader, Tony Leon, won it a substantial proportion of the white vote.

In April 2004 the ANC, won again with 69.7% of votes. However, the turn out for this election was remarkably low; just 54% of eligible voters, which was in part due to the national campaign of 'No Land! No House! No Vote!', which again was a protest to the government about lack of promised service providing since 1994. The DA again won 9.6% of the vote and retained its position in parliament as the opposition. The DA's strength has always been in the Western Cape, and in 2006, the outspoken and much-admired Helen Zille took over from Tony Leon as head of the party and was Mayor of Cape Town from 2006 to 2009; the accolade won her the title of World Mayor of the Year in 2008 for her aggressive policies against crime, drug abuse, unemployment and homelessness in Cape Town. Zille is a former journalist who famously exposed the truth about Steve Biko's death in police detention in the 1970s.

A member of the ANC since 1959, and part of its armed struggle in the early years of resistance to Apartheid, (which earned him a 10-year spell in prison on Robben Island), Jacob Zuma was elected deputy president to Mbeki in 1999 and again in 2004, so for two terms was groomed as Mbeki's successor. However, his political career stumbled on a glitch in 2005, when Mbeki sacked him because of corruption allegations over a US$5 billion arms deal in 1999. Later in 2005, he was formerly charged with corruption by the National Prosecuting Authority (in 2005 he was also charged with rape, which was later dismissed in court in 2006). After a lengthy and controversial legal battle, all charges of corruption were officially dropped in 2008, and the National Prosecuting Authority cited unlawful procedural grounds for their decision. The DA (namely Helen Zille) reacted very strongly but the decision was upheld. Despite these political and legal wranglings, Zuma was elected president of the ANC in 2007.

Just days after Zuma's trial, in September 2008, Mbeki announced his resignation after being recalled by the ANC's National Executive Committee. This followed a conclusion by a judge of his improper interference in the National Prosecuting Authority and allusions were made in the ruling to possible political interference by Mbeki and others in Zuma's prosecution. He was replaced by 'caretaker' president Kgalema Motlanthe, who headed the state until the 2009 elections. Mbeki immediately dissociated himself from politics after his abrupt and forced resignation, though he reacted strongly when Zuma publically announced that he required Mbeki to campaign for the ANC in the 2009 elections, which he refused to do. Whether Mbeki voted for the ANC or not in 2009, remains his secret.

On 6 May 2009, South Africans went to the polls. For the first time South Africans living abroad were permitted to vote, as well as those in the country that were outside their official constituency. The turnout at 76% was much higher than 2004, and about 2.5 million more people voted. The election was contested by the ANC, DA, The Congress of the People (COPE), a new party formed by breakaway members of the ANC in 2008 after Mbeki's dismissal, and a number of smaller parties. The ANC, headed by Zuma, won with a 69.69% majority (just 0.01% shy of a 70% win, which would have allowed the ANC to change anything they wanted to in the constitution – rumours were to dissolve the DA dominant Western Cape Provincial Parliament). After a vigorous campaign headed by Zille, the DA increased its position with 20 more seats in parliament and took 13.6% of the overall vote, reconsolidating its position as the opposition. In the Western Cape, however, the DA beat the ANC and took 51.2% of the vote, which instated Zille as Premier of the Western Cape, and has put her in a powerful position as leader of the opposition.

It's early days for the Zuma-led government, but like the previous post-1994 governments the main focus, and an issue that has been promised in every political campaign for the ANC, is service providing. Since the demise of Apartheid, South Africans have wanted to see their votes turned into houses, jobs, amenities, education and health care.

Economy

South Africa is often referred to as being a First and Third World economy within one country. While it is true that parts of South African society are extremely rich and the majority are extremely poor this situation is not actually that different from many other countries classified as Third World (or developing countries). The well-off sections of society are bigger than in other African countries but they are not dissimilar in size and wealth to countries such as Brazil or Argentina. The overall per capita levels of wealth in South Africa are also pretty much similar to these Latin American economies (referred to as the Higher Middle Income nations in World Bank league tables).

Structure of the economy The economy is dominated by the industries exploiting the country's extremely rich mineral resources. The mineral sector of the economy accounts for something like two-thirds of export earnings, though it employs less than 10% of the labour force. Apart from the gold and diamonds for which the country is famous it also produces a range of other mineral products, including platinum (which from 2005 has overtaken gold as an export renvue) and chromium (of which it is the major world producer). The country lacks oil, though it does have some reserves of natural gas. The scarcity of oil was a key issue in the Apartheid days, hence the conversion of coal into oil by SASOL.

Agricultural production also continues to make a significant contribution to the economy, especially if you add the food preparation secondary industries based on primary agricultural products. Almost one-third of the workforce is in agriculture, though employment in this sector is characterized by extremely low wages and seasonal unemployment. The agricultural base is very diverse and in non-drought years, the country is a net food exporter.

The manufacturing sector of the economy has tended to suffer from low productivity levels, meaning that South Africa has found it difficult to break into lucrative export markets. The southern African regional market, where South Africa does have an advantage, is constrained by low levels of consumption and is, in any case, already pretty much saturated with South African goods. The most important local manufacturing sectors include automobile assembly, machinery, textiles, iron and steel, chemicals and fertilizers.

Recent economic developments The ANC came to power in 1994 with the economy in a mess. Throughout much of the 1980s and early 1990s the economy had grown slower than population growth rates and in some years had contracted in absolute terms. Inflation rates were high, the rand was slipping against the major currencies, investment rates were low, productivity was low and unemployment rates were extremely high. Much of this was due to global isolation which had led the country down an economic dead end. Growth was low because of the limitations of the domestic market and the inaccessibility of export markets, difficulties in obtaining technology due to sanctions and an unskilled labour force due to the poor state of African education. Probably the only area in which South Africa was better placed than comparable economies was in the level of external debt: sanctions by international banks and finance organizations had prevented the government from borrowing heavily. Despite its stated objectives of reducing poverty, increasing equality and providing basic social services for all, the new ANC government also signalled its intentions to ensure macro-economic stability. The first post-Apartheid Minister of Finance, Derek Keys, was appointed from outside party politics and the subsequent budgets did not include the heavy public borrowing and increased taxation that many observers predicted before the election. Macro-economically the economy has been a qualified success, inflation has been kept under control and deficit spending and public borrowing have only risen slowly. Since 1999 the economy has experienced uninterrupted growth, and GDP has steadily risen from 2.4% in 1999 to around 5.1% in 2008. Today, in global, terms, South Africa hasn't really suffered too much in the recession, though in saying that GDP hasn't risen much either since 2008, so for some economists in South Africa, that is considered a 'recession'.

The major problem area for the economy has been unemployment. Despite the fact that the economy is growing there are still more young people entering the employment market than there are new jobs being created. Although the number of jobs being created is increasing, the growth in the population means that South Africa's unemployment rate remains stubbornly high. In 2009, it was at 21.7%.

In terms of meeting its objectives to provide basic social services for all, the government's record has been mixed. Some ministries have performed well while others barely seem to have got programmes off the ground. The much-vaulted Reconstruction and Development Programme collapsed under its own weight and its functions were parcelled out to various government agencies. The provision of clean drinking water and rural electrification programmes have both been making steady progress and in 2007 two new gas-fired power stations were commissioned in the Western Cape. Provision of new housing to meet the huge urban backlog, on the other hand, is far slower.

Ultimately, it is HIV/AIDS that may have the greatest impact on South Africa's economic future. Mining and manufacturing, the two largest segments of the South Africa economy, are estimated to be effected the most by HIV/AIDS, with absenteeism due to ill health driving down profits.

The tourism sector has been highlighted as a significant area of revenue for South Africa, with steady growth towards the 2010 FIFA World Cup™. Although the country has been hampered by its reputation for high crime rates, positive developments in the centre of Johannesburg and Cape Town have reassured many visitors. The contribution from tourism to the GDP has grown from just 4.6% in 1993 to 8.4% in 2009, and is expected to hit 12% during the World Cup. The record-breaking nine million tourists who visited South Africa in 2008 are in turn responsible for almost one million jobs.

Lesotho

Politics

With the March 1993 election Lesotho returned to a system of parliamentary democracy, suspended in 1970 after Chief Jonathan refused to hand over power to the Basotho Congress Party. The current Prime Minister is Pakalitha Mosisili, who chairs a Cabinet made up of members of Parliament. In addition to the main elected legislative lower house there is an upper house, with the power to delay and comment upon legislation, made up of the most senior chiefs and a number of appointed members. The monarch again fulfils the largely ceremonial role of Head-of-State, with a limited political role.

Despite sweeping the board in the 1993 election the Basotho Congress Party (BCP) failed to build on its strong political position. Many people in the country felt that after so many years in the wilderness the BCP came to power with surprisingly few new policies in the pipeline. Periodic political unrest has continued despite the advent of democratic elections. The first of these turmoils was in August 1994 when King Letsie III (who had succeeded his father, Moshoeshoe II, when he was exiled in November 1990) dismissed the BCP government. Though the exact links between this royal coup and the military and the opposition BNP are a little hazy it is clear that Letsie III was not acting on his own.

1998 riots and the torching of the Basotho Hat

The only blip in Maseru's history happened in 1998, when the results of the general election sparked a dispute. After the election, the Lesotho Congress of Democrats party claimed almost all the seats. This led to claims of vote rigging by the opposition who called for fresh elections. The government refused and the opposition began a long-running protest. The Southern African Development Community (SADC) became involved in mediation, but with the military becoming restive, Prime Minister Mosisili appealed to SADC to send in troops to prevent a military coup. South African troops entered Lesotho in September 1998 and confusion spread throughout the country as most people did not know exactly what was going on and were under the mistaken impression that South Africa was invading Lesotho. In response, there were widespread riots and the South African shops in Maseru and some of the other larger towns were looted and a large number of commercial buildings burnt down. In Maseru, one of these included the landmark Basotho Hat. The South African troops quickly restored order and promptly left the country.

His excuse for declaring the suspension of the government was the allegation that the leader of the BCP, Ntsu Mokhehle, had entered into talks with neighbouring heads of government to deploy a peace-keeping force because of his fears about political interference from the military. In the ensuing political unrest a number of people were shot dead and many more injured when the police and the military broke up demonstrations against Letsie's actions. Mokhehle and the BCP refused to acknowledge that the head-of-state had dismissed their government and, after direct involvement from regional heads-of-government, Letsie III eventually backed down and reinstated the elected government.

Another element in this confused political situation was that Letsie III wanted to abdicate in favour of his father, Moshoeshoe II. Moshoeshoe II had returned to Lesotho shortly before the return to democracy, but had not taken over the throne. Moshoeshoe had fairly wide domestic support and was respected by many individuals in the international development community because of his pronouncements on human rights while in exile in the early 1990s (although some of his actions while in coalition with the first military government painted a slightly different picture). This popularity explained the reason why the BCP were not altogether keen on seeing him reinstated as King, despite Letsie's actions in August 1994. Nevertheless, in February 1995, after another bout of intense political activity, Letsie did abdicate in favour of his father. Moshoeshoe II's reign on the throne proved to be short-lived, on the 16 January 1996 he was killed in a car accident.

The BCP itself has been plagued by internal political wranglings, which came to a surprising climax in June 1997. Soon after the BCP came to power two tendencies emerged within the party: one became known as the Pressure Group and the other as Majelathoko. The Pressure Group, who saw themselves as more progressive, were led by Molapo Qhobela, whilst the more conservative faction organized itself around Prime Minister Mokhehle. The division became wider when Mokhehle sidelined Qhobela in both government and the party.

In retaliation, the Pressure Group attempted to remove Mokhehle from his position as leader of the BCP, a move that under the 'Westminster system' of government would have also forced him to stand down as Prime Minister. In mid-1997 the Pressure Group seemed to be on the verge of winning this political battle when Mokhehle totally out-flanked them with a cunning political move. While Mokhehle knew there was a good chance that the party as a whole would vote against him he also calculated that he had the support of the majority of BCP members of Parliament. He therefore resigned from the BCP, registered a new political party (the Lesotho Congress of Democrats) – with him as leader, and managed to persuade 40 of the 63 elected BCP parliamentarians to join him in the new party. After a vote of confidence, his position as Prime Minister and a Lesotho Congress of Democrats (LDC) government were both confirmed, and the BCP became the official opposition party. While this move was unprecedented, it did not appear unconstitutional.

The opposition parties tried to restructure and reposition themselves to contend the 1998 general elections, which were won by the LDC under new leader Pakalitha Mosisili. Although the elections were deemed free and fair by international observers, opposition parties rejected the results, and protests intensified. This culminated in a violent demonstration outside the royal palace in August 1998. In September, junior members of the armed services mutinied, and, to prevent a full military coup, Prime Minister Mosisili appealed to the Southern African Development Community (SADC) to intervene and restore stability (see box, page 879). A military of South African and Botswana troops entered the country in September and encountered stiff resistance from the Lesotho Defence Force. Confusion spread and there followed a period of intense unrest, with looting and destruction of property. The South African shops in Maseru were looted and a large number of commercial buildings burnt down. Eventually South African and Botswana forces restored order and quelled the mutiny, and a long process of mediation began.

An interim council was established to prepare a new electoral system, under which elections are now processed. SADC troops left Lesotho in May 2000. Given Apartheid-era tensions, South Africa was uneasy about deploying troops in Lesotho, but the SADC intervention was ultimately successful in helping to maintain political stability. South Africa has set about improving relations with its neighbour, and is keen to emphasize Lesotho's sovereign equality. Elections in Lesotho in 2002 passed peacefully. The ruling LDC swept to victory and there were no signs of the instability that had followed the elections four years earlier. The LDC again comfortably won elections again in February 2007.

Swaziland

Swaziland became independent in 1968, and although the constitution guaranteed a parliamentary system when the NNLC won three seats in the 1972 election, the Swazi royal family dissolved parliament and banned all political parties. Since then political opponents have regularly been imprisoned and until 1993 attempts to reintroduce a parliamentary constitution failed. The government is now headed by the king, who is assisted by the prime minister; there are two legislative houses, the Senate and the House of Assembly. Non-party elections were held in September and October 1993, and the power of the king has been slightly reduced.

A Constitutional Review Commission was appointed by King Mswati in 1996 and while Swazis were promised that the new constitution would contain a bill of rights, it was assumed that power would remain in the hands of the king. Labour unions, banned political parties and human rights organizations boycotted the commission's work, arguing that it was un-democratic and open to manipulation by the authorities. In the absence of formal political opposition, the labour movement and the media have led the call for democratization.

Tensions between the government and the pro-democracy movement reached boiling point in 2000/2001. Protest meetings were moved to neighbouring South Africa after they were banned by Prime Minister Sibusiso Dlamini. Leaders of the trade union movement were put on trial for organizing a strike, restrictions were placed on the media, and the independence of the judiciary was effectively ended. Internal opposition and a threat by the US to take away Swaziland's trade privileges however pressured Mswati into lifting these restrictions in July 2001.

The king has been heavily criticized for his excessive spending, notably in 2002 when he spent US$45 million on a luxury jet, during a period of terrible drought and famine in the country. Tensions between Royalists and pro-democracy campaigners continue to fluctuate considerably; in 2006, the king was once again under international fire for imprisoning dozens of his opponents, and in 2007 thousands demonstrated on the streets of Manzini demanding democratic reform. For the time being, Swaziland remains Africa's last absolute monarchy.

Culture

South Africa

Population distribution

In 2009 the population was estimated to be about 49,052,000. With about 10 million, the most populous province is KwaZulu Natal, which contains a major urban area, Durban, but higher rainfall figures also means that the KwaZulu Natal countryside is able to support a greater population density than other rural areas of the country.

Gauteng, the country's smallest province in area (1.4% of the total), contains 20% of the total population, about 9.6 million, the vast majority of whom are urban residents living in the towns and cities around Johannesburg.

The Eastern Cape's 6.9 million people are less urbanized. Though the province contains a major city, Nelson Mandela Bay (Port Elizabeth), many of its people live in the area that used to comprise the homelands of Transkei and Ciskei.

The Western Cape, by contrast, never contained any homeland areas. Its 4.8 million people mainly live in and around Cape Town though there is also a significant population of farmworkers and residents of small rural towns and villages.

The next four provinces in terms of population size, Northern Province, North West, Mpumalanga and the Free State, all have their population divided between smaller industrial centres, sparsely populated white rural areas and densely populated fragments of former homelands.

Finally, the Northern Cape, the largest province in area (361,830 sq km), has a tiny population of just 1.1 million people widely dispersed across this semi-arid region.

Ethnic groups

South Africa's population is a true melting pot, with numerous races, religions, ethnicities and cultures which can be somewhat bewildering for visitors. While many people today resent being classified in terms of race and ethnicity – it was, after all, racial classifications which denied the majority of the population many of its basic human rights for many years – it is impossible to discuss modern South Africa without touching on these terms.

The Apartheid system recognized four major population groups (races) in the country: African, Asian, coloured and white (the terminology has changed over time). Despite the avowed non-racial nature of the present South African state, this fourfold classification remains profoundly important to South African life. This does not mean, however, that everyone fits neatly into these four categories: during the Apartheid era, huge numbers of people had their race altered by official decree. This could have profound impacts and often resulted in people being evicted from their homes and their children thrown out of schools. Within each of the four racial categories it is possible to make further sub-divisions on the basis of home language, tribe and geography – these sub-divisions (especially tribe) are even more fluid and open to debate than the fourfold racial classification.

African The African population makes up around 79% of South Africa's total population. The terminology used to describe this section of the population has changed over the years: in the 19th and early 20th century they tended to be referred to as 'natives' while in the 1960s the Apartheid authorities adopted the term 'Bantu'. Both these names have strong connotations of racism. The word Bantu simply comes from the Zulu and Xhosa words for people but it is resented by most South Africans because of its connection to the Apartheid institutions who adopted it in the 1960s, especially in the field of education. Today it is only acceptable to use the term when discussing languages; the Bantu group of languages includes all the African languages spoken in South Africa and related Bantu languages are spoken as far away as Somalia.

The Apartheid system also designated the African population on the basis of tribe. This was not as straightforward as it might seem. Many Africans, especially those living in urban areas and those who were long-term residents on white farms, had only weak links with any tribal authority and often did not describe themselves in terms of their tribal background. Under the Apartheid system every African was allocated to one of nine different tribes, each with a designated tribal authority and a homeland. This classification system lead to many complaints and many people claimed that they did not belong to any of the tribes or that their clan constituted a separate tribe – originally there were eight designated tribes but complaints of this nature lead to the creation of a ninth.

In terms of population, the biggest African tribal group is the Zulu. The majority of Zulus live in KwaZulu Natal or in the industrial centres of Gauteng. Rural Zulus probably have the greatest ethnic identity out of the entire African population. The second biggest ethnic group is the Xhosa. Under the Apartheid system they were ascribed two separate homelands: the Ciskie and Transkie, now incorporated into Eastern Cape. There is a large Xhosa population in Cape Town and on the farms of the Western Cape. Many of the ANC's leaders are Xhosa from the Eastern Cape, reflecting the area's long history of resistance politics and the education provided in the large number of mission schools in the region. These two groups together account for about 40% of the African population.

There are three ethnic groups in the country who are closely related to the populations of three neighbouring countries dominated by people of that tribe: the Tswana (Botswana), the Swazi (Swaziland) and the Southern Sotho (Lesotho). These three and the other four ethnic groups, the Shangana or Tsonga, the Ndebele, the Venda and the Northern Sotho have their populations dispersed in the previous homeland areas or mixed together in the towns and cities of the Highveld.

Each one of the nine ethnic groups has an official language. Many of these are more or less mutually intelligible. The major distinction is between the Nguni languages (isiXhosa, isiZulu, Swazi and isiNdebele) and those closely related to SeSotho and SeTswana.

There are distinctive cultural activities associated with each ethnic group, though these usually only come into play at times like weddings and funerals. In the urban areas, where the majority of Africans live, many of these ethnic tribal customs have been replaced by generic amalgams of different practices. Similarly a distinctive urban African language known as Tsotsi-taal containing words from all the languages plus English and Afrikaans has evolved in the urban areas.

White South Africa's white population accounts for something like 9% of the total. It can be sub-divided into two main groups on the basis of home language: English speakers and Afrikaans-speaking people. The ancestors of English-speaking white South Africans first arrived in the country in 1820 and since then there has been a steady stream of new immigrants. The first English settlers to arrive were concentrated in the Eastern Cape but today they are to be found in every town and city. They tend to be more urbanized and more metropolitan in outlook than the Afrikaners, though this is a generalization that does not always match up to reality.

The Afrikaner population are descended from the original Dutch and Huguenot settlers who came with the Dutch East India Company. The word Afrikaner simply means African in Dutch. They account for just over half of the white population. They have a reputation for being conservative, rural and more racist than the English-speaking population. In reality the vast majority live in town and you can very often only tell the difference between an English-speaking and Afrikaans-speaking white South African by their surnames.

There are a number of other smaller communities of white South Africans, including a Jewish community descended from early 20th-century immigrants from eastern Europe and a Portuguese community, many of whom came to South Africa from Mozambique and Angola in the 1970s.

Asian South Africa has a small Asian population, accounting for about 2.5% of the total. It is descended from two main groups: indentured labourers brought to the sugar cane farms of Natal in the 19th century and a number of traders and their families who followed the indentured labourers. The vast majority of the Asian population are originally from South Asia and they are also often referred to as Indian. The majority of Asians still live in KwaZulu Natal though there are small Asian communities in most towns and cities across the country, especially in Gauteng. About 70% of the Asian population are Hindu and 20% Muslim. Almost all Asians speak English as their home language.

Coloured This is probably the most contentious of the four basic racial categories used in South Africa. In some ways the coloured category just represents the rest lumped together into one group. There is a distinctive coloured cultural identity – though by no means all people classified as coloured during Apartheid would subscribe to it. Under Apartheid about 9% of the population was classified as coloured and today is about the same. The coloured population is concentrated in the Western Cape. Many of them are descended from slaves brought to work on the farms of the Cape during the era of rule by the Dutch East India Company and from slave owners and other white settlers. There are also many coloured people who are descended from the pre-colonial San and Khoi populations of the Cape. This is especially so in the Northern and Eastern Cape which never had large slave populations. Some coloured people, especially the 200,000-strong Malay community in Cape Town, have retained elements of their pre-slavery culture, including Islam.

On the whole, the coloured community is very closely linked (both culturally and through descent) with the Afrikaner community. About 80% of the coloured population speak Afrikaans as their home language: it surprises many visitors to discover that coloured Afrikaans speakers outnumber white Afrikaans speakers.

Music and dance

Most visitors will be familiar with the most famous of South African sounds, the rousing vocal harmony of Ladysmith Black Mambazo, made internationally famous by Paul Simon's *Graceland* album. It doesn't end there, though: the country has produced an incredible variety of music – little surprise given its immense range of cultures and influences. In fact, the key to understanding South African music is in realizing where it comes from. Be it the adaptation of Dutch instruments in the 17th century by Indonesian slaves, or the mutation of 1990s house music into township Kwaito, home-grown and foreign sounds mingle to produce a singularly South African sound. And like so much of South African culture, music is inextricably linked with the political upheavals of the last century.

Vocal harmony is the oldest music tradition in South Africa, with its roots in communal dances accompanied by elaborate call-and-response patterns. This movement, defined as gospel acapella (and known as Isicathamiya in Zulu), has long been popular in South Africa, but it was the band Ladysmith Black Mambazo who first propelled it into the international arena. The beginnings for the group were not easy; at their first concert in Soweto in the 1980s, they received the princely sum of R5.28 each. The band, however, became an instant hit and, when Paul Simon invited them to sing on his *Graceland* album, they were thrust into the international limelight, and they remain the most popular South African band of all time. Made up of 10 male singers, including the charismatic front-man, lead singer and original founder Joseph Shabalala, the band continue to tour, and have been going strong for 45 years.

However, few musical styles have been as influential as jazz, something of a harmonious hotbed since emerging from the Johannesburg slums in the 1920s. Today, the jazz scene is once again flourishing following a turbulent few decades when many of the biggest jazz stars left South Africa under Apartheid, and is now best experienced at the Cape Town International Jazz Festival, held every March in Cape Town. Many of the godfathers of Cape Jazz, including Abdullah Ibrahim (previously known as Dollar Brand) and Hugh Masekela can be seen performing during the three-day festival, while newcomers, using a range of influences from the harmonica of migrant west African miners, to the clubbing beats of drum 'n' bass, are also making a bit impact. Every year the South African acts are complemented by the latest international recruits.

If music is the very heartbeat of this country, then dance also features as an integral part of life for many South Africans. In KwaZula Natal tourists can be treated to a traditional Zulu ceremony, while the talented *Gumboots* dance company have toured the world with their unforgettable mix of music, dance and showmanship.

Western music is hugely popular with young South Africans, and both Durban and Cape Town have significant live rock scenes. A number of home-grown talents such as rock band Just Jinger and Freshly Ground (who won South Africa's first ever MTV award in 2006) have recently made it onto the international arena, but the most popular white musician remains Johnny Clegg. In the 1970s, Clegg began performing traditional Zulu material with Sipho Mchunu, and later added a mix of Western rock to form the band Juluka. Clegg remains something of a South African legend, and still draws thousands of fans when he performs. Known affectionately as the 'White Zulu', Clegg challenged the racial boundaries manifest in music under Apartheid, and blazed a cross-over trail which survives to this day. Although popular mainly amongst (liberal) white people, his tours are sell-outs and he remains a big influence on the music scene. In 2008 Clegg's son, Jesse Clegg, displaying a style markedly different from that of his father, released his debut album called *When I Wake Up*. As a rock musician the younger Clegg has quickly built up a following, with the album being nominated for two South African Music Awards.

Kwaito The fastest-moving force in music today is undoubtedly Kwaito, the sound of young, black Johannesburg. The style is resolutely urban, drawing on American and British house music, with slow, deep beats and electronic melodies overlaid with chanted *tsotsi* (township gangster) slang. Born from 1980s pop-influenced dance music known as bubblegum, Kwaito has a darker, edgier feel, carrying with it an unmistakable association with gangster culture. But despite its underground roots and reflection of a despondent township youth, Kwaito has become the country's definitive youth sound, led by top record label Kalawa Jazzmee and stars like Mandoza and Zola. Ubiquitous in the clubs of young black urbanites, it is also now popular in designer nightclubs – until relatively recently the reserve of the white and wealthy.

Lesotho

Lesotho's population, of just over two million, is made up almost exclusively of Basotho people, and Sesotho is the language spoken by the vast majority. There are a few Xhosa speakers in Qacha's Nek district and a handful of Asian and European settlers in the lowland towns. One of the key reasons why there are few non-Basotho settlers in Lesotho is that (officially) all land is owned communally 'by the nation'. Unofficially there is a market in land but it is very difficult for a non-Basotho to own or even lease land.

Population density in the lowlands is very high and the urban sprawl around Maseru merges into neighbouring towns and villages. In contrast the population in the mountain regions is very low and concentrated into the valleys. The high mountain tops are more or less uninhabited with the exception of the occasional herd boy. Over 80% of the population is rural, though the high density of population sometimes makes the rural/urban distinction a little hazy.

The vast majority of **Basotho**, over 80%, would classify themselves as Christians. The Catholic church is the largest and richest church in the country. In the past it received generous external funding, especially from Quebec, and indeed many of its priests were French Canadian. This has, however, dried up and efforts have been made to localize all the clergy. The Catholic Church was strongly associated with the establishment of the BNP and, though many priests were uneasy with the stance, it rarely voiced opposition to the autocratic regime of Chief Jonathan. The largest Protestant church, the Lesotho Evangelical Church (LEC), has received far less external funding and is much poorer, though its position as the first major autonomous church in Lesotho has given it prestige and strong local support. It was the first major church to ordain women and a growing number of its trainee clergy are female. The LEC frequently criticized the actions of Chief Jonathan and in return its leaders were persecuted by the government and many forced into exile. The Anglican church is also well represented in Lesotho and, as it is a diocese of the South African Anglican structure, it has good external contacts. There are also a large number of smaller churches and spiritualist movements which are receiving growing support, such as the Methodists, Pentacostalists, Zionists and Seventh Day Adventists.

Natonal dress of Lesotho

As the Basotho are one of the few African ethnic groups living in a mountainous environment, they have had to make adaptations to their living conditions. The Basotho blanket is one example. Most people in the rural areas wear colourful blankets attached at the shoulder with giant pins to form a sort of coat to provide warmth and keep the rain off. These are usually worn with well-patched gumboots, essential in the cool mountain climate. However, neither garment is produced locally and both the gumboots and blankets are imported from South Africa.

Originally, people wore clothing made from animal hides, but in 1860 European traders presented Moshoshoe with a blanket and, a decade later, demand for these blankets was insatiable. In those days the blankets were imported from the textile regions of England around Leicester and Coventry and in fact, many of the trading stores and centres in today's Lesotho started out selling blankets.

Whatever the specific church, Christianity plays an important part in the lives of most Basotho and the church is a focal point of many communal activities.

As in all societies, however, Christianity in Lesotho co-exists with other (sometimes contrary) beliefs and rituals. Many Basotho continue to include some elements of 'ancestor worship' in their religious practice and there is a strong belief in the power of witchcraft. Initiation ceremonies, including circumcision lodges for young men, still exist in many areas of Lesotho, indeed there is some evidence they have made something of a comeback in recent years.

One of Lesotho's biggest modern-day challenges is HIV/AIDS. The country has the third highest infection rate of HIV/AIDS in the world, with a prevalence rate of around 23%, which has caused a dramatic drop in national life expectancy, which is now only 40. As in South Africa, the Lesotho government has been slow to recognize the scale of the crisis, although it now has a programme of education, counselling and treatment. In late 2005, it introduced the world's first HIV/AIDS testing project for the entire population, which it hopes will reduce the stigma associated the HIV/AIDS and its treatment.

Swaziland

The population of Swaziland is put at 1.2 million, and given that it is such a little country this means that the majority of the land is densely populated. Over 80% of the population is rural. Although Western dress is widely utilized, the Swazi people have a distinctive, colourful national dress known as emahiya and this is regularly worn by men, women and children. Different accessories and head dresses are used depending on the status and age of the individual, as well as on the occasion. By tradition Swaziland is a polygamous society and men may take several wives on payment of a dowry, known as lobola, which normally entails giving cattle to the brides' parents. However, monogamous marriages, performed in the Western custom, have become more common as Swazis adopt the Western lifestyle. Swaziland's cultural heritage is deeply rooted, old Swazi traditions are carefully guarded and colourful ceremonies frequently take place to mark special occasions. These include the *Umhlanga* dance, for example, which is celebrated every two years at Loamba where the nation's young girls dance and sing in homage to the Queen Mother.

As with the rest of southern Africa, Swaziland has a high rate of HIV/AIDS infection, which at 26.1% is presently the highest of any country in the world. Anti-retrovirals were introduced in 2003, but the disease is still surrounded by taboo, which is both hindering effective education about transmission and preventing people from seeking treatment. Life expectancy in the country has now dropped from 51 (mid-1990s) to just 32 (2009).

Land and environment

South Africa

South Africa is a big country with an extremely diverse physical environment. The country's total land area amounts to 1,219,912 sq km (1,267,462 sq km including Swaziland and Lesotho). Contained within this land area are a wide mix of environments, ranging from tropical moist forest, through high mountains, rolling grasslands and temperate woodlands to sparsely vegetated areas of semi-desert. South Africa's natural scenery is world famous and rightly so. There are some amazingly beautiful areas which can take the breath away from even the most world-weary traveller. The wild and empty beaches of the south coast, the panoramic views of the Drakensberg Mountains, the wide open spaces of the Karoo and many other stunning landscapes can all leave a lasting impression.

There are also, however, some big areas of undistinguished natural scenery and the impacts of both industrialization and Apartheid have also had their toll. This is obviously worth bearing in mind when you are planning a holiday, especially if you are only going to be there for a short period of time. If your primary interest is in South Africa's natural beauty read the following sections carefully before planning your route.

Landscape

South Africa's physical geography is dominated by one feature: a massive escarpment that runs right around the subcontinent dividing a thin coastal strip from a huge inland plateau. This escarpment is clearest in the east, where it is marked by the spectacular Drakensberg Mountains, running in an arc from the Eastern Cape round to northern Mpumalanga. To the west the escarpment is confused by a jumble of beautiful mountain chains (the Cape Folded Mountains), such as the Cederberg, the Tsitsikamma, the Swartberg and the Hottentot-Hollands. The inland plateau, usually known as the Highveld, is a relatively flat plain sloping gently down towards the west and north. This plain is, however, broken up by numerous geological features, resulting in isolated steep-sided hills or longer chains of higher ground.

This interior plateau forms the southernmost tip of the massive Africa continental plateau which stretches as far north as Ethiopia. This plateau was part of the ancient landmass of Pangaea (c200 million years ago), which split in two to form Gondwanaland in the southern hemisphere and Laurasia in the north. Gondwanaland later broke up to form the continents of South America, Australasia and Africa, around 135 million years ago. As it is made up of an old continental plate many of South Africa's rocks are very old and some rocks found in the Limpopo valley, Northern Province, rank with the oldest yet discovered anywhere in the world.

Other areas, such as the Witwatersrand and Barberton complexes, are also made up of ancient Precambrian rocks, about 3000 million years old. This contrasts with rock formations in places such as the Western Cape coast which were only formed in the past

250,000 years, during the Quaternary era. Most of the country is, however, made up of sandstone and slates laid down in the Carboniferous to Jurassic periods (when Pangaea began to break up). These are commonly referred to as the Karoo sequence of rocks. The eastern portions of the Karoo sequence have been covered by an intrusion of basalt. This harder layer of rock has protected the softer Karoo sandstones from erosion and stands out as a highland area, especially in Lesotho.

The Karoo sequence is particularly rich in fossil remains. Contained in the sandstones and shales are the remains of many reptilian creatures who lived in the low-lying areas of swamps and shallow lakes. Some of these fossils have been crucial to scientists' attempts to reconstruct the way in which reptiles evolved into mammals. The best places to look for fossils is along the sides of the many steep-sided hills or koppies that dominate the Karoo landscape. The best fossils are usually found in the dull red shales, which erode easily to reveal the fossil remains.

Climate

Over most of South Africa rain falls during the southern hemisphere summer months (November to March). Rainfall tends to be in the form of intense cloud bursts, often accompanied by thunderstorms, though there can also be periods of longer rainfall. During the summer months warm and wet easterly winds sweep in from over the Indian Ocean. As these winds flow over the southeastern coast and the Drakensberg they drop much of their moisture, making these areas the wettest parts of the country with annual totals over 1000 mm. Over the Highveld the moisture-bearing winds trigger rain showers and thunderstorms. In the east of the Highveld these tend to be more regular but towards the west, especially in the Northern Cape, they are infrequent. Here average annual rainfall figures are usually below 200 mm per annum. The summer rains never reach the western coast of the Northern Cape province and rainfall levels here can be as low as 20 mm per annum. South Africa is, on the whole, a very dry country, with something like 30% of the land area receiving below 250 mm a year on average. Rain may be unpopular with visitors but it is almost always welcomed by South Africans.

The only part of the country where the major rainfall does not come from summer easterlies is the Western Cape and the extreme west of Northern Cape province. Here most rain falls during the winter months as depressions over the southern Atlantic sweep north and east bringing with them frontal systems and cool rains. Late in the winter and early spring an occasional winter storm will travel further north than usual and bring with it much needed rain to the arid northwestern coastal belt. Apart from these occasional storms this area receives its moisture from mists that roll in from the cold Atlantic during the summer months.

The winter weather systems can also sometimes skirt up along the southern coast bringing rain and even snow to the Eastern Cape, Lesotho and KwaZulu Natal. Snowfalls tend to be minor and confined to light dustings of the highest peaks, though there are occasionally significant falls of a few inches or more.

This seasonal pattern is also highly variable from year to year. This variability tends to be most pronounced in the lowest rainfall areas: here there can be some years where the rains fail entirely. The exact reasons for this variability are a matter of considerable academic debate. There does appear to be a cycle of wet and dry years in South Africa over a period of about four to eight years. This cycle is related to a frequent, but irregular, event known as the El Niño, in which ocean and air currents in the South Pacific are reversed. This, in turn, triggers changes in the circulation of air around the southern hemisphere and results in weaker easterlies and drought in South Africa. The weather system is, however, extremely complex and involves the interaction of global and local variables, so predicting exactly how something like El Niño will affect South African rainfall is impossible with any degree of accuracy. Global warming may also be further complicating the already complex weather systems. Beyond short-range forecasting all that meteorologists can predict with any degree of accuracy is that the climate is very unpredictable.

Temperatures vary according to season, altitude and distance from the moderating influence of the oceans. During the summer months the inland plateau tends to heat up considerably, especially if the rains fail. The highest daytime temperatures are to be found in the lower-lying semi-desert areas of the Northern Cape and the Lowveld regions of Mpumulanga. On the Highveld temperatures can also soar in summer, though they tend to be moderated by the higher altitudes. Fortunately in these inland regions the evenings tend to be significantly cooler, especially under clear skies. Travelling at night or in the early morning is a sensible and popular option in these regions during summer. The coastal fringes of Natal are also hot and sticky in summer and don't expect too much relief at night. The most pleasant area of the country during the summer months is the Western Cape, with hot but often breezy days and comfortable evenings.

During the winter the Western Cape can get very chilly, with frequent blustery storms and heavy rain. On the Highveld and in the Karoo stable high pressure systems result in clear skies, warm days and cold nights. It is a combination many visitors find very comfortable especially for travelling long distances. In the highest areas of the Drakensberg winter temperatures can plummet to way below freezing at night: the best time to visit these areas is during the autumn or spring. The Natal coast remains warm throughout the year, especially in the northern subtropical areas near the Mozambique border. Winter is a good time to visit the Lowveld game parks: the drier conditions make it easier to spot wildlife, especially around water holes.

Vegetation
There are a number of different ways of categorizing South Africa's vegetational zones, which are sometimes called biomes or ecozones. All these categorizations are simplifications of complex and dynamic patterns of vegetation and rarely are there clear boundaries between the different zones. Even without the influence of humans this pattern has constantly shifted with long-term trends in climate: when you add in millenniums of human impacts, mapping a set pattern of different biomes becomes an extremely difficult task.

One vegetational zone that is not difficult to classify as distinctive is the fynbos of the Western Cape. Although fynbos covers only a relatively small area it comprises one of the earth's six separate floral kingdoms. The other five floral kingdoms cover huge areas such as most of the northern hemisphere or the whole of Australia. The Cape floral kingdom is both the smallest and the richest floral kingdom in the world, with the highest known concentration of plant species per unit area. There are over 7700 different plant species within the fynbos biome and of these over 5000 are endemic to the Western Cape (ie they do not occur naturally anywhere else). The 470 sq km of the Cape Peninsula is home to 2256 different plant species – more than the whole of the UK, an area 5000 times bigger! The 60 sq km of Table Mountain alone supports 1470 species. The richness of the fynbos is well demonstrated by its ericas or heaths, of which there are over 600 different species. There are just 26 in the rest of the world. Not surprisingly the Western Cape is a magnet for plant enthusiasts.

The word fynbos comes from the Dutch for fine-leaved plants. Almost all of the woody plants have small leaves (microphyllous) which are hard, tough and leathery (sclerophyllous). True grasses are also relatively rare and as much as 5% of the biome is covered by Cape reeds (of the *Restionaceae* family). Most of the plants that fill the niches usually taken up by grasses have small, thin (ericoid) leaves. Additionally, the fynbos biome contains proteas, ericas and members of seven plant families found nowhere else in the world. These include the king protea, South Africa's national flower, the beautiful red disa, symbol of the Cape Province and the popular garden plants, pelargoniums, commonly known as geraniums. The largest family in number of species is *Asteraceae* (daisy family), with just under 1000 species, of which more than 600 are endemic. Fynbos is very rich in bulbous plants (geophytes) and many species from the family *Iridaceae* have become household names such as babiana, freesia, gladiolus, iris, moraea, sporaxis and watsonia.

As many of the endemic fynbos species have amazingly small ranges (sometimes as small as a football field), they are extremely vulnerable to extinction. One small housing project, for example, could wipe out a whole species. Given this and the fact that the Western Cape has fairly dense human population, it is not surprising that many of South Africa's threatened and rare plants are found in the fynbos. Almost 500 species are classified as rare, threatened or endangered. Fynbos species tend to grow fairly slowly. This is because they are in a winter rainfall region so during the summer months there is not enough water available and during the winter low temperatures restrict plant growth. The hot dry summer months also make fire a common occurrence in the biome. The fynbos plants are well adapted to fire and the biome is adapted to quickly re-establishing itself after naturally occurring burns. If fire is totally restricted fynbos often loses out to plant species from surrounding biomes. If fires are too frequent, however, the fynbos plants do not have time to re-establish themselves and this can lead to local extermination of species.

Soils under fynbos tend to be extremely infertile, due partially to the chemical make-up of the underlying rocks and partially to heavy leaching that has occurred over long periods. The nutrient-poor soils produce plants that are also low in nutrients and therefore of low feeding potential for grazing animals. This means that there is a relatively low density and diversity of mammals and birds in the fynbos biome.

The western coast of South Africa also has a large number of endemic plant species. This area, stretching north into Namibia, has extremely low and erratic rainfall and the plant life reflects this. Many of the plants in this region are succulents and about 200 of these are classified as rare or endangered. When rains do come to the area there is a dramatic transformation of the vegetation. Hundreds of flowering plants lying dormant during the long dry periods burst into bloom covering the whole of the landscape in a carpet of brightly coloured flowers. This is a spectacular annual event and attracts many visitors to the region every spring, but as the flowers are reliant upon unpredictable rainfall it is impossible to say exactly when and where they will appear. The rains are expected in the spring, and once the first blooms start to appear a 'Flower Hotline' can be called for the latest information. After a brief period of flowering the plants drop their seeds which then lie dormant until the next rainfall event.

The inland plateau of the Cape is dominated by Karoo types of vegetation. This is made up mainly from low-lying shrubs and succulents, though in good rainfall years grasses can also make an appearance. There tends to be a lot of open soil between the shrubs so much of the region takes on the red tinge of the underlying soils and this can lead to some wonderful sunsets and sunrises. The low density of vegetation also makes fires a less common occurrence than in better-watered regions. There are occasional areas of green alongside streams and rivers and these are the only places you will see trees in the biome.

The northern Highveld areas (along the Botswana border) and the Lowveld areas of Northern Province, Mpumalanga and Swaziland, by contrast, have a fair number of trees. This is the classic savanna formation: areas of grassland interspersed with occasional trees. In the Highveld areas the vegetation is dominated by thorny acacia woodland, often referred to as bushveld. In valley bottoms and in Lowveld areas the vegetation is often dominated by mopane, which can tolerate the extremes of waterlogging and drying encountered on heavy soils. This region tends to have fertile soils and grasses have a high nutrition content. They are, therefore, heavily populated by grazing animals (both wild and domestic). The major wildlife viewing areas fall within this biome.

The remaining Highveld, the KwaZulu Natal midlands, Lesotho and the inland areas of Eastern Cape are taken up by grasslands with few naturally occurring trees. The grasses grow vigorously during the hot and wet summer months and then remain dormant during the dry, cold winter. The grasslands are often divided into two different categories: sweet and sour veld. Sweetveld occurs in the areas with lower rainfall figures (400-600 mm per annum), especially on heavier clay soils. It tends to be more nutritious than the sour velds and is therefore popular for grazing, especially during the summer months. Sourveld tends to occur in the areas with rainfall above 600 mm per annum. Greater availability of water means that sourveld grasses grow rapidly, though they tend to have a lower nutritional content. Both these veld types intermingle and it is hard to draw a clear distinction between the two. The division between the Karoo and grassland areas is also hazy. During dry spells and in areas which have been overgrazed, Karoo-type shrubs expand into the grasslands while in wetter years or if grazing pressure is reduced they will retreat. On the Highveld much of this grassland has been converted to agriculture or covered with factories, roads and cities.

The densely populated narrow coast strip of the Eastern Cape and KwaZulu Natal was once heavily wooded. The closed canopy subtropical forests of KwaZulu Natal can still be found in a few isolated patches but most of the area has been converted to agriculture. In the Eastern Cape the evergreen temperate forest has also been largely cut down, though some small patches are left around Knysna. The forests here give some idea of what the environment would have been like before the arrival of Europeans with commercial logging: there are some beautiful trees such as the stinkwood, Cape chestnut, yellowwood and the white and red alder. In total, indigenous closed canopy woodland accounts for only 1% of South Africa's land area, with a similar amount under commercial plantations (many of these on the Drakensberg escarpment in Mpumalanga).

Urban and rural environments

Any description of the South African landscape that leaves out the impact of humans would not give a visitor any real idea about what the place actually looks like. Though Apartheid has now come to an end its legacy is often apparent in the South African landscape and the pattern of South African cities and towns. For many years some of the most striking features of Apartheid social engineering, such as the huge rural slums that sprang up around the country, were never shown on official maps. Visitors were often shocked to suddenly encounter a massive area of slum housing way out in the countryside which they could not find on their road maps and which did not appear on any road signs. Official maps and guides are now slowly catching up with reality but the landscape itself will take much longer to transform.

Agriculture While large areas of South Africa are given over to wildlife or wilderness areas most of the countryside is dominated by farming. The nature of the country's agricultural sector, therefore, has a huge impact on the landscape. The pattern of agriculture in South Africa is determined by two major factors: the physical environment and the legacy of Apartheid. Low and variable rainfall figures make arable farming an extremely risky business and only about 10% of the country is covered by arable crops. Maize is the country's staple crop. It is mainly grown in the Free State, the southern and eastern portions of North West, the western portions of Mpumalanga and those parts of Gauteng not covered by towns and industry. These areas comprise some of the least eventful countryside in South Africa. Maize and other grain crops, such as sorghum or millet, are also grown in the Eastern Cape and KwaZulu Natal. In these wetter areas the constraining factor is often not availability of water, but of sufficient flat land to plough amongst the broken topography. The most rewarding landscapes for a tourist are inevitably very different from the most rewarding landscapes for a farmer.

Other arable crops include wheat, grown mostly in the Western Cape, and sugar cane, grown mostly in KwaZulu Natal. The Western Cape is also well known for its vineyards and fruits, such as peaches and nectarines. The Lowveld areas of Mpumalanga and Northern Province are also major fruit growing areas.

The majority of the countryside is, however, given over to extensive grazing land. This accounts for something like 65% of the country's total land area, the vast majority of this given over to large enclosures of naturally occurring veld plants rather than improved and carefully managed paddocks. The wetter areas in the east, where grasses dominate over woodier Karoo shrubs, are given over mainly to cattle. The rolling hills of the KwaZulu Natal Midlands are particularly good cattle-rearing country: well watered but with sufficiently cool evenings and winters to kill off disease-bearing insects that flourish in the more tropical coastal fringes and the Lowveld regions. Further west, especially in the Karoo, livestock rearing is dominated by sheep and in the very driest areas by goats.

This pattern of agriculture is confused, however, by the legacy of Apartheid. Until very recently African farmers were not allowed to own or buy land outside certain prescribed areas. These areas, known as the homelands, comprised only 13% of the country and were supposed to provide land for an African population comprising 75% of the total. In these areas the population density is high and plots of land for agriculture are very small. Most of these plots are unproductive and yields from agricultural crops very low. Grazing in these areas is on common land owned by the local community. Though individual herds tend to be small the total animal population is high and includes a mixture of goats, sheep and cattle. As the grazing land is unfenced and communal herds will be looked after by a shepherd – usually a teenage boy – livestock will most probably be brought back to the village at night where they are kraaled to stop them wandering and to reduce the risk of theft.

This contrasts with the white farming areas where farms tend to be huge. Arable agriculture is highly mechanized and produces huge yields. Some farms, such as the fruit-growing areas, employ large numbers of seasonal labour but on the whole the number of people employed permanently on each farm is not high. On the white farms livestock are grazed in large fenced paddocks at a lower density than on the former homeland areas. Except on the dairy farms, livestock are only checked up on periodically.

These different patterns of farming produce very different-looking landscapes. The former homeland areas are more densely populated with small plots of unhealthy-looking maize interspersed amongst scattered homesteads. The grazing areas often look barren, especially towards the end of the winter dry season when all available forage has been eaten by livestock. The white farming areas, on the other hand, have large fields of arable crops or huge areas of grazing land. On the grazing land there will tend to be more vegetation available to the livestock, though in drought years these areas can also look pretty barren. It is unusual to see many people in the fields and paddocks of the white farming areas.

Though the restrictions on buying or renting land have now been lifted this pattern will remain for many years. Some African farmers who were evicted from white farming areas during the Apartheid era have been resettled on their original farms, but this process is very slow and the geography of agriculture is unlikely to change significantly in the conceivable future.

Living in the city South Africa's urban geography has been largely shaped by segregation: this pattern is now changing rapidly but the legacy of residential segregation will be apparent for a very long time to come. Under the Group Areas Act different areas of each city were reserved for one of the four major population groups (white, Indian, coloured or African). Prior to the passing of the Group Areas Act in 1950 most cities and towns were already segregated to an extent. The pattern of segregation was complicated however and there were in most cities a number of areas in which the different population groups intermingled. Under the Group Areas Act the government attempted to consolidate this pattern of segregation into bigger, clearly defined blocks of land and to do away with any areas where there was a mixture of the different races. This process continued right through to the mid-1980s. The urban environment that this system created is distinctive.

Prior to the Group Areas Act much of the poorer urban population lived in slum areas near the central business areas of industrial centres. These areas were home to large numbers of Africans, Indians and coloureds and a few 'poor whites'. Under the Group Areas Act these slum areas were knocked down and new housing for whites was built in their place. The African, Indian and coloured populations were moved to new, racially segregated, planned settlements on the outskirts of cities, known as townships. These areas tend to be some distance from the city centre and are divided from the white suburbs by areas of unoccupied land. There are often only one or two access routes into the township and the streets are wide and straight: both factors were deliberately intended to make the control of unrest and protest easier to handle. The best known of these township areas is the vast residential area called Soweto, which originally stood for South Western Townships, on the outskirts of Johannesburg.

The vast majority of Africans living in urban areas still live in these townships. They tend to be made up of large areas of small uniform houses with few local urban amenities. Many of the roads in township areas are not tarred, rubbish is strewn across the streets and air pollution is horrendous. In recent years there have been a proliferation of squatter camps within the townships on areas of open ground and many of the residential plots include not just the original house but a large number of additional shacks. These townships contrast sharply with the suburbs reserved for white populations during the Apartheid years. Houses in these areas are usually large, streets are clean and often tree-lined. The fear of crime means that in areas like Johannesburg's northern suburbs many of these houses look like mini-forts.

This pattern of residential segregation will remain for many years to come. A few rich Africans, coloureds and Indians have moved into formerly all white suburbs, but on the whole these middle-class groups tend to live in small richer enclaves in the townships.

The major change in the pattern of residential segregation over the past decade or so has been the rebirth of inner city African housing, resulting in areas such as Hillbrow in Johannesburg.

Industry and infrastructure Not surprisingly the pattern of industry and infrastructure has also been affected by Apartheid. Obviously industrial development has been influenced by matters such as the proximity to raw materials, but industrial development planning has also had an influence. The main industrial centre is Gauteng where the South African industrial revolution was centred around the gold mines on the Witwatersrand. Other important industrial centres are in the major coastal port cities of Cape Town, Nelson Mandela Bay (Port Elizabeth) and Durban and around secondary mining centres in the Free State and Mpumalanga.

During the Apartheid years some efforts were made to decentralize industrialization in order to provide jobs for the African population in areas closer to the homelands. The idea was to try to prevent rural to urban migration amongst the African population and to foster the plan of overall segregation. On the whole these decentralization policies were unsuccessful, though a number of labour-intensive industries, such as garment manufacturers, did relocate to the borders of homeland areas to take advantage of the low wages prevalent in these areas of high unemployment.

Infrastructural development tends to reflect the pattern of racial segregation. The major cities and the smaller towns and villages of the former white rural areas are well served by roads, railways and other economic infrastructure. The former homeland areas tend to be badly served by roads and railways and other infrastructure, such as piped water, is also lacking. This pattern will again take many years to rectify completely, but nevertheless spending on infrastructure continues to grow steadily.

Lesotho

Landscape
Lesotho is a small country of 30,350 sq km totally surrounded by South Africa. The country is made up of a thin lowland strip along the Clarendon River valley in the west and a high mountain plateau cut into by numerous deep valleys. The lowland strip is in reality part of the great central plateau of southern Africa and hence the lowest altitude in Lesotho is over 300 m above sea level – the highest 'low point' in the world.

The vast majority of the country's rivers drain south and east. The headwaters of the famous Orange River (known as the Senqu in Lesotho) are in the far northwest of the country and its deeply incised valley runs diagonally across the mountain area, eventually flowing into South Africa across the southeastern border. Water is one of the few resources Lesotho has in abundance and, given the growing constraints of water shortages on South Africa's economy, it is a resource that is becoming increasingly valuable. The headwaters of a number of tributaries of the Senqu River are currently being developed in the massive Lesotho Highlands Water Project to allow water to be transferred to economically important South African river systems. Phase one of the scheme was successfully completed in 1996 when the massive Katse Dam was opened. The huge weight generated by filling up the dam triggered a number of minor local earth tremors, but these problems now seem to have been overcome. The Mohole dam was operational by 2004. The transfer of water from these dams to South Africa by way of tunnels now earns a substantial foreign income for the country. Lesotho has few other natural resources.

Some diamonds have been discovered but not in profitable quantities and there is little hope of any lucrative mineral deposits.

With the exception of a few willows and fruit trees in sheltered kloofs and government sponsored woodlots, Lesotho is treeless. The lowlands and mountain valleys are planted with maize and, in the higher areas, wheat. The vast majority of the country is given over to communal grazing: the mountain grasses are considered to be some of the best sheep pasture in southern Africa.

Wildlife

Lesotho's large mammalian fauna has been decimated by hunting and displaced by agriculture. If you are very lucky you may see an eland in Sehlabathebe National Park or perhaps the occasional baboon or jackal, but there is none of the large game generally associated with southern Africa. There are, however, a number of interesting and unusual bird species, such as the bald ibis, found particularly in Mokhotlong district. The natural flora is dominated by grasses.

Swaziland

Landscape

The **Highlands** in the northwest are Swaziland's most important economic region with extensive forestry plantations and mining development. This is the coolest region of the country where the mountains, forests and streams of Malolotja and Pigg's Peak attract many visitors. The road descending through the Ezulwini Valley from Mbabane to Manzini is Swaziland's most popular region for tourists. The **Middleveld** runs through the centre of the country and is the major agricultural region covered in rolling grasslands. The **Lowveld** is a hot dry region of typical African savanna where pineapples and sugarcane are cultivated. Hlane National Park is a good example of this landscape. The **Lebombo** region is part of the escarpment rising up to 600 m which runs from Maputaland through the eastern boundaries of Swaziland and on into Mpumalanga. This is the least populated area with only two notable settlements at Big Bend and Siteki.

Game and nature reserves

The game reserves in Swaziland are rather overwhelmed by Kruger which is only a short drive away. However, the private game reserve at **Mkhaya** is one of the best places in Africa to see black rhino and **Malolotja** offers some challenging opportunities for hikers. Malolotja is a wilderness area developed for hikers with only the most basic facilities. The amazing mountain scenery is a relatively undiscovered, top hiking area, where a good network of trails has been developed. The Mbuluzi Gorge in **Mlawula Nature Reserve** is a little-visited region with over 300 recorded species of birds and a new network of hiking trails.

Books

Literature

South Africa has produced internationally recognized and award-winning novelists. Probably the best known is **John Coetzee**, whose novels include *Dusklands*, In the *Heart of the Country*, *Waiting for the Barbarians*, *Life & Times of Michael K* (winner of the 1983 Booker Prize), *Age of Iron*, *Foe* and *The Master of Petersburg*. He won the Booker Prize again in 1999 for his novel, *Disgrace*, and won the Nobel Prize for Literature in 2003, only the fourth African author to do so and the second South African after Nadine Gordimer. His style is stark and intellectual, but surprisingly accessible. He is one of the most brilliant commentators on the effects of Apartheid.

Another award-winning South African novelist is **Nadine Gordimer**. Her novels include *A Guest of Honour*, *The Conservationist* (winner of the 1974 Booker Prize), *Burger's Daughter*, *July's People*, *A Sport of Nature*, *My Son's Story*, *None to Accompany Me* and *Get a Life*. Her beautifully written work tends to concentrate on the way wider political/social events impact on individual lives, and she won the 1991 Noble Prize for Literature.

Bessie Head is a widely respected South African author, though much of her work is set in Botswana where she was exiled in 1964. She wrote 3 novels – *When Rain Clouds Gather*, *Maru* and the semi-autobiographical *A Question of Power*, a collection of short stories *The Collection of Treasures*, and *The Village of the Rain-wind*, a portrait of the Botswanan village, Serowe, where she lived and eventually died at the age of just 49.

Andre Brink is another internationally recognized author who has published in both English and Afrikaans. His novels in English include *A Chain of Voices*, *The Ambassador*, *Looking on Darkness*, *Rumours of Rain*, *An Act of Terror* and *A Dry White Season* (made into a Hollywood film). Like Coetzee he has published extensively on literary criticism as well as his own fiction.

Tom Sharpe, an Englishman who lived in South Africa throughout the 1950s, represents a very different literary genre. His novels *Riotous Assembly* and *Indecent Exposure* are both hilarious and the absurd situations and characters he conjures up seem eminently believable in the South African context.

Another novelist representing a previous generation is **Alan Paton**, internationally recognized (though some find him sentimental) for his novel *Cry the Beloved Country*, but he also published *Too Late the Phalarope* and *Ah, But Your Land is Beautiful* and a collection of short stories *Debbie Go Home*.

Olive Schreiner's *The Story of an African Farm* is another well-known South African novel. When it was first published in 1883 (under the pseudonym Ralph Iron) it received notoriety for its feminist and anti-racist message. **Rider Haggard** covered very different topics. His hugely popular novels *King Solomon's Mines* and *She* have a romantic theme with an African setting and remain popular today. More recently **John van de Ruit**'s 2006 novel *Spud* took South Africa by storm and quickly became a bestseller. It's set in 1990, the year Nelson Mandela was released and Spud Milton's first year at an elite boys-only private boarding school. This humorous book follows the adventures of the young adolescent, and is followed by *Spud – The Madness Continues* and *Spud – Learning to Fly*.

The majority of the internationally recognized South African novelists described above are white. This does not mean that there is not a tradition of novel writing amongst South Africa's African, coloured and Indian populations. The two earliest African novelists in the country were **RRR Dhlomo**, who wrote *An African Tragedy* (1928) and **Sol Plaatje**, who wrote *Mhudi*, completed in 1917 but not published until 1930.

There has also been a strong emergence of modern black creative writing since the end of Apartheid. Perhaps the most important black writer today is **Zakes Mda**, who for many years worked as a playwright and poet before turning his hand to novels. His first two novels, *She Plays with Darkness* and *Ways of Dying*, place contemporary politics in the context of family and community in modern-day South Africa. *The Heart of Redness* won the Commonwealth prize and interlaces the present with the story of Nongqawuse, a princess who brought ruin to the Xhosa people. A young author who made a significant impact before tragically committing suicide in 2005 was **K Sello Duiker**. His novels *Thirteen Cents* and *The Quiet Violence* explore, respectively, street kids in Cape Town and the life of an ostracized gay student. An insight to the physical and moral decay of life in Hillbrow is provided by the critically acclaimed **Phaswane Mpe** in *Our Hillbrow*. Far from enjoying the freedoms allowed by democracy, the book depicts the native black South Africans facing the new challenges of poverty, unemployment and HIV/AIDS. He died in 2004, of an unknown illness, presumed to be HIV related.

Autobigraphy and political writing

The autobiography that has received most attention is **Nelson Mandela**'s *Long Walk to Freedom* (London, Abacus, 1995), a fascinating insight into the struggle. A number of other ANC leaders have also published autobiographies, including a posthumous publication by **Joe Slovo**, *Slovo: the unfinished autobiography*. Autobiographies tracing the lives of less famous South Africans include **Ezekiel Mphahlele**'s *Down Second Avenue*, **Bloke Modisane**'s *Blame me on History*, and the highly recommended *Call me Woman* by **Ellen Kuzwayo**. There have also been collections of political speeches, articles and other writing by major political figures such as **Steve Biko**'s *I Write what I Like*. Others have published diaries written while in prison, such as **Albie Sachs**'s *The Jail Diary of Albie Sachs*. Another interesting diary is **Sol Plaatje**'s *Mafeking Diary: a Black Man's View of a White Man's War*.

History and biography

Recommended biographies include: **Peter Alexander**'s biography of the South African novelist and well-known liberal Alan Paton, *Alan Paton*; **William Hancock**'s biography of Jan Smuts, *The Sanguine Years, 1870-1919* and *The Fields of Force 1919-1950*; **Richard Mendelsohn**'s biography of the businessman Sammy Marks, *Sammy Marks*); **Antony Thomas**' book on Cecil Rhodes, *Rhodes: The Face for Africa*; **Donald Woods**' book on Steve Biko, *Biko* – the basis for the film *Cry Freedom*; **Ruth First**'s biography of the novelist, feminist and anti-racism campaigner *Olive Schreiner*; and finally **Brian Willan** on Sol Plaatje, the novelist and early African nationalist, *Sol Plaatje: South African Nationalist 1876-1932*. **Allister Sparks**' *Beyond the Miracle*, charters the country's first decade of democracy, giving a balanced view of the governments successes and failures. **Antjie Krog**'s *Country of My Skull*, an national bestseller, is written by the head of the SABC reporting team during the Truth and Reconciliation Commission, providing an often harrowing picture of how the commission affected those involved. **Greg Marinovich** and **Joao Silva**'s *The Bang Bang Club*, looks at South Africa's press corps, particularly photographers, as they covered the violence in South Africa during the final years of Apartheid. It is primarily about four photographers; one of them died in crossfire in a township protest and one committed suicide. A book that came out in 2008, *Playing the Enemy*;

Nelson Mandela and the Game that made a Nation, by **John Carlin** is a touching story about when South Africa won the 2005 Rugby World Cup, and Nelson Mandela presented the trophy to captain Francois Pienaar wearing a Springbok green and gold jersey. Previously rugby had been an exclusive white's game, and when Mandela embraced Pienaar, the moment melted the hearts of all South Africans. The book is currently being made into a movie directed by Clint Eastwood, starring Matt Damon as Pienaar and Morgan Freeman as Mandela. It is due to be released at the end of 2009.

Natural history and environment

Good guides to game parks and wildlife include: **Jean Dorst** and **Pierre Dandelot**, *A Field Guide to the Larger Mammals of Africa*; **Gordon Maclean Roberts**' *Birds of South Africa*, which is considered the best and has been published since 1940; **Kenneth Newman**'s *Newman's Birds of Southern Africa*; and **Braam and Piet van Wyk**, *Field Guide to the Trees of Southern Africa*.

Contents

Footnotes

Glossary

Braai Outside barbeque, usually a metal grill where you light your own fire underneath with wood or coals.

Dorp Literally meaning 'town', although usually refers to a small urban centre with just a collection of houses and a few farmers wandering around.

Jol A slang word derived from the Cape dialect which can refer to anything from a nice picnic to an all-night rave.

Lapa Thatched shelter, usually without walls, for entertaining, especially when braaiing.

Kraal Traditional African hut for living in, usually thatched with mud or stone walls.

Kopjie A hill or outcrop of rocks, which are usually balanced on top of each other and a common feature on wide open plains.

Potjiekos Three-legged cast-iron pots used for cooking over coals.

Bakkie A pickup car.

Biltong Dried meat to chew on as a snack, similar to beef jerky, often spiced.

Boerwors Spicy beef or game sausage popular for braaiing.

Robot South African term for traffic lights.

Shebeen Township pub.

Sesotho phrases

Hello *Lumela*
How are you? *U phela joang?*
I am fine *Ke phela hantle*
What is your name? *Lebitso la hau u mang?*
My name is … *Lebitso la ka ke …*
Where do you come from? *U tsoa kae?*
I come from … *Ke tsoa …*
May I have some water *Ke kopa metsi*
May I have food *Ke kopa lijo*
What is the price? *Ke bokae?*
Stay well *Sala hantle* (*salang hantle* – plural)
Thank you *Kea leboha*

Siswati

Hello *Sawubona*
How are you? *Kunjani?*
Goodbye (stay well) *Sala kahle*
Thank you *Ngiyabonga*
Yes *Yebo*
No *Cha*

Index → *Entries in bold refer to maps.*

Advertisers' index

Credits

Footprint credits

Editor: Sara Chare
Map editor: Sarah Sorensen
Colour section: Kassia Gawronski

Managing Director: Andy Riddle
Commercial Director: Patrick Dawson
Publisher: Alan Murphy
Editorial: Felicity Laughton, Nicola Gibbs, Jo Williams, Ria Gane, Jen Haddington, Alice Jell
Cartography: Robert Lunn, Kevin Feeney, Emma Bryers
Cover design: Robert Lunn
Design: Mytton Williams
Marketing: Liz Harper, Hannah Bonnell
Sales: Jeremy Parr
Advertising: Renu Sibal
Finance and administration: Elizabeth Taylor

Photography credits

Front cover: Rhino, Gordon DR Clements, AXIOM
Back cover: Ndebele Artist painting a wall with the razor shape, Robert Estall Photo Agency/Alamy
Wildlife colour section: www.naturepl.com. (Laurent Geslin, T.J Rich, Tony Heald, Anup Shah, Constantinos Petrinos, Richard du Toit, Nigel Bean, Ingo Arndt, Jose B Ruiz, Karl Ammann, Philippe Clement, Pete Oxford, John Cancalosi, Francois Savigny, Peter Blackwell, Andrew Parkinson, Peter Blackwell, Eliot Lyons)

Manufactured in India by Nutech Print Services, Delhi
Pulp from sustainable forests

Footprint feedback

We try as hard as we can to make each Footprint guide as up to date as possible but, of course, things always change. If you want to let us know about your experiences – good, bad or ugly – then don't delay and go to www.footprintbooks.com and send in your comments.

Publishing information

Footprint South Africa
10th edition
© Footprint Handbooks Ltd
November 2009

ISBN: 978 1 906098 7 04
CIP DATA: A catalogue record for this book is available from the British Library

® Footprint Handbooks and the Footprint mark are a registered trademark of Footprint Handbooks Ltd

Published by Footprint
6 Riverside Court
Lower Bristol Road
Bath BA2 3DZ, UK
T +44 (0)1225 469141
F +44 (0)1225 469461
www.footprintbooks.com

Distributed in the USA by Globe Pequot Press, Guilford, Connecticut

Every effort has been made to ensure that the facts in this guidebook are accurate. However, travellers should still obtain advice from consulates, airlines, etc about travel and visa requirements before travelling. The authors and publishers cannot accept responsibility for any loss, injury or inconvenience however caused.